S0-BNK-027

WITHDRAWN FROM
MACALESTER COLLEGE
LIBRARY

EUROPEAN HISTORICAL DICTIONARIES
Edited by Jon Woronoff

Historical Dictionary of the United Kingdom

Volume I: England and the United Kingdom

Kenneth J. Panton
and
Keith A. Cowlard

European Historical Dictionaries, No. 17

The Scarecrow Press, Inc.
Lanham, Md., & London
1997

SCARECROW PRESS, INC.

Published in the United States of America
by Scarecrow Press, Inc.
4720 Boston Way
Lanham, Maryland 20706

4 Pleydell Gardens, Folkestone
Kent CT20 2DN, England

Copyright © 1997 by Kenneth J. Panton and Keith A. Cowlard

All rights reserved. No part of this publication may be reproduced,
stored in a retrieval system, or transmitted in any form or by any
means, electronic, mechanical, photocopying, recording, or otherwise,
without the prior permission of the publisher.

British Cataloguing-in-Publication Information Available

Library of Congress Cataloging-in-Publication Data

Panton, Kenneth J. (Kenneth John), 1945–
    Historical dictionary of the United Kingdom / Kenneth J. Panton
and Keith A. Cowlard.
        p.   cm. — (European historical dictionaries ; no. 17)
    Includes bibliographical references (p.   )
    Contents: v. 1. England and the United Kingdom.
    ISBN 0-8108-3150-3 (alk. paper)
    1. Great Britain—History—Dictionaries. I. Cowlard, Keith A.
(Keith Arthur), 1946– . II. Title. III. Series.
DA34.P36 1997
941.003—dc20   96-23996

ISBN 0-8108-3150-3 (cloth : alk.paper)

♾™ The paper used in this publication meets the minimum requirements of
American National Standard for Information Sciences—Permanence of
Paper for Printed Library Materials, ANSI Z39.48–1984.
Manufactured in the United States of America.

CONTENTS

EDITOR'S FOREWORD

Of several dozen European Historical Dictionaries, including many on countries with impressive histories and, once at least, considerable influence worldwide, none has to cover quite as much ground as the *Historical Dictionary of the United Kingdom*. It must reach back into a long and eventful history, passing through numerous earlier periods and reigns until it arrives at the present day. It must also look out across what was an empire on which the sun never set and consider the remnants thereof. Finally, it has to trace two immense trajectories, one along which a relatively insignificant kingdom rose to the apogee of its power and another, even steeper, which reduced it to (almost) just another European country. Yet, even as 'just another' country, the United Kingdom is a lively and intriguing place which continues to make substantial contributions to Europe and the world.

To cover that much ground, it proved necessary to produce two volumes instead of one. This first volume deals with England and aspects common to the United Kingdom as a whole. The second volume will look more closely at Scotland, Wales and Northern Ireland. Any disadvantages in separating what has been joined are more than compensated for by permitting the authors to lavish attention on places, persons and events that would otherwise tend to be overlooked or overshadowed. And reading both volumes in conjunction will bring a broader, more rounded view.

The first volume must still present a vast span of history. That explains the numerous entries on kings and queens and lesser members of the nobility as well as the gentry and clergy, to say nothing of many ordinary people whose achievements were sometimes extraordinary. This includes a goodly number of explorers and soldiers, inventors and scientists, politicians, businesspeople and others. The book also describes essential bodies and institutions, some long since gone, others still vital, among them the parties, the courts and, especially, Parliament. Other entries treat noteworthy places and events or aspects of economic, social and cultural life. In addition, there is a handy chronology, a useful list of abbreviations and a helpful introduction to put things in their place. Particularly important, since there is so much more to know, is the comprehensive bibliography.

Generating this much information was no easy task for a team of two, although they have accomplished it extremely well. Both authors specialize in geography and know their way about the British Isles as professionals. Kenneth J. Panton is Senior Lecturer and Keith A. Cowlard is Head of the Department of Geography at London Guildhall University. But Drs Panton and Cowlard are also well versed in history and have a keen interest in other aspects of British life. Moreover, as one can readily sense from the light and easy style, writing even a work of this size was a pleasure and not a chore. May the readers find it no less enjoyable to consult than the editor!

Jon Woronoff
Series Editor

ACKNOWLEDGEMENTS

Book writing is a team sport. The authors get their names on the covers, but the final product is a combination of the hard graft and imagination of many people, some of whom contribute hours of their time, some of whom simply spark off ideas over a pint of warm beer in a country pub. We are indebted to all of them. At London Guildhall University, we relied very heavily on the knowledge and expertise of Neil Gosney, Senior Subject Librarian, who went well beyond the call of duty in his quest for the details of so many of the titles which are listed in the bibliography. Also, the cartographers in the Geography Department and the members of City Cartographic who used their technical skills to great effect: Gareth Owen prepared all of the maps while Don Shewan and Andrew Ellis took the typescript and transformed it into its present, polished form. And we have much for which to thank our families. The bulk of this text was written in our homes, at weekends, late in the evening and in the wee sma' hours of the morning, when the normal working day was over and the demands of students put aside. They have lived and breathed this dictionary as much as we have, are numbered amongst our sternest critics, and yet have been our surest support.

NOTES TO THE READER

This *Historical Dictionary of the United Kingdom* consists of two parts, one dealing with England and the United Kingdom, the other with Northern Ireland, Scotland and Wales. Such a division is necessary because the country took its present form only in 1921 and each of its component nations has preserved specific features from its past. Moreover, the strongly held sense of identity which is characteristic of the Scots, the Welsh and the Irish — and which transcends mere regionalism — means that the modern state can only be truly understood in terms of the evolution of its component parts.

Of course, many events and leaders have influenced all four territories. They are, for the most part, detailed in this first volume, which concentrates on matters which relate specifically to England — always the most powerful and influential of the quartet — and also on the politics, the economic and social developments and the international ties which have produced a united country with a considerable role in world affairs. The second volume deals more specifically with the issues, people and events which have had their greatest impact in Wales, Scotland and Northern Ireland. Most topics will, therefore, appear in one volume alone, but some will appear in both, with different emphases. To assist the reader, a list of the entries to be included in volume 2 is contained in the appendix to this book.

The present volume follows the history of England from earliest times, passing through the period of Roman control, the lengthy settlement by the Anglo-Saxons, the Viking and Norman invasions and the establishment of the Plantagenet, Tudor, Stuart and later dynasties. The country's increasing international influence (political and economic) is covered in entries dealing with conflicts in Europe and elsewhere, the Industrial Revolution and the growing Empire. More recently — and primarily in a UK context — entries reflect the impact of the two World Wars, the growth of the welfare state, declining global power and closer links with the countries of the European Union.

The following paragraphs provide fuller details of the book's format and the principles adopted in the allocation of entries to each volume.

Abbreviations

This section includes all abbreviations used in the book.

Chronologies

The chronologies provide simple checklists (in date order) of historical events and of monarchs and governments of Britain, using the precise year (or nearest relevant year) for the entry. More detailed dates, including month and day when appropriate, are noted in the relevant entries in the dictionary. Early dates are approximations from recent research publications. Later entries use the prevailing calendar of Britain for the period, with the change from the Julian to the Gregorian calendar occurring in 1752 (see dictionary entry on **CALENDAR**).

The **HISTORICAL EVENTS** Chronology includes those events described in the dictionary to which an exact or approximate date can be given. Entries correspond to the titles used in the dictionary. Events with no precise date, and references to individuals, are omitted.

The **MONARCHS** Chronology lists all monarchs of England from 1066 to 1603, England and Scotland from 1603 to 1707, Great Britain from 1707 to 1801 and the United Kingdom from 1801 to the present. Dates are the calendar years over which the monarchs reigned.

The **GOVERNMENTS, POLITICAL PARTIES AND PRIME MINISTERS** Chronology begins in 1721 (the first year in which a Prime Minister can be properly identified) and lists the dates of the elected government, the name of the Prime Minister and the title of the governing political party.

The Dictionary Section

The conventions employed in the body of the text are noted below:

Entry Conventions
Entries in this section are arranged in alphabetical order, with the title of the entry in **UPPERCASE BOLD PRINT**. When a series of entries consists of two words or more, entries which start with the same word are listed consecutively (thus, for example, **ROYAL NAVY** appears in the sequence of entries beginning with the word ROYAL and is listed before **ROYALISTS**). In some cases, entries may be listed by a word other than that used first in spoken English (for instance, all battles appear in the form **HASTINGS, BATTLE OF**, rather than **BATTLE OF HASTINGS**). All individuals, with the exception of monarchs, are listed by surname. Kings and Queens appear under their given (or Christian) name and number order.

The two volumes of the *Historical Dictionary of the United Kingdom* cover the major events in the history of Britain and the people who have helped to shape that history, particularly the monarchs, politicians and military, commercial and industrial leaders of the nation. Given the country's lengthy history, the entries are necessarily selective and that selection remains the responsibility of the authors. In particular, material related to North America has been kept to a minimum because information about Britain's involvement in that part of the world is readily available to US and Canadian readers from other sources. Also — and purely for reasons of space — there are no entries on individuals renowned for their contribution to the arts (including literature) or sport and no individual entries on former territories of the British Empire.

In addition, the allocation of material to each of the volumes is, to some extent, subjective. All material relating specifically or principally to England appears in this volume. All material relating specifically to Northern Ireland, Scotland or Wales appears in volume 2. Entries dealing with Ireland prior to 1920 (when Northern Ireland was created) are deliberately limited because a volume dealing with the Republic of Ireland will be published in this series of Historical Dictionaries.

Events and individuals which have specifically UK implications are dealt with in this volume. Matters relating to foreign relations and national policy, therefore, appear in volume 1. Individuals, with the exception of Kings, Queens and Prime Ministers, are allocated to the appropriate volume according to their place of birth.

As a help to readers, a list of entry headings in the second volume is incorporated in Appendix 1.

Cross-Referencing

Cross-references to related entries elsewhere in the dictionary are shown within the body of individual entries in **UPPERCASE BOLD PRINT** and should be consulted to obtain additional information.

Multiple Entries

In cases where the same title occurs at different dates (as, for example, when three battles occurred at the same place but in different years), the individual occurrences are given either as separate dictionary entries (for major events) or as underlined date entries within the main entry (for lesser events).

Publications

In cases where entries include reference to a publication and no separate entry for that publication exists in the dictionary, the title of that publication is shown in *lowercase italic print*.

Names

The names of ships, trains and planes are given in *italic print.*

The Bibliography

The bibliography is subdivided into chronological sections, with further thematic subdivisions for the 19th and 20th centuries. Separate sections are provided for more general introductory and reference publications. Fuller details are given in the introduction to the bibliography.

ABBREVIATIONS

AD	In the year of Our Lord (Anno Domini)
AIDS	Acquired Immune Deficiency Syndrome
am	Before noon (ante meridiem)
ANZAC	Australian and New Zealand Army Corps
ASDIC	Anti-Submarine Detection Investigation Committee
BA	Bachelor of Arts (Baccalaureus Artium)
	British Airways
BBC	British Broadcasting Corporation
BC	Before Christ
BChir	Bachelor of Surgery (Baccalaureus Chirurgiae)
BEA	British European Airways
BNP	British National Party
BOAC	British Overseas Airways Corporation
BUF	British Union of Fascists
C	Centigrade
c	circa
CBE	Commander of the Order of the British Empire
CBI	Confederation of British Industry
CENTO	Central Treaty Organization
CH	Companion of Honour
CND	Campaign for Nuclear Disarmament
CWS	Co-operative Wholesale Society
DC	District of Columbia
DORA	Defence of the Realm Acts
Dr	Doctor
DSO	Distinguished Service Order
EC	European Community
ECSC	European Coal and Steel Community
ecu	European currency unit
ed	editor
EEA	European Economic Area
EEC	European Economic Community
EFTA	European Free Trade Association
EMS	European Monetary System
ERM	Exchange Rate Mechanism
ESDA	Electrostatic Detection Apparatus
etc	etcetera
EU	European Union
EURATOM	European Atomic Energy Community
F	Fahrenheit
FD	Defender of the Faith (Fidei Defensor)
Fid Def	Defender of the Faith (Fidei Defensor)
GC	George Cross
GLC	Greater London Council
HMIP	Her (or His) Majesty's Inspectorate of Pollution
HMS	Her (or His) Majesty's Ship
ILP	Independent Labour Party
IRA	Irish Republican Army
JP	Justice of the Peace

KG	Knight of the Order of the Garter
KT	Knight of the Thistle
LCC	London County Council
LLB	Bachelor of Laws (Legum Baccalaureus)
Ltd	Limited Liability Company
MA	Master of Arts
MB	Bachelor of Medicine (Medicinae Baccalaureus)
MBE	Member of the Order of the British Empire
MC	Military Cross
MCC	Marylebone Cricket Club
MD	Doctor of Medicine (Medicinae Doctor)
MP	Member of Parliament
mph	Miles per hour
NATO	North Atlantic Treaty Organization
NEDDY	National Economic Development Council
NHS	National Health Service
OM	Order of Merit
OPEC	Organization of Petroleum Exporting Countries
OS	Ordnance Survey
plc	public limited company
PLUTO	Pipeline Under The Ocean
pm	after noon (post meridien)
PRO	Public Record Office
PSBR	Public Sector Borrowing Requirement
RADAR	Radio Detection and Ranging
RAF	Royal Air Force
RN	Royal Navy
s	shillings
SAS	Special Air Service
SDP	Social Democratic Party
SEAQ	Stock Exchange Automated Quotations System
SLDP	Social and Liberal Democratic Party
SOE	Special Operations Executive
SONAR	Sound Navigation and Ranging
STOL	Short Take-off and Landing
TUC	Trades Union Congress
TV	Television
UDI	Unilateral Declaration of Independence
UK	United Kingdom of Great Britain and Northern Ireland
UN	United Nations
US	United States of America
USA	United States of America
USSR	Union of Soviet Socialist Republics
VC	Victoria Cross
WEU	Western European Union
£	pounds sterling

CHRONOLOGY OF HISTORICAL EVENTS

Only entries of historical events and topics which can be found in the dictionary appear in this chronology. For ease of access, they follow the precise titles used in the dictionary. Dates refer to the year of the event, or the earliest year or a significant year for that topic. Only dictionary entries to which exact or significant dates can be ascribed are included and dates BC are approximations only. Entries are for events and topics, not people. Multiple entries under a single date are given in alphabetical order.

BC

500000 - 43 AD	Prehistoric Britain	878	Battle of Edington
500000 - 2500	Stone Age	891	Anglo-Saxon Chronicle
500000 - 10000	Palaeolithic Period	913	Coronation
	(Old Stone Age)	928	Royal Mint
10000 - 4400	Mesolithic Period	937	Battle of Brunanburh
	(Middle Stone Age)	991	Battle of Maldon
4400 - 2500	Neolithic Period		Danegeld
	(New Stone Age)	1016	Battle of Assandun
2750 - 1300	Stonehenge		(Ashingdon)
2500 - 800	Bronze Age	1066 - 1154	Normans
2200 -	Celts	1066	Battle of Stamford Bridge
1800	Beaker People		Battle of Hastings
1200	Hillforts		Channel Islands
800 - 43 AD	Iron Age		Curia Regis
600	Celtic Fields		Windsor Castle
100	Belgae	1066 - 1154	Normans
		1067	Freehold

AD

			Jury
		1078	Tower of London
43 - 410	Romans	1079	City of London
43	Battle of the Medway	1086	Domesday Book
	Druids	1093	Battle of Alnwick
	Villa	1095 - 99	Crusade (first)
60	Iceni	1106	Battle of Tinchebrai
122	Hadrian's Wall	1147 - 48	Crusade (second)
225	Saxon Shore Forts	1154 - 1399	Plantagenets: House of Anjou
400	Angles	1166	Assizes
	Jutes	1170	Canterbury
	Saxons	1172	Compromise of Avranches
450	Anglo-Saxons	1174	Battle of Alnwick
	Cinque Ports	1181	Assize of Arms
493	Battle of Mount Badon		Militia
514	Wessex	1189 - 92	Crusade (third)
632	Mercia	1191	Battle of Acre
664	Synod of Whitby	1192	Corporation of London
865	Vikings	1193	Ransom
871	Battle of Ashdown	1215 - 17	Barons' War

1215	Magna Carta
	Runnymede
1218 - 21	Crusade (fifth)
1222	Poll Tax
1235	Statute of Merton
1242	Battle of Saintes
1258	Oxford Parliament
	Provisions of Oxford
1259	Provisions of Westminster
	Treaty of Paris
1264 - 67	Barons' War
1264	Battle of Lewes
	Mise of Lewes
1265	Battle of Evesham
1275	Statute of Westminster
1285	Statute of Westminster
1295	Model Parliament
1301	Prince of Wales
1303	Treaty of Paris
1311	Ordinances
1337 - 1453	Hundred Years War
1337 - 1455	Free Companies
1346	Battle of Crecy
	Calais
1348 - 51	Black Death
1348	Order of the Garter
1352	Treason
1356	Battle of Poitiers
1373	Treaty of London
1376	Good Parliament
1377 - 88	Poll Tax
1380	Lollards
1381	Peasants' Revolt
1388	Battle of Otterburn
	Merciless Parliament
1390	Justice of the Peace
1399 - 1461	Plantagenets:
	House of Lancaster
1399	Duchy of Lancaster
1404	Earl
	Unlearned Parliament
1405	Battle of Shrewsbury
1407	The Merchants Adventurers
1415	Battle of Agincourt
1420	Treaty of Troyes
1424	Battle of Verneuil
1450	Battle of Formigny
	Cade's Rebellion
1455 - 85	Wars of the Roses
1455	Battle of St Albans
1459	Battle of Blore Heath
1460	Battle of Northampton

	Battle of Wakefield
1461 - 85	Plantagenets: House of York
1461	Battle of St Albans
	Battle of Towton
1464	Battle of Hexham
1467	English Trading Companies
1471	Battle of Barnet
	Battle of Tewkesbury
1476	Printing
1483	Duke
1485 - 1603	Tudors
1485	Battle of Bosworth Field
1487	Battle of Stoke
1496	Intercursus Magnus
1506	Intercursus Malus
1513	Battle of Flodden
	Battle of the Spurs
1520	Field of the Cloth of Gold
1521	Defender of the Faith
1522	Amicable Grant
1529 - 59	Reformation
1530	Star Chamber
1534	Church of England
	Act of Succession
	Act of Supremacy
1535	Court of Augmentations
1536 - 37	Pilgrimage of Grace
1536 - 41	Dissolution of the Monasteries
1536 - 43	Union of England and Wales
1536	Act of Succession
	Act of Union
	Articles of Religion
	Privy Council
	Wales
1539	Articles of Religion
1541	Free Speech
1543	Witchcraft
1544	Act of Succession
1549	Act of Uniformity
	Book of Common Prayer
	Kett's Rebellion
1551	Marquess
1552	Act of Uniformity
	Book of Common Prayer
	Recusant
1553 - 58	Marian Reaction
1553	Articles of Religion
1554	Wyatt's Rebellion
1555	Muscovy Company
1558 - 1603	Elizabethan Age
1559	Act of Supremacy
	Act of Uniformity

	War Office	1830	Georgian
1786	Anglo-French Treaty	1831	Truck Act
1787	Consolidated Fund	1832	Conservative Party
	Cricket		Parliamentary Reform
1788	Triple Alliance		Rotten Borough
1789 - 92	Carnatic War (fourth)	1833	Factory Act
1789	French Revolution	1834	Poor Law
	Mutiny on the Bounty		Quadruple Alliance
1791	Ordnance Survey		Tamworth Manifesto
1792	Gold Standard		Tolpuddle Martyrs
1793	Continental System	1835	Municipal Corporations Act
1794	Jacobinists	1836	Tithe
1798	Irish Rebellion	1837 - 1901	Victorian Age
	Battle of the Nile	1837	Marriage Act
1799 - 1800	Combination Acts	1838	Chartism
1799	Battle of Acre	1838	Public Record Office
1800	Act of Union	1839 - 42	Afghan War (first)
1801	Union of Great Britain and Ireland	1839 - 42	Opium War (first)
	United Kingdom	1839	Anti-Corn Law League
1802	Channel Tunnel		Bedchamber Crisis
	Despard Conspiracy		Durham Report
	Factory Act		Treaty of London
1803 - 15	Napoleonic Wars	1840 - 49	Hungry Forties
1803	Emmet's Rising	1840	Battle of Acre
1805	Battle of Trafalgar		Immigration
1806 - 13	Continental System		Pax Britannica
1808 - 14	Peninsular War		Penny Post
1811 - 17	Luddites		Treaty of Waitangi
1811	Battle of Albuera	1842 - 44	Rebecca Riots
	Regency	1842	Plug Riots
	Regency Period		Treaty of Nanking
1812 - 14	Anglo-American War	1844	Co-operative Movement
1812	Gas		Factory Act
	Battle of Salamanca		Poor Law
1814	Battle of Toulouse	1847 - 50	Don Pacifico Incident
	Treaty of Paris	1847	Factory Act
1815	Treaty of Ghent	1848	Football Association
	Treaty of Paris	1850	Factory Act
	Quadruple Alliance		Liberal Party
	Battle of Waterloo	1851	Great Exhibition
1816	Spa Fields Riot	1853	Factory Act
1817	March of the Blanketeers	1854 - 56	Crimean War
1819	Factory Act	1854	Battle of Alma
	Peterloo		Battle of Balaclava
	Poor Law		Battle of Inkerman
	Six Acts		Charge of the Light Brigade
1820	Cato Street Conspiracy	1856 - 57	Persian War
1825	Railways	1856 - 60	Opium War (second)
1827	Treaty of London	1856	Steel Industry
	Battle of Navarino	1857 - 58	Indian Mutiny
1829	Scotland Yard	1858	Atlantic Cable
1830 - 33	Swing Riots		Fenians

1859	Treaty of Paris	1902	Anglo-Japanese Alliance
1860	Liberal Party		Treaty of Vereeniging
1864	Factory Act	1903	North-West Passage
1865	Salvation Army	1904	Battle of Dogger Bank
1867 - 68	Abyssinian War		Entente Cordiale
1867	British North America Act	1906	Labour Party
	Dominion	1907	Anglo-Russian Entente
	Factory Act		Entente Powers
1868	Trades Union Congress		Imperial Conferences
1869	Disestablishment		Triple Entente
1870 - 1900	Great Depression (Agricultural)	1909	Osborne Judgement
1870	Home Rule	1910 -	Windsor
1872	Licensing Act	1911	Official Secrets Act
1873	Court of Appeal		Parliament Act
	Judicature Act	1912	Titanic
	Supreme Court of Judicature	1913	Cat and Mouse Act
1876	Royal Titles Act		Treaty of London
1878 - 81	Afghan War (second)	1914 - 17	Mesopotamian Campaign
1878	Berlin Congress	1914 - 18	First World War
	Electricity	1914 - 20	Conscription
1879	North-East Passage	1914	Defence of the Realm Act
	Zulu War		Battle of Dogger Bank
1880 - 81	Boer War (first)		Battle of Ypres
1884 - 85	Berlin Conference		Triple Alliance
1884 - 85	Sudanese War	1915	Defence of the Realm Act
1884	Fabian Society		Gallipoli Expedition
1885	Scramble for Africa		Treaty of London
1887	Golden Jubilee		Battle of Ypres
1888	Borough	1916	Defence of the Realm Act
	Association Football		Battle of Jutland
	London County Council		Battle of the Somme
1893	Independent Labour Party		Battle of Verdun
1894	Death Duties	1917	Balfour Declaration
1895 - 96	Jameson Raid		Rationing
1895 - 1902	Splendid Isolation		Battle of Ypres
1895	National Trust		Zimmerman Telegram
1896 - 99	Sudanese War	1918	Armistice Day
1896	Kruger Telegram		Coupon Election
1897	Suffragettes		Royal Air Force
1898	Fashoda Incident		Zeebrugge Raid
	Garden Cities	1919	Afghan War (third)
	Battle of Omdurman		Air Transport
1899 - 1900	Boxer Rebellion		Forestry Commission
1899 - 1902	Boer War (second)		Imperial Preference
1899	Anglo-German Agreement		Mandated Territories
1900	Indirect Rule		Treaty of Versailles
	Khaki Election	1920	Communist Party
	The Relief of Mafeking		League of Nations
	Yangtse Agreement		Poplarism
1901 - 10	Saxe-Coburg-Gotha	1921	Northern Ireland
1901 - 10	Wettin	1922 - 26	Hunger Marches
1901 - 14	Edwardian Age	1922	British Broadcasting

	Divorce Reform Act		Social Democratic Party
1970	Equal Pay Act	1982	British National Party
1971	Decimalization		Falklands War
1972	Crown Courts		Greenham Common
	Treaty of Accession	1983	English Heritage
1973	BEA	1985	Green Party
	British Airways	1986	Big Bang
	Oil Crisis	1988	Central Statistical Office
	Referenda	1989	Liberal Democratic Party
	Three Day Week		Guildford Four
1974	Factory Act		Secret Service
1975	Equal Opportunities Act	1990	Iraqi Supergun Affair
	Referenda		Poll Tax
	Sex Discrimination Act		Pollution Control
1976	Race Relations Act	1991	Birmingham Six
1977	Lib-Lab Pact		Citizen's Charter
1978 - 79	Winter of Discontent		Gulf War
1979	Devolution	1992	Ordination of Women
	European Monetary System	1993	European Union
	Monetarism		Maastricht
	Privatization	1994	Channel Tunnel
	Thatcherism		European Economic Area
	Referenda		Post Office
1980	Nuclear Deterrent		State Lottery
1981	The Alliance	1995	National Health Service
	Scarman Enquiry		Nationalization

CHRONOLOGY OF MONARCHS

Monarchs of England, Great Britain and the United Kingdom have rarely been of purely native stock. The Normans had French blood, as did the Plantagenets; William III was Dutch, the Hanoverians were German and the present heir to the throne is of Greek blood. The 'Europeanness' of the country's sovereigns is a remarkable story of treaty, union, war and intermarriage. The dates given are the calendar dates over which they reigned.

England 1066-1603

HOUSE OF NORMANDY

William I	1066 - 87
William II	1087 - 1100
Henry I	1100 - 35
Stephen	1135 - 41
Matilda	1141
Stephen	1141 - 54

PLANTAGENETS: HOUSE OF ANJOU

Henry II	1154 - 89
Richard I	1189 - 99
John	1199 - 1216
Henry III	1216 - 72
Edward I	1272 - 1307
Edward II	1307 - 27
Edward III	1327 - 77
Richard II	1377 - 99

PLANTAGENETS: HOUSE OF LANCASTER

Henry IV	1399 - 1413
Henry V	1413 - 22
Henry VI	1422 - 61

PLANTAGENETS: HOUSE OF YORK

Edward IV	1461 - 70
Henry VI	1470 - 71
Edward IV	1471 - 83
Edward V	1483
Richard III	1483 - 85

HOUSE OF TUDOR

Henry VII	1485 - 1509
Henry VIII	1509 - 47
Edward VI	1547 - 53
Jane	1553
Mary I	1553 - 58
Elizabeth I	1558 - 1603

England and Scotland 1603-1707

HOUSE OF STUART

James VI (of Scotland) and I (of England)	1603 - 25
Charles I	1625 - 49

[1649-1660 England was a Republic ruled by the **COMMONWEALTH** and the **PROTECTORATE**: Charles II succeeded Charles I as King of Scotland in 1649]

Charles II	1660 - 85	Mary II (with William III)	1689 - 94
James VII and II	1685 - 88		
William III (with Mary II)	1689 - 1702	Anne	1702 - 14

Great Britain 1707-1801

HOUSE OF STUART		HOUSE OF HANOVER	
Anne	1702 - 14	George I	1714 - 27
		George II	1727 - 60
		George III	1760 - 1820

United Kingdom 1801-

HOUSE OF HANOVER		HOUSE OF WINDSOR	
George III	1760 - 1820	George V	1910 - 36
George IV	1820 - 30	Edward VIII	1936
William IV	1830 - 37	George VI	1936 - 52
Victoria	1837 - 1901	Elizabeth II	1952 -

HOUSE OF WETTIN OR SAXE-COBURG-GOTHA
Edward VII   1901 - 10

CHRONOLOGY OF GOVERNMENTS, POLITICAL PARTIES AND PRIME MINISTERS 1721-1995

The office of Prime Minister did not really exist until around 1721. The concept of a political party, in modern terms, was slow to develop. Until well into the 19th century, such parties were simply loose groups of similarly minded individuals.

PERIOD	PARTY	PRIME MINISTER
1721 - 42	Whig	Robert Walpole
1742 - 43	Whig	Earl of Wilmington
1743 - 54	Whig	Henry Pelham
1754 - 56	Whig	Duke of Newcastle
1756 - 57	Whig	Duke of Devonshire
1757	Tory	Earl Waldegrave
1757 - 62	Whig	Duke of Newcastle
1762 - 63	Tory	Earl of Bute
1763 - 65	Whig	George Grenville
1765 - 66	Whig	Lord Rockingham
1766 - 68	Whig	William Pitt the Elder
1768 - 70	Whig	Duke of Grafton
1770 - 82	Tory	Lord North
1782	Whig	Marquis of Rockingham
1782 - 83	Whig	Earl of Shelburne
1783	Coalition	Duke of Portland
1783 - 1801	Tory	William Pitt the Younger
1801 - 04	Tory	Henry Addington
1804 - 06	Tory	William Pitt the Younger
1806 - 07	Whig	Baron Grenville
1807 - 09	Tory	Duke of Portland
1809 - 12	Tory	Spencer Perceval
1812 - 27	Tory	Earl of Liverpool
1827	Tory	George Canning
1827 - 28	Tory	Viscount Goderich
1828 - 30	Tory	Duke of Wellington
1830 - 34	Whig	Earl Grey
1834	Whig	Viscount Melbourne
1834 - 35	Conservative	Robert Peel
1835 - 41	Whig	Viscount Melbourne
1841 - 46	Conservative	Sir Robert Peel
1846 - 52	Liberal	Lord John Russell
1852	Tory	Earl of Derby
1852 - 55	Peelite	Lord Aberdeen
1855 - 58	Liberal	Viscount Palmerston
1858 - 59	Conservative	Earl of Derby
1859 - 65	Liberal	Viscount Palmerston

1865 - 66	Liberal	Lord John Russell
1866 - 68	Conservative	Earl of Derby
1868	Conservative	Benjamin Disraeli
1868 - 74	Liberal	William Gladstone
1874 - 80	Conservative	Benjamin Disraeli
1880 - 85	Liberal	William Gladstone
1885 - 86	Conservative	Marquis of Salisbury
1886	Liberal	William Gladstone
1886 - 92	Conservative	Marquis of Salisbury
1892 - 94	Liberal	William Gladstone
1894 - 95	Liberal	Earl of Rosebery
1895 - 1902	Conservative	Marquis of Salisbury
1902 - 05	Conservative	Arthur Balfour
1905 - 08	Liberal	Henry Campbell-Bannerman
1908 - 15	Liberal	Herbert Asquith
1915 - 16	Coalition	Herbert Asquith
1916	War Cabinet	David Lloyd George
1916 - 22	Coalition	David Lloyd George
1922 - 23	Conservative	Andrew Bonar Law
1923 - 24	Conservative	Stanley Baldwin
1924	Labour	Ramsay MacDonald
1924 - 29	Conservative	Stanley Baldwin
1929 - 31	Labour	Ramsay MacDonald
1931 - 35	Coalition	Ramsay MacDonald
1935 - 37	National	Stanley Baldwin
1937 - 40	National	Neville Chamberlain
1940 - 45	Coalition	Winston Churchill
1945	Caretaker	Winston Churchill
1945 - 51	Labour	Clement Attlee
1951 - 55	Conservative	Winston Churchill
1955 - 57	Conservative	Anthony Eden
1957 - 63	Conservative	Harold Macmillan
1963 - 64	Conservative	Alexander Douglas-Home
1964 - 70	Labour	Harold Wilson
1970 - 74	Conservative	Edward Heath
1974 - 76	Labour	Harold Wilson
1976 - 79	Labour	James Callaghan
1979 - 90	Conservative	Margaret Thatcher
1990 -	Conservative	John Major

Map 1
Major Physical Features

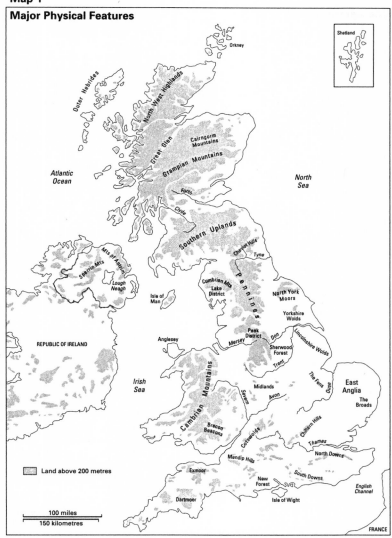

Map 2
Settlements

Map 3

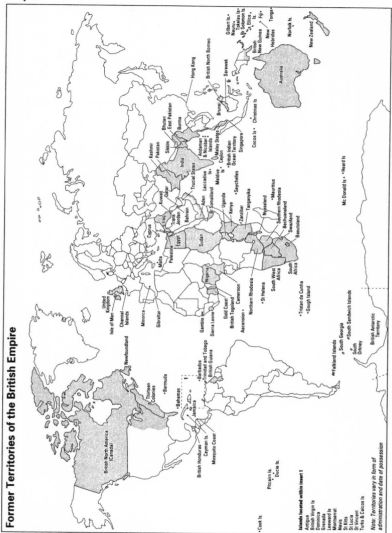

Former Territories of the British Empire

Map 4

Local Government: Pre 1974 Counties (England and Wales), Pre 1975 Counties (Scotland) and Counties (Northern Ireland)

1. Bedfordshire
2. Berkshire
3. Buckinghamshire
4. Cambridgeshire
5. Derbyshire
6. Gloucestershire
7. Hertfordshire
8. Leicestershire
9. Northamptonshire
10. Nottinghamshire
11. South Yorkshire
12. Staffordshire
13. Warwickshire
14. West Yorkshire
15. Wiltshire
G.L.C. – Greater London Council

60 miles
80 kilometres

Map 5

Local Government: Post 1974 Counties (England and Wales), Post 1975 Regions (Scotland) and Counties (Northern Ireland)

1. Bedfordshire
2. Berkshire
3. Buckinghamshire
4. Cambridgeshire
5. Derbyshire
6. Gloucestershire
7. Hertfordshire
8. Leicestershire
9. Northamptonshire
10. Nottinghamshire
11. South Yorkshire
12. Staffordshire
13. Warwickshire
14. West Yorkshire
15. Wiltshire

G.L.C. – Greater London Council

60 miles
80 kilometres

THE UNITED KINGDOM OF GREAT BRITAIN AND NORTHERN IRELAND: ENGLAND AND THE UNITED KINGDOM

The United Kingdom (UK) consists of a group of islands lying in the Atlantic Ocean close to the northwest shores of Europe. It covers some 94,525 square miles and has a population of 56.6 million (1991). Within its boundaries there are four territories associated with national groupings. England, the largest of these both in area and population, has 47.1 million people on its 50,300 square miles. Scotland (to the north) has 5.1 million people on 30,400 square miles and Wales (to the west) 2.8 million people on 8,000 square miles. Together, these three form Great Britain.

Northern Ireland is the northeast part of the island of Ireland, which lies west of the main British landmass, and has a population of 1.5 million on its 5,500 square miles.

The United Kingdom is governed as a constitutional monarchy, with succession to the throne by heredity through the male line. The modern role of the sovereign, however, is largely ceremonial. Lawmaking is the preserve of Parliament, which is divided into two chambers. The House of Commons has 651 members, each representing a single constituency and elected by adult suffrage on a simple majority of votes cast. The House of Lords consists of all peers (most of whom never attend) plus 26 Archbishops and Bishops of the Church of England and 23 Law Lords. The majority of the peers are sons of aristocratic families, who have an inherited right to sit in the Chamber. The rest are appointed for life (usually as a reward for political, or other public, services) and cannot pass either their title or its privileges to their children. Formerly the main source of legislation, the Lords now functions largely as a review body for bills originating in the Commons.

The leader of the largest political group represented in the Commons becomes Prime Minister (nominally at the invitation of the monarch) and selects a government from party representatives in both chambers. The most senior of these — usually the heads of the major departments — form the Cabinet, which shapes the administration's policy.

Geography

By world standards, the UK is a lowland country, with few points over 4,000 feet (the highest hill — Ben Nevis, in western Scotland — reaches 4,406 feet), but there is a clear differentiation between the upland north and west and the lowland south and east. Ice has been the dominant force

1

shaping the landscape in both areas. Although there are no glaciers left in Britain (the last ones vanished some 10,000 years ago), their legacy remains in the deeply scoured valleys and sculpted mountains of Scotland, Wales and the English Lake District. Beyond, the gently undulating lowlands were formed by the debris which they deposited. Only the southernmost part of the country escaped their effect.

The present-day climate is temperate, with the prevailing winds blowing from the southwest over the warm Gulf Stream. The weather is greatly influenced by depressions moving east across the Atlantic, and no settlement is more than 60 miles from the sea, so there are few extremes of temperature, with summer maxima rarely rising above 92°F (32°C) and winter minima rarely falling below 14°F (-10°C). In London, for example, January temperatures fluctuate around 41°F (5°C) and July temperatures around 65°F (18°C).

Average annual rainfall is 60 inches in the mountainous west and north but less than 30 inches in the south and east. It is fairly regularly distributed throughout the year but March to June tend to be the driest months and September to January the wettest. During May to July (the months of longest daylight), the mean daily duration of sunshine varies from eight hours along the south coast of England to five hours in northern Scotland. From November until January, it averages one hour a day in the north and two hours in the south.

The Shaping of the Kingdom

The first human inhabitants of Britain were present at least 500,000 years ago, but understanding of settlement patterns begins only with the introduction of farming during the neolithic period (which developed from about 4,400 BC) and the arrival of the Celts about 2,200 BC. A fuller picture is available after the Roman invasion of 55 BC, largely because of the introduction of writing.

The Romans extended their control throughout England to Wales and the lowlands of Scotland, basing their authority in towns (some of which — Bath, York and London, for example — survive as modern cities). Their superior technology enabled them to maintain peace over most of the area for most of the time, and their extensive empire linked the economy of the British Isles to that of the rest of Europe.

The withdrawal of the legions in 409 AD was followed by a period of unrest. The Picts raided south of the Antonine Wall, which had been the northernmost of the Roman defences in Scotland, and the Celtic peoples of Ulster (which had escaped the Roman yoke) were making forays into the mainland. Seeking help to defend themselves, the Britons enlisted the aid of Angles, Saxons and Jutes from the North German Plain. These incomers, originally employed as mercenaries, gradually established permanent colonies and pushed the native Romano-Celts into the more remote regions. They warred amongst themselves, as new kingdoms based in the north (Northumbria), the English midlands (Mercia) and the south (Wessex) strove to achieve dominance. Unity was eventually achieved, partly by conquest and partly by a need to meet the challenge of the Vikings during the 10th century. By the turn of the millenium, the Wessex dynasty had established a wide-ranging authority over most of England.

England and Wales

In 1066, the Normans crossed the English Channel to Hastings — the last successful invasion of the British Isles. Patterns of land tenure changed radically, and French became the language of the aristocracy, transforming the Germanic tongues spoken by the Anglo-Saxons. Wales remained a Celtic stronghold but was far from united, with several Princes vying for supremacy. In 1282, Edward I launched a successful campaign to bring Wales under English rule and, despite continued nationalist feelings, epitomized in the rising led by Owain Glyndwr during the early 15th century, the overlordship was maintained. Acts of Union in 1536 and 1543 united England and Wales administratively, politically and legally.

England and Scotland

When the Romans arrived, most of Scotland was inhabited by Pictish peoples. They managed to keep the invaders south of the Rivers Clyde and Forth, but, in the sixth century, migrant Scots from Ulster were able to settle in what is now Argyll, giving their name to present-day Scotland. The two groups were united under Kenneth MacAlpin during the ninth century, effectively creating a Scottish kingdom. However, the powerful and expansionist Norman monarchy in England threatened Scottish independence during the Middle Ages and conflict was frequent, even though many Scottish nobles held lands and titles south of the border and the cultural influence of English society on the Scottish court was strong. At times of peace — and on occasion to secure peace — there were marriages between the royal families of the two realms, and, in 1603, the Crowns were united when Elizabeth I of England was succeeded by James VI of Scotland, her closest heir.

Even so, the countries remained politically separate, each with its own Parliament. Moreover, they followed separate social tracks, particularly in religious matters, with the Scots Presbyterians bitterly opposed to anything which smacked of the episcopacy adopted by the English. Inevitably, that put pressure on the monarchs, who frequently found themselves faced with conflicting demands from their two Parliaments, and, in 1707, Scotland was persuaded to give up its independence and seek a new identity in a political and economic union with its old enemy. A new Parliament was formed in London (or, more accurately, the old Parliament met, augmented by Scottish representatives), and Scotland retained its own systems of law, banking, church administration and education. The Union was strained during the reigns of George I and George II, when Jacobite risings attempted to restore the Stuarts to the throne, but it survived and continues.

England and Ireland

In 1169, Henry II of England launched an invasion of Ireland after acquiring overlordship of the island from Pope Adrian IV, who wanted to bring the Irish Church into full communion with Rome. Control was secured and land transferred to the Normans, but little direct authority was exercised until the Tudor Kings determined to assert their power. Several campaigns were waged against Irish insurgents during the reign of Elizabeth I, with the main focus of rebellion centering on the northern province of Ulster.

During the 17th century, the Crown adopted a deliberate policy of anglicization, transferring English and Scots settlers to the area, and, throughout the 1700s, that brought an uneasy peace to the island. But the nationalist sentiment still simmered and successive British governments were faced with the problem of achieving stability. In 1782, the Irish Parliament was given legislative independence, leaving the Crown as the only constitutional tie with the rest of the country, but Roman Catholics were excluded from that Parliament and proved unwilling to accept anything less than complete freedom. An abortive rebellion took place in 1798, and, in response, the Westminster Government prepared legislation which fully unified Great Britain and Ireland in 1801. It was a measure which failed to solve the problem. Throughout Queen Victoria's reign, the Irish Question was a seemingly constant matter of Parliamentary debate, and, in 1886, the Liberal Government introduced a Home Rule Bill designed to give Ireland the power to run its internal affairs while reserving control over external matters to Great Britain. The move failed and caused a political crisis.

A second Home Rule Bill was introduced in 1914 and was enacted as the Government of Ireland Act, but its implementation was prevented by the outbreak of the First World War and the threat of armed rebellion by the Protestant majority in Ulster. Eventually, in 1920, an attempt was made to establish two Parliaments, one in Dublin and one in Belfast. The measure proved unacceptable, and the following year Ireland gained full independence though the six counties of Ulster opted for continued association with Great Britain, giving the United Kingdom its present structure.

The Changing Economy

At the time of the union of the Scottish and English Parliaments in 1707, England was by far the most affluent of the British nations. Most wealth took the form of land, and the gently undulating plains of the east and south, coupled with mild temperatures and adequate rainfall, facilitated the growing of crops and the pasturage of animals. In Scotland, Wales and Ireland, the steep-sided hillslopes, thin soils, short growing season and high rainfall all militated against productive agricultural economies.

The great bulk of the land was owned by the nobility. The Normans had introduced a feudal system of tenure which essentially involved distribution of estates by the sovereign to the most powerful nobles in return for dues of military service. These estates were subdivided between lesser nobles on a similar basis so the bulk of the population — the tenant farmers who worked the soil or herded the sheep — owned few possessions and occupied their smallholdings only while they fulfilled their commitments to provide arms, a proportion of their harvest or other dues to their lord.

During the 17th century, the winds of change began to blow through the economy. Forced to maximize their incomes, landowners increasingly abandoned the open field system of agriculture and replaced it with a pattern of fields bounded by hedgerows and fences. That facilitated crop rotation, increased the efficiency of machinery and clearly defined ownership but also reduced employment and created a large class of landless peasants who drifted towards the towns.

Such industry as existed was mostly small scale (as in the case of iron production in Kent and Surrey) and focussed on the home rather than the factory (pottery making, for instance, was still carried out primarily as an adjunct to farming).

However, an increasing number of entrepreneurs became convinced of the advantages of a network of canals which would allow efficient carriage of large quantities of raw materials and finished products, opening up possibilities of large-scale regional and national markets. At the same time, businessmen such as Richard Arkwright were evolving a new technology which converted the textile industry from its reliance on the spinning wheels in peasant houses to mechanized production in mills which utilized water power. Together, these developments helped to mop up surplus agricultural labour and provided the foundations for the monumental changes which were to accompany an industrial revolution based on iron, coal and steam.

The techniques of iron production had been widely known in Britain since pre-Roman times, but output was limited by resources. Charcoal was needed to fuel the blast furnaces, which had prodigious appetites. One acre of woodland was required to provide enough charcoal to produce two tons of iron, so local forests were quickly cut down (particularly so because timber was also in demand for construction, shipbuilding and fuel). Inevitably, the furnaces looked further and further afield for their supplies, but, as the road network was poor, the price of those supplies was high and that was reflected in the cost of iron. An alternative source of fuel was clearly much needed, and coal was the obvious candidate because it was readily available in many of the areas which mined the iron ores. Unfortunately, coal contains sulphur, which combines with the iron and causes it to crumble when it is being worked in the forge.

The breakthrough came in 1709 when Abraham Darby adapted his furnace to employ coke rather than coal. Coke is obtained by heating coal in a confined space: in the process the sulphur is driven off, leaving a fuel which can be used to heat iron. During the 1750s, Darby's son (also called Abraham) adapted the technique further, developing a means of using coke to produce high quality wrought iron, and from then the industry expanded rapidly. Within a few decades, Britain had made the first iron rails, the first iron bridge, the first cast-iron steam engine, the first iron boat and the first metal-framed building.

It was, however, the application of steam to the manufacturing process which was to release industry from its tie to sites suitable for waterpower and allow it to move closer to its raw materials. Workable steam engines had been available since the early 18th century, but their piston-driven action had severe limitations. James Watt's refinements during the 1770s were to pave the way for large-scale steam-driven machines using rotary action and, therefore, for the creation of a sophisticated factory-based manufacturing economy.

The technology was revolutionary but inefficient, creating great demands for coal and iron in particular. These bulky products could not be transported in quantity on horse-drawn wagons travelling unsurfaced roads so factories located close to their sources of supply. South Wales, central Scotland and the flanks of the Pennine Hills in northern England became the foci of production. Ports flourished as well. Glasgow, Liverpool, Newcastle and Cardiff all grew on the basis of a commerce which imported raw materials and exported finished products.

The need to transport these commodities between the burgeoning cities led to investment in a railway system. The Stockton-to-Darlington line, opened in 1825 and designed to carry coal from the mines to the waterways, was an immediate success and was followed by others, so by the late 1840s the major centres of population throughout the country were linked to a rail network. As a result, concepts of distance altered radically. In 1750, the 450-mile journey from Edinburgh to London took 12 days; by 1830 it took less than 2. Over the same period, the time for the 100-mile journey from London to Birmingham dropped from 2 days to 12 hours.

By midcentury, the United Kingdom was the wealthiest and most powerful nation on the face of the Earth. Its empire had expanded around the globe to incorporate great territories in India, Africa, Australasia and the Americas as well as a host of small islands, which served as military bases and refuelling posts for British ships involved in worldwide commerce. There were enormous markets for its manufactured goods, widespread sources of raw materials and an inventiveness which enabled the country to maintain its position into the second half of the 1800s.

But there were signs of trouble to come. The American Civil War cut off supplies of cotton from the Lancashire textile industry in the 1860s, causing great unemployment and poverty. In Europe, other countries were adopting the new technologies, beginning to challenge British industrial supremacy and claiming an ever larger share of the world market. At home, the cause of free trade was having a bumpy political ride, and there was constant fear of insurrection in Ireland.

The Great War of 1914-19 brought matters to a head, dislocating the economy and changing social attitudes. The industrial world which emerged in the 1920s was very different from its prewar predecessor and the industries which suffered most were those on which the Industrial Revolution had been based — iron and steel, coal, shipbuilding, chemicals and textiles. Demand for coal declined, partly because new technologies increased the output of machinery and lowered the amount of fuel needed. The world trade recession also had an impact: less trade meant fewer ships plying the oceans and that, too, reduced the market for coal. Fewer ships also meant that shipbuilders found it harder and harder to get orders and that reduced the market for steel, adding to the decline of the beleaguered coal industry.

Cotton, too, was suffering, finding that the Asian producers were undercutting the price of goods made in Britain. And profits in transport plummeted as the tonnage of commodities available for carriage slumped. The cost of basic consumer goods rose steeply and, in the climate of insecurity, labour disputes became increasingly common.

The General Strike of 1926, when coal miners, electricity workers, steel makers, transport operatives and others withdrew their labour, indicated the depth of the problem in the areas on which Britain's 19th century power had been based. But matters would become worse, with the Wall Street crash of 1929 reflecting a worldwide economic crisis which was, for the most part, to continue through the 1930s, although some new industries (notably automobile production) did thrive on the fringes of cities such as Luton, Oxford and Coventry — freed by a national electricity grid from the need to locate on the coalfields. It was not, however, until the Second World War that there was a return to full employment.

Social Change

The economic transformation wrought by the Industrial Revolution inevitably brought social change in its wake. In the early 1700s, the axis of England's population lay east to west from London across chalk and limestone vales to the port of Bristol. Two hundred years later, it stretched from southeast to northwest — from London through Birmingham and Manchester to Liverpool. Men, women and children had forsaken the land in their thousands and streamed into the industrial areas on the coalfields, augmented by boatloads of immigrants from Ireland. In Scotland, rural economies crumbled as the population concentrated in the central belt (particularly on Clydeside), and Wales experienced an influx of migrants to the coal-mining towns of the southern valleys and to the coastal ports. (The 1851 census showed that nearly 90 per cent of Cardiff's residents had been born outside the city.)

The scale of urban population growth was greater than anything experienced before. In the 70 years from 1841, Birmingham's population grew from 202,000 to 840,000, Glasgow's from 287,000 to one million and London's from 2.2 to 7.3 million. Clearly, house building could not match in-migration, so newcomers were packed into hastily constructed terraced dwellings and lodgings.

For many, the Industrial Revolution brought opportunity and consequent prosperity, but for others the poverty was extreme. Skilled workers with regular jobs saw their living standards rise as wages increased and self-help groups, such as co-operative societies, brought the benefits of bulk buying power. But, for the unskilled working class, the experience was more likely to be one of subsistence wages, overcrowded homes, a poor diet and perpetual exposure to infectious disease. For much of the 19th century, about one quarter of the British population lived in squalor, and, not surprisingly in such a situation, life expectancies were low. A child born in London in 1841 could expect to live to the age of 36, in Manchester or Liverpool to the age of 26.

There were many influential figures who were concerned at the way society was moving and who made their views known. William Blake objected to the "dark satanic mills" which pockmarked "England's green and pleasant land", William Wordsworth fulminated against the coming of the railway to the Lake District (largely because it would bring the uneducated masses in its wake), William Morris maintained that beauty could flourish in an industrial wasteland and Ebenezer Howard visualized garden cities which would give every resident access to greenery.

From the 1840s, a number of charitable organizations began to make efforts to improve the quality of life for the poor, building homes for the 'industrious classes', but they did little more than chip away at the tip of the urban housing problem because working class people simply could not afford to pay economic rents (which, at that time, included a 5 per cent return to investors). Similarly, although attempts were made to raise health levels, the measures were constantly undermined by poor sanitation, inadequate diets and a lack of knowledge about the need for hygiene.

By the last few years of the century, there were signs of improvement — compulsory education was introduced in England and Wales in 1880, a series of Housing Acts from 1890 empowered local authorities to build homes for manual workers and, in 1900, the Labour Representation Committee was formed to promote the political interests of working people — but it was not until after the First World War that there was real change. In 1918, women gained the vote after more than half a century of campaigning and, in 1919, the government introduced state subsidies for residential properties built by local authorities.

These years after the war were difficult ones, however. The economic recession affected heavy industry, so, in the areas which had been the power houses of the industrial revolution, unemployment was high. In 1932, 44.6 per cent of the adult male population of Barnsley was out of work. In Port Talbot, the figure was 48.9 per cent and, in Merthyr Tydfil, 60.9 per cent. Whole communities relied on means-tested poor relief for subsistence.

The Special Areas Act of 1934 was the first of a series of measures introduced to reverse the trend and provide jobs in the worst hit regions but the jobs which materialized were in the southeast, particularly around London, so there was a continuing movement to the towns and cities in that part of the country as the labour force no longer required by the extractive and heavy manufacturing industries sought work.

Ironically, it was the Second World War which brought a return to full employment as males were drafted into the armed forces and women took over jobs on the land and in the factories. Moreover, the conflict was seen as a justified fight against tyranny and raised the morale of the nation, which took pride in the leadership of Winston Churchill at a time of great adversity.

Events since 1945

The world which emerged afterwards was a new world. The years of austerity during the 1920s and 1930s and the hardships of the Blitz and food rationing had forged a people who were determined not to return to the old ways.

Even in the bleakest days of the Second World War, preparations were being made for reconstruction. The Barlow Report (1940) called for the decentralization of industry from congested urban areas and for the redevelopment of regions heavily dependent on the declining industries — far-reaching recommendations which implied strong centralized planning control and led to the formation of the Ministry of Town and Country Planning in 1943. The Scott Report (1943) drew attention to the problems of the rural areas and, perhaps most importantly, the Beveridge Report (1942) propounded the belief that it was the Government's responsibility to care for its citizens "from the cradle to the grave".

The 1944 Education Act, which guaranteed high school places for all children, presaged the changes to follow after the victory over the Axis powers. To great surprise, the country rejected Churchill's Conservative Party at the 1945 general election, voting for a Labour Government led by Clement Attlee and committed to state control of industry, improvements in social services (notably health care and housing provision) and full employment. However, social aspirations had to be tempered by political realities. Britain was faced with the repayment of large loans granted by the United States during the War, and, although it gained a permanent seat on the United Nations Security Council, it faced a diminishing role in world affairs. The debacle at Suez in 1956 and the conversion of an Empire composed of colonies to a Commonwealth consisting of independent sovereign states were evidence of a changing world power balance. Loss of manufacturing markets to the economic might of a rebuilt Germany, a reorganized Japan and an increasingly dominant United States caused serious problems in traditional industries.

Attitudes, however, lagged behind political and economic change. The United Kingdom shunned membership of the Common Market (which bound six western European states into a single trading bloc in 1957) and insisted on the maintenance of an independent nuclear deterrent during the Cold War. It was not until the 1970s that the inevitable restructuring occurred. Edward Heath's government took the country into the European Community in 1973 and, following years of strife between management and trade unions, Margaret Thatcher set about a wholesale spring-cleaning of the economy in 1979.

The next 11 years witnessed great reductions in the level of support to ailing industries and regions, rates of unemployment unknown since the 1920s, the introduction of a self-help ethos to replace the reliance of the individual on state support, cuts in local authority spending, the privatization of state-owned businesses, greater financial accountability in the social services and increases in the cost of health care.

The policy was condemned by many as uncaring. Not even all Conservatives approved: Edward Heath and Margaret Thatcher became implacable opponents and Harold Macmillan likened the transfer of nationalized enterprizes into private hands to a selling-off of the family silver. Loved and hated in almost equal measure at home, Mrs Thatcher was much admired internationally (even in the Soviet Union) and developed a particularly close friendship with President Ronald Reagan of the United States. She had a clear idea of where she wanted to go, providing a leadership and determination which were much in evidence at the time of the Falklands War in 1982, when she masterminded the return of the islands to British hands after an Argentinian invasion. But, as the decade progressed, she became increasingly autocratic, treating senior colleagues much as an imperious headmistress might treat her schoolchildren, and, in the end, they rebelled, replacing her with the more mild-mannered John Major in 1990.

Major adopted a more conciliatory tone, placing greater emphasis on consensus both in Europe and at home. Nevertheless, the Thatcher legacy left the United Kingdom with its share of social and economic contradictions, notably wide regional gaps in affluence, employment levels and quality of life. But the labour problems which plagued industry during the 1970s are much less evident, consumer spending is increasing and all of the major political parties are committed to membership of a growing European Union. The shape of the country in the 21st century will depend on the extent to which stability is maintained and on the way in which government and people deal with growing issues of concern, notably the importance of the environment, the provision of jobs for young people, the role of the monarchy and the problems caused by an increasingly elderly society.

THE DICTIONARY

—A—

ABDICATION CRISIS. (See **EDWARD VIII**).

ABERDEEN, EARL OF. (See **GEORGE HAMILTON- GORDON**).

ABHORRERS. This was a term applied to **TORIES** who opposed attempts by the **COUNTRY PARTY** to force **CHARLES II** to call a **PARLIAMENT.** Those attempts, which took the form of petitions sent from each Parliamentary **CONSTITUENCY**, were abhorrent to reactionaries determined to defend the rights of the **MONARCH.** (See **DIVINE RIGHT OF KINGS**).

ABJURATION, OATH OF. There were two such oaths. One early form was taken as part of the **ABJURATION OF THE REALM.** A later form was imposed, during the **CIVIL WAR**, on **ROYALIST** Roman Catholics whose property had been sequestrated. It required denial of papal supremacy, transubstantiation and imagery. Then, after payment of a fine, the property was returned.

ABJURATION OF THE REALM. Criminals who had taken advantage of the right of **SANCTUARY**, or protection from the law as long as they remained in church or churchyard, could take the **OATH OF ABJURATION**, which was an alternative to **OUTLAW**ry. A coroner would hear an oath of confession to the crime by the accused, who renounced **ENGLAND** and left for exile.

ABORTION. Abortion became illegal early in the 19th century and, in 1861, the Offences Against the Person Act (see **ACT OF PARLIAMENT**) made those who terminated pregnancies liable to life imprisonment. By 1936, the Abortion Law Reform Association was pressing for legalization of properly supervized medical abortion. The Birkett Committee recommended that the law should be changed, but the **SECOND WORLD WAR** began before action could be taken. On 27 October 1967, an Abortion Act was passed by **PARLIAMENT** after a **PRIVATE MEMBER'S BILL** had been introduced by **LIBERAL PARTY** Leader David Steel. That act allowed women to have an abortion if two doctors confirmed that it was necessary on medical grounds. It ended the activities of back-street abortionists who had performed illegal terminations and was part of a liberalization of British law at a time when attitudes to behaviour were becoming more permissive (see **FAMILY PLANNING ACT; SEXUAL OFFENCES ACT**). The Human Fertilisation and Embryology Act (1990) introduced an upper limit of 24 weeks for most abortions.

ABOUKIR BAY, BATTLE OF. (See **HORATIO NELSON; BATTLE OF THE NILE**).

ABYSSINIAN CAMPAIGN, 1935-41. An attempt by Benito Mussolini to extend the Italian Empire led to the invasion of Abyssinia in 1935. At the time, Britain declined to support the opposition expressed by the **LEAGUE OF NATIONS** but the country was forced into action when the Italians attempted to secure British Somaliland in 1940. By 1941, British forces, with local nationalist support, had driven the enemy army out of the area and reinstated Haile Selassie as Emperor of Abyssinia.

ABYSSINIAN WAR, 1867-68. British forces under Lieutenant-General Robert Napier defeated Theodore, King of Abyssinia, at Magdala and rescued diplomats and civilians who had been held prisoner.

ACCESSION, TREATY OF, 22 January 1972. The treaty by which the United Kingdom joined the **EUROPEAN COMMUNITY (EC)** followed a period during which Charles de Gaulle, the French leader, had resisted British membership. After a national referendum had approved the terms (see **REFERENDA**), the treaty was signed by Prime Minister **EDWARD HEATH**.

ACRE, BATTLES OF. Three major battles occured at this site in modern Israel. 1191: the area was retaken from Saladin, after a long siege, by King **RICHARD I** during the Third **CRUSADE**. 1799: besieged by Napoleon's Egyptian army, the Turkish defenders were helped by the British navy and Napoleon was forced to withdraw. 1840: a British/Turkish/Austrian fleet removed Mehemed Ali from Acre and restored it, and Syria, to Turkey.

ACT OF PARLIAMENT. During the 14th century, it was common for **GENTRY** to petition **PARLIAMENT** for rulings in disputes or for authority to carry out certain activities. Over the years, these rulings became codified as statutes. Now, they form the laws of the realm and are the legislative basis of the **CONSTITUTION** and **GOVERNMENT**. Acts first appear in Parliament as proposals for legislation known as **BILL**s. These may be initiated by the government (in which case they are known as Public Bills), by individual Members of Parliament (see **PRIVATE MEMBER'S BILL**) or by interest groups such as local authorities. After debate in the **HOUSE OF COMMONS**, they go to the **HOUSE OF LORDS** and then, if they are accepted, to the **MONARCH**. Once it has received the **ROYAL ASSENT**, the measure has the status of an Act of Parliament and has legal force. There is no provision for judicial review. The first Act is said to be the **STATUTE OF MERTON**, passed in 1235.

ACT OF SETTLEMENT, 1652. This **ACT OF PARLIAMENT** was intended by **OLIVER CROMWELL** to exact retribution on those involved in the **IRISH REBELLION** of 1641 by sanctioning execution of the rebels, confiscation of their estates or **TRANSPORTATION** to County Clare or County Connaught.

ACT OF SETTLEMENT, 1662. This **ACT OF PARLIAMENT** specified eligibility for **PARISH** relief under the **POOR LAW**. Overseers of the parish were able to send paupers and vagrants back to their native parish and to refuse them relief. It was a much abused law which led to the creation of an unwanted, rootless poor and the ejection from the parish of anyone not a resident who may have become chargeable on the Poor Rate.

ACT OF SETTLEMENT, 1701. This **ACT OF PARLIAMENT** ensured that succession to the English throne was limited to those of the Anglican faith (see **CHURCH OF ENGLAND**) and that anyone converting to Catholicism or marrying a Catholic was automatically barred. It also prevented the **MONARCH** from leaving **ENGLAND** without the permission of **PARLIAMENT**, provided for Parliamentary approval of declarations of war, laid the foundations for the passing of the succession to the **HANOVERIANS** and gave Parliament additional powers to restrict the royal executive. As an insurance against popery, the Act was an important complement to the Bill of Rights, but, in addition, it established the supremacy of

Parliament in deciding the succession to the monarchy and the conditions under which the Crown could be held. As a result, the House of Hanover secured the throne of Great Britain in 1714, when King **GEORGE I** succeeded Queen **ANNE.**

ACT OF SUCCESSION. Three such **ACTS OF PARLIAMENT** changed the precedence of succession to the throne of **ENGLAND.** The Act of 1534 declared Mary, daughter of King **HENRY VIII** and **CATHERINE OF ARAGON,** illegitimate and established that the rightful succession would be through the children of Henry's marriage to **ANNE BOLEYN.** The Act of 1536 replaced them with the offspring of his union with **JANE SEYMOUR** and declared other children non-successors. The Act of 1544 established the order of precedence as Edward (later **EDWARD VI**), then Mary (later **MARY I**) and, finally, Elizabeth (later **ELIZABETH I**). (See **LADY JANE GREY**).

ACT OF SUPREMACY, 1534. This **ACT OF PARLIAMENT** made the **MONARCH,** not the Pope, Supreme Head of the **CHURCH OF ENGLAND.** It was one of a series of acts which finally severed **HENRY VIII**'s allegiance to Rome, establishing Protestant power in **ENGLAND.** Repealed by **MARY I** in 1554, it was reinstated by **ELIZABETH I** in 1559 (see **ACT OF SUPREMACY,** 1559).

ACT OF SUPREMACY, 1559. This **ACT OF PARLIAMENT** reinstated the earlier Act (**ACT OF SUPREMACY,** 1534) and established Queen **ELIZABETH I** as **SUPREME GOVERNOR** of the **CHURCH OF ENGLAND.** The alteration of the title from Head to Governor changed the sovereign's powers from personal ones to those of a **MONARCH** acting through **PARLIAMENT** and so lessened the direct involvement of the monarch in ecclesiastical affairs.

ACT OF UNIFORMITY. The four Acts of Uniformity were all intended to secure the position of **PARLIAMENT** over the doctrine and acts of worship in the **CHURCH OF ENGLAND.** That of 1549 ordered the exclusive use of the **BOOK OF COMMON PRAYER,** drafted by **THOMAS CRANMER,** in all churches, with the services in English rather than Latin. The second Act, in 1552, was similar but more radical. Denying the real presence of Christ's body in the Eucharist, it enforced the use of the second Book of Common Prayer and made penalties harsher for contravention. Both this and the earlier Act were repealed under Queen **MARY I.** The Act of

1559 restored acceptance of the real presence of Christ's body and blood at the Communion service and reimposed the Book of Common Prayer. The Act of Uniformity of 1662 enforced the use of the revised Book of Common Prayer and Thirty-Nine Articles and imposed an oath of nonresistance on clergy. About 2,000 clergy lost their positions for refusing to sign this, one of the elements of the **CLARENDON CODE.**

ACT OF UNION. There have been three important Acts of Union (see **ACT OF PARLIAMENT**). That of 1536 was given **ROYAL ASSENT** by King **HENRY VIII** and joined **ENGLAND** with **WALES** so that the Welsh became subject to English laws, with new **COUNTY** or **SHIRE** administrative areas on the English model, abolishing the Welsh Marches. It imposed English as the official language and marked a key point in the decline of Welsh culture (see **UNION OF ENGLAND AND WALES**).

The Act of 1707 formed the United Kingdom of Great Britain by uniting England and Wales with **SCOTLAND**, creating a single **PARLIAMENT** and State despite opposition in Scotland. A common coinage, **STERLING**, was adopted, and Scots MPs and peers joined the British Parliament. Strictly speaking, the legislation united the two countries as equal partners (the Scots retained their own legal system, for example). The present Queen is properly, therefore, **ELIZABETH II** of England but Elizabeth I of Scotland. (See **UNION OF PARLIAMENTS**).

The Act of 1800, inspired by Prime Minister **WILLIAM PITT THE YOUNGER**, brought **IRELAND** into the Union, with the Irish Church protected. (See **UNION OF GREAT BRITAIN AND IRELAND; UNION JACK**).

ADDINGTON, HENRY (1757-1844). **PRIME MINISTER** from 1801 until 1804, Addington was born in **LONDON** on 30 May 1757, the son of Anthony Addington (a physician). He was educated at Winchester College and **OXFORD** University then, in 1784, became Member of **PARLIAMENT** for Devizes, supporting the **TORIES'** cause, led by his friend **WILLIAM PITT THE YOUNGER**, the Prime Minister.

In 1789, he became **SPEAKER** of the **HOUSE OF COMMONS**, a post which he held for 12 years, and, when Pitt resigned in February 1801, Addington replaced him. Initially he was popular, especially after the signing of the Treaty of Amiens, which brought war with France to an end in 1802, but, when conflict broke out again in May of the following year, it quickly became apparent that he had no great ability as a leader in times of unrest. On 25 April 1804, he stepped down Pitt, an outspoken opponent of Addington's policies and a much more able politician during crises, replaced him. Addington, however, retained an influence in Parliament. He could command the support of some 50 MPs and, in January 1805, became **LORD PRESIDENT OF THE COUNCIL** in a **CABINET** led by Pitt. In July, he resigned again, this time to throw his weight behind the **OPPOSITION**, and, in February 1806, accepted the post of **LORD PRIVY SEAL** in the coalition Cabinet headed by **WILLIAM WYNDHAM GRENVILLE**.

In 1807, he withdrew his support from the **GOVERNMENT** once more because his **CHURCH OF ENGLAND** leanings would not allow him to be party to plans designed to give Roman Catholics and free churchmen the right to hold commissions in the armed forces. He returned to his former post as Lord President of the Council under **SPENCER PERCEVAL** in 1812, and, after Perceval's assassination in May, was made **HOME SECRETARY** by **ROBERT BANKS JENKINSON, EARL** of Liverpool and the new Prime Minister. He faced a difficult domestic situation with problems caused by high levels of unemployment, escalating prices and civil disorder fomented both by factory owners and by the **LUDDITES**. His response was to increase the powers of the local courts, make the organization of public meetings more difficult and curtail the circulation of political propaganda. Under increasing pressure from political opponents and worn out by the stresses of the job, he withdrew from office in 1822 but (primarily at the request of **GEORGE IV**) remained in the Cabinet until 1824, when he resigned in protest against recognition of the South American republics. For the next 20 years, he took little active part in politics although he continued to speak out against Catholic emancipation. He died at Richmond Park (London) on 15 February 1844.

ADDLED PARLIAMENT, 1614. Called to vote money and supplies to **JAMES VI** and I, this **PARLIAMENT** lasted only two months (5 April to 7 June) and failed to enact any legislation or grant any monies. The members refused to cooperate with the King (particularly over his proposed taxes), an indicator of the tensions between **CROWN** and Parliament prior to the **CIVIL WAR**.

ADMIRALTY. In the 13th century, the naval forces of the **CROWN** were administered by the Keepers of the King's Ships (the first was appointed in 1214) and, by the 16th century, a Navy Board had been established (1546) to oversee the fleet and ports. That Board was abolished in 1832 and, from then until 1964 (when it became part of the Ministry of Defence), the Board of Admiralty administered the **ROYAL NAVY**.

AETHELBALD (?-757). King of **MERCIA** from 716 until his death in 757, Aethelbald held all of the provinces south of the River Humber by 731 and furthered his territorial control over the next 25 years. He occupied Somerton in **WESSEX** in 733, held **LONDON** by the same year, made war on Northumbria in either 737 or 740 and attacked the Welsh in 743. Sometime between 740 and 757, he gained overlordship of Berkshire. He was generous in his gifts to the Church and was praised by missionaries from Germany for his fair but strong rule. In 757, he was murdered by his followers.

AETHELBERT I (?-616). King of **KENT** from 560 until 616, Aethelbert was responsible for the introduction of Christianity to south-east **ENGLAND**. Although not a Christian himself, he was married to Bertha, daughter of the King of Paris, who was a devout believer. That relationship undoubtedly helps explain the tolerant reception accorded by Aethelbert to **AUGUSTINE** and his small band of followers when they arrived at Thanet in the spring of 597, sent by Pope Gregory I to bring Christ to the heathen English. The King allowed them to live in **CANTERBURY**, where the first English cathedral was founded. The King later converted to Christianity himself. Aethelbert also issued the first code of **ANGLO-SAXON** laws, which established the legal position of the clergy. He died in 616.

AETHELFRITH (?-616). King of Northumbria, Aethelfrith succeeded his father (Aethelric) as King of Bernicia in 593 and later ruled Deira as a result of his marriage to Acha, daughter of King Aelli of Deira. Between 613 and his death in 616, he defeated the Britons at Chester and extended his territorial control to such an extent that the Britons of the Kingdom of Strathclyde became separated from the Britons in **WALES**.

AETHELRED I (?-871). King of **WESSEX** from 865 until 871, Aethelred succeeded his brother, Aethelbert, at the time when the Danes began their attempt to conquer **ENGLAND** (see **VIKINGS**). He offered support to Burgred of **MERCIA** against the invaders but the Danes declined to do battle and the Mercians made peace. In 870, the Danes invaded Wessex directly and Aethelred, with his brother **ALFRED THE GREAT**, attacked them at Reading but failed to repel them. The brothers won a major victory at the **BATTLE OF ASHDOWN** (in present-day Berkshire), when Aethelred refused to start fighting until after divine service, but were defeated at Basing and Meretun. After his death in 871, Aethelred was succeeded by Alfred the Great.

AETHELRED II (968?-1016). King of **ENGLAND** from 978 until 1016, Aethelred was known as 'The Unready' (a corruption of the Old English 'unraed', meaning 'evil counsel'). The son of King **EDGAR** and Queen Aelfthryth, he succeeded to the throne on the murder of **EDWARD THE MARTYR** — his half-brother — in 978, while still a child. The story of his reign, as told in the **ANGLO-SAXON CHRONICLE**, is one of incompetence, mismanagement and defeat by the Danes (see **VIKINGS**). The invaders were bought off in 991 and on later occasions, with the price increasing each time (the payment was known as **DANEGELD**). A great victory over the Scandinavians in 1002 brought retaliation the following year, when Sweyn led a major invasion. A further invasion occurred in 1009, and, by 1013, Sweyn was accepted as King. Aethelred fled to Normandy but was invited to return after Sweyn died in 1014. The invitation contained the condition that Aethelred's standards of kingship would improve, but he had little opportunity to satisfy his subjects. **CANUTE** (Sweyn's son) led attacks against him, and war was under way when Aethelred died in London on 23 April 1016. There is, however, another side to the story. Aethlred's reign was characterized by the production of large numbers of artistic and literary works. Also, Archbishop Wulfstan of **YORK** was responsible for the formulation of a series of laws on the King's behalf. Other evidence shows that, far from being a poor manager, Aethelred possessed a considerable degree of administrative and political skill.

AETHELSTAN (?-939). Aethelstan was the first **SAXON** king to have effective rule over the whole of **ENGLAND**. The son of **EDWARD THE ELDER**, he was crowned King of **MERCIA** when his father died in 924 and King of all the English the following year. In 927, he successfully attacked Northumbria and accepted the homage of other leaders, notably Howel of Dyfed, Owain of Gwent, Constantine of the Scots and Owain of Strathclyde. Between 931 and 935, he held a series of great courts at which he forced the Welsh to promise tribute and fixed the River Wye as the boundary between England and **WALES**. In 937, Owain of Strathclyde, Constantine and Olaf Guthfrithson (claimant to the throne of **YORK**) combined against him, invaded England and were humiliatingly defeated at the **BATTLE OF BRUNANBURH** in an engagement which writers of the period regarded as the major event of Aethelstan's reign. Aethelstan also influenced politics on the European mainland, marrying his sisters to continental rulers and bringing up continental princes at his own court. He made many gifts to churches, established a single currency throughout his realm and promulgated a series of laws designed to reduce corruption and theft. He died on 27 October 939.

AETHELWULF (?-858). Aethelwulf, King of **WESSEX** from 839 until 856, was the father of **ALFRED THE GREAT**. He spent most of his reign at war with the invading Danes, gaining a major victory at Aclea in Surrey in 851 (see **VIKINGS**). A deeply religious man, he freed one-tenth of his estates from taxes so that the dues could be paid to the Church and, in 855, made a pilgrimage to Rome along with Alfred. In 856, another son, Aethelbald, seized the Wessex throne and for the rest of his life Aethelwulf ruled only in the subkingdom of **KENT**, Surrey, Sussex and Essex.

AFGHAN WARS. During the 19th and early 20th centuries, a series of conflicts occurred in southern Asia between **BRITAIN** (intent on protecting India) and Russia (seeking to expand territorial influence), with both powers attempting to impose their will on Afghanistan. The first (1839-42) led to British victory and installation of a British-supported emir, despite badly directed actions. The second (1878-1881) occurred because the emir favoured the Russians; the British again installed a pro-British emir, then withdrew from Kabul. The third (May 1919) was created by an Afghan holy war (jihad) and invasion of India in an attempt to rid Afghanistan of colonial power. The **ROYAL AIR FORCE** bombing of Kabul and the taking of the Khyber Pass led to settlement, with Britain abandoning attempts to control the country, but there was sporadic guerilla activity for some time afterwards.

AFRICA, SCRAMBLE FOR. The African continent was explored by the British, French and Germans from the 1790s, with significant contributions to knowledge of the area coming from Richard Burton and John Speke (East Africa and Lake Tanganyika), Dixon Denham (Sahara), John and Richard Lander (River Niger), David Livingstone (Central Africa, River Congo, Victoria Falls and Zambezi River), Mungo Park (West Africa) and Henry Morton Stanley (who is primarily remembered because of his search for Livingstone). Territories acquired by the European powers were used for the **SLAVE TRADE** and other forms of exploitation as colonies. The Scramble for Africa began in earnest after the attempted partitioning of the Congo and Niger river basins at the **BERLIN CONFERENCE** in 1885, with Britain, Belgium, France, Germany, Italy, Portugal and Spain all determined to add to the lands they controlled. Britain claimed, for the **BRITISH EMPIRE**, Bechuanaland (now Botswana), British East Africa (now Uganda and Kenya), Gambia, Gold Coast (now Ghana), Nigeria, Northern Rhodesia (now Zambia), Nyasaland (now Malawi), Sierra Leone, South Africa and Southern Rhodesia (now Zimbabwe). However, after the **SECOND WORLD WAR**, the trend towards **DECOLONIZATION** gathered pace and most of the British possessions gained independence during the 1950s and 1960s, joining the **COMMONWEALTH OF NATIONS**. (See Map 3 on page xxvii).

AFRICAN COMPANY. Created by Royal Charter in 1660, the Company of Royal Adventurers Trading in Africa concerned itself mainly with the **SLAVE TRADE** and the **ASIENTO**, which it held from 1713 to 1750. It was abolished in 1827. A Royal Africa Company (known as the Guinea Company of Merchants) was established in 1672 and was abolished in 1821, when the **CROWN** took control of all territorial possessions in Africa.

AGINCOURT, BATTLE OF, 25 October 1415. During the **HUNDRED YEARS WAR**, a small force of about 6,000 English archers and men-at-arms, led by King **HENRY V**, was attempting to retreat to **CALAIS** for the winter but found its way blocked by an army of about 25,000 French troops. Henry, using his 4,950 English longbowmen to great effect, won a resounding victory in little over three hours, fuelling England's military prestige, making a hero of the King and beginning attempts to gain a foothold in France. English losses were c. 400 men killed (including the **DUKE OF YORK**) whereas the French dead numbered c. 8,000 (including the Constable of France, three dukes, 90 nobles and 1,560 knights — almost half the nobility of the country).

AGRICULTURAL REVOLUTION. Between about 1760 and 1843, innovations in agricultural methods and in landowning and farming practices led to changes which transformed the countryside. New techniques were introduced, organization improved and a commercially based system of marketing produce was established.

During the 18th century, population numbers were rising and markets for food were expanding. As the prices of farmers' goods rose, the incentive to innovate and increase productivity was intense. The **OPEN FIELD SYSTEM**, with its strip plots, was replaced in southern **ENGLAND** from about 1760 by **ENCLOSURE**s which, with more consolidated landholdings, allowed better use of the improved methods and technologies. The Norfolk System introduced a four-year rotation to improve fertility, and new machines included the seed drill and horse-drawn hoe of Jethro Tull and more efficient reapers, threshers and ploughs. Scientific stock breeding began, as with Thomas Coke of Holkham Hall and Robert Bakewell, who produced new strains of sheep and cattle. Developments in the use of root crops for fodder meant greater availability of meat in the winter months as stock could be retained all year. Estate owners like "Turnip" Viscount Townsend were avid supporters of the innovatory methods, which were disseminated through local agricultural societies, the writings of Arthur Young and even the patronage of King **GEORGE III**, popularly known as "Farmer George".

Not all historians agree on the nature and dates of the Revolution. Some place it earlier (from about 1560 to 1767) while others eschew the term altogether, arguing that there was a gradual process of 18th century agrarian change which should be seen in the context of wider social and economic evolution throughout Europe. There is also a case for identifying a Second Agricultural Revolution between about 1815 and 1850, when new ideas on drainage and animal husbandry were introduced. And some scholars claim there was a Third Agricultural Revolution, based on mechanization and the development of the internal combustion engine, from about 1914 to 1930. (See **SWING RIOTS**).

AIR TRANSPORT. Developed particularly after the **FIRST WORLD WAR**, Croydon Airport was the first international airport for **LONDON**, with an inaugural commercial flight to Paris in 1919 and Imperial Airways set up in 1924. After the **SECOND WORLD WAR**, the wartime and commercial aerodromes at Heathrow and Gatwick were expanded as the capital's principal airports. **BRITISH OVERSEAS AIRWAYS CORPORATION (BOAC)** launched its first jetliner service in 1952 and the first transatlantic jet service in 1958. **CONCORDE**, the first supersonic airliner (developed as a result of cooperation between the United Kingdom and France), first flew in 1969 and entered commercial service in 1975. Between 1980 and 1990, the number of passengers carried from British airports almost doubled from 42,664,600 to 77,408,200. Stansted Airport was selected as the Third London Airport after a long period of proposals, demonstrations and public enquiries. Also, London City Airport was built in the now closed Royal Docks in London for short take-off and landing (STOL) aircraft flying short-haul flights to European destinations. Even so, there was evidence of under-capacity, and calls were made in 1993 for additional capacity at Heathrow and Stansted. (See **BRITISH AIRWAYS [BA]; BRITISH EUROPEAN AIRWAYS [BEA]**).

ALAMEIN, BATTLE OF EL, 23 October-4 November 1942. This was the decisive battle of the **SECOND WORLD WAR** in the North African front. The British Eighth Army, commanded by Lieutenant-General **BERNARD MONTGOMERY**, defeated the German Afrika Corps under Field Marshal Erwin Rommel near Alexandria. The unusual, but effective, British strategy of moving infantry forward to clear a path for tanks was decisive even though torrential rain and lack of fuel slowed the pursuit and allowed Rommel to disengage. The victory led to the collapse of Axis forces in the region, with the Germans losing 3,000 dead and 27,900 taken prisoner.

ALBERT, PRINCE (1819-61). Prince Albert was husband to **QUEEN VICTORIA** and, during a marriage of 21 years, played a significant role in advising his wife on affairs of state. Born in Rosenau, Germany, on 26 August 1819, he was the second son of Ernest, Duke of **SAXE-COBURG GOTHA**, and Princess Louise of Saxe-Gotha- Altenburg. Christened Charles Augustus Albert Emmanuel, he was educated privately in Brussels and also at the University of Bonn. His marriage to Victoria, a first cousin, was planned by their uncle, Leopold I of Belgium. At the age of 17, he visited **ENGLAND** and was introduced to his future wife. They corresponded over the next three years and, the relationship flourishing, he returned to **LONDON** on 10 October 1839. On 15 October, Victoria proposed, and they were married on 10 February, 1840.

Albert was regarded with suspicion by many people — he was a foreigner and an intellectual — and although he won over a significant number of his critics as a result of his hard work, his obvious devotion to the Queen and his diligent attempts to learn about the political and economic issues which dominated debate in his adopted country, he never dispelled the unease completely. At first, Victoria was quite adamant that her husband should have no say in **GOVERNMENT** but, after some six months, on the advice of Prime Minister **LORD MELBOURNE**, he was permitted to view despatches, then to attend meetings between the Queen and her **MINISTERS**. His role grew, and, in succeeding years, she learned from Albert the need for order in her dealings with advisers, the advantages of the aristocratic intelligence service provided as the result of the intermarriage of royal families throughout Europe and the benefits of self-discipline and diligent attendance to papers and responsibilities.

On many occasions, Victoria took her husband's advice, to good effect. For example, in 1861, during the American Civil War, the US Government stopped the British ship *Trent* during its passage to England and abducted the two Confederate envoys who were on board. At that time, the **MONARCH** played a large part in Britain's dealings with foreign nations, and Victoria responded angrily. However, Albert persuaded her to tone down her reaction in order to give the United States room for manoeuvre and, as a result, conflict between the two countries was avoided. After his death, she continued to make decisions based on what she felt her husband would have done in the same situation.

Beyond the realms of politics, Albert took a particular interest in the **ROYAL HOUSEHOLD** and properties. By 1842, he had, in effect, become Victoria's Private Secretary. By 1844, he had completely reorganized the household and, by the 1850s, had enabled the Queen to pay off her father's debts, purchase a property on the Isle of Wight and buy Balmoral Castle, where they spent their happiest times together. Despite great opposition, he was the prime mover of the **GREAT EXHIBITION** of 1851, an effort which was successfully rewarded because the event created a surplus large enough to endow the South Kensington (now the Victoria and Albert) Museum.

In 1856, Victoria pointed out that her husband had no titular rank in the United Kingdom and, the following year, he was made Prince Consort. The couple had nine children, born between 1840 and 1857. In 1861, while visiting his eldest son at **CAMBRIDGE**, Albert contracted typhoid; complications followed and he died on 14 December. After his death, many memorials were erected in his honour, notably the Albert Memorial and the Albert Hall in west London.

He is also commemorated in the Order of Victoria and Albert and in the Albert Medal for gallantry in lifesaving, both of which were instituted by a Queen who was bereft by his death and spent three years in public mourning. When she died 40 years later, she was buried beside him at Frogmore, near **WINDSOR CASTLE**.

ALBUERA, BATTLE OF, 16 May 1811. This battle was fought between an Allied army of 35,000 men (including 9,000 British troops) and a French force of 24,000 during the **PENINSULAR WAR**. The Allies won but casualties were heavy, and included some 6,200 British soldiers.

ALDERMASTON MARCHES. These annual protest marches from Trafalgar Square (**LONDON**) to the Nuclear Weapons Establishment at Aldermaston in Berkshire (the site of Britain's research into the atomic bomb during the 1950s) were organized by the **CAMPAIGN FOR NUCLEAR DISARMAMENT (CND)** from 1958. At their height, they attracted thousands of participants, but numbers declined after the signing of the nuclear test ban treaty by the United Kingdom, the Soviet Union and the United States of America in 1963.

ALFRED THE GREAT (849-99). Alfred is best known as the king who was admonished by a peasant woman for letting her cakes burn (the story dates from the 11th century), but he has more solid claims to a place in history as the conqueror of the invading Danes (see **VIKINGS**) and through his contributions to law and literature. Born at Wantage, he was the son of King **AETHELWULF** of **WESSEX** and Queen Osburh. He became King in 871, succeeding his brother **AETHELRED I** at a time when the Scandinavians were attacking his territories from the north and having to buy the invaders off with a substantial tribute. In 875, hostilities resumed, and Arthur gained victories both on land and at sea, but, in 878, the Danes captured his palace at Chippenham and he retreated to the relative safety of the Somerset marshes. Gathering a force from the surrounding shires, he emerged after seven weeks and besieged King Guthrum of Denmark at the **BATTLE OF EDINGTON** in Wiltshire. After a two-week siege, Guthrum capitulated, promising, under the terms of the Treaty of Chippenham, to withdraw from Wessex and be baptized as a Christian.

That victory was the beginning of the reconquest of the English territories taken by the Vikings. In 886, Arthur captured **LONDON** (which had been in Danish hands since 872) and placed it under the control of Aethelred, his future son-in-law. A further treaty with Guthrum, signed sometime after that success, enlarged the area he controlled and redefined the **DANELAW** (the area of Danish sovereignty) as the lands north and east of a line from London to Chester. The Scandinavians made a last attempt to invade in 892, but were repulsed and retreated to France in 896.

In establishing peace within his kingdom, Arthur developed the **BURGhal** system, reorganizing the army and defending his territories with a series of fortifications, regularly maintained and garrisoned. He codified new laws for his subjects after studying the Book of Exodus and the practices of other English kings, introducing regulations not previously known (such as a definition of the right to **SANCTUARY** and limitations to blood feud). Together, the military reforms and the legal system helped to restore the internal law and order which had been disrupted during the Danish occupation. The peace also allowed the King to promote education and scholarship. He translated several works from Latin into English, brought learned men from the European mainland and arranged that children of all social ranks at his court should be taught to read. He died on 26 October 899 and was buried at Winchester, the capital of Wessex.

ALLIANCE, THE. In September 1981, the **LIBERAL PARTY** and the **SOCIAL DEMOCRATIC PARTY (SDP)** formed an alliance to work with the same platform of policies and share out the **PARLIAMENTary CONSTITUENCIES** between them in order to increase their chances in national elections. In the 1983 **GENERAL ELECTION**, the alliance polled nearly as many votes as the **LABOUR PARTY**. That success formed the basis for the eventual merger of the two parties in 1988 as the **SOCIAL AND LIBERAL DEMOCRATIC PARTY (SDP)**, which, in 1989, became the **LIBERAL DEMOCRATIC PARTY (LDP)**.

ALMA, BATTLE OF, 20 September 1854. The first major conflict of the **CRIMEAN WAR**, this battle near the Alma River resulted in a decisive victory for Anglo-French-Turkish forces — numbering 26,000 men — over a Russian army of 35,000. The Russians were blocking the way to Sebastopol, and defeat would have meant withdrawal for the allies.

ALNWICK, BATTLES OF. There have been two major battles at

Alnwick, located in north east England near the border with Scotland.

13 November 1093: An English army defeated a Scots force, under Malcolm III, after seizing Westmorland and Cumberland.

13 June 1174: The English overcame a Scots invasion, led by King William I (the Lion), in support of a rebellion against King **HENRY II**.

AMERICAN REVOLUTION. (See **AMERICAN WAR OF INDE-PENDENCE**).

AMERICAN REVOLUTIONARY WAR (See **ANGLO- AMERICAN WAR 1812-14**).

AMERICAN WAR OF INDEPENDENCE, 1775-83. This war is still referred to in many Anglocentric texts as the American Revolution or the American Rebellion. During the 1770s, Britain's 13 colonies in North America were important markets, taking upwards of 25 per cent of the exports from the mother country. Also, the doctrine of **MERCANTILISM** strongly influenced **GOVERNMENT**s of the period, which created subservient colonial territories existing largely to provide raw materials for Britain and to take its manufactured goods. Discontent inevitably grew, fuelled by the **NAVIGATION ACTS** (which restricted colonial trade to British ships), the 1764 Sugar Tax, the 1765 Mutiny Act (which forced the colonies to pay for the British army in the region) and the 1765 **STAMP ACT** (which taxed newspapers, playing cards and legal documents) (see **ACT OF PARLIAMENT**). This last provoked the "no taxation without representation" cry, with its references to **MAGNA CARTA** and **HOUSE OF COMMONS** principles.

The State Government of Massachusetts led a boycott of British goods, only to be suspended, occasioning the Boston Massacre and the Boston Tea Party, when tea destined for Britain was thrown into the harbour. Prime Minister **FREDERICK NORTH**, failing to appreciate the seriousness of the protest, responded with the **INTOLERABLE ACTS** (1774), which merely fanned the flames of discontent. Armed clashes at Lexington and Bunker Hill in 1775 (both over control of Boston) brought British victories, but the heavy loss of manpower by the loyalists encouraged further action from the colonists. The surrender of the government forces at the Battle of Saratoga in 1777 led France, Holland and Spain to enter the conflict on the side of the rebels — a crucial development because Britain thereby lost its naval supremacy. An audacious attack at sea off Flamborough Head (in northeast England) by the Scots-born American Captain John Paul Jones, on 23 September 1779, led to the humiliation of a surrender by a British warship in British waters, and General Charles Cornwallis eventually conceded victory to the rebels at the Battle of Yorktown in October 1781. The **TREATY OF VERSAILLES**, signed on 3 September 1783, gave independent status to the colonies, while Spain regained Florida and ceded Louisiana to France. Britain retained rights of navigation on the Mississippi.

Britain was relatively weak at the time as a result of inefficient war leadership from a government which allocated too few forces to the dispute in the colonies, an overstretched navy committed also to India, Europe and the West Indies, a military system not attuned to the guerilla tactics of the colonists, the heavy use of weakly motivated German mercenary troops and the difficulties of waging war at great distance from home. Some scholars believe, however, that the loss of the American territories may have influenced Britain's move towards industrialization and led to the growth of democratic ideals in political life.

ANDREW, PRINCE (1960-). The second son and third child of Queen **ELIZABETH II** and **PHILIP, DUKE** of Edinburgh, the Prince was born in **BUCKINGHAM PALACE** on 19 February 1960 and christened Andrew Albert Christian Edward. He was educated at Gordonstoun School, Lakefield College (Ontario, Canada) and the Royal Naval College Dartmouth before joining the Royal Marines and training as a helicopter pilot. During the **FALKLANDS WAR**, he was based on HMS *Invincible* in the south Atlantic and, since 1989, has been Colonel-in-Chief of the Staffordshire Regiment. The tabloid press did much to create the impression of a fun-loving playboy with a string of girlfriends but, on 23 July 1986, he married Sarah Ferguson (daughter of Major and Mrs Ronald Ferguson) in Westminster Abbey and was created Baron Killyleagh, Earl of Inverness and **DUKE OF YORK**. The couple had two daughters Princess Beatrice Elizabeth Mary (born on 8 August 1988) and Princess Eugenie Victoria Helena (born on 23 March 1990). However, there were increasingly frequent rumours that the relationship was under strain and, on 20 and 21 August 1992, the *Daily Mirror* published photographs, taken clandestinely in the south of France, which showed the Duchess enjoying herself in the company of Mr John Brian, her American friend and financial adviser. On 19 March of the following year, Buckingham Palace announced that the Yorks were to separate, and, on 17 April 1996, divorce proceedings were initiated.

ANGEVINS. (See **PLANTAGENETS**).

ANGLES. These peoples of German origin came to Britain in the 4th and 5th centuries, possibly as auxiliaries in the **ROMAN** army. They settled mainly in northern and eastern **ENGLAND**, giving their name to the country and to the region of **EAST ANGLIA**. (See **ANGLO-SAXONS**).

ANGLO-AMERICAN WAR, 1812-14. This conflict is also referred to as the War of 1812. During the **NAPOLEONIC WARS,** Britain responded to the **CONTINENTAL SYSTEM** by blockading French ports and searching merchant ships travelling to France. The United States of America maintained that it had the right to trade without such hindrance and declared war on Britain on 19 June 1812. It also passed the Non-Intercourse Act to restrict trade with the United Kingdom and invaded Upper Canada (now Ontario), which was an area considered ripe for US expansion and where American leaders resented the British presence. The United States was victorious at York (Toronto) in April 1813 and, during the same year, established control of Lake Erie. Victories at Chippewa (Niagara) on 5 July 1814, Lundy's Lane on 25 July and Lake Champlain on 11 September heightened morale still further.

However, the end of the **PENINSULAR WAR** allowed Britain to release more troops for North America. These attacked Chesapeake Bay and burned public buildings in Washington, DC. (In the process of rebuilding, the President's home was whitewashed and named the White House.) During fighting at Baltimore, Francis Scott Key composed *The Star Spangled Banner*, now the US national anthem. At sea, American vessels inflicted heavy damage on enemy ships, but, even so, Britain's vastly superior navy controlled entry to US ports. Moreover, the United Empire Loyalists in Upper Canada remained loyal to the British **CROWN** and the American sloop *Argus* was captured in the English Channel after having attacked shipping around the coast of Britain. The war concluded with the Treaty of Ghent on 24 December 1814, when both sides declared hostilities at an end and the United States accepted the existing boundary with British Canada. (A Boundary Commission was established to settle details in disputed areas.) Coupled with the end of the Napoleonic Wars, the negotiations allowed Britain to lift the shipping blockade which had started the dispute (though there was an unsuccessful British attack on New Orleans in January 1815 before news of the peace treaty had reached America). It is argued by some authorities that the Anglo-American War and the Napoleonic Wars both helped to stimulate Britain's iron industry but adversely affected its **COTTON INDUSTRY**, which had, till then, relied on American supplies.

ANGLO-FRENCH TREATY, 1786. This trade agreement reduced French import duties on the products of the British **WOOL INDUSTRY** and **COTTON INDUSTRY** to 12 per cent, with a reciprocal arrangement for French imports to Britain. At the time, British manufactured goods of this kind were of better quality, yet cheaper than, French goods so the Treaty helped to stimulate industry in the United Kingdom during the **INDUSTRIAL REVOLUTION**.

ANGLO-GERMAN AGREEMENT, November 1899. This agreement settled rival claims to colonies in the Pacific, with Britain renouncing any right to Samoa (islands shared between Germany and the USA) in return for greater sovereignty over Tonga and the Solomon Islands. The accord was precipitated by Britain's engulfment in the **BOER WAR** and a desire to reduce tension with Germany.

ANGLO-GERMAN NAVAL AGREEMENT, 18 June 1935. Under this agreement, Germany undertook to build warships only up to 35 per cent of Britain's strength, with submarines up to 45 per cent. The arrangement was contrary to the provisions of the **TREATY OF VERSAILLES**, angered the French and was taken by Hitler as another sign of British weakness in the age of **APPEASEMENT**.

ANGLO-JAPANESE ALLIANCE, 30 January 1902. Originally designed as a defence treaty intended to reinforce British interests in China and limit Russian influence in the Far East, the Alliance was widened in 1905 and 1911 to protect British territories in India and to ensure that Japan joined the Allied side in the **FIRST WORLD WAR**. It was abrogated in 1921.

ANGLO-POLISH ALLIANCE, 25 August 1939. This agreement formalized arrangements for British military assistance to Poland if its frontiers were threatened and provided the justification for the United Kingdom's declaration of war on Germany after Hitler invaded the country on 1 September 1939. The alliance was drawn up because **NEVILLE CHAMBERLAIN** was anxious to move away from the failed **APPEASEMENT** policy and establish British opposition to German aggression.

ANGLO-RUSSIAN ENTENTE, 31 August 1907. Following rivalry between Britain and Russia in the **AFGHAN WARS**, this accord mirrored the **ENTENTE CORDIALE** of 1904 and was intended to remove all causes of misunderstanding between the two powers, particularly in Afghanistan, Tibet and Persia. In practice, it was one element in the development of political allegiances during the years prior to the **FIRST WORLD WAR** and a component of the **EAST OF SUEZ** aspect of British foreign policy.

ANGLO-SAXON CHRONICLE. This definitive history of the **ANGLO-SAXON** period was probably prepared by monks between c. 891 and 1154 and tells the story of those Germanic peoples from the time of their migration to the British Isles in the late fifth century until the **NORMANS** arrived in 1066. Possibly commissioned by **ALFRED THE GREAT**, the content is based on earlier texts (including Bede's *Ecclesiastical History of the English Nation*), folktales, lists of kings and other sources. A number of versions circulated amongst religious houses, where monks added details of important contemporary events, so copies vary in detail. Seven manuscripts survive, six in Old English and one in Latin (five are held by the **BRITISH MUSEUM**, one by the Bodleian Library [**OXFORD**] and one by Corpus Christi College [**CAMBRIDGE**]).

ANGLO-SAXONS. The **ANGLO-SAXON CHRONICLE** details the events of the period between c. 450 and 1066 when Britain was invaded and settled by **ANGLES**, **SAXONS** and **JUTES**, who collectively, by the end of the sixth century, were known as Anglo-Saxons. They pushed the native **CELTS** to the periphery of the British Isles, fought the **VIKINGS** for control of **ENGLAND** and established strong kingdoms and government in many areas, introducing a network of administrative law. They eventually succumbed to the superior strength of the **NORMANS** during the second half of the 11th century. (See **AETHELBALD; AETHELBERT I; AETHEL-FRITH; AETHELRED I; AETHELRED II; AETHELSTAN; AETHELWULF; ALFRED THE GREAT; BATTLE OF BRUNANBURH; BATTLE OF EDINGTON; BURG; EADRED; EADWIG;**

EDGAR; EDMUND I; EDMUND II; EDWARD THE CON-
FESSOR; EDWARD THE ELDER; EDWARD THE MAR-
TYR; HAROLD I; HAROLD II; HUNDRED; KENT;
MERCIA; SHERIFF; SHIRE; WESSEX; WITAN).

ANGLO-SOVIET-IRANIAN TREATY, 29 January 1942. Following
the British and Soviet occupation of Iran in 1941 to prevent Nazi
operations there, this treaty was drawn up to legitimize the presence of the two powers and guarantee Iranian independence. The
United Kingdom and the USSR were to withdraw six months after
the end of the **SECOND WORLD WAR,** but Soviet slowness to
do so resulted in heightened Cold War tensions during the late
1940s.

ANJOU, HOUSE OF. (See **PLANTAGENETS**).

ANNE (1665-1714). Queen Anne reigned during a critical period of Brit-
ish history which included the union of the Scottish and English
PARLIAMENTs, making her the first **MONARCH** to rule
GREAT BRITAIN as one country (see **TREATY OF UNION**).
She was born on 6 February 1665, the second daughter of James,
DUKE OF YORK (later **JAMES VII** and **II**), and Anne Hyde,
daughter of the Earl of Clarendon. On her twentieth birthday, she
married Prince George, the brother of King Christian V of Denmark.
A strict Protestant, she supported William of Orange (later
WILLIAM I), her brother-in-law, in the revolt which overthrew her
Roman Catholic father in 1688 and assumed the throne on William's
death in 1702. She proved to be a weak ruler, hesitant in her attempts to satisfy the conflicting claims of her religion, her concept
of duty to her country, her advisers and her friends. Ill-health, ten
miscarriages and the deaths of her five children all added to her difficulties. As a result, Parliament gained power at the expense of the
CROWN, and her reign was marked by intrigue and political tension. But science and literature flourished (though Anne was interested in neither), the **BRITISH EMPIRE** expanded and military
victories of great import (including the **BATTLE OF BLENHEIM**)
were recorded. And, in her last act as Queen, she secured the Protestant succession to the throne. She died on 1 August 1714, the last
of the **STUART** monarchs.

ANNE, PRINCESS (1950-). The second child and only daughter of
Queen **ELIZABETH II** and **PRINCE PHILIP**, the Princess was

born in Clarence House (**LONDON**) on 15 August 1950 and christened Anne Elizabeth Alice Louise. She was educated at Benenden School in **KENT** and joined her parents in many of their public engagements before developing her own schedule of duties. An accomplished horsewoman, she was a member of the British equestrian team in the early 1970s, winning a silver medal in the European Three-Day Individual Event in 1971 (the year in which she was voted **BRITISH BROADCASTING CORPORATION [BBC]** Television Sports Personality of the Year) and representing the United Kingdom at the 1976 Olympic Games in Montreal.

She met her first husband, **MARK PHILLIPS**, through a common interest in equestrian sports. The couple were married on 14 November 1973 and had two children — Peter Mark Andrew (born on 15 November 1977) and Zara Anne Elizabeth (born on 15 May 1981). However, the press carried increasingly frequent hints of friction during the 1980s, and, in 1989, **BUCKINGHAM PALACE** announced a separation. The Princess gained a divorce at an uncontested action on 23 April 1992 and, on 12 December of the same year, married Commander Timothy Laurence, RN, a former royal equerry. The ceremony was held in Crathie Church, near Balmoral Castle (Aberdeenshire), because the Church of Scotland has a more charitable policy towards the remarriage of divorcees than does the **CHURCH OF ENGLAND**.

As a young woman, the Princess earned a reputation for short temper and brusqueness, particularly in her dealings with the media, but more recently her untiring work for charity has earned her great respect and she has become one of the most popular members of the Royal Family. Much of her effort is unpublicized and contrasts with what she reportedly regards as the rather tacky publicity engineered by her sisters-in-law, **PRINCESS DIANA** and the Duchess of York (see **PRINCE ANDREW**). In particular, she has visited many Third World countries as President of the Save the Children Fund and promoted the organization's activities. In recognition of her involvement with that and other bodies, she was granted the title of **PRINCESS ROYAL** by the Queen in 1987. Princess Anne has also been President of the British Olympic Association and, in 1981, replaced the **QUEEN MOTHER** as Chancellor of the University of London. In addition, she is Patron of the Scottish Rugby Union, attends many of the international matches and knows regular players well. She has earned much affection in **SCOTLAND** because she knows the words of the somewhat nationalist anthem *Flower of Scotland* and joins in the singing before the start of each game.

ANNE OF CLEVES (1515-57). The fourth wife of **HENRY VIII**, Anne was born on 22 September 1515, the second daughter of John, Duke of Cleves (on the Dutch/German border), and his wife, Mary. Her brief union with the English King was a purely political matter. Henry was afraid that the Roman Catholic powers in Europe would combine against him and was advised by **THOMAS CROMWELL** to ally with the German Lutherans. The marriage to Anne, on 6 January 1540, was part of the political negotiations, but, in the end, the Lutherans rejected the overtures. It became clear, also, that the Catholic powers had no intention of mounting a crusade against **ENGLAND**. Henry saw little to please him in the meek, gentle Queen who could not speak English, and, with no political capital to be gained by sustaining the arrangement,**PARLIAMENT** annulled the marriage on 9 July. Granted an annuity, Anne stayed on in England until her death at Chelsea on 16 July 1557.

ANNE OF DENMARK (1574-1619). The daughter of Frederick II of Norway and Sweden and of Queen Sophia, Anne was the wife of King **JAMES VI** and **I**. She was born on 12 December 1574 and married to the King by proxy on 20 August 1589. The alliance brought no dowry but recognition of Scottish claims to the Orkney Islands and Shetland Islands and was, in part, James's gesture of independence against **ELIZABETH I**. When, in 1603, he became King of **ENGLAND** as well as **SCOTLAND** (see **UNION OF THE CROWNS**), James moved court to **LONDON** and his Queen went with him. The Scottish Calvinists had never approved of Anne's lighthearted approach to the world so London provided her with a more relaxed environment. She showed little interest in politics but spent much time and money on entertainment, dress and building. Anne died on 2 March 1619 after a lengthy illness.

ANTI-CORN LAW LEAGUE. Before the rise of the **COAL** industry and manufacturing during the **INDUSTRIAL REVOLUTION**, the cost of agricultural produce — and particularly of such basic staples as wheat, oats and barley — was an important political issue. Home producers had been protected by legislation from about 1660 and, in 1815, **PARLIAMENT** continued that policy by passing a Corn Law which prohibited wheat imports to Britain unless the price of domestic wheat reached 80 shillings a quarter bushel. That event inaugurated a protectionist period which aroused vehement opposition amongst commercial interests, employers, manufacturers and working class leaders who advocated **FREE TRADE**. As a concession, an **ACT OF PARLIAMENT** in 1828 introduced a sliding scale relating import duties to domestic prices, but the measure failed to assuage the anger of either producers or consumers as food became increasingly expensive.

The Anti-Corn Law League was set up at **MANCHESTER** in 1839, under the leadership of cotton manufacturer Richard Cobden (a cotton manufacturer) and **JOHN BRIGHT** (an MP and ardent supporter of free trade), to coordinate opposition to the hated Corn Laws and to advocate free trade. It employed a variety of techniques (including canvassing at elections) to disseminate its propaganda, resulting in much popular support. One of the first real national reform movements in Britain, it was so successful that, in 1842, Prime Minister **ROBERT PEEL** introduced new sliding scales to regulate trade in corn and ameliorate the worst price effects of the laws.

The Corn Laws were finally repealed in 1846, bringing an end to agricultural protectionism, signalling the ascendancy of free-trade principles and marking a decisive shift in the balance of political power towards middle-class opposition to the establishment. British agriculture entered a Golden Age which lasted until the importation of cheap American grain brought leaner times in 1873. (See **JOHN RUSSELL**).

APPEASEMENT. Prime Minister **NEVILLE CHAMBERLAIN** pursued an appeasement policy between 1937 and 1939, trying to halt German and Italian expansion and avert war through negotiation and concessions to Adolf Hitler and Benito Mussolini rather than by threat of force of arms. It culminated in the **MUNICH AGREEMENT** of September 1938, when Chamberlain, believing he had secured a nonaggression pact with Hitler, returned to **LONDON** and declared that he had won "peace for our time". As part of the bargain, Britain acquiesced to the Anchluss (the union of Germany and Austria) and the acquisition of the Sudetenland by Germany. The agreement was much discredited because it was soon followed by the German invasion of Czechoslovakia (March 1939) and Poland (September 1939) and by the start of the **SECOND WORLD WAR**, though some writers claim that it did give Britain extra time to rearm during a period in which the country was militarily weak.

Until about 1960, the appeasement policy was generally regarded as immoral and cowardly in the face of rising German aggression, but, since A. J. P. Taylor's book *Origins of the Second World War* was published in 1961, more works have sought to rehabilitate and explain the approach as a rational and understandable reaction to economic, political and strategic factors in a period when even the **TREATY OF VERSAILLES** was increasingly considered as unfair to Germany. These less dismissive studies point out that the British economy was in dire straits in the 1930s, that the USA had adopted an isolationist stance and that Britain could not afford military conflict at the time. (See **ANGLO-GERMAN NAVAL AGREEMENT**).

ARCADIA CONFERENCE, 22 December 1941-14 January 1942. This meeting between Britain (represented by **WINSTON CHURCHILL**) and the United States, in Washington, DC, aimed to secure continued US support for the United Kingdom during the **SECOND WORLD WAR** and, particularly in view of the Japanese attack on Pearl Harbor, to ensure that defeat for Germany in Europe took priority over operations in the Pacific. Churchill gained valuable support for Britain from the United States of America at a crucial period in the war.

ARCHBISHOP OF CANTERBURY. The archbishop is the clerical head of the **CHURCH OF ENGLAND**. The first incumbent was **ST AUGUSTINE OF CANTERBURY** and the current occupant of the post is **GEORGE LEONARD CAREY**. (See **THOMAS BECKET; THOMAS CRANMER; WILLIAM LAUD; ROBERT RUNCIE**).

ARCOS RAID, 12 May 1927. Amidst the "Reds under the bed" hysteria which followed the **GENERAL STRIKE**, the offices of Arcos Ltd, a Russian trading company based in Moorgate, **LONDON**, were raided in order to secure evidence of alleged subversive activities by the firm, which shared accommodation with a Soviet trade delegation. Nothing was proved, but diplomatic relations with the USSR were cut to justify the event.

ARKWRIGHT, RICHARD (1732-92). Arkwright has a claim to be considered one of the founding fathers of the **INDUSTRIAL REVOLUTION** through his invention of machinery which helped make the spinning of cotton yarn a factory industry (see **COTTON INDUSTRY**). Born in Preston on 23 December 1732, he trained as a barber and wigmaker but, despite a very limited formal education, interested himself in much wider matters. In 1767, he began work on the design of a new spinning machine and patented his invention in 1769. It was suitable only for the final stages of the production process but later adaptations made it possible to carry out other elements of yarn-making mechanically. In 1775, he patented a machine which combined carding, roving and spinning. In practice, few of the basic ideas were original so the 1775 patent was challenged then revoked in 1785. Arkwright's genius lay not in the development of fundamental principles but in his ability to take the theories of others and apply them to the development of technologies which would work successfully. Moreover, he had the business acumen to convert the production of cotton yarn from a cottage industry based on the traditional spinning wheel to a large-scale enterprize in factories which used water power and a skilled labour force. Other entrepreneurs followed his example and Lancashire developed as a major focus of the world textile industry in the 19th century, importing cotton from the Deep South of the United States. Arkwright was knighted in 1786 and died at Cromford on 3 August 1792, an extremely rich man.

ARMISTICE DAY, 11 November 1918. In 1918, at the 11th hour of the 11th day of the 11th month, the hostilities of the **FIRST WORLD WAR** ceased after 1,567 days of conflict and the loss of at least 908,371 lives. Prime Minister **DAVID LLOYD GEORGE** remarked that "Thus came to an end the cruellest and most terrible war. . . I hope we may say that, on this fateful morning, came to an end all wars". Every year thereafter, 11 November was celebrated as Poppy Day, deriving its name from the poppies which flowered on the battlefields of Flanders, with two minutes' silence in memory of the dead observed at 11 am. Since the **SECOND WORLD WAR**, the Sunday nearest to Armistice Day has been recognized as Remembrance Sunday, with political, civic and religious leaders laying wreaths and attending commemoration services for those who died in both conflicts.

ARMSTRONG-JONES, ANTONY CHARLES ROBERT(1930-). The first husband of **PRINCESS MARGARET**, Antony Armstrong-Jones was born in **LONDON** on 7 March 1930, the son of Mr and Mrs Ronald Armstrong-Jones. He was educated at Eton College and at **CAMBRIDGE** University, where he coxed the winning boat race crew in 1950. On 6 May 1960, he married Princess Margaret and, the following year, was created Earl of Snowdon. The couple had two children — David Albert Charles (Viscount Linley), who was born on 3 November 1961, and Lady Sarah Frances Elizabeth, born on 1 May 1964 — but the marriage ran into difficulties and was dissolved in 1978. Shortly afterwards, Lord Snowdon married Lucy Lindsay-Hogg, by whom he has one daughter.

One of Britain's leading photographers, he began work as a freelance in 1951 and developed a reputation for versatility and quality. He was appointed official court photographer in 1958 and joined the staff of the Council of International Design in 1961, continuing as a consultant until 1987. From 1961 until 1987, he was Editorial Adviser to *Design Magazine* and, from 1962 until 1990, was Artistic Adviser to Sunday Times Publications Ltd. Since 1990, he has worked with *Telegraph Magazine.* In addition, he designed the Snowdon Aviary, which was opened at London Zoo in 1965, and directed the TV film *Don't Count the Candles*, which won two Emmys in 1968. He has a particular interest in the physically disabled and has produced several television documentaries on that theme. Also, he has served on the Council of the National Fund for Research into Crippling Diseases and has chaired a Working Party on the Integration of the Disabled which produced a report in 1976. His photographs have been exhibited around the world and have particularly caught the imagination because of the ways in which he captures his subjects' personalities and draws attention to the plight of the disabled, evoking sympathy rather than pity. He is an Honorary Fellow of the Institute of British Photographers and the Royal Photographic Society and a member of several arts societies.

ARMY, BRITISH. There was no **STANDING ARMY** in **ENGLAND** until the **NEW MODEL ARMY** was formed during the **CIVIL WAR,** but, in the 18th and 19th centuries, many regiments were created to meet the country's military commitments in Europe and the colonies. During the 20th century — and particularly since the end of the **SECOND WORLD WAR**— the trend has been towards reductions of personnel. In 1990, as a result of reduced Cold War tension, the **GOVERNMENT** issued a White Paper entitled *Options for Change* and the years which followed saw a flurry of regimental mergers. By 1993, the Army consisted of 150,000 regular soldiers and 187,000 reservists. (See **ASSIZE OF ARMS; COMMISSION OF ARRAY; CONSCRIPTION; FIRST WORLD WAR; NATIONAL SERVICE; TRAINED BANDS**).

ARNHEM, BATTLE OF, 17-25 September 1944. This disastrous British, US and Polish paratroop assault attempted to take the Neder

Rijn Bridge on the River Rhine near Arnhem, behind German lines and in advance of the main forces, following the **D-DAY** landings towards the end of the **SECOND WORLD WAR**. The attack was part of **BERNARD MONTGOMERY**'s plan to establish a bridgehead on the Rhine and thereby control access to the Ruhr via the Netherlands and the Zuider Zee. The scheme was, in many ways, strategically brilliant but the supporting ground forces failed to arrive on schedule, and, as a result, the British First Airborne Division was forced to surrender on 27 September. German defence was ferocious, and led to the eventual evacuation of 2,200 Allied parachutists and the loss of 7,000 men killed or captured in the action.

ARRAY, COMMISSION OF. From the 14th until the 16th centuries, the Commission was a means of arraying (or mustering) a military force for the **MONARCH**. The practice was based on the ancient obligation of all citizens to assist in the defence of the country (see **MILITIA**). One or two prominent people in each **COUNTY** were given authority to raise troops in the King's name for national or foreign action. (See **ASSIZE OF ARMS, BRITISH ARMY, TRAINED BANDS**).

ARTHUR. Popularly known as the chivalrous head of the **KNIGHT**s of the Round Table, Arthur was probably a local chieftain who led the Britons in their struggle against the **SAXONS** early in the sixth century. To what extent the legends surrounding him have a historical basis is unclear but the seventh century Welsh poem *Y Gododdin* describes him as a great fighter and the *Historia Britonum* of Nennius, a ninth century document, gives details of 12 of his battles, including a major victory at **MOUNT BADON**. Geoffrey of Monmouth embellished these Celtic tales in his *Historia Regum Britanniae* (c. 1135), telling how Arthur added **SCOTLAND**, France and Norway to his kingdom and defeated a Roman army in Gaul. Before long, stories of his exploits and those of his knights were being told throughout Europe.

According to tradition, Arthur was the son of King Uther Pendragon and Igraine, Duchess of Cornwall. Merlin the magician (who had organised the meeting between Uther and Igraine) was the boy's tutor and faithful companion. After being crowned King, Arthur lived with the beautiful but deceiving Queen Guinevere at Camelot. There, he gathered his knights, none of whom had precedence over the others because the Round Table had neither head nor foot. The activities of one of those knights — Mordred, Arthur's treacherous nephew — led to a battle in which Mordred was killed and Arthur wounded. He was carried by barge to the magic island of Avalon to be healed and, for centuries, Britons believed that someday he would return. During the **VICTORIAN AGE**, there was a resurgence of interest in the Arthurian legends and that interest has continued to the present day, as seen, for example, in T. H. White's series of novels collected as *The Once and Future King* (1958) and the contemporary debate about the location of Camelot.

ARTICLES OF RELIGION. There were four occasions on which Articles of faith were introduced.

In <u>1536</u>, during the **REFORMATION**, King **HENRY VIII** issued ten Articles of faith and ceremony for the new **CHURCH OF ENGLAND**.

These were followed by an additional six Articles (<u>1539</u>), which furthered uniformity by attempting to impose an unmarried clergy and sustain the concept of transubstantiation.

The 42 Articles of <u>1553</u> were more Protestant than the Catholic articles of 1536, allowing only two sacraments — Eucharist and Baptism.

These were revised as the 39 Articles of <u>1571</u> which essentially established the position accepted today. Several deal with the doctrine of justification by faith; others maintain that all things necessary to achieve salvation can be learned from the scriptures. Ordained Church of England clergy must accept the articles. (See **THOMAS CRANMER**).

ARTS AND CRAFTS MOVEMENT. This 19th century movement was fired by the ideals of William Morris and John Ruskin, rejecting 19th century materialism and the poor quality and design of the products produced during the **INDUSTRIAL REVOLUTION**. It revived old crafts and romantic art.

ASHDOWN, BATTLE OF, 8 January 871. At this battle on the Berkshire Downs, **AETHELRED I** and **ALFRED THE GREAT**, leading the West **SAXONS**, defeated the **VIKING** Danes, killing one of the two enemy Kings (Bacsecg).

ASHDOWN, JEREMY JOHN DURHAM (1941-). Universally known as Paddy, Ashdown has been Leader of the **LIBERAL DEMOCRATIC PARTY (LDP)** since 1988. He was born on 27 April 1941, the son of Lieutenant-Colonel and Mrs John Ashdown, and educated at Bedford School. Much of his childhood was spent in India and **ULSTER**, but, when his parents emigrated to Australia in 1959, he joined 41 and 42 Commando Unit of the Royal Marines, rising to the rank of Captain and serving with the Special Boat Squadron in the Near East, Malaysia and **NORTHERN IRELAND**. A gifted linguist, he also acquired a First Class Honours degree in Mandarin at the University of Hong Kong.

In 1971, he joined the Diplomatic Service and acted as First Secretary with the UK Mission to the United Nations in Geneva until 1976. From then until 1978, he worked in the Commercial Manager's Department of Westland Helicopters at Yeovil and, for three years after that, was a Senior Manager with Morlands Ltd in the same town. He was a Youth Officer with Dorset **COUNTY** Council from 1981 until 1983, then won election to **PARLIAMENT** as the Member for Yeovil, previously considered a safe seat for the **CONSERVATIVE PARTY**.

He was **LIBERAL PARTY** spokesman on trade and industry until 1986 and **ALLIANCE** spokesman on **EDUCATION** and science in 1987. In 1988, he was elected leader of the **SOCIAL AND LIBERAL DEMOCRATIC PARTY (SLDP)**, a new organization formed by a merger of the Liberals and the **SOCIAL DEMOCRATIC PARTY (SDP)**, defeating Alan Beith by 41,401 votes to 16,202. Since then, he has become a well-known public figure and has skilfully reversed the decline in his party's fortunes caused by the alliance and merger confusion of the 1980s. Even disclosure of a five-month affair with his secretary — trumpeted by *The Sun* newspaper to its readers under the headline, "It's Paddy Pantsdown" — seemed to do his image more good than harm. At the 1992 **GENERAL ELECTION**, he held the Yeovil seat with a majority of 8,833.

ASIENTO. This monopoly, obtained from Spain through the **TREATY OF UTRECHT** in 1713, enabled Britain to supply African slaves, for a fee, to the Spanish colonies in the Americas. It was administered by the **AFRICAN COMPANY** from 1713 until 1750. (See **SLAVE TRADE**).

ASQUITH, HERBERT HENRY (1852-1928). Asquith was **PRIME MINISTER** between 1908 and 1916, heading a **LIBERAL PARTY GOVERNMENT** which curtailed the power of the **HOUSE OF LORDS** and introduced many major social reforms, including legislation granting pensions to the elderly (1908) and insurance to cover sickness and unemployment (1911). Born at Morley on 12 September 1852, he was the second son of Joseph Asquith, who had a small business in the **WOOL INDUSTRY**. Educated at the **CITY OF LONDON** School and **OXFORD** University, he decided to enter the law and qualified as a barrister in 1876. He was elected to **PARLIAMENT**, representing East Fife, in 1886 and continued to serve the **CONSTITUENCY** until 1918.

Asquith managed to make a success both of his legal and his political careers and, in 1892, **WILLIAM GLADSTONE** appointed him **HOME SECRETARY**, a post which he held for three years and which enhanced his reputation in the **HOUSE OF COMMONS**. By 1895, he was a major figure in Parliament, recognized both for his administrative qualities and for his debating skills, but, despite his continued success as a barrister, a lack of private wealth led him to decline the offer of Leadership of the Liberal Party (then the party in **OPPOSITION**) in 1898. In 1905, the Liberals regained power and Asquith became **CHANCELLOR OF THE EXCHEQUER** under **HENRY CAMPBELL-BANNERMAN**. In February 1908, however, Campbell- Bannerman took ill and, two months later, resigned. Asquith became Prime Minister, inheriting problems of a **CONSERVATIVE PARTY** dominated House of Lords (which, between 1906 and 1908, had consistently frustrated Liberal legislation), the danger of rebellion by the radical wing of his own Party, the growth of demands for **HOME RULE** in **IRELAND**, the debate over the disestablishment of the Welsh church and the growth of the German navy.

In 1909, in order to meet the cost of social measures and rearmament, the Liberals introduced a **BUDGET** which proposed heavy inheritance and income taxes. The House of Lords rejected the legislation but, after the **GENERAL ELECTION** of 1910 had given him a Parliamentary majority of 124 (including the 82 Irish and 40 **LABOUR PARTY** members), Asquith announced a plan to limit the powers of the Lords, allowing them to delay legislation for two years but not to veto it. The change could only be introduced if King **EDWARD VII** would create sufficient peers to get the **BILL** passed in the upper house. He agreed, on condition that Asquith fought another election on the issue. Edward died in May but his successor — **GEORGE V** — honoured the agreement and Asquith was returned at a December election with the Parliamentary balance almost unchanged. The Lords passed the bill curtailing their own power on 10 August 1911.

The period which followed was a difficult one. Asquith forced the Irish Home Rule bill through Parliament in 1914 before the outbreak of the **FIRST WORLD WAR** but opposition to his leadership increased after the start of the war and, in 1915, he was forced to form a coalition government with the Conservative Party. The following year, he resigned as Prime Minister, giving way to **DAVID LLOYD GEORGE**, with whom he differed on a number of major issues. At the end of the war, he declined Lloyd George's offer to rejoin the Government and lost his seat at the 1918 election. He returned, representing Paisley, in 1920, but never held ministerial office again. In 1924, he lost his seat once more and, the following year, accepted a peerage as Earl of Oxford and Asquith. Towards the end of his life, he was relatively impoverished and wrote a number of books to augment his income. He died in Sutton Courtenay on 15 February 1928.

ASSANDUN (ASHINGDON), BATTLE OF, 18 October 1016. Following a Scandinavian raid on London in 994 (see **VIKINGS**), a **DANEGELD** was paid, but **CANUTE** did not accept it. Raids began again in 997, and eventually **EDMUND II** was defeated in battle at Ashingdon Hill. **ENGLAND** was partitioned, with Edmund agreeing to rule in **WESSEX** while Canute controlled the north. However, only a few weeks after the understanding was reached, Edmund died and Canute took the whole kingdom into the Scandinavian empire.

ASSIZE OF ARMS. These 12th century regulations set out the weapons and armour to be held by men of different ranks under the military service requirement of the **FEUDAL SYSTEM**. The 1181 Assize of Arms made all able-bodied Freemen, and later **VILLEIN**s, liable for military service and the supply of their own arms, thus creating an early **MILITIA** force. The arrangements remained until the implementation of the Militia Act (see **ACT OF PARLIAMENT**) in 1662. (See **COMMISSION OF ARRAY**).

ASSIZES. In medieval times, this word was used primarily to mean 'seated assembly', but it could also refer to some royal declarations. In the 13th century, the practice of sending judges on circuit to adjudicate at assemblies around the country began. The Assizes, which were superior to the **QUARTER SESSIONS**, represented the government to the **SHIRE**s and advised the **PRIVY COUNCIL**. They were replaced in 1972 by the Crown (criminal) and High (civil) Courts, under the terms of the Courts Act of 1970.

(See **ACT OF PARLIAMENT; CROWN COURTS; HIGH COURT OF JUSTICE**).

ASTOR, NANCY WITCHER (1879-1964). Viscountess Astor was the first woman to sit in the **HOUSE OF COMMONS**. Born in Danville (Virginia) on 19 May 1879, she travelled to Britain in 1903 following her divorce from Robert Gould Shaw of Boston (Massachusetts) after a six-year marriage. In 1906, she married William Waldorf Astor, the **CONSERVATIVE PARTY** Member of **PARLIAMENT** for Plymouth. When William succeeded to the viscountcy (see **PEERAGE**) and relinquished his seat, Nancy was adopted as candidate. On 28 November 1919, she was elected, winning by a substantial majority and serving the **CONSTITUENCY** until her retirement in 1945. She never held **GOVERNMENT** office but took great interest in matters affecting women, advocating changes to the laws relating to illegitimacy and to the guardianship of children. In addition, she was a supporter of the temperance movement and of the campaign to raise the school leaving age. Outside Parliament, she was a leading society hostess, entertaining guests at Cliveden, her country estate. Her coterie of friends became known as the Cliveden Set and was accused of supporting **APPEASEMENT** in the face of Adolf Hitler's expansionist policies in interwar Germany. She was made a Companion of Honour in 1937 and died at Grimsthorpe Castle (Lincolnshire) on 2 May 1964.

ATHELSTAN (?-939). (See **AETHELSTAN**).

ATLANTIC, BATTLE OF THE. The term refers to the operations in the North Atlantic Ocean during the **SECOND WORLD WAR** and particularly to the engagements, from August 1940, between the U-boats of the Axis forces (commanded by Admiral Karl Doenitz) and the convoys bringing equipment and food for the war effort in Britain. The conflict lasted for 2,073 days and cost over 2,000 Allied merchant ships (mostly British), which were sunk with great loss of life.

By 1941, the U-boats were hunting in packs and attacking on the surface at night. In May of that year alone, 61 ships carrying 310,000 tons of cargo were destroyed, and the situation was relieved only briefly by the assistance of US warships as escorts. In March 1942, in a period of just 20 days, 97 vessels went down, and by June there were 150 U-boats operational in the Atlantic. The worst single disaster occurred in July 1942, when the attack on convoy

PQ 17 (on its way to Russia with supplies) resulted in 19 ships being sunk, together with their cargoes, which included 430 tanks, 210 aircraft and 3,350 vehicles.

In 1943, over 700,000 tonnes of vessel were being lost each month, and the Allied war effort was in grave danger, with Britain down to little over two months of oil supply. Special procedures were adopted, using RADAR on ships and aircraft, newly broken German cypher codes, greater numbers of escort warships (including aircraft carriers and better destroyers), long-distance spotter aircraft (particularly the Very Long Range Liberators based in Iceland from 1943) and more effective depth-charges. Also, ASDIC (the Anti-Submarine Detection Investigation Committee) developed what became SONAR. Meanwhile, the Germans had introduced acoustic torpedoes, RADAR decoy equipment and the schnorkel air circulation system, which allowed submarines to remain underwater for long periods.

The threat ended only with the Allied taking of the U-boat bases on continental Europe in 1944 although Admiral Doenitz had withdrawn his forces from the Atlantic on 24 May 1943. The total loss of life was estimated at 120,000 Allied men (including 22,000 merchant seamen), 2,200 Allied vessels (including 175 naval ships) and up to 15 million tonnes of merchant shipping. Some 28,000 German U-Boat personnel also died. This was a battle which very nearly brought Britain to the edge of disaster.

ATLANTIC CHARTER, 14 August 1941. This agreement between Britain and the USA bound both countries to strive for world freedom, national self-determination and peace. It was negotiated and signed by Prime Minister **WINSTON CHURCHILL** and President Franklin Roosevelt on a ship in Placentia Bay (Newfoundland) just before the entry of the United States of America into the **SECOND WORLD WAR**, prior to the Japanese attack on Pearl Harbor and at a time when Britain desperately needed the United States to commit its forces to Europe. Other Allied powers endorsed the accord in 1941, but it was largely a document outlining intent and propaganda rather than a treaty of substance, including declarations against territorial aggrandisement, for **FREE TRADE**, for the easing of trade barriers and for the eschewing of force to solve international disputes. The aim was that "After the final destruction of the Nazi tyranny. . . peace. . . will afford assurance that all the men in all the lands may live out their lives in freedom from fear or want". Elements of the agreement were included in the charter of the United Nations in 1945.

ATLANTIC TRIANGLE. This extremely profitable 18th century shipping route and trading system incorporated the **SLAVE TRADE.**
Britain exported cloth and iron to West Africa in return for slaves,
who were then transported to the West Indies for work on the plantations and paid for with sugar (or sugar-based products, such as
molasses), which was taken back to Britain for consumption or selling on. (See **ASIENTO**).

ATTERBURY PLOT, 1722. This Jacobite conspiracy, led by Francis
Atterbury (Bishop of Rochester) aimed to seize the **BANK OF
ENGLAND,** but the conspirators were arrested. The incident
strengthened the position of Whig Prime Minister **ROBERT
WALPOLE** by allowing him to associate the Jacobite conspiracy
with High Church **TORIES** who opposed him.

ATTLEE, CLEMENT RICHARD (1883-1967). Clement Attlee was
PRIME MINISTER of the first peacetime **GOVERNMENT** following the end of the **SECOND WORLD WAR** and was responsible for introducing the **LABOUR PARTY** legislation which provided the basis of the **WELFARE STATE.** Born in **LONDON** on
3 January 1883, he was the son of a prosperous solicitor and never
lacked financial means. He was educated at Haileybury School and
OXFORD University and qualified as a barrister in 1906 but abandoned his legal career three years later. By that time, he had taken
up residence in one of the poorest parts of east London, seeing the
extreme poverty of the working class city at firsthand and finding
his political views moving steadily leftwards. During the **FIRST
WORLD WAR,** he served with the infantry, gaining the rank of
Major, but returned to the East End on demobilization, continued
to pursue his political interests and, in 1922, was elected Member
of **PARLIAMENT** for Limehouse. He served that **CONSTITU-
ENCY** until 1950 then held the West Walthamstow seat for five
more years.

His progress in the **HOUSE OF COMMONS** was steady; he
became a member of the India Statutory Commission in 1927,
CHANCELLOR OF THE DUCHY OF LANCASTER in 1930
and **POSTMASTER GENERAL** in 1931. At the 1931 **GENERAL
ELECTION,** the Labour vote collapsed, but Attlee was reelected
and became Deputy Leader of the party under George Lansbury.
In 1935, Lansbury resigned, and Attlee succeeded him as Leader.
For the remainder of the decade, he maintained a moderate stance

on domestic issues and advocated resistance to Adolf Hitler's expansionist policies. He fully supported the declaration of war on Germany in 1939 but felt unable to join **NEVILLE CHAMBERLAIN**'s Government. In 1941, however, he was instrumental in forcing Chamberlain's replacement as coalition leader by **WINSTON CHURCHILL** and entered the War **CABINET** as **LORD PRIVY SEAL**. The following year, he became Deputy Prime Minister and **SECRETARY OF STATE** for **DOMINION** Affairs. In 1943, he was appointed **LORD PRESIDENT OF THE COUNCIL** and served in that capacity until the end of the war.

In May 1945, Attlee led the Labour Party to a surprise victory at the general election and set about the process of rebuilding the British economy in accordance with his socialist ideals. During his administration, public transport, **COAL**, the **STEEL** industry and the **BANK OF ENGLAND** were the subjects of **NATIONALIZATION**. The **NATIONAL HEALTH SERVICE** was founded, a national insurance scheme was introduced, **EDUCATION** was reformed and India, Ceylon and Pakistan were given their independence. The achievements were considerable despite great internal party conflicts; with immense skill, he held the right and left wings together and exercised control over **ERNEST BEVIN, HERBERT MORRISON, STAFFORD CRIPPS** and other colleagues who were more dominant public personalities than he.

At the 1951 general election, called after the government's Parliamentary majority had been reduced to a tenuous six seats and the resignation of Aneurin Bevan and **HAROLD WILSON** had weakened his position as Prime Minister, Attlee was narrowly defeated by the Conservatives (see **CONSERVATIVE PARTY**). He remained as Leader of the **OPPOSITION** until 1955 but resigned after the general election defeat in May of that year. He was created Earl Attlee and entered the **HOUSE OF LORDS**, where he served until his death in London on 8 October 1967.

AUGUSTAN AGE. From the early 18th until the mid-18th century, English writers were strongly influenced by the flowering of **ROMAN** culture under Emperor Augustus between 27 BC and 14 AD. Alexander Pope, Joseph Addison and their contemporaries greatly admired the work of Virgil, Ovid and Horace, imitated the order, clarity and restraint of their style and incorporated Latin allusions in their own publications. Novelists, essayists and poets frequently drew parallels between the two periods and prepared translations of classical texts. (Pope, for example, published his version of Homer's *Iliad* in six volumes between 1715 and 1720). Some references to the Augustan Age place its beginnings as early as the reign of **CHARLES II** (1660-85). Oliver Goldsmith, however, limited it to the reign of **QUEEN ANNE** (1702-14). The period is also associated with the development of **GEORGIAN** architecture, which drew heavily on the styles of Rome and Greece.

AUGUSTINE OF CANTERBURY, ST (?-c. 607). St Augustine is recognized as the founder of the Christian church in southern **ENGLAND** and the first **ARCHBISHOP OF CANTERBURY**. A monk in the monastery of St Andrew in Rome, Augustine was sent by Pope Gregory I as the leader of a mission to England, which had become largely pagan as the British Christians had retreated to the north and west in the face of the **ANGLO-SAXON** invaders. He landed at Thanet in 597 and was well received by King **AETHELBERT** of **KENT**, whose wife (Bertha) was already a Christian. Aethelbert (who was eventually baptized himself) gave Augustine land at **CANTERBURY**. In 601, Gregory made him Archbishop of Canterbury and awarded him authority over all of the Bishops in Britain, but his attempts to effect a union between his own churches and those of the **CELTS** were in vain. He died in 607. His feast day is 28 May in the United Kingdom, 26 May elsewhere.

AUSTERITY. This term is used to describe the immediate post-**SECOND WORLD WAR** period when rationing of essentials continued and Britain had a severe shortage of currency reserves. It is most notably associated with the policies of **SIR STAFFORD CRIPPS** on wage restraint, currency devaluation, exports and continued economic controls, including the reduction of rations in 1948 and 1949. Rationing of food continued until 1954.

AUSTRIAN SUCCESSION, WAR OF THE, 1740-48. Britain was a signatory of the Pragmatic Sanction (1713), which, on the death of Habsburg Emperor Charles VI (in 1740), was flouted by Bavaria, France and Prussia. These three powers declared Charles Albert of Bavaria successor to the empire over Maria Theresa, daughter of Charles VI, and seized Silesia. Britain and its allies attempted to enforce the Sanction and Britain defeated the French at the **BATTLE OF DETTINGEN** in 1743. At that time, the British and the French were already at war in North America and India, with France also encouraging the Jacobite Rebellions. In addition, the **WAR OF**

JENKIN'S EAR had broken out against Spain in 1739, widening the European conflict.

AUTHORIZED VERSION OF THE BIBLE, 1611. This translation of the Bible is also known as the King James' Version as it was **JAMES VI** and **I** who ordered it, in 1604, to replace the five largely unsatisfactory translations then in use in **ENGLAND**. Between 1607 and 1611, 50 scholars and clergy, organized into six committees, were employed to produce the text. Its beautiful prose remained unchallenged for 300 years and is still popular with many Christians. It is said to have been a factor in the rise of the **PURITANS**, who, as the **PARLIAMENTARIANS**, were later to overthrow the **STUARTS**.

AVRANCHES, COMPROMISE OF, 21 May 1172. This agreement between King **HENRY II** and the Catholic Church was reached following the murder of Archbishop **THOMAS BECKET** in **CANTERBURY** Cathedral on 29 December 1170. The King agreed to do penance at the tomb of the murdered **ARCHBISHOP OF CANTERBURY** and to remove edicts detrimental to the Church. In return, he was absolved of all blame for the incident.

—B—

BABINGTON PLOT, 1586. Anthony Babington and John Balland, both Roman Catholics, led a conspiracy to assassinate Queen **ELIZABETH I** and install Mary, Queen of Scots, on the throne of **ENGLAND**. Armed Spanish backing was promised, but the plot was discovered and the conspirators were condemned to death by hanging (until nearly dead), drawing (of entrails while still alive) and quartering (cutting into four parts). The event was one of the factors which ultimately led to the execution of Mary, who was believed to have known of the plans. (See **CAPITAL PUNISHMENT**).

BACKBENCHER. This term is applied to Members of **PARLIAMENT** who are not **MINISTER**s or **SHADOW MINISTER**s. In the **HOUSE OF COMMONS**, they occupy the benches behind those of the leading politicians.

BALACLAVA, BATTLE OF, 25 October 1854. Fought during the

CRIMEAN WAR, this battle was a conflict between Russian heavy forces and British cavalry. The British Heavy Brigade established a foothold, but later orders were misunderstood. As a result, the Light Brigade, under Lord Cardigan, charged the Russian heavy guns, and 113 cavalrymen were killed. The battle, which resulted in a repulse for the Russian attacking forces, was immortalised by Lord Tennyson in his poem about the **CHARGE OF THE LIGHT BRIGADE.** The struggle is said to be the origin of the balaclava, woollen headgear covering the whole head, apart from eyes and mouth, and supplied to troops in the Crimea.

BALDWIN, STANLEY (1867-1947). **PRIME MINISTER** during the **GENERAL STRIKE** of 1926 and the Abdication Crisis of King **EDWARD VIII** in 1936, Baldwin was a man of considerable political acumen who had the misfortune to preside over some of the most difficult episodes in the United Kingdom's recent history. He was born at Bewdley on 3 August 1867, the only son of Alfred Baldwin, Chairman of the Great Western Railway and head of Baldwin's Ltd, a large mining and **STEEL** production company. After completing his **EDUCATION** at Harrow School and **CAMBRIDGE** University, Baldwin entered his father's business, becoming responsible for its day-to-day operations when Alfred was elected Member of **PARLIAMENT** for Bewdley in 1892.

When his father died in 1908, Baldwin took his place at **WESTMINSTER**, representing Bewdley in the **CONSERVATIVE PARTY** cause. For eight years, he made little impact, but, in 1916, he was made **PARLIAMENTARY PRIVATE SECRETARY** to **ANDREW BONAR LAW** (then **CHANCELLOR OF THE EXCHEQUER**) and from that point advanced rapidly, becoming a junior Lord of the **TREASURY** in January 1917 and Joint **FINANCIAL SECRETARY** in June of the same year. In 1921, Baldwin was appointed **PRESIDENT OF THE BOARD OF TRADE** in **DAVID LLOYD GEORGE**'s coalition **CABINET** but, in 1922, in consort with Bonar Law and other Conservatives, forced Lloyd George to resign.

The Conservatives won the ensuing **GENERAL ELECTION** and Bonar Law became Prime Minister with Baldwin as his Chancellor of the Exchequer. When Bonar Law, in turn, resigned in May of the following year, Baldwin was asked to form a **GOVERNMENT**. He succeeded but, in October, announced that he would go to the country in order to seek a mandate to reverse Bonar Law's **FREE TRADE** policy. That was a considerable miscalculation and, in the general election, the Conservatives lost 107 seats.

Although still the largest party in the **HOUSE OF COMMONS**, the Conservatives faced possible defeat by a **LIBERAL PARTY-LABOUR PARTY** coalition so Baldwin resigned and **RAMSAY MACDONALD** formed a Labour government with Liberal support. After nine months, however, that government was defeated in a Commons vote, and, in the election which followed, the Conservatives were returned with a 211 seat majority over all of the other parties. Baldwin was restored as Prime Minister and formed a Cabinet which included **WINSTON CHURCHILL** as Chancellor of the Exchequer. Despite Churchill's economic reforms, the **COAL** industry was faced with recession, and the miners, refusing to accept wage cuts, went on strike on 4 May 1926. The **TRADES UNION CONGRESS** sanctioned sympathetic action by vital workers in industries such as transport, printing and engineering and Baldwin was faced by a general strike. The stoppage lasted for nine days and was marked by a freedom from violence which was due, in large part, to Baldwin's attempts not to provoke the unions. He remained as Prime Minister until 1929, when the Labour Party won the general election in a climate of increasing concern about rises in unemployment.

Baldwin was in **OPPOSITION** until 1931, when the financial crisis led to the collapse of the Labour Government and the King invited Ramsay Macdonald to form a National Government. Baldwin was made **LORD PRESIDENT OF THE COUNCIL** and, in June 1935, became Prime Minister for the third time when Macdonald retired from public life. Over the next two years, despite the German reoccupation of the Rhineland, the completion of the Italian conquest of Ethiopia (see **ABYSSINIAN CAMPAIGN**) and the beginnings of German-Italian intervention in the Spanish Civil War, he maintained a policy of isolationism which, with hindsight, failed to recognize the expansionist threat posed by Adolf Hitler and Benito Mussolini. On the other hand, faced with **EDWARD VIII**'s attachment to Mrs Wallis Simpson, he acted with great diplomacy to maintain the status of the **MONARCH**y and prevent a constitutional crisis following the King's abdication in 1936.

On 28 May 1937, Baldwin resigned and was succeeded by **NEVILLE CHAMBERLAIN**. He was created Earl Baldwin of Bewdley but played no further part in politics and died at Stourport-on-Severn on 14 December 1947.

BALFOUR, ARTHUR JAMES (1848-1930). **PRIME MINISTER**

from 1902 until 1905, Balfour was born at Whittinghame (East Lothian) on 25 July 1848, the eldest son of James Balfour and **LADY** Blanche Gascoyne-Cecil (sister of **ROBERT GASCOYNE-CECIL, MARQUESS** of Salisbury, who was to be a major influence on his political fortunes). He was educated at Eton College and **CAMBRIDGE** University then was persuaded by Salisbury to seek election to the **HOUSE OF COMMONS** and, in 1874, became MP for Hertford, representing the **CONSERVATIVE PARTY**. Four years later he was appointed Private Secretary to his uncle who, at that time, was Foreign **MINISTER**.

In 1880, he retained his seat at a **GENERAL ELECTION** which ousted the Conservatives from power and became associated with The Fourth Party, a group of four MPs (led by Lord Randolph Churchill), which was critical of official party policy. However, when the Conservatives returned in 1885, Salisbury replaced **WILLIAM GLADSTONE** as Prime Minister and made his nephew President of the Board of **LOCAL GOVERNMENT**. The administration lasted for only a few months, but, when Salisbury formed a second **GOVERNMENT** in 1886, Balfour became Secretary for **SCOTLAND** before entering the **CABINET** the following year as Chief Secretary for **IRELAND**.

That appointment seemed strange to a public accustomed to regarding the affluent, middle-aged bachelor as a man-about-town rather than a hard-bitten politician, but it proved to be inspired; implacably opposed to **HOME RULE** for Ireland, he squashed every sign of rebellion ruthlessly (earning the nickname "Bloody Balfour") but at the same time pursued enlightened social and economic policies which did much to improve living conditions on the island. (He publicly decried absentee landlords, for example.) His successes, coupled with an increasing reputation as a skilled debater, led to his promotion to First Lord of the **TREASURY** and **LEADER OF THE HOUSE OF COMMONS** in 1891 (effectively, these posts made him Deputy Prime Minister, forming a nephew-uncle combination unique in modern British politics).

The family partnership was short-lived because the **LIBERAL PARTY** won the 1892 general election. However, Balfour proved to be an effective leader of the **OPPOSITION** in the House of Commons so, when the Conservatives gained another majority in 1895, he returned to his former posts then, in 1902, replaced his uncle as Prime Minister when Salisbury resigned. Several domestic reforms (see **ACT OF PARLIAMENT**) were introduced during his ministry, notably the **EDUCATION** Act of 1902 (which rationalized secondary schooling), the Irish Land Purchase Act of 1903 (which did much to alleviate rural poverty) and the Licensing Act of 1904 (which resulted in the closure of many **PUBLIC HOUSE**s but provided compensation for the brewing firms). However, there were mistakes as well. The Education Act subsidized **CHURCH OF ENGLAND** schools and was therefore unpopular in **NONCONFORMIST** strongholds, particularly in the north of **ENGLAND**. The importation of Chinese workmen to overcome labour shortages in the mines of southern Africa was criticized both by the representatives of organized labour (who suspected a dangerous precedent) and by liberals (who believed that this mass migration was inhumane). And the proposal to abandon Britain's longstanding tradition of **FREE TRADE** and replace it with preferential treatment for imports from the colonies aroused the wrath of many members of his own party (see **IMPERIAL PREFERENCE**).

In 1905, the mounting opposition forced him to resign and the general election which followed took the Liberals back to power on the crest of a tidal wave of popular support. Balfour, however, continued to lead the Conservative Party until 1911, when, unable to stand the sniping any longer, he handed over the reins to **ANDREW BONAR LAW**. For most politicians that move would have signalled the end of a career, but when **HERBERT ASQUITH** formed his coalition Government in May 1915, some ten months after the start of the **FIRST WORLD WAR**, he invited Balfour to take the post of First Lord of the **ADMIRALTY**. The following year, when **DAVID LLOYD GEORGE** formed his War Cabinet, Balfour was included as Foreign Secretary but made limited impact except for the **BALFOUR DECLARATION** of November 1917, which formalized British support for the creation of a Jewish state in Palestine. In 1919, he was a member of the British delegation at the Versailles peace negotiations (see **TREATY OF VERSAILLES**) and, in the same year, became **LORD PRESIDENT OF THE COUNCIL** and Chancellor of Cambridge University. Three years later, he was made a Knight of the Garter (see **ORDER OF THE GARTER**) and an **EARL**. He was Lord President for a second time in **STANLEY BALDWIN**'s 1925 administration and did much to clarify the relationship between the United Kingdom and its **DOMINIONS** but, now in his seventies, was weakened by the stresses of high office and died in Woking on 19 March 1930. He never married. In 1875 he had become unofficially engaged to May Lyttleton, Gladstone's niece, but she died a few weeks later and Balfour, though he had a wide social circle, never replaced her.

BALFOUR DECLARATION, THE. On 2 November 1917, Foreign Secretary **ARTHUR BALFOUR** announced British support for the creation of a homeland for Jews in Palestine — a statement motivated by the British need to curry favour with the 75,000 Jews then living in the area. One element of the grand strategy designed to achieve victory over Germany and its allies during the later years of the **FIRST WORLD WAR** was an offensive against the Ottoman Empire. Palestine was the ideal springboard and Chaim Weizmann (a Zionist leader in Britain and later first President of Israel) persuaded Balfour to issue the declaration in the form of a letter to Lord Rothschild, a prominent British Jew, on the grounds that it would rally the support of Jews in the United States as well as those in the eastern Mediterranean. The Council of the **LEAGUE OF NATIONS** approved a British mandate over Palestine in 1922 (see **MANDATED TERRITORIES**), and the Balfour Declaration was used by supporters of Judaism to argue the case for the creation of the state of Israel. The Declaration probably stemmed from Great Britain's need of an ally state in the area of the Suez Canal. The British government made similar promises to Arab states in the region, providing a basis for future problems in foreign relations.

BANK OF ENGLAND. The Bank was created on 21 June 1694 to finance the **GOVERNMENT** of **WILLIAM III**, then in conflict with the French. The unprecedented need for funds led to the granting of wide rights to deal in bullion and bills of exchange so it quickly became the principal bank of the **CROWN**. It took over the **NATIONAL DEBT** in 1750 and, by the time it entered its current premises in 1829, was issuing notes which were accepted as legal tender. The Bank Charter Act of 1844 (see **ACT OF PARLIAMENT**) gave the Bank of England a monopoly in **ENGLAND**, phasing out the rights of other banks to issue paper money. Nationalized in 1946, the Bank is often called the "Old Lady of Threadneedle Street" after its **LONDON** location. It advises the government on monetary and financial policy, executes these policies, acts as banker to the state, manages the national gold reserves, supervizes the UK banking system, controls bank interest rates and passes directives to the major banks. The Bank of England still issues domestic notes, but coins are the responsibility of the **ROYAL MINT**.

BAREBONES PARLIAMENT, 4 July-11 December 1653. **OLIVER CROMWELL**'s army replaced the **RUMP PARLIAMENT** with an assembly of "godly chosen men" nominated by **COUNTY** churches. It failed to agree on most matters and was dissolved to make way for the **PROTECTORATE**. The Parliament gets its name from one of its members, the aptly named Praisegod Barbon (hence Barebones), a prominent Anabaptist.

BARNET, BATTLE OF, 14 April 1471. This battle, fought in heavy fog at a site near **LONDON**, resulted in defeat for the Lancastrians, led by the Earl of Warwick, at the hands of Yorkist King **EDWARD IV** during the **WARS OF THE ROSES**. The Lancastrians lost up to 1,000 men, including Warwick, who was killed while retrieving his charger. The victory left the King free to engage the Lancastrian army, led by Queen Margaret, in the west (see **BATTLE OF TEWKESBURY**).

BARON. Formerly used in **ENGLAND** to refer to a husband and in **SCOTLAND** to the owner of a freehold estate, the title has also been appropriated by tenants-in-chief of the Crown, judges and members of the nobility. It is now the lowest order in the **PEERAGE**. As with other orders, precedence depends on the date on which the title was created. The premier barony in England is de Ros (created in 1264) and that in Scotland is Forbes (created in 1424).

BARONET. The most junior of the hereditary titles in the **PEERAGE**, the term has been used by the nobility of **ENGLAND** since 1611 and by that of **SCOTLAND** since 1625.

BARONS' WARS. These were two civil wars. The first (1215-17) was between King **JOHN** and his barons after the failure of the **MAGNA CARTA** to avert confrontation. Despite initial success and support from France, the barons were eventually defeated at Lincoln. The second (1264-67) was between King **HENRY III** and his barons over the King's continual demands for money. The nobles' leader, **SIMON DE MONTFORT**, met with early success, capturing the King at the **BATTLE OF LEWES** and securing the **MISE OF LEWES**. At that period, De Montfort was in virtual control of **ENGLAND**, but the barons quarrelled and were eventually defeated at the **BATTLE OF EVESHAM**. Some scholars believe that the campaign led to constitutional change in favour of the barons under King **EDWARD I**.

BARROW. Burial sites in **PREHISTORIC BRITAIN**, barrows took two forms. Long barrows, containing the bones of several people, date from the **NEOLITHIC**, but, in the **BRONZE AGE**, burial practices changed and remains of individuals were interred in round barrows, often after cremation.

BASTARD FEUDALISM. This later medieval form of feudalism was based on service to a lord in return for money payments rather than on the landholding basis of the true **FEUDAL SYSTEM**. It stemmed from the gradual growth of landed interests and thus the need for remunerated administrators of the lord's lands and the development of a virtual standing, paid army.

BATH. A city of some 76,000 people, Bath is located in southwest **ENGLAND**, some 110 miles west of **LONDON**, and is built on a series of low hills which border the River Avon. It first became important in **ROMAN** times, when it was known as Aquae Sulis and was the focus of a luxurious lifestyle as the invaders took advantage of the bathing facilities provided by hot springs. (Bath is the only place in Britain where such springs bubble to the surface.) It experienced a second period as a fashionable resort during the 18th century, when the rich and famous went to enjoy the supposedly health-giving qualities of the local water. Many of the city's streets were laid out at that time by architect John Wood and his son (also John Wood) and their designs were copied throughout **GEOR-GIAN** England. (Royal Crescent and The Circus are considered to be their masterpieces.) Bath chairs, Bath buns and Bath olivers (a kind of biscuit) all take their name from the town. The modern city is largely residential, with its historic core protected by conservation legislation. Planning measures prevent it from being engulfed by the growth of nearby Bristol.

BEACONSFIELD, EARL OF. (See **BENJAMIN DISRAELI**).

BEAKER PEOPLE. These early **BRONZE AGE** people are named after their bell-shaped drinking vessels, which are found in Britain from about 1800 BC. They also used copper widely in ornamentation. (See **STONEHENGE**).

BECKET, ST THOMAS (A) (1118-70). At one time a royal favourite, Thomas Becket was murdered in **CANTERBURY** Cathedral by supporters of King **HENRY II** following a series of disputes over royal control of the **CHURCH OF ENGLAND**. He was born in **LONDON**, on 21 December 1118, to a **NORMAN** family. In about 1142, he joined the household of Theobald, **ARCHBISHOP OF CANTERBURY**, serving as a clerk, and was ordained as a deacon in 1154. In 1155 (or possibly at the end of the previous year), he was appointed chancellor to Henry II on Theobald's recommendation. Undoubtedly, the Archbishop hoped to insinuate a friend of the Church into royal service but he was frequently disappointed. Thomas developed a close friendship with the King and did not oppose Henry's policies on ecclesiastical matters as strongly as might have been expected. His loyalty was rewarded in 1162, when he was appointed Archbishop of Canterbury after Theobald's death. It was a position which Thomas accepted reluctantly, believing that his duty to the Church would inevitably lead to conflict with the King.

The misgivings were justified. Against Henry's wishes, Thomas resigned the post of chancellor and soon became an outspoken opponent of the **MONARCH**'s attempts to curtail ecclesiastical powers. The differences polarized in 1163, when Thomas refused to accept Henry's rulings that clerks convicted of crimes in church courts should be punished by secular authorities and that bishops should accept the King as the highest authority in the land. Counselled by Pope Alexander III, who was in considerable financial debt to Henry, Thomas became more conciliatory, but the trouble flared up again in January 1164, when the King issued the Conventions of Clarendon, which gave him the right to regulate excommunication and made him the final arbiter of all appeals over judgements relating to Church law. Initially, Thomas accepted the situation, but this time Alexander demurred and Thomas withdrew his assent. To avoid further trouble, he fled to France, where he spent the following six years continuing his struggle despite attempts by several intermediaries to effect a reconciliation.

In 1166, Thomas received wide powers from the Pope to further his cause and excommunicated many of Henry's supporters including, in 1169, the Archbishops of London and of Salisbury. In 1170, the situation worsened when, in an attempt to secure the succession, Henry arranged for his eldest son to be crowned. The **CORONATION** was carried out by the Archbishop of **YORK** — a flagrant infringement of the Archbishop of Canterbury's right to perform the ceremony. With the full authority of the Pope, Thomas suspended those Bishops who had been involved. Shortly afterwards, he returned to **ENGLAND** but angry words by the King, referring to "this turbulent priest", apparently encouraged four **KNIGHT**s to put an end to the matter. On 29 December 1170, they murdered Thomas in the cathedral at Canterbury. The act shocked Europe, and Thomas quickly took on the status of martyr. He was buried in his cathedral church and soon had a reputation for performing miracles. In 1173, he was canonized and his tomb became a popular focus of pilgrimage until it was destroyed by **HENRY VIII** during the 16th century. (See **DISSOLUTION OF THE MONASTERIES**.) His feast day is 29 December. (See **COMPROMISE OF AVRANCHES**).

BEDCHAMBER CRISIS, May 1839. Ladies of the Bedchamber are usually the wives of peers and attend the Queen at important public occasions but are not **LADIES IN WAITING**. Unable to ensure a **HOUSE OF COMMONS** majority, **VISCOUNT MELBOURNE**, Queen **VICTORIA**'s favoured **WHIG PRIME MINISTER**, attempted to resign. **ROBERT PEEL**, Leader of the **CONSERVATIVE PARTY**, was asked to form a **GOVERNMENT** but, as a condition, demanded that the Queen dismiss all Ladies of the Bedchamber who were married to Whigs in order to remove undue influence on the **MONARCH** from his political opponents. (It was said, at the time, that a Conservative cat was not so much as permitted to mew within the precincts of the Queen's Palace.) The Queen refused and asked Melbourne to continue as Prime Minister. When his government finally fell in 1841, she assented to the dismissal of three of her Ladies. This was a constitutional problem in which the Queen and the Prime Minister both acted incorrectly because Melbourne had technically offered his resignation yet continued to advise the Head of State. It did, however, establish the nonpolitical nature of the position of Ladies of the Bedchamber.

BEECHING REPORT, 1963. A report (*The Reshaping of British Railways*) by the Chairman of British **RAILWAYS** (Dr Richard Beeching), at a time when the service was running a massive deficit in revenue, proposed the elimination of 25 to 30 per cent of the rail network, closure of over 2,000 stations and a 68,000 reduction in manpower. Its implementation failed to achieve great savings and created political uproar in the more rural and remote areas, many of which lost their only transport link. The action was known as the "Beeching Axe", and the length of the rail network has declined ever since.

BELGAE. These peoples from the regions of the Rivers Rhine and Seine came to the British Isles from about 100 BC and settled mainly in the southeast of the country, forming the last wave of Celtic invasion during the **IRON AGE** (see **CELTS**). The tribes included the Catuvellauni, the Atrebates and the Cantiaci (hence **CANTERBURY**). These technically advanced people with a strong unified organization under royal houses, silver and gold coinage (which they introduced for the first time to Britain), craft and exquisite metalwork, trade and urban dwelling (as opposed to earlier **HILLFORTS**) had almost client-kingdom status with the **ROMANS** and gave southeast **ENGLAND** its early importance in the history of British civilisation.

BENTHAM, JEREMY (1748-1832).   A utilitarian philosopher and critic of legal institutions, Bentham was a major influence on the views of 19th century social and political reformers. He was born in **LONDON** in 1748 and educated at **WESTMINSTER** School and **OXFORD** University. After graduating in 1763, he entered Lincoln's Inn and was called to the Bar. Three years later, he published *Fragment on Government* (a critique of the anti-reformist opinions of legal authority Sir William Blackstone), but it was not until 1787 that *Defence of Usury* (his first treatise on economics) appeared and demonstrated his support for the views of Adam Smith. *An Introduction to the Principles of Morals and Legislation* (1789) maintained that human beings were governed by two motives — avoidance of pain and attainment of pleasure; the object of all legislation, he argued, should be to achieve "the greatest happiness of the greatest number". Modern scholars point out that his assertions in that work were based on a series of simple fallacies and that much of the argument is confusing, but, at the time, it brought Bentham international recognition. In 1791, in *Essay on Political Tactics*, he presented his views on the most effective procedures for debate in a law-making body, and, in 1818, the **HOUSE OF COMMONS** adopted a number of the suggestions he had outlined in *A Catechism of Parliamentary Reform* (1809). He died in London on 6 June 1832, and, in accordance with his wishes, his body was dissected in the presence of his friends. The skeleton was rebuilt, fitted with a wax head, dressed in his clothes and then placed in a glass case. That effigy (and his mummified head) are stored in the University of London.

BENTINCK, WILLIAM HENRY CAVENDISH (1738-1809).

PRIME MINISTER for eight months in 1783 and also from 1807 until 1809, Bentinck was born at Bulstrode on 14 April 1738, the eldest son of William, Duke of Portland. He was educated at **WESTMINSTER** School (**LONDON**) and at **OXFORD** University, succeeding to his father's title (and his place in the **HOUSE OF LORDS**) in 1762. He served as **LORD CHAMBERLAIN** during the first ministry of **CHARLES WATSON-WENTWORTH, MARQUIS** of Rockingham, between July 1765 and December 1766, then accepted the appointment of **LORD LIEUTENANT** of **IRELAND** when Rockingham became Prime Minister for the second time in April 1782. He resigned from that post four months later when **WILLIAM PETTY FITZMAURICE,** Earl of Shelburne, succeeded Rockingham, but when Shelburne, in turn, fell in February 1783, he was chosen as a compromise leader of the coalition **GOVERNMENT** in which **LORD FREDERICK NORTH** and **CHARLES JAMES FOX** were the powers behind the throne.

The coalition survived only until December, when **GEORGE III** ensured that Fox's bill, aimed at reforming the **EAST INDIA COMPANY**, would fail to get through the Lords. Bentinck was ousted and, although leading a sizeable **WHIG** faction in **PARLIAMENT**, devoted much of his time to matters outside politics until, on the outbreak of war with France in 1793, he lent his support to the Tory administration (see **TORIES**) of **WILLIAM PITT THE YOUNGER**. Under Pitt, he was **SECRETARY OF STATE** for the **HOME OFFICE** from 1794 until 1801 and then **LORD PRESIDENT OF THE COUNCIL** for four more years. Bentinck gave up that post in January 1805 but remained as a member of the **CABINET** until Pitt died in January 1806. At that point he retired but was brought back to serve a second term as Prime Minister in March 1807. His administration, however, was undermined by disagreements between **VISCOUNT CASTLEREAGH** and **GEORGE CANNING** over military strategy. Weakened by ill health and unable to paper over the cracks, he resigned in September 1809. A month later, on 30 October, he died at Bulstrode.

BERLIN, CONGRESS OF, 13 June-13 July 1898. British and Austrian opposition to Russian gains in Eastern Europe, coupled with the search for solutions to the **EASTERN QUESTION**, led to a superpower conference in Berlin. It was agreed that Bulgaria would be subdivided in order to prevent it from becoming a Russian client state, that Britain would occupy Cyprus and that Austria-Hungary would control Bosnia and Herzegovina.

Montenegro, Romania and Serbia were recognized as independent. **BENJAMIN DISRAELI** claimed the agreement as "peace with honour", a phrase reused by **NEVILLE CHAMBERLAIN** after the **MUNICH AGREEMENT** in 1938.

BERLIN CONFERENCE, 1884-85. This meeting to partition and apportion the basins of the Congo and Niger rivers in Africa was chaired by the German Chancellor, Prince Otto von Bismarck, and attended by the European colonial powers, the United States of America and Turkey. During the negotiations, Britain gained German support for its claims on Nigeria in return for recognition of German authority in the Cameroons. The conference was instrumental in setting the ground rules for the **SCRAMBLE FOR AFRICA** and in establishing many of the later colonial and national boundaries on the continent.

BESSEMER, HENRY (1813-98). The inventor of the first successful means of making **STEEL** inexpensively and in large quantities, Bessemer was born in Charlton (Hertfordshire) on 19 January 1813. The son of a type-founder, he taught himself engineering, designed improvements to typesetting machines and earned a small fortune by developing a powder which could be used to make gold paint. In 1856, at the time of the **CRIMEAN WAR,** he invented a rotating artillery shell but found that the cast **IRON** cannons of the time were too weak for it. His attempts to find a stronger material led to a series of experiments in steelmaking and eventually to a process which involved forcing hot air through molten pig iron. The result was the removal of carbon, along with other impurities, and the production of a malleable mild steel. Refinements to the technique, particularly the removal of phosphorus, added to the commercial value of the process. By 1864, it was being widely used in the United States of America and continental Europe as well as in the United Kingdom. Later, Bessemer turned his attention to the design of steamships, solar furnaces and telescopes. His contribution to industry was recognized in 1879, when he was **KNIGHT**ed. In the United States, the city of Bessemer (Alabama), founded in 1887 and a major producer of iron and steel products, was named in his honour. He died in **LONDON** on 15 March 1898. (See **INDUSTRIAL REVOLUTION**).

BEVERIDGE, WILLIAM HENRY (1879-1963). The father of Britain's **WELFARE STATE,** Beveridge was born in Rangpur (then in India, now in Bangladesh) on 5 March 1879, the son of Henry Beveridge (a judge in the Indian Civil Service) and his second wife, Annette. He was educated at Charterhouse School and **OXFORD** University, graduating in 1903 as a Bachelor of Civil Law.

In spite of the strong opposition of both parents, he turned his back on a legal career and, in 1904, took a post as Subwarden at Toynbee Hall (a charitable institution in **LONDON**), where he developed his interest in the causes and cures of unemployment. The following year, he became a leader writer with *The Morning Post* (a daily newspaper supporting the **CONSERVATIVE PARTY**) and, in 1908, joined the civil service at the **BOARD OF TRADE**. In 1909, he published *Unemployment: A Problem of Industry*, focusing on the ways in which company organization affects the labour pool. He revised his views on the basis of later experience and, in 1944, represented them in *Full Employment in a Free Society*, a work which reflected the influence of the economic theories advanced by **JOHN MAYNARD KEYNES**. From 1909 until 1916, he was Director of Labour Exchanges and prepared plans for a form of compulsory unemployment insurance. From that post, he moved to the Ministry of Food (becoming **PERMANENT SECRETARY** in 1919) and shouldered the responsibility of organizing the country's food rationing programme during the **FIRST WORLD WAR**. He returned to academic life in 1919 as Director of the London School of Economics and Political Science, turning it into a research-oriented institution with an international reputation, and, in 1937, was elected Master of University College, Oxford.

At the instigation of **WINSTON CHURCHILL**'s wartime coalition **GOVERNMENT**, he was appointed chairman of a committee on social insurance and allied services which published its recommendations in a work with the official title of *Social Insurance and Allied Services* (1942), known as **THE BEVERIDGE REPORT**. Most of the proposals, including arrangements for unemployment benefit, sickness benefit and payments to the elderly, all funded by a national insurance scheme, were implemented in the years following the end of the **SECOND WORLD WAR** and laid the foundations of the **WELFARE STATE**. In 1944, attracted by the power of **PARLIAMENT**, he left his post at Oxford and was elected to the **HOUSE OF COMMONS** as a **LIBERAL PARTY** MP representing Berwick-on-Tweed. However, his talents as an administrator were significantly greater than his skills as a politician and he was defeated at the 1945 **GENERAL ELECTION**. He was created Baron Beveridge of Tuggal in 1946 and took his place in the **HOUSE OF LORDS**. Although he served on a number of committees after that, his career was effectively over. He died in Oxford on 16 March 1963.

BEVERIDGE REPORT, THE, September 1942. Named after the Chairman of the Committee of Enquiry (**SIR WILLIAM HENRY BEVERIDGE**), this report, *Social Insurance and Allied Services,* advocated a unified social security scheme to abolish want, disease, squalor, idleness and ignorance. It proposed benefits to cushion the impact of unemployment, sickness, disability, old age and death. This was an essential plank in the **WELFARE STATE** policy of caring for citizens of the **UNITED KINGDOM** from cradle to grave. After the **SECOND WORLD WAR**, it was partially implemented through the National Insurance Scheme and the **NATIONAL HEALTH SERVICE**.

BEVIN, ERNEST (1881-1951). One of the most prominent **TRADE UNION**ists and **LABOUR PARTY** politicians during the first half of the 20th century, Bevin was born in Winsford (Somerset) on 9 March 1881. The illegitimate son of Mary Bevin, a village midwife who had separated from her husband some years previously, he grew up in conditions of great poverty. His mother died when he was only eight years old, leaving him in the care of his half-sister (Mary). Three years later, he left Hayward Boys' School, having learned only basic skills of reading, writing and arithmetic, in order to find work — and income — on a farm.

In 1894, he moved to Bristol and got a job as a mineral water deliveryman then became increasingly involved in the establishment and administration of trade unions which would represent the interests of manual workers. His first step was the foundation of a Carters' Branch of the Dockers' Union in 1910. Bevin was made a full-time official of that union the following year though the post was not formally recognized until he was given the title of Assistant General Secretary in 1920, when he appeared before a Court of Inquiry to argue the case for a guaranteed wage for his members. In 1921, sensing that size brought power, he persuaded 32 separate transport unions to amalgamate as the Transport and General Workers' Union and, from then until 1940, acted as General Secretary of the new body, turning it into the largest labour union in the world.

His high profile post made him one of the principal figures in the industrial troubles of the 1920s, particularly after he became a member of the General Council of the **TRADES UNION CONGRESS (TUC)** in 1925. He was one of the leaders of the **GENERAL STRIKE** in 1926 and, when that collapsed, persuaded the Congress to provide a mouthpiece for workers by formulating an official policy on all of the important economic issues facing the country. In 1929, he played a major role in the establishment of the TUC's Economic Committee and, the following year, was appointed to the Macmillan Committee on Finance and Industry, impressing **JOHN MAYNARD KEYNES** with his understanding of the implications of fiscal and financial policies.

At the 1918 **GENERAL ELECTION**, he had stood unsuccessfully as the Labour Party candidate in the Bristol South **CONSTITUENCY** but, during the deepening interwar economic recession, was disillusioned by the party's failure to deal with ever-increasing rates of unemployment. However, he was persuaded to represent Labour as a candidate at Gateshead in 1931. Once more he lost and this time vowed never to stand for **PARLIAMENT** again. Nevertheless, he had become convinced of the need for organized labour, in the form of trade unions, to ally itself with the Labour Party both as a means of improving wages and conditions and as a way of influencing domestic and foreign policy. During the 1930s, he became increasingly prominent as a negotiator in disputes on behalf of the dockers, the seamen and the road transport workers. On a wider canvas, he was playing a major role in the International Transport Workers' Federation and the International Labour Office so, by the time he was elected Chairman of the General Council of the TUC in 1937, he was one of the most respected (and feared) of the union bosses.

When **WINSTON CHURCHILL** formed his wartime coalition government in 1940, he turned to Bevin for help in maximizing the country's manpower resources. Deciding that the circumstances allowed him to disregard his vow never to stand for Parliament again, Bevin was elected MP for Central Wandsworth and joined the War **CABINET** as Minister of Labour and National Service. For the next five years, he made a major contribution to the war effort by directing the mobilization of service personnel and planning the transfer of workers to critical industries. As a result, his stature increased further, and, when Labour won the 1945 general election, **CLEMENT ATTLEE** appointed him Foreign Secretary. That position made him a major figure in the debates over postwar economic reconstruction. He worked to create a prosperous Europe united against communism, established strong links with the United States, helped to found the Organization for European Economic Co-operation (1948) and was one of the designers of NATO. Bevin firmly believed that his contribution to the establishment of that body in 1949 was his greatest achievement in politics. In 1950, he devised the **COLOMBO PLAN** as a means of facilitating cooperation between Commonwealth countries in south and southeast Asia (see **COMMONWEALTH OF NATIONS**), but his schemes for the Middle East were frustrated because neither the Jews nor the Arabs would support his proposal to make Palestine a joint Arab-Jewish state.

By 1951, the years of hard work had affected his health and, on 9 March, he resigned. He remained in the Cabinet as **LORD PRIVY SEAL** but died in **LONDON** on 14 April. Never embarrassed by his lack of family connections or by his limited formal education, he was a natural leader who had done much to improve the quality of life of working class Britain.

BIG BANG, 27 October 1986. The phrase was coined to describe the cataclysmic changes which occurred when the financial markets of **LONDON**, including share dealing on the **STOCK EXCHANGE**, were deregulated. The move, part of **MARGARET THATCHER**'s policy towards free markets, was intended both to secure London's position as a pivot of the world financial system, and to persuade international firms to establish themselves in the **CITY OF LONDON**, which for centuries had been renowned for its network of gentlemanly partnerships and restricted access markets. Linked to this was the computerisation of much financial dealing. A massive influx of new, mainly international, firms appeared, often paying very high salaries to its young employees. (See **THATCHERISM**).

BILL. (See **ACT OF PARLIAMENT**).

BILL OF RIGHTS, December 1689. Following the **GLORIOUS REVOLUTION**, the **CONVENTION PARLIAMENT** rejected the concept of the **DIVINE RIGHT OF KINGS**, with its arbitrary rule, and passed a Bill of Rights — the *Act Declaring the Rights and Liberties of the Subject* (see **ACT OF PARLIAMENT**). This set out the restraints on the **MONARCH** and the supremacy of **PARLIAMENT** as the law-making body in the land, free of royal interference. In effect, this legislation condemned the reign of **JAMES VII** and **II** as subversive of the Protestant religion and the laws of **ENGLAND** and ratified the accession of **WILLIAM III** and **MARY II**, barring Roman Catholics from succeeding to the throne.

BIRMINGHAM. Although it dates from **ANGLO-SAXON** times, Birmingham is essentially a product of the **INDUSTRIAL REVOLUTION.** It was linked by **CANAL** to the **COAL** fields of south Staffordshire during the 18th century and was in the forefront of subsequent technological innovation, ultimately becoming the second largest city in **ENGLAND** after **LONDON**, which lies some 100 miles to the southeast. It was formally elevated to the status of **CITY** in 1891 and, by the mid-20th century, had a highly diversified manufacturing structure with an emphasis on metalworking, including cars, machine tools, armaments, brass, railway rolling stock, tyres, jewellery and electronics. In the decades since the end of the **SECOND WORLD WAR**, much of the city has been redeveloped, with many of the older properties swept away and a new shopping centre built at the Bull Ring, a former agricultural market. Birmingham's economy suffered considerably during the recession of the 1980s, and, partly for that reason, there was a decline in population from just over one million in 1981 to 938,000 in 1991. The population of the West Midlands Metropolitan County, of which the city is the major focus, was nearly 2.5 million in 1991, a decrease of 5.5 per cent over the 1981 figure.

BIRMINGHAM SIX. In 1974, the Irish Republican Army bombed two pubs (see **PUBLIC HOUSE**) in **BIRMINGHAM**, killing 21 people and injuring 162. In August 1975, six Irishmen, including Hugh Callaghan (who later wrote an autobiography entitled *Cruel Fate*), were convicted of the bombing and given life sentences. Subsequent investigations showed that the forensic evidence may have been flawed, that the **POLICE** interrogation records may have been tampered with and that undue pressure may have been exerted on the suspects in order to obtain confessions. The Six were released in March 1991 by the **COURT OF APPEAL**, which quashed their sentences. This case mirrors those of the **MAGUIRE SEVEN** and the **GUILDFORD FOUR**: each time, unsafe verdicts were obtained by questionable methods during the period of the 1970s when IRA bombing of the mainland, and hence public outrage, was at its height.

BLACK DEATH, 1348-51. In the summer of 1349, this outbreak of bubonic plague was at its worst. It is estimated that, in that year alone, over one million people died of the Black Death in the **BRITISH ISLES** and that the population of **ENGLAND** was reduced by 33 per cent. The disease originated in China around 1333 and, by 1348, had entered southern England from the continent, probably via fleas on infected rats from ships trading out of English ports. It quickly spread northwards, hitting, in particular, urban areas, which had concentrations both of people and of rats. The disease was characterized by fever and the appearance of black spots and lumps (or buboes) in the armpits and groin. The toll of human misery was matched by a devastating effect on the largely agricultural economy; losses of labour resulted in wage rises which the Government attempted to redress, creating unrest in the form of the **PEASANTS' REVOLT**. The Black Death is said to have killed up to 30 per cent of the population of Europe, with estimates as high as 40 per cent for the losses in Britain. Later plagues in 1360 to 1362, 1369 and 1375 were more localized in extent.

BLACK HOLE OF CALCUTTA, 20 June 1756. In protest against the activities of the **EAST INDIA COMPANY**, and in an attempt to oust Britain from India while the colonial power was engaged in the **SEVEN YEARS WAR**, the Nawab of Bengal is alleged to have confined 146 British prisoners in a small room measuring 18 feet by 15 feet. It was claimed that 123 men died of suffocation in one night in the heat of the Indian summer (modern Indian scholars put the number of prisoners at 43, with 15 dead). **ROBERT CLIVE** retook Calcutta the following year and avenged the incident at the **BATTLE OF PLASSEY**. The Nawab was deposed by his own people, and Bengal passed to Britain. This was possibly an embellished story to hide administrative incompetence.

BLACK PRINCE, THE. (See **EDWARD THE BLACK PRINCE**).

BLACK ROD. The Gentleman Usher of the Black Rod is an officer of the **HOUSE OF LORDS** with duties akin to those of the **SERJEANT-AT-ARMS** in the **HOUSE OF COMMONS**, notably responsible for security, services and accommodation. He also acts as Secretary to the **LORD GREAT CHAMBERLAIN** and undertakes some ceremonial duties. While the House is sitting, the Black Rod or the Yeoman Usher (his deputy) is always present. His most public responsibility is to act as the messenger of the Sovereign when members of the **HOUSE OF COMMONS** are required to attend the State Opening of **PARLIAMENT** and hear the Queen's Speech describing **GOVERNMENT** plans for the session.

BLANKETEERS, MARCH OF THE, March 1817. This was a protest march from **MANCHESTER** to **LONDON** by handloom weavers and spinners who intended to present a petition to the Prince **REGENT** as a means of publicizing the problems in the **COTTON INDUSTRY**. It was well planned but ineffective because troops halted the marches and the leaders were imprisoned. Of the 600 starters, only one eventually reached London to present the petition. Symptomatic of the social unrest of the period, this march earned its name because the protestors carried blankets on their backs. (See **LUDDITES; PETERLOO MASSACRE; SIX ACTS; SPA FIELDS RIOT**).

BLENHEIM, BATTLE OF, 13 August 1704. At this, one of the battles of the **WAR OF THE SPANISH SUCCESSION** in Bavaria, **JOHN CHURCHILL,** Duke of Marlborough, a brilliant tactical commander with an Anglo-Austrian force of 50,000 men, defeated a Franco-Bavarian army of 60,000, thus saving Vienna and breaking the stalemate on the Danube front. A grateful nation built Blenheim Palace in Oxfordshire for the Duke after what he called "a glorious victory".

BLITZ. From 7 September 1940 to May 1941, the Luftwaffe directed heavy aerial bombardment onto **LONDON** and other British cities in a bid to break public morale. The Germans had code-named 13 August 1940 "The Day of the Eagle": 1,485 planes were sent to attack **ENGLAND** and shot down 13 fighters with a loss of 45 aircraft. That raid had marked a change in Luftwaffe tactics, with a switch from military to civilian targets, and its success probably prompted the instigation of the attacks from September which are collectively known as "The Blitz".

The first major sortie took place on 7 September, when 300 bombers attacked the capital. On the night of 29 December alone, a raid caused over 1,500 fires, mainly in the **CITY OF LONDON**. High explosive bombs, incendiaries and parachute mines were dropped. While perhaps not as unshakeable as was suggested at the time, morale did not break, even at the height of the bombing, when 3,700 Londoners died in one month and up to 600 were killed in a single night. Many buildings were damaged in the night raids, which continued for months, and residents sheltered in the underground system, Anderson Shelters (arches of corrugated iron covered in soil), Morrison Shelters (indoor steel boxes) and communal shelters in town centres. The London Underground became a place of safety for up to 177,000 people a night.

During 1941, the attacks were directed at other major cities, ports and historic towns. Coventry was raided three times, and, in May 1941, 2,000 people were killed on Merseyside (see **RIVER MERSEY**) after eight nights' bombardment. Total losses are estimated at around 43,000 dead and 51,000 injured.

Britain retaliated with the Thousand Bomber Raid on Cologne in May 1942, when only 39 planes were lost, and with the raids (with its ally, the United States of America) on the Ruhr and Berlin in 1943, using Halifax and Lancaster bombers with US Fortresses and Liberators.

The term "Blitz" derives from the German "blitzkrieg", which means "lightning war" and was a strategy developed by Heinz Guderian and Erich von Manstein.   It involved heavy bombardment, air strikes and the cutting of supply lines by rapid movements of infantry and armoured attack vehicles in land conflicts.

BLOODY ASSIZES. After the **MONMOUTH REBELLION** in 1685, the "hanging judge", George Jeffreys, tried the rebels in the west of **ENGLAND**. His **ASSIZES** got its name from the brutal and merciless way it dealt with the accused: up to 320 were hanged and over 800 were sent for **TRANSPORTATION** to the West Indies. Lady Lisle (aged 70) was sentenced to be burned to death for harbouring rebels. Judge Jeffreys was made **LORD CHANCELLOR** by King **JAMES VII** and **II** for his faithful service.

BLORE HEATH, BATTLE OF, 22-23 September 1459. This battle was fought near Market Drayton in Staffordshire during the **WARS OF THE ROSES**. A small Yorkist force, commanded by the Earl of Salisbury, defeated a Lancastrian army under Lord Audley by leading it into a hard-to-defend narrow gully. The Yorkists used field artillery for what may have been the first time in a large set-piece battle in Britain, firing cannon balls and grapeshot (composed largely of local gravel) and forcing the Lancastrian cavalry to withdraw. In August 1993, the battlefield was threatened by plans to extract gravel from the site.

BOADICEA. The wife of Prasutagas, who ruled the **ICENI** in **EAST ANGLIA** as a client king of the **ROMANS**, Boadicea led an unsuccessful revolt against the invaders. When Prasutagus died in 60 AD without a male heir, he left his wealth to his two daughters and to the Emperor Nero, hoping that the bequest to his imperial master would bring protection for his family. The plan failed. His kingdom was plundered and his family humiliated. Boadicea rebelled, raised an army and burned Colchester, Verulam and several military posts. According to Tacitus, 70,000 Roman legionaries and their British allies were massacred. The ninth legion, led by Suetonius Paulinus, the Provincial Governor, was ordered to quell the revolt and met Boadicea's force at a location thought to be near Fenny Stratford, Buckinghamshire. After a long hard battle, the Romans gained the upper hand. Thousands of British rebels were killed and Boadicea herself either took poison or died of shock.

BOARD OF TRADE. Founded in 1621, the Board is a committee of the **PRIVY COUNCIL** with responsibility, as laid down in the 1786 constitution, to consider "all matters relating to trade and foreign plantation". Initially an advisory body, it became increasingly important during the 19th century as it developed executive powers over new sectors of the economy spawned by the **INDUSTRIAL REVOLUTION** (including **RAILWAYS** and shipping). Since then, many of its areas of interest have been officially removed and allocated to new **GOVERNMENT** departments (the Ministry of Labour, for example, in 1917 and the Ministry of Transport in 1919). (See **PRESIDENT OF THE BOARD OF TRADE**).

BOBBIES. A colloquial term for **POLICE**, the word came into use in the 1830s and is taken from the first name of Sir **ROBERT PEEL** who, in 1829, established a police force for the whole of **LONDON** with the exception of the **CITY OF LONDON**. The authority of the officers stemmed from the provisions of the Metropolitan Police Act (see **ACT OF PARLIAMENT**) and their headquarters was based at Scotland Yard.

BOER WAR (first), 1880-81. Attempts by the British **GOVERN-MENT** at federation in South Africa were opposed by the Boer inhabitants of the area, who were incensed by the annexation of the Transvaal in 1877. **BENJAMIN DISRAELI** moved to safeguard the Transvaal, the Cape Colony and Natal, but the British troops were defeated at the Battle of Majuba Hill in 1881. That led to the restoration of the Transvaal Republic, with Britain retaining power over foreign relations and native affairs only. The power over native affairs was surrendered in 1884. The term "Boer" means "farmer" in Afrikaans, and the Boers were descendants of Dutch settlers.

BOER WAR (second), 1899-1902. Tensions in the Transvaal continued at a high level after the first **BOER WAR** (1880-81), especially when **CECIL RHODES** became Prime Minister of the Cape Colony and pushed for a united Africa under British rule. Also, Britain supported the Uitlanders — foreign workers in the Boer-controlled Transvaal, many of whom were British-born and had petitioned Queen **VICTORIA** because they felt that their political rights were being eroded. The Boers prepared and armed for war over for a long period, whereas Britain retained that imperious overconfidence which could be disastrous. As a result, when Natal was invaded in 1899, only 30,000 British troops were in the region and 65 per cent were colonial volunteers, not regular soldiers. The Boers gained major victories at Stormberg (10 December), Magersfontein (11 December) and Colenso (15 December) — a six-day period which became known as "Black Week" — and laid seige to Ladysmith, Kimberley and Mafeking.

The Kimberley siege was relieved on 15 February 1900 and all captured areas retaken by the end of the year as **HORATIO KITCHENER** used British, Canadian and Australian troops to push the invaders back. Transvaal and the Orange Free State were then annexed. After a period of guerilla war, systematic destruction of villages in a scorched earth policy and the establishment of concentration camps (in which up to 9,000 to 20,000 Boers, most of them children, may have died), the annexations were confirmed in 1902 by the **TREATY OF VEREENIGING** but with a promise to the Boers of eventual self-rule. The Union of South Africa was established in 1910.

British losses were estimated at 6,000 killed in battle, with perhaps 16,000 dying from wounds or disease. (See **HENRY CAMPBELL-BANNERMAN; JAMESON RAID; KRUGER TELEGRAM; RELIEF OF MAFEKING**).

BOLEYN, ANNE (c.1507-36). The second of **HENRY VIII**'s six wives, Anne was the daughter of Sir Thomas Boleyn and his wife, Elizabeth. The family moved in royal circles and she gained a number of admirers, including poet Sir Thomas Wyat and Henry Percy, heir to the Earl of Northumberland. Eventually, the King became infatuated with her, and that infatuation fuelled his desire to divorce his Queen, **CATHERINE OF ARAGON**, who had failed to give him an heir to the throne.

In 1531, Henry separated from his wife and about 25 January 1533, despite the lack of any dispensation from the Pope Clement VII (who had not sanctioned a divorce from Catherine), secretly marrried Anne.   The details of the match became public around Easter, and, in May, Archbishop of Canterbury **THOMAS CRANMER** formally recognized the marriage. Anne was crowned the following month and, in September, gave birth to a daughter (later **ELIZABETH I**). Henry, desperate for an heir, was bitterly disappointed, and that disappointment grew over the years as Anne failed to produce a male child (though a son was stillborn on 29 January 1536). Moreover, her arrogance and her animosity towards Catherine were making enemies at court.

The King's infatuation waned, and, on 2 May 1536, Anne was imprisoned in the **TOWER OF LONDON**, charged with committing adultery with several lovers, including Lord Rochford, her own brother. Ten days later, William Brereton, Henry Norris, Mark Smeaton and Sir William Weston were all found guilty of having sexual relations with her. On 15 May, a court of 26 nobles (presided over by the Duke of Norfolk, Anne's uncle) also found the Queen and her brother guilty. On 17 May, Anne's marriage to Henry was pronounced invalid by Cranmer and the men found guilty were executed.   Anne was beheaded on 19 May. To the end, she protested her innocence.

BOLINGBROKE, HENRY. (See **HENRY IV**).

BOMBER COMMAND. Following the **BLITZ** in 1941, with its concentrated air attacks on civilian targets and cities, Air Chief Marshal "Bomber" Harris (Head of Bomber Command from 1942) decided upon mass bombing of German towns in order to demoralize the civilian population and retaliate for the devastation of British cities. Attacks on German ports were followed by the Cologne raid (Operation Millenium) on the night of 30/31 May 1942, when 1,000 British planes dropped 1,455 tons of bombs in 90 minutes. Hamburg was attacked seven times in July and August of the following year, and on one occasion — Operation Gomorrah — 2,300 tons of bombs fell on the city in two hours as the new window bales of foil strip were pushed out of the aircraft to confuse enemy RADAR. The bombing of Dresden on 13/14 February 1945 (see **DRESDEN RAID**) killed upwards of 55,000 civilians. Bomber Command lost

50,000 aircrew during the raids, and there was an estimated German civilian loss of 500,000. The policy is still controversial. Some historians argue that the tying up of German resources crucially weakened the enemy, but others claim that most of the targets were civilian so the bombers failed to destroy the Nazi war machine.

BOOK OF COMMON PRAYER. The first version of this liturgy of the **CHURCH OF ENGLAND** was the work of **THOMAS CRANMER** and appeared in 1549, in English rather than Latin. A second (more Protestant) text was published in 1552 and then later redesigned during the reign of Queen **ELIZABETH I. PARLIAMENT** introduced **ACTS OF UNIFORMITY** (see **ACT OF PARLIAMENT**) to ensure that the Prayer Book was used in all religious worship in churches.

BOOTH, WILLIAM (1829-1912). The founder of the **SALVATION ARMY**, Booth was born in Nottingham on 10 April 1829. He was apprenticed to a pawnbroker at the age of 13, and, although not from an affluent background, was shocked at the poverty and degradation which he experienced day after day. In 1844, he became a committed Christian and, two years later, after listening to James Caughey (an American evangelist) began to preach at Methodist services (see **METHODISM**).

When his apprenticeship was completed in 1848, he moved to **LONDON** in an attempt to find better-paid work and was given a job by a pawnbroker in Walworth, south of the **RIVER THAMES** and close to the large working class community of the docklands. As his commitment to the ministry increased, he began to hold outdoor services, but that led to friction with other Methodist preachers so, in 1858, he transferred to the Methodist New Connection, which ordained him as a minister after he had completed a preparatory period of study. With his wife Catherine (whom he had married in 1855), he held services up and down the country. In 1861, Booth resigned from his church in order to become an itinerant evangelist, preaching to the urban poor, who had little attachment to any religious denomination.

In 1865, he returned to London and held a series of tent meetings in the Whitechapel area of the city's East End. The converts won at these revivalist crusades were formed into military-style units which, in 1878, were named the **SALVATION ARMY**. For several years, many of the members were ridiculed and persecuted (in 1884, for instance, 600 of them were imprisoned for preaching), but, by the turn of the century, the organization had earned worldwide recognition. Branches opened in the United States of America in 1879, in Australia in 1880 and in France in 1881. Over the next ten years, the movement spread throughout Europe and to territories of the **BRITISH EMPIRE** in South America, South Africa and India.

In 1890, Booth published *In Darkest England and the Way Out*, a work written with journalist W. T. Stead, which made a series of recommendations for the relief of poverty and homelessness, creation of employment and treatment of alcoholics. The proposals seemed realistic and gained considerable public support. Although greatly saddened by the death of his wife (also in 1890) and by the rift with three of his seven children, who resigned from the Army because of disagreements over discipline, Booth allowed neither personal problems nor increasing blindness to stop him from his preaching, which he continued until his death in London on 20 August 1912 at the age of 83. He was succeeded as General of the Salvation Army by Bramwell, his eldest son.

BOROUGH. The word is derived from the Old English or **ANGLO-SAXON** word **BURH**, which meant 'a fortified place with a market'. Over time, it became applied to an urban settlement with privileges in government, law, liberty, landownership or trade which had been granted by charter. The charters were awarded by the **MONARCH** (for Royal Boroughs) or by the **LORD** (for Seigneurial Boroughs). Later, **LOCAL GOVERNMENT** came to be based on the borough unit and the word *borough* became reserved for those urban districts which had legal authority to form a borough council (those which had the additional right to elect a Mayor were the Municipal Boroughs), or for places which elected a Member of **PARLIAMENT** (the Parliamentary Boroughs). The 1888 Local Government Act (see **ACT OF PARLIAMENT**) created County Boroughs, which were towns with the administrative responsibilities of a **COUNTY**. These were abolished in 1972. **LONDON** comprises 32 boroughs, plus the **CORPORATION OF LONDON**, which runs the borough that is the old City area. (See **BURGESS**).

BOSWORTH FIELD, BATTLE OF, 22 August 1485. This small-scale but extremely important battle near Leicester effectively ended the **WARS OF THE ROSES**, though it was followed by the **BATTLE OF STOKE.** It concluded with the defeat and death of **PLANTAGENET** King **RICHARD III** and led to the founding of the **TUDOR** dynasty by his victor, Henry Tudor, who used 2,000 French mercenaries in the battle and later became King **HENRY VII**. The battle restored stability to the **CROWN**, particularly because Henry then married Elizabeth, daughter of **EDWARD IV**, so ending the dynastic problems that had precipitated the Wars of the Roses.

BOUDICCA. (See **BOADICEA**).

BOUNTY, MUTINY ON THE, April 1789. Lieutenant William Bligh commanded the ship *Bounty* on a voyage to introduce breadfruit from Tahiti to the West Indies. Fletcher Christian led a mutiny against Bligh's harsh discipline, casting him adrift with 18 men in a small boat and taking the *Bounty* back to the pleasures of Tahiti, then on to Pitcairn Island, where the crew stayed with island women. Bligh reached Timor and the **ADMIRALTY** sent ships to apprehend the mutineers. In 1792, ten were court-martialled and three hanged, but Christian escaped justice.

BOW STREET RUNNERS. Henry Fielding, the author of *The History of Tom Jones*, was a magistrate at the Bow Street court. He organized this first regular **POLICE** force in **LONDON** in 1742. From 1757, it was able to operate outside the area of the **CITY OF LONDON** and eventually, in 1829, merged with the Metropolitan Police.

BOWES-LYON, ELIZABETH ANGELA MARGUERITE (1900 -). Consort of King **GEORGE VI**, the Queen Mother holds the formal titles of **LADY** of the **ORDER OF THE GARTER**, Dame Grand Cross of the Victorian Order and the Order of the British Empire, Lady of the Order of the Thistle and Dame Grand Cross of the Order of Jerusalem (see **ORDERS OF CHIVALRY**). She was born on 4 August 1900 at St. Paul's Waldenbury (Hertfordshire), the daughter of Claude Bowes-Lyon (whose family was descended from King Robert I of **SCOTLAND**) and his wife Cecilia, daughter of the Rev and Mrs Charles W. Cavendish Bentinck.

Elizabeth spent much of her childhood at Glamis Castle, the family home in Scotland, and helped nursing staff there to care for wounded servicemen during the **FIRST WORLD WAR**. She met George, **DUKE OF YORK**, in 1920 and married him in **WESTMINSTER** Abbey on 26 April 1923. The match was thoroughly approved of by the Royal Family and especially by **GEORGE V**, who had a great affection for his new daughter-in-law.

The couple set up home in **LONDON** at 145 Piccadilly and had two daughters. The first, Princess Elizabeth (later Queen **ELIZABETH II**), was born on 21 April 1926 and accompanied her parents on a tour of Australasia while she was still an infant. The second, Princess **MARGARET ROSE**, was born at Glamis on 21 August 1930. After the children were born, the Duchess of York continued to accompany her husband on his royal visits and became an increasingly influential and respected figure in royal circles. There was, however, no expectation that the Duke would ever be King. Edward, his elder brother (later **EDWARD VIII**), was heir to the throne and had been groomed for the succession. However, Edward's announcement in 1936 that he intended to marry Mrs Wallis Simpson (an American divorcee) raised difficult questions about the relationship between the **MONARCH** and the **CHURCH OF ENGLAND**. Edward was forced into abdication, and George was crowned King on 12 May 1937. Elizabeth was crowned Queen at the same ceremony and, shortly afterwards, made very successful state visits to Paris (1938) and then to the United States and Canada (1939). During the **SECOND WORLD WAR**, she remained in London with the King and was in **BUCKINGHAM PALACE** when it was attacked by the Luftwaffe in 1940. Throughout the conflict, she travelled to bomb-damaged cities with her husband and earned respect for her compassion and lack of formality. After the war was over, she returned to a schedule of domestic and foreign visits, becoming, in 1947, the only Queen-Consort to tour South Africa. In 1951 and 1952, while George was seriously ill, she undertook many of the sovereign's public duties on her own.

Her marriage had been a very happy one so she was greatly affected by her husband's death on 6 February 1952 but returned to her royal duties after a period of mourning, travelling many thousands of miles each year and becoming a much-loved and much-respected public figure. She attended her daughter's **CORONATION** in 1953 then visited Rhodesia. In 1954, she visited Canada and the United States and, in 1955, became Chancellor of the University of London, a post which she held until 1981. In 1978, she accepted the appointment of Lord Warden of the **CINQUE PORTS**, the first woman to hold the office. Also, her childhood experiences made a deep impression on her, and she retained a great affection for Scotland. She has spent much time on the restoration of the Castle of Mey (her favourite Scottish home) on the Pentland

Firth and visits Balmoral Castle in Aberdeenshire with her children, grandchildren and great grandchildren every summer. As she aged, she gradually limited her public commitments but never retired completely and, now in her nineties, still carries out a number of engagements every year.

BOXER REBELLION, 1899-1900. The expansion of British and other European control of territory and trade in China at the end of the 19th century provoked several reactions (see **OPIUM WARS**). The Boxers were young Chinese nationalists (members of the Society of Harmonious Fists, which had started as a martial arts group), who attacked churches and European legations and property (particularly in Peking and Manchuria). The 1894-95 Sino-Japanese war had precipitated rapid changes in Chinese society, encouraging hostility towards the "foreign devils" in the country, and 1,500 incomers were killed before European powers with a force of 10,000 troops under German command suppressed the rebellion. The Boxer Protocol of 7 September 1901 imposed severe restrictions on the Chinese, inluding reparations through customs payments, the execution of ten officials, garrisoning of Chinese legations and western control of the sea route from Peking. The protocol officially ended in 1943.

BRIGHT, JOHN (1811-89). One of the first of the 19th century radicals who campaigned for **PARLIAMENTARY REFORM** and attacked the vested interests of the wealthy, Bright was born in Rochdale on 16 November 1811. His father, Jacob, owned a cotton mill in the town (see **COTTON INDUSTRY**), and, after an education at a Quaker school, John went to work there in 1827. Twelve years later he became a partner. In 1833, he helped to establish a local Literary and Philosophical Society, which provided the platform for his early speeches on public issues. A natural orator, he appealed to the urban working class with vituperative criticism of the **CORN LAWS** and the landed aristocracy. He entered **PARLIAMENT** in 1843, winning a **BY-ELECTION** at Durham, and four years later took the seat at **MANCHESTER**. He quickly made an impression in the **HOUSE OF COMMONS**, advocating changes in suffrage and opposing Britain's involvement in the **CRIMEAN WAR**. However, his growing reputation in **WESTMINSTER** was not reflected in his electorate; the war was popular with the working classes and, at the **GENERAL ELECTION** of 1857, Bright was defeated.

The fall in popularity was temporary. The following year, he won at **BIRMINGHAM** and returned to his campaigning, seconding the motion which led to Viscount **HENRY PALMERSTON**'s defeat in 1858 and supporting the new **CONSERVATIVE PARTY** administration's policies of transferring the management of the **EAST INDIA COMPANY** to the **CROWN** and admitting Jews to Parliament. He continued to press for changes in the franchise and was rewarded in 1867, when **BENJAMIN DISRAELI** introduced a **BILL** which gave the vote to all householders in the **BOROUGH**s who paid their own rates. Also, he argued for an extension of **FREE TRADE** and publicly supported the north in the US Civil War (he exchanged letters with Abraham Lincoln and fervently believed in the case for the abolition of slavery).

In 1868, following the **LIBERAL PARTY** election victory, **WILLIAM GLADSTONE** offered Bright the post of **PRESIDENT OF THE BOARD OF TRADE**. He accepted but had to resign because of illness in the early winter of 1870 and remained out of office until he was made **CHANCELLOR OF THE DUCHY OF LANCASTER** in 1873. When the Conservatives won the 1874 general election, Bright returned to the **OPPOSITION** benches but continued to support Gladstone, who reappointed him to the Chancellorship in 1880. In 1882, however, the two men differed over British intervention in Egypt, and Bright resigned. Further splits occurred over the issue of **HOME RULE** for **IRELAND** (Bright was against) and eventually led to the breakup of the Liberal Party. Bright was saddened by the friction, which — along with the imperialist policies he so much despised — greatly depressed him as he aged. Troubled by ill-health, he died in Rochdale on 27 March 1889. His critics had branded him an agitator, but **JOSEPH CHAMBERLAIN** was more charitable, commenting that "he placed the happiness of the many before the interests of the few".

BRITAIN. (See **BRITISH ISLES**).

BRITAIN, BATTLE OF, 10 July-12 October 1940. During this early period of the **SECOND WORLD WAR**, **ROYAL AIR FORCE (RAF)** Fighter Command, under Sir Hugh Dowding, was heavily engaged in aerial combat with the Luftwaffe over Britain. In July 1940, the RAF had just 45 squadrons of Hurricanes and Spitfires and factories were turning out only 500 planes a month. (It was estimated that the Germans had about 2,500 aircraft to pit against just 750 British planes.) Military airfields and RADAR stations, mainly in southeast **ENGLAND**, were targeted by Hermann Goering's bombers as part of Operation Sealion, and estuaries were mined with the intention of creating German air superiority prior to invasion of the United Kingdom. At that time, Germany had 13 divisions assembled in northern France whereas Britain had only a relatively poorly trained army, recently returned from France after the **DUNKIRK** evacuation, and a volunteer defence force (later the **HOME GUARD**) to defend the country.

Large-scale attacks on airfields began in August, and, during the last days of the month and early September, the RAF was losing more men and planes than the Luftwaffe in this key struggle of the war. (The German Enigma codes had been deciphered and revealed that their strategy was to postpone invasion until "the result of the present struggle for air superiority".) On 13 August, the Luftwaffe launched Eagle Day, with 1,485 sorties flown against Britain within 24 hours, and, on 6 September alone, the RAF lost 161 planes. By 7 September, all RAF fighters in the country were stationed in the south to repel invasion.

Critically, in September the German attacked with the mass bombing of **LONDON** (see **BLITZ**) as retaliation for a raid on Berlin on 25 August. That change of strategy, made in the hope of destroying civilian morale, gave Fighter Command time to regroup. Helped by RADAR, the British lost only 915 planes compared with a German total of 1,733 in the following weeks, and, by October, Hitler had abandoned his invasion plans. At the height of the battle, **WINSTON CHURCHILL** asked "What reserves have we?", and was told "There are none." He was later to pay tribute to the young pilots of the Spitfires and Hurricanes, saying that "Never in the field of human conflict has so much been owed by so many to so few".

BRITANNIA. This ancient name for the British Isles is said to have originated from Julius Caesar's mistaken belief that the **BELGAE** invaders of Britain were Britanni. Later, the concept was used as a symbol of the **BRITISH EMPIRE** in the form of a seated female warrior holding a shield and a trident and wearing a helmet, as depicted since 1672 on British coinage. The model for Britannia was said to have been Frances Stuart, Duchess of Richmond and a mistress of King **CHARLES II**.

BRITISH AIRWAYS. This company was formed in 1973 by the merger of the **BRITISH OVERSEAS AIRWAYS CORPORATION**

(BOAC) and **BRITISH EUROPEAN AIRWAYS (BEA)**. It is now the largest European airline and a major world service provider. Even when it was established, it had 220 aircraft and 53,000 staff, carrying 14 million passengers a year. Technically innovative, it quickly became profitable and flew **CONCORDE** from its first commercial flight (see **AIR TRANSPORT**). It has expanded by takeovers and shareholdings (TAT, Qantas, USAir) but in 1992 was implicated in allegations of unethical commercial practices against Virgin Airlines. It was privatized in 1987 (see **PRIVATIZA-TION**) and, in the 1990s, carried some 25 million passengers each year on a fleet of 230 aircraft, with 50,000 employees, flying to 150 destinations in 70 countries.

BRITISH BROADCASTING CORPORATION (BBC). The BBC was founded in 1922 under the administration of the **POST-MASTER GENERAL** and with **LORD** Reith as its first Director-General. It became a public service corporation by charter, in 1926, as a national radio service financed by licence fees paid by its listeners, not a market-led company. The BBC opened its first television channel from Alexandra Palace (**LONDON**) in 1936, with colour being introduced in 1967 on a second channel. Renowned worldwide for its impartial news reporting and high public broadcasting standards, it was used to relay coded messages to the French Resistance during the **SECOND WORLD WAR** and especially before **D-DAY**. The issue of the funding of the service has been constantly under review, particularly with the launch of rival independent commercial television companies in the 1950s and satellite companies in the 1990s.

BRITISH EMPIRE. The empire consisted of territories taken and gover-ned by Britain from the 17th century (but particularly in the period 1750 to 1850) for strategic, commercial or other reasons. Virginia and New England were acquired in the 17th century, Canada after the **SEVEN YEARS WAR** and India by the **EAST INDIA COMPANY**. Large parts of Africa were gained in the late 19th century (see **SCRAMBLE FOR AFRICA**), along with Australia, New Zealand and Hong Kong.

The reign of Queen **VICTORIA** is sometimes seen as the apogee of the "Empire on which the sun never set" (so-called because it spanned the globe). By the end of the 19th century, it was the largest in history, covering up to 20 per cent of the land area of the world and 25 per cent of its people. But the proponents of **FREE**

TRADE were by then questioning the degree to which imperial possessions created wealth, and **BENJAMIN DISRAELI** was calling the colonies "millstones round our neck". In the last half of the century, the larger territories gained some measure of self-rule, many becoming **DOMINIONS**. **DECOLONIZATION** became the norm, and, in 1931, the British Empire was renamed the **COMMONWEALTH OF NATIONS**.

BRITISH EUROPEAN AIRWAYS (BEA). British European Airways was one of two state-owned airlines which concentrated on internal and European flights and amalgamated in 1973 (see **BRITISH OVERSEAS AIRWAYS CORPORATION [BOAC]**) to create **BRITISH AIRWAYS**.

BRITISH ISLES. A geographical and apolitical term, the phrase refers to the group of islands located off the northwest coast of Europe, the largest comprising **GREAT BRITAIN** and **IRELAND**. It thus includes the political entities of the **UNITED KINGDOM** and the Republic of Ireland. Its total land area is approximately 121,600 square miles. The name "Britain" is probably pre-**ROMAN** and may come from the 4th century BC Greek name for the inhabitants — the Pritani (sometimes Prettanoi), meaning figured or tattooed people. The terms *Britain* and *Great Britain* were given political significance by the **UNION OF THE CROWNS** (1603), when James VI of **SCOTLAND** became King James I of **ENGLAND** (see **JAMES VI** and **I**), because they avoided both English and Scottish nationalist sensitivities while encompassing the Welsh.

BRITISH MUSEUM. The national repository for the arts and sciences, the Museum received approval and funds from **PARLIAMENT** in 1753 and opened in 1759. It was originally based on the collections of Sir Hans Sloane, an Irish-born physician of Scottish ancestry, and of the Earls of Oxford. King **GEORGE II** moved the royal library to the museum and granted it the right to receive a copy of all published books. The current building was designed in 1823. In 1963, the Natural History Museum was hived off as a separate institution, as was the British Library in 1973.

BRITISH NATIONAL PARTY (BNP). The BNP was formed in 1982 as a breakaway group from the **NATIONAL FRONT** advocating extreme right-wing policies of repatriation for blacks and neo-Nazi racism. Membership in 1993 was believed to be about 1,000 and, on 16 September of that year, its first local councillor was elected at a **BY-ELECTION** in Millwall (east **LONDON**), where factors of isolation, poor housing and deprivation were said to have influenced voting. (See **BRITISH UNION OF FASCISTS [BUF]**).

BRITISH NORTH AMERICA. This term was applied to colonial territories in North America following the **AMERICAN WAR OF INDEPENDENCE** (1783) until the passage of the 1867 **BRITISH NORTH AMERICA ACT** (see **ACT OF PARLIAMENT**).

BRITISH NORTH AMERICA ACT, 1867. This **ACT OF PARLIAMENT** created the Confederation of Canada, uniting Ontario, Quebec, New Brunswick and Nova Scotia.

BRITISH OVERSEAS AIRWAYS CORPORATION (BOAC). The British Overseas Airways Corporation was one of two state-owned airlines developed after the **SECOND WORLD WAR**. (The other was **BRITISH EUROPEAN AIRWAYS [BEA]**) It was created in 1939 by the merger of British Airways and Imperial Airways and operated international flights (with BEA concentrating on domestic flights) using the Comet, the world's first jet airliner. In 1958, it inaugurated the first scheduled transatlantic jet service and, in 1973, was amalgamated with BEA to create a new company, **BRITISH AIRWAYS**.

BRITISH UNION OF FASCISTS (BUF). Founded in 1932 by Sir **OSWALD MOSLEY** (former **CONSERVATIVE PARTY** MP and **LABOUR PARTY** Minister) after a visit to Italy, the BUF consisted of extreme right-wing fascists who wore characteristic blackshirts and created violent confrontations at every rally. The movement was particularly strong in the East End of **LONDON**, where it fanned the flames of poor working class anti-Semitism and unemployment. (See **BRITISH NATIONAL PARTY [BNP]**). It was banned by the 1936 Public Order Act (see **ACT OF PARLIAMENT**) from public displays and outlawed under wartime regulations in May 1940.

BRONZE AGE. This period of **PREHISTORIC BRITAIN** lasted from c. 2500 BC until about 800 BC and saw the introduction of metalworking in bronze (an alloy of tin and copper), copper and gold, mostly for jewellery and trinkets rather than weapons. Trading developed, and tin mines were opened in Cornwall. Burials were in round barrows or earth mounds, and pottery developed as high quality ware. The **BEAKER PEOPLE** rebuilt **STONEHENGE** to near its current form and settled upland areas as the climate became drier and grasslands spread. Larger communities developed as agricultural production increased, and, as the population grew, new weapons (such as swords and shields) evolved. Towards the end of the period, horse riding and wheeled vehicles became more common, but growing rivalries between communities created tensions, particularly as a trend towards wetter conditions made hill farming more difficult. The period was followed by the **IRON AGE**.

BROWN, GEORGE ALFRED (1914-85). A champion of the underprivileged and a major figure in the postwar **LABOUR PARTY**, Brown was born in **LONDON** on 2 September 1914, the elder son of George Brown (a grocer's packer) and his wife, Rosina. He was educated at Grey Street Elementary School and West Square Central School, leaving at the age of 15 and taking a job as fur salesman with the John Lewis Partnership in order to supplement the family income. After his working day was over, Brown attended further **EDUCATION** classes and meetings of the Labour Party's League of Youth, eventually becoming an official of the Transport and General Workers' Union (see **TRADE UNIONS**). In 1945, he was elected Member of **PARLIAMENT** for Belper and was appointed **PARLIAMENTARY PRIVATE SECRETARY,** firstly to the **MINISTER** of Labour and National Service (1945-47) and then to the **CHANCELLOR OF THE EXCHEQUER** (1947). He became Joint **PARLIAMENTARY SECRETARY** to the Minister of Agriculture and Fisheries in 1947 and was promoted to Minister of Works in May 1951 but held the post only until the October **GENERAL ELECTION**, which took the **CONSERVATIVE PARTY** back to **DOWNING STREET**.

The 13 years of **OPPOSITION** from 1951 until 1964 were hard on Labour politicians — salaries were low, morale bruised by a series of election defeats and career prospects dim. Brown considered returning to full-time trade union work but was given financial help by Cecil King, owner of the *Daily Mirror* newspaper, and stayed on to become **SHADOW MINISTER** of Defence in 1958. He supported **HUGH GAITSKELL** against the left-wing campaign for unilateral nuclear disarmament (see **CAMPAIGN FOR NUCLEAR DISARMAMENT [CND]**) and, in 1960, was elected Vice-Chairman and Deputy Leader of the Party. Three years later, he was defeated by **HAROLD WILSON** in the contest for the leadership but, when Labour returned to power in 1964, Brown was rewarded with the posts of First **SECRETARY OF STATE** and Secretary of State for Economic Affairs.

Charged with the task of preparing a national development plan, Brown set targets for productivity, prices and incomes and established a series of Regional Planning Councils to put them into effect. In 1966, however, the **GOVERNMENT** was faced with a stark choice between devaluing **STERLING** or implementing deflationary measures. Brown argued strongly against deflation because it would mean that much of his department's work would be wasted, but Wilson decided it was the lesser of two evils and Brown, in protest, resigned from the **CABINET**. However, his decision brought an appeal to think again from over 100 Labour MPs and he agreed to steer legislation establishing statutory price and income control through Parliament. Then, in 1966, he accepted the post of Foreign Secretary. With Wilson, he visited all of the member countries of the **COMMON MARKET** in an attempt to negotiate Britain's entry, only to be baulked by the veto of President Charles de Gaulle of France. He also came close to brokering an agreement between the United States and the Soviet Union over Vietnam, but the discussions eventually broke down.

In 1968, Brown resigned for a second time, claiming that Wilson was becoming too autocratic, and returned to the back benches (see **BACKBENCHER**). Despite the differences, he continued to work hard for the Party and, in the 1972 general election campaign, travelled the country in support of local candidates. That, perhaps, was misplaced loyalty because he appeared to neglect his own **CONSTITUENCY** and was defeated at the poll. He eventually left the Labour Party in 1976, disagreeing over policies towards the **TRADE UNIONS**. By the early 1980s, his health was deteriorating, and he died of a liver complaint in Truro on 2 June 1985. Brown's abilities as an orator and administrator were widely recognized but he possessed self-destructive habits with a fiery temperament, lubricated by alcohol. He was passionate in his support for the poor and the needy, but, in the end, his unpredictability was his downfall and most of his colleagues were relieved when he finally left politics.

BRUMMELL, BEAU. (See **GEORGE BRYAN BRUMMELL**).

BRUMMELL, GEORGE BRYAN (1778-1840). A social trendsetter, Brummell was given the nickname "Beau" because of his fashionable clothes, gentlemanly manners and witty conversation. He was born in **LONDON** on 7 June 1778, son of William Brummell (Private Secretary to **LORD FREDERICK NORTH** from 1770 until 1782), and educated at Eton College and **OXFORD** University. While still a child, he was fastidious about his appearance and, as an undergraduate, cultivated a reputation as a wit. In 1794, he obtained a commission as cornet in the 10th Hussars, largely through the influence of his friend Prince George, who was later to become King **GEORGE IV**.

Having reached the rank of Captain, Brummell left the army in 1798 and took an apartment in London's socially select Mayfair district. The following year he inherited a £30,000 fortune when his father died and, often in the company of the Prince, increasingly frequented the gaming tables and salons. His attachment to royalty and his charismatic personality gave him a unique position as an arbiter of taste and determinant of fashion, but his star waned as his gambling losses increased and George grew tired of his barbed tongue. In 1816, he fled to **CALAIS** in order to escape his creditors and, for 14 years, was permanently in debt. His position improved in 1830, when he became British Consul at Caen, but that post was abolished (on his own recommendation) in 1832 and, three years later, he was imprisoned as a debtor. His former associates helped to obtain his release and provided him with a small income, but he had become a frequent victim of mental delusions and was eventually taken to the Bon Sauveur Asylum, where he died on 30 March 1840.

BRUNANBURH, BATTLE OF, 937. At an unknown site in northern **ENGLAND**, **AETHELSTAN** (King of the English), with forces from **WESSEX** and **MERCIA**, defeated a combined army of Norsemen, Scots, **PICTS** and Britons under Scottish leaders. The battle was pivotal in creating a more united nation of England as Wessex and Mercia sank their traditional rivalries (thus ensuring the supremacy of England and the south in the later politics of the British Isles). It is mentioned in the **ANGLO-SAXON CHRONICLE** that "the host from the ships fell doomed . . . the whole day the West **SAXONS** with mounted companies kept in pursuit of the hostile peoples. Grievously they cut down the fugitives from behind with their whetted swords". An unknown contemporary English poet referred to the ground as "slick with men's blood, with numberless slain among shipmen and Scots".

BRUNEL, ISAMBARD KINGDOM (1806-59). The designer of the first transatlantic steamship and a versatile **RAILWAY** engineer, Brunel was born in Portsmouth on 9 April 1806, the only son of **SIR** Marc Brunel (a French-born industrial inventor). He was educated in Caen and Paris then returned to Britain in 1822 to work with his father. In 1825, he was appointed Resident Engineer when construction started on a tunnel under the **RIVER THAMES** between Wapping and Rotherhithe (in **LONDON**). Three years later, Brunel narrowly escaped death while trying to rescue a workman trapped by a sudden flood. Sent to Bristol to recuperate, he prepared plans for a suspension bridge over the Avon Gorge at Clifton; one of his designs was accepted, but, because of lack of funds, the structure was not completed until 1864. He also planned and effected improvements to Bristol's docks, then, in 1833, was appointed Chief Engineer to the Great Western **RAILWAY** Company. The line which he planned between London Paddington and Bristol was built to a seven-foot gauge — broader than the norm — and was opened in 1841. A commercial failure, it nevertheless became noted for its relatively high speeds and stimulated investment in other railways. Brunel himself was involved in the design and construction of over 1,000 miles of track in western **ENGLAND, WALES** and **IRELAND**. In addition, he made a considerable contribution to marine transport. His *Great Western*, a wooden vessel propelled by paddles, made her maiden voyage in 1838 and became the first successful transatlantic steamship. The *Great Britain* (1845) was the world's first large iron-hulled screw steamer, and the *Great Eastern* (1858) had both paddles and screw propulsion as well as an innovative double iron hull which was incorporated into the design of 20th century ocean liners. However, although Brunel was a brilliantly creative engineer, he lacked management skills. Unwilling to delegate work to subordinates, he found that long hours and increasing strain took their toll on his health. He died in London on 15 September 1859, worn out by years of hard work.

BUCKINGHAM PALACE. The Palace has been the official residence of the **MONARCH** in **LONDON** since Queen **VICTORIA** adopted it in the mid-19th century (before that it was the family home of the sovereign). King **JAMES VI** and **I** planted mulberry trees in the gardens on the site in order to feed silkworms, but when these pleasure grounds fell into disuse the area became a well-known area for prostitutes. The original house was built in 1677 for Lord Arlington, enlarged by the Duke of Buckingham in 1702-5 and purchased in 1762 by King **GEORGE III** for £28,000 because it occupied a prestigious site overlooking The Mall. The Royal Horse Guards first "Trooped the Colours" there in 1805, and John Nash redesigned the building for King **GEORGE IV** in the 1820s. The front facade is a 20th century addition. The Palace was opened to the public for the first time on 7 August 1993 (for eight weeks), partly in order to help pay for repairs to **WINDSOR CASTLE** after the fire in 1992, and partly, perhaps, to enhance the public image of the Royal Family.

BUDGET. An annual national review and account of the financial year, the Budget is a forecast of **GOVERNMENT** expenditure for the coming twelve months and a proposal of changes to national taxes and revenues. It is presented to **PARLIAMENT** by the **CHANCELLOR OF THE EXCHEQUER**. Since the time of **WILLIAM GLADSTONE**, who created the ritual of Budget Day, it has been the pivot of the Government's economic policies and is usually presented in April, with a follow-up autumn statement on public spending targets later in the year. From 1993, however, the two events have been amalgamated into a major Unified Budget, usually in November. It has become such a traditional event that the papers are always carried to Parliament by the Chancellor in Gladstone's battered red despatch box.

BULL, JOHN. A fictional character, John Bull first appeared in a publication entitled *Law is a Bottomless Pit* by John Arbuthnot in 1712 and was described as an honest, bluff, plain-dealing fellow, choleric, bold and of a very variable temper. He became a patriotic symbol for Britain, particularly in the satirical magazine *Punch*, which depicted him as a portly, jolly fellow, usually with a bulldog for a companion.

BURG or BURH. This was a **VIKING** or **ANGLO-SAXON** settlement with a defensive area and a market. Originally a series of forts or fortified camps begun by **ALFRED**, they were important military sites, particularly in southern **ENGLAND**. Many became major towns by the 10th century. (See **BOROUGH**).

BURGESS. These individuals were free citizens of a **BOROUGH**, usually property owners and men of influence. The term has also been used to refer to a Member of **PARLIAMENT** representing a borough and to a borough councillor.

BURGHLEY, BARON WILLIAM CECIL (See **WILLIAM CECIL**).

BURKE, EDMUND (1729-97). A statesman and political theorist, Burke was a major influence on **GOVERNMENT** decision making from the 1760s until his death in 1797. He was born in Dublin in 1729, probably on 12 January, graduated from Trinity College in 1748 then moved to **LONDON** in 1750 to study law. He soon lost interest in legal matters, however, and spent some time travelling in **ENGLAND** and France. In 1756 he published anonymously *A Vindication of Natural Society . . . . in a Letter to Lord *** by a Late Noble Writer*, a satire aimed at criticism of revealed religion and at the vogue for a return to nature. *A Philosopical Enquiry Into the Origin of Our Ideas of the Sublime and Beautiful*, a tract on aesthetic theory published in 1757, added to his reputation as a writer and thinker. The following year, he began to edit *The Annual Register* (a yearly survey of world affairs) and, in 1763, he became a member of Samuel Johnson's literary club. In 1766, he entered **PARLIAMENT**, acting as Secretary to the **MARQUIS OF ROCKINGHAM** (the leader of one of the **WHIG** groups) and exerting great influence on that politician's thinking.

In the **HOUSE OF COMMONS**, Burke took issue with **GEORGE III**'s claim that the **MONARCH** should play a more active role in decision making, maintaining that **MINISTER**s should not be the favourites of the King but people approved by Members of Parliament and the public. In 1774, he was elected MP for Bristol and argued that his role was as representative of the people, not as delegate; he should consider the welfare and interests of his supporters but his job was to promote the common good, acting according to his own judgement and not according to some mandate from those who voted for him. He also struggled to gain reforms in **IRELAND**, urging greater toleration of Roman Catholics. In addition, he advocated an end to the **SLAVE TRADE** and played a large part in the investigation of misrule by the **EAST INDIA COMPANY**.

During the years before the **AMERICAN WAR OF INDEPENDENCE**, he supported the colonists and, in 1776, joined with other Whigs to submit a motion proposing the revision of all acts (see **ACT OF PARLIAMENT**) to which the settlers objected. In 1789, he adopted a stance on the **FRENCH REVOLUTION** which was in marked contrast to the general mood of the country. In *Reflections on the Revolution in France*, published in 1790, he maintained that the revolutionaries were madmen, overthrowing the established social order and devaluing tradition.

In 1780, Burke was elected MP for Malton. He resigned in 1795 but continued to write on European affairs until his death in Beaconsfield on 9 July 1797. His contribution to political theory was enormous. He explored the concept of Nature, arguing that, over time, the historical process, social conventions and social organization built up a natural harmony. He emphasized the validity of status and hierarchy, and, through his studies of events in France, provided an important stimulus to French and German counter revolutionary thought.

BUTE, EARL OF. (See **JOHN STUART**).

BUTLER, RICHARD AUSTEN (1902-82). One of the great influences on the 20th century development of the **CONSERVATIVE PARTY**, Rab Butler was born at Attock Serai (India) on 9 December 1902, the son of Sir Montagu Butler and his wife, Anne. He was educated at Marlborough College and **CAMBRIDGE** University, where he was President of the Union in 1924 and graduated with a degree in history the following year.

He became a Fellow at Corpus Christi College, Cambridge, in 1925, and, in 1929, when he entered **PARLIAMENT** as the MP for Saffron Walden. (This was a safe Conservative seat secured for him by his industrialist father-in-law, Samuel Courtauld, who arranged for him to become the Tory candidate without even being interviewed.) He was appointed **UNDER-SECRETARY OF STATE** for India in 1932 and was largely responsible for the 1935 Government of India Act (see **ACT OF PARLIAMENT**), which gave the country a measure of self-government. In 1937, he became **PARLIAMENTARY SECRETARY** at the Ministry of Labour and, in 1938, moved to the Foreign Office as Under-Secretary of State.

During the 1930s, Butler supported **NEVILLE CHAMBER-LAIN**'s policy of attempting to appease Adolf Hitler and crossed swords with the less placatory **WINSTON CHURCHILL**. The arguments were remembered, and, when Churchill became **PRIME MINISTER** and leader of the coalition **GOVERNMENT** during the **SECOND WORLD WAR**, he pushed Butler to the sidelines as President of the Board of **EDUCATION** (1941). Butler, however, refused to lie down. There had been no major changes in education for 40 years so he embarked on a series of root-and-branch reforms, which would drag teaching into the modern age. Among its provisions, the Education Act of 1944 gave every child the right to free secondary education, increased provision of nursery education, raised the school leaving age from 14 to 15 and expanded opportunities for further education.

In June 1945, Butler was made **MINISTER** of Labour but had no opportunity to make any impact before the Conservatives were defeated at the **GENERAL ELECTION** a month later. Churchill, now prepared to recognize his talents, appointed him Chairman of the Conservative Research Department and of the influential Industrial Policy Committee, roles which gave him great influence over postwar Tory policy. He became **CHANCELLOR OF THE EXCHEQUER** when his party returned to power in 1951, introducing import controls in an attempt to stabilise the economy but presenting a series of innocuous **BUDGET**s in keeping with the country's relative affluence.

In 1955, he accepted the posts of **LORD PRIVY SEAL** and **LEADER OF THE HOUSE OF COMMONS** in **ANTHONY EDEN**'s administration. That, however, was probably a mistake because these positions gave him less clout than he would have had as the head of a major government department. In 1957, when Eden resigned, he was one of the challengers for the Leadership of the Conservative Party but lost to **HAROLD MACMILLAN**, primarily because he had been opposed to Eden's Suez policies (see **SUEZ CRISIS**). Macmillan made him **HOME SECRETARY**, a job which he tackled with the same enthusiasm he had invested in education, reforming the laws on gambling, **PRISONS, PUBLIC HOUSE**s, prostitution and charities as well as introducing legislation designed to curb **IMMIGRATION**. In 1962, he became First Secretary of State and Deputy Prime Minister.

When the ailing Prime Minister resigned in 1963, it was widely expected that Butler would succeed him but Macmillan was determined to keep his old adversary out of **DOWNING STREET** and advised Queen **ELIZABETH II** to appoint **ALEC DOUGLAS-HOME** instead. Butler, bitterly disappointed, had to be content with the post of Foreign Secretary and eventually deserted politics in 1965, when **HAROLD WILSON** offered him the Mastership of Trinity College at the University of Cambridge. The first non-Trinity man to hold the post since the early 18th century, he was opposed by academics who saw his appointment as a break with tradition but he won many friends and, in 1972, 91 of the 118 Fellows voted for the maximum extension of his term of office until 1978.

Butler was also Rector of Glasgow University (1956-59), High

Steward of Cambridge University (1958-66), Chancellor of Sheffield University (1960-78) and Chancellor of Essex University (1962-82). In addition, he was President of the Modern Languages Association, the National Association of Mental Health and the Royal Society of Literature. He was awarded honorary degrees from 13 universities (including both **OXFORD** and Cambridge) and died at his home in Great Yeldham on 8 March 1982, at the age of 79. (See **BUTSKELLISM**).

BUTSKELLISM. Derived from the names of **RICHARD AUSTEN BUTLER (CONSERVATIVE PARTY)** and **HUGH GAIT-SKELL (LABOUR PARTY)**, this term was a shorthand used to describe the post-**SECOND WORLD WAR** consensus between the two major political parties on a mixed planned economy, freedom and social advancement.

BY-ELECTION. An election in a single **PARLIAMEN**Tary **CONSTITUENCY** is usually the result of the death, disqualification or resignation of the current Member of Parliament. Results, coming as they do in the midterm of a **GOVERNMENT**, are often seen as more likely to reflect local issues or a protest vote against the incumbent administration than would be the case at a **GENERAL ELECTION**.

BYE PLOT, 1603. This Roman Catholic plot to kidnap King **JAMES VI** and **I** and force him to grant toleration to Catholics was betrayed by a Jesuit. The conspirators were caught and the leader (a priest named William Watson) was executed. The event added to pressures for increased intolerance of Catholicism in **ENGLAND**. It was called the Bye Plot as if it was a minor side-issue of the contemporary **MAIN PLOT,** but they were probably unconnected.

—C—

CABAL. A cabal is a clandestine group of people (usually political in intent). The acronym is derived from the initial letters of the titles of five leading advisers to King **CHARLES II** between 1667 and 1674 — Clifford, Arlington, Buckingham, Ashley and Lauderdale. These were not, by any means, the King's only counsellors. Nor did they necassarily agree on policy. However, the word became common currency during the 17th century as a descriptive term for the King's political inner circle, which is sometimes regarded as a forerunner of **THE CABINET**.

CABINET, THE. Part of the Executive Branch of **GOVERNMENT**, the Cabinet is now the country's principal policy-making body, having replaced (except for certain activities) the **PRIVY COUNCIL** in advising the **MONARCH**. It became increasingly used in its present constitutional position from around 1720. Members are chosen by the **PRIME MINISTER** and may be heads of government departments or **MINISTER**s without portfolio (if they do not have direct responsibility for a department). The accepted principle of collective responsibility means that they speak with one voice once decisions have been taken and are responsible to **PARLIAMENT** for the conduct of government. The Cabinet draws up policy, decides the timetable of Parliamentary business, determines policy and supervises the executive. The Official **OPPOSITION** Party (that with the second-most seats in the **HOUSE OF COMMONS**) establishes its own Shadow Cabinet (see **SHADOW MINISTER**), with its members taking similar roles to those of the Cabinet proper and speaking on their allotted areas for their own party.

CADE'S REBELLION, May-July 1450. Jack Cade led a rebellion of **GENTRY** from the county of **KENT** against high taxes, corruption and military failure in Normandy. The revolt was triggered by the threat of harsh treatment from the **SHERIFF** of Kent, following the discovery of the headless body of the Duke of Suffolk on the beach at Dover. The rebels defeated King **HENRY VI**'s forces at Sevenoaks and, gathering public support, marched on **LONDON**, where they executed the Sheriff and the Lord Treasurer. The King fled to Kenilworth Castle until the rebels were routed and Cade was killed.

CALAIS. This town in northern France was the last British possession on the European continent. First taken in 1346 by King **EDWARD III** after the **BATTLE OF CRECY**, it was lost in 1558 after **MARY I**'s military excursion to Europe. Mary is said to have remarked that "when I am dead and opened, you shall find 'Calais' lying in my heart".

CALENDAR. The Earth takes 365.2422 days to complete one orbit of the Sun and the extra 0.2422 day each year creates difficulties for calendar counting of dates. The system to measure the length and structure of time in Britain was, until 1751, the Julian calendar, begun in 45 BC by Julius Caesar. This was longer than the solar year, with 46 BC being 445 days long and leap years occurring every three years. The system was refined by Augustus in 8 BC to incorporate a leap year every four years but by the 18th century was about ten days out of step. In 1752, Britain converted to the more accurate Gregorian calendar, introduced by Pope Gregory XIII in 1582 and adopted at that time by Catholic Europe. (Protestant Britain had refused to comply with any such decree from Rome.) Readjustment was necessary and 2 September 1752 (Julian) was followed next day by 14 September 1752 (Gregorian). This occasioned popular unrest with street cries of "Give us back our 11 days" as people thought 11 days of their lives had been taken away. In the same year, 1 January became New Year's Day (in **ENGLAND**, since 1155, that had occurred on 25 March). Both changes were effected by the Act of March 1751 (see **ACT OF PARLIAMENT**). Legal documents, however, are dated by the "Regnal Year" of the **MONARCH**, measured from that Monarch's day of accession to the throne, rather than by the calendar year (King **GEORGE II** had his 26th Regnal Year extended to accommodate the calendar changes in 1752). The Julian calendar is sometimes called the Old Style and the Gregorian the New Style, and, in this text, dates are given on the prevailing British system for the particular period. (By implication, other works, using the alternative system, may give different dates.)

CALLAGHAN, LEONARD JAMES (1912-). **PRIME MINISTER** from 1976 until 1979, Callaghan was born on 27 March 1912, the son of James Callaghan, a **ROYAL NAVY** Petty Officer. He was ed-ucated at Portsmouth North Grammar School, then, too poor to attend college, joined the Inland Revenue as a tax officer in 1929. Seven years later, he accepted the offer of a full-time **TRADE UNION** post as Assistant Secretary of the Inland Revenue Staff Federation. He served in the Navy during the **SECOND WORLD WAR** but turned to politics once peace was restored and, in 1945, won the working class South Cardiff **PARLIA-MENT**ary **CONSTITUENCY** for the **LABOUR PARTY**. He continued to represent that area of South **WALES** for over 30 years, holding South Cardiff until 1950, Cardiff Southeast from 1950 until 1983 and Cardiff South and Penarth from 1983 until 1987.

Callaghan's first **GOVERNMENT** post was as **PARLIA-MENTARY SECRETARY** at the Ministry of Transport from 1947 until 1950. In 1950-51, he was Parliamentary and Financial Secretary to the **ADMIRALTY** then, from 1952 until 1963, chaired the Advisory Committee on Oil Pollution of the Sea. When **HUGH GAITSKELL** died in 1963, he was one of the main contenders for the leadership of the Labour Party but was passed over in favour of **HAROLD WILSON**. Wilson, however, made him **CHANCELLOR OF THE EXCHEQUER** when Labour regained office in 1964 and, in that post, he introduced some of the most controversial fiscal measures in recent British history, including Corporation Tax and the much-loathed Selective Employment Tax, a per capita tax paid by all employers for each full-time employee and used to subsidize export-oriented manufacturing industries. He resigned in 1967, when Wilson insisted on the devaluation of **STERLING**, but was appointed **SECRETARY OF STATE** for the **HOME OFFICE** shortly afterwards and remained in that post until the Government was defeated at the 1970 **GENERAL ELECTION**.

Labour returned to power in 1974 and, when Wilson resigned two years later, Callaghan became Party Leader and Prime Minister. A far more affable, avuncular personality than his predecessor, he used his considerable diplomatic skills to steer his minority government through several months of considerable economic difficulty but, in 1977, was forced to negotiate a pact with the **LIBERAL PARTY** in order to ensure his administration's survival. Even so, country and party were unconvinced by his attempts to reduce inflation, and it was clearly only a matter of time before he fell. The end came in 1979 after **REFERENDA** on **DEVOLUTION** of government were held in Wales and **SCOTLAND**. The Welsh turned the proposals down by a majority of four to one. The Scots produced a small minority in favour but that counted as a defeat because the Devolution Act (see **ACT OF PARLIAMENT**) provided that power would be devolved only if a majority of 40 per cent voted in favour of the measure; with those who abstained added in, the total fell well below the required figure. The Scottish National Party seized the opportunity to table a motion of censure on the government, and the **CONSERVATIVE PARTY** naturally supported it. The motion was carried by 311 votes to 310; had Gerry Fitt (the Social Democratic and Labour Party representative from **NORTHERN IRELAND**) followed his usual pattern and voted for the government rather than against or if Labour had wheeled in Alfred Broughton (who was seriously ill and died a few days later), the course of British history might have been very different because the Conservatives gained a large majority of seats at the general election which followed Labour's Parliamentary defeat and Mrs **MARGARET THATCHER** became Prime Minister.

Callaghan resigned as Labour Leader in 1980 and was replaced by **MICHAEL FOOT** but remained in the **HOUSE OF COMMONS** until 1987, when he was created **BARON** Callaghan of Cardiff and took his seat in the **HOUSE OF LORDS**. His contribution to British politics has been recognized in many ways. He was made an Honorary Freeman of Cardiff in 1975, Sheffield in 1979 and Portsmouth in 1991. Universities in the United Kingdom and abroad have conferred honorary degrees on him, and, in 1986, he became President of University College, Swansea.

CAMBRIDGE. Lying just south of the flat, alluvial fenlands of **EAST ANGLIA**, Cambridge is internationally renowned as a centre of **EDUCATION**. It developed at a ford across the River Cam and archaeological evidence confirms that it was established by **ROMAN** times even though it is not mentioned in documents until 875, during the **ANGLO-SAXON** period. By 1086, the **NORMANS** had built a castle and a mint and, during the 13th century, a university was founded after a group of scholars had fled from **OXFORD** following disputes with the townsfolk. Porterhouse College was established in 1284 and was followed by seven others over the next 70 years. Nowadays, the institution dominates the city, its buildings forming the historic core of the settlement and its activities supporting the more important of the local industries, including printing and publishing, electronics and instrument making, construction and tourism. Many other tutorial colleges and language schools are situated nearby. Since the mid-1800s, the local authority has established a reputation for social innovation, particularly through its provision of public libraries and school dental services and its organization of public education. In the 1990s, it is faced with the problems of conserving its architectural heritage, and the open spaces which give character to the town, in the face of the demands of the motorist for parking spaces and the need to adapt buildings to meet modern standards and technologies. At the time of the 1991 census, Cambridge had a population of just over 88,000. (See also **UNIVERSITIES**).

CAMPAIGN FOR NUCLEAR DISARMAMENT (CND). CND was created in 1958 to agitate for disarmament and the abandonment of the **NUCLEAR DETERRENT** in Britain, with the philosopher, Bertrand Russell, as its president. Its "Ban the Bomb" slogan and symbol became well known in the 1960s, its most prominent period. From 1958, it became famous for its annual mass marches from **LONDON** to the Aldermaston Atomic Weapons Establishment site, led by Russell and Canon John Collins (see **ALDERMASTON MARCHES**). The movement declined from 1963 until the early 1980s after its more militant members broke away as the Committee of One Hundred but revived from 1 April 1983 when, during a period of widespread anti–nuclear feeling, it formed a 14-mile human chain between **GREENHAM COMMON** and Burghfield in protest against the construction of the US Cruise missile bases in Britain.

CAMPBELL-BANNERMAN, HENRY (1836-1908). **LIBERAL PARTY PRIME MINISTER** from 1905 until 1908, Campbell-Bannerman was born in Glasgow on 7 September 1836, the second son of Sir James Campbell (who was later to be Lord Provost of the city) and his wife, Janet. In 1871, he inherited property from his maternal uncle and, in gratitude, added his mother's maiden name to his own. He was educated at Glasgow High School, Glasgow University and **CAMBRIDGE** University, then worked with the family drapery and warehousing firm until 1868, when he was elected MP for Stirling, the **CONSTITUENCY** which he represented for the next 40 years. His first **GOVERNMENT** post was as Financial Secretary at the **WAR OFFICE** (1871-74), a position to which he returned in 1880 at the start of **WILLIAM GLADSTONE**'s second administration. In 1882, he became **PARLIAMENT**ary and Financial Secretary at the **ADMIRALTY** and, two years later, was made Chief Secretary for **IRELAND**.

He moved back to the War Office as **SECRETARY OF STATE** (with a seat in the **CABINET**) in 1886 and was reappointed in 1892, when Gladstone began the last of his four terms as Prime Minister. It was a post which Campbell-Bannerman occupied with considerable distinction, particularly in his dealings with the Woolwich Arsenal, where he introduced an eight-hour day in 1894. He also (in 1895) secured the resignation of the Duke of Cambridge, the Arsenal's Commander-in-Chief since 1856, without any bitterness. Cambridge had resisted reforms proposed by previous **MINISTER**s and had even annoyed his cousin, Queen **VICTORIA**, who **KNIGHT**ed Campbell-Bannerman as a reward for getting rid of him.

Four years later, Campbell-Bannerman became Leader of the Liberals in the **HOUSE OF COMMONS**, following the resignation of Sir William Harcourt, and inherited a deeply divided and demoralized party. These divisions were evident in July 1900 at a vote on the **CONSERVATIVE PARTY** Government's conduct of the second **BOER WAR**. Forty Liberal MPs supported the government, 31 condemned it and 35 (including Campbell-Bannerman) abstained. Over the next few months, however, the internal tensions eased and Campbell-Bannerman was able to unite MPs in opposition to the policy of abandoning **FREE TRADE** and in favour of **HOME RULE** for Ireland. At the same time, he was cultivating the friendship of King **EDWARD VII** so when **ARTHUR BALFOUR** resigned as Prime Minister in 1905, it was no surprise that he was invited to take over.

Forging old enemies into a united Cabinet presented serious problems, but Campbell-Bannerman was able to form a distinguished administration which included **HERBERT ASQUITH** as **CHANCELLOR OF THE EXCHEQUER** and **DAVID LLOYD GEORGE** as **PRESIDENT OF THE BOARD OF TRADE**. The **GENERAL ELECTION** in 1906 produced an enormous Liberal majority which Campbell-Bannerman utilized to push a series of domestic reforms through the Commons. The **HOUSE OF LORDS**, however, was still strongly Conservative and resisted measures passed by the lower House. The Prime Minister's response was to initiate moves which were to form the basis of the Parliament Act 1911 (see **ACT OF PARLIAMENT**) and limited the Lords' power to veto measures approved by the elected representatives of the people. Equally controversially, he granted autonomy to the Transvaal and Orange River, believing that the only way to ensure a trouble-free relationship between the Boers and **WESTMINSTER** was through the development of mutual confidence. That policy undoubtedly laid the foundations of the Union of South Africa. From 1907, however, he had to leave more and more of the administrative duties to Asquith as his health began to give way. On 22 April 1908, he died of a heart attack at 10 **DOWNING STREET**, still in office.

CANALS. During the **INDUSTRIAL REVOLUTION**, when manufacturing was developing fast, the **ROADS** in Britain proved inadequate for the transport of bulky goods and raw materials such as **COAL**, limestone, china clay and pottery. The United Kingdom has a greatly indented coastline, many rivers and a long-established coastal shipping trade so the development of canal systems (artificial navigable waterways) was a natural progression, initially to carry industrial raw materials to ports and growing towns. (For example, the Bridgewater Canal was built between 1759 and 1761 by James Brindley for the Duke of Bridgewater to carry coal from Worsley into **MANCHESTER**). These canals were a major factor in the growth of industrialization and urbanization during the early industrial revolution but were overtaken by the more efficient **RAILWAYS** after c. 1830 (the year of the opening of the world's first major rail route, between **LIVERPOOL** and Manchester). The last great project was the Manchester Ship Canal, opened by Queen **VICTORIA** on 21 May 1894. Most were nationalized in 1947 (see **NATIONALIZATION**) and placed under the management of the British Waterways Board in 1962. (See **JOSIAH WEDGWOOD**).

CANNING, GEORGE (1770-1827). **PRIME MINISTER** for four months during 1827, Canning is best remembered for his statesmanship as Foreign Secretary under **WILLIAM BENTINCK**, Duke of Portland, and later **ROBERT JENKINSON**, Earl of Liverpool. He was born in **LONDON** on 11 April 1770, but his father died exactly one year later, leaving his wife and son penniless. Mrs Canning took to the stage in an attempt to secure an income, and young George went to live with Stratford Canning, his uncle, who raised him as one of the family. He was educated at Hyde Abbey School (near Winchester) and at **OXFORD** University, graduated in 1791 and was elected MP for Newtown (Isle of Wight) in 1793. Allying himself with the **TORIES**, he was appointed **UNDER-SECRETARY OF STATE** for Foreign Affairs by **WILLIAM PITT THE YOUNGER** in 1796. Three years later, he was made Commissioner of the Board of Control then, in 1800, became Joint Paymaster of the Forces and joined the **PRIVY COUNCIL**. When Pitt resigned in 1801, Canning followed him into **OPPOSITION**, but, unwilling to approve Pitt's support for **HENRY ADDINGTON** (the incoming Prime Minister), he gave up his seat in **PARLIAMENT** and bought Tralee, one of the **ROTTEN BOROUGHS**.

In 1803, however, Pitt revised his opinion of Addington and Canning allied with him once more, getting his reward with the post of Treasurer of the Navy when Pitt formed his second **GOVERNMENT** a year later. In 1807, Portland promoted him to Foreign Secretary, a position which brought him into conflict with the Secretary for War, **ROBERT STEWART**, Viscount Castlereagh. Holding Castlereagh responsible for British defeats in the **PENINSULAR WAR**, Canning challenged him to a duel and received a thigh wound. He resigned from the administration and remained out of office until, in 1816, the Earl of Liverpool made him President of the Board of Control, with **CABINET** rank. He resigned again in 1820, this time in protest against government policy towards Queen Caroline, consort of **GEORGE IV**. Two years later, he accepted the post of **GOVERNOR GENERAL** of Bengal, but, before he could leave Britain, Castlereagh committed suicide and Canning was asked to succeed him as Foreign Secretary and **LEADER OF THE HOUSE OF COMMONS**. Unwilling to get too heavily involved in continental affairs, he took Britain out of the Holy Alliance, prevented European intervention in South America on behalf of Spain (whose colonies were in revolt), gave military aid to Portugal in its conflict with Spain and lent diplomatic weight to the Greeks in their struggle against Ottoman rule.

In 1827, Liverpool resigned following a stroke and, on 10 April, **GEORGE IV** asked Canning to form a government even though he favoured Catholic emancipation and the King was convinced that such a policy should be resisted. Many Tories refused to serve, some because of their anti-Catholic sentiments and some because of personal differences with Canning, but the **WHIGS** and most of the independent MPs supported him. He governed for only four months before his health deteriorated. Canning died at Chiswick on 8 August 1827. A sarcastic, irritable workaholic, he had made many enemies but was a brilliant orator with a sound understanding of the new commercial interests spawned by the **INDUSTRIAL REVOLUTION** and a strong sense of service to his country.

CANTERBURY. This town in **KENT** was probably first inhabited by the Cantii, one of the peoples of the **BELGAE**. It developed into a centre of **ROMAN** trade as Durovernum Cantiacorum and was the capital of Kent briefly during the **ANGLO-SAXON** period. When **ST AUGUSTINE** arrived in 597, sent by Pope Gregory to take Christianity to **ENGLAND**, he was befriended by King **AETHELBERT I** (whose wife, Bertha, was a Christian) and given land for a church at Canterbury, which became the centre of the faith in the country (see **SYNOD OF WHITBY**). After the assassination of Archbishop of Canterbury **THOMAS BECKET** in the Cathedral (1170), the town attracted many pilgrims. However, most of its religious houses were destroyed during the **DISSOLUTION OF THE MONASTERIES**, and its walls were largely demolished in the **CIVIL WARS**, when the settlement remained **ROYALIST**. It is now the seat of the **ARCHBISHOP OF CANTERBURY** and a major tourist centre.

CANUTE (c. 995-1035). King of Denmark and Norway, Canute also ruled **ENGLAND** between 1016 and 1035. In 1003, he accompanied his father — Sweyn, King of Denmark — on the campaign which led to the defeat of the English and the flight of **AETHELRED II** to Normandy in 1013. When Sweyn died in 1014, the English asked Aethelred to return, but Canute raised a fleet in Denmark and, in 1015, attempted a reconquest of his father's territories. The opposition was led by **EDMUND II**, who was defeated at the **BATTLE OF ASSANDUN** in October 1016. The two leaders negotiated a treaty which gave Edmund control of **WESSEX** and Canute control of all the lands north of the **RIVER THAMES**. However, Edmund died shortly afterwards, and Canute became undisputed King of the whole of England. In an attempt to gain the acceptance of his subjects, he married Aethelred's widow, Emma, and ruled according to native codes of law. He supported the Church and made a pilgrimage to Rome during 1026 and 1027. The story, related by Henry of Huntingdon, of Canute's attempt to control the waves is supposedly an example of his humility; he was trying to show his followers that even he was not great enough to make the oceans obey his will. His foreign policies resulted in the acquisition of Norway (which he ruled through his mistress, Aelfgifu of Northampton), the acceptance of homage from the Scots and the maintenance of peaceful relations with Normandy (despite the threat of invasion on behalf of Aethelred's sons). Canute died at Shaftesbury on 12 November 1035 and was buried at Winchester — a resting place which emphasizes his identity with the **ANGLO-SAXON** traditions of his adopted country.

CAPITAL PUNISHMENT. For centuries, death was the penalty for many offences, some of a relatively trivial nature (such as theft), and it was carried out in a variety of ways. Executions of eminent people were by sword, those of lesser nobles by axe and those of other criminals by slow strangulation or, particularly at the end of the 18th century, by hanging. Traitors (see **TREASON**) were hanged (until nearly dead), drawn (their stomachs opened and entrails removed) and quartered (cut into four pieces). Some scholars regard the drawn element as meaning the dragging to the gallows behind a horse rather than disembowelling, as with the Scot William Wallace who, in 1305, was drawn or dragged from **WESTMINSTER** to the **TOWER OF LONDON**, hanged, then disembowelled and his quarters exhibited at **NEWCASTLE-UPON-TYNE**, Stirling, Berwick and Perth. **LORD** Lovat was the last person to be executed by beheading in **ENGLAND** in 1747.

In the 1860s, the offences punishable in these ways were reduced to murder, piracy, high treason and arson. Hanging, drawing and quartering was abolished in 1870. The last public execution, always events to draw large crowds, was in 1868 and the last woman to be hanged was Ruth Ellis, in 1955, for the murder of her boyfriend. Minors under 16 years of age were no longer hanged after 1905. Increased concern at wrongful convictions led to the withdrawal of capital punishment for murder in 1965. It was abolished by **PARLIAMENT** on 18 December 1969 except for treason and piracy. The last execution in Britain was in 1964.

CAREY, GEORGE LEONARD (1935-). **ARCHBISHOP OF CANTERBURY** since 1991, Carey was born on 13 November 1935, and educated at Bifrons Secondary Modern School (Barking), the **LONDON** College of Divinity and London University. He holds the degrees of Bachelor of Divinity, Master of Theology and Doctor of Philosophy. In 1962, he was appointed Deacon at St Mary's Church, Islington, a post which he held until 1966, when he became a Lecturer at Oak Hill Theological College in Southgate. In 1970, he moved to St John's College, Nottingham, then, in 1975, forsook teaching in favour of pastoral work as Vicar at St Nicholas's Church, Durham. He returned to **EDUCATION** in 1982, accepting the appointment of Principal at Trinity College, Bristol (and acting, concurrently, as Honorary Canon at Bristol Cathedral). He was made Bishop of Bath and Wells in 1987 and, four years later, became the 103rd Archbishop of Canterbury.

Carey travelled abroad extensively and, early in 1994, made a controversial visit to Christian groups in the south of war-torn Sudan, where he met leaders of the Sudanese People's Liberation Army. A scheduled visit to Khartoum, the country's capital, was cancelled at short notice, ostensibly because Dr Carey believed that, if he stayed as guest of the Sudanese government, his action might be interpreted as a gesture of support for an administration which was persecuting people of all religions in the south. The Sudanese government, fuelled by suspicions that the Anglican Church and British politicians were behind the rebellion, responded by expelling the British ambassador, Mr Peter Streams. In a tit-for-tat move, the British government told the Sudanese ambassador, Mr Ali Osman Yassin, to leave London. A scheduled visit to Nigeria in February 1994 was cancelled due to fears that the Archbishop might be a target for Islamic extremists.

CARNATIC WARS. Between 1746 and 1792, there was a series of hostilities between the British **EAST INDIA COMPANY** and the peoples of Mysore, Hyderabad and Maratha in the Carnatic area (of the Kananese language) in India.

The First War (1746-48) involved French forces attempting to gain a foothold in the region, taking, but later returning, Madras to Britain.

The Second War (1749-54) again had British and French forces engaged over a wide front and included the **BLACK HOLE OF CALCUTTA** incident.

The Third War (1780-84), also called the Second Mysore War, continued the conflicts with little real advance.

The Fourth War (1789-92), also known as the Third Mysore War, ended with the ruler of Mysore losing half his territory to Britain, which also took Ceylon (now Sri Lanka) from the Dutch.

CASABLANCA CONFERENCE, 14-23 January 1943. At this conference, **WINSTON CHURCHILL** and US President Franklin D. Roosevelt discussed the unconditional surrender of the Axis forces in the **SECOND WORLD WAR.** They agreed to promote greater efforts in the **BATTLE OF THE ATLANTIC,** send supplies to Russia and effect greater freedom of movement for the United States of America in the Pacific (though this theatre of war remained secondary to that in Europe).

CASTLEREAGH, VISCOUNT. (See **ROBERT STEWART**).

CASTLES. These large fortified buildings (or sets of buildings) were used for defence against attackers and were normally located at strategic high points or commanding positions on routeways. They were important in British history during periods of instability and hostility. During more peaceful times, the materials employed in their construction were reused to erect houses and other buildings so that often their history is quite complex to unravel. The **CELTS' HILLFORTS** were usually simple ditches and earthworks on high ground. **ROMAN** forts were more substantial, often being built of local stone (in **KENT** of flint, taken from local chalk deposits). **ANGLO-SAXON** forts were even more impregnable, but it is to the **NORMANS** that Britain owes many of the really important early developments and structures, such as the **TOWER OF LONDON.** From the 12th century onwards, stone castles replaced the earlier "motte and bailey" form (a wooden fort on high ground, surrounded by a fenced outer courtyard). As new methods of warfare developed, so the architecture changed, with walls, bastions and towers or barbicans with star-shaped layouts being built to allow firing in more than one direction. Private castles were also constructed, but the development of gunpowder and more settled political conditions generally made such buildings less useful from the 16th century. The last great period of construction was that of the Martello Towers, built during the **NAPOLEONIC WARS.** Many castles remain as historic edifices (for example, **WINDSOR CASTLE**) and museums. (See **SAXON SHORE FORTS**).

CAT AND MOUSE ACT, 1913. The Prisoners (Temporary Discharge for Health) Act (see **ACT OF PARLIAMENT**) was used to free, under licence, recalcitrant **SUFFRAGETTES** who refused to eat. It was a means of solving a difficult problem (because of adverse public reactions to forced feeding) and was parodied in a famous poster depicting a mouse (the suffragette) in the mouth of a large cat (the **GOVERNMENT**). (See **EMMELINE PANKHURST**).

CATHERINE OF ARAGON (1485-1536). The first wife of **HENRY VIII**, Catherine failed to bear a son and the King's attempts to divorce her changed the course of English history.

Catherine was born on 16 December 1485, the daughter of Ferdinand II of Aragon and Isabella of Castile. Under the terms of the Treaty of Medina del Campo in 1489, she was betrothed to Arthur, eldest son of **HENRY VII.** The couple were married in 1501, but Arthur died the following year and plans were made for Catherine to be remarried to the King's second son, Henry (later Henry VIII). A papal dispensation was necessary because the relationship was within forbidden degrees of consanguinity, and a military alliance between Henry VII and Philip of Burgundy against Ferdinand further delayed the wedding. However, after Henry VII died in 1509, his son promptly arranged to marry Catherine the same year. Between 1510 and 1518, she gave birth to six children (two sons and four daughters) but all except one (Mary — later **MARY I** — born in 1516) were stillborn.

Henry became increasingly anxious about the lack of a male successor to the throne and created Henry Fitzroy, his illegitimate son, Duke of Richmond in order to give him precedence over his daughter. By 1526, however, he had become thoroughly infatuated with **ANNE BOLEYN** and sought papal sanction for an annulment of his marriage to Catherine on the grounds that it was within the proscribed degrees of consanguinity. Pope Clement VII procrastinated. He was unwilling to reverse the judgement of a previous Pope and, moreover, was effectively a prisoner of Catherine's nephew, Charles V, whose troops had occupied Rome. Frustrated by Clement's delaying tactics, Henry took the law into his own hands in 1531 and separated from Catherine.

The **ARCHBISHOP OF CANTERBURY (THOMAS CRANMER)** formally annulled the marriage on 23 May 1533 (some four months after Henry had secretly married Anne) and the **ACT OF SUCCESSION** (see **ACT OF PARLIAMENT**), passed the following year, formally approved the annulment, declaring Mary illegitimate and recognizing Anne's child, Elizabeth (later **ELIZABETH I**), as heiress to the throne. Belatedly, Clement declared Catherine's marriage valid in 1534.

Throughout the negotiations, Catherine steadfastly maintained that she was legally Henry's wife because the marriage to Arthur had never been consummated. She refused to accept the Act of Succession or to retire to a nunnery and, troubled by illness, died at Kimbolton (Huntingdonshire) on 7 January 1536.

CATO STREET CONSPIRACY, 1820. Arthur Thistlewood, who had served in the **AMERICAN WAR OF INDEPENDENCE** and thereby picked up revolutionary ideas, conceived a plan to assassinate the **CABINET** at dinner, parade the heads of **MINISTERS** on stakes, seize the **TOWER OF LONDON** and Mansion House and declare a republic. The plotters were arrested in Cato Street, Marylebone, **LONDON** on 23 February 1820; the leaders of the ill-planned scheme were convicted of **TREASON**, and five were hanged. This incident revealed how spies or informers (and perhaps even "agents provocateur") were used by the government to combat subversion and indicated the extent of dissatisfaction with the Tory **GOVERNMENT** in the harsh economic climate of that time. (See **LUDDITES; MARCH OF THE BLANKETEERS; PETERLOO MASSACRE; SIX ACTS; SPA FIELDS RIOT; TORIES**).

CAVALIER PARLIAMENT. This is an alternative name for the **LONG PARLIAMENT** of the **RESTORATION**, held between 1661 and 1679. It forced **NONCONFORMISTS** out of the **CHURCH OF ENGLAND** (see **ACT OF UNIFORMITY, 1662**) but was hampered by debt and was unable to pursue the **DUTCH WARS** of 1665-67 and 1672-74 as vigorously as it would have liked. For much of the time, King **CHARLES II** ruled through his **CABAL** and, in 1679, he finally dissolved the Parliament as it was becoming increasingly anti-Catholic in its attempts to prevent his son (later **JAMES VII** and **II**) from succeeding to the throne.

CAVALIERS. This term, originally derogatory, usually refers to the loyalist supporters of King **CHARLES I (ROYALISTS)** in the **CIVIL WARS** and is linked with the term **ROUNDHEADS** (used to describe Parliamentary soldiers). It derives from the use of the word "cavaliero" (or Spanish trooper) as a form of insult to a group of Royalist officers in 1641 and was meant to describe a flamboyant and overdressed individual (in contrast to the drab and plain-dressed Roundhead). Although it began as a term of abuse, the word eventually came to be regarded as a mark of honour by true Royalists.

CAXTON, WILLIAM (c. 1422-91). The first English printer, Caxton was born in **KENT** and, at the age of about 16, was employed as an apprentice by Robert Large, a mercer in the **CITY OF LONDON**. When Large died in 1441, Caxton moved to Bruges and, over the next 30 years, became a leading member of the sizeable English community in the city. In 1453, he was admitted to the livery of the Mercers' Company and, ten years later, was appointed Governor of the English Nation of **MERCHANTS ADVENTURERS** in the Low Countries (see **GUILDS**). In 1470, he moved to Cologne and, while there, learned the techniques of **PRINTING**. He bought a press and two fonts of type then, in 1475, published *The Recuyell of the Historyes of Troye*, the first book printed in English. That, and a few other texts, were produced in Bruges but, in 1476, Caxton returned to **ENGLAND** and founded a press in **WESTMINSTER**. With funding from the aristocracy, he printed a variety of works including *The Myrrour of the World* (the first illustrated encyclopaedia), Geoffrey Chaucer's *Canterbury Tales* and Thomas Malory's *Morte d'Arthur*, along with many religious studies, histories and philosophical treatises, several of which he translated from French, Dutch and Latin. Because the output was so large (numbering about one hundred books printed in multiple copies) and employed consistent conventions of spelling, punctuation and grammar, Caxton helped standardize the English language in a way that was not possible by individuals reproducing single literary works by penmanship.

CECIL, ROBERT (1563-1612). **SECRETARY OF STATE** from 1596 until 1612 and **LORD HIGH TREASURER** from 1608 until 1612, Cecil was a major political influence at the time of the **UNION OF THE CROWNS**. Born in **LONDON** on 1 June 1563, he was the son of **WILLIAM CECIL** and his wife, Mildred. He was educated at home and at **CAMBRIDGE** University then joined Gray's Inn in 1580. He entered **PARLIAMENT** in 1584 and, in 1588, went to the Spanish Netherlands with the Earl of Derby in an attempt to negotiate a peace treaty with the Duke of Parma. After Sir Francis Walsingham died in 1590, Cecil gradually took over the duties of Secretary of State but was not confirmed in that position until 1596. In 1591, he was **KNIGHT**ed and for 10 years from 1593 was the principal advocate of Queen **ELIZABETH I**'s policies in the **HOUSE OF COMMONS**. In 1601, he began a secret correspondence with James VI of **SCOTLAND** (later **JAMES VI and I**), advising him to cultivate the Queen but not to attempt to make her recognize publicly his claim to the English throne. In 1603, he was created Baron Cecil of Essendine in Rutland and, after the **UNION OF THE CROWNS**, became James's chief **MINISTER**, virtually controlling the processes of government from then until his death. In 1608, when he was appointed to the post of Lord High Treasurer, he discovered that James had run up a debt of £1,400,000. Without consulting Parliament, he introduced a series of measures which reduced that sum to £300,000, but he failed to curb the king's extravagant spending. In foreign affairs, he attempted to make **ENGLAND** the dominant force in Europe by maintaining a balance of power between Spain and France. Cecil died in Marlborough on 24 May 1612 and was buried at Hatfield near the house he had built.

CECIL, WILLIAM (1520-98). The chief government **MINISTER** during the reign of **ELIZABETH I**, Cecil was born at Bourne (Lincolnshire) on 18 September 1520. He attended the **GRAMMAR SCHOOLS** in Grantham and Stamford then went to **CAMBRIDGE** University, where he studied for six years. In 1547, he entered the service of Edward Seymour, Duke of Somerset and Lord Protector during the childhood of **EDWARD VI**. Three years later, he altered his allegiance and became Principal Secretary to John Dudley, Duke of Northumberland and Somerset's successor. In 1550, he was **KNIGHT**ed. He performed his duties efficiently but opposed the machinations which led to the exclusion of **HENRY VIII**'s daughter, Mary (later **MARY I**), from the succession and conspired with Northumberland's opponents.

When Elizabeth I succeeded Mary in 1558, she made Cecil her Principal Secretary and two years later gave him, in addition, the post of Master of the Court of Wards, a remunerative office which made him a rich man. As Principal Secretary to the Queen, Cecil was effectively the head of the Civil Service. He was responsible for the re-establishment of the **CHURCH OF ENGLAND** and for maintaining it in the face of opposition both from Roman Catholics and from **PURITANS**. Also, he supported the Protestant cause in **SCOTLAND**, thereby weakening the Catholic Mary, Queen of Scots, Elizabeth's cousin and rival for the English throne.

In 1571, he discovered a Catholic plot to unseat Elizabeth and, as a result, the Duke of Norfolk was beheaded, the Spanish Ambassador was expelled and Mary was kept in more strict confinement. For that service, he was raised to the peerage as Baron Burghley and appointed Lord Treasurer. The new post allowed him to shed much of his administrative load, but, until his death in **LONDON** on 4 August 1598, he remained the Queen's chief adviser, leading a moderate **PARLIAMENT**ary group which rejected Puritan calls for England to head a Protestant league supporting **HUGUENOT** rebels in France and Dutch rebels against Spanish overlordship of the Low Countries. In 1585, the militants were victorious, and from 1590, for the last years of his life and in his seventies, Cecil was responsible for the conduct of the war with Spain.

CELTIC FIELDS. These field systems, possibly established as early as 600 BC (and therefore, perhaps, in reality pre-Celtic) comprise regularly shaped small (usually rectangular) plots on light soils, surrounded by hedges or walls and individually cultivated. They are associated with the Celtic **BRONZE AGE** peoples and are found on hills and in highland areas. They were replaced by an **OPEN FIELD SYSTEM** introduced by the **SAXONS**. (See **CELTS**).

CELTS. First recorded in the Danube area about 6000 BC, the Celts entered Britain around 2200 BC. Their legacy is most evident in the culture and languages of **SCOTLAND**, **WALES** and **IRELAND**, which have strong affinities with northern France. A warrior-aristocratic and strongly tribal people of the **BRONZE AGE** and **IRON AGE**, they are known for elegant bronze artifacts, **HILLFORTS** and **DRUIDS**, who provided religious organization. At the onset of the **ROMAN** invasion, Celtic tribes inhabited most of Britain except the far north, with the **ICENI** in East Anglia, the Cantii in **KENT**, the Catuvellauni and Atrebates around **LONDON**, the Brigantes in Northern **ENGLAND** and the Picts and Selgovae in Scotland. People in Scotland, Ireland, Wales and Cornwall often claim Celtic descent, but after the Roman period there were great movements of population into Britain from the continent and such links, tenuous in many cases, seem to be derived from the growth of nationalistic feelings in the 19th century.

CENTRAL TREATY ORGANIZATION (CENTO). The Economic and Military Co-operation Alliance between Britain, Turkey, Iran and Pakistan, with the United States of America as an Associate Member, was created in 1959 to counter Soviet expansionism in the Middle East. Britain withdrew military forces from CENTO in 1975, and it collapsed in 1979 when Iran and Pakistan pulled out after the Iranian Revolution.

CHAMBERLAIN, ARTHUR NEVILLE (1869-1940). Remembered primarily for his attempts to appease Adolf Hitler in the years before the outbreak of the **SECOND WORLD WAR**, Chamberlain was **CONSERVATIVE PARTY PRIME MINISTER** from 1937 until 1940. He was born in Edgbaston (**BIRMINGHAM**) on 18 March 1869, the son of **JOSEPH CHAMBERLAIN** and Florence, his second wife. After studying at Rugby School and Mason College, he spent seven years in the Bahamas, attempting to make his father's sisal plantation profitable (an attempt which was in vain because of thin soils). In 1987, following his return to Britain, he found a job as manager of a metalworking firm, promoted the activities of Birmingham's Chamber of Commerce and became Chairman of the General Hospital. He was elected to the City Council in 1911, appointed **LORD MAYOR** in 1915 and established a Municipal Savings Bank the following year.

In 1916, Chamberlain was invited by Prime Minister **DAVID LLOYD GEORGE** to become Director-General of **NATIONAL SERVICE** but resigned after only seven months, claiming that he was not being given the powers which would enable him to do the job properly. The mutual dislike engendered during those weeks affected both men for the rest of their lives.

It was not until 1918, when he was nearly 50, that Chamberlain entered **PARLIAMENT** (as the Member for Birmingham Ladywood), but, once he arrived, he rose rapidly to positions of power. In 1922, he was made **POSTMASTER GENERAL** by

ANDREW BONAR LAW and, the following year, became **MINISTER** of Health (with a seat in the **CABINET**) before being offered the post of **CHANCELLOR OF THE EXCHEQUER** by **STANLEY BALDWIN**, who succeeded Law in August 1923.

The Conservative **GOVERNMENT** was ousted in January 1924 but regained power in November. Chamberlain returned to the Health Ministry and enhanced his growing reputation by introducing a system of contributory pensions for widows, orphans and the elderly in 1925. He became Chairman of the Party in 1930, by which time he was considered a potential successor to Baldwin, and joined **RAMSAY MACDONALD**'s coalition Government in 1931 (again as Minister of Health). In October, he was made Chancellor of the Exchequer for the second time and maintained a balanced budget in difficult economic circumstances, allocating funds for a programme of rearmament beginning in 1934.

In 1937, he became Prime Minister when Baldwin resigned and almost immediately entered into negotiations with Hitler in an attempt to limit German territorial expansion. His policy of **APPEASEMENT** rather than conflict was popular in many quarters so his negotiation of the **MUNICH AGREEMENT** in 1938 was welcomed by a public ready to believe that, as Chamberlain said, it guaranteed "Peace for our time". The pact had granted almost all of Hitler's territorial claims but Chamberlain was clearly aware that it might not be enough to satisfy Germany. He speeded up Britain's rearmament programme and responded to Hitler's annexation of Czechoslovakia in March 1939 with an announcement that an invasion of Poland would lead to British retaliation.

On 1 September, Nazi troops moved over the Polish border, and, two days later, Chamberlain committed the United Kingdom to war with Germany. Initially, he stayed on as Prime Minister after the outbreak of hostilities but his policies came under increasing attack from members of his own party, particularly after the failure of British attempts to force the Germans out of Norway, and, in May 1940, he tendered his resignation to King **GEORGE VI. WINSTON CHURCHILL**, his successor, formed a coalition government and invited Chamberlain to be **LORD PRESIDENT OF THE COUNCIL.** He accepted, and gave his support to the new Prime Minister, but his health was failing and on 30 September he gave up both his government office and his Chairmanship of the Conservative Party. He died at Heckfield, near Reading, on 9 November 1940.

CHAMBERLAIN, JOSEPH (1836-1914). An ardent advocate of preferential tariff rates for territories of the **BRITISH EMPIRE**, Chamberlain was born in **LONDON** on 8 July 1836, the son of Joseph Chamberlain (Master of the Cordwainers' Company) and his wife, Caroline. He was educated at University College School but showed little academic talent and left at the age of 16 to work in his father's boot and shoe business. In 1854, he moved to Nettlefold, a screw manufacturing firm in **BIRMINGHAM** owned by his maternal uncle, and remained there for 20 years, retiring at the age of 38 with a sizeable income.

Chamberlain joined the city's Liberal Association (see **LIBERAL PARTY**) in 1868 and was elected to the local Council the following year, serving as Mayor from 1873 until 1876. This involvement with **LOCAL GOVERNMENT** had far-reaching effects: he demolished slums and replaced them with parks and new thoroughfares, built a free library, established an art gallery, arranged a conference of sanitary authorities and (in 1900) founded Birmingham University. At the 1874 **GENERAL ELECTION**, he was an unsuccessful candidate for the Liberals at Sheffield but, two years later, became Member of **PARLIAMENT** for Birmingham. In 1880, he was appointed **PRESIDENT OF THE BOARD OF TRADE** in **WILLIAM GLADSTONE**'s second administration and joined the **CABINET** in 1882 as President of the Board of Local Government, arguing for more extensive social reforms than the **PRIME MINISTER** was willing to support. He resigned in 1885 when his proposals for limited devolution of power to **IRELAND** were thrown out but returned, again as President of the Local Government Board, in January 1886. In March, he resigned once more, protesting against the terms of Gladstone's Irish **HOME RULE BILL**, and, later in the year, pledged his support to the **CONSERVATIVE PARTY** on the Irish issue if the **MARQUIS OF SALISBURY**'s administration would agree to introduce the domestic reforms he believed were badly needed. That liaison led to a spate of legislation which undoubtedly improved the quality of life in Britain, particularly through the introduction of free **EDUCATION** and improvements to working class housing conditions.

When Salisbury won the 1895 general election, Chamberlain (at his own request) was made **SECRETARY OF STATE** for the colonies. A convinced imperialist, he believed that Britain's territorial possessions should be linked in a federal system which promoted trade and provided agreements for mutual defence. A conference of colonial leaders in 1902 convinced him that such a federation could only be achieved if the mother country abandoned its policy of **FREE TRADE** and introduced tariffs which would give preference to imperial possessions (see **IMPERIAL PREFER-ENCE**). The initial move, he suggested, should be remission of the duty on imported grain introduced by **CHANCELLOR OF THE EXCHEQUER**, C. T. Ritchie, in his 1902 **BUDGET**. He left for a visit to South Africa, convinced that he had persuaded the Cabinet to accept his proposal, but returned to find that Ritchie had talked senior Conservatives into retaining the status quo. In September 1903, Chamberlain resigned from the **GOVERNMENT**, believing that his campaign could best be conducted from outside the Cabinet, and undertook a series of engagements up and down the country, spelling out his case for tariff reform in public speeches and stressing the need to protect Britain's interests at a time when the United States, Germany and other countries were using import duties to shield their own agriculture and industry from foreign competition. He found much support and retained his Birmingham seat at the 1906 general election despite a crushing defeat for the Conservatives. Later that year, however, he suffered a stroke while celebrating his seventieth birthday and never spoke in public again. He died in London on 2 July 1914.

CHAMBERLAIN, JOSEPH AUSTEN (1863-1937). Foreign Secretary in **STANLEY BALDWIN**'s second **CONSERVATIVE PARTY** administration, Chamberlain was born in **BIRMINGHAM** on 16 October 1863, the eldest son of **JOSEPH CHAMBERLAIN** and his wife, Harriet. He was educated at Rugby School and **CAMBRIDGE** University then worked as Private Secretary for his father before entering the **HOUSE OF COMMONS** in 1892 as the MP for Birmingham West. In 1895, he was appointed Lord of the **ADMIRALTY** by the **MARQUIS OF SALISBURY** and, in 1900, moved to the **TREASURY** as **FINANCIAL SECRETARY**. Under **ARTHUR BALFOUR**, he expanded his experience of office, becoming **POSTMASTER GENERAL** in 1902 and then **CHANCELLOR OF THE EXCHEQUER** in 1903. During the **LIBERAL PARTY** administrations of **HENRY CAMPBELL-BANNERMAN** and **HERBERT ASQUITH**, he was a prominent figure on the **OPPOSITION FRONT BENCH** and was expected by many to become Leader when Balfour resigned in 1911. However, his colleague, Walter Long, also had considerable support so the two men agreed not to become involved in a contest which might split the Party, withdrew their candidacies and allowed

ANDREW BONAR LAW to pick up Balfour's mantle.

Chamberlain returned to **GOVERNMENT** as **SECRETARY OF STATE** for India in Asquith's coalition administration of 1915 and remained in that post when **DAVID LLOYD GEORGE** became **PRIME MINISTER** the following year. He resigned in July 1917, accepting responsibility for his Department's shortcomings in the supply of medical equipment to troops in Mesopotamia (see **MESOPOTAMIAN CAMPAIGN**), but was appointed to the War **CABINET** the following April and became Chancellor of the Exchequer for a second time in 1919. Two years later, he replaced Law as Leader of the Conservative Party and, in addition, became **LEADER OF THE HOUSE OF COMMONS** and **LORD PRIVY SEAL**.

In 1922, Chamberlain opposed the Conservative withdrawal of support from Lloyd George's coalition government and resigned the party leadership, a defiant action which kept him out of office until he returned to the fold as Foreign Secretary under Stanley Baldwin. The following year, he engineered the Locarno Pact, under which the European powers guaranteed Germany's western boundaries and paved the way for their former enemy's entry to the **LEAGUE OF NATIONS**. He was rewarded with the Nobel Peace Prize and made a **KNIGHT** of the Garter (see **ORDER OF THE GARTER**) in 1925, but, in later years, his diplomacy was less successful and his reputation suffered. In particular, relations with the Soviet Union were severed after a police raid on the **LONDON** office of its State Trading Agency (the **ARCOS RAID**) in 1927, the Conference on Naval Disarmament in Geneva (also in 1927) was a failure and negotiations with France over disarmament in 1928 were inconclusive. In August 1931, he became First Lord of the Admiralty in **RAMSAY MACDONALD**'s coalition government but resigned the following month in the wake of a mutiny over pay cuts. Though he never held office again, he continued to serve as an MP until his death in London on 16 March 1937.

CHANAK AFFAIR, September-October 1922. An Anglo-Turkish crisis followed the post-**FIRST WORLD WAR** partitioning of Turkey as Mustafa Kemal Ataturk (President of the country's National Assembly) attempted to retake former territory awarded to Greece at the 1920 Treaty of Sevres. The two armies advanced to Chanak, near the Dardanelles, but negotiations resulted in no bloodshed, the return of Eastern Thrace and Adrianople to Turkey and the ending of the Allied occupation of Constantinople. The incident led to the fall of the **GOVERNMENT** of **DAVID LLOYD GEORGE** as it almost brought Britain to war and, moreover, war for which Britain would have had neither resources nor **DOMINION** support.

CHANCELLOR OF THE DUCHY OF LANCASTER The holder of this **GOVERNMENT** office is responsible to the **MONARCH** for the efficient management of the Duchy and to the **PRIME MINISTER** for such other duties as are allocated. In **JOHN MAJOR**'s administrations, the Chancellor has been in charge of the **CITIZEN'S CHARTER**, improvement of the efficiency of the Civil Service and overview of policy on science and technology.

CHANCELLOR OF THE EXCHEQUER This office originated in the **NORMAN** period simply as Chancellor; the holder was keeper of the **GREAT SEAL** of the realm, head of the Chancery (literally, the writing house), chief clerk and custodian of the written laws of the state. By the 12th century, the Chancellor's deputy had become the head of the Exchequer (the counting house) and controller of the country's finances. The title is now held by the **CABINET** minister responsible for finance and national economic policy, including the annual **BUDGET**. The postholder is also head of the **TREASURY**.

CHANCERY, COURT OF. The Court of Chancery in **ENGLAND** and **WALES** began to develop during medieval times. By the 15th century, **COMMON LAW** had become extremely rigid and powerful lords could bribe or threaten juries (see **JURY**) and ignore court orders. In these circumstances, many litigants felt aggrieved and turned to the King for justice. The King, in turn, passed their petitions to the **LORD CHANCELLOR**, who presided over the Chancery Court and who (unlike judges in the Common Law Courts) was not bound by precedent. By the mid-17th century, the equitable judgements passed by the Court had become an accepted part of the legal system but, in 1873, the **JUDICATURE ACT** (see **ACT OF PARLIAMENT**) revolutionized the administration of justice, abolishing the separate common law and equity courts. The Chancery Court became one of the divisions of the **HIGH COURT OF JUSTICE** and now hears cases involving land sales, administration of estates, contracts, mortgages and related matters.

CHANNEL ISLANDS. A **CROWN DEPENDENCY**, the Channel Islands are located in the English Channel 10 to 30 miles off the coast of France and were the only part of the United Kingdom to be occupied by Germany during the **SECOND WORLD WAR.** They cover an area of approximately 75 square miles, with 58 per cent of the 144,000 population (1990) living on Jersey, 40 per cent on Guernsey and the remainder on the smaller islands. Part of the Duchy of Normandy by the 10th century, the islands came under the sway of the English **CROWN** in 1066 (see **NORMANS**). Now, their internal affairs are run by representative assemblies (known as States of Deliberation) and low rates of tax have turned them into a haven for the rich.

CHANNEL TUNNEL. A fixed link across the English Channel has been mooted since the early 19th century and plans have included tunnels, bridges and submerged tubes (the first scheme, in 1802, came from France). Britain, however, has always had a suspicion of the intentions of European neighbours so early proposals were attacked mostly for their impact on the security of the islands of the realm. Agreement in the 19th century eventually led to work beginning on a tunnel at Folkestone in **KENT** in 1882 but this was soon abandoned. Similar plans in the 1960s, when the United Kingdom was negotiating entry to the **EUROPEAN ECONOMIC COMMUNITY (EEC)**, were discarded by the **GOVERNMENT** on grounds of escalating costs. On 20 January 1986, Prime Minister **MARGARET THATCHER** signed an agreement with France to build a two-tunnel rail link from Folkestone to Sangatte. The official opening took place on 6 May 1994, when Queen **ELIZABETH II** and President Georges Pompidou travelled along the route. Regular services started later that year although Britain had still not upgraded the rail line through Kent to **LONDON**.

CHARLES I (1600-49). King of **GREAT BRITAIN** and **IRELAND** from 1625 until 1649, Charles was born in Dunfermline on 19 November 1600, the second son of **JAMES VI** and **I** and his wife, **ANNE OF DENMARK.** A sickly child, he was considered too ill to travel south with the royal entourage when James became King of **ENGLAND** in 1603 and did not rejoin his family until the following year. In **LONDON**, he acquired a sound education, reading widely and learning French, Italian and Spanish, but he also became increasingly aware of his stammer and short stature, regarding them as embarrassments. The death of his older brother, Henry, in 1612 and the departure of his sister, Elizabeth, on her marriage the following year left him lonely and, perhaps, account for his shy and reserved demeanour in later life. A devout man, he was attracted to the ceremony of the Anglican church (see **CHURCH OF ENGLAND**) but had little interest in politics and later was to demonstrate an ineptitude in government which ultimately led to his death.

Charles became **PRINCE OF WALES** in 1616 and succeeded to the thrones of both **SCOTLAND** and England on his father's death in 1625. Troubles with his English **PARLIAMENT** surfaced immediately, partly because the **HOUSE OF COMMONS** was largely **PURITAN** and suspicious of the King's high church leanings, and, by 1626, relationships had soured further over the cost of pursuing wars with France and Spain. In 1628, the Commons passed resolutions condemning arbitrary taxation and imprisonment. The following year, it objected to the revival of "popish practices" in the Church and to the levying of taxes without its consent. Stung by the prolonged opposition, Charles dissolved the Parliament and, for the next 11 years, ruled by himself (see **ELEVEN YEARS' TYRANNY**).

North of the border as well, antagonism was growing, partly over taxation, partly over land reform measures and partly over attempts to make the Church of Scotland more like the Anglican church. Charles's decision, in 1637, to introduce a new liturgy based on the English **BOOK OF COMMON PRAYER** met with open resistance, and, the following year, many leading nobles and churchmen signed a National Covenant to defend the Presbyterian faith whilst retaining their loyalty to the King. Charles decided to impose his measures by force but his army, faced by experienced Scottish generals, decided not to fight. A truce was agreed at Berwick in June 1639, when the King promised to summon a Scottish Parliament and hold a General Assembly of the Church. Following the truce, Charles reconvened the English Parliament in April 1640 (see **SHORT PARLIAMENT**), but it proved unwilling to support a continued campaign against the Scots and was promptly dissolved again. The war was resumed but the Scots army was able to advance as far south as Ripon before agreeing to go no further. Shocked by the ease with which it had penetrated England, Charles summoned another Parliament in November (see **LONG PARLIAMENT**); to his dismay, it continued to oppose his policies and impeached several of his ministers for **TREASON**.

Anxious to placate his critics and build up his support in the House of Commons, the King agreed to the execution of the Earl of Stafford, his Lord Deputy in **IRELAND**, in 1641 and to a measure which prohibited the **DISSOLUTION OF PARLIAMENT** without its consent. In Scotland, he accepted the full establishment of Presbyterianism. These actions failed to placate the opposition, but when, on 23 November 1641, the English Parliament issued a **GRAND REMONSTRANCE,** listing all of the King's mistakes since his accession, Charles took comfort from the knowledge that the measure was passed by only three votes and was aware that he was not without support. Divisions between the two sides deepened, and, in the summer of 1642, fighting broke out all over England, leading to a **CIVIL WAR**. During its early phase, the **ROYAL-ISTS'** cause prospered and there were rumours of disagreements in the **PARLIAMENTARIAN** ranks, but defeat at the **BATTLE OF NASEBY** in 1645, and the loss of Bristol later in the same year, led to a turning of the tide. In the spring of 1646, Charles escaped in disguise from **OXFORD**, which had been surrounded by Parliamentary troops, and headed for the Scottish covenant army, encamped at Newark. He accompanied them to **NEWCASTLE-UPON-TYNE**, but, in January 1647, the Scots came to terms with the English rebel forces and marched home, leaving the King to his fate.

After several attempts at conciliation, Charles was charged with high treason and brought before the courts on 20 January 1649. He refused to recognize the legality of the proceedings on the grounds that "a King cannot be tried by any superior jurisdiction on earth" (see **DIVINE RIGHT OF KINGS**) but was found guilty nonetheless and on 27 January was sentenced to death. The sentence was carried out in London three days later, despite the protests of the Scots that an English court had no authority to murder their sovereign.

CHARLES II (1630-85). King of **SCOTLAND** from 1649 to 1685 and of **ENGLAND** from 1660 until 1685, Charles was the eldest surviving son of **CHARLES I** and his wife, Henrietta Maria of France. Until the age of 12, he was educated at his father's court but the outbreak of the first **CIVIL WAR** in 1642 interrupted the learning process, and, eventually, he fled to the continent with his mother, seeking refuge in France and the Netherlands. Following his father's execution on 30 January 1649, he was declared King of **SCOTLAND**. England, however, had become a republic under **OLIVER CROMWELL** and Charles was determined to win the throne to which he believed he was entitled. He moved to Scotland in June 1650 and accepted the Presbyterian cause although he bitterly resented the Church's intrusions into his private affairs and never adjusted to the Calvinist lifestyle. He did, however, raise an army and invaded England in 1651, but his troops were defeated at the **BATTLE OF WORCESTER** on 3 September and he was forced to flee again. Eventually, he reached France, having evaded capture by the narrowest of margins on several occasions.

With very limited financial resources and little support on the continent, his hopes of regaining the English throne seemed limited. Cromwell's death in 1658 brought little immediate improvement to his prospects, but, by 1660, Presbyterian supporters in England had gained political control and saw the restoration of the **MONARCH**y as the only alternative to anarchy. **PARLIAMENT** agreed to open negotiations with Charles, and, on 4 April, in the **DECLARATION OF BREDA**, he expressed his belief in freedom of conscience and promised to declare a general amnesty, negotiate an equitable settlement of land disputes and honour arrears of payment to the army in full. On 8 May, he was proclaimed King (see **RESTORATION**) and, on 25 May, landed at Dover. He was crowned on 23 April 1661 and married Catherine of Braganza the following year (the dowry brought Charles over £300,000 together with the territories of Bombay and Tangier plus substantial trading rights for English merchants, thus overcoming popular distaste for a Roman Catholic consort for the monarch).

Popularly known as "The Merry Monarch", Charles earned a reputation for extravagant living and for the company of ladies, including **NELL GWYNN**. But he was plagued by debt and regularly sought Parliamentary funds for the upkeep of the army, navy and diplomatic service. Dunkirk was sold to France in 1662, partly to raise funds and partly because the royal forces were too weak to defend overseas possessions properly. War with Holland in 1665 depleted the coffers further and added to the gloom of a nation already weakened by the **GREAT PLAGUE** (1665) and the **GREAT FIRE OF LONDON** (1666). In time, he raised money from Louis XIV of France in return for a secret agreement to declare himself a Roman Catholic, restore the Catholic faith in England and declare war on the Netherlands once more.

The **DUTCH WAR** began in 1672 and, in the course of the conflict, English troops captured the colony of New Amsterdam in North America, renaming it New York. By the late 1670s, partly because of the King's willingness to permit freedom of religious expression, rumours of a Catholic insurrection were rife and Charles came under pressure to exclude from the succession his son James (later **JAMES VII** and **II**), who had converted to Catholicism in

1668 or 1669. He refused to bend and, in 1681, dissolved Parliament, ruling as an absolute monarch for the rest of his life. He died in **LONDON** on 6 February 1685 after receiving the last rites of the Roman Catholic Church, thereby smoothing James's path to the throne.

CHARLES, PRINCE (1948-). Born in **BUCKINGHAM PALACE (LONDON)** on 14 November 1948, Charles is the heir to the UK throne and oldest child of Queen **ELIZABETH II** and **PRINCE PHILIP**. Christened Charles Philip Arthur George, he was educated at Hill House School, **LONDON** (1955-57); Cheam School, Berkshire (1957-62); Gordonstoun School, **SCOTLAND** (1962-67); and Geelong Grammar School, Australia (January-September, 1966), before entering **CAMBRIDGE** University, where he studied archaeology and anthro-pology, becoming (in 1970) the first heir-apparent to receive a bachelor's degree. He also studied Welsh at University College, Aberystwyth, in preparation for his investiture as **PRINCE OF WALES** at Caernarfon Castle in 1969. He took his seat in the **HOUSE OF LORDS** in 1970 and, after a period at the **ROYAL AIR FORCE** College in Cranwell and the Royal Naval College in Dartmouth, entered the **ROYAL NAVY** (1971). By the time he left to take up royal duties full-time in 1976, he was in command of a frigate.

Unwilling to play a purely neutral role until his accession, Charles spoke his mind on social issues and frequently raised hackles. In particular, his traditionalist views on architecture have caused storms, as when he claimed that the National Theatre was "like a nuclear power station in the middle of London" and that a proposed extension to the National Gallery was "a monstrous carbuncle on the face of a well-loved building".

On 29 June 1981, he married **DIANA FRANCES SPENCER**, younger daughter of Earl Spencer and his seventh cousin once removed. The couple have two children — Prince William Arthur Philip Louis (born on 21 June 1982, and second in line to the throne after his father) and Prince Henry Charles Albert David (born on 15 September 1984). However, affections cooled, and, in December 1992, after much press speculation and amidst much rancour, Buckingham Palace announced that Charles and Diana would separate. It was widely believed that a major cause of the break was Charles's longstanding friendship with Mrs Camilla Parker-Bowles, then wife of Brigadier Andrew Parker-Bowles, Silver Stick in Waiting to the Queen. Newspapers published transcripts of an intimate telephone conversation between the two in 1989, and other evidence of their association gradually became public knowledge. Prime Minister **JOHN MAJOR** told the **HOUSE OF COMMONS** that the succession to the throne was unaffected and that there was no reason why Princess Diana should not be crowned Queen in due course. However, questions were raised about Charles's suitability as heir, particularly because of the **MONARCH**'s position as Head of the **CHURCH OF ENGLAND**, which neither sanctions adultery nor weds divorcees.

In 1994, as Charles entered the silver jubilee year of his investiture as Prince of Wales, it appeared that the Buckingham Palace publicity machine was making a concerted effort to replace the dignity and status which he had lost. Charles himself felt that his potential as British trade ambassador had been underdeveloped and that he could play a more important role in the 200 or so organizations, from farming to sport and from environment to architecture, with which he is associated. Many critics see the Prince as a dilettante, dipping into things then moving on. Others point out that he has been waiting to succeed to the throne for nearly 50 years, without any specific job to keep him occupied, and ask for Parliament to redefine the role of the heir in a modern society. In 1996, reportedly following pressure from the Queen, Charles and Diana finally began divorce proceedings.

CHARTISM. The People's Charter of 1838 declared that there should be universal male suffrage, payment of Members of **PARLIA-MENT**, abolition of MPs' property requirements for office, vote by secret ballot, annual **GENERAL ELECTION**s and equal-sized electoral **CONSTITUENCIES**. Chartism was a working class movement whose strength grew during, and was dependent on, economic recession. The period 1837-48 saw demonstrations, agitation and petitioning of Parliament (in 1839, in 1842 and in 1848) to achieve its ends. Harsh treatment of the **TOLPUDDLE MAR-TYRS**, a nascent **TRADE UNION** group, had shown many people that only political action could bring change, though poor working conditions and poor living conditions exacerbated feelings, as did anger at the 1834 reform of the **POOR LAW**. The movement collapsed in 1848, a time of revolution in Europe and fear amongst the establishment that civil riot might develop, of disagreements among Chartist leaders, of localized grievances that were hard to articulate nationally, of growing middle class opposition to its aims and of partially improving economic conditions. As industrial production grew in the 1850s and commerce revived, working class attention shifted to industrial, rather than political, action and the rise of trade unionism. The last Chartist convention was held in 1858.

CHATHAM, EARL OF. (See **WILLIAM PITT THE ELDER**).

CHEVY CHASE, BALLAD or BATTLE OF. (See **BATTLE OF OTTERBURN**).

CHIEF SECRETARY TO THE TREASURY. This **GOVERN-MENT** post ranks immediately below that of **CHANCELLOR OF THE EXCHEQUER.** In **JOHN MAJOR**'s administrations, the holder of the office was responsible for the control of public expenditure (including public sector salaries).

CHILTERN HUNDREDS. The Stewardship of the Chiltern Hundreds (see **HUNDRED**) is an ancient royal sinecure post which, as an office paid by the **CROWN**, Members of **PARLIAMENT** are barred from holding. Technically, MPs are not permitted to resign so they have to apply for the Stewardship as a device to leave the **HOUSE OF COMMONS** if they wish to give up their post at any time other than at a **GENERAL ELECTION**. The Chiltern Hundreds comprise the Buckinghamshire Hundreds of Stoke, Burnham and Desborough.

CHIVALRY, ORDERS OF. The development of chivalric associations and codes of behaviour grew during the **CRUSADES** and through the fusing of **KNIGHT**hood and religious orders. In later centuries, they became codified into a hierarchy and, subsequently, into a series of ranked orders of limited size. The **CROWN** awards membership, which now goes to individuals who have given meritorious service to the country. In order of precedence these knightly Orders are: The Most Noble **ORDER OF THE GARTER** (KG), the highest British civil or military honour, awarded to 24 Knights Companion; The Most Ancient and Most Noble Order of the Thistle (KT), which is exclusively Scottish; The Most Honourable Order of the Bath, usually awarded for outstanding military achievement; The Order of Merit (OM), for merit in public service, the arts, sciences or the armed forces; The Most Distinguished Order of St Michael and St George, usually given for achievement in foreign service; The Royal Victorian Order, for services to the Queen and awarded at her discretion; The Most Excellent Order of the British Empire, for service to government; and The Order of the Companions of Honour (CH), for service to the nation in literature and art.

CHURCH OF ENGLAND. The established church in **ENGLAND** was created in 1534, at the **REFORMATION,** by **HENRY VIII**, when he effectively nationalized the clergy, but was mostly developed under the later **TUDOR** Monarchs, **EDWARD VI** and **ELIZABETH I.** The 1534 **ACT OF SUPREMACY** (see **ACT OF PARLIAMENT**) brought the Church into existence, with the **MONARCH** as **SUPREME GOVERNOR** and Bishops sitting as of right in the **HOUSE OF LORDS**. In the 1990s, more than 27 million Britons have been baptized into the Church (usually as infants) but fewer than 9 million have been confirmed (normally that happens at about 12 years of age) and fewer than 2 million are on the official church rolls — a consequence of falling religious observance. In 1993, the Church agreed to the **ORDINATION OF WOMEN**, for the first time, causing rifts with more traditionalist interpreters of the Scriptures and several prominent Anglicans joined the Roman Catholic Church in protest. The episcopal churches in **SCOTLAND**, **IRELAND** and **WALES** are distinct from the Church of England. (See **ARCHBISHOP OF CANTERBURY**).

CHURCHILL, JOHN (1650-1722). The victor of major battles with the French during the **WAR OF SPANISH SUCCESSION**, Churchill was born in Ashe (Devon) on 26 May 1650, the son of Sir Winston Churchill and his wife, Elizabeth. He was educated at St Paul's School then became page to James, **DUKE OF YORK** (later **JAMES VII** and **II**), who arranged for him to be given a commission as Ensign in the Foot Guards in 1667. Over the next four years, he gained considerable experience in the arts of warfare, serving in Tangier (1668-70), with the English fleet in the battle against the Dutch at Solebay (1672) and with the troops sent to aid Louis XIV of France in his campaign against Holland (also in 1672). His activities earned recognition; he was made Colonel of the English Regiment by the French King in 1674, created Baron Churchill in the Scottish peerage (1682) and promoted to Colonel of the 1st Royal Dragoons (1683). Then, after the Duke of York succeeded to the throne in 1685, he was raised to the rank of Major General, created Baron Churchill and Lord of the Bedchamber in the English **PEERAGE** and won victory for the King at the **BATTLE OF SEDGEMOOR.**

However, over the next three years, he became increasingly opposed to James's pro-Catholic policies and, in 1688, transferred his allegiance to the Protestant Prince William of Orange (later **WILLIAM III**). In 1689, just before his **CORONATION**, William created Churchill Earl of Marlborough. Later that year, Churchill commanded an English brigade serving under the Prince of Walbeck in the Netherlands and, in 1690, conducted a campaign in **IRELAND**. However, despite those successes, William suspected that Marlborough had been corresponding with the exiled King James, withdrew all his offices and, albeit briefly, incarcerated him in the **TOWER OF LONDON** (1692).

Marlborough had returned to royal favour by 1696 and was appointed Commander in Chief and Plenipotentiary in Holland in 1700. When James's daughter, succeeded to the throne as Queen **ANNE** in 1702, she made him a Knight of the Garter (see **ORDERS OF CHIVALRY**), Captain General of the Forces and Master of the Ordnance. Later in the year, after a successful campaign in the Rhine region, he was created Duke of Marlborough.

By 1704, France was conducting a successful war against Austria, and Marlborough determined to intervene. The Dutch gave him permission to attack enemy forces along the Moselle River, but he went further, marched rapidly into Germany, crossed the Danube at Donauworth and met the Austrian army near Blenheim. On 13 August, the combined forces descended on the French and after a bitter battle (see **BATTLE OF BLENHEIM**) forced the enemy to retreat. The cost in lives was high, but the victory changed the balance of power in Europe, destroying Louis XIV's military might. A grateful **PARLIAMENT** rewarded him with the Manor of Woodstock and the Queen built him a palace on the land.

The success was no flash in the pan. Marlborough continued to dominate the battlefields of Europe, crushing the French at the **BATTLE OF RAMILLIES** on 23 May 1706 and again at the **BATTLE OF OUDENARDE** on 8 July 1708. On 11 September 1709, he gained another victory at the **BATTLE OF MALPLAQUET** and, on 20 October, overcame the defences at Mons. In **LONDON**, however, there was a growing belief that there was no point in further warfare, and, in 1711, Marlborough began his final campaign. He marched through France, intent on taking Le Quesnoy — the last fortress before Paris itself — but the English and Dutch Governments were involved in peace negotiations and refused to support him. His political enemies took advantage of his changed fortunes, accusing him of prolonging the war simply in order to enhance his own reputation and of misappropriating public money allocated to the building of Blenheim Palace. The charges were never proved but, even so, Marlborough was again deprived of his offices and went into exile on the continent until Queen Anne's death in 1714. He was brought back by her successor — **GEORGE I** — and his offices were returned but, in 1716, he suffered two paralytic strokes. From then, his health was continually in decline until his death at Cranbourne Lodge (Windsor) on 16 June 1722.

CHURCHILL, WINSTON LEONARD SPENCER(1874-1965). One of the outstanding British wartime leaders, Churchill was born at Blenheim Palace (Oxfordshire) on 30 November 1874, the elder son of Lord Randolph Churchill (a descendant of **JOHN CHURCH-ILL,** Duke of Marlborough) and his wife, Jennie (daughter of US financier Leonard W. Jerome). He studied at Harrow School and the Royal Military Academy Sandhurst then, in 1895, joined the 4th Queen's Own Hussars with the rank of Second Lieutenant. After a period of leave spent in the Caribbean as a foreign correspondent of the *Daily Graphic*, Churchill went with his regiment to India (1896) and later to Egypt (1898), where he took part in **HORATIO KITCHENER**'s campaign in the Sudan. He resigned his commission in 1889 and fought an unsuccessful campaign as the **CON-SERVATIVE PARTY** candidate at a **BY-ELECTION** in Oldham before going to South Africa to cover the **BOER WAR** for the *Morning Post*. Amongst his despatches were reports of his own experiences as he escaped from a prisoner of war camp.

In 1900, Churchill returned to Britain as a hero and captured Oldham for the Conservatives. Four years later, however, he transferred his allegiance to the **LIBERAL PARTY** as a protest against the policy of preferential tariffs for territories of the **BRITISH EMPIRE**, advocated by **JOSEPH CHAMBER-LAIN**. His Oldham constituency and the Conservative Party in the **HOUSE OF COMMONS** both disowned him, but, in 1906, he was elected Liberal Member of **PARLIAMENT** for **MAN-CHESTER** and was given his first **GOVERNMENT** post as **UNDER-SECRETARY OF STATE** for the colonies by Prime Minister **HENRY CAMPBELL-BANNERMAN. HERBERT ASQUITH**, Campbell-Bannerman's successor, also recognized Churchill's talents and made him **PRESIDENT OF THE BOARD OF TRADE** (1908), then **HOME SECRETARY** (1910) and finally First Lord of the **ADMIRALTY** (1911).

Aware of the possibility of war with Germany, Churchill strove to improve the effectiveness of the **ROYAL NAVY**, ordering vessels fuelled by oil rather than coal, employing heavier guns and commissioning faster battleships. His perspicacity was rewarded after the outbreak of hostilities in 1914 because the British fleet was able to contain the German threat in the North Sea from its base at Scapa Flow. However, despite that achievement, he was heavily criticized for advocating continued support for a naval offensive in the Dardanelles and demoted to **CHANCELLOR OF THE DUCHY OF LANCASTER**. His response was to resign from the government in November 1915 and join the 6th Royal Scots Fusiliers as Lieutenant Colonel.

He returned to Parliament in June 1916 and, in July of the following year, was appointed **MINISTER** of Munitions by **DAVID LLOYD GEORGE**. In 1919, he became Secretary for War, with responsibility for organizing the demobilization of servicemen, then transferred to the Colonial Office as parliamentary under-secretary in 1921.

Churchill lost his seat at the 1922 **GENERAL ELECTION** and, for the next two years, devoted much of his time to painting and writing (his account of the **FIRST WORLD WAR** — *The World Crisis* — appeared in six volumes between 1923 and 1931, earning him enough to buy Chartwell as a country home in **KENT**). In 1924, however, he was back in the House of Commons as the MP for the staunchly Conservative **CONSTITUENCY** of Epping and was immediately appointed **CHANCELLOR OF THE EXCHEQUER** by **STANLEY BALDWIN**. For five years he was in control of the country's finances, but that was a task which provided no stimulus for a man of action. He followed an orthodox line and made many mistakes, including the return to the **GOLD STANDARD** — a misjudgement which led to deflation, the **GENERAL STRIKE** of 1926 and a scathing rebuke from economist **JOHN MAYNARD KEYNES**.

When Baldwin's administration fell in 1929, Churchill went with it and soon broke with the Conservative Leadership over plans to give self-government to India, believing in slow and steady progress towards independence. For ten years he was in the political wilderness, shunned by former colleagues and losing potential allies through his support for **EDWARD VIII** during the abdication crisis of 1936 and his denunciation of **NEVILLE CHAMBERLAIN**'s **APPEASEMENT** policy in the face of German territorial expansion. However, on 3 September 1939 (the first day of the **SECOND WORLD WAR**), Chamberlain invited Churchill to join his War **CABINET** as First Lord of the Admiralty.

On 10 May of the following year, the Prime Minister resigned after learning of the German invasion of the Low Countries and advised **GEORGE VI** to appoint Lord Halifax in his place. Halifax declined the offer so Churchill was offered the post as the next best candidate. He accepted immediately and formed a War Cabinet consisting of himself, Chamberlain, Lord Halifax, Arthur Greenwood and **CLEMENT ATTLEE.** Ten days later, he faced the Commons as Prime Minister for the first time, told them that he had "nothing to offer but blood, toil, tears and sweat" and received the unanimous support of all parties.

For the next five years he was commander-in-chief of the British nation, controlling both the formulation of policy and its implementation. After the successful evacuation of soldiers stranded at Dunkerque (**DUNKIRK**) in 1940, he curbed celebration with the reminder that evacuations do not win wars and warned of the possibility of invasion, rallying the Commons with the promise that ". . . we shall fight on the beaches, we shall fight on the landing grounds, we shall fight in the fields and in the streets, we shall fight in the hills; we shall never surrender . . . ". When Hitler attacked the Soviet Union in June 1941, Churchill pledged immediate help to Premier Josef Stalin despite his condemnation of communism in prewar speeches, then, in August, travelled to Newfoundland to meet U.S. President Franklin D. Roosevelt. The **ATLANTIC CHARTER**, which the two western leaders shaped, contained no specific commitments but stressed the common goals of their countries and did much to raise morale in a beleaguered Britain.

After Germany surrendered in 1945, Churchill wanted to continue the coalition government until Japan also fell but could not convince his Cabinet colleagues, so a general election was called for 15 June 1945. Despite the Prime Minister's warning of the dire consequences of socialism, Labour swept to power under Clement Attlee and Churchill was reduced to leadership of the **OPPOSITION**. For six years he worked to rebuild party morale and, in 1951, gained a Commons majority of 26 over Labour. The following year, he went to Washington to repair the damage which he believed the Anglo-American relationship had suffered since the end of the war and, in 1953, was made a Knight of the Garter (see **ORDERS OF CHIVALRY**) and awarded the Nobel Prize for Literature.

He resigned as Prime Minister on 5 April 1955 and spent much of his last years with his brush and palette. (He had once admitted that "If it weren't for painting I couldn't bear the strain of things".) On 24 January 1965, he died peacefully in **LONDON** and a few days later, after a state funeral, was buried beside his father in the graveyard of St Martin's Church, close to Blenheim Palace.

CINQUE PORTS. A number of ports in southeast **ENGLAND** were granted legal and commercial privileges during the **ANGLO-SAXON** period in return for providing ships and men to defend the coastline from invaders (a successor to the **SAXON SHORE FORTS**). This early navy was formalized in the early 12th century by the establishment of the Cinque Ports — Hastings, Hythe, Dover, Romney and Sandwich. The original five ("cinque" is French for "five" but this was pronounced in a typically English way as "sink") were later to be joined by others. Silting of harbours, the coastline extensions around Dungeness and the eventual growth of the **ROYAL NAVY** led to the loss of charters in 1685 and now only the honorary position of Lord Warden of the Cinque Ports remains.

CITIZEN'S CHARTER. A programme introduced by **JOHN MAJOR** in 1991, the Charter was intended to make public services more accountable to their clients. It led to the growth of performance-related pay and service quality aims in public companies and utilities. **GOVERNMENT** departments, services and agencies then published their own target-led charters.

CITY. Traditionally, this honorary title was bestowed on a town because of its importance as an Anglican See or because of its eminence as a commercial or industrial centre. The title is given by right of ancient usage, by Parliamentary statute or by royal decree or charter. Only 59 towns currently have the right to call themselves City, and there is no relationship either to size or to **LOCAL GOVERNMENT** status.

CITY OF LONDON. The City, or Square Mile, is the ancient **BOROUGH** at the heart of **LONDON**. It has held a Royal Charter since 1079 and is now the business and commercial centre of the metropolis. It is managed by the **CORPORATION OF LONDON** with a **LORD MAYOR** and elected Aldermen and its ancient seat of government is the Guildhall.

CIVIL LIST, THE. An annual **PARLIAMENT**ary grant to **WILLIAM II** supplemented the **CROWN**'s hereditary incomes, but, during the reign of **GEORGE III**, Parliament sought to further restrict the powers of the **MONARCH**. By the Civil List Act of 1777 (see **ACT OF PARLIAMENT**), the King was provided with a strictly controlled royal allowance of £800,000 each year for the upkeep of the royal family and **ROYAL HOUSEHOLD**. As a result, the present Queen (**ELIZABETH II**) derives her annual income from the Civil List, from some **GOVERNMENT** departments and from private revenue. Traditionally, the Civil List was set at the beginning of a reign and remained at that level, but the Civil List Act of 1972 enabled annual increments to be made, pegged to inflation. Members of the royal family other than the monarch also draw income from the Civil List, although the **PRINCE OF WALES** derives his from Duchy of Cornwall revenues. Periodically, the Civil List is reviewed, and, in 1993, Queen Elizabeth, for the first time, agreed to pay income tax to the Inland Revenue on the sums granted.

CIVIL WAR (first), 1642-46. By 1642, King **CHARLES I** was widely unpopular. Wars with Spain and France had been underfinanced and did not command public support, particularly so because the King had levied additional charges on his subjects in order to raise funds to pay troops and manufacture weaponry. In 1629, he had decided to rule without **PARLIAMENT** (see **ELEVEN YEARS TYRANNY**), and, in 1635, he had extended the **SHIP MONEY** tax to most of **ENGLAND**. Also, Catholicism had begun to regain favour at court, with Charles using Irish and Highland Scottish Catholic armies to subdue Protestant opposition in **SCOTLAND**, but much of the country was strongly opposed to popery. The tensions between King and subjects soured debates at the start of the **LONG PARLIAMENT** and **ENGLAND** drifted into war, with Parliamentary support strong in the **LONDON** area and the main support for the **ROYALISTS** in the Midlands. Conflict began with the raising of the Royal Standard at Nottingham on 22 August 1642. Parliament, with control of London and the **ROYAL NAVY**, the support of the merchant classes and the strength of its **NEW MODEL ARMY** (a strength maintained by regular pay), gradually wore down the King's forces. The Royalists were eventually crushed at the **BATTLE OF MARSTON MOOR** (1644) and the **BATTLE OF NASEBY** (1645) and hostilities ceased in April 1646 as Charles fled north in disguise. (See

BATTLE OF CROPREDY BRIDGE; BATTLE OF EDGE-HILL; BATTLE OF LOSTWITHIEL; BATTLE OF NEWARK; BATTLE OF NEWBURY [1643 and 1644]).

CIVIL WAR (second), 1648-49. Although King CHARLES I was defeated in the first CIVIL WAR, the Scots continued to support him. Provincial risings began in South WALES, Essex, KENT and Yorkshire as the RUMP PARLIAMENT attempted to reduce the size and cost of the NEW MODEL ARMY while retaining heavy taxes, centralizing power at WESTMINSTER and maintaining military rule (see PRIDE'S PURGE). Hostilities began with a revolt in Pembrokeshire on 23 March 1648, but the uncoordinated opposition to PARLIAMENT was rapidly suppressed with, in addition, a major military victory over the Scots at the BATTLE OF PRESTON (1648). Charles was captured, found guilty of TREASON and, on 30 January 1649, executed. THE COMMONWEALTH was declared, and OLIVER CROMWELL reigned supreme. (See DIGGERS).

CLARENDON CODE. A series of ACTS OF PARLIAMENT (1661-70) named after Edward Hyde, Earl of Clarendon and LORD CHANCELLOR, the Code sought to re-establish the Anglican Church (see CHURCH OF ENGLAND) and combat NONCONFORMISM by removing the toleration of independent congregations allowed under OLIVER CROMWELL's rule. It included the 1661 Corporation Act, which excluded Nonconformists from BOROUGH offices, the 1662 ACT OF UNIFORMITY, the 1664 Conventical Act (which outlawed non-Anglican services) and the 1665 Five Mile Act (which forbade nonconformist clergy from coming within five miles of a borough boundary). Paradoxically, Clarendon was said to have been less than enthusiastic about many of these policies, adopted by the CAVALIER PARLIAMENT of CHARLES II.

CLARKE, KENNETH HARRY (1940-). CHANCELLOR OF THE EXCHEQUER in JOHN MAJOR's post-Thatcher administration (see MARGARET THATCHER), Clarke was born on 2 July 1940, the eldest child of Mr and Mrs Kenneth Clarke of Nottingham. He was educated at Nottingham High School and CAMBRIDGE University, where (while pursuing legal studies) he was Chairman of the Conservative Association (1961) and of the Union (1963). He was called to the Bar in 1963 and contested

Mansfield for the **CONSERVATIVE PARTY** at the **GENERAL ELECTION**s of 1964 and 1966, eventually winning a seat in the **HOUSE OF COMMONS** as the Member of **PARLIAMENT** for Rushcliffe in 1970.

Clarke became **PARLIAMENTARY PRIVATE SECRETARY** to the **SOLICITOR GENERAL** in 1971, Assistant Government Chief **WHIP** in 1972 and Lord Commissioner of the **TREASURY** during the last few weeks of **EDWARD HEATH**'s administration in 1974. While he was on the **OPPOSITION** benches, he was Spokesman on Social Services (1974-76) and Industry (1976-79). Then, when Mrs Thatcher led the Conservatives back into power in 1979, he became **PARLIAMENTARY SECRETARY** and later **PARLIAMENTARY UNDER-SECRETARY OF STATE** (1980-82) at the Ministry of Transport. He was **MINISTER** of Health from 1982 until 1985 and entered the **CABINET** for the first time as **PAYMASTER GENERAL** and Minister of Employment (1985-87). After a period as **CHANCELLOR OF THE DUCHY OF LANCASTER** and Minister of Trade and Industry with special responsibility for policy on the inner cities in 1987-88, he served as **SECRETARY OF STATE** for Health from 1988 until 1990 and for **EDUCATION** and Science from 1990 until 1992.

An affable politician with a liking for beer and a relish for the rough and tumble of Parliamentary life, he is widely respected for his ability to deal with high profile issues, as when he was given the task of implementing a radical reorganization of the **NATIONAL HEALTH SERVICE** in 1988. In 1989, he called in troops to man **LONDON** ambulances when the crews took industrial action as part of their campaign for better pay and conditions and, in 1991, announced plans to take sixth form colleges (which provide education for 16-18 year olds) and further **EDUCATION** colleges out of local authority control. His reputation as a political battler was undoubtedly one of the reasons for his appointment as Chancellor of the Exchequer after the sacking of Norman Lamont in 1993. He delivered his first **BUDGET** later that year with a promise to reduce government borrowing but, by early 1994, was forced to admit that taxes took a bigger bite out of family incomes than they had when the **LABOUR PARTY** was ousted from office in 1979.

CLEAN AIR ACT, 1956. Major urban centres had, since the growth of factories during the **INDUSTRIAL REVOLUTION** (and particularly with the post-**SECOND WORLD WAR** increase in numbers of vehicles on the roads), experienced bad pollution conditions, exemplified by the traditional view of fog-bound Victorian **LONDON** and the pea-soupers (very heavy fogs, likened to pea soup) of the early 1950s (that of December 1952 brought the capital to a halt and killed over 4,000 people from bronchitis and other respiratory problems). The Clean Air Act (see **ACT OF PARLIAMENT**) introduced smokeless zones and other measures to reduce emissions from factories, domestic chimneys, power stations and vehicles, dramatically improving urban air conditions. (See **POLLUTION CONTROL**).

CLIVE, ROBERT (1725-74). A soldier and statesman who was instrumental in establishing British rule in India, Clive was born on the family estate of Styche (near Market Drayton) on 29 September 1725. High-spirited as a youngster, he attended several schools but showed little academic ability and, in 1743, at the age of 18, was despatched to Madras in the service of the **EAST INDIA COMPANY**. Moody and depressed, he attempted suicide on two occasions and spent many hours reading in the library before clashes between the French and the British in the south of India gave him an opportunity to demonstrate his military talents. In 1751, he was sent to the assistance of Mohammed Ali, whose claim to the Nawabship of the Carnatic (see **CARNATIC WARS**) was contested by Chanda Sahib (who had the support of the French). Clive captured Chanda's base at Arcot then successfully withstood a 53-day siege and, over the next few months, gained a growing reputation as an outstanding strategist in guerilla warfare. He returned to Britain in 1753 but two years later, after an unsuccessful attempt to get elected to **PARLIAMENT**, was sent back to India as Governor of Fort St David.

In 1756, a dispute over Calcutta's defences precipitated the capture of the city's fort by Siraj-ud-Daula, the Nawab of Bengal. Clive was given command of a relief force, which set out in October and recaptured the city in January 1757. Initially, the Nawab and Britain agreed a peace treaty, but Clive was anxious to work with a ruler more favourable to British interests and broke with Siraj-ud-Daula, defeating him at the **BATTLE OF PLASSEY** on 23 June. Mir Jafar was installed in his stead, but Clive was the power behind the throne and was appointed Governor by the East India Company. Described by **WILLIAM PITT THE ELDER** as "a heaven-born general", he returned to Britain in 1760, was awarded an Irish peerage as Baron Clive of Plassey in 1762 and was **KNIGHT**ed in 1764 (see **ORDERS OF CHIVALRY**).

In 1765, he went back to Calcutta as Governor and Commander-in-Chief of Bengal. Negotiations with Shah Alam, the Mogul Emperor, led to an agreement which gave the East India Company the right to collect revenues in Bihar and Bengal. As a result, the company effectively controlled the two richest provinces in India and provided the foundation for the expansion of the **BRITISH EMPIRE** in the subcontinent. Clive's successes, however, were not universally acclaimed. Jealousy, accusations of corruption amongst the company's employees and prejudice against those who had made their fortune in India led to criticism. Clive was cleared by an all-night **HOUSE OF COMMONS** debate in which a majority of MPs decided that he had "rendered great and meritorious services to his country". However, the strain was too much for a man still given to depressive moodiness and, on 22 November 1774, he committed suicide at his home in **LONDON**.

CLIVE OF PLASSEY, BARON. (See **ROBERT CLIVE**).

CNUT. (See **CANUTE**).

COAL. At the beginning of the 20th century, following a massive increase in exploitation during the **INDUSTRIAL REVOLUTION**, the coal industry employed over 1 million miners and produced over 292 million tonnes per annum. Nationalized in 1947 (see **NATIONALIZATION**), it came under increasing pressure as cheaper coal was imported from overseas, as alternative fuels grew in importance (particularly gas for domestic heating) and as recession began to hit industry in the 1980s. A bitter strike by the National Union of Mineworkers during 1984-85 was met with stern opposition from **GOVERNMENT** as pits were closed. By 1991, production had dropped to 91 million tonnes and barely 57,000 miners were employed. The market for coal was reduced further through government subsidies paid for **NUCLEAR POWER**, the so-called "dash for **GAS**" after the **PRIVATIZATION** of the **ELECTRICITY** industry and the import of cheaply produced **EUROPEAN COMMUNITY (EC)** coal. In 1993, British Coal (the nationalized company controlling the mines) made a loss of £238 million. Productivity was averaging 8.76 tonnes per workshift, but, by the end of the year, only 17 pits, employing 10,500 miners, were left in operation (ten years earlier, 170 pits had employed 191,000 men). Privatization of the industry began in 1994.

COD WARS, 1958-76. Although referred to as cod wars, the differences between Britain and Iceland over fishing rights amounted to little more than skirmishes and strained relations. In 1958, Iceland unilaterally declared a 12-mile fishing exclusion zone around the country in order to preserve fish (mostly cod) stocks. Gunboats seized a Grimsby trawler, which was later freed by the **ROYAL NAVY**, and, the following year, live warning shots were fired across the bows of another trawler, occasioning vigorous protest from the British **GOVERNMENT**. The war quietened after that until a similar incident in April 1973, by which time Iceland had extended the exclusion zone to 50 miles. British frigates and Icelandic gunboats shadowed and followed each other inside the fishing fleets, and, on 19 February 1976, the two countries suspended all relations. A compromise reached later that year brought the reinstatement of full diplomatic contacts and limited Britain to 24 trawlers within the now 200 mile zone. (See **FISHERIES**).

COLOMBO PLAN. In 1951, **COMMONWEALTH OF NATIONS** negotiators drew up this agreement for economic cooperation in south and southeast Asia, with the particular aim of helping the poorer countries of the region to develop. Britain provided financial aid, training and technical expertise. Membership now includes 21 countries in the region together with the United States of America, the United Kingdom, Australia, Canada, Japan and New Zealand.

COMBINATION ACTS. The acts (see **ACT OF PARLIAMENT**) were unsuccessful attempts by the **GOVERNMENT**, in 1799 and again in 1800, to prevent the formation of "combinations" — the grouping of men into **TRADE UNIONS** to campaign for better pay and conditions of work. Any action to meet or support a combination was made punishable by imprisonment because the laws of conspiracy were applied to political agitation. Much of the fear engendered in the Establishment by the democratic tendencies of the **FRENCH REVOLUTION** found its expression in these acts, which were repealed in 1824. Legislation in that year made the unions legal (except where they employed intimidation or violence) and was followed by an upsurge in activity and membership. A further measure in 1825 restricted the unions to peaceful collective bargaining.

COMMAND PAPER. Any document formally presented to **PARLIA-MENT** on behalf of the **GOVERNMENT** is called a command paper because it is said to be presented at Her Majesty's command.

COMMON LAND. Under the **FEUDAL SYSTEM**, and later manorial forms of management (see **MANOR**), there were areas of communally owned waste and nonarable land on which tenants had the right to graze their animals in common. Much reduced by the **ENCLOSURES** and other landed class actions, this land was protected by the 1876 Commons Act and the Commons Registration Act of 1965 (see **ACT OF PARLIAMENT**). Some areas are still under threat of development so several pressure groups have formed to preserve what remains.

COMMON LAW. Since the 12th century, Common Law has been the body of law established by precedent (i.e., by the accumulation of legal judgement in the courts). The parallel body of law is derived from **ACTS OF PARLIAMENT,** (i.e., the written Statute Law). (See **JUDICIARY**).

COMMON MARKET. (See **EUROPEAN ECONOMIC COMMUNITY [EEC]**).

COMMONWEALTH, THE (1649-53). Between 30 January 1649 (when the execution of King **CHARLES I** took place) and 1660 (the year of the **RESTORATION** of **CHARLES II**), **ENGLAND** was a republic. The **RUMP PARLIAMENT** (the remnants of the **LONG PARLIAMENT**) voted to abolish the **MONARCH**y and reform the constitution. In 1649, it declared England a Commonwealth and Free State, which lasted until failure to agree on electoral reform led to its demise at the hands of **OLIVER CROMWELL** in April 1653. An attempt to continue through a nominated assembly also failed, and Cromwell took power with his Council of Officers in December 1653 to begin the **PROTECTORATE** period of the republic. The term "Commonwealth" is also applied by some scholars specifically to the periods 1649 to 1653 and 1659 to 1660 (before and after the Protectorate and before the Restoration). This period is sometimes referred to as the "Commonwealth of England". (See **INTERREGNUM**).

COMMONWEALTH OF NATIONS. The **BRITISH EMPIRE** was the largest and most successful imperial system of the 19th century and gained its maximum territorial extent after the **FIRST WORLD WAR**. Ambitions for independence in the colonies grew, and, in 1926, the **IMPERIAL CONFERENCE** declared that the United Kingdom and its self-governing **DOMINIONS** were equal and autonomous and would remain "freely associated as members of the British Commonwealth of Nations". Increasingly, however, the concept of a democracy running a subservient empire was questioned and eventually the United Kingdom negotiated **DECOLON-IZATION** of the majority of its possessions, most of which opted to join the Commonwealth upon gaining independence.

In order to eradicate the stigma of imperialism, the word "British" was dropped from the organization's title in 1949 and a permanent secretariat was established. It remains a remarkably diverse club — a loose collection of free and voluntary associates, united by colonial heritage and the English language and dedicated to mutual assistance and the encouragement of scientific, educational and economic co-operation. The Commonwealth is composed of some 50 independent states and accounts for approximately 1.4 billion people — a quarter of the world's population. In addition, it includes 14 British overseas dependencies (see **UK OVERSEAS DEPENDENCIES**) and 10 other dependencies of either Australia or New Zealand. Twenty-eight members are republics, five are monarchies and 17 recognize Queen **ELIZA-BETH II** as their head of state.

COMMUNIST PARTY. The Party was founded in 1920 and gained its first Member of **PARLIAMENT** in 1922. Requests in 1921, 1922 and 1936 to unite with the **LABOUR PARTY** were refused. Never a significant force in British politics, only ever having two MPs at any one time, it was probably eclipsed by the rise of Labour, which was strongly founded in the **TRADE UNION** movement and the working classes. It changed its name to the Democratic Left in 1991.

COMPREHENSIVE SCHOOLS. Created by the 1944 **EDUCATION** Act (see **ACT OF PARLIAMENT**), these schools were for "all secondary children (of twelve years of age and over) of all families in a given area". State secondary schools were built from the 1950s to take children of all academic abilities (that is, they were nonselective) and replace the **GRAMMAR SCHOOLS** (which selected only more able children) and the Secondary Modern schools (which had taken all others). By 1994, about 90 per cent of the pupils in the state system attended comprehensives.

CONCORDE. Britain and France agreed in 1962 to cooperate over the production of a supersonic passenger airliner. The British prototype first flew in 1969 but was dogged by problems (particularly over noise controls in what was seen as the lucrative US market) and escalating costs. The first commercial flight was made on 21 January 1976 from **LONDON** to Bahrain. Concorde remains a flagship of **BRITISH AIRWAYS** and Air France but is hardly the commercial success once envisaged.

CONFEDERATION OF BRITISH INDUSTRY (CBI). The CBI was formed in 1965 as a grouping of managers and employers which could speak for industry in talks with **GOVERNMENT** and publicize the work of industrial management.

CONSCRIPTION. Enforced statutory enlistment of civilians in the armed forces of the nation was introduced in 1916 by the Military Service Act (see **ACT OF PARLIAMENT**). It applied to all able-bodied men aged 18 to 40 because the Army demanded more front line troops during the **FIRST WORLD WAR**. At the time, it caused problems of conscience for many of the **LIBERAL PARTY**, who saw it as an infringement of personal liberties, and it was abolished in 1920. It was again applied from 1939 for the **SECOND WORLD WAR**. Essential workers (such as miners) were exempted, as were conscientious objectors (who were generally despised). From 1941, it also applied to women (under the 1941 Conscription Act, unmarried women could be directed to the forces or to essential factory work), and, after 1945, it continued as a two-year period of call-up known as **NATIONAL SERVICE.** (This was finally abandoned only in 1962.) (See **BRITISH ARMY; ROYAL AIR FORCE; ROYAL NAVY; STANDING ARMY**).

CONSERVATIVE PARTY. The Conservatives evolved gradually from the older grouping of **TORIES**, and the names are still used synonymously. The term *Conservative Party* was first employed by Prime Minister **GEORGE CANNING** in 1824 and became increasingly popular from about the time of the 1832 Reform Act (see **ACT OF PARLIAMENT**) as **ROBERT PEEL** advocated policies which retained traditional social and political institutions but allowed for development as economic and other circumstances changed. (See **TAMWORTH MANIFESTO**.) In 1886, many members of the **LIBERAL PARTY** who opposed **HOME RULE** for **IRELAND** realigned themselves with the Conservatives, then led by the **MARQUIS OF SALISBURY**, and, in 1912, the two groups formally united as the Conservative and Unionist Party, a name which is still the organization's official title.

Traditionally the party of the property-owning classes and right-wing in its policies, it has supported free market economies, free enterprize and opposition to **NATIONALIZATION**. (**BENJAMIN DISRAELI** saw it as upholding the establishment, the **BRITISH EMPIRE** and the living conditions of the people.) It was the first British political party to create a national organization, with the National Union founded in 1867 and Conservative Central Office in 1870. Currently, two-thirds of its funds come from **CONSTITUENCY** associations and individual members, the rest from company and corporation donations. It has been in power in Britain from 1979 to date (1996) and is currently led by **JOHN MAJOR**. (See **NANCY WITCHER ASTOR; STANLEY BALDWIN; ARTHUR JAMES BALFOUR; RICHARD AUSTEN BUTLER; ARTHUR NEVILLE CHAMBERLAIN; JOSEPH AUSTEN CHAMBERLAIN; WINSTON LEONARD SPENCER CHURCHILL; KENNETH HARRY CLARKE; ALEXANDER FREDERICK DOUGLAS-HOME; ROBERT ANTHONY EDEN; ROBERT ARTHUR TALBOT GASCOYNE-CECIL; EDWARD RICHARD GEORGE HEATH; QUINTIN McGAREL HOGG; DOUGLAS HURD; ANDREW BONAR LAW; NIGEL LAWSON; MAURICE HAROLD MACMILLAN; JOHN ENOCH POWELL; EDWARD GEORGE GEOFFREY SMITH STANLEY; MARGARET THATCHER; THATCHERISM**).

CONSOLIDATED FUND. The Fund is the account at the **BANK OF ENGLAND** which holds the receipts paid into the Exchequer. Dating from 1787, when it was established by **WILLIAM PITT THE YOUNGER** to consolidate income from excise and customs duties into a single fund, it is now used mainly to reduce the **NATIONAL DEBT** and fund the **CIVIL LIST**.

CONSOLIDATION BILL. These bills combine several **ACTS OF PARLIAMENT** into a single piece of legislation, thereby simplifying and refining the laws.

CONSTITUENCY. This is the geographical area represented by a Member of **PARLIAMENT**. Currently, the United Kingdom consists of 651 electoral constituencies, 524 in **ENGLAND**, 72 in **SCOTLAND**, 38 in **WALES** and 17 in **NORTHERN IRELAND**.

CONSTITUTION, BRITISH. The British Constitution is an unwritten constitution based upon legal statutes and common law, practice and precedent. It, therefore, derives from a variety of sources, particularly a) Historic Documents and Early Laws, which include the **MAGNA CARTA**, the **PETITION OF RIGHT**, the **BILL OF RIGHTS** and the **ACT OF SETTLEMENT (1701)**; b) Statutes — the extant totality of **ACTS OF PARLIAMENT**, including **HABEAS CORPUS**; c) Case Law — the rule of precedent in decisions of the **JUDICIARY**, who interpret the Statute Law; d) **COMMON LAW** — for example, those cases shaping the **ROYAL PREROGATIVE**; e) Parliamentary Law and Custom — again, by standing orders and precedent; and f) Conventions — in, for example, the **CABINET**, Parliamentary proceedings, **COMMONWEALTH OF NATIONS** relationships and the operation of the political party system. In some cases, reference is made to g) Classic Writings — for example, Walter Bagehot's *The English Constitution* (1867) and Erskine May's *Treatise upon the Law, Privileges, Proceedings and Usage of Parliament* (1815-86).

CONSTITUTIONAL MONARCHY. The **UNITED KINGDOM**'s sovereign governs by the rules of the **BRITISH CONSTITUTION** as developed since the **MAGNA CARTA** and especially following the **BILL OF RIGHTS** and 19th century **PARLIAMENTARY REFORM**. The **MONARCH** now acts as an impartial figurehead in political terms. (See **ROYAL PREROGATIVE**).

CONTINENTAL SYSTEM. This was an abortive attempt to starve Britain into submission by introducing a restrictive economic system which tried to prevent foreign merchants from trading with her. It was instigated by the French Emperor Napoleon Bonaparte after his defeat at the **BATTLE OF TRAFALGAR** but most strictly applied after 1807. Complications led to the **ANGLO-AMERICAN WAR** of 1812-14.

CONVENTICLE ACT. A conventicle was a religious gathering for worship that was not authorized. Acts (see **ACT OF PARLIAMENT**) were aimed at **RECUSANTS** and **NONCONFORMISTS**.

The Act of <u>1593</u> threatened imprisonment or **ABJURATION OF THE REALM** for those taking part in conventicles. This act was largely directed at **PURITANS**.

The Act of <u>1664</u> was part of the **CLARENDON CODE**, which forbade conventicles of more than five persons not of the same household and was intended to restrict the activities of priests defying the 1662 **ACT OF UNIFORMITY**.

CONVENTION PARLIAMENT, 1660. This **PARLIAMENT** met, without the usual royal summons, between 14 April and 29 December 1660, following the **LONG PARLIAMENT**. It approved the content of the **DECLARATION OF BREDA**, recalled **CHARLES II** to the throne (see **RESTORATION**) and granted the **MONARCH** a fixed income in lieu of **FEUDAL SYSTEM** dues. It also pardoned most offences committed over the previous 20 years.

CONVENTION PARLIAMENT, 1689. Called without a royal summons after the downfall of **JAMES VII** and **II**, this **PARLIAMENT** met from 1 to 23 February, declared the throne vacant and offered the **CROWN** to William of Orange (later **WILLIAM II**) and his wife, Mary (later **MARY II**), provided they accepted the provisions of the **DECLARATION OF RIGHTS**. (See **GLORIOUS REVOLUTION**).

COOK, JAMES (1728-79). An explorer of the Antarctic and Pacific Oceans, Cook was born in Marton-in-Cleveland (Yorkshire) on 27 October 1728, the son of a farm worker. He was educated at the village school then, at the age of 17, apprenticed to a grocer and haberdasher. However, he showed more inclination to find a job near the sea and was transferred to John Walker, a shipowner at Whitby. In 1755, he joined the navy as an Able Seaman and two years later had his own command — the 64-gun *Pembroke*, which he sailed across the Atlantic in 1758 to take part in the siege of Louisburg. Over the next decade, he was involved in surveys of the St Lawrence River, Newfoundland and Labrador and developed both a knowledge of astronomy and skill in the mathematics of navigation. (In 1767 he published a report on his method of calculating longitude by observing an eclipse of the sun and was commended by the **ROYAL SOCIETY**.)

Cook was appointed Lieutenant in command of HMS *Endeavour Bark* in 1768 and took a group of scientists to Tahiti to observe the planet Venus. Having accomplished that task, he followed his orders to sail southwards and search for the continent of Terra Australis (of which, at the time, Africa was thought to be part). Leaving Tahiti on 13 July 1769, he sighted New Zealand on 7 October and circumnavigated the islands, carrying out a survey which clearly demonstrated that any continent must lie much further south. On 1 April the following year, he left for home, charting the previously unexplored east coast of Australia en route, naming it New South Wales and claiming it for Britain.

Promoted to the rank of Commander, he suggested another voyage which would use the westerly winds in high latitudes to circumnavigate the Earth as far south as possible and establish whether there really was a continental landmass in these regions. He was given two vessels — the HMS *Resolution* and the HMS *Adventure* — and sailed on 13 July 1772. On 30 January 1774, he reached 71°10' South, further than any of his predecessors had gone. He destroyed many of the myths about a great continent but remained convinced that there must be land beyond the pack ice.

Over the next nine months, Cook covered vast areas of the oceans, visiting Easter Island, the Marquesas, the Society Islands, Niue, Tonga, the New Hebrides, New Caledonia, South Georgia and the South Sandwich Islands, adding many new territories to the **BRITISH EMPIRE**. Throughout that lengthy voyage, not one man was lost through scurvy because Cook insisted on prescribing the diet for everyone on board his ships. After he reached **ENGLAND** on 30 July 1775, he presented a paper on methods of avoiding the disease to members of the Royal Society and was awarded the institution's Copley Medal in recognition of his achievement.

On 12 July 1776, he began a third voyage, hoping to follow the Pacific shores of North America and search for a passage to the Atlantic. Again commanding the *Resolution*, and with HMS *Discovery* accompanying him, he discovered the Hawaiian islands on 18 January 1778, then made his way east to America and north from Oregon to the Bering Strait, rounding the Aleutians and reaching latitude 70° 44' North before being stopped by pack ice. He retreated to Hawaii, dropping anchor in Kealakekua Bay to repair a damaged topmast and, on 14 February 1779, was killed in a quarrel with native peoples over a stolen boat.

COOPER, ANTHONY ASHLEY (1621-83). One of the foremost opponents of the pro-Catholic policies of **CHARLES II**, Cooper was born in Wimborne St Giles (Dorset) on 22 July 1621. Son of Sir

John Cooper and his wife, Anne (daughter of Sir Anthony Ashley), he inherited large estates in southwest **ENGLAND** when his mother died in 1628 and succeeded to his father's **BARONET**cy on 23 March 1631. Educated by private tutors and at **OXFORD** University, he attended the **SHORT PARLIAMENT** of 1640 as the representative from Tewkesbury and the succeeding **LONG PARLIAMENT** as representative from Downton (Wiltshire). When the first **CIVIL WAR** began in 1642, he joined the **ROYALISTS** but changed sides in 1644 because of his Protestant beliefs. He attended the **BAREBONES PARLIAMENT** in 1653 and supported **OLIVER CROMWELL** but, by late 1654, was becoming disenchanted by the Protector's neglect of democratic procedures and began a long campaign of criticism against autocratic rule.

In 1660, Cooper was one of 12 commissioners sent by the **HOUSE OF COMMONS** to invite **CHARLES II** to return to Britain and was rewarded for his support of the Stuart cause (see **STUARTS**)with many honours, including the title of Baron Ashley and the post of **CHANCELLOR OF THE EXCHEQUER**. He used his influence in that position to secure lenient treatment for those who had followed Cromwell and earned Charles's admiration for his hard work and skilful diplomacy. Also, he developed an interest in the American colonies and, in 1663, was one of eight people given a royal grant of land, which they named Carolina after the King. Three years later, he entrusted**JOHN LOCKE** with the task of drawing up a constitution for the province based on religious tolerance and rule by the aristocracy.

By the late 1660s, however, he was becoming increasingly concerned that a Roman Catholic (James, **DUKE OF YORK** and later **JAMES VII** and **II**) would succeed to the throne, and, although he was created Earl of Shaftesbury in 1672, Cooper became more active in opposition to the King. In 1673, he supported the **TEST ACT** (which was intended to prevent Catholics from holding office under the **CROWN**) and, as a result, was dismissed from the Chancellorship although, by common consent, his period in that office had been one of considerable success. In 1674, he was removed from the **PRIVY COUNCIL** and, in 1677-78, spent a year imprisoned in the **TOWER OF LONDON** for attempting to get Parliament dissolved.

Although Cooper changed policy frequently and tended to advocate extreme views, he built up considerable support in the House of Commons and **HOUSE OF LORDS** and in 1679, 1680 and 1681 tried to use that support to secure legislation which would prevent James from becoming King. However, his attempt to get Charles's illegitimate son, James, Duke of Monmouth, recognized as the heir to the throne was seen as a means of increasing his own influence through a puppet King and his followers deserted him (see **MONMOUTH REBELLION**). On 2 July 1681, he was imprisoned in the Tower of London again, accused of high **TREASON**. The judges at his trial on 24 November found him not guilty, but 12 months later, fearing for his safety, he fled to Holland where he remained in exile until his death in Amsterdam on 21 January 1683.

COOPER, ANTHONY ASHLEY (1801-85). One of the leading social reformers of the 19th century, Cooper was born in **LONDON** on 28 April 1801, the eldest son of Cropley (a brother of the Earl of Shaftesbury) and his wife, Anne (daughter of the Duke of Marlborough). He became Lord Ashley when his father succeeded to the Earldom in 1811 and the seventh Earl of Shaftesbury when Cropley died in 1851.

Educated at Harrow School and **OXFORD** University, he entered **PARLIAMENT** in 1826 and, although broadly supportive of **CONSERVATIVE PARTY** policies, frequently pursued an independent path on lines dictated by his **NONCONFORM-IST** religious beliefs. His first major success was the passage of the Mines Act (1842), which prevented employers from sending women, girls, boys under the age of 13 and parish apprentices underground (see **ACT OF PARLIAMENT**). He was also instrumental in obtaining the passage of the Lunacy Act (1845), which defined the mentally ill as "persons of unsound mind" rather than as social outcasts. In 1847, despite the opposition of manufacturers, he rallied sufficient support to ensure **ROYAL ASSENT** for the Ten Hours **BILL**, which limited the length of the working day in mills and factories. (The legislation was strengthened by the 1874 **FACTORY ACT**, another product of Shaftesbury's campaigning.)

He was also concerned about public health and the provision of housing. In 1851, he introduced bills designed to encourage the construction of lodging houses for the working classes and for **GOVERNMENT** inspection of all such properties. He was a fervent supporter of **EDUCATION** for the poor, acting for 40 years as President of the Ragged Schools Union, which provided free classes for children of the destitute. His other interests included the Young Men's Christian Association, Working Men's Institutes, the

Bible Society and foreign missions. Shaftesbury died in Folkestone on 1 October 1885.

CO-OPERATIVE MOVEMENT. A series of co-operative groups was established following the success of the Rochdale Pioneers' store in 1844. The movement originated from the ideas of Robert Owen and aimed to sell, buy or manufacture goods for the mutual profit of its members. As it grew, it developed large retail chains which paid dividends in the form of a discount on purchases to members and, with the manufacturers' associations, agricultural co-operatives and co-operative housing societies which adopted similar principles, became particularly strong in the industrial north of **ENGLAND**. The Co-operative Wholesale Society (CWS) was established in 1863, beginning its own manufacturing ten years later. Supporters even created the Co-operative political party in 1917, allied to the **LABOUR PARTY**. With the rise of supermarket chains in the second half of the 20th century, however, 'co-ops' have declined in importance.

COPYHOLD. This feudal form of land tenure derived from the arrangement that the owner held a written copy of his legal title from the **MANOR** court. Most **VILLEIN**s had become copyholders by the 15th century as service dues were replaced by money rents. This form of tenure was abolished in 1928. (See **FEUDAL SYSTEM**).

CORN LAWS. (See **ANTI-CORN LAW LEAGUE**).

CORONATION. The ceremony of investiture and crowning of the **MONARCH** by the **ARCHBISHOP OF CANTERBURY**, as head of the established church (see **CHURCH OF ENGLAND**) and the Lords Spiritual, originated in the eighth to tenth centuries as a visible public enactment of the **DIVINE RIGHT OF KINGS**. The procedures consist of the anointing, the recognition and the taking of the oath of loyalty, the crowning and the enthronement, followed by the homage of the subjects. Since the **NORMAN** period, the ceremony has taken place in **WESTMINSTER** Abbey (**LONDON**). Queen **ELIZABETH II**'s coronation was held on 2 June 1953 and was the first to be televised. (See **CROWN**).

CORPORATION OF LONDON. This local authority governs the financial and commercial area of **LONDON** (the ancient **CITY OF**

LONDON) and is the oldest surviving corporation in the country, having appointed its first Mayor in 1192. Uniquely, it operates on an entirely nonparty political basis and is headed by a **LORD MAYOR**, who is elected annually.

COTSWOLD HILLS. This 60-mile long range of hills in the west of **ENGLAND** forms part of an escarpment of Jurassic limestone, which crosses the country from Dorset to Yorkshire (see map 1, page xxvii, for location). The average altitude is about 650 feet. From the 10th until the 18th century, the area was an important centre of the **WOOL INDUSTRY**, giving its name to a breed of sheep and generating enormous wealth still evident in the architectural heritage of settlements such as Chipping Camden and Cheltenham. The limestone rock used in the construction of local buildings is a rich creamy colour, which mellows on exposure to air and gives villages a very picturesque appearance. That picture postcard look, coupled with the absence of the trappings of modern industrialization, has turned the area into a major tourist attraction, causing considerable problems of traffic congestion during the summer. Suggestions that the Cotswolds should be turned into a **NATIONAL PARK** in order to provide some control on development have never been implemented.

COTTON INDUSTRY. The industry was first established during the 16th century by Flemish craftsmen in **EAST ANGLIA** and Lancashire as a domestic trade, with production depending on raw cotton from East Asia and, later, from the West Indies. It developed rapidly during the 19th century, with inventions stemming from the **INDUSTRIAL REVOLUTION**, making Britain the world's main producer. 'King Cotton' was the supreme example of a domestic industry transformed by factory production. Innovations such as Kay's Flying Shuttle, Crompton's Mule and Cartwright's Power Loom boosted output, and the value of exports rose from £13,000 in 1700 to over £28 million in 1830 (when cotton represented 62 per cent of all Britain's exports). At that time, Lancashire was preeminent, particularly around the **MANCHESTER** area, which specialized in spinning and had ample water supplies for production and power, the port of **LIVERPOOL** for the import of raw cotton from the United States of America and nearby **COAL** for its steam-driven machinery. However, the industry was hit by the cotton famine, caused by the disruption of imports as a result of the US Civil War during the 1860s, and then, in the 20th century, was largely supplanted by manufacture in developing countries where cheap labour was available. The last steam cotton mill in Britain closed in 1991. (See **RICHARD ARKWRIGHT**).

COUNCIL HOUSING. The concept of subsidized rental housing, built and operated by a local authority, grew out of the 19th century **ACTS OF PARLIAMENT** dealing with artisans' dwellings and slum clearance. In the interwar period (between the **FIRST WORLD WAR** and the **SECOND WORLD WAR**), **GOVERNMENT**s vied with each other to build more and more, with 1.5 million homes being constructed between 1919 and 1939. By 1980, a further 4.5 million had been added, many in high-rise tower blocks. Through the Housing Act of 1980, **MARGARET THATCHER**'s administration gave tenants the right to buy their council house or flat at a discount in order to increase home-ownership (and also, perhaps, to boost **CONSERVATIVE PARTY** votes because, traditionally, home-ownership has been equated with right-of-centre political sentiments). By 1992 1,350,000 units had been sold and restrictions on council spending had reduced new building of council dwellings to a mere 350,000 each year. In 1994, allegations were made that the ruling Conservative administration in the **LONDON BOROUGH** of **WESTMINSTER** had illegally operated its policy on council property sales and repairs to increase its electoral advantage — a modern case of gerrymandering.

COUNTRY PARTY. This Party provided the opposition to the **COURT PARTY**, which was dependent on royal patronage during the 17th and 18th centuries. Its supporters were labelled **WHIGS** or **PETITIONERS** (their opponents were the **TORIES** or **ABHORRERS**).

COUNTY. Originally an area based on the **SHIRE**, the county was an **ANGLO-SAXON** unit of **LOCAL GOVERNMENT** which was subdivided into **HUNDRED**s. The term was later adopted by the **NORMANS** to replace shire. The counties were administered by **SHERIFF**s until the 16th century, when these officials were superseded by **JUSTICES OF THE PEACE**. Later, the Local Government Act of 1888 (see **ACT OF PARLIAMENT**) created county councils as the administrative executives for the territories. The 124 counties and county **BOROUGH**s of **ENGLAND** were reorganized in 1974 and formed into 39 administrative counties. A Local Government Boundary Commission, appointed in 1992, has been reviewing these county boundaries, making proposals for implementation by 1998. In **SCOTLAND**, the 33 counties vanished completely in 1975, being replaced by a two-tier system of regions and districts. In **WALES**, the 13 counties and 4 county boroughs were replaced by eight counties but these, in turn, were abolished in 1996, when a structure of 22 unitary authorities was introduced. Each county in England and Wales now controls major services such as roads, social services and the police (see Maps 4 and 5).

COUPON ELECTION. The **GENERAL ELECTION** of December 1918 was fought by a **LIBERAL PARTY-CONSERVATIVE PARTY** coalition, whose candidates received a letter of endorsement signed by the leaders of both groups. Opponents derided this as a mere coupon. The coalition won the election, the first in which women could vote, but the arrangement accelerated the internal splits and decline of the Liberals because not all candidates of that party approved of the association with the Conservatives.

COURT OF APPEAL. In **ENGLAND** and **WALES**, the Court of Appeal is second only to the **HOUSE OF LORDS** in seniority. It has 14 regular members (known as Lord Justices of Appeal) and four ex-officio members — the **LORD CHANCELLOR**, the **LORD CHIEF JUSTICE**, the President of the Family Division of the **HIGH COURT OF JUSTICE** and the **MASTER OF THE ROLLS**. The Civil Division takes appeals from the High Court and the County Courts. The Criminal Division hears appeals from the High Court or the **CROWN COURTS**.

COURT PARTY. This party consisted of Members of **PARLIAMENT** who supported the **CROWN** from the reign of King **CHARLES II** and after the failure of the **CABAL**. **ROYALIST** as well as Anglican, it evolved into the **TORY** Party and was opposed by the **COUNTRY PARTY**, which evolved into the **WHIGS**.

CRANMER, THOMAS (1489-1556). One of the leading figures during the **REFORMATION** in **ENGLAND**, Cranmer helped **HENRY VIII** sever the ties between the **CHURCH OF ENGLAND** and the Pope. Born in Aslacton (Nottinghamshire) on 2 July 1489, he was the second son of Thomas and Agnes Cranmer. He went to **CAMBRIDGE** University in 1503 and, by 1511, had been elected to a Fellowship of Jesus College. In 1523, he was ordained as a priest and, in 1529, became embroiled in Henry's attempts to obtain papal sanction for a divorce from **CATHERINE OF ARAGON**. At a meeting with Stephen Gardiner and Edward Foxe — two of the King's advisers — Cranmer suggested that the King might strengthen his case if he sought the opinions of universities in Europe. That meeting led to an interview with Henry and to Cranmer's acceptance of a commission to prepare a treatise in support of the divorce. From that point, he became increasingly involved with the royal court and, in 1533, was appointed **ARCH-BISHOP OF CANTERBURY**.

One of his first actions was to declare Henry's marriage to Catherine invalid because it was within the proscribed degrees of consanguinity (the Queen had earlier been the wife of Henry's brother, Arthur). At the same time, he recognized **ANNE BOLEYN** as the King's lawful Queen, but, in 1536, he invalidated that match as well, citing dubious evidence for Anne's adulterous behaviour with, among others, her own brother. In 1540, he helped to arrange the annulment of Henry's marriage to **ANNE OF CLEVES** and, in 1542, played a leading role in the events which led to the beheading of **CATHERINE HOWARD** on the grounds that, when she married the King, she was not a virgin.

In 1534, **PARLIAMENT** formally recognized Henry as the supreme religious authority in the country, a break with the Vatican which made Cranmer the first Protestant Archbishop of Canterbury. Although doing as he was told over the King's marriages, Cranmer was a convinced reformer and found himself reshaping the **CHURCH OF ENGLAND** under a sovereign who had no wish for change. In consort with **THOMAS CROM-WELL**, he persuaded Henry to permit the publication of a Bible printed in English (a Bible which became compulsory in the **PARISH**es). He played a large part in the writing of the **BOOK OF COMMON PRAYER** (1549), which established the forms of worship in the Church, and the Forty-two Articles (1553) (see **ARTICLES OF RELIGION**), which became the basis of Anglican doctrine. He also abandoned a number of Roman Catholic practices (such as the use of crucifixes) and advocated a union of all the Protestant churches in Europe.

These activities made him enemies, but he retained his influence under both Henry and **EDWARD VI**. Henry, in particular, seemed to trust the Archbishop, even though Cranmer pleaded on behalf of Anne Boleyn, **THOMAS MORE** and others who had fallen out of favour. In 1553, however, under pressure from Edward, Cranmer signed a document designed to take the right of succession from Mary (later **MARY I**), Henry's daughter by Catherine of Aragon and a staunch Roman Catholic, and transfer it to the Protestant **LADY JANE GREY**. The plot failed, and he was charged with treason. In 1555, he was brought to trial on a charge of heresy and, after a long examination, condemned to death. Whilst he was awaiting sentence, Mary's government tried to break his resolve and ultimately, weak and enfeebled, he recanted his whole religious life. On 21 March 1556, he was taken to be burned at the stake and told to make his recantation in public. But, close to death, he regained his dignity and stunned his enemies by withdrawing the disavowal of his beliefs. As the flames mounted, he held his right hand — the hand which had signed the false recantations — towards them so that it would be destroyed first.

CRECY, BATTLE OF, 26 August 1346. This was a crucial battle between **ENGLAND** and France during the **HUNDRED YEARS WAR**. **EDWARD III** invaded Normandy with a force of 9,000 troops and was attacked at Crecy (near Ponthieu) by a French army of 30,000. Superior English tactics with the use of longbowmen (archers) and highly trained foot-soldiers prevailed against the larger French force and allowed the seizure of **CALAIS** the following year. Casualties were estimated at 100 English and 10,000 French dead.

CRICKET. Evidence of a bat and ball game exists from the 13th century, but it was discouraged for fear of affecting archery practices. The current national summer game developed in the 18th century, firstly at the Hambledon (Hampshire) Club's Broad Halfpenny Down ground. There is still a **PUBLIC HOUSE** on the site called the Bat and Ball, and early cricketers there are described by one commentator as "in their sky-blue waistcoats with black velvet collars, drinking their ale and singing into the evening on Halfpenny Down on Hampshire's field of dreams". Cricket's current governing body — the Marylebone Cricket Club (MCC) — was formed in 1787 and codified the rules of the game in 1835. One of the founders of the MCC was Thomas Lord, who laid out the MCC main ground, now called Lords, in 1814.

Major teams play for their **COUNTY** in a domestic competition, and the national team has played Test Matches against other nations since 1877. In 1882, Australia scored its first victory over

ENGLAND. A mock obituary in the *Sporting Times* referred to the passing of English cricket which "died at the Oval (a major **LONDON** cricket ground) on 29 August 1882" and added that "the body will be cre-mated and the ashes taken back to Aus-tralia". Since then a small urn, containing the ashes of a cricket bail (the top piece of a wicket), has been the prized trophy (known as the Ashes) of the winner of the Anglo-Australian cricket test series. This, and its rules, make cricket a curiously mystifying game to outsiders, but it remains strongly followed in many former colonies of the **BRITISH EMPIRE**.

CRIMEAN WAR, 1854-56. Turkey declared war on Russia in 1853 and saw its fleet destroyed in the same year. Fearing Tsarist in-tentions in the area, Britain and France declared war on Russia in 1854. Allied successes at the **BATTLE OF ALMA**, the **BAT-TLE OF BALACLAVA**, the **BATTLE OF INKERMAN** and at Sebastopol led to the **TREATY OF PARIS** (1856), at which the neutrality of the Black Sea, the internationalization of the River Danube and the independence of the Ottoman Empire were guaranteed to prevent Russian expansionism in the Balkans. This containment was gained at a price of 4,600 British killed and 13,000 wounded with an additional 17,500 dying from disease in the appalling conditions. Other estimates put total British losses at 45,000. **FLORENCE NIGHTINGALE** gained recog-nition as the lady with the lamp, administering nursing and strict hygiene reforms at the hospitals (and reducing the death-rate from 42 per hundred to 22 per thousand at Scutari).

The war did limit Russian influence on the area for some time, but Britain, though victorious, was not strong enough to consoli-date international power and the war proved to be the start of count-less alliances, ententes and agreements with frequent conflicts, end-ing only with the two world wars (see **FIRST WORLD WAR** and **SECOND WORLD WAR**). It was also the first major conflict to be covered by the newly invented telegraph, bringing rapid news back to Britain from the front. (See **CHARGE OF THE LIGHT BRIGADE; EASTERN QUESTION**).

CRIPPS, RICHARD STAFFORD (1889-1952). The architect of Brit-ain's post-second world war **AUSTERITY** programmes, Cripps was born in **LONDON** on 24 April 1889, the son of Charles Cripps (later Baron Parmoor) and his wife, Theresa. His mother died when he was only four, leaving instructions that her children should be raised as "undogmatic and unsectarian Christians" and taught "to love only what is true". Those ideals were to shape Cripps's entire career.

He was educated at Winchester School and won a scholarship to **OXFORD** University but was persuaded by Sir William Ramsay to study chemistry at **LONDON** University instead. He also followed a course of legal studies and was called to the Bar in 1913. Medically unfit for military service, he worked as a lorry driver with the Red Cross from 1914 to 1915 and as Assistant Superintendent of an explosives factory in **SCOTLAND** from 1915 until 1917. His hard work worsened his health still further; he was an invalid for the next two years and never fully recovered.

Cripps returned to his legal career in 1919 and specialized in patent and compensation cases, making a small fortune in fees. In 1929, he joined the **LABOUR PARTY** and (although not yet a member of the **HOUSE OF COMMONS**) was made **SOLICITOR GENERAL** by **RAMSAY MACDONALD** the following year. In 1931, he won election at Bristol East but refused to serve in MacDonald's coalition **GOVERNMENT** and sat with the majority of the Labour Party on the **OPPOSITION** benches.

Over the next few years, he became increasingly involved with left-wing groups, helping to found the Socialist League in 1932, advocating cooperation with the **COMMUNIST PARTY** in 1936 and urging a popular front against Adolf Hitler and the **APPEASEMENT** policies of **NEVILLE CHAMBERLAIN**. The Labour Party responded by expelling him in 1939, forcing him to sit as an independent Member of **PARLIAMENT** throughout the **SECOND WORLD WAR**. However, his administrative skills and agile mind were resources too valuable to waste at a time of crisis, and, in 1940, **WINSTON CHURCHILL** sent him to Moscow as British Ambassador to the Soviet Union. He returned to London early in 1942 and was appointed **LEADER OF THE HOUSE OF COMMONS, LORD PRIVY SEAL** and a member of the **CABINET**. In November, he became **MINISTER** of Aircraft Production and remained in that post until the end of the war, when he was readmitted to the Labour Party and made **PRESIDENT OF THE BOARD OF TRADE** in **CLEMENT ATTLEE**'s Cabinet. He moved to the Ministry of Economic Affairs in 1947 but after only a few weeks succeeded Hugh Dalton as **CHANCELLOR OF THE EXCHEQUER**.

From then until 1950, Cripps dominated the government's domestic reconstruction drive. His emphasis on austerity measures was unpopular initially, but the mood of the country quickly changed and his attempts to check inflation through the accumulation of large budget surpluses received widespread support. High taxation on internal consumption and imports, coupled with wage restraint, took on the trappings of a moral crusade and provided the backbone of a policy which was largely successful in overcoming the economic difficulties of the post-war years. In 1949, however, he was forced to devalue the pound and, in the House of Commons, Churchill, the Opposition Leader, told him he was unfit to run the country and should resign. In private, Churchill had congratulated him on making the correct decision and Cripps, a man of great integrity who believed totally in the importance of honesty, was devastated. Later, he declined an honorary degree offered by the University of Bristol, explaining that he was unwilling to accept it because Churchill was the institution's Chancellor.

In the summer of 1950, he sought medical treatment in Switzerland, but his poor health forced him to resign both his office and his Parliamentary seat on 20 October. He died of a spinal infection in Zurich on 21 April 1952, and his ashes were buried near Sapperton, his home in the **COTSWOLD HILLS**.

CROMWELL, OLIVER (1599-1658). Lord Protector of the **COMMONWEALTH** of **ENGLAND**, **SCOTLAND** and **IRELAND** between 1653 and 1658 (the bulk of the period when England was a **REPUBLIC**), Cromwell was born in Huntingdon on 25 April 1599, the second son of Robert Cromwell and Elizabeth Steward. He was educated at Huntingdon Free School and at **CAMBRIDGE** University, where he was steeped in **PURITAN** philosophies. In 1628, he became Member of **PARLIAMENT** for Ely and, in 1640, for Cambridge, siding on both occasions with forces against King **CHARLES I**. When the first **CIVIL WAR** broke out in 1642, he raised a troop of cavalry in Huntingdonshire and Cambridgeshire. In 1643, he was promoted to Colonel and, the following year, became second-in-command of the **PARLIAMENTARIAN** forces (known as the **ROUNDHEADS**) in eastern England, with the rank of Lieutenant-Colonel. His discipline was rigorous and his methods unorthodox — he appointed officers on the basis of ability rather than social standing, for example — but they eventually produced a highly efficient fighting machine known as the **NEW MODEL ARMY**.

On 2 July 1644, Cromwell was in command of the left wing

of the force which, at the **BATTLE OF MARSTON MOOR**, inflicted the first significant defeat on the **ROYALIST** troops and, on 14 June 1645, he led a cavalry unit at the **BATTLE OF NASEBY**. In 1646, he took part in the final stages of the siege of **OXFORD**, which brought the first phase of the Civil War to an end. Having achieved its victory, however, the Parliamentary group quickly split up into factions. Cromwell wanted to ensure freedom of worship for Christians of all sects but met stern opposition from the Presbyterians, who advocated a much more restrictive policy on religious matters. Also, he was keen to reach a settlement with the King and met Charles in the hope of negotiating an agreement, but before anything could be achieved the political situation was thrown into turmoil when, in 1647, a mob invaded the **HOUSE OF COMMONS** and the King escaped from custody. Increasingly discouraged, Cromwell felt that further discussions with Charles were unlikely to bear fruit.

In 1648, a Scottish army led by the Duke of Hamilton invaded England in the Royalist cause but was soundly defeated by Cromwell's troops and forced into surrender on 25 August (see **BATTLE OF PRESTON**). In December, the victorious force purged the House of Commons of its Presbyterian members, leaving a **RUMP PARLIAMENT** of Cromwellian supporters. King Charles was convicted of **TREASON** by the new Parliament and beheaded on 30 January 1649. England became a republic, and Cromwell was chosen as the Chairman of the Council of State which governed the country.

In August, he took his army to Ireland, where **CHARLES II** had been proclaimed King, and conducted a merciless campaign which had put down all resistance by May of the following year. He then turned his attention to Scotland, defeating the royalist troops at the Battle of Dunbar on 3 September 1650 and occupying Edinburgh the following day. After a bout of malaria, he marched south and defeated Charles's army at the **BATTLE OF WORCESTER** on 3 September 1651.

That series of victories did nothing to smooth his path in Parliament. Antagonism between the army leaders and civilian members of the House of Commons increased and, in April 1651, Cromwell forcibly dissolved the Rump Parliament. In its place, the army council selected 140 men from a list of names submitted by the churches. Variously known as the Little Parliament, the Nominated Parliament and the **BAREBONES PARLIAMENT** (after Praisegod Barbon, one of its members), it governed England until

12 December 1653. On that date, it dissolved itself and gave up its powers to Cromwell, who became Lord Protector of the **COMMONWEALTH** of England, Scotland and Ireland.

Under the new constitution, known as the Instrument of Government, Cromwell had the power to dissolve Parliament, and, in 1655, he exercised it. For the next three years he was, in effect, a dictator. In 1656, he was offered the title of King in return for his agreement to the setting up of a second house of Parliament and to the Commons controlling its own election returns. Most of his army colleagues, however, objected to the restoration of a **MONARCH**y and, in 1657, he refused the offer but accepted a new constitution (known as the Humble Petition and Advice). However, when MPs were recalled to approve the measure, it was obvious that there was a great deal of opposition. Cromwell lost his temper and dissolved Parliament again.

For then until his death, he continued his absolute rule, supporting measures that increased trade and industry and showing considerable religious tolerance. For example, he removed the ban against Jews, in effect since 1290, and allowed them to settle in the Commonwealth. Also, he concluded favourable commercial treaties with Denmark, Portugal and Sweden. Other policies were less successful; from 1655 until 1658 he fought an expensive war with Spain, gaining only Jamaica for his efforts, and grand schemes for a Protestant alliance in Europe were never realized.

Cromwell died in **LONDON**, of malaria, on 3 September 1658 and was buried in **WESTMINSTER** Abbey, but, after the **RESTORATION** of **CHARLES II**, his bones were dug up and his head placed on a pole.

CROMWELL, THOMAS (c. 1484-1540). A successful merchant and lawyer, Cromwell was a leading architect of the **REFORMATION** in **ENGLAND**. Although details of his early life are few, it is known that, by 1520, he had entered the service of Cardinal **THOMAS WOLSEY** and that, in 1523, he became a member of Gray's Inn. For the next few years, he acted as legal adviser to the Cardinal as well as furthering his activities as a wool merchant (see **WOOL INDUSTRY**) and probably also as a moneylender.

When Wolsey fell into disgrace in 1529, Cromwell entered **PARLIAMENT** as the representative for Taunton and worked assiduously in the cause of King **HENRY VIII**. In 1532, he gained office as Master of the Jewels. Two years later, he was appointed **MASTER OF THE ROLLS**; in 1536, he was made **LORD**

PRIVY SEAL. In these posts, he exerted great authority over the government of the country. He was largely responsible for the 1534 **ACT OF SUPREMACY** (which made Henry the supreme religious authority in England) and for the **DISSOLUTION OF THE MONASTERIES** and the confiscation of their estates. In 1536, he was appointed Vice-regent in Spirituals — in effect, second in command of the **CHURCH OF ENGLAND**. In that role, he advanced the cause of Protestantism, initiating a reform of the clergy and ordering that every **PARISH** should use a Bible printed in English.

In 1538, he encouraged Henry to marry **ANNE OF CLEVES** for political reasons, but, by 1540, it was clear that the rationale for the wedding (an anti-Catholic alliance with German princes) was no longer valid and the King wanted rid of his rather meek Queen and the officials who had recommended her. Cromwell did not give in easily and, in fact, was sufficiently powerful to gain the title Earl of Essex and the post of **LORD GREAT CHAMBERLAIN** in April 1540. By early summer, however, his enemies had the upper hand. He was arrested as a heretic and traitor on 10 June and condemned by act of attainder without a hearing. On 28 July, he was executed. A ruthless statesman, he nevertheless was a very competent administrator who, by rejecting the control of the Pope, turned England into a sovereign nation state. (See **COURT OF AUGMENTATIONS**).

CROPREDY BRIDGE, BATTLE OF, 29 June 1644. The last victory for King **CHARLES I** while in personal leadership of his forces during the first **CIVIL WAR**, this battle was fought for a bridge crossing of the River Cherwell. The **ROYALISTS** numbered 7,000 with a strong cavalry contingent, the **PARLIAMENTARIANS** about 6,000 but with artillery which slowed them down. It was not a great victory — the King withdrew when he learned of the approach of Parliamentary reinforcements and the **ROUNDHEADS** disintegrated in mutiny. Also, the Royalist success was marred by news of the defeat at the **BATTLE OF MARSTON MOOR.**

CROSS BENCHER. In the **HOUSE OF COMMONS**, members of the two main political parties sit facing each other. Members of the other parties sit at right-angles to these groups and are collectively known as cross benchers.

CROWN. This term is often used synonomously with **MONARCH**,

Throne, **GOVERNMENT** or state and must be interpreted in context. It is the lawful embodiment of power, which is vested in the **CONSTITUTIONAL MONARCHY**.

CROWN COLONY. These are colonies which do not possess "responsible government" and are, therefore, administered by a British governor.

CROWN COURTS. These courts were established in **ENGLAND** and **WALES** in 1972 to take over the responsibilities of the **ASSIZES** and **QUARTER SESSIONS**. They hear trials on indictment, pass sentence on defendants found guilty in lower courts and hear appeals relating to cases first heard in these lower courts.

CROWN DEPENDENCY. These territories govern their domestic affairs but the UK **GOVERNMENT** is responsible for their defence and the conduct of their international relations. (See **CHANNEL ISLANDS; ISLE OF MAN**).

CROWN LANDS (or Crown Estate). These are personal lands of the **MONARCH** on which revenues are due. They originated in the medieval period, but, in 1761, King **GEORGE III** surrendered them for the duration of the reign of the sovereign in return for payments under the **CIVIL LIST**.

CRUSADES. A series of wars which took place between the 11th and 13th centuries, the Crusades were fought by the Christian countries of western Europe against Islam in efforts to free the Holy Land from Moslem control. One consequence was the development of **ORDERS OF CHIVALRY** in England.

The first Crusade (1095-99) captured Jerusalem but had no significant English presence.

The second (1147-49) was a disaster for the west, with France and Germany failing to take Damascus after a long siege.

The third (1189-92) was led by the English King, **RICHARD I** (the Lionheart), and the Holy Roman Emperor, Frederick I (Barbarossa). They captured Acre (see **BATTLE OF ACRE**), defeated Saladin at Arsuf and almost retook Jerusalem. This was the first Crusade to have a really significant role for **ENGLAND**. Richard was captured by Duke Leopold of Austria during his return and subsequently **RANSOM**ed.

England took no part in the fourth crusade (1202-04).

The fifth Crusade (1216-21) was led by the Earl of Chester and took Damietta in 1219 but lost it again in 1221 and failed to take Cairo.

The Crusades continued but England played no further role save for the expedition in 1271 of Edward (later **EDWARD I**), which secured a decade of peace in the area.

CURIA REGIS. Originally the royal court and household of the **NORMAN** and Angevin **MONARCH**s (see **PLANTAGENETS**), the Curia Regis was the seat of all **GOVERNMENT** and immensely important to English history. It was the judicial authority which ruled on all disputes concerning the sovereign and his estates and the legislative body through which the King promulgated new laws. Also, its officers — who had considerable power and patronage — had ceremonial duties to perform. From the 13th century, it was gradually replaced by the development of specialized departments of government bureaucracy such as the **EXCHEQUER** and the civil service.

CURRENCY. British currency is based on the pound (the £ sign for which derives from *libra*, the Latin word for *pound*). Until the early 1970s, one pound consisted of 20 shillings (normally denoted by the letter *s*, derived from the Latin *solidi*). Each shilling was worth 12 pence (denoted by the letter *d* from the Latin *denarii*). Thus, the coinage was known as £sd. A farthing (which ceased to be legal tender in 1961) was one quarter of one penny. The florin (first minted in 1849) was a two-shilling coin, the half-crown was worth 2s 6d and the crown (so-called because it was stamped with a crown image) was equivalent to 5s. The guinea (which was originally made of gold from Guinea, in Africa) had a value of 21s. Other coins were the halfpenny, the threepenny bit and the sixpenny piece. On 15 February 1971, this system was swept away (see **DECIMALIZATION**) and replaced by a new metric currency based on 100 pence to the pound, much to the relief of Britons with limited arithmetical skills. (See **BANK OF ENGLAND; GOLD STANDARD; ROYAL MINT; STERLING**).

—D—

DAMBUSTERS. During the **SECOND WORLD WAR**, *617 Squadron* of the **ROYAL AIR FORCE**, flying Lancaster Bombers, was sent on the night of 16 May 1943 to destroy the dams on the Eder and Mohne Rivers in Germany, aiming to flood much of the Ruhr industrial area and destroy electricity plant. Using revolutionary five-ton bouncing bombs, the Lancasters flew at extreme low levels. Fifty-three of the 133 aircrew were killed and at least 1,200 people died on the ground, but the raid was a success. Subsequent publicity of air photos of the damage and flooding was a major propaganda boost at this period of the war, when good news was limited.

DANEGELD. Originally a tribute given to the **VIKINGS** during the 10th century in return for peace, the Danegeld was raised through taxes. It was first paid in 991 by King **AETHELRED II** and was handed over at intervals until 1016. The **NORMANS** made it a regular tax (the **DOMESDAY BOOK** was partly prepared to establish liability for payment), and it was last levied in 1162. The term is not recorded prior to 1066; until then, documents refer to *gafol*, *heregeld* (an annual tax levied between 1013 and 1052 to pay for a standing army) or tribute. (See **DANELAW**).

DANELAW. Large-scale Scandinavian settlement of **ENGLAND** began in the ninth century. Treaties effectively partitioned parts of the country, with much coming under the jurisdiction of invading **VIKING** forces and subject to Danelaw (that is, Danish rather than **SAXON** laws and customs). The area involved covered about half of the country and particularly the east from Yorkshire to Essex. The extent was largely fixed by military conquests at the **BATTLE OF EDINGTON** and the **BATTLE OF MALDON**. These lands still have remnants of the period in placenames and culture; for example, the suffix -*by* is common in settlement names in eastern England and derives from the Danish word for *village*. The reconquest of the Danelaw began during the reign of **EDWARD THE ELDER** (899-924) and was complete by that of **EADRED** (946-55). (See **DANEGELD**).

DARWIN, CHARLES (1809-82). A pioneer of the scientific study of evolution, Darwin was born in Shrewsbury on 12 February 1809, the son of Robert Darwin (a physician) and his wife, Susannah (daughter of **JOSIAH WEDGWOOD**). At the age of eight, he registered at a local day school organized by Mr Case, the Unitarian minister, but transferred to Shrewsbury School the following year. In 1825, he began medical studies at Edinburgh University but failed to complete his programme — anatomy disgusted him and the operating theatre was "horrifying". Seeking a more congenial life as a clergyman, he became a student at **CAMBRIDGE** in 1828 but developed an interest in the natural sciences (largely as a result of his friendship with Professor John Henslow of the University's Botany Department) and, after graduating in 1831, joined HMS *Beagle*, which was under the command of Captain Robert Fitzroy and charged with the task of surveying the South American coastline.

Darwin soon became engrossed, studying previously unrecorded life forms, examining fossil remains and comparing the characteristics of geographically separated species. He published some of his findings in *Journal of Researches* (1839) and *The Structure and Distribution of Coral Reefs* (1842), but it was not until 1859 that he rocked the scientific world with his work *On the Origin of Species by Means of Natural Selection, or the Preservation of Favoured Species in the Struggle for Life*, which sold all 1,250 copies on the day of issue. Darwin had recognized that individuals of the same domestic animal species have different attributes and that these attributes could be passed on by planned selective breeding (horses could be bred for speed or for strength, for example). He reasoned that the same process could occur in nature but could not identify the causes of this natural selection until he read Thomas Malthus's *Essay on the Principle of Population* (1798).

Malthus had claimed that every generation of human beings produces more children than could survive on the food supplies available. If that was true, Darwin claimed, then the natural organisms which thrived would be the ones with the characteristics most suited to their environments. He proceeded to advance a vast body of evidence to support his case, but there were many who were unconvinced. Some scientists complained that he had presented no explanation for the origin of the traits which were inherited. Others pointed out that he had merely described related species found in different places without demonstrating that intermediate forms had ever existed. And the theological establishment pilloried him because his arguments provided a self-contained scientific explanation of evolution without any need to invoke the work of God.

Darwin himself was confused by the role of the Creator, writing in 1870 that he could not look at the universe as the result of "blind chance" but neither could he see "any evidence of beneficent design". Ultimately, he became an agnostic. The principles he enunciated, however, were championed by biologist Thomas Huxley and later integrated with the work of Gregor Mendel and Ronald

Fisher on genetics to gain widespread acceptance. Darwin himself suffered from bouts of illness for the rest of his life as a result of the rigours of the *Beagle* voyage. However, his enthusiasm for study of the natural world was undiminished, and he wrote many books which qualified his arguments and attempted to refute criticism, ranging over topics such as the origin of Homo sapiens, the expression of emotions in animals, plant fertilization and the role of earthworms in the formation of soil.

He died in his home at Down (**KENT**) on 19 April 1882 and was buried in **WESTMINSTER** Abbey near fellow scientist **ISAAC NEWTON**.

D-DAY, 6 June 1944. The date of the Allied invasion of Europe during the **SECOND WORLD WAR** was code-named D-Day, the D simply being the first letter of the word "day" (in France, it is known as J-Jour for the same reason). The exact time of the invasion was H-Hour. Operation Overlord involved the transport of British, American, Canadian and other Allied forces on over 6,000 ships and aircraft to five Normandy beachheads stretching from Le Havre to the Cotentin Peninsula. By midnight, over 155,000 troops had landed, with 6,603 American, 3,000 British and 946 Canadian dead, wounded or missing and 114 Allied aircraft lost.

An earlier, abortive raid on Dieppe had shown the need to rely on other means of establishing a bridgehead than the taking of French ports so the Allies towed artificial harbours (Mulberry Harbours) across the English Channel to facilitate the movement of the enormous reserves of supplies and soldiers needed after the initial attacks (remnants of the British harbour at Arromanches can still be seen today). PLUTO (Pipeline Under The Ocean) carried oil supplies through four pipes to the bridgehead at Cherbourg from the Isle of Wight. The push inland against Nazi Germany had begun, aided by the actions of the French Resistance and Allied air superiority, with the main battlefield for the British forces centred on the strategic town of Caen.

DEATH DUTIES. Taxes on the assets in the estate of a deceased person were introduced in the 1894 Finance Act (see **ACT OF PARLIAMENT**) by the **CHANCELLOR OF THE EXCHEQUER**, Sir William Harcourt, and proved disastrous for many landed families (even Queen **VICTORIA** was said to have accused the Chancellor of spite). In 1975, when inflation was running at 21 per cent, the Capital Transfer Tax modified the duties on gifts made prior to death. This, in turn, was changed to the Inheritance Tax in 1986.

DECIMALIZATION, 15 February 1971. Until the **CURRENCY** was decimalized, **STERLING** was based on a unit of one pound, which consisted of 20 shillings. Each shilling consisted of 12 pence. After the change, each pound was equal to 100 pence and thus one new penny was worth 2.4 old pennies.

DECLARATION OF BREDA, 1660. Prior to the **RESTORATION**, **CHARLES II** issued a declaration, which paved the way for his return to the throne by promising his opponents that there would be no retribution and agreeing to an equable settlement of land disputes with **PARLIAMENT**. It also granted religious toleration and arrears of pay to the army. The declaration was instrumental in the decision to restore the **CROWN** at a time of civil unrest in the wake of the death of **OLIVER CROMWELL** and takes its name from the town in the Netherlands where Charles was based during his exile.

DECLARATION OF INDULGENCE. Four declarations (1662, 1672, 1687, 1688) during the reigns of **CHARLES II** and **JAMES VII** and II suspended the penalties on **DISSENTERS** and Roman Catholics.

DECLARATION OF RIGHTS, February 1689. Part of the **BILL OF RIGHTS** agreed between **WILLIAM III** and **MARY II** and the **CONVENTION PARLIAMENT**, the Declaration declared unconstitutional the acts of **JAMES VII and II**, established the Protestant succession and listed the rights of the new **MONARCH**s.

DECOLONIZATION. This is the name given to the process by which the **BRITISH EMPIRE** was dismantled and the colonies granted independence, most staying within the **COMMONWEALTH OF NATIONS**. Unlike other imperial nations, Britain largely achieved the breakup of its empire without major bloodshed or loss of life. The pressure to decolonize was particularly great after the **SECOND WORLD WAR**, when it became obvious that the United Kingdom could not sustain its imperial role, that nationalist movements were becoming stronger and that colonialism was no longer acceptable in political terms. The moves gathered pace in the 1960s, fuelled by **HAROLD MACMILLAN**'s warning of the "wind of change" in Africa.

DEFENCE OF THE REALM ACTS (DORA), 1914, 1915 and 1916. These acts (see **ACT OF PARLIAMENT**) gave the **GOVERNMENT** emergency powers during the **FIRST WORLD WAR**, particularly to take over factories and shape production, requisition materials, control labour relocations and impose censor-ship of the press (in addition, the 1915 Act limited alcohol sales). They were replaced in 1920 by the Emergency Powers Act, which decreed that the **CROWN** had the power to proclaim a state of emergency when necessary. That Act was used during the **SECOND WORLD WAR** after a court decision in 1942 (*Liversidge v. Anderson*) which established that the **HOME SECRETARY** could intern any individual thought to be a threat to national security. One of the consequences was a series of witchhunts against pacifists and individuals with German connections. The provisions remain part of the law.

DEFENDER OF THE FAITH. In 1521, this title was awarded to King **HENRY VIII** by the Roman Catholic Church in recognition of his book *In Defence of the Seven Sacraments (Assertio Septem Sacramentorum)*, which refuted the writings of Martin Luther. The book argued for the indissolubility of marriage, the virtues of obedience and the authority of the Papacy — ironic given the King's later break with Rome (and his divorces) at the **REFORMATION**. Pope Leo X did not authorize Henry to pass on the honour to his heirs but, in 1543, **PARLIAMENT** approved the Act of the King's Style (see **ACT OF PARLIAMENT**), which declared the words 'Fidei Defensor' to be "united and annexed for ever to the imperial **CROWN**". Since then, all British **MONARCH**s have taken the title. From the reign of King **GEORGE I**, Fid. Def. or FD (Fidei Defensor) has appeared on all British coins of the realm. In 1994, **PRINCE CHARLES** appeared to suggest in a television interview that he would prefer to be Defender of Faith, rather than of *the* Faith, in keeping with the more multireligious society of the time. (See **SUPREME GOVERNOR**).

DEMOCRATIC LEFT. (See **COMMUNIST PARTY**).

DEPENDENCIES, UK OVERSEAS. The United Kingdom still retains sovereignty over 14 overseas territories — Anguilla, Bermuda, British Antarctic Territory, British Indian Ocean Territory, British Virgin Islands, Cayman Islands, Falkland Islands, Gibraltar, Hong Kong (due to revert to China on 1 July 1997), Montserrat, Pitcairn Islands, St Helena, South Georgia and South Sandwich Islands, and the Turks and Caicos Islands. These remnants of the **BRITISH EMPIRE** have a combined population of 6 million (5.8 million of whom are in Hong Kong). (See also **CROWN COLONY**; **CROWN DEPENDENCY**).

DEPRESSION. (See **GREAT DEPRESSION**).

DERBY, EARL OF. (See **EDWARD GEORGE GEOFFREY SMITH STANLEY**).

DESPARD CONSPIRACY, 1802. An Irish colonial engineer, Edward Despard, devised a plot to occupy the **TOWER OF LONDON**, take the **BANK OF ENGLAND** and assassinate King **GEORGE III** but he was betrayed. In 1803, he was convicted of high **TREASON** and executed even though **HORATIO NELSON** spoke on his behalf. This plot occurred at a time of growing fears about revolutionary activity and sedition, of civil unrest in **IRELAND**, **EMMET'S RISING**, hostilities with France and the ever-present paranoia about French-inspired insurrection.

DETTINGEN, BATTLE OF, 27 June 1743. An engagement during the **WAR OF THE AUSTRIAN SUCCESSION**, this was the last battle which a British sovereign commanded in the field. King **GEORGE II** led a 40,000 man force of British, Hanoverian, Hessian and Austrian troops against an 80,000 strong French and Bavarian army. The King's horse threw him, but he led his soldiers on foot to a famous victory, for which he was declared a hero on his return to **LONDON**.

DEVOLUTION. The granting of **GOVERNMENT** powers to the provinces or regions of the realm, giving them local assemblies, has been a contentious issue with regard to the constituent nations of Britain (see **HOME RULE**). National **REFERENDA** in **SCOTLAND** and **WALES** under the **LABOUR PARTY GOVERNMENT** in 1979 followed the passage of the Devolution Act, 1978 (see **ACT OF PARLIAMENT**) but failed to gain the appropriate majorities for implementation. This failure was crucial because it led to the withdrawal of minority party support for the Labour Government in **WESTMINSTER** (see **LIB-LAB PACT**), where Prime Minister **JAMES CALLAGHAN** lost the consequent motion of no-confidence. The administration fell and **MARGARET THATCHER** led the **CONSERVATIVE PARTY** to victory at the ensuing **GENERAL ELECTION**. In 1992, the devolution issue was revived by the Scottish National Party in the light of the collapse of the Soviet Union and the rise of small nation-states, but it failed to excite either the voters or the main political parties. In 1994, however, Tony Blair, the Leader of the Labour Party, emphasized that it was still an important element of his policy.

DIANA, PRINCESS. (See **DIANA FRANCES SPENCER**).

DIGGERS. A radical, agrarian, communist group active during the period of the **COMMONWEALTH**, the Diggers believed in passive resistance to authority and common public ownership of land and property. In 1649, they started a commune at Weybridge, where they cultivated in simple communistic manner (hence, they were called Diggers). Led by Gerrard Winstanley, they regarded themselves as the only true **LEVELLERS**.

DIPLOMATIC REVOLUTION, 1756. In European politics, Britain had traditionally allied with Austria and France with Prussia. In 1756, however, these allegiances shifted: Britain linked with Prussia and France with Austria. The British hoped to thus ensure the **HANOVERIAN** succession, but they also became embroiled in the conflicts between Prussia and Austria during the **SEVEN YEARS WAR**.

DISARMAMENT. Adopted by **STANLEY BALDWIN**'s **GOVERN-MENT** in 1925 in an attempt to reduce defence costs after the defeat of Germany in the **FIRST WORLD WAR**, disarmament policy was abandoned in the 1930s as military threats grew in Europe but was a factor in Britain's unreadiness for war in 1939.

DISESTABLISHMENT. Formal and close links between the State and the Church were severed in 1869 in **IRELAND** and, in 1920, in **WALES**. The policy provided one of the longest words in the English language: opposition to the process is termed "antidisestablish-mentarianism".

DISRAELI, BENJAMIN (1804-81). The creator of the modern **CONSERVATIVE PARTY**, Disraeli was born in **LONDON** on 21 December 1804, grandson of an immigrant Italian Jew and son of author Isaac D'Israeli and his wife, Maria. In 1813, Isaac quarrelled with Jewish religious leaders and, as a result of that confrontation, decided to have his children baptized in the **CHURCH OF ENGLAND**. As Jews did not become eligible for election to **PARLIAMENT** until 1858, Disraeli's political career would not have been possible without that parental change of faith.

Young Benjamin was educated at schools in Blackheath and Epping then, at the age of 17, joined a firm of solicitors. By 1825, he was burdened with debt as a result of ill-advised speculations in South American mining shares and wrote *Vivian Grey*, a five-volume novel published in 1826-27, in an attempt to retrieve his financial situation. During the next four years he completed several other books, travelled through the countries of the Mediterranean and Southwest Asia and became a regular guest at society events in London. By 1831, he had decided to enter politics and contested the High Wycombe seat as an Independent twice the following year, losing on both occasions. He met the same fate in 1835 then, in the same year, fought Taunton for the **TORIES** and lost again. Finally, in 1837, he was elected as the Conservative MP for Maidstone.

Initially, he supported **ROBERT PEEL** but, humiliated by the lack of any offer to join the **GOVERNMENT** after the 1841 **GENERAL ELECTION**, turned against him. In 1845, he spoke vehemently against the **PRIME MINISTER**'s proposed repeal of the **CORN LAWS** and, the following year, helped force him into resignation after Parliamentary defeat in a vote on policies towards **IRELAND**. Disraeli became the accepted leader of the Conser-vatives and was given the post of **CHANCELLOR OF THE EXCHEQUER** in the **EARL OF DERBY**'s brief administration in 1852. He was reapppointed by Derby in 1858 and again in 1866. In 1867, he introduced a **PARLIAMENTARY REFORM BILL** which, much changed as a result of amendments made in order to ensure **LIBERAL PARTY** support, almost doubled the electorate by giving an additional one million people the right to vote.

In February 1868, when Derby retired from politics, Disraeli was the obvious successor and became Prime Minister, commenting that he had climbed to the top of a greasy pole. By the end of the year, he had slipped down again, defeated by the Liberals at an autumn general election and replaced as Prime Minister by **WILLIAM GLADSTONE**, whom he detested. For four years, he was a subdued leader of **THE OPPOSITION** but, in 1872, returned to the fray with speeches defending the **CONSTITUTIONAL MONARCHY**, the **CHURCH OF ENGLAND** and the **HOUSE OF LORDS** against perceived threats inherent in Liberal policies. Also, he advocated the expansion and strengthening of the **BRITISH EMPIRE** and the introduction of social reforms at home.

In 1874, he became Prime Minister for a second time following a decisive election victory. Supported by a strong **CABINET** and a close friendship with Queen **VICTORIA**, he promoted a series of domestic improvements affecting slum clearance, public health, working conditions in factories and the legal position of the **TRADE UNIONS**. Abroad, he purchased a controlling interest in the Suez Canal (see **SUEZ CRISIS**), giving Britain a foothold in Egypt. In 1876, he used the **ROYAL TITLES ACT** to make Victoria Empress of India while he became Earl of Beaconsfield, taking his seat in the House of Lords. The following year, he pledged support to the Turks as they attempted to repel an invasion by Russia and was rewarded in 1878 with the cession of Cyprus to Britain. In addition, Queen Victoria offered him a Dukedom, which he declined, and membership of the **ORDER OF THE GARTER**, which he accepted.

In 1878, he was the dominant force at the **CONGRESS OF BERLIN**, which curtailed Russian influence in the Balkans, but from then his fortunes declined and at the general election of 1880 the Conservatives were ousted. Disraeli, now in his late seventies, agreed to stay as leader of the Party but his health was failing and, on 19 April 1881, he died in London. Disraeli's influence had been profound. A man who enjoyed socializing and the company of women, he had shaped the Conservative Party into a powerful political force, improved the quality of life of the British people through a series of social reforms and made his country the world's major imperial power. In addition, he had carved out a career as a novelist, publishing books including *Coningsby* (1844), *Sybil* (1845) and *Daniel Deronda* (1876). Poor characterization and lengthy philosophizing detract from the literary quality of these works but they do show Disraeli's sympathy with the poor and his understanding of social politics. He was much mourned, particularly by his female friends; Queen

Victoria herself visited his family vault a few days after his funeral in order to lay a personal wreath and pay her respects.

DISSENTERS. This term refers to someone who dissents from, or disagrees with, the established **CHURCH OF ENGLAND**. The Anglican majority systematically persecuted **NONCONFORMIST** religious sects throughout the 17th century under legislation such as the **ACT OF UNIFORMITY** (see **ACT OF PARLIAMENT**) and the **CLARENDON CODE**.

DISSOLUTION OF THE MONASTERIES, 1536-41. In order to justify the elimination of monastic houses in **ENGLAND** and **WALES** during the **REFORMATION**, **THOMAS CROMWELL** collected information purporting to show their laxity and excesses. All monasteries valued at less than £200 per annum were closed, leading in part to the **PILGRIMAGE OF GRACE**, which further strengthened the case for dissolution. After 1537, the greater houses were dissolved and their properties transferred to the **CROWN**. Largely inspired by King **HENRY VIII**'s massive financial needs, the action led to the breaking up of 800 religious houses by 1540 and a massive transfer of land, wealth and power to the laity as well as the King. The policy also had political implications because it removed many religious leaders from **PARLIAMENT** and led to lay domination of the **HOUSE OF LORDS**. The **COURT OF AUGMENTATIONS** eventually sold most of the confiscated property to the landed **GENTRY**.

DISSOLUTION OF PARLIAMENT. The sovereign formally ends a **PARLIAMENT** by issuing a royal decree on the advice of the **PRIME MINISTER**. As such, this is a part of the **ROYAL PREROGATIVE**. Under the **PARLIAMENT ACT** of 1911 (see **ACT OF PARLIAMENT**), each Parliament is limited to a five-year term but dissolution can be requested at any time. A **GENERAL ELECTION** must be called shortly afterwards.

DIVINE RIGHT OF KINGS. Used much earlier, but first made explicit by **JAMES VI and I**, this theory held that the **MONARCH** was ordained by God to rule and therefore held allegiance only to God. Rebellion against a monarch was thus a sin against God. The events of the **GLORIOUS REVOLUTION** led to the replacement of a belief in the divine right of kings by the concept of a **CONSTITUTIONAL MONARCHY**, which implies that a sovereign can rule only with the consent of the people and their parliamentary representatives.

DIVORCE REFORM ACT, 1969. This legislation (see **ACT OF PARLIAMENT**) established rights to a divorce if both partners agreed that there was an irretrievable breakdown of their marriage, thus ending the need to prove the legal guilt of adultery or other offence for the match to be dissolved. The number of divorces grew rapidly and now terminate some 33 per cent of British marriages. Divorce had only become legally possible in civil actions in 1857, when the responsibility passed from the ecclesiastical courts (which had been able to annul marriages) to the secular courts through the 1857 Matrimonial Causes Act.

DOGGER BANK, BATTLES OF. Dogger Bank is a sandbank in the North Sea, about 60 miles off the northeast coast of **ENGLAND**. Three significant international incidents have occurred at the site.

The first, on 5 August 1781, was an indecisive engagement between Britain and the Netherlands during the **AMERICAN WAR OF INDEPENDENCE**.

The second, on 21 October 1904, was called The Dogger Bank Incident or The North Sea Incident and was a curious confrontation between English fishing trawlers and Russian warships on their way from the Baltic to the Russo-Japanese war theatre in East Asia. In the darkness of night, the trawlers from Hull were mistaken by the nervous Russian commander for disguised Japanese torpedoboats and fired upon, killing British fishermen and sinking one vessel. Poor Russian discipline and alarmist intelligence were to blame, and compensation was paid after French mediation. The rapid admission of responsibility and payments by the Russians eased relations between the two countries and led eventually to the **TRIPLE ENTENTE**.

The third incident, on 24 January 1915, was a minor skirmish during the **FIRST WORLD WAR** between the British fleet (under Vice-Admiral Sir David Beatty) and a German force (under Vice-Admiral Franz von Hipper) which resulted in the loss of one of the German vessels. After the confrontation, Germany adopted a more cautious approach to the deployment of its navy in the area.

DOMESDAY BOOK. Duke William of Normandy defeated King **HAROLD II** at the **BATTLE OF HASTINGS** and was crowned King of **ENGLAND** as **WILLIAM I** (William the Conqueror) on

Christmas Day 1066. In succeeding years, he extended his military power over the country and, in 1085, ordered a national survey of his estates and possessions so that he could derive the maximum from land taxes. The *Domesday Book*, completed the following year, was the most comprehensive record of its time, revealing that England had no more than 1.5 million inhabitants. The land was 35 per cent arable, 15 per cent woodland and 30 per cent pasture. Some 12,580 settlements were recorded, though **LONDON** was inexplicably omitted. The authors of the **ANGLO-SAXON CHRONICLE** wrote that "there was not a single hide nor rod of land, nor . . . an ox, a cow, a pig . . . left out". The *Domesday Book* is so called because it was said to be as authoritative as the Last Judgment on Doomsday and because *dom* meant 'assessment' in Old English.

DOMINION. A self-governing state, a Dominion is a former colony of the **BRITISH EMPIRE** which has gained its independence, joined the **COMMONWEALTH OF NATIONS** and recognized the **MONARCH** as its titular head. The term is reserved for the larger territories. It was first applied to Canada in 1867 and, since then, to Australia, the Irish Free State, New Zealand, Newfoundland and South Africa. Regularized by the **STATUTE OF WESTMINSTER** (1931), it has hardly been used since the post-second world war **DECOLONIZATION** of the Empire.

DON PACIFICO INCIDENT. (See **DAVID PACIFICO**).

DOUGLAS-HOME, ALEXANDER FREDERICK (1903-95). **PRIME MINISTER** from 1963 to 1964, Douglas-Home was born in **LONDON** on 2 July 1903, the son of the Earl of Home and Lady Lilian Home (daughter of the Earl of Durham). He was educated at Eton College and **OXFORD** University then, in 1931, won election to the **HOUSE OF COMMONS** as the Member of **PARLIAMENT** for South Lanark, supporting the **CONSERVATIVE PARTY**.

His first **GOVERNMENT** post was as **PARLIAMENTARY PRIVATE SECRETARY** to **NEVILLE CHAMBERLAIN** (1937-40), a position which left him tainted as a supporter of the Prime Minister's policy of attempting to appease Adolf Hitler and cooling his heels with no place in the **SECOND WORLD WAR** administration. He returned as **UNDER-SECRETARY OF STATE** at the Foreign Office from May until July

1945 but lost his seat at the **GENERAL ELECTION** and was out of Parliament for the next five years. In 1950, he was elected MP for Lanark but had to resign the following year when he succeeded to his father's title and took his place in the **HOUSE OF LORDS**. Over the next 12 years, he held a variety of posts — **MINISTER OF STATE** at the Scottish Office (1951-55), **SECRETARY OF STATE** for Commonwealth Relations (1955-60), Deputy Leader of the House of Lords (1956-57), **LORD PRESIDENT OF THE COUNCIL** (1957-60), Leader of the House of Lords (1957-60) and Foreign Secretary (1960-63).

In October 1963, Prime Minister **HAROLD MACMILLAN** reluctantly resigned as a result of ill health. Queen **ELIZABETH II** consulted several elder statesmen (notably **WINSTON CHURCHILL**) before appointing a successor, and it was widely believed that **RICHARD** (Rab) **BUTLER** would be offered the job. However, Macmillan was determined to ensure that his long-standing rival would not take his place and eventually, to the amazement of the political commentators, Douglas-Home was asked to form an administration. That created a constitutional problem because all Prime Ministers since the **MARQUIS OF SALISBURY** in 1902 had been members of the House of Commons, where they were answerable to the elected representatives of the people. Douglas-Home had to renounce his hereditary titles under the terms of the Peerage Act of 1963 (see **ACT OF PARLIAMENT**) and return to the Commons by way of a contrived **BY-ELECTION** at Kinross and West Perthshire.

Douglas-Home's few months as Prime Minister were unhappy ones. Uncomfortably aware of a worsening economic situation and the need to hold a general election by the end of 1964, he had some success when, as Chairman of the Commonwealth Prime Ministers' Con-ference (see **COMMONWEALTH OF NATIONS**), he negotiated an element of compromise between leaders deeply divided on racial issues. However, his aristocratic background, his upper-class accent and the undemocratic way in which he had been appointed annoyed many voters. Moreover, his cadaverous features and tweedy image created a much less positive television personality than that portrayed by the avuncular, pipe-smoking **HAROLD WILSON**, Leader of the **LABOUR PARTY**. The election contest was close but a swing against the Conservatives in several vital **CONSTITUENCIES** gave Labour a five-seat majority over the other parties. Wilson became Prime Minister, and, in 1965, Douglas-Home resigned as Leader of **THE OPPOSITION**, to be succeeded by **EDWARD HEATH**.

Ironically, Heath's appointment was based on the result of a ballot of Tory MPs (see **TORIES**), an electoral system introduced by Douglas-Home, who had been appalled by the machinations which led to his own elevation to power. Douglas-Home became Opposition Spokesman on Foreign Affairs and returned to his former post as Foreign Secretary when the Conservatives regained power in 1970. In 1974, he was created Baron Home of the Hirsel and went back to the House of Lords. He died at his house in Coldstream (Berwickshire) on 9 October 1995.

DOWNING STREET. This cul-de-sac in **WESTMINSTER (LONDON)** contains the residences of the three senior members of the **GOVERNMENT**. Number 10 is the official home of the **PRIME MINISTER**, number 11 is the official home of the **CHANCELLOR OF THE EXCHEQUER** and number 12 is the office of the Chief **WHIP**. These three buildings are all that remain of the street built around 1680 by George Downing MP. Number 10 was given by King **GEORGE II** to **ROBERT WALPOLE**, the first real Prime Minister.

DRAKE, FRANCIS (c. 1543-96). One of the foremost sea captains during the reign of **ELIZABETH I**, Drake was the second man (after Ferdinand Magellan) to sail round the world. Also, he used his naval skills to destroy much of the **SPANISH ARMADA** in its home port, giving **ENGLAND** time to augment its military resources.

Born in Tavistock, he sailed with a slave ship from Guinea to South America in 1566 (see **SLAVE TRADE**) and obtained his first command (also on a slave vessel) in the service of his cousin, Sir John Hawkins, the following year. For some time after that, he made commercial voyages to the West Indies and raided Spanish colonies in the Caribbean, gaining a reputation as a daring and successful commander. Between 1577 and 1580, he circumnavigated the globe with the twin aims of establishing trading bases and raiding the coast of South America. He set sail on 13 December 1577 in command of the 100-ton *Pelican* (later renamed the *Golden Hind*) and, accompanied by four other ships and 166 men, followed the east coast of South America, then passed through the Strait of Magellan in September 1578 At that point, he was blown south to about latitude 57°, where he discovered that the Atlantic and the Pacific met in open water and confirmed that

Tierra del Fuego is an island. From there, he turned northwards along the west coast of South America, plundering settlements and shipping as he went. It is unclear how far he travelled, but he certainly reached latitude 38° north at a point which he named New Albion. He then crossed the Pacific to the Moluccas and returned to England, arriving in Plymouth on 26 September 1580, with an enormous cargo of booty and spices.

Drake's success earned him a **KNIGHT**hood and, in addition, with his share of the profits from the venture (which amounted to some £500,000) he bought Buckland Abbey in Devon. In 1581, he served as Mayor of Plymouth and, in 1584 and 1585, sat as a Member of **PARLIAMENT**. In May 1585, however, he returned to the sea, commanding a fleet of 29 ships which attacked Spanish colonies in the Caribbean. On the return, he landed at **WALTER RALEIGH**'s Virginia settlement and took on board a number of the colonists (possibly introducing tobacco and potatoes to Britain at the same time).

In 1586, reports of Spanish preparations for an invasion of England began to arrive in **LONDON**, and, the following year, Queen Elizabeth sent Drake to harry the Armada in Cadiz harbour. In an exploit popularly known as 'The Singeing of the King of Spain's Beard', Sir Francis destroyed more than half of the ships at anchor. He then sailed to the Azores, where he captured a galleon — the *San Felipe* — which was valued at £100,000, more than twice the cost of the expedition. In 1588, he was appointed Vice-Admiral, but his plans to attack the Spanish fleet again before it left port were not approved until it was too late. On 19 July 1588, Drake was reportedly playing bowls at Plymouth when he received news that the Armada was in the English Channel; he is said to have retorted that "there's time to beat the Spaniards after" but there are no contemporary accounts to verify the story. In the ensuing battle, he captured the galleon *Rosario* and played a leading role in the attack on 29 July which effectively repulsed the Spanish threat. In 1589, Drake commanded the navy which supported Sir John Norreys's attack on Lisbon, but poor discipline and logistics contributed to an unsuccessful expedition. After that failure, Elizabeth refused to send him on another mission for five years, but, in 1595, he and Sir John Hawkins were appointed joint commanders of a fleet of 27 ships sent to raid the West Indies. During the voyage, Drake fell ill and died on 27 January 1596. He was buried at sea.

DRESDEN RAID, 13-14 February 1945. The heaviest massed bombing of a German city during the **SECOND WORLD WAR** occurred when 800 aircraft from **BOMBER COMMAND** and 450 American Flying Fortress bombers attacked Dresden on the night of 13 February 1945. This was followed by three more raids by US 8th Air Force bombers during daylight on the 14th. Estimates put the total number of phosphorous and high explosive bombs dropped at around 650,000, and German losses were estimated at 30,000 buildings and 55,000 to 400,000 casualties. Though the area was nonindustrial and known to contain many refugees, military strategists argued that it was important to strike there in order to shorten the war.

DRUIDS. The priests of the **CELTS**, the Druids headed a cult which was based on communion with nature and a knowledge of the agricultural calendar, providing a link between the divine and the human that gave them power over people. Britain was a main centre of Druidism. **ROMAN** Emperor Claudius banned the cult after 43 AD because of his concern at its human sacrifices and political influence. In a sense, the religion is still followed today because members of the Order of Druids, created in 1781, still hold solstice gatherings at **STONEHENGE**, but the modern rites are largely derived from a now discredited 17th century antiquarian study.

DUCHESS. A Duchess is either the wife (or widow) of a Duke or (more rarely) a woman who holds the rank of a Duke in her own right.

DUKE. This title is the highest rank in the **PEERAGE** (from the Latin *dux* meaning 'leader'). Medieval Kings in **ENGLAND** were reluctant to elevate subjects to dukedoms, probably because **WILLIAM I** had been Duke of Normandy before 1066 and the title was seen as the prerogative of royalty. Precedence depends on the date on which the title was created. The premier Duke in England is Norfolk (a title created in 1483) and in **SCOTLAND** Hamilton (created in 1643). (See **DUKE OF YORK**).

DUKE OF EDINBURGH. (See **PRINCE PHILIP**).

DUKE OF YORK. This title is usually bestowed on the second son of the sovereign. The current holder — **PRINCE ANDREW** — was awarded the Dukedom by Queen **ELIZABETH II** on 23 July 1986, his wedding day.

DUNES, BATTLE OF THE, 3-4 June 1658. This battle resulted in victory for **OLIVER CROMWELL**'s army, with its new French allies, over a combined Spanish and English **ROYALIST** force led by James, **DUKE OF YORK** (later **JAMES VII** and **II**), on the sand dunes near Dunkirk (now part of France but then part of the Spanish Netherlands). The subsequent cession of the area to **ENGLAND** marked the growing military power of the **PARLIA-MENTARIANS** and came barely three months before the death of Cromwell and the subsequent collapse of the **PROTECTORATE**.

DUNKIRK. During the early stages of the **SECOND WORLD WAR**, there were a number of defeats for the Allies in the west of Europe, with Belgium, Denmark, Holland and Norway falling to the Germans who, in their advance to the English Channel, trapped the British Expeditionary Force near Dunkirk (Dunkerque) on the northwest coast of France. Between 26 May and 4 June 1940, a flotilla of around 800 to 850 civilian 'little ships' and 222 naval vessels took part in Operation Dynamo and effected a mass evacuation of 346,000 troops from the French beaches in what **WINSTON CHURCHILL** called "our miracle of deliverance". Private craft of all kinds joined the operation, and they alone carried back 26,000 men. Despite the loss of armour (heavy weapons, 235 vessels and 106 planes) and 34,000 British soldiers captured, the operation was hailed in Britain as an inspirational victory of defiance against the might of the Nazi advance. Crucially, Hitler had made a strategic misjudgement by commanding the Panzers back from the Aa canal on 24 May. Worried about overstretching supply lines and wishing to defeat the French, his action gave a breathing space which allowed the defences to be strengthened at Dunkirk and, therefore, prolonged the evacuation. In addition, over 190,000 soldiers were evacuated from other ports in Normandy and from Bordeaux.

DURHAM REPORT, 1839. Formally entitled *Report on the Affairs of British North America* and compiled by the Earl of Durham while he was Governor of Canada, this document advocated colonial self-government and formed the basis of British policy towards the granting of independence to its colonies, the creation of the **DO-MINION** of Canada and the formation of the **COMMON-WEALTH OF NATIONS**. (See **DECOLONIZATION**).

DUTCH WARS. Three wars were caused by the colonial and naval rivalries of **ENGLAND** and the Netherlands.

First (1652-54): The **NAVIGATION ACT** of 1651 damaged Dutch trade, and, in response, Holland declared war on England. The English navy was defeated in a battle off Dungeness in 1652 but overcame the Dutch fleet near Texel the following year.

Second (1665-67): Colonial rivalry led to the English capture of New Amsterdam (now New York) and Holland's seizure of the English Gold Coast ports in Africa. There was also an embarrassing incident in which the Dutch fleet sailed up the River Medway and attacked the English naval dockyard at Chatham, burning four ships at anchor. The English were victorious at sea battles at Lowestoft and North Foreland.

Third (1672-74): **CHARLES I** was committed by the Treaty of Dover to support the French King Louis XIV's invasion of Holland. During the struggles, the Dutch retook New York but handed it back under the terms of the peace settlement (the Treaty of Westminster) reached in 1674.

—E—

EADRED (?-955). Son of **EDWARD THE ELDER** and Eadgifu, Eadred became King of **ENGLAND** on the assassination of his brother **EDMUND I** in 946. In 947, Archbishop Wulfstan I of **YORK** and the leaders of Northumbria pledged allegiance to him but soon changed their minds and gave their support to Eric Bloodaxe (son of Harald I of Norway). Eadred took his revenge by force, expelling Eric and demanding reparation from the Northumbrians. Eric returned to fight for Northumbrian independence but was defeated again in 954 and, by the end of his reign, Eadred was master of the whole of England. He died at Frome on 23 November 955 and was buried at Winchester, leaving in his will £16,000 so that his subjects could buy relief from famine or from heathen armies, if needed.

EADWIG (940-59). The son of **EDMUND I** and Aelfgifu, Eadwig succeeded his uncle **EADRED** to the throne of **ENGLAND** in 955, when he was 15 years of age, and ruled for only four years. The brief reign appears to have been notable largely for the animosity between Eadwig and Dunstan, Eadred's treasurer, but it is also clear that there was a widespread lack of confidence in the young King because, in 957, Mercia and Northumbria turned to his younger brother **EDGAR** and invited him to lead them. Eadwig retained his lands south of the **RIVER THAMES** but died on 1 October 959, having accomplished little.

EARL. Now indicating a level of the **PEERAGE**, the term is derived from the 11th century rulers of **SHIRE**s or, more usually, larger provinces. These were a **VIKING** introduction, the equivalent of the **ANGLO-SAXON** Ealdormen, whom they replaced throughout the land under King **CANUTE**. As 'Eorle', the word is one of the oldest known in the English language, dating from documents as early as 616 AD. Within the modern order, precedence depends on the date at which the title was created. The premier earldom of **SCOTLAND** is Mar (created in 1404) and of **ENGLAND** Shrewsbury (created in 1442).

EARLY DAY MOTION. Most motions tabled by **BACKBENCHER**s in the **HOUSE OF COMMONS** are listed for debate on "an early day". In practice, few are ever discussed because time is limited. Members of **PARLIAMENT** use this procedure as a means of expressing views under the protection afforded by **PARLIAMENTARY PRIVILEGE**. MPs approving of a motion append signatures so the popularity of the view expressed can be gauged.

EAST ANGLIA. This low-lying region of eastern **ENGLAND** includes the counties of Norfolk and Suffolk as well as parts of **CAMBRIDGE**shire, Essex and Lincolnshire. Much of the land lies below sea level and is protected from flooding by dykes and drainage schemes. East Anglia was settled by the **ANGLO-SAXONS** and, during the Middle Ages, built a considerable wealth through the manufacture of worsted cloth. More recently, the principal sources of income have been arable farming, food processing and related agricultural activities, though tourism and (decreasingly) the fishing industry also provide employment. During the 1970s and 1980s, the parts of the region closest to **LONDON** experienced considerable population expansion, partly due to a movement of people out of the city and partly due to in-migration from other parts of the United Kingdom. Norwich, Ipswich and Cambridge are the major settlements. (For location, see Map 1, page xxv.)

EAST INDIA COMPANY. A paramilitary trading company created through a royal charter granted by Queen **ELIZABETH I** in 1600, the company was awarded exclusive trading rights with the Indian subcontinent (East Indies). That monopoly gave it extensive independent powers on behalf of the **CROWN** and, with **ROBERT CLIVE**, it was instrumental in the extension of the **BRITISH EMPIRE** in the area (see **SEVEN YEARS WAR**). By 1773, however, it had come under increasing scrutiny from **PARLIAMENT** for financial irregularities and alleged oppression of native peoples. Gradually, it was subjected to increasing **GOVERNMENT** regulation, and eventually, under the provisions of the India Reform Act of 1784 (see **ACT OF PARLIAMENT**), **WILLIAM PITT THE YOUNGER** took control of India from the company. Its political and administrative powers were removed in 1858, when the India Office became responsible for the administration of the subcontinent after the **INDIAN MUTINY** had demonstrated the inability of a private company to manage the territory, and it was wound up in 1873. (See **OPIUM WARS**).

EAST OF SUEZ. This term was used from 1960 to describe British policy in the Persian Gulf and in Malaya and Singapore. Interest in these areas originally stemmed from the need to protect India (see **EASTERN QUESTION**), and the East-of-Suez policy was created even though Indian independence in 1948 had left the original reason for a British presence largely invalid. **HAROLD WILSON**'s government scaled down the country's military commitment to the region, and. though **EDWARD HEATH** attempted unsuccessfully to revive it, Britain eventually withdrew from all but Hong Kong, reducing its military involvements as its economic powers waned.

EASTERN QUESTION. This term was first used in the 19th century to refer to Britain's long-held diplomatic policy towards the control of the Balkans and the Eastern Mediterranean. The interest was stimulated by the need to protect routes to India and to counter Russian expansion in the region after the breakup of the Ottoman Empire. More generally, it has been applied to the rivalries in the eastern Mediterranean occasioned by the weakness of the Ottoman Empire, the rise of nationalist feelings in the area and the exertions of great powers to extend their influence at the expense of the Turks. Britain supported Greece in its attempts to break free from Turkey (see **BATTLE OF NAVARINO**), became involved in the **CRIMEAN WAR** and participated in diplomatic negotiations during the Balkan wars of the early 20th century, always with a policy coloured by Anglocentric views of the Ottomans as barbaric peoples and of the nationalist groups as idealists fighting for freedom.

Echoes of the Eastern Question appear in Britain's involvement in the **ANGLO-RUSSIAN ENTENTE**, the **SUEZ CRISIS**, the **GULF WAR** and even the Bosnian/Serbian conflict of the 1990s, all of which were characterized by the different attitudes of western nations and Russia over such problems as the siege of Sarajevo.

EASTLAND COMPANY. English merchants had long traded with the Baltic states and, in 1579, were incorporated as the Eastland Company in order to ensure access to the naval provisions (tar, hemp and timber) of the area and to oppose the growth of the **HANSEATIC LEAGUE** of northern traders. The company's monopoly ceased in 1673.

ECONOMIC SECRETARY TO THE TREASURY. This **GOVERNMENT** post is junior to that of **POSTMASTER GENERAL.** In **JOHN MAJOR**'s administrations, the holder has been responsible for matters relating to monetary policy and the financial system, including the banks.

EDEN, ROBERT ANTHONY (1897-1977). **PRIME MINISTER** at the time of the **SUEZ CRISIS** in 1956, Eden was born in Durham on 12 June 1897, the fourth child of Sir William Eden and his wife, Sybil. He was educated at Sandroyd School (Surrey) and Eton College, then joined the King's Royal Rifle Corps in 1915, serving as an infantry officer in France, becoming an Adjutant in 1917 and earning the Military Cross (also in 1917) for rescuing his Sergeant while under fire. In 1918, he was promoted to Brigade-Major, the youngest man to hold the rank at that time.

After the German surrender brought the **FIRST WORLD WAR** to an end, Eden went to **OXFORD** University, where he studied Asian languages and graduated with First Class Honours before entering the **HOUSE OF COMMONS** in the **CONSERVATIVE PARTY** cause as Member of **PARLIAMENT** for Warwick and Leamington in 1923. He soon gained a reputation as an expert on foreign affairs and, in 1926, was appointed **PARLIAMENTARY PRIVATE SECRETARY** to **JOSEPH AUSTEN CHAMBERLAIN**, the Foreign Secretary. His experience continued to develop under **RAMSAY MACDONALD**, who made him **UNDER-SECRETARY OF STATE** for Foreign Affairs in the coalition **GOVERNMENT** of 1931, then promoted him to **LORD PRIVY SEAL** with special responsibility for foreign affairs (1934). **STANLEY BALDWIN** appointed him **MIN-**

ISTER for **LEAGUE OF NATIONS** Affairs (June 1935) then Foreign Secretary (December 1935), a post which he retained when **NEVILLE CHAMBERLAIN** became Prime Minister in 1937. Over the next three years, he became increasingly disenchanted with Chamberlain's policy of avoiding war by negotiation with Adolf Hitler and resigned in 1938, when the Prime Minister told US President Franklin D. Roosevelt that a proposed conference to discuss the international situation should be deferred until British attempts to placate Benito Mussolini, the Italian dictator and ally of Germany, had concluded.

When the **SECOND WORLD WAR** eventually broke out in September 1939, Eden returned to the Government as **SECRETARY OF STATE** for the **DOMINION**s, then, when **WINSTON CHURCHILL** formed his coalition administration in May 1940, moved to the **WAR OFFICE**, again as Secretary of State. In December, he became Foreign Secretary once more and held the post until the 1945 **GENERAL ELECTION** swept the **LABOUR PARTY** to power. Churchill had a high regard for Eden's abilities and posted him back to the Foreign Office when the Conservatives gained a Parliamentary majority in 1951. Over the next four years, he played a major part in international affairs, helping to mediate between Italy and Yugoslavia in their quarrel over Trieste (1954), negotiating an end to war in Indochina (1954), contributing to the establishment of the South-East Asia Treaty Organization (1954) and persuading France to withdraw its objections to a series of western Europe defence agreements (1954).

In 1955, he succeeded Churchill as Prime Minister and continued his attempts to defuse potential international crises by holding meetings with Soviet leaders in **LONDON**. However, a series of decisions following Egypt's nationalization of the Suez Canal in 1956 led to his downfall. The canal provided Britain's shortest sea route to India and the East Asia, cutting out the long journey around Africa, so restrictions on its use would have a serious impact on the United Kingdom's trade and defence. Moreover, Eden had a personal interest in the affair because, in 1954, he had agreed to withdraw British troops from the Canal Zone, arguing that their removal would improve diplomatic relations with Colonel Gamal Abd-al-Nasser, the Egyptian President. In cooperation with France and against the wishes of the **UNITED NATIONS**, the army returned to the Mediterranean and an air attack was launched against Port Said. Eventually, the British and French withdrew as UN forces arrived, but the strain had taken its toll and, on 9 January 1957, following a recuperative vacation in Jamaica, Eden resigned on the grounds of illhealth. He was created Earl of Avon in 1961 and died on 14 January 1977 at his home in Alvediston, near Salisbury.

EDGAR (944-75). The son of **EDMUND I** and Aelfgifu, Edgar was King of **MERCIA** and Northumbria from 957 to 959 and King of **ENGLAND** from 959 until his death in 975. In 955, the Mercians and Northumbrians had pledged their allegiance to Edgar's elder brother, **EADWIG**, who was still only 15, but were dissatisfied with his rule and, in 957, invited 13-year old Edgar to lead them. He recalled Dunstan, who had been banished from Eadwig's court, making him Bishop of Worcester and of **LONDON** (and later installing him as **ARCHBISHOP OF CANTERBURY**). Dunstan was the power behind the throne, shaping the young King's policies, particularly towards the Church. Monasticism was encouraged, and penalties introduced for nonpayment of **TITHE**s. Trade was promoted and the administration of justice improved through the reorganization of the **HUNDRED, SHIRE** and **BOROUGH** courts. Relationships with neighbouring territories were maintained through diplomacy rather than conflict. Danish areas of England (see **VIKINGS**) were allowed to maintain their own laws, and the northern borders of the kingdom were secured through negotiations which involved the ceding of Lothian to Kenneth II of **SCOTLAND**.

As a result, Edgar's reign was marked by lengthy periods of peace and prosperity (undoubtedly furthered by the lack of any sustained Viking pressure). His **CORONATION** was delayed until 973, when he was in his thirtieth year, probably because of his religious leanings. (Priests were normally ordained at the age of 30 and Edgar almost certainly saw similarities between the duties of Kings and the duties of servants of the Church.) The crowning ceremony, held at **BATH**, was a magnificent event and was followed by a gathering at Chester, where rulers of subject kingdoms in Britain paid him homage.

He died on 8 July 975 and was succeeded by his son, **EDWARD THE MARTYR**, who had a rather different approach to monastic matters.

EDGEHILL, BATTLE OF, 23 October 1642. This was the initial large- scale engagement of the first **CIVIL WAR**, involving 12,000 **ROYALISTS**, led by King **CHARLES I**, and 10,000 **PARLIAMENTARIANS,** headed by the Earl of Essex, who was also supported by **TRAINED BANDS** from **LONDON**. The battle was indecisive because of poor leadership, panic and exhaustion, with both sides claiming victory, but it did open up the way to the capital for the King and is seen by some as a Royalist success. The battle convinced the Parliamentary side that it needed to improve the fighting skills and tactics of its forces (see **NEW MODEL ARMY**).

EDINBURGH, DUKE OF. (See **PRINCE PHILIP**).

EDINGTON, BATTLE OF, May 878. Sometimes called the Battle of Ethandun, this was a struggle on the Wiltshire Downs near Chippenham in which English troops from **WESSEX**, led by **ALFRED THE GREAT**, overcame a **VIKING** invasion force. It was a crucial engagement, which was eventually to establish Wessex as the most powerful kingdom in **ENGLAND**, and, with the **BATTLE OF MALDON**, was probably instrumental in defining the geographical extent of the **DANELAW**. The **ANGLO-SAXON CHRONICLE** says of Alfred in this battle: "in a dense, shield-locked array, (he) long maintained a stubborn fight, and at length by Divine Will obtained a victory". (His men fought in close order behind a shield wall.)

EDMUND I (c. 921-46). King of **ENGLAND** from 939 until his murder in 946, Edmund was the son of **EDWARD THE ELDER** and Eadgifu. He succeeded to the throne on the death of his half-brother, **AETHELSTAN**, with whom he had fought against the Danish, Welsh and Scots alliance at the **BATTLE OF BRUNANBURH** in 937. Olaf Guthfrithson, the King of Dublin, took the opportunity presented by Aethelstan's death to invade Northumbria and the East Midlands but, by 944, Edmund had regained all of the lost territories. The following year, he occupied Strathclyde and granted it to Malcolm I of **SCOTLAND** in return for an agreement on military support, thereby guaranteeing a secure northern frontier for his kingdom. According to the **ANGLO-SAXON CHRONICLE,** Edmund was murdered by Liofa (an exiled criminal) in his royal home in Pucklechurch (Gloucestershire) on 26 May 946. He was buried at Glastonbury.

EDMUND II (c. 988-1016). Edmund Ironside, son of **AETHELRED II** and Aelfgifu, was King of **ENGLAND** for less than eight months between April and November 1016, disputing the throne with **CANUTE**, the Danish invader (see **VIKINGS**). When Canute landed in the autumn of 1015, Edmund assembled an army to defend the country, but his men would not fight unless Aethelred was present. A similar problem arose early the following year. Meanwhile, Canute laid waste much of eastern and northern England, gaining and enforcing allegiance. Edmund returned to his father in **LONDON** and, when the King died on 23 April, was appointed his successor by local leaders. That appointment, however, did not meet with universal acceptance and, at a meeting in Southampton, the **WITAN** (the Anglo-Saxon council) chose Canute as King. Edmund continued to resist the Danes, regaining **WESSEX**, winning victories in **MERCIA** and relieving attacks on London. However, on 18 October 1016, he was defeated at the **BATTLE OF ASSANDUN** and negotiated a peace treaty under which he retained Wessex but renounced his claims to the lands north of the **RIVER THAMES**. When he died on 30 November, Canute became the undisputed King of England. Edmund was buried with his grandfather, King **EDGAR**, at Glastonbury.

EDRED. (See **EADRED**).

EDUCATION. During the **ANGLO-SAXON** period in **ENGLAND**, education was the remit of the Church, originally for its own monks or clergy but later also for lay pupils in cathedral schools and **UNIVERSITIES**. The **PURITANS** were instrumental in extending the curriculum beyond the classics. During the **INDUSTRIAL REVOLUTION**, a variety of voluntary schools, boarding schools, local private schools and **GRAMMAR SCHOOLS** developed as the nouveaux riche used their money to educate their children, and particularly their sons. The offspring of the landed classes were educated privately by tutors at home or in **PUBLIC SCHOOLS** (including Eton and Charterhouse). Grammar schools concentrated on ancient languages but later widened their curriculum, particularly after the appearance of the public examinations system, which began in 1871 with the Cambridge Local Examinations, developed further with the School Certificate of the early 20th century and eventually evolved into the current General Certificate of Secondary Education and General Certificate of Education examinations. The poor, if they had any education in the 19th century, gained it from Dame Schools run by genteel ladies, Sunday Schools, Charity Schools or Ragged Schools. The National Schools Society (Anglican) and the British Schools of the British and Foreign Society (Quaker) developed national monitor system classes where younger children were often taught by older children supplementing teachers.

State education developed during the late 19th century. The 1870 Forster Act (see **ACT OF PARLIAMENT**) introduced universal elementary education under School Boards and, in 1880, Mundella's Act made it compulsory. The 1902 Balfour Act (see **ARTHUR JAMES BALFOUR**) set up Local Education Authorities to administer the provisions. The 1907 Education Act created the system of selection for grammar schools, based on examination of pupils aged 11 to 12, which became known as the 11-plus exams, and H. A. L. Fisher's Education Act, in 1918, raised the schoolleaving age to 14. The 1944 Butler Education Act (see **RICHARD** (Rab) **BUTLER**) created universal free secondary education in grammar schools, technical schools and secondary modern schools with places depending on achievement in the 11-plus. In 1965, the **LABOUR PARTY** promoted a system of nonselective schools (known as **COMPREHENSIVE SCHOOLS**) which, by the end of the decade, had become widespread but not universal.

In the 1950s, colleges of advanced technology and of further education were introduced and, in 1960s, new **UNIVERSITIES** called **POLYTECHNICS** were created to widen higher (that is, degree level) education by improving provision of courses in applied sciences and technology. School syllabuses gradually became more inquiry-based, with decision- making elements incorporated to broaden children's skills. In 1988, the Education Reform Act introduced, for the first time, a national curriculum, detailing subjects and topics to be studied in all schools. In 1992, the **GOVERNMENT** allowed the polytechnics to change their titles and become fully independent universities. (See **SIDNEY WEBB**).

EDWARD I (1239-1307). King of **ENGLAND** from 1272 until 1307, Edward was the eldest son of **HENRY III** and Eleanor of Provence. He was born in **LONDON** on 17 June 1239 and, for much of his youth and early manhood, was a source of considerable trouble to his father. In 1255, without Henry's support, he attacked Llewelyn ap Gruffydd, Prince of Gwynnedd, following a dispute over the administration of royal estates in **WALES**, and was soundly defeated. Then, in 1259, he supported **SIMON DE MONTFORT**'s campaign for restrictions on the King's powers. Later, he deserted Simon and was forgiven by his father but was sent to Gascony in 1260 in the hope that he could be kept out of mischief. That hope was misplaced because, when he returned in

1263, he resumed his former headstrong ways. At the **BATTLE OF LEWES**, in 1264, his impetuosity contributed to Henry's defeat and his own capture by Simon's supporters. The following year, however, he escaped and gained his revenge: leading the royalist forces, he engaged the rebels at Evesham (see **BATTLE OF EVESHAM**), slew Simon and rescued his father.

Henry died in 1272, and Edward, despite his tempestuous past, became King with the full support of the English nobility. By that time, though still autocratic and intolerant of opposing views, he was somewhat older and wiser and was demonstrating considerable political skill. It was clear that feudal revenues could no longer meet all the demands made on the **MONARCH**, particularly with respect to the administration of justice. Money was needed from the new merchant class and the only way to get that was through **PARLIAMENT**. So Edward regularly called the **KNIGHT**s and **BURGESS**es to meet and advise him on important issues, with the result that Parliament increasingly became accepted as the established means of running the country, particularly from 1297, when it gained the right to vote on taxes. The reforms of the judicial system initiated by **HENRY II** were also developed. The **COURT OF CHANCERY** was established to provide redress for circumstances in which no other court was appropriate and the Courts of the King's Bench (see **QUEEN'S BENCH**), the **EXCHEQUER** and the Common Pleas were each given their own staff in order to improve their efficiency. In addition, measures were taken to limit the power of the clergy and maintain social order.

But Edward's love of action helped drain his coffers and offset much of the good he did in other spheres. In 1277, he invaded Wales and starved Llewelyn into submission. Five years later, faced by a rebellion, he invaded again, killed the Welsh prince and imposed a reorganization of government on English lines. He also attempted to incorporate **SCOTLAND** within his kingdom but those efforts met with less success. Although his puppet King, John Balliol, paid him homage, the nobles and the common people were less obeisant. In an attempt to compel submission, Edward invaded the country in 1296 and captured the Stone of Scone, on which Scottish Kings were traditionally crowned, removing it to London. However, the revolt continued, led by William Wallace, and Edward was unable to bring the northerners to heel. In addition to these conflicts, Edward warred with France between 1297 and 1299 as a result of attempts by Philip IV to acquire English lands in Gascony.

He died at Burgh by Sands, near Carlisle, on 7 July 1307, while on his way north with his army and is buried at **WESTMINSTER** in a tomb which bears the epitaph "Here lies Edward the Hammer of the Scots". (See **MODEL PARLIAMENT**).

EDWARD II (1284-1327). The son of **EDWARD I** and his first wife, Eleanor of Castile, Edward was born at Caernarvon on 25 April 1284 and was the first person to bear the title **PRINCE OF WALES**. He became King of **ENGLAND** on the death of his father in 1307 and spent most of his 20-year reign in conflict with his nobles.

A man of limited intellectual ability who scandalized court circles because of his homosexual affairs, Edward sought friends outside the normal court circle and thus antagonized those who would normally be expected to act as advisers. Conflict developed, in particular, over Piers Gaveston, a Gascon **KNIGHT** who was recalled from exile and made Earl of Cornwall even before Edward had been crowned. In 1311, Gaveston's unpopularity led a group of nobles to demand that the King should renew his exile and, in addition, agree to a limitation of the **ROYAL PREROGATIVE**s on appointments to the household, declarations of war and financial matters. Initially, Edward had to accept the demands, but he worked to draw supporters to his cause and soon had Gaveston's banishment annulled. Stung by the rebuke, the **BARON**s kidnapped Gaveston and executed him in June 1312, an action which Edward never forgave despite an apparent reconciliation with the rebels the following year.

Wars with **SCOTLAND** rubbed salt into the sores. English Kings claimed overlordship of the Scots, but the independence movement led by Robert I had successfully occupied all of the major fortifications except that at Stirling. Edward led a large army north to relieve the situation but was soundly defeated at the Battle of Bannockburn on 24 June 1314. He retreated to lick his wounds, leaving Bruce to raid England's northern frontier and further reducing his standing with the nobility, many of whom had lost sons and brothers in the fruitless campaign. His freedom of action was now so limited that he had to concede effective control of the country to his cousin Thomas, Earl of Lancaster.

By 1321, Lancaster was rousing antiroyalist opinion in the north, and Edward was able to raise an army to subdue him. The forces met at the Battle of Boroughbridge on 16 March 1322. Thomas was defeated and executed six days later.

With newfound confidence, and with the help of Hugh le

Despenser and his father, Edward began to reorganize the administration of his country in order to augment his private income. The Despensers, however, aroused antagonism as they filled their own coffers and, in particular, fuelled the fury of Edward's Queen, Isabella, whose estates in France were seized in 1324 on the grounds that a French invasion was planned. In 1325, Isabella moved to the continent, where she gathered a group of disaffected nobles around her and announced her intention to remove the Despensers. With her lover Roger Mortimore, Baron of Wigmore, she invaded England in 1326. Edward, unable to muster any support, fled with his advisers, but all three were captured. The Despensers were executed and Edward imprisoned at Kenilworth. An assembly, which called itself a **PARLIAMENT**, met on 7 January 1327, declared Edward unfit to govern and decreed his son King as **EDWARD III**. Representatives of the assembly called on Edward and forced him to abdicate, but his continued existence was seen as a threat to stability. He was moved to Berkely Castle where he was almost certainly murdered in September 1327. He was buried in Gloucester, where miracles were reportedly performed at his tomb.

EDWARD III (1312-77). The son of **EDWARD II** and his Queen, Isabella, Edward was born at **WINDSOR CASTLE** on 13 November 1312 and ruled **ENGLAND** for 50 years. His reign began on 25 January 1327, following his father's enforced abdication, though in the early years, his mother and her favourite, Roger Mortimore of Wigmore, governed in his name.

In 1330, Edward took control himself, executing Mortimore and ending Isabella's influence by banishing her to Castle Rising in Norfolk. Immediately, he attempted to reestablish the international prestige England had lost during his father's rule. Aiming to reverse the independence granted to **SCOTLAND** by the 1328 Treaty of Northampton, he supported an invasion, led by Edward Balliol, and placed him on the throne, forcing King David II to flee to France. He also advanced a claim to the French throne, largely as a ploy to retain control of Gascony and the Bordeaux wine trade but also in order to facilitate trade between English wool merchants (see **WOOL INDUSTRY**) and markets in Flanders. French resistance led to the **HUNDRED YEARS WAR** between the two countries though the dispute lasted even longer than that — until 1801, every English **MONARCH** called himself King of France. The Battle of Sluys in 1340 destroyed the French navy and gave Edward control of the English Channel. Also, victories at the **BATTLE OF**

CRECY (1346) and the **BATTLE OF POITIERS** (1356) helped his cause, but none of these successes had any long-term impact on the progress of the conflict though **CALAIS**, taken in 1347 after a 12-month siege, remained under English control for the next hundred years.

The war eventually ended in 1360 when, under the Treaty of Calais, Edward accepted Aquitaine as the price of surrendering his claim to the whole of France. In 1366, he formally rejected papal claims to feudal overlordship of England (claims stemming from King **JOHN**'s homage to Pope Innocent III in 1213), but domestic stability was threatened by the cost of the wars with France and Scotland and by the ravages of the **BLACK DEATH** from 1348 to 1350 and in 1361 and 1369. The need for funds led to attacks on the wealth of the Church and to frequent requests to **PARLIA-MENT** for financial support, requests which were granted only after bargaining over greater rights and privileges.

Increasingly, as the King aged, he left military matters in the hands of his sons, **EDWARD THE BLACK PRINCE** and **JOHN OF GAUNT**, particularly after war with France was renewed in 1368. Ultimately, Aquitaine was lost and a new truce was signed in 1375, leaving Edward with only Bayonne, Bordeaux, Brest and Calais on the continental mainland. England itself was divided by a power struggle between the two brothers, a struggle which was only resolved by the death of the Black Prince in 1376.

Edward died at Sheen on 21 June 1377. He never achieved the aims he set for himself, largely because ambition had outrun resources. Even so, he had overseen a period of major social and political change — by the end of his reign, Parliament was divided into two Houses and had an increased role in the government of the realm, English had replaced French as the language of the law courts (reflecting a declining Norman influence) and **JOHN WYCLIFFE** was promoting the Protestant cause. International ambitions had come to naught, but Edward had held his country together at a time of strife and reintroduced a self-confidence which favoured the development of trade and industry.

EDWARD IV (1442-83). King of **ENGLAND** from 1461 to 1470 and from 1471 to 1483, Edward was a much more efficient leader than his predecessor, **HENRY VI**, but his greed and his autocratic rule made him an unpopular **MONARCH** towards the end of his reign. The son of **RICHARD, DUKE OF YORK** and Cicely Neville, he was born at Rouen in France on 28 April 1442. When Richard was killed by royalist forces at the **BATTLE OF WAKEFIELD** in 1460, Edward gathered an army, defeated Henry's troops at Mortimer's Cross on 2 February 1461, then marched on **LONDON** and took the **CROWN**. He was acclaimed King at **WESTMINSTER** on 4 March.

During the early part of his reign, the struggle continued between the House of York and the House of Lancaster (a dispute known as the **WARS OF THE ROSES**), but Edward's secret wedding to Elizabeth Woodville (widow of a Lancastrian) in 1464 alienated his fellow Yorkists and particularly the Earl of Warwick, who had been negotiating a peace treaty with France to be sealed by the King's marriage to a sister-in-law of Louis XI. Warwick responded by stirring up trouble in the north of England and, in September 1470, invaded the south with help from Louis, freeing Henry from captivity and returning him to the throne. Edward fled to Holland but, with support from Charles of Burgundy, returned in March 1471.

Landing at Ravenspur, on the Humber, Edward turned south, took London and slew Warwick in the **BATTLE OF BARNET** on 14 April. A further victory at the **BATTLE OF TEWKESBURY** on 4 May made the throne secure, and, with domestic opposition defeated, he turned his attention to a revival of the English claim to France. He took a large army across the English Channel in 1475 but met French forces who were well-prepared and willing to reach an accommodation. Under the Treaty of Piquigny, he agreed to withdraw in return for the sum of 75,000 gold crowns and an annual tribute of 50,000 gold crowns for as long as he and Louis survived. These payments released Edward from dependence on Parliament for his income and augmented coffers he was filling through a reorganization of revenues on his estates, trade on his own ships and other measures. With his money, he patronized **WILLIAM CAXTON** and established a library of illuminated Flemish manuscripts. But, as he aged, he became increasingly avaricious, distrustful, cruel, promiscuous and autocratic. He died at Westminster on 9 April 1483, probably worn out by a life of debauchery, while still only 40. (See **BATTLE OF TOWTON**).

EDWARD V (1470-83). The eldest surviving son of **EDWARD IV** and Elizabeth Woodville, Edward was a King who never ruled. Sometime during 1 to 3 November 1470, he was born in **WESTMINSTER (LONDON)**, where his mother had taken refuge when his father fled to Holland to escape capture by political adversaries. On

26 June the following year, after successfully regaining the throne, Edward made his son **PRINCE OF WALES,** and the child was sent to Ludlow Castle on the border of his new estates. When the King died on 9 April 1483, young Edward set off for London in the company of a small retinue. The group was intercepted by Richard, Duke of Gloucester (later **RICHARD III**), who was acting as Regent (see **REGENCY**) and, as the boy's guardian, had responsibility for his safety. The new King was taken to the **TOWER OF LONDON**, and his mother fled once again to Westminster Abbey.

For reasons not wholly clear but certainly influenced both by threats and by cajoling, Elizabeth allowed Richard, her other son, to leave the sanctuary on 16 June and join his brother in the tower. On 25 June, **PARLIAMENT** met to consider a claim that Edward IV's marriage to Elizabeth was invalid on the grounds of a precontract with Eleanor Butler, daughter of the Earl of Shrewsbury. The claim was upheld, the children of the marriage were declared illegitimate and Richard of Gloucester was deemed to be the rightful King of **ENGLAND**. He was crowned the next day, ending Edward's brief reign.

For some weeks after that, the two boys were seen playing in the tower rooms and grounds but, in August, they vanished and, though their fate has never been satisfactorily established, it is likely that they were murdered on Richard's orders. Nearly 200 years later, in 1674, workmen in the tower discovered a wooden chest containing the remains of two children. It was assumed that these were the bones of the two princes so they were put in an urn and placed in Westminster Abbey. The urn was reopened in 1933, and forensic examinations showed that the age range of the material corresponded with the ages of the children at the time of their disappearance.

EDWARD VI (1537-53). The son of **HENRY VIII** and **JANE SEYMOUR**, Edward was born at Hampton Court Palace on 12 October 1537. Jane died 12 days after the birth, and Edward himself was a frail and sickly child. He was just nine years old when he succeeded his father in January 1547, so Edward Seymour, Duke of Somerset, was named Protector. Inevitably, however, a number of factions evolved, all attempting to gain power in the King's name, and, in 1549, John Dudley, Duke of Warwick, overthrew Somerset, effectively becoming ruler of **ENGLAND** because of his influence on the young **MONARCH**. By the spring of 1553, it was clear that Edward was dying of consumption, and Warwick (now

Duke of Northumberland) persuaded him to prepare a will which excluded his Roman Catholic half-sister Mary (later **MARY I**) from the succession and gave the **CROWN** to the "**LADY JANE GREY**'s heirs male". Lady Jane, a Protestant, was the wife of Dudley's son, Guildford. The wording of the will was changed (almost certainly by the Duke although it is clear that Edward was a committed Protestant) to read "the Lady Jane and her heirs male". Edward died in Greenwich on 6 July 1553 and was buried in **WESTMINSTER** Abbey, having had no real opportunity to stamp his authority on his country's affairs.

EDWARD VII (1841-1910). King of **GREAT BRITAIN** and **IRELAND** from 1901 until 1910, Edward was born in **LONDON** on 9 November 1841. The eldest of the four sons of Queen **VICTORIA** and **PRINCE ALBERT**, he was christened Albert Edward and was the first heir born to a reigning **MONARCH** since 1762. At birth, he was given the title of Duke of Cornwall and, when only four weeks old, was created **PRINCE OF WALES**. Until he reached the age of seven, he was educated by his governess, Sarah, Lady Lyttelton, and then by a series of tutors. He spent some time at the universities of Edinburgh, **OXFORD** and **CAMBRIDGE** and also travelled widely as a young man, visiting Europe, Canada and the United States, where he stayed with US President James Buchanan in Washington. In the summer of 1861, he served with the Grenadier Guards in **IRELAND** but news of a liaison with an Irish actress reached his mother's ears and, in her view, cast a shadow over her husband's last months. She never forgave her son, and, to his credit, Edward bore the snubs and criticism stoically for the next 40 years. In 1863, he married Alexandra, daughter of Prince Christian (later King Christian IX) of Denmark. The match had been arranged but was a happy one, although Edward is believed to have had several affairs, including one with actress Lily Langtry. The couple had six children, five of whom (two sons and three daughters) survived to adulthood. Princess Alexandra and her family spent much time at Sandringham Palace in Norfolk, but Edward enjoyed society life in London and continued his overseas travels, becoming the first heir to the throne to visit India (1875-76).

He became King when his mother died on 22 January 1901, by which time he was a grandfather nearly 60 years old. Despite his upbringing, he was concerned about the disparities of wealth and poverty in Britain and was an admirer of **WILLIAM**

GLADSTONE, whom Victoria had disliked so much. His short reign saw considerable legislation on social matters, including **BILL**s introducing secondary **EDUCATION** at state expense (1902), establishing state pensions for the elderly (1908) and creating Labour Exchanges where the unemployed could seek work (1909). His major interest, however, lay in foreign affairs, and he worked hard to strengthen his country's diplomatic power in Europe. He was fluent in both French and German and used his linguistic skills to good effect in speeches abroad, furthering a new sense of cooperation between Britain and France in particular. From 1906, his health began to fail, and he became increasingly worried by the course of affairs in Europe. He died in **BUCKINGHAM PALACE** on 6 May 1910, saddening a nation which had taken him to its heart, contrasting the fun-loving, generous Monarch with the austerity of his predecessor. (See **ENTENTE CORDIALE**).

EDWARD VIII (1894-1972). A King who was never crowned, Edward reigned for only 11 months and abdicated in order to marry an American divorcee. Born on 23 June 1894, he was the eldest child of George, **DUKE OF YORK** (later **GEORGE V**) and Princess Mary (later Queen **MARY OF TECK**). Christened Edward Albert Christian George Andrew Patrick David (the last four names being the patron saints of the constituent nations of the United Kingdom), he grew up at Sandringham Palace in Norfolk then attended the naval colleges at Osborne (1907-9) and Dartmouth (USA, 1909-10). He was admitted to the **ORDER OF THE GARTER** and invested as **PRINCE OF WALES** in 1911. After serving in the navy for three months, then travelling in Europe, he went to **OXFORD** University in 1912. In 1914, at the outbreak of the **FIRST WORLD WAR**, he joined the Grenadier Guards but, despite his objections, was kept far from the front line. As soon as the fighting was over, he embarked on a series of foreign visits, travelling to Canada, New Zealand, the Mediterranean countries, India, Ceylon, East Asia, the United States and South Africa between 1919 and 1925. In addition, he took part in official engagements at home, encouraging the economic ventures which flourished in the early 1920s.

This strenuous programme, coupled with his reputation as a sporting, fun-loving young man, made Edward immensely popular. However, rumours began to circulate about a scandalous liaison with a married woman, and these stories continued to multiply after he succeeded to the throne on the death of his father on 20 January 1936. The British press had decided not to publish the tales, but in the United States and on the European mainland there were no such scruples. The stories involved Mrs Wallis Warfield Simpson, the daughter of a Baltimore family, who had divorced her first husband (Lieutenant Winfield Spencer) in 1927 and married Ernest Simpson, a **LONDON** stockbroker, later the same year. She first met the Prince of Wales in 1930 and the two spent much time together both in Britain and abroad. In 1936, the **GOVERNMENT** became concerned when it became apparent that Mrs Simpson intended to seek a second divorce and Prime Minister **STANLEY BALDWIN** sought a series of audiences with the King. On 16 November, Edward made it quite clear to Baldwin that he intended to marry Mrs Simpson and that, if necessary, he was prepared to abdicate. Lord Rothermere proposed a morganatic solution, allowing the King to marry Mrs Simpson but withholding from her the title of Queen and excluding any children from rights of succession to the throne. **WINSTON CHURCHILL** urged caution and counselled that the King should be given time to make up his mind.

The problem was not that Mrs Simpson was a commoner nor that she was of foreign stock. The difficulty was that she was twice divorced and that both of her previous husbands were still alive. Marriage to a divorcee raised difficult questions about the **MONARCH**'s relationship with the **CHURCH OF ENGLAND**, which stood steadfastly against the whole concept of divorce. Public opinion was divided, and it became increasingly clear that, if he remained King, Edward would rule over a nation split by the controversy. He had to decide between the throne and the woman he loved — and chose the latter. On 11 December, he made a radio broadcast announcing his abdication, then left by destroyer for the continent. He was succeeded by his brother, George, who became **GEORGE VI** and, as one of his first acts, created Edward Duke of Windsor. The couple were married in France on 3 June 1937 but Mrs Simpson was refused the title of Royal Highness. The Duke was deeply hurt, and the breach between him and other members of the royal family was widened by his admiration for Hitler's Germany. That breach never healed though he attended the funeral of George VI in 1952 and of Queen Mary in 1953, and both he and his wife were present with **QUEEN ELIZABETH II** at the unveiling of a plaque commemorating Queen Mary in London in June 1967. The Duke died in Paris on 28 May 1972 and was buried at Frogmore. His wife, who died in 1986, lies beside him.

EDWARD, PRINCE (1964-). The third son and fourth child of Queen

ELIZABETH II and **PRINCE PHILIP**, Prince Edward was born at **BUCKINGHAM PALACE (LONDON)** on 10 March 1964 and christened Edward Antony Richard Louis. Like his father and elder brothers, he was educated at Gordonstoun School in **SCOTLAND**. He then spent several months as a house tutor at Wanganui School in New Zealand before going to **CAMBRIDGE** University to take a degree in history. In 1986, he joined the Royal Marines but did not enjoy the atmosphere and (reputedly much to his father's annoyance and amidst great press publicity which implied that he was something of a wimp) left the following year to begin a career in the theatre as production assistant with Andrew Lloyd Webber's Really Useful Theatre Company. An attempt to branch out on his own by forming a stage production company (Theatre Division) failed, but the Prince, undaunted, moved into television and formed Ardent Productions in December 1993. In its first year, the firm made a loss of £400,000 but the months which followed brought several commissions, including a documentary on King **EDWARD VIII** presented by Prince Edward himself on Independent Television in 1996. In the spring of 1994, tabloid press reports revealed that a girlfriend — Sophie Rhys-Jones — was living in his apartments at the Palace, reportedly with the Queen's approval. Commentators suggested that the arrangement had the support of the Royal Family because it might help to prevent the problems which had bedevilled the marriages of the Prince's brothers and sister.

EDWARD THE BLACK PRINCE (1330-76). The eldest son of **EDWARD III** and Philippa of Hainaut, Edward was one of the principal commanders of the English armies during the **HUNDRED YEARS' WAR**. He appears to have earned his nickname because he wore black armour but there are no contemporary sources which confirm that habit (the soubriquet is first used in Richard Grafton's *Chronicle of England*, which appeared in 1569). Born at Woodstock on 15 June 1330, Edward was created Earl of Chester in 1333, Duke of Cornwall in 1337 and **PRINCE OF WALES** in 1343. He served under his father at the **BATTLE OF CRECY** (1346) and won his most famous victory at Poitiers on 19 September 1356, when he captured the French king, John II, and brought him back to **ENGLAND** (see **BATTLE OF POITIERS**). Under the Treaty of Calais, in 1360, Aquitaine was ceded to England, and Edward was appointed Duke. His prowess as a soldier, however, was greater than that as a governor. He antagonized the nobles and peasantry in his dukedom, partly through the heavy taxes which he imposed in order to support his luxurious lifestyle and partly because he helped Pedro the Cruel win back the throne of Castile, from which he had been deposed by an alliance which included King Charles V of France. Edward won a major victory in Pedro's cause at Najera on 3 April 1367, but the campaign broke both his treasury and his health. Summoned to explain himself to the French Parliament in May 1369, he retorted that he would appear with 60,000 men at his back, but, despite the boasting, he was dependent for control of his dukedom on an army which he could not pay, and, in 1371, he returned to England. The details of the remainder of his life are not clear, but it appears that he worked to achieve the succession of his surviving son, Richard (later **RICH-ARD II**), and that he supported the **HOUSE OF COMMONS** at a time of political discontent, providing the focus of opposition to the administration of his brother, **JOHN OF GAUNT**. He died on 8 June 1376 and was buried at **CANTERBURY,** where his tomb and armour can be seen in the Cathedral.

EDWARD THE CONFESSOR (c. 1002-66). King of **ENGLAND** from 1042 until 1066, Edward was the son of **AETHELRED II** and Emma, daughter of Richard, Duke of Normandy. He was born at Islip but went to Normandy in 1013 (when Sweyn replaced Aethelred as King of England) and spent most of his youth and early manhood there. He returned to England in 1041 and became King the following year. His father-in-law, Godwin, Earl of **WESSEX**, had engineered his accession, and, in an attempt to balance the power held by his relatives, Edward introduced Norman advisers to important state and Church offices. That, however, lost him the sympathy of many of his leading subjects (particularly because the foreigners seemed to be making little contribution to literature, learning or other aspects of court life). Following a quarrel in 1051, Wessex and his family were dismissed from the court, but they remained a potent focus of discontent and returned the following year. In 1053, the Earl died, but his son, Harold (later **HAROLD II**), assumed the mantle of opposition and continued to gain support, particularly in the south. Constant niggling conflicts added to Edward's problems — the Dane Osgod Clapa raided Essex in 1049, the Welsh created regular trouble in the west and the Scots invaded Northumbria in 1061. On the continent, he became embroiled in the dispute between Count Baldwin V of Flanders and Henry III of Germany. The Count retaliated by providing a safe haven for English exiles. A pious, saintly man, Edward was never confident in diplomatic power struggles and too unsoldierly to impose his will by force. He died on 5 January 1066, only a week after his new abbey at **WESTMINSTER** had been dedicated, and was succeeded by Harold II. He was canonized in 1161, and his feast days are 5 January and 13 October.

EDWARD THE ELDER (?-924). Son of **ALFRED THE GREAT** and King of **WESSEX** from 899 until 924, Edward began the reconquest of the **DANELAW**. He defeated the Northumbrian Danes at Tettenhall (Staffordshire) in 910 and spent much of the next ten years trying to remove them from their bases in eastern and northern **ENGLAND**. In 917, in consort with his sister, Aethelflaed, he launched a major offensive on several fronts and within two years had gained control of **EAST ANGLIA** and the East Midlands as far north as the Humber. At the same time, he established a union of Wessex and **MERCIA** and developed an administrative structure for his estates, giving him some claim to be considered the first King of England. For the remainder of his reign, he was concerned primarily with protecting his subjects from **VIKING** incursions and pacifying territories held by the Scandinavians in Northumbria. He died at Farndon on Dee on 17 July 924, and is remembered as one of the great **SAXON** commanders.

EDWARD THE MARTYR (c. 962-78). King of the English from 975 until 978, Edward was the son of King **EDGAR** and Aethelflaed, his first wife. The short reign was initially characterized by an antimonastic policy which was the antithesis of Edgar's approach to church affairs. Eventually, however, the campaign waned, and Edward became more concerned with the claims to the throne advanced by Aethelred (later **AETHELRED II**), his younger half-brother by Edgar and his second wife, Aelfthryth. In 978, while visiting Aethelred at Corfe Castle in Dorset, Edward was assassinated. (Later rumours attributed the murder to Aelfthryth, but there is no evidence to support these tales.) Originally buried at Wareham, his remains were later moved to Shaftesbury, which, it is claimed, was the site of several miracles.

EDWARDIAN AGE. This term is properly applied to the brief reign of the genial King **EDWARD VII** (1901-10) but is usually extended to the outbreak of the **FIRST WORLD WAR** in 1914. The period was essentially transitional, one of growing freedom from **VICTORIAN AGE** restrictions, with more society elegance and glamour as the middle and upper classes, at least, enjoyed the fruits of the **INDUSTRIAL REVOLUTION** and the burgeoning **BRITISH EMPIRE**. In some ways, these were carefree years characterized by fashion and new social customs, but political unrest was growing and the Edwardian Age ultimately became a brief Indian summer of calm before the gathering of the storm clouds that broke with the First World War.

EDWY. (See **EADWIG**).

EL ALAMEIN, BATTLE OF. (See **ALAMEIN, BATTLE OF EL**).

ELECTORAL SYSTEM. The United Kingdom has universal adult suffrage at 18 years of age and utilizes a first-past-the-post system for electing Members of **PARLIAMENT**. Each Parliamentary **CONSTITUENCY** elects one MP — the candidate who polls the single largest number of votes. In turn, the opportunity to form a **GOVERNMENT** passes to the political party with the greatest number of elected MPs. It is possible, therefore, for a party to gain a majority of MPs yet have, in total, won, across the country, fewer votes than another party, and this did happen in 1951 and 1974. The system tends to produce majority governments which do not normally have to solicit support from coalition partners. (See **BY-ELECTION; GENERAL ELECTION**).

ELECTRICITY. The nature of electricity was discovered by **MICHAEL FARADAY** in 1831 while he was researching electromagnetic induction. The first voltaic cell (or battery) had been created by Alescandro Volta in 1800. Following Faraday, Joseph Swan proposed a domestic supply system in 1878 in **NEWCASTLE-UPON-TYNE**, and the first company was operating in **LONDON** by January 1882. Electricity supply was developed, like most public utilities, first through private firms and later through municipal companies. The Electricity Act of 1926 (see **ACT OF PARLIAMENT**) created a Central Electricity Board, which set up a National Grid to distribute supplies across the country (eventually completed in 1933). The industry was nationalized in 1948 (see **NATIONALIZATION**), when there were 367 municipal and 195 private companies operating. From that time the Central Electricity Generating Board took over the operation of the National Grid. **COAL** and, later, nuclear power stations (see **NUCLEAR ENERGY**) provided the base load, with hydroelectricity providing additional peak capacity.

Production returned to private hands in 1991, under the terms of the Electricity Act of 1989 (see **PRIVATIZATION**), with two competing supply companies — National Power and PowerGen — running the power stations and 12 Regional Electricity Boards supplying the consumers. Nuclear power, however, was still the responsibility of the publicly owned Nuclear Electric and the National Grid was the responsibility of a fourth company, National Grid plc. In 1994, the industry supplied 302,807 gigawatt-hours of electricity: **COAL-**, **GAS-** and **OIL**-fired stations provided 57.9 per cent of the output; nuclear stations, 27.7 per cent; gas turbines 12.1 per cent; hydroelectric stations, 1.9 per cent and others (mainly wind) 0.4 per cent. From 1961, Britain has been linked by cable across the English Channel to France so that the grids of the two countries are merged in order to share capacity.

ELEVEN YEARS TYRANNY. This describes the period from 1629 until 1640, when King **CHARLES I**, aided by Archbishop **WILLIAM LAUD**, ruled without reference to **PARLIAMENT**. Eventually, humiliation in the first of the **BISHOPS' WARS** (see **BATTLE OF NEWBURN FORD**) and the need to raise money forced him to relent and summon the **SHORT PARLIAMENT**. Charles's autocratic approach to power was one of the factors which led to the **CIVIL WAR**, but, even so, some historians have exaggerated the extent of the tyranny. (See **SHIP MONEY**).

ELIZABETH I (1533-1603). Queen of **ENGLAND** and **IRELAND** from 1558 until 1603, Elizabeth was born at Greenwich on 7 September 1533, the only child of **HENRY VIII** and **ANNE BOLEYN**. When she was only two, her mother was found guilty of adultery and beheaded. Henry's marriage to Anne was declared invalid, making Elizabeth illegitimate and thus unable to succeed to the throne. Her legitimacy was never formally reestablished, although, in 1544, she was placed by statute in the order of succession after Henry's first daughter Mary (later **MARY I**) and his son Edward (later **EDWARD VI**). As a child, she received the education expected of a Princess — she became an accomplished linguist, speaking French, Italian and Spanish, and showed considerable musical ability. She seems also to have been happy in the company of Mary and Edward though she saw little of her father, who died when she was 14. At times, her life was in danger because of her Protestant faith, as when she was imprisoned in the **TOWER OF**

LONDON in 1554, accused of plotting against Mary, who was a Roman Catholic.

However, when Mary died on 17 November 1558, Elizabeth became Queen to the acclaim of a people disheartened by setbacks in the war with France and the persecution of those who spoke out for Protestantism. She tackled the religious differences within her realm immediately, reforming the **CHURCH OF ENGLAND** in 1559 and breaking off relations with the Vatican in 1561. In 1570, Pope Pius V responded by excommunicating her and ruling that her subjects were absolved of all allegiance to her. That papal bull effectively made it impossible for any loyal Englishman to be a Roman Catholic. Increasingly, the Church of Rome's adherents claimed that Elizabeth's cousin, Mary, Queen of Scots, was the true Queen of England. Elizabeth held Mary captive from 1568 until 1587, reluctant to take other action because of the implications of beheading the crowned **MONARCH** of a neighbouring state. Nevertheless, Mary's presence in England provoked a series of assassination attempts on Elizabeth and, reluctantly, she agreed to her execution in 1587. That, coupled with fines and imprisonment of others who sought to put a Catholic Monarch on the throne, did much to contain revolt by the supporters of Rome. Elizabeth, however, was no more enamoured of the Calvinists (who argued for an independent Church) and clashed with **PURITAN** Members of **PARLIAMENT**, who attacked the principle of the episcopacy and called for the reorganization of the Church of England on Presbyterian lines. But, unlike her predecessor, she did not persecute her opponents, and, by the last decade of her reign, many Roman Catholics were willing to accept her secular authority if a way of preserving their spiritual allegiance to the Pope could be found.

Her control over foreign policy was just as tight as that over ecclesiastical matters. Within a few months of becoming Queen, Elizabeth brought the war with France to an end. Between 1559 and 1562, she took action against **SCOTLAND** to protect her country's northern border, but throughout her life she detested military conflict, preferring to achieve her aims by diplomatic means (by playing off France and Spain against each other, for example). The peace maintained by these tactics allowed England to build up its naval strength and ultimately to beat off the threat the **SPANISH ARMADA** posed in 1588. The lengthy peace during the early part of her reign also allowed her to regain control of an economy which was on the brink of disaster. By 1560, she had replaced the coinage and reduced government borrowing. Trade was promoted by regulations which directed surplus labour from the clothmaking industry to farming and introduced a tax on property owners so the unemployed received support. She encouraged commerce with other nations and backed **SIR WALTER RALEIGH**'s journeys to the Americas. (The colony of Virginia was named after Elizabeth, the virgin Queen.) Much of her success was achieved by her skill in appointing advisers for their ability rather than their noble birth. Her only major mistake was with Robert Devereux, Earl of Essex, who was a confidant for 13 years but ultimately plotted against her and was executed in 1601.

The peace and prosperity which the country experienced was reflected in a cultural renaissance known as the **ELIZABETHAN AGE** — William Shakespeare was writing plays, as were Ben Jonson and Christopher Marlowe; Francis Bacon was publishing his essays; and Edmund Spenser composed his narrative poem *The Faerie Queen*, which was dedicated to Elizabeth. In her last years, however, war with Spain led to domestic problems. Poor trading prospects and a series of bad harvests caused much poverty, and property owners protested at the level of taxes. When she died, childless, on 24 March 1603, she brought the line of **TUDOR** Monarchs to an end and the **STUART** reign began with **JAMES VI** and **I**, son of Mary, Queen of Scots, uniting England and Scotland under one **CROWN** for the first time (see **UNION OF THE CROWNS**).

ELIZABETH II (1926-). Queen of the **UNITED KINGDOM** and Head of the **COMMONWEALTH OF NATIONS**, Elizabeth was born on 21 April 1926, the eldest daughter of the **DUKE OF YORK** and the **DUCHESS** of York (later **GEORGE VI** and Queen Elizabeth, the **QUEEN MOTHER**). Educated by Marion Crawford (her governess) and by private tutors, she spent most of her teenage years at Balmoral and **WINDSOR CASTLE** while her mother and father remained in **LONDON** throughout the **SECOND WORLD WAR**. In 1947, she accompanied her parents on an official visit to South Africa, celebrating her 21st birthday in Cape Town and making a broadcast in which she dedicated her life to the service of "our great imperial family".

On her return to Britain, she became engaged to Lieutenant Philip Mountbatten (now **PRINCE PHILIP**), her third cousin and formerly Prince Philip of Greece, whom she had met at Dartmouth Naval College in 1939. The wedding in **WESTMINSTER** Abbey, on 20 November 1947, was in direct contrast to wartime **AUSTER-**

ITY (the Princess had been given an extra hundred clothing coupons for her dress [see **RATIONING**]) and touched the heart of a nation looking forward to a new world of reconstruction and peace. The bridegroom was accorded the rank of Royal Highness and created Prince Philip, Duke of Edinburgh, Earl of Merioneth and Baron Greenwich. Their first child (**PRINCE CHARLES**) was born on 14 November 1948 and their second (**PRINCESS ANNE**) on 15 August 1950. **PRINCE ANDREW** was born on 19 February 1960 and **PRINCE EDWARD** on 10 March 1964.

In 1951, with George VI seriously ill, Princess Elizabeth represented him at the official visits of the Kings of Denmark and Norway. In 1952, she and Prince Philip were at Forest Lodge, Sagana (a wedding present from the people of Kenya), when they heard the news of the King's death and flew back to London. Elizabeth was still only 25, but she was quite willing to assert her independence. When making preparations for her **CORONATION**, on 2 June 1953, she insisted, against the advice of Prime Minister **WINSTON CHURCHILL**, that the event should be televised. As a result, the ceremony was watched by 20 million people. The royal couple then embarked on a series of overseas tours, visiting the West Indies, Australia, New Zealand, Ceylon and Uganda in 1953-54, Norway in 1955, Nigeria and Sweden in 1956 and Portugal, France, Denmark, Canada and the United States in 1957. In 1959, along with U.S. President Dwight D. Eisenhower, the Queen declared the St Lawrence Seaway open.

Since then, there have been many other visits, including an audience with Pope John XIII at the Vatican in 1961, a state visit to Germany in 1965 (the first by a British **MONARCH** since the end of the Second World War) and trips to Brazil and Chile in 1968. In addition the Queen's role as Head of the Commonwealth has taken her abroad on many occasions, particularly in 1977, the year of her Silver Jubilee, when she made a 56,000-mile journey through member states. Her duties to the nations of the Commonwealth are taken seriously. She was, for example, very angry when the United States invaded Grenada (of which she is Head of State) in 1983 without any notification to her of its intentions. Similarly, she was much concerned at the bitterness which became evident when Prime Minister **MARGARET THATCHER** refused to support calls for economic sanctions against South Africa during the 1980s.

As Head of State in the United Kingdom, she has twice had to choose a successor when a Prime Minister resigned. The first occasion was in 1957, when **ANTHONY EDEN** gave up office following the **SUEZ CRISIS**. After canvassing the opinions of members of the **CABINET** and other leading political figures, she asked **HAROLD MACMILLAN** to take over in preference to **RICHARD** (Rab) **BUTLER**, who had deputized when Eden was ill. When MacMillan resigned in 1963 on grounds of ill-health, **ALEX DOUGLAS-HOME** was appointed in his place.

As a result of the spread of television and changes in the attitudes of journalists, the Queen — like all members of the royal family — is constantly in the public eye, and there have been several complaints of intrusion into her privacy. In particular, press speculation about the state of her children's marriages has caused much concern. Also, there have been attempts to reduce the distance between the Monarch and her subjects — the presentation of debutantes no longer takes place, divorcees are allowed into the royal enclosure at Ascot horse racing course and the Queen has agreed to pay tax on her income. In recent years, there has been much criticism of the expense of sustaining a Monarchy and suggestions that the Queen should resign, allowing Prince Charles to become King. The Prince's marital problems, however, have eliminated any question of abdication in the near future, and economies in the **ROYAL HOUSEHOLD** have brought the Monarchy more into line with the financial stringencies of the 1980s and 1990s.

The Queen's major recreational interest is horses. She owns several racehorses, and has visited stud farms in the United States on a number of occasions.

ELIZABETHAN AGE. This term is applied to the reign of Queen **ELIZABETH I** (1558-1603), which followed the **MARIAN RE-ACTION** and ended with successful foreign policies, victory in wars (see, for example, **SPANISH ARMADA**), colonial expansion (particularly at the expense of France, Portugal and Spain), the flourishing literature of the English Renaissance and an ever stronger economy. The established **CHURCH OF ENGLAND** was strengthened, rivals defeated and the great age of exploration was begun, with new trade routes to Africa and the East opened up (see **NORTHWEST PASSAGE**). The cultivation of the 'Gloriana' and 'Good Queen Bess' images, and the growing world status of **ENGLAND**, created a national self-confidence and a belief that this was a truly a glorious age.

EMMET'S RISING, 23 July 1803. A Protestant rising in Dublin (**IRELAND**) proclaimed the Provisional Government of the Irish Republic. It was led by Robert Emmet, who hoped for French aid and attempted to take Dublin Castle, the centre of British rule in the island. The rising failed, and Emmet was hanged and beheaded in September, becoming another martyr to the Irish cause. (See **DESPARD CONSPIRACY**).

ENCLOSURE. During the **AGRICULTURAL REVOLUTION** (and from about 1760, in particular), the process of enclosure turned the separate strip plots of the older **OPEN FIELD SYSTEM** into more manageable compact fields edged by hedges or fences. These could more easily be owned and run as a consolidated plot for crop rotation, drainage and the use of machinery. The process was usually achieved by local agreement (from the 15th century onwards) or by Enclosure Acts (see **ACT OF PARLIAMENT**), which were passed between 1760 and 1793 on a **PARISH** basis. General Enclosure Acts were passed in 1801 and 1837, and the Enclosure Commissioners were established by a similar Act in 1845 to extend coordination nationally.

Enclosures created larger, more extensive agricultural holdings and were the start of the large farm and wealthy landowner system of agriculture now characteristic of Britain compared with its European neighbours. However, they also caused much hardship through the suppression of ancient grazing rights and common activities so Britain gained its more efficient farming system at the expense of the poor villagers and small landowners. Certain historians claim that some landowners pursued enclosure in order to create reserves of cheap labour. Agricultural change was, therefore, closely linked with social change. However, because the open field system never existed in some parts of the country, the effect of the changes varied regionally.

ENGLAND. The largest part of the **BRITISH ISLES** (50,300 square miles, with 47 million population), England was an independent nation until united with **SCOTLAND** in 1707. Its land area approximates to the size of the US state of Alabama. The name is derived from the **ANGLES**, who settled in Britain from the fifth century, and was recorded in the late ninth century as "Englaland".

ENGLISH HERITAGE. The 1983 National Heritage Act (see **ACT OF PARLIAMENT**) gave English Heritage responsibility for maintaining and policing over 400 ancient monuments and historic buildings. Cost-cutting in 1992 led to controversial proposals to hand over control of many sites to **LOCAL GOVERNMENT**.

ENGLISH TRADING COMPANIES. One of the principal means by which the **BRITISH EMPIRE** emerged was through the grant of a royal charter to private trading companies, which then secured areas for the **CROWN** in return for trading privileges and profits. These companies included the **MERCHANTS ADVENTURERS** (founded in 1407), the **MUSCOVY COMPANY** (1555), the **EASTLAND COMPANY** (1579), the Guinea Company (1588), the Levant Company (1592), the Morocco Company (1595), the **EAST INDIA COMPANY** (1600), the **LONDON COMPANY** (1606), the **AFRICAN COMPANY** (1660), the **HUDSON'S BAY COMPANY** (1670) and the Plymouth Company (1696).

ENLIGHTENMENT, AGE OF. The term describes the period of intellectual freedom and cultural development which characterized much of 18th century Europe and has been viewed as a passage into the light of reason out of the darkness of tradition and prejudice. In **ENGLAND**, it began in the 17th century, when the foundations of the age were laid by men such as philosopher **JOHN LOCKE** and scientist **ISAAC NEWTON**. The new values were evident in the world of the arts, with William Blake, Percy Bysshe Shelley and others reflecting the political, religious and educational ideals of the time. Also, some scholars have argued that the new philosophies led to the growth of realism in literature and to the rise of the novel. In architecture, the formal **GEORGIAN** style was created by men such as John Wood and his son (also John Wood), who designed The Circus and Royal Crescent in **BATH**. The liberating movement was even said to have affected enlightened despots such as Frederick the Great of Prussia and Catherine the Great of Russia.

ENTENTE CORDIALE. An Anglo-French diplomatic understanding developed from a 1904 agreement to settle outstanding colonial differences and stand together against a perceived threat from Germany. It was claimed that the French were won over by the charm and personality of King **EDWARD VII** on a state visit to Paris in 1903. The Entente was extended in 1907 to include Russia (thus becoming the **TRIPLE ENTENTE**) and was instrumental in cementing the political and military cooperation alliance in the **FIRST WORLD WAR** against the Axis powers.

ENTENTE POWERS. The term applies to Britain, Russia and France between 1907 and 1917. Cooperation between the three was created by the **TRIPLE ENTENTE**, which followed the **ENTENTE CORDIALE**, and the **ANGLO-RUSSIAN ENTENTE** (particularly after September 1914, when the countries became allies in the **FIRST WORLD WAR**).

EQUAL OPPORTUNITIES COMMISSION. The Commission was created by the 1975 **SEX DISCRIMINATION ACT** (see **ACT OF PARLIAMENT**) to monitor the provisions of that and the **EQUAL PAY ACT** in an attempt to achieve equal rights for all, regardless of marital status or sex.

EQUAL PAY ACT, 1970. This act (see **ACT OF PARLIAMENT**) was intended to ensure that men and women received the same pay for the same work. Operational from 1975, it is monitored by the **EQUAL OPPORTUNITIES COMMISSION** and, though full of loopholes, has been an advance in the struggle for women's rights in Britain (see **SEX DISCRIMINATION ACT**).

ETHELBALD. (See **AETHELBALD**).

ETHELBERT I. (See **AETHELBERT I**).

ETHELFRITH. (See **AETHELFRITH**).

ETHELRED I. (See **AETHELRED I**).

ETHELRED II. (See **AETHELRED II**).

ETHELSTAN. (See **AETHELSTAN**).

ETHELWULF. (See **AETHELWULF**).

EUROPEAN COAL AND STEEL COMMUNITY (ECSC) Formed in 1952, the ECSC was designed to produce a common market in coal and steel, with international control of production. Its cooperative aims make it the earliest manifestation of what later became the **EUROPEAN ECONOMIC COMMUNITY (EEC)**.

EUROPEAN COMMUNITY (EC). The EC was created in 1957 as an organization of west European states formed by the amalgamation of the **EUROPEAN ECONOMIC COMMUNITY (EEC)**, the European Atomic Energy Community (EURATOM) and the **EUROPEAN COAL AND STEEL COMMUNITY (ECSC)**. It is committed to economic and political integration. Initially, Britain declined to participate (see **EUROPEAN FREE TRADE ASSOCIATION [EFTA]**) but applied for entry in 1961 and 1967, only to have the applications vetoed by France. Prime Minister **EDWARD HEATH** took the country into the Community in 1973 and, two years later, when Prime Minister **HAROLD WILSON** held the first national referendum in British history in order to ascertain public support for the move (see **REFERENDA**), 67 per cent of the vote was for continuation of membership.

Always an uneasy grouping for the United Kingdom, with its strong ties to the **COMMONWEALTH OF NATIONS**, its history of rivalry with European neighbours and a strong element of national identity in its psyche, the EC continues to be a subject of domestic debate. Several recent **CONSERVATIVE PARTY** policies have had an antifederalist stance, reflecting the fears of many **TORIES** that European integration implies loss of national sovereignty. However, not everyone in the party agrees with that approach, and divisions over Europe became a major element in events which led to the fall of Prime Minister **MARGARET THATCHER**. Negotiations at **MAASTRICHT** led to the evolution of the EC into the **EUROPEAN UNION (EU)** and the Single European Market, with common customs controls and increased freedom of movement for citizens, came into force in January 1994. (See **EUROPEAN ECONOMIC AREA [EEA]**).

EUROPEAN ECONOMIC AREA (EEA). The EEA was created on 1 January 1994 and linked the **EUROPEAN UNION (EU)** and the **EUROPEAN FREE TRADE ASSOCIATION (EFTA)** into a giant trading bloc, with the intention of incorporating much of EFTA into the EU by 1995. The EEA is the world's largest free trade area, joining Austria, Iceland, Finland, Norway and Sweden to the EU with a combined population of 372 million (compared to 360 million in NAFTA, the North American Free Trade Area comprising the United States of America, Canada and Mexico). The EEA covers banking, insurance, labour and public contracting but not agriculture, and it does not remove customs barriers between the EU and EFTA, nor does it replace existing trading groups.

EUROPEAN ECONOMIC COMMUNITY (EEC). The EEC or Common Market was created in 1957 as an economic association of European states. Technically, it now operates within the **EURO-PEAN COMMUNITY (EC)**, with which it is often mistakenly seen as synonymous, and deals with questions of monetary policy and union, trade and movement of labour and capital.

EUROPEAN FREE TRADE ASSOCIATION (EFTA). Britain was a founder member of EFTA, a customs association of non-members of the **EUROPEAN COMMUNITY (EC)** formed in 1960. It was intended as a rival grouping to the **EUROPEAN ECONOMIC COMMUNITY (EEC)**, unencumbered by that grouping's political implications. Britain left in 1972, when its application to join the EC was accepted. (See **EUROPEAN ECONOMIC AREA [EEA]**).

EUROPEAN MONETARY SYSTEM (EMS). The EMS was created in 1979 when member countries of the **EUROPEAN COMMU-NITY (EC)** fixed their exchange rates to a common calibrated system (known as the ERM or Exchange Rate Mechanism) which, in turn, was related to the ecu or European Currency Unit. The eventual intention was to establish a common currency throughout the EC. Britain joined the ERM in 1990 but was forced, through weak **CURRENCY**, to withdraw in 1992 and subsequently secured opt-out possibilities with respect to the moves towards a single currency.

EUROPEAN UNION (EU). The EU was created when the **MAAST-RICHT TREATY** became effective on 1 November 1993 though most specific clauses operated from January 1994. It traces its roots to the **EUROPEAN COAL AND STEEL COMMUNITY (ECSC)**, which became the **EUROPEAN ECONOMIC COM-MUNITY (EEC)**, which, in turn, became the **EUROPEAN COMMUNITY (EC)**. In 1993, the EC was transformed into the European Union. Its aims include the creation of a **EUROPEAN MONETARY SYSTEM (EMS)**, free cross-border movement for all citizens, a labour market unaffected by national boundaries, minimal customs controls and eventual economic and political union. The EU is distinguished from the EC by the addition of two further areas of cooperation — foreign/security policy and justice/home affairs. (See **EUROPEAN ECONOMIC AREA [EEA]**).

EVESHAM, BATTLE OF, 4 August 1265. At this, the final battle of the **BARONS' WARS**, the 8,000 strong **CROWN** army under

Prince Edward (later **EDWARD I**) defeated the 6,000 strong Barons' force led by **SIMON DE MONTFORT**. De Montfort was killed as Edward took terrible revenge for the events surrounding the **BATTLE OF LEWES** in this confrontation fought in a thunderstorm. It led to the release from captivity of King **HENRY III**, reestablishment of royal authority and the end of De Montfort's rule in **ENGLAND**.

EXCHEQUER. Originally the counting house and financial office of medieval **MONARCH**s, the Exchequer was superseded by the **TREASURY** from the reign of Queen **ELIZABETH I**. (See **CHANCELLOR OF THE EXCHEQUER, CURIA REGIS**).

—F—

FABIAN SOCIETY. The Society was founded in 1884 as a political association committed to gradual and democratic social reform on socialist principles. Essentially a middle class, non-Marxist, intellectual movement with moderate left-wing tendencies, it published many influential tracts on problems of the time and particularly on social reform. Led by **SYDNEY WEBB** and **BEATRICE WEBB**, it reflected the rise of socialist ideals in the late 19th century and was influential in the formation of the **LABOUR PARTY** and the founding of the **LONDON** School of Economics. It included George Bernard Shaw, Annie Besant and, later, **CLEMENT ATTLEE** amongst its members. The name derives from Fabius Maximus, the Roman general in the Punic Wars, who preferred small skirmishes to pitched battles.

FACTORY ACTS. These **ACTS OF PARLIAMENT** were intended to improve factory working conditions and protect employees from danger and excessive demands.

1802: The Health and Morals of Apprentices Act regulated the employment of pauper children in factories to 12 hours a day.

1819: This act banned employment of children under the age of nine years in the **COTTON INDUSTRY**.

1833: This act specified a maximum working week, in textile mills, of 48 hours for children aged 9 to 13 and 68 hours for those 13 to 18, with the introduction of Factory Inspectors. There was to be no night work for those under 18 years of age.

1844: These laws, applying only to textile factories, reduced hours for 8 to 13 year olds to 6.5 per day and those for women to

12 per day. They also provided for machinery protection shields.

<u>1847</u>: Parliament approved a maximum ten-hour day and a 58- hour week for children under 18 and for women.

<u>1850</u> and <u>1853</u>: The opening of textile factories was limited to a maximum of 12 hours a day in order to reduce the abuses of earlier legislation through the employment of the shift system. On Saturdays, work stopped at 2 pm.

<u>1864</u>: The earlier legislation was extended to other industries, such as pottery, and safety legislation enacted for six dangerous industries (including matches and cartridge-making).

<u>1867</u>: All previous legislation was extended to all factories employing 50 people or more.

<u>1874</u>: The minimum working age was raised to 9 years, with children under 14 years prevented from working more than half a day at a time. Further acts extended the provisions and reduced hours.

<u>1961</u>: Consolidated legislation was applied to all factories, warehouses, construction sites and docks.

<u>1974</u>: The Health and Safety at Work Act introduced comprehensive regulations and regulatory mechanisms to cover all those at work in premises above a minimum size of workforce.

FALKLANDS WAR. The Falkland Islands (480 miles from Cape Horn and 300 miles from the Straits of Magellan) had been a British **CROWN COLONY** since 1833, with the United Kingdom claiming sovereignty so that it could protect its trade routes to Australasia. Under United Nations direction, negotiations on the future of the islands had taken place between Britain and Argentina since 1966, but, on 2 April 1982, Argentina (then under the dictatorship of General Leopoldo Galtieri) invaded, capturing the garrison of 18 Royal Marines, seizing South Georgia and declaring sovereignty over "Los Islas Malvinas".

A Task Force set sail from the United Kingdom on 5 April and an exclusion zone of 200 miles was declared around the islands. South Georgia was recaptured on 25 April and, on 2 May, the Argentinean cruiser *Belgrano* was sunk. (This was the former USS *Phoenix*, a light cruiser which had survived Pearl Harbor in 1941 and was a veteran of the **SECOND WORLD WAR** in the Pacific.) Argentinean forces used Exocet missiles with devastating effect, the destroyer *Sheffield* and two British frigates being put out of action. British troops retook Goose Green, on the Falklands mainland, by the end of May and Tumbledown Hill, on the outskirts of Port Stanley (the capital), the following month.

Argentinean forces under Major-General Menendez surrendered on 14 June after the fall of Port Stanley. British dead numbered 255; Argentinean dead were estimated at 650 to 720.

This campaign was waged 8,000 miles away from the United Kingdom and used modern missile technology. Success was never certain, but Britain's professional forces (with US logistic, intelligence and diplomatic support) were decisive against a largely conscript army. Moreover, the victory was seen as a vital element in the continued political strength of **MARGARET THATCHER** at home. After the fighting ended, a policy of Fortress Falklands was adopted and, though signs of some softening of this stance appeared in the 1990s, the islands remain British.

FAMILY DIVISION. One of the three divisions of the **HIGH COURT OF JUSTICE**, the Family Division is headed by a President and hears cases dealing with adoption, wardship, marriage and related matters.

FAMILY PLANNING ACT, 1967. Formally termed the National Health Service (Family Planning) Act of 1967 (see **ACT OF PARLIAMENT**), this legislation allowed local authorities and birth control clinics to provide contraceptive advice and appliances. It was part of the liberalization of British law at a time when attitudes to behaviour were becoming generally more permissive, parallelling the **ABORTION** Act and the **SEXUAL OFFENCES ACT** of the same year.

FARADAY, MICHAEL (1791-1867). The discoverer of electromagnetic induction and formulator of the laws of electrolysis, Faraday had a limited education and no university experience but became an outstanding experimental physicist. He was born to James and Margaret Faraday in Newington (Surrey) on 22 September 1791 and apprenticed to a **LONDON** bookbinder at the age of 14. In 1813, however, he obtained a post as assistant to scientist Humphry Davy at the Royal Institution and, in 1820, made his first significant impact on the research community by discovering two previously unknown chlorides of carbon and a new compound of carbon, iodine and hydrogen. His fame spread the following year when he demonstrated that a wire carrying an electric current produces a circular magnetic field, a finding which opened routeways to the practical application of electromagnetic rotation.

Promoted to director of the laboratory at the Royal Institution in 1825, he continued to investigate the relationships between **ELECTRICITY** and magnetism, introducing the first (albeit simple) dynamo and demonstrating, in 1831, the nature of electromagnetic induction by showing that, when a wire is moved through a magnetic field, an electric current is generated. Shortly afterwards, he was able to convince sceptics that "Electricity, whatever may be its source, is identical in its nature" and that the passage of an electric current through solutions caused changes in their chemical composition. In the 1840s, pursuing a conviction that magnetism and light were connected, he proved that beams of plane-polarized light could be rotated if they were passed through a magnetic field (a phenomenon now known as the Faraday Effect).

Faraday was also an enthusiastic publicist of scientific inquiry with an ability to express complex ideas in simple language. In 1826, he instituted regular Friday evening meetings for members of the Royal Institution and began a series of special Christmas lectures for young people. He died at his home near Hampton Court (Surrey) on 25 August 1867 and is still considered by some scholars to be the greatest of all experimental scientists. The farad (a measure of an object's ability to store electrical charges) is named after him and he appears on the back of the **BANK OF ENGLAND** £10 note.

FASHODA INCIDENT, November 1898. This was the last great colonial confrontation between Britain and France. The French occupation of the British fort at Fashoda, in the Sudan, was met by a strong force of 2,600 men under **HORATIO KITCHENER**, who intended to prevent French control of this vital area on the River Nile. The French, trying to restrict British influence along the river and in Egypt, eventually withdrew without bloodshed and negotiated a deal with **LORD SALISBURY** whereby British interest in Morocco was traded for French interest in Egypt. This conflict persuaded both countries to adopt a more cooperative stance in their colonial policies and laid the foundations for the **ENTENTE CORDIALE**. (See **SUDANESE WARS**).

FATHER OF THE HOUSE. The Member of **PARLIAMENT** who has the longest record of service in the **HOUSE OF COMMONS** without a break is known as the Father of the House. The present holder of the title is **EDWARD HEATH**, who was first elected in 1950.

FAWKES, GUY. (See **GUNPOWDER PLOT**).

FENIANS. The name of this secret society was derived from the old Irish words for warriors or heroes (Fianna) and for one of that island's ancient peoples (Fene). It was founded in New York in 1858 and committed to a republican **IRELAND** to be established by revolution. Funded largely by the expatriate community in the United States of America, it found its strongest support among the working class Catholics in Ireland but was reviled by the Catholic Church. In 1867, its members created disturbances in Chester and in **LONDON**, where, on 13 December, they blew up the Clerkenwell House of Detention in an unsuccessful attempt (though it killed 12 people) to free the activist Richard O'Sullivan Burke. In general, their escapades achieved little. (Their ambitious schemes included an invasion of Canada.)

FERGUSON, SARAH. (See **PRINCE ANDREW**).

FESTIVAL OF BRITAIN, 1951. The Festival was launched to coincide with the centenary of the **GREAT EXHIBITION** of 1851, to focus rejoicing at the victory of the **SECOND WORLD WAR**, to dispel the gloom and **AUSTERITY** of the period and to act as an antidote to the depression of **RATIONING** and shortages of consumer goods. A site on the South Bank of the **RIVER THAMES** in **LONDON** was transformed and a new Royal Festival Hall built as the centre of a major arts complex. A series of exhibits celebrated British architectural, artistic, technological and industrial achievements. King **GEORGE VI** opened the Festival by saying "This is no time for despondency".

FEUDAL SYSTEM. This was a system of landholding whereby the state was run by lords, who had jurisdiction over the people who lived on their land. That land was conferred on the lords by the ruler (the term "feu" meant "free right to land in return for services"). The system originated in the **ANGLO-SAXON** period but is often claimed to have been developed by the **NORMANS**. It relied on military and political control through mutual obligations and dependencies in a strict hierarchical order, which was the basis of the **ORDERS OF CHIVALRY**. Land (known as fief) was granted to the follower (or **VASSAL**), who pledged homage and owed service (often military) or other obligations depending on his level in the hierarchy. The relationship was sealed by an act of homage to the lord, who then granted the land and his protection. Basically, the feudal pyramid was a simple structure with, at the top, the **MONARCH** who granted fiefs to his or her nobles in return for dues (money or service, often of 40 days a year). In turn, the nobles granted **MANOR**s (lesser areas of land) to their **KNIGHT**s in return for dues (usually to provide military assistance). The Knights then granted land to the peasants, either Freemen (including **YEOMEN**), who owned or rented land from the Knight, or **VILLEINS**, who worked the lord's land. Land might be held by tenure through: (1) Chivalry; such as Knight Service or Grand Sergeanty (holding an office of state); (2) Spiritual service; such as Divine Service (performing religious mass) or Frankalmoign (offering prayers for the lord); (3) Socage or Petty Sergeanty (involving personal labour) or Common Socage (involving agricultural service); or (4) Villein tenure. The system of feudal tenure was abolished in **ENGLAND** in 1661. (See **ASSIZE OF ARMS; BASTARD FEUDALISM; COPYHOLD; MILITIA**).

FIELD OF THE CLOTH OF GOLD, June 1520. This meeting at Guines (near **CALAIS**) between **HENRY VIII** of **ENGLAND** and Francis I of France was ostensibly a spectacular Renaissance summit of heads of state, but it was accompanied by such opulent and extravagant banquets as to lead some to question its intentions. Henry needed to ensure continued hostilities between Francis and the Hapsburg's Charles V, as his own military position was so weak, but the meeting was publicly supposed to promote peace between those very protagonists. Its superficiality was underlined by being followed soon afterwards by **THOMAS WOLSEY**'s treaty with Charles against France.

FIFTH MONARCHY MEN. This extremist **PURITAN** sect of the period of the **COMMONWEALTH** and **PROTECTORATE** was particularly strong in the 1650s and believed in the rule of Christ and the Saints. The Fifth Monarchy was supposed to come about after the four ancient monarchies of the Assyrians, Persians, Macedonians and Romans (see Daniel, chapter 2, in the Holy Bible). Its members supported the **BAREBONES PARLIAMENT** and the Commonwealth but became opponents of **OLIVER CROMWELL** and the Protectorate and were suppressed in 1661. Particularly influential in **WALES**, they believed in recourse to violence in order to obtain their goals.

FINANCIAL SECRETARY TO THE TREASURY. This **GOVERNMENT** post is ranked below that of **CHIEF SECRETARY TO THE TREASURY.** In Prime Minister **JOHN MAJOR**'s administrations, the holder has dealt with Inland Revenue matters and **PRIVATIZATION**.

FIRST WORLD WAR, 1914-18. The Great War was fought between the Allied powers, including Britain, and the Central European powers, led by Germany and Austria-Hungary. Britain declared war on Germany on 4 August 1914 following the German invasion of Belgium (with whom the **UNITED KINGDOM** had a defence treaty). Historians have recently reinterpreted the traditional reasoning that alliances were to blame for the war because Britain had several other reasons to wish, at that time, to reduce the power of Germany.

The United Kingdom was the only nation involved in the conflict which did not have a large standing army of trained soldiers so the British Expeditionary Force, which was sent to Belgium to halt the German advance and frustrate the Schlieffen Plan for the taking of Paris, contained fewer than 100,000 men. In the first battle, at Mons, British losses numbered 1,600 dead within nine hours. The British stalled the Germans at the River Marne and, by December 1914, both sides were dug in, with virtually the whole battle line marked by trenches. Barbed wire, new machine guns and atrocious winter weather led to heavy loss of life and very little territorial advance — 60,000 British troops died on the first day of the **BATTLE OF THE SOMME**, for example. Fighting at the **BATTLE OF YPRES** (1915 and 1917), at Passchendaele, at the **BATTLE OF VERDUN** (1916) and at the Battle of Cambrai (1917) failed to achieve a breakthrough. Both sides developed new weapons and methods in attempts to overcome the stalemate — mustard gas, airships (Zeppelins), the British tank and aerial bombardment and reconnaissance, for example. Also the **ROYAL AIR FORCE** was formed in 1918.

The Turkish front (the **MESOPOTAMIAN CAMPAIGN**) was opened in October 1914 and included the ill-fated ANZAC attack at **GALLIPOLI**. At sea, the Germans had better built and better equipped ships, including the new submarines, which inflicted heavy losses on British vessels, necessitating the development of the convoy system. (The **BATTLE OF JUTLAND** was the major naval engagement.) The United States of America entered the war in April 1917, and an armistice was signed on 11

November 1918. **BRITISH EMPIRE** losses amounted to 996,000 dead with over two million wounded.

At a time before shell shock and other disorders were recognized as consequences of battle, during horrendous events and conditions in what was probably the bloodiest conflict ever, some 307 British soldiers were shot for desertion or cowardice and a further 2,700 sentenced but later spared. Given modern knowledge, some authorities believe that many of these men should have been medically treated and argue that those executed should be pardoned. (A campaign designed to achieve that goal began in 1993.)

The war had far-reaching effects at home; the **TRADE UNIONS** gained political weight (helping the rise of the **LABOUR PARTY**), and standards of living improved. The **LIBERAL PARTY** began its decline as a result of the strains of food rationing, arguments about conscription and the rise of working class socialism. The **GOVERNMENT** introduced legislation leading to votes for women (see **SUFFRAGETTES**), better housing (the slogan from **DAVID LLOYD GEORGE** was "homes fit for heroes to live in") and other social improvements in an attempt to rebuild the fabric of the country. Thus began the inexorable drift towards greater interference in everyday life by the state, which also gradually accrued more power over the lives of all citizens, partly because of the experiences of the war and calls that it must not be repeated. (See **ARMISTICE DAY; CONSCRIPTION; ZEEBRUGGE RAID; ZIMMERMAN TELEGRAM**).

FISHERIES. In 1994, the British fishing fleet comprised some 10,300 vessels (including 450 suitable for deep sea work) and provided 59 per cent of the fish consumed in the United Kingdom. Fisheries limits extend to 200 miles from the coast or to a median line halfway between Britain and another coastal state if that is closer. British vessels have exclusive rights to fish within six miles of the United Kingdom's coastline. Since 1983, the industry has been subject to the Common Fisheries Policy of the **EUROPEAN COMMUNITY**, which prescribes catches and periods of fishing. A decommissioning policy, operated by the **GOVERNMENT**, is designed to reduce fleet size in line with catch quotas. Between 1993 and 1995, 297 vessels were scrapped, at a cost of £16.4 million. (See **COD WARS**).

FITZMAURICE, WILLIAM PETTY (1737-1805). **PRIME MIN-**

ISTER from July 1782 until February 1783, Fitzmaurice was born in Dublin on 13 May 1737, the son of John Fitzmaurice (who was created Viscount Fitzmaurice in 1751, Earl of Shelburne in 1753 and Baron Wycombe in 1760). Educated privately and at **OXFORD** University, he initially embarked upon a military career but, in 1760, was elected Member of **PARLIAMENT** for Chipping Wycombe. He was reelected the following year, but, on his father's death in May 1761, when he inherited the family titles, he forfeited his place in the **HOUSE OF COMMONS** and took his seat in the **HOUSE OF LORDS**. In 1762, he turned down the opportunity of office under the **TORIES' JOHN STUART** (Earl of Bute) but accepted the position of First Lord of Trade under his **WHIG** successor, **GEORGE GRENVILLE**, the following year. After a few months, however, he resigned and pledged his support to **WILLIAM PITT THE ELDER**, getting his reward with the post of **SECRETARY OF STATE** after the election of 1766. Two years later, he resigned again, this time following a series of differences with colleagues over policy towards the colonies, and remained out of office until he accepted the position of **HOME SECRETARY** under the **MARQUIS OF ROCKINGHAM** in 1782.

When Rockingham died in July, **GEORGE III** asked Fitzmaurice to form a **GOVERNMENT**. He was popular with the King, but his arrogance had brought him many Parliamentary enemies and his tenure as Prime Minister was limited. The Whig supporters of **GEORGE FOX** refused to serve under him and combined with **LORD FREDERICK NORTH**'s faction to defeat him in February 1783. He was succeeded by a coalition government nominally headed by the **DUKE OF PORTLAND** but that, in turn, was replaced by an administration led by Pitt in December of the same year. This time, when Pitt was appointing his **CABINET**, he omitted Fitzmaurice who, aware of his unpopularity and unwilling to embarrass his friend, accepted the situation and, for his loyalty, was created **MARQUIS** of Lansdowne in 1784. He died in **LONDON** on 7 May 1805.

FIVE BOROUGHS. These were the major **VIKING** settlements in the Midlands of **ENGLAND** under the **DANELAW** — Lincoln, Derby, Nottingham, Stamford and Leicester. They formed a federation with its own laws and were the basis of some later **SHIRE**s.

FIVE KNIGHTS. In 1627, five **KNIGHT**s were imprisoned on the direction of King **CHARLES I** for refusal to pay a forced loan. The judiciary was unable to come to a conclusion on the legality of imprisonment without cause solely on the orders of the **MONARCH**.

FIVE MEMBERS. In 1642, five Members of **PARLIAMENT** who were opponents of **CHARLES I** fled from **WESTMINSTER** into the **CITY OF LONDON** to avoid the troops intent on their **IMPEACHMENT**. Eventually, all five (John Hampden, Sir Arthur Haselrig, Denzil Holles, John Pym and William Strode) returned in triumph after the City had refused to surrender them. The incident united the **HOUSE OF COMMONS**, the **HOUSE OF LORDS** and the City against the King, and was one of the events which led to the **CIVIL WAR**.

FLODDEN, BATTLE OF, 9 September 1513. King James IV of **SCOTLAND** launched a major campaign against **ENGLAND**, supported by the French King, Louis XII, and attempting to exploit King **HENRY VIII**'s absence from the country at the **BATTLE OF THE SPURS**. At the Battle of Flodden, near Berwick in Northumberland, the Earl of Surrey's army defeated and killed James along with an estimated 10,000 Scottish soldiers, three Bishops, nine **EARL**s and 15 **LORD**s. (The dead are the "Flowers o' the Forest" in the haunting Scottish lament.) The English cannon and bowmen had proved decisive. Between 1512 and 1514, Henry VIII was at war with both Scotland and France and, despite this victory, the English **CROWN** was very soon in great financial difficulty. However, the succession of the infant King James V to the throne of Scotland weakened the Scottish position, and French hopes of reviving their traditional alliance with Scotland were dashed.

FOOT, MICHAEL MACKINTOSH (1913-). A distinguished journalist and author, Foot was Leader of the **LABOUR PARTY** between 1980 and 1983. He was born on 23 July 1913, the son of Isaac Foot (a **LIBERAL PARTY** Member of **PARLIAMENT**), and educated at Forres School (Swanage), Leighton Park School (Reading) and **OXFORD** University (where he was President of the Union in 1933). His first attempt to gain a seat in the **HOUSE OF COMMONS** — at Monmouth in 1935 — was unsuccessful so he turned to journalism while he built up his political experience. He was Assistant Editor of *Tribune* (the Labour weekly) (1937-38), Joint Editor (1948-52) and Editor (1955-56). He was also Acting Editor of the **LONDON** *Evening Standard* (1942-44) and a columnist with the *Daily Herald* (1944-64).

In 1945, he was elected MP for Devonport, Plymouth, and represented the **CONSTITUENCY** until 1955. In 1960, he won the Ebbw Vale seat and held it until 1983, when electoral areas were reorganized. From 1983 until 1992, he was MP for Blaenau Gwent. He was **OPPOSITION** Spokesman on the Power and Steel Industries (1970-71) and then on European Affairs (1971-74). Appointed **SECRETARY OF STATE** for Employment following Labour's **GENERAL ELECTION** victory in 1974, he challenged **JAMES CALLAGHAN** for the leadership of the party when **HAROLD WILSON** suddenly resigned as Prime Minister two years later. Foot lost by 176 votes to 137 and had to content himself with the position of Deputy, but Callaghan sweetened the pill by making him **LORD PRESIDENT OF THE COUNCIL** and **LEADER OF THE HOUSE OF COMMONS**, posts which he held until the **CONSERVATIVE PARTY**'s return to power at the 1979 general election.

Callaghan's resignation shortly after that Labour defeat led to another contest for the party leadership, and this time Foot won, defeating **DENNIS HEALEY**, the favourite son of the right wing, by 139 votes to 129. **MARGARET THATCHER**'s camp was delighted, believing that Foot's lack of experience in government and passionate support for nuclear disarmament were considerable weaknesses in their opponents' armoury, whereas Healey, a former Defence Secretary and **CHANCELLOR OF THE EXCHEQUER** with a considerable following in the country, would have been a much more formidable adversary. The 1983 general election proved that belief justified. The Conservatives concentrated on Foot's pacifist views and his support for the **CAMPAIGN FOR NUCLEAR DISARMAMENT**, comparing them with Mrs Thatcher's decisive military response to the Argentine's invasion of the Falkland Islands in 1982 (see **FALKLANDS WAR**). Labour's manifesto did little to help, promising withdrawal from the **COMMON MARKET** and more **NATIONALIZATION** of industry. The result was a **CONSERVATIVE PARTY** majority of 144 seats over all other parties, their biggest margin since 1935. By contrast, Labour's share of the vote — 27.6 per cent — was its lowest since the 1920s. Foot resigned the Leadership three days later and was replaced by Neil Kinnock but remained an MP until his retirement in 1992.

FOOTBALL, ASSOCIATION. The game of football has been played in Britain for centuries under a variety of local rules, often amounting to little more than gang fights and frequently discouraged because it interfered with archery practice. In 1846, representatives of the **PUBLIC SCHOOLS** met in **CAMBRIDGE** to draw up a set of standardized rules. Over the next 17 years, independent clubs emerged and, on 26 October 1863, the Football Association (FA) was established as the ruling body of the sport. (The term 'soccer' is derived from the student slang corruption of the abbreviation for 'Association' as 'Assoc'.) The first FA cup knockout competition was held in 1871 and, in 1885, the association accepted the principle of payments to players. By then, the game had grown as a spectator sport, particularly in northern working class areas, where crowds of 10,000 were not uncommon in the late 19th century. In 1888-89, a Football League was formed, with the 12 strongest clubs playing each other on a home and away basis. There are now four major divisions with a system of promotion and relegation. The season stretches from August until May.

FORESTRY. About 2,380,000 hectares of woodland remain in Britain, with 46 per cent managed by the **FORESTRY COMMISSION** and the rest in private hands. The industry supplies about 13 per cent of home needs and employs around 40,000 workers. During the 1990s, imports of timber cost the UK over £6 billion per annum.

FORESTRY COMMISSION. The commission was set up in 1919 to create forests as part of the strategic war effort after the timber shortages of the **FIRST WORLD WAR**. It now organizes **FORESTRY** education, recreational use of forests and some commercial forestry. In 1994, the **GOVERNMENT** reversed plans for **PRIVATIZATION** of the commission's woodlands but stressed that the organization would be placed on a more businesslike footing.

FORMIGNY, BATTLE OF, 15 April 1450. In this decisive battle of the **HUNDRED YEARS WAR**, the English were defeated by a superior French force as they attempted to relieve the garrison at Caen, where the troops were ill-paid and mutinous. The defeat led to the expulsion of **ENGLAND** from Normandy, leaving **CAL- AIS** as the only English possession in France.

FOUNT OF JUSTICE. Since the days of the **FEUDAL SYSTEM**, the sovereign has been accepted as the ultimate authority in the land and the basis of the laws of the realm. The situation is now only symbolic yet all governments, judges and courts are His or Her Majesty's, and all laws, under the **BRITISH CONSTITU- TION**, are derived from the **CROWN**.

FOUNTAIN OF HONOUR. This allusion to the sovereign stems from his or her role as the sole conferrer of all titles of honour and precedence (see **ORDERS OF CHIVALRY**). In practice, most are awarded on the advice of the **PRIME MINISTER**.

FOX, CHARLES JAMES (1749-1806). An implacable opponent of **GEORGE III**, Fox was the centre of controversy throughout his political career. He was born in **LONDON** on 24 January 1749 and educated at Eton College and **OXFORD** University. His father, Henry Fox (later **BARON** Holland), encouraged him to acquire dissolute habits and, in 1774, paid his gambling debts of £140,000.

He entered **PARLIAMENT** in 1768, representing Midhurst, and two years later was made a Lord of the **ADMIRALTY** but re- signed in February 1772 so that he could oppose the **ROYAL MARRIAGES ACT**. He joined the **GOVERNMENT** again in December, accepting the post of Lord of the **TREASURY**, but George, annoyed by his opposition earlier in the year, accused him of insubordination and dismissed him in February 1774. From that time, Fox pursued a personal vendetta against the King, contend- ing that the **CROWN**'s power was the major reason for Britain's ills. A friend of **EDMUND BURKE**, he soon became the ac- cepted leader of the **WHIGS** in the **HOUSE OF COMMONS**. Fired both by prejudice and by a hatred of oppression, he raged against **FREDERICK NORTH**'s policies towards the American colonies. Following Britain's defeat in the **AMERICAN WAR OF INDEPENDENCE**, North was forced into resignation in March 1782 and Fox became Foreign Secretary in the new admin- istration led by **CHARLES WATSON-WENTWORTH,** Lord Rockingham. However, in early July the **PRIME MINISTER** died and the King invited **WILLIAM PETTY FITZMAURICE**, Earl of Shelburne, to accept the premiership. Fox maintained that the **DUKE OF PORTLAND** was the logical successor, arguing that Rockingham had been Prime Minister because he had been the leader of their political group, not because he was the sovereign's favourite. Failing to get his way, he resigned, maintaining that he objected to the King's attempt to assert his authority.

Fox then allied with North in an attempt to achieve a change of leadership, and, on 2 April, George was forced to submit. Portland became the nominal Prime Minister, with Fox and North as Secretaries of State. The coalition lasted only until December, disintegrating as a result of disagreements over attempts to reform the **EAST INDIA COMPANY** by transferring control of the firm's territories to seven commissioners nominated by Parliament. The **BILL** passed through the Commons but was defeated in the **HOUSE OF LORDS** after the King announced that anyone who voted for it would be considered his enemy. **WILLIAM PITT THE YOUNGER** became Prime Minister after the ensuing election and found Fox a vociferous adversary, criticizing policies on **IRELAND**, on commercial relations with France, on the role of the **PRINCE OF WALES** during the King's period of insanity (1788-89) and on the **CORN LAW** of 1791. Fox also championed the cause of the **FRENCH REVOLUTION** against the arguments of Pitt and Burke and advocated such unpopular measures as religious freedom for Roman Catholics, Parliamentary reform and self-government for Ireland.

When Lord **WILLIAM GRENVILLE** became Prime Minister on Pitt's death in 1806, Fox was made Foreign Secretary once again, his Parliamentary support having increased and the King's animosity having weakened. In June, he persuaded the House of Commons to pass a motion committing it to the abolition of the **SLAVE TRADE** in British colonies, but, by that time, his health was failing. On 13 September, he died at Chiswick and was buried in **WESTMINSTER** Abbey, beside Pitt. The slavery bill was passed the following year.

FRANKPLEDGE. From the **NORMAN** period, householders of a **MANOR** or village were members of a frankpledge, or tithing, whereby all members were made responsible for each other's actions. This simple means of creating law and order fell into disuse with the rise of the **PARISH** and the decline of the manorial system.

FREE COMPANIES. These mercenary groups of soldiers were employed by all sides during the **HUNDRED YEARS WAR**. Drawn from many nations (particularly France, Spain and **ENGLAND**), they caused much disruption, particularly during more peaceful periods of the conflict, which lasted from 1337 until 1453.

FREE SPEECH. The right to free speech in **PARLIAMENT** was claimed by the **SPEAKER** of the **HOUSE OF COMMONS** from 1541 and secured by statute under the **BILL OF RIGHTS** in 1689. It is a privilege which remains one of the planks of parliamentary democracy. MPs are not, for example, subject to the same rules of libel when in the House as they would be outside the chamber.

FREE TRADE. Adam Smith expounded the doctrine of free trade in *The Wealth of Nations* in 1776. International commerce, he argued, should be kept free of restrictive tariffs, monopolies and quotas because, if there was no discrimination in favour of domestic markets, world trade would grow to the benefit of all. Underlying the theory was the notion that nations should specialize in the products they made or grew best, but opponents saw this as particularly dangerous because it would make countries heavily dependent on one another. Despite that criticism, it replaced **MERCANTILISM** as the dominant economic ideology of the 1700s and, in the 19th century, was embraced by the new industrialists seeking markets and the poor who wanted an end to the **CORN LAWS**. **WILLIAM PITT THE YOUNGER**, **ROBERT PEEL** and **WILLIAM GLADSTONE** all became devotees (see **ANTI-CORN LAW LEAGUE; NAVIGATION ACTS**), as did the population of Lancashire, where the **COTTON INDUSTRY** was concentrated. For a while, the philosophy served that industry well but the United States opposed it (as did the traditional ruling classes, whose wealth lay in land) and, as recession struck towards the end of the century, the trade barriers went up again, with even India attempting to defend itself against imports of British cotton. George Bernard Shaw described it as "heart-breaking nonsense", and the United Kingdom abandoned the principle in 1932, preferring the advantages of **IMPERIAL PREFERENCE** trade.

It returned to favour after the **SECOND WORLD WAR** as the proportion of the country's wealth derived from exports grew and it became clear that industrial expansion was largely a result of tariff reductions. Free trade is now an element of **EUROPEAN**

UNION (EU) policy. In the 1970s and 1980s, proponents cited the development of Hong Kong as evidence of the value of free trade, but the voices of the environmental movement have cast powerful arguments against the principle, arguing that it leads to unsustainable growth.

FREEHOLD. This form of land tenure gives virtually absolute or outright ownership of land. Under the FEUDAL SYSTEM, it was achieved by virtue of KNIGHT service or Socage (rights to land in return for agreement to perform specific services for a lord). Unfree tenures, such as COPYHOLD, were converted to freehold in 1922.

FRENCH REVOLUTION. In 1789, a mob stormed the Bastille in Paris and, by 1793, the French King (Louis XVI) had been executed, with France becoming a republic. In general, the Revolution was supported in Britain — WILLIAM PITT THE YOUNGER saw it as weakening France in Europe and the colonies — but the establishment (the TORIES and the WHIGS) feared the spread of unrest, particularly after learning of savage summary trials and executions and of the Edict of Fraternity (1792), whereby the French called on the working classes throughout Europe to rise up in rebellion against the rich. There was no uprising in Britain, but, in the long term, the revolution was certainly a factor in the push for PARLIAMENTARY REFORM and in the rise of popular radicalism and class consciousness among working people.

FRONT BENCH. In the HOUSE OF COMMONS and the HOUSE OF LORDS, Members of PARLIAMENT sit with others of the same political party and face their opponents across the floor of the House. The leading members of each party sit at the front of their group and are thus known as the Front Bench. (See BACK-BENCHER, CROSS BENCHER).

—G—

GAG ACTS. (See SIX ACTS).

GAITSKELL, HUGH (1906-63). Leader of the LABOUR PARTY from 1955 until 1963, Gaitskell was born in LONDON on 9 April 1906, the younger son of Arthur Gaitskell of the Indian Civil

Service and his wife, Adelaide (daughter of George Jamieson, who had been British Consul-General in Shanghai, China). He was educated at Winchester School and **OXFORD** University, gaining a first class honours degree in philosophy, politics and economics in 1927. Initially, he set out on a career in **EDUCA-TION**, organizing extramural classes in Nottingham (1927-28) then moving to London University as a lecturer in political economy. By the time the **SECOND WORLD WAR** had broken out in 1939, he had been promoted to Reader, but he was then persuaded by Hugh Dalton, a former university colleague, to forsake academic life for the civil service, and, throughout the conflict, he worked in the Ministry of Economic Warfare and the Board of Trade.

Gaitskell had been involved in politics while he was at Oxford, leaning towards the Labour Party but developing his own philosophy that socialism did not necessarily imply **NATION-ALIZATION** and that the true aim of a Labour **GOVERNMENT** should be the implementation of economic and social reforms which would benefit all of society. He had supported the **GEN-ERAL STRIKE** of 1926 and stood, unsuccessfully, as the Labour candidate for Chatham in 1935. As peace neared, he turned back to active politics and, in the landslide Labour victory of 1945, was elected Member of **PARLIAMENT** for Leeds South, a **CON-STITUENCY** he represented for the rest of his life. In 1947, **CLEMENT ATTLEE** made him **MINISTER** of Fuel and Power and, in 1950, **MINISTER OF STATE** for Economic Affairs. Later that year, Sir **STAFFORD CRIPPS** resigned his post as **CHANCELLOR OF THE EXCHEQUER** because of illness and Gaitskell replaced him. In his first **BUDGET**, the following spring, he introduced charges for dentures and spectacles (previously provided free under the **NATIONAL HEALTH SERVICE**) and provoked the resignation of Aneurin Bevan and **HAROLD WILSON**, his **CABINET** colleagues. After Labour's defeat at the 1951 **GENERAL ELECTION**, he became an articulate critic of government policy and so impressed his fellow socialists that, in 1955, he was chosen to succeed Attlee as Leader of the Labour Party.

Defeat at the 1959 general election was a major blow. Gaitskell had expected to win and was convinced that a commitment to nationalization, coupled with public squabbles between the party's right and left wings, had been responsible for the lack of success. He failed, however, to convince his colleagues that

Clause IV of the party's Constitution, which declared that establishment of "common ownership of the means of production" was one principal objective of a Labour Government, should be changed. The party conference at Scarborough in 1960 produced further problems when, despite advice from the National Executive, delegates voted for a policy of unilateral nuclear disarmament. Now heading a demoralized and divided Parliamentary **OPPOSITION**, Gaitskell worked ceaselessly to draw the disparate groups together and effected a reversal of the disarmament policy at the Blackpool conference the following year. In 1962, he led Labour's opposition to entry to the **COMMON MARKET** and, as the **CONSERVATIVE PARTY**'s fortunes waned, was increasingly expected to be the country's next **PRIME MINISTER**. However, he died suddenly in London on 18 January 1963, and was replaced by Harold Wilson, who took Labour on to victory at the 1964 general election.

Gaitskell presented his arguments with clinical logic and was often considered to be a cold and unemotional man, but he enjoyed an active social life. He was awarded the CBE in 1945 and received an honorary doctorate from Oxford University in 1958. (See **BUTSKELLISM**).

GALLIPOLI EXPEDITION, 25 April 1915-9 January 1916. This was a major disaster during the **MESOPOTAMIAN CAMPAIGN** of the **FIRST WORLD WAR**. A plan was devised to take the Dardanelles (between the Mediterranean and Black Seas) in order to open up communications with the Russians, launch a second front and break the trench warfare deadlock by forcing Turkey out of the war. It was audacious in design but failed largely through poor preparation, indecision, belief among generals that it was really the western front that would be decisive, and bad luck. Heatstroke, dysentery, dehydration and night frostbite all took their toll, and casualty numbers soared — over half the British force of 400,000 was killed or wounded and Turkish casualties were estimated at 500,000. The plan had been to exploit Ottoman weakness by taking the mountainous peninsula at Gallipoli and then pushing north to capture Constantinople by land, but the conflict proved to be an ominous precursor for what followed in the rest of the war: bloody, grinding trench warfare for little gain and with immense suffering and waste of human life. **WINSTON CHURCHILL** resigned from the **CABINET** after being made the scapegoat for the debacle.

GARDEN CITIES. During the 19th century, there were several proposals to create small, self-contained settlements of about 30,000 people with spacious and high-quality environments. Typical of these was Ebenezer Howard's *A Peaceful Path to Social Reform*, published in 1898 and later retitled *Garden Cities of Tomorrow*. Howard advocated the establishment of satellite towns, with rural and urban characteristics, away from large centres of congestion. The first built to his design was Letchworth Garden City (1903). Welwyn Garden City followed in 1919, and, together, they were the models for the later **NEW TOWNS**.

GARTER, ORDER OF THE. The most ancient of the **ORDERS OF CHIVALRY**, the Order of the Garter is said to be based on the **ARTHUR**ian legends of the Round Table. It was created in 1348 by King **EDWARD III**, making this the oldest **KNIGHT**hood in Europe. There is a lovely story that the blue garter worn by members of the Order originated with the loss of a garter by Joan of **KENT** (later, wife to **EDWARD THE BLACK PRINCE**) at a ball. The missing item was returned by King Edward III with the words "honi soit qui mal y pense" (evil to him who evil thinks), which became the Order's motto.

GAS. Town gas was produced from the 19th century and, on 28 January 1807, Pall Mall in **LONDON** become the first street to be illuminated by gaslight. The first company in London selling supplies to the public — the Gas, Light and Coke Company — began operations in 1812. Natural gas was first discovered at Dalkeith, in 1919, during exploration for oil supplies to support the country's forces in the **FIRST WORLD WAR**. Oil exploration in Eskdale in 1936 also found gas, and exploitation began in 1959. The industry was nationalized in 1949 (see **NATIONALIZATION**) and was later renamed the British Gas Corporation. In 1965, the first commercial deposits in the North Sea were found, and, by the 1970s, these had supplanted town gas in public supplies. By 1994, there were about 50 gasfields operating in the British sector of the North Sea and these produced over 69,960 million cubic metres of gas, making the United Kingdom the world's fifth largest producer. British Gas plc was formed when the industry was privatized in 1986 (see **PRIVATIZATION**) and expanded in the 1990s as a result of the so-called 'dash for gas', when **ELECTRICITY** generators converted to gas fired power stations as that fuel became more economic than **COAL** — a policy which became increasingly controversial as the **GOVERNMENT** unveiled plans to close many coal mines.

GASCOYNE-CECIL, ROBERT ARTHUR TALBOT (1830-1903). The last **PRIME MINISTER** to govern Britain from the **HOUSE OF LORDS**, Gascoyne-Cecil was born in Hatfield House (Hertfordshire) on 3 February 1830, the third son of James, Marquess of Salisbury, and Frances Gascoyne (his first wife). As Lord Robert Cecil, he was educated at Eton College and **OXFORD** University but left after two years with the honorary distinction of a fourth class degree in mathematics.

He set off on a world tour in 1851, returned in May 1853, and three months later became Member of **PARLIAMENT** for Stamford. His first decade in the **HOUSE OF COMMONS** was undistinguished — he wrote anonymously for the *Quarterly Review* and commented impartially on the political scene but had little direct impact on **GOVERNMENT** until 1864, when he began to show strong support for **CONSERVATIVE PARTY** policies. In 1866, he was appointed **SECRETARY OF STATE** for India by the **EARL OF DERBY** but resigned the following year because he disagreed with proposals for **PARLIAMENTARY REFORM**.

He took his seat in the **HOUSE OF LORDS** when his father died in 1868 and was persuaded by **BENJAMIN DISRAELI** to return to his India post in 1874. In 1878, he became Foreign Secretary and immediately intervened in the crisis in eastern Europe, where Turkey had been forced to place her Balkan territories under Russian suzerainty. Salisbury sent a despatch (later known as *The Salisbury Circular*) to all the major powers, insisting that the issue should be discussed at a conference of European states. As a result, the **CONGRESS OF BERLIN** was convened, and, although it did not completely resolve the political problems in the region, it greatly enhanced Salisbury's reputation.

The **LIBERAL PARTY** victory at the 1880 **GENERAL ELECTION** took **WILLIAM GLADSTONE** to **DOWNING STREET**, but, in June 1885, he resigned, following defeat in a vote on the **BUDGET**, and Queen **VICTORIA** asked Salisbury to form an administration. He accepted unwillingly, knowing that he could only govern if he was assured of support by MPs who advocated **HOME RULE** for **IRELAND**. He survived for only seven months because Gladstone promised that if he returned to power he would agree to Irish independence but became Prime Minister for a second time in July 1886, when the Liberal Home Rule **BILL** was voted down in the Commons. This time he retained power for seven years, standing aloof from European alliances (a policy which came to be known as **SPLENDID ISOLATION**) and aggressively adding some six million square miles to the **BRITISH EMPIRE**, particularly in Africa. Domestic affairs received less attention, but, even so, the **LOCAL GOVERNMENT** Act of 1888 (see **ACT OF PARLIAMENT**) had considerable repercussions, establishing **COUNTY** councils in **ENGLAND** and **WALES**, and the Free **EDUCATION** Act of 1891 introduced the principle that central government, not parents, would fund schools.

The 1892 election brought defeat, but, in 1895, the Conservatives again gained a working majority and Salisbury became Prime Minister for the third time. Once more, foreign policy dominated his agenda. He proposed a 'Concert of Europe' which would maintain peace through the cooperation of the great powers, achieved American agreement to the formation of a committee to adjudicate between Great Britain and the United States in a dispute over the location of the boundary between British Guiana and Venezuela and embroiled the country in the **BOER WAR**. Exhausted by travel and the pressures of office, he resigned in 1902 after signing a peace treaty with the Boers and died in Hatfield on 22 August the following year.

In addition to his political achievements, Salisbury was responsible for a number of advances in the sciences and particularly in practical studies of **ELECTRICITY**. (Hatfield House was the first private residence in the country to have electric lighting.) He was appointed Chancellor of Oxford University in 1869 and, although a modest man, was proud of that recognition of his scholarship.

He was succeeded as Prime Minister by his nephew, **ARTHUR BALFOUR**.

GAUNT, JOHN OF. (See **JOHN OF GAUNT**).

GENERAL ELECTION. Under the **PARLIAMENT ACT** of 1911 (see **ACT OF PARLIAMENT**), the maximum term of a **PARLIAMENT** is set at five years, after which time (or before if the **GOVERNMENT** is defeated or loses its majority, or if the **PRIME MINISTER** requests it) a General Election must be held. All Members of **PARLIAMENT** stand down, and all 651 constituencies elect a new representative. People seeking election must pay a fee of £500 and produce the signatures of ten supporters who are registered electors in the **CONSTITUENCY**. Certain individuals are ineligible to stand, notably undischarged bankrupts, members of the **HOUSE OF LORDS**, prisoners with sentences of over one year, the clergy, judges and members of the **POLICE** or armed forces. Elections are held on a single day using a first-past-the-post system — the MP is elected on a simple majority of votes cast. There are strict rules on the conduct and amounts to be spent on election campaigns — in Britain, candidates 'stand for election' in a more muted and less glitzy campaign than is common in the United States of America, where candidates 'run for election' — a commentary, perhaps, on the differing national characters of the two countries. (See **BY-ELECTION; ELECTORAL SYSTEM**).

GENERAL STRIKE, May 1926. The economic depression of the 1920s was particularly felt in the staple heavy industries and the areas associated with them. There were several reasons for the malaise — the declining competitiveness of British industry, **OIL** and **GAS** replacing **COAL** and leading to unemployment in the mines and the 1925 return to the **GOLD STANDARD** (which reduced imports). The **TRADES UNION CONGRESS (TUC)** called a General Strike on 3 May 1926 in support of the coal miners, who were already on strike and shouting the catchphrase, "Not a penny off the pay, not a minute on the day". Key sectors of the economy (such as transport, **ELECTRICITY**, the **IRON INDUSTRY**, the **STEEL INDUSTRY** and **PRINTING**) were brought to a halt. The **GOVERNMENT** enlisted the help of middle-class volunteer strikebreakers and declared a state of emergency in order to utilize troops.

The strike eventually collapsed, with the imprisonment of over 1,000 workers. Its legacy included vindictive antiunion legislation, including the 1927 Trades Disputes Act (see **ACT OF PARLIAMENT**), which made it illegal for strikes to occur in industries other than the one at the heart of the dispute. (In later years, these became known as secondary strikes.) As a failure, it was instrumental in increasing support for more moderate **TRADE UNION** leadership, but it caused disillusionment with the TUC and an overall decline in the membership of unions. The coal miners held out on strike for five months after the collapse of the general strike. (See **GREAT DEPRESSION**).

GENERAL SYNOD. This governing body of the **CHURCH OF ENGLAND** was established in 1970, replacing the Church Assembly and giving members of the Church a greater voice in decision-making processes.

GENTRY. Members of the gentry had a social rank just above **YEOMAN** but below the **PEERAGE** and were usually men whose income was derived from nonmanual sources (hence the term "landed gentry").

GEORGE I (1660-1727). When the last of Queen **ANNE**'s 17 children died in 1700, provision had to be made for the continuation of the British **MONARCH**y. Under the terms of the 1701 **ACT OF SETTLEMENT** (see **ACT OF PARLIAMENT**), it was vested in Sophia (wife of Ernest Augustus, Elector of Hanover), who was the nearest Protestant relative of the **STUARTS** (Sophia was the fifth — and only Protestant — daughter of Elizabeth of Bohemia, sole daughter of **JAMES VI and I**). Sophia herself died on 8 June 1714 and Anne on 1 August, leaving George — Sophia's eldest son — as successor to the throne, the first **HANOVERIAN** Monarch. King of Great Britain from 1714 until 1727, he was born in Hanover on 28 March 1660. By his marriage to his cousin, Sophia Dorothea, in 1682, he united the Hanoverian possessions of the House of Brunswick and became one of the most important Princes in Germany.

An unpopular ruler who had no taste for the trappings of royalty, he disliked the British, and they reciprocated. Moreover, although he had considerable knowledge of European diplomacy, he preferred to spend his time with mistresses and friends rather than in the corridors of power. His relationship with his son (later **GEORGE II**) was stormy. Primarily because of their frequent rows, the King eventually gave up attending meetings of the **CABINET** (where sovereign and prince had to sit at the same table), and took to meeting his **MINISTER**s individually. Business was conducted in French because George's command of English was very limited.

The **SOUTH SEA BUBBLE** fiasco of 1720 was a turning point both for the King and for his advisers. George, his mistresses and several supporters had invested in South Sea funds and participated in financial transactions which were, at best, dishonourable. The scandal — and financial crisis which followed — placed the Hanover dynasty in jeopardy, but the political skill of

ROBERT WALPOLE ensured that the danger was averted. George had no affection for Walpole but the incident left him little option other than to increase his authority. Walpole and his colleague, Lord Townshend, used the new power to replace political opponents with supporters and, by 1724, the King had revised his views to such an extent that he relied heavily on their advice and judgement. George died of apoplexy on 11 June 1727, while on his way to Hanover, and was succeeded by his son.

GEORGE II (1683-1760). The only son of **GEORGE I** and Sophia Dorothea, George was King of Great Britain from 1727 until 1760. He was born in Hanover on 10 November 1683 and, in 1705, married Caroline of Ansbach, who greatly influenced his political decisions. He came to Britain with his father in 1714, but the relationship was charged with animosity. When George I returned to Hanover in 1716, he refused to make his son **REGENT** in his absence and, the following year, a quarrel over family matters led to the Prince being placed under house arrest. The ill feeling was such that, when George succeeded to the throne in 1727, it was expected that he would replace all of the **MINISTER**s who had advised his father. In practice, he listened to his wife's counsel and retained some of the more able, including **ROBERT WALPOLE**.

His effectiveness as a **MONARCH**, however, was reduced by his lack of self-confidence and his limited intellect. He had great interest in military matters and organized his life with appropriate precision. As a soldier, he showed considerable courage, fighting with distinction at the **BATTLE OF OUDENARDE** in 1708 and, in 1743, at the **BATTLE OF DETTINGEN**, becoming the last British King to lead his troops into battle. He took great interest in the day-to-day business of foreign and domestic politics but preferred his ministers take the responsibility for decision making, thus strengthening the position of royal advisers. He supported Walpole's attempts to reform national finances and to refrain from intervention in foreign wars, honouring him with a pension and a title when he resigned in 1742. George then turned to Lord Carteret, who had considerable knowledge of European affairs. For two years, they pursued a foreign policy with no consideration of the views of others. Inevitably, criticism mounted, led by **WILLIAM PITT THE ELDER**, and, when Carteret decided to bring **HANOVERIAN** soldiers into the **BRITISH ARMY**, it became so strong that the King had to dismiss him. George despised Pitt and did his utmost to keep him out of office, but ultimately, faced with the possibility of a mass resignation of his ministers, he relented and, for the remaining years of his reign, Pitt dominated the political scene. As the King aged, he increasingly left political matters to his **GOVERNMENT**, who pursued an aggressive foreign policy, gaining victories and colonies in North America, the Caribbean, Africa, India and Europe. George died suddenly in **LONDON** on 25 October 1760 and was succeeded by his grandson **GEORGE III**, his eldest son (Frederick) having predeceased him in 1751.

GEORGE III (1738-1820). During a reign spanning 60 years — one of the longest in British history — George III saw his country become the world's premier industrial nation (see **INDUSTRIAL REVOLUTION**). The son of Frederick Louis, **PRINCE OF WALES**, and Princess Augusta of Saxe-Gotha, he was born in **LONDON** on 4 June 1738, the first of the **HANOVERIAN MONARCH**s to have a birthplace in **ENGLAND**. His father died when he was 12, leaving him heir to the throne, and he succeeded his grandfather, **GEORGE II**, in 1760, inheriting a **GOVERNMENT** riven by political differences and lacking an effective civil service.

He disliked the two **WHIG** leaders — **WILLIAM PITT THE ELDER** and **THOMAS PELHAM HOLLES**, Duke of Newcastle — so he replaced them with Tory friends (see **TORIES**), a policy which ensured that he gained increasing power over decisionmaking but which offended public opinion and led to much criticism in **PARLIAMENT** by a radical **OPPOSITION** led by **JOHN WILKES**. The **STAMP ACT** (pushed through, in 1765, despite Pitt's objections) added to his problems, worsening relations between Britain and its American colonies. In 1770, however, George found a Prime Minister — **LORD FREDERICK NORTH** — whom he could trust and who could command the support of the **HOUSE OF COMMONS**. The result was 12 years of political stability, during which the most critical issue was North America. George insisted that the British Parliament had supremacy over the colonies and, when war broke out in 1775, argued that, if disobedience was seen to prosper, **IRELAND** would also rise against the **CROWN**. By 1779, he had changed his tune, maintaining that the war was impossible to justify on economic grounds but still had to be fought (see **AMERICAN WAR OF INDEPENDENCE**).

The loss of the colonies in 1781 inflamed public opinion against both the King and Lord North, and the Prime Minister's credibility suffered further when, two years later, he allied with **CHARLES JAMES FOX** to produce a plan for the reform of the **EAST INDIA COMPANY**, a scheme which aroused fears that the two men intended to shore up their powerful positions by controlling eastern patronage. In an unusually authoritative show of monarchical initiative, George responded by announcing that anyone who supported the plan in the **HOUSE OF LORDS** would be considered an enemy of the King. The **BILL** failed and North resigned, to be replaced by **WILLIAM PITT THE YOUNGER.** There were no further demonstrations of royal power, however, and gradually Pitt asserted his authority whilst George's influence declined.

In the autumn of 1788, the King suffered a prolonged bout of mental illness and the attack caused a Parliamentary crisis over whether or not the **PRINCE OF WALES** (later **GEORGE IV**) should be made **REGENT**. The Prince, who supported the opposition faction led by Fox, did not help matters by ridiculing his father in public but George recovered early in 1789 and the crisis was averted. During the last decade of the century, he increasingly approved of Pitt's leadership and concerned himself more with details than with the main thrust of policy. George became more popular than at any other period in his reign, but he was ageing and the will to use his power was lacking until it was roused by Pitt's Irish policies. The Prime Minister believed that emancipation of Roman Catholics was essential if rebellion in Ireland was to be stopped but the King felt that such a reform was undesirable and eventually Pitt resigned. George opposed further attempts to reduce the severity of the laws against Catholics in 1806-7 but, by 1810, he was blind and permanently insane. In 1811, Parliament appointed the Prince of Wales as Regent and decreed that the Queen should have custody of her husband. He died at **WINDSOR CASTLE** on 29 January 1820.

GEORGE IV (1762-1830). The eldest son of **GEORGE III** and Queen Charlotte, George was born in St James's Palace (**LONDON**) on 12 August 1762. As a young man, he demonstrated a considerable ability as a linguist, but he also had a pronounced hedonistic streak; while still a teenager he admitted to being "rather too fond of women and wine". He had several mistresses before he eventually fell in love with Maria Anne Fitzherbert, an attractive and twice-widowed Roman Catholic. She refused to become his paramour so the couple were married secretly on 15 December 1785. The match was illegal under the terms of the 1772 Royal Marriage Act (see **ACT OF PARLIAMENT**), which prohibited members of the royal family under the age of 25 from marrying without the **MONARCH**'s consent. Also, the **ACT OF SETTLE-MENT** (1701) stipulated that an heir to the throne who married a Catholic lost the right to the succession. Two years later, however, George abandoned Mrs Fitzherbert, having fallen under the spell of Lady Jersey, wife of his Master of Horse. Despite that attachment, he agreed to marry his cousin, Caroline, daughter of the Duke of Brunswick and George III's sister Augusta — an arrangement which the **PRINCE OF WALES** accepted in order to induce Parliament to pay his considerable personal debts. The wedding was held in April 1795, and, the following January, Caroline gave birth to a daughter (Charlotte). But the match had been one of convenience rather than love, and a few weeks later the couple separated.

In 1810, George III became permanently insane and, the following year, his son was named as **REGENT**. By the time his father died, on 29 January 1820, the Prince had assumed all the trappings of sovereign. Caroline, however, wanted her share of those trappings. In June 1820, she returned to Britain after spending six years in Italy, but George succeeded in having her excluded from his **CORONATION** and encouraged the **EARL OF LIVER-POOL**, the **PRIME MINISTER**, to introduce a **BILL** designed to dissolve the marriage and deprive her of her title. Realizing that he could never raise a **HOUSE OF COMMONS** majority for the legislation, Liverpool eventually abandoned the attempt but arranged for Caroline to receive a maintenance grant from Parliament. She died soon afterward, on 7 August 1821, relieving the King of a major problem. Enormously unpopular with the British people because of his reputation for extravagance and promiscuous living, he inflamed political opponents through his opposition to **PARLIAMENTARY REFORM** and emancipation for Roman Catholics. He was, however, unable to prevent the **GOVERN-MENT** from conceding many of the Catholic claims in 1829.

He died at **WINDSOR CASTLE** on 26 June 1830, unlamented by his country. In its obituary, *The Times* reported that "There never was an individual less regretted by his fellows than this deceased king". A man of considerable intelligence and an acknowledged patron of the arts (he had supported architect John

Nash and recognized Walter Scott's literary genius with a **BARONET**cy, for example), he was unable to control the coarser elements of his personality and eventually alienated most of his acquaintances and Government **MINISTER**s. He was succeeded by his brother William, Duke of Clarence (later **WILLIAM IV**), because Charlotte (his only legitimate child) died in 1817. (See **GEORGE BRYAN BRUMMELL**).

GEORGE V (1865-1936). The second son of Edward, **PRINCE OF WALES** (later **EDWARD VII**), and Princess Alexandra of Denmark, George was born in **LONDON** on 3 June 1865. He was not expected to succeed to the throne and was destined for a naval career, beginning service as a cadet in 1877. He had reached the rank of Commander when, in 1892, his elder brother (the **DUKE** of Clarence and Avondale) died of pneumonia and he became heir. That same year, he was created **DUKE OF YORK**, and, in 1893, he married Princess **MARY OF TECK**, who had been his brother's fiancee. In 1901, he became Duke of Cornwall and **PRINCE OF WALES**. Over the next nine years, he made several visits to territories of the **BRITISH EMPIRE**, including Australia (where he opened the first Parliament), South Africa, Canada and India.

He became King when his father died on 6 May 1910 and inherited a constitutional crisis as well as a throne. The **HOUSE OF LORDS**, with its **CONSERVATIVE PARTY** majority, had rejected the **LIBERAL PARTY**'s **BUDGET** in 1909 — an unprecedented event — and the Liberals were seeking legislation to curb the powers of the upper house. George agreed, under pressure, to create the Liberal peers (see **PEERAGE**) necessary to ensure the **BILL**'s passage, but, after a **GENERAL ELECTION** in December 1910, the **GOVERNMENT** was returned to power and the Lords accepted the decision of the people so the King was never required to keep his promise. The arguments about **HOME RULE** for **IRELAND** also rumbled on until 1914, when the outbreak of the **FIRST WORLD WAR** interrupted a series of all-party discussions called by the King.

During the War, the King and Queen made numerous visits throughout Britain and to allied forces on the front line in France and Belgium, raising the morale of troops and civilians and earning the respect of the people. George's understanding of social conditions was also evident during the **GENERAL STRIKE** of 1926, when he wrote several times to Prime Minister **STANLEY**

BALDWIN, asking him to take steps to alleviate the problems caused by poverty and unemployment. By that time, the Irish Free State had gained its independence but other difficulties for the **MONARCH** arose both at home and abroad. **STERLING** collapsed in 1931, causing a financial crisis and bringing the Government of **RAMSAY MACDONALD** to its knees. The King intervened and was instrumental in establishing a coalition administration involving the **LABOUR PARTY**, the Conservatives and the Liberals. Territories of the Empire were becoming restless, claiming their right to be independent of Britain — a call which was reflected in the creation of the British **COMMONWEALTH OF NATIONS** in 1931. In May 1935, George celebrated his silver jubilee, with great crowds gathering outside **BUCKINGHAM PALACE**. He died of influenza at Sandringham on 20 January the following year and was buried at Windsor.

GEORGE VI (1895-1952). The younger son of **GEORGE V** and Queen **MARY OF TECK**, and (like his father) not expected to be King, George was born at Sandringham on 14 December 1895. He entered the Royal Naval College at Osborne in 1909 and transferred to Dartmouth Naval College in 1911. During the **FIRST WORLD WAR**, he was frequently affected by bouts of illness but took part in the **BATTLE OF JUTLAND** in 1916. In 1918, he was sent to France with the Royal Naval Air Service and became the first member of the royal family to gain his pilot's licence. In 1919, he entered **CAMBRIDGE** University and, in 1920, was created Duke of York, Earl of Inverness and Baron Killarney, taking his seat in the **HOUSE OF LORDS**. From that point, he developed an interest in the social conditions of his people and especially of industrial workers and their families, acting as President of the Royal Welfare Association and establishing camps where boys of all social classes could meet. In 1923, he married **LADY ELIZABETH BOWES-LYON**, becoming the first Prince of royal blood to marry a commoner since **GEORGE III** in 1761. Their first child, Princess Elizabeth (now Queen **ELIZABETH II**) was born in 1926 and their second, Princess **MARGARET ROSE**, in 1930.

George V died on 20 January 1936 and was succeeded by his eldest son as **EDWARD VIII**. However, Edward abdicated on 11 December of the same year and George became King. The early part of the reign was clouded by growing German aggression but the King and Queen visited France in 1938 and Canada and the

United States of America the following year. (As a result of the visit to the United States, George developed a close friendship with US President Franklin D. Roosevelt.) The King favoured a policy of appeasing Hitler, but, after the **SECOND WORLD WAR** broke out, the royal couple earned much respect by refusing to leave **BUCKINGHAM PALACE** throughout the **BLITZ**, by visiting munitions factories and other establishments around the country and by meeting the troops in France, North Africa, Italy and the Low Countries. After the war ended, George was disappointed to see **WINSTON CHURCHILL** defeated at the 1945 **GENERAL ELECTION**, but he was not against the principles of the reforms advocated by the new **LABOUR PARTY** government and worked well with Prime Minister **CLEMENT ATTLEE**. In 1947, he relinquished the title of Emperor of India, and, in 1949, India, along with Australia, Canada, Ceylon, New Zealand, Pakistan, South Africa and the United Kingdom recognized the King as head of the **COMMONWEALTH OF NATIONS**. By that time, George was seriously ill, initially with arteriosclerosis and later with lung cancer. He died, following a heart attack, in the early morning of 6 February 1952 and was buried at Windsor.

GEORGE, ST. The patron saint of **ENGLAND**, George was a Christian knight born near Cappadocia in Italy towards the end of the third century. From the sixth century, stories of his prowess as a warrior became widespread, and, during the late 12th century, tales of his bravery in rescuing a young woman from a dragon were told throughout much of Europe. The legends say that, while out riding, he visited the city of Sylene, which was situated near a marsh. The population of the city lived in fear of a dragon, which had set up home in the swamp, and fed it with two sheep each day in order to stop it venturing closer to their homes. When the supply of sheep was exhausted, they decided to placate the beast with human victims and elected to choose the first by drawing lots. The unfortunate loser was the beautiful daughter of the local ruler. Just as she was about to be cast to the dragon, George appeared, wounded the animal with his lance and led it into the city, where he told the people that he would kill it if they became Christians. Not surprisingly, they agreed. It is not clear how George came to be patron saint of England, although there is a story that he was seen helping the Franks at the battle of Antioch in 1098 and it is possible that the crusaders, including **RICHARD I**, came back from the east impressed by the power of his intercession.

EDWARD III put the **ORDER OF THE GARTER** under his protection and that may have emphasized his importance. At the Synod of **OXFORD** in 1222, St George's Day was included among the lesser holidays, and, in 1415, the Constitution of Archbishop Henry Chichele of **CANTERBURY** made it one of the chief celebrations of the year. His feast day was 23 April but, in 1961, the Roman Catholic Church reduced it to a commemoration. (See **UNION JACK**).

GEORGE CROSS. The United Kingdom's most distinguished award for civilian bravery was established by King **GEORGE VI** in 1940. A silver cross carrying a blue ribbon, it depicts **ST GEORGE** killing the dragon and is inscribed "For Gallantry".

GEORGIAN. This term usually refers to the reigns of Kings **GEORGE I, II, III** and **IV** and is most used to describe particular forms of elegant architecture and furniture (see **AUGUSTAN AGE**).

GHENT, TREATY OF, 24 December 1814. This was the Treaty which ended the **ANGLO-AMERICAN WAR** of 1812-14. It set up commissions to settle border disputes between the United States of America and **BRITISH NORTH AMERICA**, restored captured territories and confirmed British control of Canada. It avoided the questions of impressment into military service and the rights of neutrals, which had been at the heart of the dispute, but both nations were ready for peace so the accord began a period of cooperation and further agreements between them.

GLADSTONE, WILLIAM EWART (1809-98). One of the major British statesmen of the 19th century, Gladstone was **PRIME MINISTER** on four occasions between 1868 and 1894 and Leader of the **LIBERAL PARTY** for nearly 30 years. He was born in **LIVERPOOL** on 29 December 1809 to John and Mary Gladstone (both of whom were Scots) and was the fifth of six children. Educated at Eton College and then at **OXFORD** University, he graduated in 1831 with a double first in classics and mathematics.

Originally set on a career in the Church, he was persuaded to turn to politics and entered the **HOUSE OF COMMONS** in 1832 as the **TORIES'** Member of **PARLIAMENT** for Newark. Over the next few years, his views increasingly diverged from those of the party mainstream, but, even so, in 1841, **ROBERT PEEL**, who much admired his intellect and industry, appointed him Vice-President of the **BOARD OF TRADE**. In 1843, he was promoted to **PRESIDENT OF THE BOARD OF TRADE**, joining the **CABINET** for the first time and introducing legislation designed to improve Britain's commercial infrastructure. In 1845, he resigned over policies towards **IRELAND** but, by the end of the year, was back in the administration, this time as **SECRETARY OF STATE** for the colonies.

Peel's **GOVERNMENT** toppled in 1846 so Gladstone spent the next few years concentrating on the management of the family estates and on charitable work, particularly amongst prostitutes in **LONDON**. In 1852, he refused to join the **EARL OF DERBY**'s Cabinet but, later in the year, accepted the **EARL OF ABERDEEN**'s offer of the post of **CHANCELLOR OF THE EXCHEQUER**, a role in which he speedily established himself as the principal architect of the country's financial policy, advocating **FREE TRADE** with foreign states and a laissez-faire approach to domestic industry. When Aberdeen was replaced by the Liberals' **VISCOUNT PALMERSTON** in 1855, Gladstone accepted a place in his cabinet but resigned after only three weeks and spoke in Parliament against the government's policy of continued involvement in the **CRIMEAN WAR**. In 1859, he rejoined Palmerston (a man whom he thoroughly disliked) as Chancellor of the Exchequer, largely so that he could lend his weight to attempts to promote the unification of Italy under King Victor Emmanuel.

When Palmerston died in 1865, **EARL RUSSELL** took over as Prime Minister and Gladstone became **LEADER OF THE HOUSE OF COMMONS** as well as Chancellor. The following year, a **BILL** extending the franchise was defeated, the whole government resigned and Gladstone found himself in **OPPOSITION** once again. By 1868, however, Russell had retired from politics and the Liberals were looking to Gladstone to devise their election strategy. With a convincing victory under his belt, he accepted Queen **VICTORIA**'s invitation to become Prime Minister and, during the next six years, carried a series of far-reaching measures through Parliament. The Church of Ireland was disestablished in 1869, the **EDUCATION** Act of 1870 (see **ACT OF PARLIAMENT**) made elementary education compulsory and **TRADE UNIONS** were legalized by the Trade Union Act of 1871. Heavily defeated at the 1874 **GENERAL ELECTION** by **BENJAMIN DISRAELI**'s **CONSERVATIVE PARTY**, largely because of his policy of neutrality in foreign afffairs, he resigned the Liberal leadership but soon returned, stung by Disraeli's unwillingness to respond to the ferocity of Turkish reprisals against those involved in uprisings in the Balkans. In 1880, he returned to power and combined the role of Prime Minister with that of Chancellor of the Exchequer, leading an administration which sanctioned the invasion of Egypt in 1882 (despite a general opposition to imperialism) and, two years later, virtually doubled the franchise by giving householders in rural areas the right to vote.

In 1885, he resigned after a defeat in the Commons on financial policy but, in February of the following year, was back for a third term. This time his administration lasted for only six months before a bill granting independence to Ireland failed to get through Parliament and he resigned again. Over the next six years, he worked hard to gather support for Irish self-government. That policy, although condemned by the **GENTRY**, was enthusiastically supported by the working classes and, in 1892, he was swept back to power by the votes of the common people. By that time, however, he was 82. His health was failing, and, in 1894, after another defeat on the **HOME RULE** issue, he resigned, ostensibly because of increasing deafness and blindness. He died on the family estate at Hawarden (near Chester) on 19 May 1898 and was buried in **WESTMINSTER** Abbey. Although despised by Queen Victoria and Disraeli, he was an outstanding orator who became the great popular hero of his age and was much mourned in working-class Britain.

GLORIOUS REVOLUTION. King **JAMES VII and II**, after the suppression of the uprising led by the Protestant **DUKE** of Monmouth in 1685 (see **MONMOUTH REBELLION**), determined to return **ENGLAND** to Catholicism and began to remove restrictions laid upon those who did not conform to the established **CHURCH OF ENGLAND**. This might have been tolerated, for his heiresses were his daughters, the Protestant Mary (later **MARY II**) and Anne (later Queen **ANNE**), but, in 1688, his Queen (Mary of Modena) gave birth to a son, who took precedence in the succession and would undoubtedly be raised as a Catholic.

James's Dutch son-in-law, William, Prince of Orange (later **WILLIAM III**), sailed to Brixham in Devon, intending to march on **LONDON** and secure the Protestant succession for his wife. James panicked and fled to France. **PARLIAMENT** declared, in

January 1689, that he had abdicated the throne and, on 13 February 1689, proclaimed William and Mary joint **MONARCH**s, the only time in the history of England that this had happened. The revolution was termed 'glorious' because it had taken place by consent and without bloodshed. (For that reason it is also known as the 'Bloodless Revolution' in some texts.) It confirmed that the Monarch could only rule with the consent of the subjects of the realm, thus establishing **CONSTITUTIONAL MONARCHY**, and ensured the Protestant succession.

The Glorious Revolution of 1688 to 1691 is usually presented as an event generated by a coalition of groups opposed to James's religious practices, royal absolutism and belief in the **DIVINE RIGHT OF KINGS**. However, recent research interprets it more as a strategic invasion of England by the Dutch, during which the Dutch army replaced the English in defending London and, ultimately, the country. Its effect was to put an end to the ambitions of the French Catholic King Louis XIV's ambitions to dominate Europe and the Low Countries because it took England onto the side of his Protestant opponents. Also, it created a new balance between King and Parliament as William had to concede some traditional powers in order to ensure cooperation. Its significance, therefore, is probably understood as much in terms of European as of English views of history.

GODERICH, VISCOUNT. (See **FREDERICK JOHN ROBINSON**).

GOLD STANDARD. This monetary system is based upon free trade in gold, with currency values fixed in terms of the value of gold and the possessor of the **CURRENCY** having the right to be repaid in gold, on demand. It was the basis of **STERLING** during the 18th century but was suspended by the **BANK OF ENGLAND** during the **FRENCH REVOLUTION** and **NAPOLEONIC WARS**. Revived in 1819, it continued until 1914 and was the foundation of international trading and monetary transactions throughout the world for the remainder of the 19th century. The economic upheavals caused by the **FIRST WORLD WAR** made it impossible to sustain so Britain adopted a Gold Bullion Standard in 1925, dropping the provision for repayment of notes in the metal, and abandoned it completely in September 1931 during the **GREAT DEPRESSION**, when sterling was allowed to float and a devaluation was achieved during the financial crisis of that year. British banknotes still display the legend "I promise to pay the bearer on demand the sum of . . . ." but that now signifies only the legality of the note.

GOLDEN JUBILEE. In 1887, Queen **VICTORIA** celebrated the fiftieth year of her reign. Leaders of the self-governing territories of the **BRITISH EMPIRE** attended the first colonial conference, and the Imperial Institute (now known as the Commonwealth Institute) was established as a focus of information and to promote contacts between Great Britain's dependencies. Popular festivities in June included processions, services of thanksgiving in **WESTMINSTER** Abbey and 1,000 bonfires lit across the nation. Similar events took place in British possessions around the world.

GOOD PARLIAMENT, 1376. This **PARLIAMENT**, held at a time of heavy taxation and increasingly bad news of the war against France, led an attack on waste, corruption and inept government. It appointed Sir Peter de la Mare as its spokesman, thus creating the post of **SPEAKER** as controller of the procedures of the **HOUSE OF COMMONS**.

GORDON, CHARLES GEORGE (1833-85). Governor General of the Sudan and architect of the defence of Khartoum in 1885, Gordon was born at Woolwich on 28 January 1833, the fourth son of General H. W. Gordon of the Royal Artillery and his wife, Elizabeth. Educated in Taunton, he became an Officer Cadet at the Royal Military Academy, Woolwich, in 1848. He was commissioned as a Second Lieutenant in the Royal Engineers in 1852 then, after serving at Sebastopol during the **CRIMEAN WAR**, spent over two years as a surveyor establishing the boundary between Turkey and Russia. In 1859, he was promoted to Captain and posted to the British forces in China where, in 1863, he went with General Charles Staveley to help defend Shanghai against rebels intent on overthrowing the Manchu regime.

The U.S. mercenary, Frederick T. Ward, had raised a volunteer army of some 3,500 men (known as "The Ever-Victorious Army") to prevent the insurgents from entering the city but had been killed in September 1862. Gordon was placed in command of this raggle-taggle riffraff and turned them into a disciplined infantry, which repelled numerically superior attackers on many occasions and ultimately suppressed the insurrection. He returned to Britain in 1865 to find that his reputation had preceded him and that he had earned the nickname "Chinese Gordon". Promoted to Brevet Lieutenant Colonel and made a Companion of the Bath, he was appointed Royal Engineer Officer in charge of the naval dockyard at Gravesend. A committed Christian (though not a member of any church), he spent much of his time attempting to relieve poverty in the town by providing food, clothes and jobs. He also took the opportunity to evangelize, printing tracts which he distributed as widely as he could.

He left **ENGLAND** again in 1871 to become a member of the International Commission charged with supervizing navigation on the River Danube but a meeting with Nubar Pasha, Prime Minister of Egypt, led to an invitation to become Governor of Equatoria; in characteristically eccentric style, he accepted with one proviso — that his salary should be reduced from the proposed £10,000 to only £2000. He spent over two years in the region, during which he mapped the course of the River Nile, reduced the traffic in slaves and earned a reputation for travelling great distances by camel. He returned to Britain in 1876 but, after tossing a coin, agreed to accept the Khedive of Egypt's offer to appoint him Governor General of Sudan — an area of over one million square miles characterized by intertribal warfare, poverty, slavery and starvation. He arrived at his base in Khartoum in May 1877, but stayed for only two weeks before heading for Darfur, where some 3000 rebels besieged an army of 16,000 Egyptians. When he found the insurgents' base, he rode in, accompanied only by a small escort and an interpreter, and persuaded 1,500 of them to join him and the other 1,500 to retreat. By 1880, he had crushed both the rebellion and the slave trade, so he journeyed to Cairo, handed in his resignation and went home.

He was placed in command of the Royal Engineers in Mauritius from April 1881 until April 1882 then spent a few months in the Cape Colony, reorganizing army units based in southern Africa. For most of 1883, he was in Palestine, studying both the Bible and the landscape. In 1884, however, the British **GOVERNMENT** sent him back to Sudan, where he was instructed to organize an evacuation of civilians from Khartoum, which was in danger of falling into the hands of revolutionaries, who claimed they were fighting a holy war. He reached the town on 18 February and moved two thousand women, children and wounded men to safety before the rebels surrounded the settlement on 13 March. While the British government procrastinated, Gordon (with no European support) sustained the garrison purely by the force of his personality and an unshakeable belief that he would win out. On 26 January 1885, ten months after the siege started, a gap in the defences was breached and the occupants, including Gordon, were killed. A relief force arrived three days later. (See **HORATIO HERBERT KITCHENER**).

GORDON RIOTS, 2-9 June 1780. The 1780s was a decade of riot, rebellion and war in Europe and the United States, and the 'mob' was a part of normal life in the 18th century. In Britain, internal revolt was precipitated by the 1778 Catholic Relief Act (see **ACT OF PARLIAMENT**), which freed Roman Catholics from many of the penal regulations and restrictions to which they had been subjected since the **REFORMATION**, particularly those relating to property ownership, inheritance and the practising of religious acts. At the time, the British **GOVERNMENT** was faced with the revolt of the American colonies and rumours of a French invasion so more cynical historians interpret the act as motivated more by a desire to recruit Catholics into the army than by any wish to reinstate Catholics' rights as such.

In June 1780, Lord George Gordon, an eccentric Member of **PARLIAMENT** and leader of the Protestant Association, protested at the Relief Act and the growth of Popery, carrying a petition to the **HOUSE OF COMMONS** accompanied by 60,000 supporters. Many participants were more opposed to the economic effects of the American war than relief of the Catholics, but a riot ensued, troops were called and 235 people were said to have died in the six days of violence. Newgate Prison was demolished, Catholic chapels attacked and the mob even tried to storm the **BANK OF ENGLAND**. Gordon was tried and acquitted of **TREASON**.

GOVERNMENT. The United Kingdom is a **CONSTITUTIONAL MONARCHY** with an unwritten Constitution (see **BRITISH CONSTITUTION**). Government is the executive and consists of three parts: (1) **PARLIAMENT**, which is the legislature. This comprises a bicameral system of an upper chamber (the **HOUSE OF LORDS**) and a lower chamber (the **HOUSE OF COMMONS**). It is led by its Head of State (the **MONARCH**) and its Head of Government (the **PRIME MINISTER**); (2) the **JUDICIARY**, consisting of the judges, who interpret and enforce the law; and (3) **MINISTERS**, who are the executive of the state, administering the country according to the law and making policy. This executive branch of government comprises the Monarch, Prime Minister, **PRIVY COUNCIL** and **CABINET** Ministers. All three parts of government are held together, at least nominally, by the **CROWN** as Head of State. The party gaining most seats in a **GENERAL ELECTION** forms the government, while the party gaining the next highest number of seats forms the **OPPOSITION**.

GOVERNOR GENERAL. This official is the representative of the **CROWN** in countries of the **COMMONWEALTH OF NATIONS** which recognize the **MONARCH** as Head of State.

GRAMMAR SCHOOLS. Originally used as a name for all schools, from the 14th century the term became applied more to those specializing in Latin grammar and religious studies (particularly those associated with the **UNIVERSITIES** and monasteries). Many became public schools (private schools charging fees mainly for the wealthy), others became part of the state system of **EDUCATION**al provision and, by the 20th century, constituted the selective schools for more academically able pupils aged 12 years and over. Other children attended the Secondary Modern schools until these were superseded by the **COMPREHENSIVE SCHOOLS**. By 1990, less than 10 per cent of pupils in the state system remained in Grammar and Secondary Modern schools, but, under the Education Reform Act of 1988, individual schools may opt out of local authority control and that may change the balance.

GRAND ALLIANCE, 1689. Formed to counter the expansionist policies of King Louis XIV of France, the Alliance involved **ENGLAND**, Spain, Austria and the Netherlands. The subsequent War of the Grand Alliance is sometimes called King William's War because it crushed the Jacobite opponents of **WILLIAM III**. (See **GLORIOUS REVOLUTION**).

GRAND ALLIANCE, 1701. An alliance of **ENGLAND, SCOTLAND**, the Austrian Empire, Prussia and the Netherlands was formed to prevent the union of the French and Spanish crowns. The grouping formed the basis of the military alliance during the **WAR OF THE SPANISH SUCCESSION**.

GRAND ALLIANCE (COAL), 1726. An alliance of coalowners in northeast **ENGLAND** was formed in 1726 to create a powerful cooperative association designed to promote the **COAL** trade. By 1750, it controlled most of the production in the area and had bought land along the **RIVER TYNE** so that it could regulate water transport (and hence costs of carriage). It had declined by the early 19th century as other coal producing regions developed.

GRAND REMONSTRANCE, 1641. A comprehensive manifesto, published by the **PARLIAMENTARIANS** (led by John Pym) and passed narrowly by the **HOUSE OF COMMONS** in 1641, detailed King **CHARLES I**'s authoritarian errors, restated the achievements of the **LONG PARLIAMENT** and urged redress of grievances. An important constitutional statement, it attacked King and Church and has been said by some scholars to have hardened support for the **MONARCH**, angered moderates and demonstrated the deep divisions within **ENGLAND** at this critical period just before the **CIVIL WAR**. It was presented to Charles on 1 December 1641 and rejected on 23 December.

GREAT BRITAIN. In a geographical context, Great Britain is the main island of the **BRITISH ISLES**, covering a land area of approximately 87,820 square miles. In a political context, the term refers to the formerly independent **ENGLAND** and **WALES** (which were united by the **ACT OF UNION** in 1536 but had no official name as a union) and **SCOTLAND**. It was first employed in a royal proclamation in 1604 (after **JAMES VI** of Scotland became James I of England) and was increasingly used to describe the newly united kingdom during the 17th century but was not formally adopted until after the English and Scottish Parliaments amalgamated in 1707 (see **UNION OF PARLIAMENTS**). Some historians have suggested that the term was intended to distinguish Great Britain (**BRITANNIA** Major) from Brittany, in France, which had sometimes been referred to as Lesser, or Little, Britain (Britannia Minor). Great Britain is now part of the **UNITED KINGDOM**, for which 'Britain' is now an accepted synonym.

GREAT DEPRESSION, 1929-33. Economic collapse following the Wall Street crash of 1929 exacerbated deep problems already present in the British economy. The return to the **GOLD STANDARD** in 1925 had made exporting difficult and the decline in demand for staple industrial products was made worse by **GOVERNMENT** policies to cut expenditure, reduce the armed forces and balance domestic budgets. Unemployment rose to three million by 1931 (see **HUNGER MARCHES**) and political extremism grew (see **BRITISH UNION OF FASCISTS [BUF]**). The term has also been used in some texts to describe the Great Depression in agriculture in the latter half of the 19th century (see **GREAT DEPRESSION: AGRICULTURE**).

GREAT DEPRESSION: AGRICULTURE. The period from about 1870 until 1900 is characterized by agricultural depression and heavy falls in farm prices, occasioned by a series of poor harvests and cheap foreign imports of food. Grain prices in Britain plummeted when wheat began to arrive from the midwestern United States, Russia and the colonies as ocean transport became more viable and transcontinental railways were built. In response, British agriculture moved away from cereals towards mixed farming and pasture and the labour force on the land fell from one million in 1871 to less than 600,000 in 1901. The period also saw a slowing of industrial development, but some observers question the use of the term "Great Depression" because the economy as a whole continued to exhibit growth despite the decline in some sectors.

GREATER LONDON COUNCIL (GLC). The **CONSERVATIVE PARTY** government formed the GLC in 1965 to bring the 32 **LONDON** boroughs and the **CITY OF LONDON** into a single administrative body covering 610 square miles and with the structure and strategic responsibilities of a **COUNTY** authority. It was disbanded under the London Government Act of 1983 (see **ACT OF PARLIAMENT**) by the **MARGARET THATCHER** administration (also Conservative), ostensibly in order to make financial savings and give power back to the boroughs and people. However, it also removed a vexatious regional government, then under **LABOUR PARTY** control. (See **LOCAL GOVERNMENT; LONDON COUNTY COUNCIL [LCC]**).

GREAT EXHIBITION, 1851. An international celebration of industry, commerce and scientific achievement properly termed the Great Exhibition of the Works of Industry of All Nations, the extravaganza had been suggested by Prince **ALBERT** to celebrate the achievements of the reign of his wife, Queen **VICTORIA**, and the ascendancy of her nation as workshop of the world. It was held at the purpose-built Crystal Palace in Hyde Park, **LONDON**, designed by Joseph Paxton and with a roof of 76,000 square yards of glass and steel. The site of the exhibition is correctly, but now rarely, called Albertopolis. Some six million visitors saw the Exhibition of over 100,000 objects, most travelling by the new railway system. The profits were enormous, and some were used to build the museums complex at South Kensington.

GREAT FIRE OF LONDON. On 2 September 1666, fire broke out in a bakery in Pudding Lane, close to old **LONDON** Bridge in the **CITY OF LONDON.** It quickly spread amongst the largely wooden buildings and raged for five days over an area of 160 hectares (400 acres), destroying 87 churches and at least 13,200 dwellings. Surprisingly, fewer than 20 people lost their lives. The **LORD MAYOR** had, at first, dismissed the fire as of no consequence but, eventually, King **CHARLES II** brought in gunpowder to create firebreaks and the inferno was controlled. At the time, rumours of arson were rife, and a French priest, who confessed to starting the fire, was executed. Only later was he declared to have been insane and innocent of the crime.

Coming less than a year after the **GREAT PLAGUE,** London's economy suffered and exports were badly affected. However, the conflagration provided an opportunity to rebuild, incorporating higher standards of housing. Pressure from merchants to get back to normal quickly in order to combat Dutch trading growth led to construction in better materials but still on many of the medieval street lines, giving the City, even today, a feeling of enclosure and small intimate spaces. Many churches, including St Paul's Cathedral, were built in succeeding years.

GREAT PLAGUE, 1665. Bubonic plague killed between 65,000 and 100,000 people in **LONDON** during 1665, the equivalent of 20 per cent of the city's population. It was, without doubt, the worst year of the century for this endemic disease, though major outbreaks had occurred in 1603 (when 30,000 Londoners died) and 1625. Records confirmed that 96 of the 130 **PARISH**es of London had plague victims in 1665. Wealthy inhabitants moved out of the capital and other large cities, but the incidence of the disease was greatest in the poorest and most densely populated areas. Houses with the infection were boarded up and marked with a red cross, and burial parties took the corpses away for interment in plague-pits. Plague was a constant threat for over 350 years in the British Isles, the worst visitation being the **BLACK DEATH** of 1349. It died out after 1665 because the carrier, the black rat, was replaced by the more successful (but nonplague-carrying) brown rat, and the **GREAT FIRE OF LONDON** removed many breeding grounds.

GREAT SEAL. The **MONARCH**'s chief seal is used to authorize all royal decisions and to authenticate important state documents. It is, therefore, an important symbol of authority. Dating from the time of King **EDWARD THE CONFESSOR**, it is double-sided, showing the sovereign sitting on his throne and (on the obverse) on horseback. Wax impressions made by the seal were attached to royal and state papers as a form of authentication and are still used on **ACTS OF PARLIAMENT**. (See **LORD KEEPER OF THE GREAT SEAL**).

GREEN PARTY. In 1985, this title was adopted by a conservation-oriented political organization previously known as the People's Party (1973) and the Ecology Party (1975). It promoted environmental and peace policies, and, in the **GENERAL ELECTION** of 1987, fielded 133 candidates, none of whom was elected. It did best in the elections for the European Parliament in 1989, when it polled 15 per cent of the total British vote (2.3 million votes). In historical context, the movement can be seen as a product of the growth of environmental concern in the 1970s.

GREENHAM COMMON. In December 1982, 30,000 women held hands around the US Air Force base at Greenham Common (near Newbury) to protest about the siting of U.S.-owned and controlled Cruise missiles in the area. They set up an encampment outside the base and occupied it for 11 years. The United States removed the missiles in 1991 as part of the peace dividend resulting from the disarmament talks with the USSR. Protestors finally left the area on 27 January 1994 and the site was dismantled in 1996. (See **CAMPAIGN FOR NUCLEAR DISARMAMENT; NUCLEAR DETERRENT**).

GREENWICH MERIDIAN. The Royal Observatory at Greenwich (**LONDON**) was established by King **CHARLES II** in 1675. The Greenwich Meridian is a brass rail which, since 1884, has marked the line of longitude known as the Prime Meridian (0 degrees), from which all other lines of longitude are measured. It is an essential element in establishing geographical location on the Earth.

GRENVILLE, GEORGE (1712-70). Through his policy of taxing settlers in North America, Grenville was responsible for precipitating the **AMERICAN WAR OF INDEPENDENCE**. The son of Richard Grenville and Hester Temple, he was born on 14 October 1712 and educated at Eton and **OXFORD** University. On graduation, he trained for the Bar then entered **PARLIAMENT** as the Member for Buckingham in 1741, joining the faction which opposed the **WHIG** policies of **ROBERT WALPOLE**. In 1744, he was made Lord of the **ADMIRALTY** and, three years later, became a Lord of the **TREASURY**. He was appointed Treasurer of the Navy in 1754 but was dismissed the following year as a result of his opposition to the administration's foreign policy. **WILLIAM PITT THE ELDER** renewed the appointment in 1756, but Grenville resigned in April 1757, when Pitt was dismissed. Later that year, he was back in post again, in the ministry led by Pitt and the **DUKE OF NEWCASTLE**, and remained in office when the coalition leaders resigned in 1762. He was made Leader of the **HOUSE OF COMMONS** and **SECRETARY OF STATE** by the new Prime Minister, **JOHN STUART**, Lord Bute, but was unwilling to defend the terms of the peace treaties which the **GOVERNMENT** concluded with France and Spain so exchanged posts with the First Lord of the Admiralty later the same year.

In April 1763, Bute resigned and recommended Grenville as his successor, a recommendation which **GEORGE III** accepted. The premiership lasted for two years and was marred by dispute and tension. Grenville's relationship with the King was one of constant friction, primarily because George made a habit of conferring with Bute over major decisions. Also, the Revenue Act of 1764 and the Stamp Act of 1765 (see **ACT OF PARLIAMENT**) raised the hackles of the American colonists, who objected to taxes levied by a Parliament in which they were not represented. The prosecution of **JOHN WILKES** for libel and the **REGENCY** Act (which deliberately excluded the King's mother from the list of possible regents) added to the difficulties, the latter leading to Grenville's downfall in 1765. From then until his death in **LONDON** on 13 November 1770, he continued to support measures designed to raise taxes from the colonies.

GRENVILLE, BARON WILLIAM. (See **GRENVILLE, WILLIAM WYNDHAM**).

GRENVILLE, WILLIAM WYNDHAM (1759-1834). **PRIME**

MINISTER from January 1806 until March 1807, Grenville had as troubled a period of premiership as his father, **GEORGE GRENVILLE**, had experienced four decades earlier. Born on 25 October 1759 and educated (like his father) at Eton College and **OXFORD** University, he entered **PARLIAMENT** in 1782 as the representative for Buckingham, becoming Secretary to his brother, Earl Temple, **LORD LIEUTENANT** of **IRELAND**, later in the same year. He went out of office when the coalition administration nominally led by the **DUKE OF PORTLAND** took office in February 1783 but became Paymaster General of the Forces in the **GOVERNMENT** formed by his cousin, **WILLIAM PITT THE YOUNGER**, in December of the same year and, in 1786, was appointed Vice-President of the Committee of Trade. In January 1789, he was made **SPEAKER** of the **HOUSE OF COMMONS** but moved in June to the post of **HOME SECRETARY**. In 1790, he was created **BARON** Grenville and appointed Leader of the **HOUSE OF LORDS**. The following year, he became President of the Board of Control and retained that post when he moved to the Foreign Office later the same year.

He resigned with **WILLIAM PITT THE YOUNGER** in 1801, when **GEORGE III** refused to consider legislation dealing with the emancipation of Roman Catholics, but, thereafter, differed increasingly with him. When Pitt became Prime Minister again in 1804, Grenville declined to join his government unless **CHARLES JAMES FOX** was also included. The King refused to accede so Grenville remained in opposition until January 1806, when, following Pitt's death, he formed a coalition government which included his own supporters and those of Fox and **HENRY ADDINGTON**. The administration was marked by a conspicuous lack of success, with the solitary exception of legislation in 1807 to abolish the **SLAVE TRADE** by British vessels and prohibit the importation of slaves to British colonies. Attempts to introduce a Catholic Relief **BILL**, in March 1807, led to the King's intervention and a change of Prime Minister. Thereafter, Grenville's consistent refusal to avoid the emancipation issue kept him out of office. He died at Dropmore on 12 January 1834, the victim of a stroke.

GREY, CHARLES (1764-1845). **PRIME MINISTER** from 1830 until 1834, Grey is best remembered for his role in the passage of the 1832 **REFORM ACT** (see **ACT OF PARLIAMENT**). The son of General Sir Charles Grey (later the first Earl Grey), Charles was born at Falloden (near Alnwick) on 13 March 1764. He entered **PARLIAMENT** in 1786 as the Member for Northumberland and aligned himself with **JAMES FOX, EDMUND BURKE** and others as opponents of **WILLIAM PITT THE YOUNGER**. Particularly interested in **PARLIAMENTARY REFORM**, he attempted in 1793 and 1797 to get the matter debated at **WESTMINSTER** on the grounds that the membership of the **HOUSE OF COMMONS** did not truly represent the composition of the British people. Pitt, however, opposed these moves, and little was achieved. In 1806, the **WHIG BARON GRENVILLE** was invited by **GEORGE III** to take over as Prime Minister when Pitt died and Grey was offered the post of First Lord of the **ADMIRALTY**. Later in the year, he became Foreign Secretary and **LEADER OF THE HOUSE OF COMMONS** but the administration lasted only until March 1807. Clashes with the King over policies towards Roman Catholics escalated until Grenville refused to accede to a royal request to drop all plans for concessions, and resigned.

In the same year, Grey's father died and Charles succeeded to the title, moving to the **HOUSE OF LORDS**. From that point, the views of Grey and Grenville began to diverge. The differences arose, in particular, over policies towards France after Napoleon's return from exile in Elba in 1815, Grenville advocating military action whilst Grey argued that the French had the right to choose their own leaders. In 1820, Grey also made an enemy of the King when he opposed the **MONARCH**'s moves to divorce Queen Caroline, and, in 1827, he angered others by his opposition to Tory Prime Minister **GEORGE CANNING** (see **TORIES**). Nevertheless, when, in 1830, the **DUKE OF WELLINGTON**'s resistance to Parliamentary reform led to his defeat at a **GENERAL ELECTION**, Grey emerged as the leader of a coalition of the Whigs and the Canning faction. He was summoned by **WILLIAM IV** on 16 November and invited to become Prime Minister with a specific mandate to introduce Parliamentary reforms.

His attempts to achieve change were consistently rebuffed — even when measures had been passed by the Commons, they were rejected by the upper house. In the spring of 1832, despairing of other solutions, he asked the King to create sufficient peers to get the measures through the Lords, but William, initially keen on change, had shifted his ground and refused. On 9 May, Grey resigned, but no other political leader was able to form an administration which would command a Parliamentary majority so a week later he was recalled. The King, seeing no option, agreed to create the necessary peers but never needed to put his agreement into effect. The Lords, faced with the inevitable, passed the Reform **BILL**, which reorganized the territorial basis of seats in the House of Commons and altered the nature of the franchise. That onerous work took its toll, and, in 1834, Grey resigned and retired to his home at Howick, where he died on 17 July 1845.

GREY, EARL. (See **CHARLES GREY**).

GREY, JANE (1537-54). Queen of **ENGLAND** for only nine days, Lady Jane was the daughter of Henry Grey, **MARQUESS** of Dorset, and his wife, Frances Brandon. The great-granddaughter of **HENRY VII**, she was born in Bradgate (Leicestershire) in September 1537 and proved to be an intelligent child, becoming proficient in Greek and Latin and gaining a working knowledge of Arabic, Chaldee and Hebrew. At the age of nine, she moved to the home of Lord Seymour, who promised to arrange for her to marry his nephew, **EDWARD VI**. Seymour, however, was found guilty of **TREASON** and executed in 1549 so Jane returned to her parents. In 1552, her father was made Duke of Suffolk and gained considerable influence at the royal court. John Dudley, Duke of Northumberland and the power behind the throne, saw political advantage in an alliance with the family and arranged for Jane to marry his son, Guildford, on 21 May 1553. The match had the approval of the King, who was persuaded by Northumberland to make a will which ensured that the succession to the throne would go to the sons of Lady Jane, who was staunchly Protestant, rather than to Edward's Roman Catholic half-sister Mary (later **MARY I**). The draft of the will was manipulated to ensure that Lady Jane herself would become Queen and, when Edward died on 6 July 1553, she gained the throne.

It was a role she did not seek; when she heard the news of Edward's death and her own future, she fainted and needed much persuasion before she would agree to become sovereign. Mary, moreover, had the support of the people and of a large number of the nobility. On 19 July, the **LORD MAYOR** of **LONDON** proclaimed her Queen, to popular acclaim, and Suffolk advised his daughter to abdicate. She told him that she would willingly put the **CROWN** aside, having accepted it solely through obedience to him as her father. Suffolk and Jane were imprisoned in the

TOWER OF LONDON and, although Suffolk was pardoned, Jane was tried for treason along with her husband and other supporters. She pleaded guilty and was sentenced to death. That sentence was suspended, but Suffolk's participation in a rebellion against Mary sealed her fate (see **WYATT'S REBELLION**). She was beheaded in the Tower on 12 February 1554, still only 16.

GUILD. Sometimes known as Gilds, these organizations can trace their history to the **ANGLO-SAXON** period when associations of families were formed for mutual protection. The term is also used to denote the social or religious fraternities established during the medieval period. They evolved particularly under the **NORMAN**s when they became merchant, craft or administrative groupings of townspeople. Young boys were apprenticed to the master craftsmen of the Guild and learned their trades for seven years before they became qualified. The growth of **MERCANTILISM** and capitalism from the 16th century led to the decline of the Guilds (except for those of the **LIVERY COMPANY**) and the **INDUSTRIAL REVOLUTION** made their restrictive practices obsolete. The modern **LONDON** Guilds range from the Apothecaries and the Fishmongers to the Mercers and the Watermen.

GUILDFORD FOUR. In 1974, the Irish Republican Army bombed **PUBLIC HOUSE**s in Woolwich and Guildford. Three men and one woman were convicted in 1975 and given life sentences for the bombings. Subsequently, the written interrogation notes were found by ESDA (Electrostatic Detection Apparatus) testing to have been tampered with and allegedly altered by **POLICE** officers to secure convictions. The four were freed (and their convictions quashed) in 1989, but the subsequent cases against the officers who interrogated them were eventually dropped for lack of evidence. This case led directly to the reopening of the related case of the **MAGUIRE SEVEN** and their subsequent release, throwing suspicion on police and judicial methods during the height of the disturbances in the 1960s and 1970s. US Congressman Joe Kennedy championed the Guildford Four during their captivity, and, in June 1993, one of the released prisoners, Paul Hill, married Courtney Kennedy, sister of Joe and daughter of the assassinated Robert Kennedy. Hill was also convicted in 1975 of the murder in Belfast of Brian Shaw, a former soldier, and was freed on bail after his release for the Guildford bombings, pending an appeal which eventually also resulted in the quashing of that conviction. (See **BIRMINGHAM SIX**).

GULF WAR, 16 January-27 February 1991. On 2 August 1990, Iraq, led by Saddam Hussein, invaded Kuwait, a territory in the Persian Gulf. Six days later, he annexed the country, which was then producing around 13 per cent of the world's oil supply. Both actions were widely condemned. On 16 January 1991, a multinational force under United Nations auspices and including contingents from the United States of America, Britain, France, Egypt, Italy, Saudi Arabia and Syria, attacked at the start of Operation Desert Storm. Kuwait was freed by 24 February, and the war officially ended on 27 February. It cost Britain 17 dead (9 in an unfortunate friendly-fire incident involving US aircraft), 43 wounded and a bill of around £3 million.

GUNPOWDER PLOT, 1605. King **JAMES VI and I** failed to deliver the support expected by the advocates of the Catholic cause and, on 5 November 1605, a group of disaffected conspirators, including Guy Fawkes and Robert Catesby (the leader), attempted to kill him and his **MINISTER**s by blowing up the Houses of **PARLIAMENT** with 20 to 30 barrels of gunpowder. The conspirators were caught and executed after the Catholic Lord Monteagle was sent an unsigned cryptic note by one of his relatives (Tresham, one of the plotters), telling him to stay away from **WESTMINSTER** on 5 November. The premises were searched, and Fawkes, a Yorkshireman only recently converted to Catholicism who was the explosives expert for the plotters, was arrested in the basement of the House. His subsequent torture in the **TOWER OF LONDON** revealed the identity of the other conspirators. As a result of the torture he had to be helped onto the scaffold on 31 January 1606 to be hanged, drawn and quartered (see **CAPITAL PUNISHMENT**).

The incident led to yet further repression of Catholicism in Britain, amidst fears of **POPISH PLOT**s, and is still celebrated every Guy Fawkes night (5 November). Effigies of Fawkes are paraded on the streets and children beg "Money for the Guy". The Guy is then burnt on a bonfire and fireworks set off in this curiously English traditional celebration. Fawkes can, perhaps, be seen as the eternally unfortunate scapegoat for what was, in reality, the action of a desperate group of fanatical Catholic noblemen for whom he was simply the explosives mechanic.

GWYN, NELL (1650-87). A mistress of **CHARLES II**, Nell was born on 2 February 1650 (reputedly in an alley in Covent Garden, **LONDON**). Her father is unknown. Her mother, Helena Gwyn, ran a brothel, where Nell served brandy to the patrons. In 1664, she became an orange-seller at the King's Theatre and attracted the attention of Charles Hart, one of the leading actors. She became his mistress and embarked on a stage career, making her first appearance as Paulina in Thomas Killigrew's *Thomaso*, probably in December 1664. From 1666 until 1669 (except for a period during 1667, when she lived in Epsom as the mistress of Lord Buckhurst), she appeared regularly at the theatre, playing roles such as Florimel in John Dryden's *Secret Love* and Mirida in Robert Howard's *All Mistaken*. A fine dancer and singer, she gained a reputation for outrageous behaviour and high spirits which appealed to many people unhappy with the dour puritanism of the age (see **PURITANS**). Her last appearance was as Almahide in Dryden's two-part play *The Conquest of Granada* (1670-71), by which time she had become a mistress of the King and borne him a son. Established in a mansion in Pall Mall, she entertained the **GENTRY** but was faithful to Charles even after his death in 1685. By the time of her bereavement, she was deeply in debt, but the King had made a deathbed request that she should not starve and that wish was honoured by his successor, **JAMES VII and II**, who paid off her creditors, gave her cash gifts and granted her a sizeable pension. In March 1687, however, she was stricken by apoplexy and partially paralysed. She died on 14 November and was buried, as she had asked, at the church of St Martin's-in-the-Fields (London). At the funeral service, the vicar took as his text Luke 15: 7.

—H—

HABEAS CORPUS. Meaning, in Latin, "you should have the body", the phrase originated with 13th century writs to guarantee the presence of an accused person in court within a specified period. In the 15th century, it was used to prevent unlawful imprisonment and to identify the reasons for the detainment of citizens. As such, it became a powerful weapon against misuse of royal powers. The Habeas Corpus Act of 1679 (see **ACT OF PARLIAMENT**) strengthened the rules regarding its administrative operation and the Habeas Corpus Act of 1816 extended it from criminal charges to civil cases. It is now a major plank of civil liberties in **ENG-LAND** but has no direct equivalent in Scots law. (The Wrongous Imprisonment Act of 1701 is the closest Scottish legislation.)

HADRIAN'S WALL. A 73-mile long wall built for the **ROMAN** Emperor Hadrian between the Solway Firth and Wallsend (near South Shields, on the **RIVER TYNE**) in the first quarter of the second century AD (c. 122–27), this defensive structure was intended to control the movement of raiders across the border from **SCOTLAND** into **ENGLAND**, separate warring tribes in the area and mark the northern extent of the Roman Empire. Milecastles and turrets were built along its length, mostly of stone and cement, allowing fire signals to be sent to garrison forces whenever an incursion occurred. It was manned mainly by auxiliary troops numbering up to 11,500 at times but its role was largely replaced by the Antonine Wall, across central Scotland, about 145 AD.

HAILSHAM, VISCOUNT. (See **QUINTIN MCGAREL HOGG**).

HAMILTON-GORDON, GEORGE (1784-1860). The fourth **EARL** of Aberdeen, Hamilton-Gordon was **PRIME MINISTER** at the outbreak of the **CRIMEAN WAR** in 1854 and considered himself responsible for that conflict. Born in Edinburgh on 28 January 1784 and orphaned by the time he was 11, he was raised by his guardians — Henry Dundas (later Viscount Melville) and **WILLIAM PITT THE YOUNGER.** Educated at Harrow School and **CAMBRIDGE** University, he married Catherine, daughter of the **MARQUIS** of Abercorn, in 1805. The marriage was a happy one, but Catherine died of consumption in 1812 and, in 1815, he married the Dowager **VISCOUNT**ess Hamilton (Catherine's sister-in-law), by whom he had five children.

His political career began in 1813, when he was appointed Special Ambassador to Austria, where he played a leading role in shaping the policies which led to the defeat of Napoleon. He signed the Treaty of Toplitz in 1813, was present at the Battle of Leipzig in the same year and signed the **TREATY OF PARIS** in 1814. However, the **HOME SECRETARY (VISCOUNT CASTLEREAGH)** felt that he was being too lenient on the French and took responsibility for further negotiations himself. Hamilton-Gordon retired to his estates in Aberdeenshire, but his interest in politics was maintained and, in January 1828, he was appointed **CHANCELLOR OF THE DUCHY OF LANCAS-**

TER by the **DUKE OF WELLINGTON**. In June, he became Foreign Secretary and, over the next two years, helped settle the issue of Greek independence, maintained neutrality on Portuguese affairs and opposed France's colonial designs on Algeria. In 1830, he resigned and (apart from a brief spell in **ROBERT PEEL**'s administration [1834-35]) concerned himself more with Church affairs than national politics.

From 1841 until 1846, he served as Foreign Secretary under Peel and earned a considerable reputation as a diplomat in European affairs and in negotiations over boundary problems with the United States (his skill as a diplomat led to the formulation of the Webster-Ashburton Treaty of 1842 and the Oregon Treaty of 1846). He supported Peel on **CORN LAW** policy and resigned with him in 1846 following the Prime Minister's defeat on the Irish Coercion **BILL**. When Peel died in 1850, Hamilton-Gordon became leader of the Peelites. The following year, he led their opposition to the Ecclesiastical Titles Bill (which prevented Roman Catholic Bishops from using their territorial titles), but the legislation was so popular in the country that, when Prime Minister Lord **JOHN RUSSELL** resigned in the spring of 1852, Hamilton-Gordon was unable to accept Queen **VICTORIA**'s invitation to form the new **GOVERNMENT**.

In December of that year, however, he managed to form a coalition Government with a **CABINET** which included six Peelites, six **WHIGS** and one Radical. Despite the differing allegiances, it worked effectively on domestic matters. On international issues, however, the cracks appeared in 1853. Differences with Russia over the **EASTERN QUESTION** increased, and popular opinion favoured a declaration of war. Hamilton-Gordon delayed until 23 September, when he and his Home Secretary (Lord Clarendon), who had been upset by the Prime Minister's earlier lack of decisiveness, ordered the navy to Constantinople. They failed to consult the Cabinet, which nevertheless agreed, in December, to send the fleet to the Black Sea. War had become inevitable and was declared the following March. Hamilton-Gordon held himself responsible for the conflict, even though it became clear that he had been misled by his military advisers' poor quality of information, and an adverse vote in the **HOUSE OF COMMONS** in January 1855 forced him out of office. He was created a Knight of the Garter (see **ORDER OF THE GARTER**) and died in **LONDON** on 14 December 1860.

HANOVERIANS, 1714-1901. The **ACT OF SETTLEMENT** of 1701 (see **ACT OF PARLIAMENT**) ensured that the inheritance of the **CROWN** went to the German House of Hanover in 1714. Descended from Italian and, later, from German families, **GEORGE I** was the first Hanoverian **MONARCH** and he spoke very little English. Both he and **GEORGE II** were born in Hanover and preferred their home country but **GEORGE III** was proud of the fact that he was a true Englishman. Queen **VICTORIA** was the last of the line, succeeded by **EDWARD VII** of the House of **WETTIN** (**SAXE-COBURG-GOTHA**) in 1901. The Hanoverians ruled Britain for 123 years, a period of great social and economic change, which witnessed the **INDUSTRIAL REVOLUTION**, the **AGRICULTURAL REVOLUTION** and the **AMERICAN WAR OF INDEPENDENCE**

HANSARD. This publication contains the official verbatim record of debates in **PARLIAMENT**. In 1812, T. C. Hansard took over *Cobbett's Parliamentary Debates*, which became known by the name of its new owner. Hansard sold the business in 1889 but the title was retained.

HANSEATIC LEAGUE. During the 13th century, this association of German traders became a League of trading towns. The **LONDON** Hanse and other bases at King's Lynn, Ipswich, Hull and Boston (Lincolnshire) were the league's English arm. They supplied valuable naval stores but English traders resented them so their privileges were gradually reduced. By the 16th century they had been supplanted by the **MERCHANTS ADVENTURERS** and the **EASTLAND COMPANY**.

HARDICANUTE (c. 1017-42). The son of King **CANUTE** and his wife, Emma, Hardicanute was King of **ENGLAND** from 1040 until his death in 1042. In 1028, his father made him King of Denmark and he was in that country when Canute died in 1035. Attempts by Emma and her supporters to get Hardicanute declared King of England failed, and an alliance of Mercian (see **MERCIA**), **LONDON** and northern leaders won the appointment of Canute's illegitimate son, Harold (later **HAROLD I**), as **REGENT** until his half-brother returned. That return was postponed as Hardicanute attended to affairs in Denmark and, in 1037, Harold was confirmed as King. Emma fled into exile and Hardicanute joined her at Bruges in 1039. The following year,

Harold died and Hardicanute returned to England for a short and unpopular reign. He had his brother's body dug up and thrown into a fen, levied heavy taxes to finance his navy and burned Worcester in retaliation for the murder of two servants. He died on 8 June 1042.

HAROLD I (1017-40). The illegitimate son of King **CANUTE** and Aelfgifu of Northampton, Harold was King of **ENGLAND** from 1037 until 1040. When Canute died in 1035, Harold was appointed **REGENT** while **HARDICANUTE**, his legitimate half-brother, was attending to affairs in Denmark. Hardicanute's return was delayed and, in 1037, Harold was made King. Little is known of the events of his reign, but he does appear to have had a cruel streak. According to the **ANGLO-SAXON CHRONICLE**, he blinded, scalped and murdered members of a party, led by Alfred, son of **AETHELRED II**, which had travelled from Normandy. Also, he stole his mother's valuables and, shortly after his accession, banished her from the kingdom. He died on 17 March 1040 at **OXFORD**, but Hardicanute, on his return, dug up the body and threw it into a fen.

HAROLD II (c. 1022-66). Harold was the second son of Earl Godwin of **WESSEX** and Gytha, sister-in-law of King **CANUTE**. In 1051, along with his father, he was exiled after quarrelling with **EDWARD THE CONFESSOR**, but support for the family was considerable, particularly in the south of **ENGLAND**. In 1052, the King had little option but to allow their return. Thereafter, Harold's influence grew as Edward's lack of political acumen became increasingly evident and as continued appointment of foreign advisers alienated many potential supporters. When his father died in 1053, Harold succeeded him as Earl of Wessex and Earl of **KENT**. In 1057, he added Herefordshire to his estates. He also distinguished himself in battle, leading the English army in campaigns against rebel forces. He visited the continent in 1056 and again in 1064. During the second visit he fought for William, Duke of Normandy (see **WILLIAM I**) and, according to some authorities, swore to support William's claim to the English throne. Any such oath may, however, have been made under duress.

   Edward, on his deathbed, recommended Harold as his successor. In fact, Edgar the Aetheling, grandson of **EDMUND II**, was the nearest heir, but he was still a child and there were serious fears of civil disruption in the absence of strong rule after

Edward's weak reign. The **WITAN** (the council of **ANGLO-SAXON** leaders) therefore chose Harold as King, and he was crowned on 6 January 1066, the day after Edward's death. The circumstances of his accession, however, encouraged intervention both from Norway and from Normandy. Harold's brother Tostig, in alliance with Harald Hardrada, King of Norway, sailed up the Humber with a fleet of more than 300 ships and defeated the royal forces at Fulford on 20 September. Harold gained his revenge five days later in the **BATTLE OF STAMFORD BRIDGE**, where Tostig and Harald were both killed, but had little time to benefit from the victory. On 29 September, William of Normandy landed at Pevensey. Harold and his mounted troops returned to **LONDON** then, rather than wait for the infantry to arrive from the north or for a supporting force to join him from the southwest, decided to give battle at once. The two sides met at Senlac, seven miles northwest of Hastings, and after a struggle which lasted all day William emerged victorious (see **BATTLE OF HASTINGS**). Harold died with his brothers, Gyrth and Leofwine, killed by an arrow which pierced his eye. He was buried at Waltham and the **NORMANS** took control, changing the direction of British history.

HASTINGS, BATTLE OF, 14 October 1066. King **EDWARD THE CONFESSOR** died on 6 January 1066, and the **CROWN** passed to his brother-in-law, Harold Godwinson, who became King **HAROLD II**. Duke William of Normandy (see **WILLIAM I**), who had reputedly been named as successor by Edward two years earlier, invaded **ENGLAND** in September, landing at Pevensey and defeating the royal army at Senlac Ridge and Telham Hill, near Hastings in Sussex. The Norman force was better trained, with archers and cavalry and contingents of Normans, French, Picards, Flemings and Bretons, so they eventually overcame their opponents. Harold was killed (by tradition with an arrow in the eye) during the battle and by December the **WITAN** (the royal council of **ANGLO-SAXON** nobles) had offered the throne to William, who was crowned King at **WESTMINSTER** on 25 December. This **CORONATION** began a period of strong and secure **NORMAN MONARCH**y, which replaced the **ANGLO-SAXON** regime and lasted until the 13th century when it, in turn, was replaced by the **PLANTAGENETS**. (See **BATTLE OF STAMFORD BRIDGE**).

HASTINGS, WARREN (1732-1818). The first Governor General of India, Hastings guided affairs on the subcontinent from 1772 until 1785. He was born in the hamlet of Churchill, on the **OXFORD**shire-Gloucestershire border, on 6 December 1732. When his father moved to the West Indies in 1743, Warren joined Howard Hastings, his uncle, in **LONDON** and was sent to **WESTMINSTER** School. Howard died in 1749, and Joseph Creswicke (a distant relative) arranged for his young kinsman to join the **EAST INDIA COMPANY**. His first posting was to Bengal, where he was taken prisoner during the uprising of 1756-57. In 1758, he gained his first diplomatic post when he was appointed Resident at Murshidabad under **ROBERT CLIVE**. In 1769, he was appointed Second-in-Council at Madras and, in 1772, became Governor of Fort William in Bengal. During the next two years, he introduced a system of land revenue administration which was later to be extended throughout the **RAJ**, established a network of courts to dispense justice under civil law and instigated a series of commercial reforms (including the reorganization of arrangements for the collection of customs).

In 1773, the Regulating Act (see **ACT OF PARLIAMENT**) was passed following the Company's request to the British **GOVERNMENT** for a one million pound loan to avoid bankruptcy, creating a Governor General of Fort William and a Governing Council of four members, all to hold office for four years but with the Governor General having only a casting vote. In addition, a Supreme Court of Justice, administering English law, was to be established in Calcutta. For two years, Hastings was consistently defeated in Council, but, in 1776, one of the appointees died and the use of the casting vote became crucial. The next four years were difficult ones but, in 1780, Philip Francis, Hastings's principal adversary, returned to Britain and from then the Governor General effectively controlled policy. Much of that policy related to provision for defence and, in particular, for the control of insurrection. Hastings's most serious problems of civil disturbance occurred between 1780 and 1784, when a coalition of Indian leaders gained a series of military victories in Madras. Considerable additions of men and money to the colonial army in the region, coupled with the death of one of the Indian strategists, eventually resulted in a peace agreement. The situation remained tense, and Hastings became implicated in a number of issues which suggested, at best, a thoughtless and high-handed attitude and, at worst, interference in the course of justice. One of these involved

Nandkumar, a merchant who accused the Governor General of bribery. Hastings replied with a charge of conspiracy, but before either claim could be examined judicially another merchant accused Nandkumar of forgery. He was tried in the Supreme Court and condemned to death. Public opinion was outraged because, although the death sentence for forgery was legitimate under English law, it was unknown in India. Inevitably, Hastings was accused of putting pressure on the judges. Another controversy surrounded the treatment of Rajah Chait Singh, who was driven to rebellion in 1781 by Hastings's demands for money and was eventually defeated and dispossessed.

Hastings returned to Britain in 1785, convinced that he had no future in India and, in 1788, **WILLIAM PITT THE YOUNGER**, under pressure from **WHIG** activists led by **EDMUND BURKE** and supported by Francis, impeached him. The proceedings lasted for seven years and, though they eventually ended in acquittal on all charges, drew heavily on Hastings's financial resources. Despite the court proceedings, there were many who continued to support him. When he appeared before **PARLIAMENT** in 1813 to give evidence on Indian affairs, the **HOUSE OF COMMONS** rose to applaud him and, the following year, he was made a member of the **PRIVY COUNCIL**. For the most part, however, he lived quietly in Oxfordshire until his death on 22 August 1818.

HATTERSLEY, ROY SYDNEY GEORGE (1932-). Deputy Leader of the **LABOUR PARTY** between 1983 and 1992, Hattersley was born on 28 December 1932, the son of Mr and Mrs Frederick Hattersley. He was educated at Sheffield City **GRAMMAR SCHOOL** and at Hull University, where he studied economics. He joined the Labour Party in 1949 but worked as a journalist and a health services executive before becoming the Labour Member of **PARLIAMENT** for Sparkbrook in 1964. For the following three years, he was **PARLIAMENTARY PRIVATE SECRETARY** at the Ministry of Pensions then, in 1967, became **PARLIAMENTARY SECRETARY** at the Ministry of Labour.

Hattersley was made **MINISTER** of Defence for Administration in 1969 but, after the **CONSERVATIVE PARTY** took control of the **HOUSE OF COMMONS** in 1970, reverted to **THE OPPOSITION** benches as Spokesman on Defence (1972) and **EDUCATION** and Science (1972-74). In **HAROLD WILSON**'s administration he was **MINISTER OF STATE** for

Foreign and Commonwealth Affairs (1974-76) and under **JAMES CALLAGHAN** was **SECRETARY OF STATE** for Prices and Consumer Protection (1976-79). Later, he served as Opposition Spokesman on the Environment (1979-80) and Home Affairs (1980-83) before being elected Deputy Leader of the Labour Party under Neil Kinnock. Regarded as a right-winger, his union with the more left-wing Kinnock was seen as a 'dream ticket' which would unite all members of the Party, oust Prime Minister **MARGARET THATCHER** and take Labour to power.

Hattersley became the Opposition Spokesman on Economic Affairs and worked to isolate left-wing extremists, devise policies suited to contemporary needs and fight off the challenge of the **SOCIAL DEMOCRATIC PARTY (SDP)**, which was attempting to claim the political middle ground. Despite a glitzy campaign, Labour lost the 1987 **GENERAL ELECTION**, but both leaders were reelected the following year and Hattersley became Spokesman on Home Affairs. In the weeks before the 1992 general election, opinion polls were favouring Labour and forecasting a change of **GOVERNMENT**, but a last-minute swing to the Conservatives kept **JOHN MAJOR** in **DOWNING STREET**. Hattersley and Kinnock both resigned shortly afterwards. Outside Parliament, Hattersley has developed a considerable reputation as a historian, novelist and political commentator.

HEALEY, DENIS WINSTON (1917-). Defence **MINISTER** and **CHANCELLOR OF THE EXCHEQUER** in the **LABOUR PARTY GOVERNMENT**s of the 1960s and 1970s, Healey was born in Keighley on 30 August 1917. He was educated at Bradford Grammar School and **OXFORD** University then served with the Royal Engineers in North Africa and Italy during the **SECOND WORLD WAR**, rising to the rank of Major, earning a mention in despatches and receiving the MBE (1945).

Healey contested the **PARLIAMENT**ary **CONSTITUENCY** of Pudsey and Otley for Labour in 1945 but failed to win election and was appointed Secretary of the Party's International Department. In 1952, he became Member of Parliament for South-East Leeds but had to wait until 1964 for his first **GOVERNMENT** post, as Defence Minister in **HAROLD WILSON**'s administration. When the **CONSERVATIVE PARTY** returned to power in 1970, he was made **OPPOSITION** Spokesman on Foreign Affairs (1970-72) and then Shadow **CHANCELLOR OF THE EXCHEQUER** (see **SHADOW MINISTER**) from 1972 to 1974.

Wilson appointed him Chancellor in 1974, and he remained there until 1979 despite a series of economic crises which led to public spending cuts and accusations that he was betraying socialism by imposing monetarist policies (see **MONETARISM**). When Wilson resigned in 1976, Healey made the first of three attempts to become Leader of the Party but lost to **JAMES CALLAGHAN**. He tried again when Callaghan retired in 1980 and was unexpectedly beaten by **MICHAEL FOOT**, much to the delight of the Conservatives, who feared that the moderate policies espoused by the former Chancellor would have a more widespread appeal than the radical left-wing policies of Foot. Healey, however, became Deputy Leader and acted as Opposition Spokesman on **TREASURY** Affairs from 1979 until 1981 then on Foreign Affairs from 1981 until 1987. He made his third attempt to win the leadership in 1983 but was defeated by Neil Kinnock and eventually resigned from the Shadow **CABINET** in 1987. He was created **BARON** Healey in 1992.

HEARTH TAX, 1662. This tax (amounting to two shillings a year) was levied on the number of hearths or fireplaces in a property and was an attempt to raise assured levels of finance for the **EXCHEQUER** and replace surviving **FEUDAL SYSTEM** dues. It was crude and fiercely unpopular and was replaced by the **WINDOW TAX** in 1696.

HEATH, EDWARD RICHARD GEORGE (1916-). The **PRIME MINISTER** who successfully negotiated the United Kingdom's entry to the **EUROPEAN COMMUNITY (EC)**, Edward Heath was born in Broadstairs on 9 July 1916. He was educated at Chatham House School (Ramsgate) and at **OXFORD** University, where he was President of the Conservative Association in 1937 and of the Union in 1939. During the **SECOND WORLD WAR**, he served with the Royal Artillery, rising to the rank of Major in 1945 and earning a mention in despatches and an MBE.

Returning to civilian life, Heath worked in a merchant bank then entered the **HOUSE OF COMMONS** as the Member of **PARLIAMENT** for Bexley in 1950, one of the 'new style' supporters of the **CONSERVATIVE PARTY**, intellectual and middle class rather than aristocratic. He was appointed Assistant Chief **WHIP** in February 1951 and Lord Commissioner of **THE TREASURY** in November of the same year. In 1952, he became Joint Deputy Chief Whip and three years later was made Chief

Whip and **PARLIAMENTARY SECRETARY** to the Treasury. He was **MINISTER** of Labour (1959-60), **LORD PRIVY SEAL** (1960-63) then **SECRETARY OF STATE** for Industry, Trade and Regional Development and **PRESIDENT OF THE BOARD OF TRADE** until 1964. In 1965, he became the first Conservative Leader to be elected by a ballot of Tory MPs and, in 1970, won a surprise **GENERAL ELECTION** victory to become Prime Minister.

His four years in office were characterized by high levels of inflation and protracted **TRADE UNION** opposition to his Industrial Relations **BILL**. In 1973, with the country reduced by energy shortages to working a **THREE DAY WEEK** as a result of a confrontation with the National Union of Mineworkers, he capitulated to the demands of organized labour. Convinced of the case for European unity, he successfully negotiated the UK's entry to the **COMMON MARKET** in 1972 but, in the process, made political enemies of those who felt that closer links with Europe would lead to a loss of sovereignty. Widespread public concern about lack of economic stability and the implications of membership of the EEC led to a Conservative defeat at the general election in February 1974. With 297 seats compared to the 301 for the **LABOUR PARTY**, 14 for the **LIBERAL PARTY**, nine for the Nationalists and 12 for **NORTHERN IRELAND**, Heath struggled to form a coalition **GOVERNMENT** but failed, and **HAROLD WILSON** became Prime Minister.

A second defeat followed in October of the same year and, within a few months, he had been replaced as Leader of the Party by **MARGARET THATCHER**. However, he retained his seat in the House of Commons and, during the 1980s, became an increasingly outspoken critic of Mrs Thatcher, who excluded him from administrative posts throughout her period as Prime Minister. However, his reputation as an international statesman was undiminished, and, in 1990, he travelled to Iraq to secure the release of 33 British hostages held by Saddam Hussein. Sir Edward is also a noted yachtsman. He won the Sydney to Hobart Race in 1969, captained the British Admiral's Cup team in 1971 and 1979 and led the British Sardinia Cup team in 1980. In addition, he is an accomplished musician and has been a Member of the Council of the Royal College of Music and Chairman of the **LONDON** Symphony Orchestra Trust. He was made a Knight of the Garter in 1992 (see **ORDER OF THE GARTER**).

HEENAN, JOHN CARMEL (1905-73). A committed ecumenical, Heenan was Roman Catholic Archbishop of **WESTMINSTER** from 1963 until 1975 and was widely considered to be the spokesman for his Church in the United Kingdom. He was born in Ilford on 26 January 1905, the youngest child of four in the family of James Heenan (a civil servant in the Patent Office) and his wife, Anne. Both parents were Irish and raised their three sons and one daughter in a devoutly religious home. John made his desire to join the priesthood clear while he was still a child and was greatly encouraged by his mother and his parish priest. He was educated at St Ignatius College (**LONDON**), St Cuthbert's College (Ushaw) and the English College in Rome (where he earned doctorates in philosophy and theology). He was ordained in 1930 and, the following year, was appointed Assistant Priest at the Church of St Mary and St Ethelburga in Barking. In 1936, disguised as a psychology lecturer, he visited the Soviet Union in order to study social conditions there and on his return to **ENGLAND** was appointed Priest at St Stephen's Church in Manor Park, London.

Over the next few years, Heenan wrote a series of popular books on the Catholic faith and enjoyed a growing reputation as a public speaker. During the **SECOND WORLD WAR**, he became known as 'The Radio Priest' because of his regular wireless broadcasts. In 1947, he was invited to become Superior of the Catholic Missionary Society and, in 1951, was appointed Bishop of Leeds. By then, he had moved into television and was a regular participant in talk shows and interviews. Undoubtedly, this ability to communicate to laymen was one of the reasons for his appointment as Archbishop of **LIVERPOOL** and Metropolitan of the Northern Province in 1957. In that working-class community, with a high proportion of immigrants from **IRELAND**, he resurrected plans for the building of a cathedral and saw the structure well on the way to completion before he left the city in 1963, following his appointment as Archbishop of Westminster. He spent most of the next three years at the Second Vatican Council, where he was regarded as something of a rebel because of his espousal of religious liberty and reconciliation with the Jews. He was made a Cardinal in 1965 and, during the tempestuous years following the Council, held the Roman Catholic Church in Britain together while it adapted to changed conditions.

He died in London on 7 November 1975 and was buried in Westminster Cathedral beside the fourteenth station of the Cross.

HENRY I (1068-1135). The youngest son of **WILLIAM THE CON-QUEROR** and his wife, Matilda, Henry became King of **ENG-LAND** in 1100, following the suspicious death of his brother, **WILLIAM II**, and ruled until 1135. Over the decade after the Conqueror died in 1087, Henry switched allegiance between his two warring brothers — Robert, Duke of Normandy and William, King of England — and is widely believed to have been responsible for the 'accident' which led to William's death on 1 August 1100. With Robert still on a **CRUSADE** to the Holy Land, Henry seized the royal treasure and persuaded the bishops of **LONDON** and Hereford to crown him King on 5 August. It was an inauspicious start to a reign, but, in many ways, he proved to be a more capable leader than either of his brothers. He repealed several of William's most repressive laws and ensured peace on his northern border by marrying Matilda, daughter of King Malcolm III of **SCOTLAND**. He appointed men of comparatively humble background to positions of importance, provided they were able administrators, and extended the jurisdiction of the courts of the **SHIRE**s and **HUNDRED**s to freemen as well as feudal tenants (see **FEUDAL SYSTEM**). But justice was often harsh (albeit administered according to the tenets of law) and collection of financial dues ruthlessly applied.

Frequently, too, he was in conflict with the Church. Henry took the view that Church officials must be acceptable to the King (because they were reponsible for much wealth and often owned feudal services) so he chose the new bishops, received homage from them and invested them in their Sees. Pope Paschal II and Anselm, **ARCHBISHOP OF CANTERBURY**, attempted to persuade him to change his policy but, although he gave up the right to invest the appointees, he retained control over officials and established a pattern of authority which was to last until the 16th century.

Foreign affairs were dominated by relations with Normandy. In 1105, Henry used his brother's lack of control over dissident nobles to invade the Duchy. After a series of unsuccessful negotiations intended to avoid conflict, the two forces met at Tinchebrai on 28 September 1106 (see **BATTLE OF TINCHEBRAI**). Henry captured his brother, Robert (who spent the next 28 years in prison), and reunited England with Normandy. Robert's son, William, was the focus of several revolts over the next few years, but Henry's control over both sides of the English Channel was never seriously challenged. He established a lengthy (though expensive) peace, which he attempted to maintain by making his nobles take an oath of allegiance to Matilda, his only surviving child, as heiress to the throne. He died in Normandy on 1 December 1135, leaving 20 illegitimate children, more than any other English King.

HENRY II (1133-89). The first **PLANTAGENET** King, Henry ruled **ENGLAND** from 1154 until 1189 and became one of the most powerful **MONARCH**s in Europe. He was born at Le Mans (France) on 5 March 1133, the son of Geoffrey Plantagenet, Count of Anjou, and Matilda, daughter of **HENRY I**. In 1147, he invaded England in the hope of gaining the **CROWN** (then in the hands of **STEPHEN**) for his mother. That campaign ended unsuccessfully, but, in 1152, he married Eleanor, Duchess of Aquitaine, who brought a dowry in the form of lands which, added to his own territories in Normandy, Anjou and Maine, made him ruler of a large part of continental Europe. He returned to England in 1153, by which time Stephen had lost his wife and son and was in no mood to resist. The King meekly named Henry his heir; the young aspirant did not have long to wait for the throne because Stephen died in October of the following year. Henry's **CORONATION** was on 19 December.

His first concern was to restore order following the near-anarchy of his predecessor's reign. To that effect, he demolished **CASTLES** which nobles had built without the King's consent, reestablished the court system and raised new taxes from landholders to pay his army. In the north, he regained Cumberland, Westmorland and Northumberland, which Stephen had lost to the Scots. But the Church resented many of the ecclesistical reforms which Henry proposed, wanting more independence from secular control than the King was willing to tolerate. The result was a clash with Archbishop of Canterbury **THOMAS BECKET**. In the mid-12th century, about one in 50 of the population was a clerk in holy orders. Henry wanted any of these people convicted of crimes by the Church courts to be handed over to the secular courts for punishment. Becket refused to accept such a restriction on the Church's jurisdiction and was forced to flee to France for safety. He returned in 1170 but was murdered in **CANTERBURY** Cathedral by four of Henry's knights on 29 December.

The following years were turbulent ones for the King. In 1171, he annexed **IRELAND** and, in 1173, faced a rebellion led by his wife and sons, supported by King Louis VII of France, King William I of **SCOTLAND** and Count Philip of Flanders. He defeated the rebels in Anjou and Normandy then, in 1174, captured William at Alnwick, forcing him to accept the English King's overlordship of Scotland. The rebellion collapsed.

Henry died at Chinon (France) on 6 July 1189 while taking part in a campaign against a force led by his son Richard (later **RICHARD I**) and Philip II of France and was buried in the abbey church at Fontevrault. His empire stretched from the Tweed to the Pyrenees, and England was in a much more stable state than it had been when he inherited it. He had centralized much government activity and had removed the military obligations of the **FEUDAL SYSTEM**, replacing them with taxes which were used to pay a soldiery directly under his control. Judges administered the law in conjunction with 12 men from the local community, laying the basis of a **JURY** system of justice. And disputes over property ownership were now settled by law rather than by battle. These and related legal innovations created an organized code of practice which formed the basis of English **COMMON LAW**.

HENRY III (1207-72). Only nine years of age when he succeeded to the throne of **ENGLAND** on the death of his father, King **JOHN**, Henry was born at Winchester on 1 October 1207. In 1216, after John's death, Henry paid homage to Pope Honorius III as vassal (one of the political legacies left by his father) and was crowned on 28 October. During his minority, the country was ruled by a Council of **REGENCY** led by William Marshal, Earl of Pembroke, which gradually restored the royal authority lost during John's reign. In 1234, however, Henry took control himself, initiating a period of weak government which ultimately led to rebellion. In part, the troubles stemmed from the time following his marriage to Eleanor of Provence in 1236; the introduction of a series of Frenchmen to positions of power at his court did little to improve his popularity with England's nobility. Also, he levied heavy taxes (partly in order to refill the coffers emptied by his father, partly to finance his military campaigns and partly to pay for his extravagant lifestyle) and appointed many Italians to Church offices as a recompense for papal influence in maintaining order during the Regency, angering English churchmen. His lack of military ability added to the opposition. Eager to recover the French lands lost by his father, he attempted to force Louis IX from Poitou in 1242 but was humiliatingly defeated at the **BAT-**

TLE OF SAINTES. His political skills were equally suspect. In 1254, he made a bargain with Pope Innocent IV to finance the conquest of Sicily in return for the appointment of his son, Edmund, as King after the victory and for permission to tithe all Church revenues in his lands. English nobles could see no advantage in such a venture and deeply resented Henry's pressure on them to raise funds so, when the invasion collapsed, the King's prestige fell further and the country marched closer to civil war.

In 1258, faced with the threat of excommunication unless he fulfilled his promises to the Pope, he appealed for help to the nobles, who promised aid if he would agree to a plan to reform the government. The nobles wanted him to ensure that he took decisions only on the advice of a **PRIVY COUNCIL** of 15 members chosen by the leading families in the realm (see **PROVISIONS OF OXFORD**). The King accepted the conditions at the **OXFORD PARLIAMENT** and the proposals were put into effect — all of the **SHERIFF**s were replaced, an inquiry into the administrative misconduct of royal officials was instituted and a code of legal and administrative practice (the **PROVISIONS OF WESTMINSTER**) was drawn up. Also, in 1259, the Privy Council negotiated a peace treaty with France on Henry's behalf.

Increasingly, however, the nobles split over the implementation of the reforms. Henry added his weight to the conservatives, and Louis IX, called on to mediate, annulled the **OXFORD** agreement. The radical faction, led by **SIMON DE MONTFORT**, refused to accept the decision and went to war, capturing the King (along with his son, later **EDWARD I**) at the **BATTLE OF LEWES** in 1264. Edward escaped the following year and raised an army which defeated and killed Simon at the **BATTLE OF EVESHAM**, releasing the King from captivity. From that time, Henry handed over power to his son and exercised his kingly duties only in name. He died on 16 November 1272 in **LONDON**. A sensitive, cultured man, Henry had no aptitude whatsoever for leadership but was a great patron of the arts and particularly of church architecture. During his reign, **WESTMINSTER** Abbey was rebuilt and the plain Norman style of building was superseded by the flying buttresses and lancet windows of the Early English and Gothic styles.

HENRY IV (1366-1413). Son of **JOHN OF GAUNT** and his wife, Blanche, Henry was the first of the **LANCASTRIAN** Kings of **ENGLAND**, ruling from 1399 until 1413. He was born in

Bolingbroke Castle (Lincolnshire) on 3 April 1367, became Earl of Derby about 1377 and was created Duke of Hereford in 1397. His first foray into political matters occurred in 1387 when, with other nobles, he accused **RICHARD II's** court favourites of treason. In 1398, he was exiled following a quarrel with Thomas Mowbray, Duke of Norfolk, but returned the following year to reclaim the family lands which the King had confiscated on John of Gaunt's death. Richard was extremely unpopular at the time as a result of his policies of high taxation and disregard for the rights of **PARLIAMENT** so Henry was able to rally a great deal of support and, in September 1399, force the King to abdicate. Parliament declared its approval and proclaimed Henry King in his stead.

The reign was beset by rebellion. Determined to preserve as much power as possible for the **MONARCH**y, he quickly made enemies of many leading **KNIGHT**s. Some of his opponents advanced the claims to the throne of Richard's preferred heir, Edmund Mortimer, the Duke of Clarence. Others rallied to the flag of the Percy family, who were unhappy about their returns for defeating the Scots at the Battle of Homildon Hill in 1402. Matters came to a head at the **BATTLE OF SHREWSBURY** in 1403, when Sir Henry Percy (known as Hotspur) was killed and Thomas Percy, Earl of Worcester, captured (and later executed). In 1405, a rebellion in the north ended with the execution of the Archbishop of **YORK** (Richard Scrope) and Thomas Mowbray, Earl of Norfolk and son of the Mowbray with whom Henry had differed in 1398. The following year, a revolt in **WALES**, headed by Owain Glyndwr, was suppressed (though protests flared sporadically until 1409) and, in 1408, the Earl of Northumberland, father of Hotspur, was killed by royalist forces at Branham Moor in Yorkshire. By that time, Henry's health was deteriorating and he was finding himself under attack in Parliament over the cost of his government, a cost which was inevitably increased by the problems of keeping the peace. His son, Hal (later **HENRY V**), added his voice to the chorus of criticism, demanding greater say in the way the country was being run, and by 1410 had succeeded in getting several of his allies on to the King's council of advisers. The Prince's influence declined after 1411, but he did not have long to wait for real power because Henry died in **WESTMINSTER** Abbey on 20 March 1413. A literate and energetic monarch, he had brought an element of stability to his kingdom despite the debilitating effects of a disease which was probably syphilis, the constant threat of civil upheaval and ultimately the perfidy of his son.

HENRY V (1387-1422). The eldest son of **HENRY IV** and Mary de Bohun, Henry was King of **ENGLAND** from 1413 until his death in 1422 and earned a reputation as a military leader of great accomplishment. Born in Monmouth in August or September 1387, he was brought up in the court of King **RICHARD II** following his father's exile in 1398 and, in October the following year, was created Earl of Chester, Duke of Cornwall and **PRINCE OF WALES**. Later, he added the titles of Duke of Aquitaine and Duke of Lancaster. From 1402, he took command of the army fighting Owain Glyndwr's Welsh rebels, pursuing that campaign until 1408, when he turned his attentions more to the processes of government. After he had succeeded his father as King on 21 March 1413, he planned an invasion of France in an attempt to recapture Aquitaine, Normandy, Maine and Touraine and add other parts of the country to his empire. His experience in **WALES** stood him in good stead. The victory at the **BATTLE OF AGINCOURT** in 1415 demonstrated his ability to use a relatively small army with great effect against numerically superior forces and the Battle of the Seine, the following year, showed his strong grip on the principles of maritime control.

The reconquest of Normandy by a long process of attrition, between 1417 and early 1419, led to the **TREATY OF TROYES** (1420), which recognised Henry as heir to the French throne, but he never tasted the full fruits of his victory because he died of typhus at Bois de Vincennes on 31 August 1422. A hard, stern man, he was often ruthless but frequently showed a streak of liberality (as when he freed the Earl of March, who had been a contender for the English throne). And, in a comparatively short reign, he took England to a place among the leading nations of Europe. It is unlikely, however, that the Treaty of Troyes would have been accepted in the parts of France which remained unconquered so, had he lived, he would have found it necessary to seek additional funds from **PARLIAMENT** in order to continue the policy of territorial aggrandizement. It is quite probable that such a request would have been turned down because the conquest was taking much longer than anticipated.

HENRY VI (1421-71). The last **LANCASTRIAN** King of **ENGLAND**, Henry reigned from 1422 until 1461 and from October 1470 until May 1471. The son of **HENRY V** and Catherine de

Valois, he was only ten months old when he became **MONARCH** following his father's death on 31 August 1422. Under the terms of the **TREATY OF TROYES** (1420), he succeeded to the throne of France in October of the same year as a result of the death of his grandfather, King Charles VI. During his minority, England was ruled by a council led by the Duke of Gloucester, but, by 1437, he was considered old enough to govern for himself. He proved to be a weak and ineffectual head of state, subject to mental breakdowns and with a horror of war. His French territories were gradually lost and, by 1453, when the **HUNDRED YEARS WAR** finally ended, **CALAIS** was all that remained of the lands conquered by his father. At home, government was left largely to his advisers, who were often inefficient and more concerned with their own aggrandizement than with the affairs of England. Moreover, the King's natural generosity was exploited by members of his court, draining his resources.

The weak monarch, the loss of prestige as a result of the relinquishing of Normandy and the other French lands, poor leadership by **MINISTERS** and the increasing poverty of the **CROWN** provoked civil upheaval. Opposing factions led by the royalist Duke of Somerset and the dissident **DUKE OF YORK** engaged in a struggle for superiority which culminated in the **WARS OF THE ROSES**. In 1453, Henry suffered a bout of insanity. His wife, Margaret of Anjou, claimed the **REGENCY** but was an unpopular consort, and, in March of the following year, York was appointed Lord Protector, effectively governing in the King's name. Margaret increasingly saw York as a potential rival to the throne for her son, Edward, so, when the King recovered from his illness late in 1454, she persuaded him to restore the loyal Somerset to his court. The scene was set for conflict.

The first struggle was the **BATTLE OF ST ALBANS** on 22 May 1455 but trouble flared intermittently in the years which followed and, on 10 July 1460, Henry himself was taken captive by the Yorkists at the **BATTLE OF NORTHAMPTON**. York claimed the crown but **PARLIAMENT** refused to agree, though it did force Henry to recognize the Duke as his lawful heir. Though York was killed at the **BATTLE OF WAKEFIELD** on 30 December 1460, his forces gained the upper hand in the civil war and Henry was taken captive again at the second **BATTLE OF ST ALBANS** on 17 February 1461. The Duke of York's son, Edward, was declared King as **EDWARD IV** on 4 March and defeated the royalists, at the **BATTLE OF TOWTON** on 29 March.

Henry fled to **SCOTLAND** but returned in 1464 to support an abortive Lancastrian rising which failed to make any headway. After living in hiding for over a year, he was finally captured near Clitheroe in July 1465 and taken to the **TOWER OF LONDON**. Lancastrian successes restored him to his throne in October 1470. However, Edward re-entered **LONDON** in April the following year and, on 4 May, defeated Henry's army at the **BATTLE OF TEWKESBURY**. Prince Edward, the King's son, was killed in the fighting and the King himself taken prisoner and placed in the Tower of London. He was murdered there on the night of 21 May. A pious, generous man, he was venerated as a saint after his death and has a legacy in Eton College and King's College, **CAMBRIDGE**, both of which he founded.

HENRY VII (1457-1509). The first of the **TUDOR** Monarchs, Henry was King of **ENGLAND** from 1485 until 1509. The son of Edmund Tudor, Earl of Richmond, and Margaret Beaufort, he was born in Pembroke Castle on 28 January 1457, nearly three months after his father had died and while his mother was still only 14. Margaret was the great-granddaughter of **JOHN OF GAUNT**, whose children by Catherine Swynford were born before the couple married. **RICHARD II** legitimized the family and that legitimization was confirmed by **HENRY IV** but with the stipulation that the Beaufort line was excluded from any right to the **CROWN**. Thus, while Henry Tudor's claim to the throne was very weak, it was the best the **LANCASTRIAN** opposition to **RICHARD III** could muster.

During his youth, Henry was sent to Brittany for safety and there (supported by the French, who resented Richard's argument that he was their rightful **MONARCH**) he became the central figure in the attempts to oust the King. In 1485, he landed with an army at Milford Haven and marched east, meeting the royal forces at the **BATTLE OF BOSWORTH FIELD** on 22 August 1485. Richard's troops were defeated, the King himself was killed and Henry took the crown. On 18 January 1486, he married Elizabeth of York, daughter of **EDWARD IV**, uniting the rival houses and ending the **WARS OF THE ROSES**.

The early years of Henry's reign were marked by a series of attempts to remove him. In 1486, Lord Lovell's ill-prepared revolt was easily quelled, but, the following year, a rebellion led by Lambert Simnel was only crushed after the hard-fought **BATTLE OF STOKE**. Then Perkin Warbeck (with support at various times from France, Austria, the Netherlands and **SCOTLAND**) led three invasions from the continent before being captured in 1497. But, despite these distractions, Henry proved to be an able administrator. One of his major aims was the restoration of order after a long period of civil war — **JUSTICES OF THE PEACE** were given additional powers, advisory councils were established and arrangements were made for the poor to present cases for adjudication. Another aim was the improvement of royal finances so that the court could maintain its status — revenue from customs dues was increased through the encouragement of exports, new markets were sought (Henry helped John Cabot finance his voyages of discovery to North America in 1496, for example) and fiscal obligations were rigorously enforced. Foreign policy was similarly judicious. Realizing that war is expensive, Henry relied on diplomacy. A peace treaty was signed with France in 1492 and with the Netherlands in 1496. Dynastic marriages further cemented international relations. Henry's daughter Margaret was married to James IV of Scotland, daughter Mary to Archduke Charles (heir to the Hapsburg empire) and eldest son Arthur to **CATHERINE OF ARAGON**. And trade enhanced the political links. Commercial treaties with Denmark, Florence, the Netherlands, Spain and others greatly benefited the country's merchant community.

Henry died on 21 April 1509, leaving England one of the richest and most powerful states in Europe. In many ways, his success as a ruler reflected a popular desire for strong leadership after a long period of insecurity, but it was a result, too, of his own obsessive attention to detail and his firm control of income and expenditure.

HENRY VIII (1491-1547). King of **ENGLAND** from 1509 until 1547, Henry was a despotic, selfish **TUDOR** ruler who managed to maintain peace at a time when much of mainland Europe was in turmoil. The son of **HENRY VII** and Elizabeth of York, he was born at Greenwich on 28 June 1491. In his youth, he became an accomplished linguist, musician and sportsman before succeeding to the throne following his father's death on 21 April 1509. Initially, he left affairs of state to others, although, in 1511, he joined the Holy League (an alliance formed by Pope Julius II) and, two years later, invaded France.

It was the matter of an heir which encouraged his interest in the detail of politics. Shortly after becoming King, he had married **CATHERINE OF ARAGON** (the widow of his older brother,

Arthur). Although she had a daughter in 1516, as the years passed, it became increasingly unlikely that she would give him a son. His almoner, **THOMAS WOLSEY**, persuaded him that the Vatican would grant him a divorce on the grounds that the Church forbade marriage to a sister-in-law. Wolsey had miscalculated, however, and Pope Clement VII refused to authorize any change. Henry had Wolsey replaced by **THOMAS MORE** and took measures designed to reduce the influence of the Catholic Church in England, attempting to put pressure on Clement, but with no success. In 1531, he separated from Catherine, and the marriage was annulled in May 1533, four months after the King had secretly married **ANNE BOLEYN**. In 1534, the **ACT OF SUCCESSION** (see **ACT OF PARLIAMENT**) legitimized Anne's offspring, despite the opposition of More and others. Anne, however, fared little better than her predecessor. She produced one child (later **ELIZA-BETH I**) but, in 1536, was found guilty of adultery and beheaded.

Henry then married **JANE SEYMOUR**, who died two weeks after giving birth to the male child (later **EDWARD VI**) he so much wanted. In January 1540, he married **ANNE OF CLEVES** — a political arrangement designed to forestall a Catholic alliance against him. By June, the danger was over, and, the following month, Henry, never happy in the relationship, obtained another divorce. He then turned to **CATHERINE HOWARD** but, after only a few months, **THOMAS CRANMER**, the **ARCHBISHOP OF CANTERBURY**, informed the King of her amoral activities before the marriage; Catherine denied all charges of misconduct since her wedding but was beheaded in 1542. **CATHERINE PARR** became Henry's last wife in 1543 and survived him.

Perhaps inevitably, Henry's marital exploits have tended to overshadow other aspects of his reign. It is clear, however, that he was an astute and able ruler. His anticlerical policies, including the breakup of the great monastic estates (see **DISSOLUTION OF THE MONASTERIES, REFORMATION**), received a considerable measure of support from a population dissatisfied by the corruption amongst the clergy. And his policy of giving much of the Church's land to his supporters helped ensure loyalty and public order. Henry also brought **WALES** into full legal union with England between 1534 and 1536, successfully pacified troubles in **IRELAND** and created an effective and efficient navy which was later to challenge Spain's dominance of the seas. But his supremacy over the Church was enforced harshly, albeit within the bounds of the law, and his decision-making influenced by an inherently egotistical view that his good was England's good. He died in **LONDON** on 28 January 1547 and was buried at **WINDSOR CASTLE**. (See **ACT OF SUPREMACY; CHURCH OF ENGLAND; DEFENDER OF THE FAITH; SUPREME GOVERNOR**).

HEXHAM, BATTLE OF, 15 May 1464. This battle ended in victory for Yorkist forces during the **WARS OF THE ROSES**. The **LANCASTRIAN** commander, Lord Somerset, was captured and executed together with over 20 of his nobleman allies.

HIGH COMMISSION. This title is given to the embassy of a country which is a member of the **COMMONWEALTH OF NATIONS** in a country which is also a member. The head of the embassy is known as the High Commissioner.

HIGH COURT OF JUSTICE. A division of the **SUPREME COURT OF JUDICATURE** in **ENGLAND** and **WALES**, the High Court consists of the **COURT OF CHANCERY**, the **QUEEN'S BENCH** and the **FAMILY DIVISION**. It ranks below the **COURT OF APPEAL** but above the **CROWN COURTS**. Judges of the High Court may sit in any of the three divisions.

HILLFORTS. This term usually refers to defensive sites of ramparts, ditches and buildings constructed on hills from about 1200 BC (that is, towards the end of the **BRONZE AGE** and the beginning of the **IRON AGE**). Common throughout Britain, larger ones — some with walls up to 15 feet high — were built in the sixth century BC as population pressures increased. They were replaced by larger settlements with integral defences (oppida) from about 100 BC. (See **CASTLES**).

HOBBES, THOMAS (1588-1679). A political theorist who argued for strong central government, Hobbes was one of the major philosophers of the 17th century. He was born in Westport (Wiltshire) on 5 April 1588, the second son of Thomas Hobbes (the local Vicar), and was educated at Westport Church School, then privately and finally at **OXFORD** University. After he graduated in 1608, he became tutor to William Cavendish (later Earl of Devonshire) and, in 1610, accompanied him on a tour of Europe. On his return, he concentrated on classical studies but went back to the continent in 1629 as travelling companion to the son of Sir Gervase Clifton. In 1634, he was abroad once more, again accompanying one of the Cavendish family. The second and third visits, especially, brought him into contact with some of the leading European thinkers and stimulated his interest in philosophy, science and mathematics.

When Hobbes returned to **ENGLAND** in 1637, he prepared a treatise entitled *The Elements of Law, Natural and Politic,* which was circulating in manuscript form by 1640 and argued that peace depended on an agreement by all citizens to obey the will of an absolute sovereign power (which in 17th century Britain was, in effect, the King). His views offended royalists (who believed in the **DIVINE RIGHT OF KINGS** and resented his attempt to explain sovereignty in terms of a social contract) and Parliamentarians (who resented any argument favouring an absolute monarchy). Afraid for his life, Hobbes fled to Paris in 1640. He remained there for 11 years, tutoring the exiled **PRINCE OF WALES** (later **CHARLES II**) from 1646 until 1651, associating with French scholars and publishing further closely reasoned texts. In *De Cive* (1642), he argued that a Christian Church and a Christian state are the same body and that the sovereign who is the head of that body has the right to judge religious debates and determine the nature of public worship. His major work — *Leviathan, or the Matter, Form and Power of a Commonwealth, Ecclesiastical and Civil* — appeared in 1651 and attacked attempts both by Catholics and by Presbyterians to challenge the rights of the **MONARCH.** He argued that human beings most fear death and most desire well-being. Fear of death led to the formation of a social contract because without it life would be "solitary, poore, nasty, brutish and short". The contract gave absolute power to the sovereign, who used it to prevent men from harming each other. The will of the sovereign was law and every citizen had a duty to obey the law, although a subject had the right to desert a sovereign who could not protect him and turn to a ruler who could. His comments on Catholics were not well received in France and those on the legitimacy of deserting a sovereign raised hackles at Charles's exiled court so, increasingly friendless, he returned to England later that year.

For the remainder of his life, he was locked in controversial debates, notably with John Bramhall (Bishop of Londonderry) over free will and with scientists at Oxford University over mathematics and physics. His outspoken views made him many enemies and it became more and more difficult for him to publish. Towards the end, he turned, once again, to classical studies and had completed translations of Homer's *Iliad* and parts of the *Odyssey* before he died at Hardwick Hall (Derbyshire) on 4 December 1679, aged 91. After his death, the word *Hobbism* became widely used to describe any view that man is selfish and that absolute government is desirable. However, the idea that government is based on a social contract was incorporated into the more democratic philosophies expressed by **JOHN LOCKE** and Jean Jacques Rousseau and became basic to the concept of constitutional government.

HOGG, QUINTIN McGAREL (1907-). A senior figure in the **CONSERVATIVE PARTY** during the 1950s and 1960s, Hogg was born in **LONDON** on 9 October 1907, the son of Viscount Douglas Hailsham and his wife, Elizabeth (daughter of Judge Trimble Brown of Nashville, Tennessee). He was educated at Eton College and **OXFORD** University (where he was President of the Union in 1929) and called to the Bar in 1932. In 1938, he was elected Member of **PARLIAMENT** for Oxford City but joined the Rifle Brigade at the outbreak of the **SECOND WORLD WAR** and was wounded in the western desert. He was Joint **PARLIAMENTARY UNDER-SECRETARY OF STATE** for Air for a short period in 1945 but returned to the back benches after the **LABOUR PARTY**'s **GENERAL ELECTION** victory and, in 1950, succeeded to his father's viscountcy, taking his seat in the **HOUSE OF LORDS**. From there he held **GOVERNMENT** office as First Lord of the **ADMIRALTY** (1956-57), **MINISTER** of **EDUCATION** (January-September 1957), **LORD PRESIDENT OF THE COUNCIL** (1957-59 and 1960-64), Deputy Leader of the House of Lords (1957-60), **LORD PRIVY SEAL** (1959-60), Leader of the House of Lords (1960-63), Minister for Science and Technology (1959-64) and Minister with Responsibility for Sport (1962-64). He was also Chairman of the Conservative Party from 1957 until 1959.

During the leadership crisis which followed Prime Minister **HAROLD MACMILLAN**'s resignation in 1963, Hogg renounced his peerage and was reelected to the **HOUSE OF COMMONS** as MP for the St Marylebone **CONSTITUENCY** in west **LONDON**. He then became Minister with Responsibility for the Unemployed in the North-East and for Higher **EDUCATION**

(1963-64) and **SECRETARY OF STATE** for Education and Science (April-October 1964) before the Conservatives were ousted from office at the general election. He was made Shadow Home Office Spokesman in 1966 (see **SHADOW MINISTER**) but returned to the Lords in 1970, when he was created **BARON** Hailsham, and concluded a long political career as **LORD CHANCELLOR** under **EDWARD HEATH** (1970-74) and **MARGARET THATCHER** (1979-87). A distinguished legal scholar, he has edited Halsbury's *Laws of England* since 1972, was made a Fellow of the Royal Society in 1973 and has been Rector of Glasgow University (1959-62) and Chancellor of the University of Buckingham (1983-92).

HOLLES, THOMAS PELHAM (1693-1768). The elder son of Thomas, Lord Pelham, and his second wife, Lady Grace Holles, Thomas Holles was **PRIME MINISTER** from 1754 until 1756 and from 1757 until 1762. He inherited his mother's wealth in 1711 and that of his father the following year so he was one of the richest landowners in the country before he was out of his teens. An active supporter of **WHIG** policies, he worked hard to achieve the succession of **GEORGE I**, the first of the **HANOVERIAN** monarchs and, in 1715, was rewarded with appointments as **MARQUESS** of Clare and **DUKE** of Newcastle-upon-Tyne. In 1717, he was made **LORD CHANCELLOR** and, the following year, became a **KNIGHT** of the Garter (see **ORDER OF THE GARTER**). He was made **SECRETARY OF STATE** under **ROBERT WALPOLE** in 1724 and held the office for 30 years, exercising diplomatic skills which were central to the success of the administration of his brother, **HENRY PELHAM**, from 1743 until 1756.

His long experience of political affairs earned him much respect. In particular, he gained a reputation for his adroitness at the management of elections and at securing majorities in the **HOUSE OF COMMONS** by exercising patronage (notably through the distribution of **GOVERNMENT** posts, pensions and well-paid sinecures). When his brother died in March 1754, he succeeded him as Prime Minister, holding the post until November 1756, when he was created Duke of Newcastle-under-Lyme. He began a second period as Premier in July 1757 under an arrangement which made him responsible for the exercise of patronage and **WILLIAM PITT THE ELDER** responsible for the conduct of the **SEVEN YEARS' WAR** but was replaced in May 1762 by **JOHN STUART**, third **EARL** of Bute and a favourite of

GEORGE III. Although he held a government post as **LORD PRIVY SEAL** for a short period in 1765, for the bulk of the last six years of his life, he was in **OPPOSITION**. He died in **LONDON** on 17 November 1768.

HOME GUARD. During the **SECOND WORLD WAR**, this unpaid, volunteer civil defence militia force was formed in May 1940 to fight a possible German invasion of Britain. Initially, it was called the Local Defence Volunteers (comedians rather cruelly re-christened it 'Look, Duck and Vanish') but the name was changed to the Home Guard later in the year. By 1943, about two million men had been enrolled, many of them either too old to be conscripted or in reserved occupations such as mining. They were regarded very much as a last-ditch defence force and were poorly equipped for much of the war (one unit in Lancashire is known to have drilled with spears, and when 500,000 surplus Lee Enfield rifles arrived from the United States of America, they were issued but, for a long time, had no ammunition). They would certainly not have been a major obstacle to a landing, had it come, but they served well as security services, antiaircraft battery personnel, local defence propagandists and morale-boosters. The Home Guard was formally stood down on 1 November 1944 as a symbol that an invasion of Britain would not occur and that victory was achievable. It was disbanded on 31 December 1945.

HOME OFFICE. This **GOVERNMENT** department originated in 1782 in order to create a clear distinction between the administration of domestic and foreign affairs. Headed by the **HOME SECRETARY**, it has particular responsibility for law and order, the **POLICE**, civil defence and **IMMIGRATION**.

HOME RULE. This phrase is used to refer to the movement to repeal the **ACT OF UNION** between **GREAT BRITAIN** and **IRELAND** from about 1870 to about 1914. The Home Rule League, founded by Isaac Butt in 1870, gained 50 seats in the **GENERAL ELECTION** of 1874 and Butt was then succeeded by Charles Parnell. The Irish contingent of Members of **PARLIAMENT**, led by Parnell, held the balance of power in the **HOUSE OF COMMONS** and gained the support of **WILLIAM GLADSTONE**. Home rule **BILL**s were introduced in 1886 and in 1893, but both were rejected by the **HOUSE OF LORDS**. A third bill (in 1912) became law in 1914 but was suspended because of the **FIRST**

WORLD WAR and was bitterly opposed by Sinn Fein. The Government of Ireland Act of 1920 (see **ACT OF PARLIAMENT**) finally partitioned Ireland, with its northern and southern elements gaining separate Parliaments.

There was also a home rule movement in **SCOTLAND** during the 1880s, when nationalism grew alongside radicalism in the Highlands, leading to the establishment of a separate **SECRETARY OF STATE** for Scotland and some regional devolution. Home rule remains the official policy of the Scottish National Party and Plaid Cymru (the nationalist party in **WALES**).

HOME SECRETARY. The holder of this post — formally the **SECRETARY OF STATE** for Home Affairs — is the member of **GOVERNMENT** primarily responsible for business dealing with social affairs within the United Kingdom and is head of the **HOME OFFICE**.

HOOD, ROBIN. A legendary outlaw who lived with his band in Sherwood Forest, Robin Hood stole from the rich and gave to the poor, helped the needy and championed the oppressed. His associates included such larger-than-life figures as Little John, Friar Tuck and Will Scarlet, all of whom were opposed to the evil sheriff of Nottingham. Stories about Robin were current by the late 14th century (he is mentioned in *Piers Plowman*, an allegorical poem written by William Langland c. 1360–1400) but there is no clear evidence that he ever existed. Some writers have argued that the character is based on the Earl of Huntingdon, who was born at Locksley in 1160. Others claim that he was a **SAXON** patriot who stood firm against the **NORMANS** and came from the Wakefield district of Yorkshire, a supporter of Earl Thomas of Lancaster outlawed by **EDWARD II** or a disinherited follower of **SIMON DE MONTFORT**. It is likely that the stories originated during the 13th century, when the sheriffs were the chief local representatives of the King and were charged with upholding deeply resented laws which prevented local people from hunting in the forests. The context of these early ballads suggests that Robin was based in South Yorkshire but over the centuries the tales were much embellished. (Maid Marian, for instance, was a postmedieval introduction.) They still form the basis of movies, television series and theatre productions as well as innumerable stories and poems.

HOTSPUR. (See **HENRY PERCY**).

HOUSE OF COMMONS. Currently, the House comprises 651 Members (MPs) who are elected for a maximum of five years by universal adult (18+ years) suffrage. This lower chamber is the major element in **PARLIAMENT** and forms the base for the Parliamentary democracy of the nation, each MP representing a community-based **CONSTITUENCY**. It has its origin in the 13th century principle that taxes should be agreed by those who pay them and is the main arm of the legislature of the United Kingdom. (Statutes are passed by the Commons and nowadays only commented upon by the **HOUSE OF LORDS**.) Deliberations are overseen by the **SPEAKER**, whose job it is to interpret procedure and to regulate debates. The **GOVERNMENT** benches are faced by **THE OPPOSITION** benches, which are occupied by members of the second largest Party in the house.

HOUSE OF LORDS. The upper chamber of **PARLIAMENT** comprises unelected hereditary and life peers, two Archbishops, 23 Law lords and 24 Bishops. The title of the House was not used until the 16th century and has its basis in the advice traditionally given to the **MONARCH** by the nobility. Its powers have been much reduced over recent centuries. In particular, since 1911 it has had no rights to amend any finance **BILL**s and can only delay other bills by one year. All bills are sent from the **HOUSE OF COMMONS** to the Lords, where valuable debates can occur, though the lower House retains the real powers of the legislature. This House is still, however, the supreme court of the land and is thus the final arbiter of the judicial system (see **JUDICIARY**).

HOWARD, CATHERINE (?-1542). The fifth wife of **HENRY VIII**, Catherine was the daughter of Lord Edmund Howard, an impoverished nobleman, and Lady Howard. After her mother's death, she was raised by her paternal grandmother, Agnes, **DUCHESS** of Norfolk, and had several lovers, including Henry Mannock (her music teacher), Francis Dereham (who referred to her as his wife) and Thomas Culpepper (her cousin). Stephen Gardiner, the Bishop of Winchester, brought her to Henry's attention in 1540, at a time when Henry was becoming tired of his fourth wife, **ANNE OF CLEVES**. The marriage to Anne had been made for political reasons and, by the spring of 1540, had become an embarrassment.

Its validity was questioned and in mid-July it was annulled by Parliament, leaving Henry free to marry Catherine on 28 July. Henry appears to have been much in love with his new Queen but late in 1541 **THOMAS CRANMER**, the **ARCHBISHOP OF CANTERBURY**, drew his attention to her premarital affairs. Enquiries suggested that she had been unfaithful with Culpepper and also with Dereham, now her secretary, even after she became the King's wife. All those accused roundly rejected the charges of adultery, but **PARLIAMENT**, on 11 February 1542, declared that it was a **TREASON**able offence for an unchaste woman to marry the King. Henry, although deeply distressed, approved the **BILL** of attainder and Catherine was beheaded at the **TOWER OF LONDON** on 13 February after only 19 months as Queen.

HUDSON'S BAY COMPANY. The Company was incorporated in 1670 to exploit the fur trade in the area of Canada, draining into Hudson's Bay, which had been explored by Henry Hudson in 1610. Rivalry with France was resolved only with the **TREATY OF UTRECHT** at the end of the **SEVEN YEARS WAR** in 1713 and its monopoly territorial rights were sold to the Government of Canada in 1869. It remains a trading company — the oldest chartered company in the world — exploiting the oil found on its lands but, in 1970, transferred its headquarters from Britain to Canada.

HUGUENOTS. These French Protestant refugees came to **ENGLAND** after persecution in their homeland during the 17th century. They established many craft industries including silversmithing, lace-making and silk manufacture.

HUME, GEORGE BASIL (1923-). The leader of the UK's Roman Catholic community, Hume was born in **NEWCASTLE-UPON-TYNE** on 2 March 1923. His father — Sir William Hume, a heart specialist — was a Protestant but, even so, Hume was educated at Ampleforth, the Catholic equivalent of Eton College. From there, he went to **OXFORD** University and Fribourg University (Switzerland) and was ordained as a priest in 1950. He returned to Ampleforth as the senior modern languages master in 1952 and remained in that post until 1963, when he was made Abbot of Ampleforth. Over a period of 60 days in 1976, he was promoted from Abbot to Archbishop of **WESTMINSTER** (25 March) and then to Cardinal (24 May) — a movement up the hierarchy which is considered to be something of a record in Catholic circles. Reportedly, he was distressed to learn of his promotion to cardinal but accepted because of his duties of obedience as a monk. In 1978, he was twice among the candidates for Pope following the deaths of Paul VI and John Paul I but is now generally considered to be too old for the job. From 1957 until 1963, Hume was Magister Scholarum of the English Benedictine Congregation and, since 1979, has been President of the Roman Catholic Bishops' Conference of **ENGLAND** and **WALES**. From 1979 until 1986, he was also President of the European Bishops' Conference.

He has written a number of books and has been awarded honorary degrees by many universities including the Catholic University of America and Manhattan College, New York (both in 1980). Despite his lack of worldly experience, he is much respected, even by non-Catholics, for his tact and diplomacy. In recent years, he has frequently condemned violence by all sides in **NORTHERN IRELAND** and has indicated that members of the Anglican communion who object to the **CHURCH OF ENGLAND**'s decision to ordain women priests would be accepted into the Church of Rome. In 1994, he welcomed the conversion of the Duchess of Kent to Catholicism (the first member of the Royal Family to do so since **CHARLES II** in 1668) but refused to make capital for his Church out of the event, stressing that it was a personal decision and adding that the Duchess retained "a genuine affection" for the Church she had left.

HUNDRED. This was a **LOCAL GOVERNMENT** area for the **ANGLO- SAXONS**, part of a larger **SHIRE** (which became the **COUNTY**). The Hundreds were used as units of administration until the late 19th century and the term still survives in the **CHILTERN HUNDREDS**.

HUNDRED YEARS WAR, 1337-1453. Essentially a series of wars with differing alliances and separated by periods of comparative peace, the Hundred Years War was occasioned by the rivalry between **ENGLAND** and France and precipitated by the death, without a male heir, of Charles IV of France in 1328. England still claimed (since the 12th century union of England with Normandy, Aquitaine and **ANJOU**) the French crown and held territory in France, while France supported the Scottish nationalists and attempted to reduce English trading in Europe. England had gained Normandy by 1419 but was driven out after the **BATTLE OF FORMIGNY** and, at the end of the war in 1453, held only **CAL-**

AIS. English and British monarchs continued until 1820 to hold the title King/Queen of France and the symbol of France, the fleur de lis, remained on the English coat of arms until 1801. (See **BATTLE OF AGINCOURT; BATTLE OF CRECY; BATTLE OF POITIERS; BATTLE OF VERNEUIL; TREATY OF TROYES**).

HUNGER MARCHES. Large organized marches of the unemployed were held during the **GREAT DEPRESSION**, the best known being the Jarrow Crusade of 200 unemployed men in 1936. The **GOVERNMENT** generally dismissed the marches as a step towards civil unrest, but they created much public concern and worked as effective propaganda. The largest event was in October 1932, when 3,000 people marched with a petition containing one million signatures.

HUNGRY FORTIES. This term is applied to the 1840s as a result of a combination of the Irish potato famine, poor harvests in the late 1830s, unemployment, high food prices, the activities of the **ANTI-CORN LAW LEAGUE, CHARTISM**, the **INDUSTRIAL REVOLUTION, POOR LAWS** and poverty. The legacy of the period was widespread social discontent.

HURD, DOUGLAS (1930-). Foreign Secretary since 1989, Hurd was born on 8 March 1930, the eldest son of Baron Hurd and his wife, Stephanie. He was educated at Eton College and **CAMBRIDGE** University (where he was President of the Union in 1952) then joined the Diplomatic Service, serving in Beijing (1954-56), on the UK Mission to the United Nations (1956-60), as a Private Secretary at the Foreign Office (1960-63) and in Rome (1963-66). He joined the **CONSERVATIVE PARTY** Research Section in 1966 and became Head of its Foreign Affairs Unit two years later. In 1968, he was appointed Private Secretary to **EDWARD HEATH**, then Leader of the **OPPOSITION** and, in 1970 (when Heath became **PRIME MINISTER**), continued as Political Secretary. With that background, he was a natural Tory **PARLIAMENT**ary candidate and, in 1974, was elected to represent Mid-Oxfordshire.

He was **OPPOSITION** Spokesman on Foreign Affairs between 1976 and 1979 then occupied junior posts in **MARGARET THATCHER**'s early administrations as **MINISTER OF STATE** at the Foreign Office (1979-83) and at the **HOME OFFICE**

(1983-84). After that, resignations by a number of **CABINET** ministers contributed to speedy advancement even though he was regarded as a moderate by Thatcherite standards. He was appointed **SECRETARY OF STATE** for **NORTHERN IRELAND** in 1984 then promoted to **HOME SECRETARY** in 1985 before a surprise move to Foreign Secretary in 1989. When Mrs Thatcher resigned (1990), he entered the contest for Leadership of the Party (and, by implication, for Prime Minister) but polled only 56 votes from his fellow Conservative MPs (compared with the 185 accrued by **JOHN MAJOR**) even though he was seen by many as the man most likely to heal the splits which had developed in the organization as Mrs Thatcher had grown increasingly authoritarian. Over the next five years, he was an important British presence on the world political scene, signing the treaty by which the UK entered the **EUROPEAN UNION (EU)** (1992) and holding talks with President Carlos Menem (1993) during the first visit to Argentina by a Cabinet member since the **FALKLANDS WAR** (1982). In 1995, he announced his resignation, indicating that he wanted to spend more time with the young family of his second marriage.

—I—

ICENI. A tribe of **CELTS** based in **EAST ANGLIA**, the Iceni became a client-people of the **ROMANS** but rebelled when their overlords disarmed them, took their property and raped their King's daughters. In 60 AD, a revolt led by the warrior-Queen **BOADICEA**, with an estimated force of 120,000, destroyed Camulodunum (Colchester), overcame the ninth Legion and sacked **LONDON** but eventually succumbed to an army led by Suetonius Paulinus, the Provincial Governor. Boadicea committed suicide and the defeat left 80,000 Iceni dead.

IMMIGRATION. The United Kingdom's history is one of continued invasion and immigration, creating the multicultural society of the present day. As centre of the **BRITISH EMPIRE** and a major 19th and early 20th century world power, the country attracted waves of immigrants and refugees, many from the colonies, whose inhabitants technically had a right to British citizenship. The 1840s and 1850s saw agricultural workers fleeing the Irish potato famine, the 1880s and 1890s brought Russian Jews, the 1930s

German Jews, 1956 Hungarians and the years from the 1950s Pakistanis, Indians and West Indians. After the **SECOND WORLD WAR**, many of the migrants came from **COMMONWEALTH OF NATIONS** territories and, as a result, the early 1960s was a time of political and social tension, with the 1962 Commonwealth Immigration Act (see **ACT OF PARLIAMENT**) ultimately restricting access and creating a rush to beat the deadline of midnight on 1 July 1963. The 1968 Commonwealth Immigration Act curtailed movement further by restricting Asian immigration, particularly from Kenya. The **RACE RELATIONS ACT** (1976) attempted to control racialist excesses and the Immigration Acts (1971 and 1988), along with the British Nationality Act (1981), greatly reduced entry of non-British subjects despite opposition from Commonwealth countries such as Australia and New Zealand, which foresaw weakening ties with the mother country. In 1994, some 55,000 immigrants were accepted for settlement in Britain. Of these, about 6,240 were from Pakistan, 4,780 from India and 3,990 from the United States. (See **JOHN ENOCH POWELL**).

IMPEACHMENT. A form of trial by **PARLIAMENT** in which the **HOUSE OF COMMONS** prosecutes and the **HOUSE OF LORDS** passes judgement, impeachment is usually employed for offences against the state or because of a clamour of the people, or because of the King's word. A medieval practice, it was used by the **GOOD PARLIAMENT**, which impeached two of its officers unsuccessfully. It was never effective and, in the 17th century, became an element in the growing antagonism between **MONARCH** and Parliament. Last used in 1806, it has been superseded by more judicially acceptable processes though, technically, it is still available for high crimes and misdemeanours. It largely fell into disuse because the lower courts of the **JUDICIARY** became more effective, official corruption declined (particularly in the 19th century) and the powers of Parliament were increased to give more usable and effective means by which **MINISTERS** and other elevated persons could be kept in check. (See **WARREN HASTINGS**).

IMPERIAL CONFERENCES. Meetings of the Premiers of the **BRITISH EMPIRE**'s self-governing colonies (termed **DOMINIONS** from 1907), these conferences were held at infrequent intervals from 1887. The 1926 meeting laid the foundations of the

COMMONWEALTH OF NATIONS and the arrangements were ratified by the **STATUTE OF WESTMINSTER** in 1931.

IMPERIAL PREFERENCE. After the **FIRST WORLD WAR**, preferential tariffs and quotas were given for trade with **DOMINIONS** and colonies of the **BRITISH EMPIRE**. From 1958, the provisions also applied to members of the **COMMONWEALTH OF NATIONS**. The aim was the establishment of a self-contained commercial bloc with tariff protection. Particularly important during the **GREAT DEPRESSION**, it marked the end of **FREE TRADE** and was a sticking point in negotiations for Britain's entry into the **EUROPEAN COMMUNITY (EC)**. As the colonial territories gained independence and evolved into rival producers, rather than reciprocal trading partners with Britain, the system became increasingly unworkable and the policy was phased out during the initial stages of the UK's membership of the EC.

INCOME TAX. Originally introduced during the **NAPOLEONIC WARS**, a tax on personal incomes (including salaries and returns on investments) has been levied annually since 1842, when **ROBERT PEEL** reorganized **GOVERNMENT** finances. In the financial year from April 1996 to April 1997, the rate was 20 per cent on the first £3,900 (after allowances had been deducted), 25 per cent on incomes between £3,901 and £25,500 and 40 per cent on higher incomes.

INDEPENDENT LABOUR PARTY (ILP). Formed in 1893 by James Keir Hardie to provide a base for working class Members of **PARLIAMENT** free of their former alliance with the **LIBERAL PARTY**, the ILP declined in importance after individuals became free to join the **LABOUR PARTY** directly (rather than through the ILP) in 1918. Following policy disagreements, it disaffiliated from the Labour Party in 1932 and, although it won three seats at the 1945 **GENERAL ELECTION**, exerted little influence on political affairs in the post-**SECOND WORLD WAR** years. It lost its last MP in 1959.

INDIAN MUTINY, 1857-58. A mutiny against British rule in India began in the Bengal army of the paramilitary **EAST INDIA COMPANY**, spread to civilians and native troops and resulted in the deaths of thousands of Europeans. Its causes included religious differences (such as the suppression of suttee); hatred of the imposed western economic system; fear of land reforms; agitation based on the superstition that, as it was the centenary of the **BAT-TLE OF PLASSEY**, the then leader of Bengal (Siraj-Ud-Daula) would return to lead a fight against the British; use by the army of Enfield cartridges in weapons (the end had to be bitten off before use and — as it was rumoured to be coated in animal fat — that was seen as unclean both by Muslims and by Hindus); recent reversals for Britain in the **CRIMEAN WAR** and in Afghanistan (these defeats showed that the **BRITISH ARMY** was not invincible); and the resentment by sepoys (native soldiers) of their treatment by British officers. The mutiny broke out on 10 May 1857 at Meerut, and Delhi was seized. British forces at Cawnpore surrendered only to be massacred (as happened elsewhere in later months), but the Indians had no major leader who might have united the people. When peace was restored on 8 July 1858, heavy reprisals were exacted, with some mutineers being fired from cannons. The incident led to the 1858 Government of India Act (see **ACT OF PARLIAMENT**), whereby the territory passed from the East India Company to the **CROWN**. British citizens in the colony became even more divorced from the native peoples, building a resentment of the imperial presence which greatly influenced the later history of India.

INDIRECT RULE. First applied in Nigeria in 1900, this system of colonial rule involved the secondment of British advisers to local Chiefs, thereby maintaining native customs within the government of the colony. It was much used in the African territories of the **BRITISH EMPIRE** before **DECOLONIZATION** and can be interpreted as a form of administration which facilitated the evolution of **PROTECTORATE**s into **CROWN COLONIES** within the context of an empire of over 600 million people.

INDUSTRIAL REVOLUTION. This period of rapid economic and social change is generally accepted to have lasted from 1760 to 1860. However, the processes are hard to date and some authorities cite 1740 to 1850, others 1760 to 1830. The term *Industrial Revolution* was popularised by social reformer and economist Arnold Toynbee in the 1880s but was in use as early as the 1820s. Britain was the first country in the world to industrialize and, by the mid-19th century, had become the strongest and richest nation in Europe.

The reasons for this early development include the growth of the **BRITISH EMPIRE**, which opened up sources of raw materials and markets for production; a growing domestic population, which increased demand; a relatively free society, which encouraged experimentation; an **AGRICULTURAL REVOLUTION**, which created new opportunities and a farming system which could sustain larger urban/industrial populations; a tradition of private investment by the aristocracy and rich merchants; and a relatively efficient banking and financing network. In addition, the raw materials of **COAL** and **IRON** were available and the Protestant ethic of work, enterprize and saving was an important factor in a cultural climate favouring acquisition of wealth and investment. Britain also had a relatively stable **MONARCH**y and **GOVERNMENT** by this period and had developed a strong trading tradition in which its island status and geographical position were fundamental.

Major technological innovations occurred in the iron industry (with the development of blast furnaces and smelting techniques by men such as Abraham Darby and Henry Cort) and in the coal industry (which began working deep mines and used the Davy safety lamp). Textile output expanded, particularly in the **COTTON INDUSTRY**, and production methods changed from a largely domestic-based system to one based in large urban factories, where manufacturing could be developed more rapidly using inventions such as James Hargreave's Spinning Jenny — a device which allowed one spinner to handle many spindles. **RICHARD ARKWRIGHT**'s water-frame (water-powered machinery which led to the construction of spinning mills) and Samuel Crompton's Mule (which allowed powered manufacture of high quality yarns) stimulated the weaving industry, which was further expanded following the invention of the flying shuttle by John Kay in 1733. Thomas Newcomen, Matthew Boulton and **JAMES WATT** developed the steam engine to mechanize production and **JOSIAH WEDGWOOD** revolutionized the pottery industry at Burslem.

This was also a period of far-reaching innovation in transport fed by improvements in **CANALS**, **TURNPIKES** and **RAILWAYS** (see **ISAMBARD KINGDOM BRUNEL**). As a result, Britain urbanized rapidly, and the problems associated with that town and city growth led to changes in **LOCAL GOVERNMENT**, **PARLIAMENTARY REFORM** and the eventual development of **TOWN AND COUNTRY PLANNING** and the **WELFARE STATE**. The UK became the richest nation in the world and its trading and leading international political positions were secured.

INKERMAN, BATTLE OF, 5 November 1854. British and French forces, attempting to take Sebastopol, were attacked by a Russian army at Inkerman during the **CRIMEAN WAR**. The Allies won when French reinforcements appeared. Said to have been a soldiers' battle, the event was really a series of skirmishes and bayonet fights in thick fog rather than a set-piece engagement. Casualties from the three-hour conflict numbered 4,000 Allied dead and up to 15,000 Russians killed. The British decided, as a result of this action, that the only way to take Sebastopol was by protracted siege rather than frontal assault.

INTERCURSUS MAGNUS. In Latin, "intercursus magnus" means "the great exchange". In 1496, King **HENRY VII** concluded this treaty with Philip, Duke of Burgundy, to secure trading and fishing rights between **ENGLAND** and the Netherlands and ensure that neither country would support enemies of the other. The agreement was made at a time of great instability for the English **CROWN**, particularly following Perkin Warbeck's attempts to gain the throne by pretending to be Richard, **DUKE OF YORK** (who was one of the Princes murdered in the **TOWER OF LONDON** in 1493). It proved to be a long-lived mutual association between the two nations. (See **INTERCURSUS MALUS**.)

INTERCURSUS MALUS. In Latin, "intercursus malus" is translated as "the bad exchange". In 1506, Philip, Duke of Burgundy, was forced by a storm to shelter in **ENGLAND**, and King **HENRY VII** took advantage of the situation to renegotiate the earlier **INTERCURSUS MAGNUS** on more favourable terms, particularly in connection with trade in cloth. Philip died before he could ratify the treaty.

INTERREGNUM, THE, 1649-60. A Latin term meaning "between reigns", this phrase describes the period in English history which includes the **COMMONWEALTH** and the **PROTECTORATE**. It extends from the execution of King **CHARLES I** (30 January 1649) to the **RESTORATION** of King **CHARLES II** (8 May 1660).

INTOLERABLE ACTS. This series of coercive **ACTS OF PARLIAMENT** in 1774 was intended as retaliation on Massachusetts for the defiance of the Boston Tea Party. They revoked the state charter (creating a **CROWN COLONY**), closed Boston Harbor and permitted the billeting of British troops in American homes. Opposition in North America hardened after this display of intolerance and superiority so the legislation helped spur the colonists to rebellion and thus fuelled the **AMERICAN WAR OF INDEPENDENCE.**

IRAQI SUPERGUN AFFAIR. In April 1990, British Customs and Excise seized a consignment of machine parts — very large cylinders, which were claimed to be oil installation equipment bound for Iraq with all necessary **GOVERNMENT** clearance — at a time when tension was high and sanctions were in place to prevent exports to that part of the Middle East. Sheffield Forgemasters were involved in the manufacture of what Customs claimed to be part of a supergun project capable of firing chemical, biological or even nuclear missiles over long distances. After the **GULF WAR** evidence was found of such a construction.

IRELAND. The island of Ireland was extensively settled by the **CELTS** and, by the 12th century, was divided into a number of self-governing kingdoms. One of the Kings — Dermot MacMurrough of Leinster — was deposed in 1166 and persuaded **HENRY II** to help him win back his throne. A force of **NORMAN** soldiers was enlisted and, led by Richard de Clare, captured Dublin, restoring Dermot to his lands in 1170. When he died, in 1171, Richard succeeded him but Henry, concerned at the possible development of an alternative source of Norman power, obtained the Overlordship of Ireland from Pope Adrian IV and led an invasion force later in the year. By 1172, the major native leaders had submitted and, by the end of the century, most of the area outside the northwest and southwest was in English hands. Over the next 200 years, however, some of the land was taken back into Irish control and the Anglo-Norman hierarchy was gradually assimilated so by the end of **RICHARD III**'s reign, the Pale was confined to a relatively limited area around Dublin.

The **TUDORS** adopted an aggressive campaign to win back the island and, by the time of the **UNION OF THE CROWNS** in 1603, it was once again entirely under English jurisdiction. A Plantation policy adopted in the 16th and 17th centuries attempted to anglicize the area more fully and establish Protestantism but produced a large body of landless Roman Catholics and was bitterly resented (see **PLANTATIONS OF IRELAND**). Calls for **HOME RULE** increased but were strongly opposed by many **LONDON** politicians, and, in 1801, the all-Protestant Irish Parliament was dissolved and Ireland fully united with **GREAT BRITAIN** (see **WILLIAM PITT THE YOUNGER**). The granting of equal political rights to Catholics, in 1829, encouraged some nationalists to believe that independence could be gained through constitutional means but several attempts to push the appropriate legislation through **PARLIAMENT** failed. Moreover, it was becoming clear that a large proportion of the population of **ULSTER** wanted to remain under the British **CROWN**. **DAVID LLOYD GEORGE** tried to use the provisions of the 1920 Government of Ireland Act (see **ACT OF PARLIAMENT**) to solve the problem by attempting to establish two Irish Parliaments with equal (but limited) powers, one in Belfast and one in Dublin. However, Sinn Fein won every one of the seats for the southern assembly, with the exception of the four representing Dublin University, then refused to put it into operation. Further negotiations resulted in an Anglo-Irish Treaty (1921) which essentially conceded full independence but the six north-eastern counties immediately withdrew from the Irish Free State and opted for internal self-government as part of the United Kingdom. (See also **OLIVER CROMWELL; FENIANS; NORTHERN IRELAND**).

IRISH REBELLION, 1641. In October, a number of dispossessed Irish Catholic **GENTRY**, fearing further Protestant impositions on the island, led a protest against the plantation of settlers from other parts of the British Isles (see **PLANTATIONS OF IRELAND**). With the rebels expecting support from **CHARLES I**, several thousand English and Scottish settlers were killed. **OLIVER CROMWELL** eventually suppressed the unrest.

IRISH REBELLION, 1798. Led by the Society of United Irishmen, which wanted an independent Irish Republic and was aided by France (with whom Britain was then at war), the rebels hoped for a supporting French invasion but their rising was rapidly and viciously suppressed. The British **GOVERNMENT** had used spies to great effect, capturing a French military force at Ballinamuck and intercepting a French naval force off Donegal. Though a failure, the rebellion led **WILLIAM PITT THE YOUNGER** to address the Irish Question and was one of the factors which resulted in the eventual fusion of Britain and **IRELAND** by the **ACT OF UNION** of 1801 (see **ACT OF PARLIAMENT**).

IRON. Developments in the iron industry heralded the beginnings of the **INDUSTRIAL REVOLUTION**. Since the **ROMAN** period, ironworks had been based in forested areas, using charcoal for smelting. However, in 1709, Abraham Darby perfected the use of coke smelting to produce pig for cast iron and, in 1784, Henry Cort developed the puddling and rolling technique for wrought iron. These innovations increased iron production by a factor of 100 between 1700 and 1830 and were followed, in 1839, by James Nasmyth's steam hammer for heavy forging. Matthew Boulton's steam engines made many processes larger scale, John Wilkinson built the first iron barge and, by 1850, Britain was producing 50 per cent of the world's pig iron. As the industry developed, the older forest-based industries, such as those in the Weald of **KENT**, were replaced by coalfield-based industries and the making of iron, which was either strong but brittle (cast) or soft and malleable (wrought), developed into **STEEL** production as the demand for strong, malleable metals grew for **RAILWAY** tracks and other products.

IRON AGE. During this period in **PREHISTORIC BRITAIN**, from c. 800 BC until 43 AD, iron replaced the softer bronze as the major metal, particularly in the development of weapons in the lowlands. The climate became wetter and cooler, much like the present, and, as populations in larger settlements grew, tribal wars began so the period is characterized by the building of defensive **HILLFORTS** and large administrative settlements. Farming prospered, small trading posts developed, with European connections, and the beginnings of real regional diversity were evident in artistic and other cultural features. **DRUIDS** became powerful as links with Rome became stronger, culminating in the **ROMAN** occupation of the islands.

IRONSIDES. A cavalry regiment in **OLIVER CROMWELL**'s Parliamentary army, these soldiers were renowned for their religious fervour and military discipline. They were preeminent at the **BATTLE OF MARSTON MOOR**, during which Prince Rupert (the leader of the defeated **ROYALIST** forces) called Cromwell "Old Ironsides". The name became attached to this military unit, which played a major role in the subsequent **ROUNDHEAD** victory in the **CIVIL WAR**, but is often incorrectly attributed to the whole Parliamentary force.

ISLE OF MAN. A **CROWN DEPENDENCY** in the Irish Sea, the Isle of Man has been ruled by the Welsh (sixth to ninth centuries), the **VIKINGS** (ninth century until 1266), the Scots (1266-1765) and the British (since 1765). It covers an area of 220 square miles and has a population of 67,000 (1989). Internal affairs are managed by the Tynwald, an assembly which was originally established during the period of Viking overlordship between 1079 and 1266 and is now divided into an Upper House (the Legislative Council) and a Lower House (the House of Keys). Fiscal policies have turned the island into a tax haven.

—J—

JACOBINISTS. Extreme radical supporters of the **FRENCH REVOLUTION**, the Jacobinists advocated moves towards greater democracy in Britain. The **COMBINATION ACTS** (see **ACT OF PARLIAMENT**) and other measures were introduced to suppress all such agitation for constitutional change.

JAMES VI and I (1566-1625). The first **MONARCH** of a united **GREAT BRITAIN**, James was born in Edinburgh Castle on 19 June 1566 and proclaimed King of **SCOTLAND** on 24 July the following year after the enforced abdication of his mother, Mary, Queen of Scots. For most of his minority, he lived in Stirling Castle, where he developed interests in theology and languages, cultivating a love of learning which was to last a lifetime. At the age of 12, he took the government nominally into his own hands but, for some years after that, was buffeted by advisers and counsellors more experienced in the intricacies of Scottish politics. In 1582, he was seized by the Earl of Gowrie whilst out hunting and was imprisoned in Ruthven Castle. With the help of the Earl of Arran, he escaped in 1583 and, from that point, pursued his own political course.

It was clear that James's twin aims were to diminish the powers of the nobles and to establish his claim to succeed to the throne of **ENGLAND** on the death of **ELIZABETH I**. The first was achieved by avoiding head-on collisions, balancing opposing groups and gradually excluding powerful figures from his government, replacing them with his own appointees. The tactics were justified — by 1597, factional disputes between powerful families were rare and Scotland had entered a lengthy period of domestic peace. The second aim was achieved on 24 March 1603, when Elizabeth died childless and James was proclaimed King of England. The joint monarchy offered much potential, both domestically and on the European stage, and many of his policies initially bore fruit despite his lack of familiarity with the English political system. The war with Spain was ended the year following his accession, law and order was established on the border between England and Scotland, Scottish trade was encouraged and attempts were made to place colonists in **ULSTER** and Nova Scotia.

But he was in conflict with the Presbyterian churchmen in Scotland. James believed that kings had a divine right to rule (see **DIVINE RIGHT OF KINGS**) and therefore attempted to subject the Church to his personal authority, an authority which the increasingly democratic theologians were unwilling to accept. Through its sermons and its hold on the education system, the Church had considerable influence on the minds of the people and, therefore, was a considerable threat to the King's power. James's solution was to attempt to impose bishops, a move which was much resented by a population who felt that this was an anglicization of their worship. Further reforms, including a new liturgy and changes in ceremony (such as the obligation to kneel for communion) were similarly resisted, provoking resentment against a monarch who appeared to have abandoned his native country and earning him the title of "The Wisest Fool in Christendom".

In England, too, he had problems, notably with **PARLIAMENT**. His success in dealing with political factions was not repeated south of the border, partly because of his lack of familiarity with the English Parliamentary system, partly because his habit of lecturing assemblies on the rights of kings made his hearers wary, partly because he frequently took the law into his own hands (he summoned Parliament only twice between 1611 and 1621) and partly because his extravagances greatly added to the country's debt. Moreover, his foreign policy showed considerable disdain for English public opinion. He developed a scheme to unite the warring Protestant and Catholic nations through marriage. His daughter, Elizabeth, was wedded to the Protestant Prince Frederick V, Elector Palatine of the Rhine, and his heir, Charles (later **CHARLES I**), was intended for a daughter of the Catholic King of Spain. But if that policy was to be carried through, the

King needed money and money meant having a Parliament which could raise funds. Parliament, however, resented James and, when it was summoned in 1621, launched an attack on his government and claimed the right to dictate foreign policy. Despite the rebuff, Charles was sent to Spain in 1623 but returned with no prospect of a marriage. James, by this time an ageing figure taking less and less interest in politics, reversed his previous policies and capitulated to Parliament in 1624. On 27 March 1625, he died in **LONDON** and was buried in **WESTMINSTER** Abbey.

Historians have tended to be critical of his reign but there were mitigating circumstances. He had the misfortune to follow a popular monarch whose period of rule was later frequently seen as one of the most glorious in English history. He was an incomer, unused to the intricacies of English politics and of the Parliamentary system. And he was succeeded by a politically inept son who compounded his faults. In addition, his physical impediments — his shambling walk and constantly dribbling mouth — gave him a most unkingly appearance which made his lectures on divine rights difficult to accept. But he took Scotland from civil discord to lasting peace, he fostered the arts, and he had an unshakeable belief in his calling. His vision was often narrow, but, in many ways, he was one of the more able members of the House of Stewart. (see **ANNE OF DENMARK; STUARTS**.)

JAMES VII and II (1633-1701). King of **GREAT BRITAIN** from 1685 until 1689, James was born in St James's Palace (**LONDON**) on 14 October 1633, the second son of **CHARLES I** and Henrietta Maria (sister of Louis XIII of France). He was created **DUKE OF YORK** (the traditional title of the English **MONARCH**'s second son) in 1634 and **DUKE** of Albany (the equivalent Scottish title) in 1660. During the **CIVIL WAR**, he lived at the **ROYALIST** headquarters in **OXFORD** but, after the city surrendered in 1646, was moved by order of **PARLIAMENT** to London. In 1648, he escaped to the Netherlands and joined his mother in France the following year. He returned to Britain when Charles was restored to the throne in 1660 and was appointed Lord High Admiral of **ENGLAND**, a post for which he was well-suited after serving with both the French and the Spanish forces. He worked hard to improve the efficiency of the service and showed much interest in the development of the colonies. (When, in 1664, England seized control of the Dutch colony of New Amsterdam in North America, the King granted it to James, renaming it New York in his honour.)

Something of a rake both before and after his marriage in 1660 to Anne Hyde, daughter of the Earl of Clarendon (see **CLARENDON CODE**), he seems to have undergone a change of heart during the second half of the 1660s and, in 1668 or 1669, secretly joined the Roman Catholic Church. Knowledge of his conversion became public in 1672 and the news caused much anxiety; at the time, Catholicism was seen as the root of all evil and was associated widely with royal absolutism. The concern forced James to resign his naval position in 1673, and it increased in 1674 when (his first wife having died in 1671) he married the Roman Catholic Mary of Modena. Considerable pressure was put on the King to exclude James from the succession, but, in practice, James remained favourably disposed towards the Anglican Church, cultivated its leaders, consistently championed his own rights and gradually won the approval even of its more conservative elements. As a result, on 6 February 1685, he succeeded to the throne with little opposition.

However, rebellions by the Duke of Monmouth (see **MONMOUTH REBELLION**) and the Duke of Argyll during the summer of 1685, although unsuccessful, led to disputes between King and Parliament, largely because James appointed Roman Catholic officers to posts of influence in his expanded army. In 1686, Catholics were appointed to the **PRIVY COUNCIL** and to high offices of state, and James became increasingly estranged from his former Anglican allies. In April 1687, he issued a proclamation (usually termed the **DECLARATION OF INDULGENCE**) which suspended the laws against both Roman Catholics and Protestant dissenters. In November, it was announced that Mary of Modena was pregnant, raising the spectre of a Catholic successor to the throne. Anglicans, worried by the trends and fearful of the implications, turned in large numbers to William of Orange (later **WILLIAM III**), husband of James's elder daughter, Mary (later **MARY II**). The breaking point — and the precipitation of the **GLORIOUS REVOLUTION** — came in the spring of 1688, when the King reissued the Declaration of Indulgence, ordering that it should be read in all churches on 4 May. Seven church leaders, including the **ARCHBISHOP OF CANTERBURY**, petitioned James to withdraw the order and were charged with seditious libel. The courts acquitted the priests on 30 June, but, on the same day, a group of leading Englishmen sent a letter to William, asking him to come with an army and call a free Parliament.

William landed at Torbay on 5 November and prepared to face the royalist forces, but James's Protestant officers deserted in large numbers and he was unable to commit himself to battle. Then his younger daughter, Anne (later Queen **ANNE**), defected, and, unable to command support in the country, he escaped to France on 23 December. On 12 February 1689, the English Parliament declared that he had abdicated and offered the crown to William and Mary. The Scottish Parliament reached similar decisions on 4 April. James plotted in vain to win back his throne. In 1689, he landed in **IRELAND**, and a Parliament summoned to Dublin acknowledged him as King, but his army, composed largely of Frenchmen and Irishmen, was defeated at the Battle of the Boyne on 1 July 1690. He returned to exile in France and died at St Germain on 5 September 1701. Having, by that time, acquired something of a reputation as a holy man, his body was cut up and pieces given to those who might appreciate them — the Scots College in Paris was given his brain, the English College at St Omer his bowels.

JAMESON RAID, 29 December 1895-2 January 1896. **CECIL RHODES**, who had ambitious plans to unite southern Africa under the British flag, devized a scheme to overthrow Transvaal leader Paul Kruger by exploiting unrest in the area and creating an uprising in Johannesburg supported by an invasion of 600 men led by Leander Jameson. Transvaal was then a small Boer Republic, rich in goldfields, but many of its settlers (known as Uitlanders) had been treated as second-class citizens and taxed without representation. The raid sought to exploit the resulting unrest. It failed and led to the embarrassment of Rhodes's resignation as Prime Minister of Cape Colony, the worsening of British-Boer relations and a rise in Boer nationalism. The incident was a precursor to the **BOER WAR** of 1899. Jameson later (1904) became Premier of Cape Colony and, in 1911, a **BARONET**. (See **KRUGER TELEGRAM**).

JARROW MARCH. (See **HUNGER MARCHES**).

JENKINS' EAR, THE WAR OF, 1739-48. This conflict resulted from colonial rivalries between Britain and Spain (at that time, Britain had attempted to develop illicit trade, which was not allowed under the **ASIENTO**). The pretext for hostility was the alleged maltreatment of Captain Robert Jenkins by the Spanish navy, which allegedly severed his ear. (He exhibited the ear to **PARLIAMENT** in 1738, seven years after the incident was supposed to have happened.) Despite the fact that Jenkins was probably acting as a smuggler at the time, public opinion against the Spanish was strong and supported by a clamour from trading interests so the **GOVERNMENT** was forced to declare a war which later became part of the wider European **WAR OF THE AUSTRIAN SUCCESSION**.

JENKINSON, ROBERT BANKS (1770-1828). **PRIME MINISTER** from 1812 until 1827, Jenkinson was born on 7 June 1770, eldest son of the Earl of Liverpool. He was educated at Charterhouse School and **OXFORD** University then, in 1790, was elected Member of **PARLIAMENT** for Appleby. Between 1793 and 1812, he served under four Prime Ministers. **WILLIAM PITT THE YOUNGER** appointed him Commissioner of the India Board (1793-96) and Master of the **ROYAL MINT** (1799-1801). Under **HENRY ADDINGTON** he was Foreign Secretary (1801-4), negotiating the Peace of Amiens (1802), which brought the **NAPOLEONIC WARS** to a temporary halt. In 1803, he was created Baron Hawkesbury and, from 1804 until 1806, served as **HOME SECRETARY** in Pitt's last **GOVERNMENT**. When Pitt died, Hawkesbury was offered the post of Prime Minister but, a remarkably unambitious man for a politician, he refused, accepting the Wardship of the **CINQUE PORTS** instead. Under **WILLIAM BENTINCK**, Duke of Portland, he was Home Secretary again (1807-9) and under **SPENCER PERCEVAL** was Secretary for War and the Colonies.

When Perceval was shot dead at **WESTMINSTER** on 11 May 1812, Jenkinson was again offered the premiership and again refused. However, there were real fears that, without his leadership, the Tory Party (see **TORIES**) would fall apart and, in June, he was persuaded by colleagues to accept the post. For the next 15 years, he exercised considerable tact and diplomacy while he held together a **CABINET** dominated by such strong individuals as **GEORGE CANNING** and **VISCOUNT CASTLEREAGH** and divided over military strategy, **FREE TRADE**, emancipation of Roman Catholics and other issues. Despite the divisions, certain of his innovations enjoyed long term success. In 1819, for example, he restored the **GOLD STANDARD**, establishing the stability of **STERLING**. Also, he ensured that all **CHURCH OF**

ENGLAND appointments were made on the basis of merit rather than patronage and refused to curry Parliamentary support through the promise of **PEERAGE**s. In February 1827, a paralytic stroke forced him into retirement. He died in **LONDON** on 4 December 1828.

JOHN (1167-1216). One of the more unpopular English **MONARCH**s, John was the youngest son of **HENRY II** and Eleanor of Aquitaine. He was born in **OXFORD** on 24 December 1167, became Henry's favourite son and was granted the Lordship of **IRELAND** in 1177. When Henry died in 1189, John's elder brother, Richard, succeeded to the throne as **RICHARD II**. John was made Count of Mortain and the Lordship in Ireland was confirmed, but he had to promise that he would not enter **ENGLAND** while his brother was absent on **CRUSADE** in the Holy Land. That promise was broken when, in 1190, Richard recognized Arthur, son of Geoffrey (another of Henry's sons), as his heir. Then, when news arrived of Richard's capture by Leopold of Austria in 1193, John paid homage to King Philip II of France and made arrangements for the division of Richard's continental estates. When Richard was released in 1194, John was banished and deprived of his lands but a reconciliation was effected, some of his territories were returned and, in 1197, he was recognized as heir to the throne. He was crowned on 27 May 1199, following Richard's death the previous month.

His reign was a disaster for England. Unrest in his continental estates led to war with Philip, who was keen to take advantage of any signs of rebellion and annex the estates for himself. By 1206, Normandy, Anjou, Maine and much of Poitou had been lost. Determined to reverse his fortunes, John turned to increasing his English tax revenues in order to finance a campaign against the French King but his problems multiplied as a result of conflict with the Church. In 1206, Pope Innocent III appointed Stephen Langton to the See of **CANTERBURY** following the death of Hubert Walter. John insisted that, as King, he could name his own Archbishop. The argument escalated and, in 1209, John was excommunicated but the quarrel was diverting him from his efforts to regain his lands in France and, in 1212, he agreed to accept both Langton and the Pope's terms for his return to the Church. On 15 May 1213, he surrendered his kingdom to Innocent III, receiving it back as a vassal paying annual tribute.

The long-delayed campaign against Philip began in February

1214 and ended in failure; John was decisively defeated at
Bouvines without regaining any of his former estates. In England,
that failure added to the discontent stemming from heavy taxes,
loss of national prestige and reaction to attempts to curb the power
of the nobles. In May 1215, civil war broke out and John was
forced to accept the provisions of the **MAGNA CARTA**, which
gave the Church the right to choose its own officials, emphasized
the power of the courts by decreeing that no freeman was to be
punished except according to the law and limited the possibilities
for extortion by stating that no money was to be paid to the King
by feudal tenants without their consent. Shortly afterwards, John
appealed to the Pope, who annulled the agreement. The nobles immediately reacted, inviting Prince Louis of France (later Louis
VIII) to come to their aid. John still had the support of many leading families and strenuously resisted the rebellion but died at
Newark on 19 October 1216, before the conflict was over. His
death brought peace, ensuring the withdrawal of the French force
and the succession of his son as **HENRY III**. John was buried at
Worcester and, since then, has been cast as the archetypal evil
king but, although deceitful and callous, he was a cultured, literate
monarch who made many donations to the Church and promoted
several important administrative innovations. He was never as politically or militarily isolated as some histories have suggested.

JOHN OF GAUNT (1340-99). The fourth son of **EDWARD III**
and Philippa of Hainaut, John effectively ruled **ENGLAND**
during his father's last years and continued as **REGENT** during the minority of **RICHARD II**. Born at Ghent in March
1340, he was created **EARL** of Richmond in 1342 and, in
1359, married Blanche, daughter of the Duke of Lancaster, a
union which made him one of the richest men in the country.
Great estates in the north of England, in the midlands and in
WALES provided a strong power base.

John allied with Edward's mistress, Alice Perrers, to run the
country while his father became increasingly senile, but the administration was not particularly successful, partly because his
support for the religious reformer, **JOHN WYCLIFFE**, annoyed
orthodox churchmen and partly because the corruption of many of
his officials was widely resented. On the accession of the ten-year-
old **RICHARD II** in 1377, John became the leading figure in the
councils to which government was entrusted and, during the early
1380s, increasingly played the role of peacemaker between one

faction centred on the young King and another focusing on the Earls of Gloucester and Arundel and the Bishop of Ely. By 1386, however, he was more interested in pursuing his claim to the throne of Castile and Leon (a claim which was based on his marriage in 1371 to Constance, daughter of Pedro I, his first wife having died two years earlier). He launched a campaign aimed at winning the crown, but it failed miserably and, under the Settlement of Bayonne in 1388, he renounced any rights to the kingship, receiving a substantial sum in compensation and arranging for his daughter, Catherine, to marry Henry (son of King John I of Castile), thereby satisfying family aspirations. He returned to his old role as mediator between the power blocs in England, where the lack of his moderating influence had allowed attitudes against Richard to harden. With his support, the King was able to carry out a major purge of his enemies in 1397, but that loyalty was poorly rewarded. When he died on 3 February 1399, Richard confiscated his estates, providing an excuse for Gaunt's heir, Henry Bolingbroke, to mount a rebellion and eventually claim the crown for himself as **HENRY IV**.

JUDICATURE ACT, 1873. By the mid-19th century, the legal system in **ENGLAND** and **WALES** was bedevilled by an outmoded court structure. Most courts dated from medieval times, had jurisdictions which overlapped and were unsuited to the needs of the urban society created by the **INDUSTRIAL REVOLUTION**. The Judicature Act (see **ACT OF PARLIAMENT**) was a first step towards modernization, abolishing existing courts and replacing them with a **SUPREME COURT OF JUDICATURE** consisting of a **COURT OF APPEAL** and a **HIGH COURT OF JUSTICE**. It also enhanced the role of the **HOUSE OF LORDS** by making it the highest court of appeal in the land.

JUDICIARY. With **PARLIAMENT** and the **CABINET**, the judicial system is one of the three planks of the **GOVERNMENT** of the **UNITED KINGDOM**. The law of the land is derived from **COMMON LAW**, Rules of Equity, Statutes (**ACT OF PARLIAMENT**), Case Law, European Law and International Law. Civil Law involves action between two individuals and, in **ENGLAND** and **WALES**, is dealt with in county courts or, in more serious matters, the **HIGH COURT**. Criminal law deals with offences against the general law of the land and is handled in the magistrates' courts and, for greater offences, **CROWN COURTS**. (See

COURT OF APPEAL; JUDICATURE ACT; JURY; JUS-
TICE OF THE PEACE; LORD CHANCELLOR; LORD
CHIEF JUSTICE OF ENGLAND; LORD JUSTICE CLERK;
LORD JUSTICE GENERAL).

JURY. The term *Jury* is derived from the Latin *jurati* meaning 'sworn men' — 12 individuals who give a verdict on charges presented in a court of law. The system originated in Britain under the **NORMANS**, who reorganized judicial procedures by insisting that suspects accused of crimes had to be brought before justices by a body of local people. Trial by jury in civil cases dates from the 12th century and was extended after the abolition of **TRIAL BY ORDEAL** in 1215. Along with other cultural traits, trial by jury has spread throughout the **BRITISH EMPIRE**.

JUSTICE OF THE PEACE. These judicial posts have their origins in the 14th century, when powerful landowners, **KNIGHT**s, **LORD**s or **GENTRY**, who could command authority in their areas, were used as unpaid local governors for the **CROWN** to enforce the law. An Act of 1390 (see **ACT OF PARLIAMENT**) decreed that there should be eight JPs for each **COUNTY**, administering local justice in local courts. Nowadays, JPs sit in Magistrates' Courts where, assisted by a clerk as their legal adviser (they themselves usually having no formal legal training), they dispense justice for minor criminal offences. They are appointed by the **LORD CHANCELLOR**.

JUTES. These Germanic peoples came from Jutland and Frisia to settle in the south of **ENGLAND** (particularly in **KENT**) during the fifth century. Possibly originally brought by the **ROMANS** as auxiliary troops, they established their landholding and other customs and that accounts, in part, for the rapid and early cultural development of this area of Britain. (see **ANGLO-SAXONS**).

JUTLAND, BATTLE OF, 31 May-1 June 1916. One of the decisive naval engagements of the **FIRST WORLD WAR**, the battle was fought off the Skagerrak coast of Norway by the heavy battleships and battle cruisers of the British and German fleets. Britain lost 14 ships (including three battle cruisers) and nearly 7,000 men, the Germans only 11 ships. However, the German fleet withdrew under cover of darkness, spent the rest of the war in port and did not engage the **ROYAL NAVY** again, concentrating on U-boat action from then on. In the United Kingdom, dissatisfaction with the unimpressive Royal Navy performance greatly lowered morale.

—K—

KENT. The English **COUNTY** closest to the continent of Europe, Kent was settled in the fifth century by Hengist and his **JUTES**. The British inhabitants during the **ROMAN** period were known as the Cantiaci or Cantii (and **CANTERBURY** was named Durovernum Cantiacorum). When the area was settled by the Jutes, they became the Cantware or 'dwellers of Kent' (and Canterbury became Cantwarabyrig). King **AETHELBERT** of Kent was converted to Christianity by **AUGUSTINE** in 597, making this area the first English kingdom to formally accept the faith.

KETT'S REBELLION. A rebellion in 1549 led by Robert Kett, a Norfolk landowner, this uprising was a protest against high rents, the spread of **ENCLOSURE** and encroachments on commons in that **EAST ANGLIA**n **COUNTY**. A force of about 16,000 men was raised but defeated by the Earl of Warwick. Kett was executed.

KEYNES, JOHN MAYNARD (1883-1946). The pioneer of economic theories of full employment, Keynes was born on 5 June 1883, the eldest son of John Neville Keynes (a political economist and logician at **CAMBRIDGE** University) and his wife, Florence. He was educated at Eton College and Cambridge University, where he was President of the Liberal Club (1904) and the Union (1905). He was given a civil service post at the India Office in 1906 but returned to Cambridge as lecturer in economics in 1908 and continued to take classes there for the rest of his life. In 1913, he published his first book — *Indian Currency and Finance* — and, in 1915, became an adviser to the **TREASURY**. At the end of the **FIRST WORLD WAR,** he represented the United Kingdom at the Versailles Peace Conference but withdrew because he believed that the conditions being imposed on Germany exceeded the country's capacity to pay and threatened to disrupt the world economy. He presented his reasoning in *The Economic Consequences of the Peace* (1919), a work which sharply attacked Prime Minister **DAVID LLOYD GEORGE** and US President Woodrow Wilson, turning Keynes into a household name. In 1923, he became Chairman of *Nation* (a **LIBERAL PARTY** periodical) using it to publicize his opinions about the reconstruction of Europe and (in 1925) to berate **CHANCELLOR OF THE EXCHEQUER WINSTON CHURCHILL** for returning to the **GOLD STANDARD**, thereby (according to Keynes) making the United Kingdom a pawn of the United States.

At that time, Keynes was regarded as a conventional, albeit illustrious and controversial, economist but attitudes towards him changed radically following the publication of *A Treatise on Money* (1930) and *The General Theory of Employment, Interest and Money* (1936). Analyzing the causes of the economic depression of the 1920s and 1930s, he concluded that full employment was not an inevitable result of market forces and could only be achieved if governments and banks encouraged investment, sustained funding in public works during a recession and operated a cheap money policy. The tone of the texts was deliberately aggressive and dismissive of previous theories. Inevitably, it was heavily criticized but, in the end, the majority of economists accepted his ideas and the principles were incorporated in Franklin Roosevelt's New Deal policies in the United States of America. In 1944, Keynes played a major role in the discussions at the Bretton Woods Conference, which rejected his plan for world monetary reform through the creation of a world clearing bank for the settlement of international debts and the formation of a new international currency. Instead, the meetings adopted the US proposal for an International Monetary Fund and an International Bank for Reconstruction and Development (of which Keynes became Governor in 1946). He also negotiated a large US loan to Britain in order to fund postwar reconstruction of the economy.

In 1925, Keynes had married Lydia Lopokova, a ballerina, and thereafter turned his mind and his money to support for the arts. He helped found the Vic-Wells Ballet and establish the Cambridge Arts Theatre. Also, he conceived the idea of a **GOVERNMENT**-funded Arts Council of Great Britain, which became a reality in 1946 with the twin aims of increasing knowledge of the arts and making them more accessible to the public. He was also a Trustee of the National Gallery and Chairman of the Council for the Encouragement of Music and the Arts. He was raised to the **PEERAGE** as Baron Keynes in 1942 and died on 21 April 1946 following a heart attack at his home in Tilton.

KHAKI ELECTION, 1900. The **GENERAL ELECTION** of 1900

followed the introduction of khaki combat uniforms in the **BOER WAR** and so was named after the new attire. The **CONSERVA-TIVE PARTY GOVERNMENT** played on the patriotism of the electorate at times of conflict and managed to split the **LIBERAL PARTY** vote, already divided over **HOME RULE**.

KITCHENER, HORATIO HERBERT (1850-1916). Conqueror of the Sudan and organizer of the **BRITISH ARMY** at the start of the **FIRST WORLD WAR**, Kitchener was born in Ballylongford, County Kerry (now in the Republic of **IRELAND**), on 24 June 1850. The second son of Colonel Henry Kitchener and his wife, Anne, he was educated privately and at the Royal Military Academy in Woolwich before receiving a commission with the Royal Engineers in 1871. Over the next 12 years, as well as playing his part in the routine of army life in Britain, he spent some time on surveys of Palestine (1874-78) and Cyprus (1878 and 1880-82) and acted as Vice-Consul at Kastumini.

In 1883, he was given a posting as Second-in-Command of the Egyptian Cavalry Regiment and, in 1884-85, was with the Nile Expeditionary Force which failed to rescue General **CHARLES GORDON** and prevent the fall of Khartoum. His arrival at the settlement three days after it had been overrun by rebels made a deep impression, and he determined to avenge Gordon's death as soon as the opportunity arose. Later in 1885, he was appointed to the International Commission which delimited the territory of the Sultan of Zanzibar. In 1886, he became Governor General of the Eastern Sudan and, in 1888, Adjutant-General of the Egyptian Army. He was promoted to Commander-in-Chief of the Egyptian Army in 1892 and quickly reestablished control of the Nile Valley, driving out the supporters of Mohammed Ahmed ibn Seyyid 'Abdullah (who had been responsible for the sack of Khartoum) and his successor, Khalifa 'Abdullahi.

Gordon's death was finally avenged at the **BATTLE OF OMDURMAN** on 2 September 1898, when 10,000 Arabs were killed and a further 5,000 taken prisoner. In gratitude, Queen **VIC-TORIA** granted Kitchener a peerage. He was made Governor General of the Sudan in 1899 but spent less than a year in the post before being moved to South Africa, initially as Chief of Staff to the Commander-in-Chief, Lord Frederick Roberts, who was responsible for the conduct of the **BOER WAR**, then (from November 1900) as Commander-in-Chief himself. His approach to the campaign was ruthless (women and children were incarcerated in concentration camps, where disease was rife, and farms were burned as part of a scorched earth policy) but it was also successful and, in 1902, he was able to negotiate terms for peace.

He returned to Britain later that year and was created a **VISCOUNT** before going to India as Commander-in-Chief of the armies there. In 1904, he became enmeshed in a bitter quarrel with Lord George Curzon, the Viceroy, over control of military policy. Kitchener argued that he was in charge, Prime Minister **ARTHUR BALFOUR** agreed and Curzon resigned. In 1909, Kitchener visited Australia and New Zealand to advise on defence then, in 1911, accepted the post of Consul-General in Egypt despite disappointment at not being made Viceroy of India. In 1914, he was created Earl Kitchener of Khartoum and invited by **HERBERT ASQUITH** to join the **CABINET** as a nonpolitical **SECRETARY OF STATE** for War. Firmly convinced that the British Army was too small, out of tune with military leaders who believed that the conflict with Germany (see **FIRST WORLD WAR**) would be over in a few weeks and holding little esteem for the Territorial Army (which he thought was a thoroughly amateurish organization), he accepted the task with little relish. He put a vigorous recruitment programme in place and initiated training regimes which turned raw volunteers into professional soldiers. At the same time, he devized the military strategies for every corner of the world in which his men were fighting. That approach, of course, made enemies and, in 1915, some of the responsibility for mobilization and all of the responsibility for strategy were taken from him, much to his annoyance. The following year, he embarked on a visit to Russia but, on 5 June, the cruiser HMS *Hampshire*, on which he was travelling, struck a mine off the Orkney Islands. The vessel sank, and Kitchener drowned.

The town of Kitchener, administrative centre of Waterloo County in Ontario (Canada), was originally known as Berlin but was renamed in his honour in 1916.

KNIGHT. Originally, the knight was a mounted warrior, invested by his lord with the right to bear Arms (armorial devices) in return for payment of dues, usually military service, under the **FEUDAL SYSTEM**. His lands were known as his fee and normally consisted of a **MANOR**. Later, knights became part of the organization of **LOCAL GOVERNMENT** (see **JUSTICE OF THE PEACE**) as the growth of larger armies and standing forces led to the demise of their military power. In the modern context, they survive in terms of the **ORDERS OF CHIVALRY** and the other honours awarded by the sovereign. The coat of arms each knight is entitled to bear originated with the need to wear personal symbols so that they could be recognized in the thick of battle.

KRUGER TELEGRAM, 3 January 1896. After the British humiliation of the **JAMESON RAID**, the German Emperor, William II, sent a telegram of congratulations to the leader of the Boers in Transvaal, President Paul Kruger. That soured relations between Britain and Germany even further and was one of the incidents which led to the outbreak of the **BOER WAR** in 1899. Also, it resulted in the formation of closer ties between Britain and her former colonial rival, France.

—L—

LABOUR PARTY. The Labour Representation Committee was formed in 1900 to secure political power for the working people and was the foundation of the modern Labour Party. (The radical **INDEPENDENT LABOUR PARTY** had been formed in 1893 but split away from the **PARLIAMENT**ary Labour Party in 1932.) The title 'Labour Party' was adopted in 1906 under the leadership of the charismatic James Keir Hardie. Traditionally a left-wing socialist party, it advocated state involvement for the general good of society and in the rights of working people and the disadvantaged. However, during the 1990s, it has moved its policies towards the political middle ground in order to woo the votes of the middle-classes (for example, it has dropped its original insistence on the **NATIONALIZATION** of industries such as **STEEL** production). One quarter of party funds come from local **CONSTITUENCY** parties and individual members, the rest from **TRADE UNIONS**. (See **CLEMENT RICHARD ATTLEE; ERNEST BEVIN; GEORGE ALFRED BROWN; LEONARD JAMES CALLAGHAN; RICHARD STAFFORD CRIPPS; FABIAN SOCIETY; MICHAEL MACKINTOSH FOOT; HUGH GAITSKELL; ROY SYDNEY GEORGE HATTERSLEY; DENIS WINSTON HEALEY; JAMES RAMSAY MACDONALD; MILITANT TENDENCY; HERBERT STANLEY MORRISON; JAMES HAROLD WILSON**).

LADIES IN WAITING. This term refers to ladies, usually from the aristocracy, who routinely attend upon the Queen and other female members of the Royal Family. They provide official support and often companionship. (See **BEDCHAMBER CRISIS**).

LADY. This formal title is the female equivalent of **LORD**. It is also accorded to the wife of a lord and to the daughters of a **DUKE, MARQUESS** or **EARL**. (See **PEERAGE**).

LAKE DISTRICT. An upland area of northwest England, the Lake District covers some 850 square miles. From a mountain dome rising to just under 4,000 feet, a series of lakes spread like fingers along valleys originally shaped by ice and forming scenery which was the inspiration for much of the work of William Wordsworth and others of the **ROMANTIC MOVEMENT**. Their poetry, in particular, encouraged others to go and see the landscape for themselves, beginning a tourist industry which still flourishes. The area is now a **NATIONAL PARK**. (For location, see Map 1, page xxv).

LAMB, WILLIAM (1779-1848). **PRIME MINISTER** for four months in 1834 and again from 1835 until 1841, Lamb was born in **LONDON** on 15th March, 1779, the son of Viscount Melbourne. Something of a hedonist, Melbourne had a beautiful wife who was a leading society hostess. It was widely rumoured that she had several lovers, one of whom — Lord Egremont — was believed by some to be the child's true father. Educated at Eton and **CAMBRIDGE** University, Lamb was called to the Bar in 1804 and two years later was elected Member of **PARLIAMENT** for Leominster. By that time, he had married Lady Caroline Ponsonby, daughter of the Earl of Bessborough, but the match was disastrous. Caroline was highly-strung and frequently compromised her husband's political career, as when she had a well-publicized affair with Lord Byron in 1812–13. After a series of partings and reunions, the couple finally separated in 1825 and Caroline died three years later. Lamb, however, enjoyed female company, and some of his relationships were the source of much gossip at **WESTMINSTER**.

A **WHIG** by inclination, he gradually developed an admiration for Tory **GEORGE CANNING** (see **TORIES**), who appointed him Chief Secretary for **IRELAND** in 1827. He was retained in that post by the **DUKE OF WELLINGTON** (January

1828) but resigned after four months, ostensibly because of disagreements over the administration's foreign policy but probably also because of embarrassment caused by the increasingly public details of his affair with Lady Branden. In July, his father died, and he inherited the title of Viscount Melbourne and a seat in the **HOUSE OF LORDS**. Two years later, he was appointed **HOME SECRETARY** in **CHARLES GREY**'s administration, which was mandated by the **WILLIAM IV** to introduce **PARLIAMENTARY REFORM**. A conservative at heart, he was an unwilling supporter of change but was prepared to make concessions to the Irish and to the Roman Catholics. When Grey resigned in July, 1834, the King invited Melbourne to succeed him, but the new administration lasted only until November. William IV had little faith in several of those whom Lamb had included in his **GOVERNMENT** and objected to a number of their policies so he dismissed the Prime Minister and replaced him with **ROBERT PEEL**. Peel, however, could not command a majority in the **HOUSE OF COMMONS** so, in April 1835, Lamb was back in office. He too had trouble ensuring that he could win a Commons vote and, as a result, had to temper many of his policies to meet **OPPOSITION** demands. The **GENERAL ELECTION** of 1837 gave the two major parties virtually equal representation, complicating Melbourne's position even further. In 1839 he resigned but when **QUEEN VICTORIA** refused Peel's request to replace some of her Whig oriented **LADIES OF THE BEDCHAMBER**, Peel refused to accept the post of Prime Minister and Lamb was recalled (see **BEDCHAMBER CRISIS**). The situation failed to improve. A series of **BY-ELECTION** defeats exacerbated matters, as did an economic recession and disputes over foreign policy. Not surprisingly, the 1841 general election resulted in a **CONSERVATIVE PARTY** majority which took Peel to **DOWNING STREET**. Much of the blame for that Whig defeat lies on Melbourne's shoulders. Never a firm leader, he tended to chair **CABINET** meetings rather than direct them and his essentially reactionary approach was out of step in an age of change. A stroke suffered in the fall of 1842 virtually ended his public service. He died at Brocket (Hertfordshire) on 24 November 1848, a kind, intelligent but lonely man who had attained high office but achieved little.

LANCASTER, DUCHY OF. The Duchy is a landed estate which has been in the possession of the **CROWN** since 1399. A declaration by King **HENRY IV** decreed that it is to be kept separate from other Crown inheritances. The incomes derived go directly to the sovereign.

LANCASTRIANS. (See **WARS OF THE ROSES**).

LANSDOWNE, EARL OF. (See **WILLIAM PETTY FITZ-MAURICE**).

LAUD, WILLIAM (1573-1645). **ARCHBISHOP OF CANTER-BURY** from 1633 until his death in 1645, Laud made vigorous attempts to maintain elaborate forms of worship throughout the **CHURCH OF ENGLAND**. That led his **PURITAN** opponents to turn against him with such violence that they precipitated the **FIRST CIVIL WAR** in **ENGLAND** and the Bishops' Wars in **SCOTLAND**.

Born on 7 October 1573, the only son of William Laud, a clothier in Reading, he was educated at Reading Free School and **OXFORD** University. In 1601, he took holy orders and, two years later, became chaplain to Charles, Earl of Devonshire. In 1607, he was made Vicar of Stanford (Northamptonshire) and, the following year, Chaplain to Bishop Richard Neile. In 1611, he was appointed President of St John's College, Oxford, and, in 1614, obtained the Prebend of Buckden. In 1615, he was made Archdeacon of Huntingdon and, in 1616, Dean of Gloucester. In 1626, he gained the Bishopric of Bath and Wells and, in 1628, that of **LONDON**. In 1630, despite opposition, he was appointed Chancellor of Oxford University and, in 1633, became Archbishop of Canterbury.

Laud's views on ecclesiastical practices became clear early in his career: in his BD thesis at Oxford he wrote that "there could be no true church without diocesan bishops" and, later, he was to acknowledge Roman Catholicism as a legitimate Church but deny the Pope's infallibility. He also strenuously opposed the Roman view that Anglican bishops were not the legitimate successors to the authority of Jesus' disciples and rejected proposals to simplify Church of England ritual. The King, he maintained, ruled by divine right (see **DIVINE RIGHT OF KINGS**) and opposition to him would result in damnation. Wherever possible, Laud insisted on the use of the Prayer Book by aliens in England. He also attempted to extend his principles to Scotland but met with bitter resistance. The Scots Presbyterians saw the imposition of Anglican ways as a threat to the country's independence as well as an attack on their religion. In 1638, they raised an army and defied both Laud and King **CHARLES I.** In England, the zealousness of the Archbishop's attempts to impose his views, and the often violent treatment of those who opposed him, encouraged many Puritans to flee to the Americas and ultimately led to his own downfall. In 1640, his attempts to impose the etcetera oath, which would force people to swear perpetual allegiance to "the government of the church by archbishops, deans and archdeacons, etc," were widely condemned, and the King was forced to order its suspension.

On 18 December 1640, Laud was impeached by the antiroyalist **LONG PARLIAMENT** and, on 1 March the following year, imprisoned in the **TOWER OF LONDON**. His trial opened on 12 March 1644 and showed scant respect for elementary principles of justice (even the King's pardon, granted to him in April 1643, was rejected). Found guilty of **TREASON** by attempting to overturn religion and the law, he was beheaded at Tower Hill on 10 January 1645.

LAW, ANDREW BONAR (1858-1923). **PRIME MINISTER** in 1922 and 1923, and Leader of the **CONSERVATIVE PARTY** during the **FIRST WORLD WAR** and its immediate aftermath, Law was born in Kingston (New Brunswick, Canada) on 16 September 1858, the youngest of the four sons of James Law (a Presbyterian minister with family roots in **ULSTER**) and his wife, Elizabeth (daughter of a Glasgow iron merchant). His mother died when he was only two, and his father suffered from a form of melancholia which deepened as he grew older so, in 1870, Andrew was taken to Glasgow, where he lived with relatives. He was educated at Gilbertfield School (Hamilton) and Glasgow High School but left at the age of 16 to take a job in the family's merchant bank. In 1885, he became a junior partner in William Jacks and Company, a firm of iron merchants, and five years later was elected Conservative Member of **PARLIAMENT** for Glasgow Blackfriars.

Law was given his first **GOVERNMENT** post as **PARLIAMENTARY SECRETARY** to the **BOARD OF TRADE** in 1902 and, in that capacity, supported **JOSEPH CHAMBERLAIN**'s plans to replace **FREE TRADE** with a system of **IMPERIAL PREFERENCE**. He lost his seat at the **GENERAL ELECTION** in January 1906, beaten by the **LABOUR PARTY** candidate, but won a **BY-ELECTION** at Dulwich in May and became (with

JOSEPH AUSTEN CHAMBERLAIN) one of the leading **OP-POSITION** spokesmen on tariff reform. By 1911, he was one of the most respected figures in the party but, even so, was not considered a major candidate for the leadership when **ARTHUR BALFOUR** resigned. Newspaper correspondents predicted that the successor would be either Chamberlain or Walter Long but it became clear that neither was a clear favourite so, in order to avoid a potentially damaging split within the party, they agreed to withdraw their claims and pledge support to Law. The next three years were characterized by bitter wrangling in the **HOUSE OF COMMONS**, much of it centering on the issue of Irish **HOME RULE** (a topic about which Law, with his Scots-Irish ancestry, found it impossible to be dispassionate). However, the outbreak of the **FIRST WORLD WAR** in 1914 forced MPs of all shades of opinion to turn their attentions to other matters, and, in 1915, Law became Colonial Secretary in the coalition government headed by **HERBERT ASQUITH.** The following year, he was deeply involved in the behind-the-scenes plotting which led to the Prime Minister's resignation and **DAVID LLOYD GEORGE'**s move from the War Office to **DOWNING STREET**. Under Lloyd George, Law became **CHANCELLOR OF THE EXCHEQUER** and **LEADER OF THE HOUSE OF COMMONS** but, in 1921, a bout of illness forced him to relinquish the Chancellorship.

Over the next 12 months, the Prime Minister came under increasing pressure in Parliament and his popularity with the voters declined.   Law withdrew the Conservatives from the coalition (against the advice of many senior colleagues), and Lloyd George, no longer commanding an assured Parliamentary majority, resigned. At the general election which followed, Bonar Law was returned to power. He was in office for less than a year, insufficient to make a lasting impact on the country but long enough to face two crises. One was caused by the critical reaction to the terms negotiated by Chancellor of the Exchequer **STANLEY BALDWIN** for the settlement of Britain's war debts with the United States of America — Law felt that his colleague had driven a poor bargain and had to be persuaded not to resign. The second was a result of French occupation of the Ruhr in 1923. The action was taken because Germany had failed to pay agreed compensation for war damage on time, but Law felt that the military response was unwise so diplomatic relations with France reached a low ebb. There was no opportunity for a rebuilding of bridges. In May 1923, Law's doctors diagnosed incurable throat cancer, and he immediately tendered his resignation to King **GEORGE V**. On 30 October he died in **LONDON**.

LAWSON, NIGEL (1932-). **CHANCELLOR OF THE EXCHEQ-UER** from 1983 until 1989, Lawson was born on 11 March 1932, the son of Mr and Mrs Ralph Lawson. He was educated at **WEST-MINSTER** School and **OXFORD** University, graduating with a First Class Honours Degree in philosophy, politics and economics in 1954. He served as a Sub-Lieutenant in the Royal Naval Volunteer Reserve until 1956 then embarked on a career in journalism. From 1956 until 1960, he was on the editorial staff of the *Financial Times* and, from 1961 until 1963, was City Editor of the *Sunday Telegraph*. In 1963 and 1964, he was Special Assistant to Prime Minister **ALEC DOUGLAS-HOME** before returning to the press in 1965 as a columnist with the *Financial Times* and broadcaster with the **BRITISH BROADCASTING CORPORATION (BBC)**.

Lawson was appointed Editor of *The Spectator* in 1966 and held the post until 1970, when he unsuccessfully fought the Eton and Slough **PARLIAMENT**ary **CONSTITUENCY** for the **CONSERVATIVE PARTY**. Over the next few years, he contributed to several newspapers, notably the *Evening Standard*, **THE TIMES** and *The Sunday Times*. Then, in 1974, he was elected Member of Parliament for Blaby. His first official posts were as **OPPOSITION WHIP** (1976-77) and Spokesman on **TREAS-URY** and Economic Affairs (1977-79). In **MARGARET THATCHER**'s administrations, he was **FINANCIAL SECRE-TARY TO THE TREASURY** from 1979 until 1981, **SECRE-TARY OF STATE** for Energy from 1981 until 1983 and Chancellor of the Exchequer from 1983 until 1989. Mrs Thatcher called him "brilliant" and "unassailable" but, even so, he walked out of the **GOVERNMENT** after a series of bitter exchanges with her. On the morning of 26 October 1989, Lawson told Mrs Thatcher that his role as Chancellor was being undermined by comments made, both in public and in private, by Sir Alan Walters (her personal economic adviser), particularly with reference to the United Kingdom's membership of the **EUROPEAN MONETARY SYS-TEM**. That situation had been building up over the weeks, clearly annoying Lawson, who told the Prime Minister that either Walters went or he did. In the afternoon, Mrs Thatcher fielded a number of questions about Walters in the **HOUSE OF COMMONS** but refused to reject his criticisms of the Chancellor. Lawson saw the

PRIME MINISTER later in the day and told her he had decided to quit. After he left, he became Chairman of the Central Europe Trust and a Director of Barclays Bank. He was created Baron Lawson of Blaby in 1992.

LEADER OF THE HOUSE OF COMMONS. (See **LORD PRESIDENT OF THE COUNCIL**).

LEAGUE OF NATIONS. The **TREATY OF VERSAILLES** (1919) set up this international assembly of independent states following a suggestion made by U.S. President Woodrow Wilson. The League would monitor the peace, be an arbiter of international disputes, prevent a repeat of the **FIRST WORLD WAR** through mutual, collective security and work for disarmament, health and labour. The United Kingdom joined, along with all of the members of the **BRITISH EMPIRE**, and its first Secretary-General was the Earl of Perth. Weakened by the refusal of the United States of America to participate and the withdrawal of Japan, Italy and Germany, it failed to halt aggression in Abyssinia (see **ABYSSINIAN CAMPAIGN**) or prevent the **SECOND WORLD WAR**, though its labour and legal agencies did work well. All functions were transferred to the United Nations Organization in 1946.

LEND-LEASE. This system of primarily economic aid from the United States to the Allies in 1941 (given before the United States entered the **SECOND WORLD WAR**) was intended to allow the purchase, lease or loan of supplies in instances when such trade could be said to be in the United States of America's security interests and when the terms for repayment, which might not be in full, would be negotiated. All repayments were to be made after the war was over. Britain, then with almost exhausted reserves, gained $27 billion but had to agree not to export goods made from the aid, thus effectively ceasing to trade. However, the scheme saved the country from imminent bankruptcy. Lend-Lease ceased on 2 September 1945, with Britain accepting a debt to the United States of America of $650 million. (See **MARSHALL AID**).

LEVANT COMPANY. This company was established in 1592 by the amalgamation of the Turkey and Venice Trading Companies and built up a commerce in textiles (particularly silk and Turkish carpets), and also in tin, with the Levant (that area of the Eastern

Mediterranean which was then part of the Ottoman Empire). It ceased business in 1825.

LEVELLERS. A group of radical extremist agitators active during the **CIVIL WAR**, the Levellers advocated popular, democratic, republican government (based on the sovereignty of the people) and were therefore opposed both to King and to **PARLIAMENT**. They objected to social distinctions (hence their name) and had a strong following in **LONDON** among the ordinary soldiers of the **ROUNDHEAD** army (mutinies of Levellers in 1649 were ruthlessly put down). The term has also been used to refer to tenant farmers who protested against **ENCLOSURES** in **SCOTLAND** in the 1720s. (See **DIGGERS**).

LEWES, BATTLE OF, 14 May 1264. This battle, fought during the **BARONS' WARS**, resulted in defeat for the royal forces under Prince Edward (son of **HENRY III** and, later, **EDWARD I**) who were outsmarted by the strategic skills of **SIMON DE MONTFORT**. The conflict was precipitated when King Henry refused to accept the **PROVISIONS OF OXFORD** and ended with the capture of Edward, who was confined as surety that his father would accede to the barons' demands. Effectively, that made De Montfort ruler of **ENGLAND**. The battle was followed by the **MISE OF LEWES** and the first real **PARLIAMENT** of **KNIGHT**s so De Montfort is sometimes known as the "Father of Parliaments". (See **BATTLE OF EVESHAM; OXFORD PARLIAMENT**).

LEWES, MISE OF, 15 May 1264. Following the **BATTLE OF LEWES**, this mise (or agreement) guaranteed that those **CASTLES** which had been captured by royalist forces would be returned to their owners and that supporters of **SIMON DE MONTFORT** would be released from prison. Prince Edward (later **EDWARD I**) was held as hostage by the barons to ensure that his father (**HENRY III**) would comply with the treaty provisions.

LIBERAL PARTY. The term 'Liberal Party' gained currency only in the 19th century as a new **PARLIAMENT**ary party emerged in the 1850s from a regrouping of **WHIG** supporters. The words 'Liberal' and 'Whig' are used interchangeably for the period from 1832 to 1867, after which the older term is used to describe the landowning and upper class element of the association. The Party lost political stature in the lead-up to the **FIRST WORLD WAR** and was eclipsed in 1918 by the rise of the **LABOUR PARTY**, which appealed to the growing working class. It entered the **LIB-LAB PACT** in 1977 with the **LABOUR PARTY**, supporting the minority **GOVERNMENT** of **JAMES CALLAGHAN**, and formed an agreement with the **SOCIAL DEMOCRATIC PARTY** in 1981 to form the **ALLIANCE**. In 1988, it was restructured to form the **SOCIAL AND LIBERAL DEMOCRATIC PARTY**, which changed its name to the **LIBERAL DEMOCRATIC PARTY** the following year. During the 1990s, the Liberal Democrats have generally done better in **LOCAL GOVERNMENT** and Parliamentary **BY-ELECTIONS** than in **GENERAL ELECTIONS**. (See **HERBERT HENRY ASQUITH; HENRY CAMPBELL-BANNERMAN; DAVID LLOYD GEORGE; WILLIAM EWART GLADSTONE; ARCHIBALD PHILIP PRIMROSE ROSEBERY; JOHN RUSSELL; HENRY JOHN TEMPLE; JOHN JEREMY THORPE**).

LIBERAL DEMOCRATIC PARTY. In 1988, the **LIBERAL PARTY** merged with the **SOCIAL DEMOCRATIC PARTY** to form the **SOCIAL AND LIBERAL DEMOCRATIC PARTY**. The following year, the organization adopted its present (and shorter) title. (See **JEREMY JOHN DURHAM ASHDOWN**).

LIBERTY. A pressure group formed by Ronald Kidd in 1934 to campaign for, and defend, civil liberties, the organization was known until 1989 as the National Council for Civil Liberties.

LIB-LAB PACT. The **LIBERAL PARTY** entered a pact with the **LABOUR PARTY** in 1977 to support the minority **GOVERNMENT** led by **JAMES CALLAGHAN**. When the **DEVOLUTION** referenda failed, this pact was broken in 1979.

LICENSING ACT, 1662. Following the **ACT OF UNIFORMITY**, which had become law earlier in 1662 (see **ACT OF PARLIAMENT**), this legislation was a further imposition of censorship. It forbade publications which did not conform to **CHURCH OF ENGLAND** requirements and limited **PRINTING** to four towns only. In addition, all documents had to be registered with the Stationers' Company.

LICENSING ACT, 1872. This thoroughly unpopular act (see **ACT OF PARLIAMENT**) precipitated public riots as a result of the imposition of strict opening hours, and other limitations, on places where alcohol was sold. The new laws may also have contributed to the subsequent **GENERAL ELECTION** defeat of the already unpopular **LIBERAL PARTY** government of **WILLIAM GLADSTONE**, who remarked that "We have been borne down in a torrent of beer and gin". The laws on strict opening hours, long seen as curious by overseas visitors, were only relaxed in **ENGLAND** and **WALES** in 1988 (following earlier legislation in **SCOTLAND**) and now allow **PUBLIC HOUSE**s to open between 11 am and 11 pm.

LIGHT BRIGADE, CHARGE OF THE, 25 October 1854. At the **BATTLE OF BALACLAVA**, during the **CRIMEAN WAR**, a misunderstanding between the British commanders led the Light Brigade of cavalry, under Lord Cardigan, to charge heavily armed Russian artillery in a narrow valley (a badly worded order from Lord Raglan had taken them to the wrong location). Thirty per cent of the force was cut to pieces in this heroic but foolhardy attack, and the French commander, General Boisquet, was said to have remarked "C'est magnifique, mais ce n'est pas la guerre" ("It is magnificent, but it is not war"). In 1854, the incident inspired Alfred Lord Tennyson to write a commemorative poem, which includes the lament:

> Their's not to reason why,
> Their's but to do and die,
> Into the valley of death
> Rode the six hundred.

LIVERPOOL. One of Britain's major seaports, Liverpool is situated on the north bank of the **RIVER MERSEY**, some 200 miles northwest of **LONDON**. Initially, the settlement served as a harbour for boats crossing the Irish Sea but, during the 17th and 18th centuries, it expanded rapidly as a result of participation in the lucrative **ATLANTIC TRIANGLE** trade. Trinkets, cotton goods and other commodities were sent to the West African coast and exchanged for slaves (see **SLAVE TRADE**), who were taken to the Deep South of the United States and to the West Indies, where they were bartered or sold. The vessels returned to Liverpool with cotton, sugar and rum. In 1807, just before the commerce in slaves was abolished, 185 Liverpool-registered ships were involved, carrying nearly 50,000 slaves a year. Despite the economic setback caused by abolition, the port continued to grow, importing grain and foodstuffs, timber, tobacco, metal ores and other raw materials. The Manufactured goods were sent to all corners of the **BRITISH EMPIRE** in return. Related industries thrived, and a series of towns developed along the river, focusing on Liverpool and processing the materials imported or providing services (such as ship repair work) for the firms involved in international trade. Shipbuilding itself became a major employer but the yards were severely damaged by German bombing during the **SECOND WORLD WAR** and many closed in the 1960s and 1970s in the face of competition from Germany, Japan and the United States of America.

A dominantly working class area, the city was implacably opposed to the cuts in local authority expenditure introduced by **MARGARET THATCHER** but, in the end, was forced to capitulate as central government exercised increasingly tight control over council budgets. Also, like other large centres, it is losing population. At the time of the 1991 census, it had 436,000 residents, a drop of 13.5 per cent from the 1981 figure. The Merseyside Metropolitan County, which is effectively the Liverpool metropolitan area, had 1,367,000 people, down 9.1 per cent over the decade. (For location, see Map 2, page xxvi).

LIVERPOOL, EARL OF. (See **ROBERT BANKS JENKINSON**).

LIVERY COMPANIES. Medieval craft or trade associations in **LONDON**, the Livery Companies were successors to the **GUILD**s and had great commercial power, controlling apprenticeship rules, commercial practices and monopolies. Members wore a distinctive ceremonial dress (the livery), a practice which originated in the days of the **FEUDAL SYSTEM**, when a lord's retainers often received partial payment of their dues in the form of cloth or uniform.The organizations continue as the **CITY OF LONDON** Livery Companies.

LLOYD GEORGE, DAVID (1863-1945). One of the outstanding statesmen of the 20th century, Lloyd George was **PRIME MINISTER** from 1916 until 1922. He was born in **MANCHESTER** on 17 January 1863, the son of William George (a schoolmaster) and his wife, Elizabeth. His father died when his son was only 18 months old, leaving the family in poverty. Elizabeth Lloyd moved to Llanystum-dwy (Caernarvonshire), where her brother, a shoe-maker and Baptist minister, provided for her and the child. As a result, David grew up in a strict and impoverished household and the experiences there greatly influenced the development of his political philosophy.

In 1884, he qualified as a solicitor and, in 1890, was elected to **PARLIAMENT** as the **LIBERAL PARTY** MP for Caernar-von Boroughs, he won the seat by only 18 votes but represented the **CONSTITUENCY** for 55 years. A natural orator with the quick-witted skill of a debater, he soon made his mark in the **HOUSE OF COMMONS**, where he argued for the **NONCON-FORMIST** cause, **FREE TRADE**, social reform and Welsh inde-pendence. Also, he spoke out strongly against the **BOER WAR** and marshalled opposition to the **EDUCATION** Act of 1902, which provided **GOVERNMENT** funds for **CHURCH OF ENG-LAND** schools. In 1906, **HENRY CAMPBELL-BANNERMAN** appointed Lloyd George to his first official post — **PRESIDENT OF THE BOARD OF TRADE.** That office gave him a seat in the **CABINET** and allowed him to introduce a series of **BILL**s which led to important social and economic reforms. The Mer-chant Shipping Act of 1906 (see **ACT OF PARLIAMENT**) pre-scribed minimum living conditions for seamen, the Patents and Designs Act of 1907 closed loopholes in the law (which had al-lowed foreign countries to exploit British inventions) and the Port of **LONDON** Act of 1908 established the Port of London Author-ity to regulate the operations of the city's shipping trade.

His impact was such that, when **HENRY ASQUITH** be-came **PRIME MINISTER** in 1908, Lloyd George was made **CHANCELLOR OF THE EXCHEQUER** and applied the same enthusiasm to that job as to his previous one. In particu-lar, in 1909, he introduced a "People's **BUDGET**" which raised funds for social reform and the building of warships by imposing higher death duties, levying a super tax on incomes of over £3,000 and introducing new taxes on land values and on unearned income resulting from land sales. The **HOUSE OF LORDS** refused to approve the measures, but a **GENERAL ELECTION** in January 1910 demonstrated popular support for the Chancellor and the upper house relented. The following year, Lloyd George piloted the National Insurance Bill through Parliament despite the opposition of employers and the medical profession. That legislation provided British workers with un-employment benefits and insurance against illness — measures which foreshadowed the more encompassing legal framework on which the **WELFARE STATE** was built in the 1940s.

Following the outbreak of the **FIRST WORLD WAR**, Lloyd George was made **MINISTER** of Munitions in 1915. Calling on the assistance of managers in private industry and urging the workforce to greater effort, he increased the output of weaponry to levels which greatly enhanced the effectiveness of front line troops. In June 1916, he was moved to the War Office, where he voiced serious doubts about the conduct of the military campaign, and when Asquith resigned, in December, he became Prime Minister, supported by the **CONSERVATIVE PARTY** as well as by members of his own party. However, the change in leadership caused much bad blood, many of the leading Liberals believing that Lloyd George had, at best, been disloyal to Asquith and, at worst, had deliberately hounded him out of office. Whatever the truth of the matter, he pursued the war vigorously, appointing an Inner Cabinet of five members, speeding up decision making, cooperating closely with leaders of the **DOMINION**s and colonies and increasing the output of merchant shipping in order to replace losses to the German submarines. When the fighting ended, he opted to continue with coalition government and won public support for that policy at the 1918 election. However, many of those who advocated a return to normal party politics lost their seats (Asquith included), and, as a result, the schism in the Liberal Party widened, making Lloyd George increasingly dependent on Conservative support.

With U.S. President Woodrow Wilson and French Premier Georges Clemenceau, he was a major figure at the Versailles Peace Conference in 1919 (see **TREATY OF VERSAILLES**) and helped shape an agreement which was well received in Britain. However, peace brought problems. There were labour disputes as the economy reacted to changed conditions, rebels in **IRELAND** were violently pursuing their claims for **HOME RULE** and rumours suggested that **PEERAGE**s were being sold for large sums of money. The climax came in 1923, when critics claimed that Britain nearly became embroiled in a war with Turkey as a result of Lloyd George's support for Greek territorial expansion. The Conservatives withdrew from the coalition government and Lloyd George resigned. He remained in politics and led the Liberal Party again from 1926 until 1931, but his days of influence were over. **WINSTON CHURCHILL** asked him to join the War Cabinet in 1940, but he declined, citing age and ill health.

He was elevated to the peerage as **EARL** Lloyd George of Dwyfor in January 1945 but died at Llanystumdwy on 26 March. Shortly afterwards, Churchill told the House of Commons:
"When the history of the first quarter of the twentieth century is written, it will be found that the greater part of our fortunes in peace and war were shaped by this one man".

LLOYD'S OF LONDON. This unique Society of Underwriters originated with Edward Lloyd's coffee house, which opened in Tower Street, **LONDON**, in 1688 and became known as a good source of shipping intelligence and thus a popular meeting place for shipowners and traders. From these beginnings, Lloyd's of London grew to become the largest association of insurance underwriters in the world. It is now housed in a controversial Leadenhall Street building designed by Richard Rogers and, in recent years, has been rocked by record losses and financial scandal.

LOCAL GOVERNMENT. In the 19th century, **GOVERNMENT** in **ENGLAND** and **WALES** below that of **WESTMINSTER** comprised **COUNTY**, **BOROUGH**, urban district and rural district councils and reflected the changes of the **INDUSTRIAL REVOLUTION**, which created needs for a plethora of new authorities such as **TURNPIKE** trusts, boards of health and school boards.

During 1973 to 1975, local government in England was reorganized into 39 administrative counties (controlling major services such as roads, housing, schools and police), district councils (296 of them, a tier below the administrative county and responsible for such local services as environmental health, waste disposal and housing) and **PARISH**es (a tier below the districts and formed mainly in rural areas). Six metropolitan districts were also created but abolished in 1985. In **LONDON**, the borough councils operate most services as unitary authorities (that is, they are responsible for all functions, both district and county). A local government commission, appointed in 1992, reviewed local government in nonmetropolitan England and decided that the two tier authorities should remain, except in some of the larger cities. The changes they recommended were implemented in 1995, 1996 and 1997.

In **SCOTLAND**, local government has its roots in the burghs, shires and parishes of the medieval period. As in England, there was a multiplication of bodies following the Industrial Revolution (and also after the introduction of legislation creating the **WELFARE STATE**). By the mid-20th century, there were 33 counties, four counties of cities, 20 large burghs and 176 small burghs (those parts of the counties which did not have burgh status were known as landward areas). In 1975, these were replaced by nine regional councils, 53 second-tier district councils and three unitary authorities for the Western Isles, Orkney and Shetland. In 1996, a structure of 29 unitary councils replaced the regional and district authorities but the three island councils were retained.

In **WALES**, the 13 counties, four county boroughs and 164 district councils were replaced, in 1974, by eight counties and 36 districts. As in Scotland, there was a further wholesale change in 1996, when a new pattern of 22 unitary authorities was introduced. (See **LONDON COUNTY COUNCIL; GREATER LONDON COUNCIL; MUNICIPAL CORPORATIONS ACT**).

LOCKE, JOHN (1632-1704). The founder of the British school of empiricist philosophy (which emphasizes the importance of the senses as a source of knowledge), Locke was born in Wrington (in the west of **ENGLAND**) on 29 August 1632. His father (also John Locke) was a lawyer who arranged for his son to be educated at **WESTMINSTER** School (**LONDON**) and **OXFORD** University. After graduating with a BA degree in 1656 and an MA in 1658, he spent some time teaching, learned the principles of medicine and served as Secretary for a diplomatic mission to Cleves (1665-66). In 1667, while working as physician to **SIR ANTHONY ASHLEY COOPER** (later Earl of Shaftesbury), he published an essay on religious tolerance, questioning the theory of the **DIVINE RIGHT OF KINGS** and arguing that individuals should be free to worship whichever gods they pleased provided the exercise of that freedom did not threaten the state. The following year, he was elected Fellow of the **ROYAL SOCIETY** and, in 1671, started work on his *Essay Concerning Human Understanding*, which was ultimately published in 1690. In that treatise, he maintained that the mind of a newborn baby is a blank tablet on which knowledge is written as the child experiences the world through its senses, a claim which was directly opposed to the views of Rene Descartes and other Rationalists, who argued that ideas are innate. Also, he advocated the use of experiments as a means of accumulating knowledge.

Locke's political philosophies are most clearly stated in *Two Treatises of Government* (also published in 1690). Like **THOMAS HOBBES**, he believed that **GOVERNMENT** resulted from a social contract whereby a population accepted rule by a king. But the power of that sovereign was not absolute — if it was misused, the ruler could legitimately be overthrown. He also argued that church and state should be separate and that happiness was the natural goal and greatest good of the human race. Inevitably, his views were shaped by his experience as confidential adviser to the liberal Shaftesbury, who was **LORD CHANCELLOR** in 1672 and 1673. (Locke helped him shape the constitution of the British colony of Carolina.) He opposed the pro-Catholic policies of **CHARLES II** and **JAMES VII and II**, fleeing to Holland in 1683 and spending some time in hiding in 1685 in order to avoid arrest. In 1693, he published *Some Thoughts Concerning Education* (a work intended for the sons of the rural **GENTRY** and still one of the great texts on educational theory) and, in 1695, completed his last major study, *The Reasonableness of Christianity.* He died in Oates (Essex) on 28 October 1704.

LOLLARDS. Followers of **JOHN WYCLIFFE**, the Lollards received their name from the Flemish term *lollaerd*, meaning 'a mumbler, mutterer or one always in prayer' (and by implication a heretic). The last quarter of the 14th century was a time of great anticlerical movements. The Lollards adopted views opposed to the opulence of the Catholic Church and the worldliness of the clergy, rejecting transubstantiation (the belief that the bread and wine at the Eucharist turned into the body and blood of Christ) and campaigning for constitutional as well as religious reform. They also followed Wycliffe's insistence that the Scriptures should be available to all through the recent English translation of the Bible. King **HENRY IV** passed the *De Heretico Comburendo* statute to combat Lollardism by condemning convicted heretics to death by burning. The Lollard Rising in 1414 failed and the movement ceased to be a force from that date though many scholars consider the Lollards to have been precursors of the **NONCONFORMIST** movements of later periods.

LONDON. The capital, and major commercial centre, of the United Kingdom, London is located on the banks of the **RIVER THAMES** in southeast **ENGLAND**. The site was probably occupied by prehistoric communities (see **PREHISTORIC BRITAIN**), but its recorded history begins with the **ROMANS**, who founded a settlement, which they named Londinium, north of the river in the area now occupied by the finance houses of the **CITY**

OF LONDON. After their departure, in the early fifth century, the town lost some of its importance. Conflicts on mainland Europe reduced its foreign trade and the politics of the **ANGLO-SAXON** period moved the focus of power further west to Winchester. However, in 886, **ALFRED THE GREAT** occupied the area and rebuilt its defences in order to protect it against **VIKING** invasions. The new regime stimulated commerce and, by the time the **NORMANS** arrived in 1066, London was the largest town in the country.

Following the **CORONATION** of **WILLIAM I**, the city grew around two nodes — the royal palace at **WESTMINSTER** and the trading complex of the City and the harbour. In the early 13th century, a bridge was built across the Thames and, over succeeding decades, the port flourished. Also, as the **MONARCH**s maintained their presence, **GOVERNMENT** departments expanded and **PARLIAMENT**s regularly met at Westminster, London became recognized as the capital of England. Under the **PLANTAGENETS**, **TUDORS** and **STUARTS**, it continued to expand, with new industries (such as silk manufacture and glassmaking) established, and theatres achieving great popularity. However, the rapidly increasing population crowded into narrow streets of densely packed houses, which provided ideal conditions for the **GREAT PLAGUE** of 1665 and the **GREAT FIRE** of 1666 to wreak devastation.

During the reconstruction following the fire, brick buildings replaced wooden structures, streets were widened and sewage schemes were introduced, albeit on a piecemeal basis. Also, the population continued to rise. London was the headquarters of the **BRITISH EMPIRE**, attracting migrants who scented opportunities for wealth and fame. Between the mid-17th and the mid-19th centuries, the number of residents more than quadrupled from about 500,000 to well over 2 million.

By 1850, the docks were importing raw materials from all over the globe and exporting manufactured products. London had become the financial and commercial capital of the world. During the 20th century, however, the city has been faced with a series of problems. At the start of the **SECOND WORLD WAR**, the **BLITZ** brought havoc, destroying property and killing thousands of civilians. The damage, and changing patterns of trade, spelled decline for the docks and the rise of financial centres abroad challenged the dominance of the city. Faced with the new situation, **LOCAL GOVERNMENT** was reorganized in 1965 through the formation of a **GREATER LON-DON COUNCIL (GLC)** consisting of representatives of 12 inner city **BOROUGH**s and 20 outer boroughs. The largest urban regeneration scheme in Europe was undertaken in the docklands to breathe new life into derelict land by providing homes, offices, hotels, a marina and other facilities.

However, in 1983, **MARGARET THATCHER**'s Government disbanded the GLC, which had opposed the legislative measures introduced to control local authority spending, so London is now divided into 32 independent boroughs, plus the City of London, and coordinated planning for the whole urban area is limited. Elements of the docklands scheme have experienced financial difficulty and, during the 1990s, banks and insurance companies have reacted to new technologies and high costs by shedding staff. Also, populations have been falling. Between 1971 and 1981, all of the inner London boroughs lost more than ten per cent of their residents and five lost more than 20 per cent. In 1991, the population of the former GLC area, was 6,287,400 — nearly five per cent lower than it had been in 1981. One of the consequences has been an increasing polarization of living standards, with problems of poverty and deprivation most evident in the inner areas. London is still a major world city but its future depends on its abilities to tackle its social and economic ills. (See **LONDON COUNTY COUNCIL** and, for location, Map 2, page xxvi).

LONDON, TREATY OF. There have been several treaties of **LON-DON**.

<u>1373</u>: **JOHN OF GAUNT** had married the daughter of Portugal's King Pedro in 1372 and this treaty (confirmed through the Treaty of Windsor in 1385) reinforced that match by setting up a mutual aid agreement between **ENGLAND** and Portugal, an alliance that has never been broken.

<u>1827</u>: Britain, France and Russia signed an understanding to support the Greeks, who were seeking independence from the Ottoman Empire. It is sometimes called the London Convention. (See **EASTERN QUESTION; BATTLE OF NAVARINO**).

<u>1832</u>: This treaty established the boundaries of the new Kingdom of Greece and guaranteed its independence.

<u>1839</u>: An accord between Britain, Russia, France, Austria and Prussia affirmed the independence of Belgium and the Grand Duchy of Luxembourg. Germany and France, at British insistence, also accepted Belgian neutrality in the Franco-Prussian war. The

German invasion of Belgium in 1914 was considered to be an infringement of the treaty and was one of the reasons for Britain's entry into the **FIRST WORLD WAR**.

<u>1913</u>: This treaty ended the Balkan Wars and established the much-reduced boundaries of the Ottoman Empire.

<u>1915</u>: A secret agreement signed on 26 April 1915 by Britain, France and Russia (see **ENTENTE CORDIALE**) promised Italy territory from the Austro-Hungarian Empire if it joined the war on the side of the Allies within one month. However, the Bolshevik Russian Government revealed the existence of the treaty when it came to power in 1918, and Britain and France, under pressure from the United States of America, reneged on the terms at the end of the **FIRST WORLD WAR** so Italian gains were few.

LONDON COMPANY. The company was incorporated in 1606 and, the following year, founded the first permanent English settlement in America at Jamestown (named after King **JAMES VI and I**), Chesapeake Bay (Virginia) with 120 English settlers. Barely surviving, it became the Virginia Company in 1609 and traded in tobacco until the colony was ceded to the **CROWN** in 1624. (See **PILGRIM FATHERS**).

LONDON COUNTY COUNCIL (LCC). The LCC was created in 1888 and operated from 1889 until 1965, when it was replaced by the **GREATER LONDON COUNCIL**. It was the **COUNTY** level administration for **LONDON** and was based at County Hall, located opposite the Houses of **PARLIAMENT** on the south bank of the **RIVER THAMES**.

LONDONDERRY, MARQUIS OF. (See **STEWART, ROBERT**).

LONG PARLIAMENT, 3 September 1640-16 March 1660. This **PARLIAMENT** began as a radical body setting about constitutional and religious reform. Led by John Pym, it antagonized **CHARLES I** and the dispute led, in 1642, to **CIVIL WAR**. Purged by **OLIVER CROMWELL** in 1648, its **RUMP PARLIAMENT** twice tried to reestablish its position before being dissolved in 1660 prior to the **RESTORATION** of the **MONARCH**y. It remains the longest formal Parliament to date. (See **SHIP MONEY**).

LORD. This title can be formally applied to any **DUKE, MAR-**

QUESS, EARL, VISCOUNT or BARON. By courtesy, it is also accorded to a bishop or archbishop, a judge of the senior courts of law, the eldest son of an earl and the younger sons of a duke or marquess. (See **FEUDAL SYSTEM; ORDERS OF CHIVALRY; PEERAGE**).

LORD CHAMBERLAIN. The Head of the Royal Household, the Lord Chamberlain acts as chair of the committee which issues warrants of appointment for the supply of goods to members of the royal family. From 1843 until 1968, the Lord Chamberlain was also responsible for censorship in the theatre.

LORD CHANCELLOR. A member of the **GOVERNMENT** with a seat in the **CABINET**, the Lord Chancellor is the head of the **JUDICIARY** and presides over the **HOUSE OF LORDS**. The history of the office can be traced back to the time of **EDWARD THE CONFESSOR**, when the occupant of the post was the **MONARCH**'s Chief Secretary. (See **COURT OF CHANCERY**).

LORD CHIEF JUSTICE OF ENGLAND. The head of the **QUEEN'S BENCH** Division of the **HIGH COURT OF JUSTICE**, the Lord Chief Justice presides over the Criminal Division of the **COURT OF APPEAL**. The occupant of the post is junior only to the **LORD CHANCELLOR** in the legal hierarchy and is appointed by the **CROWN** on the nomination of the **PRIME MINISTER**.

LORD GREAT CHAMBERLAIN. This official has general responsibility for the Palace of **WESTMINSTER** and particularly for the **HOUSE OF LORDS**. The post was established by the **NORMANS** and is now largely concerned with ceremonial duties (such as the introduction of new peers to the Lords).

LORD HIGH STEWARD. This post was established by the **NORMANS** and was largely honorific in nature although the holder had jurisdiction in some courts. It ceased to be a permanent office during the reign of **HENRY IV**. Thereafter, a steward was appointed only when required to preside over the court which assessed petitioners' claims to be represented at a **CORONATION**, to perform certain ceremonial duties or to act as judge at the trial of a peer accused of a serious crime.

LORD HIGH TREASURER. This official was responsible for the finances of the later **SAXON** kings but it was not until the 16th century that the title came into general use. In 1612, the duties were allocated to a board headed by the First Commissioner, also known as First Lord of the **TREASURY**. Formally, the **PRIME MINISTER** is now First Lord, with the **CHANCELLOR OF THE EXCHEQUER** Second Lord.

LORD KEEPER OF THE GREAT SEAL. King **EDWARD THE CONFESSOR** adopted the practice of attaching the **GREAT SEAL** of **ENGLAND** to important state documents. Gradually, it became the custom to entrust guardianship of the seal to one individual, who was officially known as the Lord Keeper. The post was abolished in 1757. (See **LORD PRIVY SEAL**).

LORD LIEUTENANT. This was the official title of the **VICEROY** of **IRELAND** until 1922, when that territory ceased to be part of Great Britain. It is also conferred on the individual who acts as the sovereign's representative in a region of the **UNITED KINGDOM**. The duties of that official are now largely ceremonial.

LORD MAYOR. The holder of this post is the chief magistrate and leading civic dignitary of certain larger cities and **BOROUGHS** in **ENGLAND, NORTHERN IRELAND** and **WALES**.

LORD PRESIDENT OF THE COUNCIL. One of the great officers of state, the Lord President presides over meetings of the **PRIVY COUNCIL** and is responsible for the work of the Council's office. The holder of the post acts as leader of the **HOUSE OF COMMONS**, arranging **GOVERNMENT** business and supervizing the legislative programme.

LORD PRIVY SEAL. A member of the **GOVERNMENT** with a seat in **THE CABINET**, the Lord Privy Seal was formerly responsible for the security of the Privy Seal, a personal seal introduced by King **JOHN** of **ENGLAND** to authenticate documents relating to his domestic affairs. Under later **MONARCH**s, the duties of the seal's keeper increased and the holder of the post became one of the most powerful of the sovereign's advisers. The Privy Seal Office was abolished in 1884, but the title of Lord Privy Seal was retained and is conferred by the **PRIME MINISTER** on the individual responsible for the conduct of the governing party's business in the **HOUSE OF LORDS**. (See **LORD KEEPER OF THE GREAT SEAL**).

LORD STEWARD. In theory, the Lord Steward is responsible for the day-to-day management of the **ROYAL HOUSEHOLD** and finances. In practice, the holder of the post (which has its roots in the organization of the royal court during the 13th century) now has solely ceremonial duties.

LOSTWITHIEL, BATTLE OF, 2 September 1644. Following heavy losses at the **BATTLE OF MARSTON MOOR** during the **CIVIL WAR**, King **CHARLES I** was able to regroup and lead his forces to victory over the **PARLIAMENTARIANS** at Lostwithiel (Cornwall) two months later. That success secured **ROYALIST** support in the west of **ENGLAND** and gave the King the opportunity to attack **LONDON**. The Earl of Essex fled from the battlefield and the subsequent rout of the **ROUNDHEAD**s' most experienced troops was one of the factors which led to the eventual reorganization of the Parliamentarian forces into the **NEW MODEL ARMY**.

LUDDITES. Named after a mythical character (who may have been based on Ned Lud, a real person), the Luddites were allegedly led by General or King Ludd and were responsible for violence and destruction of machinery in the midlands and north of **ENGLAND** during the period from 1811 to 1817. The troubles were particularly evident in Nottinghamshire and Lancashire, where frame-knitters and loom workers formed the basis of the textile industry and destroyed machines which they believed were taking their jobs during this period of depression, unemployment and low wages, which was partly caused by the **NAPOLEONIC WARS**. Troops were used to control the dissidents' activities and machine-breaking was made a capital offence. The term is now applied to anyone opposed to technological advance

—M—

MAASTRICHT TREATY, 1992. The Dutch town of Maastricht was the location for the signing, by the members of the **EUROPEAN COMMUNITY**, of an agreement to create a **EUROPEAN UNION** which would work towards economic and political integration, a common currency, common citizenship and common travel arrangements. It caused a furore in **PARLIAMENT**, particularly over questions about the sovereignty of the nation, the Social Chapter (which dealt with working practices and welfare support and from which Britain secured an opt-out agreement) and the currency arrangements. The ruling **CONSERVATIVE PARTY** was divided and ratification was protracted, finally being approved in 1993.

MacDONALD, JAMES RAMSAY (1866-1937). The first **LABOUR PARTY** Prime Minister, Macdonald was born in Alves (near Lossiemouth) on 12 October 1866, the illegitimate son of Anne Ramsay (a farm worker) and John MacDonald (a head ploughman). He was educated at Drainie School but left for a few months at the age of 15 before returning as a pupil teacher. In 1885, he moved to Bristol, where he helped to run a boys' club and became involved with socialist politics, but returned to **SCOTLAND** before the end of the year, taking the little he had saved out of his small income. In 1886, he travelled to **LONDON**, tramped the streets looking for work and eventually found a job with the Cyclists' Touring Club (reputedly on the day his last shilling was spent). However, much of his pay was used to buy books and attend evening classes, leaving little for food, and eventually the strain told, his health broke down and he went home yet again. In 1888, he was back in London, working as Secretary to Thomas Lough, a supporter of **WILLIAM GLADSTONE** and **PARLIAMENT**ary candidate for Islington. MacDonald unsuccessfully contested Southampton for the **INDEPENDENT LABOUR PARTY** in 1894 then worked hard to persuade the **TRADE UNIONS** to sponsor a new political organization independent of the **LIBERAL PARTY** and the **CONSERVATIVE PARTY**. The **TRADES UNION CONGRESS** of 1899 supported his campaign and, the following year, the Labour Representative Committee was established.

At the 1900 **GENERAL ELECTION**, MacDonald was a candidate at Leicester West and was heavily defeated, but, in 1906, he got his revenge, becoming Member of Parliament for the **CONSTITUENCY** with a greatly increased vote. In 1911, he was appointed Chairman of the Party, but he made enemies three years later when, at the outbreak of the **FIRST WORLD WAR**, he advocated pacifism. He behaved with great dignity throughout the conflict, but his popularity declined and, in 1918, he lost his

HOUSE OF COMMONS seat by over 14,000 votes, returning in 1922 as the representative for Aberavon (a Welsh mining constituency) and soon afterwards becoming leader of **THE OPPOSITION**. Always the voice of moderation, he made his respect for the traditions of British institutions clear as his standing in the country increased. In 1923, after Prime Minister **ANDREW BONAR LAW** had resigned because of ill health and been replaced by **STANLEY BALDWIN**, the Conservatives called a general election which was, in essence, a vote on the party's policy of replacing **FREE TRADE** with a tariff system which favoured members of the **BRITISH EMPIRE** (see **IMPERIAL PREFERENCE**). The proposed reforms were unpopular in many quarters and Baldwin himself had been under attack the previous year for negotiating an agreement for the repayment of Britain's war debts to the United States which was seen as deeply disadvantageous to the country's interests. The result was the decimation of the Conservatives' Parliamentary majority. After the election, they were still the largest party in the Commons, but the country had clearly voted against empire preference.

With the support of the Liberals, MacDonald became Prime Minister early in 1924, the first Labour politician to attain that office. He also assumed the role of Foreign Secretary, recognizing the communist government in the Soviet Union, negotiating an agreement with Germany over the nature and extent of reparations for wartime activities and working with France to establish the Geneva protocol for security and disarmament. But a botched attempt to prosecute the Editor of the communist *Workers' Weekly* for attempting to influence the discipline of the army led to a Commons defeat and the **DISSOLUTION OF PARLIAMENT**. Just before the ensuing general election, newspaper revelations that Grigori Zinoviev, Chairman of the Executive Committee of the Communist International, had sent a letter to the British **COMMUNIST PARTY** urging it to undertake subversive activities which would lead to an overthrow of the British system of government fuelled fears of a Bolshevik takeover and led to a massive Conservative vote (see **ZINOVIEV LETTER**). As a result, Conservative representation in the Commons rose from 258 to 413 and Labour's fell from 191 to 151.

MacDonald returned to the opposition benches but regained power in 1929, when Labour became the largest party in the House. This time, although there were successes in foreign policy (notably a naval treaty reached with the United States of America in 1930), the **GOVERNMENT** was faced with mounting unemployment and an unfavourable balance of trade. In 1931, MacDonald and Philip Snowden, his **CHANCELLOR OF THE EXCHEQUER**, sought to meet the crisis through a series of economy measures, but their colleagues would not agree to reductions in unemployment benefit and MacDonald offered his resignation to King **GEORGE V** on 24 August. The following day he formed a coalition government with Conservative and Liberal support, but, as the Conservatives had a majority in the **CABINET**, they inevitably dominated policy making and MacDonald was regarded as a traitor by his former colleagues. Despite the obloquy and the interparty tensions, he remained in office but his health deteriorated and, in 1935, he resigned again, changing posts with Baldwin and becoming **LORD PRESIDENT OF THE COUNCIL**. He died at sea on 9 November 1937 while on a recuperative voyage to South America.

MACMILLAN, MAURICE HAROLD (1894-1986). **PRIME MINISTER** from 1957 until 1963, Macmillan was born in **LONDON** on 10 February 1894, the son of Maurice Macmillan and his wife, Helen. He was educated at Eton College and at **OXFORD** University, interrupting his studies for service with the Grenadier Guards during the **FIRST WORLD WAR**, in which he was wounded on three occasions and won the Military Cross. In 1919–20 he was Aide-de-Camp to the Duke of Devonshire (**GOVERNOR-GENERAL of CANADA**), fell in love with his daughter (Lady Dorothy Cavendish) and married her. On his return to Britain, he joined the family publishing business but the lure of politics was stronger than the lure of commerce and, in 1924, he was elected **CONSERVATIVE PARTY** Member of **PARLIAMENT** for Stockton-on-Tees. He lost the seat in 1929 but was reelected in 1931 and held it until 1945.

In his early days, he was seen by the Party leaders as something of a rebel, advocating state control of industry and services as a means of reducing unemployment and criticizing **NEVILLE CHAMBERLAIN**'s **APPEASEMENT** policy towards Nazi Germany. As a result, he got no official post until **WINSTON CHURCHILL** made him **PARLIAMENTARY SECRETARY** to the Ministry of Supply in 1940. Two years later, he became Colonial **UNDER-SECRETARY OF STATE** but, after a few weeks, was posted to North Africa as **MINISTER** Resident at Allied Headquarters. He was **SECRETARY OF STATE** for Air for a time in 1945 but lost his Stockton seat at the May **GENERAL ELECTION** and remained outside Parliament until he won a **BY-ELECTION** at Bromley in November.

Macmillan was appointed Minister of Housing when the Conservatives regained power in 1951 and successfully kept a promise to build 300,000 new homes every year, confounding those who claimed his programme was too ambitious. In 1954, he became Minister of Defence, then had a nine-month spell as Foreign Secretary from April the following year before being appointed **CHANCELLOR OF THE EXCHEQUER** in December. Following **ANTHONY EDEN**'s resignation in 1957, he emerged, in **RAB BUTLER**'s somewhat ambiguous phrase, as "the best Prime Minister we have". The appointment was not popular with those who believed that, after an initial hawkish stance on the Suez issue in 1956, he had deserted Eden (see **SUEZ CRISIS**). Others argued that his grouse-moor aristocratic image was out of touch with the times. However, Macmillan did have an infectious confidence and an air of integrity which, coupled with a policy of economic expansion, eventually swung the public behind him and earned him the soubriquet 'Supermac'.

One of his first tasks in foreign affairs was the healing of wounds which differences over Suez had inflicted on Britain's relationship with the United States. He also visited Nikita Khruschev in Russia during 1959 in an effort to act as intermediary between the United States of America and the Soviet Union during the frigidity of the Cold War. In addition, he gained much respect for his political bravery, notably as a result of a speech in Cape Town on 3 February 1960, when he reemphasized the UK's opposition to apartheid, recognized growing demands for political independence in the colonies and angered members of the South African Parliament with an assertion that "The wind of change is blowing through this continent". At home, he had won the 1959 general election with the slogan "You've Never Had It So Good", but the early 1960s were hard times for many as the rate of inflation rose, unemployment levels increased and statistics showed that Britain's industrial output was lagging behind that of its foreign competitors. Attempts to restore the economy through a limitation on wage increases in 1961 were deeply unpopular and led Macmillan to attempt a change of direction by sacking seven **CABINET** ministers and 16 other members of his **GOVERNMENT** the following year (a political bloodbath which the press gleefully reported with references to "Mac The Knife"). Problems mounted as attempts to take Britain into the **EUROPEAN COM-MUNITY** were frustrated by French President Charles de Gaulle and the sexual peccadilloes of John Profumo, the **SECRETARY OF STATE** for War, led to allegations of breaches in security (see **PROFUMO SCANDAL**).

Macmillan had health problems to cope with as well and, on 10 October 1963, following a prostrate gland operation, reluctantly informed Queen **ELIZABETH II** that he intended to resign. In 1984, on his ninetieth birthday, he was created Earl of Stockton, and, in the **HOUSE OF LORDS,** continued a lifetime's tradition of failing to toe the party line, upbraiding **MARGARET THATCHER** for her **PRIVATIZATION** policies. He remained active, serving as President of Macmillan Ltd from 1974 and as Chancellor of the University of Oxford from 1960 until his death on 29 December 1986.

MAFEKING, THE RELIEF OF, 13 October 1899-17 May 1900. During the **BOER WAR (second)**, this British garrison in Cape Province (later Cape Colony and then Botswana) was besieged by a Boer army of 5,000. The occupants of the settlement — 700 troops and 600 civilians led by Colonel Robert Baden-Powell (the founder of the Boy Scout movement) — held out for seven months before the enemy gave up. The incident was of little military significance (though it did tie down large forces which could have caused problems elsewhere) but its fate was much written about in the press and its eventual relief after 217 days on 17 May 1900 caused patriotic celebrations in **LONDON**, with **THE TIMES** alluding to the "fundamental grit of the breed".

MAGNA CARTA. King **JOHN** lost control of **LONDON** to a rebellion of his **BARON**s in May 1215, after a protracted dispute over the powers of the **CROWN**, and the rebels presented their demands to him at **RUNNYMEDE**, close to Windsor, in the form of the Magna Carta. This "Great Charter of Liberties" was signed on 15 June 1215 and safeguarded the privileges of the Church, the nobles and free men of the kingdom, with clauses which defined obligations under the **FEUDAL SYSTEM**, limited royal rights, prevented the King from committing administrative and legal abuses of power, restricted the raising of taxes and ensured the importance of the Barons' advice on all important matters. It included clauses that "no free man shall be taken or imprisoned or disseised (seized) or exiled, or in any way destroyed, except by the lawful judgement of his peers or by the law of the land" (the basis of **HABEAS CORPUS**) and that "to none will we sell, to none will we deny or delay right of justice". The event was an early step towards limitations on the powers of the **MONARCH**y and guaranteed justice to all as well as safety from illegal interference with the property of free men. (See **BRITISH CONSTITUTION**).

MAGUIRE SEVEN. In 1976, seven people, including four Maguires from the same family, were convicted of bombing **PUBLIC HOUSE**s in Guildford and Woolwich as part of the Irish Republican Army (IRA) campaign of violence on the British mainland two years earlier. The prosecution case was based on forensic evidence that the accused had handled nitroglycerine but, in June 1991, that evidence was reviewed and the verdict changed. The six remaining defendants (one having died in prison) were then released and a total of £1,100,000 was paid by the **HOME OFFICE** in compensation. This was one of a series of convictions for IRA activities in the 1960s and 1970s which were later overturned. (See **GUILDFORD FOUR**).

MAIN PLOT, 1603. This plot to depose King **JAMES VI and I** and replace him with his cousin, Lady Arabella Stuart, was unsuccessful. The leader of the plot, Henry Brooke, and **SIR WALTER RALEIGH** (his alleged supporter) were both imprisoned in the **TOWER OF LONDON**. The incident was called the Main Plot because it was said to be related to the lesser **BYE PLOT** of the same year, but they were probably unconnected.

MAJOR, JOHN (1943-   ). The successor to **MARGARET THATCHER** as **PRIME MINISTER**, John Major has an unlikely background for a 'high-flying' member of the **CONSERVATIVE PARTY**. He was born on 29 March 1943. His father, Thomas Major, had been a trapeze artist in a circus and raised his family in Brixton, one of the poorest areas in **LONDON**, with a high proportion of West Indian immigrants.

John attended Rutlish School but left at the age of 16. After a period of unemployment, he found a job with Standard Chartered Bank in 1965 and worked with the firm in a variety of posts until 1979. He had joined the Conservative Party in 1960 and was an active member of its Brixton Branch over the next ten years, chairing it from 1970 to 1971. He was also elected to Lambeth

BOROUGH Council, serving from 1968 until 1971 and leading the Housing Committee in his final year. His first attempts to get into **PARLIAMENT** — at the St Pancras **CONSTITUENCY** in the February and October **GENERAL ELECTION**s of 1974 — were unsuccessful but in 1979 he won at Huntingdonshire. His first **GOVERNMENT** post was as **PARLIAMENTARY PRIVATE SECRETARY** to Timothy Raison and **PATRICK MAYHEW, MINISTER**s **OF STATE** at the **HOME OFFICE**, from 1981 until 1983. He then became Assistant Government **WHIP** (1983-84), Lord Commissioner of **THE TREASURY** (1984-85), **UNDER-SECRETARY OF STATE** for Social Security (1985-86) and Minister of State for Social Security (1986-87). Having impressed Prime Minister **MARGARET THATCHER** in these offices, his rise thereafter was meteoric. He was **CHIEF SECRETARY TO THE TREASURY** from 1987 until 1989, Foreign Secretary from July to October of 1989, **CHANCELLOR OF THE EXCHEQUER** in 1989-90 and Prime Minister in 1990 at the age of 47, the youngest occupant of the post this century.

Major had had his share of luck, getting the Foreign Secretary's post after Geoffrey Howe had walked out of the Government and becoming Chancellor when **NIGEL LAWSON** resigned in similarly acrimonious circumstances. So, when Mrs Thatcher was persuaded to step down in November 1990, he was well-known in the party and one of three candidates for her office, emerging victorious from a poll of Conservative MPs by winning 185 votes compared with 131 for Michael Heseltine and 56 for **DOUGLAS HURD**. For many people, his principal attribute was his unassuming nature and moderate stance on major issues — considerable contrasts with the hectoring style and extremist views which Margaret Thatcher had adopted, particularly in the later years of her administration. Others, however, argued that his lack of personality made him a grey man, without the charisma needed to win votes. For some days after his election, he continued his habit of dropping into his local McDonald's for breakfast, but eventually his bodyguards convinced him of the security risk. It was more difficult for him to change his placid approach to life: when a mortar bomb exploded in **DOWNING STREET** on 7 February 1991, just 40 feet from where he was chairing a **CABINET** meeting, he is said to have kept cool and suggested, "I think we had better start again somewhere else". In the early months, he undoubtedly lived in the shadow of Mrs Thatcher, who made several criticisms of new policies which departed from her preferred line and called him "arrogant and wrong" for refusing to hold a referendum on the case for a single European currency. However, he earned public confidence through his handling of the **GULF WAR** with Iraq (1991) and his competent chairmanship of the Group of Seven conference of the leading in-dustrial nations (also in 1991).

He steered his party to an unexpected but nevertheless emphatic victory in the 1992 general election but, by late 1993 and early 1994, was beset by problems stemming from the sexual and financial activities of colleagues and by the news that personal taxation under his administration had risen to a higher proportion of family income than it had been when the **LABOUR PARTY** was in power during the late 1970s. The collapse of the Conservative vote at the 1995 **LOCAL GOVERNMENT** elections added to his woes, but he insisted that he had no intention of resigning.

Criticism of his leadership mounted, and, in 1995, he responded by resigning the leadership of the party and challenged his opponents to face him in an election for the position. The result justified the risk — he defeated his only challenger (John Redwood, formerly **SECRETARY OF STATE** for Wales and champion of the right wing) by 218 votes to 89 (Conservative MPs constituted the electorate). According to press commentators, that victory meant that he would lead the **TORIES** into the next General Election.

MALAYAN EMERGENCY, 1948-60. Communist guerilla activity began in **MALAYA** in 1948, and a state of emergency was declared. **COMMONWEALTH OF NATIONS** forces from Britain, **AUSTRALIA** and **NEW ZEALAND** were sent to the peninsula. Their commander, General **SIR** Harold Biggs, proposed cutting the insurgents' supply lines by settling villagers in new defended villages (to isolate them from communist influence) and heavy use of helicopters. This strategy resulted in the withdrawal of the communist forces. The worst of the troubles were over by 1954, but the state of emergency was not formally ended until 31 July 1960. (See **EAST OF SUEZ**).

MALDON, BATTLE OF, 11 August 991. Defeat for a British force at the hands of an invading **VIKING** army established Danish supremacy over **EAST ANGLIA** and set the maximum extent of the **DANELAW** because the Danes established control in Essex but **WESSEX** remained supreme in the south. It resulted in the first payment of **DANEGELD** and thus encouraged more frequent raids by the Vikings. (See **BATTLE OF EDINGTON**).

MALPLAQUET, BATTLE OF, 11 September 1709. This battle during the **WAR OF THE SPANISH SUCCESSION** was fought between the French and a combined British and Holy Roman Empire force, led by the **DUKE OF MARLBOROUGH** and Prince Eugene of Savoy. The fighting ended in a victory for the allies, but the casualties were enormous, numbering over 31,000 men, and the carnage gave ammunition to the movement for peace back home — so much so that Marlborough was recalled to **ENGLAND** two years later.

MANCHESTER. Although Manchester's history dates from the days of the **CELTS**, its growth was a product of the **INDUSTRIAL REVOLUTION**, which transformed it from a market town to a manufacturing centre during the late 18th and 19th centuries. The city lies at the confluence of the Rivers Irk, Irwell and Medlock, some 180 miles northwest of **LONDON**. In 1761, one of the first **CANALS** in the country facilitated the transport of **COAL** to the settlement and, in 1789, the first steam engine designed for spinning cotton (see **COTTON INDUSTRY**) was constructed in the town. The manufacturing of cotton goods quickly became a major source of employment and spawned a great range of ancillary activities, including spinning, weaving, bleaching, dyeing, printing, packing and warehousing. Migrants seeking work moved into the area from other parts of the country and, as demand increased, nearby towns flourished, with Manchester itself providing the bulk of the financial, legal and other services which the new firms required.

The opening of a ship canal in 1894 gave access to the sea for vessels of up to 15,000 tons deadweight, effectively making the city an inland port. However, trade suffered during the recessions of the 20th century and textiles, in particular, were hit by the development of cheaper manufacturing centres in India and the Far East. Manchester was heavily bombed during the **SECOND WORLD WAR** and, in the years that followed, a major slum clearance programme was undertaken. New housing was built at lower densities and that, coupled with a preference for suburban and small town living, has resulted in a decline in the city's population. At the time of the 1991 census, it had 384,600 residents (a decrease of 12.1 per cent over the 1981 figure). The Greater

Manchester Metropolitan County, of which Manchester is the major centre, had 2,435,000 people, 5.5 per cent fewer than in 1981. (See **PETERLOO MASSACRE** and, for location, Map 2, page xxvi).

MANDATED TERRITORIES. By **LEAGUE OF NATIONS** mandate, former German or Turkish colonies were placed under the control of one of the victorious nations after the **FIRST WORLD WAR**. Britain secured the trusteeship of Iraq, Palestine, Tanganyika, Transjordan, Togoland and part of Cameroon.

MANOR. A form of land tenure introduced by the **NORMANS** (the word is derived from the Old French *manoir*, meaning 'dwelling place'), the manor was held according to the regulations of the **FEUDAL SYSTEM.** It was usually divided into the noble's land (or **DEMESNE**), which was farmed by his unfree tenants (the **VILLEINS**), and the rest, farmed by free tenants who owed service or dues to the Lord of the Manor by virtue of their tenure. Many manorial organizations developed (including the manorial court), and land was held in fee simple (that is, on the death of the lord it passed automatically to his eldest son or heir). Manors survived as units of **LOCAL GOVERNMENT** into the 18th century and the term has been used since then to denote a landed estate of some size.

MANSFIELD JUDGEMENT, 1772. Granville Sharp, a clergyman's son, fought a successful legal test case for James Somerset, a slave from Virginia, to establish the principle that "as soon as any slave sets foot on English ground, he becomes free". The judgement, delivered by Lord Mansfield in 1772, set free between 10,000 and 14,000 negro slaves then held in **ENGLAND**. (See **SLAVE TRADE**).

MARGARET ROSE, PRINCESS (1930-). Sister of Queen **ELIZA-BETH II**, Margaret was born in Glamis Castle on 21 August 1930, the second daughter of the Duke and Duchess of York (later King **GEORGE VI** and Queen Elizabeth, now usually known as the **QUEEN MOTHER**). She was the first child in the direct line of succession to the throne to be born in **SCOTLAND** for 300 years. Her childhood and youth were spent mainly in **LONDON** but she accompanied her parents on many public engagements and, as she grew older, carried out a number of duties in her own right. In 1955, she made clear that she wished to marry Group Captain Peter Townsend but his earlier marriage had been dissolved and the match was frowned on both by the **CHURCH OF ENGLAND** and by members of the Royal Family. Under pressure, the Princess terminated the relation-ship, but, on 6 May 1960, married **ANTONY ARMSTRONG-JONES**, a society photographer, who was created Earl of Snowdon the following year. The couple had two children — David Albert Charles (Viscount Linley), born on 3 November 1961, and Lady Sarah Frances Elizabeth, born on 1 May 1964 — but the marriage ran into problems and the couple separated. In 1978, they were divorced. Since that time, the tabloid press has printed several speculative stories about romantic attachments, but the Princess has never re-married. She carries out a number of public engagements every year and acts as patron to several charities but, by current royal standards, keeps a low profile.

MARIAN REACTION, 1553-58. As a reaction against the **REFOR-MATION**, Queen **MARY I** attempted to reinstate the Roman Catholic faith in **ENGLAND**. The 1549 and 1552 **ACTS OF UNIFORMITY** were repealed (see **ACT OF PARLIAMENT**), clergy who had married were removed from their livings and, by 1554, all anti-Papal legislation had been removed. In 1555, the Catholic doctrine was restored and some 300 Protestant recalcitrants (including **ARCHBISHOP OF CANTERBURY THOMAS CRANMER**) were burned to death. This persecution (which earned the Queen the title "Bloody Mary") and her marriage to Philip of Spain ultimately fuelled anti-Papal feelings and a rise of nationalism which came to fruition under **ELIZABETH I** and led to the reversal of the Marian Reaction.

MARLBOROUGH, DUKE OF. (See **JOHN CHURCHILL**).

MARQUESS. This title is the second most senior in the **PEER-AGE**, below that of **DUKE**. Within the order, seniority reflects the date on which the title was created. The premier Marquess in **ENGLAND** is that of Winchester (created in 1551) and the premier Marquess in **SCOTLAND** is that of Huntly (created in 1599). The wife of a Marquess is accorded the title of Marchioness. (See **MARQUIS**).

MARQUESS OF SALISBURY. (See **ROBERT ARTHUR**

TALBOT GASCOYNE-CECIL).

MARQUIS. This is an alternative spelling of **MARQUESS** preferred by some holders of the title.

MARRIAGE ACT, 1753. This act (see **ACT OF PARLIA-MENT**), sometimes known as Hardwicke's Act after its proposer, made marriages in the established **CHURCH OF ENGLAND**, or by special licence, the only ones valid in the eyes of the law. Marriage under the age of 21 was forbidden without parental consent, and all weddings had to be recorded in the **PARISH** Register, now an immensely important source for historians. Intended to prevent abuse of minors and other transgressions, the act did not recognize **COMMON LAW** marriages (effected simply by consent before witnesses). Only Jews and Quakers were exempt from its provisions.

MARRIAGE ACT, 1837. This **ACT OF PARLIAMENT** recognized marriages solemnized according to the rites of religious groups other than the **CHURCH OF ENGLAND** (with the exception of Quakers) and also permitted marriage by a Civil Registrar.

MARSHALL AID. This European Recovery Program, which ran from 1948 to 1951, was proposed by General George C. Marshall, the US Secretary of State after the **SECOND WORLD WAR**. The United States of America agreed to help the rebuilding of Western Europe and a $12 billion programme began on 1 July 1948 with loans and grants to 18 countries, Britain receiving the lion's share ($980 million). It was in both the American and European interests to expand trade quickly and to restore the ability of the Allied nations to reduce their dollar deficits. One unforeseen consequence of the scheme may have been an accelerated division of Europe into East and West because the Soviet Union refused to participate and the Plan became increasingly perceived as a means of containing communism through economic cooperation.

MARSTON MOOR, BATTLE OF, 2 July 1644. The **ROYALIST** defeat in this, one of the most decisive battles of the **CIVIL WAR**, critically damaged **CHARLES I**'s power base in the north of **ENGLAND** (fought near **YORK**, it was one of the largest battles of the war). The 27,000 **PARLIAMENTARIANS** (both English and Scottish), led by **OLIVER CROMWELL**, used their cavalry to great effect and overcame Prince Rupert's 19,000 troops. The King's side suffered heavy casualties, with up to 4,000 killed and 1,500 taken prisoner, including many experienced officers. Prince Rupert was said to have referred to Cromwell as "Old Ironsides" and the **ROUNDHEADS'** elite cavalry subsequently became known as the **IRONSIDES**.

MARTIAL LAW. The suspension of normal legal processes during times of grave crisis and the use of military courts to try civilians without a **JURY** system has been used by **GOVERNMENT**s to counter the **PILGRIMAGE OF GRACE**, the Jacobite threat and the **GORDON RIOTS**. Martial law has also been invoked in **IRELAND** (1920), and on a number of occasions in the colonies, to counter civil unrest.

MARY I (1516-58) The only child of **HENRY VIII** and **CATHERINE OF ARAGON** to survive infancy, Mary was Queen of **ENGLAND** from 1553 until 1558. She was born in Greenwich on 18 February 1516 and, at the age of two, was betrothed to the Dauphin of France. Three years later, that engagement was broken, and, under the terms of the Treaty of Windsor (1522), she was matched with Charles V, the Holy Roman Emperor. In 1525, Charles withdrew from the agreement, and two years later an arrangement was made for her to marry either Francis I of France (the Dauphin's father) or Henry, Duc d'Orleans (Francis's second son). At that point, Henry began to seek papal consent for a divorce from Catherine and, from 1531, kept Mary apart from her mother.

In 1534, the **ACT OF SUCCESSION** recognized **ANNE BOLEYN** as Queen and her daughter, Elizabeth (later **ELIZABETH I**), as heiress to the throne. It also formally annulled Henry's marriage to Catherine and declared Mary illegitimate. Mary refused to acknowledge that status; in reprisal, her household was broken up and she was despatched to act as lady-in-waiting to the infant princess who had replaced her in the line of succession. Her health deteriorated but, even then, Henry refused to allow her mother to visit her. When Catherine died in 1536, Mary was forbidden to attend the funeral. Undoubtedly, the enforced separation from her mother and the stigma of illegitimacy embittered her, but, in the spring of 1536, Anne Boleyn was beheaded and Mary was encouraged to seek a reconciliation with her father. The terms were humiliating — she had to renounce the Roman Catholic

Church, accept Henry as the supreme religious authority in England and admit her illegitimacy by accepting that the King's marriage to Catherine was "incestuous and unlawful". The reconciliation did restore many of her privileges but, after Henry's death in 1547, she was subject to further pressure while his successor, **EDWARD VI**, was on the throne. Edward himself was kind to her but his advisers were actively promoting Protestantism and inevitably that led to clashes; Mary, for example, insisted on having a Latin mass although services conducted in English were being imposed throughout the realm.

Just before the King died in July 1553, he prepared a will which was manipulated to ensure that the succession passed to the Protestant Lady **JANE GREY** and her heirs rather than to Mary. Lady Jane did rule for nine days but the mood of the country was very much on Mary's side and she became Queen to popular acclaim. However, shortly after her accession, she announced her engagement to Prince Philip of Spain. As Spain was England's major trading competitor, that match proved unpopular. The **HOUSE OF COMMONS** advised her to cancel the wedding, but she refused, sparking a rebellion by Sir Thomas Wyatt in 1554 (see **WYATT'S REBELLION**). Undaunted, Mary went ahead with her plans and married Philip on 25 July 1554. Later the same year, she stirred up opposition by abolishing the **CHURCH OF ENGLAND**, reestablishing papal authority throughout her realm and reviving the laws of heresy. Her decision, in 1557, to allow England to be drawn into war with France as an ally of Spain further alienated many of her subjects because, the following year, she suffered the ignominy of losing **CALAIS**, her country's last foothold on the mainland of Europe.

Protestants responded to the banishing of their religion by holding services in secret and circulating anti-Catholic pamphlets. Over the next four years, Mary, convinced that hers was the only true faith, burned nearly 300 of her opponents at the stake, including John Hooper (the Bishop of Gloucester) and **THOMAS CRANMER** (the **ARCHBISHOP OF CANTERBURY**). The burnings continued until her death on 17 November 1558 and earned her the soubriquet 'Bloody Mary'. She died childless, leaving a reputation as a harsh ruler, but she showed much kindness to the poor and clemency towards the Jane Grey faction. Her unhappy childhood seems to have strengthened her religious zeal, leading her to believe that strict treatment of heretics was necessary in order to save souls. (See **MARIAN REACTION**).

MARY II (1662-94). The elder daughter of **JAMES VII** and **II** by his first wife, Anne (daughter of the Earl of Clarendon), Mary ruled Great Britain jointly with her husband **WILLIAM III** from 1689 until her death in 1694. Born in **LONDON** on 30 April 1662, she was raised as a Protestant and, in 1677, was married to her cousin, William of Orange. Her father had become a convert to Roman Catholicism in the late 1660s and, after his accession to the throne in 1685, had increasingly antagonized his subjects by granting Catholics freedom of worship and appointing them to government posts. In 1688, when James's wife (Mary of Modena) produced a son and heir, fears of a Catholic succession led many influential British figures to ask William to invade and depose the King. Mary supported that policy, partly because she felt it to be her duty as a Protestant and partly because she believed that there had been a deception over the birth of James's son. (Mary of Modena had produced five children between 1675 and 1682; none of them had survived.) William landed at Brixham in November 1688 and marched unopposed to London. Mary joined him in February the following year and, rejecting all suggestions that she should become Queen by herself, accepted the proposal that the **MONARCH**y should be held jointly. The Scots made a similar deal.

When William was at home, Mary happily left politics to him but, while he was absent with his troops in **IRELAND** and in Europe, she governed by herself. As a Monarch, she was popular with her people but she never settled in **ENGLAND**, was constantly worried by her father's situation and quarrelled with relatives over political issues. In 1694, after only five years on the throne, she contracted smallpox and died in London on 28 December. The nation, as well as her husband, grieved deeply. Despite her short reign, she left her mark. Her charitable works included Greenwich Hospital for Seamen, and she was closely involved in the rebuilding of Kensington Palace and Hampton Court Palace, taking a particular interest in the design of the gardens, which she modelled on Dutch lines. (See **GLORIOUS REVOLUTION**).

MARY OF TECK (1867-1953). Consort of King **GEORGE V**, Queen Mary was born in Kensington Palace (**LONDON**) on 26 May 1867, the eldest child and only daughter of Francis, Prince (and later Duke) of Teck, and Princess Mary Adelaide, granddaughter of **GEORGE III**. Her parents were not rich by aristocratic standards so May (as she was called before she was married) learned the skills of budget management and the value of money from her mother. The Prince and Princess took little interest in their daughter's formal education, but she mastered French and German; at the age of 16, she went to Florence for two years and developed an interest in art which was to last throughout her life.

In London, Queen **VICTORIA** had plans for her future, believing that she would make a good wife for the Duke of Clarence, elder son of the **PRINCE OF WALES** and, therefore, second in the line of succession to the throne. The couple became engaged in 1891, but the Duke died suddenly the following year and, in 1893, May accepted a proposal from his younger brother, George, **DUKE OF YORK**. They were married in the chapel of St James's Palace on 6 July 1893 — a match that was clearly a matter of political convenience but which developed into a devoted relationship. Their first child (later **EDWARD VIII**) was born on 23 June 1894 and their second (later **GEORGE VI**) on 14 December 1895. Their other children were Princess Mary (born on 25 April 1897), Prince Henry (31 March 1900), Prince George (20 December 1902) and Prince John (12 July 1905).

Despite the frequent pregnancies and her growing family, May and her husband carried out many public engagements together, including a visit to Australia for the opening of the federal Parliament in 1901 and a tour of India in 1905. When George succeeded to the throne on the death of his father (**EDWARD VII**) in 1910, the new Queen became known as Queen Mary. During the **FIRST WORLD WAR**, she set up organizations to find work for women, visited hospitals, took considerable interest in the welfare of the armed forces and ensured that the **ROYAL HOUSEHOLD** shared in the austerity which affected her subjects. The couple's silver wedding celebrations in 1918 coincided with the end of the war and brought an increase in the number of commitments, with the Queen showing her understanding of poverty in visits to major industrial cities around the country. When George fell ill in 1928, she shouldered much of the burden of royal duties on her own and, after his death in 1935, maintained a full schedule of activities.

The next few years proved to be ones of great strain caused by the grief which followed the loss of her husband, the abdication of her eldest son (to whom she was deeply devoted), an automobile accident which permanently damaged her eyesight in May 1939 and the outbreak of the **SECOND WORLD WAR** later the same year. She spent much of the war at Badminton (her niece's home) and became a familiar figure in the surrounding towns, particularly in those which had suffered from bombing. Frequently, she ordered her chauffeur to stop so that she could give a lift to servicemen making their way along the country lanes. She renewed her national commitments when the war ended but was greatly shocked by the death of George VI in 1952 and made few public appearances afterwards.

She died in London on 24 March 1953 and was buried beside her husband at Windsor. A product of Victorian England, in some ways she was reluctant to move with the times (she never spoke on the telephone, for instance), but she was a brave and kindly woman who brought a uniquely human touch to the **MONARCH**y and was much mourned.

MASTER OF THE ROLLS. The lawyer holding this office is head of the Civil Division of the **COURT OF APPEAL**. His title derives from his historical role as custodian of the Court record (or rolls).

MAU MAU UPRISING, 1952-60. Extreme violence by members of the Mau Mau secret society in **KENYA** led to a state of emergency being declared in 1952. The conflict originated in the refusal of white settlers to concede political representation to the black majority in the country and in anticolonial nationalism. Ninety-five whites and 13,000 blacks died in the disturbances. Their leader, Jomo Kenyatta, was imprisoned from 1953 to 1961 and became first Prime Minister of the independent state of Kenya in 1963.

MEDWAY, BATTLE OF THE, 43 AD. The first major battle between the invading **ROMAN** forces under Aulus Plautius and Vespasian (with four legions and 20,000 supporting auxiliary troops) and the Britons (or **BELGAE**), led by Caractacus and his brother Togodumnus (with a strength of 60,000 to 80,000 men), was fought at a crossing of the River Medway in **KENT**. The two-day struggle ended in defeat for the Britons. They had assumed that the Romans would need to build a bridge across the river but, instead, the invaders sent detachments upstream to a ford and confounded the British strategy. The conflict marked the beginning of the conquest of Britain by the Roman legions, with Emperor Claudius later entering Camulodunum

(Colchester) in triumph on an elephant.

MELBOURNE, VISCOUNT. (See **WILLIAM LAMB**).

MERCANTILISM. Popular from the 16th until the 18th century, the economic doctrine of mercantilism held that a favourable balance of trade was essential, that self-sufficiency was to be encouraged, that imports should be reduced by tariffs and that the inflow of precious metals was a basic necessity for a strong commercial nation. All of these, it was believed, could be achieved by **GOVERNMENT** regulation. Adoption of the philosophy resulted in a nationalistic and state-controlled approach to colonial and trade management (as, for example, with the **NAVIGATION ACTS**) and was attacked by Adam Smith in *The Wealth of Nations* (1776). It had its greatest influence from about 1650 until about 1780 but was replaced by the policies of **FREE TRADE** during the 19th century.

MERCHANTS ADVENTURERS. During the 14th century, a number of **GUILD**s combined in an association trading in cloth. Their organization was incorporated in **LONDON** in 1407 as an **ENGLISH TRADING COMPANY** intended to rival the **HANSEATIC LEAGUE**, which it supplanted as major trader in **ENGLAND** by the 16th century (at that time it controlled 75 per cent of English foreign trade). It held a series of European bases including Bruges, **CALAIS** and Antwerp (where it gained from the **INTERCURSUS MAGNUS**) but lost its English charter in 1689 and was finally dissolved as a European company in 1808. It had been an important commercial influence on English foreign policy, imperial ambitions and trade. (See **PILGRIM FATHERS**).

MERCIA. A kingdom created by **ANGLES**, who settled in the west-central parts of **ENGLAND** from the fifth century, the area became the frontier between the **ANGLO-SAXONS** (to the east) and the British (to the west, in what later became **WALES**). A strong dynasty developed the penny coinage and expanded its territory, building **OFFA**'s Dyke as a boundary marker (the term 'Mercia' comes from the Old English *Merce* meaning 'the boundary peoples'). It was a rival society to that of **WESSEX** but they formed an alliance to fight the **BATTLE OF BRUNANBURH**. Mercia was eventually overthrown by Danish invaders. (See

AETHELBALD; AETHELSTAN).

MERCILESS PARLIAMENT, 1388. At the Battle of Radcote Bridge (December 1387), **RICHARD II** had suffered a military defeat at the hands of the dissident nobles. In February 1388, the Lords Appellant (opponents of the King's advisers) called a **PARLIAMENT** to try royalist supporters for treason and to execute **KNIGHT**s who had fought for the **MONARCH**. Two were put to death, but few people considered the action just, hence the adjective 'merciless'.

MERSEY, RIVER. The Mersey is formed at Stockport (Lancashire) by the confluence of the Goyt and the Tame, which rise on the western flanks of **THE PENNINES**. From there, it flows some 70 miles to the Irish Sea, draining the Cheshire-Lancashire plain. The inner estuary has rapid tidal movements which greatly reduce the need for dredging and facilitated the development of **LIVERPOOL** as a deep water port. During the 18th and 19th centuries, the river was joined by **CANAL**s to other waterways and rapidly became industrialized along much of its length. (For location, see Map 1, page xxvii).

MERTON, STATUTE OF, 1235. Said to be the first **ACT OF PARLIAMENT**, this statute was issued at the Great Council meeting at Merton in Surrey. It allowed lords of the **MANOR** to enclose their common lands after protecting the pasture rights of freemen and declared that children born before marriage were illegitimate, even after the subsequent marriage of the parents.

MESOLITHIC. This period of **PREHISTORIC BRITAIN** followed the **PALAEOLITHIC** and is sometimes called the Middle Stone Age (*mesos* is Greek for 'middle', *lithos* means 'stone'). During this time (c. 10,000 BC-4,400 BC, or 8,000 BC-3,500 BC in some texts) people began to establish semipermanent settlements but still had no knowledge of agricultural techniques (that came with the **NEOLITHIC**). By 10,000 BC the climate was improving (the ice having retreated northwards) and becoming warmer and drier. Woodland was replacing the earlier tundra vegetation and more sophisticated weapons were being developed to hunt animals. About 6,000 BC-8,000 BC, the land link with Europe was lost as glacial melting caused sea levels to rise and the English Channel formed to produce the **BRITISH ISLES**. By 7,000 BC, bows and arrows had evolved, sewn garments were being produced and the forests cleared (by burning) to allow animals to feed and breed in the better vegetation which replaced the trees. Tribal organization probably also began during this period as population grew and rivalries developed. Archaeological sites from this period include Star Carr (Yorkshire), which has been recently dated to 8,700 BC (by radiocarbon methods) and contains artifacts preserved in the waterlogged soil.

MESOPOTAMIAN CAMPAIGN, 1914-17. Mesopotamia — the part of the Ottoman Empire which now comprises Iraq — was a major focus of British action during the **FIRST WORLD WAR**. Then, as more recently (see **GULF WAR**), the aim was to secure vital oil supplies but victory was also necessary for political reasons. After the failure of the **GALLIPOLI EXPEDITION**, the UK **GOVERNMENT** badly needed a victory over the Turks and ordered an advance on Baghdad which went disastrously wrong, with 10,000 troops captured at Kut al Amara. The area was eventually taken with a force in excess of 300,000 men, but 16,000 Anglo-Indian troops lost their lives in the process.

METHODISM. Founded by **JOHN WESLEY** and **CHARLES WESLEY** in the 18th century, this offshoot of the **CHURCH OF ENGLAND** had a strong central authority coupled with a methodical routine of prayer and work which appealed to the working classes, particularly in the industrial north of **ENGLAND**. Characterized initially by evangelistic zeal and mass open-air meetings which emphasized individual salvation, it separated from the Anglican Church in 1795 and now has about 7,500 places of worship.

MILITANT TENDENCY. An extreme left pressure group, the Tendency was formed in the 1960s to infiltrate the **LABOUR PARTY** and the **TRADE UNIONS**. Under Derek Hatton, it controlled **LIVERPOOL** City Council in the 1980s but its members were publicly expelled from the Labour Party in 1983 in an attempt to rid the organization of its association with the hard left.

MILITIA. There is an ancient obligation on all able-bodied males between the ages of 15 and 60 to muster arms in defence of the realm (property owners had carried such obligations from the days of the **FEUDAL SYSTEM**). In the 16th century, the term *militia* referred to the non-professional defence forces maintained by the counties (see **COUNTY**) and raised by the **LORD LIEUTEN-ANT**. The **LONG PARLIA-MENT** took powers to appoint the Lord Lieutenants and so gain control of the militia in 1642 but, by 1661, the authority had reverted to the **CROWN**. The militia ceased to exist in 1907 on the establishment of the Territorial Army, a part-time volunteer reserve force. (See **ASSIZE OF ARMS; TRAINED BANDS**).

MILL, JOHN STUART (1806-73). A liberal thinker who argued the case for individual freedom and social reform, Mill was born in **LONDON** on 20 May 1806, the eldest son of philosopher James Mill and his wife, Harriet. He was educated by his father and, by the age of ten, had read Herodotus, Plato and other classical writers in the original Greek and Latin. In 1823, he became a clerk at India House (headquarters of the **EAST INDIA COMPANY**) and formed the Utilitarian Society, a group which admired **JEREMY BENTHAM**'s doctrine that the chief aim of society should be to promote the greatest happiness for the greatest number of people. In 1826, however, he underwent a personal crisis, unsure of his aims and his beliefs. He emerged with a deepened interest in poetry (especially that of William Wordsworth) and a more moderate view of the nature of human happiness. Essays in *The London and Westminster Review* on Bentham (1838) and Samuel Taylor Coleridge (1840) demonstrated how he diverged from orthodox utilitarian doctrine and *The System of Logic* (1843) outlined his approach to scientific investigation. His evolving views on the relationship between production and consumption and between profits and wages are evident in *Essays on Some Unsettled Questions on Political Economy* (1844) and *Principles of Political Economy* (1848). In many ways, these views were shaped by Harriet Taylor, whom he met in 1831, saw constantly over the next 20 years and eventually married, in 1851, after the death of her husband. The exact nature of her influence is often unclear, but she certainly inspired the essay on *Enfranchisement of Women* which appeared in *Dissertations and Discussions* (1859).

During the 1850s, Mill's output declined as the pressure of his job at India House increased (he was in charge of the East India Company's relations with the Indian states from 1836 until 1856 and had to prepare a defence of its government of India prior to its dissolution in 1858). Shortly after the Company was disbanded, Harriet died in Avignon and Mill, distraught, spent much of the remainder of his life there. He published a series of books on political and ethical themes which had been written in collaboration with her (notably the essay *On Liberty*, published in 1859) then, in the early 1860s, turned again to the wider issues which he had considered in *The System of Logic*. Throughout his life, Mill had used his philosophical writings to argue the case for practical reforms including the abolition of slavery in North America, universal suffrage, equality for women, free **EDUCATION** and self-government for the **DOMINION**s. In 1865, he was elected to **PARLIAMENT** as the independent representative for **WESTMINSTER** and took a leading part in debates on the 1866–67 Reform Bills (see **PARLIAMENTARY REFORM**), land tenure in **IRELAND**, the **NATIONAL DEBT** and Britain's duty to intervene on the side of freedom in international disputes. He was elected Rector of St Andrews University in 1867 and, in 1873, published his *Autobiography*, which documents his changing views from youth through maturity. He died in Avignon on 8 May 1873.

MINISTER. This term is applied to any member of the **HOUSE OF COMMONS** or **HOUSE OF LORDS** holding **GOVERNMENT** office.

MINISTER OF STATE. This **GOVERNMENT** post is immediately junior to that of the **SECRETARY OF STATE**, who delegates specific departmental responsibilities to the holder. **MINISTER**s of State do not normally have **CABINET** rank.

MINT, THE ROYAL. The coinage of the realm is manufactured at the Royal Mint under the authority of **THE TREASURY** and the **GOVERNMENT**. From the 13th century, local mints were restricted and eventually only the Royal Mint, in the **CITY OF LONDON**, was empowered to make coinage. In 1811, it was moved from the **TOWER OF LONDON** across the road to premises at Tower Hill and, in 1968, transferred to Llantrisant in South **WALES** as part of a government attempt to encourage offices to relocate outside **LONDON**. The mint also makes medals and foreign coinage but banknotes are the province of the **BANK OF ENGLAND**. (See **CURRENCY; DECIMALIZATION; STERLING**).

MODEL PARLIAMENT, 1295. This **PARLIAMENT** was called by

King **EDWARD I** to raise money for military expeditions against France and **WALES**. It was given its name during the 19th century by historians who considered it to be the most representative Parliament ever held, with **EARL**s, **BARON**s, Archbishops and Bishops, **KNIGHT**s and even city representatives and elected commoners participating.

MONARCH, THE. The United Kingdom has a **CONSTITU-TIONAL MONARCHY** in which the powers of the sovereign have been reduced over the centuries by statute and convention to the extent that nowadays the Queen (or King) acts solely on the advice of the **PRIME MINISTER**. The monarch gives **ROYAL ASSENT** to legislation, appoints Prime Ministers, creates peers (see **PEERAGE**) and makes Orders in Council advised by the **PRIVY COUNCIL**. In practice, these procedures are formal and ceremonial rather than independent of other wings of **GOVERN-MENT**. (For details of individual reigns, see the *Chronology of Monarchs* on pages xxiii–xxiv and the entries in the dictionary for each monarch).

MONETARISM. A philosophy particularly derived from the ideas of the American economist Milton Friedman (who argued that socialism stifled initiative and freedom and that control of the money supply was the best way to direct the economy), monetarism greatly influenced the policies espoused by **MARGARET THATCHER** (see **THATCHERISM**). It led to cuts in public spending, targets for **GOVERNMENT** borrowing requirements, high rates of interest (up to a crippling 17 per cent in 1980) and reliance on market forces. One of the consequences was a steep rise in unemployment but, even so, the approach was believed by its advocates to be the only way to transform the British economy for the better.

MONMOUTH REBELLION, 1685. The Protestant **DUKE** of Monmouth, an illegitimate son of **CHARLES II**, denounced the accession of **JAMES VII and II** and raised a 5,000-strong army to install himself as **MONARCH**. A capable soldier, he had convinced himself that he could rally the Protestant cause, but his army was ill-disciplined and composed of many untrained elements and the King was not yet unpopular, having only recently gained the throne. Monmouth landed at Lyme Regis on 11 June with 82 supporters and raised his troops in the west of **ENG-**

LAND but was defeated at the **BATTLE OF SEDGEMOOR** and later executed. Judge George Jeffreys, at the **BLOODY ASSIZES**, hanged over 300 of the insurgents and a further 800 were deported as slaves to Barbados. (See **TRANSPORTATION**).

MONTFORT, SIMON DE (c. 1208-65). As Earl of Leicester, Simon led a revolt against **HENRY III** between 1259 and 1265. Born on the Ile de France, he was French both by birth and by education but re-nounced his family estates and revived the Montfort claim to the earldom. He crossed to **ENGLAND** in 1229 and paid homage to Henry two years later though his case was not fully recognized until 1236. Initially, Henry and Simon got on well together, and the King arranged for his sister, Eleanor, widow of the Earl of Pembroke, to marry his favourite on 7 January 1238. That, however, infuriated the nobles, who were not consulted about the wedding and, alarmed by the protest, Henry turned on the couple and forced them out of England in 1239. Returning in 1242, Simon was reconciled with the King during the Poitevan campaign but fell out of favour again as a result of his ruthless rule as Henry's representative in Gascony between 1248 and 1252. That experience convinced him that the King was unfit to govern, a conviction made absolutely certain by Henry's agreement, at the request of Pope Innocent IV, to finance an invasion of Sicily in 1254. His views were by no means unique and, in 1258, he and other leading nobles forced Henry to accept a number of restrictions on his power, including an agreement that he would rule only on the advice of a **PRIVY COUNCIL**.

By 1259, however, cracks were beginning to appear in the reformers' ranks. One group, led by the Earl of Gloucester, wanted simply to prevent abuses of royal power but another, led by Simon, wanted far more stringent controls on the King's decision making. In 1260, Henry accepted Gloucester's position, dividing the opposition and leaving Simon at the head of an extremist faction. Arbitration by Louis IX of France in 1263 failed to resolve the differences and the two sides went to war, with Simon winning the first round at the **BATTLE OF LEWES** (1264), when Henry was captured along with his son Edward (later **EDWARD I**). With the King confined, Simon attempted to establish a legal basis for his position by summmoning **PARLIAMENT** and negotiating with royal supporters but he failed and was forced to rule England as a military dictator. Eventually, he alienated Gilbert de Clare, his chief ally, who deserted to the King's side and helped Edward escape from his captivity in Hereford in May 1265. Edward immediately went to the head of his army and, with considerable skill, defeated the rebels at the **BATTLE OF EVESHAM** on 4 August, killing Simon and the majority of his followers. The revolt was crushed, but Simon is remembered by modern writers as one of the first advocates of limitations on the power of the **MONARCH**y through elected representatives and as a very capable military leader.

MONTGOMERY, BERNARD LAW (1887-1976). One of the most gifted of the **SECOND WORLD WAR** commanders, Montgomery was born in **LONDON** on 17 November 1887, the son of Bishop H. H. Montgomery, and was educated at St Paul's School and the Royal Military Academy Sandhurst. He entered the army in 1908 and served with distinction during the **FIRST WORLD WAR,** winning the DSO in 1914 and earning a reputation for leadership. By the outbreak of the **SECOND WORLD WAR**, he had reached the rank of Major-General and, after **DUNKIRK**, was given responsibility for British forces in southeast **ENGLAND** in anticipation of a German invasion. In 1942, **WINSTON CHURCHILL** placed him in command of the 8th Army in north Africa, where morale was low following a series of setbacks. He restored confidence, won a major victory at the **BATTLE OF EL ALAMEIN** then pursued the German regiments to a surrender at Tunis (May 1943). After that, he pushed through Sicily and up the east coast of Italy before being recalled to lead the invasion of France in June 1944. From Normandy he marched to the Rhine and, on 4 May 1945, received the Nazi capitulation at Luneburg Heath. Following the war, Montgomery was made a **VISCOUNT** (1946) and served as Chief of the Imperial General Staff (1946-48), Chairman of the Permanent Defence Organization of the **WESTERN EUROPEAN UNION (WEU)** (1948-51) and Deputy Supreme Allied Commander Europe (1951-58). Never a man to act hastily, Montgomery unvaryingly insisted on complete readiness of men and materials before he entered battle. That was a policy which exasperated his superior officers (including Dwight D. Eisenhower) but brought great success and made him very popular with his men. He died at Alton on 24 March 1976.

MORE, THOMAS (1478-1535). **LORD CHANCELLOR** of **ENGLAND** from 1529 to 1532, More was martyred for refusing to accept **HENRY VIII** as his country's supreme religious authority.

Born in **LONDON** on 7 February 1478, he went to **OXFORD** University about 1492 and studied law, entering New Inn about 1494. He sat in **PARLIAMENT** from 1504 and became a member of the Company of Mercers in 1508, the year in which he was appointed Under-**SHERIFF** of London. In 1512, he represented the Merchants of the Staple in negotiations with the **MERCHANTS ADVENT-URERS** and, in 1521, was **KNIGHT**ed. Two years later, he was chosen for the post of **SPEAKER** of the **HOUSE OF COMMONS** and, in 1525, became **CHANCELLOR OF THE DUCHY OF LANCASTER**

When **THOMAS WOLSEY** fell from grace in 1529, More succeeded him as Lord Chancellor. Initially, he and Henry got on well together (in 1520, for example, he helped the King to write an attack on the theology of Martin Luther, a treatise for which Pope Leo X awarded Henry the title of **DEFENDER OF THE FAITH** which is still claimed by British **MONARCH**s). However, More, a staunch Catholic, could not support Henry's attempts to have his marriage to **CATHERINE of ARAGON** annulled and, in 1532, in an attempt to avoid a quarrel, resigned the Chancellorship and retired to the country, pleading ill health. Two years later, he was called to London to confirm, by oath, the **ACT OF SUCCESSION** (see **ACT OF PARLIAMENT**), which declared the King's marriage to Catherine void and that with **ANNE BOLEYN** valid. More agreed to recognize Anne on the grounds that she had already been anointed Queen but declined to take the oath because it included a repudiation of papal authority.

The **ACT OF SUPREMACY**, also passed in 1534, made the Monarch supreme head of the **CHURCH OF ENGLAND** — refusal to recognize that title was an act of **TREASON**. More, however, continued to insist that he would not take the oath and was eventually brought to trial in the Palace of **WESTMINSTER** on 1 July 1535. In his defence, he maintained that he had never spoken against the King's supremacy and that, under **COMMON LAW**, silence implied consent so he could be deemed to have approved Henry's position. The jury refused to accept the argument and found him guilty. In response, More maintained that a layman could not be head of a spiritual body and that the Christian Church was a unity so one country could not make laws affecting it without the consent of all others. He was beheaded on 6 July, declaring on the scaffold that he "died the King's good servant but God's first". His head was placed in public view on **LONDON BRIDGE**. (His daughter, Margaret Roper, later interred it in a church in **CANTERBURY**.) Considered a martyr by the Roman Catholic Church, he was beatified in 1886 and canonized in 1935. His feast day is 9 July.

In addition to his reputation as a man willing to die for his beliefs, More has a claim to fame as a writer. In 1516, he published *Utopia*, a description (in Latin) of a search for the best possible form of government. (The word 'Utopia' means 'no place': it was coined by More and is an enduring contribution to the English language.) Other works include *Dialogue* (a refutation of the writings of **WILLIAM TYNDALE,** published in 1528) and a history of **RICHARD III**, published in 1543. Both were written in English. Robert Bolt's play *A Man for all Seasons*, dealing with More's relationship with Henry, was made into a successful film in 1960.

MORRISON, HERBERT STANLEY (1888-1965). One of the principal political architects of Britain's economic and social recovery from the effects of the **SECOND WORLD WAR**, Morrison was born in Brixton (**LONDON**) on 3 January 1888, the youngest of the seven children in the family of Mr Henry Morrison (a policeman) and his wife, Priscilla. He was educated at St Andrews **CHURCH OF ENGLAND** School but left at the age of 14 to become an errand boy then worked as a shop assistant, a switchboard operator and the circulation manager for the *Daily Citizen* before becoming Secretary of the London **LABOUR PARTY** (which he had helped to found) in 1915. From then, his life was devoted to the socialist cause.

Morrison was opposed to British involvement in the **FIRST WORLD WAR**: even though he would not have been accepted for military service because he had been blind in one eye since birth, he registered as a conscientious objector and was sent to work in a market garden in Hertfordshire. In 1919, he was elected Mayor of Hackney, one of the poorest of the London **BOROUGH**s, and three years later joined the **LONDON COUNTY COUNCIL** as the representative for East Woolwich (another working class community). He became Leader of the Council in 1934 and between then and 1939 did much to improve the quality of life in the city, notably through administrative improvements to the transport network, reforms to public assistance programs, slum clearance and the designation of a Greenbelt around the built-up area.

He was elected to **PARLIAMENT** as the MP for South Hackney (1923-24, 1929-31 and 1935-39). A strong supporter of

RAMSAY MacDONALD, he was MINISTER of Transport from 1929 until 1931 and devised the Road Traffic Act of 1930 (see ACT OF PARLIAMENT) and the London Passenger Transport Board, established in 1933. In 1935, he stood unsuccessfully against CLEMENT ATTLEE for Leadership of the Labour Party and, for the next 20 years, worked closely with him in a sometimes tempestuous marriage of convenience. During the SECOND WORLD WAR, he was Minister of Supply from May until October 1940 and then both HOME SECRETARY and Minister of Home Security until 1945.

It was Morrison who was largely responsible for writing the manifestoes which took Labour to victory in the first postwar GENERAL ELECTIONs (1945 and 1950), promising a new and better society in a restructured Britain. Elected as MP for South Lewisham, he served under Attlee as Deputy PRIME MINISTER, LORD PRESIDENT OF THE COUNCIL and LEADER OF THE HOUSE OF COMMONS, carrying much of the burden of a heavy legislative program as well as the arrangements for the FESTIVAL OF BRITAIN (1951). In 1951, he replaced ERNEST BEVIN as Foreign Secretary but had no real feel for international affairs and was blamed for mishandling a dispute with Persia which resulted in the expulsion of British personnel working with the Anglo-Iranian Oil Company. After the CONSERVATIVE PARTY's general election victory in the late summer, Morrison returned to his former post of Deputy Leader of the Labour Party but resigned after being defeated by HUGH GAITSKELL in the contest for the leadership which followed Attlee's retirement in 1955. Rejecting all efforts to persuade him to stay on, he was awarded a life PEERAGE as Lord Morrison of Lambeth in 1959. He became President of the British Board of Film Censors the following year. Morrison was cremated following his death in Sidcup on 6 March 1965, and his ashes were strewn on the RIVER THAMES.

MOSLEY, OSWALD (1896-1980). Leader of the British Fascist movement during the 1930s, Mosley was born in LONDON on 16 November 1896, the eldest son of Oswald and Katharine Mosley. He was educated at Winchester School and the Royal Military Academy Sandhurst then joined the 16th Lancers at the outbreak of the FIRST WORLD WAR in 1914. His military career, however, was terminated two years later by a flying accident, and he spent the last years of the conflict behind desks at the Ministry of

Munitions and the Foreign Office. In 1918, he won the Harrow **PARLIAMENT**ary **CONSTI-TUENCY** for the **CONSERVA-TIVE PARTY** but differed with the **GOVERNMENT** (particularly over its policy on **IRELAND**), became an Independent then, in 1924, joined the **LABOUR PARTY**. In 1929, he was appointed **CHANCELLOR OF THE DUCHY OF LANCASTER** in **RAMSAY MACDONALD**'s administration but resigned the following year because his plans to stimulate the country's economic recovery were rejected by the **CABINET**.

Two years later, Mosley visited Italy and, impressed by developments there, launched the **BRITISH UNION OF FASCISTS (BUF)** soon after his return. By dint of personality and a persuasive oratorical style, he dominated mass meetings but middle class right-wingers increasingly distanced themselves from him as violence and anti-semitism became an important part of his platform. Interred at the start of the **SECOND WORLD WAR**, he was released because of illness after four years. In 1948, he launched the Union Movement, which promoted European unity on racial grounds but his attempts to return to Parliament at West Kensington in 1959 and Shoreditch in 1966 resulted in heavy defeats and it was clear that his influence on mainstream politics was over. He died at Orsay (France) on 3 December 1980.

MOUNT BADON, BATTLE OF, c. 493 AD-516 AD. At an unknown site, a Romano-British army, supposedly led by King **ARTHUR**, defeated an invasion force of **ANGLO-SAXONS**. The struggle was important because it held up further invasions in the southwest of England for nearly 200 years but information about the battle is scanty.

MOUNTBATTEN, LOUIS FRANCIS ALBERT VICTOR NICHOLAS (1900-79). The only member of the Royal Family to have been killed by the Irish Republican Army (IRA), Mountbatten was born on 25 June 1900, the son of Prince Louis Alexander of Battenberg (who took the name Mountbatten in order to lose the Germanic sound of the family title during the **FIRST WORLD WAR**) and Princess Victoria of Hesse-Darmstadt. A second cousin of **GEORGE VI** and uncle of **PRINCE PHILIP**, Mountbatten attended Lockyer's Park School (Hertfordshire) then entered the Naval Training College at Osborne as a Cadet in 1913. In 1916, he joined HMS *Lion* as a Midshipman and, over the next three years, served on the *Queen*

Elizabeth, on submarines and on torpedo boats. In 1922, he married heiress Edwina Ashley and, during the interwar years, earned a reputation as an aristocratic playboy with a love of fast cars, speedboats and polo.

Mountbatten continued to develop his naval career and, in 1939, just before the outbreak of the **SECOND WORLD WAR**, became Captain of the destroyer *Kelly*. The vessel was sunk in the Mediterranean in May 1941, and he survived only by swimming away from the ship as it turned over. The following year, he was made Chief of Combined Operations and, in 1943, was appointed Supreme Allied Commander in southeast Asia. In 1945, he accepted the formal surrender of the Japanese at Singapore and, in 1947, was made Viceroy of India, with the task of partitioning the subcontinent into the independent countries of India and Pakistan. That job completed, he returned to **LONDON** and, in 1952, resumed naval duties as Commander-in-Chief of the Mediterranean Fleet. Two years later, he was appointed First Sea Lord then, in 1956, was promoted to Admiral of the Fleet. He was Chief of the UK Defence Staff between 1959 and 1965 before retiring and turning his energies to support for a large number of charitable organizations. His main form of relaxation was his annual vacation at Classiebawn Castle, his Irish home. On 27 August 1979, a family party went out in a fishing boat to collect lobster pots. The vessel was destroyed by a bomb planted by the IRA and Mountbatten was killed instantly.

MUNICH AGREEMENT, 29 September 1938. A pact designed to prevent the outbreak of the **SECOND WORLD WAR** was negotiated by Prime Minister **NEVILLE CHAMBERLAIN** with Adolf Hitler and with the leaders of Italy and France really nominal signatories, for this was an Anglo-German accord. It led to the surrender of 20 per cent of the lands of the state of Czechoslovakia (which was not at Munich) to Germany, along with fortifications, economic resources and one-quarter of the German-speaking peoples of the Sudetenland. Seeing it as part of a policy of **APPEASEMENT**, later discredited, Chamberlain regarded this sacrifice of Czechoslovakia as a price to pay for "peace for our time . . . peace with honour" and the accord included a statement that the two countries would "never go to war with one another again". However, by March 1939 Hitler had annexed what remained of Czechoslovakia and conflict was inevitable. **WINSTON CHURCHILL** referred to the agreement as "a defeat without war" and the word 'Munich' has entered the English language as a synonym for acts of cowardly capitulation.

MUNICH AIR TRAGEDY, 6 February 1958. An air crash in snowy conditions at Munich airport killed seven players of the highly successful Manchester United **FOOTBALL** team. Four of those who died had international honours but the survivors included Matt Busby (the Manager) and Bobby Charlton (who later played many times for **ENGLAND**).

MUNICIPAL CORPORATIONS ACT, 1835. This act (see **ACT OF PARLIAMENT**) established the structure of **LOCAL GOV-ERN-MENT** for Victorian **ENGLAND** by accepting the changes wrought in the great towns as a result of the **INDUSTRIAL REVOLUTION** and by doing away with ancient, outmoded and often corrupt forms of urban government. It created 178 municipal councils (elected by all ratepayers), which were gradually given more powers to control the **POLICE**, highways and public health. The Act did not apply to the **CITY OF LONDON**.

MUSCOVY COMPANY. In 1555, following Richard Chancellor's attempt to find the **NORTHEAST PASSAGE** to Asia, an **ENG-LISH TRADING COMPANY** was created to develop commerce with Russia. It traded in fish, timber and furs until the Russian Revolution in 1917.

—N—

NANKING, TREATY OF, 29 August 1942. This Treaty ended the **OPIUM WARS** and led to Britain gaining **HONG KONG** along with trading rights in four Chinese ports. It also marked the beginnings of a growth in western influence in China and the subsequent development of local resentment against that influence.

NAPOLEONIC WARS, 1803-15. Napoleon Bonaparte's expansionist policies in France intensified conflict with Britain, particularly because he adopted the **CONTINENTAL SYSTEM** of protectionism, which decreed that no British ships would be allowed into any country in Europe and that neutral ships entering British ports would be seized by France. Napoleon gained the support of Prussia and Austria and the tacit agreement of other states but

Britain retaliated in kind and used its naval power to enforce a blockade on French harbours (the **PENINSULAR WAR** occurred because Portugal supported Britain and refused to cooperate with Napoleon). Victory over the French at the **BATTLE OF TRAFALGAR** was followed by the **DUKE OF WELLINGTON**'s defeat of Napoleon's forces in Spain. Paris fell in 1814 and Napoleon was exiled first to Elba then, after his brief return and defeat at the **BATTLE OF WATERLOO**, to St Helena, where he died in 1821. (See **ANGLO-AMERICAN WAR; MARTELLO TOWERS**).

NASEBY, BATTLE OF, 14 June 1645. The most decisive battle of the first **CIVIL WAR** ended with defeat of the 7,500–10,000 strong **ROYALIST** army, led by King **CHARLES I** and Prince Rupert, by the larger (14,000) and tactically superior **PARLIAMENTARIAN** force under **SIR** Thomas Fairfax and **OLIVER CROMWELL**. It was the first successful test of the **NEW MODEL ARMY** and convincingly demonstrated Cromwell's decisive use of his **IRONSIDES** cavalry regiment. Five thousand prisoners were taken and captured papers were said to have revealed the King's foreign intrigues, notably his plans to bring an Irish army to **ENGLAND** and to plot with European countries against the realm. The battle effectively destroyed the Royalist cause in the midlands and, since the **BATTLE OF MARSTON MOOR** had crushed the Royalists in the north, can be seen as the most significant conflict of the civil war. Recent research has revealed that the site of the struggle is some way north of its earlier supposed position. Contemporary works, such as Joshua Sprigg's *Anglia Rediviva* (1647), use pictorial maps with misleading perspective so the location has always been hard to define precisely (also, at that period, it was common for each soldier in battle formation to be at least three feet from his nearest companion, thus the battle line was probably over 1.3 miles long). The new information made nonsense of the protests when the building of the A1-M1 link road in 1992 was thought to have destroyed this historic battlefield.

NASSAU AGREEMENT, 18 December 1962. Under the terms of a nuclear collaboration pact between Britain and the USA, the United States agreed to sell Polaris missiles for use in British submarines which formed part of the NATO defence force but Britain had to agree to US approval before they were used. The UK also agreed to abandon its own Blue Streak missile programme. The Treaty was said to have convinced President Charles de Gaulle of France that Britain was more committed to the special relationship with the USA than to links with Europe and, therefore, was one of the factors which caused him to veto Britain's application to join the **EUROPEAN COMMUNITY (EC)**. It also inflamed domestic anti-nuclear opinion (see **ALDERMASTON MARCHES; CAMPAIGN FOR NUCLEAR DISARMAMENT**) and weakened Britain's independent **NUCLEAR DETERRENT**.

NATIONAL ANTHEM. The official anthem of the United Kingdom begins with the words "God save our gracious Queen (or King)" and has been used as a patriotic song in theatres since the Jacobite Rebellions of the 18th century. Its origins are obscure but allusions to celebrations after the **GUNPOWDER PLOT** and to music sung for King Louis XIV of France in 1686 are part of its history. The constituent nations of the UK also have anthems which are used at appropriate occasions (such as sporting events). **WALES** has *Mae Hen Wladd Fy Nhadau (Land of My Fathers)*, **NORTHERN IRELAND** has *Danny Boy* (also known as *Londonderry Air*) and **SCOTLAND** has *Flower of Scotland*.

NATIONAL DEBT. The **GOVERNMENT** borrows from creditors and the national debt is the sum total of its debt in any one year. It originated with the war against France in 1692, when £1 million was borrowed. Two years later, the **BANK OF ENGLAND** lent further sums following the Government **BILL** which pledged the receipts of beer and liquor taxes to secure the original £1 million. A **SINKING FUND** was set up in 1717 to repay the debt and, in 1719, the South Sea Company took over the obligation until the **SOUTH SEA BUBBLE** caused the company's collapse. The Bank of England formally took over the management of the whole national debt in 1750. By 1840, the sum amounted to over £800 million. It then declined but was pushed up again by the **FIRST WORLD WAR**, the **GREAT DEPRESSION** and the **SECOND WORLD WAR**. By 1920, it stood at £8 billion and by 1945 was £21 billion. The national debt is now about 50 per cent of Gross Domestic Product (a measure of the nation's goods and services).

NATIONAL ECONOMIC DEVELOPMENT COUNCIL (NEDDY). NEDDY was created in 1962 as a forum for discussions between **GOVERNMENT, TRADE UNIONS** and management on national economic strategy but was disbanded in 1982 by **MARGARET THATCHER** as relations between the parties deteriorated.

NATIONAL FRONT. An extreme right-wing party formed in 1967, the National Front wants repatriation of immigrants, an end to all coloured immigration and strong penalties for criminals. In the **GENERAL ELECTION** of 1970, it received its largest-ever proportion of the total vote (3.6 per cent), but no candidates have ever been elected to **PARLIAMENT**. The organization's only political success was the election of two **LOCAL GOVERNMENT** councillors in Blackburn (Lancashire) in the 1970s. In 1982, it was transformed into the **BRITISH NATIONAL PARTY**. (See **BRITISH UNION OF FASCISTS**).

NATIONAL HEALTH SERVICE (NHS). The NHS was created by **ACT OF PARLIAMENT** in 1946 to provide free medical care for all (medical care included services offered by opticians, dentists, general practitioners and hospitals). It was an important element of the **WELFARE STATE** envisaged by the **BEVERIDGE REPORT** (1942), which, with National Insurance and deduction of contributions from wages, provided one of the most comprehensive social support systems in the world. In 1990, reforms stemming from the National Health Service and Community Care Act led to budget-holding status for general practitioners and the creation of Hospital Trusts, which made some hospitals self-governing. Both measures reflected attempts to introduce market principles to the NHS and reduce overall costs. In 1995, frustration with the changes, coupled with annoyance over low salaries, led nurses to vote for strike action for the first time.

NATIONAL LOTTERY. (See **STATE LOTTERY**).

NATIONAL PARKS. Created by the 1949 National Park and Access to the Countryside Act (see **ACT OF PARLIAMENT**), these areas of environmental or scenic importance enjoy special protection and planning controls in order to ensure their proper management and sympathetic development. Much of the land is still owned by private individuals, not by the state, and the public have no automatic right of access but, even so, the Parks are supposedly controlled for the public benefit. The largest are those in the Lake District, Snowdonia, the Peak District, the Yorkshire Dales and the North York Moors. There are no National Parks in **SCOT-LAND**. (See **TOWN AND COUNTRY PLANNING**).

NATIONAL SERVICE. The **CONSCRIPTION** of males over the age of 18 into the armed services prior to the **SECOND WORLD WAR** was continued by the 1947 National Service Act (see **ACT OF PARLIAMENT**) in the form of a compulsory year of military service. The obligation was extended to two years in 1950 but abolished in 1960. From 1939 until 1960, over 5.3 million men worked their National Service. (See **BRITISH ARMY; ROYAL AIR FORCE; ROYAL NAVY; STANDING ARMY**).

NATIONAL TRUST. Created in 1895 by Octavia Hill as a voluntary body dedicated to the preservation of buildings of historic or architectural interest, or land of natural beauty, for the public good, this is a private charity. The 1907 National Trust Act (see **ACT OF PARLIAMENT**) made its property inalienable, with rights in perpetuity, so no **GOVERNMENT** or other agency can compulsorily acquire its holdings without the express will of **PARLIAMENT**. In 1992, membership of the **ENGLAND, WALES** and **NORTHERN IRELAND** Trust was about 1.7 million and it received more voluntary donations than any other charity in the country. It is also bequeathed, or given, property and may carry out purchases on its own behalf. Now the largest private landowner in Britain, it owns ninety great houses, 15 per cent of the coastline and large parts of the biggest **NATIONAL PARKS**. There is a separate National Trust for **SCOTLAND**.

NATIONALIZATION. In 1918, the **LABOUR PARTY** introduced a policy of compulsorily purchasing industrial and commercial properties and utilities from their private owners in order to bring activities essential to the nation's well-being under **GOVERNMENT** control and make them more efficient. From 1945, it was applied vigorously, first by the **CLEMENT ATTLEE**'s administration, to the **BANK OF ENGLAND** (1946), **COAL** (1947), **GAS** (1949), **RAILWAYS** (1947), **ELECTRICITY** (1947), civil aviation (1947) and other sectors of the economy. Between 1945 and 1951, 20 per cent of British industry was nationalized (**IRON** and **STEEL** were returned to private control by the **CONSERVATIVE PARTY** and then re-nationalized by **HAROLD WILSON**'s Labour Government in 1964). **PRIVATIZATION**, the policy of selling back these state-owned corporations to private shareholders and companies, was energetically pursued by **MARGARET THATCHER** and reversed the trend during the 1980s. In 1995, the Labour Party dropped the commitment to nationalization from its Constitution in order to increase its attractiveness to the electorate.

NAVARINO, BATTLE OF, 20 October 1827. In the last full-scale battle involving sailing ships, an Egyptian-Turkish fleet was defeated in the Bay of Navarino by a combined flotilla of British, French and Russian vessels supporting the Greek revolt against the Ottoman Empire. Involvement was justified by the terms of the 1827 **TREATY OF LONDON**. Greek independence was eventually recognized through the Treaty of London (1832).

NAVIGATION ACTS. A series of 17th and 18th century **ACTS OF PARLIAMENT** was intended to secure monopoly trade between Britain and its colonies so that the colonies would take manufactured goods while providing raw materials. No other countries could trade with the territories and all transport had to be in British ships. The legislation stemmed from the economic doctrine of **MERCANTILISM** and was effected through tariffs and quotas, but it proved vexatious, particularly to the burgeoning American possessions.

The Act of <u>1651</u> was aimed at producing a unified imperial trade system, to the exclusion of the Dutch, and at building a merchant marine force capable of underpinning British naval power.

The Act of <u>1663</u> restricted the cattle trade and colonial trade with **IRELAND**.

The Act of <u>1671</u> prevented New World products from entering Britain via Ireland.

The Act of <u>1731</u> allowed restricted trade between Ireland and the American colonies.

The laws were easily broken, as was evident by the growth of illicit trade with the American colonies through foreign vessels.

NELSON, HORATIO (1758-1805). One of the great naval strategists, Nelson won major victories at the **BATTLE OF THE NILE**, the Battle of Copenhagen and the **BATTLE OF TRAFALGAR**, ensuring Britain's supremacy at sea during the **NAPOLEONIC WARS**. He was born at Burnham Thorpe (Norfolk) on 29 September 1758, the son of Edmund Nelson (Rector of the parish) and his wife, Catherine Suckling. At the age of 12, he joined the navy, initially serving under his uncle (Captain Maurice Suckling) then gaining experience in the East Indies, the Arctic and the West Indies. In 1777, he was promoted to Lieutenant and, the following year, was given command of his first warship, the *Badger*. From 1784 until 1787, he was senior officer at the Leeward Islands Naval Station (where he enforced the **NAVIGATION ACTS**). Towards the end of his service, he married Frances Nisbet, the widow of a doctor who had worked on the neighbouring island of Nevis. The couple returned to **ENGLAND** together but Nelson found himself without a command until 1793, when he was appointed to the 64-gun *Agamemnon* following the outbreak of war with France.

From then until 1800, Nelson was on almost continuous active service. From 1793 until 1797, he was in the Mediterranean, where he met Emma Hamilton, who was to become his mistress. In April and May 1794, he was engaged in the capture of Bastia, and, in June, July and August, in the taking of Calvi, both on Corsica. During the action at Calvi he was wounded in the right eye, which gradually lost its sight, but the impairment had no effect on his career. In 1797, he was involved in the Battle of St Vincent, commanding the 74-gun *Captain*, one of 15 warships under Admiral Sir John Jervis. In February, a fleet of 27 Spanish vessels was attacked off Cape St Vincent in Portugal. When it seemed that the majority of the enemy ships would escape unscathed, Nelson acted without orders and engaged the 130-gun *Santissima Trinidad*, blocking the Spanish route to safety. As a result, four Spanish men-of-war were captured and the remainder put to flight. Nelson was knighted and promoted to the rank of Rear Admiral in recognition of his contribution to the victory. In July 1797, he made an unsuccessful attempt to capture Santa Cruz de Tenerife in the Canary Islands. The attack, made during the night, resulted in heavy losses and Nelson himself, shot through the elbow, had to have his arm amputated in semidarkness. The action in the Battle of the Nile, in April 1798, resulted in a another wound, this time to the forehead, but, even so, he won a major victory, which gave Britain control of the Mediterranean and thereby prevented Napoleon from putting his plans to conquer Egypt and India into effect.

Early in 1800, Nelson returned to England on leave. The stay was short but, nevertheless, gave him sufficient time to separate from his wife and father a child by Emma Hamilton. In 1801, he was promoted to Vice-Admiral and appointed second in command of a fleet, led by Sir Hyde Parker, which was charged with breaking the armed neutrality of the Baltic powers. During an attack on the Danish navy off Copenhagen on 2 April, Parker signalled his junior officer to disengage; Nelson put a telescope to his blind eye and, claiming that he could see no signal, fought on. As a result the Danish fleet was destroyed, and Nelson, on his return to England, was made a **VISCOUNT**.

During 1802 and early 1803, he lived quietly with the Hamiltons in Surrey but, in May, war broke out with France once again and he was given command of the Mediterranean Fleet. In July 1803, he began a blockade of the French at Toulon but, in March 1805, the enemy ships slipped out and headed for the West Indies in an attempt to join the Spanish navy and then invade Britain. Nelson chased the French back and forth across the Atlantic, eventually bringing them to battle on 21 October off Cape Trafalgar, south of Cadiz. Signalling that "England expects every man to do his duty", he deployed his ships in two groups, sending each one through the enemy fleet. The Franco-Spanish navy was destroyed but Nelson himself was struck by a bullet while standing on the quarterdeck of *Victory*, his flagship. His spine was broken and, although he continued to ask for details about the progress of the battle, it was clear that he would not recover. As his sight dimmed he told his officers "Thank God I have done my duty" then passed away. His body was taken back to **LONDON** and buried in St Paul's Cathedral. His statue, at the centre of Trafalgar Square, is one of the city's best known landmarks, and HMS *Victory* is preserved as a tourist attraction at Portsmouth.

NEOLITHIC. During this period of **PREHISTORIC BRITAIN** lasting from c. 4,400 BC until 2,500 BC, stone was used for grinding and polishing. The period is also known as the New Stone Age (*neos* is Greek for 'new', and *lithos* means 'stone'). The cultivation of agricultural crops (especially wheat) began and the domestication of animals (cattle, goats, pigs and sheep) led to a more sedentary life in permanent settlements. Dolmen and portal graves were built as stone tombs were constructed and later the long **BARROW**s, a more elaborate and much larger collective burial monument, developed. Mines for stone, and especially the hard and sharp flint (prized as a weapon), were established (for example, at Grimes Graves in Norfolk) and pottery became more sophisticated. Warrior chieftains began to lead rival tribes, especially in the more densely settled south of **ENGLAND**. The building of **STONEHENGE** was begun during this period, which was followed by the **BRONZE AGE**.

NEW MODEL ARMY. The New Model Army Ordinance of 27 January 1645 reorganized the whole Parliamentary army (see **PARLIA-MENTARIANS**) along the lines of **OLIVER CROMWELL**'s **IRONSIDES** after the defeat at the **BATTLE OF LOSTWITHIEL**. New regiments were created with a total strength of 22,000 men, most of whom were expected to be volunteers, and **SIR** Thomas Fairfax was made Commander-in-Chief. The restructuring was an attempt to create a permanent national force of well-trained soldiers with regular pay and professional administration. In the short term, the New Model Army opposed the **ROYALIST** troops of **CHARLES I** (which were recruited and retained on more traditional grounds) and proved to be a decisive element in the **CIVIL WAR**, making its mark first at the **BATTLE OF NASEBY**. In the longer term, it brought standardized uniforms, a high order of discipline and training and carefully conceived tactics to British soldiery.

NEW TOWNS. These free-standing urban developments were derived from the earlier **GARDEN CITIES** and were conceived as self-contained, socially balanced towns to take overspill (or excess) population from the overcrowded cities of Britain. The 1946 New Towns Act (see **ACT OF PARLIAMENT**) became a cornerstone of post-**SECOND WORLD WAR TOWN AND COUNTRY PLANNING** as the United Kingdom attempted to regulate the size of its largest settlements by relocating families in New Towns constructed up to 30 miles from the boundaries of the metropolitan areas. The programme was gradually wound up in the 1970s and 1980s as views on cost-effectiveness changed and population pressures reduced in political importance. The grand scheme was typical of the post-1945 view that almost anything, on whatever scale, could be achieved. (See **WELFARE STATE**).

NEWARK, BATTLE OF, 21 March 1644. During the **CIVIL WAR**, a battle was fought at this fortified stronghold of the **ROYALISTS**. Prince Rupert won and allowed the defeated **PARLIAMENTARIANS** to march away after capturing their baggage train and 3,000 muskets.

NEWBURN FORD, BATTLE OF, 28 August 1640. At this short and virtually bloodless battle, a force of 20,000 men from **SCOT-**

LAND overcame an English army of 4,000 which was trying to protect a crossing of the **RIVER TYNE** on the route to **NEW-CASTLE-UPON-TYNE**. The importance of the event has only recently been stressed by scholars, who believe that the defeat of **CHARLES I** was instrumental in forcing him to abandon his attempt to rule without **PARLIAMENT** during the **ELEVEN YEARS OF TYRANNY**.

NEWBURY, BATTLES OF. There were two battles at Newbury (Berkshire) during the **CIVIL WAR**.

The first was on <u>20 September 1643</u> and was inconclusive though the Earl of Essex, commanding the Parliamentary Militia (see **PARLIAMENTARIANS**), forced the withdrawal of **CHARLES I** after the King failed to take the strategic Round Hill, which was occupied by the **LONDON TRAINED BANDS**. Total losses were in the region of 6,000–8,000 men.

The second was fought on <u>27 October 1644</u>, when King **CHARLES I** was confronted by no fewer than three separate Parliamentary armies (one led by **OLIVER CROMWELL**). The battle was bloody but also inconclusive, the Parliamentarians failing, through mismanagement, to drive home their undoubted advantage in numbers. That failure was one of the factors which led to the decision to form the **NEW MODEL ARMY**. In 1993, there was controversy over a planned bypass road which would bisect the site of this battle, though recent research has revealed some doubt about the exact location of the conflict.

NEWCASTLE-UPON-TYNE. The major settlement on the North Sea coast of northeast **ENGLAND**, Newcastle dates at least from **ROMAN** times but its great period of expansion came with the **INDUSTRIAL REVOLUTION. COAL** had been mined in the area since the 13th century and the years of experience provided a basis for a vastly increased trade after the development of steam power. Newcastle, located on the **RIVER TYNE** 275 miles north of **LONDON**, became one of the country's principal ports and developed a variety of ancillary industries, including shipbuilding, glassmaking, chemical production, flour milling and the manufacture of machinery. Five major bridges were built across the Tyne between 1849 and 1928, and a large urban complex developed downstream, incorporating such subsidiary centres as Gateshead, Jarrow (see **HUNGER MARCHES**) and South Shields. The economic recessions of the 1920s and 1980s seriously affected the area and unemployment rates reached levels well above the national average on both occasions, but Tyneside is still a major focus of sea-borne commerce with the Scandinavian countries.   At the time of the 1991 census, Newcastle had a population of 252,000 (a decrease of 7.5 per cent over the 1981 count) and the Tyne and Wear Metropolitan County, of which it is the major focus, had 1,074,000 (down 5.5 per cent over the decade). (For location, see Map 2, page xxvi).

NEWCASTLE, DUKE OF. (See **THOMAS PELHAM HOLLES**).

NEWTON, ISAAC (1642-1727). One of the dominant figures in the history of science, Newton was born in Woolsthorpe on Christmas Day 1642. His father had died two months earlier, and, in 1645, his mother remarried, moved to her new husband's home and left Isaac in the care of his maternal grandmother. Following his stepfather's death in 1656, he rejoined his mother to help run the family farm but preferred mathematics to husbandry so, in 1660, was sent back to school. He entered **CAMBRIDGE** University in 1661 and graduated with a BA degree in 1665, but, in the autumn of that year, the University was closed as a result of the **GREAT PLAGUE** and he returned to Woolsthorpe. Over the next 18 months, he laid the foundations of his stream of discoveries in mathematics and physics, developing the binomial theorem and the fluxions (a form of differential calculus), discovering (by experiment) that white light is composed of all the colours of the spectrum and reasoning that the moon is held in orbit round the earth by the force of gravity. The last of these discoveries, he claimed, was the result of seeing an apple fall (he argued that there must be some force pulling the apple down to the Earth and that the same force would attract the moon sufficiently to keep it in orbit rather than fly off into space).

Newton returned to Cambridge when the University reopened in 1667 and shortly afterwards was created Lucasian Professor of Mathematics but found his theories under strong attack from fellow scientists. His response was to carry out further investigations which led to the development of the corpuscular theory of light (that is, that light consists of tiny particles, or corpuscles, which have different properties for different colours and are guided by waves). He also proposed a law relating the radius of a bright ring to the colour of light (and pointed out that, because the radius is a function of the colour, when a ring of white light is used, an observer will see concentric rings of different colours round a black core, a phenomenon now termed 'Newton's Rings'). An account of his work and its implications was published in 1687 as *Philosophiae Naturalis Principia Mathematica* (*Mathematical Principles of Natural Philosophy*), which claimed that a single mathematical law could explain the motion of the stars and planets as well as account for the rise and fall of tides and the movement of natural forces on the Earth. The work is now considered to be one of the major pillars on which modern scientific investigation was built.

Elected Member of **PARLIAMENT** for Cambridge University in 1689, Newton returned to his studies of mathematics after the **DISSOLUTION OF PARLIAMENT** the following year. He was ill with a nervous complaint between 1692 and 1694 but recovered sufficiently to take up the post of Warden of **THE ROYAL MINT** in 1695. Four years later, he became Master, with responsibility for introducing means of maintaining the value of **CURRENCY**. In 1701, he resigned his professorship and moved to **LONDON**, becoming President of the **ROYAL SOCIETY** in 1703. The following year, he published *Opticks*, a summary of his work on light and colour which, in later editions (and particularly that of 1717), included appendices dealing with electrical, chemical and magnetic phenomena. He was knighted in 1705 but, after that, lived the life of a recluse, involved in scientific quarrels. (Both he and G.W. Liebniz claimed to have invented the calculus, for instance.) He became seriously ill early in 1727, died on 20 March and was buried in **WESTMINSTER** Abbey eight days later.

NIGHTINGALE, FLORENCE (1820-1910). The founder of modern nursing, Florence Nightingale is best known for her work with soldiers injured during the **CRIMEAN WAR** but also made major contributions to public health care. Born in Florence (Italy) on 12 May 1820, the daughter of William and Florence Nightingale, she decided (despite a wealthy background) that God had called her to serve and, in 1844, opted to fulfill that calling as a nurse. Her parents were shocked — nursing was low grade, unskilled labour often performed by drunken prostitutes and clearly no job for a woman from an affluent family. Because of their opposition, she was unable to gain any experience until 1851, when she worked for a while in Germany, but two years later she found a post in **LONDON** as Superintendent of the Institution for the Care of

Sick Gentlewomen in Distressed Circumstances. Her management of that organization was so successful that, in 1854, she was asked by Sidney Herbert, the **SECRETARY OF STATE** for War, to supervize nursing at the British hospitals in the Crimea. With a staff of 38, she provided care for 5,000 men and, despite the squalor and lack of equipment, greatly reduced the hospital death rate by improving hygiene and sanitary conditions, structuring provision and working extremely long hours. Her patients christened her 'The Lady with the Lamp', and tales of her efforts turned her into a national heroine.

When she returned to Britain in 1855, Florence continued her work with the army, analyzing the supply of housing, food and health services for soldiers, improving the efficiency of hospitals and introducing training for nurses. Those interests led her into a consideration of public health and, in 1860, using money raised by public subscription, she founded the Nightingale School and Home for Nurses at St Thomas's Hospital, London. She was also much in demand as a consultant, developed the network of district (or local visiting) nurses, became an expert on India and wrote prodigiously even though the strain of the workload damaged her own health. In 1907, she was awarded the Order of Merit (becoming the first woman to receive the honour) and, on 13 August 1910, died in London. In 1934, the Florence Nightingale International Foundation, a postgraduate institute for nurses, was established in her memory.

NILE, BATTLE OF THE, 1 August 1798. Also called the Battle of Aboukir Bay, this naval engagement was fought during the **NAPOLEONIC WARS. HORATIO NELSON** defeated the French fleet at the mouth of the River Nile, destroying all but two of its 13 ships of the line and inflicting between 4,000 and 6,000 casualties. As a result, Britain regained the initiative lost with the French seizure of Malta and effectively blocked Napoleon's ambitions in the Mediterranean.

NINETEEN PROPOSITIONS, 1 June 1642. The propositions were a series of political demands made by the **LONG PARLIAMENT** to King **CHARLES I** following the **GRAND REMONSTRANCE.** They included insistence that **PARLIAMENT** should approve the appointment of officers of state, supervize the education of the **MONARCH**'s children, control the **MILITIA** and, crucially, strictly enforce anti-Catholic legislation. The King rejected all of the proposals, an action which led directly to the **CIVIL WAR**.

NONCONFORMISTS. A Protestant **DISSENTER** who did not conform to the canons and doctrines of the **CHURCH OF ENGLAND** was persecuted under, for example, the 1593 **CONVENTICLE ACT** (see **ACT OF PARLIAMENT**) and the **CLARENDON CODE** (1661-70). Such Nonconformists were allowed to worship in their own way only after the passage of the **TOLERATION ACT** (1689). (See **RECUSANT**).

NORMANS, 1066-1154. The House of Normandy (France) gained the throne of **ENGLAND** in 1066 at the **BATTLE OF HASTINGS**. **WILLIAM I** (the Conqueror) was crowned on Christmas Day 1066, and his dynasty reigned until 1154, when it was replaced by the **PLANTAGENETS**. The Norman period ended English isolation from mainland Europe, introduced the **FEUDAL SYSTEM** and left, as a legacy, a distinctive architectural style characterized by the great round-topped arches of major cathedrals and other buildings. Also, many elements of **GOVERNMENT** and law date from this time. For example, the British sovereign is still invested as **DUKE** of Normandy at the accession to the throne though Normandy itself was lost in 1205: the **CHANNEL ISLANDS**, which were part of this duchy, still owe allegiance to the British **MONARCH** through the title. (See **HENRY I; STEPHEN; WILLIAM I–II**).

NORTH, FREDERICK (1732-92). **PRIME MINISTER** during the **AMERICAN WAR OF INDEPENDENCE**, North was born in **LONDON** on 13 April 1732. He was educated at Eton College and **OXFORD** University then, at the age of 22, was elected Member of **PARLIAMENT** for Banbury, supporting the **TORIES**. In 1759, he was made a Lord of **THE TREASURY** and, in 1766, became **PAYMASTER GENERAL** and a member of the **PRIVY COUNCIL**. The following year, he was appointed **CHANCELLOR OF THE EXCHEQUER** and, in 1770, succeeded the **DUKE** of Grafton as Prime Minister, a post which he held for 12 years. He had the confidence of **GEORGE III** and was an able orator but frequently found himself defending measures of which he did not approve and crossing swords with opponents of the calibre of **CHARLES JAMES FOX** and **EDMUND BURKE**.

His most difficult times occurred during the American Revolution.   One of his first acts was to announce the retention of the Tea Duty, a decision which inflamed the colonists and led to the Boston Tea Party. Underestimating the settlers' strength of feeling and powers of resistance, he attempted both to coerce and cajole with little success. Easily depressed, he often felt that there was little chance of his troops winning the war, and, in March 1782, he resigned after hearing of Lord Cornwallis's surrender at Yorktown.   In April of the following year, he formed a coalition with Fox, under the leadership of the **DUKE OF PORTLAND**, and held office as Secretary of State but, in December, the understanding dissolved in the wake of the defeat of Fox's India Bill (see **ACT OF PARLIAMENT**) in the **HOUSE OF LORDS**.   For the following three years, North was an ally of Fox in opposition but, in 1786, he retired from politics on the grounds of failing eyesight. In 1790, he succeeded to the hereditary title of Earl of Guilford and, on 5 August 1792, died in London.

NORTH, LORD. (See **FREDERICK NORTH**).

NORTHAMPTON, BATTLE OF, 18 July 1460. This battle was fought between Yorkist and Lancastrian armies during the **WARS OF THE ROSES**. The Lancastrian forces lost, with heavy casualties and the capture of King **HENRY VI** (after barely 30 minutes of struggle). Their powder was wet from an earlier rainstorm and, during the short fight, Lord Edmund Grey treacherously allowed the Yorkists to penetrate the trench defences, as a consequence of which Lord Buckingham and many prominent Lancastrian nobles were killed.

NORTH BRITON. A periodical published from 5 June 1762 until 23 April 1763 by **JOHN WILKES**, the *North Briton* criticized the **MONARCH** and the **GOVERNMENT**, calling King **GEORGE III** a liar. It particularly parodied the publication of *The Briton*, which had promulgated the policies of the **PRIME MINISTER**, the **EARL OF BUTE**. Wilkes was tried in May 1763 for sedition and acquitted, the judge ruling that as he was a Member of **PARLIAMENT** (MP) he should be able to criticize. However, in November 1763, MPs condemned issue Number 45 as seditious libel and Wilkes fled to Paris. In 1768, he was again arrested for publishing the *North Briton* and a pornographic *Essay on Woman*. Public support led to the St George's Day Massacre at which troops killed five demonstrators but Wilkes was fined £1,000 and sentenced to 22 months' imprisonment. "Wilkes and Liberty" was the cry on the streets and the freedom of the press became an issue for Government.

NORTHEAST PASSAGE. During the 16th century, there was an intensive search for a sea route from the Atlantic to the Pacific along the northern Eurasian coast. Many expeditions were sponsored by the **MUSCOVY COMPANY**, but, although the voyages of Richard Chancellor and others secured trade with Russia for naval stores, the first successful Atlantic/Pacific voyage did not take place until 1879.

NORTH-SOUTH DIVIDE. Much used in the 1980s, this term was coined to describe the growing disparity in living conditions between the relatively poor north of **ENGLAND**, with its **INDUSTRIAL REVOLUTION**-based declining industries, and the increasing prosperity of **LONDON** and the south of England due to the expansion of finance houses, service industries and activities based on high technology.

NORTHWEST PASSAGE. The search for a short sea passage through the Arctic Sea from the Atlantic to the Pacific Oceans much exercised mariners from the 15th century. Attempts were made by Sebastian Cabot, Martin Frobisher and Henry Hudson but, although they opened up northern Canada and Hudson's Bay, they failed to find an ice-free route. The first successful voyage was by Roald Amundsen between 1903 and 1905.

NORTHERN IRELAND. When Eire gained its independence in 1921, the six northeastern counties of the island of **IRELAND** formed a federal relationship with the United Kingdom (preferring to remain outside the new republic). Northern Ireland was given its own Parliament for domestic affairs, but, in 1972, that was abolished as civil disruption in the Province increased and, in 1974, the **SECRETARY OF STATE** for Northern Ireland was made responsible for the government of the territory. Its 1.5 million people live in an area of 5,500 squre miles and return 17 Members of **PARLIAMENT**. After the 1992 **GENERAL ELECTION**, 13 of the **CONSTIT-UENCIES** were held by the Unionist groups, the remainder by the Social Democratic and Labour Party. (See **ULSTER**).

NORTHERN REBELLION, 1569. A rebellion by the northern **EARL**s of Northumberland and Westmorland (and originally also Norfolk, who tried to reduce the power of the Cecil family at the court of **ELIZABETH I**) was promised Spanish aid to return the realm to Roman Catholicism and release the imprisoned Mary, Queen of Scots. However, the revolt was easily suppressed by the Queen's forces and, although the leaders fled to **SCOTLAND**, some 800 of the nobles' followers were executed. This was, by far, the most serious domestic challenge to Elizabeth's **MONARCH**y.

NUCLEAR DETERRENT. Britain developed nuclear technology at the end of the **SECOND WORLD WAR**, detonating its first atomic bomb in 1952 and its first hydrogen bomb in 1957. The United Kingdom's development then fell behind that of the United States of America and the USSR and the **NASSAU AGREEMENT** (1962) tied its nuclear weapons to US control through the purchase of American Polaris missiles. Official papers, declassified by the **PUBLIC RECORD OFFICE (PRO)** in 1994, reveal that scientists at Aldermaston (see **ALDERMASTON MARCHES**) mounted an elaborate bluff in the late 1950s with respect to the success of Britain's nuclear programme. Three bombs (codenamed Short Granite, Purple Granite and Orange Herald) were tested in 1957 and two failed to explode; the third did, but all were publicised as successful H-bomb tests at the time (the press was told that all were hydrogen bombs but the one which exploded was actually a less powerful atomic bomb). It has also now been revealed that the United States of America provided blueprints to the British scientists, who were eventually successful in 1958. The hoax was probably a patriotic gesture at a time when possession of a nuclear deterrent was vital to this country's international prestige. Later agreements to have United States controlled Cruise missiles on American bases in Britain, making the United Kingdom the first country to do so in Europe, enraged the **CAMPAIGN FOR NUCLEAR DISARMAMENT** and led to the **GREENHAM COMMON** demonstrations in June 1980. (See **OFFICIAL SECRETS ACT**).

NUCLEAR ENERGY. The world's first fully operational nuclear power station — at Windscale, near Calder Hall in Cumberland — was opened in 1956, utilising a magnox power installation which had been designed at the Harwell Laboratory, established in 1946.

As well as providing **ELECTRICITY**, it produced plutonium for the Aldermaston Atomic Weapons Establishment (see **ALDERMASTON MARCHES, NUCLEAR DETERRENT**) and, in 1952, began the reprocessing of spent nuclear fuel. The plant, now called Sellafield (a name change adopted after a nuclear overheat accident there in October 1957), remains a controversial installation because of allegations that it is responsible for an unnaturally high incidence of some cancers in the area. From 1976, British nuclear stations were based on Advanced Gas Cooled reactors, but, in 1979, the **GOVERNMENT** decided to adopt the American Pressurized Water Power System. By 1993, Britain had 14 nuclear power stations, with the industry divided between Nuclear Electric (which administers the power stations) and British Nuclear Fuels (which was split off in 1971 as a state-owned enterprize for the reprocessing of nuclear waste). The research and monitoring Atomic Energy Authority was identified for **PRIVATIZATION** in 1994 and the power stations themselves the following year (though the ageing magnox stations remained in state hands). In 1995, British Energy (the new private company) announced that it was abandoning plans to build further nuclear generating plant.

—O—

OBSCENE PUBLICATIONS ACT, 1959. This act (see **ACT OF PARLIAMENT**) introduced, to legal rulings on pornography, the concept of 'public good' — such literary, artistic or scientific merit in a publication as could be cited to prevent it being condemned as "likely to corrupt or deprave" (the general definition of obscenity). A prosecution involving D. H. Lawrence's *Lady Chatterley's Lover* was the first case to test the new law. In November 1960, the novel, released by Penguin Publishers, was legally acquitted of obscenity, an indicator of the changing public morality in Britain evident in the vogue for realistic and working class fiction and cinema and the growing popularity of satirical humour in print and on television. The book became an immediate best-seller.

OFFA (?-796).   King of **MERCIA** from 757 until 796, Offa seized power in the civil war which followed the murder of his cousin **AETHELBALD**. Despite strong resistance in some areas (notably **KENT**), he established control over the whole of **ENGLAND** south of the River Humber and extended his influence further by marrying one daughter to Aethelred (King of Northumbria) and another to Beorhtric (King of **WESSEX**). He also introduced a new form of currency and was probably responsible for the construction of an earthwork (Offa's Dyke), along the western boundary of his territory, marking the end of his jurisdiction and the start of the area occupied by Welsh tribes. The **ANGLO-SAXON CHRONICLE** records that he passed away in 796.

OFFICIAL SECRETS ACT, 1911. The act (see **ACT OF PARLIA-MENT**) provides for the protection of knowledge which may be prejudicial to the state if divulged. Members of the Civil Service are obliged to sign the act (to prohibit them from revealing information). It was used during the 1980s against **GOVERNMENT** officials leaking information about Cruise missiles.

OIL. The first major discovery of oil in Britain was at Nottingham in 1939. However, from the 1960s onwards, the major focus of the industry has been the exploitation of the enormous reserves in the North Sea, which is shallow (at 160 feet average) compared with other oceanic sources of the fuel and therefore accessible. The first oil from these fields came ashore in 1975, a critical year because Britain had, until then, relied wholly on imports and the new resources were to help immensely after the **OIL CRISIS**. By 1980, the country was both self-sufficient and the world's sixth largest producer. Output peaked at 125 million US tons in 1985 though new deposits are still being found. In 1990, Britain was the ninth largest producer overall and the second largest offshore producer, with 44 crude oil fields in the North Sea. The industry has, therefore, become an important element of the British economy, estimated to be worth £20 million each day in 1992 and with reserves sufficient to let the United Kingdom remain a significant producer well into the 21st century. (See **GAS**).

OIL CRISIS. The world economic problems in the late 1960s and early 1970s were largely the result of difficulties with **OIL** supplies as consumption rose and Arab producers increased prices through their cartel, the Organisation of Petroleum Exporting Countries (OPEC), which had growing political muscle. The situation was further complicated by the Yom Kippur Arab-Israeli war and the closure of the Suez Canal. In 1973, Britain was heavily dependent on imported oil, North Sea supplies not then being sufficiently developed, and **EDWARD HEATH**'s **GOVERNMENT** was beset by industrial unrest over a hardening prices and incomes policy, major industrial action by the **COAL** miners, railwaymen and **ELECTRICITY** workers and a slump in manufacturing output, so much so that press commentators considered the economic situation to be the worst since the end of the **SECOND WORLD WAR**. Government action to cope with the reduction in oil supplies included cuts in public spending, a 50 mph speed limit on roads, credit controls, an enforced television closedown at 10.30 pm to save electricity, the issue of ration books for fuel and, eventually, the imposition of a **THREE-DAY WEEK** to reduce fuel consumption. Inevitably, there were political repercussions and, by March 1974, the **CONSERVATIVE PARTY** had lost power, the **LABOUR PARTY** had taken over and **HAROLD WILSON** had become **PRIME MINISTER**.

OMBUDSMAN. Since 1967, **PARLIAMEN**tary Commissioners (or ombudsmen) have been appointed to investigate citizens' complaints of maladministration by central or **LOCAL GOVERNMENT** departments, the health service or public bodies. Cases have to be referred to the Commissioners by MPs. The term comes from the Swedish concept of a representative and this British version is properly called "Parliamentary Commissioner for Administration".

OMDURMAN, BATTLE OF, 2 September 1898. This was the key battle in **HORATIO KITCHENER**'s campaign to retake the Sudan from the forces of the Khalifa. With an Anglo-Egyptian army of 26,000 armed with Maxim automatic guns, Kitchener took Omdurman and inflicted casualties in excess of 10,000 men in a victory seen at the time as revenge for the death of General **CHARLES GORDON** at Khartoum. The success, coupled with the results of negotiations over Fashoda (see **FASHODA INCIDENT**), brought the Sudan back under British control. (See **SUDANESE WARS**).

OPEN FIELD SYSTEM. In this ancient farming system, open (or unhedged) fields were divided into strip plots and each tenant had a mixture of strips on good and poor land. Usually, there were three large open fields farmed in rotation, with one lying fallow each year. Common rights existed for forage and grazing of ani-

mals on meadows and woodlands. It was most common in southern and midland **ENGLAND**. Though the system was equitable, it
needed constant democratic decision making to make it work and
was unsuited to mechanization, large-scale production and the
other changes brought by the **AGRICULTURAL REVOLU-
TION**. It stifled innovation and discouraged attempts to improve
land quality because there were no hedges to fence in animals and
all tenants had to follow the **PARISH** traditions. As a result, it
virtually vanished during the **ENCLOSURE** movement of the
18th and 19th centuries. The village of Laxton in Nottinghamshire
is probably the only surviving area with an intact three field system. There, the medieval farmland survived enclosure and landowner disputes and 483 acres of land are still administered by the
Court Leet (or village court). The fields are divided into strips and
the Court can still impose fines for agricultural offences.

OPIUM WARS, 1839-1842 and 1856-1860. During the 18th century,
China took only silver in return for its agricultural and manufactured products (tea, porcelain and silk) but, in the early 19th century, merchants persuaded Chinese traders to accept opium, which
the British had banned in India and which now needed an alternative outlet. This questionable, but highly profitable, barter trade
was organized by the **EAST INDIA COMPANY**. In 1839, however, the Chinese seized all the opium stored in British ships and
warehouses in Canton in order to reduce the disastrous effects of
the drug, bring some of the immense profits from the trade into
Chinese hands, restore silver imports and rid Chinese soil of foreigners. In response, the British took control of Canton in 1841 and
Shanghai the following year. In 1842, China agreed to pay an in-
demnity of £6 million, open more ports to European traders and
cede Hong Kong to Britain on a 150-year lease. (See **TREATY
OF NANKING**).

Chinese seizure of the British ship *Arrow* in 1856 led to renewed hostilities. This war ended in 1860 after a British/French
force took Peking (Beijing). An agreement was signed in October of that year giving British merchants access to five 'treaty
ports' in China.

OPPOSITION, THE. As part of the development of
PARLIAMENTary democracy during the 19th century, party
politics became the norm, replacing temporary coalitions of individual Members of Parliament. The second largest party became

known as Her (or His) Majesty's Loyal Opposition, with the duty of opposing the **GOVERNMENT** in debate and therefore acting as a check on the **PRIME MINISTER** and the **CABINET**. The Leader of the Opposition is elected by members of the party but is paid by the state.

ORDINANCES, 1311. The Lords Ordainers established 41 Ordinances in an attempt to secure control of **GOVERNMENT** for the Barons and limit the powers of the **MONARCH**. King **EDWARD II** was forbidden to leave the country without the consent of the nobles and his finances were limited. **PARLIAMENT** was to be called at least twice a year and the King's Italian bankers were arrested. A move towards greater royal accountability to Parliament rather than an effort to promote constitutional change, the Ordinances were revoked in 1322. Strictly, an ordinance is legislation passed by Parliament but lacking **ROYAL ASSENT**.

ORDINATION OF WOMEN. In 1985, the **GENERAL SYNOD** of the **CHURCH OF ENGLAND** allowed women to become Deacons, able to officiate at all but the most sacred of ceremonies. In 1992, it went further and decided in favour of the ordination of women as priests, causing a rift with those who held to the traditional view of female roles in the Church and the defection to Roman Catholicism of some prominent Anglicans, including Members of **PARLIAMENT**. On 22 February 1994, the General Synod approved the final promulgation of canons amending ecclesiastical law to allow women to be ordained in **ENGLAND**. The first ladies with full authority to administer the sacraments became priests at Bristol on 13 March of that year. In April 1994, the Anglican Province of **WALES** voted against the ordination of women.

ORDNANCE, BOARD OF. During the **TUDOR** period (1485-1603), a Board was created to supply ordnance or munitions to the armed forces of the realm. It was based in the **TOWER OF LONDON** until it became part of the **WAR OFFICE** in 1855.

ORDNANCE SURVEY (OS). As its name suggests, Britain's official mapmaking organization had military origins. It was founded in 1791 to meet the need for accurate maps for the artillery (ordnance), who were preparing to repel the threatened invasion from Napoleon Bonaparte, but had its real beginnings earlier in General

William Roy's surveys for roads planned in Highland **SCOTLAND** so that troops could quell the rebellious Jacobite supporters. The first maps were at a scale of one inch to one mile, and the first published sheet (in 1801) covered part of **KENT**. Areas of **LONDON** were mapped at a massive scale of 60 inches to 1 mile by the mid-19th century and gradually coverage extended over the whole country. By 1873, the OS had become part of the Civil Service. After the **SECOND WORLD WAR**, a National Grid was created to facilitate precise geographical reference. OS maps were metricated in 1969 and are now revised from aerial and satellite survey with, by 1993, fully computerized sales of digitized maps. The maps are regarded as accurate and reliable, so much so that, during the **SECOND WORLD WAR**, the Luftwaffe issued overprinted OS maps to its bomber crews. In 1990, the OS was converted into an executive agency and expected to fund itself from profits.

OSBORNE JUDGEMENT, December 1909. W.V. Osborne, Secretary of the Walthamstow Branch of the Amalgamated Society of Railway Servants, secured a judgement outlawing the use of **TRADE UNION** dues for political purposes. The result was a large drop in funds for the **LABOUR PARTY** and this led, in 1911, to state salaries being paid to Members of **PARLIAMENT** to ensure democracy. Eventually, the Trade Union Act of 1913 (see **ACT OF PARLIAMENT**) legalized such use of levies but allowed individual members to opt out of payments earmarked for political activities.

OTTERBURN, BATTLE OF, 19th August 1388. A Scottish force returning home with plunder after a foray into Northumberland was engaged by English troops under **HENRY PERCY**. After a lengthy night-time struggle, the Scots emerged victorious, capturing Percy, but their leader — James, Earl of Douglas — was killed. The fight is sometimes known as the Battle of Chevy Chase (the *Ballad of Chevy Chase* includes the lines: "Of fifteen hundred archers of **ENGLAND**, Went away but fifty-three; Of twenty hundred spearmen of **SCOTLAND**, But even five and fifty").

OUDENARDE, BATTLE OF, 11 July 1708. This battle, fought in the Netherlands during the **WAR OF THE SPANISH SUCCESSION**, brought victory for the **DUKE OF MARLBOROUGH** over the French army. It restored the strategic position of the allies, who eventually went on to other victories. (See **BATTLE OF MALPLAQUET**).

OUTLAW. The final legal step in placing a felon outside the protection of the law was to declare him an outlaw in his absence from criminal proceedings. Prior to the **NORMAN** period, the outlaw was said to be *caput lupinum* ('bearing the wolf's head'), and it was lawful for any person to kill him, but by the 14th century only the **SHERIFF** could take his life. All of the outlaw's property was seized by the authorities. Outlawry was abolished in civil proceedings in 1879 and in criminal proceedings in 1938.

OWEN, DAVID ANTHONY LLEWELLYN (1938-). A cofounder of the short-lived **SOCIAL DEMOCRATIC PARTY (SDP)**, Owen was born in Plympton on 2 July 1938, the son of Dr John Owen (a general practitioner) and his wife, Mary. He was educated at Bradfield College, **CAMBRIDGE** University and St Thomas's Hospital (**LONDON**), graduating BA, MB, BChir. He held various appoint-ments at St Thomas's for two years from 1962 then became Neuro-logical and Psychiatric Registrar in 1964. He unsuccessfully cont-ested the **PARLIAMENT**ary **CONSTITU-ENCY** of Torrington for the **LABOUR PARTY** in 1964 but was elected for Plymouth Sutton in 1966. **PRIME MINISTER HAROLD WILSON** immediately made him **PARLIAMEN-TARY PRIVATE SECRETARY** at the Ministry of Defence and promoted him to **UNDER-SECRETARY OF STATE** in 1968. He was appointed **OPPOSITION** Spokesman on Defence in 1970 but resigned in 1972 as a protest against Labour's decision to turn its back on the **EUROPEAN COMMUNITY**.

When the Party returned to power in 1974, Owen accepted the post of Under-Secretary of State at the Department of Health and Social Security, becoming **MINISTER OF STATE** later in the year. **JAMES CALLAGHAN** moved him to the Foreign Office (again as Minister of State) in 1976 and made him Foreign Secretary (the youngest for over 40 years) in 1977. By then, however, it was evident that he was becoming increasingly at odds with Labour policies and particularly with the decision to allow Members of Parliament only ten per cent of the votes in elections for the Party Leadership. After the **CONSERVATIVE PARTY** victory at the 1979 **GENERAL ELECTION**, he served as Opposition Spokesman on Energy but left Labour in 1981 (along with Roy Jenkins, Bill Rodgers and Shirley

Williams) to found the Social Democratic Party, which aimed to capture the political middle ground.

He was Deputy Leader of the Party (1982-83) and Leader from 1983 until 1987, when he objected to the merger of the SDP and the **LIBERAL PARTY** as the **SOCIAL AND LIBERAL DEMOCRATIC PARTY (SLDP)** and resigned (taking a few colleagues with him). Opinion polls showed that his personal standing with the voters was high but his Party was humiliated in a **BY-ELECTION** at Bootle in May 1990, when the SDP polled only 155 votes (the Monster Raving Loony Party got 418) and in June it disbanded: with only 6,200 members it was too small to function properly. Owen decided not to fight as a candidate in the 1992 general election and was made Co-Chairman of the European Community's Peace Conference on Yugoslavia. On 20 January 1994, the European Parliament voted to dismiss him, partly because he had achieved nothing and partly because he wanted to divide Bosnia-Herzegovina on ethnic grounds even though it was a member of the United Nations. However, Prime Minister **JOHN MAJOR** and Hans van den Broek (the **EUROPEAN UNION**'s Foreign Policy Commissioner) both backed Owen publicly but he resigned in June 1995. Later that year, he was appointed executive director of Middlesex Holdings, a company with aluminium, oil and coal interests in the former Soviet Union.

OXFORD. Known internationally as a centre of **EDUCATION**, Oxford is situated at the confluence of the **RIVER THAMES** and the River Cherwell, 60 miles northwest of **LONDON**. It is first mentioned in documents as part of the estate of **EDWARD THE ELDER** in 912 but the development of the university appears to begin in the 12th century. The first colleges to be founded were University (in 1249) and Balliol (about 1263). From that period, a series of royal charters favoured the institution's growth and, by the 14th century, it effectively controlled the settlement, which functioned as a market town. **PARLIAMENT** met in Oxford in 1258 and 1641 and, during the **CIVIL WAR**, the town became the headquarters of King **CHARLES II** but otherwise it played little part in politics and experienced limited expansion until the 19th century, when printing and jam-making became major industries. In 1912, William Morris built his first car at Cowley, south-east of the town, and, in succeeding years, automobile manufacture and related trades provided much employment. Motor vehicles, pressed steel, publishing and the making of preserves turned Oxford into an industrial city with a historic core centred on the university. In addition, many tutorial colleges and language schools were established, trading on the city's reputation for educational excellence. In 1991, the population numbered 106,470. (See **OXFORD PARLIAMENT** [1258]; **OXFORD PARLIAMENT** [1641]; **OXFORD MOVEMENT**; **PROVISIONS OF OXFORD,** and, for location, Map 2, page xxvi).

OXFORD AND ASQUITH, EARL OF. (See **HENRY HERBERT ASQUITH**).

OXFORD PARLIAMENT, 1258. King **HENRY III** was forced to call this **PARLIAMENT** to secure finances during a period when the Barons were reluctant to accede to his demands and growing stronger in opposition to the **CROWN**. The King received his money in return for an acceptance of some reform in the **PROVISIONS OF OXFORD**.

OXFORD PARLIAMENT, 1641. The last **PARLIAMENT** of King **CHARLES I** was called in **OXFORD** to debate the succession to the throne and the position of James, **DUKE OF YORK**. It failed to agree and was dissolved by the King, who called it a "mongrel Parliament".

—P—

PACIFICO, DAVID (1784-1854). The catalyst in the Don Pacifico Incident, which nearly ended the political career of **VISCOUNT PALMERSTON**, Pacifico was a Jew born in Gibraltar and, therefore, a British subject even though his parents were Portuguese. In 1847, his Athens home was burned down during anti-Semitic disturbances which the police did nothing to quell. He claimed compensation from the Greek Government, citing both the loss of goods and the destruction of records of money owed to him. These claims were disputed because Pacifico had a shady reputation and was believed to have exaggerated the sums involved but Palmerston, the British Foreign Secretary, took advantage of the opportunity to put pressure on a foreign administration markedly less liberal than he would have liked. Although Britain had a joint agreement with Russia and France over the protection of Greece, he acted unilaterally, seizing Greek vessels and ordering the

ROYAL NAVY to blockade the port of Piraeus. As a result, although the Greeks paid only a small portion of Pacifico's claim relating to the loss of his records they were forced to meet the full demand resulting from the damage to goods. Palmerston's intervention, condemned both at home and abroad, resulted in his censure by the **HOUSE OF LORDS**. In the **HOUSE OF COMMONS**, however, he survived a similar motion with a majority of 46 after an eloquent speech in which he argued that, as a result of his show of strength, "a British subject, in whatever land he may be, shall feel confident that the watchful eye and the strong arm of **ENGLAND** will protect him against injustice and wrong". Eventually, Palmerston recovered from the criticism and, in 1855, became **PRIME MINISTER**. Pacifico moved from Athens to **LONDON** and died there on 12 April 1854.

PALAEOLITHIC. The period of **PREHISTORIC BRITAIN** sometimes called the Old Stone Age gets its name from the Greek words *palaios* (meaning 'old') and *lithos* (meaning 'stone'). During this time (c. 500,000 BC to c. 10,000 BC), Britain was joined to mainland Europe, allowing migration on foot, and the climate fluctuated between arctic conditions (during which much of the country was glaciated) and relative warmth. The earliest settlers, perhaps as early as 500,000 BC, would have been Homo Erectus hunters and gatherers, who used simple stone implements known as palaeoliths. They probably settled in **EAST ANGLIA**, where they may have hunted rhinoceros and elephant. Their settlements in **KENT**, as at Swanscombe, show wide-spread use of flint tools. These people were followed, probably around 225,000 BC, by Homo Neanderthalensis, who found refuge in places such as Cheddar Gorge in Somerset. Homo Sapiens arrived at the end of the period, between about 34,000 and 12,000 BC, when a warmer climate and lusher vegetation developed. These groups obtained their food by using hafted stone weapons, traps and fishing equipment. A Late Palaeolithic site at Newark in Nottinghamshire, dated at 12,000 BC to 11,000 BC and covering eight acres, has shown that extensive communities of people, living in tents or huts, existed in this period and that the image of Early Stone Age peoples dwelling in caves is probably derived from Victorian misconceptions.

PALMERSTON, VISCOUNT. (See **HENRY JOHN TEMPLE**).

PANKHURST, EMMELINE (1858-1928). A militant advocate of women's suffrage, Emmeline Pankhurst was born in **MANCHESTER** on 14 July 1858, the third of 11 children born to calico printer Robert Goulden and his wife, Sophia. She was educated at private schools in Manchester and Paris then, in 1879, married Richard Marsden, a radical barrister who drafted the Married Women's Property Acts of 1870 and 1882 (see **ACT OF PARLIAMENT**). Both resigned from the **LIBERAL PARTY** in 1884, when **WILLIAM GLADSTONE** refused to include measures giving women the right to vote in his Reform Bill.

After her husband's death in 1898, Emmeline had to raise her family of two sons and two daughters on her own, becoming registrar of births, marriages and deaths for Rusholme in order to earn an income. Five years later, despite the demands of work and young children, she formed the Women's Social and Political Union as a means of coordinating the activities of all those struggling to secure the female franchise. The organization first gained widespread publicity in 1905, when Emmeline's daughter (Christabel) and her friend (Annie Kenney) were ejected from a Liberal Party meeting because they heckled the speaker (Sir Edward Grey) with demands for votes for women. Outside the hall, they became involved in a fracas and were arrested on a charge of assaulting the police. Both refused to pay their fines and were sent to prison — Christabel for seven days, Annie for three. The incident attracted considerable press coverage and convinced Mrs Pankhurst of the value of publicity, so, in 1906, she moved to **LONDON** in order to devote more of her time to the campaign.

Believing that the Liberals were the great obstacle to women's suffrage, she and her supporters interrupted their meetings, stood against them at **PARLIAMENT**ary elections, organized demonstrations, broke windows, set fire to railway stations and chained themselves to railings in order to keep their cause in the public eye. In 1908, she was sent to prison for three months after being found guilty of encouraging fellow campaigners to disrupt the **HOUSE OF COMMONS**. In 1912, she was back, this time on a charge of conspiracy, but was released after she went on a hunger strike. One of the results of that action was the introduction of the Prisoner (Temporary Discharge for Ill-Health) Act of 1913 (the **CAT AND MOUSE ACT**), which allowed courts to release wrongdoers who refused to eat then re-arrest them when they had regained their health. Mrs Pankhurst and her followers suffered because of that act on many occasions. Shortly after it became law, she was convicted on a charge of incitement to violence and sent to Holloway Prison. She refused meals, rejected liquids and deprived herself of sleep so her condition quickly became serious. At that point she was released but, when she had recovered, she was returned to gaol. Over the next year, she was released and re-arrested 12 times, serving a total of 30 days of her sentence.

At the outbreak of the **FIRST WORLD WAR** in 1914, Mrs Pankhurst stopped her activities, and the **GOVERNMENT** released all prisoners held for **SUFFRAGETTE** offences. Four years later, some of her demands were met in the form of the Representation of the People Act (1918), which gave limited voting rights to women, and, in 1919, she left for Canada, where she worked as a speaker on the need for hygiene and child welfare. On her return to Britain in 1926, she was chosen to represent the **CONSERVATIVE PARTY** at an election in Whitechapel but died in London on 14 June 1928 before she had an opportunity to contest the seat. A month later, Parliament passed the Representation of the People Act (1928), which gave women the same voting rights as men.

PARIS, TREATY OF. There were seven treaties of Paris.

In 1259, a treaty was signed by King **HENRY III** and Louis IX of France whereby Henry renounced his claim to territories in France (with the exception of Gascony and Aquitaine), thus effectively ending the European **ANGEVIN** Empire.

In 1303, King **EDWARD I** and Philip IV of France agreed a Treaty which allowed **ENGLAND** to regain its French territories and which betrothed Edward's son (the future **EDWARD II**) to Philip's daughter.

A Treaty in 1763 ended the **SEVEN YEARS WAR** and defined British and French colonial jurisdictions, with Britain gaining much of Canada, Florida, Minorca and some Caribbean islands. This agreement established the primacy of Britain as the major colonial power in North America.

In 1783, the **AMERICAN WAR OF INDEPENDENCE** ended with a Treaty under which Britain recognized the independence of the United States and its boundaries (including the Mississippi River in the west). East and West Florida were ceded to Spain but Canada remained under British sovereignty.

The 1814 Treaty is sometimes called the Peace of Paris and followed the abdication of Napoleon Bonaparte. It set the boundaries of France, with Britain returning some territories taken during the **NAPOLEONIC WARS**.

The Treaty of <u>1815</u>, which followed the **BATTLE OF WATERLOO** and Napoleon's final defeat, is often known as the Second Peace of Paris. It excluded Napoleon's son from succeeding to the dukedom of his mother's Italian possessions.

In <u>1856</u>, a treaty (also confusingly called the Peace of Paris) ended the **CRIMEAN WAR**. Russian influence was contained (see **EASTERN QUESTION**) by Britain guaranteeing the boundaries of Turkey.

PARISH. As a unit of **LOCAL GOVERNMENT**, the parish evolved from 7th century administrative areas around some churches (monastic communities centred on these churches were entitled to receive dues from the farmers in the areas). It later became more widespread and coterminous with settlements, the inhabitants of which paid **TITHE**s (or tenths) of their produce for its upkeep and that of its vicar or priest. The parish formally became a unit of government in the 16th century. Since the reorganization of local government from 1973 to 1975, councils with jurisdiction in rural areas known as civil parishes have had responsibility for the provision of recreational facilities, community infrastructure and footpaths. There are over 7,000 of these parish councils. The older ecclesiastical parish is now an areal unit in the Anglican Church organized by a vicar or priest and part of a larger **DIOCESE**.

PARLIAMENT. The word 'Parliament' is derived from the **NORMAN** French *parler* meaning 'to talk'. The institution emerged from the **CURIA REGIS** and was first called in the 13th century to give counsel and advice to the **MONARCH**. Members were drawn from the powerful Lords and meetings usually involved attempts by the **CROWN** to secure funds (normally taxes) for military operations. It now comprises two Houses, or chambers, (plus the Monarch) which together constitute the legislative branch of **GOVERNMENT**, making law through **ACT**s **OF PARLIAMENT**. The upper chamber is the **HOUSE OF LORDS** and the lower chamber is the **HOUSE OF COMMONS**.

Parliament has unlimited power and decides its own proceedings. Members are elected at **GENERAL ELECTIONS** and **BY-ELECTIONS** under the **PARLIAMENT ACT** (1911) for a maximum period of five years. Strictly, the term 'Parliament' refers to 'The Queen in Parliament' and includes the Monarch and the two Houses of Parliament while the term 'government' refers to the majority political party and **MINISTER**s acting as the executive. The shortest Parliament was that at **WESTMINSTER** which lasted just one day in 1306 (30 May) while the lengthiest was the **LONG PARLIAMENT** between 3 September 1640 and 16 March 1660. The longest sitting of the **HOUSE OF COMMONS** was 41.5 hours from January 31 to February 2 1881, when it debated measures relating to the protection of people and property in **IRELAND**. (See **BILL OF RIGHTS; MAGNA CARTA; PETITION OF RIGHT**).

PARLIAMENT ACT, 1911. The **HOUSE OF LORDS** rejected the **BUDGET**s of the **LIBERAL PARTY GOVERNMENT** in 1909 and was forced, on threat of the creation of sufficient Liberal peers (see **PEERAGE**) to secure its passage, to accept an Act (see **ACT OF PARLIAMENT**) which would curtail its own powers. From that time, the House of Lords has been able to delay legislation by only one month in the case of Finance **BILLS** and two years in the case of all other Public Bills. The Act also reduced the term of a **PARLIAMENT** from seven to five years (the Triennial Acts of 1641–94 had fixed it at three years and the Septennial Act of 1716 had changed that to seven years). The measure led to the supremacy of the elected **HOUSE OF COMMONS** in Parliament. (See **HERBERT ASQUITH; GEORGE V**).

PARLIAMENTARIANS. The supporters of the Parliamentary faction in the **CIVIL WAR** (often known as **ROUNDHEADS**) opposed attempts by King **CHARLES I** to maintain and enhance the traditional powers and rights of the sovereign.

PARLIAMENTARY PRIVATE SECRETARY. Individual **MINISTER**s choose **BACKBENCHER** Members of **PARLIAMENT** from their own party to assist them in their duties. These Parliamentary Private Secretaries receive no payment for their work and are not formally part of **GOVERNMENT**. However, the post is seen as a stepping stone to greater responsibility.

PARLIAMENTARY PRIVILEGE. The **HOUSE OF COMMONS** and the **HOUSE OF LORDS** both have special privileges which allow them to carry out their work properly. The most critical of these are the rights to undertake enquiries into matters of public concern, make witnesses attend those enquiries and produce whatever documents are needed, regulate

PARLIAMENTary business free from interference by the courts, publish papers without being subject to action for defamation and punish members found guilty of a breach of privilege. The privileges accorded to individual Members of Parliament have been reduced over the years and now amount largely to freedom of speech in the debating chambers and committee rooms, exemption from jury service and the right to disobey subpoenas. In practice, many aspects of Parliamentary privilege are unclear so each House has a Committee of Privileges to help clarify individual situations.

PARLIAMENTARY REFORM. Before 1832, the geographical pattern of PARLIAMENTary CONSTITUENCIES did not reflect the reality of population distribution, with large towns such as MANCHESTER and BIRMINGHAM having no Members of Parliament, a concentration of the franchise in the hands of the landed classes and few voting rights for the growing industrial masses. The period from 1832 to 1885 brought major changes. Reform was demanded by the self-made industrialists, merchants and financiers and, increasingly, by the working men in the factories and mills. The traditional landowning establishment opposed erosion of its power and unrest grew in the 1820s as a result (see CHARTISM).

A series of ACTS OF PARLIAMENT gradually followed to redress the balance.

The Catholic Emancipation Act (1829) weakened the TORIES' opposition to reform at a time when the economy was in a downturn, JEREMY BENTHAM was extolling his views on "philosophic radicalism" for intellectuals and revolutions in Europe were showing what could happen to the establishment if concessions were not made.

The 1832 Reform Act abolished 56 ROTTEN BOROUGHS (also known as pocket BOROUGHs, these settlements either had negligible populations or were in the patronage of one man). The legislation created 34 new COUNTY seats, added 42 in the new industrial centres and widened the franchise to householders and freeholders of larger properties. This Act helped to create a middle class power base, increased the electorate by 40 per cent and led the way to more radical change.

By the 1860s, reform was again a political issue. The growing industrial working classes were still voteless, the TRADE UNIONS were agitating for reform, the US Civil War was seen as a symbol of the trend towards equal rights and a visit by Guiseppe Garibaldi (champion of liberal reform and hero of unification in Italy) led to the formation of the Reform League in 1865.

The 1867 Reform Act created more urban seats and extended the franchise in the boroughs to all ratepayers and lodgers paying a rent of £10 per annum, creating an electorate of 2.5 milion people.

The Reform and Redistribution Acts of 1884 and 1885 greatly increased borough representation in **LONDON** and created more seats elsewhere.

The Representation of the People Act of 1884 widened the franchise in urban and county areas to householders paying rates (property taxes), lodgers occupying property with an annual rent in excess of £10 and others with land worth £10 per year. By 1885, the UK electorate numbered 5.6 million people.

In 1928, a further Representation of the People Act gave women the same voting rights as men (see **EMMELINE PANKHURST, SUFFRAGETTES**).

PARLIAMENTARY SECRETARY. This **GOVERNMENT** post is the most senior rank below the Head at the **LORD CHANCEL-LOR**'s office, the Ministry of Agriculture and the Office of Public Service and Science.

PARLIAMENTARY UNDER-SECRETARY OF STATE This is the most junior of positions in **GOVERNMENT** departments. The duties of the holder are allocated by the appropriate **SECRETARY OF STATE.**

PARR, CATHERINE (1512-48). The daughter of Sir Thomas Parr and Lady Parr, Catherine was the sixth and last of **HENRY VIII**'s wives. She had two husbands — Edward Borough (who died c. 1529) and Lord Latimer (who died in 1542 or 1543) — before she married Henry on 12 July 1543. During the last year's of the King's reign, she provided a stabilising and gentle influence, ensuring that his children — Edward (later **EDWARD VI**), Mary (later **MARY I**) and Elizabeth (later **ELIZABETH I**) — were properly educated, and attempting to limit religious persecution in **ENGLAND**. While Henry was fighting in France in 1544, she acted as **REGENT**. After the King's death in 1547, she married Lord Seymour of Sudeley but died on 7 September 1548, a week after giving birth to a daughter.

PASSCHENDAELE, BATTLE OF. (See **BATTLE OF YPRES**).

PAX BRITANNICA. This term was first used by **JOSEPH CHAMBERLAIN** in the 19th century to mean the peace ('pax' in Latin) imposed on the world by the **BRITISH EMPIRE**, which was considered so vast that the sun never set on its colonies. It is considered most apposite to the period from 1815 until 1914, during which time Britain maintained global supremacy and world power status.

PAYMASTER GENERAL. This **GOVERNMENT** post is junior to that of **FINANCIAL SECRETARY TO THE TREASURY**. In **JOHN MAJOR**'s administrations, the holder has been responsible for matters relating to Customs and Excise and to the **EUROPEAN UNION** budget.

PEASANTS' REVOLT, 1381. General unrest stemming from economic and social conditions (and particularly a sequence of poor harvests after the **BLACK DEATH** and the **POLL TAX**) led to a series of uprisings by agricultural labourers and artisans. Widespread attacks on landed **GENTRY**, clergy and tax- collectors occurred, with demands for the ending of **VILLEIN**age and the **POLL TAX**. The best known incident is that involving Wat Tyler, who sacked Rochester Castle in **KENT** and marched on **LONDON**, joined by an Essex band led by Jack Straw. The **TOWER OF LONDON** was occupied and the Chancellor and **ARCHBISHOP OF CANTERBURY** executed. King **RICHARD II** regained control by promising to meet the demands of a petition received at Mile End on 14 June but, nine days later, he changed his mind, declaring, "Villeins ye are and villeins ye shall remain". The **LORD MAYOR** of London had his men attack the peasants and killed Tyler at Smithfield although the King had promised the rebels that there would be no reprisals. The event was the first large-scale public protest recorded in **ENGLAND**.

PEEL, ROBERT (1788-1850). **CONSERVATIVE PARTY PRIME MINISTER** for five months in 1834-35 and from 1841 until 1846, Peel was a major figure in British politics during the first half of the 19th century, steering his country through the ferment of social and economic change which accompanied the **INDUSTRIAL REVOLUTION**. He was born in Bury on 5 February 1788, the first son of Sir Robert Peel, a wealthy manufacturer of cotton goods (see **COTTON INDUSTRY**). Young Robert was educated at Harrow School and **OXFORD** University (where he demonstrated his intellectual abilities by becoming the first person to get a double first in mathematics and classics). He entered **PARLIAMENT** in 1809, representing the Irish seat of Cashel, and allied himself with the **TORIES**. In 1810, he was made **UNDER-SECRETARY OF STATE** for War and the Colonies by **SPENCER PERCEVAL** and, two years later, moved to the difficult post of Chief Secretary for **IRELAND**, distinguishing himself as an effective and efficient administrator. In an attempt to control crime, he introduced legislation which established the Royal Irish Constabulary (colloquially known as the Peelers) and, in 1817, reduced the effects of the potato famine by arranging a system of food distribution. Also in 1817, he nailed his colours to the mast in a speech opposing measures which would have allowed Roman Catholics to become Members of Parliament.

In 1818, Peel left Ireland and, in 1819, was given the task of chairing the committee which was to return Britain's financial base to the **GOLD STANDARD**, a move which, his opponents argued, contributed to the economic woes of the 1820s. In 1820, he married Julia, daughter of General Sir John Floyd, built a **LONDON** house and began to acquire a series of Dutch, Flemish and English paintings which was to become one of the most notable private collections in the country. Two years later, he accepted the post of **HOME SECRETARY** under the **EARL OF LIVERPOOL** and was faced with the task of redrafting the criminal justice code. Much of that simply involved the repeal of obsolete legislation but it was also necessary to reduce the complexities of the court system and introduce new measures to meet new circumstances. One of his most novel proposals, effected by means of the Metropolitan **POLICE** Act (see **ACT OF PARLIAMENT**), was the formation of a police force for the whole of London, with the exception of the **CITY OF LONDON** (the police officers quickly became known as 'bobbies' after their founder).

In 1827, when **GEORGE CANNING** (who favoured Catholic emancipation) became Prime Minister, Peel (still adamantly opposed) resigned but returned to office the following year in the **DUKE OF WELLINGTON**'s administration, accepting the posts of Home Secretary and **LEADER OF THE HOUSE OF COMMONS**. In May 1828, the House voted in favour of a motion supporting concessions to Catholics and Peel tendered his resignation. Persuaded by Wellington to stay on, he introduced the Emancipation **BILL** to the **HOUSE OF COMMONS** but, inevitably, was accused of being a turncoat. He regained some of his former prestige during the 1833 and 1834 Parlia-ments, in which he acted as a force for moderation during the period following the reforms introduced by **EARL GREY**, and, when **VISCOUNT MEL-BOURNE**'s **GOVERNMENT** was dismissed by **WILLIAM IV** in November 1834, he was called on to form an administration. His situation was always precarious, however, because he could not be sure of a Parliamentary majority, and, in April 1835, he re-signed after a defeat at the hands of an **OPPOSITION** coalition.

During the next six years, he worked assiduously to build more solid support but, in 1839, declined an invitation from Queen **VICTORIA** to become Prime Minister because she would not replace her **WHIG** Ladies of the Bedchamber with attendants more to his political liking (see **BEDCHAMBER CRISIS**). The 1841 **GENERAL ELECTION** gave him a working majority in the Commons and this time he accepted the post, forming an administration which included six men who had been, or would become, Prime Ministers. Their poli-cies included establishment of peace abroad, encouragement to industry and commerce, an improvement in the living condi-tions of the working classes and a less volatile financial sys-tem. These were to be achieved by revision of the banking laws, the use of income tax to increase revenue, the reduction of import duties and a more conciliatory approach towards France and the United States (with both of whom relations had been strained). In the east of North America, the disputed boundary between Maine and New Brunswick was settled in 1842 and, in the west, the extension of the 49th parallel to the Pacific Ocean (with a deviation which incorporated Vancouver Island into Canada) was agreed in 1846. The **CORN LAWS**, repealed in 1846, brought cheaper food to industrial workers in the cities.

These programmes, however, made Peel many enemies and, in the end, split his party. On June 25 1846, the Govern-ment was defeated on an Irish Bill by a coalition of Whigs and others. Peel resigned four days later and, though he continued his political activities, never held office again. He died in Lon-don on 2 July 1850 as a result of injuries received when thrown from his horse. An intellectual with a flair for administration, he has been regarded by many scholars as the outstanding Par-liamentarian of his age. (See **TAMWORTH MANIFESTO**).

PEERAGE. Membership of the peerage, the highest social rank below the **CROWN**, is conferred by the **MONARCH** (usually on the advice of the **PRIME MINISTER**). All peers have the right to sit in the **HOUSE OF LORDS** and are barred from membership of the **HOUSE OF COMMONS** under the terms of the 1963 Peerage Act (see **ACT OF PARLIAMENT**). However, they may renounce their title and, having done so, can seek election as Members of **PARLIAMENT** (in 1963, **ALEXANDER DOUGLAS-HOME** took that step in order to succeed **HAROLD MACMILLAN** as Prime Minister). In descending order of precedence, the titles in the peerage are: **DUKE**/Duchess, **MARQUESS** (or **MARQUIS**)/Marchioness, **EARL**/Countess, **VISCOUNT**/Viscountess and **BARON**/Baroness. The spiritual peerage consists of the Archbishops and Bishops of the **CHURCH OF ENGLAND**. Traditionally, the right to a nonspiritual title passes to the eldest male descendant of the holder, but, since 1958, life peerages have been awarded to individuals who have rendered political or other service to the country; these honours cannot be inherited. The term *peer* comes from the Latin *pares* (meaning 'equal'), and peers have the right to be tried for misdemeanours by their fellow peers.

PELHAM, HENRY (1696-1754). **PRIME MINISTER** from 1743 until 1754, Pelham was the son of Thomas, Lord Pelham, and Lady Grace Holles, his second wife. He was educated at **WESTMINSTER** School and **OXFORD** University then served in the army for a short time before being elected Member of **PARLIAMENT** (MP) for Seaford in 1717. Five years later, he was reelected as the MP for Sussex, a **CONSTITUENCY** which he represented until his death. He was a staunch supporter of the **WHIG** policies of **ROBERT WALPOLE** and was rewarded in 1721 with the post of Lord of the **TREASURY**. In 1724, he became Secretary of War and, in 1730, was appointed Paymaster to the Forces. In 1743, he became Prime Minister and **CHANCELLOR OF THE EXCHEQUER**, heading an administration which was to survive under his leadership for 11 years. In many ways, the success of Pelham's ministry was a result of the diplomatic skills of his older brother **THOMAS PELHAM HOLLES**, Duke of Newcastle (although the two were frequently at loggerheads). The political unity enabled him to oust particular favourites of **GEORGE II** including, in 1744, John Carteret, Earl Granville, who wanted a more aggressive approach to the **WAR OF THE**

AUSTRIAN SUCCESSION. Two years later, the entire **CABINET** resigned (the first time such an event had happened) in an attempt to force the King to accept the appointment of people such as **WILLIAM PITT THE ELDER**, whom he disliked. Pelham's principal administrative contributions to his country's development lay in his attempts to reduce the national debt. He died in **LONDON** on 6 March 1754.

PENAL LAWS. This general term is applied to legislation designed to suppress **RECUSANT** activities from about 1570 to the 18th century until repealed under the **TOLERATION ACTS**.

PENINSULAR WAR, 1808-1814. Portugal's support of Britain when Napoleon Bonaparte imposed his **CONTINENTAL SYSTEM** of trade embargoes led to the invasion of that country by the French in 1807 (see **NAPOLEONIC WARS**). The following year Spain, too, was taken. Under the terms of the **TREATY OF LONDON** (1373), Britain went to Portugal's aid. The struggle between France and Britain to control the Iberian Peninsula led **SIR ARTHUR WELLESLEY** (later the **DUKE** of Wellington) to a victory at Vineiro (21 August 1808) which heralded the start of a campaign to drive France from the region, an aim which was achieved by the spring of 1814. The six year war was called "the Spanish ulcer" by Napoleon, who saw his resources drained away by the constant fighting. (See **BATTLE OF TOULOUSE**).

PENNINES, THE. These hills form the backbone of **ENGLAND**, stretching from the Scottish border south to Derbyshire and determining the course of many major rivers. The rocks date from the Carboniferous period and form an anticline, which has been dissected by river action into a series of ranges. The rolling uplands reach a maximum height of just under 3,000 feet and are largely treeless sheep pasture, heather moor and peat bog, forming an open landscape characterized by stone-walled fields on the lower slopes. The streams and rivers, which flow from the hills, provided the power for textile mills in the early days of the **INDUSTRIAL REVOLUTION**, with the west specializing in the **COTTON INDUSTRY** and the east in the **WOOL INDUSTRY**. Also, with increasing demands for **COAL**, mines and pits were established along both flanks of the Pennines and several large towns developed, including **MANCHESTER**, Sheffield, Leeds and Bradford. The hills themselves, however, remained largely unpopulated and, increasingly, became a recreational resource for people escaping from the built-up areas. Parts of the area are incorporated in the Northumberland, Peak District and Yorkshire Dales **NATIONAL PARKS**. (For location, see Map1, page xxv).

PENNY POST. A national postal service was introduced by Sir Rowland Hill in 1840. The **POST OFFICE** had, until then, operated a system based on the weight of the letter or the parcel and the distance travelled, causing considerable administrative work for its staff and often exorbitant costs for the consumer. The new charge was one penny for one half-ounce letter, prepaid by the sender through the purchase of an adhesive stamp, which bore the head of Queen **VICTORIA** and became known as the Penny Black. There was no increase in price until 1918. The innovation led to great improvements in both the organization and the profitability of the Post Office. In 1838 around 75 million letters were posted; in 1864 about 642 million.

PENRUDDOCK'S RISING, March 1655. Colonel John Penruddock led a revolt of **ROYALISTS** against the **PROTECTORATE**, capitalizing on general unrest in the army. With a force of only 200 men, he took Salisbury (Wiltshire) but found little local support and was pursued into Dorset by a **PARLIAMENTARIAN** force. The rebels were quickly defeated and the leaders executed or transported. (See **TRANSPORTATION**).

PERCEVAL, SPENCER (1762-1812). **PRIME MINISTER** from 1809 until 1812, Spencer was born in **LONDON** on 1 November 1762, the second son of John Perceval, **EARL** of Egmont. He was educated at Harrow School and **CAMBRIDGE** University, called to the bar in 1786 and appointed King's Counsel in 1796. Also in 1796, he entered the **HOUSE OF COMMONS** as Member of **PARLIAMENT** for Northampton, supporting the Tory administration of **WILLIAM PITT THE YOUNGER** (see **TORIES**). In 1801, when **HENRY ADDINGTON** became Prime Minister, Perceval accepted the post of **SOLICITOR GENERAL**. The following year, he was appointed **ATTORNEY GENERAL**, a role which he maintained until Pitt's death in 1806. In 1807, when **GEORGE III** dismissed **LORD WILLIAM WYNDHAM GRENVILLE**'s administration and made **WILLIAM BENTINCK**, Duke of Portland, Prime Minister,

Perceval became **CHANCELLOR OF THE EXCHEQUER** and **CHANCELLOR OF THE DUCHY OF LANCASTER** In September 1809, when Portland resigned because of ill-health and dissension within his administration, Perceval replaced him. Although scholars have often him considered him ineffective, he vigorously pursued the **NAPOLEONIC WARS** despite deep divisions within his **CABINET** and rigorously suppressed the civil unrest which stemmed from the difficult economic circumstances of the early 19th century (see **LUDDITES**). On 11 May 1812, he was shot dead in the lobby of the House of Commons by John Bellingham, a bankrupt who had several times unsuccessfully petitioned him for help. Bellingham was declared insane but, even so, was hanged for his crime on 18 May.

PERCY, HENRY (1364-1403). The son of Henry, Earl of Northumberland, Percy was a powerful political force during the later 14th century. From 1384, he was Warden of the March, defending **ENGLAND** against invasion by the Scots and earning the nickname 'Hotspur' for the zeal with which he carried out his duties. In 1399, he joined Henry of Lancaster (later **HENRY IV**) in his successful campaign for the throne and, in 1401, led the royal army sent to subdue the Welsh. In 1402, he defeated Scots troops under the Earl of Douglas at Homildon Hill but the victory marked the opening of a rift with the King, who refused him permission to keep Douglas as his personal prisoner. That rebuff, coupled with the lack of reimbursement for the expenses incurred in subduing the insurrection in **WALES**, led the Percys to rebellion. The armies met at the **BATTLE OF SHREWSBURY** on 21 July 1403, Hotspur was killed and the rebellion crushed. (See **BATTLE OF OTTERBURN**).

PERSIAN WAR, 1856-57. Britain responded to Persian incursion into Afghanistan by declaring war on 1 November 1856 in order to protect its imperial interests in India. The fighting ended when the Shah of Persia agreed to withdraw.

PETERLOO MASSACRE, 16 August 1819. A peaceful crowd of between 50,000 and 80,000 people who had gathered to hear Orator (Henry) Hunt speak for **PARLIAMENTARY REFORM** at St Peter's Fields in **MANCHESTER** was broken up by panicking, sabre-wielding troops sent by local magistrates, who feared trouble during this hot summer of fear and disorder (see **ANTI-**

CORN LAW LEAGUE, LUDDITES). Eleven people were killed and over 400 injured. The term "Peterloo" is a derogatory reference to the **BATTLE OF WATERLOO** and reflects the popular view that the incident was an example of **GOVERNMENT** repression of a defenceless people at a time of very real establishment fear of revolutionary uprising. This was one of the most famous events at which there was a reading of the **RIOT ACT** to disperse a gathering. (See **SIX ACTS; SPA FIELDS RIOT**).

PETITIONERS. The supporters of the **COUNTRY PARTY** organized petitions in an attempt to force King **CHARLES II** to call a Parliament. These **WHIGS** were thus called Petitioners and those **TORIES** who were said to abhor this action were called **ABHORRERS**.

PETITION OF RIGHT, 1628. In April 1628, **PARLIAMENT** presented King **CHARLES I** with a statement of its own rights and liberties and those of English citizens (including protection from billeting of soldiers without consent, a practice which had become vexatious). It was drawn up by Sir Edward Coke and included declarations that Parliament alone had the right to levy taxes and that individuals could only be committed to prison after a proper court hearing, assertions which challenged the view that the **MONARCH** could rule as he or she wished (see **DIVINE RIGHT OF KINGS**). The King agreed on 7 June because he needed money from Parliament but when an attempt was made to enforce the provisions the following year he responded by dissolving the legislature. The petition was an important element in the development of the **BRITISH CONSTITUTION**.

PHILIP, PRINCE (1921-). The consort of Queen **ELIZABETH II**, Philip was born at Mon Repos (Corfu) on 10 June 1921, the son of Prince Andrew of Greece and Denmark and Princess Alice (granddaughter of Queen **VICTORIA**). At that time, the Greek Royal Family was in exile so Philip was educated at Cheam, Baden (Germany), Gordonstoun and the Royal Naval College Dartmouth. During the **SECOND WORLD WAR**, he served with the Mediterranean Fleet and with the British Pacific Fleet, taking part in the action at Cape Matapan (1941) and the landings on Sicily (1943). On 28 February 1947, he became a British citizen, renounced his claim to the Greek and Danish thrones and adopted his mother's surname of Mount-batten. (His father's surname was Schleswig-Holstein-Sonderburg-Glucksburg.) On the eve of his marriage to Princess Elizabeth on 20 November of the same year, he was designated a Royal Highness, created a Knight of the Garter (see **ORDER OF THE GARTER**) and given the titles of Baron Greenwich, Earl of Merioneth and Duke of Edinburgh.

Philip continued on active service with the **ROYAL NAVY**, commanding the frigate *Magpie*, until Elizabeth's accession to the throne on 6 February 1952. Since then, he has shared many of the Queen's official engagements and has carried out his own schedule of public duties. In 1957, he was accorded the dignity and style of a Prince of the Realm. Well known for his outspoken views (he once told the British people, at a time of recession, to take their collective finger out), he supports many charities and is a keen environmentalist. In 1956, he founded the Duke of Edinburgh's Award Scheme, which encourages community service and the development of skills and a sense of adventure in young people. It now operates in over 40 countries. The Duke and the Queen have four children — **PRINCE CHARLES** (born on 14 November 1948); **PRINCESS ANNE** (15 August 1950), **PRINCE ANDREW** (19 February 1960); and **PRINCE EDWARD** (10 March 1964).

PHILLIPS, MARK ANTONY PETER (1948-). The first husband of **PRINCESS ANNE**, Mark was born in Tetbury on 22 September 1948, the only son of Major Peter Phillips and Anne Phillips. He was educated at Marlborough College and the Royal Military Academy Sandhurst then, in 1969, joined the 1st Queen's Dragoon Guards, with whom he was on regimental duty until 1974, when he returned to Sandhurst as a Company Instructor. In 1977 and 1978, he was a member of the Ministry of Defence's Army Training Directorate. Between 1970 and 1976, Phillips was a regular member of the British equestrian team and won a gold medal at the 1972 Olympic Games in Munich. He also gained a silver medal at the 1988 Games in Seoul. In addition, he was in the three-day event team which won the World Championships in 1970 and the European Championships in 1972. He won the Badminton three-day event in 1971, 1972, 1974 and 1981. Since 1988, he has been Managing Director of the Gleneagles Mark Phillips Equestrian Centre. He met Princess Anne through a common interest in equestrian sports and married her on 14 November 1973. The couple had two children — Peter Mark Andrew (born on 15

November 1977) and Zara Anne Elizabeth (born on 15 May 1981) — but separated in 1989 and were divorced in 1992. The tabloid press has since carried several stories of romantic links with other women, but he has not remarried.

PHONEY WAR. During the period from the declaration of war on Germany by Britain on 3 September 1939 until well into 1940, British troops moved to France, the French took positions behind their Maginot Line and the Germans strengthened defences behind their Siegfried Line. There were 110 Allied divisions in the front line but an almost complete lack of action and the British and French Governments seemed curiously lethargic in the face of German aggression. The armies often became bored, and, in the United Kingdom, some of the people evacuated from the large towns began to return home. In **LONDON**, practice air raids and restrictions on normal life became irritants to the population and enthusiasm for the war waned, with half of those who had joined the Auxiliary Fire Service resigning. The Phoney War ended when Germany invaded Scandinavia in April 1940 and France the following month. The first British serviceman was killed in December. (See **SECOND WORLD WAR**).

PILGRIMAGE OF GRACE, 1536-37. A series of Roman Catholic rebellions broke out in Lincolnshire and Yorkshire, protesting against **THOMAS CROMWELL,** his role in the reform of the Church in **ENGLAND** and particularly the **DISSOLUTION OF THE MONASTERIES,** agrarian change and taxes. The leader, Robert Aske, called for a pilgrimage to restore Christ's Church after the **REFORMATION** and a rebel force of 30,000 took **YORK**, but the violence was stopped when the **DUKE** of Norfolk promised concessions. These promises were never honoured and the insurrection was bloodily suppressed.

PILGRIM FATHERS. This group of **NONCONFORMISTS** chose exile in the New World in order to escape religious persecution and sailed from **ENGLAND** in 1620 aboard the *Mayflower* to found the colony of New Plymouth (Massachusetts). The 102 emigrants included 35 **PURITANS**, who had first gone to Holland and secured rights to develop a settlement which became known as Plimoth Plantation, gaining the financial backing of the **MERCHANTS ADVENTURERS** in return for an agreement on a seven-year monopoly trading right. The pioneers were known as

Old Comers by their contemporaries and as Forefathers by their successors. The term "Pilgrim Fathers" did not become common until the 1790s and gained currency from 1819, when a Pilgrim Society was formed as a means of honouring the original group.

PITT THE ELDER, WILLIAM (1708-78). One of the great 18th century British statesmen, Pitt was born in **LONDON** on 15 November 1708, the son of Robert Pitt and his wife, Harriet Villiers. The fourth child in a family of seven, he received his schooling at Eton College then moved to **OXFORD** University, which he left after one year (partly because of the persistent gout from which he suffered). He spent some time studying law at the University of Utrecht then, in 1731, was appointed Cornet in the King's Own Regiment of Horse. He entered the **HOUSE OF COMMONS** in 1735, representing Old Sarum, one of the most rotten of the **ROTTEN BOROUGHS**, and soon became a prominent member of the group opposed to **ROBERT WALPOLE** and the **WHIG GOVERNMENT**. (His maiden speech thoroughly annoyed Walpole, who retaliated by depriving him of his army commission.) The **PRINCE OF WALES** made him a Groom of the Bedchamber in 1737, and in **PARLIAMENT** he received support from the rising merchant class, whose interests he promoted. His talents for oratory were used to good effect, and he soon became known as 'The Great Commoner' because he frequently sought out public opinion before taking sides on an issue.

In February 1746, Pitt was appointed Joint Vice-Treasurer of **IRELAND** and, two months later, became Paymaster General of the Forces. His refusal to use these public offices for personal gain earned him an enduring reputation for honesty. He held the Paymaster post for nine years and left it still a relatively poor man, but a legacy of £10,000 from the Duchess of Marlborough put his finances on a firm footing: he bought South Lodge in Enfield and indulged in landscape gardening then, in 1754, married Hester Grenville, with whom he had an enormously happy home life.

The outbreak of the **SEVEN YEARS WAR** provided Pitt with a real opportunity to influence the course of history. He was the only politician to command the support of the nation and was called on by **GEORGE II** to lead the government. In 1757, he formed a ministry with his rival, **THOMAS HOLLES**, Duke of Newcastle, who had strong support in the House of Commons. Newcastle accepted the situation on the understanding that he controlled all the patronage and that Pitt was responsible for the conduct of the war, a division of labour which suited both men. Pitt reorganized the army and the navy, replacing old leaders with keen young officers. He made strenuous efforts to unite public opinion behind his policies and, rather than conduct a costly campaign on the continent, subsidized the armies of Frederick the Great of Prussia (Britain's main European ally) and focussed his own troops' attentions on French interests in North America and India. The result was that, under the terms of the **TREATY OF PARIS** in 1763, Britain became the chief power in both places, held Minorca as a Mediterranean base and gained territories in the West Indies and Africa.

Pitt's strategy had earned his country a greatly expanded empire but, before the war was over, he was forced into resignation. In 1760, **GEORGE III** became King. Determined to bring the conflict to an expeditious end and to restore the power of the **MONARCH**y, he began to undermine Pitt's authority. Pitt himself had made many enemies because he had concentrated the whole conduct of government in his own hands and had treated his colleagues with haughty aloofness. In 1761, he resigned when he failed to get approval to declare war on Spain and again became a leading member of **THE OPPOSITION** faction in the Commons. He attacked the terms of the Treaty of Paris as an inadequate recognition of Britain's worldwide success in the war and, in 1766, took the side of the American colonists on the "no taxation without representation" issue. In July 1766, the King asked Pitt to form a Government drawn from all sections of Parliament. He agreed but shortly afterwards accepted a peerage as Earl of Chatham and moved to the **HOUSE OF LORDS**. Without his control, the all-party ministry dissolved into factions and, in 1768, it fell. Pitt was becoming susceptible to fits of insanity, and, as a result, his influence declined. He appeared in the Lords on a few occasions over the next decade to plead for a more generous treatment of North America but spent most of his time in seclusion. He died at Hayes on 11 May 1778 and was buried in **WESTMINSTER** Abbey.

PITT THE YOUNGER, WILLIAM (1759-1806). **PRIME MINISTER** from 1783 until 1801 and from 1804 until 1806, Pitt was born at Hayes on 28 May 1759, the second son of **WILLIAM PITT THE ELDER**, Earl of Chatham, and his wife, Lady Hester Grenville. Because of his delicate health and his father's dislike of **PUBLIC SCHOOLS**, he was educated at home then, from the age of 14, studied at **CAMBRIDGE** University. He was an able undergraduate but, in 1776, ill health induced him to make use of the privilege which allowed the sons of noblemen to graduate without examination. He entered Lincoln's Inn and was called to the Bar in 1780 but, the following year, was elected to the **HOUSE OF COMMONS** as the Member of **PARLIAMENT** for Appleby. Joining the **TORIES** in **OPPOSITION** under the **EARL OF SHELBURNE**, he made his maiden speech on 26 February, supporting **EDMUND BURKE**'s reform proposals. In March 1782, when **FREDERICK NORTH**'s **GOVERNMENT** was on its last legs, he announced that he would not accept any subordinate appointment in the next administration and did, in fact, decline the post of Vice-Treasurer of **IRELAND** offered by **CHARLES WATSON-WENTWORTH**, Marquess of Rockingham, North's successor.

Following Rockingham's death in July 1782, Shelburne became Prime Minister and Pitt was made **CHANCELLOR OF THE EXCHEQUER** at the tender age of 23. On 24 February 1783, Shelburne resigned, defeated by a coalition led by North and **CHARLES FOX. GEORGE III** invited Pitt to form a government but, realizing that he would not command a majority in Parliament, he declined and the King had to capitulate to the coalition group. In December, however, the attempt by Fox and North to reform the **EAST INDIA COMPANY** was defeated in the **HOUSE OF LORDS** after the King had announced that anyone voting for the **BILL** (which had already been passed in the Commons) would be considered his enemy. George at once dismissed the coalition and, on 19 December, again offered Pitt the post of Prime Minister. This time, he accepted.

A liberal by inclination, Pitt had the support of the reform groups and, during the first years of his administration, worked hard to promote **FREE TRADE** (tariff duties were reduced and an agreement on freedom of commerce signed with France, for example). Also, a more equitable system of taxation was introduced and duties on imports lowered in order to limit smuggling. In 1785, he attempted to keep his pledge to reform the House of Commons but the move was heavily defeated and, from that time, he virtually abandoned the cause. Foreign policy centred on the colonies. A bill was introduced to establish greater Government reponsibility for the administration of the East India Company while adopting a noninterventionist approach to the affairs of the Indian Princes. Also, Quebec was divided into predominantly French and predominantly British provinces, with the French Canadians given the opportunity to preserve their own way of life. Alliances were made with Holland and Prussia and the support of the latter allowed Pitt to triumph over the Spanish in the Nootka Sound dispute when they attacked British vessels at Vancouver Island. The victory, political rather than military, effectively destroyed Spanish claims to a monopoly of trade and settlement on the western seaboard of North America and enabled Canada to expand to the Pacific.

By 1792, it was clear that war in Europe was becoming increasingly likely. The aristocracy feared the spread of revolutionary doctrines advocating democratic rule and watched French military aggression with dismay but Pitt clung to a policy of noninvolvement until France declared war on Britain and Holland in 1793. Stringent sedition laws were drafted, the writ of **HABEAS CORPUS** was suspended and labour unions were outlawed, significant blows to those favouring social reform. Rebellion in Ireland in 1798 added to the Prime Minister's problems and was quickly suppressed but it convinced Pitt that a legislative union of Britain and Ireland was necessary to ensure order. That was achieved in 1800 (see **UNION OF GREAT BRITAIN AND IRELAND**)but only because large scale corruption carried the measure through the Irish Parliament and promises were made that Roman Catholics would be allowed to hold public office. George III, however, refused to consider any form of Catholic emancipation, and, on 3 February 1801, Pitt resigned. He was succeeded by his friend, **HENRY ADDINGTON**, who made peace with France in 1802 but found himself at war again the following year.

On 25 April 1804, Addington withdrew and the King invited Pitt to take up the reins again. This second ministry was weaker than the first for the Addington faction went into Opposition and, despite Admiral **HORATIO NELSON**'s victory at the **BATTLE OF TRAFALGAR**, Pitt was dealt a serious blow when Napoleon's armies were victorious at Austerlitz. Moreover, his health — always a matter of concern — was deteriorating, and, by the winter of 1805, his friends were attempting to persuade him to resign in order to preserve his life. He died in Putney on 23 January the following year and was buried in **WESTMINSTER**. A motion for a grant of £40,000 to pay his debts was carried unanimously by Parliament.

PLACE ACTS. A series of **ACTS OF PARLIAMENT** in the 17th and 18th centuries was designed to remove **PLACEMEN** from **PARLIAMENT** and so curtail undue **CROWN** or **GOVERN-MENT** influence over the **HOUSE OF COMMONS.**

PLACEMEN. These Members of **PARLIAMENT** derived their seats from the operation of patronage in the 17th and 18th centuries. Some held offices of profit under the **CROWN**; others were given financial inducements to support the **GOVERNMENT.** The **PLACE ACTS** progressively removed them.

PLANNING, TOWN AND COUNTRY. The organization of the layout or design of buildings, the development of land and control of that development are relatively recent phenomena which grew from the attempts in the 19th century to deal with two particular problems created by the **INDUSTRIAL REVOLUTION** — poor urban housing conditions and low standards of public health. Urban management evolved incrementally through legislation and experiments, such as the **GARDEN CITIES** concept promoted by Ebenezer Howard. The 1909 Housing, Town Planning etc Act (see **ACT OF PARLIAMENT**) brought the intervention of **LOCAL GOVERNMENT** into supervision of land use. The Town and Country Planning Act of 1947 was a far-reaching socialist enactment which placed development under the control of public authorities and strictly regulated changes. In the post-**SECOND WORLD WAR** euphoria, such draconian legislation was accepted and, until deregulation in the 1980s and 1990s, gave the United Kingdom one of the most centralized planning systems in the world. (See **NATIONAL PARKS, NEW TOWNS**).

PLANTAGENETS, 1154-1485. Rulers of **ENGLAND** for over 300 years, the Plantagenets derived their name from the piece of the Broom plant (planta genista) that Geoffrey, Count of Anjou, wore in his cap. The dynasty consisted of three houses — Anjou (1154-1399), Lancaster (1399-1461) and York (1461-1485). It came to power with King **HENRY I** (Geoffrey was the husband of Matilda, Henry's daughter) and saw the imposition (by King **HENRY II**) of a court system to replace **TRIAL BY BATTLE**, the beginnings of democracy with the **MAGNA CARTA** and the development of printing by **WILLIAM CAXTON.** The dynasty was characterized by strife and dissension, particularly through the simmering dispute between the Yorkists and the Lancastrians (see **WARS OF THE ROSES**), the **HUNDRED YEARS WAR** and the loss of English territories in France. **RICHARD III** was the last of the line, dying at the **BATTLE OF BOSWORTH FIELD** in 1485. (See **EDWARD I-V; HENRY III-VI; JOHN; RICHARD I-II**).

PLANTATIONS OF IRELAND. During the 16th and 17th centuries, English and Scottish families settled in **IRELAND** as a result of attempts by the English Government to secure the area by transferring land from Irish ownership, Anglicizing the population and increasing the numbers of loyal subjects in the region (for example, the **CITY OF LONDON** sent colonists to newly named Londonderry and this settlement came to epitomise the hated process for the Irish, who, to this day, refer to it as Derry). The policy undoubtedly secured the area for English rule, but it also sowed the seeds of the longstanding Irish problem.

PLASSEY, BATTLE OF, 23 June 1757. Victory by **ROBERT CLIVE** secured Bengal for Britain and thus ensured British power in India. With a force of only 3,200 men, drawn mainly from the paramilitary **EAST INDIA COMPANY**, against a combined Bengali-French army of 50,000, he used bribery, corruption and naval supremacy on the rivers of the area to great effect. The action was regarded as a reprisal for the **BLACK HOLE OF CALCUTTA**.

PLUG RIOTS. After the rejection of the Chartist petition to **PARLIAMENT** in 1842 (see **CHARTISM**), strikers in the midlands and north of **ENGLAND** knocked out the plugs on the boilers of machines to immobilize them. The action was suppressed by the **GOVERNMENT**.

POCKET BOROUGHS. (See **ROTTEN BOROUGHS**).

POITIERS, BATTLE OF, 19 September 1356. **EDWARD, THE BLACK PRINCE**, with a force of 7,000 and using his English bowmen to good effect, crushingly defeated the French army (and captured its leader, King John II) in this battle fought during the **HUNDRED YEARS WAR**. In consequence, the French requested a truce which lasted for seven years.

POLICE. Before the 18th century, the maintenance of law and order was the responsibility of unpaid constables appointed by the **JUS-**

TICES OF THE PEACE and the local watchmen. The first force was established in **LONDON** (see **BOW STREET RUNNERS**) in 1757 and they, with the nightwatchmen, provided policing for the capital until the 1829 Metropolitan Police Act (see **ACT OF PARLIAMENT**) created the first professional security system. The **MUNICIPAL CORPORATIONS ACT** of 1835 made **BOROUGH**s set up similar forces and the **COUNTIES** followed, four years later, with provision for rural areas. By 1856, such forces, reporting to the **HOME OFFICE**, were made obligatory in all administrative regions and a decentralized organizational system evolved, remaining relatively unchanged ever since. Recently, proposals for restructuring have been considered in an attempt to reduce costs and meet the challenge posed by criminals who operate on a regional or national scale. (See **BOBBIES; ROBERT PEEL; SCOTLAND YARD**).

POLL TAX. A poll tax was levied on all adults over 14 years of age in 1222 in an attempt to meet the costs of the Holy Land **CRU-SADES** but was widely evaded. Three similar measures were introduced between 1377 and 1381, causing rioting and the **PEAS-ANTS' REVOLT** (four pence per lay adult had been levied in 1377 to prosecute a French war: the addition of a further 1 shilling in 1381 led directly to the Revolt, as a result of which King **RI-CHARD II** almost lost his crown).

Another unwelcome Poll Tax was authorized in 1641 by the **LONG PARLIAMENT**, and poll taxes imposed during the reign of **WILLIAM III**, in 1698, occasioned great bitterness amongst his subjects.

On 31 March 1990, a further poll tax (formally titled the Community Charge) was approved by the **CONSERVATIVE PARTY GOVERNMENT** of Prime Minister **MARGARET THATCHER** to replace Rates (the local property taxes). It was first imposed in **SCOTLAND** in 1989 amidst much protest but without violence. When levied in **ENGLAND**, however, it led to mass demonstrations in **LONDON** and provincial cities, rioting in other parts of the country and widespread evasion of payment, contributing to Mrs Thatcher's eventual resignation. On 1 April 1993, it was replaced by the Council Tax, a local tax based on banded residential property values.

POLLUTION CONTROL. Since 1990, pollution control has been under the general direction of Her Majesty's Inspectorate of Pollu-

412 / POLYTECHNICS

tion (HMIP) and subject to **EUROPEAN COMMUNITY** directives. Air pollution was greatly eased by the 1956 **CLEAN AIR ACT** (see **ACT OF PARLIAMENT**) though gaseous emissions from power stations remain a problem. Photochemical smog in towns during the summer regularly exceeds the World Health Organization's permitted level of 120 parts per billion and acid rain affects 67 per cent of British trees. The National Rivers Authority polices water pollution in rivers, and sea pollution has been a controversial issue, particularly because of the discharge of sewage effluent into coastal waters. Pesticide use is heavily controlled through legislation, but nitrogen levels have increased with the widespread use of artificial fertilizers.

POLYTECHNICS. During the 19th century, the polytechnics were essentially technical colleges but, following the Robbins Report in 1963, 30 new institutions were created, with a specialized practical orientation towards industry and the professions and with powers to train students at undergraduate and postgraduate levels. Funded by **LOCAL GOVERNMENT**, they took the brunt of the 1970s and 1980s expansion of higher **EDUCATION** and, under the 1992 Further and Higher Education Act (see **ACT OF PARLIAMENT**), were enabled to change their titles to ones including the term University, thus abolishing a distinction which had become known as the 'binary line'. (See **UNIVERSITIES**).

POOR LAW. There were three major periods during which systems of relief for the poor were introduced.

Legislation in 1572, 1597 to 1598, and 1601 created the first attempt at social welfare by raising a Poor Rate tax in each **PARISH** to provide relief for the indigent. The Overseers of the Parish used the proceeds to erect workhouses and provide work for paupers, with "outdoor relief" in their own homes for the old and infirm (in the form of provision of tools and materials) and "indoor relief" in the workhouses for the able-bodied. Idle rogues and vagrants could be sent to the House of Correction (that is, to prison). Under the terms of the 1662 **ACT OF SETTLEMENT** (see **ACT OF PARLIAMENT**), those without work who could not prove residence in the Parish could be forcibly removed.

Legislation in 1819, 1834 and 1844 gave property owners (the main payers of the Poor Rate) more say in the administration of relief as the burden of caring for the impoverished continued to increase due to agricultural depression and rising birthrates. Moreover, the **SWING RIOTS** galvanized opinion for reform. The Poor Law Amendment Act of 1834 created a central board which amalgamated parishes into unions to organize union workhouses and outdoor relief. The regime in the workhouses was deliberately harsh in order to discourage applications for aid and the deserving poor were separated from the undeserving in an attempt to encourage a self-help principle. A further Act in 1844 gave electors and ratepayers more power over the Guardians of the workhouses.

Under the terms of the Poor Law Act of 1930, the Poor Law was renamed Public Assistance and only the infirm and old could apply for workhouse relief. The National Assistance Act of 1948 finally abolished the Poor Law provisions completely, providing a system of payments to the less affluent members of society. National Assistance is now known as Income Support.

POPISH PLOT, September 1678. A supposed Jesuit conspiracy to murder King **CHARLES II**, massacre Protestants and use Irish and French forces to put the Catholic **DUKE OF YORK** (later **JAMES VII and II**) on the throne was fabricated by Titus Oates and Israel Tonge, creating panic and anti-Catholic hysteria. Thirty-five people were executed for alleged complicity in the plot before it was revealed as false. One of the consequences was the 1678 **TEST ACT**.

POPLARISM. This term, referring to policies founded upon fairness to the disadvantaged and on local control of state benefits for local people, is derived from the work of Member of **PARLIAMENT** George Lansbury in the poor **LONDON** East End **BOROUGH** of Poplar during the 1920s.

PORTLAND, DUKE OF. (See **WILLIAM HENRY CAVENDISH BENTINCK**).

POSTMASTER GENERAL. This was the title of the **MINISTER** appointed as Head of the **GOVERNMENT**'s **POST OFFICE** department until its abolition in 1969.

POST OFFICE. The Office was established by King **CHARLES I** in 1635 as the General Post Office with monopoly rights to deliver mail. The **PENNY POST** led to greatly increased activity from 1840 and, in 1969, it was converted from a **GOVERNMENT** department into an executive agency. Plans for the **PRIVATIZA-**

TION of some of its activities were abandoned in 1994 after **TRADE UNIONS** warned that the move could result in the loss of 50,000 jobs and 5,000 rural post offices and a small group of **CONSERVATIVE PARTY** Members of **PARLIAMENT** threatened to vote against the proposals in the **HOUSE OF COMMONS**.

POTSDAM CONFERENCE, 17 July-2 August 1945. This was the final summit meeting held by **WINSTON CHURCHILL** (Britain), Harry S Truman (United States of America) and Joseph Stalin (USSR) near Berlin to arrange for the drawing up of peace treaties with Germany's allies and the imposition of reparations for Nazi war crimes and actions. Churchill was replaced by his successor **CLEMENT ATTLEE** during the negotiations. The Potsdam Declaration on 26 July 1945 demanded the unconditional surrender of Japan, threatening utter destruction for noncompliance. Soviet hegemony in the east was accepted, and the terms discussed led eventually to the partitioning of Germany and the start of the Cold War.

POTTERIES, THE. The term is applied to the area of Staffordshire which became visually distinctive from the 17th century due to its increasing numbers of bottle-kilns and which was the centre of the British ceramics industry during the **INDUSTRIAL REVOLUTION**. It includes the towns of Burslem, Tunstall, Hanley, Stoke-on-Trent, Longton and Fenton, which merged as Stoke-on-Trent in 1910. The factories of **JOSIAH WEDGWOOD**, Josiah Spode, Thomas Minton and Henry Doulton were founded there. This area also provided the setting for Arnold Bennett's novels. (For location of Stoke-on-Trent, see Map 2, page xxvi).

POWELL, JOHN ENOCH (1912-   ). A thorn in the side of the **CONSERVATIVE PARTY** during the 1960s and 1970s, Powell was born in Stechford on 16 June 1912, the son of Albert Powell and his wife, Ellen. He was educated at King Edward's School (**BIRMINGHAM**) and at **CAMBRIDGE** University then accepted a post as Professor of Greek at Sydney University (Australia) in 1937. He returned to the United Kingdom at the outbreak of the **SECOND WORLD WAR** in 1939 and enlisted as a Private in the Royal Warwickshire Regiment, earning the MBE in 1943 and rising to the rank of Brigadier. He joined the Conservative Party in 1946 and was elected Member of **PARLIAMENT** (MP) for Wolverhampton four years later.

Powell's first **GOVERNMENT** post was as **PARLIA-MENTARY SECRETARY** at the Ministry of Housing (1955–57). In 1957, he moved to **THE TREASURY** as **FINANCIAL SECRETARY** but resigned the following year when proposals to curb inflation by cutting expenditure were turned down by **HAROLD MACMILLAN**'s **CABINET**. He was appointed **MINISTER** of Health in 1960 and, over the next three years, made a series of speeches calling for restrictions on the **IMMI-GRATION** of coloured people to the UK. He resigned in 1963 in protest against the appointment of **ALEX DOUGLAS-HOME** as **PRIME MINISTER** and never held office again.

An intellectual with an ability to analyse situations coldly and logically, he annoyed many Conservatives because of his outspoken views on racial integration. Support was voiced only by right-wingers although many others who felt sympathy for his cause undoubtedly kept quiet, knowing that association with Powell would damn their political careers. He entered the contest for Leadership of the Party when Douglas-Home resigned in 1965 but made little impression, polling only 15 votes from other MPs compared with the 150 cast for **EDWARD HEATH** and the 133 for Reginald Maudling. He was appointed **SHADOW MINISTER** for Defence but was sacked by Heath in 1968 after a speech which took senior Tories by surprise and in which he claimed that he looked ahead with foreboding. "Like the Roman," he said, "I seem to see the River Tiber foaming with much blood" as a result of racial conflict. Liberals and representatives of the immigrant communities condemned his racist stance, but he insisted that he had chosen his words carefully. A Gallup poll showed that 74 per cent of the population was broadly in agreement with him.

Powell was opposed to membership of the **EUROPEAN ECONOMIC COMMUNITY** and refused to stand at the 1974 **GENERAL ELECTION** in order to make his point but returned to Parliament as the **ULSTER** Unionist Party MP for South Down later that year. He resigned his seat in 1985 because he disagreed with the Anglo-Irish Agreement, which allowed the Government of the Republic of **IRELAND** to influence policy in Ulster, but was reelected in January 1986, claiming that his success was a reflection of the voters' rejection of the deal. He was defeated at the 1987 general election and has played no part in politics since. A classical scholar of great repute, he has published several translations of Herodotus and written a series of historical studies.

PREHISTORIC BRITAIN. The earliest human remains found in Britain were unearthed in a Sussex quarry in 1994 and dated at 520,000 to 480,000 years old. It is likely, therefore, that the first settlers arrived from Europe sometime in the warm postglacial period which followed the Pleistocene Ice Age. The subsequent prehistory of Britain can be divided into three basic periods, though different scholars provide different chronological boundaries. Broadly, the **STONE AGE** lasted from c. 500,000 BC until c. 2,500 BC and can be divided into the Old Stone Age (or **PALAEOLITHIC**) from c. 500,000 BC until c. 10,000 BC), the Middle Stone Age (or **MESOLITHIC**) from c. 10,000 BC until c. 4,400 BC and the New Stone Age (or **NEOLITHIC**) from c. 4,400 BC until c. 2,500 BC. The **BRONZE AGE** lasted from c. 2,500 BC until c. 800 BC and the **IRON AGE** from c. 800 BC until 43AD. The arrival of the **ROMANS** (and the art of writing) in 43AD is conventionally considered the end of British prehistory even though Iron Age cultures continued under the invaders' rule. (See **CELTIC FIELDS; CELTS; DRUIDS; HILLFORTS; ICENI; STONEHENGE**).

PRESCOTT, JOHN LESLIE (1938-   ). Deputy Leader of the **LA-BOUR PARTY** since 1994, Prescott is a left-wing trade unionist who appeals to the traditional working class voter and, according to the media, blends well with the more articulate and more right-wing Party Leader, Tony Blair. Born on 31 May 1938, the son of John and Phyllis Prescott, he was educated at Ellesmere Port Secondary Modern School, Ruskin College (**OXFORD**) and Hull University. He joined the merchant navy in 1955 and, in 1968, became an official with the National Union of Seamen. Two years later, he was elected Member of **PARLIAMENT** for Hull East and, in 1974, was appointed **PARLIAMENTARY PRIVATE SECRETARY** to the **SECRETARY OF STATE** for Trade. He served successively under (Leonard) **JAMES CALLAGHAN**, **MICHAEL FOOT**, Neil Kinnock and John Smith as **OPPOSITION** Spokesman on Transport (1979-81, 1983-84 and 1988-93), Regional Affairs and Devolution (1981-83), Employment (1984-87 and 1993-94) and Energy (1987-88). Following Smith's death in 1994, he stood against Blair for the party leadership but was never seriously expected to win and gained only 24 per cent of the vote. However, he was more successful in the contest for the Deputy Leadership, a post which he had long coveted, gaining 56 per cent of the poll and defeating Margaret Beckett. In the past,

Prescott and Blair have sometimes failed to see eye to eye (Prescott once commented that Blair was a man of warm words rather than definite policies) but commentators now believe that the two men get on reasonably well and that Prescott's relish for Parliamentary rough and tumble complements his Leader's more polished approach.

PRESIDENT OF THE BOARD OF TRADE. This is the formal title of the political head of the **GOVERNMENT**'s Department of Trade and Industry. The **MINISTER**, who has overall responsibility for the work of the Department, is also **SECRETARY OF STATE** for Trade and Industry and has a seat in the **CABINET**.

PRESTON, BATTLE OF. There were two important battles near Preston.

On 17 to 19 August 1648, **OLIVER CROMWELL** secured a crushing victory over an invading Scots force under the **DUKE** of Hamilton, who had hoped to advance the cause of **CHARLES I**. The demonstration of power established the primacy of the army as the dominant power in **ENGLAND**, able to impose its will on **PARLIAMENT**.

A struggle between 12 and 14 November 1715 saw the brief occupation of the city by Jacobite forces on 9 November. The English forces lost over 200 men in attempts to storm the barricades and settled down for a lengthy siege but, on 14 November, the Jacobites surrendered — internal indecision and recriminations in their camp had robbed them of success. The event ended both 1715 Jacobite Rebellion.

PRIDE'S PURGE, 6 December 1648. Colonel Thomas Pride orchestrated the exclusion, and forced expulsion, from **PARLIAMENT** of 140 MPs who supported **CHARLES I** in the **CIVIL WAR**. The remaining legislators formed the **RUMP PARLIAMENT**.

PRIME MINISTER. Strictly speaking, the head of the British **GOVERNMENT** is Prime Minister and First Lord of **THE TREASURY** because it has always been accepted that the **MONARCH** should be most closely advised by the State Treasurer. The title has become popular since 1820 (prior to that **GOVERNMENT**s had their Principal Minister). The Prime Minister is the head of the majority party in the **HOUSE OF COMMONS** and is appointed to that position according to the rules of that party, not by the popular vote of the British people (for example, after **MARGARET THATCHER**'s resignation in 1990, **JOHN MAJOR** was appointed as her successor following a ballot of **CONSERVATIVE PARTY** Members of **PARLIAMENT**). Prime Ministers choose and chair the **CABINET**, select each **MINISTER** and **SECRETARY OF STATE**, initiate policy developments, provide a link between Parliament and Monarch, advise the sovereign on the exercise of the **ROYAL PREROGATIVE** (the appointment of a Prime Minister is itself part of that Prerogative), play a leading role in the House of Commons and lead a political party. In the modern political context, this is the most powerful position in the land, but maintenance of that position depends on the holder's ability to command a Commons majority and party support.

PRINCE OF WALES. King **EDWARD I**, having conquered **WALES**, decreed to the Welsh Barons that he would give them a Prince who could claim a birthplace in Wales. This was his son, Edward (later **EDWARD II**), who had been born in Caernarfon. In 1301, he was invested with the lands of the **PRINCIPALITY**. From the time of **EDWARD III**, the **MONARCH**'s eldest son, the heir apparent, has usually been created Prince of Wales. The title has attracted its share of notoriety. **EDWARD II** brought ignominy to the monarchy through homosexual affairs. Frederick, son of **GEORGE II**, was called the "lowest stinking coward in the world" by his father, and George, son of **GEORGE III**, was involved in a sexual and financial scandal, causing the **CIVIL LIST** to be created to avoid rows between monarch and **GOVERNMENT**. Edward, son of **VICTORIA** (and later **EDWARD VII**), lived riotously, with a playboy image, known to all as 'Bertie'. (He was christened Albert Edward.) **PRINCE CHARLES**, the current incumbent, has attracted much press attention as a result of his self-confessed extramarital affair with Camilla Parker-Bowles and the breakdown of his marriage to Princess **DIANA** (see **DIANA SPENCER**).

PRINCESS DIANA. (See **DIANA FRANCES SPENCER**).

PRINCESS OF WALES. (See **DIANA FRANCES SPENCER**).

PRINCESS ROYAL. This title may be conferred on the **MONARCH**'s eldest daughter. In 1987, Queen **ELIZABETH II**

granted the title to **PRINCESS ANNE** in recognition of her charitable work, particularly in her capacity as President of the Save the Children Fund, which focusses on Third World countries.

PRINTING. Printing with moveable type originated with Johann Gutenberg in Germany c. 1440 and was introduced to **ENGLAND** in 1476 by **WILLIAM CAXTON**, who had a printing house in the grounds of **WESTMINSTER** Abbey. His successor moved to Fleet Street, which later became the centre of the **LONDON** printing and newspaper trade. Steam presses came with the **INDUSTRIAL REVOLUTION**, phototypesetting in the 1950s and computerised desk top publishing in the 1980s.

PRISONS. Long-term imprisonment, except for debt, was unusual in Britain until the 19th century as most felons were executed (see **CAPITAL PUNISHMENT**) or transported (see **TRANSPORTATION**). By the end of the 18th century, a movement proposing a reform of conditions was growing as, by then, Newgate Prison and the Fleet Prison (both in **LONDON**) were notorious and conditions often poor and dependent on bribery. Most towns had only a small gaol or lock-up and, at times of war, old ship hulks were pressed into service as temporary cells. During the 19th century, Elizabeth Fry and John Howard campaigned for change, and gradually, as the number of offences punishable by capital punishment was reduced, more prisons were built (**ROBERT PEEL**'s Gaol Act of 1823 obliged **COUNTIES** to operate a prison which would be inspected regularly and which would provide correction and secure holding). Pentonville in London (1842), one of the prisons which grew rapidly as a result of the ending of the transportation policy in 1853, was built to **JEREMY BENTHAM**'s Panopticon design around a central observation area.

The **HOME OFFICE** took over management of the prisons in 1877, and, as penal offences attracted shorter sentences, the convict population swelled. Many 19th century prisons still remain in use, often causing riots (as at Strangeways in 1991) and concern has been expressed about overcrowding. The first experimental private prison began operating in 1992.

PRIVATE BILL. These **BILL**s are introduced to **PARLIAMENT** with the intention of benefiting a specific individual or interest group. Local authorities use them as a means of gaining permission to carry out public works, sometimes in order to circumvent the restrictions of the **TOWN AND COUNTRY PLANNING** system. (See **ACT OF PARLIAMENT**).

PRIVATE MEMBER'S BILL. These **BILL**s are introduced to the **HOUSE OF COMMONS** by individual Members of **PARLIAMENT** rather than by **MINISTER**s acting for the **GOVERNMENT**.

PRIVATIZATION. Strictly, this term is applied to the sale of shares in publicly owned industries or corporations (see **NATIONALIZATION**), but it is more frequently used with reference to **MARGARET THATCHER**'s policy of reducing the role of the state in industry and commerce and replacing it with a philosophy governed more by market forces and an enterprize ethic. The changes involved contracting out to private tender some of the work previously done by **LOCAL GOVERNMENT** (such as street cleaning), abolishing the monopolies enjoyed by public bodies (municipal transport, telephones and broadcasting, for instance) and selling shares in such public corporations and enterprizes as British Aerospace, **BRITISH AIRWAYS**, British **GAS**, Britoil and the Trustee Savings Bank. Although the policy stemmed partly from ideological roots (see **THATCHERISM**), it also served to increase **GOVERNMENT** income.

PRIVY COUNCIL. The Council originated in 1536, in the early part of the reign of **HENRY VIII**, when noble attendants in the King's Privy (or private) Chamber were able to influence the **MONARCH** while attending to his personal needs. **THOMAS CROMWELL** reduced this King's Council to a smaller, 20-strong group of influential advisers who wielded exceptional influence and were the source of executive power before the institution of **CABINET** government in the 18th century. The Privy Council now advises the Monarch on Royal Proclamations and other matters and consists of all present and past Cabinet **MINISTER**s, leaders of the main political parties, archbishops, judges and some **COMMONWEALTH OF NATIONS** representatives. Because of its composition, it rarely meets as a full body. It is also the final court of appeal from ecclesiastical courts and **UK OVERSEAS DEPENDENCIES**.

PRIVY SEAL. The seal was used from the 11th century to authenticate, by impression into red wax, important state papers and letters. The Privy Seal Office was abolished in 1884, but **LORD PRIVY SEAL** is still an official **GOVERNMENT** post and its holder is a member of the **CABINET**.

PROFUMO SCANDAL, 1963. John Profumo was **SECRETARY OF STATE** for War and was revealed to have had an association with Christine Keeler (a high-class prostitute), who was at the same time having an affair with Eugene Ivanov, a Soviet Naval Attache. The scandal involved not only sex and a potential security problem but also rumours of involvements with other **MINISTER**s and lies to the **HOUSE OF COMMONS**. Profumo was eventually censured by the House and resigned on 4 July. Lord Denning mounted an inquiry, and the scandal discredited the **CONSERVATIVE PARTY GOVERNMENT** of **HAROLD MACMILLAN** beyond repair.

PROTECTORATE. Territories which are administered by local rulers but given military protection (and special trading agreements) by Britain, protectorates have often become **CROWN COLONIES**.

PROTECTORATE, THE, 1653-1659. After the dissolution of the **BAREBONES PARLIAMENT**, **OLIVER CROMWELL** ruled **ENGLAND** as Lord Protector, using his **ROUNDHEAD MAJOR GENERALS** for **LOCAL GOVERNMENT** after **PENRUD-DOCK'S RISING**. Cromwell refused the **CROWN** and, after his death in 1658, was succeeded by his son, Richard, until he, in turn, was deposed by the army and the **RUMP PARLIAMENT** was recalled to reestablish the **COMMONWEALTH** the following year.

PROVISIONS OF OXFORD, 1258. Radical reforms of government and restrictions on the activities of the **MONARCH** were imposed by a committee of 24 members of the **OXFORD PARLIAMENT** on King **HENRY III**. The committee set up a council of 15 advisers to the King and they, in effect, became the real rulers of the country, along with a legislative commission of 12 members. Related to the **PROVISIONS OF WESTMINSTER**, the reforms were rescinded in 1266.

PROVISIONS OF WESTMINSTER, 1259. Less revolutionary than the preceding **PROVISIONS OF OXFORD**, these reforms of local government and royal financial controls were the result of the power invested in the council of 15 advisers established by the earlier Provisions. Their major aims were to redress the grievances of the Barons and reimpose the provisions of the **MAGNA CARTA**. (See **HENRY III**).

PUBLIC HOUSE. The Pub developed mainly in the cities of the **VICTORIAN AGE** as a licensed drinking place and social meeting house, similar to bars and cafes elsewhere but strictly controlled by the 1872 **LICENSING ACTS** (see **ACT OF PARLIAMENT**). Often they were given distinctive names and bore an external sign so they could be identified easily. From 1988, they have been able to stay open for longer periods (between 11 am and 11 pm), and most now sell food as well as alcohol.

PUBLIC RECORD OFFICE (PRO). The PRO was created in 1838 as the national repository and archive of **GOVERNMENT** and legal records. It contains material dating from the **DOMESDAY BOOK** to the present and is an unrivalled source for historical research. Its creation ensured the survival of ancient records, many of which had been the responsibility of the **MASTER OF THE ROLLS** since 1290, but it by no means ensures the level of freedom of information which exists in the United States. Under the provisions of the 1967 Public Records Act (see **ACT OF PARLIAMENT**), state documents usually have a 30-year embargo on release to the public. In the case of royal documents and the census returns for individual households, that period is extended to 100 years. The PRO is based in Chancery Lane (**LONDON**), but, in 1977, a second site was opened at Kew in order to cope with the growing archives.

PUBLIC SCHOOLS. Modern descendants of the medieval **GRAMMAR SCHOOLS**, the public schools are theoretically open to all academically able pupils whose parents can pay the tuition and other fees. The quality of **EDUCATION** varies widely but the best have a worldwide reputation. Originally designed for one or other of the sexes, most are now coeducational even if only with the older age groups. They include institutions such as Eton, Harrow and Marlborough, which have been nurseries for generations of **CABINET** ministers.

PUBLIC SECTOR BORROWING REQUIREMENT. The Requirement is the difference between the amount **GOVERNMENT** spends and the amount it raises in taxes.

PURITANS. An extreme Protestant movement, which evolved in the 16th and 17th centuries, Puritanism was divided into a number of sects, whose members wanted to distance themselves more completely from Popism than was acceptable even in the post-**REFORMATION CHURCH OF ENGLAND,** which had retained the episcopy and much of the ceremonial, ritual and ornate vestments of the Roman Catholics. The emphasis, according to the Puritans, who derived their theology from Calvin, should be on pure worship, free of bishops and ceremony. Followers of the doctrine were prominent in the **CIVIL WAR** as **LEVELLERS** and **FIFTH MONARCHY MEN,** supporters of the **PARLIAMENTARIANS** and members of the **NEW MODEL ARMY.** (See **PILGRIM FATHERS**).

—Q—

QUADRUPLE ALLIANCE. There were three quadruple alliances.

In 1718, Britain, the Netherlands, Austria and France allied to prevent the expansion of Spain into Italy and to impose the **TREATY OF UTRECHT** (1713). Spain had supported the Jacobite Rebellion of 1715 but capitulated to the demands of the allies in 1720.

In 1815, Britain, Russia, Austria and Prussia allied to guarantee the **TREATY OF PARIS** (1814) on the defeat of Napoleon.

In 1834, Britain, Portugal, France and Spain allied to banish the pretenders to the thrones of Spain and Portugal from their territories.

QUANGO. This acronym is derived from Quasi-Autonomous Non-**GOVERNMENT**al Organization. These bodies are not part of the civil service, are funded through the patronage of government **MINISTER**s and operate in many areas of British life. They grew rapidly in the 1960s and 1970s, were reduced in number while **MARGARET THATCHER** was **PRIME MINISTER** but increased again in the 1990s as **PRIVATIZATION** and related policies removed many functions from government departments. Seen by some as insidious forms of government control (10,000 appointments were made by ministers in 1992, and it is estimated that there are more appointees to quangos than employees in **LOCAL GOVERNMENT**), quangos are regarded as cheap ways of getting essential activities done. Many deal with important areas of public life such as the **BANK OF ENGLAND**, British **COAL**, the Civil Aviation Authority and the Monopolies and Mergers Commission.

QUARTER SESSIONS. These courts were held quarterly (that is, every three months) to hear cases relating to minor infringements of the law and were presided over by the **JUSTICE**s **OF THE PEACE**. In 1972, they were superseded by the **CROWN COURTS**.

QUEEN MOTHER. (See **ELIZABETH ANGELA MARGUERITE BOWES-LYON**).

QUEEN'S BENCH. Formerly a court at which the **MONARCH** presided, the Queen's Bench is now a Division of the **HIGH COURT OF JUSTICE**. In medieval times, it heard cases which involved the sovereign or, the great nobles, who could be tried only by the **MONARCH**. Gradually, however, it lost this royal connection and became a court of **COMMON LAW** exercising its jurisdiction over criminal as well as civil cases. Under the provisions of the **JUDICATURE ACT** of 1873 (see **ACT OF PARLIAMENT**), it became part of the High Court. Its 25 judges, headed by the **LORD CHIEF JUSTICE**, hear cases involving tort (that is, wrongs which can be compensated by the award of damages), contract, some crimes and appeals from lower courts. When the monarch is a King, this court is known as the King's Bench.

QUIBERON BAY, BATTLE OF, 20 November 1759. The British navy, led by Admiral Edward Hawke, gained a victory over the French off the Brittany coast during the **SEVEN YEARS WAR**. Nine of the 21 enemy vessels were destroyed — a tremendous blow to France, which was attempting to redress the losses it had sustained in North America and the West Indies and launch an invasion of **ENGLAND**

—R—

RACE RELATIONS ACT, 1976. The 1976 Act (see **ACT OF PARLIAMENT**) repealed Acts of 1965 and 1968 and set up the Commission for Racial Equality in an attempt to end discrimination against coloured groups. (See **IMMIGRATION**).

RAILWAYS. Collieries developed tramroads with horse-drawn wagons in the 18th century, and Richard Trevithick built a steam carriage by 1801, but the first modern railway was the Stockton and Darlington line, constructed for the carriage of **COAL** in 1825. It was closely followed by the **LIVERPOOL** and **MANCHESTER** (running **GEORGE STEPHENSON**'s *Rocket*) in 1830 and the **LONDON** to **BIRMINGHAM** in 1838. The years from 1844 to 1847 are generally recognized as a period of 'railway mania', with large numbers of firms formed and investment gathering momentum, financed by **JOINT-STOCK COMPANIES**. The most famous promoter of the time was George Hudson of **YORK**, dubbed the 'Railway King', who built extensively until losing his money in 1849. In 1843, there were 1,952 miles of track, but, by 1900, the tentacles of the system had lengthened to 18,000 miles. This growth of the network was a major factor in the **INDUSTRIAL REVOLUTION**, the expansion of towns and ports and the movement of people. Also, during the second half of the 19th century, the railways began to develop as a form of leisure transport. However, the idea of a national, organized pattern of routes was anathema to a Victorian society which believed in a laissez-faire economy and free enterprize so it was only really with the Railway Act of 1921 (see **ACT OF PARLIAMENT**) that Britain began to combine the regional and rival companies into four major areas. These came under direct **GOVERNMENT** control in 1947 (see **NATIONALIZATION**). As passenger numbers declined in the face of competition from the motor car and freight operations turned to road transport, the **BEECHING REPORT** of 1963 attempted to rationalize the network, closing uneconomic routes and stations. Under **JOHN MAJOR**, the Government has adopted a policy — much contested — of returning the railways to private ownership. There are currently 10,500 miles of railway track in the UK.

RAJ. This term is given to the period of British rule in India. It is derived from the Hindi and Sanskrit words meaning 'king'.

RALEIGH, WALTER (1554-1618). A soldier, seaman, explorer and author, Raleigh was one of the favourites of **ELIZABETH I** and an advocate of English colonization of the Americas. The son of Sir Walter Raleigh and his wife, Katherine, he was born at Hayes Barton (Devon) in 1554 (or possibly 1552). In 1572, he was at **OXFORD** University and, by 1575, had become a member of the Middle Temple. He went to **IRELAND** in 1580, fighting against rebel troops, but returned to **ENGLAND** in 1581. According to legend, he gained Elizabeth's attention by throwing his cloak over a puddle so that she would not get her feet wet as she passed. There is no evidence to support the tale, but it is clear that, by 1582, he was well established at the royal court.

Raleigh was knighted in 1585 and, two years later, became Captain of the Queen's Guard. By that time, he was a rich man, with large estates in Ireland and a considerable income from the sale of wine licences and the export of broadcloth. He used some of that capital to sponsor a series of expeditions to North America, naming Virginia in honour of the 'virgin queen'. Although he never set foot on his New World territories, he was keen to exploit their resources and introduced tobacco to England. (It is also claimed that he was responsible for taking the potato to Britain but the plant is not indigenous to Virginia and there is no contemporary account which authenticates the story.) From 1584, he sat in **PARLIAMENT**, advocating increased taxes so that the country's defences could be improved and championing the cause of the poor. In 1592, however, he fell out of favour. His sin was to marry, in secret, Elizabeth Throckmorton (one of the Queen's **LADIES IN WAITING**). Elizabeth I would not countenance such disloyalty by one of her favourites and imprisoned the couple in the **TOWER OF LONDON**. Raleigh remained in captivity until the following year, when his ships captured the Portuguese galleon *Madre de Dios*, one of the richest prizes ever taken by English seamen. With the booty, he bought his release. In 1595, he made his first visit to the Americas, travelling up the Orinoco River in search of El Dorado but finding only quartz and mahogany.

In 1596, Sir Walter Raleigh allied with Robert Devereux, Earl of Essex and a competitor for Elizabeth's favours, in an attack on the Spanish stronghold of Cadiz, returning in 1597 to harry the Azores. From then, he grew closer to the Queen as Essex's star waned. In 1600, he was made Governor of Jersey and improved the island's defences, introduced a property register and promoted trade. In 1601, he was officer in charge of the soldiers at Essex's execution (the price of unsuccessful rebellion against the Queen), but the death of Elizabeth in 1603 and the accession of **JAMES VI and I** was the beginning of the end. **ROBERT CECIL** and Lord Henry Howard persuaded the King that he had been involved in a plot to put the Roman Catholic Arabella Stuart (James's cousin) on the throne. It is most unlikely that the charges were justified, but Raleigh was convicted of high **TREASON** and condemned to death.

James granted a reprieve just before the sentence was carried out but, for the next 13 years, Raleigh was confined to the Tower. During that time, he conducted a series of chemical experiments and wrote a history of the world, the first (and only) volume of which was published in 1614. In 1616, he was released, having persuaded the King to allow him to lead an expedition to Guiana and promising that, if he did not discover a mountain covered with gold and silver, the commander of the fleet could cut off his head. James agreed, provided that nothing was done to offend the Spaniards, but the venture was plagued by ill fortune from the start. Because of Raleigh's precarious situation, only the most desperate of seamen would join his crews, the outward voyage was dogged by bad weather and Raleigh himself fell ill in Trinidad. Then Lawrence Keymis, his lieutenant, attacked the Spanish fortress of San Thome, which guarded the approach to Guiana. And there was no gold. Raleigh returned to England empty-handed and was beheaded at **WESTMINSTER** on 29 October 1618.

RAMILLIES, BATTLE OF, 22-23 May 1706. At this battle, fought in the Flanders area of the Netherlands during the **WAR OF THE SPANISH SUCCESSION**, the **DUKE OF MARLBOROUGH**, with his efficient cavalry and full force of 62,000 men, used his brilliant tactical mind to overcome a French army numbering 60,000 (and inflicting heavy casualties numbering some 15,000 men). Marlborough was unhorsed and ridden over by the enemy cavalry but survived. The victory led to further successes, the defeat of France in this theatre of war by Britain and its Dutch ally and the eventual taking of the Spanish Netherlands. (See **BATTLE OF OUDENARDE**).

RANSOM. Payment for the release of persons or property was common following warfare at the time of the **FEUDAL SYSTEM**. The best known example was the ransom of 150,000 marks paid to release King **RICHARD I** from imprisonment by Emperor Henry VI in 1194.

RATIONING. Systems for controlling consumption of food and clothing have been common during times of national emergency. In the modern era, they have usually taken the form of coupons issued by **GOVERNMENT** and used to purchase defined goods. During the **FIRST WORLD WAR**, rationing was introduced in 1917 but was much evaded. Reinstated in January 1940, following the outbreak of the **SECOND WORLD WAR**, it covered basic foodstuffs and clothing and was more effective. The restrictions remained in force during the **AUSTERITY** years after the war, partly because of the economic crisis of 1947, which forced rationing back to severe war-time levels. However, clothes and sweets were removed from rationing in 1949 and other commodities in 1954 (ritual burnings of ration books took place in celebration of the event). A more restricted rationing of petrol was planned and ration books issued (though never used) during the **OIL CRISIS** following the Arab-Israeli war of 1973.

RECUSANT. This term refers to citizens who refused to attend services of the **CHURCH OF ENGLAND** at a time when such attendance was compulsory. Most were Roman Catholics although Protestants were included. Legislation attempted to bring them into line, subjecting them to fines under the 1552 and 1559 **ACTS OF UNIFORMITY**. In 1580, these fines were increased to an enormous £20 per month and, by 1587, up to 66 per cent of a recusant's property could be seized. The increasing harshness corresponded with growing political fears of Catholic uprisings. (See **TOLERATION ACTS**).

REFERENDA. The use of a direct popular vote on specific issues is uncommon in British history because of a longstanding acceptance of the view that the electoral system creates a body of representative and democratically elected Members of **PARLIAMENT** who should decide on policy. Referenda have been used only in 1973 (in **NORTHERN IRELAND**), in 1975 (on continued **EUROPEAN COMMUNITY** membership) and in 1979 (on **DEVOLUTION** of **GOVERNMENT** to **SCOTLAND** and **WALES**).

REFORM ACTS. (See **PARLIAMENTARY REFORM**).

REFORMATION. The 16th century European movement to reform the Roman Catholic Church acted as a catalyst for political and social change in Britain. In 1531, **HENRY VIII** was refused a divorce from **CATHERINE OF ARAGON** by Pope Clement VII and declared himself **SUPREME HEAD** of the Church in **ENGLAND.** The Pope then excommunicated Henry, who set about the **DISSOLUTION OF THE MONASTERIES** (thereby occasioning the **PILGRIMAGE OF GRACE**) and, in 1534, approved the **ACT OF SUPREMACY** (see **ACT OF PARLIAMENT**), which broke the power of the Church of Rome in England and established the **CHURCH OF ENGLAND.** ACTs **OF UNIFORMITY** imposed new forms of worship during Henry's reign but more particularly in those of his children, **EDWARD VI** and **ELIZABETH I.** Catholics found themselves increasingly ostracized despite the brief relief of the **MARIAN REACTION** while **MARY I** was on the throne. Elizabeth, for example, introduced a further **ACT OF SUPREMACY** (1559), adopted a redesigned **BOOK OF COMMON PRAYER** and saw, during her reign, a growth in the influence of **PURITAN** sects. Henry VIII had broken with Rome yet accepted the Catholic doctrines: his successors completed the Reformation. (See **ARTICLES OF RELIGION; THOMAS CROMWELL**).

REGENCY. Occasionally, it has been necessary to invest royal authority in a person who is not the **MONARCH.** Technically, the monarchy can never die so there cannot be an interregnum when the powers of the sovereign are not exercised. The need for a regent (an individual or body invested with the interim authority of the head of state) normally arises when the sovereign is a minor or incapacitated or otherwise absent. In **ENGLAND**, the procedure has been used during the reigns of **HENRY III, RICHARD II, EDWARD V, HENRY VI, EDWARD VI** and **GEORGE III.** Following the onset of George's mental illness, the 1811 Regency Act (see **ACT OF PARLIAMENT**) named the **PRINCE OF WALES** as Regent for his failing father. Further Acts of 1937, 1943 and 1953 confirmed arrangements for the appointment of a Regent and limited the powers that individual would hold. (See **REGENCY PERIOD**).

REGENCY PERIOD. This term is applied to the period at the beginning of the 19th century, from 1811, when the Prince Regent (later King **GEORGE IV**) took over royal duties from his insane father,

King **GEORGE III**. It was seen as a time of great style, particularly in architecture, furniture and other decorative arts as well as in literature, and was characterized by ostentation, gaiety and aristocratic extravagance. (See **GEORGE BRYAN BRUMMELL**).

REGENT. (See **REGENCY**).

REPUBLIC, 19 May 1649. After the execution of King **CHARLES I**, **ENGLAND** was effectively a Republic though it is more usually referred to as the **COMMONWEALTH**.

RESTORATION. A rise in pro-**ROYALIST** feelings, caused by the excesses of the **PURITANS** during the **INTERREGNUM**, led to General George Monk (army commander in **SCOTLAND**) briefly ruling **ENGLAND** as Captain-General (replacing Richard Cromwell after the fall of the **PROTECTORATE**) before calling the **CONVENTION PARLIAMENT**. Following the **DECLARA-TION OF BREDA** (1660), in which **CHARLES II** assured his opponents that they would be pardoned, **PARLIAMENT** agreed to restore the **CROWN** to him, accompanying it with a settlement guaranteeing a considerable income, control of the army and a statement accepting the **DIVINE RIGHT OF KINGS** but retaining many powers for itself.

REVOLUTIONARY WAR. (See **AMERICAN WAR OF INDE-PENDENCE**).

RHODES, CECIL JOHN (1852-1902). A statesman and entrepreneur who wanted to see British colonies in Africa stretch 'from Cape to Cairo', Rhodes was born at Bishop's Stortford on 5 January 1853. The fifth son of F.W. Rhodes (a Hertfordshire vicar) and his wife, Louisa, he was educated at the local **GRAMMAR SCHOOL** but left at the age of 16 to join his older brother, Herbert, a cotton grower in Natal. News of the discovery of diamonds at Kimberley attracted both men, and, in 1872, they discarded farming for mining.

Over the next few years, Cecil divided his time between academic study and business. He entered **OXFORD** University in 1873 but took ill the following year and, with the doctors giving him only six months to live, returned to Africa, where he recovered his health. He went back to Oxford in 1876 and graduated with a BA degree in 1881. During his undergraduate programme, he became convinced that people of northwest European stock were the ultimate achievement of God's plan for human evolution and that he had a responsibility to ensure the spread of British influence in Africa (see **SCRAMBLE FOR AFRICA**). In 1873, he formed a partnership with C. D. Rudd and (with financier Alfred Beit) began to purchase claims to potential diamond sites. By 1891, he had the entire industry under his control in De Beers Consolidated Mines Ltd. In 1881, he had become a member of the Cape Parliament, representing the rural area of Barkly West, and he used that position to extend British control in southern Africa. In 1885, he persuaded the **GOVERNMENT** in **LONDON** to make northern Bechuanaland a British **PROTECTORATE** and southern Bechuanaland a **CROWN COLONY** in order to prevent Germany from linking its Namaqualand-Damaraland Protectorate with Transvaal and blocking British expansion northwards.

Then, in 1888, Rhodes negotiated with Lobengula, Chief of the Matabele, to get a gold prospecting monopoly in Mashonaland in exchange for £1,200 per annum, 1,000 rifles and an armed steamboat on the Zambesi River. The following year, his British South Africa Company was set up to carry out the work and given a Royal Charter (effectively making it the Government's official representative in southern Africa). By 1893, it had extended its control over the whole of the area which, two years later, was formally named Rhodesia in his honour. Also, in 1891, he arranged for Nyasaland to become a British Protectorate, pledging that his company would donate £10,000 annually for the territory's upkeep and that he would donate a similar sum privately. As part of the bargain, it was agreed that the British South Africa Company would adminster the area north from the Zambesi River to Lake Tanganyika.

While these business interests were expanding, Rhodes was also extending his political influence. In 1890, he became Prime Minister of the Cape Colony, with the declared aim of uniting British and Dutch interests against Germany, the common enemy. He ruled according to standard British principles of colonization, introducing the Franchise and Ballot Act in 1892 in order to guarantee that only black Africans who were literate and could earn a labourer's wage would have a right to vote and take part in government. He also dreamed of a federation of South African states within the **BRITISH EMPIRE** but President Paulus Kruger of Transvaal resisted political and economic pressures to join. Eventually, in 1895, Rhodes lost patience when Kruger made a speech which contained friendly gestures towards Germany. He authorized an attempt by an armed force from the British South Africa Company, led by his friend Leander Jameson, to overthrow the Transvaal Government but the episode was a fiasco (see **JAMESON RAID**). On 2 January 1896, Jameson surrendered and, a few days later, Rhodes resigned his post of Prime Minister. In later years, he arranged for a rail link between Salisbury and Lake Tanganyika as a step towards his dream of a Cape to Cairo railroad. He died at Muizenberg (now in South Africa) on 26 March 1902 and (never having married) left a large portion of his fortune to provide funds for foreign students to study at Oxford University. These Rhodes Scholarships have become prestigious awards, administered by eight trustees who ensure that, in keeping with his wishes, recipients are of high moral character as well as academically able.

RICHARD I (1157-99). The son of **HENRY II** and Eleanor of Aquitaine, Richard ruled **ENGLAND** from 1189 until 1199 but spent only some six months in the country. For much of the remainder of the time, he was involved in European military campaigns and in the third **CRUSADE** to the Holy Land, earning a reputation as a warrior which made him the hero of innumerable stories told throughout the continent.

Richard was born in Chalus (France) on 8 September 1157 and became **DUKE** of Aquitaine in 1168 and Duke of Poitiers in 1172. With his brothers, he took part in the rebellion against Henry in 1173 and 1174 but later received his father's pardon. In 1189, however, in alliance with King Philip II of France, he turned against him again and when, on 6 July, Henry died in the midst of the campaign, Richard succeeded to the throne. He immediately turned his attention to the Holy Land, hoping to recapture Jerusalem, which the Moslem leader, Saladin, had taken in 1187. In order to raise money for the venture, he sold the rights to many offices of state, ransomed King William I of **SCOTLAND** (who had been captured by Henry at Alnwick in 1174) and dipped deeply into his treasury. England was seen solely as a source of revenue (Richard is reputed to have said that he would sell **LONDON** if a buyer could be found). He set off for Palestine in 1190, wintered in Sicily then travelled on to the Holy Land, capturing Cyprus en route. He joined the seige of Acre in 1191 (see **BATTLE OF ACRE**) but showed the brutal side of his nature after the city had fallen; believing that Saladin had broken the terms of the surrender, he killed 2,500 men, women and children, whom he had held prisoner, in order to assert his authority.

He also captured Arsuf and marched on to Jerusalem, but the European coalition was beginning to crack because leaders from the west were quite ruthless in their attitude towards the infidels whereas those from the east were more tolerant and disputes over policy were becoming increasingly common. Eventually, several of the commanders, including Philip of France, turned for home, leaving Richard in undisputed charge of the Crusade. With depleted troops, he was unable to drive the Moslem force from Jerusalem and, in 1192, entered a truce with Saladin which allowed Christian pilgrims free access to their holy places. He sailed for home shortly afterwards but was blown ashore near Venice during a storm and taken captive by his former Crusade ally Leopold of Austria, who sold him to Emperor Henry VI. For 14 months he was held in a secret castle until, so the legends say, he was discovered by his minstrel, Blondel. Henry demanded an enormous **RANSOM** for Richard's release in 1194; the money was raised by taxation and stands testimony to the prosperity of 12th century England.

Richard's remaining years were largely spent at war with King Philip, to whom his brother, **JOHN**, had sworn homage in return for Richard's lands. Whilst laying seige to the castle at Chaluz in 1199, he was wounded. He died on 6 April and was buried in the church at Fontevrault, close to his father. Richard had brought great honour to England, enormously increasing the country's prestige in Europe, but he was fortunate that domestic affairs lay in the hands of capable administrators who were able to maintain prosperity and order in the absence of a **MONARCH**.

RICHARD II (1367-1400). King of **ENGLAND** from 1377 until 1399, Richard was the son of **EDWARD THE BLACK PRINCE** and Joan of **KENT**. Born in Bordeaux (France) on 6 January 1367, he succeeded to the throne on the death of his grandfather, **EDWARD III**, on 21 June 1377, while still only ten years of age and at a time of considerable social unrest. During his minority, government was largely in the hands of his uncle, **JOHN OF GAUNT**, but, during the **PEASANTS' REVOLT** over wage restraint and high taxes in 1381, he showed great courage and remarkable political skill in persuading a group of rebels who had destroyed John's **MANOR** in the **CITY OF LONDON** to return to their homes in Essex. As he grew older, however, he increasingly alienated the most powerful members of the nobility as a result of his unwillingness to accept criticism, his arrogance and his choice of advisers (who became renowned for their greed and their expensive lifestyles). John of Gaunt provided a moderating influence but, when he left England in 1386 to pursue his claim to the throne of Castile and Leon, matters came to a head. **PARLIAMENT** attempted to blame the Earl of Suffolk, the King's Chancellor, for a series of unpopular policies but Richard came to his official's defence, saying that he would not remove a scullion from his kitchen at Parliament's request. However, the pressure on the **MONARCH** was too great and eventually Suffolk was dismissed. The following year, Richard's opponents went further, demanding the arrest of several favourites, including Robert de Vere, Earl of Oxford and the King's closest friend. The King allowed his allies to escape but, in 1388, they were impeached by Parliament and found guilty of **TREASON**. The return of John of Gaunt in 1389 brought an apparent reconciliation between the two sides but Richard used the uneasy peace to garner new support. An expedition to **IRELAND** in 1394 and 1395, and a conciliatory approach which ended the lengthy conflict with France in 1396, enhanced his prestige so, by 1397, he felt sufficiently powerful to attack his opponents openly; the Duke of Gloucester was murdered, the Earl of Arundel was executed and the Earl of Warwick was exiled. The opposition apparently weakened, he embarked on a policy of high taxation to support a luxurious court.

When John of Gaunt, one of the richest men in England, died, in 1399, Richard confiscated his estates. Henry Bolingbroke, John's son and later **HENRY IV**, rebelled and found much support in a kingdom tired of the onerous tax structure and disregard of the rights both of individuals and of Parliament. On 30 September, Richard was forced to abdicate. He was taken to Pontefract Castle, where he died on 14 September 1400, probably of starvation. The last of the monarchs from the House of Anjou (see **PLANTAGENETS**), Richard was a sensitive man who supported literature and the arts, giving gifts to writers such as Geoffrey Chaucer and rebuilding **WESTMINSTER** Hall, but he was uninterested in military matters and that, as much as anything, alienated him from leading nobles during his youth. Later, his self-interest and malice made him enemies, and his reign collapsed quickly after the death of John of Gaunt, who had worked tirelessly and with much skill to prevent confrontation. (See **MERCILESS PARLIAMENT**).

RICHARD III (1452-85). King of **ENGLAND** from 1483 until 1485, Richard was the youngest son of **RICHARD, DUKE OF YORK,** and Cicely Neville. He was born at Fotheringhay Castle on 2 June 1452 and created Duke of Gloucester in 1461. He served in the Yorkist armies during the **WARS OF THE ROSES** and was probably involved in the murder of Lancastrian **HENRY VI** in 1471, earning the post of Lieutenant Governor in the north of England for his loyalty. In 1483, his brother, **EDWARD IV,** died leaving a young son, **EDWARD V.** The boy had been brought up by the Nevilles but Richard, wary of the family's influence, took him to **LONDON.** Edward IV's wife, Elizabeth Woodville, feared for her safety and sought protection for herself and her family in **WESTMINSTER** Abbey. On 25 June 1483, **PARLIAMENT** decreed that Edward's marriage to Elizabeth was invalid on the grounds of an earlier contract with Eleanor, daughter of the Earl of Shrewsbury. His children were declared illegitimate and Richard was acknowledged as the rightful King. His reign began the following day. Some weeks later, Elizabeth was persuaded to allow Richard, her other son, to join his brother in the **TOWER OF LONDON.** In August, they disappeared, and although there is no evidence to show Richard's involvement, it was widely believed that they were murdered on the King's orders.

Richard proved to be an efficient administrator — he promoted trade, introduced a series of financial reforms, built churches and supported learning, but he had alienated so many of the nobility that his power base was limited. Henry Tudor (later **HENRY VII**) provided a rallying point in France for the opposition. On 7 August 1485, their combined force landed at Milford Haven and, on 22 August, they met the royal army at the **BATTLE OF BOSWORTH FIELD.** Richard was killed in the fighting and buried in Leicester.

RICHARD COEUR DE LION. (See **RICHARD I**).

RICHARD, DUKE OF YORK (1411-60). The father of **EDWARD IV** and **RICHARD III,** the **DUKE OF YORK** laid claim to the throne of **ENGLAND** in a political power struggle which led to the **WARS OF THE ROSES.** Born on 21 September 1411 to Richard, Earl of Cambridge, and Anne Mortimer, he succeeded his uncle, Edward, as Duke of York in 1415. Ten years later, on the death of the Earl of March, he inherited considerable estates in England, **WALES** and **IRELAND.** He served in **HENRY VI's**

armies on the continent and was rewarded with the posts of Lieutenant-General and Governor of Normandy and France.

At home, the **GOVERNMENT**, controlled mainly by members of the Beaufort family, was becoming increasingly dissatisfied with the conduct of the war and Richard threw his weight behind its chief opposition, Humphrey, Duke of Gloucester. When Gloucester died in 1447, York was moved to Ireland as Lieutenant, a post intended as an exile but one in which he earned considerable praise. He returned to England in 1450 and then, as well as in 1452, attempted to remove Henry's chief minister, Edmund Beaufort, Duke of Somerset, by armed force. He failed to achieve that goal but took his opportunity to gain power following the King's bout of mental illness in 1453.

Queen Margaret claimed the **REGENCY**, but she was widely disliked and, in March of the following year, York was chosen as Protector and Defender of the Realm Increasingly, however, Margaret viewed Richard as a possible usurper to the throne, preventing her son, Edward, from becoming King, so when Henry recovered his sanity, in 1454, she persuaded him to dismiss York and reinstate Somerset. The following year, York again sought Somerset's removal, gaining considerable support from his wife's family (the Nevilles). The two nobles brought their armies to St Albans on 22 May 1455 (see **BATTLE OF ST ALBANS**): Somerset was killed and York took control of government. Margaret, however, continued her opposition, rebuilding her army, and further conflict seemed inevitable. In 1459, Richard fled to Ireland because his soldiers refused to fight against the King in person but the Nevilles, along with York's son, Edward, defeated the royalist force at the **BATTLE OF NORTHAMPTON** on 10 July 1460, and took Henry prisoner.

York returned from Ireland and claimed the **CROWN** on the basis of his priority by descent (he could prove ancestry from Lionel, the third son of **EDWARD III**, whereas Henry was descended from **JOHN OF GAUNT**, the fourth son). Most of the **HOUSE OF LORDS** opposed the claim, but Henry himself, wanting to avoid confrontation, agreed to recognize the Duke as his heir. In response, Margaret raised yet another force and York went north to meet it. On 30 December 1460, showing a complete lack of strategic judgement, he left his castle at Sandal with a small company to meet a much larger opposition and was killed (see **BATTLE OF WAKEFIELD**). His head, bearing a paper crown, was displayed in **YORK** until his son removed it after the

BATTLE OF TOWTON on 4 March the following yeart. The Duke's remains were finally interred at Fotheringhay in 1476.

RICHARD THE LIONHEART. (See **RICHARD I**).

RIDOLFI PLOT, 1571. A plot by Roberto Ridolfi (an Italian banker) and the **DUKE** of Norfolk to assassinate Queen **ELIZABETH I** and bring Mary Queen of Scots to the throne of **ENGLAND** (with the aid of a force from Spain) was uncovered by **WILLIAM CECIL** and his network of spies. Norfolk was executed and Mary's cause much maligned by this complicated and unworkable scheme which was said to involve the Pope.

RIOT ACT, December 1715. A response to the Jacobite rebellion and the public disorders following the accession of the **HANOVERIANS**, this act (see **ACT OF PARLIAMENT**) decreed that individuals involved in riotous assemblies of more than 12 persons could be arrested as felons if they did not immediately disperse after a **GOVERNMENT** official had read aloud the terms of the legislation in public. The penalty could be life imprisonment and repetition of the offence could be punishable by death. The act was famously used at the **PETERLOO MASSACRE** and was repealed in 1973. It survives in the phrase 'To read the Riot Act' meaning 'To warn someone of severe treatment'.

RIPON, EARL OF. (See **FREDERICK JOHN ROBINSON**).

ROADS. Roads in **PREHISTORIC BRITAIN** were usually paths along high ground, clear of forests and the potential for ambush. The **ROMANS** built the first coordinated system of routeways to link their towns and forts and to supply their imperial possessions. For strategic reasons, these were often well made, with ditches and a camber, so that chariots and other wheeled traffic could travel at speed (the legacy of that network explains the modern pattern of trunk roads radiating from **LONDON** to old established settlements and avoiding the later centres of the **INDUSTRIAL REVOLUTION**). In the 16th century, each **PARISH** was responsible for its own routes and, in addition, a series of drove roads which provided a means of getting cattle and sheep to the market towns. However, lack of investment resulted in a poor state of repair, with considerable implications for the development of commerce. Thus, during the late 17th and 18th centuries, a series of **TURNPIKES** was created, the Turnpike Trusts being charged with improving the roads with funds gained from tolls. Engineers such as Thomas Telford, Blind Jack of Knaresborough and John Macadam (inventor of tarmac) turned their talents to road-building and the 1835 Highways Act (see **ACT OF PARLIAMENT**) made **COUNTY** Councils responsible for highway maintenance.

The 19th century love affair with the **RAILWAYS** diverted attention away from roads until the development of motorized transport in the late 1800s and early 1900s fuelled a resurgence of interest. **GOVERNMENT** responsibility for the national route pattern was accepted through the creation, in 1920, of the Ministry of Transport and, since 1934, a network of main trunk roads has been established, with A, B and C class roads (in descending order of importance) taking local traffic from the interregional motorways. In recent years, proposals to develop new roads have been heavily attacked by environmentalist groups and there have been calls for more efficient use of the private motor car, transfer of freight to the railways and investment in public transport systems. Some authorities (in **NATIONAL PARKS**, for example) have experimented with bans on car travel in certain areas. There are currently 225,600 miles of paved highway in the United Kingdom.

ROBIN HOOD. (See **HOOD, ROBIN**).

ROBINSON, FREDERICK JOHN (1782-1859). **PRIME MINISTER** from August 1827 until January 1828, Robinson was born in **LONDON** on 1 November 1782. The son of Thomas Robinson, Baron Grantham, he was educated at Harrow School and **CAMBRIDGE** University. Owing his political advancement to his friendship with **VISCOUNT CASTLEREAGH** and his kinship with Philip Yorke, Earl of Hardwicke and **LORD LIEUTENANT** of **IRELAND** (whom he served as Private Secretary from 1804 until 1806), he was made **UNDER-SECRETARY OF STATE** for War and the Colonies by **SPENCER PERCEVAL** in 1809 and, the following year, became Lord of the **ADMIRALTY**. In 1812, he was appointed Lord of **THE TREASURY** by the **EARL OF LIVERPOOL**, in 1813 became joint **PAYMASTER GENERAL** and, in 1818, was made **PRESIDENT OF THE BOARD OF TRADE**. He was promoted to **CHANCELLOR OF THE EXCHEQUER** in 1823, assisting in the dismantling of the **NAVIGATION**

ACTS as the **GOVERNMENT** adopted a policy favouring **FREE TRADE**, then served under **GEORGE CANNING** as **SECRETARY OF STATE** for War and the Colonies in 1827.

As Viscount Goderich, he also acted as Leader of the **HOUSE OF LORDS** for Canning, whom he succeeded as Prime Minister in August 1827. In that role, he was (by his own admission) a failure, unable to prevent the **TORIES** from disintegrating, and was dismissed by **GEORGE IV** in January 1828. **EARL GREY** gave him a second spell as Secretary for War and the Colonies in 1830. Three years later he was created Earl of Ripon and made **LORD PRIVY SEAL**. In 1834, he resigned and transferred his allegiance to Sir **ROBERT PEEL**, with whom he served as President of the Board of Trade from 1841 until 1843 and as President of the India Board from 1843 until 1846. He died in Putney on 28 January 1859.

ROCKINGHAM, MARQUIS OF. (See **WATSON-WENTWORTH, CHARLES**).

ROMANS. Julius Caesar raided Britain in 55 BC and 54 BC, but it was not until Emperor Claudius sent four legions in 43 AD that the conquest began. Landing at Richborough (**KENT**), Aulus Plautius, the commander, quickly subdued the south of **ENGLAND** and began to spread control over the native **CELTS**. **BOADICEA**, Queen of the **ICENI**, led an unsuccessful revolt in 61 AD and **WALES** was conquered by 78 AD. In **SCOTLAND**, the Romans defeated the Caledonians at the Battle of Mons Graupius and, in the same year, they destroyed the **DRUID** settlement on Anglesey. However, they had difficulty holding the outer parts of **BRITANNIA**, particularly in the north and west, where disaffection with the conquerors led to the building of **HADRIAN'S WALL** and the Antonine Wall to distinguish between the southern civil zone and the northern military zone.

Within the area of Roman control, towns were used as centres of administration. Military barracks, tax offices and legal buildings were sited in settlements, many of which (**BATH**, **CANTERBURY**, Chester and **YORK**, for instance) are still important regional foci. **ROADS** such as Ermine Street (the later A1), Watling Street (between **LONDON** and Wales) and the Fosse Way (from the southwest to the northeast) were built to connect the settlements and link them with military units at the frontier. Agriculture flourished (notably close to **VILLA**s) and the mining of silver, lead, tin, iron and gold developed, as did wheat growing in south-central England and even viticulture in more sheltered southern areas.

The Romans never did subdue all of Britain and, by 350 AD, the Empire as a whole was straining under increased barbarian attacks (particularly from **IRELAND** and Denmark). Legions were withdrawn from Britain to defend France against the Gauls, Foederati (auxiliary troops) increasingly pressed into service to defend imperial interests and the **SAXON SHORE FORTS** built. In 410 AD, the people who had arrived as conquerors abandoned this outpost of empire, leaving it to sort out its own destiny but endowing it with a legacy of sophisticated writing, legal systems, engineering, towns, roads and trade which was to last for two millenia. (See **SAXONS**).

ROMANTIC MOVEMENT. A literary movement which lasted from 1770 until about 1840, Romanticism was a reaction to the **EN-LIGHTENMENT** inspired by the French and American Revolutions and by the wars of independence in Spain, Greece and Poland. It stressed the importance of individual experience, the spiritual effects of the natural landscape and the value of imagination. Politically, it was reflected in support for progressive reforms (such as improvements to the rights of women), but it could also invoke despair when hopes for such reforms were dashed. The central figures tended to be people who found solace and stimulus in the great outdoors — climbers, walkers and sea bathers, for example. They included George Byron, Percy Bysshe Shelley and William Wordsworth.

ROSEBERY, ARCHIBALD PHILIP PRIMROSE (1847-1929). An aristocrat who became **PRIME MINISTER** more by accident than by ambition, Rosebery was born in **LONDON** on 7 May 1847, the son of Archibald, fourth Earl of Rosebery, and his wife, Catherine (daughter of Philip, Earl Stanhope). He was educated at Eton College and **OXFORD** University, took his seat in the **HOUSE OF LORDS** in 1868 and was **UNDER-SECRETARY OF STATE** at the **HOME OFFICE** from 1881 until 1883 in **WILLIAM GLADSTONE**'s second **LIBERAL PARTY** administration. His chief contribution during those years was to insist that Scottish interests should be given special attention by **GOVERNMENT**, an insistence which ultimately led to the formation of the Scottish Office in 1885. An ultrasensitive individual, he resigned in 1883, unwilling to accept criticism even over minor issues, and set off for a tour round the world. When he returned, he spent a short period as **LORD PRIVY SEAL** (March-June 1885) and then, at Queen **VICTORIA**'s suggestion, was appointed Foreign Secretary in February 1886, serving until the **CONSERVATIVE PARTY** victory at the **GENERAL ELECTION** in July. While the Liberals were in **OPPOSITION**, he concentrated more on local than national affairs, chairing **LONDON COUNTY COUNCIL** for 18 months from its inception in January 1889 until July 1890.

In November 1890, his wife, Hannah (daughter of Baron Meyer de Rothschild), died of typhoid fever; she left an £800,000 fortune but that was little consolation to Rosebery, who had relied heavily on her advice. In his grief, he wanted to retire from politics but was persuaded to continue and, much against his better judgement, agreed to accept the post of Foreign Secretary in Gladstone's fourth administration (1892-94). The appointment did neither much good because they differed fundamentally on many aspects of policy (Gladstone wanted Britain to give up control of Uganda, for example, but Rosebery wanted to maintain imperial influence in East Africa). Moreover, Rosebery had no flair for international politics (he seemed oblivious to the implications of the 1894 Franco-Russian Alliance for the balance of power in Europe, for instance). His grasp on domestic matters was stronger, and, as a result, he was able to act as arbitrator in a dispute between management and labour in the **COAL** industry during 1893.

In the same year, Rosebery and Gladstone crossed swords in an argument over funds for the **ROYAL NAVY** (Rosebery favoured an increase; Gladstone did not) and that issue eventually led to the Prime Minister's resignation the following year. Gladstone recommended Lord Spencer as his successor and the general public favoured the radical Sir William Harcourt but Queen Victoria exercised her **ROYAL PREROGATIVE** and asked Rosebery to form a government. The administration lasted from March 1894 until June 1895 and was notable primarily for its lack of impact on anything. That ineffectiveness was not entirely of Rosebery's making because the House of Lords was dominated by Conservatives and therefore unwilling to pass legislation proposed by Liberals in the **HOUSE OF COMMONS**. On the other hand, his limited powers of leadership meant that he failed to deal with a deeply divided **CABINET** and, when he was defeated in a **PARLIAMENT**ary vote on **WAR OFFICE** policy in June 1895, he was only too happy to resign.

There was one outstanding achievement during those years — the racing stable which he had founded, while still an undergraduate, won the Derby in 1894 and again in 1895, but these successes merely confirmed the **NONCONFORMIST** view that he was an affluent hedonist. Rosebery resigned the Liberal leadership in 1896 and, from that point, began to drift away from his former colleagues, finally withdrawing completely from the Party in 1905 with a declaration that he could no longer support moves for Irish **HOME RULE**. He intervened on only two issues after that; in 1909, he condemned **DAVID LLOYD GEORGE**'s **BUDGET**, claiming that it was socialist, and, in 1910, he proposed that the powers of the House of Lords should be increased (a view which gained little support in a Commons which wanted a weakened second chamber rather than a stronger one). In later years, he did much to recruit soldiers to fight in the **FIRST WORLD WAR** and turned his home at Dalmeny, near Edinburgh, into a hospital for injured servicemen but, just before the conflict ended, suffered a stroke which left him crippled. He died at The Durdans, his country home near Epsom, on 21 May 1929 and was succeeded as Earl by Albert, his eldest son.

ROSEBERY, EARL OF. (See **ARCHIBALD PHILIP PRIMROSE ROSEBERY**).

ROSES, WARS OF THE. This term was coined by Walter Scott, in his romanticized novels, to describe the domestic troubles in **ENGLAND** between 1455 and 1485. English politics were shaped by a dynastic struggle for the **CROWN** between two **PLANTAGENET** families — the House of York (which sported a white rose emblem) and the House of Lancaster (which had a red rose). The bitter rivalry began during the minority reign of the Lancastrian **HENRY VI**, who was less than one year old when he came to the throne in 1422. England was governed by a council of nobles and was subjected to internecine killings and ineffectual leadership in later years. The factions were led by the royalist Duke of Somerset and the dissident **RICHARD, DUKE OF YORK**, who declared himself King after he had captured Henry at the **BATTLE OF NORTHAMPTON**. **PARLIAMENT** refused to accede and, after the **BATTLE OF ST ALBANS** (1461), supported the claims of his son, who became **EDWARD IV**.

In the later 1460s, the influential Richard Neville, Earl of Warwick, rebelled against Edward and, as the political pendulum swung, Henry was restored to the throne (in 1470) but, following a crushing defeat at the **BATTLE OF TEWKESBURY**, was put to death in the **TOWER OF LONDON** (1471). Edward returned to the throne and ruled until he died in 1483, leaving his 12-year old son to succeed him as **EDWARD V**. Richard, Duke of Gloucester and brother of Edward IV, had Edward V and his younger brother imprisoned in the Tower (the young Princes of the Tower were never seen again) and usurped the throne as King **RICHARD III**.

In the 30 years from 1455, only about 60 weeks of armed conflict actually occurred but these culminated in victory for the Lancastrians at the **BATTLE OF BOSWORTH FIELD** (1485), where Richard was killed. His victor, Lancastrian Henry **TUDOR**, became **HENRY VII** and established the Tudor line, which lasted until the **UNION OF THE CROWNS** in 1603. The struggles almost destroyed the principle of hereditary succession to the Crown. (See **BATTLE OF STOKE; BATTLE OF TOWTON; BATTLE OF WAKEFIELD**).

ROTTEN BOROUGHS. This term originated with a remark by **WILLIAM PITT THE ELDER** that the representation of **BOROUGHS** was the "rotten part of the Constitution". By the early 19th century, a number of long-established boroughs had been depopulated, or had become part of a gentleman's country estate, yet still returned Members of **PARLIAMENT**. They were thus in the control of one individual or a small group of influential people. (Rotten boroughs were sometimes called pocket boroughs because they were 'in the pocket' of a patron.) Examples included Old Sarum (which had no residents), Dunwich (which had been submerged by the sea for centuries) and Gatton (a country residence). They were abolished by the 1832 Reform Act (see **ACT OF PARLIAMENT**) as part of the movement for **PARLIAMENTARY REFORM**.

ROUNDHEADS. This term is used to describe the **PURITAN PARLIAMENTARIAN** soldiers of the **CIVIL WAR** and **COMMONWEALTH**. It is usually linked with the term **CAVALIERS** (which denotes the more colourful, royalist supporters of King **CHARLES I**) and originated in 1641 when a party of loyal officers fought with a group of apprentices. The close-cropped hair of the apprentices led to the abusive term 'roundhead'.

ROYAL AIR FORCE (RAF). The Royal Flying Corps (part of the **BRITISH ARMY**) was formed on 13 April 1912 and merged with the Royal Naval Air Service (part of the **ROYAL NAVY**) on 1 April 1918 to form the Royal Air Force, independent of both of the other services. The merger created the world's first independent air force. The **FIRST WORLD WAR** had transformed the role of airplanes in hostilities from simple reconnaissance to a fighting arm of the nation but, even so, the decision to create the RAF was extraordinarily far-sighted for its time, establishing a combat unit which could operate without reference to the other services and which was capable of commanding vast areas of land and sea. During the **SECOND WORLD WAR** and the **BATTLE OF BRITAIN**, it proved its worth as an effective first line of defence as well as in an aggressive role (see **BOMBER COMMAND**). In 1964, it was put under the control of the Ministry of Defence and now comprises Strike Command, Support Command and RAF Germany. Strike Command has about 850 aircraft ranging from Tornado fighters to Harrier jump-jets and Nimrod reconnaissance planes. Support Command provides logistics, signals and maintenance while RAF Germany serves Supreme Allied Command Europe. In 1992, the RAF had approximately 83,000 personnel, including 7,000 women. (See **DAMBUSTERS**).

ROYAL ASSENT. By this action (normally a signature), the **MONARCH** gives royal approval to a **BILL**. Technically, that approval can be refused but, in modern times, **PARLIAMENT** (rather than the sovereign) is the supreme law-making authority so Assent is a formality (the last time it was refused was in 1707, when Queen **ANNE** was on the throne). As soon as it is given, the Bill becomes an **ACT OF PARLIAMENT** and therefore part of the law of the land.

ROYAL FINANCES. The finances of the sovereign now comprise the **CIVIL LIST**, Grant in Aid for the upkeep of palaces and other structures, the Privy Purse (from the income of the **DUCHY OF LANCASTER**) to meet semiofficial expenses and the **MONARCH**'s personal income (which is now subject to income tax). There are also other sums set by **GOVERNMENT** departments (for example, to maintain the Royal Yacht).

ROYAL HOUSEHOLD. The Household, which consists of the **MONARCH**'s followers and advisers, was the basis of **GOVERNMENT** from the 12th century and originally included the **EXCHEQUER** and **THE TREASURY**. Gradually, it came to be responsible only for the sovereign's support, official administration and ceremonial. (See **BEDCHAMBER CRISIS; CIVIL LIST; CURIA REGIS**).

ROYAL MARRIAGES ACT, 1772. King **GEORGE III** was said to be furious that two of his relatives had married commoners. This act (see **ACT OF PARLIAMENT**) attempted to bring them into line by making it illegal for any member of the Royal Family directly descended from **GEORGE II** to marry without the sovereign's consent unless they were over 25 years of age. Others could marry only if one year's notice was given to the **PRIVY COUNCIL** and there were no objections from **PARLIAMENT**.

ROYAL NAVY. King **ALFRED THE GREAT** created a navy in the ninth century, and by the 16th century the Board of **ADMIRALTY** was in control of this ancient armed service. It was reorganized by Samuel Pepys for King **CHARLES II**, who wrote: "It is upon the navy under the good providence of God that the safety, honour and welfare of this realm do chiefly depend". Thus the Senior Service came about. It is now administered from Northwood (Middlesex) while shore-based facilities are run from Portsmouth. The Royal Marines is a military wing which has its separate structure. The fleet consists of submarines (including Polaris-carrying vessels), guided missile destroyers and frigates. In 1992, they were operated by 54,000 personnel, including 4,000 women, but the so-called 'peace dividend' at the end of the Cold War led to the introduction of a programme of reductions both in manpower and craft. It now has fewer than 30 readily available destroyers and frigates and some newly built submarines are being leased to other nations (as recently as 1953, there had been 44 frigates, 25 destroyers, eight cruisers, seven aircraft carriers and one battleship).

ROYAL PREROGATIVE. These are the rights, powers and privileges enjoyed by the **MONARCH** and recognized by law. They were virtually unlimited in the medieval period but were increasingly challenged, initially by the **MAGNA CARTA** but more particularly from the 17th century (see **BILL OF RIGHTS, CIVIL**

LIST, PARLIAMENTARY REFORM, PETITION OF RIGHT). Remaining rights, most exercised under the advice and control of **GOVERNMENT**, include the appointment of a **PRIME MINISTER**, formal approval of a Government, the creation of life peers (see **PEERAGE**) and the granting of other honours, the summoning and dissolution of **PARLIAMENT**, the dismissal of Government (a prerogative not used since King **WILLIAM IV** replaced **VISCOUNT MELBOURNE** with **ROBERT PEEL** in 1834) and the making of war and peace. (See **DIVINE RIGHT OF KINGS**).

ROYAL TITLES ACT, 1876. The brainchild of Prime Minister **BENJAMIN DISRAELI**, this act (see **ACT OF PARLIA-MENT**) declared Queen **VICTORIA** Empress of India in an attempt to establish a clear distinction between British and native rulers in the subcontinent.

ROYALISTS. A term applied to all supporters of the **MONARCH**, the word is usually used specifically with reference to followers of King **CHARLES I** and King **CHARLES II**. These people, also termed **CAVALIERS**, included the leading landowners and Catholics of the time. (See **CAVALIER PARLIA-MENT; CIVIL WAR; GRAND REMONSTRANCE; PENRUDDOCK'S RISING**).

RUMP PARLIAMENT, 1648-1653 and 1659-1660. The remnants of the **LONG PARLIAMENT**, left after **PRIDE'S PURGE** tried and condemned **CHARLES I**, abolished the **HOUSE OF LORDS** and declared **ENGLAND** a **COMMONWEALTH**. Attempts to enforce strict **PURITAN** standards evoked much criticism and eventually Members were forcibly ejected by the army on the orders of **OLIVER CROMWELL**. It was succeeded by the **BAREBONES PARLIAMENT** but was recalled in 1659 after the collapse of the **PROTECTORATE**. It dissolved itself the following year and was followed by the **CON-VENTION PARLIAMENT**.

RUNCIE, ROBERT ALEXANDER KENNEDY (1921-). **ARCH-BISHOP OF CANTERBURY** throughout the social and economic change of the 1980s, Runcie was born on 2 October 1921, the son of Robert Runcie and his wife, Ann. Educated at Merchant Taylor's School in Crosbie and at **OXFORD** and **CAMBRIDGE**

Universities, he served with the Scots Guards during the **SEC-OND WORLD WAR**, earning the Military Cross in 1945. He was ordained as a deacon in 1950 and as a priest the following year. From 1950 until 1952, he was Curate at All Saints, Gosforth, then, from 1953 to 1954, served as Chaplain at Westcott House, Cambridge. He was promoted to Vice-Principal in 1954 and held the post until 1956, when he was appointed Fellow, Dean and Assistant Tutor at Trinity Hall (also in Cambridge). In 1960, he became Vicar of Cuddesdon and Principal of Cuddesdon Theological College (Oxford) and, in 1970, was consecrated Bishop of St Albans. From 1973 until 1979, he chaired Television's Central Religious Advisory Committee and, in 1980, was made Archbishop of Canterbury.

The next decade was to be a period of great turmoil in Britain and Runcie was at the heart of it. In 1982, he welcomed Pope John Paul II to **CANTERBURY** and, in a dramatic gesture of reconciliation between the Roman Catholic and Anglican Churches, knelt beside him in the Cathedral for prayer. He also presided at a service following the end of the **FALKLANDS WAR** and reportedly annoyed Prime Minister **MARGARET THATCHER** by stressing the need to build bridges with Argentina rather than glory in victory. In later years, he was involved in the debate over homosexuality in the priesthood and the arguments about the ordination of women. He retired in 1990 and, the following year, was appointed High Steward of the University of Cambridge and raised to the **PEERAGE** as Baron Runcie.

RUNNYMEDE, 1215. In this meadow alongside the **RIVER THAMES** in Surrey, between Windsor and Staines, King **JOHN** agreed the terms of the **MAGNA CARTA** with his Barons. The site now has an acre of land, given to the United States of America by the people of Britain, which has a monument to John F. Kennedy and an excerpt from his inaugural address which echoes the Magna Carta: "We shall pay any price, bear any burden, meet any hardship, support any friend and oppose any foe in order to assure the survival and success of liberty".

RUSSELL, EARL. (See **JOHN RUSSELL**).

RUSSELL, JOHN (1792-1878). **LIBERAL PARTY PRIME MINISTER** from 1846 until 1852 and from October 1865 until June 1866, Russell was born in **LONDON** on 18 August 1792, the third son of the Duke of Bedford. He was educated privately and at **WESTMINSTER** School and Edinburgh University then, in 1813, entered **PARLIAMENT** and began a political career marked by support for social change and particularly for **PARLIAMENTARY REFORM.**

His first **GOVERNMENT** job was as **PAYMASTER GENERAL** under **EARL GREY** in 1830. The new Prime Minister appointed a committee to prepare legislation aimed at changing the composition of the **HOUSE OF COMMONS.** Russell was included and, after he had moved the first reading of the bill (see **ACT OF PARLIAMENT**) in March 1831, increasingly became recognized as the man who had shaped the new political structure. In 1835, he was appointed to the dual post of **HOME SECRETARY** and **LEADER OF THE HOUSE OF COMMONS** by **VISCOUNT MELBOURNE,** much to the chagrin of **WILLIAM IV**, who was no supporter of his reformist ideals. In 1839, he became **SECRETARY OF STATE** for War and the Colonies but, two years later, was removed from office by a **GENERAL ELECTION** which brought the **CONSERVATIVE PARTY**, led by Sir **ROBERT PEEL**, to power.

In 1846, he supported Peel's repeal of the **CORN LAWS**, an action which split the Conservatives, led to Peel's resignation and brought a Liberal Government, headed by Russell, to **DOWNING STREET**. As Prime Minister, he had mixed success. In 1847, his policy of importing US corn to alleviate famine in **IRELAND** did little to solve a problem caused more by overpopulation than lack of food, but, in 1848, he was much more effective in his dealings with the **CHARTISTS**. In the end, his administration toppled because of differences with **VISCOUNT PALMERSTON**, his Foreign Secretary. Palmerston had a habit of acting on his own initiative and, in 1851, sent a message to the French conveying Britain's approval of the coup d'état led by Louis Napoleon. Neither Queen **VICTORIA** nor Russell had been consulted and, embarrassed, the Prime Minister sacked his Minister. Palmerston, however, got his revenge the following year, helping to bring down the Government.

When the **EARL OF ABERDEEN** became Prime Minister in 1852, leading a coalition administration, Russell was given the post of Foreign Secretary (December 1852-February 1853) then, from June 1854, acted as **LORD PRESIDENT OF THE COUNCIL**. In early 1855, he resigned, differing with his colleagues over an inquiry established to examine the Government's handling of the **CRIMEAN WAR,** and, later that year, made a series of errors while acting as British representative at the Vienna Conference designed to negotiate peace and bring an end to the War. In both cases, he was widely accused of political misjudgement and, as a result, remained out of office until he was recalled as Foreign Secretary by Palmerston in 1859. In 1861, he was awarded an earldom but again his political activities met with mixed success (he made a number of mistakes over policies relating to the US Civil War, for instance).

When Palmerston died on 18 October 1865, Russell became Prime Minister for the second time, but his tenure lasted only until June of the following year, when his Government was defeated in a vote on a new Reform Bill. Now 73, he retired from politics and died at Pembroke Lodge in Surrey on 28 May 1878.

—S—

ST ALBANS, BATTLES OF. There were two major battles at St Albans during the **WARS OF THE ROSES**.

On 22 May 1455, a Lancastrian force supporting **HENRY VI** was heavily defeated by a rebel army led by **RICHARD, DUKE OF YORK**. This followed Richard's attempt to take control of the country as Protector and Chief Counsellor. Henry was wounded and captured, allowing Richard to strengthen his dictatorial powers over **ENGLAND**.

On 17 February 1461, the Lancastrian forces of Queen Margaret were successful, defeating Richard Neville, Earl of Warwick, and rescuing Henry. But the cruelty and pillage which followed, coupled with the unpopularity of alliances with the Scots and the French (both traditional enemies of England), turned the country against them. On 4 March, Henry was deposed and York's son declared King as **EDWARD IV**.

SAINTES, BATTLE OF, 21 July 1242. The French forces gained a victory over the forces of King **HENRY III**, who was attempting to retrieve the lost territory of Poitou (in France). Protracted negotiations with allies and difficulty in raising funds had dogged the escapade and Henry was left only with the occupation of Gascony in mainland France.

SALAMANCA, BATTLE OF, 22 July 1812. In one of the decisive battles of the **PENINSULAR WAR**, the **DUKE OF WEL-LINGTON** defeated a French force in only 40 minutes, inflicting massive casualties numbering over 15,000. He said of the battle, "Everything went as it should. There never was an army so beaten in so short a time".

SALISBURY, MARQUIS OF. (See **ROBERT ARTHUR TALBOT GASCOYNE-CECIL**).

SALVATION ARMY. This evangelical religious movement was founded by **WILLIAM BOOTH** in the East End of **LONDON** in July 1865. Its quasi-military organization, with generals and other ranks, dates from its reorganization from the earlier Christian Revival Association into the Salvation Army in 1878. An international movement by the 1880s, its mission was to provide succour for the poor and destitute as well as to hold simple religious services and worship.

SANCTUARY. From early Christian times in **ENGLAND**, church and churchyard provided a place of refuge for fugitives. They could not be removed but, after 40 days, were forced to take the **OATH OF ABJURATION** and leave the country. Sanctuary for traitors (see **TREASON**) was removed in 1486, for criminals in 1623 and for civil offenders in 1697 and 1723.

SAXE-COBURG-GOTHA, 1901-10. **EDWARD VII** was the only **MONARCH** of the Saxe-Coburg-Gotha line, which is more properly referred to by its family name as the House of **WETTIN**. Edward was the child of **PRINCE ALBERT**, Consort of Queen **VICTORIA** and son of Ernest, Duke of Saxe-Coburg-Gotha. (See **WINDSOR**).

SAXONS. Germanic invaders of Britain during the fifth and sixth centuries, the Saxons came mainly from Frisia and settled in the south and east of the country. By the seventh century, Saxon kingdoms and bretwaldaships (or overkingships) had been established, notably in **WESSEX**. The major opposing power was **MERCIA**, established by the **ANGLES**. (See **ANGLO-SAXONS; SAXON SHORE FORTS**).

SAXON SHORE FORTS. From about 225 AD, Britain came under increasing attack from coastal pirates, barbarians and **SAXON** invaders. In response, the **ROMANS** constructed a series of 14 massive stone forts (the last at Pevensey in 330 AD) along the coast of south and east **ENGLAND**, from the Isle of Wight to Norfolk. They were commanded by the Count of the Saxon Shore and remnants of many remain.

SCARMAN ENQUIRY, 1981. This committee, chaired by **LORD** Scarman, was set up to inquire into the factors involved in a series of inner city riots during 1981, particularly in St Paul's (Bristol), Brixton (**LONDON**), Toxteth (**LIVERPOOL**) and Moss Side (**MANCHESTER**). It made several recommendations, some of which were implemented by **MARGARET THATCHER**'s **GOVERNMENT**.

SCOTLAND. The most northerly part of the **BRITISH ISLES**, Scotland has a population of 5.1 million (1991), covers an area of 30,400 square miles and can be divided into three physical areas — the highlands, the central valley and the southern uplands. Population and settlement are concentrated in the second of these areas. Although often considered by the kings of **ENGLAND** to be part of their realm, Scotland maintained a fierce independence of its southern neighbour until the **UNION OF THE CROWNS** under **JAMES VI** and I in 1603 and the **TREATY OF UNION** in 1707. It still has separate education and legal systems, its own banks and a Presbyterian established church (the Church of Scotland). In the **HOUSE OF COMMONS**, it is allocated 72 seats. After the 1992 **GENERAL ELECTION**, 49 of these were held by the **LABOUR PARTY**, 11 by the **CONSERVATIVE PARTY**, nine by the **LIBERAL DEMO-CRATIC PARTY** and three by the Scottish Nationalist Party.

SCOTLAND YARD. The Yard was the headquarters of the Metropolitan **POLICE** from 1829 until the 1960s, when the force was rehoused in purpose-built accommodation at New Scotland Yard, near the Houses of **PARLIAMENT**. The area acquired its name during the 10th century, when King **EDGAR** gave King Kenneth MacAlpin of **SCOTLAND** land on which to build a palace.

SCOTT, ROBERT FALCON (1868-1912). Leader of the second expedition to reach the South Pole, Scott was born in Devonport on 6 June 1868, the second son of John and Hannah Scott. He was educated at Stoke Damerel and Stubbington then, in 1880, joined

HMS *Britannia* as a Naval Cadet. Over the next two decades he rose through the ranks until, by 1899, he was Torpedo-Lieutenant on HMS *Majestic*, flagship of the Channel Squadron. In 1900 (on the recommendation of Sir Clements Markham, President of the Royal Geographical Society), he was appointed Leader of the National Antarctic Expedition, which explored South Victoria Land and the interior of the Antarctic continent between 1901 and 1904, adding much to scientists' understanding of meteorology, biology and magnetism. On his return, he was made a Commander of the Royal Victorian Order and promoted to Captain. He spent the next five years in command of HMS *Victorious*, HMS *Essex* and HMS *Bulwark* but had been smitten by his polar experiences. In 1909, Scott announced that he intended to take another expedition to the Antarctic and become the first person to reach the South Pole.

He sailed from Britain in June 1910 and, on 24 October 1911, set off across the ice from Cape Evans with four companions. On 17 January 1912, after a sledge journey of 1,842 miles, he reached his destination, only to find a note from Roald Amundsen telling him that a Norwegian party had arrived on 14 December. On the return journey, the group was beset by bad weather, illness and a lack of food. On 4 February, Petty Officer Edgar Evans fell and suffered concussion. On 17 February he died. On 17 March, Captain L. E .G. Oates, suffering from frostbite and too ill to travel further, walked out into a blizzard believing that, by sacrificing his own life, he might save his com-panions. Scott wrote in his journal that "It was the act of a brave man and an English gentleman — we all hope to meet the end with a similar spirit". The depleted band struggled on for another four days but was forced by a blizzard to camp just 11 miles from a food depot. They were still there on 29 March, when Scott made the last entry in his diary: "Every day we have been ready to start for our depot but outside the door of our tent it remains a scene of whirling drift . . . We shall stick it out to the end . . . and the end cannot be far". On 12 November, a search party found the tent and the bodies of Scott, Lieut H. R. Bowers and E. A. Wilson (the expedition doctor).

Although there had been much mismanagement of the arrangements for the long trek, in Britain the men were seen as heroes. Scott's widow was accorded the rank of the wife of a Knight Commander of the Bath by Queen **VICTORIA** and **GOVERNMENT** pensions were awarded to relatives of those who died. In 1920, a Polar Institute was founded in **CAMBRIDGE** to commemorate Scott's achievements. (See

ERNEST HENRY SHACKLETON).

SEBASTOPOL, SIEGE OF, October 1854-September 1855. A long siege by British and French forces eventually resulted in the taking of Sebastopol during the **CRIMEAN WAR**. This port and its arsenal were vital strategic locations during the conflict.

SECOND WORLD WAR, 1939-45. This war was fought between the Allies (including Britain) and the Axis powers of Germany and Italy, and Japan. Its origins lay in the failure of the **TREATY OF VERSAILLES** (which ended the **FIRST WORLD WAR**) to secure peace in Europe and the inability of the great powers to make the **LEAGUE OF NATIONS** a significant force in the face of aggressive calls from Adolf Hitler's Nazi Germany for lebensraum (or 'living space'). Austria was occupied in 1938, and the British **APPEASEMENT** policy failed abysmally to halt further aggression. Czechoslovakia was invaded in March 1939 and Poland in September.

Britain formally declared war on Germany on 3 September 1939. After France fell in 1940, a major rescue operation had to be mounted to get members of the British Expeditionary Force home from **DUNKIRK**. The **BATTLE OF BRITAIN** foiled German plans to invade the UK, but there were heavy civilian casualties, who suffered from bombing and rocket attack, particularly during the **BLITZ**. The **BATTLE OF THE ATLANTIC** launched the counterattack and continued against the U-boat threat until 1943. The **D-DAY** invasion of Europe started on 6 June 1944, beginning a push against the main German forces which was ultimately to lead them to surrender on 7 May the following year.

In the Pacific, the Japanese attack on Pearl Harbor (Hawaii) on 7 December 1941 brought the United States of America into the War, opening up a second front (until then, the Allies had received American aid in **LEND-LEASE** and intelligence). Over the next four years, many areas of the **BRITISH EMPIRE** were overrun as the Japanese extended control in Asia but the single atomic bomb, dropped by a US B-29 bomber on Hiroshima on 6 August 1945, quickly resulted in capitulation.

The six years of fighting had resulted in the deaths of 60,595 civilians, 264,433 members of the British armed forces and 30,248 merchant seamen — with a total of 484,472 British and **COMMONWEALTH OF NATIONS** dead. The effects of the war were far-reaching in Britain — a remarkable postwar altruism and the strongly centralist **GOVERNMENT** of wartime provided a climate for great social change (see **BEVERIDGE REPORT; EDUCATION; TOWN AND COUNTRY PLANNING; WELFARE STATE**). But the strains of the war effort meant economic ruin and loans from the United States were needed in order to rebuild manufacturing and other industry (see **MARSHALL AID**). The socialist **LABOUR PARTY** was in the political ascendancy, despite **WINSTON CHURCHILL**'s war leadership, and government in general seemed more powerful, enabling it to have a radical impact on the life of British citizens. (See **BATTLE OF EL ALAMEIN; ARCADIA CONFERENCE; ARMISTICE DAY; BATTLE OF ARNHEM; ATLANTIC CHARTER; CLEMENT ATTLEE; BOMBER COMMAND; CASABLANCA CONFERENCE; NEVILLE CHAMBERLAIN; CONSCRIPTION; DAMBUSTERS; DRESDEN RAID; BERNARD LAW MONTGOMERY; PHONEY WAR; POTSDAM CONFERENCE; RATIONING; SPECIAL OPERATIONS EXECUTIVE; BATTLE OF TOBRUK**).

SECRETARY OF STATE. This title is accorded to government **MINISTER**s who head major departments (thus, for example, the **HOME SECRETARY** is formally Secretary of State for the Home Department). These senior ministers have a seat in the **CABINET**.

SECRET SERVICE. The existence of a British Secret Service was only officially revealed in 1991 under Prime Minister **JOHN MAJOR**'s policy of open **GOVERNMENT** but the state has used spies and informers for centuries. Intelligence was collected from agents in the **TUDOR** period and, by the time of the **BOER WAR**, the **WAR OFFICE** and the Foreign Office had both established sophisticated networks of agents, including many travellers and journalists. A Secret Service Bureau was formed in 1909 and, in July 1993, for the first time, M15 (the counter-espionage arm, which concentrates largely on the domestic sphere) produced a public document containing information on its activities. This revealed that 70 per cent of the organization's resources were used to combat terrorism, of which 44 per cent was domestic and particularly Irish and Middle Eastern in focus (MI5 was the Division 5 of the British Directorate of Military Intelligence). MI6 is responsible for intelligence work in foreign countries and the Government Communications Headquarters monitors radio transmissions. All information is channelled through the Joint Intelligence Committee which reports to **MINISTER**s. (See **SPECIAL OPERATIONS EXECUTIVE**).

SEDGEMOOR, BATTLE OF, 6 July 1685. Fought near Bridgewater (Somerset), this battle ended the **MONMOUTH REBELLION** against King **JAMES VII and II**. The Duke of Monmouth's army was an ill-disciplined force of 5,000 and no match for the King's efficient troops. Up to 1,400 rebels were killed in the fighting or in the later pursuit. This was the last pitched battle on English soil and savage reprisals (see **BLOODY ASSIZES**) were visited on the west country — 250 of Monmouth's followers were executed and a further 850 transported (see **TRANSPORTATION**). Monmouth himself was executed at Tower Hill in **LONDON** on 15 July 1685.

SELECT COMMITTEE. The members of these Committees of **PARLIAMENT** are selected from the **HOUSE OF COMMONS** or the **HOUSE OF LORDS**. They are appointed to enquire into specific matters of public interest (such as broadcasting).

SERJEANT-AT-ARMS. The **HOUSE OF COMMONS** and the **HOUSE OF LORDS** each has a Serjeant-at-Arms, appointed by the **MONARCH**, who is responsible for security, for the efficient organization of support services and for certain ceremonial duties.

SEVEN YEARS WAR, 1756-63. The conclusive war for empire between Britain and France was fought on the battlegrounds of Europe, India and North America while, at the same time, Prussia and Austria clashed in Europe. Early British losses (such as Minorca in 1756) caused initial despondency but were later overshadowed by successes in the West Indies and victories for **ROBERT CLIVE** at the **BATTLE OF PLASSEY** (1757) and for **JAMES WOLFE** at the Battle of Quebec (1759). Montreal, and with it all French Canada, was surrendered to Britain on 8 September 1760. In 1762, war was declared on Spain and Britain seized Havana and Manila. A combination of naval and land supremacy, along with the subsidies of powerful European allies (such as Frederick the Great of Prussia), overwhelmed opposing powers, destroying French imperial plans and laying the foundations of the **BRITISH EMPIRE**. However, at the same time, the jealousies and emnities engendered created conditions conducive to European, and especially French, support for the rebellious colonists during the **AMERICAN WAR OF INDEPENDENCE.** The Seven Years War ended with the **TREATY OF PARIS** (10 February 1763), which gave Britain effective control of Canada, all of French America, islands in the West Indies, Senegal, India and a string of small islands and dependencies.

SEVERN, RIVER. The longest river in the United Kingdom, the Severn rises in the mountains of mid-**WALES** and follows a semicircular, 215-mile route to the Bristol Channel, flowing southeast initially and then turning towards southwest **ENGLAND.** During the 18th and 19th centuries, it was connected to the **RIVER THAMES** by the Kennet and Avon **CANAL** and to the industrial West Midlands by other links but these waterways are now largely disused or maintained only as recreational resources. The upper section of the river has been dammed to form Lake Vyrnwy, which supplies much of **LIVERPOOL**'s drinking water. At the other end, there is a tidal bore (or wave) some five feet in height and there have been proposals to use the energy for **ELECTRICITY** generation. However, the schemes have been strongly criticized on grounds of cost and the destruction which would be caused to the habitats of wading birds. The Severn is navigable by small barges as far as Welshpool, about 180 miles from its mouth. (For location, see Map 1, page xxv.)

SEX DISCRIMINATION ACT, 1975. This legislation (see **ACT OF PARLIAMENT**) made it unlawful to discriminate between the sexes in education, training, employment and the provision of services and goods. It also banned discriminatory advertising. The **EQUAL OPPORTUNITIES COMMISSION** enforce its provisions and those of the **EQUAL PAY ACT**, which came into effect the same year.

SEXUAL OFFENCES ACT, 1967. This act (see **ACT OF PARLIAMENT**) made homosexual acts between consenting male adults over 21 years of age legal in **ENGLAND** and **WALES** for the first time. It was part of the liberalization of the law at a period when attitudes to behaviour were generally becoming more permissive. (See **ABORTION; FAMILY PLANNING ACT; STREET OFFENCES ACT; WOLFENDEN REPORT**).

SEYMOUR, JANE (c. 1509-37). **HENRY VIII**'s third Queen, Jane was the eldest daughter of Sir John and Lady Margaret Seymour of Savernake (Wiltshire). She became lady-in-waiting to **CATHERINE OF ARAGON** and then to **ANNE BOLEYN** but, when Henry began to pay court to her in 1535, two years after his marriage to Anne, she refused to become his mistress — an attitude which undoubtedly hastened the Queen's downfall. Anne was executed on 19 May 1536 and, 11 days later, Henry and Jane wed privately. Though she played little part in affairs of state, she was popular with her subjects and the marriage seems to have been a happy one but she died on 24 October 1537 as a result of complications in the birth of the son (later **EDWARD VI**) which Henry had longed for.

SHACKLETON, ERNEST HENRY (1874-1922). The leader of two Antarctic expeditions, Shackleton was born in Kilkee on 15 February 1874, the son of Henry Shackleton, MD, and his wife, Henrietta. He was educated privately in **IRELAND** then at preparatory school in Sydenham and at Dulwich College (where he was described as backward for his age). He became an apprentice in the merchant navy at the age of 16 and, by 1901, when he joined **ROBERT FALCON SCOTT**'s National Antarctic Expedition, had risen to the rank of Sub-Lieutenant in the Royal Naval Reserve. With Scott and Edward Wilson, he took part in a sledge journey over the Ross Ice Shelf to latitude 82°16' South, but his health suffered and he had to return to Britain in 1903, a year before his colleagues. However, in 1908, he was appointed Leader of a second British Antarctic Expedition and, after wintering on Ross Island in McMurdo Sound, took a sledge party to within 97 miles of the pole. He was bitterly disappointed at having to turn back but the Expedition was considered a success because another group, led by T.W. Edgeworth David, reached the South Magnetic Pole and the Victoria Land Plateau was claimed for Britain and named after the Queen. In recognition of his achievements, Shackleton was **KNIGHT**ed and made a Commander of the Royal Victorian Order.

In 1914, he was in charge of the British Imperial Trans-Antarctic Expedition, which intended to cross the continent from the Weddell Sea to the Ross Sea, visiting the South Pole en route. However, in January 1915, his ship (HMS *Endurance*) became icebound and drifted until 27 October, when it was crushed by pack ice and had to be abandoned, 200 miles from land and 1,000 miles from the nearest settlement. The expedition members camped on ice floes until April 1916 then escaped in lifeboats to the South Shetland Islands, landing on Elephant Island. From there, Shackleton and five colleagues sailed 800 miles to South Georgia Island in a 22-foot whaleboat in order to get help for his stranded crew. He returned to Antarctica for a fourth time in 1921 but died in South Georgia on 5 January 1922, after suffering an attack of angina. His name is commemorated by Shackleton Inlet and Shackleton Ice Shelf in Antarctica and by the two Mount Shackletons in the Canadian Rockies and Greenland.

SHADOW MINISTER. In the **HOUSE OF COMMONS, OPPOSITION** Parties appoint spokesmen to lead the attack on **GOVERNMENT MINISTER**s. These spokesmen are frequently termed Shadow Ministers in the press.

SHAFTESBURY, EARL OF. (See **ANTHONY ASHLEY COOPER** [1621–83]).

SHAFTESBURY, EARL OF. (See **ANTHONY ASHLEY COOPER** [1801–85]).

SHELBURNE, EARL OF. (See **WILLIAM PETTY FITZMAURICE**).

SHERIFF. From the 11th century, the Shire Reeve replaced the **EARL** as the chief official in the **SHIRE**s, responsible largely for the management of royal properties and the collection of taxes. In **ENGLAND** and **WALES**, the office declined in importance from the 15th century and now carries responsibilities relating only to the organization of **PARLIAMENT**ary elections and the execution of legal writs. In **SCOTLAND**, however, the sheriff still presides over local criminal courts.

SHIP MONEY. In 1634, during the **ELEVEN YEARS TYRANNY**, a tax was imposed by King **CHARLES I** on maritime towns and **SHIRE**s to pay for the naval defence of the realm against Dutch and French threats. In imposing the tax, Charles was exercising an ancient **ROYAL PREROGATIVE** (enabling him to impose fiscal measures without the approval of **PARLIAMENT**) but, nevertheless, the action was interpreted as an attempt to rule without reference to Parliament. When it was extended, in 1635, to inland districts and then made an annual levy, it caused immense resentment although the income was vital to the King as he was spending up to half his income on the **ROYAL HOUSEHOLD** and was faced with falling returns from other sources. Ship Money was eventually declared illegal by the **LONG PARLIAMENT** in 1641.

SHIPBUILDING. King **ALFRED THE GREAT** is usually considered to be the father of the **ROYAL NAVY**, having created a fleet during the 9th century. From then, **ENGLAND** relied heavily on its naval strength and its merchant marine for commercial and imperial success and that reliance provided the basis of a large shipbuilding industry. The **NAVIGATION ACT** of 1381 (see **ACT OF PARLIAMENT**) encouraged the building of military and merchant vessels by restricting trade in English waters to English ships and, in the 16th century, legislation protected the timber, hemp and flax production on which the building of ships depended. Further Navigation Acts in the 17th century boosted trade and shipbuilding further by ensuring that the colonies would use English ships for all seaborne trade, adding to the demand for large, capacious vessels. By the late 19th century, Britain was supplying some 80 per cent of the world's ships, using the new technologies of the **INDUSTRIAL REVOLUTION**. While shipbuilding was badly affected by the **GREAT DEPRESSION** and the damage caused by enemy action during the **FIRST WORLD WAR**, demand held and yards remained relatively busy until the 1950s, when foreign firms (particularly in the Far East) began to undercut British costs inflated by antiquated equipment and poor labour practices. By 1994, the shipbuilding industry was all but dead, with only one major yard still in business. Britain's merchant marine fleet now comprises only 290 ships and ranks 33rd in the world.

SHIRE. The precursor of the Norman **COUNTY**, this **ANGLO-SAXON** administrative area was subdivided into **HUNDRED**s and named after its principal town. The shire was the **LOCAL GOVERNMENT** unit which organized defence, internal security, taxation and justice and its court was presided over by the **SHERIFF**, who was the key official. Rural counties are still sometimes referred to as 'Shire Counties', particularly those in the Midlands of **ENGLAND** whose names ended in '-shire' (as, for example, Leicestershire).

SHORT PARLIAMENT, 1640. In 1640, King **CHARLES I** recalled **PARLIAMENT** for the first time since 1629 because he urgently needed to raise money to support his army in **SCOTLAND**. When, after only three weeks, the Parliament refused to grant his request until its grievances had been addressed, Charles dissolved it. The action led to a prolonged dispute over the relative rights of the **MONARCH** and his subjects which continued in the **LONG PARLIAMENT** later in the year.

SHREWSBURY, BATTLE OF, 21 July 1403. **HENRY IV**'s forces defeated the rebel Sir **HENRY PERCY** (also known as Hotspur), killing him in the struggle. Afterwards, the King founded a church and monastery on the site. Kings are generally very visible in battles but, in this encounter, several volunteers dressed up in royal armour to deceive the enemy while Henry himself fought in a normal **KNIGHT**'s armour.

SIDMOUTH, VISCOUNT. (See **HENRY ADDiNGTON**).

SINKING FUND. First established by **ROBERT WALPOLE** in 1717, this was a fund into which excess **GOVERNMENT** revenues were placed in order to reduce the **NATIONAL DEBT**. However, the finances were often diverted to more pressing problems and the last fund was established in 1928.

SIR. This prefix is used before the first name of a **KNIGHT** or **BARON** to indicate his place in the **PEERAGE**.

SIX ACTS, 1819. The **GOVERNMENT**'s legislative answers to the events which led to the **PETERLOO MASSACRE,** the **CATO STREET CONSPIRACY,** the **SPA FIELDS RIOT,** the **MARCH OF THE BLANKETEERS** and other agitation for social and political reform were designed to suppress radicalism and were known, therefore, as the 'Gag Acts' (see **ACT OF PARLIAMENT**). They introduced rights to search property without a warrant, prevent individuals from petitioning except in their own **PARISH**, cancel public meetings unless six days notice had been given to the authorities and try political offences without a **JURY**. The laws were draconian but effective.

SLAVE TRADE. Trade in slaves, the personal property of an owner, had been common in **ANGLO-SAXON** times between Britain and **IRELAND** but died out until revived with the settlement of the American colonies during the 17th century. A three-way **AT-LANTIC TRIANGLE** commerce developed — slaves from West Africa were taken to the West Indies and exchanged for sugar, coffee, cotton and mahogany, which went to the British market; the proceeds of their sale were invested in cloth, muskets, iron and gunpowder, which were sent to Africa and bartered for slaves. Under the terms of the **TREATY OF UTRECHT** (1713), Britain gained the right to sell African slaves in the Spanish South American colonies (see **ASIENTO**). Slaves in Britain gained their freedom in 1772 (see **MANSFIELD JUDGEMENT**) but the trade remained a main plank in the development of the **BRITISH EMPIRE** until well into the 19th century. The Abolition of Slavery Society (founded in 1787), religious groups and powerful individuals (notably Member of Parliament **WILLIAM WILBERFORCE**) pressured against slavery in all its forms and succeeded in getting the import of slaves to the colonies made illegal and slave trading by British ships banned in 1807. In 1833, the Abolition of Slavery Act (see **ACT OF PARLIAMENT**) freed slaves throughout the Empire, despite opposition from sugar traders in the West Indies who feared a loss of advantage to the United States of America, which still retained slaves. Under the terms of the Act, slaves were to be freed within one year and then indentured to their owners as apprentices for up to seven years in order to ease the transition from a slave to a wage economy. (See **WAR OF THE SPANISH SUCCESSION**).

SNOWDON, LORD. (See **ANTONY CHARLES ROBERT ARMSTRONG-JONES**).

SOCIAL AND LIBERAL DEMOCRATIC PARTY. (See **LIBERAL PARTY, SOCIAL DEMOCRATIC PARTY**).

SOCIAL DEMOCRATIC PARTY (SDP). The SDP was formed in 1981 by four disaffected **LABOUR PARTY** Members of **PARLIAMENT** (MPs), Roy Jenkins, **DAVID OWEN**, Bill Rodgers and Shirley Williams (who were quickly dubbed 'The Gang of Four' by the press). Opposing Labour's left-wing drift and its anti-**EUROPEAN COMMUNITY** stance, they issued a statement, in January 1981, supporting close links with Europe, multilateral nuclear disarmament and electoral reform through the introduction of proportional representation (the so-called 'Limehouse Declaration'). **BY-ELECTION**s helped the new Party to win its maximum number of 27 seats in the **HOUSE OF COMMONS** over the next two years but most of these were lost at the **GENERAL ELECTION** in 1983. In its early days, it had formed an **ALLIANCE** with the **LIBERAL PARTY** in order not to split the middle-of-the-road vote and, in 1988, reduced to a rump of five MPs, merged with its ally as the **SOCIAL AND LIBERAL DEMOCRATIC PARTY (SLDP)**. A small group of members (including Owen) attempted to retain the SDP's identity as a separate unit but failed to gain significant support and disbanded in 1990. (See **LIBERAL DEMOCRATS**).

SOLICITOR GENERAL. One of the **GOVERNMENT**'s chief legal officers, the holder of this post deals with matters delegated by the **ATTORNEY GENERAL.**

SOMME, BATTLE OF THE, 1 July 1916-18 November 1916. This, the first major frontal attack by British and French forces during the **FIRST WORLD WAR**, involved the storming of strongly defended German positions in heavy rain and thick mud and quickly deteriorated into a battle of attrition, with neither side gaining real territorial advantage or strategic position. Tanks were used for the first time in war and casualties were enormous; estimates vary but are in the region of 420,000 British, 195,000 French and 450,000–660,000 German dead. In the first 24 hours of the conflict, 19,000 Britons lost their lives and over 57,000 were wounded — the greatest losses in a single day ever suffered by the **BRITISH ARMY**. The effect on troop morale was devastating and, although the battle probably saved the French from annihilation at Verdun, the fighting all but destroyed the new 1st Army and became synonomous with the waste and futility of warfare. In retrospect, however, it may also have been a real turning-point in the conflict because it severely weakened the German forces.

SOUTH AFRICAN WAR. (See **BOER WAR [second], 1899-1902**).

SOUTH SEA BUBBLE, 1720. A **JOINT-STOCK COMPANY**, the South Sea Company was created in 1711 and much promoted by politicians as a means of reducing the **NATIONAL DEBT** through a monopoly of trade with the Spanish Americas. Its value appreciated considerably, rising tenfold in a few months, causing a run on investment and fuelling wild speculation in the financial markets so that, when the bubble burst, thousands of investors from all walks of life lost heavily. The episode caused a financial and political crisis until **ROBERT WALPOLE**, then **PAYMASTER GENERAL**, successfully intervened.

SPA FIELDS RIOT, 2 December 1816. A meeting at Spa Fields in Islington (**LONDON**) demanded **PARLIAMENTARY REFORM**. Part of the crowd, induced by agitators, marched on the Royal Exchange in the **CITY OF LONDON** and confronted the **LORD MAYOR** but was dispersed by the **POLICE**. The incident was indicative of the general unrest at a time of popular demand for social and political change. (See **ANTI-CORN LAW LEAGUE; CATO STREET CONSPIRACY; LUDDITES; MARCH OF THE BLANKETEERS; PETERLOO MASSACRE; SWING RIOTS**).

SPANISH ARMADA, 1588. The Armada was supposed to destroy the English fleet, thereby allowing Spain to invade **ENGLAND**, end **ELIZABETH I**'s support for the Protestant Dutch and reimpose Roman Catholicism. A flotilla of 128 ships, with 19,000 soldiers on board, embarked from Lisbon but failed to pick up the 30,000 strong Spanish army units in the Netherlands and was attacked by English vessels in the Channel. Defeated at the Battle of Gravelines on 29 July, the surviving members of the fleet attempted to escape around the northern coast of more friendly **SCOTLAND** but further losses were encountered due to bad weather. The English navy was commanded by Lord Howard of Effingham with Sir **FRANCIS DRAKE** second in command. The romantic story that Drake refused to engage the Armada until he had finished a game of bowls is pure legend, but his daring raid on the Spanish fleet at Cadiz in 1587 (an exploit known as 'singeing the King of Spain's beard') had delayed the sailing of the invasion fleet by at least ten months. Queen Elizabeth I was said to have stirred her troops at Tilbury with the words: "I have come . . . in the midst and heat of battle, to live and die amongst you . . . I know I have the body of a weak and feeble woman, but I have the heart and stomach of a King".

SPANISH CIVIL WAR, 1936-39. The war began in July 1936 with the uprising led by General Francisco Franco against the Republican Government in Spain. Formally, the United Kingdom remained neutral and a member of the Non-Intervention in Spain

Agreement, signed in **LONDON** in September of that year, but unofficial aid collections were made and British citizens joined the International Brigades fighting on the Republican side. These brigades attracted many prominent intellectuals, such as George Orwell and W.H. Auden.

SPANISH SUCCESSION, WAR OF THE, 1702-13. In 1701, King Charles II of Spain died childless after having named Philip, grandson of King Louis XIV of France, as his heir. Fearful of the emergence of a new power bloc, **ENGLAND** joined Austria, Prussia and the Netherlands in a **GRAND ALLIANCE** to prevent the unification of France and Spain under a single ruler. In 1711, however, Austrian Emperor Joseph died and the British changed sides in order to prevent the union of the Hapsburg Empire, the Holy Roman Empire and Spain under his successor (and brother), the Archduke Charles. Britain's support for Philip was conditional on his renunciation of all claim to the French throne. Under the **TREATY OF UTRECHT** (1713-15), which ended the hostilities, Britain gained Gibraltar, Minorca, Nova Scotia and **SLAVE TRADE** rights in the **ASIENTO**. (See **BATTLE OF BLENHEIM; JOHN CHURCHILL; BATTLE OF MALPLAQUET; BATTLE OF OUDENARDE; BATTLE OF RAMILLIES**).

SPEAKER, THE. The Speaker is the elected Member of **PARLIAMENT** in charge of proceedings in the **HOUSE OF COMMONS**, including the maintenance of order and adherence to established practice. The occupant of the post is chosen by Members of the House and is expected to act impartially. (See **GOOD PARLIAMENT**).

SPECIAL AIR SERVICE (SAS). The SAS is an elite, secretive **BRITISH ARMY** unit trained in anti-terrorist and related activities. Its roots lie in the **SECOND WORLD WAR** commando unit which operated in North Africa under Colonel David Stirling. Over the years, the Service has earned a reputation for ruthless efficiency as a result of exploits in Europe to create confusion in the lead-up to **D-DAY**, in **NORTHERN IRELAND**, the **FALKLANDS WAR** and the **GULF WAR**. Most of its activities are unpublicized but, in 1988, it was accused of a shoot to kill policy when it encountered a group of suspected Irish Republican Army terrorists in Gibraltar.

SPECIAL OPERATIONS EXECUTIVE (SOE). A **SECRET SERVICE** unit formed in July 1941 to stimulate resistance in areas occupied by the Axis powers during the **SECOND WORLD WAR** and to fuse intelligence and propaganda services, the SOE proved to be a highly efficient sabotage group. It operated clandestinely, mainly in Germany, and was disbanded in January 1946.

SPENCER, DIANA FRANCES (1961-). Former consort of **PRINCE CHARLES**, heir to the throne, Diana was born at Sandringham on 1 July 1961. The third child of Viscount Althorp and his first wife, Frances (daughter of Baron Fermoy), she became Lady Diana when her father succeeded to the Spencer earldom in 1975. Following her parents' divorce in 1969, she stayed in **SCOTLAND** with her mother during summer vacations but, prior to that, had spent much of her holidays playing with **PRINCE ANDREW** and **PRINCE EDWARD** on the Sandringham estate. She was educated at Riddlesworth Hall (Thetford) and at West Heath School (Sevenoaks) then went to finishing school at Chateau d'Oex in Switzerland, where she honed her French and became an able skier. When she returned to **LONDON**, she rented an apartment in South Kensington with three other women and took a post as kindergarten teacher at the Young England School. Her social activities brought renewed acquaintance with the Royal Family and, during 1980, she became particularly friendly with Prince Charles. Romance blossomed, and the couple were engaged on 24 February 1981 then married in St Paul's Cathedral on 29 July. Their first son (Prince William Arthur Philip Louis) was born on 21 June 1982 and became second in line to the throne after his father. Another son — Prince Henry Charles Albert David — was born on 15 September 1984.

During the late 1980s, there were increasingly frequent rumours that Charles and Diana were growing apart, and, in 1992, Andrew Morton revealed in his book *Diana: Her True Story* that the Princess had attempted to commit suicide on five occasions because of her husband's uncaring attitude and his association with Camilla Parker-Bowles, wife of Brigadier Andrew Parker-Bowles, one of Queen **ELIZABETH II**'s aides. It was widely believed that the book was published with the Princess's permission. On 14 August 1992, the *Sun* newspaper added fuel to the flames by printing what purported to be extracts from a confidential telephone conversation between Diana and Mr James Gilbey, a close friend, and, on 9 December, **BUCKINGHAM PALACE** formally confirmed the break-up, commenting that "We are not suggesting that the media are to blame but the cumulative effect of years of intrusive coverage has created an atmosphere that makes life intolerable". Both parents were to be involved in the raising of their sons and both were to continue their programmes of public engagements. Diana, in particular, received high profile coverage, notably for her work with AIDS victims.

In November 1995, the Princess admitted, during a television interview, that she had had an adulterous affair with James Hewitt, and, the following year, she and Prince Charles began divorce proceedings.

SPLENDID ISOLATION. This term is used to describe British foreign policy during the period from 1895 until 1902 when the country used the strengths of the **ROYAL NAVY** and **BRITISH EMPIRE** to stand back from major alliances while most other European powers were dividing into opposing blocs. Usually, it is ascribed to the policies of the **MARQUESS OF SALISBURY**'s administration in particular but the term originally came from Canada and was published in *THE TIMES* before it was adopted by Salisbury.

SPURS, BATTLE OF THE, 16 August 1513. This battle was fought at Guinegate after King **HENRY VIII** had invaded France with the support of troops from the Holy Roman Empire and the backing of Pope Julius II, who wished to drive the French out of Italy. It received its name from the hasty retreat of the French cavalry: riders urged their horses to go faster and some, it is said, lost their spurs in the flight. Coming in the same year as the **BATTLE OF FLODDEN**, the victory marked the high point of Henry's military achievements.

STAMFORD BRIDGE, BATTLE OF, 25 September 1066. **HAROLD II** defeated the Norwegian forces of Harold Hardrada at this battle near **YORK**, killing the Scandinavian King. After the victory, Harold marched south with his exhausted troops in an attempt to counter the invasion of the **NORMANS**, whom he met at the **BATTLE OF HASTINGS**.

STAMP ACTS. There were two major Stamp Acts.

The Act of 1712 (see **ACT OF PARLIAMENT**) introduced

the first tax on official papers and periodicals.

Similar legislation in <u>1765</u> created intense resentment in the American colonies where, as the first direct tax on the colonists, it provoked riots. The measure was intended to cover the costs of holding the territories in the New World but the settlers preferred to raise their own monies and, amidst opposition at home and abroad, it was repealed one year later.

STANDING ARMY. A Standing Army is a professional military force maintained by the **EXCHEQUER** to defend the realm and is supported in times of peace as well as war. It developed in **ENGLAND** in the 17th century. Prior to that, the **MONARCH**y relied on armies raised periodically under the **FEUDAL SYSTEM** and on mercenaries, the **MILITIA**, the **ROYAL NAVY** and **TRAINED BANDS**, mustering men only when required. (See **BRITISH ARMY; CONSCRIPTION; NATIONAL SERVICE**).

STANLEY, EDWARD GEORGE GEOFFREY SMITH (1799-1869). **PRIME MINISTER** on three occasions, Stanley was born in Knowsley on 29 March 1799, the son of Lord Stanley. Educated at Eton College and **OXFORD** University, he was elected to **PARLIAMENT** in 1820, supporting the **WHIGS**. His first political post was as **UNDER-SECRETARY OF STATE** for War and the Colonies in **VISCOUNT GODERICH**'s **GOVERNMENT** of 1827-28. **EARL GREY** made him Chief Secretary for **IRELAND** in 1830 then, in 1833, **SECRETARY OF STATE** for War and the Colonies (a position which involved him in the introduction of legislation designed to abolish the **SLAVE TRADE** throughout the **BRITISH EMPIRE**). In 1834, however, he resigned his **CABINET** post, disagreeing with colleagues over plans to direct revenues of the Irish church towards non-ecclesiastical uses. His sympathies moved increasingly towards the **TORIES** and, when Sir **ROBERT PEEL** became Prime Minister in 1841, Stanley returned to his former job as Secretary for War and the Colonies. He performed his duties competently but, in 1845, became a lone voice in the Cabinet, objecting to legislation repealing the **CORN LAWS**. Utilizing his brilliant oratorical skills, he soon became the leader of a faction determined to retain protectionism, with **BENJAMIN DISRAELI** presenting the arguments in the **HOUSE OF COMMONS**.

In 1851, Stanley's father died and he succeeded to the title, becoming the fourteenth Earl of Derby. In February of the following year, after the fall of Lord **JOHN RUSSELL**'s Government, he became Prime Minister for the first time and formed an overtly protectionist administration which included Disraeli as **CHANCELLOR OF THE EXCHEQUER**. The ministry lasted only until December, when it was defeated in the House of Commons in a vote on the **BUDGET**. Derby became Prime Minister once more in 1858 but again his term of office was limited. A **BILL** designed to introduce further **PARLIAMENTARY REFORM** was defeated in the Commons and a **GENERAL ELECTION** in the summer of 1859 left the **CONSERVATIVE PARTY** with too few seats to ensure a majority against a coalition of opponents. In **OPPOSITION**, Derby turned his attention to the alleviation of the effects of the industrial crisis in Lancashire's **COTTON INDUSTRY**. The US Civil War had virtually halted imports of raw materials, causing much poverty and misery in northeast **ENGLAND**. Derby contributed several thousand pounds to relief efforts and solicited revenues from others, earning the respect and gratitude of the mill owners and workers.

In 1866, he went back to **DOWNING STREET**, following the rejection of Lord John Russell's Reform Bill. This time, the administration lasted for two years and succeeded in introducing legislation reforming Parliament, largely because of Disraeli's ability to keep the Government Bill intact despite numerous efforts to introduce amendments. Derby, however, had little opportunity to enjoy the success. Troubled by ill health, he resigned in February 1868 and died at Knowsley on 23 October 1869.

STAR CHAMBER. This court of law originated in the 14th century. During the 1530s and 1540s, it met in the Star Chamber at **WESTMINSTER** under the leadership of Cardinal **THOMAS WOLSEY** and ruled on disputes about interference in local courts and on property matters. It was greatly distrusted because it gave considerable powers to the sovereign and his **PRIVY COUNCIL** (who comprised the original membership) and was not subject to the same constraints as other courts. It was widely used by the **TUDORS** and King **CHARLES I** but abolished in 1640 by the **LONG PARLIAMENT**.

STATE LOTTERY. The first effective state lottery (the Million Lottery) was established in 1693-94 under **PARLIAMENT**ary auspices. Brief lotteries had been used by the **CROWN** to raise money before then but this one was held 126 times between 1694 and 1826 and was part of a period of considerable reorganization of state finances which included the establishment of the **BANK OF ENGLAND** and the **STOCK EXCHANGE**. Subscribers received **GOVERNMENT** annuities and revenues were used, amongst other things, to pay the costs of the **AMERICAN WAR OF INDEPENDENCE**. In 1787, competitive tendering was introduced for companies wishing to run the lottery and, until 1821, the drum containing the tickets was protected by the **POLICE** and **BRITISH ARMY** Grenadiers. It was abolished in 1826, following great public disquiet at the management of the scheme and a more general concern with public morals (gaming had by then become popular with the poor and with the clergy). In 1993, the government announced a new state lottery and chose contractors to run it in May 1994. The successful bid was from a consortium of multi-national companies including Cadbury Schweppes, Racal, ICL and De La Rue.

STATUTE OF MERTON. (See **MERTON, STATUTE OF**).

STEEL. Steel is stronger and more versatile than **IRON** but also more expensive so its use until the 19th century was confined to the manufacture of high cost products (such as those of the cutlery trade in Sheffield) by domestic methods. Mass production came from **HENRY BESSEMER**'s converter in 1856, the open hearth process developed by William Siemens in 1869 and the Thomas-Gilchrist process for utilizing phosphoric ores which was perfected in the 1870s. These all enabled the use of hot gases to regulate the carbon content of the base iron and therefore produce high-grade steel which could be employed in the construction of **RAILWAY** track and engines, bridges, ships, machinery and buildings. By 1918, it had outstripped the production of the iron industry and become the base material for 20th century economies. In 1870, Britain produced 300,000 tons of steel. By 1900, output had increased to 5 million tons and, by 1970, reached its peak of 28 million tons. Foreign competition led to tariff barriers and, ultimately, state control through **NATIONALIZATION** in the form of the British Steel Corporation (1967). Even so, output by 1985 had fallen to 16 million tons and, in 1988, reeling from world recession, the industry was returned to private ownership (see **PRIVATIZATION**) as British Steel. Plant closures followed as production was rationalized and, as a result, the company is now in profit but only four steel plants remain (at Scunthorpe, Teesside, Llanwern and Port Talbot).

STEPHEN (c. 1097-54). While **HENRY I** was on the English throne, he made the nobility swear an oath of fealty to his daughter, Matilda, in an attempt to ensure that she would become Queen when he died. However, the concept of a female **MONARCH** was repugnant to the **NORMANS**, who also distrusted her husband, Geoffrey of Anjou, and, following Henry's death in 1135, they invited Stephen, son of **WILLIAM THE CONQUEROR**'s daughter (Adela) and her husband (Count Stephen of Blois and Chartres) to become King. Stephen had grown up in the royal circle, was a popular and charming courtier and had strong support amongst churchmen. But as a ruler he was a disaster, proving unable to control the nobles or maintain law and order. His weaknesses became obvious soon after his **CORONATION** in December 1135. In 1136, despite having a large force at his command, he conceded Cumbria to an invading Scottish army. And, in 1137, he failed to take the opportunity of unrest in Normandy to wrest the duchy from Matilda, an error which was to have serious consequences for the peace of his realm.

In 1138, Earl Robert of Gloucester, having originally pledged allegiance to Stephen but frustrated by his ineptitude, openly supported Matilda's claim to the throne. Others followed and, encouraged, Matilda crossed to **ENGLAND** the following year. Stephen, instead of imprisoning her, courteously provided her with an escort to Bristol, which became the centre of antiroyalist activity. The country slipped into civil war, with nobles exercising absolute authority over their own lands and often failing to keep the peace. Never, according to the **ANGLO-SAXON CHRONICLE**, did a country endure greater misery.

Early in 1141, it seemed as though the situation would be resolved — the royalist forces were attacked at Lincoln, Stephen was taken prisoner and Matilda prepared for her coronation. But there was still opposition. Matilda's arrogance had offended many of her supporters and her attempts to impose taxes on the citizens of **LONDON** were so resented that she had to flee to **OXFORD** for safety. Stephen's queen (Matilda of Boulogne) took advantage of the situation to defeat an Angevin army at Winchester, capturing Earl Robert. King and Earl were exchanged shortly afterwards and a lengthy period of stalemate followed, with neither side able to gain the upper hand. Eventually, in 1147, Robert died and

Matilda left for Normandy, leaving Stephen recognized as King over most of the land south of the **RIVER TYNE**. In 1149 and 1153, however, Matilda's son Henry (later **HENRY II**) attempted to gain the **CROWN** for the House of Anjou (see **PLANTAGENETS**). Stephen, depressed by the death of his Queen and his son Eustace, had no will to fight. In November 1153, he reached agreement with the Angevins that he would retain the throne until his death but that Henry would be recognized as his heir. He died at Dover less than a year later on 25 October 1154. A kindhearted, brave and chivalrous man, he never had the ruthlessness required to rule a Norman nobility bent on self-aggrandizement.

STEPHENSON, GEORGE (1781-1848). The inventor of the first steam-powered **RAILWAY** engine designed both for freight and for passenger transport, Stephenson was born in Wyland (Northumberland) on 9 June 1781, the son of Robert Stephenson (a colliery fireman) and his wife, Mabel. Unable to read or write until he taught himself at the age of 17, he found his first job as a brakesman at Black Callerton Colliery. In 1802, he became an engineman at Willington Ballast Hill mine, earning extra cash by repairing watches in his spare time, and, ten years later, obtained a post as engine-wright at High Pit Colliery, where he designed a safety lamp for underground workers. On a much larger scale, he invented a steam-driven engine which began work in 1815, taking wagons from the pit to the port where the **COAL** was loaded on to ships. In 1822, while the railway between Stockton and Darlington was under construction, he used that success to persuade the directors of the company to invest in steam rather than in animal power and, the following year, opened an engine-building works in **NEWCASTLE-UPON-TYNE** in partnership with his cousin, Thomas Richardson, and a friend, Edward Pease. The world's first passenger train ran between the two towns on 27 September 1825, reaching speeds of 16 miles an hour and pulled by Stephenson's eight ton locomotive (named *Active* at the time but later re-christened *Locomotion*).

The engines were unreliable and expensive to maintain but, even so, Stephenson managed to convince directors of the **LIVERPOOL** and **MANCHESTER** Company's railroad that they, too, should use steam power. In 1829, a competition was held to find a suitable engine and Stephenson won with *Rocket*, which performed better than earlier designs because it used a multiple fire-tube boiler rather than single flue boilers. Eight locomotives were ready for the opening of the line on 15 September 1830, all of them built at his construction yard. Over the next 15 years, Britain was gripped by railway mania and lines were constructed in most parts of the country. Stephenson was the designer of many of them and acted as consultant to foreign companies as well, particularly in Spain and Belgium. He retired in 1845 and died at Tapton House, his Chesterfield home, on 12 August 1848, far removed from the poverty in which he had been raised.

STERLING. Silver is considered to be of sterling quality if it contains no more than 7.5 per cent of any other metal. The use of the word with reference to British **CURRENCY** stems from the days when the coinage was made of precious metals and there was no paper money: a silver coin was worth its face value if it reached sterling (that is, standard) quality, containing the appropriate proportion of the metal. (See **BANK OF ENGLAND; ROYAL MINT**).

STEWARTS. (See **STUARTS**.)

STEWART, ROBERT (1769-1822). Foreign Secretary for over a decade, Stewart used his considerable diplomatic skills to advance British interests at the peace conferences following the **NAPO-LEONIC WARS**. The son of Robert Stewart and his first wife, Lady Sarah Frances Seymour-Conway, he was born in Dublin on 18 June 1769 and educated in Armagh and at **CAMBRIDGE** University. Known by the courtesy title of Viscount Castlereagh from 1796, he succeeded his father as Marquis of Londonderry in 1816. Elected to the Irish Parliament as an independent in 1790, he was appointed Keeper of the Privy Seal in 1797 and, the following year, made Acting Chief Secretary to the **LORD LIEUTENANT** of **IRELAND**. He strongly supported the union of Ireland with Great Britain in 1800 and advocated speedy attention to the question of Catholic emancipation by the new Parliament.

When **WILLIAM PITT THE YOUNGER** failed to get **GEORGE III**'s approval for any form of emancipation, he resigned and Stewart went with him. However, Castlereagh continued to advise the **GOVERNMENT** on Irish questions and, in 1802, **HENRY ADDINGTON** made him President of the Board of Control for Indian Affairs. Pitt was appointed **PRIME MINIS-TER** again in 1804 and, the next year, appointed him to the post of **SECRETARY OF STATE** for War. He left office following

Pitt's death in 1806 but returned under **WILLIAM BENTINCK**, Duke of Portland, in 1807. Committed to a war against Napoleon Bonaparte, he reorganized Britain's defences and increased the size and efficiency of army units. In 1809, he sent troops to defend Portugal against Spanish incursion and planned an attack on Napoleon's naval base at Antwerp. **CABINET** procrastination, however, delayed that attack and many soldiers took ill and died on the island of Walcheren. Responsibility for the deaths lay with the commander, the Earl of Chatham, who had disobeyed Castlereagh's instructions, but **GEORGE CANNING**, the Foreign Secretary, placed the blame squarely on Stewart's shoulders. The two men fought a duel then resigned office.

Castlereagh returned to Government as Secretary for Foreign Affairs under **SPENCER PERCEVAL** in 1812 but offered to resign the post after Perceval's assassination in order to allow Canning to enter the administration. Canning refused, unwilling to accept his old rival as **LEADER OF THE HOUSE OF COMMONS**. Confirmed in the position, Stewart held together the opposition to Napoleon as the War drew to a close then, when the conflict ended, ensured, through the **TREATY OF PARIS** (1814), that British demands for the recognition of the Low Countries as an independent kingdom and the replacement of the Bourbon Monarchy in France were met. At the Congress of Vienna (1814-15), he resisted the territorial demands of Prussia and Russia and attempted to strengthen the militarily weak Germany and Italy. He also laid great stress on regular meetings of the major powers, preferring diplomacy through discussion to other forms of peacekeeping. When independence for Greece and for Spain's American colonies became an issue in the early 1820s, Stewart made it clear that Britain would recognize any Governments established by revolution. At home, however, his international diplomacy was over-shadowed by domestic crises. As Leader of the House, he was associated in the public mind with the **PETERLOO MASSACRE** in 1819 and with Government attempts to effect a divorce between **GEORGE IV** and his consort, Queen Caroline. The criticism and the pressure of work appeared to unhinge his mind and, on 12 August 1822, he committed suicide.

STOCK EXCHANGE. JOINT-STOCK COMPANIES originated in the 17th century, with the **MUSCOVY COMPANY** being the first to issue shares. These were bought and sold in the coffee houses of **LONDON** until the Stock Exchange was established as the national centre of stock and share trading in 1773. It was deregulated at the **BIG BANG** in 1986 and most trade is now by computer through SEAQ (the Stock Exchange Automated Quotations System).

STOKE, BATTLE OF, 16 June 1487. This was the final battle of the **WARS OF THE ROSES.** The rebel Yorkist army was supported by 2,000 German mercenaries and had crowned Lambert Simnel, a ten-year-old pretender to the English throne, as 'King Edward VI' (Simnel claimed to be the Earl of Warwick, who was actually in the **TOWER OF LONDON** at the time). King **HENRY VII**'s forces defeated them near Newark, the leaders were killed and Simnel was sent to work as a royal kitchen servant (an astute move to discredit the Yorkist conspirators).

STONE AGE. This period of **PREHISTORIC BRITAIN,** dating from 500,000 BC to 2,500 BC, is conventionally divided into the **PALAEOLITHIC, MESOLITHIC** and **NEOLITHIC** and is characterized by the use of stone implements and weapons. Domestication of animals, cereal production and permanent settlement became increasingly common from about 4,400 BC. (See **STONEHENGE**).

STONEHENGE. Stonehenge is probably the most famous prehistoric site in Europe and makes a considerable visual impact on the landscape of Salisbury Plain in Wiltshire. A stone circle surrounded by a ditch and bank, it was constructed in six phases between 3,200 BC (or, according to some texts, 2,750 BC) and 1,800 BC by **NEOLITHIC** and **BRONZE AGE** peoples. The main period of building probably occurred about 2,100 BC, when a circle of sarsens was put in place and a horseshoe of five trilithons erected in the centre. Most of the stones (some of them over 20 feet high and weighing up to 45 tons) were from local sources but it is believed that the smaller bluestones may have been brought nearly 250 miles from the Preseli Hills in south-west **WALES**. The sarsens were dressed by masons to ensure a smooth curve round the circle and the lintels were locked in place by mortice and tenon joints.

Although popularly connected with **DRUIDS**, Stonehenge was built some two millenia before they came to Britain; the connection seems to be a figment of the imagination of 18th century writers. The real function of the building is unknown though it is believed to have been the centre both of religious activities and of astronomical observations. Because of damage to the stones and erosion of the land around the monument, the general public have not been able to gain close access to Stonehenge since the late 1970s and there are controversial proposals to build a new visitors' centre a mile from the site in order to reduce the pressures even further.

STREET OFFENCES ACT, 1959. Following the recommendations of the **WOLFENDEN REPORT** (1957), this legislation (see **ACT OF PARLIAMENT**) criminalized all street soliciting by prostitutes, increased the penalties for procuring and living off the earnings of prostitutes and imposed heavier fines on those who allowed prostitutes to pick up clients in **PUBLIC HOUSE**s and similar places.

STUART, JOHN (1713-92). The third Earl of Bute, Stuart was a confidant of **GEORGE III**, leader of the **TORIES**, Prime Minister and a powerful political figure during the early 1760s. The son of James, second Earl of Bute, and Lady Anne Campbell (daughter of the first Duke of Argyll), he was born in Edinburgh on 25 May 1713 and succeeded to the peerage on his father's death in 1723. In 1736, he married Mary, daughter of Edward and Lady Mary Wortley Montagu, and later controlled the large fortune she inherited when her father died. He was elected as a representative peer for **SCOTLAND** in 1737 and, in 1738, was made a Knight of the Thistle (see **ORDERS OF CHIVALRY**).

In 1747, when rain prevented Frederick, **PRINCE OF WALES**, from going to the horse racing at Egham, Bute was summoned to his tent to make up a whist party. The two men became firm friends, and, in 1750, Stuart was appointed a Lord of the Bedchamber. The Prince died in 1751 but Bute became a constant companion of his son, George, who, when he succeeded to the throne as **GEORGE III** in 1760, made him a Privy Councillor (see **PRIVY COUNCIL**), Groom of the Stole and First Gentleman of the Bedchamber. Bute was the only person in whom the King had real confidence and was his most trusted adviser on policies designed to end the **SEVEN YEARS WAR** and oust from power those **MINISTER**s with whom George disagreed. On 3 November 1761, he appeared in the **HOUSE OF LORDS** (which he had not attended for 20 years) as First Minister but was not popular because of his Scottish background, his situation as a King's favourite and his role in the events which had led to the resignation of **WILLIAM PITT THE ELDER** earlier that year. He could not appear in the streets without the protection of body-guards. Jack boots (a pun on his name) and petticoats (representing the Princess of Wales, George's mother, with whom, according to **JOHN WILKES**, Bute was having a scandalous relationship) were burned in public.

In January 1762, Stuart was forced to reverse his previous policy and declare war on Spain and, in May, succeeded the Duke of Newcastle as the First Lord of **THE TREASURY** and thus as **PRIME MINISTER**. Eager to achieve peace with France, he conducted negotiations secretly and eventually the discussions led to an agreement ratified on 10 February 1763 (see **TREATY OF PARIS**). That success did not make him more acceptable at home, however, because opinion was inflamed by his imposition of a cider tax, which placed great burdens on farmers in west and south-west **ENGLAND** and added to the system of taxation by excise, which was seen as an infringement of liberties. In the end, unable to cope any longer with the animosity, suffering from ill-health and fearing that his unpopularity would affect the **MONARCH**y, he resigned on 8 April 1763. For a time, he retained influence with the King, but **GEORGE GRENVILLE** (who was appointed as his successor) insisted on the sovereign's full confidence. Failing to obtain Grenville's dismissal, Bute withdrew from court on 28 September. He continued to correspond with George until May 1765, when Grenville persuaded the King that his former adviser should have no further influence on public affairs. During the next few years he spoke on a number of issues in the House of Lords but, in 1778, refused to play any part in a proposed alliance with Pitt.   He died in **LONDON** on 10 March 1792 and was buried in Rothesay, on the Isle of Bute.

STUARTS, 1603-1714. Between 1371 and 1603, this House produced the **MONARCH**s of **SCOTLAND**. In 1603, James VI of Scotland also became King of **ENGLAND** (as **JAMES I**) in the line of succession from **ELIZABETH I** (see **UNION OF THE CROWNS**) and began the Stuart period of rule, which was to last for the next 111 years (they ruled Scotland for 232 years). It was a troubled time, witnessing **CIVIL WAR**, the execution of **CHARLES I** and the **GLORIOUS REVOLUTION**, but it also brought the growth of empire, with expansion into North America,

India and Africa. The Stuarts were succeeded by the **HANOVER-IANS** in 1714. In Scotland, the family name was usually spelt 'Stewart' but the form 'Stuart' became more common after James's accession to the English throne. (See **ANNE; CHARLES II; JAMES VII and II; MARY II; WILLIAM III**).

SUDANESE WARS, 1884-85 and 1896-99. In 1884, the Sudan, a territory of Egypt, rose under the leadership of the Mahdi, a religious fanatic. General **GEORGE GORDON** was sent by Prime Minister **WILLIAM GLADSTONE** to evacuate Egyptian officials. Defying his orders, he remained in Khartoum, intent on defeating the Mahdi, and was besieged. A relief force was eventually sent but arrived too late to save him. Records released in 1993 seem to support the view that Gladstone's **LIBERAL PARTY** government was discredited by their failure to relieve Gordon — they believed that he was not dead but a hostage and so delayed sending reinforcements — and that this was a major factor in the fall of the administration within months. **HORATIO KITCHENER** defeated the Sudanese in the second conflict at the **BATTLE OF OMDURMAN** (1898) and gained joint Anglo-Egyptian control of the area, an important step towards British supremacy in this part of Africa.

SUEZ CRISIS, 1956. The Suez Canal opened in 1869 and proved to be a lifeline for the **BRITISH EMPIRE**, shortening the journey from India and the Far East by 4,000 miles. In 1875, **BENJAMIN DISRAELI** purchased a half share in the Canal for Britain and, in 1936, treaty negotiations allowed the United Kingdom to continue to station troops on the Canal after Egypt gained its independence. The Suez Crisis was precipitated by the cancellation of that arrangement when Colonel Gamal Nasser became leader of Egypt in 1952. On 26 July 1956, he nationalized the Canal, ostensibly to pay for the Aswan High Dam project. Prime Minister **ANTHONY EDEN**, worried by possible support for Nasser from the Soviets, planned an attack on the routeway in a combined operation with the French and the Israelis (the Israelis were to attack Egypt, thus giving Britain and France the excuse to go in). British troops landed in Suez and Port Said on 5 November and occupied the area with little difficulty. However, political opposition was fierce, both domestically through the **LABOUR PARTY** and internationally through the USA and the United Nations, so Eden was forced to make way for a UN peacekeeping force on 7 November. The

United Kingdom had lost both an important trade route and diplomatic prestige in an embarrassing episode which emphasized its slide from its former position as a world power. Allied losses were 33 killed and 129 wounded and the incident was a major factor in the eventual resignation of the Prime Minister in 1957.

SUFFRAGETTES. The word 'suffragette' is derived from the Latin *suffrogium* meaning 'a vote'. The predecessors of the modern feminists were a key element in the political and social battle to improve the status of females in Britain. Mary Wollstonecraft had published the *Vindication of the Rights of Women* in 1792 but, although there had been some steps towards emancipation over the next 100 years, there was still widespread discrimination in politics, work and **EDUCATION**. The National Union of Women's Suffrage Societies was formed in 1897 by Millicent Fawcett as part of a campaign to win equal voting rights for women and the more militant Women's Social and Political Union was founded in 1903 by **EMMELINE PANKHURST** and her daughter, Christabel. Supporters chained themselves to railings, smashed windows and heckled at public meetings in order to draw attention to their struggle and Emily Davidson died when she threw herself in protest under the King's horse at the Derby race in 1913. When arrested, the women often began hunger strikes, and force-feeding added to the public outcry, leading to the 1913 **CAT AND MOUSE ACT**, which allowed temporary release of prisoners whose health was affected. The 1918 Representation of the People Act gave married women, women householders and female graduates over the age of 30 the right to vote (largely in recognition of their contribution during the **FIRST WORLD WAR**), but it was not until 1928 that all adult women achieved full and equal franchise with men.

SUPREME COURT OF JUDICATURE. Originally established in 1873 under the provisions of the **JUDICATURE ACT** (see **ACT OF PARLIAMENT**) and reorganized following the Courts Act (1971), the Supreme Court has authority in **ENGLAND** and **WALES** and consists of the **COURT OF APPEAL** (which has a civil and a criminal division), the **HIGH COURT OF JUSTICE** and the **CROWN COURTS**. It ranks below the **HOUSE OF LORDS**, which is the final court of appeal.

SUPREME GOVERNOR. This title was assumed by King

HENRY VIII at the **REFORMATION**, giving him ecclesiastical and temporal authority over the **CHURCH OF ENGLAND** in a jurisdictional rather than sacramental sense. (See **DEFENDER OF THE FAITH**).

SWING RIOTS, 1830-33. During the **CHARTIST** period, violent disturbances erupted in agricultural districts of southern **ENGLAND**. Uncoordinated and concentrated mainly amongst the very poor, they took their name from the fictitious Captain Swing, who was reputed to be involved in violent protest, in poison-letter writing and particularly in hay-rick burning in **KENT**, especially during 1831. The troubles were probably a function of frustration as a result of extreme poverty rather than any co-ordinated political movement.

SYNOD OF WHITBY, 664. At the Synod (or general gathering of clerics) at Whitby (**YORK**shire) in 664, Roman Christianity triumphed over Irish (Celtic) Christianity, particularly in the debate on the dating of Easter and the leadership of the Church in **ENGLAND**. The meeting was a turning point in the history of Christianity in Britain, aligning it with the rest of Europe.

—T—

TAMWORTH MANIFESTO, 1834. An address by **ROBERT PEEL** to his constituents in Tamworth, before the 1835 **GENERAL ELECTION**, espoused the cause of **PARLIAMENTARY REFORM** and is said to mark the emergence of the **CONSERVATIVE PARTY** from its traditional (and narrower) base of the **TORIES** because it appealed to the landed classes as well as those seeking moderate change.

TEMPERANCE MOVEMENT. The movement to restrict the sale and consumption of alcohol flourished with the formation of Temperance Societies in the 1820s and drew strength from **NONCONFORMISTS** and **METHODISM**. Amongst the middle classes, it became particularly strong after the passage in 1830 of the Beerhouse Act (see **ACT OF PARLIAMENT**), which tried to curb excessive drinking. By 1853, the United Kingdom Alliance was promoting its cause and persuading people to sign the pledge against the demon drink. Its power led to the passage of the 1872 and 1902 **LICENSING ACT**s, which have only recently been relaxed. (See **PUBLIC HOUSE**).

TEMPLE, HENRY JOHN (1784-1865). The dominant figure in mid-19th century British politics, Temple was **PRIME MINISTER** for nine years, Foreign Secretary for 16 and a Member of **PARLIAMENT** for 58. He was born in **LONDON** on 20 October 1784, the elder son of Henry, Viscount Palmerston, and his wife, Mary. From Harrow School, he went to Edinburgh University and attended classes taught by philosopher Dugald Stewart, with whom he lived during his student days. He succeeded to the viscountcy on his father's death in 1802, studied at **CAMBRIDGE** University from 1803 until 1806 and, in 1807, entered Parliament as the member for Newport (Isle of Wight). His first **GOVERNMENT** office was Lord of the **ADMIRALTY**, under the **DUKE OF PORTLAND**, from 1807 until 1809. **SPENCER PERCEVAL** wanted to make him **CHANCELLOR OF THE EXCHEQUER** in 1809 but Palmerston turned the post down, preferring the more junior position of **SECRETARY OF STATE** for War. He remained in that job for 19 years while five Prime Ministers came and went, proving to be a thoroughly efficient administrator but having little impact on Government policy.

In 1828, he found himself at odds with the **DUKE OF WELLINGTON** over foreign affairs and resigned from the **CABINET**, returning in 1830 as Foreign Secretary under **EARL GREY** and remaining in office for 11 years, except for a short break during 1834-35. Forthright and often tactless, he earned his respect through hard work, a command of European languages, mastery of Foreign Office business and a detailed knowledge of international politics. Within a year, he had engineered Belgium's independence from Holland and, by 1834, had ensured the continuation of constitutional monarchy in Spain. In 1839, he played a major role in uniting the western European powers in support of the independence of Turkey (which was threatened by Mohammed Ali, Pasha of Egypt) and, in 1841 (through the Straits Convention), ensured that large warships would be denied peacetime entry to the Bosporus and the Dardanelles. Also, he was a principal architect of the **TREATY OF NANKING** (which ended war with China and ceded Hong Kong to Britain in 1842) though it was signed after he left office in June 1841 at the **DISSOLUTION OF PARLIAMENT**, which followed a vote of no confidence in **VIS-**

COUNT MELBOURNE.

For five years, Palmerston languished in **OPPOSITION**, spending much time on personal and domestic interests, but he returned to his old post as Foreign Secretary in Lord **JOHN RUSSELL**'s admin-istration, formed in 1846. In 1848, during a series of civil disturbances in Europe, he argued that peace could be better maintained by the continued existence of large power blocs than by the fragmentation of existing states, but his natural inclinations were often with the underdog and, in 1850, he supported the dubious claims of **DAVID PACIFICO** against the Greek Government, primarily because it was more authoritarian than Palmerston wanted. That support took the form of naval action and was roundly condemned both by foreign Governments and by the **HOUSE OF LORDS** but he survived a censure motion in the **HOUSE OF COMMONS** after an eloquent speech supporting the need for the state to protect its citizens.

The reprieve was temporary. Palmerston had become increasingly highhanded in his dealings with colleagues, habitually making decisions without consulting them. Even Queen **VICTORIA** took umbrage, annoyed by his failure to keep her informed of Foreign Office business and his habit of altering despatches without consulting her. Thus, when, in 1851, he communicated Britain's approval of a coup d'état in France to the French Ambassador without any discussion with other **MINISTER**s, Russell took the opportunity to dismiss him. Despite the criticism, however, he had a large group of supporters in Parliament and, in December 1852, was made **HOME SECRETARY** in the **EARL OF ABERDEEN**'s coalition Government. In that post, he displayed the same industry and ability which had characterized his work in the international arena, promoting prison, penal and social reforms and gaining new political allies in the process. As a result, when the coalition administration collapsed in February 1855, it was clear that he was the logical choice as the next Prime Minister. In 1856, his standing in the country increased as a result of the successful conclusion of the **CRIMEAN WAR** and he was awarded the **ORDER OF THE GARTER**, a rare distinction for an MP. When **WILLIAM GLADSTONE, BENJAMIN DISRAELI** and others defeated him in the Commons over his aggressive policies towards China in 1857, he simply dissolved Parliament, called a **GENERAL ELECTION** and routed the opposition.

In 1858, the tide began to turn and, the following year, he was forced into resignation after a defeat on policies dealing with conspiracy to murder but he bounced back in 1859 and remained as Prime Minister until his death six years later. During that period, he supported the French invasion of Italy (1859) and opposed the construction of the Suez Canal. In 1861, he advocated British neutrality during the American Civil War and, in 1864, attempted to uphold the independence of Denmark in the face of Prussian aggression. At home, he clashed with Gladstone over **FREE TRADE** and the extension of the franchise but introduced little in the way of social or fiscal change. He died on 18 October 1865 at Brocket Hall, near Hatfield, shortly after winning a general election but before the new Parliament had met.

TEST ACTS. There were a number of Test Acts (see **ACT OF PAR-LIAMENT**) which required **GOVERNMENT** officeholders to swear allegiance to the **CROWN**, receive Anglican Holy Communion and repudiate Catholicism (thereby passing a test of appropriateness for the post).

The 1673 Act prevented Catholics from holding public office.

The 1675 Act declared resistance to the **MONARCH** unlawful.

The 1678 Act excluded all Catholics, except the **DUKE OF YORK**, from **PARLIAMENT**.

TEWKESBURY, BATTLE OF, 4 May 1471. This decisive victory for the Yorkist faction in the **WARS OF THE ROSES** secured the throne of **ENGLAND** for **EDWARD IV**. Queen Margaret (wife of the imprisoned **HENRY VI**) and her son, Prince Edward, crossed from France and made for **WALES** with the Lancastrian army, aiming to join up with the forces of Jasper **TUDOR**. The King defeated the 6,000 Lancastrians, commanded by the Duke of Somerset, at Tewkesbury and Prince Edward was among the casualties. His mother took refuge in a religious house, claiming **SANCTUARY**, but the claim was not respected and she was taken into captivity. Somerset was executed two days later and Henry's murder in the **TOWER OF LONDON** completed the rout. The battle site was threatened in 1993 by plans to build a housing estate at the location where Margaret set her camp.

THAMES, RIVER. The Thames is the longest river wholly within **ENGLAND** and second in length only to the **RIVER SEVERN** in the United Kingdom. Four tributaries rise in the **COTSWOLD HILLS** and unite at Lechlade to form the Thames proper. From there, the river flows east for some 210 miles, passing through

OXFORD, Reading and **LONDON** before reaching the North Sea. Above Oxford, it is also known as the Isis. For most of the route, its banks are characterized by meadows, woodlands and arable crops and the river's primary uses are as a drainage channel and focus for recreational activities. Beyond London, however, and particularly on the north bank, the soft clays were easily dug out and harbour facilities constructed, allowing the city to develop as a major international trading centre. In certain weather conditions, these low lying areas were liable to flooding but the construction of a flood barrier has limited that risk. (For location, see Map 1, page xxv).

THATCHER, MARGARET HILDA (1925-   ). The United Kingdom's first woman **PRIME MINISTER**, Margaret Thatcher was born in Grantham on 13 October 1925. Her father, Alfred Roberts, had a small, but prosperous, grocery store in the High Street and, as mayor of the town, introduced his daughter to politics while she was still a youngster. She was educated at Kesteven and Grantham Girls' High School and at **OXFORD** University, where she studied chemistry and was President of the **CONSERVATIVE PARTY** Association. After graduation in 1947, she worked as a research chemist but retained her interest in public affairs and, in 1950 and 1951, stood unsuccessfully at the **PARLIAMENT**ary elections for Dartford. Also in 1951, she married Denis Thatcher and began legal studies, taking her Bar finals in 1953, the year in which her twin son and daughter (Mark and Carol) were born. She then practised as a taxation lawyer until 1959, when she was elected MP for Finchley. Two years later, Mrs Thatcher was given her first **GOVERNMENT** post — **PARLIAMENTARY SECRETARY** to the **MINISTER** of Pensions and National Insurance — and held it until the Conservative defeat at the **GENERAL ELECTION** in 1964. While in **OPPOSITION**, she was given the Pensions and National Insurance Brief (1964), followed by Housing and Land (1965-66), **TREASURY** Affairs (1966-67), Power (1967) and Transport (1969-70). When the Conservatives returned to office in 1970, she was made **SECRETARY OF STATE** for **EDUCATION** in **EDWARD HEATH**'s administration, causing much controversy when she ended the provision of free milk to schools. After the **LABOUR PARTY**'s election victory in 1974, she acted as Shadow **CHANCELLOR OF THE EXCHEQUER** (see **SHADOW MINISTER**) and, the following year, was elected Party Leader, defeating Heath by 130 votes to 119 in a poll of

Conservative MPs.

In 1979, she became Prime Minister and, positioned on the right wing of the party and with a 42-seat majority in the **HOUSE OF COMMONS**, introduced a series of measures designed to reduce state ownership of industry, encourage private enterprize and maintain tight control over public expenditure in order to regulate money supply. The result was a reduction in the rate of inflation and levels of unemployment higher than at any time since the 1930s. In 1983, she led her Party to victory for a second time on a wave of popularity generated by her decisive action during the **FALKLANDS WAR** the previous year. By then, she was firmly established on the international scene and the Soviets had christened her 'The Iron Lady' because of her intransigent stance on foreign issues.

Her career was almost brought to a premature end in 1984 when a bomb exploded in the Grand Hotel, Brighton, during the annual Conservative Party conference. However, Mrs Thatcher emerged unscathed and continued to pursue her aims of **PRIVATIZATION** of such state-owned businesses as **GAS** and **ELECTRICITY** supply, tight fiscal control and increased responsibility for the individual citizen — an approach which the press had christened **THATCHERISM**. She also widened her attempts to curb **TRADE UNION** power, forcing the **COAL** miners to return to work in 1985 after a year-long strike, which had often erupted into violence. In international relations, she refused to accept many of the policies of the **EUROPEAN COMMUNITY** and forged increasingly strong links with US President Ronald Reagan.

By 1987, the economy was leaner and fitter than it had been when Mrs Thatcher took control eight years earlier, but unemployment was still high and many commentators were arguing that Thatcherism was favouring the better-off at the expense of the poor. Nevertheless, the opposition parties were in disarray so the Conservatives won the 1987 General Election with a majority of 100 seats. The following year, Mrs Thatcher became the longest-serving Prime Minister this century and pushed ahead with radical legislation covering health care and education. She also introduced powers to limit **LOCAL GOVERNMENT** spending and make authorities sell their council houses to any tenant who wished to buy. But disaffection was growing, even in the ranks of the Conservative Party, as she became increasingly autocratic, often rapping her ministers over the knuckles in public. The much hated **POLL TAX** exacerbated matters further and, in 1989, **NIGEL LAWSON**, her Chancellor of the Exchequer, resigned, complaining that Mrs Thatcher listened more closely to her personal advisers than to him. The following year, Geoffrey Howe (her Deputy Prime Minister and longest-serving **CABINET** member) also departed and, on 13 November, made a speech in the House of Commons which deprecated the Prime Minister's attitude to European integration.

The next day, Michael Heseltine, a former Defence Minister, announced his intention to challenge Mrs Thatcher for the Party Leadership. He lost but gained sufficient support to rattle the Prime Minister, who returned from a visit to Paris, consulted with close colleagues and then, on 22 November, announced her decision to stand down. She was replaced by **JOHN MAJOR** (the successor she favoured) and, in 1991, announced her intention not to seek reelection to the Commons. The following year, she accepted a life **PEERAGE** and entered the **HOUSE OF LORDS** as Baroness Thatcher (see **BARON**). She has also received many other honours, including the Presidential Medal of Freedom in the United States of America (1991), the Chancellorship of the United Kingdom's only private university, the University of Buckingham (1992), and the Chancellorship of the College of William and Mary in Virginia (1993). (See **THREE-DAY WEEK**).

THATCHERISM. This doctrine, associated with the Premiership of **MARGARET THATCHER**, places an emphasis on strict **MONETARISM**, market forces, **FREE TRADE**, strong defence and law and order. It led to **PRIVATIZATION** and an aggressive form of conviction-led politics, allowing little softening of the harsh social side-effects of market forces and involving the removal of major obstacles without mercy (see, for example, **COAL; GREATER LONDON COUNCIL**). The approach resulted in the development of tough, uncompromising policies which deepened social divisions but created what its proponents believed was an economic miracle in its impact on the British economy during the 1980s.

THIRTY YEARS WAR, 1618-48. This European conflict was fought between Protestant and Catholic powers. **ENGLAND** became embroiled in 1624, opposing Spain, and suffered defeat the following year in a maritime battle off Cadiz. Simultaneously, the **HUGUE-**

NOT rebels of La Rochelle were given support in their struggle against persecution in France. Peace was made with France in 1629 and Spain in 1630. After that, lack of money ensured that there was no further English part in the war, particularly as the **CIVIL WAR** and strife in **SCOTLAND** and **IRELAND** focussed attention on more domestic issues.

THORPE, JOHN JEREMY (1929-). The Leader of the **LIBERAL PARTY** from 1967 until he resigned in 1976 following allegations about his private life, Thorpe was born on 29 April 1929, to Mr J.H. Thorpe (a former **CONSERVATIVE PARTY** Member of **PARLIAMENT**) and his wife, Ursula, daughter of Sir John Norton-Griffiths (who had also been a Conservative MP). He was educated at Rectory School in Connecticut (USA), Eton College and **OXFORD** University, where he was President of the Union in 1951. In 1954, he was called to the Bar and, the following year, unsuccessfully contested the North Devon Parliamentary **CONSTITUENCY** for the Liberal Party. In 1959, however, he won the seat and held it for 20 years. Thorpe became Leader of the Liberal Party in 1967 and was offered a **CABINET** post by **EDWARD HEATH** during moves to form a coalition **GOVERNMENT** in 1974 but resigned in 1976 following allegations that he had indulged in a homosexual relationship with Norman Scott, a male model. In 1979, shortly after losing his seat at the **GENERAL ELECTION**, he was acquitted at the Central Criminal Court of charges of conspiracy and incitement to murder Scott. Since 1984, he has been Chairman of Jeremy Thorpe Associates, Development Consultants in the Third World.

THREE-DAY WEEK. On 13 November 1973, a state of emergency was declared after the miners in the **COAL** industry banned overtime and the power workers followed suit, thus making provision of full **ELECTRICITY** supplies impossible. On 1 January 1974, the **GOVERNMENT** restricted provision of electricity to industry to just three days each week. The confrontation was instrumental in the downfall of Prime Minister **EDWARD HEATH** and created the impression of powerful **TRADE UNIONS** holding the country to ransom. That, in turn, became a key element in **MARGARET THATCHER**'s rise to power on an anti-union ticket.

THROCKMORTON PLOT, 1583. Under torture, Francis

Throckmorton revealed a plot to use French and Spanish forces, led by Henry, Duc de Guise, to replace Queen **ELIZABETH I** with Mary, Queen of Scots, and restore papal authority in **ENGLAND**. Throckmorton was executed for **TREASON** and the Spanish Ambassador, who was implicated in the scheme, was expelled.

TIMES, THE. The oldest national daily newspaper in **ENGLAND** began in 1785 as the *Daily Universal Register*, changing to its present title in 1788. It was nicknamed 'The Thunderer' after an impassioned editorial in 1830 during the debates on **PARLIAMENTARY REFORM**. In 1981, it became part of Rupert Murdoch's publishing empire.

TINCHEBRAI, BATTLE OF, 28 September 1106. When **WILLIAM I** of **ENGLAND** died, his eldest son, Robert, received the **CROWN**'s Normandy estates and son William received the English estates (becoming **WILLIAM II**). The two men struggled constantly for control of each other's lands. After William's suspicious death in 1100, Henry (William I's youngest son) became King as **HENRY I** and continued the campaign, defeating Robert at Tinchebrai and thus reuniting the territories.

TITANIC, **THE**, April 15 1912. The White Star Cunard liner, pride of the British merchant fleet, hit an iceberg on its maiden voyage from Southampton to New York and sank. The steamer (supposedly unsinkable because of its new double-bottom hull and airtight compartments) went down some 95 miles south of the Grand Banks, Newfoundland, in just over two hours with the loss of 1,517 lives. There were 711 survivors. It was revealed later that there had been insufficient lifeboat spaces available for the complement of passengers the vessel was carrying. Following the tragedy, the US Government imposed regulations designed to improve safety on steamships, including requirements to provide lifeboats for everyone and keep 24-hour radio watches. The wreck of the *Titanic* was found in 1985 and attempts to raise it in 1996 were unsuccessful.

TITHE. Payments of one-tenth of earnings or produce to support the **PARISH** and its priest were made compulsory by King **EDGAR** during the 10th century. In later centuries, they became much hated, particularly when the **INDUSTRIAL**

REVOLUTION brought urban growth into rural areas to which these taxes were attached. The 1836 Tithes Commutation Act (see **ACT OF PARLIAMENT**) replaced tithes in kind with money rents, based on the price of corn, and that fuelled further town development by releasing land owners from agricultural responsibilities. The Tithe Redemption Commissioners were charged with drawing up accurate maps of land holdings and properties so that dues could be properly assessed and the resultant Tithe Maps have become a valuable research source for scholars. All tithes were abolished in 1936.

TOBRUK, BATTLE OF, May-June 1942. During the **SECOND WORLD WAR**, the Germans, under Field Marshal Erwin Rommel, took the port of Tobruk (Libya) after bitter fighting, capturing 35,000 British troops. That success posed a real threat to Egypt and the Suez Canal but the city was retaken in November of the same year after the Allied victory at the **BATTLE OF EL ALAMEIN**.

TOLERATION ACTS. These **ACTS OF PARLIAMENT** ended the legal discrimination against **NONCONFORMISTS** and **RECUSANT**s prescribed by **PENAL LAWS** such as the **CLARENDON CODE.** The 1689 Act followed the **GLORIOUS REVOLUTION** and gave rights of free worship, and designation of places of worship, to the Nonconformist sects. Further Acts removed or repealed restrictive legislation through the 19th century.

TOLPUDDLE MARTYRS, 1834. Six farm labourer members of a **TRADE UNION** from the Dorset village of Tolpuddle campaigned against wage reductions and were convicted, on slender and dubious evidence, of having sworn illegal and seditious oaths. Despite petitions and public unrest, which only exacerbated the authorities' fear of the rise of trade unionism, they received sentences of **TRANSPORTATION** to Australia for seven years. Eventually, they were pardoned and returned to **ENGLAND** in 1836 but the severity of their treatment led many to espouse the cause of the working man against the propertied and owner classes and was a factor in the rise of the **CHARTISTS.** The harsh sentences are now seen as a symptom of growing **GOVERNMENT** fears of uprising and the potential role of organized labour in opposing the state.

TORIES. The word *Tory* is derived from the Irish Gaelic *toraidhe* meaning 'bandit' or 'brigand' and was first used as a term of abuse. Originally, it emerged after the **POPISH PLOT** to describe supporters of the status quo, hereditary succession, the **CHURCH OF ENGLAND**, unreformed **PARLIAMENT**, landownership and royal power. These were people who, having been frightened by the **FRENCH REVOLUTION**, believed unswervingly in law and order. In the early 1800s the word was applied to the **COURT PARTY**, which evolved into the **CONSERVATIVE PARTY** later that century. Modern Conservatives are still often called 'Tories'. (See **ABHORRERS**).

TOULOUSE, BATTLE OF, 10 April 1814. This battle brought victory for Britain (led by the **DUKE OF WELLINGTON**) over the French at a site near the River Garonne. It was the last major confontation of the **PENINSULAR WAR**.

TOURISM. Britain's history and heritage are great attractions for tourists, with over 21 million visitors from abroad coming to the country in 1994 and spending an estimated £10 billion. About 63 per cent of the travellers come from the **EUROPEAN UNION** and 17 per cent from North America. The industry, the country's second largest, employs 1.5 million people and earns annually about £33 billion. However, the United Kingdom has shown a deficit on tourism since 1985 because Britons are deserting domestic resorts in their millions and spending vacations abroad.

TOWER OF LONDON. The original White Tower, which now forms the centrepiece of the Tower of **LONDON**, was built from 1078 by King **WILLIAM I** both to protect London (his capital) and its **RIVER THAMES** approaches and to protect his interests from London, then an uncertain element in the new King's realm. Other defences were added in later centuries and, after the **TUDOR** period, it was used to house eminent prisoners (including **ELIZABETH I, THOMAS MORE** and **ANNE BOLEYN**) as well as more notorious individuals (such as the **SECOND WORLD WAR** Nazi Rudolf Hess, for a brief period in May 1941). By the 17th century, defence of the **MONARCH** was less critical and the Tower lost its royal residence function. It is now a major museum and tourist attraction. Since 1303, it has been the repository of the English Crown Jewels.

TOWTON, BATTLE OF, 29 March 1461. In a massive ten-hour battle (reputed to be the bloodiest on English soil) fought in a blinding snowstorm near Leeds during the **WARS OF THE ROSES**, the Lancastrians were defeated and suffered heavy casualties (upwards of 28,000 according to Yorkist heralds but probably nearer to 10,000 on each side). **EDWARD IV** went on to take **YORK**, thereby winning control of northern **ENGLAND**.

TRADE UNIONS. These associations of workers in particular trades or sets of related trades, organized to protect their collective interests, were a product of the **INDUSTRIAL REVOLUTION**. Early in the period, such groups had been responsible for the weavers' riots in Tiverton (1720), the **WOOL INDUSTRY** wage dispute (1723) and the **LIVERPOOL** seamen's strike (1762) so they were greatly feared by the establishment and legislation such as the **COMBINATION ACTS** (see **ACT OF PARLIAMENT**) attempted to repress them. Robert Owen's proposed countrywide organization, the Grand National Consolidated Trade Union, reinforced these concerns and resulted in the anti-subversion actions of the **GOVERNMENT** against the **TOLPUDDLE MARTYRS**.

In the mid-19th century, however, trade unions became more widespread. As the economy grew, they were developed by the **COAL** miners (1841), the engineers (1851) the carpenters and joiners (1862) and other industrial craftsmen. The national **TRADES UNION CONGRESS (TUC)** was formed in 1868 to coordinate their activities and, under the 1871 Trades Union Act, its affiliated organizations gained legal recognition. After the depression of the last quarter of the 19th century, unions were formed for workers in unskilled jobs (notably in the **RAILWAYS**, agriculture and the docks) and the movement became more militant. Increasingly, also, it became associated with the **LABOUR PARTY**.

The number of trade unions peaked around 1920, when there were 1,384 with a total membership of 8,348,000. Membership reached an all-time record in 1979, when there were 13,498,000 members in 454 unions. Since then, registration has fallen as a result of recession and de-industrialization in the British economy so, by 1991, only some 50 per cent of the workforce was registered with the unions. (See **CHARTISM; GENERAL STRIKE; WINTER OF DISCONTENT**).

TRADES UNION CONGRESS (TUC). The TUC was founded in

MANCHESTER in 1868 as a national association of affiliated **TRADE UNIONS** aiming at the reform of laws relating to industrial relations. It now operates to assist member unions, monitor legislation and act politically for the union cause. Its annual conference is seen as its policy-making body. (See **GENERAL STRIKE; LABOUR PARTY; WINTER OF DISCONTENT**).

TRAFALGAR, BATTLE OF, 21 October 1805. Britain declared war on France on 17 May 1803, following the violations of the Treaty of Amiens by Napoleon Bonaparte. Lord **HORATIO NELSON** engaged a combined French and Spanish fleet under Admiral Pierre de Villeneuve at Cape Trafalgar, off Cadiz, on 21 October 1805 and issued his famous order that "England expects every man will do his duty". A brilliant tactician, he split the enemy fleet in two and destroyed 18 ships in close-quarter fashion to win an historic victory, which shattered the naval power of France. During the battle, he was shot and killed by a French sniper but his achievement reduced the threat of invasion and secured sea supremacy for Britain for more than a century. The battle was the last great naval action involving sailing ships.

TRAINED BANDS. In 1573, after the **NORTHERN REBELLION** and the threat of invasion by the **SPANISH ARMADA**, Queen **ELIZABETH I** ordained that Trained (or Train) Bands should be organized in every **COUNTY**. These bands consisted of local citizens and could be amalgamated to form military forces in time of need (the **LONDON** Trained Band, in particular, had a great reputation as a fighting force). As a **MILITIA**, they were of limited use but they were deployed during the **CIVIL WAR**, when their members were referred to as 'soldiers of place'.

TRANSPORTATION. The deportation of convicted criminals to a penal colony of the **BRITISH EMPIRE** was a form of punishment (at its height over 160 offences carried sentences involving transportation) but it was also a means of populating imperial possessions. Introduced in the 17th century (from 1666, criminals were "transported to any of His Majesty's Dominions in North America"), it was often used as an alternative to execution, especially during the 1700s. At first, many of the convicts were sent to North America but, after the **AMERICAN WAR OF INDEPENDENCE**, that became impossible and they went instead to Botany Bay (Australia). The number of people exiled in this way was greatest in the 19th century, when between 1,093 and 6,871 were sent to Australia each year. Transportation was abandoned by 1868.

TREASON. A criminal offence, treason is the violation of allegiance owed by a citizen to a **MONARCH** or **GOVERNMENT**. The Statute of Treasons (1352) listed six high treason offences, including plotting a Monarch's death, assisting enemies of the state, violating the Queen, killing a judge and counterfeiting money. The penalty was hanging (until almost dead), drawing (the cutting out of entrails) and quartering (dividing the body into four pieces). That sentence was changed in 1795 to beheading and, in 1870, to hanging (see **CAPITAL PUNISHMENT**). Through the centuries, the definitions of treason have varied. For example, the Treason Act of 1534 (see **ACT OF PARLIAMENT**) added the use of words as well as deeds to the offence and incorporated the denying of "the dignity, title or name of royal estates, or the royal supremacy" (that legislation was used against **THOMAS MORE** and other opponents of **HENRY VIII**). In this century, several spies have been charged under the treason laws, which still, technically, carry the death penalty.

TREASURY, THE. The department of **GOVERNMENT** responsible for the management of the economy was removed from the **EXCHEQUER** in 1653. During the 18th century, the First Lord of the Treasury gradually also became **PRIME MINISTER** and that is still nominally the case today. Since 1833 (when the Exchequer was abolished), the Treasury has been led by the **CHANCELLOR OF THE EXCHEQUER**.

TRENT, RIVER. The third longest river in the United Kingdom, the Trent flows eastwards for 170 miles from Biddulph Moor (Staffordshire) to join the River Humber and, ultimately, the North Sea. During the **INDUSTRIAL REVOLUTION**, it became built up along much of its course as it passed through Stoke-on-Trent (the heart of **THE POTTERIES**), Burton-on-Trent (a major centre of the brewing industry) and Nottingham (where textile mills, pharmaceutical companies and tobacco processors became major employers). In addition, a series of **CANALS** linked the river to other waterways, including the **RIVER MERSEY**. However, with the decline of manufacturing industry during the second half of the 20th century, the Trent has lost much of its former commercial importance. (For location, see Map 1, page xxvii).

TRIAL BY BATTLE. Introduced by the **NORMANS**, this form of trial was an alternative to **TRIAL BY ORDEAL** and involved a court appearance followed by armed struggle. If the case involved criminal charges, the litigants had to fight in person but in civil cases they could appoint champions. The last trial by battle took place in 1817. Two years later, it was abolished.

TRIAL BY ORDEAL. An ancient **ANGLO-SAXON** method of legal decision-making, trial by ordeal involved an appeal to God's judgement within a church. The method varied according to the status of the accused. A Freeman could hold or walk on hot iron and was adjudged innocent if free of wounds after three days. An Unfreeman could thrust an arm into hot water: an absence of wounds proved his innocence. Alternatively, he could be bound then lowered into a river: if he floated he was not guilty. A clergyman could swallow a 'cursed morsel' (food with a feather in it): if he did not choke he was adjudged innocent. The alternative of **TRIAL BY BATTLE** was introduced by the **NORMANS** and replaced trial by ordeal in 1215.

TRIANGULAR TRADE. (See **SLAVE TRADE**).

TRIPLE ALLIANCE. There have been three international triple alliances and one national triple alliance.

In 1668, **ENGLAND** joined Sweden and the Netherlands in opposition to King Louis XIV of France.

In 1717, Britain, the Netherlands and France formed an alliance in opposition to Spain.

In 1788, a treaty signed by **WILLIAM PITT THE YOUNGER** and the governments of the Netherlands and Prussia was designed to limit the influence of Austria, preserve the preeminent trading position of **LONDON** and maintain the international status quo. After the **AMERICAN WAR OF INDEPENDENCE**, Britain found herself without allies and with many enemies so the alliance stabilized foreign affairs for a period.

The term 'Triple Alliance' has also been used to describe a mutual support agreement reached, in 1914, by the three powerful **TRADE UNIONS** representing workers on the **RAILWAYS**, in other forms of transport and in the **COAL** industry. This was a time of increasing trade union membership and militancy in the labour movement but the **FIRST WORLD WAR** intervened before the Alliance could get properly organized and it collapsed on 15 April 1921 (Black Friday), when the miners failed to persuade the other partners to mount sympathetic strikes in support of their dispute with the pit owners.

TRIPLE ENTENTE, 1907. A cooperative agreement between Britain, France and Russia grew out of the **ENTENTE CORDIALE** and formed the basis of the opposition to the Central Powers in the lead-up to the **FIRST WORLD WAR**. Motivated essentially by fear of the growing strength of Germany and her allies, it was broken only by the assumption of power in Russia by the Bolsheviks. The three countries became known as the **ENTENTE POWERS** (and later as the Allies) as a result. (See **BATTLES OF DOGGER BANK**).

TROYES, TREATY OF, 21 May 1420. Under an agreement between King **HENRY V** and Charles VI of France during the **HUNDRED YEARS WAR**, Henry married Catherine (Charles's daughter) and, in return, was recognized as heir to the throne of France. It was a diplomatic triumph for **ENGLAND** which never realized its potential because Henry died of dysentery in 1422. His successor, **HENRY VI**, did, however, inherit the dual **MONARCH**y and so was able to lay claim to territories on the European mainland for future English sovereigns.

TRUCK ACT, 1831. Under the truck system, employers profited at the expense of their workers by paying them in goods or by giving them trade tokens, which could only be used at the company store (or 'tommy shop'). The 1831 Act (see **ACT OF PARLIAMENT**) was designed to remove the worst features of this system. Under its terms, wages had to be paid wholly in currency (except in the case of domestic servants).

TUDORS, 1485-1603. The Tudor line claimed descent from the Romano-British Chief of the 4th century, Coel Hen Godebog (known to generations of children as the nursery rhyme character Old King Cole) and ruled **ENGLAND** for 118 years. **HENRY VII**, the first of the **MONARCH**s, took the **CROWN** from **RICHARD III** at the **BATTLE OF BOSWORTH FIELD** (1485), an event sometimes considered to mark the end of the Middle Ages because it resulted in considerable changes to the **FEUDAL SYSTEM**, which was dependent on the hegemony of the many nobles who died in the **WARS OF THE ROSES**. The period which followed was one of expansion and social change, the Renaissance and the development of **PRINTING**, the **REFORMATION** and the growth of exploration and trade in the **ELIZABETHAN AGE**. The Tudors were succeeded by the **STUARTS** in 1603. (See **EDWARD VI; ELIZABETH I; HENRY VIII; MARY I**).

TURNPIKES. The word 'turnpike' refers to a swinging bar which blocked progress along a routeway until a fee was paid: it was often shaped like a pike. By the late 17th century, the **ROADS** of Britain were in disrepair, many not having been upgraded since the days of the **ROMANS**. The responsibility for maintenance had been with each **PARISH** but little had been done so Turnpike Trusts — private companies given the responsibility of building and maintaining specific road projects and levying tolls for their use — were created by legislation in the late 18th century. Over 700 Turnpike Trust Acts (see **ACT OF PARLIAMENT**) were passed between 1750 and 1836, the largest number being for Lancashire and Yorkshire. The Trusts employed their own workers and hired engineers such as Blind Jack (John Metcalf), John Rennie, John Macadam (inventor of the macadamized or, tarmac, road surface) and Thomas Telford, perhaps the most successful of the road and bridge builders of the 18th and 19th centuries. Their turnpikes allowed the development of the Royal Mail coach system on policed roads, free of footpads and highwaymen, and contributed to the growth of the **INDUSTRIAL REVOLUTION** in many areas of Britain. The last turnpike toll was collected in 1895.

TYNDALE, WILLIAM (c. 1494-1536). A leading clergyman during the **REFORMATION** in **ENGLAND**, Tyndale was the translator of the first Bible to be printed in English. Born in Gloucestershire, he studied at **OXFORD** University and was influenced by the works of some of the major figures in the reform movement, including **JOHN WYCLIFFE** and Martin Luther. In 1522 and 1523, he worked as a tutor in the home of Sir John Walsh and became involved in discussions with churchmen who were guests at the house. Those discussions convinced him of the need to translate the Vulgate Bible from Latin into English so that it would be more accessible to the common people. He sought support from Cuthbert Tunstal, Bishop of **LONDON**, but the response was disappointing and, as a result, he left England to continue his work on the continent. By the summer of 1525, he had submitted a manuscript version of his translation to a printer in Cologne. However, Johannes Cochlaeus — one of Luther's opponents — heard about the plans and told the authorities. Tyndale escaped in the nick of time and found another printer in Worms. In 1526, an octavo edition of 3,000 copies was issued. Some of those which reached England were burned at the instigation of Tunstal, who also bought up many of the later editions in an attempt to prevent their distribution. As a result, only two copies remain, one which the British Library purchased from Bristol Baptist College for £1 million in 1994 and the other in the library of St Paul's Cathedral.

Having completed the New Testament, Tyndale set to work on a translation of the Old. The Pentateuch was published in 1530 and, by the time of his death, he had got as far as Nehemiah (with Jonah also finished). The papers were incorporated by John Rodgers into the Matthews version of the Old Testament and from there into the **AUTHORIZED VERSION OF THE BIBLE** In addition to these translations, Tyndale wrote a number of tracts, including *The Parable of the Wicked Mammon* (an argument for the doctrine of justification by faith, published in 1528), *Obedience of the Christian Man* (a treatise on the authority of the Scriptures and the rights of the individual, also published in 1528) and *An Answere Unto Sir Thomas Mores Dialogue* (published in 1530). In 1535, while on the continent, he was arrested for heresy and imprisoned in Vilvoorde Castle, near Brussels. In October 1536, he was taken into the courtyard and strangled. His body was burned.

TYNE, RIVER. Although only 30 miles long, the Tyne was of major economic significance during the **INDUSTRIAL REVOLUTION**. It rises in the rolling uplands of Northumberland, flows eastwards to the North Sea and, in its lower reaches, is navigable to ocean-going ships. The soft clays along its banks were easily dug out and, as a result, a major shipbuilding complex developed at its seaward end. In addition, **COAL** exporting firms became major employers and **NEWCASTLE-UPON-TYNE** rapidly expanded both as a port and as the major commercial centre in northeast **ENGLAND**. The decline in UK manufacturing activity in recent decades has, however, greatly reduced the Tyne's significance in national and international trade. (For location, see Map 1, page xxv).

—U—

ULSTER. The most powerful of the five ancient kingdoms of **IRE-LAND** by the fifth century, Ulster retained its independence until the **PLANTATIONS** of the 17th century. It became part of the United Kingdom as the Province of **NORTHERN IRELAND** when the island was partitioned in 1921.

UNDER-SECRETARY OF STATE. (See **PARLIAMENTARY UNDER-SECRETARY OF STATE**).

UNILATERAL DECLARATION OF INDEPENDENCE (UDI). UDI was declared by Premier Ian Smith in Southern Rhodesia on 11 November 1965 in order to prevent the introduction of majority black rule in this self-governing colony. Britain retaliated with ineffective economic sanctions and, by 1974, black nationalist groups had begun a campaign of guerilla warfare. Talks on **DECOLONIZATION** in 1979 and 1980 resulted in free elections for the independent state of Zimbabwe, led by Robert Mugabe.

UNION, TREATY OF, 1707. The **STUART MONARCH**s experienced great difficulty in coping with the frequently conflicting demands of two Parliaments after the **UNION OF THE CROWNS** (1603) and matters came to a head when, in 1701, the Scots refused to accept the **HANOVERIAN** succession. Political pressure resulted in acceptance by both legislatures of a Treaty of Union, which created what was technically a new **PARLIAMENT** for Great Britain but, in practice, was simply the former English Parliament with an additional 45 Scots in the **HOUSE OF COMMONS** and 16 in the **HOUSE OF LORDS**. Under the terms of the Treaty, **SCOTLAND** retained its own established church and its own legal system.

UNION OF THE CROWNS. In 1603, King James VI of **SCOTLAND**, became King of **ENGLAND** (see **JAMES VI and I**), thus uniting the **CROWN**s of the two countries. He moved the royal court to **LONDON** but the Scots Parliament remained independent of the English **PARLIAMENT** and continued to meet in Edinburgh. Attempts were made to unite the countries politically but these were not successful. Similar moves during the **PROTECTORATE** were also short-lived but political union finally came in 1707 (see **ACT OF UNION**) though Scotland still retains separate legal, educational and religious systems.

UNION OF ENGLAND AND WALES. The two countries had effectively, though not officially, been combined when **EDWARD I** created the first **PRINCE OF WALES** in 1301 and a series of **ACTS OF PARLIAMENT** between 1536 and 1543 formalized the situation. By the **ACT OF UNION** (1536), the Principality became part of **ENGLAND**. Both sets of citizens had equal rights and the Welsh gained representation in **PARLIAMENT** (no new name was created for the united state; Wales was simply absorbed by England). The final Act, in 1543, imposed English legal codes on the Welsh **SHIRE**s.

UNION OF GREAT BRITAIN AND IRELAND. At a time of rebellion in **IRELAND** and hostilities with France, **WILLIAM PITT THE YOUNGER** introduced the 1800 **ACT OF UNION** (see **ACT OF PARLIAMENT**) to unite Ireland with Great Britain and secure the rule of **WESTMINSTER** in the Province as part of a new United Kingdom, formed in 1801. This Union (properly known as the United Kingdom of Great Britain and Ireland) was eventually beset by the movement for **HOME RULE**, the success of which led to the partition of Ireland and the formation of the **UNITED KINGDOM OF GREAT BRITAIN AND NORTHERN IRELAND** in 1922. (See **UNION JACK**).

UNION OF PARLIAMENTS. (See **TREATY OF UNION**).

UNION JACK. The national flag combines, on a blue background, the vertical red cross of **ST GEORGE** (the patron saint of **ENGLAND** since 1277) edged in white (its original field), the diagonal (saltire) white cross of St Andrew (the patron saint of **SCOTLAND**) on its blue field and the diagonal (saltire) red cross of St Patrick (the patron saint of **IRELAND**) on a white field. The Welsh dragon does not appear because Wales had been united with England in 1536 and so was already part of the country when King **JAMES VI** and **I** created the first Union Flag in 1606 (then incorporating only the crosses of St George and St Andrew) after the **UNION OF THE CROWNS**. Known as the Union Flag or the Union Jack, the current version dates from the **UNION OF GREAT BRITAIN AND IRELAND** in 1801, when the Irish cross was placed on top of the Scottish one. By making the amount of white on each arm broader on one side than the other, the design emphasized the fact that the saltire formed part of St Andrew's cross and was not merely background to the Irish one. Strictly, the flag should be known only as a Union Jack when it is flown from the bow of a ship (a jack being a ship's flag) but the usage has now become common.

UNITED KINGDOM (UK). The UK comprises **ENGLAND, WALES, SCOTLAND** and **NORTHERN IRELAND** and is properly called the United Kingdom of Great Britain and Northern Ireland. It has an area of 94,525 square miles (244,820 square kilometres) and a population (at the time of the 1991 census) of 56.6 million people. Strictly speaking, the United Kingdom is the sovereign state, Scotland and England are formerly independent countries which combined (see **UNION OF THE CROWNS, TREATY OF UNION**), Wales is a Principality and Northern Ireland is a Province. The country was created as the United Kingdom of Great Britain and **IRELAND** in 1801 and adopted its current title on the formation of the Irish Free State in 1921. (See **UNION OF ENGLAND AND WALES; UNION OF GREAT BRITAIN AND IRELAND**).

UNIVERSITIES. The earliest British universities (such as **OXFORD** and **CAMBRIDGE**) evolved, like many medieval universities in Europe, from schools attached to monasteries and cathedrals during the 12th century. Others (such as Edinburgh) followed after the **REFORMATION** but it was not until the 19th century and, in particular, the 20th century that the number of institutions expanded significantly. Many were established during the **INDUSTRIAL REVOLUTION**, particularly in the north of **ENGLAND**, where settlements were growing and technology was advancing rapidly (**LIVERPOOL**, for example, gained its Charter in 1903, Leeds the following year). In **LONDON**, University College was created in 1826 and was followed quickly by King's College (which was founded to expound the philosophies of the established Church). These two combined in 1836 to form the University of London. More university foundations followed after the **SECOND WORLD WAR** and especially in the 1960s (**EAST ANGLIA**, Essex, Keele, Lancaster, Stirling and others were all products of a growth in demand for higher **EDUCATION** at that time and became known as 'redbrick universities' because of their modern buildings). Also, in 1974, the Open University was started, using radio and television to take part-time distance learning to mature students: it rapidly became the largest university in the country. In 1992, the **POLYTECHNICS** — originally created in 1967 to provide broader, more vocational degree-level syllabuses, which would be an alternative to the courses offered by traditional centres of learning — were granted university status. There are now 83 universities in the United Kingdom. With the exception of the University of Buckingham, all are state funded.

UNLEARNED PARLIAMENT, 1404. This Parliament was held at Coventry by King **HENRY IV**, who needed to raise revenues in order to finance his military expeditions at home and abroad. It received its name because the King excluded all members who had legal training in the hope that this would shorten discussion and create an amenable outcome.

UTRECHT, TREATY OF, 1713. Nine treaties (sometimes collectively referred to as the Peace of Utrecht) were agreed by the European powers between 1713 and 1715 at the end of the **WAR OF THE SPANISH SUCCESSION**. As a result, Britain gained French territories in Canada (including Hudson's Bay and Acadia), Spanish territories in Minorca and Gibraltar and the rights to the **ASIENTO**. (See **SLAVE TRADE**).

—V—

VASSAL. A vassal was a tenant who held land under the **FEUDAL SYSTEM** in return for swearing homage and fealty (loyalty) to his (or, rarely, her) lord.

VERDUN, BATTLE OF, February-July 1916. An attempt by German forces to break through the French lines near Paris during the **FIRST WORLD WAR** was repulsed by British troops at the **BATTLE OF THE SOMME**. The action prevented German reinforcement at Verdun and their offensive was eventually neutralized.

VEREENIGING, TREATY OF, 31 May 1902. The treaty ended the second **BOER WAR**, affirming Britain's annexation of Orange Free State and Transvaal and leading eventually to **DOMINION** status for South Africa in 1910.

VERNEUIL, BATTLE OF, 17 August 1424. In this, the greatest of **ENGLAND**'s victories during the **HUNDRED YEARS WAR**, a combined French and Scottish army numbering 15,000 was annihilated by an Anglo-Burgundian force of 9,000 under the Duke of Bedford.

VERSAILLES, TREATY OF, 1783. This treaty, which ended the **AMERICAN WAR OF INDEPENDENCE,** recognized the independent sovereignty of the United States, ended maritime hostilities with Spain, France and the Netherlands and returned Florida to Spain. Britain retained Quebec and rights to navigate the Mississippi. King **GEORGE III** had no regrets about the loss of territory in North America. "Knavery seems to be so much the striking feature of its inhabitants", he said, "that it may not, in the end, be an evil that they become aliens to this kingdom"!

VERSAILLES, TREATY OF, 1919. This treaty concluded the **FIRST WORLD WAR** and aimed to prevent Germany from ever again threatening European stability. For Britain, it brought peace and a commitment to occupation of the demilitarized Rhineland until 1926. The **LEAGUE OF NATIONS** was proposed by a Covenant of the Treaty.

VICTORIA (1819-1901). Queen of Great Britain and Ireland from 1837 until 1901, Victoria was born in **LONDON** on 24 May 1819. The only child of Edward, Duke of Kent and fourth son of **GEORGE III**, she succeeded to the throne because the two daughters of **WILLIAM IV** (her predecessor) did not survive their infancy. Her father died when she was only eight months old so she was brought up by her mother (Princess Mary Louisa Victoria of **SAXE-COBURG-GOTHA**) and her governess (Louise Lehzen). She became Queen, on 20 June 1837, while still only 18 years old and at a time when the role of the **MONARCH**y in British politics was unclear.

Victoria became devoted to **VISCOUNT MELBOURNE,** the Whig **PRIME MINISTER** and her chief adviser, who encouraged her to appoint **LADIES IN WAITING** who were of the same political persuasion. In what became known as the **BED-CHAMBER CRISIS**, when Melbourne resigned in 1839 she refused to agree to a request made by his potential successor, the **TORIES**' Sir **ROBERT PEEL**, that the Ladies be removed. Faced with the Queen's intransigence, Peel declined to take office and Victoria had to persuade Melbourne to return.

In October 1839, she was equally forthright in proposing to her cousin **PRINCE ALBERT** of Saxe-Coburg. They were married on 10 February 1840 and had four sons and five daughters who wedded into European aristocracy, extending British influence throughout the continent. Initially, Victoria tried to prevent Albert from taking any part in **GOVERNMENT** but gradually his role increased until he was handling most of the affairs of state. For her part, the Queen was happiest when living outside London in the Isle of Wight or at Balmoral Castle in **SCOTLAND**. Scotland was her particular favourite — her journals show that she esteemed the highland way of life and that she preferred Scottish church services (provided the sermons were short). Despite the distractions of travel, however, she was extremely conscientious and, under Albert's guidance, learned how to organize her duties and encourage her **MINISTER**s to explain issues simply but with detail. As a result, when her consort died of typhoid in 1861, she was able to pick up the reins, attempting to take the decisions she believed he would have made.

Despite her sense of duty, Victoria appeared in public rarely for several years after Albert's death, missing her helpmate greatly. Many of her subjects resented that seclusion, feeling that she should display the pomp and majesty appropriate to the head of the world's first industrial nation, with its growing empire. It was **BENJAMIN DISRAELI** who gave her the confidence to emerge from her grieving in the late 1870s. Dizzy, as she called him, was a staunch advocate of overseas expansion and earned Victoria's gratitude when he sponsored a **BILL** naming her Empress of India in 1876. Relations with **WILLIAM GLADSTONE**, who was Prime Minister on four occasions during her reign, were less cordial. Gladstone held Victoria in great awe, treated her stiffly and wrote her ponderous missives about his **LIBERAL PARTY** policies, for which she had little sympathy. In particular, she would not support schemes designed to meet the grievances of the Irish, an issue which occupied much of Gladstone's time. Increasingly, she insisted on being consulted by her Prime Ministers, even on relatively trivial issues, leading **JOSEPH CHAMBERLAIN** to comment in exasperation that "The Queen does interfere constantly". Her lengthy reign inevitably gave her considerable experience of the affairs of government and she took every opportunity to give her advisers the benefit of that experience.

For the British people, she increasingly became a symbol of power and progress so there was genuine sadness when she died, on 22 January 1901, after a short illness. She had ruled with dignity over a century of enormous social and economic change and provided stability to a Monarchy which had fallen into some disrepute because of the failings of her immediate predecesors.

Victoria was buried beside Albert at Frogmore, not far from **WINDSOR CASTLE**, as she had wished.

VICTORIA CROSS (VC). The United Kingdom's premier distinction for gallantry in battle was established by Queen **VICTORIA** in 1856. In 1902, **EDWARD VII** decreed that it could be awarded posthumously. The VC carries the royal crest (a lion standing on a crown) and is inscribed "For Valour". The ribbon is dark crimson. As other medals for bravery were introduced during the late 18th and early 19th centuries, the standards required for the award of the Victoria Cross rose so far fewer were awarded during the **SECOND WORLD WAR** than during the **FIRST WORLD WAR**.

VICTORIAN AGE. Like the **ELIZABETHAN AGE**, the reign of Queen **VICTORIA** (1837-1901) is often seen as a glorious period in British history. It was a time of growing world influence and extension of the **BRITISH EMPIRE**, developing technology and science, and burgeoning industrial cities and commerce. The **INDUSTRIAL REVOLUTION** made the United Kingdom the world's major political power and a cult of individuality, tempered by strict social morality, replaced the more overt conformism of the **GEORGIAN** period. In the decorative arts, heavily ornate styles were characteristic in furniture and architecture and, in literature, authors such as George Eliot, Charles Dickens and William Wordsworth found enormous audiences. The period also brought the beginnings of a social conscience which was ultimately to result in the extension of the franchise to women (see **SUFFRAGETTES**) and other legislative change in the 20th century.

VIKINGS. Scandinavian seafaring traders and raiders of the eighth to 11th centuries used fast and strong narrow boats (known as longships) for coastal and river penetration. The techniques were employed to great effect in 865, when an invasion by the Danish Great Army destroyed the English kingdoms, with the exception of **WESSEX**. These Danes settled mostly in eastern and southern **ENGLAND** (see **DANELAW**), with Norsemen (Norwegians) in **SCOTLAND** and the northern islands. For a short time, the kingdoms of England, Norway and Denmark were within one empire, at least in terms of allegiance to King **CANUTE**. The **ANGLO-SAXON CHRONICLE**, recording events of the time, refers to the Vikings as "the force" and "the heathen". (See **ALFRED THE GREAT; BATTLE OF ASSANDUN; DANEGELD; BATTLE OF EDINGTON; BATTLE OF MALDON**).

VILLA. A landed estate of the **ROMAN** period which was owned by Romans (or by British aristocracy who accepted Roman rule and custom), the villa was essentially an agricultural unit, although sometimes it also had an industrial element. It was the mainstay of Roman farming in Britain and frequently incorporated substantial dwellings with mosaic floors and hypocaust heating systems.

VILLEIN. Under the **FEUDAL SYSTEM**, the villein (or villager) was an unfree peasant who owed services of labour (rather than tenurial obligations) to the lord of the **MANOR**. Virtually (but not actually) a slave, he was bought and sold, held few legal rights and worked the demesne of his lord.

VIRGINIA COMPANY. (See **LONDON COMPANY**).

VISCOUNT. Originally the administrative deputy of an **EARL**, a viscount has (since 1440) been recognized as one of the peers of the realm (see **PEERAGE**). A viscountess may be either the wife of a viscount or a lady holding a viscountcy in her own right.

—W—

WAITANGI, TREATY OF, 1840. An agreement with the Maoris of New Zealand granted land rights to the local chiefs who, in turn, accepted British sovereignty. The United Kingdom's failure to honour the agreement led to Maori Uprisings between 1843 and 1848, and from 1860 to 1870. Maori leaders still contest the Treaty, arguing that Britain has never honoured the land rights of the native peoples of New Zealand.

WAKEFIELD, BATTLE OF, 30-31 December 1460. One of the

critical encounters during the **WARS OF THE ROSES**, the battle resulted in defeat for the Yorkists and death for their leader, Richard **PLANTAGENET** (challenger to **HENRY VI** for the English throne). Some 2,800 Yorkists were killed and the heads of their leaders were hung by the Lancastrians on Micklegate Bar in **YORK** so that "York might look upon York".

WALES. The name of this part of the **BRITISH ISLES** is derived from the Old English word *walh* which meant 'foreigner' and was used by the **ANGLO-SAXONS** to describe the alien **CELTS** who inhabited the area. Wales was incorporated into **ENGLAND** in 1536 (see **UNION OF ENGLAND AND WALES**) but retains many distinctive cultural characteristics though it has no legal or financial independence. It has a land area of approximately 8,000 square miles and a population (in 1991) of 2.8 million, with most of its industry concentrated in the south. In the 1979 referendum on devolution of power (see **REFERENDA**), the Welsh electorate voted 11.9 per cent for devolution with 46.9 per cent against. The Principality returns 38 representatives to the **HOUSE OF COMMONS**. After the 1992 **GENERAL ELECTION**, the **LABOUR PARTY** held 27 of these, the **CON-SERVATIVE PARTY** six, Plaid Cymru (the Welsh National Party) four and the **LIBERAL DEMOCRATIC PARTY** one.

WALPOLE, ROBERT (1676-1745). Walpole, who is usually regarded as the first British **PRIME MINISTER**, was born in Norfolk on 26 August 1676, the third son of Colonel Robert Walpole and his wife, Mary. He was educated at Eton College and **CAMBRIDGE** University but his studies were cut short in 1698 when he returned to **EAST ANGLIA** in order to administer the family estate after the death of his elder brother, Edward. When his father died in 1700, he inherited the family's **PARLIAMENT**ary seat for the **ROTTEN BOROUGH** of Castle Rising but, in 1702, transferred to nearby King's Lynn, which he represented for the next 40 years. In the **HOUSE OF COMMONS**, Walpole sided with the **WHIGS** and quickly gained a reputation as a forceful speaker. In 1708, he became **SECRETARY OF STATE** for War and, two years later, Treasurer of the Navy. At the 1710 **GENERAL ELECTION**, however, the **TORIES** won control of Parliament and impeached many of the Whig leaders in an attempt to destroy the **OPPOSITION** party. Walpole was among the accused: in 1712, he was found guilty of corruption and imprisoned in the **TOWER OF LONDON**.

He regained office in 1714, when **GEORGE I** became King and the Whigs returned to power. Walpole was initially made **PAYMASTER GENERAL** of the Forces but, in 1715, was promoted to First Lord of **THE TREASURY** and **CHAN-CELLOR OF THE EXCHEQUER**. He resigned in 1717, claiming that other **MINISTER**s were sacrificing their country's interests in order to curry favour with the new King, and for the next three years consistently opposed the **GOVERN-MENT**. A reconciliation with George was effected in 1720, enabling Walpole to return to his former post of Paymaster General, but he was no sooner back in office than he got caught up in the **SOUTH SEA BUBBLE** scandal. He had actually invested in the scheme but had been saved from ruin by the foresight of his banker, Robert Jacomb, and, in Parliament, used his considerable political skill to stabilize the nation's finances and preserve the **HANOVERIAN MONARCH**y. The King had little love for Walpole, but his achievements required a reward which came in the form of his reappointment as First Lord and Chancellor, posts which he held until 1742.

His position and power, in effect, meant that he controlled Parliament. Gradually, he ousted his opponents from office and used his administrative skills to reform the country's finances, supported by George I and his successor, **GEORGE II**. A **SINK-ING FUND** was established in order to reduce the **NATIONAL DEBT** and a policy of low taxation endeared him to the landed **GENTRY**, helping to gain him support in the Commons. In foreign affairs he was a pacifist, preferring diplomacy to war and thus encouraging prosperity at home. His schemes, however, made enemies who felt that the use of patronage to make appointments to official posts was a form of corruption, that the reluctance to go to war was a betrayal of national interests and that the financial manoeuverings were of little value.

His opponents had an opportunity to assail him in 1733, when he announced his intention to impose a tax on wines and tobacco in order to control smuggling and customs frauds. In the end, Walpole withdrew the measure but his position was weakened and, in 1739, he met further trouble. Disputes with Spain over West Indian trade could not be solved by negotiation and he had to declare war. He proved to be an indifferent wartime leader and, though he won the general election of 1741, resigned on 2 February 1742. George II created him Earl of Orford, enabling him to play an influential role in the **HOUSE OF LORDS** until his death in **LONDON** on 18 March 1745.

WAR OF 1812. (See **ANGLO-AMERICAN WAR**).

WAR OFFICE. This Department of **GOVERNMENT** was responsible for the **BRITISH ARMY** from its formation in 1785 until it was absorbed into the Ministry of Defence in 1964.

WATERLOO, BATTLE OF, 18 June 1815. This battle, which ended the **NAPOLEONIC WARS**, took place at the village of Waterloo, near Brussels in Belgium, when the Duke of Wellington (see **ARTHUR WELLESLEY**) led a combined British and Prussian force against the army of Napoleon Bonaparte. Paris had fallen to Britain on 30 March 1814 and Napoleon had returned from exile on Elba on 1 March the following year, intent on avenging the loss of the French capital by taking the allied forces by surprise in Belgium and attacking the Prussians at Ligny. The hard-fought battle which ensued could have resulted in victory for either side but eventually brought success for the Iron Duke, who regarded it as "the nearest run thing you ever saw in your life". French losses amounted to 25,000 men and over 15,000 of the British troops were dead or wounded, including all of Wellington's personal staff. Some 8,000 Prussians also lost their lives. It is said that the horror of the experience led Wellington to politics and, thereafter, to seek to avoid full-scale conflict. Napoleon was again exiled, this time to the island of St Helena in the South Atlantic, and abdicated on 22 June 1815.

WATSON-WENTWORTH, CHARLES (1730-1782). **WHIG PRIME MINISTER** from July 1765 until July 1766 and from March until July 1782, Watson-Wentworth was born on 13 May 1730, the fifth son of Thomas Watson-Wentworth, who was created Marquis of Rockingham in 1746. He left home in 1745 to fight against the Jacobite army, led by Charles Edward Stuart, and, in September 1750, was created Baron Malton and Earl Malton in the peerage of **IRELAND**. In December of the same year, he succeeded to his father's title and to the family estates in Northamptonshire, Yorkshire and Ireland. In 1751, he became Lord of the Bedchamber to **GEORGE II** but resigned in 1762 as an act of sympathy with his friend, William Cavendish, Duke of Devonshire, on his dismissal from the post of **LORD CHAMBER-**

LAIN. In July 1765, Watson-Wentworth accepted an invitation from the King to form an administration to replace that of **GEORGE GRENVILLE** but, from the beginning, his **CABINET** was riven by internal disagreement and, moreover, failed to gain the support of **WILLIAM PITT THE ELDER** in the **HOUSE OF COMMONS**. Attempts to appease the growing protests of the American colonists reduced his popularity even further and, in July 1766, he resigned, to be replaced by Pitt. For the next six years, he led the **PARLIAMENT**ary **OPPOSITION**, voicing strong condemnation of the war against the American colonists (see **AMERICAN WAR OF INDEPENDENCE**) and, in March 1782, was again appointed Prime Minister following the resignation of Lord **FREDERICK NORTH** in the wake of the British defeat in North America. Over the next 16 months he opened peace negotiations with the American rebels, gave legislative independence to the Irish Parliament and introduced a programme of economic reforms. His ministry, however, was cut short by his death on 1 July 1782.

WEBB, BEATRICE (1858-1943). With her husband, **SIDNEY WEBB**, Beatrice was deeply involved in advocating social reforms which would benefit the poor. Born in Gloucester on 22 January 1858, one of the nine daughters of Richard Potter and his wife, Laurencina, she was educated at home. After her mother died in 1882, she increasingly acted as a travelling companion to her father who, as President of the Great Western **RAILWAY**, had to attend meetings in various parts of the country. She also became his hostess at the family home in **LONDON** and took responsibility for the collection of rents on his estates. In 1887, she began to help her cousin, Charles Booth, with his investigation of urban poverty, the results of which were published between 1889 and 1903 as the 17-volume *Life and Labour of the People of London.*

This involvement with Booth and other members of his radical circle led to a meeting with Sydney Webb and, in 1892, to marriage. Their commitment to reform was such that their honeymoon was spent at the annual conference of the **TRADES UNION CONGRESS** in Glasgow and their wedding rings were inscribed "Pro Bono Publico". For the rest of their lives, they worked closely together, and their home in Grosvenor Road, London, became a meeting place for socialist philosophers and activists from all over the country. In 1905, Beatrice became a member of the Royal Commission on the **POOR LAW**s and, four years later, presented a cogently argued minority report challenging the basis of the system, which was designed to look after those who did not have the means to look after themselves. The Webbs argued that this palliative approach should be replaced by measures which would stop poverty occurring and, in particular, by the establishment of specialized social service units which would attend to individual aspects of need. They campaigned strongly for acceptance of the minority report but failed (though many aspects of it were reflected in the **WELFARE STATE** infrastructure developed after the **SECOND WORLD WAR**).

While Sidney was working with the **LABOUR PARTY** and in the **HOUSE OF COMMONS** between 1914 and 1931, Beatrice wrote articles, pamphlets and books, which advocated greater attention to the needs of the poor, and served on numerous **GOVERNMENT** committees, including the Statutory War Pensions Committee (1916-17), the Reconstruction Committee (1917-18), the Committee on the Machinery of Government (1917-19) and the War Cabinet Committee on Women in Industry (1918-19). When, in 1929, her husband allowed himself to be cajoled into joining **RAMSAY MACDONALD**'s second administration and had to accept the title of Baron Passfield (thereby getting a seat in the **HOUSE OF LORDS**, from which he could act as **SECRETARY OF STATE** for the **DOMINION**s and Colonies), Beatrice refused to accept the title of Lady Passfield. They visited Russia in 1932 and were greatly impressed, documenting their reactions in the two-volume *Soviet Communism: a New Civilisation?*, published in 1935. From then, the Soviet Union become their greatest interest.

Beatrice died at home in Liphook on 30 April 1943, and her ashes were placed in **WESTMINSTER** Abbey. She and her husband had a prolific output of coauthored books, notably *History of Trade Unionism* (1894), *Industrial Democracy* (1897), *English Local Government* (three vols, 1906-29) and *English Poor Law Policy* (1910). Of the works she wrote on her own, the most important were *The Co-operative Movement in Great Britain* (1891) and *My Apprenticeship* (1926).

WEBB, SIDNEY (1859-1947). A passionate advocate of social reform, Webb was born in **LONDON** on 13 July 1859, the son of Mr and Mrs Charles Webb. He was educated privately in Switzerland and Germany and at Birkbeck Institute and the **CITY OF**

LONDON College. In 1875, he joined a firm of brokers as a Clerk then, three years later, passed the Civil Service entrance examinations and was given a similar job in the **WAR OFFICE**. In 1879, following another examination success, he obtained a post with the Surveyor of Taxes and, after a further two years, was promoted to the Administrative Grade and moved to the Colonial Office. In 1885, he became a barrister and also joined the **FABIAN SOCIETY**, a socialist organization dedicated to the restructuring of community life "in accordance with the highest moral possibilities". In 1886, he was awarded an LLB by London University and, five years later, resigned from the Civil Service in order to campaign for election to the newly- formed **LONDON COUNTY COUNCIL**, winning election on an overtly left-wing ticket as the Progressive member for Deptford.

At about the same time, Webb met Beatrice Potter, the daughter of industrialist Richard Potter, and, in 1892, they married (see **BEATRICE WEBB**). From then, they worked closely together (so closely that Beatrice referred to them as "the firm of Webb"). The main focus of Sidney's LCC activities was the administration of the city's **EDUCATION**al services: he did much to shape the structure of provision in London at all levels and was instrumental in framing the 1903 London Education Act (see **ACT OF PARLIAMENT**), which made London County Council responsible for all public education in the city. Also, he arranged London University's conversion from a purely examining body to a teaching institution and helped to establish scholarship schemes which enabled children to progress from elementary to secondary schools. In 1910, he resigned his Council post but remained active in politics and maintained a steady output of books and articles, many produced jointly with his wife.

In 1913 (with his wife), he founded the *New Statesman*, a socialist weekly aimed at educated readers, and, the following year, was appointed to the **LABOUR PARTY**'s War Emergency Committee. In 1915, he joined the Party's National Executive and wrote the manifesto — *Labour and the New Social Order* — on which it fought the **GENERAL ELECTION**s in 1918, 1922 and 1924. He was elected Member of **PARLIAMENT** for Durham Seaham in 1922 by a margin of 12,000 votes and, two years later, became **PRESIDENT OF THE BOARD OF TRADE** in the first (and short-lived) Labour **GOVERNMENT**, led by **RAMSAY MACDONALD**. He resigned his **HOUSE OF COMMONS** seat in 1928 but was persuaded to return to government a few months later, a decision which (because he was no longer an MP) required him to swallow his pride and accept the title Baron Passfield then take his place in the **HOUSE OF LORDS**. MacDonald appointed him **SECRETARY OF STATE** for the **DOMINION**s and Colonies (1929), but he resigned after only two years. He was awarded the Order of Merit in 1944 and died in Liphook on 13 October 1947. His ashes were placed in **WEST-MINSTER** Abbey.

WEDGWOOD, JOSIAH (1730-95). The creator of a world renowned ceramics company, Wedgwood converted pottery production from a small-scale cottage industry to large-scale factory-based manufacturing by investing in the construction of the Trent and Mersey **CANAL** (see **RIVER MERSEY**; **RIVER TRENT**). He was born in Burslem on 12 July 1730, the son of Thomas Wedgwood (himself a potter) and his wife, Mary. He received some education locally but, when his father died in 1739, he had to leave school and work at the family business. Five years later, he was apprenticed to Thomas, his elder brother, and, in 1754 (after surviving an attack of smallpox), entered into a partnership with Thomas Whieldon, one of the most respected of the Staffordshire potters. In 1759, he set up on his own account and carried out a series of experiments, working with various types of clay and developing new glazes in an attempt to diversify his range of products. One of the results was a cream-coloured earthenware, which became known as 'Queen's Ware' because it was much admired by Queen Charlotte, consort of King **GEORGE III**. It proved to be very hard wearing and gave Wedgwood an international market.

In 1762, a new partnership with **LIVERPOOL** merchant, Thomas Bentley, led to the development of ornamental ware. Designs reflected the vogue for classical allusions in **GEORGIAN** Britain and consisted of raised figures on contrasting backgrounds. However, demand consistently outstripped supply because production was constrained by the poor transport infrastructure. Rivers were too shallow to permit bulk carriage either of clay imports or of finished merchandise and the unsurfaced **ROADS** resulted in a high proportion of breakages. Plans to build a canal between the River Trent and the River Mersey offered a means of overcoming these problems because barges could carry large quantities of clay and move pottery undamaged from producer to consumer. In 1769, Wedgwood opened a factory beside the still unfinished canal at a site he named Etruria after the home of Etruscan pottery in northern Italy. As the canal opened over the next decade, his business expanded and other manufacturers followed his example. Research into glazes continued and artists were commissioned to design tableware and ornamental pottery, allowing the company to develop quality products which commanded high prices. Production remained at the Etruria site until 1940, when it was relocated in more modern premises at Barlaston, five miles south of Stoke-on-Trent. Wedgwood was elected a Fellow of the Royal Society in 1783 and of the Society of Antiquaries in 1786. He died in his home at Etruria on 3 January 1795. (See **THE POTTERIES**).

WELFARE STATE. This term, coined in 1941 by William Temple (**ARCHBISHOP OF CANTERBURY**) to describe the development of a comprehensive system of social welfare provided through taxation and national insurance, is now used to describe the post-**SECOND WORLD WAR** 'cradle to grave' state-provided community care envisaged in the **BEVERIDGE REPORT** (1942). The activities of late 19th century social workers such as **BEATRICE WEBB** and **SYDNEY WEBB**, the pressure of politicians such as Aneurin Bevan and the introduction of legislation such as the 1911 National Health Insurance Act (see **ACT OF PARLIAMENT**) laid the foundations of the Welfare State but its infrastructure was most fully developed by the **LABOUR PARTY** administration formed under **CLEMENT ATTLEE** after the 1945 **GENERAL ELECTION**. As well as implementing the 1944 **EDUCATION** Act, the **GOVERNMENT** adopted a programme which provided family allowances, maternity grants, sickness and unemployment benefits, death grants, retirement pensions, a free health service (see **NATIONAL HEALTH SERVICE**), a free education service and public housing. The system came under increasing political pressure from the late 1970s, especially during the governments of **MARGARET THATCHER**, who began the deconstruction of an edifice seen by those on the right wing of the **CONSERVATIVE PARTY** as patronizing, destructive to self-help and, above all, a drain on the public purse. Opposition to the subsequent changes came particularly from the elderly (who are on limited incomes but are heavy users of welfare state provisions), the medical profession (which resisted the erosion of cheap medical care) and the Church (which argued that change would widen the gap between rich and poor).

WELLESLEY, ARTHUR (1769-1852). **PRIME MINISTER** and

the principal strategist behind Britain's successes in the **NAPO-LEONIC WARS**, Wellesley was born in Dublin (then part of Britain), probably on 1 May 1769. The fifth son of Garrett Wesley, Earl of Mornington, he was educated at local schools in **IRELAND**, at Eton College and at the French Military Academy at Angers. In 1787, he enlisted as an Ensign with the 73rd Highland Regiment and purchased his way through the ranks with money loaned by his brother, Richard. He saw action against the French in the 33rd Foot Brigade with the **DUKE OF YORK**'s troops in Flanders (1794-95) and, in 1796, sailed with his regiment to India. Disenchanted by the mismanagement of the Flanders campaign, he set himself the task of becoming proficient in the arts of war and, in 1800, led an army of British and Indian troops to restore the chief of Mahratta to his throne, winning victories at Poona, Assaye and Argaum. His success was rewarded with a **KNIGHT**hood.

Wellesley returned to Europe in 1805 and became Member of **PARLIAMENT** for Rye the following year. In 1807, he was selected as the Member for the St Michael **CONSTITUENCY** in Cornwall and accepted the post of Chief Secretary for Ireland under the **DUKE OF PORTLAND**. His administrative duties were soon curtailed, however, because in the summer of 1807 he was sent to deal with the Danish fleet, which the **GOVERNMENT** thought might be used to support Napoleon. In 1808, after the outbreak of the **PENINSULAR WAR**, he led a British force ordered to oppose a French invasion of Portugal and won a major victory at Vimeiro, near Lisbon, on 21 August. The effect of that success was diminished by his superior officer, Sir Harry Burrard, who allowed the enemy to withdraw rather than force them into surrender. Furious, Wellesley returned to his Irish post but, in 1809, he was back, charged with the task of driving the 23,000 French troops from Portugal. He succeeded within a month and withstood an enemy counterattack at Talavera de la Reina, in Spain, on 28 July. The popularity of those victories with the British public was reflected in the award of a Viscountcy with the designation Wellington of Talavera.

Despite the acclaim, Wellesley realised that the military situation was still uncertain and constructed a series of fortifications (known as the lines of Torres Vedras) between the River Tagus and the sea. That was supplemented by a scorched earth policy: Napoleon's armies lived off the land and Wellington intended to weaken them through starvation. The strategy was successful, compelling the French to withdraw and enabling Wellington to recapture a series of fortresses which guarded the major routes into Spain. On 22 July 1812, he defeated the French once again at the **BATTLE OF SALAMANCA** then occupied Madrid and, in the spring of the following year, began a northward advance towards the Pyrenees. He gained another major victory at the Battle of Vitoria (21 June), an achievement which resulted in his promotion to Field Marshal and the award of the **ORDER OF THE GARTER**. He pushed on into France and, on 12 April 1814, after the **BATTLE OF TOULOUSE**, was told of Napoleon's abdication. The grant of a Dukedom followed in May. From August 1814, until January 1815, he served as British Ambassador to France but then left Paris to replace **VISCOUNT CASTLEREAGH** at the Congress of Vienna. Discussions there were interrupted in March by news that Napoleon had escaped from his exile on Elba and landed in France. Wellington was given command of the allied troops and met the French on 18 June at the **BATTLE OF WATERLOO**. Napoleon was defeated, but the cost was enormous. In this, his last battle, Wellington lost 23,000 men and wept at the news.

He remained in command of the occupying army in northern France until its withdrawal in 1818, when he resumed his political career. His appointment to the post of Master-General of the Ordnance, in December 1818, gave him a seat in the **CABINET** under the **EARL OF LIVERPOOL** and, for the next nine years, he represented Britain at international meetings and took particular interest in the country's foreign policies, disagreeing vehemently with the views of Foreign Secretary **GEORGE CANNING**. In January 1827, he was made Commander in Chief of the army but, three months later, resigned in protest against Canning's appointment as Prime Minister.

Canning lasted for only four months and his successor — **VISCOUNT GODERICH** — proved incompetent. **GEORGE IV**, determined to find a leader with mettle, appointed Wellington to the post in January 1828. Wellington accepted partly out of duty and partly because he wanted to reunite a Tory party (see **TORIES**) weakened by internal differences. Those hopes were unfulfilled. Fundamental schisms over foreign policy led to the resignation of some of the more able members of the Cabinet and, in 1829, the passage of legislation giving votes to Roman Catholics made the Duke many enemies. There were calls for further constitutional reform. Wellington refused but the opposition was such that he resigned in November 1830, following the Government's defeat in the **HOUSE OF COMMONS**. He remained out of office until 1834, when **WILLIAM IV** dismissed the **WHIG** Government of **VISCOUNT MELBOURNE**.

Wellington was, once again, asked to form a Government but, arguing that the Prime Minister should be a member of the House of Commons, declined. He did, however, agree to serve as Foreign Secretary under Tory **ROBERT PEEL**. When Peel resigned in April 1835, Wellington went with him. The Tories were returned to office in 1841 and Wellington (though 72) accepted a seat in the Cabinet without any specific portfolio. In 1842, he was made Commander-in-Chief again but, when Peel resigned for the second time in 1846, Wellington followed and played little further part in public life. He died at Walmer Castle (**KENT**) on 14 September 1852 and was buried in St Paul's Cathedral beside **HORATIO NELSON**.

WELLINGTON, DUKE OF. (See **ARTHUR WELLESLEY**).

WESLEY, CHARLES (1707-1788). Co-founder of **METHODISM** along with his brother, **JOHN WESLEY**, Charles was born in Epworth on 18 December 1707, the third son of Samuel Wesley (an Anglican vicar) and his wife, Susanna (daughter of a **NONCONFORMIST** minister). He was educated at **WESTMINSTER** School and at **OXFORD** University, where he formed the Holy Club, a group of undergraduates who tried to live a Christian life through methodical study and prayer (hence the term 'Methodists', which was often used disparagingly). He graduated with a BA in 1730 and took an MA in 1733 then, in 1735, agreed to travel to America with his brother and act as Secretary to Colonel James Oglethorpe, founder of the Colony of Georgia. In order to perform that duty effectively, he was ordained as a priest of the **CHURCH OF ENGLAND** but he found the rigours of the New World both physically and spiritually sapping so it was with great relief that he left in May 1736, carrying despatches to Britain on behalf of his master.

Over the next two years, Wesley had considerable contact with the Moravian community, who introduced him to the doctrine of justification, by which sinners are reconciled with their Creator. That induced a sense of being "at peace with God", a situation which he recognized on 21 May 1738. For the next 17 years he helped his brother organize Methodist groups within the Anglican

Church, broadcasting an evangelical doctrine which stressed personal experience of salvation through faith in God. His ministry concentrated on **LONDON** and Bristol (partly because poor health limited his mobility) and made a strong impact on the urban working classes, who had been neglected by the established church. His greatest contribution, however, was his prodigious output of hymns — well over 4,000 in more than 100 different verse forms and including many which are still popular, such as *Love Divine All Loves Excelling, Hark the Herald Angels Sing* and *Jesus, Lover of My Soul* (the last of which John Wesley felt was too sentimental).

Gradually, an element of mutual antipathy crept into the brothers' relationship. In part, that was because, in 1749, Charles persuaded John's fiancee (Grace Murray) to marry another man, convincing her that the match would affect the growth of Methodism. In addition, however, he became increasingly afraid that John's decision to ordain ministers (taken in 1784) would lead to a schism between the Methodists and the Church of England. Rather than indulge in a public squabble, he deliberately stepped into the background and attempted to temper those of John's policies which he felt were too extremist. He continued to write his hymns until his death in London on 29 March 1788. (See **JOHN WESLEY**).

WESLEY, JOHN (1703-91). John and **CHARLES WESLEY** were the founders of **METHODISM**. John was born in Epworth on 17 June 1703, the second son of Samuel Wesley (a **CHURCH OF ENGLAND** vicar) and his wife, Susanna (daughter of a **NONCONFORMIST** minister). He was educated at Charterhouse School and **OXFORD** University, graduated with a BA in 1724 and the following year became a Deacon in the Anglican Church. For four years he worked with his father in the parish of Epworth and Wroot then, in 1728, was ordained as a priest. He returned to Oxford in 1729 in order to fulfill the residential requirements for his University Fellowship and became leader of the Holy Club, a society of undergraduates which had been formed by his brother and which met regularly for religious study and devotions (the methodical and regular approach to their studies earned them the nickname 'Methodists').

In 1735, Wesley sailed for America with Colonel James Oglethorpe, Governor of the Colony of Georgia, intending to look after the spiritual needs of the settlers and attempt to convert the

Indians. He met with little success, largely because his flock objected to his strict observance of high church rituals and his condemnation of strong drink and slavery. Somewhat chastened, he returned to Britain in 1737 and met Peter Bohler, a Moravian, who convinced him that all he needed in order to obtain salvation was faith. On 24 May 1738, he attended a Moravian meeting in **LONDON** and, according to his journal, felt a strange warmth in his heart as the preacher talked of the changes God works in individuals who believe in the Christian doctrine.

From then, Wesley felt, his mission should be to help others achieve this personal experience of religious conversion. That, however, involved a form of individualistic evangelism which many orthodox clergymen abhorred. As a result, he was refused access to the churches and held his services in fields and marketplaces and barns — anywhere people could gather and listen. His style was quiet and logical — more academic than emotional — but it attracted those who found no comfort in the formality of the Church of England and frequently drew audiences of many hundreds, as on 1 April 1739, when over 3,000 people turned up to hear him in Bristol.

For half a century, Wesley travelled the country, covering well over 5,000 miles a year and delivering an average of 15 sermons a week. As he went, he encouraged his listeners to form small groups which could meet regularly under lay preachers and, in 1743, published rules for these groups, detailing the evils to be avoided and the good works which should be done. The following year, he invited the preachers to a conference at which matters both of faith and of organization were discussed: the meeting was considered a great success and became an annual event.

Wesley consistently maintained that the Methodists were part of the Anglican communion but his response to the consequences of the **AMERICAN WAR OF INDEPENDENCE** resulted in a separation which had long been expected. Methodism had spread to North America during the 1860s but it had been carried largely by loyal Britons who returned home when the rebellion began. When the English Bishops refused to ordain ministers to serve America's Methodists in 1784, Wesley carried out the ceremony himself. In the same year, he assigned the government of his local groups to the Methodist Conference. Effectively, the break with the Church of England had been made. In addition to his preaching and administrative duties, Wesley published many books, advocated reform of the prison system and founded orphanages and schools for the poor. He died in London on 2 March 1791, leaving some 300 itinerant preachers and 72,000 society members. (See **CHARLES WESLEY**).

WESSEX. An **ANGLO-SAXON** kingdom of the peoples of West Sussex from the 6th century, Wessex was a rival power to **MERCIA**, which subjugated it in the late eighth century but had been forced out again by 838. **ALFRED THE GREAT** led Wessex against the Danes in 878 and, by 926, Aethelstan ruled all **ENGLAND** through uniting the two dynasties. (See **AETHELRED I; AETHELWULF; BATTLE OF BRUNANBURH**).

WESTERN EUROPEAN UNION. This defence organization was created in 1955 as a result of the refusal of the United Kingdom and France to join a European defence community. Its members include Britain, France, Belgium, Germany, Italy, Luxembourg and the Netherlands and its original aims were to collaborate in economic, social, and cultural affairs as well as in military matters. Most of its activities were later transferred to the **EUROPEAN UNION** or NATO but it was reactivated by Britain in 1984 to improve military cooperation and, in 1991, the EU agreed to develop it as a defence force.

WESTMINSTER. The building in which the Houses of **PARLIAMENT** are located is the Palace of Westminster (**LONDON**). The name is now widely used as a synonym both for Parliament and for **GOVERNMENT**.

WESTMINSTER, STATUTE OF. There have been four statutes.

That of <u>1275</u> corrected legal malpractices, imposed **JURY** trial and began to lay out common rights before the law. It also set a limit to legal memory (confirming that precedents and customs from before a set date, 6 July 1189, could not be cited in court). That date is the beginning of "time immemorial" — "from time whereof the memory of man runneth not to the contrary".

The enactment at **WESTMINSTER** in <u>1285</u> required settlements in **ENGLAND** to appoint watchmen to keep the peace and strengthened the laws of inheritance through its article entitled *De Donis Conditionalibus*, which established entail of property whereby sale and bequests could not restrict the inheritance of land by heirs.

The Statute of <u>1290</u>, *Quia Emptores*, revised the principles of land tenure to make land a marketable commodity and loosen some of the rigidities of the **FEUDAL SYSTEM**.

Under the Statute of <u>1931</u>, the self-governing **DOMINION** territories were granted full legislative independence and equal status with Britain in the **COMMONWEALTH OF NATIONS**. The document covered Australia, Canada, the Irish Free State, Newfoundland, New Zealand and South Africa. It also gave **PARLIAMENT**ary ratification to the creation of the Commonwealth in 1926.

WETTIN, 1901-10. Queen **VICTORIA**, last of the **HANOVERIAN MONARCHS**, was succeeded by **EDWARD VII**, who was from the House of Wettin (or **SAXE-COBURG-GOTHA**). The House of Wettin became the House of **WINDSOR**, by decree, in 1917 to lose the German connection in the name. (See **GEORGE V**).

WHIGS. This loosely structured **PARLIAMENT**ary Party of the 17th century dominated politics by the early 1700s and evolved into the **LIBERAL PARTY** in the 1800s. Standing for Parliamentary freedoms and Protestantism while supporting merchant and banking interests and the **NONCONFORMISTS**, this **COUNTRY PARTY** opposed the views of its opponent **COURT PARTY** (the **TORIES**). The **GLORIOUS REVOLUTION** is seen by some as the epitome of Whig principles of paternalist, moderate reform and opposition to **MONARCH**ical powers and patronage. The term originated during the reign of King **CHARLES II** as a corruption of 'whiggamore' — a derogatory word meaning 'cattle thief', which was used to describe Scots Presbyterians during the **CIVIL WAR**. (See **PETITIONERS**).

WHIP. A Whip is a member of the **HOUSE OF COMMONS** or the **HOUSE OF LORDS** who is given the responsibility of ensuring that others of his or her political party are available to vote when required. In practice, **GOVERNMENT** and **OPPOSITION** Whips arrange a system of pairing: if one individual is ill or unavoidably absent from **WESTMINSTER** when a vote is called, his partner in the other party refrains from voting, thereby maintaining a balance and allowing Members to undertake other activities. On occasions when the system has not operated, Members of **PARLIAMENT** have been treated to the undignified sight of colleagues being brought from hospital beds to vote.

WILBERFORCE, WILLIAM (1759-1833). A philanthropist and politician, Wilberforce was one of the principal driving forces behind British withdrawal from the West Indian **SLAVE TRADE**. Born in Hull on 24 August 1759, he was educated at the city's **GRAMMAR SCHOOL** and at **CAMBRIDGE** University, where he began a friendship with **WILLIAM PITT THE YOUNGER** which was to last a lifetime. A man of considerable inherited wealth, he was elected Member of **PARLIAMENT** for Hull in 1780, for Yorkshire in 1784 and for Bramber (Sussex) in 1812.

Never associated with any political party for long, Wilberforce was a staunch supporter of Pitt's policies but became increasingly conservative on issues involving Roman Catholic emancipation after the **FRENCH REVOLUTION** and spoke in favour of the **CORN LAWS** after 1815. His stance on slavery was rooted in his religious beliefs. Converted to Evangelical Pietism in the 1780s, largely through the influence of Isaac Milner (one of his schoolmasters), he founded a Committee for the Abolition of the Slave Trade in 1787 and began a Parliamentary campaign to bring British involvement in the marketing of captive Africans to an end. It was a considerable time before his efforts bore fruit but, in 1806, the **HOUSE OF COMMONS** adopted a **BILL** prohibiting British merchants from providing slaves to the colonies and banning the import of slaves to newly-acquired British possessions. The following year, further legislation prohibited slave trading by British vessels and made importation of slaves to all British colonies illegal.

For the remainder of his life, Wilberforce continued to work for complete abolition of slavery throughout the **BRITISH EMPIRE**, becoming Vice-President of the Antislavery Society in 1823. He retired from Parliament as a result of ill health in 1825 and died on 29 July 1833, just a month before the Emancipation Act (see **ACT OF PARLIAMENT**), which effectively freed all slaves in British-held territories, became law. Wilberforce had also been keenly interested in moral welfare, establishing a Society for the Reformation of Manners in 1787 and, in 1797, publishing *A Practical View of the Prevailing Religious System of Professed Christians in the Higher and Middle Classes of this Country Contrasted with Real Christianity.* He used his fortune to promote his ideals and became much respected for his diplomatic skills and able, persuasive oratory.

WILKES, JOHN (1725-97). A politician, journalist and outspoken advocate of a free press, Wilkes was born in **LONDON** on 17 October 1725, the second son of a Clerkenwell distiller. He was educated at John Worsley's Dissenting Academy in Hertford then privately and at Leiden University. Something of a hedonist by nature, Wilkes was one of the Medmenham monks, a group which held orgies in the ruins of St Mary's Abbey, Medmenham. In 1757, after an election campaign in which he bribed many of the voters, he was elected Member of **PARLIAMENT** for Aylesbury and hoped to repay some of his growing debts through the political patronage of **WILLIAM PITT THE ELDER** and Earl Temple. In 1762, as author of the newsheet **NORTH BRITON**, he began to support Temple's campaign against **JOHN STUART**, Lord Bute, making scandalous allegations about his relationship with Princess Augusta, **GEORGE III's** mother. He continued the vituperative attacks on **GEORGE GRENVILLE**, Bute's successor, and was eventually arrested, incarcerated in the **TOWER OF LONDON** for a week then released by Lord Chief Justice Pratt on the grounds that the arrest was a breach of **PARLIAMENTARY PRIVILEGE**.

Lord Sandwich, **SECRETARY OF STATE** and a former friend of Wilkes, plotted to remove the obstacle to imprisonment by ousting Wilkes from the **HOUSE OF COMMONS**. Philip Webb, Solicitor to **THE TREASURY**, obtained (through bribery and theft) a copy of *Essay on Woman* (an obscene and blasphemous parody of Alexander Pope's *Essay on Man*), which had been written by Wilkes and Thomas Potter some years earlier. In November 1763, Sandwich read the work to fellow members of the **HOUSE OF LORDS**, which declared it a libel and a breach of privilege. At the same time, the House of Commons voted that the attacks on Grenville in the *North Briton* were also libellous and in breach of privilege so it was no surprise that, in January 1764, a motion for Wilkes' expulsion was carried. By that time, he had absconded to Paris but he was tried in his absence, found guilty of libel and declared an **OUTLAW**.

For the next few years, Wilkes lived the life of a rake on the continent, hoping in vain that a change of ministry would allow him to return. In 1768, however, his debts in Europe mounting, he travelled to London in order to seek reelection to Parliament as a champion of public liberty. The tide was in his favour because feeling against the **GOVERNMENT** was high, and he returned to the Commons as the MP for Middlesex. Waiving his Parliamentary privilege, he accepted the two year gaol sentence and £1,000 fine on the libel charges for which he had been tried after his flight but then campaigned for a pardon and arraigned **MINISTER**s who did not support his case.

Wilkes was expelled from the Commons for a second time on 3 February 1769, but the popularity of his stand against the Government secured his reelection on the 16th. He was expelled once more but re-elected on 16 March and again on 13 April after further expulsions. By that time, Parliamentary patience had been stretched to its limits and the House declared that Henry Luttrell, the defeated candidate, was the duly elected Member. Supporters of Wilkes rallied to pay his debts and further his anti-Government campaign. He was elected as an Alderman in the **CITY OF LONDON** in 1769, **SHERIFF** in 1771 and finally **LORD MAYOR** in 1774. Also in 1774, he was elected MP for Middlesex once again and spoke against the **AMERICAN WAR OF INDEPENDENCE** on several occasions. In 1782, he was successful in getting the details of his expulsions removed from Parliamentary records but his reputation was waning and he was increasingly accused of insincerity. His popularity on the decline, he did not fight the election in 1790 and died in London on 26 December 1797.

WILLIAM I (c. 1027-87). William led the **NORMAN** invasion of **ENGLAND** in 1066 and changed the course of British history, strengthening the power of the **MONARCH**y, altering social relationships, introducing continental lifestyles and reshaping the language. The son of Duke Robert I of Normandy and his mistress, Arlette, William had designs on the English throne. It seems likely that **EDWARD THE CONFESSOR** (who had spent much of his youth in Normandy) had promised him the Crown but, shortly before his death, he publicly named Harold, Earl of **WESSEX** (later **HAROLD II**) as his heir. Arguably, Edgar the Aetheling, grandson of **EDMUND II**, also had a strong claim by descent through the royal line but, when Edward died on 5 January 1066, Harold was preferred, primarily because Edgar was still a child and the nobles believed that the country badly needed firm rule after Edward's ineffectual reign. The uncertainty over the succession was William's excuse for invasion though he took the precaution of getting approval from Pope Alexander II, who was concerned about irregularities in English church affairs.

The Normans landed at Pevensey on 28 September 1066 and met Harold's army near Hastings on 14 October (see **BATTLE OF HASTINGS**). The battle was closely fought but William's cavalry and archers eventually defeated the English infantry, Harold was killed and William marched on to **LONDON**, where he was crowned on Christmas Day. The rule which followed was strict and frequently, by modern standards, cruel. Minor offences were punished by heavy fines and sometimes by mutilation (for example, anyone caught poaching deer was blinded). And when he quelled a rebellion in Northumbria in 1069, William devastated the countryside from Cheshire to **YORK**, leaving the population to die of hunger as he emphasized the might of the invading army. But he earned a reputation as an upright, church-fearing man capable of leading a nation and imposing peace and order.

The estates of the English nobles were confiscated and awarded to William's supporters so, by the time of his death, the landowning classes were almost entirely Norman and provided the military support which he needed to pacify rebels and deter crime. A major survey of property (see **DOMESDAY BOOK**) was carried out in 1086 in order to establish the extent and value of the royal demesne. Also, during that same year, nobles were forced to take the Oath of Salisbury, which decreed that loyalty to the monarch was paramount over loyalty to all other lords and did much to reduce domestic strife. In addition, William supervized a series of church reforms which included the establishment of new cathedrals and led to acknowledgment of the **ARCHBISHOP OF CANTERBURY**'s role as head of the religious community in England.

In 1087, he left the country on a campaign designed to reconquer Vexin, which had been annexed by Philip I of France. After destroying Mantes, he was riding through the ruins of the town when his horse reared after treading on a hot cinder. He suffered a serious internal injury and died at Rouen on 9 September. An entry in the **ANGLO-SAXON CHRONICLE** records his achievements and notes that he brought peace and order to his kingdom "so that a man of any substance could travel unmolested throughout the country with his bosom full of gold".

WILLIAM II (c. 1056–1100). Known as Rufus because of his ruddy complexion, William was the third son of **WILLIAM I** and his wife, Matilda. The Conqueror left Normandy to Robert, his eldest son. The second son, Richard, died early, and William inherited **ENGLAND**. He was crowned on 26 September 1087, 17 days after his father's death in Rouen, and was never popular with the **NORMAN** nobility, who would have preferred the easygoing

Robert to the more restrictive and anti-Christian William. Rebellion surfaced within a year of the **CORONATION**. Early in 1088, Bishop Odo of Bayeux, Earl of Kent, led a series of uprisings by Norman lords in **EAST ANGLIA**, **KENT**, Leicestershire and the Welsh borderlands. Rufus appealed to the English for help, promising restoration of the forests for hunting and a new tax structure. They rallied in such numbers that he was able to put down the revolt but he failed to keep the promises, alienating many of his supporters. A second rebellion, led by Robert de Mowbray, Earl of Northumberland, in 1095, was also repulsed. In addition, **WALES** was invaded in 1093, and a series of **CASTLES** built to impose Norman rule.

Cumbria was taken from the Scots in 1092 and **SCOTLAND** itself brought under William's overlordship through the appointment of **VASSAL** Kings. His main interest, however, was the acquisition of Normandy. In 1090, he mounted an invasion which forced Robert to cede him large parts of the Duchy the following year but his real opportunity arose in 1096, when Robert mortgaged his entire demesne to William in return for the money which he needed in order to finance his participation in the first **CRUSADE** to the Holy Land. William raised the money through heavy taxes and by directing Church revenues into his own coffers. For the next four years, he ruled both countries, reconquering Maine (which Robert had lost) and starting negotiations to purchase Aquitaine. It is clear that he had every intention of retaining Normandy when Robert returned but the expected dispute between the brothers never materialized. While he was hunting in the New Forest on 1 August 1100, William was killed by an arrow. It was never established how the death occurred, but the modern consensus is that it was engineered by William's younger brother, Henry (later **HENRY I**), who seized the throne immediately afterwards. The King left many enemies, notably amongst the leading landowning families and the Church, which he had neglected and robbed, but he had achieved wide popularity with the common people through his admiration for feats of arms and the maintenance of the peace and discipline which his father had imposed.

WILLIAM III (1650-1702). William, Prince of Orange, was born at The Hague on 14 November 1650 and married his cousin, Mary, daughter of **JAMES VII** and **II**, in 1677. By the 1680s, James was antagonizing so many of his subjects through his pro-Catholic policies that several leading figures in Britain were urging

William to intervene. In 1688, the birth of James's son brought matters to a head and William was asked to invade and restore the Protestant succession. He landed at Brixham on 5 November and advanced almost unopposed to **LONDON**. James fled to France and, the following year, the Scottish and English Parliaments both declared that he had forfeited the right to the **CROWN**. William and Mary were declared joint **MONARCH**s in both countries in April 1689.

In **ENGLAND**, the **GLORIOUS REVOLUTION** had been achieved without bloodshed, but, in **SCOTLAND**, there was re-sistance and throughout the reign the country was unsettled. The monarchy was perceived of as a contract between the Scots and the monarchs. James' flight had destroyed the notion that the monarch held the **DIVINE RIGHT OF KINGS** to rule (in essence, he had been deposed because he had not ruled in the country's interests) and the throne was given to William and Mary on the understanding that they were subject to the laws of Scotland and bound to uphold the freedoms of the Scottish people. As a result, the Presbyterian church was restored without an episcopacy (and late 17th-century Scotland earned an almighty reputation for religious intolerance).

In **IRELAND**, rebellion erupted in 1690 but William, with French support, successfully defeated the insurgents at the Battle of the Boyne on 1 July and was able to turn his attention to European affairs. He brought England into a **GRAND ALLIANCE** with Austria, the Netherlands, Spain and a group of the German states against Louis XIV of France and spent much time campaigning on the continent. A peace treaty was signed in 1697 but the succession to the Spanish throne remained uncertain and William believed that trouble would soon break out again. That suspicion proved justified because, in 1701, when the exiled James passed away, Louis proclaimed James's son King of England and stoked the flames of English enthusiasm for war. However, on 19 March 1702, William also died, following a riding accident, before a conflict began.

During his reign, William had attempted to promote religious freedom and had furthered the stability of the state by making the judiciary independent of **CROWN** and **PARLIAMENT**. Moreover, his foreign policies had laid the foundation for British power in Europe during the 18th and 19th centuries. But, although the mass of the people viewed him as a Protestant saviour, he was never accepted by the aristocracy and, in Scotland, was always seen as a King who favoured English interests.

WILLIAM IV (1765-1837). King of **GREAT BRITAIN** and **IRELAND** from 1830 until 1837, William was the third son of **GEORGE III** and Queen Charlotte. Born in **LONDON** on 21 August 1765, he joined the navy as a midshipman at the age of 13 and, in 1785, was given his first command. In 1789, he was created Duke of Clarence and, in 1790, left the service. He was promoted to Vice-Admiral in 1794 and to Admiral in 1799 but these titles were purely nominal, his father having refused to allow him to rejoin the fleet when the **FRENCH REVOLUTION** broke out in 1793.

In 1791, William took up residence in Richmond with actress Dorothea Jordan, who gave him ten children between 1794 and 1807. By 1811, however, his attentions were wandering, and he was showing considerable interest in heiress Catherine Tylney-Long. To his great disappointment, she preferred another suitor and William was left to make proposals of marriage to several other ladies before eventually being accepted by Adelaide of Saxe-Meiningen in July 1818, by which time he was nearly 53 years old. Adelaide bore him two daughters, but both died in infancy.

On 26 June 1830, he succeeded his brother, **GEORGE IV**, as King. At the time, **PARLIAMENTARY REFORM** was the major issue in domestic politics. A Reform **BILL** passed through the **HOUSE OF COMMONS** in 1831, piloted by **WHIG** Prime Minister **EARL GREY**, but the **HOUSE OF LORDS**, defending its hereditary interests, rejected the measures. William refused to create the 50 new peers necessary to ensure a majority in the upper house so Grey and his colleagues resigned. The **TORIES**, however, were unable to form an administration and the King was forced to recall Grey to office. The Prime Minister then extracted a written promise from William that the new peers would be created if necessary and, faced by the inevitable, the Lords' opposition crumbled. The Bill eventually became law in 1832, extending the vote to the middle classes on the basis of property ownership.

Other events during William's reign emphasized the decrease in the power of the **MONARCH**y. In November 1834, the King (distrusting the reformist policies of the Whigs) dismissed the Prime Minister, **VISCOUNT MELBOURNE**, and appointed Tory Sir **ROBERT PEEL** in his stead. In the **GENERAL ELEC-**

TION of January 1835, Peel's Party gained insufficient seats to establish an overall majority in the Commons and, after a series of embarrassing defeats, resigned. William was forced to recall Melbourne, demonstrating that the sovereign no longer had the means to determine the course of politics through patronage. However, whereas other European Monarchies crumbled before the power of the masses, Britain retained its long tradition of kingship.

William died at **WINDSOR CASTLE** on 20 June 1837 and was succeeded by his niece, Princess Victoria (later Queen **VICTORIA**). *The Spectator* summed up the majority view: William, it said, "was a weak, ignorant commonplace sort of person (but) a popular sovereign". That popularity, however, "was acquired at the price of something like public contempt".

WILLIAM THE CONQUEROR. (See **WILLIAM I**).

WILLIAM RUFUS. (See **WILLIAM II**).

WILSON, JAMES HAROLD (1916-). Labour Party **PRIME MINISTER** from 1964 until 1970 and from 1974 until 1976, Wilson was the son of Mr and Mrs Herbert Wilson. He was born in Huddersfield on 11 March 1916 and educated at Milnsbridge Council School, Royds Hall **GRAMMAR SCHOOL**, Wirral Grammar School and **OXFORD** University, where he gained a First Class Honours degree in philosophy, politics and economics. He accepted an economics lectureship at Oxford in 1937 but was drafted into the Civil Service at the outbreak of the **SECOND WORLD WAR** and, in 1941-42, worked with the War **CABINET** Secretariat. In 1941, he was made Director of Economics and Statistics at the Ministry of Fuel and Power and, in 1945, became the Labour Member of **PARLIAMENT** for Ormskirk in the landslide **GENERAL ELECTION** victory. He held the seat until 1950, when he was elected for Huyton, a **CONSTITUENCY** which he represented for the next 33 years.

His first **GOVERNMENT** post was as **PARLIAMENTARY SECRETARY** in the Ministry of Works from 1945 until 1947. He then became **SECRETARY OF STATE** for Overseas Trade but, after only a few weeks, was promoted to **PRESIDENT OF THE BOARD OF TRADE**. He resigned from that office in April 1951, protesting against the introduction of **NATIONAL HEALTH SERVICE** charges and Government policies on rearmament, an action which propelled him towards leadership of the left wing of the Party. In 1954, he was appointed Shadow **CHANCELLOR OF THE EXCHEQUER** (see **SHADOW MINISTER**) and thus chief **OPPOSITION** Spokesman on Economic Affairs. From 1959 until 1963, he was Chairman of the **HOUSE OF COMMONS'** Public Accounts Committee and, in 1960, unsuccessfully challenged **HUGH GAITSKELL** for the Leadership of the Party. Despite that defeat, his standing was such that, when Gaitskell died suddenly in 1963, he was elected Leader and took Labour to a narrow general election victory of only four seats in 1964. The tiny majority was a constant concern but, even so, he introduced a series of social and fiscal reforms and established himself as a major figure in world politics through visits to Washington, Paris and other capitals.

Wilson's programme was clearly popular with the British people and, at the 1966 election, he was returned by a healthy margin of 97 seats. However, the last years of the 1960s were to prove difficult. Rhodesia's **UNILATERAL DECLARATION OF INDEPENDENCE** forced Wilson to impose increasingly harsh economic sanctions on the colony. In France, General de Gaulle continued to oppose the UK's entry to the **EUROPEAN COMMUNITY** and, at home, the weak economy required firm direction. The **TRADE UNIONS** and many members of his party resented the introduction of a statutory incomes policy and, because of vociferous opposition, proposals for industrial relations reforms had to be shelved. Official support for US policies towards Vietnam and the imposition of tighter controls on **IMMIGRATION** reduced his standing in other quarters but, even so, Labour's popularity increased during 1969 and defeat at the 1970 general election came as a surprise. For four years, Wilson led the Opposition in the House of Commons before returning to power in 1974.

Wilson renegotiated the UK's terms of entry to the EC (with the terms confirmed by a national referendum in 1975) but suddenly resigned in 1976 at a time of worsening economic crisis and when his Party had a precarious majority in Parliament. He remained in the House of Commons until 1983, when he was created Baron Wilson of Rievaulx and died in **LONDON** in 24 May 1995.

WINDOW TAX. First imposed in 1696 to replace the **HEARTH TAX**, the Window Tax was scaled according to the number of windows in a dwelling (those with fewer than seven were exempted in 1792). It reached its heaviest level in 1808. In order to avoid payments, property owners bricked-up windows (some can still be seen) and houses were constructed with as few windows as possible. The measure became thoroughly hated, particularly after the steep rises occasioned by the hostilities surrounding the **FRENCH REVOLUTION**. It was replaced in 1851 by a house duty.

WINDSOR (1910-). King **GEORGE V**, when he acceded to the throne in 1910, was a scion of the House of **WETTIN** (or **SAXE-COBURG-GOTHA**), a dynasty stemming from Prince **ALBERT**. On 17 July 1917, however, he adopted the name Windsor for his family in recognition of the intense anti-German feelings evident in the country during the **FIRST WORLD WAR** and out of respect for the symbolic place **WINDSOR CASTLE** holds in the story of the British **MONARCH**y. In 1960, Queen **ELIZABETH II** decreed that her male descendants would be known by the name Mountbatten-Windsor. (See **PRINCE ANDREW; PRINCESS ANNE; PRINCE CHARLES; EDWARD VIII; PRINCE EDWARD; GEORGE VI; LOUIS MOUNTBATTEN**).

WINDSOR CASTLE. A principal royal residence, and arguably one of the best known symbols of the British **CROWN**, Windsor Castle is located west of **LONDON** on the **RIVER THAMES**. It has been in continuous royal occupancy since the **NORMANS** built a **CASTLE** at that location on the site of an earlier **ANGLO-SAXON** fortification. The Round Tower was rebuilt in stone by King **HENRY II** in the 1170s and the apartments were extended by King **EDWARD III** in the 1360s. St George's Chapel, the great gothic structure, was constructed from the 15th century. The building was partially remodelled for King **CHARLES II** in the 1670s, when its military features were less needed, but its current crenellated appearance is the result of a redesign in the 1820s by King **GEORGE IV** and his architect, Sir Jeffry Wyatville. Its importance as a royal symbol is evidenced by King **GEORGE V**'s decision, in 1917, to change the name of the Royal Family from **SAXE-COBURG-GOTHA** to Windsor. A fire on 20 November 1992 extensively damaged the Castle and St George's Chapel, leading to the public opening of **BUCKINGHAM PALACE** to help pay for the estimated £40 million restoration.

WINTER OF DISCONTENT. The winter of 1978 to 1979 was one of general worker opposition to the **LABOUR PARTY** government's policy of limiting pay increases for public sector employees to five per cent at a time when private industry was granting 15 per cent and inflation was running at ten per cent per annum. There were strikes in many public service industries (notably hospitals, **RAILWAYS** and water works) and rubbish remained uncollected on the streets as municipal workers downed tools. Ford employees went on strike in the private sector, joined by lorry and petrol tanker drivers. Even the dead lay unburied and the situation was made worse by bad winter weather, the worst for 16 years. Matters were further inflamed by Prime Minister **JAMES CALLAGHAN**'s supposed remark (actually a headline in the *Sun* newspaper) "Crisis, what crisis?" and his intimation of even more restraint in the throw-away line "You ain't seen nothing yet!". The events created much long-lasting anti-**TRADE UNION** feeling in the country and were key factors in the fall of the Government, **MARGARET THATCHER**'s **GENERAL ELECTION** victory in 1979 and the subsequent legislation restricting the actions of labour unions in industrial disputes. The description of the period is taken from William Shakespeare's *Richard III* ("Now is the winter of our discontent").

WITAN. This assembly, or council, was appointed by the **ANGLO-SAXON MONARCH**s to tender advice and witness legislation. Its name is derived from the Old English word *wita* which meant 'one who knows'. Membership was by invitation of the King and meetings were held at his request, normally at one of the royal manors. The heads of leading families were usually summoned, along with representatives of the Church and the chief officials of the royal household. Their duty was to advise on any issues which he brought to their attention: matters relating to new taxes, new laws and land grants were frequently considered. The character of the assembly changed little throughout the Anglo-Saxon period although its size increased somewhat as Kings enlarged their territories and, towards the end of the period, it acquired a number of ceremonial duties (such as holding feasts to celebrate major Christian festivals). A similar body — the burgh-witan — met to consider the local governance of towns.

WITCHCRAFT. Women (and, less frequently, men) who were elderly or deformed, or in some way different, have often been accused of misusing magic to harm people or blamed for local disasters. Punishable from the **NORMAN** period, witchcraft was a felony from 1543 and a capital offence in **ENGLAND** from 1563. Witchhunting was common, particularly during the mid-17th century, and many women were executed after summary justice. 'Witch-Finder General' Matthew Hopkins toured eastern England after 1644, hanging many unfortunate women until he was himself hanged for being a wizard. The last trial for witchcraft in England was in 1712, when Jane Wenham was acquitted of flying as a witch after the judge ruled that there was no law against flying. The last execution was in 1706 at Huntingdon and the legislation was repealed in 1736. Accusations of witchcraft are often interpreted by modern scholars as intercommunal or familial expressions of tensions and local hysteria. Modern covens are known to exist in many parts of the country.

WOLFE, JAMES (1726-59). The commander of the British troops who took Quebec from the French in 1759, Wolfe was born in Westerham (**KENT**) on 22 December 1726, the elder son of Lieutenant-Colonel Edward Wolfe and his wife, Henrietta. He was educated at Swinden's Academy (Greenwich) then, in 1741, was commissioned as a Second Lieutenant in the 12th Foot, his father's regiment. He saw active service against the French at the **BATTLE OF DETTINGEN** (1743) and the Battle of Laffeldt (1747) and against the Jacobites at the Battle of Falkirk and the Battle of Culloden (both in 1746). His courage and tactical skills earned him promotion to Brigade Major (1745). In 1749, he was given Acting Command of the 20th Foot and, the following year, awarded the rank of Lieutenant Colonel. Between 1750 and 1756, he was with his regiment in **SCOTLAND** and southern **ENGLAND**, then, in 1757, took part in the unsuccessful attack on the French fortress at Rochefort. His forthright criticisms of the strategy adopted for that action were noted by the **PRIME MINISTER — WILLIAM PITT THE ELDER —** who arranged for him to be attached as Brigadier to the staff of Major General Sir Jeffrey Amherst.

In 1758, Wolfe played a large part in Amherst's assault on Louisburg (Cape Breton Island) and, on his return to Britain, was awarded the acting rank of Major General, with instructions to invade French Canada and take Quebec. In June 1759, he sailed up the St Lawrence River with 9,000 men and captured Isle d'Orleans then bombarded the Marquis de Montcalm's army from the adjacent mainland while he searched for a weakness in the settlement's defences. Over the summer, he became ill with tuberculosis and, towards the end of August, publicly accepted the advice of his senior officers to land his force several miles above Quebec. However, while they led their men upriver on 12 September, Wolfe climbed the Heights of Abraham with a force of infantrymen during the night, surprised the French the following morning and took the fortress after a struggle lasting only a few minutes. He was wounded three times and died on the battlefield. Montcalm, also injured, died the next day. Wolfe's body was taken back to England and buried in the family vault at St Alfege's Church, Greenwich, on 20 November 1759.

WOLFENDEN REPORT, 1957. Sir John Wolfenden chaired a **GOVERNMENT**-appointed committee which recommended that private homosexual acts between consenting males over the age of 21 should be legalized. The Report was a turning point in attitudes towards homosexuality and was reflected in the provisions of the **SEXUAL OFFENCES ACT** of 1967 (see **ACT OF PARLIAMENT**). Its proposals on the regulation of prostitution were incorporated in the **STREET OFFENCES ACT** (1959).

WOLSEY, THOMAS (c. 1473-1530). Cardinal Wolsey, as **LORD CHANCELLOR** and Papal Legate, greatly influenced the course of secular and religious life in **ENGLAND** from about 1515 until 1529. Educated at **OXFORD** University, he was ordained in 1498. His energy and eye for detail ensured advancement and, in 1509, he was appointed Royal Almoner to **HENRY VIII**. In February 1514, he became Bishop of Lincoln and, in September of the same year, Archbishop of **YORK**. In 1515, he was made a Cardinal by Pope Leo X and **LORD CHANCELLOR** by Henry.

The King's lack of interest in politics meant that Wolsey exercised great control over both domestic and foreign policy. In his attempt to gain papal approval, he directed English affairs along lines which would enhance his reputation at the Vatican, exercising his diplomatic talents in the corridors of European power in an attempt to achieve peace throughout the Christian realm. He also greatly influenced the work of the Court of the **STAR CHAMBER** but his concentration on politics and the administration of justice left him insufficient time to instigate the reforms of the Church for which the Vatican had granted him powers as Legate. He fell from royal favour in 1529, partly because he was unable to secure papal approval for Henry's divorce from **CATHERINE**

OF ARAGON, partly because his foreign policies had left England virtually without allies in Europe and partly because his plans for reorganizing the administration of the Church had come to nought. A writ of praemunire was issued against him on 9 October and he was removed from office and deprived of all his ecclesiastical preferments except York. In November 1530, he intended to become enthroned as Archbishop of York but Henry, informed that he was corresponding with foreign powers, became wary of his influence and arrested him.

On 29 November, while on his way to **LONDON** for a meeting with the King, Wolsey died at Leicester Abbey. One of the last clerics to influence affairs of state, he was a greedy and ruthless man in his prime but repented many of his actions in later life and wore a hair shirt as a penance.

WOOL INDUSTRY. Prior to the **INDUSTRIAL REVOLUTION**, wool had been Britain's primary industry, concentrated in **EAST ANGLIA**, the West Country and West Yorkshire. In the Middle Ages it was a major source of wealth: many towns owe their churches and other facilities to this trade, particularly those areas with water which could supply power to the mills. Steam and mechanization in the 19th century led to concentration in the West Riding of Yorkshire as the older areas resisted change. Wool textiles suffered competition as a result of the rise of the **COTTON INDUSTRY** and, during the 20th century, through the development of artificial fibres but have developed a modern market for high quality knitwear. (See **WOOLSACK**).

WOOLSACK. In the **HOUSE OF LORDS**, a sack filled with wool from **ENGLAND, NORTHERN IRELAND, SCOTLAND, WALES** and the countries of the **COMMONWEALTH OF NATIONS** is placed in front of the throne. During debates, the **LORD CHANCELLOR**, as **SPEAKER** (or Chairman), sits on the Woolsack beside the mace, which is the symbol of the sovereign's authority.

WORCESTER, BATTLE OF, 3 September 1651. **OLIVER CROMWELL**'s crowning glory, this battle resulted in the defeat of a 14,000 strong Scottish invasion force led by the future King **CHARLES II** (the invasion had been a response to the **PARLIAMENTARIAN** victory in the **CIVIL WAR**). Charles, pursued by Cromwell, fled in disguise and hid in an oak tree near the **RIVER**

SEVERN to evade capture, eventually escaping to France. This was the decisive victory which secured Cromwell's power.

WYATT'S REBELLION, 1554. Sir Thomas Wyatt led a force of 3,000 to 4,000 men from **KENT** to **LONDON** in protest over the treaty for the marriage of Queen **MARY I** to King Philip of Spain. They intended to release Princess Elizabeth (later Queen **ELIZA-BETH I**) from custody and proclaim her Queen, but were unsuccessful, and many rebels, including Wyatt, were eventually put to death. The unfortunates included Lady **JANE GREY** — who has never been adequately linked with the rebel uprising and was probably executed more to appease Philip of Spain (whom Mary hoped to marry in order to secure the return of Britain to Roman Catholicism) than because of any direct link with the rebellion.

WYCLIFFE, JOHN (c. 1330-84). One of the major figures in the early **REFORMATION** movement, Wycliffe greatly influenced opposition to the teachings of the Roman Catholic Church. He was born about 1330, possibly in Yorkshire, and studied at **OXFORD** University where, by 1372, he had earned a doctorate. He held a number of ecclesiastical offices from 1361 but increasingly criticized the growing secularism in the Church and advanced a realist metaphysical philosophy which contradicted orthodox theological teaching. Many of his proposals for curbing abuses by the clergy were incorporated in legislation laid before **PARLIAMENT** in 1376 but, early the following year, he was called to appear before the Bishop of **LONDON** to explain his views. His supporter, **JOHN OF GAUNT**, appeared to defend him but a scuffle developed between the Bishop and Henry Percy, Marshal of **ENG-LAND**, bringing the inquisition to an abrupt conclusion.

In May 1377, Pope Gregory XI cited 18 erroneous opinions advanced by Wycliffe and ordered his imprisonment. However, neither Oxford University nor the government would carry out the command and gradually his writing became more extreme. In *De veritate scripturae* (1378), he demanded that the Scriptures should be made freely available to the laity, not confined to churchmen, and in *De eucharistia* (1379) he rejected the doctrine of transubstantiation, contending that it was philosophical nonsense and arguing that Christ did not replace the substance of the bread and the wine in the Eucharist but was simply present with them. In *De potestate papae*, also written about 1379, he claimed that there was no Biblical basis for the

Pope's authority and in other works he criticized the concept of celibacy, the veneration of saints and other practices.

The outbreak of the **PEASANTS' REVOLT** in 1381 undoubtedly helped Wycliffe's opponents, who were able to identify sections in his treatises which justified attacks on private property even though he played no direct part in fomenting the troubles. Much of his support deserted him, concerned both by the violence of the revolt and by the increasingly heretical nature of his views. He retired to his rectory at Lutterworth and completed a summary of his teachings (the *Trialogus*) which was ultimately published in Basle in 1525. Towards the end of 1384, he suffered a stroke and died on 31 December. In 1415, the Council of Constance rejected his teachings, and, in 1428, his bones were dug up and burned. His views, however, influenced John Huss and, through him, John Calvin and Martin Luther. They also inspired the **LOLLARDS** and thus paved the way for the Reformation in England.

—Y—

YALTA CONFERENCE, 4-11 February 1945. This meeting in the Crimea (Ukraine) between **WINSTON CHURCHILL**, Josef Stalin and Franklin D. Roosevelt towards the end of the **SECOND WORLD WAR** was held to discuss postwar reparations, disarmament and arrangements for the dismemberment of Germany.

YANGTSE AGREEMENT, 10 October 1900. This agreement between Britain and Germany was designed to give both countries an open door to China via the Yangtse River. All other nations were excluded and the signatories would take joint action against them if necessary. The strategy was part of British measures to secure Chinese trade and counter Russian designs on the area.

YEOMEN. Yeomen were owner-occupiers or (later) tenant farmers with very small land or property holdings. The term was also applied to a form of farming for profit by small freeholders and, socially, described an individual just below the **GENTRY** rank. The yeomen disappeared with the **INDUSTRIAL REVOLUTION** and the **ENCLOSURE** movement as farms in Britain developed larger and more commercial forms.

YORK. Lying at the confluence of the Rivers Ouse and Foss, York is just under 200 miles north of **LONDON** and, historically, is the ecclesiastical capital of northern **ENGLAND**. The **ROMANS** built a fort on the site in 71 AD, naming it Eboracum and using it as a military base until they withdrew from Britain during the fifth century. In 625, Paulinus became the first Archbishop of York and, in 627, King Edwin of Northumbria built a church on the site of the present cathedral. The medieval town flourished as a market centre, concentrating, in particular, on the wool trade, the profits of which were used to endow some 40 religious establishments, including the Minster, which was built from the 13th to the 15th centuries and is the largest Gothic church in the country. The agricultural trade remains important in the modern city, but the manufacture of railway carriages, shock absorbers, glass containers, optical instruments and confectionery have superseded it as sources of employment. In 1984, a thunderbolt (traditionally a sign of divine wrath) struck the minster only a week after the consecration of the controversial David Jenkins as the Bishop of Durham (Jenkins had suggested that the Virgin Birth and the Three Wise Men were mythological fallacies). The damage cost over £1 million to repair. At the time of the 1991 census, York had a population of 101,400. (For location, see Map 2, page xxvi).

YORKISTS. (See **WARS OF THE ROSES**).

YPRES, BATTLES OF. Three battles were fought at Ypres (Flanders) during the **FIRST WORLD WAR**.

Between 12 October and 22 November 1914, German attempts to reach the coast were thwarted but at a cost of casualties in excess of 50,000 men.

From 22 April to 25 May 1915, the first use of poison chlorine gas in war led to the retreat of Allied forces and 59,000 British casualties.

The major conflict, which took place between 31 July and 10 November 1917, is also known as the Battle of Passchendaele and involved major British assaults on German lines for three months in appalling conditions of mud, created by bad weather, and constant bombardment. Estimates put losses at 245,000–250,000 British casualties for a gain of barely five miles of territory.

—Z—

ZIMMERMAN TELEGRAM, 16-19 January 1917. A coded telegram from the German Foreign Secretary, Arther Zimmerman, was sent to his Minister in Mexico, urging an alliance between Mexico and Germany if the United States of America entered the **FIRST WORLD WAR**. It also implied that Germany would attempt to persuade Japan to attack the United States, provide Mexico with financial aid and arrange for the return of territories in Arizona, New Mexico and Texas after the victory. The telegram was intercepted by the British Naval **SECRET SERVICE** and was instrumental in inducing the USA to enter the war with Germany on 6 April 1917.

ZINOVIEV LETTER, 25 October 1924. A letter allegedly written by Grigori Zinoviev, Chairman of the Communist Third International, to the British **COMMUNIST PARTY** advocated armed insurrection and sedition and gave advice on revolution. Revealed in the *Daily Mail* and other **CONSERVATIVE PARTY**-oriented newspapers just prior to the 1924 **GENERAL ELECTION**, it was probably intended to discredit the **LABOUR PARTY**, whose **GOVERNMENT,** under **RAMSAY MACDONALD,** had been trying to improve relations with the Bolsheviks. Equally probably it did not, by itself, bring about Labour's subsequent election defeat. The letter was revealed as a forgery in 1966.

ZULU WAR, 1879. Britain demanded the establishment of **PROTECTORATE** status over Zululand in South Africa in order to protect Natal from the Zulus. However, Chief Cetewayo and 20,000 Zulu warriors heavily defeated the British at Isandhlwana, killing over 1,600 men and threatening the Transvaal. The Africans were finally suppressed at Ulundi on 4 July 1879 after the arrival of 10,000 British reinforcements. Zululand was occupied and became a Protectorate in 1887. It was absorbed into Natal later the same year. The removal of the Zulu power base encouraged the Boers in their struggle with Britain in the Transvaal and thus may have contributed to the later **BOER WARS**.

BIBLIOGRAPHY

There is a voluminous body of literature on the history of the United Kingdom so, in a work of this size, some (essentially arbitrary) decisions are necessary in order to keep the list of bibliographical citations within bounds. No journal articles have been included, and all the books are written in English (though some are in translation). In addition, the emphasis is placed on more recent publications, partly because they are more readily obtainable and partly because many contain references to the earlier material. Because of limitations of space, it has not been possible to include the publishing history of each of the citations but the date attributed is that of the most recent edition known to the authors. The list also contains references to reprinted or reissued texts; in such cases the date is that of the reprint or reissue, not of the original publication.

To help the user identify potential sources of information, the texts are listed alphabetically within a chronological sequence which is widely accepted by scholars. In addition, works relating to the 19th and 20th centuries are further subdivided on a thematic basis. However, any classification is imperfect because it imposes boundaries on the continuum of historical process. Some books, for example, are relevant to more than one time period and are, therefore, cited in each. Also, readers are advised to scan the references given for time periods before or after the one in which they are interested in order to ensure that they maximize the coverage of relevant material. Similarly, those focusing on the past 200 years may find that perusal of listings under more than one theme will add to potential sources of information.

It may also be appropriate, for some purposes, to turn to material other than that listed below. The four quality daily newspapers (*The Daily Telegraph*, *The Guardian*, *The Independent* and *The Times*) and the specialist *Financial Times* contain contemporary accounts of events of national importance, along with obituaries of political and other notable figures, and are now available in nonpaper forms (such as microfiche). There are, in addition, several periodicals (*The Economist*, *New Society* and *The New Statesman*, for example) which have reflected public debate and provided fora for all shades of opinion over the years.

Academic journals provide more sober analyses of patterns and processes. Some (such as the *Transactions of the Royal Historical Society*) are the official publications of learned institutions; others (such as the *English Historical Review*) reflect disciplinary interests within the scholarly community. All are widely available in university libraries throughout the English-speaking world.

Over the years, government departments have produced a mountain of reports by Royal Commissions, Committees of Inquiry and other bodies. Many of these are published by Her Majesty's Stationery Office (49 High Holborn, London WC1V 6HB: Telephone 171-873-0011), which will provide details of material still available. In addition, the Office of Population Censuses and Surveys has produced decennial statistical returns outlining the demographic and social characteristics of the British people ever since 1801 (with the exception of 1941, when the Second World War prevented any survey from being undertaken). These reports have become increasingly detailed since computerization of data processing began during the 1960s and present figures for a variety of administrative areas, including counties and parliamentary constituencies as well as the country as a whole. Also, the maps of the Ordnance Survey have charted the transformation of the British landscape since before the Industrial Revolution and provide an unsurpassed resource.

The material cited below opens the door to these alternative sources and enables the student, amateur or professional, to widen the search for suitable information.

General Works

Ade Ajayi, J. F., and J. D. Y. Peel, ed. *People and Empires in African History: Essays in Memory of Michael Crowder.* London: Longman, 1992.

Afigbo, A., E. Ayandele et al. *The Making of Modern Africa.* 2 vols. London: Longman, 1990.

Armitage, Michael. *The Royal Air Force: An Illustrated History.* London: Arms and Armour Press, 1993.

Armstrong, A. *The Church of England, the Methodists and Society.* London: University of London Press, 1973.

Armytage, W. H. G. *Four Hundred Years of English Education.* London: Cambridge University Press, 1970.

Barber, Charles. *The English Language: A Historical Introduction.* Cambridge: Cambridge University Press, 1993.

Barker, Rodney. *Politics, Peoples and Government: Themes in British Political Thought since the Nineteenth Century.* Basingstoke, England: Macmillan, 1994.

Barker, T. C., and Dorian Gerhold. *The Rise and Fall of Road Trans-*

port, 1700–1990. Basingstoke, England: Macmillan, 1993.

Beckett, J. C. *The Making of Modern Ireland, 1603–1923.* London: Faber, 1981.

Bence-Jones, Mark, and Hugh Montgomery-Massingberd. *The British Aristocracy.* London: Constable, 1979.

Benson, John. *The Rise of Consumer Society in Britain, 1880–1980.* London: Longman, 1994.

Black, Jeremy. *Convergence or Divergence?: Britain and the Continent.* Basingstoke, England: Macmillan, 1994.

Bowle, John. *The Imperial Achievement: The Rise and Transformation of the British Empire.* London: Secker and Warburg, 1974.

Brand, C. F. *The British Labour Party: A Short History.* Stanford, Calif.: Hoover Institution Press, 1974.

Briggs, Asa. *A Social History of England.* London: Weidenfeld and Nicolson, 1983.

Bryant, Arthur. *Freedom's Own Island: The British Oceanic Expansion.* London: Collins, 1986.

———. *A History of Britain and the British People.* 2 vols. London: Grafton, 1985 (vol 1) and 1986 (vol 2).

———. *A Thousand Years of British Monarchy.* London: HarperCollins, 1975.

Cain, P. J., and A. G. Hopkins. *British Imperialism: Crisis and Deconstruction, 1914–1990.* London: Longman, 1993.

———. *British Imperialism: Innovation and Expansion, 1688–1914.* London: Longman, 1993.

Cannon, J., and R. Griffiths. *The Oxford Illustrated History of the British Monarchy.* Oxford: Oxford University Press, 1988.

Challis, C. E., ed. *A New History of the Royal Mint.* Cambridge: Cambridge University Press, 1992.

Champion, A. G., and A. R. Townsend. *Contemporary Britain: A Geographical Perspective.* London: Edward Arnold, 1990.

Christopher, A. J. *The British Empire at Its Zenith.* London: Croom Helm, 1988.

Clarke, P. F. *Liberals and Social Democrats.* Cambridge: Cambridge University Press, 1978.

Coleman, David, and John Salt. *The British Population: Patterns, Trends and Processes.* Oxford: Oxford University Press, 1992.

Cook, Chris. *A Short History of the Liberal Party, 1900–1992.* Basingstoke, England: Macmillan, 1993.

Cook, Chris, and I. Taylor. *The Labour Party.* Harlow, England: Longman, 1983.

Darwin, John. *Britain and Decolonisation: The Retreat from Empire in the Post-War World.* Basingstoke, England: Macmillan, 1988.

Deane, P., and W. A. Cole. *British Economic Growth, 1688–1959: Trends and Structure.* Cambridge: Cambridge University Press, 1969.

Evans, David. *A History of Nature Conservation in Britain.* London: Routledge, 1991.

Ferrier, R. W. *A History of the British Petroleum Industry.* Cambridge: Cambridge University Press, 1982.

Fleure, H. J., and M. Davies. *A Natural History of Man in Britain.* London: Bloomsbury, 1989.

Floud, Roderick, and Donald McCloskey. *The Economic History of Britain since 1700.* 3 vols. Cambridge: Cambridge University Press, 1994.

Foster, R. F. *The Oxford History of Ireland.* Oxford: Oxford University Press, 1992.

Fraser, Antonia, ed. *The Lives of the Kings and Queens of England.* London: Weidenfeld and Nicolson, 1993.

Fraser, Derek. *The Evolution of the British Welfare State: A History of Social Policy since the Industrial Revolution.* London: Macmillan, 1984.

Gibson-Jarvie, Robert. *The City of London: A Financial and Commercial History.* Cambridge: Woodhead-Faulkner, 1979.

Girouard, Mark. *The English Town.* London: Guild, 1990.

Goudie, Andrew. *The Landforms of England and Wales.* Oxford: Blackwell, 1993.

Gregg, Pauline. *A Social and Economic History of Britain, 1760–1972.* London: Harrap, 1973.

Hall, John M. *Metropolis Now: London and Its Region.* Cambridge: Cambridge University Press, 1990.

Halliday, F. E. *England: A Concise History.* London: Thames and Hudson, 1989.

Hanson, M. *2000 Years of London.* London: Country Life, 1967.

Harvey, J. *How Britain is Governed.* London: Macmillan, 1983.

Haswell, Jock. *The British Army: A Concise History.* London: Thames and Hudson, 1975.

Havinden, Michael, and D. Meredith. *Colonialism and Development: Britain and Its Tropical Colonies, 1850–1960.* London: Routledge, 1993.

Haydon, Peter. *The English Pub: A History.* London: Robert Hale, 1994.

Hennessy, E. *A Domestic History of the Bank of England.* Cambridge: Cambridge University Press, 1992.

Hennessy, Peter. *The Hidden Wiring: Unearthing the British Constitution*. London Gollancz, 1995.

Hibbert, Christopher. *The English: A Social History, 1066–1945*. London: Grafton, 1987.

————. *The Story of England*. London: Phaidon, 1992.

Higham, Robert, and Philip Barker. *Timber Castles*. London: Batsford, 1992.

Hoskins, W. G. *The Making of the English Landscape*. Harmondsworth: Penguin, 1970.

Irwin, John L. *Modern Britain: An Introduction*. London: Routledge, 1994.

James, Lawrence. *The Rise and Fall of the British Empire*. London: Little, Brown, 1994.

Jenkins, J. Geraint. *The Wool Textile Industry in Britain*. London: Routledge, 1972.

Johnson, Paul. *The Offshore Islanders: A History of the English People*. London: Orion, 1992.

Johnson, Paul, ed. *Twentieth-Century Britain: Economic, Social and Cultural Change*. London: Longman, 1994.

Johnston, R. J., and Vince Gardiner, eds. *The Changing Geography of the United Kingdom*. London: Routledge, 1991.

Judd, Denis, and Peter Slinn. *The Evolution of the Modern Commonwealth, 1902–80*. London: Macmillan, 1982.

Kennedy, Paul M. *The Rise and Fall of British Naval Mastery*. London: Fontana, 1991.

King, D. J. Cathcart. *The Castle in England and Wales: An Interpretative History*. London: Croom Helm, 1988.

Kushner, Tony, ed. *The Jewish Heritage in History: Englishness and Jewishness*. London: Frank Cass, 1993.

Lasdun, Susan. *The English Park: Royal, Private and Public*. London: Deutsch, 1991.

Lawson, Philip. *The Imperial Challenge*. London: UCL Press, 1994.

Lawton, Richard, and C. G. Pooley. *Britain, 1740–1950: An Historical Geography*. London: Edward Arnold, 1992.

Laybourn, Keith. *The Rise of Labour: The British Labour Party, 1890–1979*. London: Edward Arnold, 1988.

Lloyd, Christopher. *The British Seaman, 1200–1860*. London: Collins, 1968.

Lloyd, T. O. *The British Empire, 1558–1983*. Oxford: Oxford University Press, 1984.

————. *Empire, Welfare State, Europe: English History, 1906–*

1992. Oxford: Oxford University Press, 1993.

Longford, Elizabeth. *The Royal House of Windsor.* London: Weidenfeld and Nicolson, 1984.

Longmate, Norman. *Defending the Island: From Caesar to the Armada.* London: Hutchinson, 1989.

———. *Island Fortress: The Defence of Great Britain, 1603–1945.* London: Hutchinson, 1991.

Lowe, Peter. *Britain in the Far East.* London: Longman, 1981.

May, Trevor. *An Economic and Social History of Britain, 1760–1970.* London: Longman, 1987.

McCrum, Robert, William Cran, and Robert MacNeil. *The Story of English.* London: Faber, 1986.

McFarlane, Anthony. *The British in the Americas, 1480–1815.* London: Longman, 1994.

Michie, R. C. *The City of London: Continuity and Change, 1850–1990.* London: Macmillan, 1992.

Mingay, G. E. *The Gentry: The Rise and Fall of a Ruling Class.* London: Longman, 1976.

———. *Land and Society in England, 1750–1980.* London: Longman, 1994.

Monckton, H. A. *A History of the English Public House.* London: Bodley Head, 1969.

More, Charles. *The Industrial Age: Economy and Society in Britain, 1750–1985.* London: Longman, 1989.

Morgan, D. J. *The Official History of Colonial Development.* 5 vols. London: Macmillan, 1979.

Morgan, Kenneth O. *The Oxford Illustrated History of Britain.* Oxford: Oxford University Press, 1984.

Morris, James. *Farewell the Trumpets: An Imperial Retreat.* Harmondsworth, England: Penguin, 1979.

———. *Heaven's Command: An Imperial Progress.* Harmondsworth, England: Penguin, 1979.

———. *Pax Britannica: The Climax of an Empire.* Harmondsworth, England: Penguin, 1979.

Morris, Richard. *Churches in the Landscape.* London: Dent, 1989.

Pearce, Malcolm, and Geoffrey Stewart. *British Political History, 1867–1990: Democracy and Decline.* London: Routledge, 1992.

Pelling, Henry. *A Short History of the Labour Party.* Basingstoke, England: Macmillan, 1993.

Perkin, Harold. *The Origins of Modern English Society.* London: Routledge, 1985.

Pimlott, Ben, and Chris Cook. *Trade Unions in British Politics: The*

First 250 Years. London: Longman, 1991.

Pollard, Sidney. *The Development of the British Economy, 1914–1990*. London: Edward Arnold, 1992.

Porter, Bernard. *Britannia's Burden: the Political Evolution of Modern Britain, 1851–1990*. London: Edward Arnold, 1994.

————. *The Lion's Share: A Short History of British Imperialism, 1850–1983*. London: Longman, 1984.

Porter, R. *London: A Social History*. London: Hamish Hamilton, 1994.

Pounds, N. J. G. *The Culture of the English People: Iron Age to the Industrial Revolution*. Cambridge: Cambridge University Press, 1994.

Pugh, Martin. *State and Society: British Political and Social History, 1870–1992*. London: Edward Arnold, 1994.

Punnett, R. M. *British Government and Politics*. Aldershot, England: Gower Press, 1987.

Rasmussen, S. E. *London: The Unique City*. Cambridge, Mass.: MIT Press, 1982.

Reed, Michael. *The Landscape of Britain*. London: Routledge, 1990.

Reynolds, David. *Britannia Overruled: British Policy and World Power in the Twentieth Century*. London: Longman, 1991.

Richards, Denis, and J. W. Hunt. *An Illustrated History of Modern Britain, 1783–1980*. Harlow, England: Longman, 1983.

Richards, Sandra. *The Rise of the English Actress*. Basingstoke, England: Macmillan, 1993.

Riddall, J. G. *Introduction to Land Law*. London: Butterworth, 1993.

Robbins, Keith. *The Eclipse of a Great Power: Modern Britain, 1870–1992*. London: Longman, 1994.

Rose, Tessa. *The Coronation Ceremony of the Kings and Queens of England and the Crown Jewels*. London: Her Majesty's Stationery Office, 1992.

Royle, Edward. *Modern Britain: A Social History, 1750–1985*. London: Edward Arnold, 1987.

Schweinitz, K. de. *The Rise and Fall of British India*. London: Methuen, 1983.

Shaw, A. G. L. *Convicts and the Colonies*. London: Faber, 1966.

Smellie, K. B. *A History of Local Government*. London: Allen and Unwin, 1968.

Somerset, A. *Ladies-in-Waiting: From the Tudors to the Present Day*. London: Weidenfeld and Nicolson, 1984.

Speck, W. A. *A Concise History of Britain, 1707–1975*. Cambridge: Cambridge University Press, 1993.

Thompson, E. P. *The Making of the English Working Class.* Harmondsworth, England: Penguin, 1980.

Tidrick, Kathryn. *Empire and the English Character.* London: I. B. Tauris, 1990.

Tomlinson, R. *Divine Right: The Inglorious Survival of British Royalty in the Twentieth Century.* London: Little, Brown, 1994.

Trevelyan, G. M. *English Social History: A Survey of Six Centuries — Chaucer to Queen Victoria.* Harmondsworth, England: Penguin, 1967.

Tucker, R. W., and D. C. Hendrickson. *The Fall of the First British Empire.* Baltimore, Md.: Johns Hopkins University Press, 1983.

Van Thal, H. *The Prime Ministers: Russell to Heath.* London: Allen and Unwin, 1975.

Walvin, J. *Passage to Britain: Immigration in British History and Politics.* Harmondsworth, England: Penguin, 1984.

———. *The People's Game: A Social History of British Football.* London: Allen Lane, 1975.

Whittow, John. *Geology and Scenery in Britain.* London: Chapman and Hall, 1992.

Prehistoric Britain

Ashbee, P. *The Ancient British: A Social-Archaeological Narrative.* Norwich, England: Geo Abstracts, 1978.

Atkinson, R. J. C. *Stonehenge.* Harmondsworth, England: Penguin, 1990.

Bord, Janet, and Colin Bord. *A Guide to Ancient Sites in Britain.* London: Paladin, 1979.

Bradley, Richard. *The Prehistoric Settlement of Britain.* London: Routledge, 1978.

———. *The Social Foundations of Prehistoric Britain.* London: Longman, 1984.

Bradley, Richard, and Mark Edmonds. *Interpreting the Axe Trade: Production and Exchange in Neolithic Britain.* Cambridge: Cambridge University Press, 1993.

Burl, Aubrey. *Prehistoric Avebury.* New Haven, Conn.: Yale University Press, 1979.

Castleden, Rodney. *Neolithic Britain: New Stone Age Sites of England, Scotland and Wales.* London: Routledge, 1992.

———. *The Stonehenge People: An Exploration of Life in Neolithic Britain, 4700–2000 BC.* London: Routledge, 1987.

Chadwick, Nora. *The Celts*. Harmondsworth, England: Penguin, 1971.

Chippindale, Christopher. *Stonehenge Complete*. London: Thames and Hudson, 1994.

Cole, S. M. *The Neolithic Revolution*. London: British Museum (Natural History), 1961.

Cummins, W. A. *King Arthur's Place in Prehistory: The Great Age of Stonehenge*. Stroud, England: Alan Sutton, 1992.

Cunliffe, Barry. *Iron Age Communities in Britain*. London: Routledge, 1974.

―――. *Wessex to AD 1000*. London: Longman, 1993.

Darvill, T. *Prehistoric Britain*. London: Batsford, 1987.

Drewett, Peter, David Rudling, and Mark Gardiner. *The South East to AD 1000*. London: Longman, 1988.

Ellis, Peter Beresford. *The Druids*. London: Constable, 1994.

Fleure, H. J., and M. Davies. *A Natural History of Man in Britain*. London: Bloomsbury, 1989.

Ford, Boris, ed. *Early Britain*. Cambridge: Cambridge University Press, 1992.

Fowler, P. *The Farming of Prehistoric Britain*. Cambridge: Cambridge University Press, 1983.

Harding, D. W. *The Iron Age in Lowland Britain*. London: Routledge, 1974.

Hawkins, Gerald S. *Stonehenge Decoded*. London: Souvenir Press, 1966.

Higham, Nick. *The Northern Counties to AD 1000*. London: Longman, 1986.

Laing, Lloyd. *Celtic Britain*. London: Routledge, 1979.

Laing, Lloyd, and Jennifer Laing. *The Origins of Britain*. London: Paladin, 1982.

MacKie, Euan W. *Science and Society in Prehistoric Britain*. London: Elek, 1977.

Megaw, J., and D. Simpson. *An Introduction to British Prehistory*. Leicester, England: Leicester University Press, 1979.

Merriman, Nick. *Prehistoric London*. London: Her Majesty's Stationery Office, 1990.

Morrison, A. *Early Man in Britain and Ireland*. London: Croom Helm, 1980.

Powell, T. G. E. *The Celts*. London: Thames and Hudson, 1989.

Renfrew, Colin. *British Prehistory: A New Outline*. London: Duckworth, 1974.

Richards, J. *The English Heritage Book of Stonehenge*. London:

Batsford, 1991.

Roe, D. A. *The Lower and Middle Palaeolithic Periods in Britain.* London: Routledge, 1981.

Ross, Anne. *Pagan Celtic Britain: Studies in Iconography and Tradition.* London: Constable, 1992.

Simmons, I. G., and M. Tooley. *The Environment in British Prehistory.* London: Duckworth, 1981.

Thomas, C. *Celtic Britain.* London: Thames and Hudson, 1986.

Thomas, N. *A Guide to Prehistoric England.* London: Batsford, 1976.

Todd, Malcolm. *The South West to AD 1000.* London: Longman, 1987.

Roman Britain

Bedoyere, Guy de la. *Roman Villas and the Countryside.* London: Batsford, 1993.

Birley, A. R. *The People of Roman Britain.* London: Batsford, 1979.

Breeze, D. J., and B. Dobson. *Hadrian's Wall.* London: Allen Lane, 1976.

Cunliffe, Barry. *Wessex to AD 1000.* London: Longman, 1993.

Dark, Kenneth R. *Civitas to Kingdom: British Political Continuity, 300–800.* London: Pinter, 1994.

Drewett, Peter, David Rudling, and Mark Gardiner. *The South East to AD 1000.* London: Longman, 1988.

Ford, Boris, ed. *Early Britain.* Cambridge: Cambridge University Press, 1992.

Frere, S. *Britannia: A History of Roman Britain.* London: Pimlico, 1991.

Higham, Nick. *The Northern Counties to AD 1000.* London: Longman, 1986.

Johnson, S. *Later Roman Britain.* London: Routledge, 1980.

Legg, Rodney. *Romans in Britain.* London: Heinemann, 1983.

Margary, I. D. *Roman Roads in Britain.* London: John Baker, 1973.

Merrifield, Ralph. *London: City of the Romans.* London: Batsford, 1983.

Ottaway, Patrick. *Roman York.* London: Batsford, 1993.

Richmond, I. A. *Roman Britain.* Harmondsworth, England: Penguin, 1963.

Rivet, A. L. F. *Town and Country in Roman Britain.* London: Hutchinson, 1975.

Salway, Peter. *The Oxford Illustrated History of Roman Britain.* Oxford: Oxford University Press, 1993.

Scott, J. M. *Boadicea.* London: Constable, 1975.

Scullard, H. H. *Roman Britain: Outpost of the Empire.* London: Thames and Hudson, 1979.

Todd, M. *Roman Britain, 55 BC–AD 400.* London: Fontana, 1981.

Wacher, John. *The Coming of Rome.* London: Routledge and Kegan Paul, 1979.

———. *Roman Britain.* London: Dent, 1978.

———. *The Towns of Roman Britain.* London: Batsford, 1975.

Anglo-Saxon and Viking Britain

Alcock, Leslie. *Arthur's Britain: History and Archaeology, AD 367–634.* Harmondsworth, England: Penguin, 1989.

Ashe, Geoffrey. *The Discovery of King Arthur.* Garden City, N.Y.: Anchor Press, 1985.

———. *The Kings and Queens of Early Britain.* Chicago: Academy, 1982.

Ashe, Geoffrey, ed. *The Quest for Arthur's Britain.* London: HarperCollins, 1968.

Bassett, Steven. *The Origins of the Anglo-Saxon Kingdoms.* London: Pinter, 1990.

Blair, Peter Hunter. *An Introduction to Anglo-Saxon England.* Cambridge: Cambridge University Press, 1977.

Britnell, R. H. *The Commercialisation of English Society, 1000–1500.* Cambridge: Cambridge University Press, 1992.

Brook, C. N. L. *From Alfred to Henry III, 871–1272.* Edinburgh: Nelson, 1961.

Brooks, Nicholas. *The Early History of the Church in Canterbury.* London: Pinter, 1984.

Bruce-Mitford, Rupert. *The Sutton Hoo Burial: A Handbook.* London: British Museum, 1979.

Burton, Janet. *Monastic and Religious Orders in Britain, 1000–1300.* Cambridge: Cambridge University Press, 1994.

Campbell, J. *The Anglo-Saxons.* Oxford: Phaidon, 1982.

Clark, John. *Saxon and Norman London.* London: Her Majesty's Stationery Office, 1989.

Coghlan, Ronan. *The Encyclopaedia of Arthurian Legends.* Shaftesbury, England: Element, 1991.

Crossley-Holland, Kevin. *The Anglo-Saxon World.* Woodbridge,

England: Boydell, 1982.

Cubitt, Catherine R. E. *Anglo-Saxon Church Councils, 650–850*. London: Pinter, 1994.

Cunliffe, Barry. *Wessex to AD 1000*. London: Longman, 1993.

Dark, Kenneth R. *Civitas to Kingdom: British Political Continuity, 300–800*. London: Pinter, 1994.

Dornier, A. *Mercian Studies*. Leicester, England: Leicester University Press, 1977.

Drewett, Peter, David Rudling, and Mark Gardiner. *The South East to AD 1000*. London: Longman, 1988.

Duckett, E. S. *Alfred the Great and His England*. London: Collins, 1992.

Evans, A. C. *The Sutton Hoo Ship Burial*. London: British Museum, 1992.

Finberg, H. P. R. *The Formation of England, 540–1042*. London: HarperCollins, 1976.

Fisher, D. J. V. *The Anglo-Saxon Age, c.400–1042*. Harlow, England: Longman, 1976.

Ford, Boris, ed. *Early Britain*. Cambridge: Cambridge University Press, 1992.

Garmonsway, G. N., translator. *The Anglo-Saxon Chronicle*. London: Dent, 1972.

Goodrich, Norma Lorre. *King Arthur*. New York: Watts, 1986.

Higham, Nick. *The Northern Counties to AD 1000*. London: Longman, 1986.

Hill, D. *An Atlas of Anglo-Saxon England*. Oxford: Blackwell, 1981.

Jenkins, Elizabeth. *The Mystery of King Arthur*. New York: Coward, McCann and Geoghegan, 1975.

Lawson, M. K. *Cnut: The Danes in England in the Early Eleventh Century*. London: Longman, 1993.

Lees, Beatrice Adelaide. *Alfred the Great: The Truth Teller, Maker of England, 848–899*. New York: Lemma, 1972.

Loyn, Henry. *Anglo-Saxon England and the Norman Conquest*. London: Longman, 1991.

———. *The Governance of Anglo-Saxon England, 500–1087*. London: Edward Arnold, 1984.

———. *The Vikings in Britain*. London: Batsford, 1977.

Mapp, Alf J. *The Golden Dragon: Alfred the Great and His Times*. La Salle, Ill.: Open Court, 1975.

Markale, Jean. *King Arthur, King of Kings*, translated by Christine Hauch. London: Gordon and Cremonesi, 1977.

Marsden, John. *The Fury of the Northmen: Saints, Shrines and Sea-*

Raiders in the Viking Age. London: Kyle Cathie, 1993.

Morris, John. *The Age of Arthur: A History of the British Isles from 350 to 650.* London: Weidenfeld and Nicolson, 1973.

Newton, S. *The Origins of Beowulf and the Pre-Viking Kingdom of East Anglia.* Cambridge: D.S. Brewer, 1993.

Plummer, Christopher. *The Life and Times of Alfred the Great.* New York: Haskell House, 1970.

Richards, Julian. *Viking Age England.* London: Batsford, 1991.

Ridyard, Susan J. *The Royal Saints of Anglo-Saxon England: A Study of West Saxon and East Anglian Cults.* Cambridge: Cambridge University Press, 1989.

Roesdahl, E. *The Vikings.* Harmondsworth, England: Penguin, 1992.

Rumble, Alexander. *The Reign of Cnut: The King of England, Denmark and Norway.* London: Pinter, 1994.

Saklatavala, Beram. *Arthur, Roman Britain's Last Champion.* New York: Taplinger, 1967.

Savage, A. *The Anglo-Saxon Chronicles.* London: Heinemann, 1982.

Sims-Williams, Patrick. *Religion and Literature in Western England, 600–800.* Cambridge: Cambridge University Press, 1990.

Stenton, Sir Frank. *Anglo-Saxon England.* Oxford: Oxford University Press, 1989.

Todd, Malcolm. *The South West to AD 1000.* London: Longman, 1987.

Whitelock, Dorothy. *The Beginnings of English Society.* Harmondsworth, England: Penguin, 1974.

Wood, Michael. *In Search of the Dark Ages.* Harmondsworth, England: Penguin, 1994.

Woodruff, Douglas. *The Life and Times of Alfred the Great.* London: Weidenfeld and Nicolson, 1974.

Yorke, Barbara. *Wessex in the Early Middle Ages.* London: Pinter, 1994.

The Normans (1066–1154)

Amt, Emilie. *The Accession of Henry II in England: Royal Government Restored, 1149-1159.* Woodbridge, England: Boydell Press, 1993.

Appleby, John T. *The Troubled Reign of King Stephen.* New York: Barnes and Noble, 1970.

Ashley, Maurice. *The Life and Times of William I.* London: Weidenfeld and Nicolson, 1973.

Barlow, Frank. *The Feudal Kingdom of England, 1042–1216.* London: Longman, 1988.

———. *Thomas Becket.* London: Weidenfeld and Nicolson, 1986.

———. *William Rufus.* London: Methuen, 1983.

Britnell, R. H. *The Commercialisation of English Society, 1000–1500.* Cambridge: Cambridge University Press, 1992.

Brook, C. N. L. *From Alfred to Henry III, 871–1272.* Edinburgh: Nelson, 1961.

Brown, R. Allen. *The Normans.* Woodbridge, England: Boydell, 1984.

———. *The Normans and the Norman Conquest.* Woodbridge, England: Boydell, 1985.

Bryant, Arthur. *The Medieval Foundation.* London: Collins, 1966.

Burton, Janet. *Monastic and Religious Orders in Britain, 1000–1300.* Cambridge: Cambridge University Press, 1994.

Campbell, Bruce M. S., and Richard H. Britnell, ed. *A Commercialising Economy: England 1086–c1300.* Manchester: Manchester University Press, 1993.

Carpenter, D. A. *The Minority of Henry III.* London: Methuen, 1990.

Cassady, Richard F. *The Norman Achievement.* London: Sidgwick and Jackson, 1986.

Chrimes, S. B. *An Introduction to the Administrative History of Medieval England.* Oxford: Blackwell, 1966.

Clanchy, M. T. *England and Its Rulers, 1066–1272: Foreign Lordship and National Identity.* London: HarperCollins, 1989.

Clark, John. *Saxon and Norman London.* London: Her Majesty's Stationery Office, 1989.

Coss, Peter. *Lordship, Knighthood and Locality: A Study in English Society, c1180–c1280.* Cambridge: Cambridge University Press, 1991.

Cronne, H. A. *The Reign of Stephen, 1135–54: Anarchy in England.* London: Weidenfeld and Nicolson, 1970.

Crosby, Everett U. *Bishop and Chapter in Twelfth–Century England: A Study of the Mensa Episcopalis.* Cambridge: Cambridge University Press, 1994.

Dalton, Paul. *Conquest, Anarchy and Lordship: Yorkshire, 1066–1154.* Cambridge: Cambridge University Press, 1994.

Darby, H. C., and G. R. Versey. *Domesday Gazetteer.* Cambridge: Cambridge University Press, 1975.

Davis, R. H. C. *King Stephen, 1135–1154.* London: Longman, 1990.

Finn, R. W. *Domesday Book: A Guide.* London: Phillimore, 1973.

Fleming, Robin. *Kings and Lords in Conquest England.* Cambridge:

Cambridge University Press, 1991.

Ford, Boris, ed. *Medieval Britain*. Cambridge: Cambridge University Press, 1992.

Galbraith, V. H. *The Making of the Domesday Book*. Oxford: Clarendon Press, 1961.

Garmonsway, G. N., translator. *The Anglo–Saxon Chronicle*. London: Dent, 1972.

Garnett, George, and John Hudson, eds. *Law and Government in Medieval England and Normandy: Essays in Honour of Sir James Holt*. Cambridge: Cambridge University Press, 1994.

Golding, Brian. *Conquest and Colonisation: The Normans in Britain, 1066–1100*. Basingstoke, England: Macmillan, 1991.

Green, Judith. *The Government of England Under Henry I*. Cambridge: Cambridge University Press, 1989.

Hallam, Elizabeth, ed. *Chronicles of the Crusades*. London: Weidenfeld and Nicolson, 1989.

Harvey, Barbara. *Living and Dying in England, 1100–1540: The Monastic Experience*. Oxford: Clarendon Press, 1993.

Hutchinson, Gillian. *Medieval Ships and Shipping*. London: Pinter, 1994.

Kealey, Edward J. *Harvesting the Air: Windmill Pioneers in Twelfth–Century England*. Woodbridge, England: Boydell Press, 1987.

Kenyon, John R. *Medieval Fortifications*. London: Pinter, 1991.

Le Patourel, J. *The Norman Empire*. Oxford: Clarendon Press, 1976.

Lewis, A. R. *Nomads and Crusaders, AD 1000–1368*. Bloomington, Ind.: Indiana University Press, 1988.

Lloyd, T. H. *England and the German Hanse, 1157–1611: A Study of Their Trade and Commercial Diplomacy*. Cambridge: Cambridge University Press, 1991.

Loyn, H. R. *The Norman Conquest*. London: Hutchinson, 1982.

Miller, Edward, and John Hatcher. *Medieval England: Rural Society and Economic Change, 1086–1348*. London: Longman, 1978.

Morillo, Stephen. *Warfare under the Anglo-Norman Kings, 1066–1135*. Woodbridge, England: Boydell, 1994.

Poole, R. L. *The Exchequer in the 12th Century*. London: Frank Cass, 1973.

Pounds, N. J. G. *The Medieval Castle in England and Wales: A Political and Social History*. Cambridge: Cambridge University Press, 1993.

Reeves, A. C. *The Marcher Lords*. Llandybie, Wales: C. Davies, 1983.

Riley-Smith, J. *Atlas of the Crusades*. London: Times Books, 1991.

Rowley, Trevor. *The High Middle Ages, 1200–1500*. London: Routledge and Kegan Paul, 1986.

Saul, Nigel. *England in Europe, 1066–1453*. London: Collin and Brown, 1994.

Stenton, Doris Mary. *English Society in the Early Middle Ages, 1066–1307*. Harmondsworth, England: Penguin, 1965.

Stringer, Keith J. *The Reign of Stephen: Kingship, Warfare and Government in Twelfth Century England*. London: Routledge, 1993.

Warren, Wilfred Lewis. *The Governance of Norman and Angevin England, 1086–1272*. London: Edward Arnold, 1987.

———. *Henry II*. London: Eyre Methuen, 1973.

The Plantagenets (1154–1485)

Acheson, Eric. *A Gentry Community: Leicestershire in the Fifteenth Century, c1422–1485*. Cambridge: Cambridge University Press, 1992.

Allmand, C. T. *The Hundred Years War: England and France at War, c1300–c1450*. Cambridge: Cambridge University Press, 1988.

Amt, Emilie. *The Accession of Henry II in England: Royal Government Restored, 1149–1159*. Woodbridge, England: Boydell Press, 1993.

Ashley, Maurice. *The Life and Times of King John*. London: Weidenfeld and Nicolson, 1972.

Bailey, Mark. *A Marginal Economy?: East Anglian Breckland in the Later Middle Ages*. Cambridge: Cambridge University Press, 1989.

Barber, Richard. *The Devil's Crown: Henry II, Richard I, John*. London: British Broadcasting Corporation, 1978.

———. *Edward, Prince of Wales and Aquitaine: A Biography of the Black Prince*. London: Allen Lane, 1978.

———. *Henry Plantagenet*. Ipswich, England: Boydell Press, 1972.

Barlow, Frank. *The Feudal Kingdom of England, 1042–1216*. London: Longman, 1988.

———. *Thomas Becket*. London: Weidenfeld and Nicolson, 1986.

Bennett, Michael. *The Battle of Bosworth*. Stroud, England: Alan Sutton, 1993.

Bevan, B. *King Richard II*. London: Rubicon Press, 1990.

Bingham, Caroline. *The Crowned Lions: The Early Plantagenet*

Kings. Newton Abbot, England: David and Charles, 1978.

————. *The Life and Times of Edward II.* London: Weidenfeld and Nicolson, 1973.

Blake, N. F. *Caxton: England's First Publisher.* London: Osprey, 1976.

Bonney, Margaret. *Lordship and the Urban Community: Durham and Its Overlords, 1250–1540.* Cambridge: Cambridge University Press, 1990.

Brewer, Derek. *Chaucer.* Harlow, England: Longman, 1973.

————. *Chaucer and His World.* London: Eyre Methuen, 1978.

Brewer, Derek, ed. *Geoffrey Chaucer.* Woodbridge, England: D. S. Brewer, 1990.

Britnell, R. H. *The Commercialisation of English Society, 1000–1500.* Cambridge: Cambridge University Press, 1992.

Brook, C. N. L. *From Alfred to Henry III, 871–1272.* Edinburgh: Thomas Nelson, 1961.

Brooke, Z. M. *The English Church and the Papacy: From the Conquest to the Reign of John.* Cambridge: Cambridge University Press, 1989.

Bruce, M. L. *The Usurper King: Henry of Bolingbroke, 1366–99.* London: Rubicon, 1986.

Bryant, Arthur. *The Age of Chivalry.* London: Collins, 1963.

————. *The Medieval Foundation.* London: Collins, 1966.

Burton, Janet. *Monastic and Religious Orders in Britain, 1000–1300.* Cambridge: Cambridge University Press, 1994.

Campbell, Bruce M. S., and Richard H. Britnell, eds. *A Commercialising Economy: England, 1086–c1300.* Manchester: Manchester University Press, 1994.

Carpenter, Christine. *Locality and Polity: A Study of Warwickshire Landed Society, 1401–1499.* Cambridge: Cambridge University Press, 1992.

Carpenter, D. A. *The Minority of Henry III.* London: Methuen, 1990.

Chancellor, John. *The Life and Times of Edward I.* London: Weidenfeld and Nicolson, 1981.

Cheetham, Anthony. *The Life and Times of Richard III.* London: Weidenfeld and Nicolson, 1972.

Chrimes, S. B. *An Introduction to the Administrative History of Medieval England.* Oxford: Blackwell, 1966.

Clanchy, M. T. *England and Its Rulers, 1066–1272: Foreign Lordship and National Identity.* London: HarperCollins, 1989.

Clive, Lady Mary. *This Sun of York: A Biography of Edward IV.* London: Macmillan, 1973.

Coghill, Neville. *The Poet Chaucer.* London: Oxford University Press, 1967.

Cole, Hubert. *The Black Prince.* London: Hart-Davis MacGibbon, 1976.

Coss, Peter. *Lordship, Knighthood and Locality: A Study in English Society, c1180–c1280.* Cambridge: Cambridge University Press, 1991.

Coulton, G. G. *Chaucer and His England.* London: Bracken, 1993.

Crosby, Everett U. *Bishop and Chapter in Twelfth-Century England.* Cambridge: Cambridge University Press, 1994.

Crouch, David. *William Marshal: Court, Career and Chivalry in the Angevin Empire, 1147–1219.* London: Longman, 1990.

Curry, Anne. *The Hundred Years War.* Basingstoke, England: Macmillan, 1993.

Deacon, Richard. *A Biography of William Caxton: The First English Editor, Printer, Merchant and Translator.* London: Muller, 1976.

Dickinson, H. T. *Bolingbroke.* London: Constable, 1970.

Dobson, R. B., ed. *The Peasants' Revolt of 1381.* Basingstoke, England: Macmillan, 1983.

Doe, Norman. *Fundamental Authority in Late Medieval English Law.* Cambridge: Cambridge University Press, 1991.

Duffy, Eamon. *The Stripping of the Altars: Traditional Religion in England, 1400–1580.* New Haven, Conn.: Yale University Press, 1992.

Dyer, Alan. *Decline and Growth in English Towns, 1400–1640.* Basingstoke, England: Macmillan, 1991.

Dyer, Christopher. *Standards of Living in the Later Middle Ages: Social Change in England, c1200–1520.* Cambridge: Cambridge University Press, 1989.

Earle, Peter. *The Life and Times of Henry V.* London: Weidenfeld and Nicolson, 1972.

Emerson, Barbara. *The Black Prince.* London: Weidenfeld and Nicolson, 1976.

Falkus, Gila. *The Life and Times of Edward IV.* London: Weidenfeld and Nicolson, 1981.

Ford, Boris, ed. *Medieval Britain.* Cambridge: Cambridge University Press, 1992.

Fowler, K. *The Hundred Years War.* London: Macmillan, 1971.

Gardner, John. *The Life and Times of Chaucer.* New York: Knopf, 1976.

Garnett, George, and John Hudson, eds. *Law and Government in Me-*

dieval England and Normandy: Essays in Honour of Sir James Holt. Cambridge: Cambridge University Press, 1994.

Gillingham, J. *Richard the Lionheart.* London: Weidenfeld and Nicolson, 1978.

Given-Wilson, Chris. *Chronicles of the Revolution, 1397–1400: The Reign of Richard III.* Manchester: Manchester University Press, 1993.

Goodman, Anthony E. *John of Gaunt: The Exercise of Princely Power in Fourteenth-Century Europe.* Harlow, England: Longman, 1992.

————. *The Wars of the Roses.* London: Routledge, 1981.

Griffiths, Ralph A. *The Reign of Henry VI: The Exercise of Royal Authority, 1422–1461.* London: Benn, 1981.

Hall, Louis Brewer. *The Perilous Vision of John Wyclif.* Chicago: Nelson-Hall, 1983.

Hallam, Elizabeth, ed. *The Chronicles of the Crusades.* London: Weidenfeld and Nicolson, 1989.

————. *The Chronicles of the Wars of the Roses.* London: Weidenfeld and Nicolson, 1988.

————. *The Plantagenet Chronicles.* London: Weidenfeld and Nicolson, 1986.

————. *The Plantagenet Encyclopaedia.* London: Weidenfeld and Nicolson, 1990.

Hammond, P. W. *The Battles of Barnet and Tewkesbury.* Stroud, England: Alan Sutton, 1993.

Harding, Alan. *England in the Thirteenth Century.* Cambridge: Cambridge University Press, 1993.

Harriss, G. L. *Henry V: The Price of Kingship.* Stroud, England: Alan Sutton, 1993.

Harvey, Barbara. *Living and Dying in England, 1100–1540: The Monastic Experience.* Oxford: Clarendon Press, 1993.

Harvey, John. *The Black Prince and His Age.* London: Batsford, 1976.

————. *The Plantagenets.* London: Severn House, 1976.

Harvey, Margaret M. *England, Rome and the Papacy, 1417–1464.* Manchester: Manchester University Press, 1993.

Hibbert, Christopher. *Agincourt.* London: Batsford, 1978.

Holt, J. C. *Magna Carta.* Cambridge: Cambridge University Press, 1992.

Holt, Richard, and Gervase Rosser, eds. *The Medieval Town: A Reader in English Urban History, 1200–1540.* London: Longman, 1990.

Horrox, Rosemary. *The Black Death*. Manchester: Manchester University Press, 1994.

———. *Richard III: A Study of Service*. Cambridge: Cambridge University Press, 1991.

Houlbrook, Ralph A. *The English Family, 1450–1700*. London: Longman, 1984.

Howard, Donald R. *Chaucer: His Life, His Works, His World*. New York: Dutton, 1987.

Hudson, A. M., ed. *Selections from English Wycliffite Writing*. Cambridge: Cambridge University Press, 1978.

Hutchinson, Gillian. *Medieval Ships and Shipping*. London: Pinter, 1994.

Hutchinson, Harold F. *Edward II: The Pliant King*. London: Eyre and Spottiswoode, 1971.

———. *King Henry V: A Biography*. New York: Doubleday, 1967.

Hutton, Ronald. *The Rise and Fall of Merry England: The Ritual Year, 1400–1700*. Oxford: Oxford University Press, 1994.

Johnson, P. A. *Duke Richard of York, 1411–1460*. Oxford: Clarendon Press, 1988.

Kealey, Edward J. *Harvesting the Air: Windmill Pioneers in Twelfth-Century England*. Woodbridge, England: Boydell Press, 1987.

Kenyon, John R. *Medieval Fortifications*. London: Pinter, 1991.

Kirby, John Lavan. *Henry IV of England*. London: Constable, 1970.

Labarge, Margaret Wade. *Henry V: The Cautious Conqueror*. London: Secker and Warburg, 1975.

———. *Simon de Montfort*. London: Eyre and Spottiswoode, 1962.

Lander, J. R. *The Wars of the Roses*. Stroud, England: Alan Sutton, 1990.

Lewis, A. R. *Nomads and Crusaders, AD 1000–1368*. Bloomington, Ind.: Indiana University Press, 1991.

Lindsay, Philip. *The Devil and King John*. Bath, England: Cedric Chivers, 1972.

Lloyd, Alan. *The Hundred Years War*. London: Hart—Davis MacGibbon, 1977.

———. *King John*. Newton Abbot: David and Charles, 1973.

Lloyd, T. H. *England and the German Hanse, 1157–1611: A Study of Their Trade and Commercial Diplomacy*. Cambridge: Cambridge University Press, 1991.

Maddicott, J. R. *Simon de Montfort*. Cambridge: Cambridge University Press, 1994.

Mathew, G. *The Court of Richard II*. London: John Murray, 1969.

McIntosh, Marjorie Keniston. *Autonomy and Continuity: The Royal*

Manor of Havering, 1200–1500. Cambridge: Cambridge University Press, 1986.

Meale, Carol M., ed. *Women and Literature in Britain, 1150–1500.* Cambridge: Cambridge University Press, 1993.

Miller, Edward, and John Hatcher. *Medieval England: Rural Society and Economic Change, 1086–1348.* London: Longman, 1978.

Mortimer, Richard. *Angevin England, 1154–1258.* Oxford: Blackwell, 1994.

Myers, A. R. *England in the Late Middle Ages.* Harmondsworth, England: Penguin, 1978.

Neillands, Robin. *The Wars of the Roses.* London: Cassell, 1992.

Oman, C. *The Great Revolt of 1381.* Oxford: Clarendon Press, 1969.

Ormrod, W. M. *The Reign of Edward II: Crown and Political Society in England, 1327–1377.* New Haven, Conn.: Yale University Press, 1993.

Packe, Michael. *King Edward III.* London: Routledge and Kegan Paul, 1983.

Painter, George D. *William Caxton: A Quincentenary Biography of England's First Printer.* London: Chatto and Windus, 1976.

Pallister, A. *Magna Carta: The Heritage of Liberty.* Oxford: Clarendon Press, 1971.

Parsons, John Carmi. *Eleanor of Castile.* Basingstoke, England: Macmillan, 1994.

Pollard, A. J. *Richard III and the Princes in the Tower.* Stroud, England: Alan Sutton, 1991.

———. *The Wars of the Roses.* Basingstoke, England: Macmillan, 1988.

Poole, R. L. *The Exchequer in the 12th Century.* London: Frank Cass, 1973.

Poos, L. R. *A Rural Society after the Black Death: Essex, 1350–1525.* Cambridge: Cambridge University Press, 1991.

Potter, Jeremy. *Good King Richard?: An Account of Richard III and His Reputation.* London: Constable, 1983.

Pounds, N. J. G. *The Medieval Castle in England and Wales: A Political and Social History.* Cambridge: Cambridge University Press, 1993.

Preston, Raymond. *Chaucer.* New York: Greenwood Press, 1969.

Prestwich, Michael. *Edward I.* London: Methuen, 1988.

———. *English Politics in the Thirteenth Century.* Basingstoke, England: Macmillan, 1990.

Richards, Jeffrey. *Sex, Dissidence and Damnation: Minority Groups in the Middle Ages.* London: Routledge, 1991.

Riley-Smith, J. *Atlas of the Crusades.* London: Times Books, 1991.

Ross, Charles Derek. *Edward IV.* London: Eyre Methuen, 1974.

———. *The Wars of the Roses: A Concise History.* London: Thames and Hudson, 1976.

Rowley, Trevor. *The High Middle Ages, 1200–1500.* London: Routledge and Kegan Paul, 1986.

Saul, Nigel. *England in Europe, 1066–1453.* London: Collin and Brown, 1994.

Schlight, John. *Henry II Plantagenet.* New York: Twayne, 1973.

Seward, Desmond. *Henry V as Warlord.* London: Sidgwick and Jackson, 1987.

Shrewsbury, F. J. D. *A History of the Bubonic Plague in the British Isles.* Cambridge: Cambridge University Press, 1970.

Starkey, David. *The English Court: From the Wars of the Roses to the Civil War.* London: Longman, 1987.

Stenton, Doris Mary. *English Society in the Early Middle Ages, 1066– 1307.* Harmondsworth, England: Penguin, 1965.

Swanson, R. N. *Catholic England: Faith, Religion and Observance before the Reformation.* Manchester: Manchester University Press, 1993.

Thomson, John A. F. *The Transformation of Medieval England 1370-1529.* London: Longman, 1983.

Treharne, R. *The Glastonbury Legends.* London: Cresset Press, 1967.

Trevelyan, George Macaulay. *England in the Age of Wycliffe.* New York: AMS Press, 1975.

Turner, Ralph. *King John.* London: Longman, 1994.

Vaughan, Richard. *The Illustrated Chronicles of Matthew Paris: Observations of Thirteenth Century Life.* Stroud, England: Alan Sutton, 1993.

Ward, Jennifer C. *English Noblewomen in the Later Middle Ages.* London: Longman, 1992.

Warren, Wilfred Lewis. *The Governance of Norman and Angevin England, 1086–1272.* London: Edward Arnold, 1987.

———. *Henry II.* London: Eyre Methuen, 1973.

———. *King John.* London: Eyre Methuen, 1978.

Waugh, S. L. *England in the Reign of Edward III.* Cambridge: Cambridge University Press, 1991.

Weir, Alison. *The Princes in the Tower.* London: Bodley Head, 1992.

Wilkinson, B. *The Later Middle Ages in England, 1216–1485.* London: Longman, 1977.

Winston, R. *Thomas Becket.* London: Constable, 1967.

Ziegler, Philip. *The Black Death.* Stroud, England: Alan Sutton, 1991.

The Tudors (1485–1603)

Adamson, Jack H., and Harold Freeze Folland. *The Shepherd of the Ocean: An Account of Sir Walter Ralegh and His Times.* London: Bodley Head, 1969.

Andrews, K. R. *Trade, Plunder and Settlement: Maritime Enterprise and the Genesis of the British Empire, 1480–1630.* Cambridge: Cambridge University Press, 1984.

Ayris, Paul, and David Selwyn, ed. *Thomas Cranmer: Churchman and Scholar.* Woodbridge, England: Boydell and Brewer, 1993.

Barry, Jonathan, ed. *The Tudor and Stuart Town: A Reader in English Urban History, 1530–1688.* London: Longman, 1990.

Barry, Jonathan, and Christopher Brooks, eds. *The Middling Sort of People: Culture, Society and Politics in England, 1550–1800.* London: Macmillan, 1994.

Baskerville, Stephen. *Not Peace But a Sword: The Political Theology of the English Revolution.* London: Routledge, 1993.

Beckingsale, B. W. *Thomas Cromwell: Tudor Minister.* Totowa, N.J.: Rowman and Littlefield, 1978.

Beier, A. L. *The Problem of the Poor in Tudor and Early Stuart England.* London: Methuen, 1983.

Belloc, Hilaire. *Cranmer, Archbishop of Canterbury.* New York: Haskell House, 1973.

Bennett, M. *The Battle of Bosworth.* Gloucester, England: Alan Sutton, 1985.

———. *Lambert Simnel and the Battle of Stoke.* Gloucester, England: Alan Sutton, 1987.

Bonney, Margaret. *Lordship and the Urban Community: Durham and Its Overlords, 1250–1540.* Cambridge: Cambridge University Press, 1990.

Boughner, Daniel C. *The Devil's Disciple: Ben Jonson's Debt to Machiavelli.* New York: Philosophical Library, 1968.

Bowle, John. *Henry VIII: A Biography.* Newton Abbot, England: David and Charles, 1973.

Brenner, Robert. *Merchants and Revolution, Commercial Change, Political Conflict and London's Overseas Traders, 1550–1653.* Cambridge: Cambridge University Press, 1993.

Brooke, Z. M. *The English Church and the Papacy: From the Con-

quest to the Reign of John. Cambridge: Cambridge University Press, 1989.

Brooks, Peter Newman. *Thomas Cranmer's Doctrine of the Eucharist.* Basingstoke, England: Macmillan, 1994.

Bruce, Marie Louise. *Anne Boleyn.* London: Collins, 1972.

———. *The Making of Henry VIII.* London: Collins, 1977.

Bryant, Arthur. *The Medieval Foundation.* London: Collins, 1966.

Burgess, Anthony. *Shakespeare.* London: Cape, 1970.

Burgess, Glenn. *British Political Thought: From Reformation to Revolution.* Basingstoke, England: Macmillan, 1994.

Carpenter, Christine. *Locality and Polity: A Study of Warwickshire Landed Society, 1401–1499.* Cambridge: Cambridge University Press, 1992.

Chapman, Hester W. *Anne Boleyn.* London: Cape, 1974.

———. *Lady Jane Grey, October 1537–February 1554.* London: Cape, 1962.

———. *The Last Tudor King: A Study of Edward VI , October 12th, 1537–July 6th, 1553.* Bath, England: Cedric Chivers, 1973.

Chrimes, S. B. *Henry VII.* London: Eyre Methuen, 1972.

———. *An Introduction to the Administrative History of Medieval England.* Oxford: Blackwell, 1966.

———. *Lancastrians, Yorkists and Henry VII.* London: Macmillan, 1966.

Chute, Marchette. *Ben Jonson of Westminster.* London: Souvenir Press, 1978.

Collinson, Patrick. *The Birthpangs of Protestant England: Religious and Cultural Change in the Sixteenth and Seventeenth Centuries.* Basingstoke, England: Macmillan, 1988.

Colman, D. C. *Industry in Tudor and Stuart England.* Basingstoke, England: Macmillan, 1975.

Coote, Stephen. *A Play of Passion: The Life of Sir Walter Raleigh.* Basingstoke, England: Macmillan, 1993.

Crawford, Patricia. *Women and Religion in England, 1500–1720.* London: Routledge, 1993.

Daniell, David. *William Tyndale: A Biography.* New Haven , Conn.: Yale University Press, 1994.

Davis, Michael Justin. *The Landscape of William Shakespeare.* Exeter, England: Webb and Bower, 1987.

Dickens, A. G. *The English Reformation.* London: Batsford, 1989.

———. *Thomas Cromwell and the English Reformation.* London: English Universities Press, 1967.

Dickens, A. G., and Dorothy Carr. *The Reformation in England to the Accession of Elizabeth I.* London: Edward Arnold, 1967.

Dolan, Frances E. *Dangerous Familiars: Representations of Domestic Crime in England, 1550–1700.* Ithaca, N.Y.: Cornell University Press, 1994.

Doran, Susan. *Elizabeth I and Religion, 1558–1603.* London: Routledge, 1993.

Duffy, Eamon. *The Stripping of the Altars: Traditional Religion in England, 1400–1580.* New Haven, Conn.: Yale University Press, 1992.

Durant, D. N. *Ralegh's Lost Colony: The Story of the First English Settlements in America.* London: Weidenfeld and Nicolson, 1981.

Dyer, Alan. *Decline and Growth in English Towns, 1400–1640.* Basingstoke, England: Macmillan, 1991.

Dyer, Christopher. *Standards of Living in the Later Middle Ages: Social Change in England, c1200–1520.* Cambridge: Cambridge University Press, 1989.

Edwards, Brian. *William Tyndale, the Father of the English Bible.* Farmington Hills, Mich.: William Tyndale College, 1982.

Elton, G. R. *England Under the Tudors.* London: Routledge, 1991.

———. *Reform and Reformation: England, 1509–1558.* London: Edward Arnold, 1977.

———. *Thomas Cromwell.* Bangor, Wales: Headstart History, 1991.

Erickson, Carolly. *Anne Boleyn.* London: Macmillan, 1984.

———. *Bloody Mary.* London: Dent, 1978.

———. *The First Elizabeth.* New York: Summit Books, 1983.

———. *Great Harry.* London: Dent, 1980.

Fecher, Constance. *The Last Elizabethan: A Portrait of Sir Walter Raleigh.* New York: Farrar, Straus and Giroux, 1972.

Fideler, Paul, and T. F. Mayer. *Political Thought and the Tudor Commonwealth: Deep Structure, Discourse and Disguise.* London: Routledge, 1992.

Ford, Boris, ed. *16th Century Britain.* Cambridge: Cambridge University Press, 1992.

Foster, Andrew. *The Church of England, 1570–1640.* London: Longman, 1994.

Fox, Alistair. *Thomas More: History and Providence.* Oxford: Basil Blackwell, 1982.

Fraser, Antonia. *The Six Wives of Henry VIII.* London: Weidenfeld and Nicolson, 1992.

Fraser, G. M. *The Steel Bonnets.* London: Barrie and Jenkins, 1971.

Frye, Susan. *Elizabeth I: The Competition for Representation.* New

York: Oxford University Press, 1993.

Gosse, Edmund. *Raleigh.* Norwood, Pa.: Norwood Editions, 1977.

Grant, Alexander. *Henry VII.* London: Methuen, 1985.

Graves, Michael A. R. *The Tudor Parliaments: Crown, Lords and Commons, 1485–1603.* London: Longman, 1985.

Griffiths, Paul, Adam Fox, and Steven Hindle, ed. *The Experience of Authority in Early Modern England.* Basingstoke, England: Macmillan, 1994.

Griffiths, Ralph A. *The Making of a Tudor Dynasty.* Stroud, England: Alan Sutton, 1994.

Gunn, S. J., and P. G. Lindley, ed. *Cardinal Wolsey: Church, State and Art.* Cambridge: Cambridge University Press, 1991.

Guy, John. *The Public Career of Sir Thomas More.* New Haven, Conn.: Yale University Press, 1980.

———. *Tudor England.* Oxford: Oxford University Press, 1988.

Gwyn, Peter. *The King's Cardinal: The Rise and Fall of Thomas Wolsey.* London: Barrie and Jenkins, 1990.

Hackett, Helen. *Virgin Mother, Maiden Queen: Elizabeth I and the Cult of the Virgin Mary.* Basingstoke, England: Macmillan, 1994.

Haigh, Christopher. *Elizabeth I.* London: Longman, 1988.

———. *The Reign of Elizabeth I.* Basingstoke, England: Macmillan, 1985.

Halliday, F. E. *Shakespeare.* London: Thames and Hudson, 1986.

Harris, Tim. *Popular Culture in England, c1500–1850.* London: Macmillan, 1993.

Harvey, Barbara. *Living and Dying in England, 1100–1540: The Monastic Experience.* Oxford: Clarendon Press, 1993.

Harvey, Nancy Lenz. *Elizabeth of York; The Mother of Henry VIII.* New York: Macmillan, 1973.

———. *Thomas Cardinal Wolsey.* New York: Macmillan, 1980.

Haynes, Alan. *Robert Cecil, Earl of Salisbury, 1563–1612: Servant of Two Sovereigns.* London: Owen, 1989.

Heal, Felicity, and Clive Holmes. *The Gentry in England and Wales, 1500–1700.* Basingstoke, England: Macmillan, 1994.

Heard, Nigel. *Edward VI and Mary: A Mid-Tudor Crisis?.* London: Hodder and Stoughton, 1990.

———. *Tudor Economy and Society.* London: Hodder and Stoughton, 1992.

Hibbert, Christopher. *The Virgin Queen: The Personal History of Elizabeth I.* London: Viking, 1990.

Hinton, R. W. K. *The Eastland Trade and the Common Weal in the*

Seventeenth Century. Cambridge: Cambridge University Press, 1972.

Holt, Richard, and Gervase Rosser, ed. *The Medieval Town: A Reader in English Urban History, 1200–1540.* London: Longman, 1990.

Hopkins, Eric. *Britain in the Widening World: British History, 1485–1763.* London: Nelson, 1967.

Hoskins, W. G. *The Age of Plunder: The England of Henry VIII, 1500– 1547.* London: Longman, 1976.

Houlbrooke, Ralph A. *The English Family, 1450–1700.* London: Longman, 1984.

Houston, R. A. *The Population History of Britain and Ireland,1500–1750.* Basingstoke, England: Macmillan, 1992.

Hutton, Ronald. *The Rise and Fall of Merry England: The Ritual Year, 1400–1700.* Oxford: Oxford University Press, 1994.

Ives, E. W. *Anne Boleyn.* Oxford: Blackwell, 1986.

Jenkins, Elizabeth. *Elizabeth and Leicester.* London: Gollancz, 1961.

Johnson, Paul. *Elizabeth I: A Study in Power and Intellect.* London: Weidenfeld and Nicolson, 1974.

Jordan, W. K. *Edward VI, the Young King: The Protectorship of the Duke of Somerset.* London: Allen and Unwin, 1968.

Keay, John. *The Honourable Company: A History of the English East India Company.* London: HarperCollins, 1991.

Keen, Maurice. *English Society in the Later Middle Ages.* Harmondsworth, England: Allen Lane/The Penguin Press, 1990.

Kenyon, Timothy. *Utopian Communism and Political Thought in Early Modern England.* London: Pinter, 1989.

Kerridge, Eric. *Agrarian Problems in the Sixteenth Century and After.* London: Allen and Unwin, 1969.

Laurence, Anne. *Women in England, 1500–1700:A Social History.* London: Weidenfield and Nicolson, 1994.

Lawson, Philip. *The East India Company: A History.* London: Longman, 1993.

Lloyd, Christopher. *Sir Francis Drake.* London: Faber, 1979.

Lloyd, T. H. *England and the German Hanse, 1157–1611: A Study of Their Trade and Comercial Diplomacy.* Cambridge: Cambridge University Press, 1991.

Loades, D. M. *The Mid-Tudor Crisis, 1545–1565.* Basingstoke, England: Macmillan, 1992.

———. *The Reign of Mary Tudor.* London: Longman, 1991.

Lockyer, Roger. *Tudor and Stuart Britain, 1471–1714.* Harlow, England: Longman, 1985.

Logan, George M., Robert M. Adams, and Clarence H. Miller, ed. *More: Utopia.* Cambridge: Cambridge University Press, 1994.

Lotherington, John, ed. *The Tudor Years.* London: Edward Arnold, 1994.

Luke, Mary M. *Catherine the Queen.* New York: Coward-McCann, 1967.

————. *Gloriana: The Years of Elizabeth I.* New York: Coward, McCann and Geoghegan, 1973.

————. *The Nine Days Queen: A Portrait of Lady Jane Grey.* New York: Morrow, 1986.

MacCafrey, Wallace. *Elizabeth I.* London: Edward Arnold, 1993.

MacCulloch, Diarmaid. *The Later Reformation in England, 1547–1603.* Basingstoke, England: Macmillan, 1990.

MacCurtain, Margaret. *Tudor and Stuart Ireland.* Dublin: Gill and Macmillan, 1972.

Marius, Richard. *Thomas More: A Biography.* New York: Knopf, 1984.

Marshall, R. K. *Elizabeth I.* London: Her Majesty's Stationery Office, 1991.

————. *Mary I.* London: Her Majesty's Stationery Office, 1993.

Martienssen, Anthony. *Queen Katherine Parr.* London: Secker and Warburg, 1973.

Mathew, David. *Lady Jane Grey: The Setting of the Reign.* London: Eyre Methuen, 1972.

Mattingley, G. *The Defeat of the Spanish Armada.* London: Cape, 1983.

McFarlane, Anthony. *The British in the Americas, 1480–1815.* London: Longman, 1994.

McIntosh, Marjorie Keniston. *Autonomy and Community: The Royal Manor of Havering, 1200–1500.* Cambridge: Cambridge University Press, 1986.

Meroff, Deborah. *Coronation of Glory: The Story of Lady Jane Grey.* London: Pickering and Inglis, 1979.

Merriman, Roger Bigelow. *Life and Letters of Thomas Cromwell.* 2 vols. Oxford: Clarendon Press, 1968.

Miles, Rosalind. *Ben Jonson: His Life and Work.* London: Routledge and Kegan Paul, 1986.

Muller, J. A. *Stephen Gardiner and the Tudor Reaction.* New York: Octagon Books, 1970.

Myers, A. R. *England in the Late Middle Ages.* Harmondsworth, England: Penguin, 1978.

O'Day, Rosemary. *The Debate on the English Reformation.* London:

Routledge, 1986.

———. *The Longman Companion to the Tudor Age.* London: Longman, 1994.

O'Sullivan, Dan, and Roger Lockyer. *Tudor England, 1485–1603.* London: Longman, 1994.

Outhwaite, R. B. *Dearth, Public Policy and Social Disturbance in England, 1550–1800.* Basingstoke, England: Macmillan, 1991.

Palliser D. M. *The Age of Elizabeth: England under the Late Tudors, 1547–1603.* London: Longman, 1992.

Palmer, John. *Ben Jonson.* Port Washington, N.Y.: Kennikat Press, 1967.

Paul, Leslie. *Sir Thomas More.* Freeport, N.Y.: Books For Libraries Press, 1970.

Perry, Maria. *Elizabeth I: The Word of a Prince; A Life From Contemporary Documents.* London: Folio Society, 1990.

Platt, Colin. *The Great Rebuildings of Tudor and Stuart England: Revolutions in Architectural Taste.* London: UCL Press, 1994.

Plowden, Alison. *Elizabeth Regina: The Age of Triumph, 1588–1603.* London: Macmillan, 1980.

———. *Elizabeth Tudor and Mary Stewart — Two Queens in One Isle.* Totowa, N.J.: Barnes and Noble, 1984.

———. *Lady Jane Grey and the House of Suffolk.* New York: F. Watts, 1986.

Pocock, J. G. A., Gordon J. Schochet, and Lois G. Schwoerer, ed. *The Varieties of British Political Thought, 1500–1800.* Cambridge: Cambridge University Press, 1994.

Pollard, Albert Frederick. *Henry VIII.* London: Longman, 1968.

———. *Wolsey.* Westport, Conn.: Greenwood Press, 1978.

Pomfret, J. E., and F. M. Shumway. *Founding the American Colonies, 1583-1660.* New York: Harper and Row, 1970.

Poos, L. R. *A Rural Society After the Black Death: Essex, 1350–1525.* Cambridge: Cambridge University Press, 1991.

Porter, Roy. *Disease, Medicine and Society in England, 1550–1860.* Basingstoke, England: Macmillan, 1993.

Prior, Mary, ed. *Women in English Society, 1500–1800.* London: Methuen, 1985.

Pythian-Adams, Charles. *Societies, Cultures and Kinship, 1580–1850: Cultural Provinces and English Local History.* London: Pinter, 1993.

Quennell, Peter. *Shakespeare: The Poet and His Background.* London: Weidenfeld and Nicolson, 1963.

Quinn, D. B. *The Elizabethans and the Irish.* Ithaca, N.Y.: Cornell

University Press, 1966.

————. *England and the Discovery of America, 1481–1620.* New York: Knopf, 1974.

Randell, Keith. *Elizabeth I and the Government of England.* London: Hodder and Stoughton, 1994.

————. *Henry VIII and the Government of England.* London: Hodder and Stoughton, 1991.

————. *Henry VIII and the Reformation in England.* London: Hodder and Stoughton, 1993.

Read, C. *Lord Burghley and Queen Elizabeth.* London: Cape, 1960.

Rees, David. *The Son of Prophecy: Henry Tudor's Road to Bosworth.* London: Black Raven, 1985.

Rex, Richard. *Henry VIII and the English Reformation.* Basingstoke, England: Macmillan, 1993.

Richardson, R. C. *The Debate on the English Revolution Revisited.* London: Routledge, 1989.

Ridley, Jasper. *Elizabeth I.* London: Constable, 1987.

————. *Henry VIII.* London: Constable, 1984.

————. *The Life and Times of Mary Tudor.* London: Weidenfeld and Nicolson, 1973.

————. *Statesman and Saint: Cardinal Wolsey, Sir Thomas More and the Politics of Henry VIII.* New York: Viking Press, 1983.

Riggs, David. *Ben Jonson: A Life.* Cambridge, Mass.: Harvard University Press, 1989.

Rogers, Caroline. *Henry VII.* London: Hodder and Stoughton, 1991.

Rowley, Trevor. *The High Middle Ages, 1200–1500.* London: Routledge and Kegan Paul, 1986.

Rowse, A. L. *Court and Country: Studies in Tudor Social History.* Athens, Ga.: University of Georgia Press, 1987.

————. *Sir Walter Raleigh: His Family and Private Life.* Westport, Conn.: Greenwood Press, 1975.

————. *William Shakespeare: A Biography.* London: Macmillan, 1963.

Sargent, Daniel. *Thomas More.* Freeport, N.Y.: Books For Libraries Press, 1970.

Scarisbrick, John Joseph. *Henry VIII.* London: Eyre and Spottiswoode, 1968.

Schoenbaum, S. *Shakespeare's Lives.* Oxford: Clarendon Press, 1991.

Sharpe, J. A. *Crime in Early Modern England, 1550–1750.* London: Longman, 1984.

————. *Early Modern England: A Social History, 1550–1760.* London: Edward Arnold, 1987.

Simmons, R. C. *The American Colonies from Settlement to Independence.* London: Longman, 1981.

Slack, Paul. *The English Poor Law, 1531–1782.* Basingstoke, England: Macmillan, 1990.

———. *Poverty and Policy in Tudor and Stuart England.* London: Longman, 1988.

Smith, A. G. R. *The Emergence of the Nation State: The Commonwealth of England, 1529 to 1660.* London: Longman, 1984.

Smith, Lacey Baldwin. *Elizabeth Tudor: Portrait of a Queen.* London: Hutchinson, 1976.

———. *Henry VIII: The Mask of Royalty.* London: Cape, 1971.

Somerset, Anne. *Elizabeth I.* London: Weidenfeld and Nicolson, 1991.

Starkey, David. *The English Court: From the Wars of the Roses to the Civil War.* London: Longman, 1987.

Starkey, David, ed. *Privilege and Power: Lives of the Great Tudor Dynasties.* Basingstoke, England: Macmillan, 1990.

Stebbing, William. *Sir Walter Ralegh: A Biography.* New York: Lemma, 1972.

Stone, Lawrence. *The Causes of the English Revolution, 1529–1642.* London: Routledge, 1986.

Strathmann, Ernest A. *Sir Walter Ralegh: A Study in Elizabethan Skepticism.* New York: Octagon, 1973.

Sugden, J. *Sir Francis Drake.* London: Barrie and Jenkins, 1990.

Thirsk, John. *England's Agricultural Regions and Agrarian History, 1500–1750.* Basingstoke, England: Macmillan, 1987.

Thomson, George Malcolm. *Sir Francis Drake.* New York: Morrow, 1972.

Thomson, John A. F. *The Early Tudor Church and Society: 1485–1529.* London: Longman, 1993.

———. *The Transformation of Medieval England, 1370–1529.* London: Longman, 1983.

Todd, M. *Reformation to Revolution.* London: Routledge, 1994.

Waldman, Milton. *The Lady Mary: A Biography of Mary Tudor, 1516–1558.* London: Collins, 1972.

Warnicke, R. M. *The Rise and Fall of Anne Boleyn.* Cambridge: Cambridge University Press, 1989.

Warren, John. *Elizabeth I: Religion and Foreign Affairs.* London: Hodder and Stoughton, 1993.

Weinstein, Rosemary. *Tudor London.* London: Her Majesty's Stationery Office, 1994.

Weir, Alison. *The Six Wives of Henry VIII.* London: Pimlico, 1992.

Williams, Neville. *The Cardinal and the Secretary: Thomas Wolsey and Thomas Cromwell.* New York: Macmillan, 1976.

––––––. *Elizabeth I, Queen of England.* London: Weidenfeld and Nicolson, 1967.

––––––. *Francis Drake.* London: Weidenfeld and Nicolson, 1973.

––––––. *Henry VIII and His Court.* London: Weidenfeld and Nicolson, 1971.

––––––. *The Life and Times of Elizabeth I.* London: Weidenfeld and Nicolson, 1972.

––––––. *The Life and Times of Henry VII.* London: Weidenfeld and Nicolson, 1973.

Williams, Norman Lloyd. *Sir Walter Raleigh.* London: Cassell, 1988.

Williams, P. *The Tudor Regime.* Oxford: Clarendon Press, 1979.

Williamson, Hugh Ross. *Sir Walter Raleigh.* Westport, Conn.: Greenwood Press, 1978.

Williamson, James A. *The Tudor Age; 1485–1603.* London: Longman, 1979.

Winton, John. *Sir Walter Ralegh.* New York: Coward, McCann and Geoghegan, 1975.

Woodward, G. W. O. *The Dissolution of the Monasteries.* London: Blandford Press, 1966.

Wrightson, Keith. *English Society, 1580–1680.* London: Routledge, 1982.

The Stuarts (1603–1714)

Abernethy, Cecil. *Mr Pepys of Seething Lane.* London: White Lion, 1974.

Adamson, Jack H., and Harold Freeze Folland. *The Shepherd of the Ocean: an Account of Sir Walter Ralegh and His Times.* London: Bodley Head, 1969.

Albert, W. *The Turnpike Road System in England, 1663–1840.* Cambridge: Cambridge University Press, 1972.

Andrews, K. R. *Trade, Plunder and Settlement: Maritime Enterprise and the Genesis of the British Empire, 1480-1630.* Cambridge: Cambridge University Press, 1984.

Ashley, Maurice. *Charles I and Oliver Cromwell: A Study in Contrasts and Comparisons.* London: Methuen, 1987.

––––––. *Charles II: The Man and the Statesman.* London: Weidenfeld and Nicolson, 1971.

————. *England in the Seventeenth Century*. London: Hutchinson, 1978.

————. *The English Civil War: A Concise History*. Stroud, England: Alan Sutton, 1990.

————. *The House of Stuart: Its Rise and Fall*. London: Dent, 1980.

————. *James II*. London: Dent, 1977.

Ashley, Maurice, ed. *Cromwell*. Englewood Cliffs, N.J.: Prentice-Hall, 1969.

Ashton, Robert. *Counter-Revolution: The Second Civil War and Its Origins, 1646–8*. New Haven, Conn.: Yale University Press, 1994.

Ayers, Michael. *Locke*. London: Routledge, 1993.

Aylmer, G. E. *The Levellers in the English Revolution*. London: Thames and Hudson, 1975.

Bakeless, John. *Christopher Marlowe*. New York: Haskell House, 1975.

Barnett, Correlli. *Marlborough*. London: Eyre Methuen, 1974.

Barry, Jonathan, ed. *The Tudor and Stuart Town: A Reader in English Urban History, 1530–1688*. London: Longman, 1990.

Barry, Jonathan, and Christopher Brooks, ed. *The Middling Sort of People: Culture, Society and Politics in England, 1550–1800*. London: Macmillan, 1994.

Baskerville, Stephen. *Not Peace but a Sword: The Political Theology of the English Revolution*. London: Routledge, 1993.

Bax, Clifford. *Pretty Witty Nell: An Account of Nell Gwyn and Her Environment*. New York: Blom, 1969.

Baxter, S. B. *William III*. London: Longman, 1966.

Beatty, Edward Corbyn Obert. *William Penn as Social Philosopher*. New York: Octagon, 1975.

Beddard, R. *A Kingdom without a King*. Oxford: Phaidon, 1988.

Beier, A. L. *The Problem of the Poor in Tudor and Early Stuart England*. London: Methuen, 1983.

Belloc, Hilaire. *Milton*. Westport, Conn.: Greenwood Press, 1970.

Bevan, Bryan. *Marlborough the Man: A Biography of John Churchill, First Duke of Marlborough*. London: Hale, 1975.

Bingham, Caroline. *James I of England*. London: Weidenfeld and Nicolson, 1981.

Black, Jeremy. *The Politics of Britain, 1688–1800*. Manchester: Manchester University Press, 1993.

————. *A System of Ambition?: British Foreign Policy, 1660–1793*. London: Longman, 1991.

Boughner, Daniel C. *The Devil's Disciple: Ben Jonson's Debt to*

Machiavelli. New York: Philosophical Library, 1968.

Bowen, Catherine Drinker. *Francis Bacon: The Temper of a Man.* London: Hamish Hamilton, 1963.

Bowle, John. *Charles I: A Biography.* London: Weidenfeld and Nicolson, 1975.

Bradford, Gamaliel. *Samuel Pepys.* New York: Haskell House, 1975.

Brailsford, H. N. *The Levellers and the English Revolution.* Nottingham, England: Spokesman Books, 1983.

Brailsford, Mabel Richmond. *The Making of William Penn.* Freeport, N.Y.: Books For Libraries Press, 1970.

Brenner, Robert. *Merchants and Revolution: Commercial Change, Political Conflict and London's Overseas Traders, 1550–1653.* Cambridge: Cambridge University Press, 1993.

Brewer, John. *The Sinews of Power: War, Money and the English State, 1688–1783.* London: Unwin Hyman, 1989.

Bridenbaugh, C., and R. Bridenbaugh. *No Peace Beyond the Line: The English in the Caribbean, 1624–1690.* New York: Oxford University Press, 1972.

Bryant, Arthur. *Samuel Pepys.* London: Panther, 1984.

Burgess, Anthony. *Shakespeare.* London: Cape, 1970.

Burgess, Glenn. *British Political Thought: From Reformation to Revolution.* Basingstoke, England: Macmillan, 1994.

———. *The Politics of the Ancient Constitution: An Introduction to English Political Thought.* Basingstoke, England: Macmillan, 1994.

Bush, Douglas. *John Milton: A Sketch of His Life and Writings.* New York: Macmillan, 1964.

Cain, P. J., and A. G. Hopkins. *British Imperialism: Innovation and Expansion, 1688–1914.* London: Longman, 1993.

Cain, T. G. S., and Ken Robinson. *Into Another Mould: Change and Continuity in English Culture, 1625–1700.* London: Routledge, 1992.

Cannon, John. *Parliamentary Reform, 1640–1832.* London: Cambridge University Press, 1972.

Capie, Forrest H. *History of Banking, 1650–1850.* 10 vols. London: William Pickering, 1994.

Carlton, Charles. *Archbishop William Laud.* London: Routledge and Kegan Paul, 1987.

———. *Charles I: The Personal Monarch.* London: Routledge and Kegan Paul, 1983.

———. *Going to the Wars: The Experience of the British Civil Wars, 1638–1651.* London: Routledge, 1992.

Chandler, David. *Marlborough as Military Commander.* New York: Scribner, 1973.

Chapman, Hester W. *Mary II, Queen of England.* Leicester, England: F. A. Thorpe, 1974.

Chappell, Vere. *The Cambridge Companion to Locke.* Cambridge: Cambridge University Press, 1994.

Chaudhuri, K. N. *The Trading World of Asia and the English East India Company, 1660–1760.* Cambridge: Cambridge University Press, 1978.

Chute, Marchette. *Ben Jonson of Westminster.* London: Souvenir Press, 1978.

Clancy, Thomas H. *A Literary History of the English Jesuits: A Century of Books, 1615–1714.* San Francisco: Catholic Scholars Press, 1994.

Clark, J. C. D. *English Society, 1688–1832.* Cambridge: Cambridge University Press, 1985.

———. *Samuel Johnson: Literature, Religion and English Cultural Politics From the Restoration to Romanticism.* Cambridge: Cambridge University Press, 1994.

Cliffe, Trevor. *Puritan Gentry Besieged, 1650–1700.* London: Routledge, 1993.

———. *Puritans in Conflict.* London: Routledge, 1988.

Collinson, Patrick. *The Birthpangs of Protestant England: Religious and Cultural Change in the Sixteenth and Seventeenth Centuries.* Basingstoke, England: Macmillan, 1988.

Colman, D. C. *Industry in Tudor and Stuart England.* Basingstoke, England: Macmillan, 1975.

Condren, Conal. *The Language of Politics in Seventeenth-Century England.* Basingstoke, England: Macmillan, 1994.

Cook, Harold J. *Trials of an Ordinary Doctor: Joannes Groenevelt in 17th-Century London.* Baltimore, Md.: Johns Hopkins University Press, 1994.

Cope, Esther S. *Politics Without Parliaments, 1629–1640.* London: Allen and Unwin, 1987.

Coote, Stephen. *A Play of Passion: The Life of Sir Walter Raleigh.* Basingstoke, England: Macmillan, 1993.

Coward, Barry. *The Early Stuart Age.* London: Longman, 1994.

———. *Oliver Cromwell.* London: Longman, 1991.

———. *The Stuart Age: England, 1603–1714.* Harlow, England: Longman, 1994.

Cowie, L. W. *Plague and Fire, London, 1665–6.* London: Wayland, 1970.

Cowles, Virginia. *The Great Marlborough and His Duchess.* New York: Macmillan, 1983.

Cragg, Gerald R. *The Church and the Age of Reason, 1648–1789.* Harmondsworth, England: Penguin, 1960.

Cranston, Maurice. *John Locke: a Biography.* Oxford: Oxford University Press, 1985.

Crawford, Patricia. *Women and Religion in England, 1500–1720.* London: Routledge, 1993.

Currier-Briggs, N. *English Adventurers and Colonial Settlers.* London: Phillimore, 1971.

Curtis, Gila. *The Life and Times of Queen Anne.* London: Weidenfeld and Nicolson, 1972.

Cust, Richard and Ann Hughes, ed. *Conflict in Early Stuart England: Studies in Religion and Politics, 1603–1642.* London: Longman, 1989.

Davies, K. G. *The North Atlantic World in the Seventeenth Century.* Minneapolis, Minn.: University of Minnesota Press, 1974.

Dawson, Terence, and Robert S. Dupree, ed. *Seventeenth-Century English Poetry: The Annotated Anthology.* Hemel Hempstead, England: Harvester Wheatsheaf, 1994.

Deane, Phyllis, and W. A. Cole. *British Economic Growth, 1688–1959: Trends and Structure.* Cambridge: Cambridge University Press, 1969.

Derry, T. K., and M. G. Blakeway. *The Making of Britain: Life and Work Between the Renaissance and the Industrial Revolution.* London: John Murray, 1969.

Dewhurst, Kenneth. *John Locke, 1632–1704, Physician and Philosopher.* New York: Garland, 1984.

Dobry, Bonamy. *William Penn, Quaker and Pioneer.* Folcroft, Pa.: Folcroft Library Editions, 1978.

Dodd, Alfred. *Francis Bacon's Personal Life-Story.* London: Rider, 1986.

Dolan, Frances E. *Dangerous Familiars: Representations of Domestic Crime in England, 1550–1700.* Ithaca, N.Y.: Cornell University Press, 1994.

Downes, Kerry. *Christopher Wren.* London: Allen Lane, 1971.

Du Maurier, Daphne. *The Winding Stair: Francis Bacon, His Rise and Fall.* London: Gollancz, 1976.

Dunn, Mary Maples. *William Penn, Politics and Conscience.* Princeton, N.J.: Princeton University Press, 1967.

Durston, Christopher. *James I.* London: Routledge, 1993.

Dyer, Alan. *Decline and Growth in English Towns, 1400–1640.*

Basingstoke, England: Macmillan, 1991.

Dyos, H. J., and D. H. Aldcroft. *British Transport: An Economic Survey from the Seventeenth Century to the Twentieth.* Leicester: Leicester University Press, 1969.

Earle, Peter. *The Life and Times of James II.* London: Weidenfeld and Nicolson, 1972.

Endy, Melvin B. *William Penn and Early Quakerism.* Princeton, N.J.: Princeton University Press, 1973.

Falkus, Christopher. *The Life and Times of Charles II.* London: Weidenfeld and Nicolson, 1972.

Fantel, Hans. *William Penn: Apostle of Dissent.* New York: Morrow, 1974.

Fecher, Constance. *The Last Elizabethan: A Portrait of Sir Walter Ralegh.* New York: Farrar, Strauss and Giroux, 1972.

Ferguson, Moira. *Subject to Others: British Women Writers and Colonial Slavery, 1670–1834.* London: Routledge, 1992.

Fincham, Kenneth, ed. *The Early Stuart Church, 1603–1642.* Basingstoke, England: Macmillan, 1993.

Firth, C. H. *Cromwell's Army.* London: Methuen, 1962.

Fissel, M. C. *The Bishops' Wars.* Cambridge: Cambridge University Press, 1994.

Flathman, Richard E. *Thomas Hobbes: Skepticism, Individuality, and Chastened Politics.* London: Sage, 1993.

Fletcher, Anthony. *The Outbreak of the English Civil War.* London: Edward Arnold, 1985.

Ford, Boris, ed. *17th Century Britain.* Cambridge: Cambridge University Press, 1992.

Foster, Andrew. *The Church of England, 1570–1640.* London: Longman, 1994.

Foster, Elizabeth Read. *The House of Lords, 1603–1649.* Chapel Hill, N.C.: University of North Carolina Press, 1983.

Fraser, Antonia. *Cromwell, Our Chief of Men.* London: Weidenfeld and Nicolson, 1973.

———. *King Charles II.* London: Mandarin, 1990.

———. *King James VI of Scotland, I of England.* London: Weidenfeld and Nicolson, 1974.

———. *The Weaker Vessel: Woman's Lot in Seventeenth-Century England.* London: Mandarin, 1993.

French, J. Milton. *The Life Records of John Milton.* 5 vols. New York: Gordian Press, 1966.

Garnett, Richard. *Life of John Milton.* New York: AMS Press, 1970.

Gillingham, John. *Cromwell: Portrait of a Soldier.* London:

Weidenfeld and Nicolson, 1976.

Gosse, Edmund. *Raleigh.* Norwood, Pa.: Norwood Editions, 1977.

Gotch, John Alfred. *Inigo Jones.* New York: Blom, 1968.

Gould, Heywood. *Sir Christopher Wren: Renaissance Architect, Philosopher and Scientist.* New York: Watts, 1970.

Graham, Walter, ed. *The Letters of Joseph Addison.* St. Clair Shores, Mich.: Scholarly Press, 1976.

Greaves, Richard L. *Enemies Under His Feet: Radicals and Nonconformists in Britain, 1664–1677.* Stanford, Calif.: Stanford University Press, 1990.

Green, A. Wigfall. *Sir Francis Bacon.* New York: Twayne, 1966.

Green, David. *Queen Anne.* London: Collins, 1970.

Gregg, Edward. *Queen Anne.* London: Routledge and Kegan Paul, 1980.

Gregg, Pauline. *King Charles I.* London: Dent, 1981.

———. *Oliver Cromwell.* London: Dent, 1988.

Griffiths, Paul, Adam Fox, and Steven Hindle, ed. *The Experience of Authority in Early Modern England.* Basingstoke, England: Macmillan, 1994.

Halliday, F. E. *Shakespeare.* London: Thames and Hudson, 1986.

Hamilton, Elizabeth. *William's Mary: A Biography of Mary II.* London: Hamish Hamilton, 1971.

Hammond, Brean S. *Pope.* Brighton, England: Harvester Press, 1986.

Hampton, Jean. *Hobbes and the Social Contract Tradition.* Cambridge: Cambridge University Press, 1987.

Hanford, James Holly. *Milton: Poet and Humanist.* Cleveland, Ohio.: Press of Western Reserve University, 1966.

Harris, Ian. *The Mind of John Locke: A Study of Political Theory in Its Intellectual Setting.* Cambridge: Cambridge University Press, 1994.

Harris, Tim. *Politics under the Later Stuarts: Party Conflict in a Divided Society, 1660–1715.* London: Longman, 1993.

———. *Popular Culture in England, c1500–1850.* London: Macmillan, 1993.

Hart, James S. *Justice upon Petition: The House of Lords and the Reformation of Justice, 1621–1675.* London: Routledge, 1991.

Haswell, Jock. *James II: Soldier and Sailor.* London: Hamish Hamilton, 1972.

Haynes, Alan. *Robert Cecil, Earl of Salisbury, 1563–1612: Servant of Two Sovereigns.* London: Owen, 1989.

Heal, Felicity and Clive Holmes. *The Gentry in England and Wales,*

1500–1700. Basingstoke, England: Macmillan, 1994.

Hearsey, John E. N. *Young Mr. Pepys.* London: Constable, 1973.

Heathcote, T. A. *The Military in British India: the Development of British Land Forces in South Asia, 1600–1947.* Manchester: Manchester University Press, 1994.

Hibbert, Christopher. *Cavaliers and Roundheads: The English at War 1642–1649.* London: HarperCollins, 1993.

Hill, Christopher. *The Century of Revolution 1603–1714.* London: Routledge, 1991.

————. *God's Englishman: Oliver Cromwell and the English Revolution.* New York: Dial Press, 1970.

————. *The World Turned Upside Down: Radical Ideas during the English Revolution.* Harmondsworth, England: Penguin, 1975.

Hirst, Derek. *Authority and Conflict: England, 1603–1658.* London: Edward Arnold, 1986.

Holmes, G. S. *Britain after the Glorious Revolution, 1689–1714.* London: Macmillan, 1969.

————. *The Making of a Great Power: Late Stuart and Early Georgian Britain, 1660–1722.* London: Longman, 1993.

Hopkins, Eric. *Britain in the Widening World: British History, 1485–1763.* London: Nelson, 1967.

Horle, Craig W. *The Quakers and the English Legal System, 1660–1688.* Philadelphia, Pa.: University of Pennsylvania Press, 1988.

Horne, Thomas A. *Property Rights and Poverty: Political Argument in Britain, 1605–1834.* Chapel Hill, N.C.: University of North Carolina Press, 1990.

Houlbrooke, Ralph A. *The English Family, 1450–1700.* London: Longman, 1984.

Houston, R. A. *The Population History of Britain and Ireland, 1500–1750.* Basingstoke, England: Macmillan, 1992.

Howell, Roger. *Cromwell.* Boston, Mass.: Little, Brown, 1977.

Hughes, Ann. *The Causes of the English Civil War.* Basingstoke, England: Macmillan, 1991.

Hull, William Isaac. *William Penn: A Topical Biography.* Freeport, N.Y.: Books For Libraries Press, 1971.

Hutchings, Donald, ed. *Late Seventeenth Century Scientists.* Oxford: Pergamon Press, 1969.

Hutchinson, Francis Ernest. *Milton and the English Mind.* New York: Haskell House, 1974.

Hutton, Ronald. *The British Republic, 1649–1660.* Basingstoke, England: Macmillan, 1990.

————. *The Rise and Fall of Merry England: The Ritual Year,*

1400– 1700. Oxford: Oxford University Press, 1994.

Israel, J. *The Anglo-Dutch Moment.* Cambridge: Cambridge University Press, 1991.

Jones, Esmor. *Milton.* Glasgow, Scotland: Blackie, 1977.

Jones, G. H. *Convergent Forces: Immediate Causes of the Revolution of 1688 in England.* Ames, Iowa.: Iowa State University Press, 1990.

Jones, J. R. *Britain and the World, 1649–1815.* London: Fontana, 1980.

———. *Charles II: Royal Politician.* London: Allen and Unwin, 1987.

———. *Country and Court: England, 1658–1714.* London: Edward Arnold, 1978.

———. *Marlborough.* Cambridge: Cambridge University Press, 1993.

———. *The Revolution of 1688 in England.* London: Weidenfeld and Nicolson, 1972.

Keay, J. *The Honourable Company: A History of the English East India Company.* London: HarperCollins, 1991.

Kenyon, F. W. *Glory and the Dream: the Story of John Churchill, 1st Duke of Marlborough.* London: Hutchinson, 1972.

Kenyon, J. P. *The Civil Wars of England.* London: Weidenfeld and Nicolson, 1988.

———. *The Popish Plot.* London: Heinemann, 1972.

———. *Stuart England.* Harmondsworth, England: Penguin, 1985.

———. *The Stuarts.* London: Severn House, 1977.

King, Preston, ed. *Thomas Hobbes: Critical Assessments.* 4 vols. London: Routledge, 1992.

Kishlansky, M. *The Rise of the New Model Army.* Cambridge: Cambridge University Press, 1979.

Knoppers, Laura Lunger. *Historicizing Milton: Spectacle, Power and Poetry in Restoration England.* Athens, Ga.: University of Georgia Press, 1994.

Lamont, William, ed. *Baxter: A Holy Commonwealth.* Cambridge: Cambridge University Press, 1994.

Laslett, Peter, ed. *Locke: Two Treatises of Government.* Cambridge: Cambridge University Press, 1988.

Laurence, Anne. *Women in England, 1500–1760: A Social History.* London: Weidenfeld and Nicolson, 1994.

Lawson, Philip. *The East India Company: A History.* London: Longman, 1993.

Lee, Stephen J. *The Thirty Years War.* London: Routledge, 1991.

Levack, B. P. *The Formation of the British State: England, Scotland and the Union, 1603–1707.* Oxford: Clarendon Press, 1987.

Linklater, Eric. *Ben Jonson and King James.* Port Washington, N.Y.: Kennikat Press, 1972.

Little, Bryan. *Sir Christopher Wren: A Historical Biography.* London: Hale, 1975.

Lloyd, S. A. *Ideals as Interests in Hobbes 'Leviathan': The Power of Mind over Matter.* Cambridge: Cambridge University Press, 1992.

Lloyd, T. H. *England and the German Hanse, 1157–1611: A Study of Their Trade and Commercial Diplomacy.* Cambridge: Cambridge University Press, 1991.

Lockyer, Roger. *The Early Stuarts: A Political History of England, 1603–1642.* London: Longman, 1989.

———. *Tudor and Stuart Britain, 1471–1714.* Harlow, England: Longman, 1985.

Lubbock, Percy. *Samuel Pepys.* Folcroft, Pa.: Folcroft Library Editions, 1974.

Lynch, Michael. *The Interregnum: 1649–60.* Abingdon, England: Hodder and Stoughton, 1994.

MacCurtain, Margaret. *Tudor and Stuart Ireland.* Dublin: Gill and Macmillan, 1972.

MacGregor-Hastie, R. *Nell Gwyn.* London: Robert Hale, 1987.

Mack, Maynard. *Alexander Pope: a Life.* New Haven, Conn.: Yale University Press, 1985.

Manuel, Frank E. *A Portrait of Isaac Newton.* London: Oxford University Press, 1968.

Marshall, John. *John Locke: Resistance, Religion and Responsibility.* Cambridge: Cambridge University Press, 1994.

Mathew, David. *James I.* London: Eyre and Spottiswoode, 1967.

McFarlane, Anthony. *The British in the Americas, 1480–1815.* London: Longman, 1994.

Miles, Rosalind. *Ben Jonson: His Life and Work.* London: Routledge and Kegan Paul, 1986.

Miller, John. *Charles II.* London: Weidenfeld and Nicolson, 1991.

———. *James II: A Study in Kingship.* London: Methuen, 1991.

———. *The Life and Times of William and Mary.* London: Weidenfeld and Nicolson, 1974.

———. *Seeds of Liberty: 1688 and the Shaping of Modern Britain.* London: Souvenir Press, 1988.

Minchington, W. *The Growth of English Overseas Trade in the Seventeenth and Eighteenth Centuries.* London: Methuen, 1969.

Molesworth, W., ed. *Collected Works of Thomas Hobbes.* 12 vols. Bristol: Thoemmes Press, 1992.

Monod, P. K. *Jacobitism and the English People, 1688–1788.* Cambridge: Cambridge University Press, 1989.

Morrill, John. *The Nature of the English Revolution.* London: Longman, 1993.

Morrill, John, ed. *Oliver Cromwell and the English Revolution.* London: Longman, 1990.

Mullett, Michael. *James II and English Politics, 1678–1688.* London: Routledge, 1994.

Newman, P. R. *Atlas of the English Civil War.* London: Croom Helm, 1985.

——. *The Battle of Marston Moor, 1644.* Chichester, England: Bird, 1981.

——. *Companion to the English Civil Wars.* New York: Facts on File, 1990.

——. *The Old Service: Royalist Regimental Colonels and the Civil War, 1642–1646.* Manchester: Manchester University Press, 1993.

Nicholls, M. *Investigating Gunpowder Plot.* Manchester: Manchester University Press, 1991.

O'Connor, D. J. *John Locke.* New York: Dover, 1967.

Ollard, Richard. *The Image of the King: Charles I and Charles II.* London: Pimlico, 1993.

——. *Pepys: A Biography.* London: Hodder and Stoughton, 1974.

Outhwaite, R. B. *Dearth, Public Policy and Social Disturbance in England, 1550–1800.* Basingstoke, England: Macmillan, 1991.

Palmer, John. *Ben Jonson.* Port Washington, N.Y.: Kennikat Press, 1967.

Palmer, Tony. *Charles II: Portrait of an Age.* London: Cassell, 1979.

Parkin, Rebecca Price. *The Poetic Workmanship of Alexander Pope.* New York: Octagon, 1966.

Parry, R. H. *The English Civil War and After, 1642–1658.* London: Macmillan, 1970.

Peck, Linda Levy. *Court Patronage and Corruption in Early Stuart England.* London: Routledge, 1993.

Platt, Colin. *The Great Rebuildings of Tudor and Stuart England: Revolutions in Architectural Taste.* London: UCL Press, 1994.

Plumb, J. H. *The Growth of Political Stability, 1675–1725.* London: Macmillan, 1967.

Pocock, J. G. A., Gordon J. Schochet, and Lois G. Schwoerer, eds. *The Varieties of British Political Thought, 1500–1800.* Cambridge: Cambridge University Press, 1994.

Pomfret, J. E., and F. M. Shumway. *Founding the American Colonies, 1583–1660.* New York: Harper and Row, 1970.

Porter, Roy. *Disease, Medicine and Society in England, 1550–1860.* Basingstoke, England: Macmillan, 1993.

Prall, Stuart E. *The Bloodless Revolution: England, 1688.* Madison, Wisc.: University of Wisconsin Press, 1985.

Prior, Mary, ed. *Women in English Society, 1500–1800.* London: Methuen, 1985.

Pythian-Adams, Charles. *Societies, Cultures and Kinship, 1580–1850: Cultural Provinces and English Local History.* London: Pinter, 1993.

Quennell, Peter. *Alexander Pope: the Education of Genius, 1688–1728.* New York: Stein and Day, 1968.

———. *Shakespeare: The Poet and His Background.* London: Weidenfeld and Nicolson, 1963.

Quinn, D. B. *England and the Discovery of America, 1481–1620.* New York: Knopf, 1974.

Quintrell, Brian. *Charles I: 1625–1640.* London: Longman, 1993.

Reik, Miriam M. *The Golden Lands of Thomas Hobbes.* Detroit, Mich.: Wayne State University Press, 1977.

Richardson, R. C. *The Debate on the English Revolution Revisited.* London: Routledge, 1989.

Richardson, R. C., ed. *Town and Countryside in the English Revolution.* Manchester: Manchester University Press, 1993.

Riggs, David. *Ben Jonson: A Life.* Cambridge, Mass.: Harvard University Press. 1989.

Rogers, H. C. B. *Battles and Generals of the Civil War, 1642–1651.* London: Seeley, 1968.

Rogow, Arnold A. *Thomas Hobbes: Radical in the Service of Reaction.* New York: Norton, 1986.

Roots, Ivan Alan, ed. *Cromwell: A Profile.* New York: Hill and Wang, 1973.

Roseveare, Henry. *The Financial Revolution, 1660–1760.* Longman: London, 1991.

Rowse, A. L. *Sir Walter Ralegh: His Family and Private Life.* Westport, Conn.: Greenwood Press, 1975.

———. *William Shakespeare: A Biography.* London: Macmillan, 1963.

Ruffhead, Owen. *The Life of Alexander Pope.* Hildesheim, West Germany: Olms, 1968.

Russell, C. *The Causes of the English Civil War.* Oxford: Clarendon

Press, 1990.

Russo, John Paul. *Alexander Pope: Tradition and Identity.* Cambridge, Mass.: Harvard University Press, 1972.

Schoenbaum, S. *Shakespeare's Lives.* Oxford: Clarendon Press, 1991.

Schultz, P. *Isaac Newton: Scientific Genius.* Champaign, Ill.: Garrard, 1972.

Seaward, Paul. *The Restoration, 1660–1688.* Basingstoke, England: Macmillan, 1991.

Shapin, Steven. *A Short History of Truth: Civility and Science in Seventeenth Century England.* Chicago: University of Chicago Press, 1994.

Sharpe, J. A. *Crime in Early Modern England, 1550–1750.* London: Longman, 1984.

———. *Early Modern England: A Social History, 1550–1760.* London: Edward Arnold, 1987.

Sharpe, Kevin. *The Personal Rule of Charles I.* New Haven, Conn.: Yale University Press, 1992.

Sharpe, Kevin, and Peter Lake, ed. *Culture and Politics in Early Stuart England.* Basingstoke, England: Macmillan, 1994.

Simmons, R. C. *The American Colonies from Settlement to Independence.* London: Longman, 1981.

Slack, Paul. *The English Poor Law, 1531–1782.* Basingstoke, England: Macmillan, 1990.

———. *Poverty and Policy in Tudor and Stuart England.* London: Longman, 1988.

Slater, Victor L. *Noble Government: The Stuart Lord Lieutenancy and the Transformation of English Politics.* Athens, Ga.: University of Georgia Press, 1994.

Smith, A. G. R. *The Emergence of the Nation State: The Commmonwealth of England 1529 to 1660.* London: Longman, 1984.

Sommerville, J. P. *Politics and Ideology in England, 1603–1640.* London: Longman, 1986.

———. *Thomas Hobbes: Political Ideas in Historical Context.* Basingstoke, England: Macmillan, 1992.

Sorrell, Tom. *Hobbes.* London: Routledge, 1991.

Speck, W. A. *Tory and Whig: The Struggle in the Constituencies, 1701–1715.* London: Macmillan, 1970.

Starkey, David. *The English Court: From the Wars of the Roses to the Civil War.* London: Longman, 1987.

Stebbing, William. *Sir Walter Ralegh: A Biography.* New York:

Lemma, 1972.

Stephen, Leslie. *Alexander Pope.* New York: AMS Press, 1968.

———. *Hobbes.* Bristol: Thoemmes Press, 1991.

Stevenson, John. *Popular Disturbances in England, 1700–1832.* London: Longman, 1992.

Stone, Lawrence. *The Causes of the English Revolution, 1529–1642.* London: Routledge, 1986.

Stone, Lawrence, ed. *An Imperial State at War: Britain From 1689–1815.* London: Routledge, 1994.

Strathmann, Ernest A. *Sir Walter Ralegh: A Study in Elizabethan Skepticism.* New York: Octagon, 1973.

Sturt, Mary. *Francis Bacon: A Biography.* Norwood, Pa.: Norwood Editions, 1975.

Tanner, J. R. *Mr. Pepys: An Introduction to the Diary Together with a Sketch of His Later Life.* Westport, Conn.: Greenwood Press, 1971.

Thirsk, John. *England's Agricultural Regions and Agrarian History, 1500–1750.* Basingstoke, England: Macmillan, 1987.

Thorpe, James. *John Milton: The Inner Life.* San Marino, Calif.: Huntington Library, 1983.

Tite, C. G. C. *Impeachment and Parliamentary Judicature in Early Stuart England.* London: Athlone Press, 1974.

Toynbee, M., and P. Young. *Cropredy Bridge, 1644: The Campaign and the Battle.* Kineton, England: Roundwood Press, 1970.

Trevor, Muriel. *The Shadow of a Crown: the Life Story of James II of England and VII of Scotland.* London: Constable, 1988.

Trevor-Roper, Hugh. *Archbishop Laud, 1573–1645.* Basingstoke, England: Macmillan, 1988.

Tuck, Richard, ed. *Hobbes: Leviathan.* Cambridge: Cambridge University Press, 1991.

Tully, James. *An Approach to Political Philosophy: Locke in Contexts.* Cambridge: Cambridge University Press, 1993.

Ubbelohde, C. *The American Colonies and the British Empire, 1607–1763.* London: Routledge, 1968.

Underdown, D. *Pride's Purge.* Oxford: Clarendon Press, 1971.

Van Der Zee, Barbara. *William and Mary.* London: Macmillan, 1973.

Walsh, John, Colin Haydon, and Stephen Taylor, eds. *The Church of England c1689–c1833: From Toleration to Tractarianism* New York: Cambridge University Press, 1993.

Watson, David Robin. *The Life and Times of Charles I.* London: Weidenfeld and Nicolson, 1972.

Weatherill, Lorna. *Consumer Behaviour and Material Culture in*

Britain 1660–1760. London: Methuen, 1988.

Wedgwood, C. V. *The King's Peace, 1637–1641*. Harmondsworth, England: Penguin, 1983.

———. *The Thirty Years War*. London: Methuen, 1981.

Weinbrot, Howard D. *Britannica's Issue: The Rise of British Literature From Dryden to Ossian*. Cambridge: Cambridge University Press, 1993.

Weir, Rosemary. *The Man Who Built a City: A Life of Sir Christopher Wren*. New York: Farrar, Straus and Giroux, 1971.

Westfall, Richard S. *Never At Rest: A Biography of Isaac Newton*. Cambridge: Cambridge University Press, 1980.

Wheatley, Henry B. *Samuel Pepys and the World He Lived In*. New York: Haskell House, 1975.

Whinney, Margaret. *Christopher Wren*. New York: Praeger, 1971.

Wildes, Harry Emerson. *William Penn*. New York: Macmillan, 1974.

Willey, Basil. *The Seventeenth Century Background: Studies in the Thought of the Age in Relation to Poetry and Religion*. London: Routledge, 1986.

Williams, Charles. *Bacon*. Norwood, Pa.: Norwood Editions, 1978.

Williams, Norman Lloyd. *Sir Walter Raleigh*. London: Cassell, 1988.

Williamson, Hugh Ross. *Sir Walter Raleigh*. Westport, Conn.: Greenwood Press, 1978.

Wilson, Adrian. *The Making of Man-Midwifery: Childbirth in England, 1660-1770*. London: UCL Press, 1994.

Wilson, Charles. *England's Apprenticeship, 1603–1763*. London: Longman, 1984.

Winton, John. *Sir Walter Ralegh*. New York: Coward, McCann and Geoghegan, 1975.

Woolrych, Austin. *Battles of the English Civil War*. London: Batsford, 1961.

———. *England without a King*. London: Routledge, 1983.

Wormald, B. H. G. *Francis Bacon: History, Politics and Science, 1561– 1626*. Cambridge: Cambridge University Press, 1993.

Wrightson, Keith. *English Society, 1580–1680*. London: Routledge, 1982.

Young, Peter. *Edgehill, 1642: The Campaign and Battle*. Kineton, England: Roundwood Press, 1968.

———. *Naseby, 1645: The Campaign and the Battle*. London: Century, 1985.

Young, P., and R. Holmes. *The English Civil War*. London: Eyre Methuen, 1974.

Zakai, A. *Exile and Kingdom: History and Apocalypse in the Puri-

tan Migration to America. Cambridge: Cambridge University Press, 1992.

The Georgians (1714–1830)

Abel-Smith, B., and R. Stevens. *Lawyers and the Courts: A Sociological Study of the English Legal System, 1750–1965.* London: Heinemann, 1967.

Addy, John. *The Agrarian Revolution.* Harlow, England: Longman, 1972.

Ainsworth, William Harrison. *Beau Nash, or, Bath in the Eighteenth Century.* Bath: Chivers, 1977.

Albert, W. *The Turnpike Road System in England, 1663–1840.* Cambridge: Cambridge University Press, 1972.

Anderson, M. S. *The Eastern Question, 1774–1923.* London: Macmillan, 1966.

Andrews, Allen. *The King Who Lost America: George III and Independence.* London: Jupiter, 1976.

Andrews, Malcolm. *The Search for the Picturesque: Landscape Aesthetics and Tourism in Britain, 1760–1800.* Aldershot, England: Scolar Press, 1989.

Anstey, R. T. *The Atlantic Slave Trade and British Abolition, 1760–1810.* London: Macmillan, 1975.

Ashley, P. *The Glorious Revolution of 1788.* London: Hodder and Stoughton, 1966.

Ashton, T. S. *The Industrial Revolution, 1760–1830.* Oxford: Oxford University Press, 1968.

Ashton, T. S., and J. Sykes. *The Coal Industry of the Eighteenth Century.* Manchester: Manchester University Press, 1964.

Aspin, Chris. *The Cotton Industry.* Aylesbury, England: Shire Publications, 1981.

Atkinson, Charles Milner. *Jeremy Bentham: His Life and Work.* New York: AMS Press, 1971.

Ayling, Stanley. *Edmund Burke: His Life and Opinions.* London: John Murray, 1988.

———. *The Elder Pitt, Earl of Chatham.* London: Collins, 1976.

———. *Fox: the Life of Charles James Fox.* London: John Murray, 1991.

———. *George the Third.* London: Collins, 1972.

———. *John Wesley.* London: Collins, 1979.

Baker, Frank. *John Wesley and the Church of England.* Nashville,

Tenn.: Abingdon Press, 1970.

Barker, T. C., and Dorian Gerhold. *The Rise and Fall of Road Transport, 1700–1990.* Basingstoke, England: Macmillan, 1993.

Barnett, Correlli. *Marlborough.* London: Eyre Methuen, 1974.

Barry, Jonathan, and Christopher Brooks, eds. *The Middling Sort of People: Culture, Society and Politics in England, 1550–1800.* London: Macmillan, 1994.

Bassett, D. K. *British Trade and Policy in Indonesia and Malaysia in the Late Eighteenth Century.* Zug, Switzerland: Inter Documentation Company, 1971.

Bate, W. Jackson. *Samuel Johnson.* New York: Harcourt Brace Jovanovich, 1977.

Bayly, C. A. *Imperial Meridian: the British Empire and the World, 1780–1830.* London: Longman, 1989.

Beaglehole, J. C. *The Life of Captain James Cook.* Stanford, Calif.: Stanford University Press, 1974.

Beaglehole, J. C., ed. *The Journals of Captain James Cook on His Voyages of Discovery.* 4 vols. Cambridge: Cambridge University Press, 1955-1974.

Beckett, John. *The Rise and Fall of the Grenvilles: The Dukes of Buckingham and Chandos, 1710 to 1921.* Manchester: Manchester University Press, 1994.

Bence-Jones, Mark. *Clive of India.* New York: St Martin's Press, 1975.

Bennett, George. *The Concept of Empire: Burke to Attlee, 1774–1947.* London: Black, 1962.

Bevan, Bryan. *Marlborough the Man: A Biography of John Churchill, First Duke of Marlborough.* London: Hale, 1975.

Birch, Alan. *Economic History of the Iron and Steel Industry, 1784–1879.* London: Frank Cass, 1967.

Black, Jeremy. *Pitt the Elder.* Cambridge: Cambridge University Press, 1992.

———. *The Politics of Britain, 1688–1800.* Manchester: Manchester University Press, 1993.

———. *Robert Walpole and the Nature of Politics in Early Eighteenth Century Britain.* Basingstoke, England: Macmillan, 1990.

———. *A System of Ambition?: British Foreign Policy, 1660–1793.* London: Longman, 1991.

Borsay, Peter, ed. *The Eighteenth Century Town: a Reader in English Urban History, 1688–1820.* London: Longman, 1990.

Brewer, John. *The Sinews of Power: War, Money and the English State, 1688–1783.* London: Unwin Hyman, 1989.

Briggs, Asa. *The Age of Improvement, 1783–1867.* London: Longman, 1979.

———. *Iron Bridge to Crystal Palace.* London: Thames and Hudson, 1979.

Brooke, John. *The Chatham Administration, 1766–1768.* Westport, Conn.: Greenwood Press, 1976.

———. *The House of Commons, 1754–1790.* London: Oxford University Press, 1968.

———. *King George III.* London: Constable, 1972.

Brown, P. A. *The French Revolution in English History.* London: Frank Cass, 1965.

Brown, Peter Douglas. *William Pitt, Earl of Chatham: The Great Commoner.* London: Allen and Unwin, 1978.

Brown, Richard. *Church and State in Modern Britain, 1700–1850.* London: Routledge, 1991.

———. *Society and Economy in Modern Britain, 1700–1850.* London: Routledge, 1991.

Burnett, John. *The Experience of Unemployment, 1790–1990.* London: Routledge, 1994.

Burns, J. H., and H. L. A. Hart, ed. *Jeremy Bentham: A Fragment on Government.* Cambridge: Cambridge University Press, 1988.

Burton, Anthony. *Josiah Wedgwood: A Biography.* London: Deutsch, 1976.

Busch, B. C. *Wars and Revolutions: Britain, 1760–1815.* London: Edward Arnold, 1982.

Cain, P. J., and A. G. Hopkins. *British Imperialism: Innovation and Expansion, 1688–1914.* London: Longman, 1993.

Cameron, R. *Banking in the Early Stages of Industrialization.* London: Oxford University Press, 1967.

Cannon, John. *Parliamentary Reform, 1640–1832.* London: Cambridge University Press, 1972.

———. *The Whig Ascendancy: Colloquies on Hanoverian England.* London: Edward Arnold, 1981.

Capie, Forrest H. *History of Banking, 1650–1850.* 10 vols. London: William Pickering, 1994.

Carswell, J. *The South Sea Bubble.* Stroud, England: Alan Sutton, 1993.

Case, S. C. *The Industrial Revolution.* London: Evans Brothers, 1975.

Cashin, Edward J. *Governor Henry Ellis and the Transformation of British North America.* Athens, Ga.: University of Georgia Press, 1994.

Chamberlain, Muriel E. *Pax Britannica?: British Foreign Policy, 1789–1914*. London: Longman, 1988.

Chambers, J. D., and G. E. Mingay. *The Agricultural Revolution, 1750–1880*. London: Batsford, 1966.

Chandler, David. *Marlborough as Military Commander*. New York: Scribner, 1973.

Chapman, S. D. *The Cotton Industry in the Industrial Revolution*. Basingstoke, England: Macmillan, 1987.

Chaudhuri, K. N. *The Trading World of Asia and the English East India Company, 1660–1760*. Cambridge: Cambridge University Press, 1978.

Chaudhuri, Nirad C. *Clive of India: A Political and Psychological Essay*. London: Barrie and Jenkins, 1975.

Christie, Ian R. *Crisis of Empire: Great Britain and the American Colonies, 1754–1783*. London: Edward Arnold, 1966.

———. *Wars and Revolutions: Britain 1760–1815*. London: Edward Arnold, 1982.

Christie, Ian R., and Benjamin W. Labaree. *Empire or Independence, 1760–1776*. New York: Norton, 1976.

Claeys, Gregory, ed. *Utopias of the British Enlightenment*. Cambridge: Cambridge University Press, 1994.

Clark, J. C. D. *English Society, 1688–1832*. Cambridge: Cambridge University Press, 1985.

Clarke, John. *The Life and Times of George III*. London: Weidenfeld and Nicolson, 1972.

Coats, Alice Margaret. *Lord Bute: an Illustrated Life of John Stuart, Third Earl of Bute, 1713–1792*. Aylesbury, England: Shire Publications, 1975.

Cole, Hubert. *Beau Brummell*. London: Granada, 1977.

Colley, Linda. *Britons: Forging the Nation, 1707–1837*. London: Pimlico, 1994.

Cormack, Malcolm. *Constable*. Oxford: Phaidon, 1986.

Cowie, Leonard W. *Edmund Burke, 1729–1797: A Bibliography*. Westport, Conn.: Greenwood Press, 1994.

Cowles, Virginia. *The Great Marlborough and His Duchess*. New York: Macmillan, 1983.

Cragg, Gerald R. *The Church and the Age of Reason, 1648–1789*. Harmondsworth, England: Penguin, 1960.

Crawford, Patricia. *Women and Religion in England, 1500–1720*. London: Routledge, 1993.

Curtin, P. D. *The Image of Africa: British Ideas and Action, 1780–1850*. London: Macmillan, 1965.

Davie, Donald. *The Eighteenth–Century Hymn in England.* Cambridge: Cambridge University Press, 1993.

Deane, Phyllis. *The First Industrial Revolution.* Cambridge: Cambridge University Press, 1979.

Deane, Phyllis, and W. A. Cole. *British Economic Growth, 1688–1959: Trends and Structure.* Cambridge: Cambridge University Press, 1969.

Derry, John. *Politics in the Age of Fox, Pitt and Liverpool.* Basingstoke, England: Macmillan, 1990.

Derry, T. K., and M. G. Blakeway. *The Making of Britain: Life and Work Between the Renaissance and the Industrial Revolution.* London: John Murray, 1969.

Dickerson, O. M. *The Navigation Acts and the American Revolution.* New York: Barnes, 1963.

————. *The Politics of the People in Eighteenth–Century Britain.* Basingstoke, England: Macmillan, 1994.

Dickinson, H. T. *British Radicalism and the French Revolution, 1789– 1815.* Oxford: Blackwell, 1985.

————. *Walpole and the Whig Supremacy.* London: English Universities Press, 1973.

Dickson, P. G. M. *The Financial Revolution in England.* London: Macmillan, 1967.

Digby, Anne. *Making a Medical Living: Doctors and Patients in the English Market for Medicine, 1720–1911.* Cambridge: Cambridge University Press, 1994.

Dyos, H. J., and D. H. Aldcroft. *British Transport: An Economic Survey from the Seventeenth Century to the Twentieth.* Leicester: Leicester University Press, 1969.

Edwardes, Michael. *British India, 1772–1947.* London: Sidgwick and Jackson, 1967.

————. *Clive, The Heaven-Born General.* London: Hart-Davis MacGibbon, 1977.

Edwards, Michael M. *The Growth of the British Cotton Trade, 1780– 1815.* Manchester: Manchester University Press, 1967.

Ehrman, J. *The Younger Pitt.* 2 vols. London: Constable, 1969.

Elbourne, R. *Music and Tradition in Early Industrial Lancashire, 1780–1840.* Woodbridge, England: Brewer, 1980.

Emsley, Clive. *British Society and the French Wars, 1793–1815.* London: Macmillan, 1979.

————. *Crime and Society in England, 1750–1900.* London: Longman, 1987.

Evans, Eric. *The Forging of the Modern State: Early Industrial Brit-*

ain, 1783–1870. London: Longman, 1983.

———. *Political Parties in Britain, 1783–1867.* London: Methuen, 1985.

Ferguson, Moira. *Subject to Others: British Women Writers and Colonial Slavery, 1670–1834.* London: Routledge, 1992.

Fitton, R. S. *The Arkwrights: Spinners of Fortune.* Manchester: Manchester University Press, 1989.

Flinn, M. W. *The Origins of the Industrial Revolution.* London: Longman, 1966.

Ford, Boris, ed. *18th Century Britain.* Cambridge: Cambridge University Press, 1992.

Fraser, John Lloyd. *John Constable, 1776–1837: The Man and His Mistress.* London: Hutchinson, 1976.

Frost, Alan. *Convicts and Empire: A Naval Question, 1776–1811.* Melbourne, Australia: Oxford University Press, 1980.

Fulford, Roger. *Hanover to Windsor.* London: Batsford, 1960.

Furniss, Tom. *Edmund Burke's Aesthetic Ideology: Language, Gender and Political Economy in Revolution.* Cambridge: Cambridge University Press, 1993.

Garnett, Jane, and Colin Matthew, ed. *Revival and Religion since 1700: Essays for John Walsh.* London: Hambledon Press, 1993.

Garrett, Richard. *General Wolfe.* London: Barker, 1975.

———. *Robert Clive.* London: Barker, 1976.

Gascoigne, John. *Joseph Banks and the English Enlightenment: Useful Knowledge and Polite Culture.* Cambridge: Cambridge University Press, 1994.

Gatrell, V. A. C. *The Hanging Tree: Execution and the English People, 1770–1868.* Oxford: Oxford University Press, 1994.

Gauldie, Enid. *Cruel Habitations: A History of Working-Class Housing, 1780–1918.* London: Allen and Unwin, 1974.

Gibson, William. *Church, State and Society, 1760–1850.* Basingstoke, England: Macmillan, 1994.

Griffiths, Paul, Adam Fox, and Steven Hindle, ed. *The Experience of Authority in Early Modern England.* Basingstoke, England: Macmillan, 1994.

Hadfield, Charles. *The Canal Age.* Newton Abbot, England: David and Charles, 1968.

Hammond, Brean S. *Pope.* Brighton, England: Harvester Press, 1986.

Harris, Ian, ed. *Burke: Pre-Revolutionary Writings.* Cambridge: Cambridge University Press, 1993.

Harris, J. R. *The British Iron Industry, 1700–1850.* Basingstoke,

England: Macmillan, 1988.

Harris, Tim. *Popular Culture in England, c1500–1850.* London: Macmillan, 1993.

Hartwell, R. M. *The Causes of the Industrial Revolution in England.* London: Methuen, 1967.

———. *The Industrial Revolution.* Oxford: Blackwell, 1970.

———. *The Industrial Revolution and Economic Growth.* London: Methuen, 1971.

Hattersley, Roy. *Nelson.* New York: Saturday Review Press, 1974.

Hatton, Ragnild. *George I: Elector and King.* London: Thames and Hudson, 1978.

Haydon, Colin. *Anti–Catholicism in Eighteenth–Century England: A Political and Social Study.* Manchester: Manchester University Press, 1993.

Hayes, J. *The Drawings of Thomas Gainsborough.* 2 vols. London: Zwemmer, 1970.

Heathcote, T. A. *The Military in British India: The Development of British Land Forces in South Asia, 1600–1947.* Manchester: Manchester University Press, 1994.

Hempton, David. *Methodism and Politics in British Society, 1750–1850.* London: Hutchinson, 1984.

Hibbert, Christopher. *Africa Explored: Europeans in the Dark Continent, 1769–1889.* London: Allen Lane, 1982.

———. *Nelson: A Personal History.* London: Viking, 1994.

———. *The Personal History of Samuel Johnson.* Harlow, England: Longman, 1971.

———. *Redcoats and Rebels: The War for America, 1770–1781.* London: Grafton, 1990.

Hills, Richard L. *Power From Steam: A History of the Stationary Steam Engine.* Cambridge: Cambridge University Press, 1993.

Hobsbawm, Eric. *Industry and Empire.* London: Weidenfeld and Nicolson, 1968.

Holmes, G. S. *The Making of a Great Power: Late Stuart and Early Georgian Britain, 1660–1722.* London: Longman, 1993.

Holmes, Geoffrey, and Daniel Szechi. *The Age of Oligarchy: Pre-Industrial Britain, 1722–1783.* London: Longman, 1993.

Hoobler, Dorothy, and Thomas Hoobler. *The Voyages of Captain Cook.* New York: Putnam, 1983.

Hopkins, Eric. *Britain in the Widening World: British History, 1485–1763.* London: Nelson, 1967.

Horne, Thomas A. *Property Rights and Poverty: Political Argument in Britain, 1605–1834.* Chapel Hill, N.C.: University of North

Carolina Press, 1990.

Hough, Richard. *Captain Bligh and Mr Christian: The Men and the Mutiny.* New York: Dutton, 1973.

————. *Captain James Cook: Prince of Navigators.* Abingdon, England: Hodder and Stoughton, 1994.

Howarth, David, and Stephen Howarth. *Lord Nelson: The Immortal Memory.* New York: Viking, 1989.

Hudson, Pat. *The Industrial Revolution.* London: Edward Arnold, 1992.

Humble, Richard. *Captain Bligh.* London: Barker, 1976.

Humphreys, A. R. *The Augustan World: Life and Letters in Eighteenth Century England.* London: Methuen, 1964.

Jain, Nalini, and John Richardson. *Eighteenth-Century English Poetry: The Annotated Anthology.* New York: Harvester Wheatsheaf, 1994.

Jarrett, Derek. *Pitt the Younger.* New York: Scribner, 1974.

Jenkins, D. T., and K. G. Ponting. *The British Wool Textile Industry, 1770–1914.* London: Heinemann, 1982.

Johnson, Nichola. *Eighteenth Century London.* London: Her Majesty's Stationery Office, 1991.

Jones, J. R. *Britain and the World, 1649–1815.* London: Fontana, 1980.

————. *Marlborough.* Cambridge: Cambridge University Press, 1993.

Keay, John. *The Honourable Company: A History of the English East India Company.* London: HarperCollins, 1991.

Kemp, B. *Sir Robert Walpole.* London: Weidenfeld and Nicolson, 1976.

Kennedy, Gavin. *Bligh.* London: Duckworth, 1978.

Kenyon, F. W. *Glory and the Dream: The Story of John Churchill, 1st Duke of Marlborough.* London: Hutchinson, 1972.

Kerridge, Eric. *The Agricultural Revolution.* London: Allen and Unwin, 1967.

Klein, Lawrence E. *Shaftesbury and the Culture of Politeness: Moral Discourse and Cultural Politics in Early Eighteenth–Century England.* Cambridge: Cambridge University Press, 1994.

Laurence, Anne. *Women in England, 1500–1760: A Social History.* London: Weidenfeld and Nicolson, 1994.

Lawford, James Philip. *Clive, Proconsul of India: A Biography.* London: Allen and Unwin, 1976.

Lawson, Philip. *The East India Company: A History.* London: Longman, 1993.

————. *The Imperial Challenge: Quebec and Britain in the Age of the American Revolution.* London: UCL Press, 1994.

Leppert, R. *Music and Image: Domestic Ideology and Socio-Cultural Formation in Eighteenth Century England.* Cambridge: Cambridge University Press, 1988.

Leslie, Michael, and Timothy Raylor. *Culture and Cultivation in Early Modern England.* Leicester, England: Leicester University Press, 1992.

Levack, B. P. *The Formation of the British State: England, Scotland and the Union, 1603–1707.* Oxford: Clarendon Press, 1987.

Lindsay, Jack. *Thomas Gainsborough: His Life and Art.* London: Granada, 1981.

Lipsky, Abram. *John Wesley: A Portrait.* New York: AMS Press, 1971.

Lloyd, Alan. *The Wickedest Age: The Life and Times of George III.* Newton Abbot, England: David and Charles, 1971.

Macfie, A. L. *The Eastern Question, 1774–1923.* London: Longman, 1989.

Mack, Maynard. *Alexander Pope: A Life.* New Haven, Conn.: Yale University Press, 1985.

Marlow, Joyce. *The Life and Times of George I.* London: Weidenfeld and Nicolson, 1973.

Marshall, Dorothy. *Eighteenth Century England: 1714–1784.* London: Longman, 1974.

————. *Industrial England, 1776–1851.* London: Routledge and Kegan Paul, 1982.

Marshall, J. D. *The Old Poor Law, 1795–1834.* London: Macmillan, 1985.

McCord, Norman M. *Free Trade: Theory and Practice from Adam Smith to Keynes.* Newton Abbot, England: David and Charles, 1970.

McFarlane, Anthony. *The British in the Americas, 1480–1815.* London: Longman, 1994.

McKelvey, James Lee. *George III and Lord Bute: The Leicester House Years.* Durham, N.C.: Duke University Press, 1973.

Miller, P. *James.* London: Allen and Unwin, 1971.

Minchington, W. *The Growth of English Overseas Trade in the Seventeenth and Eighteenth Centuries.* London: Methuen, 1969.

Mingay, G. E. *Land and Society in England, 1750–1980.* London: Longman, 1994.

Monod, P. K. *Jacobitism and the English People, 1688–1788.* Cambridge: Cambridge University Press, 1989.

Moore, Robert L. *John Wesley and Authority: A Psychological Perspective.* Missoula, Mont.: Scholars Press, 1979.

Morgan, Marjorie. *Manners, Morals and Class in England, 1774–1858.* Basingstoke, England: Macmillan, 1994.

Morley, John. *Walpole.* Westport, Conn.: Greenwood Press, 1971.

Morris, R. J. *Class and Class Consciousness in the Industrial Revolution, 1780–1850.* London: Macmillan, 1979.

Morris, R. J., and John Langton. *Atlas of Industrializing Britain, 1780–1914.* London: Routledge, 1986.

Mui, Hoh-Cheung, and Lorna Mui. *Shops and Shopkeeping in Eighteenth Century England.* Kingston, Ontario, Canada: McGill-Queen's University Press, 1989.

Neale, Jonathan. *The Cutlass and the Lash: Mutiny and Discipline in Nelson's Navy.* London: Pluto Press, 1985.

Nicolson, Harold. *The Age of Reason, 1700–1789.* London: Constable, 1960.

Noble, Iris. *Rivals in Parliament: William Pitt and Charles Fox.* New York: Messner, 1970.

O'Brien, Patrick, and Roland Quinault, ed. *The Industrial Revolution and British Society.* Cambridge: Cambridge University Press, 1993.

O'Gorman, F. *The Whig Party and the French Revolution.* London: Macmillan, 1967.

Oldfield, J. R. *Popular Politics and British Anti-Slavery: The Mobilisation of Public Opinion against the Slave Trade.* Manchester: Manchester University Press, 1994.

Outhwaite, R. B. *Dearth, Public Policy and Social Disturbance in England, 1550–1800.* Basingstoke, England: Macmillan, 1991.

Pakenham, T. *The Year of Liberty: the History of the Great Irish Rebellion of 1798.* London: Hodder and Stoughton, 1969.

Palmer, Marilyn, and Peter Neaverson. *Industry in the Landscape, 1700–1900.* London: Routledge, 1994.

Parekh, Bhikhu. *Jeremy Bentham: Critical Assessments.* 4 vols. London: Routledge, 1993.

Parkin, Rebecca Price. *The Poetic Workmanship of Alexander Pope.* New York: Octagon, 1966.

Pearson, Hesketh. *Johnson and Boswell: The Story of Their Lives.* London: Cassell, 1987.

Perry, Keith. *British Politics and the American Revolution.* Basingstoke, England: Macmillan, 1990.

Pimlott, Ben, and Chris Cook. *Trade Unions in British Politics: The First 250 Years.* London: Longman, 1991.

Plumb, J. H. *The Growth of Political Stability, 1675–1725.* London: Macmillan, 1967.

Pocock, J. G. A., Gordon J. Schochet, and Lois G. Schwoerer, eds. *The Varieties of British Political Thought, 1500–1800.* Cambridge: Cambridge University Press, 1994.

Pocock, Tom. *Sailor King: The Life of William IV.* London: Sinclair-Stevenson, 1991.

Pollock, John. *John Wesley.* Wheaton, Ill.: Victor Books, 1989.

———. *Wilberforce.* London: Constable, 1977.

Porter, Roy. *Disease, Medicine and Society in England, 1550–1860.* Basingstoke, England: Macmillan, 1993.

Prior, Mary, ed. *Women in English Society, 1500–1800.* London: Methuen, 1985.

Pythian-Adams, Charles. *Societies, Cultures and Kinship, 1580–1850: Cultural Provinces and English Local History.* London: Pinter, 1993.

Quennell, Peter. *Alexander Pope: The Education of Genius, 1688–1728.* New York: Stein and Day, 1968.

Read, D. *Press and People, 1790–1850.* London: Edward Arnold, 1960.

Reilly, Robin. *Pitt the Younger, 1759–1806.* London: Cassell, 1978.

———. *Wolfe of Quebec.* London: White Lion Press, 1973.

Robertson, Sir Charles Grant. *Chatham and the British Empire.* Westport, Conn.: Greenwood Press, 1984.

Rodger, Richard. *Housing Urban Britain, 1780–1914.* Basingstoke, England: Macmillan, 1989.

Rose, Michael E. *The English Poor Law, 1780–1930.* Newton Abbot, England: David and Charles, 1971.

Rosebery, Lord. *Pitt.* New York: Haskell House, 1968.

Rosenthal, Michael. *Constable.* London: Thames and Hudson, 1987.

Roseveare, Henry. *The Financial Revolution, 1660–1760.* London: Longman, 1991.

Royle, Edward. *Modern Britain: A Social History, 1750–1985.* London: Edward Arnold, 1987.

Rubinstein, W. D. *Capitalism, Culture and Decline in Britain, 1750-1990.* London: Routledge, 1993.

Rudé, G. *The Crowd in History: A Study of Popular Disturbance in France and England, 1730–1848.* New York: Wiley, 1964.

———. *Wilkes and Liberty.* Oxford: Clarendon Press, 1962.

Ruffhead, Owen. *The Life of Alexander Pope.* Hildesheim, West Germany: Olms, 1968.

Rule, John. *Albion's People: English Society, 1714–1815.* London:

Longman, 1992.

———. *British Trade Unionism, 1750–1850.* London: Longman, 1988.

———. *The Labouring Classes in Early Industrial England, 1750–1850.* London: Longman, 1986.

———. *The Vital Century: England's Developing Economy, 1714–1815.* Harlow, England: Longman, 1992.

Russo, John Paul. *Alexander Pope: Tradition and Identity.* Cambridge, Mass.: Harvard University Press, 1972.

Sanderson, Michael. *Education, Economic Change and Society in England, 1780–1870.* Basingstoke, England: Macmillan, 1991.

Schultz, P. *Isaac Newton: Scientific Genius.* Champaign, Ill.: Garrard, 1972.

Schwartz, Hillel. *The French Prophets: The History of a Millenarian Group in Eighteenth–Century England.* Berkeley, Calif.: University of California Press, 1980.

Schweizer, Karl. *William Pitt, Earl of Chatham, 1708–1778: A Bibliography.* Westport, Conn.: Greenwood Press, 1993.

Scull, A. T. *The Most Solitary of Afflictions: Madness and Society in Britain, 1700–1900.* London: Allen Lane, 1993.

Semmell, B. *The Methodist Revolution.* New York: Basic Books, 1973.

———. *The Rise of Free Trade Imperialism.* Cambridge: Cambridge University Press, 1970.

Sharpe, J. A. *Crime in Early Modern England, 1550–1750.* London: Longman, 1984.

———. *Early Modern England: A Social History, 1550–1760.* London: Edward Arnold, 1987.

Sherrard, O. A. *Lord Chatham: Pitt and the Seven Years' War.* Westport, Conn.: Greenwood Press, 1975.

Simmons, R. C. *The American Colonies: From Settlement to Independence.* London: Longman, 1981.

Slack, Paul. *The English Poor Law, 1531–1782.* Basingstoke, England: Macmillan, 1990.

Smith, Charles Daniel. *The Early Career of Lord North, the Prime Minister.* London: Athlone Press, 1979.

Solkin, David H. *Painting for Money: The Visual Arts and the Public Sphere in 18th–Century England.* New Haven, Conn.: Yale University Press, 1993.

Somerset, Anne. *The Life and Times of William IV.* London: Weidenfeld and Nicolson, 1980.

Spear, P. *Master of Bengal: Clive and His India.* London: Thames and Hudson, 1975.

Speck, W. A. *Stability and Strife: England, 1714–1760.* London: Edward Arnold, 1977.

———. *Tory and Whig: The Struggle in the Constituencies, 1701–1715.* London: Macmillan, 1970.

Stephen, Leslie. *Alexander Pope.* New York: AMS Press, 1968.

Stevenson, John. *Popular Disturbances in England, 1700–1832.* London: Longman, 1992.

Stewart, Maaja A. *Domestic Realities and Imperial Fictions: Jane Austen's Novels in 18th-Century Contexts.* Athens, Ga.: University of Georgia Press, 1993.

Stone, Lawrence, ed. *An Imperial State at War: Britain From 1689–1815.* London: Routledge, 1994.

Thirsk, John. *England's Agricultural Regions and Agrarian History, 1500–1750.* Basingstoke, England: Macmillan, 1987.

Thomas, John. *The Rise of the Staffordshire Potteries.* Bath, England: Adams and Dart, 1971.

Thomas, Peter D. G. *Lord North.* London: Allen Lane, 1976.

Thomis, Malcolm, and Peter Holt. *Threats of Revolution in Britain, 1789–1848.* London: Macmillan, 1977.

Thompson, Allan. *The Dynamics of the Industrial Revolution.* London: Edward Arnold, 1973.

Trench, Charles Chevenix. *George II.* London: Allen Lane, 1973.

Turner, Michael E. *Enclosure in Britain, 1750–1830.* London: Macmillan, 1984.

Tuttle, Robert G., Jr. *John Wesley: His Life and Theology.* Grand Rapids, Mich.: Zondervan, 1978.

Tyson, John R., ed. *Charles Wesley: A Reader.* New York: Oxford University Press, 1989.

Ubbelohde, C. *The American Colonies and the British Empire, 1607–1763.* London: Routledge, 1968.

Urbank, Albion M. *Religion and Society in a Cotswold Vale: Nailsworth, Gloucestershire, 1780–1865.* Berkeley, Calif.: University of California Press, 1990.

Valentine, Alan. *Lord North.* Norman, Okla.: University of Oklahoma Press, 1968.

Villiers, Alan. *Captain James Cook.* New York: Scribner, 1967.

Vincent, David. *Literacy and Popular Culture: England 1750-1914.* Cambridge: Cambridge University Press, 1989.

Vulliamy, C. E. *John Wesley.* Westwood, N.J.: Barbour, 1985.

Wain, John. *Samuel Johnson.* London: Macmillan, 1974.

Walsh, John, Colin Haydon, and Stephen Taylor, ed. *The Church of*

England c1689–c1833: From Toleration to Tractarianism New York: Cambridge University Press, 1993.

Walvin, James. *Slaves and Slavery: The British Colonial Experience.* Manchester: Manchester University Press, 1992.

Ward, W. R. *Religion and Society in England, 1790–1850.* London: Batsford, 1972.

Warner, Oliver. *A Portrait of Lord Nelson.* Harmondsworth, England: Penguin, 1987.

Weatherill, Lorna. *Consumer Behaviour and Material Culture in Britain, 1660–1760.* London: Methuen, 1988.

Weinbrot, Howard D. *Britannica's Issue: The Rise of British Literature From Dryden to Ossian.* Cambridge: Cambridge University Press, 1993.

Whinney, Margaret. *Wren.* London: Thames and Hudson, 1971.

White, Stephen K. *Edmund Burke: Modernity, Politics and Aesthetics.* Thousand Oaks, Calif.: Sage, 1994.

Wilberforce, Robert Isaac, and Samuel Wilberforce. *The Life of William Wilberforce.* 5 vols. Freeport, N.Y.: Books For Libraries Press, 1972.

Williams, Basil. *The Life of William Pitt, Earl of Chatham.* 2 vols. New York: Octagon, 1966.

———. *The Whig Supremacy, 1714–1760.* Oxford: Clarendon Press, 1962.

Wilson, Adrian. *The Making of Man–Midwifery: Childbirth in England, 1660–1770.* London: UCL Press, 1994.

Wilson, Charles. *England's Apprenticeship, 1603–1763.* London: Longman, 1984.

Woodhouse, C. M. *The Battle of Navarino.* London: Hodder and Stoughton, 1965.

Worman, Isabelle. *Thomas Gainsborough: A Biography.* Lavenham, England: Dalton, 1976.

Wren, C. *Parentilia: or Memoirs of the Family of Wrens.* Farnborough: Gregg, 1965.

Wright, D. G. *Popular Radicalism: The Working-Class Experience, 1780– 1880.* London: Longman, 1988.

The Nineteenth Century

Biography and Autobiography

Ackroyd, Peter. *Dickens.* London: Sinclair-Stevenson, 1990.

Agassi, Joseph. *Faraday as a Natural Philosopher.* Chicago: University of Chicago Press, 1971.

Allen, Walter. *George Eliot.* New York: Macmillan, 1964.

Appleman, Philip, ed. *Darwin.* New York: Norton, 1979.

Aronson, Theo. *Heart of a Queen: Queen Victoria's Romantic Attachments.* London: John Murray, 1991.

————. *Victoria and Disraeli: The Making of a Romantic Partnership.* London: Cassell, 1977.

Atkinson, Charles Milner. *Jeremy Bentham: His Life and Work.* New York: AMS Press, 1971.

Baden-Powell, Heather. *Baden Powell: A Family Album.* Glouceste, Englandr: Alan Sutton, 1986.

Baker, Alfred. *The Life of Sir Isaac Pitman.* London: Pitman, 1980.

Barker, Juliet. *The Brontes.* London: Weidenfeld and Nicolson, 1994.

Barker, Michael. *Gladstone and Radicalism.* Hassocks, England: Harvester Press, 1975.

Battiscombe, Georgina. *Shaftesbury: A Biography of the Seventh Earl, 1801–1885.* London: Constable, 1974.

Baumann, Arthur Anthony. *The Last Victorians.* Freeport, N.Y.: Books For Libraries Press, 1970.

Beckett, John. *The Rise and Fall of the Grenvilles: The Dukes of Buckingham and Chandos, 1710 to 1921.* Manchester: Manchester University Press, 1994.

Bennett, Daphne. *King without a Crown: Albert, Prince Consort of England, 1819–1861.* London: Heinemann, 1977.

Blake, Robert. *Disraeli.* London: Eyre and Spottiswoode, 1966.

Bloom, Ursula. *Edward and Victoria.* London: Hale, 1977.

Bloomfield, Paul. *William Morris.* Folcroft , Pa.: Folcroft Library Editions, 1973.

Bolitho, Hector. *Albert, Prince Consort.* London: David Bruce and Watson, 1970.

Bolton, Sarah. *Famous English Statesmen of Queen Victoria's Reign.* Freeport, N.Y.: Books For Libraries Press, 1972.

Bowlby, John. *Charles Darwin: A New Life.* New York: Norton, 1991.

Bowler, Peter J. *Charles Darwin: the Man and His Influence.* Oxford: Blackwell, 1990.

Bradford, Sarah. *Disraeli.* London: Weidenfeld and Nicolson, 1982.

Brent, Peter. *Charles Darwin: A Man of Enlarged Curiosity.* London: Heinemann, 1981.

————. *Lord Byron.* London: Weidenfeld and Nicolson, 1974.

Brooke, John. *King George III.* London: Constable, 1972.

Brundage, Anthony. *The People's Historian: John Richard Green and the Writing of History in Victorian England.* Westport, Conn.: Greenwood Press, 1994.

Bullett, Gerald William. *George Eliot, Her Life and Books.* Westport, Conn.: Greenwood Press, 1971.

Bush, Douglas. *Matthew Arnold: A Survey of His Poetry and Prose.* New York: Macmillan, 1971.

Butler, David. *Disraeli, Portrait of a Romantic.* New York: Warner, 1980.

Campbell, Olwen. *Shelley and the Unromantics.* New York: Russell and Russell, 1966.

Cantor, Geoffrey. *Michael Faraday — Sandemanian and Scientist: A Study of Science and Religion in the Nineteenth Century.* London: Macmillan, 1991.

Cary, Elisabeth Luther. *William Morris, Poet, Craftsman, Socialist.* Norwood, Pa.: Norwood Editions, 1977.

Cassar, George H. *Kitchener: Architect of Victory.* London: Kimber, 1977.

Cecil, David. *A Portrait of Jane Austen.* London: Constable, 1978.

Chancellor, John. *Charles Darwin.* London: Weidenfeld and Nicolson, 1973.

Charlot, Monica. *Victoria: The Young Queen.* Oxford: Blackwell, 1991.

Cole, Hubert. *Beau Brummell.* London: Granada, 1977.

Cole, Margaret, ed. *The Webbs and Their Work.* Westport, Conn.: Greenwood Press, 1985.

Collini, Stefan, ed. *J. S. Mill: On Liberty.* Cambridge: Cambridge University Press, 1989.

Collins, Irene. *Jane Austen and the Clergy.* London: Hambledon Press, 1993.

Collins, Philip. *Dickens: the Critical Heritage.* London: Routledge, 1971.

Compton, Piers. *The Last Days of General Gordon.* London: Hale, 1974.

Compton-Rickett, Arthur. *William Morris: A Study in Personality.* Folcroft, Pa.: Folcroft Press, 1969.

Constantine, Stephen. *Lloyd George.* London: Routledge, 1992.

Coote, Stephen. *William Morris: His Life and Work.* London: Garamond, 1990.

Cormack, Malcolm. *Constable.* Oxford: Phaidon, 1986.

Cowling, Maurice. *Mill and Liberalism.* Cambridge: Cambridge University Press, 1990.

Darby, Elizabeth. *The Cult of the Prince Consort.* London: Yale University Press, 1983.

Davis, Hunter. *A Biographical Study of the Father of Railways, George Stephenson, on the Occasion of the 150th Anniversary of the Opening of the World's First Public Railway, the Stockton and Darlington, 1825–1975, Including an Account of Railway Mania and a Consideration of Stephensonia Today.* London: Weidenfeld and Nicolson, 1975.

Davis, Richard W. *Disraeli.* London: Hutchinson, 1976.

Desmond, Adrian, and James Moore. *Darwin.* New York: Warner, 1992.

Dickens, Mamie. *My Father As I Recall Him.* New York: Haskell House, 1974.

Dodd, Valerie A. *George Eliot: An Intellectual Life.* New York: St Martin's Press, 1990.

Dowden, Edward. *The Life of Percy Bysshe Shelley.* New York: Barnes and Noble, 1966.

Duff, David. *Albert and Victoria.* London: Muller, 1972.

Dugdale, Blanche Elizabeth Campbell. *Arthur James Balfour, First Earl of Balfour, K.G., O.M., F.R.S.* Westport, Conn.: Greenwood Press, 1970.

Egremont, Max. *Balfour: A Life of Arthur James Balfour.* London: Collins, 1980.

Evans, Eric J. *Sir Robert Peel: Statesmanship, Power and Party.* London: Routledge, 1991.

Eyck, Erich. *Gladstone,* translated by Bernard Miall. New York: A. M. Kelley, 1968.

Eyck, Frank. *The Prince Consort: a Political Biography.* Bath, England: Chivers, 1975.

Feiling, Sir Keith Grahame. *Sketches in Nineteenth Century Biography.* Folcroft, Pa.: Folcroft Library Editions, 1972.

Feuchtwanger, E. J. *Gladstone.* Basingstoke, England: Macmillan, 1988.

Fielding, K. J. *Charles Dickens: A Critical Introduction.* FolcroftPa.: Folcroft Library Editions, 1977.

Finlayson, Geoffrey B. A. M. *The Seventh Earl of Shaftesbury, 1801–1885.* London: Eyre Methuen, 1981.

Foot, M. R. D., and H. C. G. Matthew, ed. *The Gladstone Diaries.* 4 vols. Oxford: Clarendon Press, 1968–74.

Fraser, John Lloyd. *John Constable, 1776–1837: The Man and His Mistress.* London: Hutchinson, 1976.

Fulford, Roger. *Hanover to Windsor.* London: Batsford, 1960.

Furneaux, Robin. *William Wilberforce.* London: Hamish Hamilton, 1974.

Garrett, Richard. *General Gordon.* London: Barker, 1974.

Gash, Norman. *Mr. Secretary Peel: The Life of Sir Robert Peel to 1830.* London: Longman, 1985.

————. *Sir Robert Peel: The Life of Sir Robert Peel after 1830.* Totowa, N.J.: Rowman and Littlefield, 1972.

Gatrell, Simon. *Hardy the Creator: A Textual Biography.* Oxford: Clarendon Press, 1988.

Gerin, Winifred. *Anne Bronte.* London: Nelson, 1959.

————. *Charlotte Bronte: The Evolution of Genius.* Oxford: Clarendon Press, 1967.

————. *Emily Bronte.* Oxford: Clarendon Press, 1971.

Gittings, Robert. *The Older Hardy.* London: Heinemann, 1978.

————. *Young Thomas Hardy.* London: Heinemann, 1975.

Gladstone, Penelope. *Portrait of a Family: The Gladstones, 1839–1889.* Ormskirk, England: Lyster, 1989.

Glassman, Peter. *J. S. Mill: The Evolution of a Genius.* Gainesville, Fla.: University of Florida Press, 1985.

Goldie, Sue M., ed. *I Have Done My Duty: Florence Nightingale in the Crimean War, 1854–56.* Iowa City, Iowa.: University of Iowa Press, 1987.

Gordon, Charles George. *The Journals of Major-General C. G. Gordon, C.B., at Kartoum: Printed From the Original Manuscript.* London: Darf, 1984.

Grant, Neil. *Benjamin Disraeli: Prime Minister Extraordinary.* New York: F. Watts, 1969.

Gribble, Francis Henry. *The Romantic Life of Shelley and the Sequel.* New York: Haskell House, 1972.

Griffith, Paddy. *Wellington: Commander: The Iron Duke's Generalship.* Chichester, England: Bird, 1985.

Haight, Gordon S. *George Eliot: A Biography.* Oxford: Oxford University Press, 1978.

Hammond, J. L., and Barbara Hammond. *Lord Shaftesbury.* Hamden, Conn.: Archon, 1969.

Hardy, Evelyn. *Thomas Hardy: A Critical Biography.* Folcroft, Pa.: Folcroft Library Editions, 1973.

Hardy, Florence Emily. *The Life of Thomas Hardy, 1840–1928: Compiled Largely from Contemporary Notes, Letters, Diaries and Biographical Memoranda.* Hamden, Conn.: Archon Books, 1970.

Hartman, Geoffrey H. *Wordsworth's Poetry, 1787–1814.* New Haven, Conn.: Yale University Press, 1964.

Harvey, Charles H. *Matthew Arnold, a Critic of the Victorian Period.* Hamden, Conn.: Archon, 1969.

Harvey, Charles and Jon Press. *William Morris: Design and Enterprise in Victorian England.* Manchester: Manchester University Press, 1991.

Hattersley, Roy. *Nelson.* New York: Saturday Review Press, 1974.

Hawkins, Desmond. *Hardy: Novelist and Poet.* London: Macmillan, 1981.

Henderson, Philip. *William Morris: His Life, Work and Friends.* Harmondsworth, England: Penguin, 1973.

Hibbert, Christopher. *Disraeli and His World.* New York: Scribner, 1978.

——. *George IV, Prince of Wales, 1762–1811.* Harlow, England: Longman, 1972.

——. *George IV, Regent and King, 1811–1830.* London: Allen Lane, 1974.

——. *The Making of Charles Dickens.* Harmondsworth, England: Penguin, 1983.

——. *Nelson: A Personal History.* London: Viking, 1994.

Hinde, Wendy. *George Canning.* London: Collins, 1973.

Hobhouse, Hermione. *Prince Albert: His Life and Work.* London: Hamish Hamilton, 1983.

Hogg, Thomas Jefferson. *The Life of Percy Bysshe Shelley.* St. Clair Shores, Mich.: Scholarly Press, 1970.

Honan, Park. *Matthew Arnold, a Life.* New York: McGraw-Hill, 1981.

Howarth, David, and Stephen Howarth. *Lord Nelson: The Immortal Memory.* New York: Viking, 1989.

Howe, Irving. *Thomas Hardy.* New York: Macmillan, 1967.

Huxley, Elspeth. *Florence Nightingale.* London: Weidenfeld and Nicolson, 1975.

Hyman, Anthony. *Charles Babbage: Pioneer of the Computer.* Oxford: Oxford University Press, 1982.

Irvine, William. *Walter Bagehot.* Hamden, Conn.: Archon, 1970.

Ivy, Judy Crosby. *Constable and the Critics, 1802–1837.* Woodbridge, England: Boydell, 1991.

James, Robert Rhodes. *Albert, Prince Consort: A Biography.* London: Hamish Hamilton, 1983.

Jarrett, Derek. *Pitt the Younger.* New York: Scribner, 1974.

Jeal, Tim. *Baden-Powell.* London: Century, 1989.

Jenkins, Roy. *Gladstone.* London: Macmillan, 1995.

Judd, Denis. *Palmerston.* London: Weidenfeld and Nicolson, 1975.

————. *Radical Joe: A Life of Joseph Chamberlain.* London: Hamish Hamilton, 1977.

Kamm, Josephine. *The Story of Emmeline Pankhurst.* New York: Meredith Press, 1968.

Kaplan, Fred. *Dickens: A Biography.* New York: Morrow, 1988.

Kelvin, Norman, ed. *The Collected Letters of William Morris.* 2 vols. Princeton, N.J.: Princeton University Press, 1984, vol 1, and 1987, vol 2.

Komroff, M. *Disraeli.* New York: Messner, 1963.

Laski, Marghanita. *Jane Austen.* London: Thames and Hudson, 1986.

Lindsay, Jack. *William Morris: His Life and Work.* London: Constable, 1975.

Lloyd, Alan. *The Wickedest Age: the Life and Times of George III.* Newton Abbot, England: David and Charles, 1971.

Longford, Elizabeth. *Victoria R.I.* London: Pan, 1983.

————. *Wellington.* 2 vols. London: Weidenfeld and Nicolson, 1969, vol 1, and 1972, vol 2).

Lowry, Howard Foster, ed. *The Letters of Matthew Arnold to Arthur Hugh Clough.* Philadelphia, Pa.: West, 1977.

MacCarthy, Fiona. *William Morris: A Life for our Time.* London: Faber and Faber, 1994.

MacDonald, James Ramsay, and Margaret MacDonald. *A Singular Marriage: A Labour Love Story in Letters and Diaries.* London: Harrap, 1988.

Mackay, Ruddock F. *Balfour: Intellectual Statesman.* Oxford: Oxford University Press, 1985.

MacKenzie, Norman, and Jeanne MacKenzie. *Dickens: A Life.* Oxford: Oxford University Press, 1979.

Machin, Ian. *Disraeli.* London: Longman, 1994.

Marlow, Joyce. *Mr and Mrs Gladstone: An Intimate Biography.* London: Weidenfeld and Nicolson, 1977.

Marquand, David. *Ramsay MacDonald.* London: Cape, 1977.

Marsh, Peter T. *Joseph Chamberlain: Entrepreneur in Politics.* New Haven, Conn.: Yale University Press, 1994.

Marshall, Dorothy. *The Life and Times of Victoria.* London: Weidenfeld and Nicolson, 1992.

————. *Lord Melbourne.* London: Weidenfeld and Nicolson, 1975.

Matthew, H. C. G. *Gladstone 1809–1874.* Oxford: Clarendon Press, 1986.

Medwin, Thomas. *The Life of Percy Bysshe Shelley.* St. Clair Shores,

Mich.: Scholarly Press, 1971.

Middleton, Charles S. *Shelley and His Writings.* 2 vols. Folcroft, Pa.: Folcroft Library Editions, 1972.

Mill, John Stuart. *Autobiography.* London: Oxford University Press, 1971.

Millgate, Michael. *Thomas Hardy: A Biography.* Oxford: Oxford University Press, 1982.

Monypenny, William Flavelle, and George Earle Buckle. *The Life of Benjamin Disraeli, Earl of Beaconsfield.* 4 vols. New York: Russell and Russell, 1968.

Moore, Doris Langley. *The Late Lord Byron: Posthumous Dramas.* New York: Harper and Row, 1977.

———. *Lord Byron: Accounts Rendered.* London: John Murray, 1974.

Moorman, Mary. *William Wordsworth: A Biography.* 2 vols. Oxford: Clarendon Press, 1957, vol 1, and 1965, vol 2.

Morley, John. *The Life of William Ewart Gladstone* . 3 vols. New York: Greenwood Press, 1968.

Moseley, Maboth. *Irascible Genius: The Life of Charles Babbage.* Chicago: Regnery, 1970.

Muggeridge, Kitty. *Beatrice Webb: A Life, 1858–1943.* Chicago: Academy Publishers, 1983.

Newton, Scott, and Dilwyn Porter. *Joseph Chamberlain, 1836–1914: A Bibliography.* Westport, Conn.: Greenwood Press, 1994.

Nicolson, Nigel. *The World of Jane Austen.* London: Weidenfeld and Nicolson, 1991.

Noble, Iris. *Rivals in Parliament: William Pitt and Charles Fox.* New York: Messner, 1970.

Nord, Deborah Epstein. *The Apprenticeship of Beatrice Webb.* Amherst, Mass.: University of Massachusetts Press, 1985.

Nye, Robert. *Memoirs of Lord Byron.* London: Hamish Hamilton, 1989.

O'Neill, Michael. *Percy Bysshe Shelley: A Literary Life.* New York: St. Martin's Press, 1990.

Palmer, Alan. *The Life and Times of George IV.* London: Weidenfeld and Nicolson, 1972.

Pankhurst, Emmeline. *My Own Story.* London: Virago, 1979.

Partridge, Michael S., and Karen E. Partridge. *Lord Palmerston, 1784– 1865: A Bibliography.* Westport, Conn.: Greenwood Press, 1994.

Pearson, Hesketh. *Dizzy: The Life and Personality of Benjamin Disraeli, Earl of Beaconsfield.* London: White Lion, 1974.

Peck, Walter Edwin. *Shelley, His Life and Work.* Folcroft, Pa.: Folcroft Library Editions, 1973.

Pinto-Duschinsky, Michael. *The Political Thought of Lord Salisbury, 1854–68.* London: Constable, 1967.

Plowden, Alison. *The Young Victoria.* London: Weidenfeld and Nicolson, 1981.

Pollock, John. *Shaftesbury: The Poor Man's Earl.* London: Hodder and Stoughton, 1985.

———. *Wilberforce.* Tring, England: Lion, 1978.

Pound, Reginald. *Albert: A Biography of the Prince Consort.* London: Michael Joseph, 1973.

Powell, J. Enoch. *Joseph Chamberlain.* London: Thames and Hudson, 1977.

Prest, John. *Lord John Russell.* London: Macmillan, 1972.

Radice, Lisanne. *Beatrice and Sidney Webb: Fabian Socialists.* London: Macmillan, 1984.

Ramsay, A. A. W. *Sir Robert Peel.* London: Constable, 1971.

Read, Donald. *Cobden and Bright.* London: Edward Arnold, 1967.

Redinger, Ruby V. *George Eliot: The Emergent Self.* New York: Knopf, 1975

Rees, J. *Jane Austen: Woman and Writer.* New York: St. Martin's Press, 1976.

Reiman, Donald H. *Percy Bysshe Shelley.* New York: Twayne, 1969.

Reynolds, Graham. *Constable: The Natural Painter.* London: Cory, Adams and MacKay, 1965.

Richardson, Joanna. *Victoria and Albert: A Study of a Marriage.* London: Dent, 1977.

Ridley, Jane. *The Young Disraeli: 1804–1846.* London: Sinclair Stevenson, 1995.

Robinson, Virgil E. *William Booth and His Army.* Mountain View, Calif.: Pacific Press Publishers Association, 1976.

Rolo, P. J. V. *George Canning.* London: Macmillan, 1965.

Rolt, L. T. C. *Isambard Kingdom Brunel.* Harmondsworth, England: Penguin, 1970.

———. *The Railway Revolution: George and Robert Stephenson.* New York: St. Martin's Press, 1962.

Rose, John Holland. *William Pitt and the Great War.* Westport, Conn.: Greenwood Press, 1971.

Rosebery, Lord. *Pitt.* New York: Haskell House, 1968.

Rosenthal, Michael. *The Character Factory: Baden-Powell and the Origins of the Boy Scout Movement.* New York: Pantheon, 1986.

———. *Constable.* London: Thames and Hudson, 1987.

Rowse, A. L. *Matthew Arnold: Poet and Prophet.* Lanham, Md.: University Press of America, 1986.

Royle, Trevor. *The Kitchener Enigma.* London: Michael Joseph, 1985.

Salter, Richard. *Peel, Gladstone and Disraeli.* Basingstoke, England: Macmillan, 1991.

Sells, Iris Esther. *Matthew Arnold and France: the Poet.* New York: Octagon, 1970.

Shannon, Richard. *Gladstone.* London: Hamish Hamilton, 1982.

Sharp, William. *Life of Percy Bysshe Shelley.* Port Washington, N.Y.: Kennikat Press, 1972.

Sitwell, Edith. *Victoria of England.* London: Hutchinson Education, 1987.

Skeat, W. O. *George Stephenson: The Engineer and His Letters.* London: Institute of Mechanical Engineers, 1973.

Skorupski, John. *John Stuart Mill.* London: Routledge, 1989.

Smiles, Samuel. *The Life of George Stephenson, Railway Engineer.* Ann Arbor, Mich.: Plutarch Press, 1971.

Smith, F. B. *Florence Nightingale: Reputation and Power.* New York: St. Martin's Press, 1982.

Smith, George Barnett. *Shelley: A Critical Biography.* New York: Haskell House, 1974.

Sprague, Rosemary. *George Eliot: A Biography.* London: Chilton, 1968.

Stansky, Peter. *Gladstone: A Progress in Politics.* London: Norton, 1979.

Stewart, J. I. M. *Thomas Hardy: A Critical Biography.* New York: Dodd, Mead, 1971.

Strachey, Lytton. *Eminent Victorians.* London: Penguin, 1986.

———. *Queen Victoria.* London: Chatto and Windus, 1969.

Strange, G. Robert. *Matthew Arnold: The Poet As Humanist.* Princeton, N.J.: Princeton University Press, 1967.

Taylor, Robert. *Lord Salisbury.* New York: St. Martin's Press, 1975.

Thompson, E. P. *William Morris: Romantic to Revolutionary.* New York: Pantheon, 1977.

Thompson, Paul. *The Work of William Morris.* London: Heinemann, 1967.

Thursfield, James R. *Peel.* Freeport, N.Y.: Books For Libraries Press, 1972.

Todhunter, John. *A Study of Shelley.* Folcroft, Pa.: Folcroft Press, 1969.

Tomalin, Claire. *Shelley and His World.* New York: Scribner, 1980.

Trench, Charles Chevenix. *The Road to Khartoum: A Life of General Charles Gordon.* New York: Norton, 1979.

Trevor, Meriol. *The Arnolds: Thomas Arnold and His Family.* New York: Scribner, 1973.

Trilling, Lionel. *Matthew Arnold.* Oxford: Oxford University Press, 1982.

Trueblood, Paul Graham. *Lord Byron.* Boston, Mass.: Twayne, 1977.

Vaughan, Adrian. *Isambard Kingdom Brunel: Engineering Knight Errant.* London: John Murray, 1991.

Vicinus, Martha, and Bea Nergaard, ed. *Ever Yours, Florence Nightingale: Selected Letters.* London: Virago, 1989.

Vincent, John R., ed. *Disraeli, Derby and the Conservative Party: Journals and Memoirs of Edward Henry, Lord Stanley, 1849–1869.* New York: Barnes and Noble, 1978.

Walton, John K. *Disraeli.* London: Routledge, 1990.

Warner, Oliver. *A Portrait of Lord Nelson.* Harmondsworth, England: Penguin, 1987.

Warner, Philip. *Kitchener: The Man Behind the Legend.* London: Hamish Hamilton, 1985.

Watts, Duncan. *Joseph Chamberlain and the Challenge of Radicalism.* London: Hodder and Stoughton, 1992.

Weber, Carl J. *Hardy of Wessex, His Life and Literary Career.* New York: Columbia University Press, 1965.

Weintraub, Stanley. *Victoria: An Intimate Biography.* New York: Dutton, 1987.

Weller, Jac. *Wellington at Waterloo.* London: Longman, 1967.

Wilberforce, Robert Isaac, and Samuel Wilberforce. *The Life of William Wilberforce.* 5 vols. Freeport, N.Y.: Books For Libraries Press, 1972.

Williams, L. Pearce. *Michael Faraday: A Biography.* New York: Basic Books, 1965.

Wilson, Angus. *The World of Charles Dickens.* London: Secker and Warburg, 1972.

Winstanley, Michael J. *Gladstone and the Liberal Party.* London: Routledge, 1990.

Woodham-Smith, Cecil. *Queen Victoria: Her Life and Times.* London: Hamish Hamilton, 1972.

Young, Kenneth. *Arthur James Balfour: The Happy Life of the Politician, Prime Minister, Statesman and Philosopher, 1848–1930.* London: Bell, 1963.

Zastoupil, Lynn. *John Stuart Mill and India: The Map of Civilisation on the Mind.* Cambridge: Cambridge University Press, 1994.

Zebel, Sydney H. *Balfour: A Political Biography.* London: Cambridge University Press, 1973.

Ziegler, Philip. *Addington: A Life of Henry Addington, First Viscount Sidmouth.* London: Collins, 1965.

———. *Melbourne: A Biography of William Lamb, 2nd Viscount Melbourne.* London: Collins, 1976.

Culture and Society

Abel-Smith, B., and R. Stevens. *Lawyers and the Courts: A Sociological Study of the English Legal System, 1750–1965.* London: Heinemann, 1967.

Anderson, R. D. *Universities and Elites in Britain Since 1800.* Basingstoke, England: Macmillan, 1992.

Anstey, R. T. *The Atlantic Slave Trade and British Abolition, 1760–1810.* London: Macmillan, 1975.

Begg, Paul, Martin Fido, and Keith Skinner. *The Jack the Ripper A to Z.* London: Headline, 1994.

Benson, John. *The Rise of Consumer Society in Britain, 1880–1980.* London: Longman, 1994.

———. *The Working Class in Britain, 1850–1939.* London: Longman, 1989.

Berrol, Selma. *East Side/East End: Eastern European Jews in London and New York, 1870–1920.* London: Greenwood, 1994.

Best, G. *Mid-Victorian Britain, 1851–75.* London: Weidenfeld and Nicolson, 1971.

Birley, Derek. *Sport and the Making of Britain.* Manchester: Manchester University Press, 1993.

Bourne, John. *Patronage and Society in Nineteenth–Century England.* London: Edward Arnold, 1986.

Breach, R. W., and R. M. Hartwell. *British Economy and Society, 1870– 1970.* London: Oxford University Press, 1972.

Briggs, Asa. *The Age of Improvement, 1783–1867.* London: Longman, 1979.

———. *Victorian Cities.* London: Odhams, 1963.

———. *Victorian People.* Chicago: University of Chicago Press, 1972.

Brown, Richard. *Church and State in Modern Britain, 1700–1850.* London: Routledge, 1991.

———. *Society and Economy in Modern Britain, 1700–1850.* London: Routledge, 1991.

Brown, R., and C. Daniels. *Nineteenth Century Britain.* London: Macmillan, 1980.

Bruce, M. *The Coming of the Welfare State.* London: Batsford, 1968.

Bryant, Arthur. *The Age of Elegance, 1812–1822.* London: Collins, 1975.

Burnett, John. *Idle Hands: The Experience of Unemployment, 1790–1990.* London: Routledge, 1994.

Bynum, W. F. *Science and the Practice of Medicine in the 19th Century.* Cambridge: Cambridge University Press, 1994.

Carter, Harold, and C. R. Lewis. *An Urban Geography of England and Wales in the Nineteenth Century.* London: Edward Arnold, 1991.

Checkland, S. G. *The Rise of Industrial Society in England, 1815–1885.* London: Longman, 1964.

Cherry, Gordon E. *Cities and Plans: the Shaping of Urban Britain in the 19th and 20th Centuries.* London: Edward Arnold, 1988.

Chesney, K. *The Victorian Underworld.* London: Temple Smith, 1970.

Cheyette, Bryan. *Constructions of "The Jew" in English Literature and Society: Racial Representations, 1875–1945.* Cambridge: Cambridge University Press, 1993.

Clapp, B. W. *An Environmental History of Britain since the Industrial Revolution.* London: Longman, 1994.

Clapson, Mark. *A Bit of a Flutter: Popular Gambling in England, c1823–1961.* Manchester: Manchester University Press, 1992.

Clark, J. C. D. *English Society, 1688–1832.* Cambridge: Cambridge University Press, 1985.

Colley, Linda. *Britons: Forging the Nation, 1707–1837.* London: Pimlico, 1994.

Daunton, M. J. *House and Home in the Victorian City: Working-Class Housing, 1850–1914.* London: Edward Arnold, 1983.

Davies, Andrew, and Steven Fielding, ed. *Workers' Worlds: Cultures and Communities in Manchester and Salford, 1880–1939.* Manchester: Manchester University Press, 1992.

Dennis, Richard J. *English Industrial Cities of the 19th Century: A Social Geography.* Cambridge: Cambridge University Press, 1984.

Digby, Anne. *British Welfare Policy: Workhouse to Workfare.* London: Faber, 1989.

———. *Making a Medical Living: Doctors and Patients in the English Market for Medicine, 1720–1911.* Cambridge: Cambridge University Press, 1994.

Douglas, Arthur. *Will the Real Jack the Ripper.* Chorley, England: Countryside Publications, 1979.

Dowling, Linda. *Hellenism and Homosexuality in Victorian Oxford.* Ithaca, N.Y.: Cornell University Press, 1994.

Drescher, Seymour. *Capitalism and Antislavery: British Mobilization in Comparative Perspective.* London: Macmillan, 1987.

Driver, F. *Power and Pauperism: The Workhouse System, 1834– 1884.* Cambridge: Cambridge University Press, 1993.

Dyos, H. J. *The Victorian Suburb.* Leicester, England: Leicester University Press, 1973.

Dyos, H. J., and Michael Wolff. *The Victorian City.* 2 vols. London: Routledge, 1973.

Edwards, Amy. *The Prison System in England and Wales, 1878– 1978.* London: Home Office Prison Department, 1978.

Elbourne, R. *Music and Tradition in Early Industrial Lancashire, 1780– 1840.* Woodbridge, England: Brewer, 1980.

Emsley, Clive. *British Society and the French Wars, 1793–1815.* London: Macmillan, 1979.

———. *Crime and Society in England, 1750–1900.* London: Longman, 1987.

Englander, David. *A Documentary History of Jewish Immigrants in Britain, 1840–1920.* Leicester, England: Leicester University Press, 1994.

———. *Landlord and Tenant in Urban Britain, 1838–1918.* Oxford: Clarendon Press, 1983.

Ferguson, Moira. *Subject to Others: British Women Writers and Colonial Slavery, 1670–1834.* London: Routledge, 1992.

Fido, Martin. *The Crimes, Detection and Death of Jack the Ripper.* London: Weidenfeld and Nicolson, 1987.

Foster, R. F. *Paddy and Mr Punch: Connections in Irish and English History.* London: Allen Lane, 1993.

Fraser, Derek. *The Evolution of the British Welfare State: A History of Social Policy Since the Industrial Revolution.* London: Macmillan, 1984.

Garnett, Jane, and Colin Matthew, ed. *Revival and Religion Since 1700: Essays for John Walsh.* London: Hambledon Press, 1993.

Gash, Norman. *Aristocracy and People: Britain, 1815–1865.* London: Edward Arnold, 1979.

Gatrell, V. A. C. *The Hanging Tree: Execution and the English People, 1770–1868.* Oxford: Oxford University Press, 1994.

Gauldie, Enid. *Cruel Habitations: A History of Working-Class Housing, 1780–1918.* London: Allen and Unwin, 1974.

Gibson, William. *Church, State and Society, 1760–1850.* Basingstoke, England: Macmillan, 1994.

Gilmour, Robin. *The Victorian Period: Intellectual and Cultural Context, 1830–1890.* London: Longman, 1994.

Gordon, Peter. *The Victorian School Manager: A Study in the Management of Education, 1800–1902.* Ilford, England: Woburn Press, 1974.

Greenslade, William. *Degeneration, Culture and the Novel, 1880–1940.* Cambridge: Cambridge University Press, 1994.

Hadfield, A. M. *The Chartist Land Company.* Newton Abbot, England: David and Charles, 1970.

Harris, Jose. *Private Lives, Public Spirit — a Social History of Britain, 1870–1914.* Oxford: Oxford University Press, 1993.

Harris, Melvin. *The Ripper File.* London: W. H. Allen, 1989.

Harris, Tim. *Popular Culture in England, c1500–1850.* London: Macmillan, 1993.

Harrison, Brian. *Drink and the Victorians.* London: Faber, 1971.

Harrison, J. F. C. *Late Victorian Britain, 1875–1901.* Glasgow, Scotland: Fontana, 1990.

Harrison, Paul. *Jack the Ripper: the Mystery Solved.* London: Hale, 1991.

Harrison, S. *The Diary of Jack the Ripper.* London: Smith Gryphon, 1993.

Hempton, David. *Methodism and Politics in British Society, 1750–1850.* London: Hutchinson, 1984.

Hewett, Edward, and W. F. Axton. *Convivial Dickens: The Drinks of Dickens and His Times.* Athens, Ohio.: Ohio University Press, 1983.

Higgs, Edward. *Making Sense of the Census: The Manuscript Returns for England and Wales, 1801–1901.* London: Her Majesty's Stationery Office, 1989.

Holmes, Colin. *John Bull's Island: Immigration and British Society, 1871–1971.* Basingstoke, England: Macmillan, 1988.

Hopkins, Eric. *Childhood Transformed: Working-Class Children in Nineteenth Century England.* Manchester: Manchester University Press, 1994.

Howkins, Alun. *Reshaping Rural England: A Social History, 1850–1925.* London: HarperCollins Academic, 1991.

Hughes, Kathryn. *The Victorian Governess.* London: Hambledon Press, 1993.

Inglis, K. C. *Churches and the Working Classes in Victorian England.* London: Routledge, 1963.

Jenkins, Jennifer, and Patrick James. *From Acorn to Oak Tree: The Growth of the National Trust, 1895–1994.* Basingstoke, England: Macmillan, 1994.

Jones, G. Stedman. *Outcast London: A Study in the Relationship between Classes in Victorian Society, 1830 to 1855.* Oxford: Clarendon Press, 1971.

Kain, Roger, and Hugh C. Prince. *The Tithe Surveys of England and Wales.* Cambridge: Cambridge University Press, 1985.

Kearns, G., and C. W. J. Withers, ed. *Urbanising Britain: Essays on Class and Community in the Nineteenth Century.* Cambridge: Cambridge University Press, 1991.

Kellett, J. R. *The Impact of Railways on Victorian Cities.* London: Routledge, 1969.

Kitson-Clark, G. S. *The Making of Victorian England.* London: Methuen, 1962.

Knight, Stephen. *Jack the Ripper: The Final Solution.* London: Treasure, 1984.

Leask, Nigel. *British Romantic Writers and the East: Anxieties of Empire.* Cambridge: Cambridge University Press, 1992.

Liddington, Jill. *The Road to Greenham Common: Feminism and Anti-Militarism in Britain Since 1820.* Syracuse, N.Y.: Syracuse University Press, 1991.

Longmate, Norman. *The Workhouse.* London: Temple Smith, 1974.

Lowerson, John. *Sport and the English Middle Classes, 1870–1914.* Manchester: Manchester University Press, 1993.

Lyons, F. S. L. *Ireland Since the Famine.* London: Fontana, 1973.

MacKenzie, John M. *Propaganda and Empire: The Manipulation of British Public Opinion, 1880–1960.* Manchester: Manchester University Press, 1986.

Mangan, J. A., ed. *The Imperial Curriculum: Racial Images and Education in the British Colonial Experience.* London: Routledge and Kegan Paul, 1993.

Marsden, Gordon, ed. *Victorian Values: Personalities and Perspectives in Nineteenth-Century Society.* London: Longman, 1990.

Marsden, W. E. *Educating the Respectable: A Study of Fleet Road Board School, Hampstead, 1879–1903.* Ilford: Woburn Press, 1991.

———. *Unequal Educational Provision in England and Wales: The Nineteenth-Century Roots.* Ilford, England: Woburn Press, 1987.

Marshall, J. D. *The Old Poor Law, 1795–1834.* London: Macmillan, 1968.

Mason, Tony. *Association Football and English Society, 1863–1915.*

Brighton: Harvester Press, 1980.

McLeod, Hugh. *Religion and the Working Class in Nineteenth-Century Britain.* London: Macmillan, 1984.

Mingay, G. E. *Land and Society in England, 1750–1980.* London: Longman, 1994.

Mitchell, Sally. *Victorian Britain: an Encyclopedia.* New York: Garland Press, 1988.

Morgain, Thais E., ed. *Victorian Sages and Cultural Discourse: Renegotiating Gender and Power.* New Brunswick, N.J.: Rutgers University Press, 1991.

Morgan, Marjorie. *Manners, Morals and Class in England, 1774–1858.* Basingstoke, England: Macmillan, 1994.

Morris, R. J. *Cholera 1832: The Social Response to an Epidemic.* London: Croom Helm, 1976.

———. *Class and Class Consciousness in the Industrial Revolution, 1780–1850.* London: Macmillan, 1979.

Morris, R. J., and Richard Rodger, ed. *The Victorian City: A Reader in British Urban History, 1820–1914.* London: Longman, 1993.

Musgrave, P. W. *Society and Education in England Since 1800.* London: Methuen, 1968.

Nash, David. *Secularism, Art and Freedom.* London: Pinter, 1989.

Neale, Jonathan. *The Cutlass and the Lash: Mutiny and Discipline in Nelson's Navy.* London: Pluto Press, 1985.

Norman, E. R. *Anti-Catholicism in Victorian England.* London: Allen and Unwin, 1968.

O'Brien, Patrick K., and Roland Quinault, ed. *The Industrial Revolution and British Society.* Cambridge: Cambridge University Press, 1993.

Oldfield, J. R. *Popular Politics and British Anti-Slavery: The Mobilisation of Public Opinion against the Slave Trade.* Manchester: Manchester University Press, 1994.

Panayi, Panikos. *Immigration, Ethnicity and Racism in Britain, 1815–1945.* Manchester: Manchester University Press, 1994.

———., ed. *Racial Violence in Britain, 1840–1950.* Leicester: Leicester University Press, 1993.

Parsons, Gerald, and James R. Moore, ed. *Religion in Victorian Britain.* 4 vols. Manchester: Manchester University Press, 1988.

Pearsall, Ronald. *The Worm in the Bud: The World of Victorian Sexuality.* London: Pimlico, 1993.

Porter, Roy. *Disease, Medicine and Society in England, 1550–1860.* Basingstoke, England: Macmillan, 1993.

Pugh, Martin. *State and Society: British Political and Social History,*

1870–1992. London: Edward Arnold, 1994.

————. *Women's Suffrage in Britain, 1867–1928.* London: Historical Association, 1980.

Pythian-Adams, Charles. *Societies, Cultures and Kinship, 1580–1850: Cultural Provinces and English Local History.* London: Pinter, 1993.

Read, Donald. *The Age of Urban Democracy: England 1868–1914.* Harlow, England: Longman, 1994.

Reid, Alastair J. *Social Classes and Social Relations in Britain, 1850–1914.* Basingstoke, England: Macmillan, 1992.

Robinson, Fred Miller. *The Man in the Bowler Hat: His History and Iconography.* Chapel Hill, N.C.: University of North Carolina Press, 1993.

Rodger, Richard. *Housing Urban Britain, 1780–1914.* Basingstoke, England: Macmillan, 1989.

Rose, Michael E. *The English Poor Law, 1780–1930.* Newton Abbot, England: David and Charles, 1971.

Rosen, Andrew. *Rise Up Women!* London: Routledge, 1974.

Royle, Edward. *Modern Britain: A Social History, 1750–1985.* London: Edward Arnold, 1987.

Rubinstein, W. D. *Capitalism, Culture and Decline in Britain, 1750–1990.* London: Routledge, 1993.

Rudé, G. *The Crowd in History: A Study of Popular Disturbance in France and England, 1730–1848.* New York: Wiley, 1964.

Rule, John. *Albion's People: English Society, 1714–1815.* London: Longman, 1992.

————. *The Labouring Classes in Early Industrial England, 1750–1850.* London: Longman, 1986.

Russell, D. *Popular Music in England, 1840–1914: A Social History.* Manchester: Manchester University Press, 1987.

Sanderson, Michael. *Education, Economic Change and Society in England, 1780–1870.* Basingstoke, England: Macmillan, 1991.

————. *From Irving to Olivier: A Social History of the Acting Profession in England, 1880–1983.* London: Athlone Press, 1984.

Scola, Roger. *Feeding the Victorian City: The Food Supply of Manchester.* Manchester: Manchester University Press, 1992.

Scull, A. T. *The Most Solitary of Afflictions: Madness and Society in Britain, 1700–1900.* London: Allen Lane, 1993.

Semmel, Bernard. *The Methodist Revolution.* New York: Basic Books, 1973.

Shiman, Lilian Lewis. *Women and Leadership in Nineteenth-Century England.* Basingstoke, England: Macmillan, 1992.

Simon, Brian. *Education and the Labour Movement, 1870–1920.* London: Lawrence and Wishart, 1965.

Sindall, Rob. *Street Violence in the Nineteenth Century.* Leicester: Leicester University Press, 1993.

Smith, Malcolm. *British Politics, Society and the State Since the Late Nineteenth Century.* London: Macmillan, 1990.

Spiers, Edward M. *The Late Victorian Army, 1868–1902.* Manchester: Manchester University Press, 1992.

Stedman-Jones, G. *Outcast London: a Study of the Relationships Between Classes in Victorian Society.* Oxford: Clarendon Press, 1971.

Stevenson, John. *Popular Disturbances in England, 1700–1832.* London: Longman, 1992.

Sturgis, Matthew. *Passionate Attitudes: The English Decadence of the 1890s.* London: Macmillan, 1995.

Swift, Roger, and Sheridan Gilley, ed. *The Irish in Britain: 1815–1939.* London: Pinter, 1989.

Taylor, A. J. *The Standard of Living in the Industrial Revolution.* London: Methuen, 1975.

Taylor, Rogan. *Football and Its Fans: Supporters and Their Relations With the Game, 1885–1985.* Leicester, England: Leicester University Press, 1992.

Thomas, Terence, ed. *The British: Their Religious Beliefs and Practices.* London: Routledge, 1988.

Thomis, M. I. *The Luddites.* Newton Abbot, England: David and Charles, 1973.

Thompson, E. P. *The Making of the English Working Classes.* London: Gollancz, 1963.

Thomson, David. *England in the Nineteenth Century.* Harmondsworth, England: Penguin, 1978.

Tobias, J. J. *Crime and Industrial Society in the Nineteenth Century.* London: Batsford, 1967.

Turner, Frank M. *Contesting Cultural Authority: Essays in Victorian Intellectual Life.* Cambridge: Cambridge University Press, 1993.

Urdank, Albion M. *Religion and Society in a Cotswold Vale: Nailsworth, Gloucestershire, 1780–1865.* Berkeley, Calif.: University of California Press, 1990.

Vincent, David. *Literacy and Popular Culture: England 1750–1914.* Cambridge: Cambridge University Press, 1989.

Walsh, John, Colin Haydon, and Stephen Taylor, ed. *The Church of England c1689–c1833: From Toleration to Tractarianism.* New York: Cambridge University Press, 1993.

Walton, John K. *Fish and Chips and the British Working Class, 1870–1940.* Leicester, England: Leicester University Press, 1992.

Walton, John K., and Alastair Wilcox, ed. *Low Life and Moral Improvement in Mid-Victorian England: Liverpool Through the Journalism of Hugh Shimmin.* Leicester, England: Leicester University Press, 1993.

Walvin, James. *Slaves and Slavery: the British Colonial Experience.* Manchester: Manchester University Press, 1992.

———. *Victorian Values.* London: Deutsch, 1987.

Ward, W. R. *Religion and Society in England, 1790–1850.* London: Batsford, 1972.

Weeks, Jeffrey. *Sex, Politics and Society: The Regulation of Sexuality Since 1800.* London: Longman, 1989.

Weiner, M. J. *English Culture and the Decline of the Industrial Spirit, 1850–1980.* London: Cambridge University Press, 1981.

Wheeler, Michael. *English Fiction of the Victorian Period, 1830–1890.* London: Longman, 1994.

White, R. J. *Life in Regency England.* London: Batsford, 1963.

Wood, Anthony. *Nineteenth Century Britain, 1815–1914.* Harlow, England: Longman, 1982.

Woodham-Smith, Cecil. *The Great Hunger: Ireland 1845–1849.* Harmondsworth, England: Penguin, 1991.

Woods, Robert. *The Population of Britain in the Nineteenth Century.* Basingstoke, England: Macmillan, 1992.

Yates, Nigel. *The Oxford Movement and Anglican Ritualism.* London: Historical Association, 1983.

Yeo, Richard R. *Defining Science: William Whewell, Natural Knowledge and Public Debate in Early Victorian Britain.* Cambridge: Cambridge University Press, 1993.

Politics

Adelman, Paul. *The Rise of the Labour Party, 1880–1945.* London: Longman, 1986.

Barker, Michael. *Gladstone and Radicalism: The Reconstruction of Liberal Policy in Britain, 1885–94.* New York: Barnes and Noble, 1975.

Barker, Rodney. *Politics, People and Government: Themes in British Political Thought Since the Nineteenth Century.* Basingstoke, England: Macmillan, 1994.

Barnes, D. G. *A History of the English Corn Laws.* London: Frank

Cass, 1961.

Behagg, Clive. *Chartism*. Harlow, England: Longman, 1993.

————. *Labour and Reform: Working Class Movements, 1815–1914.* Abingdon, England: Hodder and Stoughton, 1991.

Belchem, John. *Orator Hunt: Henry Hunt and English Working-Class Radicalism.* Oxford: Clarendon Press, 1985.

Bentley, M. *The Climax of Liberal Politics.* London: Edward Arnold, 1987.

Birch, Lionel. *The History of the TUC, 1868–1968.* London: General Council of the TUC, 1968.

Blake, Robert. *The Conservative Party From Peel to Thatcher.* London: Methuen, 1985.

Boyce D. G. *The Irish Question and British Politics, 1868–1986.* Basingstoke, England: Macmillan, 1988.

Brock, Michael. *The Great Reform Act.* London: Hutchinson, 1973.

Brown, R., and C. Daniels. *Nineteenth Century Britain.* London: Macmillan, 1980.

Brundage, A. *The Making of the New Poor Law.* London: Hutchinson, 1978.

Burns, J. H., and H. L. A. Hart, ed. *Jeremy Bentham: A Fragment on Government.* Cambridge: Cambridge University Press, 1988.

Cannon, John. *Parliamentary Reform, 1640–1832.* London: Cambridge University Press, 1972.

Chamberlain, Muriel E. *Pax Britannica?: British Foreign Policy, 1789–1914.* London: Longman, 1988.

Christie, Ian R. *Wars and Revolutions: Britain 1760–1815.* London: Edward Arnold, 1982.

Clegg, Hugh A. *A History of British Trade Unions Since 1889.* 3 vols. Oxford: Clarendon Press, 1964-1994.

Cole, Margaret. *The Story of Fabian Socialism.* London: Heinemann, 1961.

Colley, Linda. *Britons: Forging the Nation, 1707–1837.* London: Pimlico, 1994.

Cowling, M. *1867: Disraeli, Gladstone and Revolution.* Cambridge: Cambridge University Press, 1967.

Derry, John. *Politics in the Age of Fox, Pitt and Liverpool.* Basingstoke: Macmillan, 1990.

Dickinson H. T. *British Radicalism and the French Revolution, 1789–1815.* Oxford: Blackwell, 1985.

Douglas, Roy. *The History of the Liberal Party, 1895–1970.* London: Sidgwick and Jackson, 1971.

Emsley, Clive. *British Society and the French Wars, 1793–1815.* London: Macmillan, 1979.

Evans, Eric. *The Forging of the Modern State: Early Industrial Britain 1783–1870*. London: Longman, 1983.

———. *The Great Reform Act of 1832*. London: Methuen, 1983.

———. *Political Parties in Britain, 1780–1867*. London: Methuen, 1985.

Feuchtwanger, E. J. *Democracy and Empire: Britain, 1865–1914*. London: Edward Arnold, 1985.

Foster, R. F. *Paddy and Mr Punch: Connections in Irish and English History*. London: Allen Lane, 1993.

Fraser, Derek. *The Evolution of the British Welfare State: A History of Social Policy Since the Industrial Revolution*. London: Macmillan, 1984.

Fulford, Roger. *Hanover to Windsor*. London: Batsford, 1960.

Goldfrank, David M. *The Origins of the Crimean War*. London: Longman, 1994.

Hadfield, Alice Mary. *The Chartist Land Company*. Newton Abbot, England: David and Charles, 1970.

Hempton, David. *Methodism and Politics in British Society, 1750–1850*. London: Hutchinson, 1984.

Hibbert, Christopher. *The Court of St James's: the Monarch at Work from Victoria to Elizabeth II*. London: Weidenfeld and Nicolson, 1979.

Hilton, Boyd. *Corn, Cash, Commerce — The Economic Policies of the Tory Governments, 1815–30*. Oxford: Oxford University Press, 1977.

Hobley, L. F. *The Trade Union Story*. Glasgow, Scotland: Blackie, 1969.

Hobsbawm, Eric J., and George Rudé. *Captain Swing*. London: Lawrence and Wishart, 1969.

Hoppen, K. Theodore. *Ireland Since 1800*. London: Longman, 1989.

Horne, Thomas A. *Property Rights and Poverty: Political Argument in Britain, 1605–1834*. Chapel Hill, N.C.: University of North Carolina Press, 1990.

Howell, David. *British Workers and the Independent Labour Party, 1888–1906*. Manchester: Manchester University Press, 1983.

Hume, Leslie Parker. *The National Union of Women's Suffrage Societies, 1897–1914*. New York: Garland Press, 1982.

Hunt, E. H. *British Labour History, 1815–1914*. London: Weidenfeld and Nicolson, 1981.

Hutt, Allen. *British Trade Unionism: A Short History*. London: Lawrence and Wishart, 1975.

James, Robert Rhodes. *The British Revolution: British Politics, 1880–1939.* 2 vols. London: Hamish Hamilton, 1976, vol 1, and 1977, vol 2.

Jenkins, T. A. *The Liberal Ascendancy, 1830–1886.* Basingstoke, England: Macmillan, 1994.

Jones, David. *Chartism and the Chartists.* London: Allen Lane, 1975.

Jones, Raymond A. *The British Diplomatic Service, 1815–1914.* Gerrards Cross, England: Smythe, 1983.

Knaplund, Paul. *Gladstone and Britain's Imperial Policy.* Hamden, Conn.: Archon, 1966.

———. *Gladstone's Foreign Policy.* Hamden, Conn.: Archon, 1970.

Lane, P. *Radicals and Reformers.* London: Batsford, 1973.

Laybourn, Keith. *The Rise of Labour: The British Labour Party, 1890–1979.* London: Edward Arnold, 1988.

Lee, Stephen J. *Aspects of British Political History, 1815–1914.* New York: Routledge, 1994.

Lewis, Michael. *The Navy in Transition, 1814–1864.* London: Hodder and Stoughton, 1965.

Lovell, J., and B. C. Roberts. *A Short History of the TUC.* London: Macmillan, 1968.

Mackenzie, Norman, and Jeanne Mackenzie. *The First Fabians.* London: Weidenfeld and Nicolson, 1977.

Mansergh, P. N. S. *The Irish Question, 1840–1921.* London: Allen and Unwin, 1975.

Marlow, Joyce. *The Peterloo Massacre.* London: Rapp and Whiting, 1969.

———. *The Tolpuddle Martyrs.* London: Deutsch, 1971.

McCord, Norman. *The Anti-Corn Law League.* London: Allen and Unwin, 1968.

———. *British History, 1815–1906.* Oxford: Oxford University Press, 1994.

———. *Free Trade: Theory and Practice from Adam Smith to Keynes.* Newton Abbot, England: David and Charles, 1970.

Morgan, D. *Suffragists and Liberals: The Politics of Women's Suffrage in England.* Oxford: Blackwell, 1975.

Morton, Grenfell. *Home Rule and the Irish Question.* London: Longman, 1980.

Musson, A. E. *British Trade Unions, 1800–1875.* London: Macmillan, 1972.

Nicholson, Peter P. *The Political Philosophy of the British Idealists: Selected Studies.* Cambridge: Cambridge University Press, 1990.

Nicolson, Harold. *The Congress of Vienna: A Study of Allied Unity,*

1812–1822. London: Cassell, 1989.

Oldfield, J. R. *Popular Politics and British Anti-Slavery: The Mobilisation of Public Opinion Against the Slave Trade.* Manchester: Manchester University Press, 1994.

Park, Joseph Hendershot, ed. *British Prime Ministers of the Nineteenth Century: Policies and Speeches.* Freeport, N.Y.: Books For Libraries Press, 1970.

Pearce, Malcolm, and Geoffrey Stewart. *British Political History, 1867–1990: Democracy and Decline.* London: Routledge, 1992.

Pearce, Robert, and Roger Stearn. *Government and Reform, 1815–1918.* Abingdon, England: Hodder and Stoughton, 1994.

Pease, Edward R. *The History of the Fabian Society.* London: Frank Cass, 1963.

Pelling, Henry. *A History of British Trade Unionism.* London: Macmillan, 1992.

———. *The Origins of the Labour Party, 1880–1900.* Oxford: Clarendon Press, 1965.

Phillips, Gordon. *The Rise of the Labour Party, 1893–1931.* London: Routledge, 1992.

Pimlott, Ben, and Chris Cook. *Trade Unions in British Politics: The First 250 Years.* London: Longman, 1991.

Porter, Bernard. *Britannia's Burden: The Political Evolution of Modern Britain, 1851–1990.* London: Edward Arnold, 1994.

Powell, David. *British Politics and the Labour Question, 1868–1990.* Basingstoke, England: Macmillan, 1992.

Pugh, Martin. *State and Society: British Political and Social History, 1870–1992.* London: Edward Arnold, 1994.

———. *The Tories and the People, 1880–1935.* Oxford: Blackwell, 1985.

———. *Women's Suffrage in Britain, 1867–1928.* London: Historical Association, 1980.

Read, Donald. *The Age of Urban Democracy: England 1868–1914.* Harlow, England: Longman, 1994.

Richardson, Joanna. *The Regency.* London: Collins, 1973.

Robbins, Keith. *The Eclipse of a Great Power: Modern Britain, 1870–1992.* London: Longman, 1994.

Rosen, Andrew. *Rise Up Women!* London: Routledge, 1974.

Royle, Edward. *Chartism.* London: Longman, 1986.

Rule, John. *British Trade Unionism, 1750–1850.* London: Longman, 1988.

Saville, John. *1848: The British State and the Chartist Movement.* Cambridge: Cambridge University Press, 1987.

Searle, G. R. *The Liberal Party: Triumph and Disintegration, 1886–1929*. Basingstoke, England: Macmillan, 1992.

Shannon, Richard. *The Age of Disraeli, 1867–1881: The Rise of Tory Democracy*. London: Longman, 1992.

Sheldrake, John. *Industrial Relations and Politics in Britain, 1880–1989*. London: Pinter, 1991.

Simon, Brian. *Education and the Labour Movement, 1870–1920.* London: Lawrence and Wishart, 1965.

Smith, E. A. *The House of Lords in British Politics and Society, 1815–1911*. Harlow, England: Longman, 1992.

Smith, F. B. *The Making of the Second Reform Bill.* Cambridge: Cambridge University Press, 1966.

Stevenson, John. *Popular Disturbances in England, 1700–1832.* London: Longman, 1992.

Stewart, Robert. *The Foundation of the Conservative Party, 1830–1867*. London: Longman, 1978.

———. *Party and Politics, 1830–1852*. Basingstoke, England: Macmillan, 1989.

Stone, Lawrence, ed. *An Imperial State at War: Britain from 1689–1815*. London: Routledge, 1994.

Thomis, Malcolm. *The Luddites*. Newton Abbot, England: David and Charles, 1970.

Thomis, Malcolm, and Peter Holt. *Threats of Revolution in Britain, 1789–1848*. London: Macmillan, 1977.

Thompson, Dorothy. *The Chartists*. London: Temple Smith, 1984.

Thompson, P. *Socialists, Liberals and Labour: The Struggle for London, 1885–1914*. London: Routledge, 1967.

Vincent, John R. *The Formation of the British Liberal Party, 1857–1868*. Hassocks, England: Harvester Press, 1976.

Walmsley, Robert. *Peterloo: the Case Reopened.* Manchester: Manchester University Press, 1969.

Walton, John K. *The Second Reform Act*. London: Methuen, 1987.

Ward, J. T. *Chartism*. London: Batsford, 1973.

———. *Popular Movements, c1830–1850.* London: Macmillan, 1970.

Winstanley, Michael J. *Ireland and the Land Question, 1800–1922.* London: Methuen, 1984.

Wright, D. G. *Popular Radicalism: The Working-Class Experience 1780–1880*. London: Longman, 1988.

International Relations

Adams, P. *Fatal Necessity: British Intervention in New Zealand, 1830–1847.* Auckland, New Zealand: Auckland University Press, 1977.

Ally, Russell. *Gold and Empire: The Bank of England and South Africa's Gold Producers, 1886–1926.* London: UCL Press, 1994.

Anderson, M. S. *The Eastern Question, 1774–1923.* London: Macmillan, 1966.

Anstey, R. T. *The Atlantic Slave Trade and British Abolition, 1760–1810.* London: Macmillan, 1975.

Barthorp, Michael. *The Zulu War: A Pictorial History.* Poole, England: Blandford Press, 1984.

Bartlett, C. J. *Defence and Diplomacy: Britain and the Great Powers, 1815–1914.* Manchester: Manchester University Press, 1993.

———. *Great Britain and Sea Power, 1815–1853.* Oxford: Clarendon Press, 1963.

Bates, Darrell. *The Fashoda Incident of 1898: Encounter on the Nile.* Oxford: Oxford University Press, 1984.

Bayly, C. A. *Imperial Meridian: The British Empire and the World, 1780–1830.* London: Longman, 1989.

Belich, James. *The New Zealand Wars and the Victorian Interpretation of Racial Conflict.* Auckland (New Zealand): Auckland University Press, 1986.

Bennett, George. *The Concept of Empire: Burke to Attlee, 1774–1947.* London: Black, 1962.

Bradford, Ernle. *Gibraltar — The History of a Fortress.* London: Hart-Davis, 1971.

Burroughs, Peter. *Britain and Australia, 1831–1855: A Study in Imperial Relations and Crown Lands.* Oxford: Oxford University Press, 1967.

Busch, B. C. *Britain and the Persian Gulf, 1894–1914.* Berkeley, Calif.: University of California Press, 1967.

———. *Wars and Revolutions: Britain 1760–1815.* London: Edward Arnold, 1982.

Cain, P. J., and A. G. Hopkins. *British Imperialism: Innovation and Expansion, 1688–1914.* London: Longman, 1993.

Chamberlain, Muriel E. *Pax Britannica?: British Foreign Policy, 1789–1914.* London: Longman, 1988.

———. *The Scramble for Africa.* London: Longman, 1974.

Christopher, A. J. *The British Empire at its Zenith.* London: Croom Helm, 1988.

Clark, Manning. *A History of Australia.* 6 vols. Carlton, Australia: University of Melbourne Press, 1962–1987.

Clayton, G. D. *Britain and the Eastern Question.* London: University of London Press, 1971.

Cook, Adrian. *The Alabama Claims, American Politics and Anglo-American Relations, 1865–1872.* Ithaca, N.Y.: Cornell University Press, 1975.

Craton, Michael. *Sinews of Empire: A Short History of British Slavery.* London: Temple Smith, 1974.

Curtin, P. D. *The Image of Africa: British Ideas and Action, 1780–1850.* London: Macmillan, 1965.

Davis, R. *The Industrial Revolution and British Overseas Trade.* Leicester, England: Leicester University Press, 1979.

Edwardes, Michael. *British India, 1772–1947.* London: Sidgwick and Jackson, 1967.

Eldridge, C. C. *Victorian Imperialism.* London: Hodder and Stoughton, 1978.

Farwell, Byron. *Queen Victoria's Little Wars.* London: Allen Lane, 1973.

Feuchtwanger, E. J. *Democracy and Empire: Britain, 1865–1914.* London: Edward Arnold, 1985.

Fieldhouse, D. K. *Economics and Empire, 1830–1914.* London: Weidenfeld and Nicolson, 1973.

Frost, Alan. *Convicts and Empire: A Naval Question, 1776–1811.* Melbourne, Australia: Oxford University Press, 1980.

Galbraith, John S. *Crown and Charter: The Early Years of the British South Africa Company.* Berkeley, California: University of California Press, 1974.

Hall, Christopher D. *British Strategy in the Napoleonic War.* Manchester: Manchester University Press, 1992.

Havinden, Michael, and D. Meredith. *Colonialism and Development: Britain and its Tropical Colonies, 1850–1960.* London: Routledge, 1993.

Heathcote, T. A. *The Military in British India: The Development of British Land Forces in South Asia, 1600–1947.* Manchester: Manchester University Press, 1994.

Hibbert, Christopher. *Africa Explored: Europeans in the Dark Continent 1769–1889.* London: Allen Lane, 1982.

———. *The Great Mutiny: India 1857.* London: Allen Lane, 1978.

Hobsbawm, E. J. *The Age of Empire, 1875–1914.* London: Weidenfeld and Nicolson, 1987.

Holt, Edgar. *Protest in Arms.* London: Putnam, 1960.

Howard, Christopher. *Splendid Isolation.* London: Macmillan, 1967.

Hyam, Ronald. *Britain's Imperial Century, 1815–1914.* Basingstoke, England: Macmillan, 1993.

———. *Empire and Sexuality: The British Experience.* Manchester: Manchester University Press, 1990.

Jones, J. R. *Britain and the World, 1649–1815.* London: Fontana, 1980.

Judd, Denis. *Balfour and the British Empire: A Study in Imperial Evolution 1874–1932.* London: Macmillan, 1968.

———. *The Boer War.* London: Hart-Davis MacGibbon, 1977.

———. *The Crimean War.* London: Hart-Davis MacGibbon, 1975.

———. *The Victorian Empire, 1837–1901.* London: Weidenfeld and Nicolson, 1970.

Knaplund, Paul. *Gladstone and Britain's Imperial Policy.* Hamden, Conn.: Archon, 1966.

———. *Gladstone's Foreign Policy.* Hamden, Conn.: Archon, 1970.

Koss, S. *The Pro-Boers: The Anatomy of an Anti-War Movement.* Chicago: University of Chicago Press, 1973.

Lee, Edwin. *The British as Rulers Governing Multi-Racial Singapore, 1867–1914.* Singapore: Singapore University Press, 1991.

Longford, Elizabeth. *Jameson's Raid: The Prelude to the Boer War.* London: Weidenfeld and Nicolson, 1982.

Macfie, A. L. *The Eastern Question, 1774–1923.* London: Longman, 1989.

MacKenzie, John M. *Propaganda and Empire: The Manipulation of British Public Opinion, 1880–1960.* Manchester: Manchester University Press, 1986.

Mahon, John K. *The War of 1812.* New York: Da Capo Press, 1991.

Martin, Ged. *Britain and the Origins of Canadian Confederation, 1837–67.* Basingstoke, England: Macmillan, 1994.

McDonough, Frank. *The British Empire, 1815–1914.* Abingdon, England: Hodder and Stoughton, 1994.

McFarlane, Anthony. *The British in the Americas, 1480–1815.* London: Longman, 1994.

McLean, D. *Britain and Her Buffer State: The Collapse of the Persian Empire, 1890–1914.* London: Royal Historical Society, 1979.

Medlicott, W.N. *The Congress of Berlin and After: A Diplomatic History of the Near Eastern Situation, 1878–80.* London: Frank Cass, 1963.

Merk, F. *The Oregon Question.* Cambridge, Mass.: Belknap Press, 1967.

Metcalf, Thomas R. *Land, Landlords and the British Raj: Northern India in the Nineteenth Century.* Berkeley, Calif.: University of California Press, 1979.

Miller, Rory. *Britain and Latin America in the Nineteenth and Twentieth Centuries.* London: Longman, 1993.

Millman, Richard. *Britain and the Eastern Question.* Oxford: Clarendon Press, 1979.

Neillands, Robin. *Wellington and Napoleon: Clash of Arms, 1807–1815.* London: John Murray, 1994.

Norris, J. A. *First Afghan War, 1838–1842.* Cambridge: Cambridge University Press, 1967.

Pakenham, Thomas. *The Boer War.* London: Weidenfeld and Nicolson, 1979.

———. *The Scramble for Africa.* London: Weidenfeld and Nicolson, 1991.

Palmer, Alan. *The Crimean War.* New York: Dorset Press, 1992.

Porter, A. N. *Atlas of British Overseas Expansion.* London: Routledge, 1991.

———. *The Origins of the South African War: Joseph Chamberlain and the Diplomacy of Imperialism.* Manchester: Manchester University Press, 1980.

Porter, Bernard. *The Lion's Share: A Short History of British Imperialism, 1850–1983.* London: Longman, 1984.

Rich, Norman. *Why the Crimean War?* Hanover, N.H.: University Press of New England, 1985.

Rickard, John. *Australia: A Cultural History.* London: Longman, 1988.

Robbins, Keith. *The Eclipse of a Great Power: Modern Britain, 1870–1992.* London: Longman, 1994.

Robinson, Ronald, and John Gallagher. *Africa and the Victorians: The Official Mind of Imperialism.* London: Macmillan, 1981.

Searing, James F. *West African Slavery and Atlantic Commerce.* Cambridge: Cambridge University Press, 1993.

Shaw, A. G. L. *Convicts and the Colonies.* London: Faber, 1966.

———. *Great Britain and the Colonies, 1815–65.* London: Methuen, 1970.

Smith, I. R. *The Origins of the South African War, 1899–1902.* London: Longman, 1994.

Stone, Lawrence, ed. *An Imperial State at War: Britain from 1689–1815.* London: Routledge, 1994.

Turnbull, C. M. *The Straits Settlements, 1826–67: Indian Presidency to Crown Colony.* London: Athlone Press, 1972.

Verdier, Daniel. *Democracy and International Trade: Britain, France and the United States, 1860–1990.* Princeton, N.J.: Princeton University Press, 1994.

Walvin, James. *Slaves and Slavery: The British Colonial Experience.* Manchester: Manchester University Press, 1992.

Warwick, Peter, ed. *The South African War: The Anglo-Boer War 1899–1902.* Harlow, England: Longman, 1980.

Watson, Bruce. *The Great Indian Mutiny.* New York: Praeger, 1991.

Weigall, David. *Britain and the World, 1815–1986.* London: Batsford, 1987.

Woodhouse, C. M. *The Battle of Navarino.* London: Hodder and Stoughton, 1965.

Yapp, M. E. *Strategies of British India: Britain, Iran and Afghanistan, 1798–1850.* Oxford: Clarendon Press, 1980.

Youngs, Tim. *Travellers in Africa: British Travelogues, 1850–1900.* Manchester: Manchester University Press, 1994.

Industry and Commerce

Addy, John. *The Agrarian Revolution.* Harlow, England: Longman, 1972.

Albert, W. *The Turnpike Road System in England, 1663–1840.* Cambridge: Cambridge University Press, 1972.

Ally, Russell. *Gold and Empire: The Bank of England and South Africa's Gold Producers, 1886–1926.* London: UCL Press, 1994.

Anstey, R. T. *The Atlantic Slave Trade and British Abolition, 1760–1810.* London: Macmillan, 1975.

Ashton, T. S. *The Industrial Revolution, 1760–1830.* Oxford: Oxford University Press, 1968.

Ashworth, William. *An Economic History of England, 1870–1939.* London: Methuen, 1960.

Aspin, Chris. *The Cotton Industry.* Aylesbury, England: Shire Publications, 1981.

Barker, T. C., and Dorian Gerhold. *The Rise and Fall of Road Transport, 1700–1990.* Basingstoke, England: Macmillan, 1993.

Barnes, D. G. *A History of the English Corn Laws.* London: Frank Cass, 1961.

Benson, John. *The Rise of Consumer Society in Britain, 1880–1980.* London: Longman, 1994.

Birch, Alan. *Economic History of the Iron and Steel Industry, 1784–1879.* London: Frank Cass, 1967.

Birch, Lionel. *The History of the TUC, 1868–1968.* London: General Council of the TUC, 1968.

Birchall, Johnston. *Co-op: the People's Business.* Manchester: Manchester University Press, 1994.

Breach, R. W., and R. M. Hartwell. *British Economy and Society, 1870–1970*. London: Oxford University Press, 1972.

Briggs, Asa. *The Age of Improvement, 1783–1867*. London: Longman, 1979.

————. *Iron Bridge to Crystal Palace*. London: Thames and Hudson, 1979.

Brown, Richard. *Society and Economy in Modern Britain, 1700–1850*. London: Routledge, 1991.

Cameron, R. *Banking in the Early Stages of Industrialization*. Oxford: Oxford University Press, 1967.

Capie, Forrest H., ed. *History of Banking, 1650–1850*. 10 vols. London: William Pickering, 1994.

Case, S. C. *The Industrial Revolution*. London: Evans Brothers, 1975.

Chambers, J. D. *The Workshop of the World: British Economic History from 1820 to 1880*. London: Oxford University Press, 1968.

Chambers, J. D., and G. E. Mingay. *The Agricultural Revolution, 1750–1880*. London: Batsford, 1966.

Chapman, S. D. *The Cotton Industry in the Industrial Revolution*. Basingstoke, England: Macmillan, 1987.

Claeys, Gregory. *Machinery, Money and the Millenium: The New Moral Economy of Owenite Socialism, 1815–60*. Princeton, N.J.: Princeton University Press, 1987.

Clegg, Hugh A. *A History of British Trade Unions Since 1889*. 3 vols. Oxford: Clarendon Press, 1964-1994.

Crouzet, F. *Capital Formation in the Industrial Revolution*. London: Methuen, 1972.

Davis, R. *The Industrial Revolution and British Overseas Trade*. Leicester: Leicester University Press, 1979.

Deane, Phyllis. *The First Industrial Revolution*. Cambridge: Cambridge University Press, 1979.

Deane, Phyllis, and W. A. Cole. *British Economic Growth, 1688–1959: Trends and Structure*. Cambridge: Cambridge University Press, 1969.

Dyos, H. J., and D. H. Aldcroft. *British Transport: An Economic Survey from the Seventeenth Century to the Twentieth*. Leicester, England: Leicester University Press, 1969.

Edwards, Michael M. *The Growth of the British Cotton Trade, 1780–1815*. Manchester: Manchester University Press, 1967.

Evans, Eric J. *The Contentious Tithe*. London: Routledge, 1976.

————. *The Forging of the Modern State: Early Industrial Britain, 1783–1870*. London: Longman, 1983.

Fieldhouse, D. K. *Economics and Empire, 1830–1914.* London: Weidenfeld and Nicolson, 1973.

Fitzgerald, Robert. *British Labour Management and Industrial Welfare, 1846–1939.* London: Croom Helm, 1988.

Flinn, M. W. *The Origins of the Industrial Revolution.* London: Longman, 1966.

Gledhill, D. *Gas Lighting.* Aylesbury, England: Shire Publications, 1981.

Hadfield, Charles. *British Canals.* Newton Abbot, England: David and Charles, 1979.

———. *The Canal Age.* Newton Abbot, England: David and Charles, 1968.

Harris, J. R. *The British Iron Industry, 1700–1850.* Basingstoke, England: Macmillan, 1988.

Hartwell, R. M. *The Causes of the Industrial Revolution in England.* London: Methuen, 1967.

———. *The Industrial Revolution.* Oxford: Blackwell, 1970.

———. *The Industrial Revolution and Economic Growth.* London: Methuen, 1971.

Hawke, G. R. *Railways and Economic Growth in England and Wales, 1840–1870.* Oxford: Clarendon Press, 1970.

Heaton, Herbert. *The Yorkshire Woollen and Worsted Industries.* Oxford: Oxford University Press, 1965.

Hills, Richard L. *Power From Steam: A History of the Stationary Steam Engine.* Cambridge: Cambridge University Press, 1993.

Hobley, L. F. *The Trade Union Story.* Glasgow, Scotland: Blackie, 1969.

Hobsbawm, Eric. *Industry and Empire.* London: Weidenfeld and Nicolson, 1968.

Hobsbawm, E. J., and George Rudé. *Captain Swing.* London: Lawrence and Wishart, 1969.

Hope, Ronald. *A New History of British Shipping.* London: John Murray, 1990.

Hudson, Pat. *The Industrial Revolution.* London: Edward Arnold, 1992.

Hunt, E. H. *British Labour History, 1815–1914.* London: Weidenfeld and Nicolson, 1981.

Hutt, Allen. *British Trade Unionism: A Short History.* London: Lawrence and Wishart, 1975.

Jenkins, D. T., and K. G. Ponting. *The British Wool Textile Industry, 1770–1914.* London: Heinemann, 1982.

Jenkins, John G. *The Wool Textile Industry in Great Britain.* London:

Routledge, 1972.

Jones, E. L. *The Development of English Agriculture, 1815–1873.* London: Macmillan, 1968.

Kain, Roger. *The Tithe Surveys of England and Wales.* Cambridge: Cambridge University Press, 1985.

Keay, John. *The Honourable Company: A History of the English East India Company.* London: HarperCollins, 1991.

Keeble, S. P. *The Ability to Manage: A Study of British Management, 1890–1990.* Manchester: Manchester University Press, 1992.

Kellett, John R. *The Impact of Railways on Victorian Cities.* London: Routledge, 1969.

Kerridge, Eric. *The Agricultural Revolution.* London: Allen and Unwin, 1967.

Kirby, M. W. *The British Coalmining Industry, 1870–1946.* London: Macmillan, 1977.

Kynaston, David. *The City of London: A World of Its Own, 1815–1890.* London: Chatto and Windus, 1994.

Lane, Peter. *The Industrial Revolution: The Birth of the Modern Age.* London: Weidenfeld and Nicolson, 1978.

Lawson, Philip. *The East India Company: A History.* London: Longman, 1993.

Lovell, J., and B. C. Roberts. *A Short History of the TUC.* London: Macmillan, 1968.

Marshall, Dorothy. *Industrial England, 1776–1851.* London: Routledge and Kegan Paul, 1982.

Mathias, Peter. *The First Industrial Nation.* London: Routledge, 1988.

McCord, Norman M. *Free Trade: Theory and Practice From Adam Smith to Keynes.* Newton Abbot, England: David and Charles, 1970.

Morris, R. J., and John Langton. *Atlas of Industrializing Britain, 1780–1914.* London: Routledge, 1986.

Musson, A. E. *British Trade Unions, 1800–1875.* London: Macmillan, 1972.

Palmer, Marilyn, and Peter Neaverson. *Industry in the Landscape, 1700–1900.* London: Routledge, 1994.

Payne, Peter L. *British Entrepreneurship in the Nineteenth Century.* Basingstoke, England: Macmillan, 1988.

Pelling, Henry. *A History of British Trade Unionism.* London: Macmillan, 1992.

Perkin, Harold. *The Age of the Railway.* London: Panther, 1970.

Pimlott, Ben, and Chris Cook. *Trade Unions in British Politics: The First 250 Years.* London: Longman, 1991.

Pollard, Sidney. *Britain's Prime and Britain's Decline: The British Economy, 1870–1914.* London: Edward Arnold, 1990.

Pollard, Sidney, and Paul Robertson. *The British Shipbuilding Industry, 1870–1914.* Cambridge, Mass.: Harvard University Press, 1979.

Raistrick, A. *Quakers in Science and Industry.* Newton Abbot, England: David and Charles, 1968.

Reed, M. C. *Railways and the Victorian Economy.* Newton Abbot, England: David and Charles, 1969.

Robbins, Michael. *The Railway Age.* London: Routledge, 1962.

Rule, John. *British Trade Unionism, 1750–1850.* London: Longman, 1988.

————. *The Vital Century: England's Developing Economy, 1714–1815.* Harlow, England: Longman, 1992.

Sekers, David. *The Potteries.* Princes Risborough, England: Shire Publications, 1981.

Semmell, Bernard. *The Rise of Free Trade Imperialism.* Cambridge: Cambridge University Press, 1970.

Sheldrake, John. *Industrial Relations and Politics in Britain, 1880–1989.* London: Pinter, 1991.

Simmons, Jack. *The Railway in England and Wales, 1836–1914.* Leicester, England: Leicester University Press, 1978.

Thomas, John. *The Rise of the Staffordshire Potteries.* Bath, England: Adams and Dart, 1971.

Thomis, M. I. *The Luddites.* Newton Abbot, England: David and Charles, 1973.

Thompson, Allan. *The Dynamics of the Industrial Revolution.* London: Edward Arnold, 1973.

Thompson, E. P. *The Making of the English Working Classes.* London: Gollancz, 1963.

Timmins, Geoffrey. *The Last Shift: The Decline of Handloom Weaving in Nineteenth-Century Lancashire.* Manchester: Manchester University Press, 1993.

Turner, Michael E. *Enclosure in Britain, 1750–1830.* London: Macmillan, 1984.

Ward, John T. *The Factory Movement, 1830–1855.* London: Macmillan, 1962.

————. *The Factory System.* 2 vols. Newton Abbot, England: David and Charles, 1970.

Warren, K. *The Geography of British Heavy Industry Since 1800.* London: Oxford University Press, 1976.

Weiner, M. J. *English Culture and the Decline of the Industrial Spirit,*

1850–1980. London: Cambridge University Press, 1981.

Williams, T. I. *A History of the British Gas Industry.* Oxford: Oxford University Press, 1981.

The Twentieth Century

Biography and Autobiography

Addison, Paul. *Churchill on the Home Front, 1900–1955.* London: Cape, 1992.

Anderson, Bruce. *John Major: The Making of the Prime Minister.* London: Fourth Estate, 1991.

———. *Margaret Thatcher: A Study in Power.* London: Hamish Hamilton, 1984.

Arnold, Harry. *Charles and Diana.* London: New English Library, 1981.

Aronson, Theo. *The King in Love: King Edward VII's Mistresses — Lillie Langtry, Daisy Warwick, Alice Keppel, and Others.* New York: Harper and Row, 1988.

Arthur, Jane. *The Princess and the Duchess.* London: Hale, 1990.

Ashdown, Paddy. *Beyond Westminster.* London: Simon and Schuster, 1994.

Aster, Sidney. *Anthony Eden.* London: Weidenfeld and Nicolson, 1976.

Baden-Powell, Heather. *Baden Powell: A Family Album.* Gloucester, England: Alan Sutton, 1986.

Balen, Malcolm. *Kenneth Clarke: a Biography.* London: Fourth Estate, 1994.

Barker, Elisabeth. *Churchill and Eden at War.* London: Macmillan, 1978.

Bartram, Peter. *David Steel: His Life and Politics.* London: W. H. Allen, 1981.

Beaverbrook, Lord. *The Decline and Fall of Lloyd George: And Great Was the Fall Thereof.* Westport, Conn.: Greenwood Press, 1981.

Beckett, John. *The Rise and Fall of the Grenvilles: Dukes of Buckingham and Chandos, 1710 to 1921.* Manchester: Manchester University Press, 1994.

Benedictus, David. *Lloyd George.* London: Weidenfeld and Nicolson, 1981.

Bessell, Peter. *Cover-Up: The Jeremy Thorpe Affair.* Wilmington: Simons Books, 1980.

Bloch, M., ed. *Wallis and Edward: Letters 1931–1937.* London: Weidenfeld and Nicolson, 1974.

Bloom, Ursula. *The Great Queen Consort.* London: Hale, 1976.

Boothroyd, Basil. *Philip: An Informal Biography.* Harlow, England: Longman, 1971.

Bradford, S. *George VI.* London: Weidenfeld and Nicolson, 1989.

Bradley, John. *Churchill and the British.* London: Watts, 1990.

Brendon, Piers. *Winston Churchill: A Brief Life.* London: Secker and Warburg, 1984.

Brent, Peter. *Captain Scott and the Antarctic Tragedy.* London: Weidenfeld and Nicolson, 1974.

Brooks, Stephen, ed. *Montgomery and the Eighth Army: A Selection From the Diaries, Correspondence and Other Papers of Field Marshal the Viscount Montgomery of Alamein, August 1942 to December 1943.* London: Bodley Head, 1991.

Brough, James. *Margaret, the Tragic Princess.* New York: Putnam, 1978.

Brown, George. *In My Way: The Political Memoirs of Lord George Brown.* London: Gollancz, 1971.

Bullock, Alan. *The Life and Times of Ernest Bevin.* 3 vols. London: Heinemann, 1960–1983.

Burridge, T. *Clement Attlee.* London: Cape, 1985.

Butler, David. *Lord Mountbatten: The Last Viceroy.* London: Methuen, 1985.

Butler, Mollie. *August and Rab.* London: Weidenfeld and Nicolson, 1987.

Butler, R. A. *The Art of the Possible.* London: Hamish Hamilton, 1971.

Callaghan, James. *Time and Chance.* London: Collins, 1987.

Campbell, John. *Lloyd George: The Goat in the Wilderness, 1922–31.* London: Cape, 1977.

Campbell, Judith. *Queen Elizabeth: A Biography.* New York: Crown, 1980.

Campbell, Lady Colin. *Diana in Private: The Princess Nobody Knows.* London: Smith Gryphon, 1992.

Campbell-Johnson, Alan. *Eden: The Making of a Statesman.* Westport, Conn.: Greenwood Press, 1976.

Carey, George. *I Believe.* London: SPCK, 1991.

Carlton, David. *Anthony Eden: A Biography.* London: Allen Lane, 1981.

Carpenter, Humphrey. *The Life of W. H. Auden: A Biography.* London: Allen and Unwin, 1981.

Carter, Violet Bonham. *Winston Churchill As I Knew Him.* London:

Eyre and Spottiswoode, 1965.

Cassar, George H. *Kitchener: Architect of Victory.* London: Kimber, 1977.

Cathcart, Helen. *Anne, the Princess Royal: A Princess for Our Times.* London: W. H. Allen, 1988.

————. *Charles: Man of Destiny.* London: W. H. Allen, 1988.

————. *Her Majesty the Queen: The Story of Elizabeth II.* New York: Dodd, Mead, 1966.

————. *Lord Snowdon.* London: W. H. Allen, 1968.

————. *The Married Life of the Queen.* London: W. H. Allen, 1970.

————. *Princess Margaret.* London: W. H. Allen, 1974.

————. *The Queen Herself.* London: W. H. Allen, 1982.

————. *The Queen Mother: Fifty Years a Queen.* London: W. H. Allen, 1986.

Chalfont, Alun. *Montgomery of Alamein.* London: Weidenfeld and Nicolson, 1976.

Charmley, John. *Churchill: The End of Glory.* Hodder and Stoughton, 1992.

Cherry-Garrard, Apsley. *The Worst Journey in the World: Antarctic, 1910–13.* Harmondsworth, England: Penguin, 1979.

Chester, Lewis, Magnus Linklater, and David May. *Jeremy Thorpe: A Secret Life.* London: Fontana, 1979.

Churchill, Randolph S. *Winston S. Churchill.* vols 1, and 2. London: Heinemann, 1966, vol 1 and 1967, vol 2.

Cole, Margaret, ed. *The Webbs and Their Work.* Westport, Conn.: Greenwood Press, 1985.

Collis, Maurice. *Nancy Astor.* London: Futura, 1982.

Constantine, Stephen. *Lloyd George.* London: Routledge, 1992.

Cosgrave, Patrick. *Margaret Thatcher: A Tory and Her Party.* London: Hutchinson, 1978.

Courtney, Nicholas. *Princess Anne: A Biography.* London: Weidenfeld and Nicolson, 1986.

Cregier, Don M. *Bounder From Wales: Lloyd George's Career Before the First World War.* Columbia, Mo.: University of Missouri Press, 1976.

Crick, Bernard. *George Orwell: A Life.* London: Secker and Warburg, 1980.

Davies, Nicholas. *Diana: A Princess and Her Troubled Marriage.* New York: Carol, 1992.

————. *The Unknown Maxwell: The Disgraced Tycoon's Secret Lives.* London: Pan, 1993.

Dempster, Nigel. *H.R.H. The Princess Margaret: A Life Unfulfilled*

London: Quartet, 1981.

Dimbleby, Jonathan. *The Prince of Wales.* London: Little, Brown, 1994.

Donaldson, Frances. *Edward VIII.* London: Weidenfeld and Nicolson, 1974.

———. *King George VI and Queen Elizabeth.* London: Weidenfeld and Nicolson, 1977.

Douglas-Home, Alec. *Letters to a Grandson.* London: Collins, 1983.

———. *The Way the Wind Blows: An Autobiography.* New York: Quadrangle/New York Times, 1976.

Duff, David. *Elizabeth of Glamis.* London: Muller, 1973.

———. *George and Elizabeth: A Royal Marriage.* London: Collins, 1983.

———. *Queen Mary.* London: Collins, 1985.

Dugdale, Blanche Elizabeth Campbell. *Arthur James Balfour, First Earl of Balfour, K.G., O.M., F.R.S.* Westport, Conn.: Greenwood Press, 1970.

Dunlop, Janice. *Charles and Diana: A Royal Romance.* New York: Dell, 1981.

Eden, Anthony, Earl of Avon. *Another World.* Garden City, N.Y.: Doubleday, 1977.

———. *Facing the Dictators: The Eden Memoirs.* London: Cassell, 1962.

———. *Full Circle: The Memoirs of the Rt. Hon. Sir Anthony Eden.* London: Cassell, 1960.

———. *The Reckoning: The Eden Memoirs.* London: Cassell, 1965.

Edgar, Donald. *The Queeen's Children.* London: Barker, 1978.

Edmonds, Robin. *The Big Three: Churchill, Roosevelt and Stalin in Peace and War.* London: Hamish Hamilton, 1991.

Edwards, Anne. *Matriarch: Queen Mary and the House of Windsor.* London: Hodder and Stoughton, 1984.

———. *Royal Sisters: Elizabeth and Margaret, 1926–1956.* London: Collins, 1990.

Egremont, Max. *Balfour: A Life of Arthur James Balfour.* London: Collins, 1980.

Ellis, Nesta Wyn. *John Major: An Authorized Biography.* London: Futura, 1991.

Evans, Harold. *Downing Street Diary: The Macmillan Years, 1957–1963.* London: Hodder and Stoughton, 1981.

Fisher, Graham. *Charles: the Man and the Prince.* Long Preston, England: Magna, 1984.

———. *Consort: The Life and Times of Prince Philip.* London: W. H.

Allen, 1980.

Fisher, Graham, and Heather Fisher. *Charles and Diana: Their Married Life.* London: Hale, 1984.

———. *Monarch: The Life and Times of Elizabeth II.* London: Hale, 1985.

———. *Prince Andrew.* London: W. H. Allen, 1981.

———. *The Queen's Life and Her Twenty–Five Years of Monarchy.* London: Hale, 1976.

Fisher, Nigel. *Harold Macmillan: A Biography.* London: Weidenfeld and Nicolson, 1982.

Flamini, Roland. *Sovereign: Elizabeth II and the Windsor Dynasty.* New York: Delacorte Press, 1991.

Frischauer, Willi. *Margaret: Princess Without a Cause.* London: Michael Joseph, 1977.

Fulford, Roger. *Hanover to Windsor.* London: Batsford, 1960.

Fyvel, T. R. *George Orwell: A Personal Memoir.* London: Weidenfeld and Nicolson, 1982.

Gardiner, George. *Margaret Thatcher: From Childhood to Leadership.* London: Kimber, 1975.

Gatrell, Simon. *Hardy the Creator: A Textual Biography.* Oxford: Clarendon Press, 1988.

George, W. R. P. *Lloyd George: Backbencher.* Llandysul, Wales: Gomer Press, 1983.

Gilbert, Bentley Brinkerhoff. *David Lloyd George, a Political Life.* 2 vols. London: Batsford, 1987, vol 1, and 1992, vol 2.

Gilbert, Martin. *Churchill: A Life.* London: Heinemann, 1991.

———. *In Search of Churchill: A Historian's Journey.* London: HarperCollins, 1994.

———. *Winston S. Churchill.* Vols 3-8. London: Heinemann, 1971–1986.

Gittings, Robert. *The Older Hardy.* London: Heinemann, 1978.

Grigg, John. *Lloyd George: From Peace to War, 1912–1916.* London: Methuen, 1985.

———. *Lloyd George: The People's Champion, 1902–1911.* London: Minerva, 1991.

Grimond, Jo. *Memoirs.* London: Heinemann, 1979.

Hailsham of St Marylebone, Lord. *A Sparrow's Flight.* London: Collins, 1990.

Hall, Unity. *Philip: The Man Behind the Monarchy.* London: O'Mara, 1987.

Hamilton, Alan. *The Real Charles.* London: Collins, 1988.

Hamilton, Mary Agnes. *J. Ramsay MacDonald.* Freeport, N.Y.: Books

For Libraries Press, 1971.

Hamilton, Nigel. *Monty: The Battles of Field Marshal Bernard Law Montgomery*. London: Hodder and Stoughton, 1994.

————. *Monty: The Field Marshal 1944–1976*. London: Hamish Hamilton, 1986.

————. *Monty: The Making of a General, 1887–1942*. London: Hamish Hamilton, 1981.

Hardy, Evelyn. *Thomas Hardy: A Critical Biography*. Folcroft, Pa.: Folcroft Library Editions, 1973.

Hardy, Florence Emily. *The Life of Thomas Hardy, 1840–1928: Compiled Largely from Contemporary Notes, Letters, Diaries and Biographical Memoranda*. Hamden, Conn.: Archon Books, 1970.

Harris, Jose. *William Beveridge: A Biography*. Oxford: Clarendon Press, 1977.

Harris, Kenneth. *Attlee*. London: Weidenfeld and Nicolson, 1985.

————. *The Queen*. London: Weidenfeld and Nicolson, 1994.

————. *Thatcher*. London: Weidenfeld and Nicolson, 1988.

Harrison, Rosina. *Rose: My Life in Service*. New York: Viking Press, 1975.

Hattersley, Roy. *Goodbye to Yorkshire*. London: Gollancz, 1976.

————. *A Yorkshire Boyhood*. London: Chatto and Windus, 1983.

Hawkins, Desmond. *Hardy: Novelist and Poet*. London: Macmillan, 1981.

Heald, Tim. *The Duke: A Portrait of Prince Philip*. London: Hodder and Stoughton, 1991.

Hibbert, Christopher. *Edward, the Uncrowned King*. London: Macdonald, 1972.

————. *Edward VII, a Portrait*. London: Allen Lane, 1976.

Higham, Charles, and Roy Moseley. *Elizabeth and Philip: The Untold Story of the Queen of England and Her Prince*. New York: Doubleday, 1991.

Hillman, Judy, and Peter Clarke. *Geoffrey Howe: A Quiet Revolutionary*. London: Weidenfeld and Nicolson, 1988.

Hoey, Brian. *Anne, the Princess Royal: Her Life and Work*. London: Grafton, 1989.

————. *Mountbatten: The Private Story*. London: Sidgwick and Jackson, 1994

Holden, Anthony. *Charles: a Biography*. London: Weidenfeld and Nicolson, 1988.

Horne, Alistair. *Macmillan*. 2 vols. London: Macmillan, 1988, vol 1, and 1989, vol 2.

Hough, Richard Alexander. *Winston and Clementine: The Triumph of the Churchills*. London: Bantam, 1990.

Howard, Anthony. *Rab: The Life of R. A. Butler*. London: Cape, 1987.

Howarth, Patrick. *George VI: A New Biography*. London: Hutchinson, 1987.

Howe, Geoffrey. *Conflict of Loyalty*. London: Macmillan, 1994.

Howe, Irving. *Thomas Hardy*. New York: Macmillan, 1967.

Hoyle, Fred. *The Small World of Fred Hoyle: An Autobiography*. London: Michael Joseph, 1986.

Hutchinson, George. *Edward Heath: A Personal and Political Biography*. Harlow, England: Longman, 1970.

————. *The Last Edwardian at No 10: An Impression of Harold Macmillan*. London: Quartet, 1980.

Hutchinson, Roger, and Gary Kahn. *A Family Affair: The Margaret and Tony Story*. New York: Two Continents, 1977.

Huxley, Elspeth. *Scott of the Antarctic*. London: Weidenfeld and Nicolson, 1977.

Hyde, H. Montgomery. *Baldwin: The Unexpected Prime Minister*. London: Hart-Davis MacGibbon, 1973.

Hynes, Samuel. *The Auden Generation*. London: Bodley Head, 1976.

James, Paul. *Anne: The Working Princess*. London: Piatkus, 1987.

————. *Margaret: A Woman of Conflict*. London: Sidgwick and Jackson, 1990.

————. *Prince Edward: A Life in the Spotlight*. London: Piatkus, 1992.

James, Robert Rhodes. *Churchill: A Study in Failure, 1900–1939*. London: Weidenfeld and Nicolson, 1970.

————. *Anthony Eden*. London: Weidenfeld and Nicolson, 1986.

James, Robert Rhodes, ed. *Winston Churchill: His Complete Speeches, 1897-1963*. 8 vols. New York: Chelsea House Publishers, 1974.

Jeal, Tim. *Baden–Powell*. London: Century, 1989.

Jenkin, J., ed. *John Major, Prime Minister*. London: Bloomsbury, 1990.

Jenkins, Roy. *Asquith*. London: Collins, 1986.

————. *Baldwin*. London: Collins, 1987.

————. *A Life at the Centre*. London: Macmillan, 1991.

————. *Mr Balfour's Poodle: An Account of the Struggle Between the House of Lords and the Government of Mr Asquith*. London: Collins, 1968.

Jordan, Ruth. *Princess Margaret and Her Family*. London: Hale, 1974.

Judd, Denis. *The Life and Times of George V*. London: Weidenfeld and Nicolson, 1973.

————. *King George VI: 1895–1952*. London: Michael Joseph, 1982.

————. *Prince Philip: A Biography.* London: Michael Joseph, 1980.

Junor, Penny. *Charles.* London: Sidgwick and Jackson, 1987.

————. *Diana, Princess of Wales: A Biography.* London: Sidgwick and Jackson, 1982.

————. *Margaret Thatcher: Wife, Mother, Politician.* London: Sidgwick and Jackson, 1983.

Kamm, Josephine. *The Story of Emmeline Pankhurst.* New York: Meredith Press, 1968.

Kellner, Peter. *Callaghan: The Road to Number Ten.* London: Cassell, 1976.

King, Peter. *The Viceroy's Fall: How Kitchener Destroyed Curzon.* London: Sidgwick and Jackson, 1986.

Kinross, Lord. *The Windsor Years: The Life of Edward, as Prince of Wales, King and Duke of Windsor.* New York: Viking Press, 1967.

Koss, Stephen Edward. *Asquith.* London: Allen Lane, 1976.

Lacey, Robert. *Majesty: Elizabeth II and the House of Windsor.* London: Hutchinson, 1977.

Laing, Margaret. *Edward Heath, Prime Minister.* London: Sidgwick and Jackson, 1972.

Laird, Dorothy. *Queen Elizabeth the Queen Mother and Her Support to the Throne during Four Reigns.* London: Coronet, 1975.

Lane, Peter. *Prince Charles: A Study in Development.* London: Hale, 1988.

————. *The Queen Mother.* London: Hale, 1979.

Langhorne, Elizabeth. *Nancy Astor and Her Friends.* London: Barker, 1974.

Lawson, Nigel. *The View from Number 11: Memoirs of a Tory Radical.* London: Bantam Press, 1992.

Lewin, Ronald. *Churchill as Warlord.* London: Batsford, 1973.

————. *Montgomery as Military Commander.* London: Batsford, 1971.

Lloyd George, Frances. *Lloyd George: A Diary.* London: Hutchinson, 1971.

Longford, Elizabeth. *Elizabeth R: A Biography.* London: Weidenfeld and Nicolson, 1983.

————. *The Queen Mother.* London: Weidenfeld and Nicolson, 1981.

————. *Winston Churchill.* London: Sidgwick and Jackson, 1974.

Lynch, Michael. *Lloyd George and the Liberal Dilemma.* London: Hodder and Stoughton, 1993.

Mackay, Ruddock F. *Balfour: Intellectual Statesman.* Oxford: Oxford University Press, 1985.

MacLeod, Iain. *Neville Chamberlain.* London: Muller, 1961.

Macmillan, Harold. *At the End of the Day, 1961–1963.* New York: Harper and Row, 1973.

———. *Pointing the Way, 1959–1961.* London: Macmillan, 1972.

———. *Riding the Storm, 1956–1959.* New York: Harper and Row, 1971.

———. *Tides of Fortune, 1945–1955.* New York: Harper and Row, 1969.

———. *War Diaries: Politics and War in the Mediterranean: January 1943–May 1945.* London: Macmillan, 1984.

———. *Winds of Change, 1914–1939.* New York: Harper and Row, 1966.

Magnus, Philip. *King Edward the Seventh.* London: John Murray, 1964.

Marquand, David. *Ramsay MacDonald.* London: Cape, 1977.

Marsh, Peter T. *Joseph Chamberlain: Entrepreneur in Politics.* New Haven, Conn.: Yale University Press, 1994.

Martin, Ralph G. *Charles and Diana.* New York: Putnam, 1985.

Masters, Anthony. *Nancy Astor: A Life.* London: Weidenfeld and Nicolson, 1981,

Maxwell, S. *The Princess of Wales.* London: Queen Anne Press, 1982.

Mayer, Allan J. *Madam Prime Minister: Margaret Thatcher and Her Rise to Power.* New York: Newsweek Books, 1979.

McDermott, Geoffrey. *Leader Lost: A Biography of Hugh Gaitskell.* Princeton, N.J.: Vertex, 1971.

McSmith, Andy. *Kenneth Clarke: A Political Biography.* London: Verso, 1994.

Metcalfe, James. *All the Queen's Children.* London: W. H. Allen, 1982.

Middlemas, Keith. *The Life and Times of Edward VII.* London: Weidenfeld and Nicolson, 1972.

———. *The Life and Times of George VI.* London: Weidenfeld and Nicolson, 1974.

Middlemas, Keith, and John Barnes. *Baldwin: A Biography.* London: Weidenfeld and Nicolson, 1969.

Millgate, Michael. *Thomas Hardy: A Biography.* Oxford: Oxford University Press, 1982.

Minogue, Kenneth, and Michael Biddiss, ed. *Thatcherism: Personality and Politics.* Basingstoke, England: Macmillan, 1987.

Montgomery-Massingberd, Hugh. *Her Majesty the Queen.* London: Collins, 1985.

Morgan, Austen. *Harold Wilson: A Life.* London: Pluto Press, 1991.

———. *J. Ramsay MacDonald.* Manchester: Manchester University

Press, 1987.

Morgan, Kenneth O. *Lloyd George*. London: Weidenfeld and Nicolson, 1974.

Morpurgo, J. E. *Barnes Wallis: A Biography*. London: Ian Allan, 1981.

Morrow, Ann. *The Queen*. London: Granada, 1983.

————. *The Queen Mother*. London: Granada, 1984.

Mortimer, Penelope. *Queen Elizabeth: A Life of the Queen Mother*. Harmondsworth, England: Viking, 1986.

Morton, Andrew. *Diana: Her True Story*. London: O'Mara, 1993.

Morton, Andrew, and Mick Seamark. *Andrew, the Playboy Prince*. London: Severn House, 1983.

Mosley, Sir Oswald. *My Life*. London: Nelson, 1968.

Muggeridge, Kitty. *Beatrice Webb: A Life, 1858-1943*. Chicago: Academy Publishers, 1983.

Neville, Peter. *Neville Chamberlain: A Study in Failure*. London: Hodder and Stoughton, 1992.

Newton, Scott, and Dilwyn Porter. *Joseph Chamberlain, 1836–1914: A Bibliography*. Westport, Conn.: Greenwood Press, 1994.

Nord, Deborah Epstein. *The Apprenticeship of Beatrice Webb*. Amherst, Mass.: University of Massachusetts Press, 1985.

Ogden, Chris. *Maggie: An Intimate Portrait of a Woman in Power*. New York: Simon and Schuster, 1990.

Owen, David. *David Owen: Personally Speaking to Kenneth Harris*. London: Weidenfeld and Nicolson, 1987.

————. *Time to Declare*. London: Michael Joseph, 1991.

Paget, Gerald. *The Lineage and Ancestry of HRH Prince of Wales*. 2 vols. Edinburgh: Skilton, 1977.

Pankhurst, Emmeline. *My Own Story*. London: Virago, 1979.

Parker, John. *Prince Philip: A Critical Biography*. London: Sidgwick and Jackson, 1990.

————. *The Princess Royal*. London: Hamish Hamilton, 1989.

Pearce, Edward. *The Quiet Rise of John Major*. London: Weidenfeld and Nicolson, 1991.

Pelling, Henry. *Winston Churchill*. London: Macmillan, 1989.

Pimlott, Ben. *Harold Wilson*. London: HarperCollins, 1992.

Pope-Hennessy, James. *Queen Mary, 1867–1953*. London: Unwin, 1987.

Pound, Reginald. *Scott of the Antarctic*. London: Cassell, 1966.

Pugh, Martin. *Lloyd George*. London: Longman, 1988.

Radice, Lisanne. *Beatrice and Sydney Webb: Fabian Socialists*. London: Macmillan, 1984.

Regan, Simon. *Margaret: A Love Story*. London: Everest, 1977.

Rippon, Angela. *Mark Phillips: The Man and His Horses.* Newton Abbot, England: David and Charles, 1982.

Robbins, Keith. *Churchill.* London: Longman, 1992.

Rosenthal, Michael. *The Character Factory: Baden-Powell and the Origins of the Boy Scout Movement.* New York: Pantheon, 1986.

Roth, Andrew. *Heath and the Heathmen.* London: Routledge, 1972.

Rothwell, V. H. *Anthony Eden: Political Biography, 1931–57.* Manchester: Manchester University Press, 1992.

Rowland, Peter. *Lloyd George.* London: Barrie and Jenkins, 1975.

Royle, Trevor. *The Kitchener Enigma.* London: Michael Joseph, 1985.

Sampson, Anthony. *Macmillan: A Study in Ambiguity.* London: Allen Lane, 1967.

Satchell, Tim. *Royal Romance: Prince Andrew and Sarah Ferguson.* Sevenoaks, England: New English Library, 1986.

Scott, R. F. *Scott's Last Expedition: The Personal Journals of R. F. Scott.* London: Tandem, 1973.

Seward, Ingrid. *Diana.* London: Grafton, 1989.

———. *Prince Edward.* London: Century, 1995

———. *Sarah: Duchess of York.* London: Fontana, 1992.

Sinclair, David. *Queen and Country: The Life of Elizabeth the Queen Mother.* London: Dent, 1979.

———. *Snowdon: A Man for Our Times.* London: Proteus, 1982.

———. *Two Georges: The Making of the Modern Monarchy.* London: Hodder and Stoughton, 1988.

Skidelsky, Robert. *Oswald Mosley.* London: Macmillan, 1990.

Slater, Ian. *Orwell: The Road to Airstrip One.* New York: Norton, 1985.

Smith, Ronald A. *The Premier Years of Margaret Thatcher.* London: Kevin Francis, 1991.

Snowdon, Antony Armstrong-Jones, Earl of. *Snowdon: A Photographic Autobiography.* New York: Times Books, 1979.

Soames, Mary. *Winston Churchill; His Life as a Painter: A Memoir by His Daughter.* London: Collins, 1990.

Stansky, Peter. *Churchill: A Profile.* New York: Hill and Wang, 1973.

Stansky, Peter, and William Abrahams. *The Unknown Orwell.* New York: Knopf, 1972.

St Aubyn, Giles. *Edward VII: Prince and King.* London: Collins, 1979.

Stewart, J. I. M. *Thomas Hardy: A Critical Biography.* New York: Dodd, Mead, 1971.

Sykes, Christopher. *Nancy: The Life of Lady Astor.* New York: Harper and Row, 1972.

Taylor, Robert. *Lord Salisbury.* New York: St. Martin's Press, 1975.

Terraine, John, ed. *The Life and Times of Lord Mountbatten.* New York: Holt, Rinehart and Winston, 1980.

Thatcher, Margaret. *The Downing Street Years.* London: Harper Collins, 1993.

―――. *The Revival of Britain: Speeches on Home and European Affairs, 1975–1988*, compiled by Alastair B. Cooke. London: Aurum, 1989.

Thompson, R. W. *Montgomery, the Field Marshal: The Campaign in North-West Europe, 1944/45.* New York: Scribner, 1970.

Thornton, Michael. *Royal Feud: The Queen Mother and the Duchess of Windsor.* London: Michael Joseph, 1985.

Trukhanovskii, V. G. *Anthony Eden,* translated by Ruth English. Moscow, Soviet Union: Progress Publishers, 1984.

Turner, John. *Macmillan.* London: Longman, 1994.

Wade, Judy. *Charles and Diana: Inside a Royal Marriage.* London: Angus and Robertson, 1987.

Waite, Terry. *Taken on Trust.* London: Hodder and Stoughton, 1993.

Wapshott, Nicholas, and George Brock. *Thatcher.* London: Macdonald, 1983.

Ward, Stephen R. *James Ramsay MacDonald: Low Born among the High Brows.* New York: Lang, 1990.

Warner, Philip. *Kitchener: The Man behind the Legend.* London: Hamish Hamilton, 1985.

Warwick, Christopher. *Debrett's Queen Elizabeth II.* Exeter, England: Webb and Bower, 1986.

―――. *King George VI and Queen Elizabeth: A Portrait.* New York: Beaufort, 1985.

―――. *Princess Margaret.* New York: St. Martin's Press, 1983.

Weber, Carl J. *Hardy of Wessex, His Life and Literary Career.* New York: Columbia University Press, 1965.

Williams, Philip M. *Hugh Gaitskell: A Political Biography.* London: Cape, 1979.

Williams, Philip M., ed. *The Diary of Hugh Gaitskell, 1945–1956.* London: Cape, 1983.

Wilson, Harold. *The Making of a Prime Minister, 1916–1964.* London: Michael Joseph, 1986.

Windsor, Duchess of. *Wallis and Edward: Letters 1931–37: The Intimate Correspondence of the Duke and Duchess of Windsor.* London: Weidenfeld and Nicolson, 1986.

Winter, Denis. *Haig's Command: A Reassessment.* London: Viking, 1991.

Woodcock, George. *The Crystal Spirit: A Study of George Orwell.*

Boston, Mass.: Little, Brown, 1966.

Young, G. M. *Stanley Baldwin.* Westport, Conn.: Greenwood Press, 1979.

Young, Hugo. *One of Us: a Biography of Margaret Thatcher.* London: Pan Books, 1993.

Young, Kenneth. *Arthur James Balfour: The Happy Life of the Politician, Prime Minister, Statesman and Philosopher, 1848–1930.* London: Bell, 1963.

———. *Sir Alec Douglas-Home.* London: Dent, 1970.

———. *Stanley Baldwin.* London: Weidenfeld and Nicolson, 1976.

Zebel, Sydney Henry. *Balfour: A Political Biography.* London: Cambridge University Press, 1973.

Ziegler, Philip. *King Edward VIII: The Official Biography.* London: Collins, 1990.

———. *Mountbatten: The Official Biography.* London: Collins, 1985.

———. *Wilson: The Authorized Life of Lord Wilson of Rievaulx.* London: Weidenfeld and Nicolson, 1993.

Ziegler, Philip, ed. *Personal Diary of Admiral the Lord Louis Mountbatten, Supreme Allied Commander, South-East Asia, 1943–1946.* London: Collins, 1988.

Industry and Commerce

Aldcroft, Derek H. *British Transport Since 1914.* Newton Abbot, England: David and Charles, 1975.

———. *Education, Training and Economic Performance, 1944–1990.* Manchester: Manchester University Press, 1992.

———. *The Inter-War Economy: Britain 1919–1939.* London: Batsford, 1970.

Alford, B. W. E. *British Economic Performance, 1945–1975.* Basingstoke, England: Macmillan, 1988.

———. *Depression and Recovery?: British Economic Growth, 1918–1939.* London: Macmillan, 1972.

Ally, Russell. *Gold and Empire: The Bank of England and South Africa's Gold Producers, 1886–1926.* London: UCL Press, 1994.

Armstrong, Mark, Simon Cowan, and John Vickers. *Regulatory Reform: Economic Analysis and British Experience.* London: MIT Press, 1994.

Ashworth, William. *An Economic History of England, 1870–1939.* London: Methuen, 1960.

Bacon, R., and W. Eltis. *Britain's Economic Problem: Too Few Pro-*

ducers. London: Macmillan, 1976.

Ball, Michael, Fred Gray, and Linda McDowell. *The Transformation of Britain: Contemporary Social and Economic Change.* London: Fontana, 1989.

Barker, T. C., and Dorian Gerhold. *The Rise and Fall of Road Transport, 1700–1990.* Basingstoke, England: Macmillan, 1993.

Barry, E. Eldon. *Nationalisation in British Politics.* London: Cape, 1965.

Bennett, Robert J., Peter Wicks, and Andrew McCoshan. *Local Empowerment and Business Services: Britain's Experiment with Training and Enterprise Councils.* London: UCL Press, 1994.

Benson, John. *The Rise of Consumer Society in Britain, 1880–1980.* London: Longman, 1994.

Beresford, Tristram. *We Plough the Fields.* Harmondsworth, England: Pelican, 1975.

Berthoud, R., and T. Hinton. *Credit Unions in the United Kingdom.* London: Policy Studies Institute, 1989.

Birch, Lionel. *The History of the TUC, 1868–1968.* London: General Council of the TUC, 1968.

Birchall, Johnston. *Co-op: the People's Business.* Manchester: Manchester University Press, 1994.

Boddy, M. *The Building Societies.* London: Macmillan, 1981.

Bonavia, Michael R. *The Birth of British Rail.* London: Allen and Unwin, 1979.

———. *British Rail: The First 25 Years.* Newton Abbot, England: David and Charles, 1981.

Bowler, I. *Government and Agriculture: A Spatial Perspective.* London: Longman, 1979.

Breach, R. W., and R. M. Hartwell. *British Economy and Society, 1870–1970.* London: Oxford University Press, 1972.

Brown, Richard. *Society and Economy in Modern Britain.* London: Routledge, 1991.

Buxton, Tony, Paul Chapman, and Paul Temple. *Britain's Economic Performance.* London: Routledge, 1994.

Cairncross, Alec. *The British Economy since 1945: Economic Policy and Performance, 1945–1990.* Oxford: Blackwell, 1992.

Calvocoressi, Peter. *The British Experience, 1945–75.* London: Bodley Head, 1978.

Charlesworth, George. *A History of British Motorways.* London: Thomas Telford, 1984.

Chisholm, Michael, and G. Manners, ed. *Spatial Policy Problems of the British Economy.* London: Cambridge University Press, 1971.

Church, Roy. *The Rise and Decline of the British Motor Industry.* Basingstoke, England: Macmillan, 1994.

Clegg, Hugh A. *The Changing System of Industrial Relations in Great Britain.* Oxford: Blackwell, 1979.

————. *A History of British Trade Unions Since 1889.* 3 vols. Oxford: Clarendon Press, 1964–94.

Clutterbuck, David, and Stuart Crainer. *The Decline and Rise of British Industry.* London: W. H. Allen, 1988.

Curran, James, and Robert Blackburn. *Small Firms and Local Economic Networks: The Death of the Local Economy?* London: Paul Chapman, 1994.

Davies, Michael. *Belief in the Sea: State Encouragement of British Merchant Shipping and Shipbuilding.* London: Lloyds of London, 1992.

Deane, Phyllis, and W. A. Cole. *British Economic Growth, 1688–1959: Trends and Structure.* Cambridge: Cambridge University Press, 1969.

Donaldson, J. G. S., and Frances Donaldson (in association with Derek Barber). *Farming in Britain Today.* Harmondsworth, England: Penguin, 1972.

Dyos, H. J., and D. H. Aldcroft. *British Transport: An Economic Survey from the Seventeenth Century to the Twentieth.* Leicester, England: Leicester University Press, 1969.

Ferrier, R. W. *A History of the British Petroleum Industry.* 2 vols. Cambridge: Cambridge University Press, 1982, vol 1 and 1994, vol 2.

Fieldhouse, D. K., *Economics and Empire, 1830–1914.* London: Weidenfeld and Nicolson, 1973.

Fitzgerald, Robert. *British Labour Management and Industrial Welfare, 1846–1939.* London: Croom Helm, 1988.

Fothergill, S., and G. Gudgin. *Unequal Growth: Urban and Regional Employment Change in the United Kingdom.* London: Heinemann, 1982.

Gale, Walter K. V. *The British Iron and Steel Industry.* Newton Abbot, England: David and Charles, 1967.

Gamble, Andrew. *Britain in Decline.* Basingstoke, England: Macmillan, 1994.

Gentle, Christopher J. S. *The Financial Services Industry.* Aldershot, England: Avebury, 1992.

Gibb, R., ed. *The Channel Tunnel: A Geographical Perspective.* Chichester, England: John Wiley, 1994.

Gimbel, John. *The Origins of the Marshall Plan.* Stanford, Calif.:

Stanford University Press, 1976.

Glasson, John. *An Introduction to Regional Planning.* London: Hutchinson, 1978.

Gledhill, D. *Gas Lighting.* Aylesbury, England: Shire Publications, 1981.

Glucksmann, Miriam. *Women Assemble: Women Workers and the New Industries in Inter-War Britain.* London: Routledge, 1990.

Goddard, J. B., and A. G. Champion. *The Urban and Regional Transformation of Britain.* London: Methuen, 1983.

Gourvish, Terry, and Alan O'Day. *Britain since 1945.* Basingstoke, England: Macmillan, 1988.

Gregg, Pauline. *The Welfare State: An Economic and Social History of Great Britain From 1945 to the Present Day.* London: Harrap, 1967.

Guiseppi, John. *The Bank of England.* London: Evans, 1966.

Hann, Danny. *Government and North Sea Oil.* London: Macmillan, 1986.

Hannington, W. *Unemployed Struggles, 1919–1936.* London: Lawrence and Wishart, 1977.

Harbury, Colin, and Richard G. Lipsey. *An Introduction to the U.K. Economy.* London: Pitman, 1993.

Haresnape, Brian. *British Rail, 1948–83: A Journey by Design.* Shepperton, England: Ian Allan, 1983.

Harrison, Shirley. *The Channel.* Glasgow, Scotland: Collins, 1986.

Hennessy, Elizabeth. *A Domestic History of the Bank of England, 1930– 1960.* Cambridge: Cambridge University Press, 1992.

Hobley, L. *The Trade Union Story.* Glasgow, Scotland: Blackie, 1969.

Hogan, Michael J. *The Marshall Plan: America, Britain and the Reconstruction of Western Europe, 1947–1952.* Cambridge: Cambridge University Press, 1987.

Holliday, I., G. Marcou, and R. Vickerman. *The Channel Tunnel: Public Policy, Regional Development and European Integration.* Chichester, England: John Wiley, 1991.

Hope, Ronald. *A New History of British Shipping.* London: John Murray, 1990.

Howells, Peter, and Keith Bain. *Financial Markets and Institutions.* London: Longman, 1994.

Howson, H. F. *London's Underground.* London: Ian Allen, 1986.

Hunt, E. H. *British Labour History, 1815–1914.* London: Weidenfeld and Nicolson, 1981.

Hutt, Allen. *British Trade Unionism: A Short History.* London: Lawrence and Wishart, 1975.

Jenkins, D. T., and K. G. Ponting. *The British Wool Textile Industry, 1770–1914.* London: Heinemann, 1982.

Jenkins, John G. *The Wool Textile Industry in Great Britain.* London: Routledge, 1972.

Johnson, Christopher. *The Economy under Mrs Thatcher, 1979–1990.* Harmondsworth, England: Penguin, 1991.

Johnson, N., and A. Cochrane. *Economic Policy-Making by Local Authorities in Britain and Western Germany.* London: Allen and Unwin, 1981.

Johnson, Paul, ed. *Twentieth-Century Britain: Economic, Social and Cultural Change.* London: Longman, 1994.

Kay, Diana. *Refugees or Migrant Workers?: European Volunteer Workers in Britain, 1946–1951.* London: Routledge, 1992.

Keeble, D. E. *Industrial Location and Planning in the United Kingdom.* London: Methuen, 1976.

Keeble, S. P. *The Ability to Manage: A Study of British Management, 1890–1990.* Manchester: Manchester University Press, 1992.

Keeling, B. S., and A. E. G. Wright. *The Development of the Modern British Steel Industry.* London: Longman, 1964.

Kelf-Cohen, R. *British Nationalisation, 1945–1973.* London: Macmillan, 1973.

Kelly, John, and Edmund Heery. *Working for the Union: British Trade Union Officers.* Cambridge: Cambridge University Press, 1994.

Kingsford, Peter. *The Hunger Marchers in Britain, 1920–1939.* London: Lawrence and Wishart, 1982.

Kirby, M. W. *The British Coalmining Industry, 1870–1946.* London: Macmillan, 1977.

Laybourn, Keith. *The General Strike of 1926.* Manchester: Manchester University Press, 1993.

Lever, W. F., ed. *Industrial Change in the United Kingdom.* Harlow, England: Longman, 1987.

Lewis, Jim, and Alan Townsend. *The North-South Divide: Regional Change in Britain in the 1980s.* London: Chapman, 1989.

Leyshon, A., N. Thrift, and M. Justice. *A Reversal of Fortune?: Financial Services and the Southeast of England.* London: Seeds, 1993.

Lovell, J., and B. C. Roberts. *A Short History of the TUC.* London: Macmillan, 1968.

Marchington, Mick, and Philip Parker. *Changing Patterns of Employee Relations in Britain.* London: Harvester Wheatsheaf, 1990.

Mathias, Peter. *The First Industrial Nation.* London: Methuen, 1983.

McCord, Norman M. *Free Trade: Theory and Practice From Adam Smith to Keynes.* Newton Abbot, England: David and Charles, 1970.

Milward, Alan S. *The Reconstruction of Western Europe, 1945–1951.* London: Methuen, 1984.

Minns, R. *Pension Funds and British Capitalism.* London: Heinemann, 1980.

Morgan, E. Victor, and W. A. Thomas. *The Stock Exchange.* London: Elek, 1969.

Morris, M. *The General Strike.* Harmondsworth, England: Penguin, 1976.

Morris, R. J. and John Langton. *Atlas of Industrializing Britain, 1780–1914.* London: Routledge, 1986.

Pelling, Henry. *A History of British Trade Unionism.* London: Macmillan, 1992.

Phillips, G. A. *The General Strike: The Politics of Industrial Conflict.* London: Weidenfeld and Nicolson, 1976.

Pimlott, Ben, and Chris Cook. *Trade Unions in British Politics: The First 250 Years.* London: Longman, 1991.

Pollard, Sidney. *Britain's Prime and Britain's Decline: The British Economy, 1870–1914.* London: Edward Arnold, 1990.

———. *The Development of the British Economy, 1914–1970.* London: Edward Arnold, 1992.

———. *The Gold Standard and Employment Policies between the Wars.* London: Methuen, 1970.

Pollard, Sidney, and Paul Robertson. *The British Shipbuilding Industry, 1870–1914.* Cambridge, Mass.: Harvard University Press, 1979.

Rees, Goronwy. *The Great Slump.* London: Weidenfeld and Nicolson, 1970.

Renshaw, Patrick. *The General Strike, 1926.* London: Eyre Methuen, 1975.

Roberts, J., D. Elliott, and T. Houghton. *Privatising Electricity: The Politics of Power.* Chichester, England: John Wiley, 1991.

Sampson, Anthony. *The Changing Anatomy of Britain.* London: Hodder and Stoughton, 1982.

Saul, S. B. *The Myth of the Great Depression.* London: Macmillan, 1985.

Schenk, Catherine R. *Britain and the Sterling Area: From Devaluation to Convertibility in the 1950s.* London: Routledge, 1994.

Scott, Andrew. *Willing Slaves?: British Workers under Human Resource Management.* Cambridge: Cambridge University Press, 1994.

Sekers, David. *The Potteries.* Princes Risborough, England: Shire Publications, 1981.

Sheldrake, John. *Industrial Relations and Politics in Britain, 1880–1989.* London: Pinter, 1991.

Simmons, Jack. *The Railway in England and Wales, 1836–1914.* Leicester, England: Leicester University Press, 1978.

Skelley, Jeffrey, ed. *The General Strike, 1926.* London: Lawrence and Wishart, 1976.

Smith, David. *From Boom to Bust: Trial and Error in British Economic Policy.* Harmondsworth, England: Penguin, 1992.

Smith, Justin Davis. *The Attlee and Churchill Administrations and Industrial Unrest, 1945–55.* London: Pinter, 1990.

Starkie, D. N. M. *The Motorway Age: Road and Traffic Policies in Post War Britain.* Oxford: Pergamon Press, 1982.

Stevenson, John. *Britain in the Great Depression.* London: Longman, 1994.

Terry, M., and P. Edwards, ed. *Shopfloor Politics and Job Controls: the Post-War Engineering Industry.* Oxford: Blackwell, 1988.

Townsend, Alan R. *The Impact of Recession.* London: Croom Helm, 1983.

Vaizey, John. *The History of British Steel.* London: Weidenfeld and Nicolson, 1974.

Warren, K. *The Geography of British Heavy Industry since 1800.* London: Oxford University Press, 1976.

Weiner, M. J. *English Culture and the Decline of the Industrial Spirit, 1850–1980.* London: Cambridge University Press, 1981.

Westall, Oliver. *The Provincial Insurance Company, 1903–1938: Family, Markets, Competitive Growth.* Manchester: Manchester University Press, 1993.

Widlake, Brian. *In the City.* London: Faber and Faber, 1986.

Williams, Richard, and Barry Wood. *Urban Land and Property Markets in the UK.* London: UCL Press, 1994.

Williams, T. I. *A History of the British Gas Industry.* Oxford: Oxford University Press, 1981.

Willman, Paul, Timothy Morris, and Beverly Aston. *Union Business: Trade Union Organisation and Financial Reform in the Thatcher Years.* Cambridge: Cambridge University Press, 1993.

Politics

Adams, R. J. Q. *British Politics and Foreign Policy in the Age of Appeasement, 1935–39.* Basingstoke, England: Macmillan, 1993.

Addison, Paul. *The Road to 1945: British Politics and the Second*

World War. London: Pimlico, 1994.

Adelman, Paul. *Britain's Domestic Politics, 1939–64.* Abingdon, England: Hodder and Stoughton, 1994.

————. *The Decline of the Liberal Party, 1910–1931.* London: Longman, 1981.

————. *The Rise of the Labour Party, 1880–1945.* London: Longman, 1986.

Adonis, Andrew, and Tim Hames, ed. *A Conservative Revolution?: The Thatcher-Reagan Decade in Perspective.* Manchester: Manchester University Press, 1993.

Ambrose, Peter. *Urban Process and Power.* London: Routledge, 1994.

Atkinson, Bob, and Graham Moon. *Urban Policy in Britain: The City, the State and the Market.* Basingstoke, England: Macmillan, 1994.

Barber, James. *The Prime Minister since 1945.* Oxford: Blackwell, 1991.

Barber, Michael. *The Making of the 1944 Education Act.* London: Cassell, 1994.

Barker, Anthony. *Quangos in Britain: Government and the Networks of Public Policy-Making.* London: Macmillan, 1982.

Barker, Rodney. *Politics, Peoples and Government: Themes in British Political Thought since the Nineteenth Century.* Basingstoke, England: Macmillan, 1994.

Barry, E. Eldon. *Nationalisation in British Politics.* London: Cape, 1965.

Bartlett, C. J. *British Foreign Policy in the Twentieth Century.* Basingstoke, England: Macmillan, 1989.

————. *A History of Postwar Britain, 1945–1974.* London: Longman, 1977.

————. *'The Special Relationship': A Political History of Anglo-American Relations since 1945.* London: Longman, 1992.

Behagg, Clive. *Labour and Reform: Working Class Movements, 1815–1914.* Abingdon, England: Hodder and Stoughton, 1991.

Benewick, Robert. *The Fascist Movement in Britain.* London: Allen Lane, 1972.

Bennett, R. *The Black and Tans.* London: Four Square, 1961.

Bentley, Michael. *The Climax of Liberal Politics.* London: Edward Arnold, 1987.

Bessell, Peter. *Cover-Up: The Jeremy Thorpe Affair.* Wilmington, Del.: Simons Books, 1980.

Birch, Lionel. *The History of the TUC, 1868–1968.* London: General Council of the TUC, 1968.

Birchall, Johnston, ed. *Housing Policy in the 1990s.* London:

Routledge, 1992.

Blackman, Tim. *Urban Policy in Practice.* London: Routledge, 1994.

Blake, Robert. *The Conservative Party from Peel to Thatcher.* London: Methuen, 1985.

Blythe, R. *The Age of Illusion: England in the Twenties and Thirties, 1919–1940.* London: Hamish Hamilton, 1963.

Bowler, I. *Government and Agriculture: A Spatial Perspective.* London: Longman, 1979.

Boyce, D. G. *The Irish Question and British Politics, 1868–1986.* Basingstoke, England: Macmillan, 1988.

Brand, C. F. *The British Labour Party: A Short History.* Stanford, Calif.: Hoover Institution Press, 1974.

Branson, Noreen. *Poplarism, 1919–1925: George Lansbury and the Councillors' Revolt.* London: Lawrence and Wishart, 1979.

Brewer, John D. *Mosley's Men: The British Union of Fascists in the West Midlands.* Aldershot, England: Gower Press, 1984.

Brivati, Brian, and Harriet Jones, ed. *From Reconstruction to Integration: Britain and Europe since 1945.* Leicester, England: Leicester University Press, 1993.

Brooks, David. *The Age of Upheaval: Edwardian Politics, 1899–1914.* Manchester: Manchester University Press, 1993.

Browning, Peter. *The Treasury and Economic Policy, 1964–1985.* London: Longman, 1986.

Bruce-Gardyne, Jock. *Ministers and Mandarins: Inside the Whitehall Village.* London: Sidgwick and Jackson, 1986.

Bull, D., and P. Wilding. *Thatcherism and the Poor.* London: Child Poverty Action Group, 1983.

Burgess, Tyrrell, and Tony Travers. *Ten Billion Pounds: Whitehall's Takeover of the Town Halls.* London: Grant McIntyre, 1980.

Butcher, Hugh, Ian G. Law, Robert Leach, and Maurice Mullard. *Local Government and Thatcherism.* London: Routledge, 1990.

Butler, David, Andrew Adonis, and Tony ⌐avers. *Failure in British Government: The Politics of the Poll Tax.* Oxford: Oxford University Press, 1994.

Buxton, R. *Local Government.* Harmondsworth, England: Penguin, 1973.

Byrne, Tony. *Local Government in Britain.* Harmondsworth, England: Penguin, 1990.

Cairncross, Alec. *The British Economy Since 1945: Economic Policy and Performance, 1945–1990.* Oxford: Blackwell, 1992.

———. *Years of Recovery: British Economic Policy, 1945–51.* London: Methuen, 1985.

Carlton, David. *Britain and the Suez Crisis.* Oxford: Blackwell, 1988.

Cathcart, Brian. *Test of Greatness: Britain's Struggle for the Atom Bomb.* London: John Murray, 1994.

Cesarani, David, and Tony Kushner, ed. *The Internment of Aliens in 20th Century Britain.* London: Frank Cass, 1993.

Chamberlain, Muriel E. *Pax Britannica?: British Foreign Policy, 1789–1914.* London: Longman, 1988.

Charmley, John C. *Chamberlain and the Lost Peace.* London: Hodder and Stoughton, 1989.

Chester, Lewis, Stephen Fay, and Hugo Young. *The Zinoviev Letter.* London: Heinemann, 1967.

Childs, David. *Britain since 1939.* Basingstoke, England: Macmillan, 1994.

Clarke, P. F. *Liberals and Social Democrats.* Cambridge: Cambridge University Press, 1978.

Clegg, Hugh A. *A History of British Trade Unions since 1889.* 3 vols. Oxford: Clarendon Press, 1964-1994.

Cloke, Paul, ed. *Policy and Change in Thatcher's Britain.* Oxford: Pergamon, 1992.

Cockett, Richard. *Twilight of the Truth: Chamberlain, Appeasement and the Manipulation of the Press.* London: Weidenfeld and Nicolson, 1989.

Coffey, Thomas M. *Agony at Easter: The 1916 Irish Uprising.* London: Harrap, 1970.

Cole, Margaret. *The Story of Fabian Socialism.* London: Heinemann, 1961.

———, ed. *The Webbs and Their Work.* Westport, Conn.: Greenwood Press, 1985.

Colville, John. *The Fringes of Power: Downing Street Diaries, 1939–1955.* London: Hodder and Stoughton, 1985.

Coogan, Tim Pat. *The I.R.A.* London: Fontana, 1987.

Cook, Chris. *A Short History of the Liberal Party, 1900–1992.* Basingstoke, England: Macmillan, 1993.

Cook, Chris, and John Ramsden. *By-Elections in British Politics.* London: Macmillan, 1973.

———. *Trends in British Politics since 1945.* London: Macmillan, 1978.

Cook, Chris, and I. Taylor. *The Labour Party.* Harlow, England: Longman, 1983.

Coopey, Richard., Steven Fielding, and Nick Tiratsoo, ed. *The Wilson Governments, 1964–70.* London: Pinter, 1993.

Cosgrave, Patrick. *The Strange Death of Socialist Britain: Postwar*

British Politics. London: Constable, 1992.

Crossman, Richard. *The Diaries of a Cabinet Minister.* 3 vols. London: Hamish Hamilton, 1975–77.

Crouch, Colin, and David Marquand, ed. *The New Centralism: Britain out of Step in Europe.* Oxford: Blackwell, 1989.

Crowther, Anne. *Social Policy in Britain, 1914–1939.* Basingstoke, England: Macmillan, 1988.

Deakin, Nicholas. *The Politics of Welfare.* New York: Harvester Wheatsheaf, 1994.

Denver, David. *Elections and Voting Behaviour in Britain.* London: Harvester Wheatsheaf, 1992.

Derbyshire, J. Denis, and Ian Derbyshire. *Politics in Britain from Callaghan to Thatcher.* Edinburgh: Chambers, 1990.

Digby, Anne. *British Welfare Policy: Workhouse to Workfare.* London: Faber, 1989.

Dockrill, M. *British Defence since 1945.* Oxford: Blackwell, 1988.

Donaldson, Frances. *The British Council: The First Fifty Years.* London: Cape, 1984.

Donnison, D., and P. Soto, ed. *The Good City: A Study of Urban Development and Policy in Britain.* London: Heinemann, 1980.

Donoghue, Bernard. *Prime Minister: The Conduct of Policy under Harold Wilson and James Callaghan.* London: Cape, 1987.

Douglas, Roy. *The History of the Liberal Party, 1895–1970.* London: Sidgwick and Jackson, 1971.

Dunleavy, Patrick, Andrew Gamble, Ian Holliday, and Gillian Peele, ed. *Developments in British Politics.* Basingstoke, England: Macmillan, 1983.

Edwards, J., and R. Batley. *The Politics of Positive Discrimination: an Evaluation of the Urban Programme, 1967–77.* London: Tavistock, 1978.

Eisenschitz, Aram, and Jamie Gough. *The Politics of Local Economic Policy: The Problems and Possibilities of Local Initiative.* Basingstoke, England: Macmillan, 1993.

Elcock, Howard. *Local Government Policy and Management in Local Authorities.* London: Routledge, 1994.

Evans, L., and P. L. Pledger. *Contemporary Sources and Opinions in Modern British History.* London: Warne, 1967.

Feuchtwanger, E. J. *Democracy and Empire: Britain, 1865–1914.* London: Edward Arnold, 1985.

Fraser, Derek. *The Evolution of the British Welfare State: A History of Social Policy Since the Industrial Revolution.* London: Macmillan, 1984.

Fulford, Roger. *Hanover to Windsor.* London: Batsford, 1960.

Gilbert, B. B. *British Social Policy: 1914–1939.* London: Batsford, 1970.

Gilbert, Martin. *The Roots of Appeasement.* London: Weidenfeld and Nicolson, 1966.

Gilbert, Martin, and Richard Gott. *The Appeasers.* London: Weidenfeld and Nicolson, 1967.

Gorst, Anthony, Lewis Johnman, and W. Scott Lucas, ed. *Contemporary British History, 1931–1961: Politics and the Limits of Policy.* London: Pinter, 1991

Gourvish, Terry, and Alan O'Day. *Britain since 1945.* Basingstoke, England: Macmillan, 1991.

Grove, E. J. *Vanguard to Trident: British Naval Policy since World War Two.* London: Bodley Head, 1987.

Gyford, John, Steve Leach, and Chris Game. *The Changing Politics of Local Government.* London: Unwin Hyman, 1989.

Hall, S., and M. Jacques, ed. *The Politics of Thatcherism.* London: Lawrence and Wishart, 1983.

Ham, Christopher. *Health Policy in Britain: The Politics and Organisation of the National Health Service.* Basingstoke, England: Macmillan, 1992.

Hann, D. *Government and North Sea Oil.* London: Macmillan, 1986.

Harvey, J. *How Britain is Governed.* London: Macmillan, 1983.

Headey, Bruce. *British Cabinet Ministers: The Roles of Politicians in Executive Office.* London: Allen and Unwin, 1974.

Hennessy, Peter. *The Hidden Wiring: Unearthing the British Constitution.* London: Gollancz, 1995.

———. *Whitehall.* London: Secker and Warburg, 1989.

Hibbert, Christopher. *The Court of St James's: The Monarch at Work from Victoria to Elizabeth II.* London: Weidenfeld and Nicolson, 1979.

Himmelweit, Hilde T., Patrick Humphreys, and Marianne Jaeger. *How Voters Decide.* Buckingham, England: Open University Press, 1985.

Hobley, L. F. *The Trade Union Story.* Glasgow, Scotland: Blackie, 1969.

Holmes, Martin. *The First Thatcher Government, 1979–1983: Contemporary Conservatism and Economic Change.* Brighton, England: Harvester Wheatsheaf, 1985.

Holt, Edgar. *Protest in Arms: The Irish Troubles, 1916–1923.* London: Putnam, 1960.

Hoppen, K. Theodore. *Ireland since 1800.* London: Longman, 1989.

Howell, David. *British Workers and the Independent Labour Party, 1888–1906.* Manchester: Manchester University Press, 1983.

Howson, Susan. *British Monetary Policy, 1945–51.* Oxford: Oxford University Press, 1993.

Hume, Leslie Parker. *The National Union of Women's Suffrage Societies, 1897–1914.* New York: Garland Press, 1982.

Hunt, E. H. *British Labour History, 1815–1914.* London: Weidenfeld and Nicolson, 1981.

Hutt, Allen. *British Trade Unionism: A Short History.* London: Lawrence and Wishart, 1975.

James, Robert Rhodes. *The British Revolution: British Politics, 1880–1939.* 2 vols. London: Hamish Hamilton, 1976, vol 1, and 1977, vol 2.

Jeffrey, Kevin. *The Attlee Governments, 1945–51.* London: Longman, 1992.

———. *The Labour Party since 1945.* London: Macmillan, 1993.

Jenkins, Peter. *Mrs Thatcher's Revolution: The Ending of the Socialist Era.* London: Cape, 1987.

Jenkins, Simon. *Accountable to None: The Tory Nationalisation of Britain.* London: Penguin, 1996.

Johnson, Christopher. *The Economy under Mrs Thatcher, 1979–1990.* Harmondsworth, England: Penguin, 1991.

Johnson, N., and A. Cochrane. *Economic Policy-Making by Local Authorities in Britain and Western Germany.* London: Allen and Unwin, 1981.

Jones, Bill, and Linton Robins, ed. *Two Decades in British Politics.* Manchester: Manchester University Press, 1992.

Jones, Raymond A. *The British Diplomatic Service, 1815–1914.* Gerrards Cross, England: Smythe, 1983.

Judd, Denis, and Peter Slinn. *The Evolution of the Modern Commonwealth, 1902–80.* London: Macmillan, 1982.

Kavanagh, D., ed. *The Politics of the Labour Party.* London: Allen and Unwin, 1982.

Keith-Lucas, B., and P. Richards. *A History of Local Government in the Twentieth Century.* London: Allen and Unwin, 1978.

Kelly, John, and Edmund Heery. *Working for the Union: British Trade Union Officers.* Cambridge: Cambridge University Press, 1994.

Kendall, Walter. *The Revolutionary Movement in Britain, 1900–1921.* London: Weidenfeld and Nicolson, 1969.

Keohane, Dan. *Labour Party Defence Policy since 1945.* London: Pinter, 1993.

Kingdom, John. *Local Government and Politics in Britain.* London:

656 / Bibliography

Philip Allan, 1991.

Kinnear, Michael. *The Fall of Lloyd George: The Political Crisis of 1922.* London: Macmillan, 1973.

Klein, Rudolph. *The Politics of the National Health Service.* London: Longman, 1989.

Lagroye, J. and P. Wright, ed. *Local Government in Britain and France.* London: Allen and Unwin, 1979.

Lane, Peter. *The Conservative Party.* London: Batsford, 1973.

————. *The Liberal Party.* London: Batsford, 1973.

Laybourn, Keith. *The General Strike of 1926.* Manchester: Manchester University Press, 1993.

————. *The Rise of Labour: The British Labour Party, 1890–1979.* London: Edward Arnold, 1988.

Lawless, Paul. *The Evolution of Spatial Policy: A Case Study of Inner City Policy in the United Kingdom, 1968–81.* London: Pion, 1986.

Lee, Stephen J. *Aspects of British Political History, 1815–1914.* London: Routledge, 1994.

Leigh, David. *The Wilson Plot: The Intelligence Services and the Discrediting of a Prime Minister.* London: Heinemann, 1988.

Lenman, Bruce P. *The Eclipse of Parliament: Appearance and Reality in British Politics since 1914.* London: Edward Arnold, 1992.

Lewis, D. S. *Illusions of Grandeur: Mosley, Fascism and British Society, 1931–81.* Manchester: Manchester University Press, 1987.

Lindsay, T. F., and Michael Harrington. *The Conservative Party, 1918–1979.* London: Macmillan, 1979.

Lloyd, T. O. *Empire, Welfare State, Europe: English History, 1906–1992.* Oxford: Oxford University Press, 1993.

Loewenheim, Francis L., ed. *Peace or Appeasement?: Hitler, Chamberlain and the Munich Crisis.* Boston, Mass.: Houghton Mifflin, 1965.

Loney, M. *Community against Government: The British Community Development Project, 1968–1978.* London: Heinemann, 1983.

Longford, Elizabeth. *Royal Throne: Future of the Monarchy.* Sevenoaks, England: Hodder and Stoughton, 1993.

Lovell, J., and B. C. Roberts. *A Short History of the TUC.* London: Macmillan, 1968.

Lunn, Kenneth, and Richard Thurlow, ed. *British Fascism.* London: Croom Helm, 1980.

MacKenzie, Norman, and Jeanne MacKenzie. *The First Fabians.* London: Weidenfeld and Nicolson, 1977.

Macmillan, Harold. *The Past Masters: Politics and Politicians, 1906–1939.* New York: Harper and Row, 1975.

Mansergh, P. N. S. *The Irish Question, 1840–1921.* London: Allen and Unwin, 1975.

Marr, Andrew. *Ruling Britannia.* London: Michael Joseph, 1995.

Massie, Robert K. *Dreadnought.* London: Cape, 1992.

McColgan, John. *British Policy and the Irish Administration, 1920–22.* London: Allen and Unwin, 1983.

McCord, Norman. *Free Trade: Theory and Practice from Adam Smith to Keynes.* Newton Abbot, England: David and Charles, 1970.

McCrone, Gavin. *Regional Policy in Britain.* London: Allen and Unwin, 1969.

McInnes, Colin. *Trident: The Only Option?* London: Brassey's, 1986.

McKibbin, R. *The Evolution of the Labour Party, 1910–24.* London: Oxford University Press, 1975.

McKie, D., and Chris Cook. *The Decade of Disillusion: British Politics in the Sixties.* London: Macmillan, 1972.

McLellan, G., D. Held, and S. Hall, ed. *State and Society in Contemporary Britain.* Oxford: Polity Press, 1984.

Medlicott, W. N. *Britain and Germany: The Search for Agreement, 1930–37.* London: Athlone Press, 1969.

Mendelssohn, Peter de. *The Age of Churchill.* London: Thames and Hudson, 1961.

Mohan, John, ed. *The Political Geography of Contemporary Britain.* London: Macmillan, 1989.

Morgan, D. *Suffragists and Liberals: The Politics of Women's Suffrage in England.* Oxford: Blackwell, 1975.

Morgan, Kenneth O. *The Age of Lloyd George.* London: Allen and Unwin, 1971.

———. *The People's Peace: British History, 1945–1990.* Oxford: Oxford University Press, 1992.

Morton, Grenfell. *Home Rule and the Irish Question.* London: Longman, 1980.

Mount, Ferdinand. *The British Constitution Now: Recovery or Decline.* London: Mandarin, 1993.

Norris, Pippa. *British By-Elections: The Volatile Electorate.* Oxford: Clarendon Press, 1990.

Norton, Philip, ed. *Parliament in the 1980s.* Oxford: Blackwell, 1985.

Ovendale, Ritchie, ed. *British Defence Policy since 1945.* Manchester: Manchester University Press, 1994.

Overy, Richard, and Andrew Wheatcroft. *The Road to War.* London: Macmillan, 1989.

Parker, R. A. C. *Chamberlain and Appeasement: British Policy and the Coming of the Second World War.* Basingstoke, England:

Macmillan, 1993.

Pearce, Malcolm, and Geoffrey Stewart. *British Political History, 1867–1990: Democracy and Decline.* London: Routledge, 1992.

Pearce, Robert. *Attlee's Labour Governments, 1945–51.* London: Routledge, 1994.

———. *Britain: Domestic Politics, 1918–39.* Abingdon, England: Hodder and Stoughton, 1992.

Pearce, Robert, and Roger Stearn. *Government and Reform, 1815–1918.* Abingdon, England: Hodder and Stoughton, 1994.

Pease, Edward R. *The History of the Fabian Society.* London: Frank Cass, 1963.

Peden, G. C. *British Economic and Social Policy: Lloyd George to Margaret Thatcher.* Hemel Hempstead, England: Philip Allan, 1991.

———. *Keynes, the Treasury and British Economic Policy.* Basingstoke, England: Macmillan, 1988.

Pelling, Henry. *The British Communist Party.* London: Black, 1975.

———. *A History of British Trade Unionism.* London: Macmillan, 1992.

———. *A Short History of the Labour Party.* Basingstoke, England: Macmillan, 1993.

Phillips, G. A. *The General Strike: The Politics of Industrial Conflict.* London: Weidenfeld and Nicolson, 1976.

———. *The Rise of the Labour Party, 1893–1931.* London: Routledge, 1992.

Pimlott, Ben, and Chris Cook. *Trade Unions in British Politics: The First 250 Years.* London: Longman, 1991.

Pirie, Madson. *Privatization: Theory, Practice and Choice.* Aldershot, England: Wildwood House, 1988.

Porter, Bernard. *Britannia's Burden: The Political Evolution of Modern Britain, 1851–1990.* London: Edward Arnold, 1994.

Powell, David. *British Politics and the Labour Question, 1868–1990.* Basingstoke, England: Macmillan, 1992.

Prestwich, Roger, and Peter Taylor. *Introduction to Regional and Urban Policy in the United Kingdom.* Harlow, England: Longman, 1990.

Proudfoot, M. *British Politics and Government, 1951–70.* London: Faber, 1974.

Pugh, Martin. *State and Society: British Political and Social History, 1870–1992.* London: Edward Arnold, 1994.

———. *The Tories and the People, 1880–1935.* Oxford: Blackwell, 1985.

————. *Women's Suffrage in Britain, 1867–1928.* London: Historical Association, 1980.

Punnett, R. M. *British Government and Politics.* Aldershot, England: Gower Press, 1967.

Raeburn, Antonia. *The Militant Suffragettes.* London: Michael Joseph, 1973.

Ranelagh, John. *Thatcher's People: An Insider's Account of the Politics, the Power and the Personalities.* London: HarperCollins, 1991.

Read, Donald. *The Age of Urban Democracy: England, 1868–1914.* Harlow, England: Longman, 1994.

————. *Edwardian England, 1901–1915: Society and Politics.* London: Harrap, 1972.

Redcliffe-Maud, Lord, and B. Wood. *English Local Government Reformed.* London: Oxford University Press, 1974.

Reiner, Robert. *The Politics of the Police.* New York: Harvester Wheatsheaf, 1992.

Reynolds, David. *The Creation of the Anglo-American Alliance, 1937–41.* London: Europa, 1981.

Rhodes, R. A. W. *Beyond Westminster and Whitehall: The Sub-Central Governments of Britain.* London: Unwin Hyman, 1988.

Richards, Peter G. *The Reformed Local Government System.* London: Allen and Unwin, 1978.

Riddell, Peter. *The Thatcher Era and Its Legacy.* Cambridge, Mass.: Blackwell, 1991.

Robbins, Keith. *The Eclipse of a Great Power: Modern Britain, 1870–1992.* London: Longman, 1994.

Roberts, J., D. Elliott, and T. Houghton. *Privatising Electricity: The Politics of Power.* Chichester, England: John Wiley, 1991.

Robson, Brian. *Those Inner Cities: Reconciling the Social and Economic Aims of Urban Policy.* Oxford: Clarendon Press, 1988.

Rock, William R. *British Appeasement in the 1930s.* London: Edward Arnold, 1977.

Rosen, Andrew. *Rise Up Women!* London: Routledge, 1974.

Rothwell, V. *British War Aims and Peace Diplomacy, 1914–1918.* Oxford: Clarendon Press, 1971.

Saggar, Shamit. *Race and Politics in Britain.* New York: Harvester Wheatsheaf, 1992.

Sampson, Anthony. *The Essential Anatomy of Britain: Democracy in Crisis.* London: Hodder and Stoughton, 1992.

Sanders, David. *Losing an Empire, Finding a Role: British Foreign Policy since 1945.* Basingstoke, England: Macmillan, 1990.

Searle, G. R. *The Liberal Party: Triumph and Disintegration, 1886–1929.* Basingstoke, England: Macmillan, 1992.

Sheldrake, John. *Industrial Relations and Politics in Britain, 1880–1989.* London: Pinter, 1991.

Simon, Brian. *Education and the Labour Movement, 1870–1920.* London: Lawrence and Wishart, 1965.

———. *The Politics of Educational Reform, 1920–1940.* London: Lawrence and Wishart, 1974.

Sked, Alan, and Chris Cook. *Post-War Britain: A Political History.* London: Penguin, 1993.

Skelley, Jeffrey, ed. *The General Strike, 1926.* London: Lawrence and Wishart, 1976.

Skidelsky, Robert. *Politicians and the Slump: The Labour Government of 1929–31.* London: Macmillan, 1967.

Smith, David. *From Boom to Bust: Trial and Error in British Economic Policy.* Harmondsworth, England: Penguin, 1992.

Smith, E. A. *The House of Lords in British Politics and Society, 1815–1911.* Harlow, England: Longman, 1992.

Smith, Justin Davis. *The Attlee and Churchill Administrations and Industrial Unrest, 1945–55.* London: Pinter, 1990.

Smith, Malcolm. *British Politics, Society and the State since the Late Nineteenth Century.* London: Macmillan, 1990.

Stevenson, John. *Britain in the Great Depression.* London: Longman, 1994.

Stevenson, John, and Chris Cook. *Britain in the Depression: Society and Politics, 1929–39.* London: Longman, 1994.

Stoker, Gerry. *The Politics of Local Government.* Basingstoke, England: Macmillan, 1991.

Sullivan, Michael. *Modern Social Policy.* New York: Harvester Wheatsheaf, 1994.

Swenarton, Mark. *Homes Fit For Heroes: The Politics and Architecture of Early State Housing.* London: Heinemann Educational, 1981.

Taylor, A. J. P. *English History, 1914–1945.* Oxford: Clarendon Press, 1992.

Theakston, Kevin. *Junior Ministers in British Government.* Oxford: Blackwell, 1987.

Thompson, P. *Socialists, Liberals and Labour: The Struggle for London, 1885–1914.* London: Routledge, 1967.

Thomson, David. *England in the Twentieth Century.* Harmondsworth, England: Penguin, 1965.

Thornley, Andrew. *Urban Planning under Thatcherism: The Chal-*

lenge of the Market. London: Routledge, 1993.

Thurlow, Richard. *Fascism in Britain: A History, 1918–1985.* Oxford: Blackwell, 1987.

Tiratsoo, Nick, ed. *The Attlee Years.* London: Pinter, 1991.

Tomlinson, R. *Divine Right: the Inglorious Survival of British Royalty in the Twentieth Century.* London: Little, Brown, 1994.

Townshend, Charles. *The British Campaign in Ireland, 1919–1921: The Development of Political and Military Policies.* London: Oxford University Press, 1978.

Verrier, Anthony. *Through the Looking Glass: British Foreign Policy in an Age of Illusions.* London: Cape, 1983.

Watkins, Alan. *A Conservative Coup: The Fall of Margaret Thatcher.* London: Duckworth, 1991.

Watts, Duncan. *Tories, Unionists and Conservatives, 1815–1914.* Abingdon, England: Hodder and Stoughton, 1994.

Willcocks, Arthur John. *The Creation of the National Health Service: a Study of Pressure Groups and a Major Social Policy Decision.* London: Routledge and Kegan Paul, 1967.

Willman, Paul, Timothy Morris, and Beverly Aston. *Union Business: Trade Union Organisation and Financial Reform in the Thatcher Years.* Cambridge: Cambridge University Press, 1993.

Wilson, Harold. *Final Term: the Labour Government, 1974–1976.* London: Michael Joseph, 1979.

———. *The Labour Government, 1964–70.* London: Michael Joseph, 1971.

Wilson, Theodore A. *The First Summit: Roosevelt and Churchill at Placentia Bay.* Boston, Mass.: Houghton-Mifflin, 1969.

Wilson, Trevor. *The Downfall of the Liberal Party, 1914–1935.* London: Collins, 1966.

Winstanley, Michael J. *Ireland and the Land Question, 1800–1922.* London: Methuen, 1984.

Wood, Sydney. *The British Welfare State, 1900–1950.* Cambridge: Cambridge University Press, 1982.

Wynn, Humphrey. *RAF Strategic Nuclear Deterrent Forces: Their Origins, Roles and Deployment, 1946–1969: A Documentary History.* London: Her Majesty's Stationery Office, 1994.

Young, Hugo, and Anne Sloman. *The Thatcher Phenomenon.* London: BBC Publications, 1986.

Young, John W. *Britain and European Unity, 1945–92.* Basingstoke, England: Macmillan, 1993.

Culture and Society

Abel, R. L. *The Legal Profession in England and Wales.* Oxford: Blackwell, 1988.

Abel-Smith, B., and R. Stevens. *Lawyers and the Courts: A Sociological Study of the English Legal System, 1750–1965.* London: Heinemann, 1967.

Alderman, Geoffrey. *Modern British Jewry.* Oxford: Clarendon Press, 1992.

Aldous, Tony. *Battle for the Environment.* London: Fontana, 1971.

Anderson, R. D. *Universities and Elites in Britain since 1800.* Basingstoke, England: Macmillan, 1992.

Annan, Noel. *Our Age: The Generation That Made Post War Britain.* London: Weidenfeld and Nicolson, 1990.

Ball, Michael, Fred Gray, and Linda McDowell. *The Transformation of Britain: Contemporary Social and Economic Change.* London: Fontana, 1989.

Bannister, Roger. *The Four-Minute Mile.* New York: Dodd, Mead, 1981.

Benning, Keith. *Edwardian Britain: A Society in Transformation.* Glasgow, Scotland: Blackie, 1980.

Benson, John. *The Rise of Consumer Society in Britain, 1880–1980.* London: Longman, 1994.

———. *The Working Class in Britain, 1850–1939.* London: Longman, 1989.

Berrol, Selma. *East Side/East End: Eastern European Jews in London and New York, 1870–1920.* London: Greenwood, 1994.

Birley, Derek. *Sport and the Making of Britain.* Manchester: Manchester University Press, 1993.

Blacksell, Mark, and Andrew Gilg. *The Countryside: Planning and Change.* London: Allen and Unwin, 1981.

Blacksell, M., K. Economides, and C. Watkins. *Justice outside the City: Access to Legal Services in Rural England.* Harlow, England: Longman, 1991.

Blythe, R. *The Age of Illusion: England in the Twenties and Thirties, 1919–1940.* London: Hamish Hamilton, 1963.

Booker, Christopher. *The Neophiliacs: The Revolution in English Life in the Fifties and Sixties.* London: Pimlico, 1992.

Bourke, Joanna. *Working Class Cultures in Britain, 1890–1960: Gender, Class and Ethnicity.* London: Routledge, 1994.

Breach, R. W., and R. M. Hartwell. *British Economy and Society, 1870–1970.* London: Oxford University Press, 1972.

Briggs, Asa. *The BBC: The First 50 Years.* Oxford: Oxford University Press, 1985.

————. *The History of Broadcasting in the UK.* 4 vols. London: Oxford University Press, 1961–1979.

Brown, Richard. *Society and Economy in Modern Britain.* London: Routledge, 1991.

Brownill, Sue. *Developing London's Docklands: Another Great Planning Disaster?* London: Paul Chapman, 1990.

Bugler, Jeremy. *Polluting Britain: A Report.* Harmondsworth, England: Penguin, 1972.

Burnett, John. *Idle Hands: The Experience of Unemployment, 1790–1990.* London: Routledge, 1994.

Canter, David, Miriam Comber, and David L. Uzzell. *Football in its Place: an Environmental Psychology of Football Grounds.* London: Routledge, 1989.

Catterall, Peter, and James Obelkevich. *Understanding Post-War British Society.* London: Routledge, 1994.

Champion, Tony, ed. *Population Matters: The Local Dimension.* London: Paul Chapman, 1993.

Champion, Tony, and Charles Watkins, ed. *People in the Countryside: Studies of Social Change in Rural Britain.* London: Paul Chapman, 1991.

Cherry, Gordon E. *Cities and Plans: The Shaping of Urban Britain in the 19th and 20th Centuries.* London: Edward Arnold, 1988.

Cheyette, Brian. *Constructions of "The Jew" in English Literature and Society: Racial Representations, 1875–1945.* Cambridge: Cambridge University Press, 1993.

Childs, David. *Britain since 1939.* Basingstoke, England: Macmillan, 1994.

Clapp, B. W. *An Environmental History of Britain since the Industrial Revolution.* London: Longman, 1994.

Clapson, Mark. *A Bit of a Flutter: Popular Gambling in England, c1823–1961.* Manchester: Manchester University Press, 1992.

Clarke, Michael, David Smith, and Michael McConville. *Slippery Customers: Estate Agents, the Public and Regulation.* London: Blackstone Press, 1994.

Cohen, Philip, and Harwant S. Bains, ed. *Multi-Racist Britain.* Basingstoke, England: Macmillan, 1988.

Constantine, Stephen. *Social Conditions in Britain, 1914–1939.* London: Routledge, 1983.

Cooke, Philip, ed. *Localities: The Changing Face of Urban Britain.* London: Routledge, 1989.

Crow, Graham, and Graham Allan. *Community Life: An Introduction to Social Relationships.* New York: Harvester Wheatsheaf, 1993.

Cullingworth, J. Barry, and Vincent Nadin. *Town and Country Planning in Britain.* London: Routledge, 1994.

Daunton, M. J. *House and Home in the Victorian City: Working Class Housing, 1850–1914.* London: Edward Arnold, 1983.

Davidson, Joan, and Gerald Wibberley. *Planning and the Rural Environment.* Oxford: Pergamon, 1977.

Davies, Andrew, and Steven Fielding, ed. *Workers' Worlds: Cultures and Communities in Manchester and Salford, 1880–1939.* Manchester: Manchester University Press, 1992.

Digby, Anne. *Making a Medical Living: Doctors and Patients in the English Market for Medicine, 1720–1911.* Cambridge: Cambridge University Press, 1994.

Donnison, D. and P. Soto, ed. *The Good City: A Study of Urban Development and Policy in Britain.* London: Heinemann, 1980.

Douglas, J. W. B. *The Home and the School: A Study of Ability and Attainment in the Primary School.* London: MacGibbon and Kee, 1964.

Dunning, Eric, Patrick Murphy, and John Williams. *The Roots of Football Hooliganism: An Historical and Sociological Study.* London: Routledge, 1988.

Edwards, Amy. *The Prison System in England and Wales, 1878–1978.* London: Home Office Prison Department, 1978.

Edwards, J., and R. Batley. *The Politics of Positive Discrimination: An Evaluation of the Urban Programme, 1967–77.* London: Tavistock, 1978.

Englander, David. *A Documentary History of Jewish Immigrants in Britain, 1840–1920.* Leicester, England: Leicester University Press, 1994.

————. *Landlord and Tenant in Urban Britain, 1838–1918.* Oxford: Clarendon Press, 1983.

Fainstein, Susan S., Ian Gordon, and Michael Harloe, ed. *Divided Cities: New York and London in the Contemporary World.* Oxford: Blackwell, 1992.

Finnegan, Ruth. *The Hidden Musicians: Music-Making in an English Town.* Cambridge: Cambridge University Press, 1989.

Ford, J. *Consuming Credit: Debt and Poverty in the United Kingdom.* London: Child Poverty Action Group, 1991.

Foster, R. F. *Paddy and Mr Punch: Connections in Irish and English History.* London: Allen Lane, 1993.

Frankenberg, Ronald. *Communities in Britain: Social Life in Town and*

Country. Harmondsworth, England: Penguin, 1965.

Fuchs, Sir Vivian. *Of Ice and Men: The Story of the British Antarctic Survey, 1943–73.* Oswestry, England: Nelson, 1982.

Garnett, Jane, and Colin Matthew, ed. *Revival and Religion since 1700: Essays for John Walsh.* London: Hambledon Press, 1993.

Gasiorek, Andrzej. *Postwar British Fiction: Realism and After.* London: Edward Arnold, 1994.

Gauldie, Enid. *Cruel Habitations: A History of Working-Class Housing, 1780–1918.* London: Allen and Unwin, 1974.

Gilg, Andrew. *Countryside Planning.* Newton Abbot, England: David and Charles, 1978.

Goldsmith, Edward, and Nicholas Hildyard, ed. *Green Britain or Industrial Wasteland.* Cambridge: Polity, 1986.

Goldsmith, F. B., and A. Warren. *Conservation in Progress.* Chichester, England: Wiley, 1993.

Gorst, Anthony, Lewis Johnman, and W. Scott Lucas, ed. *Post War Britain, 1945–64: Themes and Perspectives.* London: Pinter, 1989.

Gourvish, Terry, and Alan O'Day. *Britain since 1945.* Basingstoke, England: Macmillan, 1991.

Graham, Hilary. *Hardship and Health in Women's Lives.* New York: Harvester Wheatsheaf, 1993.

Green, B. *Countryside Conservation.* London: Allen and Unwin, 1981.

Greenslade, William. *Degeneration, Culture and the Novel, 1880–1940.* Cambridge: Cambridge University Press, 1994.

Gregg, Pauline. *The Welfare State: An Economic and Social History of Great Britain From 1945 to the Present Day.* London: Harrap, 1967.

Gregory, Adrian. *The Silence of Memory: Armistice Day, 1919–1946.* Oxford: Berg, 1994.

Gregson, Nicky, and Michelle Lowe. *Servicing the Middle Classes: Class, Gender and Waged Domestic Labour in Contemporary Britain.* London: Routledge, 1994.

Hall, John M. *Metropolis Now: London and its Region.* Cambridge: Cambridge University Press, 1990.

Hall, Peter. *Urban and Regional Planning.* London: Routledge, 1992.

Hamnett, Chris, Michael Harmer, and Peter Williams. *Safe as Houses: Housing Inheritance in Britain.* London: Paul Chapman, 1991.

Hannington, W. *Unemployed Struggles, 1919–1936.* London: Lawrence and Wishart, 1977.

Harris, Jose. *Private Lives, Public Spirit — a Social History of Britain, 1870–1914.* Oxford: Oxford University Press, 1993.

Havighurst, Alfred F. *Modern England, 1901–1984.* Cambridge: Cambridge University Press, 1987.

Hennessy, Peter. *Never Again: Britain, 1945–1951.* London: Cape, 1992.

Hillman, Mayer. *The Social Consequences of Rail Closures.* London: Policy Studies Institute, 1980.

Hills, J., ed. *Income and Wealth in Modern Britain.* Cambridge: Cambridge University Press, 1995.

Hogarth, R. *London: A New Metropolitan Geography.* London: Hodder and Stoughton, 1991.

Holmes, Colin. *John Bull's Island: Immigration and British Society, 1871–1971.* Basingstoke, England: Macmillan, 1988.

———. *A Tolerant Country: Immigrants, Refugees and Minorities in Britain.* London: Faber and Faber, 1991.

Howkins, Alun. *Reshaping Rural England: A Social History, 1850–1925.* London: HarperCollins Academic, 1991.

Hudson, R., and A. Williams. *Divided Britain.* Chichester, England: John Wiley, 1994.

Imrie, Rob, and Huw Thomas. *British Urban Policy and the Urban Development Corporations.* London: Paul Chapman, 1993.

Jenkins, Jennifer, and Patrick James. *From Acorn to Oak Tree: The Growth of the National Trust, 1895–1994.* Basingstoke, England: Macmillan, 1994.

Johnson, J. H., ed. *Suburban Growth.* London: John Wiley, 1974.

Johnson, Paul, ed. *Twentieth-Century Britain: Economic, Social and Cultural Change.* London: Longman, 1994.

Jones, Stephen G. *Sport, Politics and the Working Class: Organised Labour and Sport in Inter-War Britain.* Manchester: Manchester University Press, 1992.

Keith, Michael. *Race, Riots and Policing: Lore and Disorder in a Multi-Racist Society.* London: UCL Press, 1993.

Knox, E. G., C. MacArthur, and K. J. Simon. *Sexual Behaviour and AIDS in Britain.* London: Her Majesty's Stationery Office, 1993.

Lane, Peter. *A History of Post-War Britain.* London: Macdonald, 1971.

Lawless, Paul. *The Evolution of Spatial Policy: A Case Study of Inner City Policy in the United Kingdom, 1968–81.* London: Pion, 1986.

Lawless, Paul, and Frank Brown. *Urban Growth and Change in Britain: an Introduction.* London: Paul Chapman, 1986.

Lawless, Paul, and Colin Raban, eds. *The Contemporary British City.* London: Paul Chapman, 1986.

Lenon, Barnaby. *London.* London: Unwin Hyman, 1988.

Lewis, Peter. *The Fifties.* London: Heinemann, 1978.

Liddington, Jill. *The Road to Greenham Common: Feminism and Anti-*

Militarism in Britain since 1820. Syracuse, N.Y.: Syracuse University Press, 1991.

Loney, M. *Community Against Government: The British Community Development Project, 1968–1978.* London: Heinemann, 1983.

Lowe, R., and W. Shaw. *Travellers: Voices of the New Age Nomads.* London: Fourth Estate, 1993.

Lowerson, John. *Sport and the English Middle Classes, 1870–1914.* Manchester: Manchester University Press, 1993.

Lunn, Kenneth, and Richard Thurlow, ed. *British Fascism.* London: Croom Helm, 1980.

MacEwen, A., and M. MacEwen. *National Parks: Conservation or Cosmetics.* London: Allen and Unwin, 1982.

MacKenzie, John M. *Propaganda and Empire: The Manipulation of British Public Opinion, 1880–1960.* Manchester: Manchester University Press, 1986.

Mack, J., and S. Lansley. *Poor Britain.* London: Allen and Unwin, 1985.

Martin, David. *A Sociology of English Religion.* London: Heinemann, 1967.

Marwick, Arthur. *Britain in the Century of Total War — War, Peace and Social Change, 1900–1967.* London: Bodley Head, 1968.

———. *British Society since 1945.* Harmondsworth, England: Penguin, 1982.

———. *The Deluge: British Society and the First World War.* Basingstoke, England: Macmillan, 1991.

Mason, Tony. *Association Football and English Society, 1863–1915.* Brighton, England: Harvester Press, 1980.

Massa, Ann, and Alistair Stead. *Forked Tongues?: Comparing Twentieth-Century British and American Literature.* London: Longman, 1994.

McArthur, Colin. *Television and History.* London: British Film Institute, 1978.

McLellan, G., D. Held, and S. Hall, ed. *State and Society in Contemporary Britain.* Oxford: Polity Press, 1984.

Merrett, S. *Owner-Occupation in Britain.* London: Routledge and Kegan Paul, 1982.

Mingay, G. E. *Land and Society in England, 1750–1980.* London: Longman, 1994.

Morgan, Kenneth O. *The People's Peace: British History, 1945–1990.* Oxford: Oxford University Press, 1990.

Morris, R. J., and Richard Rodger, ed. *The Victorian City: A Reader in British Urban History, 1820–1914.* London: Longman, 1993.

Mowat, C. L. *Britain between the Wars, 1918–1940.* London: Methuen, 1968.

Murphy, Robert. *Smash and Grab: Gangsters in the London Underworld, 1920–60.* London: Faber, 1993.

Musgrave, P. W. *Society and Education in England since 1800.* London: Methuen, 1968.

Nelson, G. K. *Seen and Not Heard: Memories of Childhood in the Early 20th Century.* Stroud, England: Alan Sutton, 1993.

Ogden, Philip, ed. *London Docklands: The Challenge of Development.* Cambridge: Cambridge University Press, 1993.

Panayi, Panikos. *Immigration, Ethnicity and Racism in Britain, 1815–1945.* Manchester: Manchester University Press, 1994.

———, ed. *Racial Violence in Britain, 1840–1950.* Leicester, England: Leicester University Press, 1993.

Parsons, Gerald, ed. *The Growth of Religious Diversity: Britain from 1945.* 2 vols. London: Routledge, 1993, vol 1, and 1994, vol 2.

Patmore, J. Allan. *Land and Leisure.* Harmondsworth, England: Penguin, 1972.

Pimlott, J. A. R. *The Englishman's Holiday.* Hassocks, England: Harvester Press, 1976.

Pope, Rex. *War and Society in Britain, 1899–1948.* London: Longman, 1991.

Pugh, Martin. *State and Society: British Political and Social History, 1870–1992.* London: Edward Arnold, 1994.

Rasmussen, Steen Eiler. *London: The Unique City.* Cambridge, Mass.: MIT Press, 1982.

Read, Donald. *The Age of Urban Democracy: England, 1868–1914.* Harlow, England: Longman, 1994.

———. *Edwardian England, 1901–15: Society and Politics.* London: Harrap, 1972.

Reid, Alastair J. *Social Classes and Social Relations in Britain, 1850–1914.* Basingstoke, England: Macmillan, 1992.

Rex, J., and S. Tomlinson. *Colonial Immigrants in a British City.* London: Routledge and Kegan Paul, 1979.

Robson, Brian. *Those Inner Cities: Reconciling the Social and Economic Aims of Urban Policy.* Oxford: Clarendon Press, 1988.

Rodger, Richard. *Housing Urban Britain, 1780–1914.* Basingstoke, England: Macmillan, 1989.

Rosenthal, Michael. *The Character Factory: Baden-Powell and the Origins of the Boy Scout Movement.* New York: Pantheon, 1986.

Royle, Edward. *Modern Britain: A Social History, 1750–1985.* London: Edward Arnold, 1987.

Rubinstein, W. D. *Capitalism, Culture and Decline in Britain, 1750–1990*. London: Routledge, 1993.

Russell, D. *Popular Music in England, 1840–1914: A Social History*. Manchester: Manchester University Press, 1987.

Rydin, Yvonne. *The British Planning System*. Basingstoke, England: Macmillan, 1993.

Sampson, Anthony. *The Essential Anatomy of Britain: Democracy in Crisis*. London: Hodder and Stoughton, 1992.

Sanderson, Michael. *From Irving to Olivier: A Social History of the Acting Profession in England, 1880–1983*. London: Athlone Press, 1984.

———. *The Missing Stratum: Technical School Education in England, 1900–1990*. London: Athlone Press, 1994.

Scannell, Paddy. *A Social History of British Broadcasting, vol 1, 1922–1939*. Oxford: Blackwell, 1990.

Schaffer, F. *The New Town Story*. London: MacGibbon and Kee, 1970.

Seabrook, Jeremy. *Unemployment*. London: Quartet, 1982.

Seaman, L. C. B. *Post-Victorian Britain, 1902–1951*. London: Methuen, 1966.

Shattock, Michael. *The UGC and the Management of British Universities*. Buckingham, England: Open University Press, 1994.

Short, J. *Housing in Britain: The Post-War Experience*. London: Methuen, 1982.

Simon, Brian. *Education and the Labour Movement, 1870–1920*. London: Lawrence and Wishart, 1965.

———. *Education and the Social Order, 1940–1990*. London: Lawrence and Wishart, 1991.

Smith, Lesley M. *The Making of Britain: Echoes of Greatness*. Basingstoke, England: Macmillan, 1988.

Smith, Malcolm. *British Politics, Society and the State since the Late Nineteenth Century*. London: Macmillan, 1990.

Solomos, John. *Race and Racism in Contemporary Britain*. Basingstoke, England: Macmillan, 1989.

Spencer, Frank. *Piltdown: A Scientific Forgery*. London: Natural History Museum, 1990.

Stevenson, John. *Britain in the Great Depression*. London: Longman, 1994.

Stevenson, John, and Chris Cook. *Britain in the Depression: Society and Politics, 1929–39*. London: Longman, 1994.

Stone, M. *The Education of the Black Child in Britain*. London: Fontana, 1981.

Swift, Roger, and Sheridan Gilley, ed. *The Irish in Britain, 1815–1939*.

London: Pinter, 1989.

Taylor, Rogan. *Football and Its Fans: Supporters and Their Relations with the Game, 1885–1985.* Leicester, England: Leicester University Press, 1992.

Thomas, Terence, ed. *The British: Their Religious Beliefs and Practices.* London: Routledge, 1988.

Thompson, Paul. *The Edwardians: The Remaking of English Society.* London: Routledge, 1992.

Thomson, David. *England in the Twentieth Century.* Harmondsworth, England: Penguin, 1965.

Thornley, Andy, ed. *The Crisis of London.* London: Routledge, 1992.

Thorpe, Andrew. *The Longman Companion to Britain in the Era of the Two World Wars, 1914–45.* London: Longman, 1994.

Tillyard, S. K. *The Impact of Modernism, 1900–1920: Early Modernism and the Arts and Crafts Movement in Edwardian England.* London: Routledge, 1988.

Vincent, David. *Literacy and Popular Culture: England, 1750–1914.* Cambridge: Cambridge University Press, 1989.

Walton, John K. *Fish and Chips and the British Working Class, 1870–1940.* Leicester, England: Leicester University Press, 1992.

Ward, Colin, and Dennis Hardy. *Goodnight Campers: The History of the British Holiday Camp.* London: Mansell, 1986.

Ward, Stephen V. *Planning and Urban Change.* London: Paul Chapman, 1994.

Weeks, Jeffrey. *Sex, Politics and Society: The Regulation of Sexuality since 1800.* London: Longman, 1989.

Weidiger, Paula. *Gilding the Acorn: Behind the Facade of the National Trust.* London: Simon and Schuster, 1994.

Weiner, M. J. *English Culture and the Decline of the Industrial Spirit, 1850–1980.* London: Cambridge University Press, 1981.

Welsby, Paul A. *A History of the Church of England, 1945–1980.* Oxford: Oxford University Press, 1986.

Western, John. *A Passage to England: Barbadian Londoners Speak of Home.* London: UCL Press, 1992.

Wilding, Richard. *The Care of Redundant Churches: A Review of the Operation and Financing of the Redundant Churches Fund.* London: Her Majesty's Stationery Office, 1990.

Williams, John, and Stephen Wagg, ed. *British Football and Social Change: Getting Into Europe.* Leicester, England: Leicester University Press, 1991.

Williamson, Bill. *The Temper of the Times: British Society Since World War II.* Oxford: Blackwell, 1990.

Wilson, Elizabeth. *Only Halfway to Paradise: Women in Postwar Britain, 1945–1968.* London: Tavistock, 1980.

Wolfe, John. *The Growth of Religious Diversity in Britain from 1945.* London: Edward Arnold, 1993.

Wood, Anthony. *Nineteenth Century Britain, 1815–1914.* Harlow, England: Longman, 1982.

Ziegler, Philip. *Elizabeth's Britain: 1926 to 1986.* London: Country Life, 1986.

International Relations

Adams, R. J. Q. *British Politics and Foreign Policy in the Age of Appeasement, 1935–39.* Basingstoke, England: Macmillan, 1993.

Alastos, Dores. *Cyprus Guerilla: Grivas, Makarios and the British.* London: Heinemann, 1960.

Aldrich, R. J. *British Intelligence, Strategy and the Cold War, 1945–51.* London: Routledge, 1992.

Ally, Russell. *Gold and Empire: The Bank of England and South Africa's Gold Producers, 1886–1926.* London: UCL Press, 1994.

Anderson, M. S. *The Eastern Question, 1774–1923.* London: Macmillan, 1966.

Bartlett, C. J. *British Foreign Policy in the Twentieth Century.* Basingstoke, England: Macmillan, 1989.

———. *Defence and Diplomacy: Britain and the Great Powers, 1815–1914.* Manchester: Manchester University Press, 1993.

———. *"The Special Relationship": A Political History of Anglo-American Relations Since 1945.* Harlow, England: Longman, 1992.

Baylis, John. *Anglo-American Defence Relations.* London: Macmillan, 1984.

———. *The Diplomacy of Pragmatism: Britain and the Formation of NATO, 1942–49.* Basingstoke, England: Macmillan, 1993.

Beck, P. *The Falkland Islands as an International Problem.* London: Routledge, 1988.

Bell, P. M. H. *John Bull and the Bear: British Public Opinion, Foreign Policy and the Soviet Union, 1941–1945.* London: Edward Arnold, 1990.

Bennett, George. *The Concept of Empire: Burke to Attlee, 1774–1947.* London: Black, 1962.

Black, Jeremy. *Convergence or Divergence?: Britain and the Continent.* Basingstoke, England: Macmillan, 1994.

Blake, R. *A History of Rhodesia.* London: Eyre Methuen, 1977.

Bradford, Ernle. *Gibraltar — the History of a Fortress.* London: Hart-Davis, 1971.

Brivati, Brian, and Harriet Jones, ed. *From Reconstruction to Integration: Britain and Europe since 1945.* Leicester, England: Leicester University Press, 1993.

Brome, V. *The International Brigades: Spain, 1936–39.* London: Heinemann, 1965.

Bulmer-Thomas, Victor, ed. *Britain and Latin America: A Changing Relationship.* Cambridge: Cambridge University Press, 1989.

Busch, B. C. *Britain and the Persian Gulf, 1894–1914.* Berkeley, Calif.: University of California Press, 1967.

Cain, P. J., and A. G. Hopkins. *British Imperialism: Crisis and Deconstruction, 1914–1990.* London: Longman, 1993.

———. *British Imperialism: Innovation and Expansion, 1688–1914.* London: Longman, 1993.

Calvert, Peter. *The Falklands Crisis: The Rights and the Wrongs.* London: Pinter, 1982.

Carlton, David. *Britain and the Suez Crisis.* Oxford: Blackwell, 1988.

Catterall, Peter, and Christine Morris, ed. *Britain and the Threat to Stability in Europe, 1918–47.* London: Leicester University Press, 1993.

Chamberlain, Muriel E. *Decolonization: The Fall of the European Empires.* Oxford: Blackwell, 1985.

———. *Pax Britannica?: British Foreign Policy, 1789–1914.* London: Longman, 1988.

Freedman, Lawrence. *Britain and the Falklands War.* Oxford: Blackwell, 1988.

Geraghty, Tony. *Who Dares Wins: The Story of the Special Air Service.* London: Arms and Armour Press, 1980.

Gilbert, Martin. *The Roots of Appeasement.* London: Weidenfeld and Nicolson, 1966.

Gilbert, Martin, and Richard Gott. *The Appeasers.* London: Weidenfeld and Nicolson, 1967.

Gimbel, John. *The Origins of the Marshall Plan.* Stanford, Calif.: Stanford University Press, 1976.

Gowing, Margaret, and Lorna Arnold. *Independence and Deterrence: Britain and Atomic Energy, 1945–1951.* 2 vols. London: Macmillan, 1974.

Grimal, Henri. *Decolonization: The British, French, Dutch and Belgian Empires, 1919–1963.* London: Routledge, 1978.

Hardie, Frank M. *The Abyssinian Crisis.* London: Batsford, 1974.

Hargreaves, J. D. *Decolonization in Africa.* Harlow, England: Longman, 1988.

Hastings, Max, and Simon Jenkins. *The Battle for the Falklands.* London: Michael Joseph, 1983.

Havinden, Michael, and D. Meredith. *Colonialism and Development: Britain and its Tropical Colonies, 1850–1960.* London: Routledge, 1993.

Heathcote, T. A. *The Military in British India: The Development of British Land Forces in South Asia, 1600–1947.* Manchester: Manchester University Press, 1994.

Henderson, Nicholas. *The Birth of NATO.* London: Weidenfeld and Nicolson, 1982.

Henig, Ruth B. *The League of Nations.* Edinburgh: Oliver and Boyd, 1973.

Hetherington, Penelope. *British Paternalism and Africa, 1920–40.* London: Frank Cass, 1978.

Hobsbawm, E. J. *The Age of Empire, 1875–1914.* London: Weidenfeld and Nicolson, 1987.

Hogan, Michael J. *The Marshall Plan: America, Britain and the Reconstruction of Western Europe, 1947–1952.* Cambridge: Cambridge University Press, 1987.

Holland, Robert. *The Pursuit of Greatness: Britain and the World Role, 1900–1970.* London: Fontana, 1991.

Hyam, Ronald. *Britain's Imperial Century, 1815–1914.* London: Macmillan, 1993.

Hyam, Ronald, ed. *The Labour Government and the End of Empire, 1945–1951.* 4 vols. London: Her Majesty's Stationery Office, 1992.

Johnson, N., and A. Cochrane. *Economic Policy-Making by Local Authorities in Britain and Western Germany.* London: Allen and Unwin, 1981.

Judd, Denis. *Balfour and the British Empire: A Study in Imperial Evolution, 1874–1932.* London: Macmillan, 1968.

Judd, Denis, and Peter Slinn. *The Evolution of the Modern Commonwealth, 1902–80.* London: Macmillan, 1982.

Kelling, G. H. *Countdown to Rebellion: British Policy in Cyprus, 1939–1955.* Westport, Conn.: Greenwood Press, 1990.

Kennedy, Paul M. *The Rise and Fall of British Naval Mastery.* London: Allen Lane, 1976.

Kent, John. *British Imperial Strategy and the Origins of the Cold War.* London: Pinter, 1993.

Kolinsky, Martin. *Law, Order and Riots in Mandatory Palestine,*

1928–35. Basingstoke, England: Macmillan, 1993.

Lagroye, J., and P. Wright, ed. *Local Government in Britain and France.* London: Allen and Unwin, 1979.

Lee, Edwin. *The British as Rulers Governing Multi-Racial Singapore, 1867–1914.* Singapore: Singapore University Press, 1991.

Leffler, Melvyn P., and David S. Painter. *The Origins of the Cold War.* London: Routledge, 1994.

Lo, C. P. *Hong Kong.* London: Belhaven, 1992.

Loewenheim, Francis L., ed. *Peace or Appeasement?: Hitler, Chamberlain and the Munich Crisis.* Boston, Mass.: Houghton Mifflin, 1965.

Louis, William Roger. *The British Empire in the Middle East, 1945–51.* Oxford: Clarendon Press, 1984.

———. *Great Britain and Germany's Lost Colonies, 1914–1919.* Oxford: Clarendon Press, 1967.

Lowe, Peter C. *Great Britain and Japan, 1911–15.* London: Macmillan, 1969.

Macfie, A. L. *The Eastern Question, 1774–1923.* London: Longman, 1989.

MacKenzie, John M. *Propaganda and Empire: The Manipulation of British Public Opinion, 1880–1960.* Manchester: Manchester University Press, 1986.

Malone, Peter. *The British Nuclear Deterrent.* London: Croom Helm, 1984.

Mangan, J. A., ed. *The Imperial Curriculum: Racial Images and Education in the British Colonial Experience.* London: Routledge and Kegan Paul, 1993.

McDonough, Frank. *The British Empire, 1815–1914.* Abingdon, England: Hodder and Stoughton, 1994.

McLean, D. *Britain and Her Buffer State: The Collapse of the Persian Empire, 1890–1914.* London: Royal Historical Society, 1979.

Medlicott, W. N. *Britain and Germany: The Search for Agreement, 1930–37.* London: Athlone Press, 1969.

Miller, Rory. *Britain and Latin America in the Nineteenth and Twentieth Centuries.* London: Longman, 1993.

Millman, Richard. *Britain and the Eastern Question.* Oxford: Clarendon Press, 1979.

Milward, Alan S. *The Reconstruction of Western Europe, 1945–1951.* London: Methuen, 1984.

Monroe, Elizabeth. *Britain's Moment in the Middle East, 1914–56.* London: Chatto and Windus, 1981.

Northedge, F. S. *Descent from Power: British Foreign Policy, 1945–*

1973. London: Allen and Unwin, 1974.

Nunnerley, David. *President Kennedy and Britain.* New York: St Martin's Press, 1972.

Nutting, Anthony. *No End of a Lesson: The Story of Suez.* London: Constable, 1967.

Osgood, R. E. *NATO: The Entangling Alliance.* Chicago: University of Chicago Press, 1962.

Overy, Richard, and Andrew Wheatcroft. *The Road to War.* London: Macmillan, 1989.

Paget, Julian. *Last Post: Aden, 1964–1967.* London: Faber, 1969.

Pakenham, Thomas. *The Boer War.* London: Weidenfeld and Nicolson, 1979.

Parker, R. A. C. *Chamberlain and Appeasement: British Policy and the Coming of the Second World War.* Basingstoke, England: Macmillan, 1993.

Pelly, M. E., H. J. Yasamee, and K. A. Hamilton, ed. *Documents on British Policy Overseas: Eastern Europe, August 1945–April 1946.* London: Her Majesty's Stationery Office, 1991.

Pocock, Tom. *East and West of Suez: The Retreat from Empire.* London: Bodley Head, 1986.

Polyviou, Polyvios S. *Cyprus: Conflict and Negotiations, 1960–80.* London: Duckworth, 1980.

Porter, A. N., and A. J. Stockwell. *British Imperial Policy and Decolonization, 1938–1964.* 2 vols. Basingstoke, England: Macmillan, 1987, vol 1, and 1989, vol 2.

Porter, Bernard. *The Lion's Share: A Short History of British Imperialism, 1850–1983.* London: Longman, 1984.

Rathbone, Richard, ed. *British Documents on the End of Empire.* 2 vols. London: Her Majesty's Stationery Office, 1992.

Reynolds, David. *Britannia Overruled: British Policy and World Power in the Twentieth Century.* London: Longman, 1991.

———. *The Creation of the Anglo-American Alliance, 1937–41.* London: Europa, 1981.

Rickard, John. *Australia: A Cultural History.* London: Longman, 1988.

Robbins, Keith. *The Eclipse of a Great Power: Modern Britain, 1870–1992.* London: Longman, 1994.

———. *Munich, 1938.* London: Cassell, 1968.

Rock, William R. *British Appeasement in the 1930s.* London: Edward Arnold, 1977.

Rothwell, Victor. *Britain and the Cold War, 1941–1947.* London: Cape, 1982.

Sanders, David. *Losing an Empire, Finding a Role: British Foreign*

Policy since 1945. Basingstoke, England: Macmillan, 1990.

Schenk, Catherine R. *Britain and the Sterling Area: From Devaluation to Convertibility in the 1950s.* London: Routledge, 1994.

Short, Anthony. *The Communist Insurrection in Malaya, 1948–60.* London: Muller, 1975.

Silverfarb, Daniel. *The Twilight of British Ascendancy in the Middle East: A Case Study of Iraq, 1941–1950.* Basingstoke, England: Macmillan, 1994.

Singh, Anita Inder. *The Limits of British Influence: South Asia and the Anglo-American Relationship, 1947–56.* London: Pinter, 1993.

Small, Melvin and Otto Feinstein, ed. *Appeasing Fascism.* Lanham, Md.: University Press of America, 1991.

Smith, I. R. *The Origins of the South African War, 1899–1902.* London: Longman, 1994.

Thomas, Hugh. *The Suez Affair.* London: Weidenfeld and Nicolson, 1986.

Tilchin, William N. *Theodore Roosevelt and the British Empire: A Study in Presidential Statecraft.* Basingstoke, England: Macmillan, 1994.

Verdier, Daniel. *Democracy and International Trade: Britain, France and the United States, 1860–1990.* Princeton, N.J.: Princeton University Press, 1994.

Verrier, Anthony. *Through the Looking Glass: British Foreign Policy in an Age of Illusions.* London: Cape, 1983.

Wainwright, A. Martin. *Inheritance of Empire: Britain, India and the Balance of Power in Asia, 1938–55.* Westport, Conn.: Greenwood Press, 1994.

Walder, David. *The Chanak Affair.* London: Hutchinson, 1969.

Waley, Daniel P. *British Public Opinion and the Abyssinian War, 1935–6.* London: Temple Smith, 1975.

Walker, Martin. *The Cold War and the Making of the Modern World.* London: Fourth Estate, 1993.

Warwick, Peter, ed. *The South African War: The Anglo-Boer War, 1899–1902.* Harlow, England: Longman, 1980.

Wasserstein, Bernard. *The British in Palestine.* Oxford: Blackwell, 1991.

Watkins, K. W. *Britain Divided: The Effect of the Spanish Civil War on British Public Opinion.* London: Nelson, 1963.

Weigall, David. *Britain and the World, 1815–1986.* London: Batsford, 1987.

Whelan, Richard. *Drawing the Line: The Korean War, 1950–1953.* London: Faber, 1990.

Wilson, H. S. *African Decolonization*. London: Edward Arnold, 1994.

Wilson, Theodore A. *The First Summit: Roosevelt and Churchill at Placentia Bay*. Boston, Mass.: Houghton Mifflin, 1969.

Windrich, Elaine. *Britain and the Politics of Rhodesian Independence*. London: Croom Helm, 1978.

Woodcock, George. *Who Killed the British Empire?* London: Cape, 1974.

Yasamee, H. J., and K. A. Hamilton, ed. *Documents on British Policy Overseas: Korea, June 1950–April 1951*. London: Her Majesty's Stationery Office, 1991.

Young, John W. *Britain and European Unity, 1945–92*. Basingstoke, England: Macmillan, 1993.

———. *The Longman Companion to Cold War and Detente, 1941–1991*. London: Longman, 1993.

The First and Second World Wars

Adamthwaite, Anthony. *The Lost Peace*. London: Edward Arnold, 1980.

Addison, Paul. *The Road to 1945: British Politics and the Second World War*. London: Pimlico, 1994.

Aronson, Theo. *The Royal Family at War*. London: John Murray, 1993.

Babington, Anthony. *For the Sake of Example: Capital Courts-Martial, 1914–1920*. London: Leo Cooper, 1983.

Barker, Elisabeth. *Churchill and Eden at War*. London: Macmillan, 1978.

Barker, Rachel. *Conscience, Government and War: Conscientious Objection in Great Britain, 1939–1945*. London: Routledge, 1982.

Barnett, Corelli. *The Battle of El Alamein: Decision in the Desert*. London: Macmillan, 1964.

Bates, L. M. *The Thames on Fire*. Lavenham, England: Dalton, 1985.

Batt, Reg. *The Radar Army: Winning the War of the Airwaves*. London: Robert Hale, 1991.

Bekker, Cajus. *The Luftwaffe War Diaries*. Garden City, N.Y.: Doubleday, 1968.

Belfield, Eversley, and H. Essame. *The Battle for Normandy*. London: Pan, 1965.

Beloff, M. *Wars and Warfare: Britain, 1914–1945*. London: Edward Arnold, 1984.

Bennett, G. *Battle of Jutland*. London: Batsford, 1964.

Bickers, Richard Townsend. *The Battle of Britain*. London: Salamander, 1990.

―――. *The First Great Air War*. London: Hodder and Stoughton, 1988.

Bond, Brian. *The First World War and British Military History*. Oxford: Clarendon Press, 1991.

Bourne, John. *Britain and the Great War, 1914–1918*. London: Edward Arnold, 1989.

Bracco, Rosa Maria. *Merchants of Hope: British Middlebrow Writers and the First World War, 1919–1939*. Oxford: Berg, 1993.

Breur, W. B. *Hoodwinking Hitler: The Normandy Deception*. Westport, Conn.: Praeger, 1993.

Brickhill, Paul. *The Dam Busters*. London: Evans Brothers, 1977.

Brooks, Stephen, ed. *Montgomery and the Eighth Army: A Selection from the Diaries, Correspondence and Other Papers of Field Marshal the Viscount Montgomery of Alamein, August 1942 to December 1943.* London: Bodley Head, 1991.

Brown, Malcolm. *The Imperial War Museum Book of the First World War: A Great Conflict Recalled in Previously Unpublished Letters, Diaries and Memoirs*. London: Sidgwick and Jackson, 1991.

Brown, Malcolm, and Shirley Seaton. *Christmas Truce: The Western Front, December 1914*. London: Leo Cooper, 1984.

Calder, Angus. *The Myth of the Blitz*. London: Cape, 1991.

―――. *The People's War: Britain 1939–45.* London: Cape, 1969.

Cantwell, John D. *The Second World War: A Guide to the Documents in the Public Record Office*. London: Her Majesty's Stationery Office, 1993.

Clemens, D. S. *Yalta*. New York: Oxford University Press, 1970.

Cooper, Alan. *Free To Fight Again: RAF Escapes and Invasions, 1940–1945*. Wellingborough: William Kimber, 1988.

Costello, John, and Terry Hughes. *The Battle of the Atlantic*. London: Collins, 1977.

Coultass, Clive. *Images for Battle: British Film and the Second World War, 1939–1945*. Newark, Del.: University of Delaware Press, 1989.

Cruickshank, Charles. *The German Occupation of the Channel Islands*. Stroud, England: Alan Sutton, 1990.

Deighton, Len. *Battle of Britain*. London: Cape, 1980.

Divine, David. *The Nine Days of Dunkirk*. London: White Lion, 1976.

Dockrill, Michael L., and J. Douglas Goold. *Peace without Promise: Britain and the Peace Conferences, 1919–1923.* London: Batsford, 1981.

Douglas, Roy. *In the Year of Munich.* London: Macmillan, 1977.

Dyer, Geoff. *The Missing of the Somme.* London: Hamish Hamilton, 1994.

Edmonds, Robin. *The Big Three: Churchill, Roosevelt and Stalin in Peace and War.* London: Hamish Hamilton, 1991.

Ellis, John. *The World War II Databook.* London: Aurum Press, 1993.

Evans, A. S. *Beneath the Waves: A History of HM Submarine Losses, 1904–1971.* London: William Kimber, 1986.

Farrar-Hockley, A. H. *The Somme.* London: Batsford, 1964.

Feis, H. *Between War and Peace: The Potsdam Conference.* Princeton, N.J.: Princeton University Press, 1960.

———. *Churchill, Roosevelt, Stalin.* Princeton, N.J.: Princeton University Press, 1967.

Frankland, N. *The Bombing Offensive against Germany.* London: Faber, 1965.

Gardiner, Juliet. *"Over Here": The GIs in Wartime Britain.* London: Collins and Brown, 1992.

Garlinski, Jozef. *Hitler's Last Weapons.* London: Friedman, 1978.

Garrett, Stephen A. *Ethics and Airpower in World War II: The British Bombing of German Cities.* Basingstoke, England: Macmillan, 1994.

Gates, Eleanor M. *End of the Affair: The Collapse of the Anglo-French Alliance, 1939–40.* London: Allen and Unwin, 1981.

Gelb, Norman. *Ike and Monty: Generals at War.* London: Constable, 1994.

Gilbert, Martin. *First World War.* London: Weidenfeld and Nicolson, 1994.

———. *Second World War.* London: Weidenfeld and Nicolson, 1989.

Glover, Michael, ed. *The Fateful Battle Line: The Great War Journals and Sketches of Captain Henry Ogle MC.* London: Leo Cooper, 1993.

Gregory, Adrian. *The Silence of Memory: Armistice Day, 1919–1946.* Oxford: Berg, 1994.

Harrisson, T. *Living through the Blitz.* London: Collins, 1976.

Hastings, Max. *Bomber Command.* London: Michael Joseph, 1987.

Haythornthwaite, Philip J. *A Photohistory of World War I.* London: Arms and Armour Press, 1993.

Higgins, Trumbull. *Winston Churchill and the Second Front, 1940–1943.* Westport, Conn.: Greenwood Press, 1974.

Hinsley, F. H. *British Intelligence in the Second World War.* 4 vols. London: Her Majesty's Stationery Office, 1979-1984.

Horne, Alistair. *The Price of Glory: Verdun, 1916.* London:

Macmillan, 1962.

Hough, Richard. *The Longest Battle: The War at Sea, 1939–1945.* London: Weidenfeld and Nicolson, 1986.

Inglis, Ruth. *The Children's War: Evacuation, 1939–1945.* London: Collins, 1988.

James, Robert Rhodes. *Gallipoli.* London: Macmillan, 1989.

James, Robert Rhodes, ed. *Winston S. Churchill: His Complete Speeches, 1897–1963.* Vols. 6 and 7. New York: Chelsea House Publishers, 1974.

Joll, James. *The Origins of the First World War.* London: Longman, 1992.

Jones, Matthew. *Britain, the US and the War in the Mediterranean, 1942–44.* Basingstoke, England: Macmillan, 1994.

Kimball, Warren F. *The Most Unsordid Act: Lend-Lease, 1939–41.* Baltimore, Md.: Johns Hopkins Press, 1969.

Lash, Joseph P. *Roosevelt and Churchill, 1939–41: The Partnership That Saved the West.* London: Deutsch, 1977.

Lewin, Ronald. *Churchill as Warlord.* London: Batsford, 1973.

Liddell-Hart, B. H. *History of the First World War.* London: Pan, 1972.

———. *History of the Second World War.* London: Cassell, 1970.

Liddle, Peter H. *The Airman's War, 1914–1918.* Poole, England: Blandford Press, 1987.

———. *Gallipoli, 1915: Pens, Pencils and Cameras at War.* London: Brassey's, 1985.

Loewenheim, Francis L., Harold D. Langley, and Manfred Jonas, ed. *Roosevelt and Churchill: Their Secret Wartime Correspondence.* London: Barrie and Jenkins, 1975.

MacDonald, Lyn. *1915: The Death of Innocence.* London: Headline, 1993.

———. *Somme.* London: Michael Joseph, 1983.

———. *They Call It Passchendaele.* London: Michael Joseph, 1978.

Macintyre, Donald. *The Battle of the Atlantic.* London: Batsford, 1961.

Marwick, Arthur. *The Deluge: British Society and the First World War.* Basingstoke, England: Macmillan, 1991.

McCarthy, Chris. *The Somme: The Day-by-Day Account.* London: Arms and Armour Press, 1993.

McKee, Alexander. *Caen — Anvil of Victory.* London: Souvenir Press, 1964.

———. *Dresden, 1945: The Devil's Tinderbox.* London: Souvenir Press, 1982.

———. *El Alamein: Ultra and the Three Battles.* London: Souvenir

Press, 1991.

Medlicott, W. N. *Britain and Germany: The Search for Agreement, 1930–37.* London: Athlone Press, 1969.

Messinger, Gary S. *British Propaganda and the State in the First World War.* Manchester: Manchester University Press, 1992.

Middlebrook, Martin. *The First Day on the Somme.* London: Allen Lane, 1971.

Moore, William. *A Wood Called Bourlon: The Cover-up after Cambrai, 1917.* London: Leo Cooper, 1988.

Morgan, David, and Mary Evans. *The Battle for Britain: Citizenship and Ideology in the Second World War.* London: Routledge, 1993.

North, P. *Eagles High: An Illustrated History of the Battle of Britain.* London: Leo Cooper, 1990.

Occleshaw, Michael. *Armour against Fate: British Military Intelligence in the First World War.* London: Columbus, 1989.

Overy, Richard. *The Air War, 1939–1945.* London: Europa, 1980.

Overy, Richard, and Andrew Wheatcroft. *The Road to War.* London: Macmillan, 1989.

Parker, R. A. C. *Chamberlain and Appeasement: British Policy and the Coming of the Second World War.* Basingstoke, England: Macmillan, 1993.

Pelling, Henry. *Britain and the Second World War.* London: Collins, 1970.

Ramsay, Winston G. *The War in the Channel Islands: Then and Now.* London: Battle of Britain Prints International, 1981.

Reynolds, David. *The Creation of the Anglo-American Alliance, 1937–41.* London: Europa, 1981.

Reynolds, David, Warren F. Kimball, and A. O. Chubarian, ed. *Allies at War: The Soviet, American and British Experience, 1939–1945.* Basingstoke, England: Macmillan, 1994.

Richards, Denis. *The Hardest Victory: RAF Bomber Command in the Second World War.* London: Hodder and Stoughton, 1994.

Rimell, Richard Laurence. *The Airship VC: The Life of Captain William Leefe Robinson.* Bourne End, England: Aston, 1989.

———. *Zeppelin!: A Battle for Air Supremacy in World War I.* London: Conway Maritime Press, 1982.

Roach, Peter. *The 8.15 To War: Memoirs of a Desert Rat — El Alamein, Wadi Haifa, Tunis, Salermo, Garigliano, Normandy and Holland.* London: Leo Cooper, 1982.

Rothwell, V. *British War Aims and Peace Diplomacy, 1914–1918.* Oxford: Clarendon Press, 1971.

Ruge, Friedrich. *Scapa Flow, 1919.* Shepperton, England: Ian Allan,

1973.

Ryan, Cornelius. *The Longest Day: June 6, 1944*. London: Gollancz, 1960.

Sainsbury, Keith. *Churchill and Roosevelt at War: The War They Fought and the Peace They Hoped To Make*. Basingstoke, England: Macmillan, 1994.

Shackleton, Richard. *The Second World War*. London: Historical Association, 1991.

Sharp, Tony. *The Wartime Alliance and the Zonal Division of Germany*. Oxford: Clarendon Press, 1975.

Sheffield, G. D., and G. I. S. Inglis. *From Vimy Ridge to the Rhine: The Great War Letters of Christopher Stone, DSO, MC*. Marlborough, England: Crowood Press, 1989.

Siepmann, Harry. *Echo of the Guns: Recollections of an Artillery Officer, 1914–18*. London: Hale, 1987.

Slader, John. *The Red Duster at War: A History of the Merchant Navy during the Second World War*. London: William Kimber, 1988.

Smithers, A. J. *Cambrai: The First Great Tank Battle, 1917*. London: Leo Cooper, 1992.

Smithies, Edward, ed. *War in the Air*. London: Viking, 1990.

Stafford, David. *Britain and European Resistance, 1940–1945*. London: Macmillan, 1979.

Stansky, Peter, and William Abrahams. *London's Burning: Life, Death and Art in the Second World War*. London: Constable, 1994.

Steiner, Zara S. *Britain and the Origins of the First World War*. London: Macmillan. 1977.

Taylor, A. J. P. *The First World War*. London: Hamish Hamilton, 1963.

———. *The Origins of the Second World War*. London: Penguin, 1964.

———. *The Second World War*. London: Hamish Hamilton, 1975.

Taylor, Telford. *Munich: The Price of Peace*. London: Hodder and Stoughton, 1979.

Terraine, John. *Business in Great Waters: The U-boat Wars, 1916–1945*. London: Leo Cooper, 1989.

———. *The Right of the Line: The Royal Air Force in the European War, 1939–1945*. London: Hodder and Stoughton, 1985.

Thorne, Christopher. *Allies of a Kind: The United States, Britain and the War against Japan, 1941–1945*. Oxford: Oxford University Press, 1978.

———. *The Approach of War, 1938–39*. London: Macmillan, 1967.

Townsend, Colin, and Eileen Townsend. *War Wives*. London: Grafton,

1989.

Travers, Tim. *The Killing Ground: the British Army, the Western Front and the Emergence of Modern Warfare, 1900–1918.* London: Unwin Hyman, 1990.

Turnbull, P. *Dunkirk: Anatomy of a Disaster.* London: Batsford, 1978.

Turner, E. S. *The Phoney War.* New York: St. Martin's Press, 1962.

Turner, L. C. F. *Origins of the First World War.* London: Edward Arnold, 1970.

Watt, Donald Cameron. *How War Came: The Immediate Origins of the Second World War, 1938–1939.* London: Macmillan, 1990.

Whitaker, Denis, and Shelagh Whitaker. *Dieppe: Tragedy to Triumph.* London: Leo Cooper, 1992.

Whiting, Charles. *The Poor Bloody Infantry, 1939–1945.* London: Stanley Paul, 1987.

Willis, J. *Churchill's Few: The Battle of Britain Remembered.* London: Michael Joseph, 1985.

Wilson, Theodore A. *The First Summit: Roosevelt and Churchill at Placentia Bay, 1941.* Boston, Mass.: Houghton Mifflin, 1969.

Winton, John, ed. *The War At Sea, 1939–45.* London: Pimlico, 1994.

The Welfare State

Aldridge, M. *The British New Towns.* London: Routledge and Kegan Paul, 1979.

Baldwin, Sally, and Jane Falkingham. *Social Security and Social Change: New Challenges to the Beveridge Model.* Hemel Hempstead, England: Harvester Wheatsheaf, 1994.

Barber, Michael. *The Making of the 1944 Education Act.* London: Cassell, 1994.

Beloff, Max. *Wars and Welfare: Britain, 1914–1945.* London: Edward Arnold, 1984.

Benn, Caroline, and Brian Simon. *Half Way There: Report on the British Comprehensive School Reform.* Harmondsworth, England: Penguin, 1972.

Berry, Fred. *Housing: the Great British Failure.* London: C. Knight, 1974.

Birchall, Johnston, ed. *Housing Policy in the 1990s.* London: Routledge, 1992.

Blackman, Tim. *Urban Policy in Practice.* London: Routledge, 1994.

Bruce, Maurice. *The Coming of the Welfare State.* London: Batsford, 1968.

Bull, D., and P. Wilding. *Thatcherism and the Poor.* London: Child Poverty Action Group, 1983.

Byrne, D., B. Williamson, and B. Fletcher. *The Poverty of Education.* Oxford: Martin Robertson, 1975.

Cannan, Crescy. *Changing Families, Changing Welfare: Family Centres and the Welfare State.* London: Harvester Wheatsheaf, 1992.

Coates, Ken, and Richard Silburn. *Poverty: The Forgotten Englishmen.* Harmondsworth, England: Penguin, 1970.

Cole, Ian, and Robert Furbey. *The Eclipse of Council Housing.* London: Routledge, 1993.

Constantine, Stephen. *Social Conditions in Britain, 1918–1939.* London: Routledge, 1983.

Crowther, Anne. *Social Policy in Britain, 1914–1939.* Basingstoke, England: Macmillan, 1988.

Culyer, A. J., Alan Maynard, and John Posnett, ed. *Competition in Health Care.* London: Macmillan, 1990.

Dale, R. *Contemporary Education Policy.* London: Croom Helm, 1983.

Davie, Ronald, Neville Butler, and Harvey Goldstein. *From Birth to Seven: A Report of the National Child Development Study.* London: Longman, 1972.

Deacon, A., and J. Bradshaw. *Reserved for the Poor: The Means-Test in British Social Policy.* Oxford: Blackwell, 1983.

Deakin, Nicholas. *The Politics of Welfare.* New York: Harvester Wheatsheaf, 1994.

Digby, Anne. *British Welfare Policy: Workhouse to Workfare.* London: Faber, 1989.

Douglas, J. W. B. *The Home and the School: A Study of Ability and Attainment in the Primary School.* London: MacGibbon and Kee, 1964.

Edwards, J., and R. Batley. *The Politics of Positive Discrimination: An Evaluation of the Urban Programme, 1967–77.* London: Tavistock, 1978.

Evans, Hazel, ed. *New Towns: The British Experience.* London: Charles Knight, 1972.

Flynn, Norman. *Public Sector Management.* New York: Harvester Wheatsheaf, 1993.

Forrest, Ray, and Alan Murie. *Selling the Welfare State: The Privatisation of Council Housing.* London: Routledge, 1990.

Fraser, Derek. *The Evolution of the British Welfare State: A History of Social Policy Since the Industrial Revolution.* London: Macmillan, 1984.

George, V. *Social Security: Beveridge and After.* London: Routledge and Kegan Paul, 1968.

Gilbert, B. B. *British Social Policy: 1914–1939.* London: Batsford, 1970.

Glasson, John. *An Introduction to Regional Planning.* London: Hutchinson, 1978.

Glendinning, Caroline, and Jane Millar, ed. *Women and Poverty in Britain: the 1990s.* New York: Harvester Wheatsheaf, 1992.

Glendinning, Miles, and Stefan Muthesius. *Tower Block: Modern Public Housing in England, Scotland, Wales and Northern Ireland.* New Haven, Conn.: Yale University Press, 1994.

Glennerster, Howard. *Paying for Welfare: The 1990s.* New York: Harvester Wheatsheaf, 1992.

Golding, P., ed. *Excluding the Poor.* London: Child Poverty Action Group, 1987.

Gordon, Peter, Richard Aldrich, and Dennis Dean. *Education and Policy in England in the Twentieth Century.* Ilford, England: Woburn Press, 1991.

Graham, Hilary. *Hardship and Health in Women's Lives.* New York: Harvester Wheatsheaf, 1993.

Gregg, Pauline. *The Welfare State: An Economic and Social History of Great Britain from 1945 to the Present Day.* London: Harrap, 1967.

Ham, Christopher. *Health Policy in Britain: The Politics and Organisation of the National Health Service.* Basingstoke, England: Macmillan, 1992.

Harris, J. *The Welfare State.* London: Batsford, 1973.

Havighurst, Alfred F. *Modern England, 1901–1984.* Cambridge: Cambridge University Press, 1987.

Hay, J. R. *The Development of the British Welfare State, 1880–1975.* London: Edward Arnold, 1978.

Hill, Dilys M. *Citizens and Cities: Urban Policy in the 1990s.* New York: Harvester Wheatsheaf, 1994.

James, Adrian L., and Will Hay. *Court Welfare in Action: Practice and Theory.* New York: Harvester Wheatsheaf, 1993.

Johnson, Norman. *Reconstructing the Welfare State: A Decade of Change, 1980–1990.* Hemel Hempstead, England: Harvester Wheatsheaf, 1990.

Jones, Helen. *Health and Society in Twentieth-Century Britain.* London: Longman, 1994.

Kincaid, J. *Poverty and Inequality in Britain.* Harmondsworth, England: Penguin, 1973.

Klein, Rudolph. *The Politics of the National Health Service.* London: Longman, 1989.

Land, Andrew, Rodney Lowe, and Neal Whiteside. *The Development of the Welfare State, 1939–1951: A Guide to Documents in the Public Record Office.* London: Her Majesty's Stationery Office, 1992.

Lane, Peter. *A History of Post-War Britain.* London: Macdonald, 1971.

Leathard, Audrey. *Health Care Provision: Past, Present and Future.* London: Chapman and Hall, 1990.

Levitt, Ruth, and Andrew Wall. *The Reorganised National Health Service.* London: Chapman and Hall, 1992.

Lowe, Rodney. *The Welfare State in Britain since 1945.* London: Macmillan, 1993.

Mack, J., and S. Lansley. *Poor Britain.* London: Allen and Unwin, 1985.

Mitchell, B. R. *The State and Higher Education.* London: Woburn Press, 1994.

Musgrave, P. W. *Society and Education in England since 1800.* London: Methuen, 1968.

Newton, J. *All In One Place: The British Housing Story, 1971–1990.* London: Catholic Housing Aid Society, 1991.

Pater, John E. *The Making of the National Health Service.* London: King Edward's Hospital Fund For London, 1981.

Paton, Calum. *Competition and Planning in the National Health Service: The Danger of Unplanned Markets.* London: Chapman and Hall, 1992.

Peden, G. C. *British Economic and Social Policy: Lloyd George to Margaret Thatcher.* Hemel Hempstead, England: Philip Allan, 1991.

Rose, Michael E. *The English Poor Law, 1780–1930.* Newton Abbot, England: David and Charles, 1971.

Rutter, Michael, Barbara Maughan, Peter Mortimore, and Janet Ouston. *Fifteen Thousand Hours: Secondary Schools and Their Effects on Children.* London: Open Books, 1979.

Salter, Brian, and Ted Tapper. *The State and Higher Education.* Ilford, England: Woburn Press, 1994.

Schaffer, F. *The New Town Story.* London: MacGibbon and Kee, 1970.

Seaman, L. C. B. *Post-Victorian Britain, 1902–1951.* London: Methuen, 1966.

Short, J. *Housing in Britain: The Post-War Experience.* London: Methuen, 1982.

Simon, Brian. *Bending the Rules: The Baker "Reform" of Education.*

London: Lawrence and Wishart, 1988.

——. *Education and the Social Order, 1940–1990*. London: Lawrence and Wishart, 1991.

Spurgeon, Peter, ed. *The Changing Face of the National Health Service in the 1990s*. Harlow, England: Longman, 1990.

Strong, Philip. *The NHS: Under New Management*. Milton Keynes, England: Open University Press, 1990.

Sullivan, Michael. *Modern Social Policy*. New York: Harvester Wheatsheaf, 1994.

Swenarton, Mark. *Homes Fit For Heroes: The Politics and Architecture of Early State Housing*. London: Heinemann Educational, 1981.

Thornley, Andy. *Urban Planning under Thatcherism: the Challenge of the Market*. London: Routledge, 1991.

Timmins, Nicholas. *The Five Giants: A Biography of the Welfare State*. London: Harper Collins, 1995.

Townsend, Peter. *Poverty in the United Kingdom*. Harmondsworth, England: Penguin, 1979.

Vincent, David. *Poor Citizens: The State and the Poor in Twentieth Century Britain*. London: Longman, 1991.

Walker, Carol. *Managing Poverty: The Limits of Social Assistance*. London: Routledge, 1993.

Walters, Vivienne. *Class Inequality and Health Care: The Origins and Impact of the National Health Service*. London: Croom Helm, 1980.

Widgery, David. *The National Health: A Radical Perspective*. London: Hogarth, 1988.

Wilding, Paul, ed. *In Defence of the Welfare State*. Manchester: Manchester University Press, 1986.

Willcocks, Arthur John. *The Creation of the National Health Service: A Study of Pressure Groups and a Major Social Policy Decision*. London: Routledge and Kegan Paul, 1967.

Williams, K., and J. Williams, ed. *A Beveridge Reader*. London: Allen and Unwin, 1987.

Wood, Sydney. *The British Welfare State, 1900–1950*. Cambridge: Cambridge University Press, 1981.

Yelling, J. A. *Slums and Redevelopment: Policy and Practice in England, 1918–45, with particular reference to London*. London: UCL Press, 1992.

Reference Works

Ajayi, J. F. Ade, and Michael Crowder, ed. *Historical Atlas of Africa.* Harlow, England: Longman, 1985.

Barnwell, P. S., and A. T. Adams. *The House Within: Interpreting Medieval Houses.* London: Her Majesty's Stationery Office, 1994.

Barraclough, G., ed. *The Times Atlas of World History.* London: Times Books, 1989.

Bayly, C. A., ed. *Atlas of the British Empire.* London: Hamlyn, 1989.

Baynton-Williams, Ashley. *Town and City Maps of the British Isles, 1800–1855.* London: Studio Editions, 1992.

Beaver, Paul. *Encyclopaedia of the Fleet Air Arm since 1945.* Wellingborough, England: Patrick Stephens, 1985.

Brett, Denis. T. *The Police of England and Wales: A Bibliography.* Basingstoke, England: Police Staff College Library, 1979.

Brooke-Little, J. P. *Boutell's Heraldry.* London: Frederick Warne, 1983.

Burke's Genealogical and Heraldic History of the Landed Gentry. 3 vols. London: Burke's Peerage, 1965–72.

Butler, David, and Gareth Butler. *British Political Facts, 1900–1994.* Basingstoke, England: Macmillan, 1994.

Catalogue of British Parliamentary Papers. Blackrock, Ireland: Irish University Press, 1977.

Catchpole, B. *A Map History of the British People.* London: Heinemann Educational, 1975.

Central Office of Information. *Britain: an Official Handbook.* London: Her Majesty's Stationery Office. Published annually.

———. *The Monarchy.* London: Her Majesty's Stationery Office, 1991.

Central Statistical Office. *Annual Abstract of Statistics.* London: Her Majesty's Stationery Office. Published annually.

———. *Economic Trends.* London: Her Majesty's Stationery Office. Published monthly.

———. *Family Spending: A Report on the Family Expenditure Survey.* London: Her Majesty's Stationery Office. Published annually.

———. *Financial Statistics.* London: Her Majesty's Stationery Office. Published monthly.

———. *Guide to Official Statistics.* London: Her Majesty's Stationery Office, 1990.

———. *Regional Trends.* London: Her Majesty's Stationery Office. Published annually.

———. *Social Focus on Children.* London: Her Majesty's Stationery

Office, 1994.

———. *Social Trends*. London: Her Majesty's Stationery Office. Published annually.

———. *United Kingdom Balance of Payments: The Pink Book*. London: Her Majesty's Stationery Office. Published annually.

———. *United Kingdom Business and Social Statistics*. London: Her Majesty's Stationery Office. Published annually.

———. *United Kingdom National Accounts: The Blue Book*. London: Her Majesty's Stationery Office. Published annually.

Champion, A. G., and C. Wong. *Population of Britain in the 1980s: Social and Economic Atlas*. Oxford: Oxford University Press, 1995.

Checklist of British Parliamentary Papers. Blackrock, Ireland: Irish University Press, 1972.

Cheney, C. R., ed. *Handbook of Dates for Students of English History*. London: Royal Historical Society, 1991.

Chronicle of Britain. Farnborough: Chronicle Communications, 1992.

Clout, Hugh. *The Times London History Atlas*. London: The Times, 1991.

Cook, Chris, ed. *Sources in British Political History, 1900–1951*. 6 vols. London: Macmillan, 1975-1985.

Cook, Chris, Jane Leonard, and Peter Leese. *The Longman Guide to Sources in Contemporary British History: vol 2 — Individuals*. London: Longman, 1994.

Cook, Chris, and John Stevenson. *The Longman Handbook of Modern British History, 1714–1987*. London: Longman, 1988.

Cook, Chris, and David Waller. *The Longman Guide to Sources in Contemporary British History: vol 1 — Organisations and Societies*. London: Longman, 1994.

Craig, F. W. S. *British Parliamentary Election Results, 1950–1973*. Chichester, England: Parliamentary Research Services, 1983.

———. *British Parliamentary Election Statistics, 1918–1970*. Chichester, England: Political Reference Publications, 1971.

Craig, F. W. S., ed. *British Election Manifestoes, 1959–1987*. Dartmouth, England: Parliamentary Research Services, 1990.

———. *British Electoral Facts, 1832–1987*. Dartmouth, England: Parliamentary Research Services, 1989.

Crewe, Ivor, Neil Day, and Anthony Fox. *The British Electorate, 1963–1987: A Compendium of Data from the British Election Studies*. Cambridge: Cambridge University Press, 1991.

Debrett's Peerage and Baronetage. London: Debrett's Peerage and Macmillan, 1990.

Dictionary of National Biography. Oxford: Oxford University Press.

Dod's Parliamentary Companion. London: Dod's Parliamentary Companion. Published annually.

Dolphin, Philippa, Eric Grant, and Edward Lewis. *The London Region: An Annotated Geographical Bibliography.* London: Mansell, 1981.

Drabble, Margaret, ed. *The Oxford Companion to English Literature.* Oxford: Oxford University Press, 1990.

Edwards, R. D. *An Atlas of Irish History.* London: Methuen, 1981.

Ekwall, Eilert. *The Concise Oxford Dictionary of English Place-Names.* Oxford: Oxford University Press, 1960.

Faragher, John Mack. *The Encyclopaedia of Colonial and Revolutionary America.* New York: Facts on File, 1990.

Field, John. *A History of English Field Names.* London: Longman, 1993.

Foote, Geoffrey. *A Chronology of Post War British Politics.* London: Croom Helm, 1988.

Freeman, Michael, and Derek Aldcroft. *The Atlas of British Railway History.* London: Croom Helm, 1985.

Gelling, Margaret. *Place-Names in the Landscape: The Geographical Roots of Britain's Place-Names.* London: Dent, 1993.

Gilbert, Martin. *British History Atlas.* London: Weidenfeld and Nicolson, 1968.

Guide to Sources for British History: Papers of British Cabinet Ministers, 1782–1900. London: Her Majesty's Stationery Office, 1982.

Guide to Sources for British History: Papers of British Churchmen, 1780–1940. London: Her Majesty's Stationery Office, 1987.

Guide to Sources for British History: Papers of British Politicians, 1782–1900. London: Her Majesty's Stationery Office, 1989.

Guide to Sources for British History: Papers of British Scientists, 1600–1940. London: Her Majesty's Stationery Office, 1982.

Guide to Sources for British History: Private Papers of British Colonial Governors, 1782–1900. London: Her Majesty's Stationery Office, 1986.

Guide to Sources for British History: Private Papers of British Diplomats, 1782–1900. London: Her Majesty's Stationery Office, 1985.

The Guinness UK Data Book. Enfield, England: Guinness Publishing, 1992.

Habgood, Wendy, ed. *Chartered Accountants in England and Wales: A Guide to Historical Records.* Manchester: Manchester University Press, 1994.

Hawkings, David T. *Criminal Ancestors: A Guide to Historical Crimi-*

nal Records in England and Wales. Stroud, England: Alan Sutton, 1992.

Hey, David. *Family History and Local History in England.* London: Longman, 1987.

Hoskins, W. G., and David Hey. *Local History in England.* London: Longman, 1984.

Keesing's U.K. Record. Cambridge: CIRCA Reference.

Kerr, D. G. *Historical Atlas of Canada.* Don Mills, Canada: Nelson, 1975.

King, A. C. *British and Irish Archaeology: A Bibliographical Guide.* Manchester: Manchester University Press, 1994.

Kinross, J. *Walking and Exploring the Battlefields of Britain.* Newton Abbot, England: David and Charles, 1993.

Knowles, David, and R. Neville Handcock. *Medieval Religious Houses: England and Wales.* London: Longman, 1994.

Land, Andrew, Rodney Lowe, and Noel Whiteside. *The Development of the Welfare State, 1939–1951: A Guide to Documents in the Public Record Office.* London: Her Majesty's Stationery Office, 1992.

McKinley, R. A. *A History of British Surnames.* London: Longman, 1990.

Milner, J. Edward. *The Green Index: A Directory of Environmental Organizations in Britain and Ireland.* London: Cassell, 1994.

Mitchell, B. R. *British Historical Statistics.* Cambridge: Cambridge University Press, 1988.

Mitchell, Sally. *Victorian Britain: An Encyclopedia.* New York: Garland Press, 1988.

Morris, R. J., and John Langton. *Atlas of Industrialising Britain, 1780–1914.* London: Routledge, 1986.

Mort, David, and Marcus Woolley, ed. *The Counties and Regions of the UK: Economic, Industrial and Social Trends in Local Authority Areas.* Aldershot, England: Gower, 1994.

Natkiel, Richard. *Atlas of Twentieth Century History.* London: Hamlyn-Bison, 1982.

Office of Population Censuses and Surveys. *General Household Survey.* London: Her Majesty's Stationery Office. Published annually.

Palmer, Alan, and Veronica Palmer. *The Chronology of British History: From 250,000 BC to the Present Day.* London: Century, 1982.

Pope, Rex, ed. *Atlas of British Social and Economic History since c1700.* London: Routledge, 1990.

Porter, A. N., ed. *Atlas of British Overseas Expansion*. London: Routledge, 1991.

Rathbone, Richard, ed. *British Documents on the End of Empire.* 2 vols. London: Her Majesty's Stationery Office, 1992.

Record Repositories in Great Britain: A Geographical Directory. London: Her Majesty's Stationery Office, 1991.

Ritchie, L. A., ed. *The Shipbuilding Industry: A Guide to Historical Records.* Manchester: Manchester University Press, 1992.

Robbins, Keith, ed. *The Blackwell Biographical Dictionary of British Political Life in the Twentieth Century.* Oxford: Blackwell, 1990.

Schwartzberg, Joseph E., ed. *A Historical Atlas of South Asia.* New York: Oxford University Press, 1992.

Smurthwaite, David. *The Complete Guide to the Battlefields of Britain.* London: Mermaid, 1993.

UK Christian Handbook. London: MARC Europe, 1991.

Waller, Robert. *The Almanac of British Politics.* London: Routledge, 1991.

West, John. *Town Records.* Chichester, England: Phillimore, 1983.

Who's Who. London: A. and C. Black. Published annually.

Who Was Who. London: A. and C. Black. Published decenially.

APPENDIX

Entries in Volume 2

Buchan, John
Burgh
Burns, Robert
Bute, Marquis of
Buttington, Battle of
Caledonia
Callanish
Calvinistic Church of Wales
Cameron Commission
Cameronians
Campaign for Democracy in Ulster (CDU)
Campaign for Social Justice (CSJ)
Cardiff
Carham, Battle of
Carnegie, Andrew
Carson, Edward Henry
Casket Letters
Cattle Acts
Celtic Church
Celtic Fringe
Celtic Revival
Central Citizens' Defence Committee (CCDC)
Chalmers, Thomas
Charles, Thomas
Chichester-Clark, James
Church in Ireland
Church of Scotland
Church in Wales
Circulating Schools
Claim of Right
Clan
Clarsach
Claverhouse, John Graham of
Clearances, The Highland
Clegg Affair, The Private Lee
Clyde, River
Colnbrook, Lord
Columba, St
Combined Loyalist Military Command (CLMC)

Commonwealth Labour Party (CLP)
Community Councils (Wales)
Company of Scotland
Congregation, Lords of The
Convention of Royal Burghs
Convention of Scottish Local Authorities
Countryside Council for Wales
Court of Justiciary
Court of Session
Court of the Four Burghs
Covenanters, The
Craig, James (1744-1795)
Craig, James (1871-1940)
Crofting
Crown Office
Culloden, Battle of
Culzean Castle
Curling
Curragh Incident
Currency
Cyfraith Hywel Dda
Cymmrodorion, Society of
Dafyyd ap Gruffudd
Dafydd ap Gwilym
Dafydd ap Llywelyn
Dalriada
Darien Settlement
Darnley, Henry Stewart
David I-II
David, St
Davies, Clement
Democratic Unionist Party (DUP)
Development Board for Rural Wales
Devlin, Bernadette Josephine
Devolution
Diplock Commission
Diplock Courts
Direct Rule
Disruption of the Church of

Otterburn, Battle Of
Owen, Robert
Paisley, Ian Richard Kyle
Palatine Counties
Park, Mungo
Partition of Ireland
Patagonia
Paterson, William
Patrick, St
Peace People
Peace Wall
Penal Code
Pentland Rising
Perth, Treaty of
Philiphaugh, Battle of
Phoenix Park Murders
Pibroch
Picts
Pinkerton, Allan
Pinkie, Battle of
Piper Alpha Disaster
Plaid
Plaid Cymru
Plantations of Ulster
Porteous Riots
Potato Famine, Irish
Poynings' Act
Presbyterian Church in Ireland
Presbyterian Church of Wales
Presbyterians
Prestonpans, Battle of
Prince of Wales
Principality
Prior, James Michael Leathe
Pym, Francis Leslie
Radical War
Ramsay, Allan
Ramsay, William
Rebecca Riots
Red Clydeside
Red Hand Commando
Rees, Merlyn

Republican Labour Party (RLP)
Restoration Settlement
Revolution Settlement
Rhodri Mawr
Rhondda Valleys
Rhuddlan, Statute of
Richard, Henry
Rifkind, Malcolm Leslie
Robert I-III
Rob Roy
Rough Wooing
Rowland, Daniel
Royal and Ancient Golf Club
Royal Ulster Constabulary (RUC)
Runrig
Ruthven, Battle of
Ruthven Raid
Salesbury, William
Salmond, Alexander Elliot Anderson
Scapa Flow
Scotia
Scott, Walter
Scottish Arts Council
Scottish Civic Trust
Scottish Enterprise
Scottish Episcopal Church
Scottish National Party (SNP)
Scottish Natural Heritage
Scottish Office
Scottish Power
Scottish Respresentative Peers
Secretary of State for Northern Ireland
Secretary of State for Scotland
Secretary of State for Wales
Settlement Acts
Sgian Dubh
Sheriff
Sheriff Courts
Sheriffmuir, Battle of
Shetland Islands

ABOUT THE AUTHORS

KENNETH J. PANTON is a graduate of the University of Edinburgh and of King's College, University of London. A journalist before entering academic life, he has taught with the Open University, Kansas State University. He is now senior lecturer in geography at London Guildhall University and the University of Southern Mississippi with research interests in education and religion. In recent years, he has published several interdisciplinary analyses of study abroad programmes with faculty based at universities in the United States.

KEITH A. COWLARD is head of the Department of Geography at London Guildhall University. He took his bachelor's degree and doctorate at the University of Leeds. Publications reflect his research interest in urban history and town planning, focusing on the identification of social class areas in 19th century cities and on the economic transformation of London's Docklands. He has also been a director of Planning Aid for London and is active in the promotion of international education.

DEC 1 8 200

CANCELLED

CANCELLED

CHILL FACTOR

A Detective Inspector Charlie Priest mystery

Super-salesman Tony Silkstone wreaks a terrible revenge when he discovers his wife dead, apparently strangled by her lover. The top brass of the Heckley police want to wrap up the case with a manslaughter charge, but Charlie Priest is the investigating officer and is not convinced the murder is as cut and dried as it seems. When links are found between Mrs Silkstone's killer and the murder of a young girl in another part of the country, Charlie follows the trail, only to find he is faced with difficult questions about his friends and his feelings towards them...

CHILL FACTOR

CHILL FACTOR

by

Stuart Pawson

CANCELLED

Macquarie
Regional Library

Magna Large Print Books
Long Preston, North Yorkshire,
BD23 4ND, England.

British Library Cataloguing in Publication Data.

Pawson, Stuart
    Chill factor.

    A catalogue record of this book is
    available from the British Library

    ISBN   0-7505-1947-9

First published in Great Britain in 2001 by Allison & Busby Limited

Copyright © 2001 by Stuart Pawson

Cover illustration © Anthony Monaghan

The right of Stuart Pawson to be identified as the author of this work
has been asserted by him in accordance with the Copyright, Designs
and Patents Act, 1988

Published in Large Print 2003 by arrangement with
Allison & Busby Limited

All Rights reserved. No part of this publication may be reproduced,
stored in a retrieval system, or transmitted in any form or by any
means, electronic, mechanical, photocopying, recording or otherwise
without the prior permission of the Copyright owner.

Magna Large Print is an imprint of Library Magna Books Ltd.

Printed and bound in Great Britain by
T.J. (International) Ltd., Cornwall, PL28 8RW

This novel is a work of fiction.
Names, characters, places and events
are used fictitiously and any resemblance to
actual persons, living or dead,
is entirely coincidental.

Chapter 1

Scott Walker had just reached the poetic bit – *Loneliness ... is the cloak you wear* – when a movement in the wing mirror caught my attention.

'They're here,' I said. *Emptiness ... follows everywhere.* I reached out and cut him off before he could break my heart.

'Aw, I like the next bit,' Detective Constable Annette Brown complained without conviction, twisting round in the driver's seat to see through the back window.

'I'll sing it to you later.' I clicked the transmit button on my RT three times and spoke into it: 'Charlie to Young Turks. Wake up, we're in business.'

'Promises, promises,' Annette mumbled quietly

'And you can put it back on Radio Four,' I told her. We were sitting in my car in the short-stay car-park outside Heckley station – that's railway, not police – with Annette in the driving seat. It's fifty pence for twenty minutes, except that the barrier was fixed in the upright position with all the covers off the electrical boxes so that it looked as if it were faulty. There were five other unmarked police cars nearby, including a couple of hastily arranged armed response vehicles, awaiting the connection from Manchester that had just arrived. It would have looked bad if we'd all had to stop, one by one, and put a fifty pence

9

piece in the box before we could follow our suspect, so I'd arranged for the barrier to be out of order for an hour. That's the sort of power I have. Impressive, eh?

A trickle of people were leaving the concourse: businessmen with briefcases; younger people with sports bags, heading for the taxis and buses or looking for somebody meeting them. 'Hey,' Annette suddenly remarked. 'You never told us about the sales conference. Did you learn anything?'

'Some,' I replied. 'It was interesting to see our man in action, and I'm now an expert on how to sell double glazing.'

'Which might come in handy,' she reminded me, 'after today.'

The warbling of my mobile phone prevented me from dwelling on that prospect. 'Priest,' I said into it.

'He's off the train and will be with you any second,' a voice with a London accent told me. 'He's wearing a blue leather blouson, fawn slacks and carrying a huge Adidas bag. I suggest you lift him as soon as he's clear of the building.'

'Understood,' I replied, and broke the connection. 'And ignored,' I added, quietly.

'Boss...' Annette began, 'are you sure this is wise?'

'Oh, it's Boss now, is it?'

'Charlie, then.'

'Um, Sugar Plum?' I ventured.

'Get stuffed.'

'Here he comes.' I put the radio to my mouth again. 'Young Turks, Young Turks, Robin leaving

10

concourse now. Wearing a blue leather blouse and carrying a big Adidas bag.' The most wanted man on our books stepped through the automatic doors and looked around him. 'And,' I added, 'a suntan like George Hamilton III.'

Six cars along from us a blue BMW moved forward. 'We were right,' Annette said. 'It's the BMW.'

The telephone was warbling again. I switched it off and threw it in the glovebox.

Annette started the engine. 'Charlie...' she tried once more.

'I know, I know,' I told her. 'You're right, it's not *wise*. But what's *wise* got to do with it? I didn't get where I am today–' I gestured expansively towards the raised barrier, symbol of my power, '–by being *wise*, so let's do it.' The BMW had pulled out of the car-park and stopped at the kerb in front of the station entrance. Robin exchanged a quick word with the driver and climbed in the back, throwing his bag in first. I clicked the RT. 'Charlie to Jeff and Pete,' I said, more urgently than before. 'Robin just leaving in blue BMW. We'll do it my way, so he's all yours.'

'Got him,' and 'Understood,' came back to me, and a motorbike and a rusty Ford Fiesta parked in the road outside the station moved off. The car looked grotty, but there was a turbo-charged sixteen hundred engine under the bonnet, and the tyres were extraordinarily wide.

'Besides,' I said to Annette, 'we don't have enough firepower. He wasn't expected to get off at Heckley, and he wouldn't hesitate to shoot himself out of trouble.'

11

'Oh God!' she exclaimed. 'I've just seen Batman.'

Batman was our contact, and he'd been following Robin for the last eight hours. I turned to look. A big man with the beginnings of a beer gut had emerged from the station. He was wearing Burberry check shorts that came to just below his knees, a Desperate Dan T-shirt and some chunky sandals that could have been made by Land Rover. With socks.

'Jee-sus,' I hissed.

Batman stabbed a finger at the mobile phone he was holding and shouted something at it. My phone, in the glove box, remained resolutely silent. He did a little war-dance, shooting glances from one side to the other, as if his feet were on fire and the man with the bucket of water hadn't turned up.

'Charlie...' Annette tried again.

'No,' I told her.

Batman pushed a woman away from the door of the first taxi in the queue and climbed in. The Asian driver tried to remonstrate with him but Batman was in no mood for an argument and the force of his personality, reinforced by a warrant card, prevailed. Besides, the driver had always dreamed of the day that a top cop would climb into his cab and tell him: 'Follow that car.'

'Flippin' 'eck, I've always wanted to do that,' I declared. Annette looked across at me, sighed and shook her head. She's shaken her head quite a few times, recently. 'Charlie to Young Turks,' I said into the radio. 'Move off, move off. ARV1 in front, ARV2 behind me. Let's go, and note that

12

it's the taxi we're stopping. Have you got that?'

The ARVs were an afterthought, at the super's insistence, and not completely in on the plan. 'The taxi?' one of them queried. 'You mean the BMW?'

'No, the taxi. Not the BMW. Understood?'

'Batman? We're stopping Batman?'

'Affirmative, Batman.'

After a long silence one of them said: 'Understood,' and the other grudgingly admitted: 'You're the boss.'

It almost went perfectly. When I gave the signal we boxed-in the taxi and forced it to a standstill. Annette squealed to a stop alongside him, leaving my wing mirror parked neatly behind his, but with no room for me to open the door. She leapt out, slamming the door at her side behind her. As I unbuckled my seat belt the driver glared across at me, his eyes wide with fright.

I had to climb over the centre console, avoiding the gear lever and handbrake, and slide the driver's seat back before I could push the door open, so everything was under control when I finally arrived on the scene. The ARV gunmen had Batman spread-eagled across the bonnet of the taxi, their Glock 9mm self-loading pistols aimed at his head. They'd pulled on their chic little baseball caps with the black and white checks, especially for the occasion. 'OK, boys,' I said as I negotiated my way around the jammed-together cars, 'put them away, he's one of us.'

The ARV officers lowered their guns and stared at me, mystified. Batman stretched upright and turned round. He looked a lot uglier than before, and had developed a twitch at the corner of his mouth. From the colour of his face his blood pressure wasn't too good, either. I said: 'DI Charlie Priest, Heckley CID,' by way of introduction, but decided that a handshake was probably a trifle over-familiar.

For a few seconds he couldn't speak, his breath rasping in his throat as if he'd just completed the four hundred metres hurdles, his shoulders rising and falling as he fought to drag air into his lungs. When he did his voice had a cracked, bluesy tone, a bit like Tom Waits. 'Detective ... Chief Inspector ... Moynihan,' he eventually gasped as he turned in my direction. 'Metropolitan Police ... Regional Crime Squad.' His arm slowly raised until it pointed straight at me, his fingertip an inch from my nose. I stared along the length of it, straight into his piggy eyes as he hissed: *'And if it's the last thing ... I ever do ... I'm going to have ... your fucking head on a plate.'*

Chapter 2

It is a truth universally acknowledged that if a man wishes to maintain a long and happy marriage he should refrain, as often as is possible, from arriving home from work early.

He was having a sod of a week. It wasn't just a sod, it was a complete meadow of sods of a week. Like the one before it and all the ones before that since the government brought in the new legislation. He was Northern Area manager – 'Uh!' he snorted at the thought of it – of Trans Global Finance, and he'd spent all week on the road, chasing clients when he should have been chasing sales staff.

TGF, as the company was known, was formed by the few directors of a Far Eastern bank who were still free to walk the streets undisguised after the bank crashed and left thousands, some say millions, of their customers penniless. As most of them were of Oriental extraction the collapse caused academic concern in the financial pages of the heavier papers but aroused no desire among the greater public to help out. The CEO and mastermind behind the bank received a derisory jail sentence but fled abroad while awaiting his appeal hearing, and two of his co-conspirators vanished without a trace. Not to be deterred by this small hiccup, and seeking a new venture in which to invest their ill-gotten millions, the remaining European directors created Trans Global Finance.

Thanks to aggressive sales techniques and a range of financial products that regularly invoked the comment 'too good to be true,' which was an accurate description, TGF blossomed like a garden centre on Good Friday. Salesmen – sales *executives* – made money to match their mobile phone numbers, and spent it as quickly as they earned it, because, they were told, the good life was theirs for the taking and success breeds success. Nobody loves a loser. To them that have, it shall be given. If you've got it, flaunt it.

Then came the pensions scandal, and they were in the thick of it. Thousands of working people with perfectly good company pension schemes were exhorted to change to TGF, with promises of higher, index-linked pensions when they retired. Promises that nobody, particularly a company that paid its directors and sales people like TGF did, could keep.

The government, in an uncharacteristic fit of guilt because it had led the exhortations to change, ordered the financial houses – and there were several of them – to pay heavy compensation. TGF was nearly crippled, but not quite. They pulled in their horns, downscaled, rationalised and regrouped. It was going to be a long slog, but for those who stayed the rewards could be immense. The days of Rolexes and Porsches, if not Ferraris, would be back.

But not just yet. It's the manager's prerogative to see the most promising clients. The riffraff are sent to talk to the ones that the tele-sales girls churn out: the ones who reluctantly agree to let a financial consultant call at their homes – without obligation – because the girl on the phone has a come-to-bed voice and there's always the chance she will visit you herself. The manager calls during office hours on the small and medium-sized companies who are thinking of expanding and might be interested in a variety of packages that are on offer. And on the lottery winners whose only previous experience of investment has been via the little shop on the high street with the sporting prints on the blacked-out windows.

But even these were wise, nowadays. Three hundred and twenty miles of driving and four appointments had left him with two *I'll think about its*, one *I'll have to ask my brother-in-law, who works for Barclays*, and one *Are you that lot who went bankrupt? The Sunday Times says you are.* Cruel experience, fashioned in the crucible of double-glazing selling, had taught him that all of these were just variations of a straight forward *No way, Jose.*

'Closing,' he said to himself. That's what it was all about. Closing a deal. Backing the punter into a corner by asking him what he liked about the product, what he was looking for, and then giving it to him in such a way that he couldn't retract. Once he'd been the master. He'd sold double-glazing to people who lived in council flats and to people who lived in caravans. He'd sold double-glazing to people who already *had* double-glaz-ing.

'Do you prefer the aluminium or the UPVC, Sir?'

17

'Oh, the UPVC, don't we, Elsie?'

'That's right, Joe. Easy to clean, eh?'

'Precisely my sentiments, Elsie. Life's too short for cleaning window frames. And you won't say no to the free patio door, will you?'

And they didn't. And they signed the bottom of the complicated form that was hastily explained to them and slid across the table, pen laid invitingly across it. And when the windows and the 'free' patio door were fitted they thought they were wonderful, because double-glazing in a climate like Britain's is essential. And they never knew that they could have bought the same deal for a third of the price if they had shopped around, because they were lazy, and inexperienced, and kind, and he'd been such a nice man. And they didn't discover until it was too late that the ten-year guarantee was worthless, because it was the company's policy to go bankrupt every five years.

The Prince of Closing, someone had christened him at a conference, and he was regularly asked to lecture on the subject. But times change, and punters were becoming streetwise to the language of the salesman. Say one wrong word, a single misrepresentation, and they'd have you on some consumer programme, explaining that it was a simple oversight not to mention that the quoted interest rate was monthly, not annual. A change of tactics was required; the books needed re-writing. He burped and tasted bile. He'd grabbed a ham sandwich for lunch, gulped down with two pints of Tetley's – beer, not tea – and his stomach and bladder were protesting. The big roundabout was approaching. Left for Heckley and home, right for the next appointment, another twenty miles away. He glanced at the clock: nearly half past three. The sixth form college would be letting out soon and he hadn't seen her for three weeks. He turned left, reaching for the phone to cancel the appointment, and slowed to a crawl.

Schoolchildren were walking towards him, some purposefully, some in desultory groups; and others, the smaller ones, fooling around. The girls wore blue skirts and white blouses, the boys grey slacks, with a few of them carrying blazers. She'd be going in the opposite direction. He drove past the end of the street that led to the school and hoped he hadn't missed her.

There she was. Her skirt was grey and short, a gesture of defiance against a school regime ill-equipped to deal with young women like her, and her blouse hung outside it. She was tall, about five eight, he guessed, and stacked like whoever made her enjoyed his work. Black tights held legs that would never have to do the chasing, and her skirt curled under her bum so that the afternoon sun's shadows delineated its curves. He imagined his hands resting on those hips, holding her close, before sliding upwards on to the arch of her waist and her cool, young skin.

He squirmed in the driving seat, making himself more comfortable, and cast a sideways glance at her as he drove by. The expression on her puffy face was miserable or sultry, depending on your standpoint. As he watched her hand came up to her mouth and she took a puff of a cigarette, rocking her head back in pleasure as she drew upon it, her breasts rising as she inhaled. He swallowed and reluctantly looked back at the road. In ten years, perhaps less, she'd be over the hill, he thought, but right now she was perfect. Just perfect.

A hundred yards beyond her there was a small shopping precinct. He swung into it and jumped out of the car. As she reached the precinct he was coming from the newsagent's shop, peeling the cellophane off a packet of Benson and Hedges. He walked out on to the pavement on a collision course.

''Scuse me, love,' he said to her. 'I seem to have lost my matches, Could you give me a light, please?'

'Mmm, 'course I can,' she replied, raising her stunted cig to the fresh one between his lips. Glowing tip met tobacco and transferred its fire as he inhaled, his eyes on her. Her lashes were short and brown, and there were whiteheads at the sides of her nose. She was wearing cheap perfume, lots of it, and he wondered what a classroom full of that would do to a man.

'Thanks,' he sighed, smoke streaming from his nose and mouth. 'I was ready for that.'

'No problem,' she replied with a smile. She looked radiant when she smiled.

He turned, as if to leave, then said: 'Sorry, love, can I give you one?' and held the packet towards her.

'No, I'm all right,' she told him, blushing ever so slightly.

He walked in the wrong direction, away from

20

his car, for a few yards, then turned in time to see her cross the road and walk up a street on the right. Her feet were walking, but her arse was doing the samba. She vanished into a development of houses built at the height of the boom: all Elizabethan gables, Georgian windows and Thatcherite mortgages.

Back in the car he wound the window down and lit another B and H. They were shorter than they used to be, he thought. Once they were a luxury cigarette, the epitome of coolness, but now they were just a device for getting nicotine into your system as economically as possible. He held it outside in a half-hearted attempt to stop the car's interior smelling like a public bar.

It had been a long time. He inhaled deeply, wrapping his tongue around the smoke like a grazing cow, and felt it fill his lungs, inflating every little bronchiole and alveolus, finding its way into corners where oxygen had never ventured. Distillations of nicotine were absorbed into his bloodstream and transported to the brain, where receptors, lying redundant for millions of years until Sir Walter Raleigh brought tobacco from the New World, eagerly latched on to them and converted them into an electro-chemical signal. A signal that said: 'Ah! That's good.'

Yes sir, it had been a long time. But the urge never left you. Once tasted, you were hooked. He remembered the date and did a quick calculation. Fifteen years and six months, almost to the day, since the last time. It hadn't been easy, for the yearning, the hunger, was always there, waiting to catch you out. And lately it was stronger than ever. He'd allowed the genie out of its bottle, and once on the loose he knew it had to be obeyed. The thought scared and excited him. He flicked the smouldering stub on to the car-park and started the engine.

Home was a four-bedroomed detached house built with just six others on a spare patch of land between a farm and the canal. The service road was block-paved, with speed humps, and the gardens were open plan. There was a paddock to the rear, but his neighbour had jumped in first and bought that, much to his annoyance. Each house had a double garage but they all left their vehicles outside. It's not conspicuous consumption if you hide it away. On a Sunday morning, when everyone was at home, the development resembled a four-wheel-drive regatta, just before the judging of the *concourse d'elegance*.

His wife's Suzuki Vitara was on the drive, with a Citroen Xantia behind it. 'What's he doing here?' he wondered, parking in the street and swinging his legs wearily out. He collected his jacket from the Armani hanger behind the driving seat and his briefcase from the boot.

The wind chimes welcomed him as if he were entering a Buddhist monastery, but he broke the illusion by shouting:

'I'm here. Cut it out, whatever you're doing,' as he moved through the kitchen and hallway, towards the parlour.

His wife was sitting on the settee and the visitor in an easy chair, an empty cup and saucer perched demurely on his knees. A compilation

22

CD of music from television adverts was playing in the background, very softly. The track was *Bailero*, from the *Songs of the Auvergne*, but he only knew it as the Kenco coffee tune.

'Hello, darling,' his wife said. 'You're home early.'

He stooped to give her a peck on the cheek and turned to the visitor. 'So this is what you get up to while the boss is working his butt off, eh?'

'Oh, not every week,' the visitor replied with a grin.

He placed his briefcase on the floor and draped his jacket over it. 'Will you excuse me,' he asked them, moving back towards the door he'd just entered through, 'but I'm bursting for a piss.'

They listened to his footsteps climb the stairs, looking at each other. She with an expression of relief, he guiltily. The bathroom door closed and he opened his mouth to speak, but she silenced him by putting a finger to her lips. It was possible, she knew, that her husband had closed the door but remained outside it. It wasn't until she heard the sound of flushing that she dared to whisper: 'Phew! That was close.'

'What are we going to do?' he hissed.

'I'll ring you,' she replied.

He placed the cup and saucer on a low table and rose to his feet as footfalls sounded on the stairs again. The husband went straight into the kitchen and was looking in the refrigerator as the visitor passed through. 'I'm off,' he said.

'Why not stay and eat with us, Peter,' the husband offered.

'Thanks all the same, but no,' he replied. 'I've

things to do. I was in the vicinity so I thought I'd come and have a cuppa with the little woman.'

'OK. See you tomorrow, then.'

'God willing. 'Bye Margaret,' he called. 'Thanks for the coffee.'

'You're welcome,' she called back.

When he'd gone the husband poured himself an orange juice and rejoined his wife. 'What did he want?' he asked.

'You've been smoking,' she accused, ignoring the question.

'Just the one,' he replied. 'A client ... you know how it is.'

'Good God, you're pathetic,' she told him.

'I asked you what he wanted.'

'Nothing,' she replied. 'Like he said, he was just passing.'

'Does he make a habit of just passing?'

'That's about the second time this year, but Peter's welcome any time. He's a good friend.'

'He's a bloody awful salesman. What time's supper?'

'I haven't thought about it. I wasn't expecting you for another two hours.'

He resisted the temptation to say: 'Evidently.' Scoring meaningless points wasn't his style. 'Let's eat out, then,' he suggested.

'We can't afford it.'

'It's two for one at the Anglers before six.'

'The Anglers!' she sniffed.

'Well bloody-well cook something. I'm starving.'

'Oh, very well,' she said, standing up. 'Let's go to the Anglers.'

24

Chapter 3

Nine o'clock Wednesday morning somebody mugged a *Big Issue* seller in Heckley town centre. He'd never get rich that way but he made four pounds – enough for a heroin wrap or a few tueys; or some bush, bute, bhang, boy, blow, Bolivian or B-bombs to see him through the day. I ticked the report and slid it into my You'll be Lucky tray.

I was reading the list of overnight car thefts when there was a knock at the door of my partitioned-off domain in the corner of the CID office and big Dave 'Sparky' Sparkington walked in. He's a DC and my best pal.

'It looks lovely out,' he announced.

'Well leave it out, then,' I told him. We'd lost a Fiesta XR3 and an elderly Montego to enemy action. Both crashed and burned, both somebody's pride and joy. Two more people would be braving the rigors of public transport this morning, or arranging for neighbours to take the kids to school and grandma to her appointment at the hospital, while they sorted the insurance.

'Somebody mugged a *Big Issue* seller,' he said.

'I know. I've seen the report from downstairs. Any ideas?'

'No, but I could borrow a couple of bags and a dog, and we could have a day in the field, under-cover, while the weather's nice.'

I looked down at my jeans and check shirt. I

dress the same nowadays as I did when I was an art student, before the Flood. 'I wouldn't have to borrow any clothes,' I said, before he could.

'That's true,' he confirmed, adding: 'or have a haircut.'

I changed the subject. 'Where's young Jamie Walker these days?'

'Ah,' Dave began. 'You've noticed the small blip in the stolen vehicles chart, with the emphasis on older cars with low-tech ignition systems.'

'So where is he?'

'He finished his youth custody yesterday. Jeff and Annette have gone round to his mam's to see if he's there.'

'The little bastard,' I hissed. 'We could do without him ballsing up all our figures and budgets.'

Jamie Walker was fourteen years old and weighed seven stones. Our file on him was so thick he couldn't see over it. He'd spent nearly all his short life in care and his disregard for the law was total. We couldn't touch him, couldn't hurt him. He'd never had anything so he didn't know what loss was. His mother was a slag who only remembered his dad as an obligatory but unsatisfactory tumble with a lorry driver in his cab on the way back from a Gary Glitter concert.

Jamie was bright and cocky. The uniformed boys would slip him a fag while he was in the cells, and have a chat with him. They talked about cars and football, man to man, and invited him to the youth club for a game. He said he'd come, but he never did. Table tennis and five-a-side can't compete with handbrake turns and police chases. Milky coffee doesn't give you the

26

same buzz as Evostick.

I hated him. Dave and the others saw the victims as they sat in their homes, shell-shocked, and asked: 'Why?' Why was he so mindlessly destructive? Why did he have to torch their car? Why did magistrates allow him out on the streets to commit offence upon offence? It was nothing for Jamie to be arrested while on bail, while on probation, while awaiting to appear before the youth court, for a string of separate offences. More than once his hearing had ground to a halt because the prosecution thought they were in court for a stolen car, the defence were all wound up about a burglary and the child psychiatrist had spent most of her weekend analysing why a fourteen-year-old brought up by his grandma would steal her pension book. We had a computer programme dedicated solely to sorting his progress through the system because it was too complicated for the human mind. He was on first-name terms with all the duty solicitors and they loved him.

I didn't. He made a mockery of my overtime budgets, ruined my clear-up statistics and wasted resources that could have been used to solve proper crime. Or what I thought of as proper crime. I hated him, but not for that. Not for any of that. I had other reasons to hate him.

'Fancy going for a pint tonight?' Dave was asking.

'Oh, er, yeah. Good idea,' I replied. We went for a pint nearly every Wednesday night.

'We could go to the Spinners Arms,' he suggested.

'That'll make a nice change,' I said, because we always went to the Spinners Arms. 'Ring Nigel and tell him we'll see him there,' I added. Nigel Newley was one of my hotshot proteges who'd recently moved on to HQ in the quest for fame and glory.

'I've tried, but he's on holiday. Shirley said she might come.' Shirley was Dave's wife, who didn't usually come out with us but it was all right by me.

'OK,' I said.

'And Sophie might, too.'

'Good,' I said, trying not to sound too pleased. Sophie was his daughter, my goddaughter, who I regard as my nearest family. She would be going to university in October and she is tall, graceful and beautiful. When God smiles on some people he really gives them the works. Sophie coming along was definitely all right by me, but I didn't let it show. Dads can be touchy about their daughters. I shuffled the remaining papers on my desk into a neat bundle and shoved them back into the in-tray. 'Tell you what,' I began, 'let's do some proper policing for the rest of the day.'

But I didn't get a chance. The phone rang and I spent the next hour talking to a Prosecution Service solicitor about some evidence we had on a serial thief who specialised in stealing underwear from washing lines. It doesn't sound great crime, but it unnerves the victims, and can lead to other things. We'd marked some stuff and left it hanging out in his usual area of operations and he'd risen to the bait. Trouble was, the underwear we used was bought from the back room at the

Oxfam shop, and it was hot stuff. Open crotches, black and red frills, suspender belts. Phew! Now the CPS solicitor was saying that unnecessary temptation might be a good defence. He wasn't keen, but I persuaded him to let it run. We might not get a conviction, but we'd be sending out the right messages.

Five o'clock the War Cabinet was having a cup of proper coffee in the super's office when the phone rang. He listened, looked at me, said: 'He's here,' and grunted a few times. The word *ominous* flashed through my mind as he replaced the phone.

The War Cabinet comprises of Gilbert Wood, the superintendent and overall boss at Heckley nick; Gareth Adey, my uniformed counterpart; and me; plus any sergeant or other rank who didn't escape quickly enough at the end of his shift. We try to meet at the end of the day for a relaxing cuppa, a general chinwag and to discuss the state of play with the villains and population in general on our corner of God's Own Country. Today we discussed Jamie Walker, our one-small-person crime wave, and regretted not having the power to drive him to a remote corner of the country and push him out of the car. Cape Wrath would do nicely. Sometimes, in the absence of possible avenues of action, we descend to fantasy.

'Go on,' I invited Gilbert. 'Tell me the worst.'

'Right up your street,' he replied. 'Chap rung in to say he's done a murder. They're making it easy for you, these days.'

Gareth rose to his feet asking: 'Is somebody on their way?'

29

'It's Marlborough Close, on the West Woods,' Gilbert told him, 'and there's a car handy.'

The West Wood estate was the first flush of post-war private housing to hit Heckley, back in the sixties. They were mainly semis, bought by young couples who believed that marriage came before children, even though this was supposed to be the permissive age. The real revolution in morality came twenty years later, but nobody sang about it. They all had kids at the same time and for a while the place became one giant playground. But youngsters have this habit of growing into teenagers, and the West Woods featured more and more in our statistics, until they all eventually matured, like the leylandii trees in their gardens, moved on and had kids of their own. Things evened out, and now the estate is a pleasant backwater, with a good mix of ages and races.

'I'll go down to control,' Gareth announced, finishing his coffee in a gulp and leaving us. He likes to create an aura of efficiency and bustle, but mostly he just makes splashes.

'Get the biscuits out, please, Gilbert,' I said. 'The chocolate digestives you keep in the bottom drawer. I've a feeling that I might not be eating for a while.'

Eight minutes and four biscuits later the phone rang again. Gilbert listened for a while then told them that we were on our way. 'It's genuine,' he told me. 'Grab your coat.' Going down the stairs I learned that there was one dead male at the house on Marlborough Close, with another male, alive, sitting in a chair saying he did it.

We went in separate cars with me leading the way, and were there in less than fifteen minutes. One of our Escorts was parked outside number 15, the corner house at the end of a cul-de-sac with a PC standing in the gateway. He stepped forward and opened my door as I coasted to a standstill.

'Hi, Jim,' I said, climbing out. 'What've we got?'

'Hello, Mr Priest,' he replied. 'We've got a murder. One bloke dead, in the kitchen, and a guy in the front room saying he did it.'

Gilbert had joined us. 'Hello, er, John,' he said. 'What have we got?'

'Hello, Mr Wood,' Jim said, and repeated what he'd told me.

'Let's go have a look then, shall we?' Gilbert suggested, moving towards the house. A woman was standing in next door's garden, watching us, and another woman from further along came out to join her.

'You're sure he's dead, Jim?' I asked.

'Yeah, they don't come any deader,' he replied, 'but not for very long.'

'A wild guess at how long?' I invited.

'One or two hours. No rigor, and the blood's hardly dry.'

'Great,' I said to him. 'It's nearly six o'clock. If this body lived here his family might be coming home any time now. Have a word with those two,' I nodded towards the neighbours, 'and see what you can find out.'

'Right, Boss,' he replied, then hesitated. 'Er, how much can I tell them?' I'd known Jim a long time. First in Halifax, and now at Heckley. He

31

had about twenty years in and was solid and dependable, but unimaginative. This wasn't the first dead body he'd attended.

'Say it's a suspicious death,' I told him. 'Find out who lives here, what they look like. Then radio in and see who's on the electoral roll for this address.'

'Right,' he repeated, and headed towards the women.

The house looked sad and seedy with unwashed windows and weeds growing in the borders. The lawn had been mown recently, but the grass cuttings were still lying on it, as if the owner felt that clearing them up was a task too far. I wondered if mine looked like this to a casual visitor and vowed to have a crash clean-up, when I had the time. The two cars parked on the drive didn't look neglected. There was a Citroen Xantia tight up against the garage door and an Audi A8 behind it, at a slight angle, with the driver's door not fully closed. The front door of the house was wide open. I stepped over the threshold and that old feeling hit me, like the smell of a bacon sandwich on a frosty morning. Some primordial instinct was being tapped: the thrill of the chase, and all that. At times like these, when news of a murder is breaking, I wouldn't change my job for any in the world. At others, when there are names and faces to fill in the blank spaces, and I've lived with the grief that people cause each other, I could walk out of it at a moment's notice. Except that someone else would have to do it. There's always an *except that*.

I was in a hallway that faced straight on to a

staircase, with a grubby biscuit-coloured carpet on the floor, nice but impractical, and Victorian bird prints on the walls. One of the first things I look at in someone else's home is their pictures. It's usually depressing and today was no exception.

Gilbert was in the front room, to my left, and I heard him say: 'Do you live here, sir?' I peeked in and saw a man slumped in an easy chair, head down, his elbows on his knees. Gilbert was sitting facing him, his back to me, and another PC was standing nearby. The PC saw me and I winked at him. There was a glass door, slightly ajar, at the end of the hall. I placed the knuckle of my forefinger against it and eased it open.

I was in a kitchen of the type they grandly call a galley which is probably one of the finer examples of the estate agent's art. Cooking might be the rock 'n' roll of the nineties, but back when these houses were built they had the real thing and food was something you grabbed between living. Somebody had been preparing dinner. A pan was on the worktop, lid alongside it, and a spaghetti jar was standing nearby One gas ring was burning at full blast, and it was hotter than Hades in there. The floor was done in brown and cream carpet tiles, and spread-eagled across them was the body of a man. A turkey carver was sticking out of his chest, in the approximate vicinity of the heart. That's the way to do it, I thought. He was wearing a white shirt, before someone ruined it, with the sleeves loosely rolled halfway up his forearms. That's how middle class people turn them up. Workers, proper workers,

33

take them right over the elbow. The man in the parlour, talking to Gilbert, was wearing a blue suit.

It looked to me as if the person lying dead on the kitchen floor had lived here, and the one in the other room with Gilbert was a visitor. It takes years of experience to make deductions like that.

The PC came to join me standing in the doorway to the kitchen. 'Shall I take over outside, Mr Priest?' he asked.

'Oh, er, hello Martin,' I replied. 'Yes, if you will please. How much has laddo told you?' I took three careful steps across the kitchen and turned the gas off.

'Not a great deal. His opening words were: 'I killed him,' but since then he's clammed up, refused to answer any questions.'

I backed out again, trying to place my feet on the same brown squares. 'Right. I'll radio for the team if you'll take up station on the gate and log all visitors, please. There might be someone – family – coming home from work anytime, so watch out for them and don't let them in.'

'So will you do a full enquiry?' he asked.

'We'll have to,' I told him.

'What? SOCOs and all that?'

'You bet.'

'Even though you know who did it?'

I tapped my nose with a finger and said: 'Something's fishy.'

'Blimey,' he replied, and went outside.

When I stepped into the front room Gilbert looked up at me and shook his head. 'This is Detective Inspector Priest,' he said to the man, enunciating the words as if he were addressing a foreigner. 'Perhaps you would like to talk to him.'

It looked to me as if the chief suspect was playing dumb. 'Maybe we should let Sam have a look at him,' I suggested. Sam Evans is the police surgeon, and we needed him to certify the victim dead, but when a witness or suspect is in any sort of a state it's always useful to have a medical opinion, if only for self-defence at a later date.

'Good idea,' Gilbert said, rising to his feet. 'I'll send for him while you...' he gestured towards the man, '...try to have a word.'

'I haven't sent for the team, yet,' I said to his back.

'I'll do it,' he replied.

The team was comprised of the collection of experts we had on duty round the clock, plus a few others that we always called in for a murder enquiry. They'd be at home now, tucking into their fish fingers and chips or playing with the kids, but they'd grab their jackets with unseemly haste and be out of the door before their wives could ask what time they'd be back. We needed SOCOs and a photographer to record the murder scene before anything was moved, exhibits and statements officers, and sundry door-knockers. Then there was the duty DCS at region, the coroner and the pathologist to inform. I dredged up the checklist from the recesses of my mind and ticked off the procedures.

The man was smartly dressed, with slip-on shoes that gleamed and a gaudy silk tie dangling between his knees. The top of his head was facing me and he was completely bald, his scalp as shiny

35

as his shoes. I placed my hands on his lapels and eased him upright.

'Could you just sit up please,' I said to him, 'so I can see you.'

He didn't resist, and flopped against the chair back. His eyes were red, as if he'd been crying, or rubbing his knuckles into them, and there was blood on his fingers.

'That's better,' I said. There were stains on the front of his jacket, too, but I couldn't be sure what they were. 'Like my superintendent told you,' I began, 'I'm DI Priest from Heckley CID. Now could you please tell me who you are?'

He didn't reply and the corner of his mouth began to curl into the beginnings of a sneer. He shook his head, ever so slightly and leaned back, staring up at the ceiling.

'Your name, sir,' I tried. 'Who are you?'

He mumbled something I couldn't catch.

'Could you repeat that?' I asked.

He looked at me and said: 'It doesn't matter.'

'What doesn't matter?'

'All of this. Who I am. It doesn't matter.'

Before he could protest I reached forward, pulled his jacket open and whipped his wallet from his inside pocket. The secret is to make sure you go for the correct side. He made a half-hearted attempt to grab it back, then resumed his slumped position in the chair.

It was just a thin notecase, intended for credit cards and a few tenners for emergencies. I didn't count them but there looked to be about ten. I read the name on a Royal Bank of Scotland gold card and checked it against the others. They were

36

all the same.

'Anthony Silkstone,' I said. 'Is that you?'

He didn't answer at first, just sat there, looking at me with a dazed, slightly contemptuous expression. I didn't read anything into it; I'm not sure what the correct expression is for when you've just impaled someone with the big one out of a set of chef's knives.

'I killed him,' he mumbled.

Well that was easy I thought. Let's just have it in writing and we can all go home. 'You killed the man in the kitchen?' I asked him.

'Yes,' he confirmed. 'I told the others. How many times do I have to say it.'

'Just once more, for the record. And your name is Anthony Silkstone?'

He gave a little nod of the head. I handed him his wallet back and said: 'Stand up, Mr Silkstone. We're taking you down to the station.' He placed it back in his pocket and rose shakily to his feet.

I held his arm and guided him down the driveway and out into the street. A small crowd had gathered but Martin was doing sterling work holding them back. I sat Silkstone in the back of the police car and gestured for Martin to join me.

'Anthony Silkstone,' I began, 'I am arresting you for the murder of a person so far unknown...' He sat expressionless through the caution and obligingly offered his wrists when I produced the handcuffs. 'Take him in as soon as some help arrives,' I told Martin. 'I'll tell the custody sergeant to expect you.'

At the station they'd read him his rights and find him a solicitor. Then they would take all his clothes and possessions and label them as evidence. Even his socks and underpants. Finger-prints and DNA samples would follow until the poor sod didn't know if he was a murder suspect or a rat in a laboratory experiment. He'd undress, sit down, stand up, say 'Yes' at the appropriate times and meekly allow samples of his person to be taken. Then, dressed like a clown in a village play he'd be locked in a cell for several hours while other people determined his fate and came to peep at him every fifteen minutes.

Gilbert and Jim joined me on the driveway. 'You've arrested him,' Gilbert commented.

'It's a start,' I said, turning to Jim. 'Any luck?'

'Yes, Boss,' he replied. 'A bloke called Peter Latham lives here. He's single, lives alone, and works as some sort insurance agent. Average height, thin build, dark hair. Sounds like the man on the floor.'

'He does, doesn't he. Single. Thank God for that.'

'Somebody'll love him,' Gilbert reminded us as his mobile phone chirruped into life. He placed it to his ear and introduced himself. After a few seconds of subservience from the super I deduced that it was the coroner on the phone. Gilbert outlined what we'd found, told him I was on the job and nodded his agreement at whatever the coroner was saying. Probably something along the lines of: 'Well for God's sake don't let Charlie touch anything.' Gilbert closed his phone and told us: 'We can move the body when we're ready.'

'We haven't certified the poor bloke dead yet,' I

38

informed him.

'Well he'd just better be,' he replied.

A white van swung into the street, at the head of a convoy. 'Here come the cavalry,' I said. 'In the nick of time, as always.'

As soon as Sam Evans, the doctor, confirmed that the man on the kitchen floor was indeed dead, and had been so for about an hour, we let the photographer and scene of crime loose in the place. They tut-tutted and shook their heads disapprovingly when I confessed to turning off the gas ring. Sam's opinion, only given when requested, was that death was possibly induced by the dagger sticking out of the deceased's heart. Police doctors and pathologists are not famed for their impetuous conclusions.

I asked Sam if he'd go to the station and give an opinion about the state of mind of Anthony Silkstone, the chief suspect, and he agreed to. The doc's an old pal of mine. I've plenty of old pals. In this job you gather them like burrs. Some stick, some irritate, most of them fall off after a while.

As we hadn't set up an incident room we had our initial team meeting with lowered voices in the late Mr Latham's back garden. I sent the enquiry team, all three of them, knocking on doors to find out what they could about the dead man. Except that they wouldn't have to knock on any doors because everybody was outside, standing around in curious groups, wondering if this was worth missing Coronation Street for or if it was too late to light the barbecue. We wanted to know if anybody had seen anything within the

39

last three or four hours, the background of the deceased, and anything about his lifestyle. Visitors, girlfriends, boyfriends, that sort of thing. I was assuming that the dead man was the householder. As soon as someone emerged who was more than just a neighbour I'd ask them to identify the body.

We knew that Silkstone had the opportunity, now we needed a motive and forensic evidence. He might retract his confession, say he called in to see an old friend and found him dead. Maybe he did, so if he wasn't the murderer we needed to know, fast. Gilbert went back to the station to set up all the control staff functions: property book, diary, statement reader, etcetera, plus vitally important stuff like overtime records, while I stayed on the scene to glean what I could about a man who aroused passions sufficiently to bring about his elimination.

The SOCO was doing an ESFLA scan on the kitchen floor, looking for latent footprints, so I had a look around the upstairs rooms. It was a disappointment. There was nothing to indicate that he was anything other than a normal, hetero-sexual bloke living on his own. No gay literature, no porn, no inflatable life-size replicas of Michel-angelo's David. Except that the bed was made. His duvet was from Marks and Spencer and his wallpaper and curtains probably were too. It all looked depressingly familiar. I promised myself that from now on I'd lead a tidier life, just in case, and dispose of the three thousand back issues of *Big Wimmin* that were under my bed.

There were ten suits in his wardrobe. 'That's

nine more than in mine,' I said to myself, slightly relieved to discover a discrepancy in our life-styles. And he had more decent shirts than me. The loo could have been cleaner but wasn't too bad, and the toilet paper matched the tiles. He'd changed his underpants recently because the old ones were lying on the bathroom floor, with a short-sleeved shirt. There was a sprinkling of water in the bottom of the bath, and the towel hanging over the cold radiator was damp. At a guess he'd showered and changed before meeting his maker, which would be a small comfort to his mother. In his bathroom cabinet I found Bonjela, Rennies and haemorrhoid cream. Poor sod didn't have much luck with his digestive tract, I thought.

I gravitated back into the master bedroom. That's where the clues to Mr Peter Latham's way of living and dying lay I was sure. Find the lady, I was taught, and there were framed photographs of two of them on a chest of drawers, opposite the foot of the bed. I stood in the window and looked down on the scene outside. Blue and white tape was now ringing the garden and the street was blocked with haphazardly parked vehicles. Neighbours coming home from work were having to leave their cars in the next street and Jim, the PC, was having words with a man carrying a briefcase who didn't think a mere death should come between him and his castle. I gave a little involuntary smile: he'd get no change out of Jim.

The first photograph standing on the chest of drawers in a gilt frame was one of those wedding

41

pictures you drag out, years afterwards, to amuse the kids. It was done by a so-called professional, outside a church in fading colour. The bride was taller than the groom, with her hair piled up to accentuate the difference. She looked good, as all brides should. This was her day. Wedding dresses don't date, but men's suits do, which is what the kids find so funny. His was grey with black edging to the floppy lapels of his frock coat. The photographer had asked him to turn in towards his new wife, in a pose that nature never intended, and we could see the flare of his trousers and the Cuban heels. Dark hair fell over his collar in undulating cascades. He'd have got by in a low budget production of *Pride and Prejudice*. It wouldn't have stood as a positive ID but I was reasonably confident that the groom and the man lying on the kitchen floor were one and the same. So where was she, I wondered? The second picture was smaller, black and white, in a simple wooden frame. It showed a young girl in a pair of knickers and a vest, taken at a school sports day She'd be ten or twelve, at a guess, but I'm a novice in that department. Some men would find it sexy, I knew that much. Her knickers were tight fitting and of a clingy material, with moderately high cut legs; and a paper letter B pinned to her vest underlined the beginnings of her breasts. It was innocent enough, I decided, but she'd be breaking hearts in four or five years, that was for sure. Maybe a niece or daughter. At either side of her you could just see the elbows and legs of two other girls, and I reckoned that she'd been cut from a group photograph. A relay team, perhaps.

As with the other picture, I wondered if this young lady might come bounding up the garden path anytime now.

'Boss?'

I turned round to see the SOCO who was standing in the bedroom doorway still dressed in his paper coveralls. I hadn't put mine on, because the case had looked cut and dried.

'Yes!' I replied, smartly.

'We've finished in the kitchen,' he said. 'We just need the knife retrieving.'

'I'll have a look before anybody touches it,' I told him.

'Oh. We, er, were hoping that you'd, er, do it.'

'Do what?'

'Well, retrieve it.'

'You mean ... pull it out?'

'Mm.'

'That's the pathologist's job. He'll want to do it himself.'

'Ah. We have a small problem there. He's on his way back from London and his relief is nowhere to be found, but he's spoken to Mr Wood and he's happy for you to do it if we take a full record of everything.'

'I see. What does it look like for prints.'

'At a guess, covered in 'em.'

'Good. What do you make of those?' I asked, nodding towards the photographs.

'The pictures?' he asked.

'It looks like their wedding day.'

'I'd gathered that. Do you think it's him?'

'Um, could be.' He looked more closely adding: 'Yeah, I'd say it was.'

43

'Good. What about the other?'

'The girl? Could be their daughter,' he replied. 'The hair colour's similar, and they both look tall and thin.'

'Or the bride as a schoolgirl,' I suggested.

The SOCO bent down to peer at the picture. After a few seconds he said: 'I don't think so.'

'Why not?'

'Because the timings wrong.'

'You've lost me,' I told him.

'Can't be sure,' he went on, 'but they both look as if they were taken around the same time. About fifteen or twenty years ago, at a guess. Maybe a bit less for that one.' He pointed towards the schoolgirl.

'How do you work that out,' I asked, bemused.

'The knickers,' he replied. 'Long time ago they'd be cut straight across. Now they wear them cut higher. These are in-between.'

'I take it you have daughters,' I said.

'Yep. Two.'

'Some men would find a picture like that provocative,' I told him.

'I know,' he replied. 'And you can see why, can't you?'

I suppose that was as close as we'd ever get to admitting that it was a sexy image. 'I don't find it sexy,' we'd say 'but I can understand how some men might.'

'Why,' I asked him, 'do the knicker manu-facturers make them with high-cut legs when they know that they are intended for children who haven't reached puberty yet?'

'Because that's what the kids want. There's a

demand for them.'

'But why?'

'So they can be like their mothers.'

'Oh.'

All knowledge is useful. Knowledge catches crooks, I tell the troops. But there are vast landscapes, whole prairies and Mongolian plains, which are a foreign territory to me. They're the bits surrounding families and children and relationships that have stood the test of time. My speciality, my chosen subject, is ones that have gone wrong. Never mind, I consoled myself; loving families don't usually murder each other.

We went downstairs into the kitchen. Peter Latham hadn't moved, but there was a thin coating of the fingerprint boys' ally powder over all his possessions. 'We decided not to do the knife *in situ*,' one of them told me.

'So you want me to pull it out?'

'Please.'

'Great.'

'But don't let your hands slip up the handle.'

'Maybe we should use pliers,' I suggested, but they just shrugged their shoulders and pulled faces.

'Have we got photos of it?' I asked. We had.

'And measurements?' We had.

'Right, let's have a look, then.'

Sometimes, you just have to bite the bullet. Or knife, in this case. I stood astride the body and bent down towards the sightless face with its expression cut off at the height of its surprise, a snapshot of the moment of death. Early detectives believed that the eyes of the deceased would

45

capture an image of the murderer, and all you had to do was find a way to develop it.

I felt for some blade, between the handle and the dead man's chest, and gripped it tightly with my thumb and forefinger. It didn't want to come, but I resisted the temptation to move it about and as I increased the pressure it moved, reluctantly at first, then half-heartedly like the cork from a bottle of Frascati, until it slipped clear of the body. The SOCO held a plastic bag towards me and I placed the knife in it as if it were a holy relic.

'Phew!' I said, glad it was over. I could feel sweat on my spine.

'Well done,' someone murmured.

My happy band of crime-fighters started to arrive, wearing the clothes they'd intended spending the rest of the evening in. Annette Brown was in jeans and a Harlequins rugby shirt, and my mouth filled with ashes when I saw her. She's been with us for about a year, and was now a valuable member of the team. For a long while she'd kept me at a distance, not sure how to behave, but lately we'd been rubbing along quite nicely. She was single, but I'd never taken her out alone, and as far as I knew nobody else had. Inevitably, there were rumours about her sexual inclination. She has wild auburn hair that she keeps under control with a variety of fastenings, and the freckles that often go with that colour. I looked at my watch, wondering if we'd have the opportunity to go for that drink later, and ran my tongue over my teeth. No chance, I thought, as I saw the time.

I sent Sparky and Annette to talk to the house-

to-house boys, collating whatever they'd discovered, and asked Jeff Caton to do some checks
on the car numbers and the two people in the
house. At just before ten the undertaker's van
collected the body. We secured the house, leaving
a patrol car parked outside, and moved *en masse*
to the incident room that Mr Wood had hopefully
set up at the nick.

The coffee machine did roaring service. As
soon as I'd managed to commandeer a cup I
called them all to order. 'Let's not mess about,' I
said. 'With a bit of luck we'll still be able to hit
our beds this side of midnight. First of all, thank
you for your efforts. First indications are that the
dead man might be called Peter Latham. What
can anybody tell me about him?'

Annette rose to her feet. 'Peter John Latham,'
she told us, 'is the named householder for
number 15, Marlborough Close, West Woods. He
is also the registered keeper of the Citroen
Xantia parked on the drive. Disqualified for OPL
in 1984, otherwise clean. Latham's description
tallies with that of the dead man, and a woman at
number 13 has offered to identify the body. She's
a divorcee, and says they were close.'

'Do you mean he was doing a bit for her,
Annette?' someone called out.

'No, close as in living in the adjoining semi,' she
responded, sitting down.

'Thanks Annette,' I said, raising a hand to
quieten the laughs. 'It appears,' I went on, 'that
Latham was killed with a single stab wound to
the heart. We'll know for certain after the post
mortem.'

47

'Arranged for eight in the morning,' Mr Wood interrupted. He was on the phone in his office when I'd started the meeting, organising the PM, and I hadn't seen him sneak in.

'Thanks, Boss,' I said. 'It doesn't appear to have been a frenzied attack, but all will be revealed tomorrow. You OK for the PM, Annette?'

She looked up from the notes she was making and nodded.

'The man who claims to have done it,' I continued, 'is called Anthony Silkstone. What do we know about him?'

Jeff flipped his notebook open but spoke without consulting it. 'Aged forty-four,' he told us. 'Married, comes from Heckley and has a string of driving convictions, but that's all. His address is The Garth, Mountain Meadows, wherever that is.'

I knew where it was, but didn't admit it.

'Yuppy development near the canal, on the north side of town,' Gareth Adey interrupted. 'We've had a car there, but the house is in darkness and the door locked. Presumably the key is in Silkstone's property.'

Jeff waited until he'd finished, then went on: 'He shares the place with a woman called Margaret Silkstone, his wife, I imagine, and drives an Audi A8 with the same registration as the one parked outside the dead man's house.'

'Nice car,' someone murmured.

'What's it worth?' I asked.

'They start at about forty grand,' we were informed.

'So he's not a police officer. OK. Number one

48

priority is find Mrs Silkstone – we'd better get someone round to the house again, pronto – get the key from Silkstone's property. Then we need next of kin for the dead man.

'We're on it, Charlie,' Gareth Adey said.

'Cheers, Gareth. And we need a simple statement for the press.' He nodded to say he'd take that on, too.

The door opened and the afternoon shift custody sergeant came in, wearing no tie and a zipper jacket over his blue shirt to indicate that he was off duty and missing a well-earned pint.

'Just the man,' I said. 'Has our friend been through the sausage machine?'

'He's all yours, Mr Priest,' he replied. 'He's co-operating, and beginning to talk a bit. Dr Evans says there's no reason why he shouldn't be questioned, and he's not on any medication.'

'We think there's a wife, somewhere. Has he asked for anybody to be informed?'

'No, Boss, just his solicitor. I've never heard of them, but apparently they're an international firm with a branch in Manchester, and someone's coming over.'

'Tonight?'

'That's what they said.'

'They must be able to smell a fat fee.' I turned to the others. 'Right, boys and girls,' I said. 'Anybody short of a job, see me. Otherwise, go home to bed and we'll meet again at eight in the morning. With a bit of luck we'll have this sewn up by lunchtime.'

They drifted away or talked to the sergeants to clarify their tasks. Sparky found me and said:

'Well that mucked up our nice quiet drink, didn't it?'

'And I could use one,' I replied.

'If you get a move on we might manage a swift half over the road,' he said.

'You go,' I told him. 'I'll hang about a bit in case anybody wants a word.' I like to make myself available. They might be detectives, but some of them are not as forthcoming as others. There's always someone who seeks you out to discuss an idea or a problem, or to ask to be allocated to a certain task. This time it was Iqbal, who was on a fortnight's secondment with us from the Pakistan CID and who never stopped smiling. He was lodging with Jeff Caton, and apparently had come in with him.

'Where would you like me to go, Inspector Charlie?' he asked.

For over a week he'd followed me round like a bad cold, and I was tempted to tell him, but he outranked me and the big grin on his face made me think that his provocative phrasing was deliberate.

'Ah! Chief Inspector Iqbal,' I said. 'Just the man I'm looking for. Tomorrow you can help me with the submission to the CPS. That should be right up your street.'

'The dreaded MG forms,' he replied.

'Precisely.'

Before I could continue Annette came by and said: 'Goodnight, Boss. See you some time in the morning.'

'Er, we were thinking of trying to grab a quick drink at the Bailiwick,' I told her. 'Fancy one?

Dave's paying.'

'Ooh,' she replied, as if the thought appealed to her, then added: 'I'd better not. I don't want to feel queasy at the PM. Thanks all the same.'

'The PM!' I exclaimed, as enlightenment struck me. 'What a good idea. How do you feel about taking Iqbal along with you?'

Whatever she felt, she declined from expressing it. I don't know how Iqbal felt about watching a body being cut open, but I suspected he'd rather eat a whole box of pork scratchings than be shown around by a woman. He tipped his head graciously and they arranged to meet at the General Hospital, early.

As they left us Sparky said: 'Annette's a nice girl, isn't she?'

'She is,' I replied. 'Very sensible. But she will insist on calling me Boss all the time.'

He grinned and shook his head.

'What did I say?' I demanded.

'Nothing,' he replied.

A couple of others came to clarify things with me and it was about ten to eleven as we walked along the corridor towards the front desk. Some of the team had already gone across to the pub. The duty constable was talking to a short man in a raincoat, and when he saw me he indicated to the man that I was the person he needed.

'This is Mr Prendergast, Mr Silkstone's solicitor,' the constable told me, before introducing me as the Senior Investigating Officer. Prendergast didn't offer a handshake, which was OK by me. I'm not a great shaker of hands.

He didn't waste time with unnecessary preliminaries or pleasantries. 'Have you charged my client?' he asked.

'No,' I replied. 'We haven't even interviewed him, yet.'

'So he is under arrest and the clock is running?'

'Yes.'

'Since when?'

'Since about six forty-five this evening. The precise time will be on the custody sheet.' He was a keen bugger, no doubt about it. I mentally slipped into a higher gear, because he'd know every dodge in the book and screw us if we made the slightest mistake.

'And when do you propose to interview him?' he demanded.

'In the morning,' I replied. 'We normally allow the prisoner to sleep at night. He's been offered food and drink, and given the opportunity to inform another person of his arrest, but he has declined to do so.'

'Yes, Yes,' Prendergast said, swapping his brief-case from his left hand to his right. 'I'm sure you know the rules, Inspector, but I would prefer it if you interviewed him tonight, then perhaps we can explain away this entire sorry event.'

'I think that's unlikely, but I'm happy to interview him if he's willing.' I turned to Sparky who was hovering nearby, and said: 'Looks like we're in for a late night, Sunshine. You'd better ring home.'

'Right,' he replied, grimly. Anybody who keeps Sparky away from that desperately needed pint is walking near the edge. We took the brief through into the custody suite to have words with the sergeant, then locked him in the cell with his client, so they could get their story straight. After ten minutes we knocked on the door, but he asked for another ten minutes. We didn't wait idly while they were conferring. Phone calls to friends in the business told us that Prendergast specialised in criminal law for a big firm of solicitors based in Luxembourg who worked for several large companies with tendencies to sail close to the wind. It was nearly midnight when Sparky pressed the red button on the NEAL interview recorder and I made the introductions.

Tony Silkstone, as he called himself, was of barely average height but built like a welterweight. I could imagine him working out at some expensive health club, wearing all the right gear. The stuff with the labels on the outside. His pate still glistened, so I decided he was a natural slaphead and not one from choice. He had a suntan and his fingernails were clean, even and neatly cut. Apart from that, his paper coverall was pale blue and a trifle short in the arms.

'Today,' I began, after the formalities had been committed to tape, 'at about five p.m., police officers were called to number 15, Marlborough Close, Heckley. Did you make that call, Mr Silkstone?'

'Yes,' he replied in a firm voice, and Prendergast nodded his approval.

'When they arrived there,' I continued, 'they found the body of a man believed to be one Peter Latham. He was lying dead in the kitchen. Did you kill Mr Latham?'

That threw them into a tizzy but I wasn't in a

53

mood for tiptoeing round the issue. I wanted it sewn up, so I could go home. Silkstone had been offered a meal; Prendergast had probably dined lavishly on smoked salmon and seasonal vegetables, washed down by a crisp Chardonnay; I'd had a Cornish pasty twelve hours ago. And, I remembered, four chocolate digestives in Gilbert's office. Prendergast grabbed his client's arm and told him not to answer, as I'd expected.

'That's a rather leading question, Inspector,' he said.

'And I'd like a leading answer,' I replied.

'I think I'd like to confer with my client.'

'Mr Prendergast,' I said. 'It is after midnight and I am tired. Your client has had a stressful day and is probably tired, too. Do you not think it would be in his interest to conduct this interview in the morning, when we all have clear heads? If you are constantly asking for adjournments we could be here until the day after tomorrow.'

Except, of course, that there would be other places where Prendergast would prefer to be tomorrow. Like the golf course, or entertaining one of his corporate clients who was having alimony problems. Silkstone himself came to the rescue. He ran his hand over the top of his head and massaged his scalp with his fingers, before saying: 'It's all right, Mr Prendergast. I'd like to answer the inspector's questions.'

'In which case,' I stated, 'I would like it on record that this interview is continuing at your insistence and not under any duress from me.'

Prendergast put the top on his fountain pen and sat back in his plastic chair.

'Why did you make that phone call, Mr Silkstone,' I asked.

'Because Peter was dead.'

'You knew he was dead?'

'I was fairly certain.'

'You didn't send for an ambulance?'

'There was nothing anybody could do for him.'

'Who killed him?'

'I did.'

Prendergast sat forward in an involuntary reaction, then relaxed again.

'Tell me about it.'

'I followed him home. We had words and I pulled a knife out of the set of carvers that just happened to be on the worktop. I stabbed him with it, in the chest, and he fell down. He moved about for a bit, then lay still. I could tell he was dead.'

'What did you do then?' I asked.

'I sat in the other room for a while. Driving there I'd been seeing red. Literally. I always thought it was just an expression, but it isn't. I'd been mad, raging mad, but suddenly I was calm again. I could see what I'd done. After about ten minutes I rang the police.'

'So you are confessing to killing Peter Latham, by stabbing him in the chest?'

'Yes. I did it.'

'And the man is indeed Peter Latham?'

'Yes, it's Peter.'

'You knew him well?'

'Yes.'

'So why did you kill him?'

Silkstone put his face in his hands and leaned

55

forward until his forehead rested on the little table that separated us.

I said: 'Why did you follow him home and stab him?' and he mumbled something through his fingers.

'I'm sorry?' I said.

He sat up, his eyes ringed with red. 'He killed her,' he told us.

So that was it, I thought. Some old score settled. Some grudge over an old sweetheart, real or imagined, that had festered away for years until it could be contained no longer. I'd seen it all before. I even held one myself. 'Who did he kill?' I demanded.

'My wife. He killed my wife.'

I leaned forward until my elbows were on the table. 'When was this?' I asked. 'When are we talking about?'

'Today. This afternoon. He ... he ... he raped her. Then he strangled her.'

There was a 'clump' as the front legs of Sparky's chair made contact with tiled floor, and Prendergast's eyes nearly popped out. I interlaced my fingers and leaned further forward.

'You're saying that Latham killed your wife this afternoon, Mr Silkstone?' I said, softly.

He looked up to see if there was a clock on the wall, but it was behind him. 'Yes,' he replied.

'Where exactly did this take place?'

'At my house. I came home early and saw him leaving. She ... Margaret ... she was upstairs, on the bed. He'd ... he'd done things to her. So I followed him home and killed him.'

I looked across at Sparky. 'Sheest!' he mumbled.

'Interview terminated while further investigations are made,' I said, reading off the time and nodding for him to stop the tape. I rose to my feet and glanced at the hotshot lawyer who looked as if he was trying to run uphill with his shoelaces tied together. 'I think it's safe to say we'll be holding your client for a while, Mr Prendergast,' I told him.

'I'm not surprised, Inspector,' he responded, shaking his head.

Chapter 4

The estate agent's advert had said that Mountain Meadows was a pleasant development on a flat strip of land alongside the canal. There were only seven houses, all detached and with decent gardens. Sparky and myself went to investigate, in my car, after ringing Mr Wood with the latest bombshell. The roads were empty and I drove fast. Soon we were clear of the streetlamps, tearing along through the night.

'You seem to know where you're going,' Dave observed.

'I came to look at them, once,' I replied.

'What? You were thinking of moving?'

'Mmm.'

'You kept that quiet.'

'I don't tell you everything.'

A cat darted halfway across the road, then stopped and stared into my headlights. I hit the brakes and the front of the car dipped and pulled to the right as a wheel locked. The moggie regained the power of movement and leapt to safety.

After a silence Dave said: 'You and Annabelle?'

'Yeah. We could have afforded one reasonably comfortably if we'd pooled our resources.'

Annabelle was my last long-term relationship. We were together for about five years, which was a personal best for me, but she decided the grass

58

was greener when seen through the windscreen of a Mercedes. I live in the house I inherited from my parents, and she owned an old vicarage. When things were good between us we'd done the tour of a few places, including Mountain Meadows. On paper it had looked ideal, but a quick visit one summer's evening destroyed the dream. The smoke from all the barbecues and the incessant drinky-poos with the neighbours would have ruined our lungs and livers. Then she left me, so it was just as well that we hadn't moved.

Except, maybe, if we had... Ah well, we'd never know.

'So what do you think,' Dave asked, changing the subject.

'We'll soon find out,' I replied. 'This is it.'

I turned off the lane and slowed down for the speed humps, hardly recognising the place. The darkness was almost absolute, broken only by an occasional lighted window, and all the twigs with garden centre labels on them that had dotted the open plan gardens were now luxuriant shrubs and trees. As my headlights swung around, probing the shadows, we saw that the conservatory salesman had done a roaring trade, and since my last visit the registration letters on the cars parked outside every house had progressed two places along the alphabet. Two houses, next to each other, had speedboats. Tony Silkstone had told us that his house, The Garth, was the last one on the right. 'The one with the converted gas lamps along the drive,' he'd added. Somebody's million-watt security light flicked on behind us, turning night into day.

59

The panda sent by Inspector Adey was parked outside The Garth. We'd radioed instructions for them to guard and contain the property until we arrived. I freewheeled to a standstill behind it, yanked the brake on and killed the lights as the two occupants opened their doors and stretched upright. 'Got the key?' I asked the driver.

'Right here, Boss,' he replied.

'Thanks. Hang around, we might need you.'

The converted gas lamps were not switched on and a Suzuki Vitara stood on the drive, nose against the garage door. The house was in total darkness, although all the curtains were pulled back. Dave put the key in the Yale latch, turned it and pushed the door open. When Silkstone dashed out he hadn't locked the door deliberately; he'd just pulled it shut, or it had slammed behind him. Mr Yale had done the rest. So far, so good.

As we stepped inside a wind chime broke into song above our heads. 'I could do without that,' I hissed.

The feeble illumination from a digital clock was enough to tell us that we were in a kitchen, and it was a good deal larger than the last one we'd stood in. Edges of implements and utensils in chrome and stainless steel reflected its glow. Unblinking green and red pilot lights watched us, like animals in the jungle, wondering who the intruders were, and a refrigerator added a background hum.

I found a light switch and clicked it on. The shapes became Neff appliances and the jungle animals lost their menace. Dave handed me a

60

rolled-up coverall and I started to pull it over my feet. I wasn't sure if it was necessary, but I was playing safe. Sometimes I cut corners, occasionally I'm reckless, but never where forensics are concerned. Hunches are no good in this game. A hunch never swayed a jury or earned the sympathy of a judge. Motive, opportunity, witnesses, forensic. They're what convict criminals, with the emphasis on the forensic. You can fudge the other three, but not the forensic. That's what I'd always believed, and, so far, it had done well for me. That was the received wisdom, as taught at Staff College.

We had a lot to learn.

'Close the door,' I said, and Dave pushed it shut with an elbow. We pulled latex gloves on to our hands and eased our feet into over-socks. We didn't bother to pull the hoods over our heads. My mouth was dry and I could feel my heart banging against my ribs. The thrill of the chase had long since degenerated into the drudgery of killing, the sordidness of death. It always does. Apart from the occasional gangland shooting there's no such thing as a good murder. This wasn't a straightforward, cut-and-dried jealous husband killing any more; it was something squalid. A clock was ticking somewhere in the room, measuring each second with well-oiled precision.

'OK?'

'OK?'

'C'mon, then.'

The interior door opened on to a hallway. I wasn't there to admire the furnishings and look

61

at the pictures – that would come later – but I couldn't help doing it. I switched the light on and absorbed the scene.

The Axminster carpet was covered in swirly patterns and felt as heavy as leaf mould under the feet. Facing us was an oil painting of a vaguely European city scene on a rainy day, churned out on a production line in Taiwan, hanging over an antique captain's desk that I'd have accepted as a week's salary anytime. The wallpaper was red, cream and gold stripes and a grandfather clock modelled on Westminster stood in a corner. Here, I thought, lived a man who knew what he liked. I found another switch and illuminated the staircase.

It's the boss's prerogative to lead the way. I climbed the stairs slowly, keeping well over to the left in case we needed to do a footprint check on them, and Dave followed. 'Silkstone said first door on the right,' he reminded me.

The door was open, and we could already see what we'd expected by the glow from the landing lights. I reached around the doorframe and found the bedroom switch, just to do the job properly.

She was lying face down on the bed and appeared to be naked below the waist. I stepped forward into the room and stooped beside her, looking into my second dead face that night. There was a pair of tights knotted round her neck, and the bulging eyes and pig's liver of a tongue lolling from her mouth confirmed that she'd died by throttling. I'd have preferred the knife in the heart, anytime. I scanned her body

62

feeling like the worst sort of voyeur and noticed that she was, in fact, wearing a short skirt that had been pulled up around her waist. My eyes went into the routine, as they had done too many times in the past, and the questions popped up one by one like the indicators on an old-fashioned cash register: Signs of a struggle? Anything under the fingernails? Bruising or bleeding? Is this where the attack took place?

Dave was standing just outside the room, to one side, and I rejoined him. 'Seen enough?' I asked, and he nodded. We stepped carefully down the stairs and retraced our path back out to my car. I rang Gilbert and told him the news. He'd contact the coroner and the pathologist and off we'd go again. We decided to get the SOCOs on the job immediately and leave everything else until after the morning meeting. Which was, I noticed, looking at the car clock, just six hours away.

'You didn't really want to live here, did you?' Dave asked as we sat waiting.

'It was just a thought,' I replied.

'You wouldn't have been happy.'

'I'm not happy now.'

'Unhappy with money in the bank is better than unhappy skint,' he replied.

'I suppose so.'

'This'll bring the property prices down,' he added, looking out of the window.

'That's a consolation.'

The SOCO's white van came swaying round the corner, bouncing over the speed humps and triggering the big security light. 'Looks like Michael

Schumacher's on duty tonight,' Dave observed as we opened our doors. I pointed to a spot behind me and the SOCO parked there and doused his lights.

He's young, fresh faced, and can still boogie 'til dawn then appear in court bright as a squirrel. 'Hi, Mr Priest,' he said, slamming the van door. 'What's going on? Is it two-for-the-price-of-one night, or something?'

'First of all, it's Charlie,' I told him. 'Secondly there are people in bed and I'd prefer them to stay there, and thirdly don't be so bloody cheerful at this time in the morning.' We told him what we'd found, and a few minutes later another patrol car came into the estate, followed by the other SOCO and the photographer. Bedroom lights came on in the neighbouring houses and curtains twitched. We were having an operational meeting, in hushed voices, when we heard a police siren in the distance, gradually growing louder. A minute later a traffic car, diverted off the motorway, careered round the corner and nearly took off over the humps. Somebody had dialled 999. I had words with the driver, persuaded him to turn his blue lights off, and sent him back to cruising the M62. A man from one of the houses joined us, saying he was chairman of the local Neighbourhood Watch, demanding to know what was going on. He wore a flying-officer moustache and a dressing gown over pyjamas. I ushered him to one side and asked him – 'just between the two of us' – what he knew about the people who lived at The Garth, adding that I'd be very grateful if he could put it all in writing for me, before nine o'clock in the morning. He wandered off composing a hatchet job on the neighbour with the ghastly street lamps in his garden.

That was all we could do. Priorities were identification of the bodies and times and causes of death. These would be checked against Silkstone's story and we'd see if anything else we discovered supported or disputed the facts. If he were telling the truth the Crown Prosecution solicitors would decide the level of the charge against him; if he were lying I had a job on my hands.

We left the experts doing their stuff, with the uniformed boys outside to keep the ghouls at bay, and went home. Come daylight, we'd be back in force.

While I was addressing the troops about the killing of Peter Latham, young Jamie Walker was practising the new scam he'd learned at the detention centre. He'd strolled into a pub in the town centre, one he knew the layout of because they had no scruples about serving juveniles, and sidled his way towards the toilets, carefully avoiding being seen by the bar staff. When nobody was looking he'd slipped upstairs to the landlord's living quarters and rifled them. Pub landladies collect gold jewellery like some of us collect warm memories, and he made quite a haul. He escaped in a Mini taken from the car-park and celebrated by driving it through the town centre flat out. The traffic car that came to Silkstone's house had earlier chased young Jamie for a while, but he escaped by driving along the towpath. Two of our pandas spent the rest of the night driving from one reported sighting to another, without success. We know it was Jamie because he left fingerprints in the pub and in the mini, which he had to abandon before he could torch it.

I found all this out much later. When I arrived home I took off all my clothes, found a fresh set for next day and cleaned my teeth. I slipped under the duvet and closed my eyes.

The house Annabelle and I nearly bought was two along from Silkstone's, backing on to a rocky field that the estate agent called a paddock. It had a double garage that dominated the front aspect, with an archway over the path and a wrought iron gate. Inside were four bedrooms, two with *en suite* bathrooms, and a study. The downstairs rooms had dado rails and patio doors, and the next door neighbours were members of the National Trust. They introduced themselves, saying we'd be very happy there, and gave us some membership forms. Annabelle said they were sussing us out.

We could have been happy there. The house was warm and dry and airy, with decent views over the fells; and pissing-off the neighbours would have been no problem. We could have locked the doors and closed the curtains, and played her Mozart and my Dylan to our hearts' content. I'm sure we'd have been very happy there if we both hadn't been such bloody reverse snobs.

Today – no, yesterday – I pulled a carving knife out of a dead body, standing astride it as if I were

66

harvesting carrots. Play the film in reverse and you'd see the knife going in, feeling its way between rib and cartilage, following the line of least resistance as it severed vein, nerve and muscle. A dagger in the heart doesn't kill you. It's not like an electrical short circuit that immediately blows a fuse and cuts off the power. Blood stops flowing, or pumps out into the body's cavities instead of following its normal well-ordered path, and the brain dies of starvation.

Today it was strangulation. A pair of tights knotted around the neck, stopping the flow of air and blood until, again, the brain dies. A pair of tights: aid to beauty; method of concealing identity favoured by blaggers; murder weapon. She had black hair and white skin, and may have been attractive, once. Before fear twisted her features and the ligature tightened, building up the pressure in her skull until her eyeballs and tongue tried to escape from it.

Murder doesn't come stalking its victim at night, skulking from shadow to shadow, whispering unheard threats. It comes in the afternoon, with the sun casting shadows on the wall and the curtains blowing in the breeze. It comes from familiar hands, that once were loving.

The collared doves that live in next door's apple tree were tuning up like a couple of novice viola players, and my blackbird was doing his scales prior to the morning concert. I got out of bed and staggered to the bathroom for a shower. I put on the clean clothes, brushed my hair and opened the curtains.

The sky was light, with Venus the palest speck

67

on the horizon, not quite drained of its glow by the advancing sun. Above it was the disc of the moon, a duller blue than the sky, one edge dipped in cream. They hovered there like the last two reluctant guests to leave a party. I picked up the alarm clock and went downstairs to grab an hour's rest on the settee.

The night 'tec was sitting at my desk when I arrived in the office, reading the morning paper. 'Hi, Rodge, anything in about us?' I asked, slipping my jacket off.

'Morning, Charlie. No, not yet,' he replied, moving out of my chair.

'Pity. I was hoping they'd have it sorted for us.'

'You've had a busy night.'

'Oh, just two murders,' I replied. 'Nothing special. And you?'

'Sex or money?'

'Sex. Sex all the way.'

We only have one detective on duty through the night, in case the uniformed boys come across anything that requires a CID presence. He slid a typed report across to me, saying: 'Jamie Walker. He was out causing grief again but we've got some dabs – I had to borrow a SOCO from City because ours were otherwise engaged. Hopefully we'll pick him up today.'

'And as soon as we put him in front of the mags they'll give him bail,' I said. 'God, I could do without him.'

I told him to carry on looking after the stuff outside the murder enquiries, adding that we'd have them sorted as soon as the PM results came through to confirm what we already knew. He went home to breakfast with his wife, a nightshift staff nurse at the General, and I read his report. 'Jamie Walker, aged fourteen, why do I hate you?' I said to myself as I slid it into the *Pending* tray.

The team, plus a few reinforcements from HQ CID, reassembled at eight in the small conference room and there were gasps of disbelief when Mr Wood told them about the developments. After his pep talk I split them into two groups and appointed two sets of control staff, as if the murders were separate enquiries, and sent the troops back out on to the streets. Priorities were the backgrounds of the three leading players and their relationships with each other. The neighbours would be given their opportunity to dish the dirt, so that might throw up something, and we needed the post mortem results desperately. I told the Latham team to reconvene at three and the Silkstone team at four.

We could hold him in custody without charging him for twenty-four hours, and then ask for extensions, but we're supposed to charge a prisoner as soon as is practicable. We decided to do him for a section 18 assault, that's GBH with intent, purely as a holding charge, and let the CPS lawyers decide at their leisure whether to go for murder or manslaughter. He appeared in front of a magistrate that morning and our man explained the seriousness of the offence. It's not necessary to present any evidence at this stage. The magistrate obligingly remanded Silkstone into our custody for seven days while we completed our enquiries. After that period he would appear again and hopefully be committed to appear before the crown court at sometime in the remote future. We booked his solicitor, Prendergast, for eleven a.m., when the fun would begin.

Dave and I made a return visit to Silkstone's house at Mountain Meadows. The sun was shining after a shower as we turned into the development, and it looked good. Several of the gardens had weird trees with twisted branches and dangling fronds, like you see in Japanese watercolours, and pampas-grass was popular. There were two panda cars outside The Garth and blue 'keep out' tape stretched across the driveway.

The PC in charge showed me the visitors' book and entered our names in it. I saw that the undertakers had called at six a.m. to take the body away, and a reporter from the *Gazette* had been tipped off by a friendly neighbour. We stepped over the tape and walked down the drive.

It looked different in the daylight. Allowing for the Silkstones' crap taste, it looked highly desirable. Everything they had was expensive, top of the range, and they had everything. We stood in the kitchen, where we'd stood with such different feelings a few hours earlier, and took it all in. The wind chime gave a single, hollow, *boing* but I reached up and disabled it before it could run through its repertoire. There were Toulouse-Lautrec prints on the walls and a rope of garlic hanging behind the door.

'Not bad,' Dave admitted. From him, that's an Oscar.

I sniffed the garlic, then felt it. 'Plastic,' I said. 'No wonder it didn't work.'

'Work?'

'It's supposed to keep evil at bay.'

He looked at me without turning his head, and said: 'Er, listen, Charlie. I wouldn't put that in your report if I were you. One or two people have been saying things about you, recently...'

The sitting room was a surprise. With its two leather chesterfields and dark wood it looked more like a gentlemen's club than a room in a suburban house. The fireplace was polished stone, complete with horse brasses, and a photograph of the householder took pride of place above it. A beaming Silkstone was standing next to a much taller and slightly embarrassed man who looked remarkably like Nigel Mansell, former World Formula 1 champion.

'He moves in fast company,' I remarked.

'Golf tournament,' Dave said, which was fairly obvious from the single gloves, silly trousers and the clubs they were leaning on. 'Probably a charity do, or something.'

'Right. What do you think of the room?' The carpet was plain blue and vertical blinds covered the windows. There were no flowers or frills, no Capo di Monte shepherd boys – *Alleluia* for that small mercy – and not a single pot plant. The wallpaper was blue and cream stripes, edged in gold, on all four walls.

'It's a bit austere,' Dave remarked, turning round in a circle. He paused, then said: 'The wife wanted me to put one of them up.'

'One of what?'

He pointed. 'A dildo rail.'

I said: 'It's called a dado rail,' not sure if I'd

71

fallen into a trap.

'Is it? I'm sure she said dildo.'

'Maybe you misunderstood.'

'Sounds like it.'

'C'mon,' I told him. 'Let's go upstairs. That's where the story of Tony and Margaret begins and ends.'

The path we'd pioneered the night before was designated with blue tape so we stayed with it, although it wasn't necessary. In the bedroom little adhesive squares with green arrows on them indicated items of interest that were invisible to my eyes. They were scattered randomly over the carpet near the bed, and concentrated around the disturbed surface of the duvet. Dave bent down and examined the area.

'Doesn't look like blood,' he announced, straightening up.

'Other bodily fluids,' I suggested. The SOCO had probably found spots and splashes by using an ultra violet lamp or Luminol spray.

Next door was the woman's room, all done in pink and lace, with a dressing table crowded with the things some ladies need to apply before they can face the world. She wore Obsession perfume and Janet Reger undies. A wedding photograph, similar in style to the one in Latham's room, stood on the dressing table but pushed to the back, behind all the jars and bottles and aerosols. It was lightly covered with powder either from her compact or left by the fingerprint experts. In it, Silkstone was wearing a morning suit and his wife a traditional white dress. They were a hand-some couple and it was impossible to date this one, unlike Mr and Mrs Latham's.

The husband had his own room. It was furnished in a mock tartan material that looked pretty good and the bookcase was filled with coffee-table manuals about cars. We had classic cars, the world's fastest cars, the most expensive cars, Ferraris, Porsches, and so on. There were yearbooks about the Grands Prix going back about ten years and a collection of Pirelli and Michelin calendars for a similar period. They were all big glossy books, heavy on pictures, light on words.

I found his reading books on the bottom shelf. They were by people like Dale Carnegie and Mark McCormack, and had titles such as *How To Sell Crap To People Who Didn't Know They Needed It*; and *What To Do With That Second Million*. When this is over, I thought, I could do worse than read one or two of these. Or perhaps even write one.

There was a framed photograph of Silkstone on the wall behind the bed, and another of Nigel Mansell, autographed, on the facing wall. Silkstone was posing beside a Mark II Jaguar and looked about twenty. It was a snapshot, blown up to poster size, and was badly focused, but the numberplate was legible. He had a faint blond fuzz on his head, like a peach, which for a young bloke was seriously bald. Dave joined me as I was staring at it.

'Not as nice as your Jag,' he said.

'It's not, is it.'

'Ever regret selling it?'

'Mmm, now and again.' I turned to face the

other picture. 'What do you reckon to that one?'
I asked.

'It's great. Our Daniel would love it.' Daniel
was his son, a couple of years younger than
daughter Sophie.

'Why Mansell? He's not a gay icon, is he?'

'No, of course not. He's a happily married
man.'

'He has the moustache.'

'So has Saddam Hussein.'

'He *is* gay.'

'Yeah, as gay as a tree full of parrots. Listen,'
Dave said. 'Mansell was the greatest driver of his
day, and lots of other days, because he was such
a fierce competitor. He liked to win. At everything. That's why people like Silkstone look up to
him. He's a winners' icon, not a gay one.'

'Mmm, makes sense,' I agreed.

Dave looked at his watch, saying: 'It's time we
were off.'

The friendly neighbourhood spy had informed
his contact at the *Gazette* that I was on the scene,
and a reporter was waiting for us as we emerged
from The Garth. She had spiky red hair, a ring
through her nose and a bullish manner.

'Are you the investigating officer?' she demanded.

'Yes,' I told her, resigning myself to making
some sort of statement. 'And just who are you?'

She rattled off one of those names that rhymes
with itself, like Fay Day or Carol Barrel, as if it
were self-evident who she was and only a
parochial fool like myself wouldn't know. This
woman was ambitious, going places, and a small-

74

town murder meant nothing more to her than a by-line. Next week she'd either be applying for Kate Adie's job or back on hospital radio. 'And is the raid on this house related to the murder last evening at West Woods?' she asked.

News travels fast, I thought. I drew a big breath and launched myself into it: 'We are investigating a suspicious death at a residence in the West Woods estate,' I told her, 'and have arrested a person. Our enquiries have brought us here, where we have found the body of a woman. At this point in the investigation we are not looking for anybody else. Our press office will release further information as and when it becomes available.' I can reel out the cop-speak with the best of them, when I don't want to say what I'm thinking.

She couldn't believe her luck. 'You mean there's still a body in there?' she demanded, her eyes gleaming.

'No,' I said. 'It was removed earlier this morning, for post mortem examination. Now if you'll excuse me.'

She produced a mobile phone – it was hanging on a thong around her neck – and called for a photographer, *House of Death* headlines buzzing through her head.

The PC on duty asked if I wanted the integrity of the scene maintaining and I said I did. We had a quick word with the house-to-house people, but they had no great revelations for us, and drove back to the nick.

On the way Dave said: 'You're not happy with this, are you?'

'Just playing safe, Dave,' I replied.

'What's the problem?'

'No problem. According to Silkstone, Latham killed his wife so he killed Latham. Motive – revenge. Taking into consideration the balance of his mind, and all that, he'd be done for manslaughter and could be free in a year.'

'That's true,' Dave said. 'And if he was on remand for a year he could be released straight after the trial.'

'But what if,' I continued, 'they were both in on it? What if they were both there when Mrs Silkstone died? That could mean a life sentence. This way, he's put all the blame on Latham, who is in no position to defend himself.'

Dave thought about it, before saying: 'You mean, they were having some sort of three-in-a-bed sex romp, and it all went wrong?'

I glanced sideways at him. 'Do people do such things in Heckley?' I asked.

'Not to my knowledge,' he replied.

'Maybe they were over enthusiastic,' I suggested, 'and she died. They invented some sort of story but Silkstone thought of a better one. He killed Latham and came to us.'

'It's a possibility,' Dave agreed.

'Alternatively,' I began, exploring the possibilities, 'perhaps Silkstone did them both, all alone and by himself. It'd be cheaper than a divorce.'

'And tidier,' Dave added.

'And possibly even profitable,' I suggested. 'That's something to look at.'

'We're getting ahead of ourselves,' Dave cautioned. 'Let's wait for the DNA results.' He was silent for the rest of the way. As we turned into the car-park he said: 'The bloke's lost his wife, Charlie. Don't forget that.'

'I know,' I replied, adding: 'I think I'll ask the professor to look at the crime scene, see what he thinks.' The professor is the pathologist at Heckley General Hospital, and at that very moment he was turning his blade towards the fair skin of Mrs Margaret Silkstone, subject of our debate. I locked the car doors and we headed for the entrance.

There was a message from Annette waiting for me at the front desk. A neighbour had positively identified Peter Latham, who had died from a single knife wound to the heart. Time of death between three and six o'clock, Wednesday afternoon. I passed it to Dave and asked if Prendergast had arrived yet. He was locked in the cell with his client, I learned, discussing strategies, defences and tactics. The truth was outside his remit.

''Ello, Mr Priest,' a squeaky voice said, behind me. I spun round and faced two traffic cops straight in the eye. They were wearing standard-issue Velcro moustaches and don't-do-that expressions, but neither had a ventriloquist's dummy sitting on his arm. I tilted my gaze downwards forty-five degrees and met that of a grubby angel standing between them.

'Jamie!' I exclaimed, treading an uneasy path between disapproval and surprise. 'What are you doing here?'

'Bin invited in to 'elp you wiv enquiries, 'aven't I?' he replied.

'And can you 'elp – help – us?'

'Nah. Don't know nowt about it, do I?'

'Well do your best.' I turned back to the desk, but he said: ''Ere, Mr Priest. Is it right you used to 'ave a knee-type Jag?'

'That's right,' I told him. 'A red one.'

'Cor!' he replied. 'Best car on t'road.'

They took him away to feed him on bacon sandwiches while he fed them a pack of lies, and we arranged to interview Silkstone in ten minutes. I went to the bog and washed my face. There was a mounting pile of reports on my desk, but they'd have to wait. I always read them all, but on every murder enquiry we have a dedicated report reader who siphons off the important stuff. I like to read all the irrelevant details, too: the minutiae of the lives of the people who pass through our hands. Sometimes, they tell me things. As Confucius say, wisdom comes through knowledge.

Prendergast was wearing a blue suit and maroon tie, and could have been about to deliver a budget speech. He didn't. He launched straight into the attack by complaining about our treatment of his client, who was, he reminded us, traumatised by the sudden and violent death of the woman he loved.

I apologised if we had appeared insensitive, but reminded them that Mr Silkstone had, by his own admission, killed a man and we were conducting a murder enquiry. We'd collect some of his own clothes for him, I promised, as soon as the crime scene was released, and I told him that his wife's body had been taken to the mortuary.

We needed Silkstone to formally identify the body later, and he agreed.

'Will he be taken there in handcuffs, Inspector?' Prendergast asked.

'As Mr Silkstone surrendered himself voluntarily I don't think that will be necessary,' I conceded. I must be getting soft.

The preliminary fencing over, we started asking questions. Silkstone stuck to his story, saying that he'd come home to see Latham leaving his house. Inside, he'd found Margaret lying on the bed with a ligature around her neck. He'd attempted to remove it, but quickly realised that she was dead. The rest was a bit vague, he claimed. It always is. He agreed that he must have followed Latham home and gone in the house after him. He suddenly found himself standing in the kitchen, with Latham's body lying on the floor, between his feet. There was a knife sticking out of Latham's chest, and on the worktop there was one of those wooden blocks with several other knives lodged in it. He did not dispute that he stabbed Latham, but claimed to have no memory of the actual deed.

When he realised the enormity of what he'd done he sat in the front room for a while – about ten minutes, he thought – then dialled 999. Prendergast made sympathetic noises about the state of his client's mind and suggested that Unlawful Killing might be an appropriate charge.

'Do you think there was any sort of relationship between your wife and Latham?' I asked, and Silkstone's shrug suggested that it was a possibility. The tape doesn't pick up shrugs, but I let it

79

go. 'Could you explain, please,' I asked.

He stubbed his cigarette in the tin ashtray and left the butt there with the other three he'd had. Only prisoners are allowed to smoke in the nick. 'I wondered if they were having an affair,' he said. He thought about his words for a while, then added: 'Or perhaps Peter – Latham – wanted to start one, and Margaret didn't. Last week, last Wednesday I went home early and he was there, talking to her. He said he'd just called in for a coffee, and she said the same. But there was a strained air, if you follow me. They seemed embarrassed that I caught them together. Maybe, you know, he was trying it on.'

'How well did Margaret know him?' I asked, adding: 'Officially, so to speak.'

'Quite well,' he replied. 'We – that's Peter and I – married two sisters, back in 1975, and he came to work for me. Neither marriage lasted long, but we stayed friends.'

'What line of work are you in?'

'I'm Northern Manager of Trans Global Finance, and Peter is – was – one of my sales executives.'

'Wasn't he working yesterday?'

'No. He often sees clients at weekends, when it's convenient for them, and takes a day off through the week.'

'Is it usually Wednesday?'

'Yes, it is.'

'And Margaret? Did she work?'

'For me. TGF is heavily into e-commerce, and Margaret acted as my secretary, working from home.'

80

'E-commerce?' I queried, vaguely knowing what he meant.

'Electronic commerce.'

'In other words, your company doesn't have a huge office block somewhere.'

'That's right, Inspector. We have very small premises, just an office and a typist, in Halifax and various other towns. Our HQ is in Docklands, but that's quite modest. Our parent company resides in Geneva.'

I exhaled, puffing my cheeks out, and tapped the desk with my pencil. Dave took it as his cue and came in with: 'Mr Silkstone, you said that Latham was at your house the previous Wednesday, when you arrived home early.'

'Yes.' He reached into his pocket and removed a Benson and Hedges packet.

'What time was that?' Dave asked.

'About four o'clock. Perhaps a few minutes earlier.'

'Was it unusual for you to come home at that time?'

'Yes. Very unusual.'

'So Latham could have been there the week before, and the week before that, and you wouldn't have known.'

He lit a cigarette with a gold lighter borrowed from his brief and took a deep draw on it. 'Yes,' he mumbled, exhaling down his nose. There were four of us in the tiny interview room and three of us were passively smoking the equivalent of twenty a day, thanks to Silkstone. The atmosphere in there would have given a Greenpeace activist apoplexy. Carcinogenic condensates were

81

coagulating on the walls, evil little particulates furring-up the light fittings. What they were doing to our tubes I preferred not to imagine but I vowed to sue him if I contracted anything.

'But yesterday you came home early again,' Dave stated.

Good on yer, mate, I thought, as our prisoner sucked his cheeks in and felt round the inside of his mouth with his tongue.

'That's true,' Silkstone admitted.

'Twice in eight days. Very unusual, wouldn't you say?'

'Gentlemen,' Prendergast interrupted. 'My client is senior management with an international company His hours are flexible, not governed by the necessity to watch a clock. He works a sixty-hour week and takes time off when he can. I'm sure you can imagine the routine.'

'But still unusual,' Dave insisted.

'He's right,' Silkstone agreed, talking to his lawyer. Turning to Dave he added: 'Last week I wasn't feeling very well, so I skipped my last appointment and came home early. It wasn't business, just calling on one of my staff for a pep talk. Yesterday–' he shrugged his shoulders. 'I finished early and went home. That's all.'

Dave stroked his chin for a few seconds before asking: 'Are you sure that's all?'

Prendergast jumped in again, saying this speculation was leading nowhere, like any good lawyer would have done. What he meant was that if his client went home early because he thought he might catch his wife in bed with her lover, we could tell the court that his actions were premeditated. And that meant murder.

Silkstone moved as if to stub the cigarette out, realised it was only half smoked and took another drag on it. 'I don't know,' he replied, ignoring his brief's protestations. 'I've been wondering that myself. Did I expect to find them together again? Is that why I left the afternoon free? You know, subconsciously I don't think I did. I loved my wife, trusted her, and she loved me. If I'd really expected to catch them together I'd have returned home even earlier, wouldn't I?' He took another long draw on the cigarette while we pondered on his question. 'Truth is,' he continued, 'I've been worrying about the old ticker a bit, lately. Decided to cut my workload. That's why I came home early.'

Which, I thought, was a good point. I quizzed him about how he'd felt as he drove to Latham's house; how he gained entry; about the knife and any conversation he had with Latham. It was a waste of time. Everything was obscured by the thick red mist of convenient memory loss. There's a lot more of it about than you'd ever believe, especially among murder suspects. 'Interview terminated,' I said, looking up at the clock and reading off the time. Dave reached out and stopped the tape.

'Your case papers will be sent to the crown prosecutors,' I told Silkstone, 'who will determine the level of charge against you. Assuming the results of the forensic tests validate what you say they may decide to go for a charge of manslaughter. If not, I shall be pressing for a murder charge. You will be committed for trial at crown

83

court and we shall be applying for you to be remanded in custody until then. Is there anything you wish to ask me?'

Silkstone shook his head. Prendergast said: 'I have explained the procedure to my client, Inspector. We will be making our own clinical and psychiatric reports and demand full access to any forensic procedures that are being undertaken. It goes without saying that we will be applying for bail.'

'You do that,' I replied, sliding my chair back and standing up.

We grabbed a bacon sandwich in the canteen and drove to Latham's house on the West Wood estate. There are no trees at the West Woods, because the landscape around Heckley does not suit them. The ground is rocky, the winters harsh and the sheep omnivorous. Archaeologists following the builders' excavators found remnants of a forest in the patch of peat bog they were building on, and an imaginative sales person did the rest. There is no North, South or East Wood.

We wandered around his home from room to room, looking in drawers, feeling through the pockets of his suits, like a couple of vultures picking over a carcass. Wilbur Smith's *Elephant Song* was lying on a shelf within reach of his easy chair, with a bookmark at about the halfway point. In the smallest bedroom, filled with junk, there was a big bag of fishing rods and a box of tackle. I hadn't marked him as a fisherman.

On his fridge-freezer door, held in place by a magnetic Bart Simpson, was a postcard showing a painting that I recognised. I eased it off and looked at the back, but it was blank. 'Gauguin,' I said, flapping the card towards Dave.

'You'd know,' he replied.

I replaced it exactly where I'd found it and opened the fridge door. He ate ready meals from the supermarket, supplemented with oven chips, and was seriously deficient in vegetables.

'He didn't eat properly,' I said.

'You'd know,' Dave repeated.

I was drawn, as always, to the bedroom. I was sitting on the edge of the bed, looking at the two photographs, when Dave joined me.

'Who do you reckon she is?' I asked.

He looked at the picture of the young girl without handling it. 'Mmm, interesting,' he mused. 'Taken a while ago. Could be his wife, assuming that's them in the other picture. Is it, er, a bit on the salacious side, or is that just me?'

'It's just you,' I told him, untruthfully.

'I don't think it's a daughter or niece,' he continued.

'Why not?'

'Well, I wouldn't frame a similar picture of our Sophie and have it on display and she'd certainly have something to say about it if I did. I reckon it's his wife, when she was at school. They keep it there for a laugh, or a bit of extra stimulation. I don't know, you're the one with all the experience. I'm just a happily married man.'

'The SOCO reckons it was taken about the same time as the wedding photo,' I said, 'which means it's not the wife.'

'Fair enough,' he replied, adding: 'Maybe all

will be revealed at the meeting, when we learn something about his background.'

'Let's hope so,' I said. We left, locking the door behind us, and told the PC on duty that we still wanted the crime scene maintaining.

In the car Dave said: 'That photo.'

'Mmm.'

'Of the young girl.'

'Mmm.'

'Maybe it's just a curio type of thing. The sort of picture you might pick up at a car boot sale, or something. Know what I mean?'

'I think so,' I said. 'A collector's item. Like some dirty old Victorian might have drooled over.'

'Yeah. Voluptuous innocence and all that crap.'

'Lewis Carroll and Alice,' I suggested.

'Exactly. He used to photograph children in the nude, you know.'

'Crikey,' I said. 'So where did he keep his spare films?'

We'd told the Latham team to assemble at three, but the Mrs Silkstone investigators were there too, keen to learn the big picture. Annette and Iqbar were sitting in the front row, and she passed me a foolscap sheet of the PM findings. That was what I'd wanted most of all. I perused it as everybody found seats and joshed with each other. The small conference room doubles as a lecture theatre, and is equipped with all the usual paraphernalia like overhead projectors and CCTV. At one minute to three I picked up the wooden pointing stick and rattled it against the floor, calling out: 'OK, boys and girls, let's have some order.'

As the hubbub died down Mr Wood entered the room. 'Keeping them entertained, Charlie?' he said.

'Just doing a few quick impressions, Boss,' I replied.

'I see. Any chance of you impersonating a police officer for the rest of the day?' He has a vicious tongue, at times.

Gilbert told the troops that HQ had sanctioned their overtime payments, which is what they wanted to hear, and thanked them for their efforts before handing over to me. I started by adding my appreciation for their work. A murder enquiry is always disruptive to the private lives of the investigators, as well as the principal characters. 'This is a double murder enquiry,' I told them, 'and the eyes of the world are upon us, so it's important that we show them what we can do. As always, you have responded to the challenge, and we are grateful.' I outlined the bare bones of the case, and then asked about the identity of the first body.

Inspector Adey said: 'First body confirmed to be that of Peter John Latham. We contacted his ex-wife – he's a divorcee – who lives in Pontefract. She was reluctant to come over to ID him because she has young children, and showed little interest in knowing when the funeral might be. Eventually we asked a neighbour, Mrs Watson, who was friendly with him, and she positively identified him.'

'Any other next of kin?' I asked.

'His mother in Chippenham, if she's still alive. She vacated her last known address to move into a nursing home, but we're trying to find her.'

'Thanks Gareth. We might as well do the other one now,' I said. 'Any volunteers?'

A uniformed constable raised his hand and uncoiled from his chair. He'd taken Mr Silkstone to the mortuary at the General Hospital, he told us, where Silkstone had positively identified the body of a woman as being that of his wife, Margaret. I thanked him and he sat down.

'Was he suitably grief stricken?' I asked him.

'Yes sir.'

Gareth Adey rose to his feet, saying: 'Point of order, Mr Priest.'

I was expecting it. Asking a murderer to identify an associated body was a trifle unusual, if not bizarre. 'Yes, Gareth,' I said.

'Do you not think, Mr Priest,' he waffled, 'that we might be leaving ourselves open to criticism by inviting the accused to ID a body allegedly murdered by the victim of his revenge killing?'

'Good point, Gareth,' I told him. 'We need a second opinion. Could I leave that with you, and I'd be grateful if you'd do the usual with next of kin.'

He smiled contentedly and sat down.

'Cause of death,' I said, pointing to Annette.

She was wearing jeans and a white blouse, her jacket draped over the back of the chair. She stood up, unsmiling, and brushed her hair off her face. 'Peter Latham was killed by a single knife-wound to the heart,' she told us. 'The knife found in him would be identical to the one missing

88

from the set in his kitchen. The blade entered his chest between the fifth and sixth ribs on an upward trajectory, puncturing the left ventricle. This indicates an underhand blow from someone of approximately the same height. Latham was only a hundred and sixty-eight centimetres tall. That's five feet six inches. The blade missed the ribs and unusual force would not be required.'

'Time of death?' I asked.

'Between three and six p.m.,' Annette replied.

'We can narrow that down,' I declared. 'Silkstone rang nine-double-nine at seventeen ten hours, saying he'd done it. Let's call it between three and five.' Doc Evans had said between four and five, I remembered, and he was on the scene quite quickly. The professor was working from a cold cadaver, sixteen hours after the event. 'On second thoughts, make it between four and five,' I told them. Sometimes, knowing the precise time of death can be crucial.

Annette had taken her seat again, but I said: 'Go on, Annette, you might as well tell us about the other one.'

She rose, brushing the offending hair aside, and launched straight into it. She was a young attractive woman, one of only four in a room with thirty men, and I wondered if I'd been fair, sending her to the post mortems. She said: 'Margaret Silkstone died as a result of strangulation. There was a pair of tights knotted around her throat but there was also bruising caused by manual strangulation, apparently from behind. She'd recently had anal and vaginal intercourse, and semen samples have been recovered and sent for analysis.'

89

'How recently,' I asked.

'At about the time of death,' she replied. 'The professor's preliminary conclusions are that vaginal intercourse took place before death, and anal possibly after, but he wants to do a more considered examination.'

'And when was the time of death?'

'Between two and six p.m.'

'Right. Thanks for doing the gory stuff, Annette,' I told her. 'I appreciate it.'

She gave me the briefest of smiles and sat down. After that I invited the team to let us know what they had discovered about the background of the deceased.

They all came from Gloucestershire. Silkstone had been a big wheel in a company based in Burdon Manor, variously known as Burdon Home Improvements, Burdon Engineering and Burdon Developments; and Latham was one of his salesmen. Back in 1975 they'd married two sisters but neither marriage had lasted. When the receiver finally pulled the plug on Burdons, Silkstone went to work for the now-defunct Oriental Bank of Commerce, or OBC, a name that sent a chill up the spine of every financial manager in the world. Now he was Northern big-cheese for a company called Trans Global Finance, and had been married to the late Margaret for ten years. Silkstone had five speeding convictions and two for careless driving. Latham had one for OPL and Margaret was clean.

'So now,' I told the throng of eager, upturned faces, 'you know all about them. Any questions?'

'Yes Sir,' someone said. 'Will you have the DNA results tomorrow?'

'No. Saturday,' I replied.

There was nothing else, so I terminated the meeting. Someone brewed up in the big office and I carried a mug of tea into my little den in the corner. I opened an A2 drawing pad and divided the sheet into several boxes. Dave came in, followed by Annette. In Box 1 I wrote:

Silkstone telling truth. Latham killed Margaret, then Silkstone killed Latham, in a rage.

'What next?' I asked.

'Three in a bed romp,' Dave suggested. In Box 2 I wrote:

Sex game gone wrong. Latham and Silkstone killed Margaret. Silkstone killed Latham to cover his tracks.

'Hmm, that's interesting,' Annette said.

'Charlie's idea,' Dave told her. 'I don't know about such things. What next?'

In Box 3 I wrote:

Margaret and Latham having an affair. Silkstone killed them both in a jealous rage.

Dave said: 'I reckon that's the obvious explanation.'

'It's the favourite,' I agreed, 'but how about this?' I wrote:

All a plot by Silkstone

and numbered it Box 4.

'What, like, cold blooded?' Dave asked. 'You think he planned it all?'

'I don't think that. We just have to consider it. What if Silkstone killed Margaret for personal reasons and threw the blame on Latham? The

91

whole thing might be a pack of lies. We need to know if he gains financially in any way.' I turned to Annette. 'That's a little job for you, Annette. Find out if he had her insured. How much do they owe on the house and will the insurance company pay out for her death, if you follow me?'

'You mean, if they had a joint life policy,' she replied.

'Do I?'

'She's a clever girl,' Dave said.

Annette picked up her still steaming mug of tea and walked out. I gazed at the door she'd closed behind her and said to it: 'I didn't mean right now!'

I wrote M, O and F in each box, meaning motive, opportunity and forensic, and ticked them where appropriate. I didn't bother with W for witnesses, because the only one we had was Silkstone himself. 'That's as far as we can go, Sunshine,' I declared, 'until we get some results from the lab and find out who spread his seed all over the crime scene.' The phone rang before I could put cornices on all the capital letters and generally titivate the chart. It was the professor, replying to the message I'd left for him earlier in the day.

'It's The Garth, Mountain Meadows,' I told him.

'What, no number?'

'No, but there's only seven houses.'

'Pretentious twats. I'll see you there at five. You can have half an hour.'

'Great, Prof. I appreciate it.'

Annette came in as I was replacing the phone.

I looked at her, bemused by the rapid departure and return. She said: 'Silkstone paid nearly two hundred thousand for the house, and still owes over a hundred and fifty K on it. And yes, the mortgage is insured joint life, first death, so if he didn't kill Margaret himself they'll have to pay out.'

It took me a few seconds to speak. Eventually I asked: 'How did you find all this so quickly?'

'I went down and asked him,' she replied, smiling. 'Took him a cup of tea. It's not secret information. As he said, joint life is fairly stand-ard practice, not necessarily sinister, but yes, he does come in for a handy payout.'

'Told you she was a clever girl,' Dave declared. He drained his mug, adding: 'I'll leave you to it; there's work to be done.'

When he'd gone Annette said: 'And I've had a word with the Met. Asked them to contact the head office of Trans Global Finance just to con-firm things.'

'Brilliant, we'll make a detective of you yet.' I told her about the call from the prof., and as Dave had vanished I suggested she come along with me to hear what he had to say. She seemed pleased to be asked, and went off to do her paperwork.

At twenty to five I gathered up a set of photo-graphs of the Mountain Meadows crime scene, plus my new chart of possible scenarios, and let Annette drive us there in her yellow Fiat. The professor arrived at about five past. He greeted Annette like a long-lost relative, then said: 'Right, let's get on with it.'

I laid out a set of photographs on the worktop in the kitchen, telling him what we'd found but not passing any opinions nor making any speculations. The prof. nodded and sniffed a few times, peering at the photos through his half-spectacles, and asked to be shown the bedroom.

The bed was made up with a duvet in a floral pattern, but still bore the impression of the action that had taken place there, highlighted by the SOCO's little arrows. In the twenty-four hours since the killing the smell of neglect had pervaded the room. The cocktail of perfumes: her make-up, somebody's sweat and other fluids, flowed uneasily through the nostrils. I breathed through my mouth to avoid it. We had a pre-liminary report from the scientific boys, saying what had been found where, but no definitive DNA evidence to say from whom it all came. The professor examined the sites marked by the arrows, checking with the report after each one.

'We'll leave you to it,' I said, and led Annette downstairs. It was the first time she'd been in the house and her eyes scanned everything, sweeping over the furniture, pausing to examine the decorations more closely. Partly I supposed, from the professional point of view, partly as a woman in another woman's house. 'Have a good look round,' I invited, seating myself on a leather settee that was as hard as a park bench.

A coffee table book about Jaguar cars was propped in an alcove adjoining the fireplace. I reached for it and flipped through until I found the E-type. They'd photographed a red one, same as mine, from low down at the front. I'm not a car person, but the E-type was special and I felt a pang of regret for selling it.

'I had one like that,' I said to Annette as she returned, holding the double-page spread open for her to see.

'What? An E-type?' she exclaimed, smiling wider than I'd ever seen her.

'Mmm.'

'Cor! I wish I'd known you then.'

'Everybody said it was a good bird-puller.'

'And was it?'

I smiled at the memories. 'I suppose so. My dad bought it as a pile of scrap and restored it. When he died it came to me.'

'I'm sorry,' Annette said, sitting in an easy chair.

'Sorry?'

'About your dad. He was a policeman, wasn't he?'

'That's right. A sergeant at Heckley. He was a nice man.'

'Yes, I can imagine.' She stood up abruptly and walked over to the window. I watched her, wanting to join her there. It would have been the most natural thing in the world to slip my hand around her waist and stand with her, looking out over the garden. It might also have earned me a knee in the groin. Her hair was tied in a wild bundle behind her head. Difficult to manage, I thought, and smiled. 'What's the verdict on the house?' I asked.

Annette turned to face me. Her cheeks were pink. 'This house?'

'Mmm.'

'The house is OK. Not sure about the occupants.'

'I really meant the occupants.'

'Right. The place speaks volumes about them. I'd say they were well off, but lacking in taste. He's a control freak, hasn't grown up yet. What sort of man...'

The professor was clomping down the stairs and Annette stopped speaking. He came into the room with a worried expression on his face, which meant nothing because his features were set that way. Anybody's would be, with his job. He pulled his spectacles off, wiped his eyes with a big white handkerchief, and flopped onto the other Chesterfield. It flinched slightly and creaked under his weight.

'Fancy a coffee, Prof.?' I asked.

Annette said: 'I'll make us...'

'No, no,' the professor insisted, flapping a hand. 'Kind of you, but I'd rather not. Too busy.'

'Right. So what can you tell us?'

'Not a great deal,' he began. 'Without the DNA results we're barking into the dark somewhat. She was killed on the bed, either during or just after sexual intercourse; and that's about it. You can definitely rule out her being killed elsewhere.'

'One man or two?'

'Dunno. The lab should be able to tell us, though.'

'Up to the point of death, was she a willing participant?'

'Good question. Apparently so, or to put it another way, she wasn't dragged kicking and

96

screaming into the room. That doesn't mean that there wasn't some duress applied.'

'Like, at knifepoint, for example?'

'Yes. Precisely.'

I turned to my new partner. She was definitely more attractive than Sparky, but I didn't know how she'd be in a fistfight. 'Anything, Annette?' I asked.

'Yes,' she began. 'From your earlier examinations, Professor, and what you've seen here, could you say if any violence was used during the acts of intercourse?'

'The actual penetration, you mean?'

'Er, yes.'

'Difficult to interpret. Yes, entry was quite violent, but one man's – or woman's – violence is another's big turn-on. It was rough intercourse, but I cannot interpret the victim's feelings about that.'

'How rough?' I asked.

'Some damage to the mucous membranes, but not excessively so.'

'Both ends?'

'More so in the anus, but that's quite usual.'

I spread my chart on the arm of the settee and explained it to the professor. We all agreed that what he had determined at the house fitted perfectly with Silkstone's story but I argued that it could also support the sex romp theory.

'Did you find any other supportive evidence?' the professor asked.

'Such as?'

'Well, for instance, did you find any pornography? Sex aids? Bondage paraphernalia? That

97

sort of thing.'

'No,' I reluctantly admitted.

'Then I'd say it was unlikely.'

My pet theory had just prised the bars open and escaped. 'Unless the DNA tests show that they were both there,' I argued.

'I suppose so,' the professor said, in a tone that suggested I shouldn't hold my breath.

'How about Silkstone killing them both in a jealous rage?' I suggested, tapping Box 3 with the blunt end of my pen. 'That's probably what we would have concluded had it not been for his admissions.'

'Ye-es, I'd wondered about that,' the professor replied, 'but I'm not sure that what I've seen validates it. Force was undoubtedly used against Mrs Silkstone, but she wasn't knocked about and there are few signs of a struggle. There's no bruising to her face, but her arms bear evidence of being tightly gripped. It was a controlled force, in my opinion, by someone who knew exactly what he was doing.'

'Was she a willing partner, in the sex?'

'Willing? Probably not. Reluctant, I'd say. She certainly didn't fight for her life until she had no chance.'

'Are you suggesting that the motive for the assault was rape, pure and simple,' I asked, 'and killing her was an afterthought?'

'It's a possibility,' he agreed, 'although I'm not sure about the pure and simple. Assaults of this nature are not necessarily for sexual gratification – they're about inflicting humiliation on the victim. Which, I suppose, when you think about it, enhances the gratification. He's a control freak, likes to dominate – that's what stimulates him. I'm rambling a bit, Charlie. That side of it is not my field, thank goodness, I'm just the plumber.'

I pointed to the fourth box on my chart. 'And then there's the possibility that Silkstone orchestrated the whole thing,' I said. 'He killed them both but put the blame for Margaret on to Latham. That way he comes out of it with a fairly hefty financial gain.'

The professor pursed his lips, deep in thought. He has a face like a desiccated cowpat, but always looks as fresh and clean as a newly bathed baby. His talcum smelled of roses or some other garden flowers. 'It'd be a bugger to prove, Charlie,' he concluded. 'Let's wait and see what the DNA says, eh?'

We thanked the prof. and drove away in silence. I wasn't equipped to have a meaningful conversation with an attractive woman about the merits of rough sex, so I kept my thoughts to myself, but Annette had no such inhibitions. 'Why do men – some men – want to do that?' she asked.

'Um, do what?' I enquired.

'Inflict humiliation. Why isn't the sex act enough in itself?'

'Good question,' I said, stalling for time. 'It's probably something deep in our psyche, in our genes.'

'You mean all men are like that?'

'Well, um, I wouldn't say all men. I don't know, perhaps we are. At a very subconscious level. Most of us have never recognised it in ourselves,

99

but it's probably in there, somewhere.'

'Really?' She twisted in her seat to face me and nearly drove into the kerb.

'Put it like this,' I said, checking my seatbelt. 'Most men, I'm sure you know, find a woman in her underwear sexier than a woman in a bikini. Why do you think that is?'

'No idea. It's a mystery to me.'

'Well, most men wouldn't know, either, if you asked them. But it could be because a woman in her underwear is at a disadvantage. You've caught her partially dressed. However, the same woman in a bikini is fully dressed and completely in charge of the situation.'

'Gosh! I'd never have thought of that.'

'Whereas most men,' I pronounced, holding my hands aloft, 'rarely think of anything else.'

There was a pub called the Anglers Rest about half a mile down the road, with an A-board outside saying that they did two-for-the-price-of-one meals before six o' clock. We'd missed that, but it reminded me that I was starving.

'Are you hungry?' I asked.

'Ravishing,' Annette replied, and giggled.

'I can see that,' I told her. 'I asked if you were hungry.'

'Mmm. Quite.'

'Fancy a Chinese?'

She looked across at me. 'Yes. That sounds like a good idea.' Her cheeks were pink again.

'Take us to the Bamboo Curtain then, please,' I suggested, and settled back into the seat feeling uncommonly content. Things were moving along quite nicely, and the enquiry wasn't going too badly, either.

I ate with chopsticks, to show how sophisticated I am, and we drank Czech beer, which I insisted in pouring into glasses. A glass is essential if you want to experience the full flavour of the drink. Itsy-bitsy sips from the bottle are a waste of time. I insisted on Annette doing several comparisons, and she politely conceded that I might have had a point. Drinking from the bottle, I told her, is an affectation encouraged by the brewing industry to save them the trouble and expense of washing glasses, that's all. Apart from that, the bottles have been stored for months outside some warehouse, and the security man's dog probably cocked its leg over them several times each night as they did their rounds. She smiled and humoured me.

Women in the police have a hard time. Be one of the lads and you get a reputation as a slapper; stay aloof from all that and you're a lesbian. Times are changing and a new breed of intelligent, confident women are coming into the service, but old attitudes take a long time to be pensioned off. I like working with women, and they make good detectives. Traditionally we've always given them the jobs with an emotional content – child abuse, rape, that sort of thing – but they can be surprisingly hard at times. Harder than a man. Stereotypes and prejudices, I thought. The more you work at them, the deeper the hole you dig for yourself.

As far as anyone knew Annette had never been out with another copper, so the inevitable whispers had gone round the locker room. I'm as

101

guilty as all the rest, and wouldn't have been surprised to learn they were true. Disappointed, but not surprised. We talked about the case, the job and the E-type, but steered clear of personal chat. We'd both considered teaching when we were younger. I had a degree in Art and she had one in Physics.

'A proper degree,' I declared, sharing out the last of the beer.

'That's right,' she agreed across the top of her glass, holding my gaze.

Mr Ho, the proprietor, brought me the customary pot of green tea, on the house, and I asked him for the bill. Annette produced a tenner and slid it across to me.

'Is that enough?' she asked.

'It's OK,' I said. 'I'll get these.'

'No, I'd rather pay my way,' she insisted. Men handle these things much better than women. Any of the male DCs would have said: 'Cheers, I'll get them next time,' but they wouldn't have spent all evening analysing my every word, waiting for the boss to proposition them.

'I'll arm wrestle you for it,' I said.

'Please?'

'If you insist.' I reached for the note and put another with it. 'That's a one pound sixty tip,' I said. 'Alright with you?'

'Yes.'

'Good.'

It was a short drive back to the station, where my car was parked. No opportunity for an invitation in for coffee there. She parked the Fiat behind my Ford, without stopping the engine.

Eyes would be upon us from within the building.

'That was very pleasant, Annette,' I told her, opening the door.

'Yes, it was. Thank you,' she replied.

They say the moon was formed when another planet strayed close to the fledgling Earth and its gravity tore a great chunk from us. I know the feeling. The car door was open, beckoning, and this beautiful lady was eighteen inches away, her face turned to me, her perfume playing havoc with my senses. I felt lost, pulled apart. Salome was dancing, but was it for me or was I in for the chop?

Just a kiss. That's all I wanted. Just a kiss. A simple token of affection after a harrowing day. No harm in that, is there? The scientists don't know it, but there's one force out there in the universe far more powerful than gravity. It's called rejection. I wrenched myself away, saying: 'See you in the morning.'

'Yes,' she replied. 'See you in the morning. Boss.'

Chapter 5

It was no big deal. I drove home and collected the mail from behind the door. Six items, all junk. I put the kettle on and hung my jacket in the hallway. It wasn't nine o' clock yet but I was tired and felt like going to bed. There'd be no red faces in the office tomorrow, no mumbled apologies as we crossed paths in the corridor. We'd be able to continue working together as a team, and that was a big consolation.

I had loosely promised myself to clean the microwave oven tonight, but it could wait. There'd been a slight accident with an exploding chicken Kiev at the weekend, and the kitchen stunk of garlic, but I couldn't face pulling on another pair of rubber gloves and setting to work with the aerosol of nitric acid, or whatever it was I'd bought for the job. I was sure it said *self-cleaning* when I bought the oven, but it isn't. You just can't believe anything these days.

I made a pot of tea – more tea – and settled down with Dylan on the turntable, unaware of the fiasco being enacted in the town centre. *Last night I danced with a stranger, but she just reminded me you are the one.* Spot on, Bob. Spot on.

Dick Lane stretches down to the canal in a part of the town that has been heavily redeveloped. Legend has it that the street gets its name from a worker in the woollen industry who could carry bigger bales of wool than anybody else. Twenty-five stones, or some other mind-boggling figure. More mischievous sources say the name is derived from the row of cast-iron posts that runs across the end of the street. A now defunct Methodist church stands on the corner, and the posts were possibly placed there to deter the carters from taking a short cut to the loading wharves. They were erected by the minister of the day, and it is hard to believe that the foundry that moulded them was not having a joke at his expense, for the posts look remarkably like huge, rampant male members. The developers wanted to remove them, but the council, in its wisdom, slapped a preservation order on them. Dick Lane still has its dicks.

More important than all that is the fact that the posts are exactly sixty-four inches apart. There's no known reason, practical or mystical, for this. Nobody has come up with the theory that it's the distance between the Sphinx's eyes, or the exact width of the Mark IV Blenkinsop loom. It probably just looked about right to the bloke who installed them, nearly two hundred years ago.

At about half past eight young Jamie Walker, now on the run, stole a Ford Fiesta; his favourite car. The owner saw him drive off in it and phoned the police. He was a known drugs user and peddler on the Sylvan Fields estate and demanded to know what we were doing about the theft of his only means of continuing in business. Control circulated the description, filed a report and went back to the Sun crossword. Ten minutes later one of the patrol cars, conveniently parked in the town centre where they could ogle the talent making its way to the various pubs, saw a green Fiesta with a white bonnet and red passenger door tearing the wrong way through the pedestrian precinct. It was Jamie. They did a seven-point turn and gave chase.

The rules of engagement say follow the target vehicle until the driver is well aware that you require him to stop. Then, if he continues to flee, drop back but try to remain in visual contact until assistance can be organised. The patrol car, siren and lights a-go-go, positively identified the registration number and was backing off when Jamie turned into Dick Lane.

'Gorrim!' declared the driver of the patrol car.

Jamie's Ford Fiesta was sixty-three inches wide, which gave him a clearance of half an inch each side as he slotted it neatly between the posts at the bottom of Dick Lane. That's an ample margin when you are escaping arrest, in somebody else's vehicle. He wiped the wing mirrors off, but he never used them anyway. The pursuing officers saw the Fiesta slow to a crawl and make a right turn on to the towpath, towards freedom.

What was actually said between the driver and his observer is open to speculation, as their stories conflicted at the resulting enquiry. What is known is that: a) They decided to continue the chase; and b) A Ford Escort of the type they were driving is sixty-six inches wide. The iron posts neatly redesigned the front wings of the police car, in a process known to engineers as extrusion, and then held it fast. Alpha Foxtrot Zero Three juddered to a standstill with the posts jammed solid halfway along its front doors.

The advent of closed circuit television has been, it is generally agreed, a wondrous breakthrough in the policing of town centres. Tonight it was to prove a curse. Two very large police officers trying to extricate themselves through the rear doors of a fairly small car makes very good television. The CCTV cameras recorded the build-up and several local yuppies with palm-sized Sonys committed the rest of the story to magnetic tape in much greater detail, negotiating contracts with Reuters and Associated Press via their mobile phones even as they filmed.

After doing some much-needed tidying in the kitchen I made myself a peanut butter, honey and banana sandwich and ate it in the bath, accompanied by Rachmaninov's Piano Concerto number 2 played very loud on the CD. It's not one of my favourites, but it includes the *Brief Encounter* music, which amused me. I dried myself and fell into bed feeling reasonably wound down considering the day I'd had, totally oblivious of Jamie's latest exploits.

'Boss wants you. *Now*,' I was told as I passed the front desk early Friday morning.

'What's he doing in at this time?'

'Don't ask.'

I ran straight up the stairs to Mr Wood's office on the top floor. First thought in my head was that Silkstone had topped himself in the cells.

'Morning, Gilbert,' I said, after knocking and walking in. 'You're in early.'

'You haven't seen it then?' he asked without returning my greeting.

'Seen what?'

'Breakfast TV.'

'I'd rather fart drawing pins. What's happened?'

'Watch this.'

He went over to the monitor on another desk and pressed a few buttons. After a snowstorm of blank tape a well-polished couple with colour-coordinated hair flickered into view. I stayed silent, not knowing what to expect, but it was looking like a Martian invasion at the very least. The Chosen Two shared a joke which we couldn't hear because the sound was off and the picture changed to black and white.

'That's Heckley,' I said, recognising the scene. 'Down near the canal.'

'Dick Lane,' Gilbert stated.

'That's right.'

A car jerked towards the camera in ten yard steps, like an early movie. The clock in the bottom right-hand corner said 2123.

'Driven by Jamie Walker,' Gilbert informed me.

'Oh,' I replied. 'Last night?'

'Mmm.'

There were some posts across the end of the street. The car – it looked like a Fiesta – was stopped by the camera as it reached them and in the next frame it was through and bits were flying off it. It exited to the left, narrowly avoiding falling into the canal, and another car jumped into the top of the picture.

'Watch,' Gilbert ordered.

'One of ours?'

'Alpha Foxtrot Zero Three.'

'Who up?'

'Lockwood and Stiles.

Jim Lockwood and Martin Stiles were first on the scene when we arrested Tony Silkstone. I felt uneasy, expecting their car to go into the water and drown them both, or roll over and burst into flames. All it did was get stuck between the posts. The coloured picture came back on, with the Golden Couple laughing just enough not to ruffle their coiffures or flake their make-up. I tried to stifle a giggle, but failed.

'You've got to laugh, Gilbert,' I chuckled.

'What's so funny about it?' he demanded.

'It just is.'

'We're a bloody laughing stock! It won't be funny when the Chief Constable sees it, I'll tell you that.'

'Yeah, you're right,' I admitted. 'Nobody was hurt, that's the main thing. I was expecting to see someone hurt. What's happening?'

'I'm having them in at nine o'clock. I'll have to ground them, Charlie. And the car's probably a write-off. Jamie-fucking-Walker! I'd like to take the little scrote and ... and ... oh, what's the point?'

'Who's investigating it?' I asked. He told me the name of a chief inspector from HQ who I hardly knew.

The super was right: it wasn't funny. Wrecking a police car is a serious matter. Lockwood and Stiles would be taken off driving while a senior

109

officer made preliminary enquiries. It was back to the beat for them. If he'd committed a prosecutable offence it could be the end of the driver's career. 'Were this a member of the public would further action be taken?' was the question that the investigating officer would be asking. Meanwhile, we'd lost the use of two men and a car.

'The point is, Charlie,' Gilbert said, 'we need young Jamie in custody. Number one priority, everybody on it. Right?'

'I *am* conducting a double murder enquiry,' I reminded him.

'Forget it. Get Jamie. Anyhow, it's all sewn up, isn't it?'

'Everybody seems to think so except me. I've got my doubts.'

'Here we go again!' he complained, putting his hands on his head. 'Listen, Charlie: Silkstone's confessed; Latham did the other. It all makes sense, no loose ends. Put it to bed, for God's sake, and concentrate on getting Jamie. We're going to be asked some searching questions about that young man before this is over, mark my words, so let's have him in. Understood?'

'If you say so.'

'I do.'

I said: 'Fourteen years old, top of our Most Wanted list. Not bad, eh? He'll be dining out on that for the rest of his life, if anybody tells him.'

'He'll be dining out in Bentley Prison maximum security unit for the rest of his life if I can help it,' Gilbert responded. 'Just ... *find him.*'

110

We had an informal meeting in the office and I wound down the murder enquiry until Monday. Even the smallest investigation soon develops branches until it looks like some ancient tree, every fork representing a Yes and a No answer to a simple question. 'Did you know your wife was having an affair, Sir?' Go left for Yes, right for No. This one was no exception, but we'd have the DNA results in the morning and that would enable us to do some drastic pruning. Then, hopefully, we'd be able to file the whole thing until the wheels of justice came to rest against the double yellow lines of Her Majesty's Crown Court, or something. I handed the Jamie Walker case over to Jeff Caton, one of my DSs, and gave him full control of all the troops. What more could be done?

Annette went off to find Jamie's mother. I was hoping to have a quick word with Annette when nobody else was around, just: 'Hello, how's things?' to maintain the momentum, but it didn't work out. She was wearing jeans with a scarlet blouse and looked breathtaking. Sparky came in as I eyed the pile of paper in my in-tray.

'I'm off looking for Jamie's mates,' he said. 'Anything you want to know before I go?'

'No, I don't think so,' I replied. 'I'll have a go at this lot and then start on a submission to the CPS.'

'What are you doing over the weekend?'

'Housework, and coming here in the morning. Why?'

'I just wondered. You're not ... you know...?'

'I'm not what?' I demanded.

111

'You're not, you know, taking Annette out?'

'No, I'm not. Whatever gave you that idea?'

'Nothing. I just thought you might be.'

'Is that why you rather pointedly left us alone together yesterday?'

'Just trying to help an old mate.'

'Well don't bother, thank you. Never get involved with a colleague, Dave. That's my motto.'

'She's an attractive woman.'

'Yes, I had noticed.'

'And she obviously fancies you like mad.'

'Does she? That's news to me.'

'Because you're blind. So you're free on Saturday night?'

'Sadly, as a bird.'

'Right,' he said. 'Sophie finished her A-levels yesterday, and says she's happy with the way they went, so we're taking her for a celebratory steak. And, of course, they say it wouldn't be the same without you. Can't think why.'

'Oh, that's brilliant,' I declared. 'Well done Sophie. Is she in? I'll give her a ring.'

'No, she's gone into Leeds with her mum. I heard Harvey Nicks mentioned, so it could cost me. All she has to do now is get the grades, then it's Cambridge, here we come. The kid's worked hard, Charlie. Harder than I ever have.'

'I know. And think of the pressure, too.'

'Well, we've never pressurised her. Encouraged her, but win or lose, we don't mind as long as she's happy. So shall I put you down for a T-bone?'

'You bet.'

'And, er, will you be bringing a friend?'

112

'A friend? No, I don't think so,' I replied.

'But you'll come?'

'Try stopping me.'

'Why don't you ask Annette? You might be surprised.'

'Wouldn't that make Sophie jealous?' I joked. She had a crush on me when she was younger, but I imagined she was long grown out of it. Now she'd see me for the old fogey I really was.

'No, not really. I told her about your prostate problems and she went off you. Oh, and I told her that you bought your clothes at Greenwoods. That clinched it.'

'Thanks. Greenwoods do some very nice jackets.'

'So will it be steak for one or two?'

'One please.'

'Go on, ask her.'

'I'll see.'

'OK.'

He went off to find his villains and I thought about Sophie. My previous girlfriend was called Annabelle, and she and Sophie became good friends. Sophie copied her style and mannerisms, even to the point of calling me by my Sunday name, Charles. I smiled at the memories. And soon she'd be off to Cambridge.

The internal phone rang. 'Priest,' I said into it.

'Just letting you know that the Deputy Chief Constable has arrived, Charlie,' the desk sergeant informed me in a stage whisper.

'Thanks,' I said. 'In that case, I'm off.'

I went down the back stairs and into the main office. Every major crime has an appointed ex-

113

hibits officer and a connected property store, which in this case was a drawer in a filing cabinet. It's essential that a log is kept of every piece of evidence, accounting for all its movements and recording the names of everyone who has had access to it. There's no point in telling the court that a knife had fingerprints on it if the defence can suggest – just suggest – that the defendant may have handled it after he was arrested. I didn't want the knife, just the keys to Silkstone's house. I said a silent apology to Gilbert for leaving him in the clutches of the DCC and drove back to Mountain Meadows.

The panda cars and the blue tape had gone and the street had resumed its air of respectability. The Yellow Pages delivery man had done his rounds and the latest edition was sitting on the front step of several houses, neatly defining who was at home and who wasn't. I'd had Silkstone's Audi taken from Latham's house to our garage for forensic examination, so there was plenty of room for me to park on the drive alongside the Suzuki. I picked up the directory and let myself in.

First job was a coffee. They drank Kenco instant, although there was a selection of beans from Columbia and Kenya. I watched the kettle as it boiled and carried my drink – weak, black and unsweetened – through into the lounge. I sat on the chesterfield and imagined I was at home.

It was a difficult exercise. This was the most uncomfortable room I'd ever been in, outside the legal system. The furnishings were good quality, expensive, but everything was hard-edged and

114

solid. No cushions or fabrics to soften things. Focal point of the room was a Sony widescreen television set big enough to depict some of TV's smaller performers almost lifesize. I shuddered at the thought. After about ten minutes the wallpaper started dancing and weaving before my eyes, like a Bridget Riley painting. I stood up and went exploring.

There was a toilet downstairs, a bathroom upstairs with a bath shower and rowing machine, and one *en suite* with the room where we'd found Mrs Silkstone. A room under the stairs with a sloping ceiling was their office, where a Viglen computer and seventeen-inch monitor stood on an L-shaped desk. I sat in the leather executive chair and opened the first drawer.

An hour later I was in the kitchen again. I examined all the messages on the pin board and made a note of several phone numbers. The cupboard under the sink was a surprise: there was still some room in it. I spread a newspaper – the *Express* – on the floor, emptied their swing bin on to it and poked around in the tea bags and muesli shrapnel like I'd seen TV cops do. Then I went outside, dragged the dustbin into the garage and did it again, big time.

I washed my hands and had another coffee, sitting in the captain's chair at the head of their dining room table. It was all mahogany in there, with more striped wallpaper. The only picture on the walls was a limited edition signed print of Damon Hill winning the British Grand Prix. Number fifty-six of eight million. His room again, I thought.

I had a pee in the downstairs loo. It was the standard type, like the one in my 1960's house. I pulled the lever and watched the water splash about and subside. I'd have thought that a house as modern as this one would have had those low-level ones, where you watch everything swirling around, convinced it will never all go down that little hole. Personal preference, I supposed. I might even have chosen the same ones myself. I went upstairs into the master bedroom and, lo and behold, the *en suite* bog was the modern type, in coral pink. I did a comparison flush and decided that maybe these were better after all, but it wasn't a convincing victory. Just for the record I looked in the main bathroom. Old type, in stark white. Flushed first time, like the others. I didn't write any of this in my notebook.

I sat in one of the hard leather chairs for half an hour, thinking about things. I enjoy being alone with my thoughts, and the seat was more comfortable than I expected. You had to sit well back and upright, but it wasn't too bad. Probably good for the posture, I thought. Next time I saw Silkstone I'd check his posture. A brandy and a cigar would have gone down well, or perhaps a decent port.

Jim Lockwood and Martin Stiles were coming out of the front door as I arrived back at the nick. Jim was wearing a suit and tie, Martin a short-sleeved shirt and jeans. They looked worried men.

'How'd it go?' I asked.

'He's sacked us,' Martin blurted out.

'We're suspended,' Jim explained.

116

'He can't sack you,' I replied.

'He wants us sacked,' Martin declared.

I looked at Jim. 'Yeah,' he confirmed. 'He made that clear. Mr Wood tried to stand up for us, but the DCC went 'airless. Said we'd made a mock'ry of the force, and all that. It was on TV again this morning, apparently.'

'Well he can't sack you,' I repeated. 'You know that. And next time you're in for an interview make sure you have the Federation rep with you. Don't let them two-one you.'

'Right, Mr Priest,' Martin replied.

'Meanwhile,' I flapped a hand at the sky, 'make the best of the decent weather. Paint the outside of the house, or something. It'll be a nine-day wonder, you'll see.'

'Thanks, Boss,' Jim said, and they skulked away like two schoolboys caught peeing off the bike shed roof.

I made a pot of tea – all that coffee makes you thirsty – and ate the M & S cheese and pickle sandwich I'd bought on the way back. The lab at Wetherton confirmed that I'd have the DNA results tomorrow, but otherwise they had nothing to tell me. I rang the CPS and agreed to a meeting with them on Monday afternoon.

The hooligans down in the briefing room had a recording of the Dick Lane Massacre and were delighted to show it to me. It was worse than I expected. Some local chancer had recorded the whole thing on his camcorder and networked it. He took up the story as Jim and Martin were trying to extricate themselves from the jammed car. Unable to climb into the back, they even-

117

tually reclined their seats and crawled out of the rear doors on hands and knees. It wasn't a picture of noble policemen fighting crime against impossible odds with courage and dignity. It was a fourteen-year-old twocker making two fully-grown cops look complete pillocks. The only good thing was that Jamie wasn't named. That would have made a folk-hero of him. Jim and Martin's so-called colleagues jeered and cat-called throughout the showing, relieved they weren't the subjects of such ridicule.

'If the car had caught fire and they'd been burnt to cinders, we'd be saying they were heroes,' I said. I stomped back upstairs, wondering if that was the reason why I hated Jamie Walker.

The troops filtered back, empty handed. Dave called into my office and asked if I'd had a report on the DNA.

'Tomorrow,' I replied. 'You know they said tomorrow.'

'Just thought you might have rung them and asked.'

'I did. They still said tomorrow. What about you? Find anything?'

'Nah. Waste of time. His mates think he might be in Manchester, but the little toe-rag's screwing a bird from the Sylvan Fields, so they say he won't stay away long.'

'Video games and sex,' I said. 'Kids today have it all.'

'What did we have?' Dave asked. 'Train spotting and snowball fights. Makes yer fink, do'n it?'

'Do'n it just.'

118

'I called at this house in the Sylvan Fields estate,' he said, 'and there was this great big Alsatian in the garden, barking an' slavering. A woman was leaning out of an upstairs window and she shouted: "It won't hurt you, love. Just kick its balls for it." So I went in and kicked it in the balls and it ran away yelping and the woman shouted down: "No, not them! Its rubber balls that it plays with."'

I laughed, against my wishes, and said: 'You'd think they'd learn, wouldn't you?'

Annette knocked and came in, just as Dave said: 'Well, I'd better report to Jeff. Hi, Annette.'

'Hello Dave,' she replied, holding the door for him. 'Find anything?'

'Mmm. Ronald Biggs did the Great Train Robbery. Nothing on Jamie, though.'

'Perhaps he's hiding in Brazil,' she said.

'Could be. See you.'

Dave went and I waved towards the spare chair. She sat in it and crossed her ankles. Her jacket was tweed, what might have been called a sports coat or hacking jacket a few years ago, and her blouse spilled from the sleeves and unbuttoned front in splashes of colour. She looked carelessly dishy, with extra mayonnaise.

'Hard day?' I asked.

'Waste of time,' she replied. 'Running about after a will o' the wisp. Word is that he's gone to Manchester. When he was in care his best pal was a youth from there called Bernie, so all we have to do is track down all the Bernards who were in care at the same time as our Jamie. Methinks he'll resurface long before then.'

119

'Methinks you're right,' I agreed. She was wearing a ring on the third finger of her right hand. A delicate gold one with a tiny diamond. Wrong hand, I thought.

'So,' Annette began, 'I was just wondering if anything had come through from Wetherton about the samples?'

'No, they said tomorrow,' I told her.

'Oh. I thought you might not be able to resist giving them a ring and asking if they'd found anything.'

'I couldn't,' I admitted, 'but they haven't. We should have the full report at about ten in the morning.'

'Right.'

She uncrossed her ankles, as if to stand up and leave. I said: 'Thanks for coming with me last night, Annette. It was nice to have some company for a change.'

'I enjoyed it,' she replied. 'Thanks for inviting me.' She smiled one of her little ones, barely a movement of the corners of her mouth, but her cheeks flushed slightly.

'As a matter of fact,' I went on, 'tomorrow night I'm going to the Steakhouse with Dave and his family It's a bit of a celebration. If you're not doing anything I'd love for you to come along.'

'Saturday?' she asked.

'Mmm.'

'No, I'm sorry, I can't make it.'

'Oh, never mind. His daughter has just finished her A-levels, and she's been accepted for Cambridge if she gets the grades, so we're taking her out. They do good steaks there. That's the Steakhouse, not Cambridge, I think she needs two As and a B. Sophie's my goddaughter. And other stuff, if you're not a steak eater.' I waffled away. See if I care.

'Sophie?' Annette asked. 'Dave's daughter Sophie?'

'Yes. Have you met her?'

'Of course I have. She used to come on the walks.'

'That's right, she did. You'd just joined us. I used to wonder what you kept in that great big rucksack you carried.'

'Did you?'

'Yes.'

She stood up, saying: 'Remember me to Sophie, please, Boss, and give her my congratulations.'

I pulled a pained face and said: 'Annette. Could you please call me Charlie once in a while? Everybody else does. I shan't read anything into it, honestly. It just helps maintain the team spirit. That's all.'

She sat down again, and this time the smile was fulsome. 'Sorry,' she said. 'Charlie.'

'That's better. I hope you have a good weekend. If you ring me I'll tell you the results of the tests.'

'Oh, I'll come here first, in the morning,' she asserted.

'You've no need to, if you're going away. Anywhere special?'

'Um, York, to a friend's, that's all. I'll come here first, for the results.'

'If you say so.'

She went off to report to Jeff about Jamie's
121

movements, leaving a faint, tantalising reminder of her presence in my office. Annabelle came on some of the walks we'd organised, and the two of them had surely met. Annabelle – Annette, I thought, Annette – Annabelle. A man would have to be careful with two names like that, in a passionate situation. Not that one was ever likely to arise. I wondered about the mystery friend in York and growled at the next person to come into the office.

The forecast for the weekend was good so I told the troops that we'd have a meeting about the murders on Monday. Most of them said they'd pop in Saturday morning, for the results. I still do a few paintings, when the mood takes me or someone commissions one. I only charge for materials. Mr Ho at the Bamboo Curtain had asked for one, for on his staircase, so I decided to make a start on it. It was going to be six feet by four feet six inches, abstract but with a Chinese theme. On the way home I called in the library and borrowed a book on Chinese art.

I had a trout for tea, with microwave oven chips and peas. Not bad. Chinese art is big on impossible cliffs and bonsai trees. I hinted at a few terracotta warriors and coolie hats, for the human touch, and a couple of tanks to show where the power lay. By midnight I'd done the underpainting and it was looking good. What a way to spend Friday night, but better than cleaning the oven. The next part, laying on the colour straight out of the tubes, was the best bit. Therapeutic. I had a shower and went to bed.

I couldn't sleep. Maybe it was the trout, maybe it was the enquiry. If the DNA results were as expected we'd have that sewn up tomorrow, so no problem there. Maybe I was thinking about the sad life I was drifting into. Maybe I was thinking about a woman. Maybe I should set it to music.

I listened to the World Service for a while, then switched to the local station. There'd been a bad accident on the Heckley bypass, something about a jack-knifed lorry, and traffic disruption was expected to last into the morning. Six o'clock I went downstairs and made some tea.

I was lying on the settee using the remote control to pick out my favourite tracks on *The Bootleg Series* when the phone rang, right in the middle of *Blind Willie McTell*. Anybody who interrupts *Blind Willie* had better have a good reason.

It was the night 'tec. 'Sorry to ring you at this time, Charlie,' he began.

'No problem, Rodger.' He doesn't telephone me lightly and his voice was strained. 'What've you got?'

'There's been a bad RTA on the bypass.'

'I know. I'm up and heard it on the radio. What happened?'

'Head on, between a Mini and a milk tanker. The Mini's jammed underneath.'

'God, that sounds nasty.' I visualised the carnage. 'How many in the Mini?'

'Just one, as far as we can tell. I'm pretty sure it's Jamie Walker.'

I didn't speak for a while. 'You still there, Charlie?' Rodger asked.

'Yeah, I'm still here,' I replied. 'Dead, I assume?'

'Instantly.'

'Was he being chased?'

'No. We didn't even know he was in the area.'

'Thank God for that. You got some help?'

'Everybody and his dog's here. Just thought you'd like to know.'

'Right. Thanks for ringing, Rodge, and stay with it, please.'

Jamie Walker, aged fourteen, wouldn't be stealing any more cars, and our figures would resume their steady downward path after the recent hiatus. Jamie Walker, who I hated, was eliminated from the equation. I had cornflakes and toast for breakfast and went into the garage to look at the painting. It looked as good as I remembered. At seven, because I couldn't think of anything else to do, I drove to the nick.

By the time the troops arrived at our office on the first floor they'd all heard about Jamie. It was mainly smiles all round, because Jamie had killed himself. All too often it's someone completely innocent who pays the price. Rodger came in, looking completely shagged out, and told us the details. Jamie had come round a bend on the wrong side of the road and hit the tanker at a combined speed of about a hundred and ten. The tanker driver was unhurt but in hospital under sedation.

'He'd stolen the Mini from the bloke who lives next door to where he was staying,' Rodger told us. 'This bloke works for a security firm, on about eighty quid a week. He has two daughters who are asthmatic, and he runs the car so he can take them to the coast every weekend. Someone told him sea air would do them good. Don't ask me to weep for Jamie Walker, because I can't. Good riddance to the little bastard, I say.'

'Go home, Rodger,' I said. 'You've had a tough night. Take whatever it is that makes you sleep and snuggle up to your Rosie.' But I doubted if there'd be any sleep for him today, or tomorrow, or even the next day. He walked away, jacket slung over his shoulder, and we looked at our watches, waiting for the mail to arrive.

Gilbert rang from home, asking for news, and I promised to let him know as soon as we had anything. Annette came in, wearing a shortish skirt and high heels, which was unusual. Her working clothes are practical, and she only wears a skirt for court appearances. I gave her a wink and was rewarded with a smile. At five past ten a traffic car arrived, with the report. I opened the envelope and read the resume that preceded the detailed stuff.

'What does it say?' someone asked.

'Wait,' I told them, reading.

'They close at four,' someone complained.

'Shurrup!'

'Sorry.'

'That's all right. OK, it's as we expected.' I handed the report to Annette, who was sitting directly in front of me. 'The semen samples are all from Peter Latham. Hairs were found in the bed from all three of them.'

'Which isn't surprising, as it was Silkstone's bed,' Dave told us.

'Pubic hair, in his case, I presume,' someone added.

125

'Yes,' I agreed, 'It does say that.' They started chattering between themselves, so I hushed them, saying: 'There is just one more thing.' When they were silent I told them: 'According to the lab, traces of a spermicidal lubricant, as used on condoms, were also found in Mrs Silkstone. That's something for us to think about.'

'In where? Does it say?' someone asked.

'Not sure,' I replied, looking at Annette. She thumbed through the pages, there were about ten, scanning each briefly as she shook her hair away from her face.

'Can you find it?'

'Yes, it's here. It says: 'Traces of a spermicidal lubricant, of a type commonly used on condoms, were found in the anus and rectum.''

'Does it say if any was found on Latham's dick?'

Annette turned the pages back, looking for the information.

'Is it there?'

'Yes, I think this is it.' She studied the report for a few seconds then read out aloud: 'A spermicidal lubricant of a similar type as that found in the female body was found on the subject's penis.'

I thanked her, saying to the rest of them: 'If any of you has a theory about how all this came about, I'll treat the information in the strictest confidence. Meanwhile, we'll prepare a condensed version and do the necessary. Any questions that won't wait until Monday?'

Nobody had one, so I thanked them for coming in and telephoned Gilbert.

126

'So Silkstone's story holds water,' he concluded, when I finished.

'It looks like it,' I admitted.

'Good. Let's have it sewn up, then. And young Walker won't be causing us any more trouble, I hear.'

'Unless his mother sues us for not arresting him.'

'Bah! Bloody likely, too. But we'll cross that bridge when we come to it. Meanwhile, I'm off for an hour's fishing. Fancy coming, Charlie? Do you good.'

'No thanks, Gilbert. Sticking a hook through a small creature's nose is not my idea of entertainment.'

'You wouldn't catch anything!' Gilbert retorted. 'What makes you think you'd catch anything?'

'I meant the maggots,' I replied. 'Maggots have feelings, too.'

I would have fallen hopelessly, crazily, desperately in love with Sophie as soon as I saw her, except that I already was. She was wearing a blue silk dress and her hair was piled up in a sophisticated style that I'd never seen her wear before. 'You look sensational,' I said, pecking her on the cheek. 'Cambridge won't know what's hit them.'

'She's gonna be a spy,' her younger brother, Daniel, informed me. 'That's where they train them all.'

'Well that's better than being a traitor,' she retorted, referring to Danny's ambition to play football for Manchester United and not Halifax Town.

We went in my car. I'd have to drive home afterwards, so this meant that Dave could have a few drinks. His wife, Shirley, said: 'Hey, this is all right, being chauffeured about by the boss.'

'Let's get one thing clear,' I told her as we set off. 'Tonight I am taking my favourite god-daughter out for a meal. You three are just hangers-on.'

'I'm your only goddaughter, Uncle Charles,' Sophie reminded me, and her brother jumped straight in with: 'You don't think you'd be his favourite if there was another, do you?'

'It's going to be one of those evenings,' Shirley remarked.

I'd made a bit of an effort with my appearance, for once, and was glad I had. Blue jacket with a black check, black trousers, blue shirt and contrasting tie. Dark clothes suit me and add to that air of mystery. I'd even put some aftershave on.

'You look handsome tonight,' Shirley had told me when I arrived. 'Dave said you might bring a friend.'

'He speak with forked tongue,' I'd replied.

'Annette Brown. He reckons she has the hots for you. She's a lovely girl.'

'Tomorrow, he die.' I explained that she wasn't my type; I didn't want to be involved with another officer and as far as I knew she was already in a perfectly happy relationship.

'So you asked her.'

'I didn't say that!'

Four of us had fillet steak and Dave had the speciality mixed grill, which includes a steak and

128

just about every other bovine organ known to science. Two bottles of a Banrock Shiraz helped it down quite nicely. We talked about Jamie Walker and the Silkstone case, without being too explicit, and I had my favourite apple pie for pudding. I asked Sophie why she'd chosen Cambridge and not Oxford, and she said: 'Everybody goes to Oxford.'

We had more coffee back at their house and sat talking until midnight, when the kids went to bed. Dave fell asleep on the settee, snoring with his mouth wide open, which I took as a good time to leave. It was a warm evening, and Shirley walked out to the car with me.

'Thanks for inviting me, Shirley,' I said. 'It was considerate of you.'

'You're part of the family, Charlie,' she replied. 'You were married to Dave before I was.'

'Well, I wouldn't have put it quite like that, but I appreciate it.'

At the gate I said: 'He was quiet tonight. Not his usual self.'

'No,' she replied, 'he wasn't, was he?'

'Has the Jamie Walker business upset him?'

'A little, perhaps. Daniel was that age not too long ago, but I think it's mainly because of Sophie.'

'Sophie?'

'Mmm. Going to university, leaving the nest and all that. If it's not Cambridge it will be somewhere else. She's just finished with her first boyfriend, but there'll be more. Danny was always my son, but Sophie is Dave's daughter, and he's losing her. It hurts. You worry about them,

129

Charlie. The temptations, the pressures, the mistakes they'll make. You want to live their lives for them, but you can't. You have to step back and let them do it their way, and sometimes it's painful.'

'It's called love,' I told her.

'Yes, it is.'

We kissed cheeks and said goodnight.

At home I cleaned my teeth and hung up my clothes. I poured a glass of the plonk that was open, to catch up with the others, put Vaughan Williams on the CD and went to bed with the curtains open, so I could watch the clouds drifting past the window, like the backdrop of a silent movie. There was a new moon, and it and Thomas Tallis gave magic to the night. The wine and my thoughts probably helped.

But there's a dark side to the moon, and clouds are fickle. New faces came to me, pushing aside the ones I cherished. Young Jamie Walker was dead, and I didn't care. His death had lifted a weight off me, eased the tourniquet that tightened around my spleen whenever I'd heard his name. Monday morning someone would come out with a Jamie Walker joke – 'What does Jamie Walker have on his cornflakes?' – and I'd laugh with the rest of them. I didn't hate him for being a thief. I didn't hate him for the grief and misery he caused people who were as poorly off as he was. I didn't give a shit about our crime figures. I hated him for making me not care about his death. For doing that to me, I could never forgive him.

Sunday I gave the microwave a wash and brush-up. The fine spell was holding and the weather forecasters were predicting a good summer because the swallows were flying high and the grasshoppers were wearing Ray-Bans. I went to the garden centre to buy some new blades for the hover mower and had to park in the next field. Forget banks, knock-off a garden centre.

In the evening I watched a video about the space race that Daniel had loaned me. Apparently the USA bagged Mars first, so Russia decided to concentrate on Venus. They didn't know until they sent the first probe there that the atmosphere was comprised largely of sulphuric acid. As my mother used to say; 'There's always someone worse off than yourself.' Danny is envious that his dad's generation witnessed the moon landings, as they happened. To him it's just another event in history, like World War II or the Battle of Hastings. I'm eternally grateful to the Americans for taking a television camera on the trip. OK, they did it for self-publicity, because they needed public approval for all that expenditure, but it was a brave thing to do. It could have all gone dreadfully wrong.

I have a photograph of Daniel and Sophie, standing alongside my old E-type. It was taken at Heckley Gala a couple of summers ago, after we'd taken part in the grand cavalcade, and published in the *Heckley Gazette*. I knew roughly where it was and soon found it. Sophie was all legs, posing elegantly with one hand on the car door, and Danny was wearing his trade-mark grin. The photo was in black and white, ten by

131

eight, and slightly over-exposed. I turned it over and looked at the Gazette's rubber stamp mark on the back. The copyright was theirs and a serial number was written in ink in the appropriate box. The date space was empty I propped it against the clock and wondered about framing it.

Margaret Silkstone had consenting sex with Peter Latham on her marital bed. He wore a condom initially but removed it later. A disagreement arose between them and he strangled her. That was about as much as we could be sure of.

'Maybe she objected to him removing the condom,' Gilbert suggested.

'Or to his, er, sexual proclivities,' the CPS lawyer said, adding, 'putting it another way, she didn't want it up her bum.'

'Why does other people's love-making always sound so bloody sordid?' I asked.

'Because you're not getting any,' Gilbert stated.

Putting it another way! I like that,' the lawyer chuckled. He was young and bulky, in a charcoal suit that bulged and gaped like the wrapping of a badly made, slightly leaky, parcel. Prendergast would eat him for breakfast, but he was the best we had. I looked at him and wondered who the anonymous genius was who coined the phrase *big girl's blouse*.

'Whichever it was,' Gilbert stated, 'we'll never know. But it does look as if Peter Latham murdered Margaret Silkstone. All agreed?'

'Yes, I think we can be certain about that,' the lawyer replied.

Gilbert was looking at me over his spectacles,

132

defying me to launch into a conspiracy theory. 'Yep, the evidence points that way,' I concurred.

'Good. Now what about Tony Silkstone?'

'We have one witness, namely Silkstone himself, and some forensic,' the lawyer told us, 'and all the forensic indicates that he is telling the truth. Have you anything to the contrary, Mr Priest?'

I shook my head. 'Nope.'

'So we go for manslaughter.'

'Except I don't believe it,' I said.

'What you believe, Charlie,' Gilbert snapped, 'is neither here nor there. It's evidence that sways a court.'

'Evidence,' I repeated. *Evidence.* I wish I'd known that. I'd have brought some along.'

'What makes you think it's murder?' the lawyer asked.

For murder we needed to prove a degree of premeditation, or an intention to kill. Silkstone had almost admitted that he thought his wife might be having an affair, during that first interview when he was trying to show us what a forthright fellow he was, but his brief would have soon made him aware of that folly. I thought about him, images from the little I knew about the man lining up for inspection and moving on as the next one popped up. All that surfaced was that he had a photograph of Nigel Mansell on his wall. Hardly damning. 'Nothing,' I replied. 'Let's go for manslaughter.'

'Oppose bail?' the lawyer asked.

'Definitely,' I insisted, as if the alternative were unthinkable.

'On what grounds?'

Bail is rarely granted in murder cases, but is fairly common for manslaughter. The accused has to show the court that he is unlikely to abscond, interfere with the course of justice or commit another crime. As Silkstone had a clean record up to now, was in gainful employment and could reside in the area once we had deemed his house no longer a crime scene, he'd probably be granted it.

'Psychiatric reports,' I said. 'He's pleading some sort of mental aberration, red mist and all that rubbish. Of a temporary nature, of course, from which he has now miraculously recovered. We need to show that either he never had it or it's still there. I don't mind which.'

'Our expert witness will be a registrar from the General on a flat fee,' the lawyer told me. 'His will be a whiz kid from Harley Street who lights his cigars with ten-pound notes.' His tie had little Mickey Mouses on it, and a faded patch where he'd removed a stain.

'But Silkstone has killed someone,' I said. 'Sticking a knife in somebody's heart takes a lot of explaining away. They'll let him out eventually, but let's hold him for as long as we can.'

The lawyer agreed and said he'd do his best. I felt sorry for him, but not as sorry as I felt for Margaret Silkstone.

'So?' Dave asked when I arrived back in the office.

'Manslaughter,' I told him. 'As we expected.'

'Fair enough,' he replied.

134

'It's not fair enough if he planned the whole thing,' I retorted. 'Involuntary manslaughter and he could be out in a year. He might not even go to jail at all.'

'But Latham was shagging his wife,' Dave stated.

'Oh, so that makes it OK, does it? What law's this, Sparkington's law?'

'You know what I mean.'

'No I don't.'

'Mc-whatsit made the laws. What does he say about it?'

'The McNaughton Rules? He says that to establish a defence against murder they have to prove that the defendant was off his trolley, which they probably can do. He came home and found his wife dead in bed, murdered and raped by one of his employees. It's strong stuff, if that's what happened. I think we'd best resign ourselves to calling this a double clean-up and get on with keeping the streets safe.'

'Everybody else is happy with that, Charlie. You're the one wanting to make a meal of it.'

'Yeah, well,' I said.

I went downstairs to find the custody officer. He was in the briefing room, listening to one of the other sergeants, a new guy, regaling the troops with stories from his holiday in Florida. He had a suntan and a big mouth, and was thrust upon us by HQ for reasons we knew not.

'And this hostess was coming down the aisle,' he was telling them. 'Typical American – all tits and teeth. "Would you like some TWA coffee, sir?" she asked. "No," I told her, *"–but I wouldn't mind some TWA tea!'"*

They laughed as only a captive audience can. I caught the custody sergeant's gaze and he followed me into his purpose-designed domain.

'He's in fine form,' I said.

'Isn't he just.'

'Have a brotherly word with him, Bill, or I might have to.'

'Right.'

'We've decided to do Silkstone for manslaughter.'

'Good,' he replied, opening a drawer in one of his filing cabinets. 'In that case we'd better ring his brief and get on with the paperwork.'

Something was troubling me. Nothing I could name or explain or put in a report to show what a clever boy I was at a later date. There was a loose end – less than that, more like a draught around the edge of a closed window – that was making me feel uneasy. I collected the keys from the connected property store and drove to number 15, Marlborough Close, home of the late Peter Latham.

The spaghetti jar still stood on his worktop, next to the pan lid, as if the cook had been interrupted by the ringing of the telephone, and a carton of milk was making unhealthy smells. I took it outside and dropped it in his dustbin. The woman next door peered at me shamelessly, but didn't come to investigate. The pile of mail behind the door looked depressingly familiar, with not a single hand-written envelope amongst it all. I toyed with the idea of writing: *Dead, return to sender* on everything, but resisted the temptation. They'd probably all send it back asking for it to go to the next of kin.

The bird prints on his walls were Audubons, and good quality. Maybe I'd underestimated Peter Latham. I climbed the stairs slowly listening for creaks, wondering if he'd ever led Mrs Silkstone up them, tugging at her hand. If walls could speak, what would they tell us? The door to his bedroom was ajar. I pushed it open and went in.

The sun cast a big geometric patch of light across the bed and wall, showing off the room as if in an advertising brochure. There's something inviting and evocative about sunlight spilling across a made-up bed. Three tiny Zebra spiders scurried across the windowsill, alarmed by my intrusion, but a dead or sleeping wasp ignored me. The photograph of the young girl was still there, smiling shyly, self-consciously, as she had done for God-knew how many years, and the new Mrs Latham was still gazing down into his eyes. But it was the girl I was interested in.

I sat on the bed and removed a pair of latex gloves and my Swiss Army knife from a jacket pocket. The room was chilly but the sunlight warmed my legs. I wriggled my fingers into the gloves and tried to open the big blade of the knife. Couldn't do it. My thumbnail wouldn't engage with the little groove. I removed one glove, opened the knife and replaced the glove. You live and learn.

Carefully, I eased back the metal sprigs that held the photo in the frame. There was a stiff

137

backing card, a sheet of acid-free paper to stop the picture discolouring, and then the photo itself. Something about it had reminded me of the one I owned with Sophie and Daniel on. Both pictures were black and white, and exposed to the same degree. Mine was taken and printed by the *Heckley Gazette*.

This one had a similar stamp on the back. Both sides were trimmed to isolate this girl only, and one edge of the stamp had gone, but it told me that the photographer had worked for the *Burdon and Frome Exp* ... and the serial number was 2452...? We were in business.

Five minutes later I was on Latham's phone, dialling a Somerset number. A small intuitive leap had told me that the picture came from the *Burdon and Frome Express* and I was right first time. Sometimes, you have to trust your instincts.

'Gillian McLaughlin,' a voice said, after I'd asked to be put through to the editor in charge. I introduced myself and asked if she were the editor.

'Deputy editor,' she stated. 'Mr Binks is not in at the moment. How can I help you?'

'In the course of an enquiry,' I began, 'we have come across a photograph which apparently comes from your paper.' I explained what it was and told her the number on the back.

'Shouldn't be a problem, Inspector,' she replied, and went on to tell me that the number was the edition number and only the digits which identified the actual page and photograph were missing. They were now up to edition 3,582.

'So this picture was taken just over a thousand

editions ago,' I stated.

'Um, yes, which is about, um...'

'Are you a weekly?'

'Yes, we are.'

'About twenty years, then.'

'Um, yes. Twenty years,' she agreed.

She also agreed to extricate the full article from the archives and fax me a copy. I told her that we were trying to track down a dead person's relatives, and we suspected this girl might be one of them. If there was a story in it, I assured her, she'd be the first to know.

Nothing was spoiling back at the nick so I went home. My house wasn't as tidy as Latham's, I decided, so I made the bed, just in case, and washed and dried a two-day pile of crockery. When you live alone you don't notice how the sloppy habits slowly overtake you. The decay starts in the unseen corners, then spreads like mould on a bowl of fruit. For tea I had boil-in-the-bag cod with pasta. If you put the pasta in the same pan as the cod it saves on washing up. The telly cooks never tell you useful stuff like that.

Big Jim Lockwood was leaving the car-park as I arrived on Tuesday morning, wheeling an upright bicycle that was last used when *Whitehall one-two one-two* was the number you dialled after the villains had said: 'It's a fair cop, Guv.' I wound the window down and spoke to him.

'Back with us, eh, Jim?'

'Looks like it, Mr Priest,' he replied, 'but we're still grounded.'

'Have they said how long for?'

139

'Indefinitely. Calling it a new initiative. Bobbies in the community and all that. It'll get me fit, lose some weight.'

'That's one way of looking at it.' I drove into my space, shaking my head at the stupidity of it.

Gillian McLaughlin's fax was waiting for me when I came out of the morning prayer meeting. 'Come and dig this,' I said to all and sundry as I bore it into the office. They gathered round and peered at it. There were four girls on the photo, all carrying the letter B on their chests. They were, the text told us, the victorious Under 13s relay team at the recent Burdon schools sports day and the girl second from the left was called Caroline Poole.

'Caroline Poole,' I heard Annette whisper. 'Where are you now?'

'With looks like that,' someone said, 'I'm surprised she's not on t'telly. I bet she grew up into a right cracker.'

'She's certainly a bonny 'un,' another agreed.

'Let's find her, then,' I suggested. 'And the others. Should be easy enough. They'll be in their early thirties, now.' I turned to Annette. 'Can I leave that with you, Ms Brown?'

She smiled, saying: 'No problem, Boss.'

'No hurry,' I told her. 'There's nothing in it for us, more than likely. She's probably a relative of Latham's, that's all.'

Four of us, including Annette, went down to the canteen for bacon sandwiches. 'Mr Wood's sent Jim Lockwood and Martin Stiles out on the beat, on bikes,' Jeff Caton stated.

'It wasn't Mr Wood,' I disclosed. 'The order

140

came down from above.'

'What, God?'

'His deputy.'

'Bloody crackers, if you ask me.'

'It's a new initiative. Get the bobby back on the beat.'

'On a 1930s bike that weighs half a ton and has rotting tyres. They'll be laughing stocks.'

'They became that when they got the car stuck.'

We chuckled at the memory. 'You've got to admit it was bloody funny,' Jeff said.

Annette and Dave came back from the counter carrying the teas. Annette placed a mug in front of me, saying: 'No milk or sugar for you, Charlie.'

'Wait a minute. Wait a minute,' Jeff demanded. 'How come you know that the boss doesn't take milk or sugar?'

'The same way as you know,' she told him, without hesitation.

'Oh. And did you know he liked his belly rubbed with baby oil?'

'Cut it out,' I said. 'You might not be embarrassing Annette but you're embarrassing me. I don't want everybody in the station knowing my little foibles.'

I was sitting with my back to the canteen counter, and a phone started ringing behind me. I raised a finger in a *listen* gesture, and after a few seconds was rewarded with a call of: 'Mr Priest, it's for you,' from the office manageress.

The other three stirred, with mumbles of 'I'll get it,' but I beat them to it.

'Priest here,' I said.

'Detective Inspector Priest?' The voice was new to me.

'That's right. How can I help you?'

'This is George Binks, editor of the *Burdon and Frome Express*. I've just discovered that my deputy has faxed you a photograph that you were interested in.'

'Hello, George. That's right. Ms McLaughlin found what I wanted. Pass on my thanks to her, please.'

He said he would, and asked me why I was interested. I gave him the sanitised version, without mentioning dead bodies, and then he explained why he'd rung. I was sprawling across the canteen counter, leaning on my elbows because the phone cord wasn't long enough. 'Wait a second,' I told him, putting the phone down and going behind the counter. I picked it up again, found a seat and said: 'Go on.'

Annette had said something funny and they all laughed out loud as I approached the table. They quietened as they saw me and Jeff pushed a chair towards me with his feet.

'Are you all right, Chas?' Dave asked. 'You look as if you've seen a ghost.'

I shook my head and sat down.

'What is it, Charlie, bad news?' Annette added, concerned.

'That was the editor of the *Burdon and Frome Express*,' I told them. 'He's just seen a copy of the fax on his desk. Apparently the girl in the photograph ... Caroline Poole ... four years later, in 1984, when she was sixteen ... she was raped and strangled. Nobody was ever done for it.'

Annette said: 'Oh God no!' and her hand reached out and covered mine. She pulled it back as I said: 'I'm afraid so. We'd better take another long hard look at Peter John Latham.'

Chapter 6

I rang my opposite number in Somerset. His euphoria evaporated when I told him that Latham was dead, so there was little point in coming to Yorkshire to interview him. However, we did have the man who killed Latham in our cells, and the two of them went back a long time. Maybe he could throw some candle power on Latham's movements at the time of Caroline's death. It had been a big hunt. Caroline had grown into a beauty, as predicted, and her face had captured the public's imagination. We all remembered her when we saw the later picture that they'd used during the search.

Two detectives from Somerset said they would drive up and interview Silkstone some time on Wednesday. Wednesday morning they rang to say that they'd been delayed and they'd now be with us on Thursday. They confirmed that Latham did not appear to be related to Caroline in any way. Late Wednesday afternoon they said they were on their way and could we have Silkstone and his brief primed for a ten a.m. interview. They sounded keen.

Trouble was, Thursday morning I'd been requested to attend a high-power committee meeting, about catching murderers, chaired by the Deputy Chief Constable. I insisted that someone from Heckley sit-in on the Silkstone interview, and nominated Dave Sparkington.

The DCC considers himself an expert at murder enquiries. Early in his career he arrested a drunken husband who'd stabbed his wife to death in the middle of a bus queue, and that became the launch pad for his rise to fame. Fact is, the best collar he's felt in the last twenty-five years is on his dinner jacket. He'd resigned himself to never having the top job, so he wanted to make his mark by creating the definitive programme for a murder enquiry. Something that would bear his name and be used by police forces world-wide as a template – his word – in their quests to solve the most dastardly crimes of all. His name – Pritchard – would be in all the textbooks, alongside those of Bertillon, Jeffreys and Kojak. And he wanted me to help put it there.

They'd been meeting for months, unknown to me, and had commissioned a video showing how to examine the crime scene during those first, crucial minutes. It was good, which wasn't surprising considering that the combined salaries of those involved would have paid for a battleship. They'd watched a lot of television, and remembered or made notes on how it was done. I couldn't fault it.

'You all know Charlie,' the DCC told them. 'Charlie has caught more murderers than anyone in the division, and I'm sure you'll all be interested to know what he thinks of our little enterprise. Over to you, Charlie. What have we forgotten?'

I stood up, mumbling something, and told them how impressed I was with the film. As Mr

Pritchard had said, those first few minutes were crucial and recording evidence without destroying other evidence was the essence of the early enquiry. 'I thought the way the film demonstrated the importance of reading the complete crime scene, the overall picture, was particularly well demonstrated,' I told them, and the collective glow they radiated nearly ignited my shirt. 'However,' I continued, 'perhaps there is one small point that you've overlooked,' and they shuffled in their seats. All I needed now was to think of one.

I wasn't knocking them. Some of us like to be out on the streets, some of us are more suited to administrative jobs. He couldn't have done mine as effectively as I do, and I couldn't have done his. Put me in charge of discipline and complaints and anarchy would reign. Give me the budget and we'd be bankrupt in a month.

'Context,' I said.

'Context?' the DCC murmured, his head tipped to one side, one finger pressed to his chin.

'Mmm, context,' I repeated. While we were watching their film I'd been thinking about the space video young Daniel had loaned me, and it had come to my rescue. 'The first men on the moon,' I began, 'stuffed their pockets with the first rocks they found and brought them home. Frankly, they were a bit of a disappointment. On the last expedition, Apollo 17, they sent a geologist. He looked for rocks that were out of context, and found some interesting stuff. If you are looking for meteorites, here on earth, you don't look on a beach. You'd never recognise them amongst all those different stones. You go to one of the big deserts, or better still, Antarctica, and set up your stall there. If you find a rock in the middle of an ice field it is out of context, and chances are it came from outer space.' I swept my gaze across them, one by one. Eye contact, that's what it's all about. They were all listening.

'In a murder enquiry,' I continued, 'we do something similar. We look for the unusual, the everyday item that is in the wrong place. If you look in the dead man's shoe cupboard – or the accused's shoe cupboard – and find shoes, no problem. If you look in his shirt cupboard, and there's a pair of shoes tucked under there, start asking questions. One of the suspects in the case I'm on at the moment is as bald as a coot. If I'd found a comb in his pocket I'd have wanted to know about it.'

'For his eyebrows?' someone suggested and everybody roared with laughter.

'I'd've accepted that,' I replied, nodding, and they laughed even more.

It was the buzzword they were looking for. 'Context,' they mumbled as we gathered our papers and prepared to leave. 'Context,' 'Context,' 'Context.'

Bollocks, I thought.

'Charlie,'

It was the DCC. 'Yes, Boss,' I replied.

'Any chance of you giving me a lift to Heckley? My car's in for a service.'

'Sure, no problem. What have we done to deserve a visit?' As if I didn't know.

'I'm wearing my D and C hat, seeing those two prats who got the car stuck between the bollards. Lockwood and Smiles, isn't it? He won't be smiling when I've finished with him, I'll tell you that much.'

'Stiles,' I told him. 'Lockwood and Stiles.'

'Is it? Oh.'

I opened his door but didn't wait to close it behind him, and threw my briefcase on the back seat. On the bypass a speed limit sign went by at well over the stated figure and I eased off the accelerator. If you think being followed by a police car is bad, you should try having the Deputy Chief Constable sitting in your passenger seat with his discipline and complaints hat on. I said: 'Bit over the top, isn't it, Sir, suspending them and you handling it personally?'

'High profile, Charlie,' he explained. 'The media are involved. Made a laughing stock of the whole force. I'm seeing them at two.'

'Right,' I said, nodding in slow motion to indicate how I understood his position.

To change the subject I told him about the Latham case and how young Caroline Poole had suddenly come into the picture, complicating things. He saw it as two clear-ups, with a possible third. We're very extravagant with our clear-up figures. Jamie Walker's death would allow us to put every stolen car for the period he was out of detention down to him, and therefore solved. We'd just have to be careful not to have him doing two at the same time, in different parts of town. Perhaps we'd be able to put Caroline's murder down to Latham. Somerset would close the file, issue a statement saying that they were not looking for anybody else. There might even be a crumb of comfort in it for her parents.

After a silence Pritchard said: 'Never took you for an astronomer, Charlie. Interested in that Star Trek stuff, are you?'

'No, that's fantasy,' I replied. 'I'm more interested in the real thing. Science in general, I suppose. Sometimes it comes in useful, like today.'

'I'm sure you're right, I'm sure you're right. And it's good to have an outside interest. Too much work, and all that.'

'Yep. That's what I think.'

Another long silence, then I decided to give him the works. I said: 'Back in the early seventies, when the space race was in full flow, the Americans sent an unmanned craft to Mars and took a few photographs so the Russians, determined to match or outdo the Yanks, decided to send one to Venus. Unfortunately for them the atmosphere was so hot that the lens cap melted on the front of the camera, and they didn't get any pictures.'

'Ah! Serves the buggers right,' he commented.

'Being Russians,' I continued, 'they announced it as a glorious triumph for the Soviet people and vowed to continue the exploration of space on their behalf. The scientists involved were invited to sit on Lenin's tomb for the next May Day parade. The following year they sent another probe up, at a cost of a few more zillion roubles, but this time with a high melting-point lens cap on the camera. It also carried a device to scoop

149

up some soil from the surface of Venus and analyse it.'

'Clever stuff,' the DCC said. 'Marvellous what they can do, these days.'

'It is, isn't it. And this time, everything worked perfectly. The lens cap flew off and the camera took a photo of Venus's soil, which looked very much like any other soil. Then the arm stretched out and the scoop picked up a sample and brought it back on board for analysis.' I paused to let the pictures form in his mind, then went on: 'Trouble was, the scoop had picked up the lens cap. They spent all that money, travelled a hundred million miles, to analyse something they took with them.'

He looked across at me. 'You're kidding!' he scoffed.

'According to the telly,' I replied.

'The daft buggers.'

'It was hailed as another Soviet success story,' I told him, 'and the scientists were awarded the Order of Lenin and given free holidays on the Black Sea.' We'd arrived at the nick. I freewheeled into my space and yanked the handbrake on.

'Ha ha,' he chuckled. 'That's a good story, Charlie. A good story. With a moral in it, too. Learn from other people's mistakes, eh.'

'That's right, Mr Pritchard,' I said, adding: 'And you've got to admit, it makes writing-off a Ford Escort sound small beer, don't you think?'

He called me a devious sod, but he was grinning as he said it. I hoped I'd done Big Jim and Martin a favour, but I wasn't sure.

Dave and the two 'tecs from Somerset were in

Gilbert's office, waiting for me. They were a DI and a DS, and were a little taken aback when I introduced Pritchard to them. He'd insisted on being present and they weren't used to their top brass being so accessible. After handshakes all round and mugs of tea for me and the DCC, Gilbert said: 'Apparently, Charlie, Latham is totally unrelated to Caroline Poole and there is no obvious reason why he should have that photograph of her.'

Dave said: 'The picture came from the *Burdon and Frome Express*, as we know, but they have no record of the buyer. If it was paid for in cash, in advance, and collected in person, they wouldn't have.'

'Or he could have used a false name,' the DCC suggested, eager to help, but failing.

'So what does Silkstone have to say?' I asked.

The DI was a huge man in a light grey suit, with a clipped moustache and nicotine-stained fingers. He said: 'We'll start before that, if you don't mind. The reason that we decided not to come up yesterday morning was because we'd done some preliminary investigations in the Caroline Poole files. Or, to be more precise, Bob here had.'

Bob, the DS, nodded.

'Bob discovered that the names Latham and Silkstone were in there, would you believe.'

'Go on,' I invited. It had been a big case, and probably every male in Somerset was in there.

'A car was seen in the vicinity of the last sighting of Caroline. A dark one, British Leyland, possibly a Maestro. In the next three months the owners of eighteen thousand dark Maestros were

151

interviewed, without any success. Two of them belonged to Latham and Silkstone. Or, to be more accurate, to the company they worked for: Burdon Home Improvements.'

When we talk to people in large numbers like that, there's not a great deal you can ask. 'Where were you on...' is about it. We insist on an answer, and then ask if anyone was with them, to confirm the story. If there was, and they do, that person is eliminated from enquiries, as we professionals say.

'This is where it gets interesting,' the DI was saying.

'Just one thing,' the DCC interrupted, to prove he was awake, and interested, and really on top of things. 'Are the files computerised?'

'After a fashion,' Bob replied. 'It's an ancient system, from before the mouse was invented, but it works, once you find someone who knows about these things. At the moment, because it was an unsolved case, it's all being updated to the latest HOLMES standard.'

'Good, good. Sorry to chip in.'

'That's OK, Sir. Like I was saying, this is where it gets interesting. Caroline was last seen walking home from a school play, at about nine fifteen. Latham said he was in a pub at the time in question, twenty miles away. He gives one Tony Silkstone as his alibi, plus two women they just happened to talk to. When Silkstone was interviewed he gave Latham's name, plus the two women.'

'Were the women traced?' I asked.

'Yep. It's all here.' He rattled his knuckles

against the file on the desk.

'But you won't have had time to find them again?'

The DI shook his head but didn't speak.

'Right. So what does Silkstone say *now*?'

'Silkstone says,' he began, 'that he was out with his current girlfriend at the time in question, a lady called Margaret Bates. He was a married man, and this was an illicit affair. He later left his wife and married Margaret. She became the late Mrs Silkstone.'

'*Cherchez la femme*,' the DCC mumbled, nodding as if everything was suddenly clear. I was beginning to wish I hadn't brought him. Gilbert caught my eye and winked.

'Meanwhile Latham, we are informed, was playing fast and loose with another woman, called Michelle Webster, who was a friend of Margaret Bates. According to Silkstone he was terrified that his wife would find out, but Michelle was his only alibi for the night Caroline disappeared. He asked Silkstone to say that he was with him, and that they just happened to meet two women in a pub outside Frome, The Lord Nelson. Silkstone agreed, he says, and persuaded the two women to say that they'd all met, briefly, at the pub.'

Dave said: 'They were married to two sisters, weren't they?'

'Yes,' the DI confirmed.

'And then they were knocking off two mates?'

'That's right.'

'It all sounds a bit cosy.'

'It does, doesn't it? But the important thing is

that Silkstone's story tallies with what's in the files. He was with Latham, Latham was with him, in the Lord Nelson. The two women confirmed seeing them there. Bingo – eliminated from enquiries, even though it's a pack of lies.'

'Margaret Silkstone's dead,' I said. 'What about the other one?'

'Michelle Webster?' Bob replied. 'We haven't found her yet, but she's our next priority.'

'It'll be interesting to hear what she has to say,' I stated.

'Ye-es, very interesting,' the DCC agreed.

It was Iqbal's last day with us, Allah be praised, and Annette came to tell me that the troops were meeting in the Bailiwick at home time, to give him a send-off. I told her to make two coffees for us, and bring herself back to my office. Maybe she'd appreciate the assertive approach.

When she was seated opposite me I told her all about the Silkstone interview. She listened gravely, and offered the opinion that lack of alibi and possession of a photograph was hardly enough to convict a man for murder.

'Except that he went on to kill again,' I said.

'That's not evidence,' she stated.

'No,' I agreed, 'but the Somerset boys can go back and look at the case again, with Latham in mind. We haven't seen the file. There might be a load of stuff in there that will all fall into place, now.'

Annette was right, though. We have to be careful. You can't arrest a man because he has a scar on his cheek, and then announce to the court that he has a scar on his cheek, just like the witness said. Latham was only in the frame for Caroline because he possessed her photograph. We couldn't then use that piece of non-evidence to clinch his guilt. I heaved a big sigh and took a bite of chocolate biscuit.

'You look tired, Charlie,' she observed.

'Yeah, a bit.'

'So where does all this leave us?'

'Us?' I queried.

'I meant the Latham case. Our Latham case.'

'Everybody agrees that it's sewn up,' I told her. 'Latham killed Mrs S. Mr S came home and found her, then he killed Latham. Balance of mind, manslaughter, three years top whack, free in one.'

'I thought you weren't happy about it.'

'I'm happy,' I protested. 'The evidence is good. Why does everybody want me to be out of line?'

Her face lit up in a smile. 'Because that's where you belong,' she said.

We sipped our coffee in silence for a few moments, her left hand absentmindedly straightening the papers near the corner of my desk until they were exactly parallel to the edges. 'Do you think of Georgina Dewhurst very often?' she asked.

I wasn't expecting it, and it took me a few moments to reply. Georgina was a little girl, murdered by her stepfather. 'Yes,' I admitted. 'Probably more often than is healthy.'

'I was a WPC on that case,' Annette told me.

'I know. You were with the Child Protection Unit.'

'Good grief!' she exclaimed. 'I'm amazed you noticed.'

I grinned, saying: 'As SIO, it was part of my remit to keep a fatherly eye on all the young WPCs.'

Her smile was warm and comfortable, the best I'd ever seen her give. 'That's when I decided I wanted to be a detective,' she said. 'Not just be a detective, I wanted ... well ... oh, never mind.'

'Wanted what?'

Her smile was still there, fighting to be seen through the blush that crept over her face like a desert sunset. 'Oh, nothing,' she said.

I didn't insist on an answer. People with red hair and freckles blush easily, but it was strange that she never did when answering questions about our clients that some people would find embarrassing. Then, she was totally professional. It was only when... Ah, well, it was something for me to ponder over.

'Tonight,' I began, 'after we've given Iqbal a send-off. We could go for a Chinese again, if you've nothing on. Or a curry. I'm just as well-known in the Last Viceroy as I am in the Bamboo Curtain. You missed a good steak on Saturday, by the way.'

She nodded and said: 'Right. See you in the pub.'

I did paperwork and made phone calls until after half-past six, then walked over the road to the Bailiwick. The lab had done a micro-analysis of various samples taken from the Silkstone bedroom and their report was in the post. Expecting me to wait for it was like asking a child

156

to wait until Easter for his Christmas presents. I asked for a condensed version over the phone.

They'd found skin flakes from all three involved, but not too many from Tony Silkstone. The sheet and duvet cover were probably clean on that day which had made things easier. The footprint scans were relatively straightforward, too, as the whole house had been thoroughly vacuumed. All three of the protagonists had climbed up and down the stairs a couple of times, and last one down was Silkstone himself. No signs of a struggle, no tracks left by trailing heels. All good stuff, which led us nowhere. Mrs Silkstone liked a tidy house and clean sheets for when her lover called, and that was about it. The jammy sod, I thought. Pity about the dagger in the heart.

Jeff and Iqbal were sitting in a corner, behind half-empty glasses, the barman was reading the *Mirror* and the cat was asleep on the jukebox. All-day opening has closed more pubs than any temperance society ever did.

'Ah, Inspector Charlie!' Iqbal exclaimed as I entered. 'What can I purchase for you?'

'Oh, a pint of lager would go down nicely, please,' I replied, and Iqbal went over to the bar.

'Where is everybody?' I whispered to Jeff.

'Dunno. Playing hard to get, by the look of it.'

'Annette said she'd be here.'

'I saw her leave, in her car.'

'Oh.' I tried not to sound disappointed.

Iqbal returned with my drink. He placed it carefully in front of me, saying: 'Jeffrey was just explaining how the legal system in your country,

157

and therefore in mine also, dates back to the twelfth century, and that there are still several anomalies in the statutes book that have no relevance to the modern world.'

'So they say, Iqbal,' I replied, adding: 'Cheers,' and taking a long sip of Holland's major contribution to international goodwill. It was an old chestnut that poor Jeff had dug up to keep the conversation flowing.

'For instance,' he continued, 'Jeffrey tells me that it is still permissible, due to an oversight or perhaps lack of time in Parliament, for the driver of a vehicle who is taken short to urinate against the front offside wheel of the aforementioned vehicle. Is that really so?'

'Not quite,' I told him. 'It's the front nearside wheel.'

'Offside,' Jeff asserted.

'Nearside,' I argued.

'Offside.'

'Uh-uh. Nearside.'

'It's the offside. I looked it up.'

'Are you sure?'

'Positive.'

'Oh heck. No wonder I got some funny looks in the High Street this morning.' One or two of the others arrived, so Iqbal's send-off wasn't a complete disaster. I was just starting my third pint, which is about double my normal intake, these days, when Annette arrived. She was wearing a blue pinstripe suit with a shortish skirt and high heels. I smiled at her and moved along to make some room, but didn't speak. I wasn't sure I could control what might come out if I tried to talk. Someone fetched her an orange juice.

At half past eight people started to make excuses and drift away. We all shook hands with Iqbal, telling him what a delight his stay with us had been, wishing him well for the future. I pointedly asked Annette if she'd like a Chinese, and she said: 'What a good idea.'

I opened the invitation to the others but they all politely declined. Dave had eaten, he said; some had meals waiting for them, and Jeff had defrosted a vegetarian lasagne for himself and Iqbal. 'Just us, then,' I told Annette, and our ears were burning like stubble fires as we walked away from them all.

'Your reputation is now in tatters, you know,' I said as I fastened my seatbelt in her Fiat.

'That's what reputations are for,' she replied, clunking the car into first gear.

We went through the menu and had fun. I introduced Annette to wontons and Mr Ho introduced both of us to various other delicacies he kept bringing from the kitchen. 'Umm, delicious, what is it?' Annette would giggle, and he would reply in Chinese.

'What's that in English?' she'd demand.

'You no rike if I tell you in Engrish,' he'd laugh.

I grabbed the bill when it came. 'This was my idea, and I earn more than you,' I told her, not allowing her the chance to object.

'Oh, er, right, thanks,' she said.

'My pleasure. Any chance of a lift home?'

She wouldn't come in for coffee. We were sitting outside my house with the car's headlights still on and the engine running. Switching off, stopping the engine, would have been a statement of intent. It didn't come.

'At the risk of being politically incorrect,' I began, 'you look stunning, Annette.'

'Oh, I can take political incorrectness like that,' she replied with a smile.

'Good. I've enjoyed tonight.'

'Mmm, me too.'

After a silence I said: 'Are you going away this weekend?'

The smile slipped away and she fiddled with a button on the front of her jacket. 'Yes,' she replied, very softly.

One of the neighbours came walking down the pavement with his little dog on a lead, returning from its evening crap at the other end of the street. I have very considerate neighbours. 'Is he a good bloke?' I asked.

Annette turned to face me. 'How do you know it's a bloke?' she asked.

I shook my head. 'I don't, but it usually is.'

'Normally. You mean normally.'

'Usually, normally. They're just words.'

'I'm the station dyke, Charlie,' she replied. 'Surely you know that.'

'You're a great police officer and I'm very fond of you. That's all I know.'

'Would it bother you if I were?'

'What? Gay?'

'Mmm.'

'No.'

'Why not?'

I was tired. I hadn't thought out my arguments. Or my feelings. 'I don't know. It just wouldn't,'

160

was the best I could manage.

The button came off in her fingers and she gave a tiny snort of dismay. 'They don't make them like they used to,' I said.

'It's been loose all night,' she replied.

'You could've had that coffee, and I could've sewn it back on for you.'

The smile came back. 'Role reversal,' she said. 'I'm all in favour of that.'

'They teach you to sew buttons on in the SAS,' I told her.

'Were you in the SAS?'

'Mmm. Under twelve's branch. They threw me out because I wouldn't wear the oblong sunglasses.'

She laughed, just a little, and called me a fool. And Charlie. 'You are a fool, Charlie' she said, in the nicest possible way.

'Thank you for a pleasant evening, ma'am,' I said, opening the door. 'Don't be late, in the morning.'

'What time do you want picking up?' she asked.

'God!' I exclaimed, pulling the door closed again. 'My car's still outside the nick, isn't it. Um, in that case, whenever.'

'About twenty to eight?'

'Yeah, that's fine, If I can get up. I think I'm slightly pissed.'

I opened the door just enough for the interior light to come on. Annette said: 'For the record, yes, he is a good bloke.'

'Your friend in York?'

'Mmm.'

'Does he deserve you?'

161

'I think so. He's a schoolteacher, and has two daughters, seven and nine.'

'Divorced?'

'Widower.'

'Rich?'

'He's a schoolteacher.'

'Right,' I said. 'Right.' I felt hollow inside. A schoolteacher I could deal with. I'd ask the local boys to waste him and arrange for the coastguard to drop his weighted body off the edge of the continental shelf. Not the girls, though. I couldn't be that much of a bastard.

'Annette...' I began.

'Mmm.'

'Would you be willing to ... you know ... make allowances for my intoxicated state if I ... sort of ... transgressed, type of thing?'

'I'm not sure,' she replied, warily. 'What do you have in mind?'

'Um, well, I was just wondering, er, if there was any chance of, um, a goodnight kiss?'

She leaned over and gave me a loud peck on the cheek, completely catching me off guard. It wasn't quite what I had in mind, but it was a start. 'There,' she said.

'Thank you,' I told her, pushing the door wide.

'Charlie...'

I twisted back to face her. 'Mmm.'

'You should get pissed more often.'

Friday morning I put eggs, bacon and tomatoes from the fridge out on the worktop, together with corn flakes, bread, marmalade, a tub of Thank Christ It's Not Butter, the frying pan and the

162

toaster. It was my attempt at humour, but Annette waited in the car for me. I finished my coffee and went out.

'Another day, another collar,' I said, winding myself into the Fiat's passenger seat. Italian cars make no concessions towards the different body shapes of their European neighbours. Short legs and long arms – take it or leave it. 'Thank you, Ms Brown. The office, please.'

But there were no collars to feel, that day. Some of the team were out looking at burglary scenes, others, me included, caught up with paperwork and reading. Dave went out for sandwiches at lunchtime, and brought me hot pork in an oven bottom cake, with stuffing. They don't do them like that in M & S. And at a fraction of their price.

In the afternoon the remains of Jamie Walker, loosely arranged in some sort of order, were buried with full Christian pomp. His mother prostrated herself on the coffin, for the *Gazette*'s photographer, then repeated the scene, with sound effects, when local TV arrived. Practice makes perfect. He was a good son, she told them: everybody loved him and his mischievous ways. This wouldn't have happened if the police had been more firm with him, and she was considering taking legal action against them. Nobody from the job went to the funeral, under orders, but we all caught it on TV later that evening.

Last phone call before I left work was from Bob, the Somerset DS. 'We've traced Michelle Webster,' he told me. 'She married and changed

163

her name, but she's now divorced and has reverted back to her maiden name.'

You can't revert forward, I thought. 'Have you spoken to her?' I asked.

'No, Mr Priest. She's living in Blackpool, would you believe. Our chief super's making noises about expenses and thinks there's no need for us to see her ourselves. He said to let someone local interview her. He wants to wait until after the inquests then issue a statement saying that we are not looking for anybody else, and that would be the Caroline Poole case cleared up.'

'Which would please the relatives, I suppose.'

'That's what he said.'

'How would you feel if someone from here nipped across and had a word with Michelle?'

'No problem, Mr Priest. That's partly why I'm ringing you. You're a couple of hundred miles nearer to her than we are.'

'Call me Charlie, Bob. Everybody else does.'

'Oh, right.'

'Give me the address. I'll try to send someone next week, and let you know the outcome.'

'We'd appreciate that, Charlie. Thanks for your help.'

'My pleasure.'

And it would be, too. Blackpool might be the last resort, but a day there with Annette sounded a good way of adding the finishing touches to the Latham case. I straightened my blotter, washed my mug and went home.

Jamie's funeral, on TV, made me angry. 'You should get pissed more often,' Annette had told

164

me. No way. I'd staggered down that road a long time ago, and didn't like the scenery. My Sony rasta-blaster holds three CDs. I chose carefully, then carried it into the garage where the unfinished painting leaned against the wall. I laid the tubes of colour out in the same order I always use and screwed the caps off. Yellow ochre, to start with, I decided. I squeezed a six-inch worm of it onto the palette and dipped a number twelve filbert into the glistening pigment.

The knock on the garage door came about halfway through the second playing of Mahler's Symphony No. 5. The neighbour was standing there with his little dog. I stared at him, brush in one hand, palette knife in the other.

'Um, er, your radio's on a bit loud, Mr Priest, if you don't mind me saying so.'

It was. That's how you listen to Mahler. 'I'm sorry,' I said. 'I didn't know you could hear it outside.'

'Well you can, and it's keeping Elsie awake.'

'I really am sorry,' I repeated, because I was. I like to consider myself the invisible neighbour. 'I was painting. What time is it?'

'About ten to one.'

'What!' I exclaimed. 'I didn't realise it was so late.'

'She's been in bed since just after the play ended. It's her waterworks, you know.'

'Really. Well it won't happen again.' I moved back into the garage and switched off the CD. He stepped into the vacant space in the doorway and his gaze settled on the nearly-finished picture. 'It's supposed to represent China,' I explained, as

I wiped away the blob of cerulean blue that I'd accidentally dabbed on the Sony.

'China?' he repeated.

'Mmm.'

'China China?'

'That's right.' As opposed to cup-and-saucer china, I think he meant. 'That's the Great Wall, and that's a panda.' I pointed to the images, some strong, some barely hinted at, and read them off. 'The Long March, Tiananmen Square, coolie hats, bonsai, typical scenery, Chairman Mao.'

'I don't like this modern stuff,' he declared.

'This is hardly modern,' I told him. 'I don't like much of the really modern stuff.' I manoeuvred him outside and walked him towards the gate. 'And apologise to your wife about the noise, please. It won't happen again.'

'The wife? She's stone deaf, like me. Neither of us ever hears a thing once we switch off.'

'Oh. You said, er, Elsie.'

'Elsie.' He tugged the dog's lead. 'This is Elsie.'

'Right. Er, right.'

Next morning at ten a.m. I rang Michelle Webster, provider of alibi for a child murderer, and arranged to see her in the afternoon. Don't ask me why, but sometimes I feel more at ease when dealing with the criminally insane.

The rain started as soon as I passed over the tops and began the long descent into Lancashire. Having Annette with me would have been pleasant, but she was in York with her friend, and the thrill of the chase was more than I could resist. I was quite pleased about the rain – maybe

166

it would keep the traffic down. It didn't, and we had the usual stop-go on the M6. There's this crackpot idea that the more roads you build, the more traffic you create. It all started after they opened the M25. Two million Londoners apparently said: 'Ooh, good, they've built a new road. Let's dash out and buy a car.' It's now used as an argument for not making new roads or widening existing ones, and the M6 is doomed to permanent gridlock.

Michelle Webster had given me extremely detailed directions, which I hadn't listened to, and sounded determined that I shouldn't get lost. All I recorded was that she was on the south side, but not quite St Anne's. There's posh, I thought, as I looked at the map: they've retained the apostrophe.

When I was in the general vicinity I asked, and soon was creeping along a street of respectable, if slightly dilapidated, pre-war semis. They had shingled bay windows and mature trees in the gardens. I saw the number and parked between an ageing Range Rover and a Toyota Celica with a dented corner. Michelle Webster opened her front door before my finger was off the button, halfway through the second bar of *Strangers in the Night*.

She looked sixty, pushing nine. Little girls like to dress up in their mother's clothes, I'm told. This was serious role reversal. She was wearing a pink micro skirt, black silk blouse, black tights and black suede boots that would have come well above her knees had not the tops been turned down, cavalier fashion. I remembered the joke

167

about the woman who went to the doctors complaining of thrush. He gave her a prescription to take to the cobblers, to have two inches taken off the top of her boots.

'Mrs Michelle Webster?' I asked. I'd done a calculation on the way over and reckoned she'd be in her mid forties.

'It's *Miss* Webster,' came the reply, as she stood to one side to let me through with hardly a glance at my ID. A little dog came yapping towards me out of the gloom of the hallway. Michelle said: 'Hush, Trixie,' and picked it up. It had lots of hair, and looked as if it had just escaped from a serious accident with a tumble drier. 'There-there darling, it's only a nice policeman come to see Mummy,' she told it, planting a kiss into the middle of the ball of fur, and for a moment their hair merged like two clouds of noxious gasses after a chemical spillage.

'So what's he done now?' Michelle asked with a touch of glee in her voice, when we were seated in her front room, which I suspected was called the parlour. She'd moved a menagerie of fluffy toys to make room for me, and straightened the antimacassars on the chair arms. There were pictures on the walls of various stars of stage and screen, with autographs scrawled across them by a girl with a rubber stamp in an office in Basingstoke.

'Who?' I asked.

'Greg, my ex. It's about him. Isn't it?'

It wasn't, but I did some gentle probing. Greg was part owner of a club in town, and into all sorts of wheeling and dealing. She could tell me stuff that would make my hair curl. Mafia? Don't talk to her about the Mafia.

So I didn't. 'You were in showbusiness?' I asked, flapping a hand towards the photos and recognising Roy Orbison in a central position amongst all the bouffant hair and gleaming teeth of the ones who didn't make it to his level.

'Not on the performing side.' She smiled and crossed her legs, which was difficult with the footwear she had on. 'Not enough talent, unfortunately,' she explained with a modest shrug. 'No, Greg and I were more into management and promotions.'

'You were evidently successful at it.' The house was probably hers, and prices in Blackpool are no doubt above average.

'Oh, we were, we were. They were great days. And then the shit ran off with a dancer from the Tower whose cup size was as far as she ever made it through the alphabet. The fat little cow.'

'I haven't come to talk about Greg,' I told her, anxious to steer the conversation back on course. 'I want to talk to you about people you knew when you lived in Burdon, back in the eighties.'

'Burdon? That was a long time ago.'

'1984, to be precise. Did you know a man called Peter Latham?'

She pretended she wasn't sure – 'There were so many, Inspector' – until she realised that I wasn't going to be more forthcoming. Then she remembered him. I told her that he was dead, as was her friend Margaret Silkstone, nee Bates, under suspicious circumstances, and we'd be very grateful for any help she could give. After a little weep it

169

all came out.

They were a foursome: she and Peter Latham; Margaret and Tony Silkstone. They met three nights a week at a pub near Frome – the Nelson – where there was music and dancing, and paired off when the alcohol and hormones started to work. Peter, she said, was kind and relaxed. Unlike Silkstone, who was a show-off, always wanting to have more, do better than anyone else. They were married to two sisters, which was why they knew each other. Peter's wife, Michelle said, was a 'hatchet-faced cow, and frigid with it.' I remembered the wedding photo I'd seen, of a tall brittle blonde who towered over him, and decided that the description could be accurate.

The affair came to an end when Latham was breathalysed and banned from driving. They struggled to meet for a while, playing gooseberry with Silkstone and Margaret, but Michelle came to Blackpool for a holiday and met Greg. End of a beautiful friendship.

'He was a lovely man,' she sobbed, for the tears had started again. 'He knew the names of things. Birds and flowers an' stuff like that. And poetry. He knew whole poems. Not the ones you did at school. Daft ones, that you can understand, by him from Liverpool. Paul McCartney's brother.'

And had a penchant for sex with young girls. I thought.

'Not like Tony,' she continued. 'All he knew was the price of cars.' She sniffed and dabbed her nose with a tissue. 'I married Greg because he was a bit in-between, if you follow me. Except with him it was show-biz.'

I wasn't sure I did follow, but I skipped asking for an explanation. 'You were obviously fond of him,' I said. 'I'm sorry I had to bring you bad news.' But now for the *bad* news. I said: 'Do you remember when a girl called Caroline Poole went missing?'

She did. Nobody who lived in Burdon would ever forget it. 'It was the biggest manhunt ever held in Somerset,' I told her. 'Everybody was questioned, including Tony and Peter. According to the records they said they were with you and Margaret that night. Do you remember?'

She pursed her lips and shrugged, warily, and I imagined her growing pale under the makeup. Lipstick was beginning to bleed away from the corners of her mouth like aerial views of the Nile delta. 'I never asked you if you'd like a drink!' she exclaimed, pulling herself to her feet. 'What must you think of me?' Trixie, who was curled up on her lap, fell to the floor.

There was a bar in the corner of the room, behind me, with a quilted façade and optics on the mirrored wall. A personal replica of the real thing for those times when you can't face the world. I twisted in my seat as she poured clear liquid from a decanter. 'What would you like, Chief Inspector?' she asked.

There was no coffee percolator quietly gurgling on the counter. 'Not for me, thank you,' I said. Glass clinked against glass, suede swish-swashed against suede and she resumed her seat, slowly easing herself down into it like a forklift truck lowering a crate of eggs. If it was gin she now held in her hand she'd be talking in hieroglyphics

171

before she was halfway through it. 'Whose idea was it to lie?' I asked, getting straight to the point.

She took a long drink, slurped, gurgled and coughed. 'I don't know.' The end of Trixie that didn't have a curly tail looked up at her, then decided not to bother. The dog sloped off and crashed out on a folded sheepskin rug near the fireplace.

'Did Peter ask you?'

'Ask me what?'

'Did he ask you to say he was with you?'

'No. I don't think so. I'd stopped seeing him by then.'

'By when?'

'By when the police were asking questions. It was months after the girl was murdered.'

'Was it Silkstone, then?'

'I don't know. It was a long time ago. I used to drink a lot...' She downed half of the tumbler to demonstrate how it was done and re-crossed her legs.

'Was it Margaret's idea. Did she persuade you to say that you saw Peter and Tony in the Lord Nelson, that night?'

'I was never very good at times, and days of the week.'

'Was it Margaret's idea?'

'I think so.'

'What did she say?'

She downed the last of whatever it was and stared gloomily at the empty glass. Her legs uncrossed themselves, as if she were about to go for another, but she decided not to and sank back in the chair. There'd be plenty of time for that when

172

the nice policeman had gone.

'She said that Peter was scared stiff that his wife would find out about, you know, me an' 'im. We used to go to the Nelson to hear this group. They were called the Donimoes ... the Dominoes. Gerry and the Donimoes. They did all Roy's stuff. When Gerry sang In Dreams they used to dim all the lights, an' the group, they used to turn their backs to the audience, as if to say that this was 'is spot. All 'is.' She closed her eyes and the savage lips melted into a smile.

'*In dreams I walk with you,*' she sang, very softly, her head weaving gently from side to side. '*In dreams I talk to yo-ou.*'

'It's a lovely song,' I said. 'Do you like it?'

'Mmm. You were telling me what Margaret said to you?'

She looked at the glass, realised it was still empty and leaned forward to place it on the coffee table. Her fingers fumbled, lost their grip, and it rolled on to the floor. It was a heavy tumbler, cut glass, and the rug was luxurious, so it didn't break. I picked it up and placed it just out of her reach.

'What did she say?'

'She shaid ... she said ... that Peter had told Tony that he didn't 'ave a ... a ... a nalibi for the night that little girl went missing. He was wiv me, she shaid, she ... said, bur 'e couldn't tell the police that, cos 'is wife would find out.'

'What did she tell you to do?'

'Just that we saw 'em in the pub. The Nelson. I was wiv Margaret, an' we saw these two blokes, called Peter and Tony. They dint buy us a drink

173

or anything, but we spoke to them. If the police came and asked where I was on that Wednesday night, I'd to say I was in the Nelson, wiv 'er.'

'And did they?'

'Did what?'

'Did the police ask you where you were?'

'Yes, but ages after. I could 'ardly remember.'

'And was Peter with you, that Wednesday night?'

'That's the funny fing. I didn't realise until I fought about it. We went to the Nelson free times a week, when the Donimoes ... the Dominoes ... were playing. But they were on a Sunday and on a Tuesday and on Thursday nights. Not We'ns-days. We never went on We'nsdays. It was old time dancing on We'nsdays.'

I made her a black coffee, but I couldn't do much about the brewery in the corner. Leaving her alone with her real or imagined memories, a CD of Roy Orbison's greatest breakdowns and a gallon of spirits was like playing Russian Roulette with her, but I didn't see what else I could do. Hopefully she'd collapse and sleep it off. She must have been half cut when I arrived, so she knew the score.

The rain drove all the day-trippers away early, so it was a twenty-minute crawl to reach the motorway. I stopped at the Birch services for a meal but changed my mind when I saw the prices. I always do. Instead it was a trout from Sainsbury's, with Kenyan green beans and new potatoes, followed by half a pint of strawberry Angel Delight. I did the trout under the grill, with lashings of butter, and it was delicious.

I hadn't lied to Michelle. I saw Roy Orbison, once, at Batley Variety Club, and he was brilliant. I took Vanessa, my wife, soon to be ex-wife. He sounded exactly the same live as he did on record, which is more than you can say for most of them. I went upstairs to the spare bedroom, humming *Pretty Woman*, and logged on to the computer that lives in there.

'Michelle Webster admitted that she lied when asked by the investigating officer if Peter Latham was with her on the night Caroline Poole disappeared,' I typed. I expanded the story, with all the dates and legal-speak to make it sound professional. As an afterthought, I added that she was totally kettled when I interviewed her, and was an unreliable witness, open to manipulation. When it was finished I ran off two copies and deleted the file.

Monday morning I'd post it to Somerset, augmented with a phone call. They'd use the information to pin a sixteen-year-old girl's murder on Latham, and close the case. It wasn't much, but he had, after all, gone on to commit another murder up in Yorkshire, hadn't he?

Meanwhile, we'd reinforce our case against the man by regarding him as someone who had killed before, down in Somerset. It wasn't what might be called a Catch 22, but there ought to be a name for it. Ah well, I thought, the coroners will have to sort that one out.

Latham did leave his sperm all over Margaret Silkstone's thighs, I remembered as I logged off, and felt happier. Were he still alive he'd be having

175

difficulties arguing that small fact away. Thank God for sperm samples – where would we all be without them? Jeff Caton had loaned me the video of Ridley Scott's *Blade Runner*, with Harrison Ford, and I watched it while sipping lager I'd brought from the supermarket. It was the later version, the director's cut, with the voice-over removed. Sorry, Mr Scott, but you ruined it. Sometimes, the man in charge just doesn't know best. You can be so close to something that you don't see the wet fish coming until it slaps you in the chops.

Monday morning I followed a double-decker bus all the way into town. Since the buses were regulated – or was it de-regulated? – they've started painting them in fancy colours and allowing different companies to sponsor individual buses. Sometimes you don't know if it's the one you want coming down the road or a bunch of New Age travellers, On the back of most of them, covering the panel that conceals the engine, it states: *Bus advertising works. You're reading this, aren't you?*

Dave's and Annette's cars were already in their places when I swung into the station yard. Latham's ex-wife, who lives in Pontefract, started work at the local hospital at ten a.m., and they'd arranged to drive over and catch her early. I filled them in with my weekend discoveries but suggested they concentrate initially on our enquiry, not Somerset's. The Caroline Poole case was muddying the waters, and it wasn't fair to Latham to use it to pre-judge him.

Dave said: 'Where's our rock, then?' to change the subject. What he meant was don't tell your grandma how to suck eggs.

'What rock?'

'Our Blackpool rock. You had a day at the seaside and you didn't bring us any rock back?'

'It was raining. I didn't hang about.'

He turned to Annette. 'Shows how much he thinks of us.'

Annette looked thoughtful. She said: 'So Latham didn't have an alibi for the Caroline Poole job.'

'No, he didn't.'

'Which means, of course, that Silkstone probably didn't have one, either.'

'Yes, Annette,' I agreed. 'That thought had occurred to me, too.'

'Unless he was alone with Margaret at the time,' Dave suggested.

'But she's dead,' Annette and I replied, simultaneously.

They went off to Pontefract and I went upstairs for the morning prayer meeting. Gilbert huffed and puffed and thought I was wasting time on details when the big picture was as plain as a gravy stain. The Caroline Poole case wasn't ours. End of story. Latham killed Margaret. Silkstone killed Latham. End of story.

'But we don't know that Silkstone wasn't involved with Margaret's death,' I argued.

'Well if he was he's got away with it. Good luck to the bloke, we can't win 'em all, Charlie.'

Gareth Adey offered his considered opinion, which agreed with Gilbert's. It always does. 'I think Mr Wood is right, Charlie,' he told me. 'Good grief, two murders cleared up is pretty good going by anybody's standards. Well done, I say, and I bet the Chief Constable is thinking the same way. Now, can we talk about the new CCTV in the market place?'

So we did. Three minutes about two murders, half an hour about his poxy TV cameras. 'Well done, Charlie. Two murders cleared up. Maybe you'll get a commendation.' And what about frigging justice, I thought?

I rang Michelle Webster when I was back in my office, to satisfy myself that she was OK. 'I was worried about you,' I told her, after the formalities. 'That was rather a large G and T you made yourself.' She giggled, saying that there was no T in it, and hoped that she had behaved herself. We chatted for a while, had a laugh and said goodbye. She never asked about Latham or his funeral, never mentioned the man who killed him, never asked how her friend Margaret had died. I replaced the phone and wondered why I'd bothered.

Somerset were more interested, when I rang them, and thanked me for my efforts. As Gilbert said, they were regarding it as a clear-up. In the middle of our conversation someone in the big office held up a phone and mouthed: 'For you,' at me, through the glass. I shook my head and waved the one I was holding.

He took a message then came to deliver it, leaning in the doorway of my little office until I'd finished. 'That was the Jeff from the court,' he said. 'The magistrate has remanded Silkstone in

178

custody and he's been taken to Bentley. His solicitor has intimated that they'll be pleading guilty to manslaughter, with provocation and lashings of mitigating circumstances.'

'Hey, that's good news,' I said. 'I expected him to be let loose. Good for the CPS, for once.'

'A short, sharp shock,' he replied. 'Teach him what he's in for. They'll free him next time.'

'Yep,' I agreed.

We had a loose-ends meeting at four o'clock. Annette placed a huge bag of Pontefract cakes and one of all-sorts on the table in front of me. 'Where did you get these?' I asked.

'Pontefract.'

'They do sell them in the supermarket,' I argued.

'Not fresh ones, straight from the oven.'

I found a coconut mushroom and popped it into my mouth, saying: 'Dese are by faborites,' as I passed the bag across the table.

'There's a castle there,' Dave said.

'Where Richard the Second was murdered,' Annette added.

'It's an interesting place.'

'And stinks of liquorice.'

'But it's quite a pleasant smell, really.'

'And every other building is a pub.'

'OK, OK, spare me the travelogue,' I protested as I sucked a piece of coconut from between my teeth. 'Next weekend we'll all have a day out in Pontefract. Now can we talk about you-know-what, please.'

Other information had come in and been

179

collated. Most significant were the facts that Silkstone and his wife had blazing rows and were in severe financial difficulties. The car was leased and he'd slipped behind a couple of times with his mortgage payments. His salary, we discovered, was quite modest, and the hefty commissions that he was used to weren't coming his way. Margaret's death had given him a timely leg-up out of the shit creek.

Neighbours confirmed that Latham was a regular Wednesday afternoon visitor. No bedroom curtains were pulled across after he arrived, but it wasn't possible for anyone to see into the room.

'Actually,' Dave confided, 'between us and these four walls, it's quite pleasant in the afternoon, with the curtains open.'

'Put that in your report,' I told him. The phone in my office rang and I went to answer it. It was the CPS solicitor to ask if I'd received the news about Silkstone. I said I had and congratulated him on a minor victory. I suspected that was what he wanted to hear. When I went back into the main office Dave was in full swing.

'...and my dad told me to keep a big sweet jar under the bed,' he was saying, 'and to put a dried pea in it every time we made love. And then, after I was forty, to take one out every time we made love. He said that nobody ever emptied the jar.'

'Subject normal,' Annette explained as I resumed my seat.

'And have you emptied it?' somebody asked.

'Not yet,' I interrupted, 'but I'm helping him. Where were we?'

Latham's wife had married, and divorced, for a second time. Silkstone had given her husband a job as a salesman, first in double glazing, then in the financial sector, but he did it very reluctantly. It just wasn't his scene, she'd said, but the money was good. Apparently his affable manner took punters by surprise, and they trusted him, so he did reasonably well without trying too hard. Silkstone came north because of the job, and Latham followed him, but his marriage failed soon after.

'What went wrong?' I asked.

'Partly boredom, partly the affair,' Annette replied. 'She was attracted to him because of his laid back approach to life, but it quickly paled. At first she couldn't believe that he'd had enough go in him to have an affair. Coming up here was a fresh start, but it didn't work out.'

'And what about Caroline Poole? Did you get round to her?'

'Yes, Boss. She remembered, with a bit of prompting, that Peter's car was the same type that we were looking for. She thinks she mentioned it to him and he just shrugged it off. They never discussed it again.'

'But Latham wasn't at home with her on the night in question?'

'She doesn't think so, and he didn't ask her for an alibi. It was all a non-event as far as she was concerned.'

'Anything else?'

'Yes. She doesn't believe that he killed Margaret. He was the least-violent person imaginable, she said.'

181

'She couldn't believe he was having an affair, either,' I pointed out.

'I know,' Annette agreed, with a shrug.

Dave said: 'I reckon that's about as far as we can go with this, Chas. We've done our bit.'

'Yep,' I replied, ' that just about sews it up. Now answer me this. If bus advertising works, why do they have to advertise it on the backs of all the buses?'

Dave said: 'Eh?' and Annette's expression implied something similar.

'Why,' I repeated, 'do they have to advertise bus advertising? It obviously doesn't work, otherwise they'd advertise something that pays them, like Coca-Cola or Fenning's Fever Cure, wouldn't they?'

'Is that what you've been thinking about all day?' Dave grumbled.

'It was just a thought, troubling my enquiring mind,' I replied, but neither of them looked convinced, 'OK,' I continued, clapping my hands briskly, 'reports on my desk by nine in the morning, please. Then we can concentrate on keeping the streets of Heckley safe for the good burghers of this town. Mr Wood wants us to restore the times when you could drop your wage packet on the pavement and it would still be there when you went back for it.'

'It would now,' Dave said. 'Lost in all the rubbish. And nobody would recognise a wage packet, these days.'

'What's Fenning's Fever Cure?' Annette asked.

Chapter 7

A couple of years ago Annabelle and I had a lightning drive down to London to see an exhibition of Pissarro's work at the Barbican. I like him, the reviews were good, and it was an excuse for a day out. On the way home, late that night, Annabelle was making conversation to keep me awake. 'If you could have one painting,' she began, 'just one, to hang above your fireplace, which would it be?'

'Of Pissarro's?' I asked.

'No. Anybody's'

'Oh, in that case, a Picasso. Any Picasso.'

'Except him.' She knew I was a Picasso freak.

'Right.' I gave it a long thought. We were approaching Leicester Forest services and I asked if she wanted to stop. She didn't. 'I think it would be a Gauguin,' I told her.

'A Gauguin? I've never heard you championing him before.'

'Oh, I'm very fond of him,' I said, 'but there's one in particular that gets me.' I thumped my chest for emphasis, saying: 'Right here.'

'I know!' she exclaimed. 'One with lots of nubile South Sea Islanders showing their breasts.'

'Where do you get these ideas about me?' I protested. 'Actually, it's a self portrait. Gauguin is just coming home from a walk, and his

183

landlady is greeting him at the garden gate. It's called *Bonjour, Monsieur Gauguin*. He captures the moment beautifully. Haven't you ever seen it?'

'No, I don't think I have.'

'You'll like it. The colours glow like a stained glass window. I have it in a book somewhere.'

The conversation was preserved in my mind with almost every other word that passed between us, but I hadn't expected it to be recalled in this way. The Bart Simpson fridge magnet was drawing my thoughts back to Peter Latham's house, or, more precisely, to the postcard that it pinned against the cold metal. It was the same picture as I'd told Annabelle I'd like to have on my wall, before all others: Gauguin's self portrait, *Bonjour, Monsieur Gauguin*.

There was no message written on the back, no pinhole through it. It was as blank as a juror's expression. Cards like that are only available in galleries. Had Latham bought it for himself, because he liked it above all the other offerings on show? That was something for me to ponder over.

Tuesday morning we hit the headlines. The *UK News*, Britain's foremost tabloid, written for Britons by Britons, with lots of white British bosoms for red-blooded British men, carried yet another world exclusive. Yesterday it had been the convent schoolgirl with the fifty-two inch bust – *Only another seven days to her sweet sixteenth, then all will be revealed!* – today it was: *Why is this man in jail?* above a near life-size

184

photograph of a tearful Tony Silkstone.

Silkstone, we were told when we turned to page five, was living in a prison hell because he had rid the world of a scumbag. Latham was a child killer and rapist who had gone on to kill Silkstone's wife. Cue blurred holiday snap of Margaret, wearing a bikini. Silkstone had done what any good citizen would have done – what the courts should have done years ago – and made sure Latham wouldn't be raping or murdering anybody else. Good riddance to him, but meanwhile poor Silkstone had to wait in an overcrowded prison, three to a cell, while the geriatric legal system, aided and abetted by a police force only interested in statistics, argued what to do with him. *Give him a medal, says the UK News!* On the next page was a picture of Caroline Poole – not the sports day one, thank God – and all the gory details of how her violated young body was found, back in 1984.

Prendergast! I thought. Bloody Prendergast! The courts are supposed to be isolated from public opinion, but if you believe that you probably still think that Christmas is the time of goodwill to all men. And why shouldn't the public have their say, you may argue: it's the public's law, after all. And while we are at it, let's bring back lynching.

Wednesday I went to the Spinners with Dave and we had a good chinwag. We've lapsed a few times, lately. Thursday night I ate at home, alone. I didn't have the opportunity to ask Annette if she fancied a Chinese, and I didn't go looking for her. No point in appearing eager.

Summer fell on the third of July. Otherwise, it slipped by in the usual mixture of showers and mild days. As the saying goes: If you don't like the English weather, just wait ten minutes. I did some walking, finished the painting and one Saturday, in an unprecedented burst of enthusiasm, dug all the shrubs out of the garden. They weren't as labour-saving as I'd planned, so decided to sow annuals from now on.

It was the silly season. A family in Kent – Mum, Dad and two kids – changed their names so that their initials matched the numberplate on their Mitsubishi Shogun. It was easier and cheaper than doing things the other way round. Heckley's first space probe exploded on the launch pad up on the moors, and a man was drowned trying to sail across the Channel in a shopping trolley.

In the job, we had the opportunity to catch up with burglaries and muggings, and made a few good arrests. A female drug dealer whose home we were raiding one morning drove over Dave's foot while trying to escape. There were all the usual 'hopping mad' jokes, and for a few days he came to work with it heavily bandaged, minus shoe. I appointed him office boy, and the troops started calling him Big Foot behind his back. The new CCTV cameras were installed in the market place and soon earned their keep, and the chief constable's daughter was fined and banned for driving while pissed. That cheered everybody up.

Annette took two weeks' leave. I didn't ask her if she was going away, but a card from the Dordogne appeared on the office notice board.

The day she was due back I booked into my favourite boarding house in the Lakes. The weather stayed fine, sharpened by the first suggestions of an early autumn, and I bagged a few good peaks.

'Nice holiday?' I asked, when I saw her again.

'Mmm,' she nodded, without too much enthusiasm. Ah well, I thought, she has been back at work for a whole week. 'And you?' she asked.

'Mmm,' I echoed, adding: 'You caught the sun.' Her freckles were in full flush against a background hue several shades deeper than usual.

She blushed, adding to the rainbow effect. 'I try to stay out of it,' she said, 'but you caught it, too.'

'The weather,' I explained. 'I caught the weather.'

On August 19th Sophie learned that she'd earned three straight As, and the following day a magistrate allowed Tony Silkstone out on bail. Swings and roundabouts. We knew he was likely to be released but we'd opposed it, and I'd gone to court in case the magistrates had any questions. They didn't. Silkstone was unlikely to abscond as he'd phoned the police himself to confess, and psychiatric reports were available which said that he was sane and unlikely to offend again. Coming home twice to find your wife murdered and raped by your best friend would be downright bad luck. What probably clinched it was the fact that he had a job to go to. Heckley magistrates' court hadn't tried anyone with a job for nearly two years. Silkstone had been inside on remand for eight weeks, which would be deducted from any sentence he was given, and there were conditions to his bail. He had to surrender his passport, reside at The Garth, Mountain Meadows, and report to Heckley nick twice per week. We wouldn't be inviting him to stay for tea and biscuits.

While I was slogging up Dollywagon Pike, sweating off a hangover, the troops had collared a burglar who put his hand up to just about every outstanding blag on our books. I saw it as making the citizens of Heckley safer in their beds at night, to Gilbert it was an opportunity to make our clear-up figures look better than Olga Korbut's on a good day. Dave and Annette sat him in the front seat of Dave's car and took him for a ride. He took pride in his work, liked to show off about his nefarious deeds. Put him in the company of an attractive lady and he sang like the Newport Male Voice Choir the time they beat the All Blacks. I didn't like using Annette that way, didn't like the thought of his hungry eyes dragging over her contours, stripping her naked, but sometimes I have to act like a grown-up. It's not easy for me.

'A hundred and nineteen,' she sighed, five fifteen Thursday evening, as she flopped into the spare chair in my office.

'That'll do,' I told her. 'No more days out for Laddo with my glamorous assistant. Do they all check out?'

'The ones we've looked at do. He remembers how he got in, what he took, the make of every-thing and how much he sold it for. A hundred and nineteen householders are going to find out that their burglary – *their* burglary – has been taken into consideration. All that grief, and he walks. He doesn't give a toss about any of them. It doesn't seem fair, Boss.'

She was right. He'd stand trial for the one we caught him for and, if found guilty, the judge would be informed of the other offences. The TICs. They'd make a marginal difference to his sentence, his slate would be wiped clean and our figures would look good. Everybody happy except the victims. But villains don't commit crimes against individuals, they commit them against society. It might be your house that is burgled, your car that is stolen and torched, but the crime is against the state, so tough luck.

'It's not fair,' I agreed, 'but that's the law, and our job ends when we nab him and gather the evidence. Don't worry about it, Annette. If he gets a light sentence and never does another crime, then the system has worked. If he keeps on blagging, we'll keep on catching him. His cards are well-marked.'

'I suppose so. Sorry to be a moan, Boss.'

'No problem.'

She bent forward, as if to rise from the chair, then stopped. 'Um, it's Thursday, today,' she said, looking me straight in the face.

'Yep, I had noticed.'

'Well, after four days of him I don't feel like going home and cooking. Fancy a Chinese? I owe you one.'

I pursed my lips, sucked in my cheeks. Anything to look noncommittal. I failed, miserably. 'Um, yeah,' I said. 'Smashing.'

'What time?' she asked, rising to her feet.

'Er, now?' I wondered, following her up.

She wanted to go home and change, and it wasn't a bad idea for me to do the same. At seven thirty, clean shaven and crisply attired, I parked outside her downstairs flat on the edge of the town. Annette saw me arrive and came out, wearing jeans and a Berghaus fleece over a T-shirt. Her hair was tied back, where it exploded from out of a black band in an untamed riot. I wanted to sit there and tell her how good she looked, but I didn't.

I settled for: 'Hi Kid, still Chinese?'

'Yes, please.'

'We could have a change, if you'd prefer it.'

'No, Chinese is fine.'

'OK.' I put the car in first gear and eased away from the kerb. 'If I remember rightly,' I told her, 'it's my turn to get you drunk.'

Mr Ho wasn't there, so we didn't have a cabaret or free tea, but it gave us a chance to talk. The holiday had been good but I gained the distinct impression that something about it wasn't too brilliant. The company, perhaps? They'd canoed down the river for four days, staying at campsites and imbibing copious amounts of local produce. It sounded heaven to me. She didn't want to talk about it, and her friend was never mentioned by name. When I ventured to ask if the two girls had enjoyed themselves the first flicker of enthusiasm came into her eyes and she said they had. Inevitably, the conversation found its way back to the job.

190

'I saw Silkstone this morning,' Annette said, 'when he came to sign the bail book. He was larger than life and twice as cheerful.'

'Cocky little sod,' I replied. 'I haven't seen him since he was given bail. Anybody would think he'd won the welterweight championship, the way he was jumping up and down, shaking hands with his brief.'

'He wants to change his day next week, because he's talking at a sales conference.'

'Has his solicitor applied to the court?'

'Yes. He was asking if we'd had notification.'

'Did they let him?'

'I imagine so.'

'Well they shouldn't have.' I adopted my stern expression and growled.

'You think he's got away with it, don't you, Charlie?'

'I don't know, Annette. I really don't know.'

'The famous intuition?'

I shook my head. 'No, definitely not. I have no sense of intuition. I study the picture, weigh the facts. All the facts, including the seemingly irrelevant.'

She tipped her head to one side and rested it against her fist. 'Such as what?' she asked.

The waiter brought the portion of toffee bananas we'd decided to share and I spooned a helping on to my side plate. 'These are delicious,' I told her, passing the remainder across the table.

'Mmm!' she agreed after the first mouthful.

'What do you do with junk mail?' I asked.

'Throw it away, usually,' she replied.

'No. In detail, please. Step by step.'

'Step by step? Well, I look at the envelopes, then usually put it all to one side.'

'So you don't throw it straight in the bin?'

'Um, no.'

'Go on.'

'It stays on the hall table until I have an idle moment. Then I open it, read it a bit ... and ... that's when I chuck it in the bin!'

'What about charity stuff?'

'Charity stuff? That hangs about a bit longer. I usually save it until I have a clear out, then it goes the way of the rest, I'm afraid.'

'Do you reply to any?'

'Not as much as I should. Mum has bad arthritis, and I'm scared of it, so I usually send them something. And children's charities. One or two others, perhaps, but not very often.'

'I'd say you were a generous, caring person,' I told her. 'You probably feel uncomfortable about not helping more, but sometimes resent being blackmailed by the more emotional appeals.'

'Yes, I think I do.'

'There were four items of junk mail in Latham's dustbin, two of them from charities. He'd opened them all and the return envelope and payment slip from one of the charities – the World Wildlife Fund – was pinned on his kitchen noticeboard. Silkstone, on the other hand, handled things more efficiently. There were two items in his bin, both of them unopened. One of them, from ActionAid, was postmarked the day before the killings, so it had probably only arrived that morning.' I grinned, saying: 'Of the two of them, I'd rather pin it on Silkstone.

Wouldn't you?'

She smiled and carefully lifted a spoonful of toffee banana towards her mouth. I watched her lips engulf it and the spoon slide out from between them. 'So...' she mumbled, chewing and swallowing, 'So ... if you were a psychiatrist, doing a profile of whoever had killed Mrs Silkstone, you'd go for the person who dumped his junk mail, unopened.'

'Every time.'

'What about the evidence?'

'We're just talking profiles. You used the word, I try to avoid it.'

'Why?'

'Because most of it is common sense. I don't need a psychiatrist on seventy grand to pinpoint crime scenes on a map for me and say: "He lives somewhere there".'

'It might be common sense to you, Charlie. It's mumbo-jumbo to most of us.'

'It'll come. There's no substitute for experience.'

'So how did Latham's semen get to be all over Mrs Silkstone?' Annette asked.

I shrugged and flapped a hand. I suspect I blushed, too. 'In the usual manner?' I suggested.

'So he was there when she died?'

'It looks like it.'

'But you think Silkstone was with him?'

'I don't know, Annette,' I sighed. 'What do some people get up to behind their curtains? It's all a mystery to me. Profiling isn't evidence. It should be used to indicate a line of enquiry, and you should always bear in mind that it might be the wrong line. When you do it backwards, like we've done, it's next to worthless.'

She smiled, saying: 'That was interesting. Thank you.'

'You're welcome, ma'am.' A waiter placed the bill in front of me but Annette's arm reached out like a striking rattlesnake and grabbed it.

'My treat,' she said.

Light rain was falling when we hit the street, and I guided Annette under the shelter of the shop canopies, my hand in the small of her back. 'Shall we have a drink somewhere?' I asked.

'Mmm. Where?'

'Dunno.' I was out of touch with the town-centre pubs. Most of them were good, once, but *yoof* culture had taken them over and the music made thinking, never mind conversation, impossible. Annette might not mind that, I thought, and something gurgled in the pit of my stomach. I didn't have a calculator in my pocket, but elementary mental arithmetic said she was nineteen years younger than me. Nowhere would that gap be more evident than in a town-centre pub.

Across the road there blinked the neon sign of the Aspidistra Lounge, Heckley's major night-spot. Formerly the Copper Banana, formerly Luigi's Nite Scene, formerly Mad John's Fashion Emporium, formerly the Regal Kinema. The later two of these enterprises were run by Georgie Casanove, formerly George Hardwick. Georgie was our town's answer to Pete String-fellow, but without the finesse.

'We could try there,' I said, nodding towards

the lights.

'The Aspidistra Lounge?'

'Mmm. We could call it work, claim on our expenses. Georgie, the proprietor, isn't exactly a Mr Big, but I think he could finger a few people for us, if he were so inclined. Let's put some pressure on him.'

'Right!' she said. 'I'm game.'

We dashed across the road, avoiding the puddles, and stepped through the open doorway of the disco. A bouncer with a shaven head and Buddy Holly spectacles was leaning on the front desk, chatting to the gum-chewing ticket girl. He straightened up and stepped to one side, taken off-guard by the sudden rush of customers, and tried to look menacing. I've seen more menace on the back of a cornflakes box.

'Two, please,' I said to the girl, not sure whether to speak under, over or through the armoured glass that surrounded her. We could have flashed our IDs like TV cops would have done, and they would have let us in, but I preferred it this way.

The words: 'Ladies are free before ten,' came out of her mouth in a haze of peppermint that evaporated in the air somewhere between her and the bouncer, who she was gazing towards.

'Oh, I'll take three, then,' I answered.

'That'll be seven pounds fifty.'

I pushed a tenner towards her and she slid my change and two cloakroom tickets under the window. 'Thank you.' The bouncer strode over to a door and yanked it open. I ushered Annette forward and said: 'Cheers,' to him. We were in.

I know one tune that's been written in the last

ten years by any of the so-called Brit-Pop stars I see on the front pages of the tabloids, and the DJ was playing it.

I leaned towards Annette and said: 'Verve,' into her ear. She stared at me, her eyes wide. *'Bitter Sweet Symphony,'* I added, determined to exploit my sole opportunity to swank. It's a simple catchy rhythm, repeated ad nauseum. I nodded my head in time with it: *Dum-dum-dum, dum-dum-dum, dum-dum-dum-dum, dum-dum-dum.* Once heard, it's ringing through your brain for days, a bit like Canon in D.

'I'm amazed!' she gasped, and I rewarded her with a wink.

Our brains slowly modified our senses to accommodate the sudden change in environment. Irises widened to dispel the jungle gloom and nerves in our ears adjusted their sensitivity to just below the pain barrier. Noses twitched, seeking out pheromones from anyone of the opposite sex who was ripe for mating. Four million years of evolution, and this was what it was all leading to.

'It's a bit quiet,' I shouted above the battery of chords bouncing through my body.

'It's early,' Annette yelled back at me, in explanation.

It was the same as every other disco I remembered from my younger days. A bright, small dance floor; bored DJ sorting records behind a console straight from NASA; pulsating lights and lots of red velvet. OK, so we didn't have lasers and dry ice then, but they're no big deal. Still permeating everything was that same old feeling of despair. These places always look a dump when you see them with the house lights up. This looked a dump in semi-darkness. When I was a kid we called it the Bug Hutch, and came every Saturday to catch up with Flash Gordon's latest adventures.

Georgie himself was behind the bar, attired like a cross between Bette Davis on a bad night and Conan the Barbarian. 'It wouldn't cost much to convert this back to a cinema, George,' I told him, flapping a hand in the direction of the auditorium.

'Hello, Mr Priest,' he growled, managing to sound threatening and limp simultaneously. 'Not expecting any trouble, are we?'

'Who could cause trouble in an empty house?'

'It's early. We'll fill up, soon as the pubs close.'

'Two beers, please.' The locks on his head were platinum blond, but those cascading through the slashed front of his satin shirt were grey.

'What sort?'

I looked at Annette and she leaned over the bar, examining the wares. 'Foster's Ice, please,' she said.

'Two,' I repeated.

He popped the caps and placed the bottles on the counter. 'That'll be four pounds fifty,' he told me.

I passed him another tenner, asking: 'How much is there back on the bottles?'

'Isn't he a caution,' he said to Annette as he handed me my change.

We walked uphill, away from the bar and the speakers, feeling our way between the empty tables to where the rear stalls once were. It was much quieter back there, and a few other people were sitting in scattered groups, arranged according to some logic based on personal territory. As the place filled territories would shrink and a pecking order emerge. There were two couples, three men presumably from out of town, and a group of girls. We looked for a table equidistant from the girls and the couples, but before we could sit down one of the girls waved to me.

It was Sophie, with three of her friends. I nudged Annette and gestured for her to follow. The girls moved their chairs to make room for us, removing sports bags from the vacant ones.

'It's Charles, he's my uncle,' Sophie told her friends, a big smile illuminating her face.

'Hello, Uncle Charles,' they chorused.

I introduced Annette to them, and Sophie rattled off three names that I promptly forgot. She and Sophie renewed their acquaintance.

'You don't do this for amusement, do you?' I asked, looking around at the decor.

'We've been playing badminton at the leisure centre,' someone informed me.

'We just come in for a quick drink and a dance,' another added.

'It's free before ten,' Sophie said.

'Right,' I nodded. Apart from the price of the drinks, it sounded a reasonable arrangement. I gritted my teeth and asked them what they'd have.

'Thanks, Uncle Charles,' they all said when I returned, six bottles dangling from between my fingers. One of the girls, dark-haired, petite and vivacious, said: 'Can I call you Charlie, Uncle Charles? I already have an Uncle Charles.'

'I'd prefer it if you all called me Charlie. Uncle Charles makes me feel old.'

'How old are you?'

'Twenty-eight,' I lied, glancing up at the ceiling.

'Gosh, that is old.'

They were in high spirits, the adrenaline still pumping after a couple of hours on court, and I began to wonder if joining them had been such a good idea. Four confident young women at the crossroads: left for marriage and a family; right for a career in whatever they chose; straight on for both. I didn't feel old – I felt fossilised.

The music paused, the DJ spoke for the first time, and when it started again the four of them jumped to their feet, prompted by some secret signal.

'We dance to this.'

'Come on, Annette. Can you dance, Charlie?'

'Can I dance? Can I dance? *Watch my hips.*'

I had a quick sip of lager, for sustenance, and followed them on to the floor. The difference in rhythm or melody was invisible to me, but this was evidently danceable, what had gone before wasn't. I joined the circle of ladies, swivelled on one leg and wondered about joint replacements.

The style of dancing hadn't changed, so I didn't make a complete fool of myself. The girls put on a show, swaying and gyrating, lissom as snakes, but I gave them a step or two. Fifteen minutes later the DJ slowed it down and the floor emptied again, faster than a golf course in a thunderstorm.

We finished our tasteless beer and left. There was a street vendor outside, selling hot dogs. The girls' ritual was to have one each then make their ways home. I couldn't have eaten one if Delia Smith herself was standing behind the counter in her wimple. Just the smell of them made me want to dash off and bite a postman's leg. We stood talking as they wolfed them down. Young appetites, young tastes, young digestive systems. Here we go again, I thought.

Annette shared my views on hot dogs, and declined one. When we'd established that nobody needed a lift we left. 'That was fun,' Annette said as we drove off.

'It was, wasn't it.'

'Sophie's grown up.'

'I had noticed.'

'The little dark one – Shani – took a shine to you.'

'Understandably.'

'And not a size ten between them,' she sighed.

I freewheeled to a standstill outside her flat, dropping on to sidelights but leaving the engine running. 'Thanks for the meal, Ms Brown,' I said.

'You're welcome, Mr Priest,' she replied. 'I've enjoyed myself.'

'Good. That's the intention.'

'Well it worked.'

After a moment's uncomfortable silence I asked: 'Are you ... are you going away, this weekend.'

'Yes,' she mumbled.

'Right.'

She pulled the catch and pushed the door open. 'Charlie...' she began, half turning back towards me.

'Mmm?'

'Oh just, you know ... thanks for ... for being, you know ... a pal. A friend.'

'A gentleman. You mean a gentleman.'

'Yes, I suppose I do.'

'Just as long as you understand one thing.'

She looked puzzled, worried. 'What's that?'

'That it's bloody difficult for me.'

'Is it?'

'Yes.'

Her smile made me want to plunder a convent. 'Goodnight, Charlie,' she said.

'Goodnight, Annette.'

The house was in darkness, blind and forlorn. The outside light is supposed to turn itself on at dusk, but it looked as if the bulb had blown again. The streetlights illuminate the front, but the side door is in shadow. I avoided the milk bottle standing on the step and felt for the key-hole with a finger, like drunks do, before inserting the key. It was cold inside, because a front had swept in from Labrador and the central heating was way down low. I turned the thermo-stat to thirty and the timer to constant. That'd soon warm things up. I made some tea and lit the gas fire. I was too alert to sleep, too many thoughts and rhythms tumbling around in my head. The big CD player was filled with Dylan, but that wasn't what I needed:

I know that I could find you, in somebody's room.

It's a price I have to pay: you're a big girl all the way.

Not tonight, Bob, thank you. I flicked through the titles until one flashed a light in my brain. Gorecki's third; a good choice. Sometimes, the best way to deal with a hurt, real or imaginary, is to overwhelm it with somebody else's sadness. I slipped the gleaming disc from its cover and placed it on the turntable.

'What do some people get up to, behind the curtains?' I'd asked Annette. 'Profiling isn't evidence,' I'd said. They get up to everything you could imagine, and plenty of things you couldn't, and that's the truth. Read the personal column in your newspaper; look at the magazines on the top shelf in any newsagents; explore the internet; look at the small ads in the tabloids. That's the visible bit.

We don't stop when we prove that someone committed a murder. We carry on until we prove that everybody else involved didn't commit it. Sometimes, with some juries, nothing less will do.

If it wasn't for the evidence, we'd have arrested Silkstone for the murder of his wife. Everything pointed to him, except the evidence. That's a big except. The evidence, and the witness, pointed to Latham. That witness, of course, was Silkstone, and Latham was in no position to defend himself. The obvious solution was that Silkstone killed them both after discovering that they were lovers, but that's not what he said happened, and he was the only witness. Next favourite, for me, was that Silkstone killed Latham out of self-preservation, because they were both there when Margaret died, but, like the professor said, it would be a bugger to prove. Perhaps they did the Somerset job together, too. Sadistic murdering couples were usually a male and a female, with the male the dominant partner, but there were exceptions. Some people think the Yorkshire Ripper didn't always act alone, and the Railway Rapist almost certainly had an accomplice. And even if they're wrong, there's got to be a first time. There's always got to be a first time.

My job is to catch murderers. It's a dirty job, and dirt rubs off. Like the men who empty my dustbin, I come home with the smell of it following me. To catch a jackal you must first study its ways. Before you can look a rat in the eyes it is necessary to get down on your belly and roll in the dirt. Silkstone and Latham had known each other for a long time; married two sisters; committed adultery with two women who were friends. No doubt they'd shared a few adventures. Had they shared their women, too?

How does it start? A casual boast, man to man, after a few pints? A giggled comment between the wives after one too many glasses of wine? Expressions of admiration, followed by a tentative suggestion? Jaded senses find new life, curiosity is aroused, objections dismissed. 'If we all agree, nobody gets hurt, do they?' Next thing you know, you're alone with your best friend's partner, undoing those buttons that you've looked at so often across the table, revealing the mysteries that they conceal.

Is that what happens? Don't ask me. I thought

203

Fellatio was a character in *Romeo and Juliet* until I was thirty-two. I awoke to Dawn Upshaw in full voice, and on that pleasant note crawled up the stairs to bed.

Monday morning I rang the clerk to the court who had granted Silkstone a variation to his bail conditions. 'I believe he's supposed to be speaking at a sales conference,' I said.

'That's what his solicitor told us in the application, Mr Priest.'

'Did he say what time?'

'Yes, I have the letter here. He's speaking at two p.m., for half an hour, but he asked if he could spend the full day at the conference. We saw no reason to object and we've told him to report tomorrow, instead. It's not our intention to interfere with his employment.'

'No, that's fair enough. And where is this conference, exactly?'

'Um, here we are: the Leeds Winchester Hotel.'

'Good. Thanks for your help.'

'Is there a problem, Mr Priest? Would you have preferred it if we'd contacted you earlier?'

'No, no problem at all. I was just thinking that I might go along and listen to him.'

The troops had plenty to catch up on, and the super was more interested in his monthly fly-fishing magazine, so I didn't tell him my intentions. Just before one I walked out of the office and drove to Leeds.

The Winchester Hotel is part of the revitalised riverside area, to the south of town, near the new Royal Armouries. Leeds has an inner ring road, which is only half a ring, and something called the Loop, which doesn't join up with it. I missed the hotel, drove into the city centre and came out again following the M1 signs, except that the M1 is now called the M621 and the new M1 is not what I wanted. I drove back into the city centre and tried again.

This time I found it. The Winchester chain of hotels caters for business trade working to a budget. It's room-only accommodation, without the frills. No Corby trouser press, no complimentary shower cap. If you want to eat, there's a restaurant on the ground floor. I pushed my way through the door at a few seconds before two, just as the tail end of a group of people disappeared into the lift. The doors closed, leaving me stranded. I looked around for a sign saying where the conference was being held, but there wasn't one. Presumably it wasn't necessary. Ah well, I'm not a detective for nothing. The illuminated indicator above the lift door had flicked through the lower numbers and was now stationary at number five. That must be it, I thought, pressing the button.

There was a movement beside me and I turned to see a little man standing there, his face moist with perspiration. The indicator over the lift door to my left stopped at G, something pinged and the door opened. I gestured for the man to enter first. You never know, maybe there'd been a failure of electronics and the lift wasn't really there. He didn't fall to his death so I followed him in.

'Five?' I asked.

'Yes please.' He was seriously overweight and appeared to be wearing a skirt over his blue-check trousers. A name badge declared that he was called Gerald Vole.

'Er, napkin,' I whispered, nodding towards his nether regions.

'Oh God!' he exclaimed, snatching it from his belt. He managed a nervous smile, saying: 'The service was terrible in the restaurant,' by way of explanation.

'It always is,' I confirmed, airily.

The door pinged and opened, and I gestured him forward. 'Enjoying the conference?' I asked.

'Yes, very much. There's so much to learn, though. Are you with the company?'

'Yes, for my sins,' I lied.

'Sales?'

'Head office,' I told him, adding: 'Personnel,' because it felt good.

'Gosh!' he replied, impressed.

'Charlie Priest,' I said, offering him my hand.

'Gerry Vole,' he squeaked as I crushed his clammy fingers. 'Pleased to meet you.'

'Welcome to TGF, Gerry,' I said.

The door we entered through was at the back of the room, fortunately. The conference facilities consisted of one side of the whole fifth floor being left empty, the space divided into three by sliding partitions. Trans Global Finance had booked the lot, so all the partitions were retracted. The place was nearly full, but we found chairs on the end of the back row and sat down. Gerry produced a typist's pad from a pocket and rested it on his knee. I stared at row after row of shaven necks poking from blue suit collars. It could have been a Mormon revivalist meeting. Gerry's checks and my sports jacket were the only discordant notes. Gerry would have to learn to conform; I make a speciality of not doing so.

The door behind me closed with a bang and I took a sly peep back. A man and woman who would have looked completely at home on local-network breakfast TV were standing there, and he'd pulled the door shut. She had nice knees, and I'd seen her type a hundred times before. Sometimes she, or her sister, was in the precinct, handing out freebies for the local newspaper; other times she was there in her clingy T-shirt and Wonder Bra extolling the virtues of holidays in Cornwall or Tenerife. A promotions girl. Anxious to shake the dust of Heckley from her stilettos but not good looking enough to be a model, not bright enough to be a holiday rep. Promises of riches galore had brought her into the finance industry, and today she was a cheerleader.

'Welcome back!' a voice boomed from the front. The owner had oddly luxuriant grey hair and could easily have done Billy Graham on *Stars in Their Eyes*. 'And now for the session you're all waiting for,' he proclaimed. 'It's my proud duty to introduce the man we all think of as the Prince of Closing. The man who can, literally, walk on water...'

Boy, this I've got to see, I thought. Gerry Vole beside me was wriggling in his seat, trying to make himself taller.

'Ladies and gentlemen...'

207

'No! No! No!' Silkstone was there, waving his arms as he dashed on to the stage to interrupt the eulogy, but just too late, of course, and the rest of it was drowned by the applause. It started behind me in a burst of small explosions and rattled through the audience like machine gun fire. 'Good afternoon!' Silkstone shouted.

'Good afternoon,' we yelled back.

'I didn't hear you! GOOD AFTERNOON!'

'GOOD AFTERNOON!' This time they heard us in Barnsley.

'Right on!' I added as the reverberations faded away, and nudged Gerry with my elbow.

'Yeah!' he shouted, recovering his balance and punching the air with a podgy fist.

'What is that magical quality that converts a lead into a sale?' Silkstone demanded of us.

'Closing!' The word jumped around the auditorium like a firecracker.

'What are the three golden bullets in the salesman's armoury?'

'Closing, closing, closing.'

'You don't seem sure!' he shouted. 'So I'll tell you!' There was a table and chair on the low stage, with a glass and water jug on the table. Silkstone leapt up on to the chair and shouted: 'Number one – closing!' Long pause for effect as he made eye contact with the front rows. 'Number two – closing!' Another leap took him on to the table. 'Number three – CLOSING!'

Gerry, beside me and beside himself, was busy scribbling. He'd written: *3 golden bullets: 1 – closing, 2 – closing, 3 – closing!!!*

Silkstone, still up on the table, was launching

into an anecdote about how Bill Gates got to be the world's richest man. Presumably, I thought, because gates are good at closing. After five minutes I'd had enough. I reached out and took Gerry's pad from him. On it I wrote: *4 – treat every client as if he might be an eccentric millionaire* and winked as I passed it back. 'I'm off,' I said, rising to my feet. 'Good luck.' He read what I'd written and stared at me, eyes wide, mouth open, as if I'd just given him the co-ordinates of the Holy Grail.

I yanked the door open and took a last look at Silkstone. He had one foot on the floor, one on the chair when the movement at the back of the room caught his eye. He froze in mid-stride and fell silent as he recognised me. Other heads turned my way. I stepped out through the opening and closed the door behind me. 'That'll give him something to think about,' I mumbled to myself as I headed towards the lift.

Gwen Rhodes played netball for England and hockey for Kent. I had trials with Halifax Town as a goalkeeper, but wasn't signed up. I considered myself a sportsman, years ago, although I never reached the heights that Gwen did. We sit on a committee together, and have talked about the value of sport over a cup of coffee in the canteen. These days, the only place you can regularly see honesty, courage, passion is on the playing field. Out there, with the sting of sweat in your eyes and the taste of blood in your mouth, where you come from and who you know is of no help at all.

So when I saw the note on my desk saying that she wanted me to ring her I didn't wait. 'The Governor, please,' I said, when the switchboard at Bentley Prison answered.

'Who wants her, please?'

'Detective Inspector Priest, Heckley CID.'

'One moment.'

I waited for the music, wondering what might be appropriate – *Unchained Melody? Please release me, let me go?* – but none came. 'Hello, Charlie. Thanks for ringing,' Gwen's plummy voice boomed in my ear.

'My pleasure, Gwen. Long time no see. Shouldn't we be having a meeting soon, or did you ring to tell me I'd missed it?'

'Between you and me, Charlie, I think that committee has probably quietly faded away. We didn't achieve much, did we?'

'Lip service, Gwen, that's what it's all about. Make it look as if you are doing something. So what can I do for you? I'm available, Saturday morning, if you need a goalie.'

'Oh, those were the days. I may have some information for you, Charlie, but first of all, an apology.'

'Go on.'

'You know that we monitor inmates' calls, tape-record them for transcription at a later date.'

'Mmm.'

'Well, we've rather fallen behind lately, so this weekend I put one of my officers on to them, and he's come up with something that might be of interest to you.'

'I'm all ears, Gwen.'

'Does the name Chiller mean anything?'

'Chiller?'

'Yes.'

'No.'

'You disappoint me.'

'I'm sorry.'

'He's supposed to be the most wanted man in Britain, according to the tabloids.'

'Chiller?'

'That's his nickname, a contraction.'

I repeated the name softly, to myself: 'Chiller-Chiller-Chiller,' until it hit me. 'Chilcott!' I pronounced. 'Kevin Chilcott!'

'That's the man.'

'He's a cop killer,' I said, suddenly alert. 'What can you tell me?'

'Just that one of our inmates, a hard case called Paul Mann, telephoned a London number, four weeks ago, asking for a message to be sent to someone called Chiller about 'a job'. Since then there has been a quantity of rather enigmatic traffic, but the name was never mentioned again. Sums were quoted. There's lots of other stuff which may or may not be related.'

'Chilcott's a hitman,' I said. 'Maybe someone's putting some work his way.'

'That's what my man thought. He's ex-Pentonville, and was there at the same time as Kevin Chilcott. He said everybody called him Chiller, and he rejoiced in the name.'

'When can I come over and see this stuff?'

'I should be free about four-thirty,' she replied.

'Right, put the kettle on. Will you make it right for me at the gate, please?' Getting into prisons is

211

harder than getting out of them.

'It's a long time since you were here' she observed. 'I'm over the road, now. Just ask and they'll point you in the right direction.'

I did some thinking before I went down to Control to find someone authorised to interrogate the computer systems. The CRO would tell us Chilcott's record, the PNC would have other stuff about him. Confidential stuff. Trouble was, his name would be tagged in some way, and any enquiry we made would be relayed straight to Special Branch and NCIS. They were on our side, I decided, so I did it anyway.

The print-outs didn't make pleasant reading. Chilcott started young, served the usual apprenticeship. He had a full house of cautions, followed by probation and youth custody. As an adult he'd served two years for robbery and eight for armed robbery. After that, it was all hearsay. A series of building society raids were put down to him, as was a bank heist that netted over half a million and left a security guard shot dead. I was wrong about one thing – he wasn't a cop killer. A uniformed PC, under-experienced and over-diligent, walked into a stake-out that nobody had told him about and was shot for his troubles. He didn't die, but in his shoes I'd have preferred it. The bullet fractured his spine, high up, and left him a quadriplegic. Chilcott escaped and fled the country. Nothing had been heard of him since 1992, but rumour linked him with a string of gangland killings. Maybe the money was running out, I thought.

Her Majesty's Prison Bentley sits four-square on a hill just outside Halifax. It's a Victorian-Gothic pile, complete with battlements, crenellated turrets and fake arrow-slits, but with the proportions of a warthog. The architect was probably warned about the gales that howl down from the north, so he built it squat and solid. It strikes terror in my heart every time I visit the place. I swung into the car-park, mercifully empty because we were outside visiting hours, and gazed up at the gaunt stone walls, wondering if Mad King Ludwig ever had a skinhead brother.

Gwen had told the gatehouse to expect me, but they put a show on before accompanying me to her office. Doublecheck my ID, a quick frisk and then through the metal detector. She runs a tight ship. She has to; Bentley houses some of the most dangerous men in the country, as well as remand prisoners.

I'd forgotten how handsome she is, in a Bloomsbury-ish sort of way. Strong features, hair pinned back, long elegant fingers. No faded delicacy with Gwen, though. At a shade under six feet tall she'd be a formidable opponent, tearing towards you brandishing a hockey stick. We shook hands and pretended to kiss cheeks, and I flopped into the leather chair she indicated.

I told her she looked well and she said I looked tired. That made it twice, recently. One of her officers, male, approaching retirement age, knocked and poked his head round the door to ask if I preferred tea or coffee. Gwen thanked him, calling him Thomas. He called her ma'am.

213

'These are the transcripts,' she said, reaching across the polished top of her desk to pull a sheaf of loose sheets towards us. She'd joined me at the wrong side of it, where you stood to receive her wrath; or words of encouragement; or the news that your wife and the bloke you didn't grass on had run away to Spain with all the money. 'I've highlighted the relevant bits,' she added, pulling her chair closer to mine, so we could both read them. I detected the merest hint of her perfume, which was heavy and musky and put me off balance for a moment or two.

I studied the lists, then said: 'I never realised just how much work was entailed with these, Gwen.' Someone had to obtain a printout of all the calls, with times and numbers, and then transfer that information to a transcript of all the tape-recorded conversations that somebody else had prepared.

'It's a bind, Charlie. And all for so little return.'

'Now and again you come up with gold,' I said. 'Maybe this is one of those times. How do you know who made the calls?'

'The hard way. An inmate has to ask to use the phone, and we keep a book.'

'Which wing is whatsisname on?'

'Paul Mann? A-wing.'

Maximum security, for long term prisoners in the early years of their sentences, and the nutcases. 'What'd he do?'

'Poured paraffin over his girlfriend and ignited it. It burns deeper than petrol, apparently.'

'She died?'

'Eventually.'

'Mr Nice Guy.' I read the scraps of conversation from the sheet, next to the London number he'd dialled:

V1: Billy?
V2: Yeah.
V1: S'me. Can't talk for long. Only got one f– card. Tell Davy I need a job doing, don't I. [Indecipherable] S'important.
V2: A job? What sort of f– job.
V1: Never you f– mind. Just tell him I know someone who wants to buy a Roller.
V2: A f– Roller? What you on about?
V1: Listen, c–. Ask Davy to have a word with Chiller about it. And don't ask no f– questions.
V2: Oh, right.
V1: I'll ring you Tuesday.
V2: OK. S'long.
V1: S'long.

Tuesday's conversation was even less fulsome:

V1: Billy?
V2: Yeah.
V1: You talk to Davy?
V2: Yeah.
V1: What's he say?
V1: He says a decent f– Roller is hard to come by these days. Could be f– expensive. Cost your friend a packet.
V1: How expensive?
V2: Fifty big ones, plus expenses. Number f– plates, an'all.
V1: [Indecipherable]

215

V2: You what?
V1: I said tell him I'll f– think about it.

Two days later we had:

V1: That you, Billy?
V2: Yeah. Listen. Davy can do your friend the Roller, at the price agreed, including all expenses, if you can arrange accommodation. No f– problem. And he wants to know when he'd like to take delivery. He says sooner the f– better.
V1: Right. Right. Tell him we might have a f– deal.

Thomas came in with the teas, on a tray with china cups and a plate of biscuits. We both thanked him and Gwen poured the tea. I reached for a bourbon, saying: 'Whoever transcribed this cares about your sensibilities.'

She beamed at me. 'Sweet, isn't he?'

'What's Mann's tariff?' I asked.

'Thirty years,' she replied, easing an over-filled cup in my direction.

'So ordering a Rolls Royce would seem a little premature?'

'I'd say so.'

'And would you say that fifty thousand pounds was a reasonable price for killing a man?'

The cup was halfway to her lip. She paused and lowered it back to its saucer. 'Mann killed his girlfriend because the baby was crying,' she told me.

I bit half off the biscuit and slowly chewed it. When my mouth was empty I asked: 'What did he do with the baby?'

'The baby? Oh, the room was on fire, so he tried to save the baby. He threw her out of the window. Says he forgot they were on the seventh floor.'

'Jee-sus,' I sighed.

Chapter 8

The prisons have a dilemma. It doesn't take long
for a hierarchy to form, with men like Mann and
Chiller as the kingpins. They build up a coterie of
acolytes and prey on the weaker inmates. Contrary to popular opinion, for most prisoners once
is enough. All they want to do is put their heads
down, serve their time and never come back.
Faced with someone like Mann, they back down,
accept the bottom bunk, hand over their phone
cards and cigarettes. The men at the top never
want for drugs, booze, cigarettes or sex. They still
run their outside empires through a network of
contacts, and anyone who steps out of line gets
hurt. The occasional broken leg, slashed face or
crushed hand is amazingly good for business.

So the prison governors move them. They allow
the hard men to become established and then
transfer them to the other end of the country,
with maximum inconvenience. It's called ghost-
ing. He eats his breakfast in Brixton, full of the
joys of life, and at lunchtime finds himself
hobbling out of the van in Armley, squinting up
at the coils of razor wire above the walls, wondering who the top cat is. On any Monday morning
prison vans, usually accompanied by the local
police, are criss-crossing the country like worker
bees seeking out new feeding grounds.

There is a down-side, of course. The constant

exchange of prisoners creates an unofficial inter-jail communications network that cannot be improved upon. When the inmates of Hull decide to have a dirty protest, or to hurl tiles down from the roof, it's no coincidence that the prisoners in Strangeways, Bentley and Parkhurst choose exactly the same time to do exactly the same thing. The great revolution of the late twentieth century has been in communications, and the prison population is leading the field.

Some of it is high-tech, some of it lower than you'd believe people could go. Phone cards, not snout, are the new currency, but the big porcelain phone in the corner is available to everyone with a strong stomach. The days of slopping out are over because most cells now have a toilet. The prisoners are not as overjoyed about this as you might expect. Once they had a room, now they have a shithole in the corner of the cell, behind an aluminium sink unit to give a modicum of privacy when you're sitting there. What no one envisaged was the communications opportunities this created. What no one realised was the ingenuity of caged men.

All the toilets lead down to a common drain. Take a small receptacle – your cellmate's drinking cup will do fine – and drain all the water out of the toilet u-bend. Pour it down the sink. You are now connected to the drain. If somebody else does the same thing elsewhere in the prison, even in another wing, you can now have a conversation without raising your voice above a whisper. There may be interruptions of a nature that BT users never experience, but you'll never be left hanging on through three movements of the Four Seasons. To break the line, terminate the call, you simply flush the toilet.

I didn't feel hungry. I'd had no lunch but the thought of having a long and meaningful conversation with your head down the pan, listening to all the extraneous noises, savouring the odours, is a wonderful appetite suppressant. Perhaps I could sell the concept to Weight Watchers and never have to work again. I won twenty-five thousand pounds in a quiz programme on television, then had a long hot soak in the bath. Freshly scrubbed, I managed a tin of chicken soup, with some decent bread, followed by a few custard creams. In deference to all the people who think I looked tired I went to bed early and, unusual for me, slept like a little dormouse.

'Where were you, yesterday?' Gilbert asked at the morning prayer meeting.

'Bentley prison,' I replied, sliding a chair across and placing my mug of tea on a beer mat on his desk. 'I left word.' There were only the two of us, because Gareth Aidey had a court appointment and was polishing the buttons on his best tunic.

'So you really went to Bentley?'

'Of course I did. Where did you think I was – having a round of golf?'

'I don't know what you get up to. I'm only the super. Regional Crime Squad were after you, said that Special Branch had tipped them off that you were on to something.'

'Christ, that was quick.'

'Nobody had a clue what it was all about. I felt

220

a right wally.'

'Sorry, Gilbert, but I didn't know myself until after five o'clock. I was at Bentley until nearly seven.'

'So what was it about?'

I found the transcripts in my briefcase and laid them on his desk. 'It looks as if someone in Bentley prison is trying to organise a hitman to do a job, and the hitman is a certain Kevin Chilcott. Remember him?'

'Kevin Chilcott? He killed a police officer, didn't he, ten or twelve years ago?'

'As good as. I consulted the PNC about him and SB must have picked it up.'

'Humph!' he snorted. 'Makes you wonder what else they pick up. So what have you got?' Gilbert read the excerpts, running his finger along the lines like a schoolchild. He mumbled to himself and turned the page over.

'That's just the usual stuff,' I told him.

'What do you call the usual stuff?'

'Oh, you know...' – I adopted a whining voice – *'That you Sharron? Yeah. I love you. I love you. How's your mum. She's all right. Tell her I love her. She sez she love's you. How's your Tracy? She's all right. Tell her I love her. She's pregnant. Is she? Yeah. Whose is it? Dunno. When's it due? January. It can't be mine, then.'*

Gilbert said: 'OK, OK, I get the message. So this stuff stands out, then.'

'Like a first-timer at a nudist colony.'

'You'd better let RCS know.'

'I'll do it now.'

Gilbert stood up and retrieved his jacket from

behind the door. 'I'm off to headquarters,' he told me. 'Monthly meeting. You're in charge. What can I report about the Margaret Silkstone case?'

'Solved,' I replied.

'Good. And the Peter Latham job?'

'Solved.'

'Good. As long as you remember you said it. Do you want me to tell them about this?' He waved a hand towards the papers on his desk.

'Might as well,' I replied. 'Give you something to talk about.'

Special Branch are not a band of super-cops, based in London. Every Force has an SB department, quietly beavering away at god-knows what. They have offices at all the airports and other points of entry, and keep an eye on who comes in and goes out of the country. Anti-terrorism is their speciality, but they keep a weather-eye open for big-league criminals on the move. If you don't mind unsociable hours and have a high boredom threshold it could be the career for you. Special Branch don't feel collars, they gather information. The Regional Crime Squads specialise in heavy stuff like organised crime, the syndicates and major criminals. They are experts at covert surveillance, tailing people and using informers. They move about, keep a low profile, infiltrate gangs. Dangerous stuff.

'So where is he?' I asked an RCS DI in London when I finally found myself talking to someone with an interest in the case.

'Wish we knew,' he confessed. 'Over the last five years we've had sightings in Spain, Amsterdam and Puerto Rico. He moves around. What we do know, though, is that the money must have run out by now, even if he's living very modestly. Half a million sounds a lot, but when someone charges you thirty per cent for converting it to used notes or a foreign currency, and someone else charges you for their silence, and so on, it soon depletes.'

'In the transcripts he says make it quick,' I told him.

'Sounds like he's getting desperate, then. We'll dig out a new description of him and circulate it to all points of entry. After that, we can only hope that someone spots him. Which district are you?'

'Number three.'

'So that will be our Leeds office?'

'That's right.'

'Any chance of you getting the transcripts over there? If the conversations took place a month ago we might be too late already.'

''Fraid not. I'll address them to you and leave them behind the front desk.' It was their baby, so they could do the running around.

'OK. I'll arrange for them to be collected, and thanks for the information.'

'My pleasure.' I asked him to keep us informed and replaced the receiver. Another satisfied customer, I thought, as I delved into Gilbert's filing cabinet where he keeps his chocolate digestives.

After two of them I rang Gwen Rhodes at HMP Bentley and told her that the hard men were now on the Chiller case and that they had promised to keep us informed, but don't hold your breath. People say they will, then don't bother. It's a mistake. I always make a point of saying my thank-yous, letting people know what happened. They remember, and next time you want something from them you get it with a cherry on the top.

Gwen said: 'So the message was definitely for Chilcott, was it?'

'They think so, Gwen. Apparently his money should have run out by now, and they're expecting him to make a move. This might be it.'

'Good,' she said. 'Good. Glad we could be of assistance.'

'Listen, Gwen,' I said. 'While you're on the line, there's something else I'd like to ask you.'

'Ye-es, Charlie,' she replied, in a tone that might have been cautious, may even have been expectant. What was I going to ask her? How about dinner sometime? The theatre?

'A few weeks ago you had a remand prisoner of mine called Anthony Silkstone,' I said. 'I was wondering how he took to life on the inside.'

'Silkstone,' she repeated, downbeat. 'Tony Silkstone?'

'That's the man.'

'Killed his wife's murderer?'

'That's him. Anything to report about his behaviour?'

'I read about him in the papers but I didn't realise he was one of yours, Charlie. Knew we had him, and he certainly didn't cause any problems. Let's see what the oracle says...' I heard the patter of keys as she consulted the computer terminal that sat on her desk, followed by a soft: 'Here we are,' to herself, and a long silence.

'Gosh,' she said when she came back on the

224

line. 'You can send us as many like him as you can find, Charlie. A golden prisoner by any standards.'

'Oh,' I said. 'What did he do?'

'It's all here. First of all the other inmates, the remandees that is, regarded him as some sort of folk hero. It explains that the person Silkstone killed had murdered his – Silkstone's – wife and was also a sex offender. Is that true? Was he a sex offender?'

'Um, it looks like it.'

'So that gave him a big pile of kudos, in their eyes. You know what they all think of nonces. It goes on to say that Silkstone took an active part in the retraining programme we're conducting, and became a popular lecturer in salesmanship. He even promised one or two of them an interview with his company, when they were all released. We need more like him, Charlie. Send us more, please.'

'That sounds like my man. He's a little treasure, no mistake.'

'He certainly is. Anything else you'd like to ask?'

Dinner? The theatre? 'No, Gwen,' I replied, 'but thanks a lot.'

Wednesday morning Sophie Sparkington received a letter from the admissions tutor at St John's College, Cambridge, where she would be reading history, and I received one from the matron of the Pentland Court Retirement Home, Chipping Sodbury.

Mine was handwritten on headed paper, and

225

was addressed to the senior detective at Heckley Police Station. It said:

Dear Sir
One of our clients, Mrs Grace Latham, who is elderly and frail, dictated this letter to me and asked for it to be forwarded to you. If you have any queries please do not hesitate to contact me.
Yours faithfully
Jean Hullah (Mrs) (Matron)

Stapled behind it was another sheet of the same paper, with the same handwriting. This one read:

Dear Sir,
My name is Grace Latham and I am the mother of Peter John Latham who was murdered. Now that he is dead the papers are saying terrible things about him. These are not true but he cannot defend himself. Peter was a good son and I know he could not have done these terrible things. He was kind and gentle, and wouldn't hurt a fly, and was always good to me. Please catch the proper murderer and prove that my son, Peter, did not do it.
Yours faithfully
Jean Hullah (Mrs)(Matron)
p.p. Grace Latham

Dave came in and I handed him the letters. He read them in silence and shrugged his shoulders.
  'Mothers,' I said.
  'Yeah,' he replied.
  'Which would you rather be: the murderer's

parent or the victim's parent?'

'Don't ask me. I wonder if Hitler's mother said that she always knew he'd turn out to be a bastard, or if she loved him right to the end. What do you want to do with it?'

'Drop her a reply, please. Not the card. Make it a letter, in my name. Then show it to Annette and stick it in the file.'

'OK. Nigel rang,' Dave said. 'Wants to know if we're going to the Spinners tonight. He says long-time-no-see.'

'What did you tell him?'

'Eight thirty.'

'Looks like we are, then.'

'Oh, and he says not to laugh, but he's grown a moustache.'

'A moustache?'

'That's what he says.

'Nigel?'

'Mmm.'

'This I've got to see.'

But I didn't, because he never came. We've developed a new routine for our Wednesdays out. The Spinners is about two miles from each of our houses, so we walk there. It's a half-hour power walk and that first pint slides down like snow off a roof when you stroll into the pub and lean on the bar. Towards closing time Dave's wife, Shirley, comes in the car for an orange juice and takes us home.

Dave had arrived first and was sitting in our usual corner. I collected the pint he'd paid for and joined him.

'Sophie heard from Cambridge this morning,'

227

he told me before I was seated. 'We're going down at the weekend to look at her accommodation.'

'Fantastic. I'll have to buy her a present. Don't suppose there's any point in asking you what she might want.'

He looked glum. 'Just about everything. Pots, pans, microwave. You name it, she needs it. Then there's a small matter of books, tuition fees, meals, rent. It's never-ending.'

'That's the price of having brainy kids,' I said.

'Brainy *kid*. Daniel wants to be a footballer or snooker star.'

'He could be in for a rude awakening,' I warned.

'He'll take it in his stride. We did.'

'That's true.' We were both failed footballers. Dave had his trial with Halifax Town the same time as me, with a similar result: don't call us, we'll call you.

'This beer's on form,' I said, enjoying a long sip.

'It is, isn't it.'

'So where's Golden Balls with this flippin' moustache?' But at that very moment Detective Sergeant Nigel Newley's full attention was elsewhere. He was gazing into the green eyes of Marie-Claire Hollingbrook, her face framed by the riot of golden hair heaped upon her pillow, her full lips parted and her naked body languidly spread-eagled across the bed. They were the first green eyes Nigel had ever seen, and he was stunned by their beauty. They were unable to return his gaze, because Marie-Claire had been strangled, several hours earlier.

'Do you ever regret not making it as a foot-baller?' Dave asked me.

'Nah,' I replied. 'This is a lot better. Do you? They'd have taken you on if you hadn't fluffed that goal.'

'No, I don't think so. Can't imagine how I missed it though. An open goalmouth in front of me, and I kicked it over the bar.'

'As I remember it, you kicked it over the grandstand.'

'It was a wormcast. The ball hit a wormcast and bobbed up, just as I toe-ended it. The rest, as they say, is history.'

'Sentenced to a lifetime of ignominy by a wormcast.' I said.

'I know,' he replied, glumly raising his glass and draining it.

'Just think,' I continued. 'Of all the millions of worms in the world, if that one particular speci-men hadn't crapped on that one particular square centimetre of grass on that one particular day, you might have married one of the Beverly sisters.'

'Blimey Frightenin', innit?' he replied.

'Innit just. Same again?'

'Please.'

'Pork scratchings?'

'Cheese and onion crisps.'

I went to the bar to fetch them.

The phone call we were hoping for but not ex-pecting came next morning, just as I was having my elevenses. I went downstairs to control, to catch the action. Arthur, a wily old sergeant, was in the hot seat. He slid a filled-in message form towards me as I moved a spare chair alongside him.

'Anything come in about the dead girl in Halifax?' I asked. There'd been a report about it on the local news.

'Just the bare details, pulled off the computer. We haven't been asked to assist, yet.'

'Our young Mr Newley will be up to his neck in that one,' I said, secretly wishing that I was there, too.

'Ah! Nigel'll find 'em.'

'So what have we here?'

'From the Met Regional Crime Squad,' he said as I read. 'One of their men thinks he's seen Kevin Chilcott at the Portsmouth ferry terminal. He rang in from a phone box and is now trying to follow him. Last report came from the arrivals concourse at 10:37 hours.'

'So what do they expect us to do?' I asked.

'Be alert, that's all. He could be going anywhere.'

I explained to Arthur that we were responsible for raising the APW on Chilcott, because of the messages from Bentley prison, but the phonecalls were to London, and that was probably where he was heading. 'Stay with it,' I told him, 'and keep me informed. I'll be in the office.'

I went back upstairs and finished my coffee. One by one, for no reason that I could think of, I rang Dave, Annette, Jeff and three others on their mobiles and told them what was happening. 'Keep in touch,' I told them, 'he might be coming this way.'

The super was unimpressed when I told him.

'He'll be heading for London,' he declared, dismissively.

'Yeah, you're probably right,' I agreed.

But he wasn't. Arthur rang me on the internal at 14:20 hours, saying that Chilcott, with the RCS chief inspector tagging along behind him, had boarded the 13:30 express from Kings Cross to Leeds. I went downstairs again and spoke directly to the RCS control, in London. Their man, I was told, was starting his holiday, but had found his way into the arrivals section hoping to meet his parents, who were coming home. He'd seen Chilcott come off the boat and followed him. They caught the train to Waterloo and transferred to Kings Cross, where Chilcott had purchased a single to Leeds. The DCI was unable to communicate from the Portsmouth train, but he could from this one. He was, they said, wearing holiday clothes, which made him somewhat conspicuous.

Our own Regional Crime Squad, based in Leeds, went on to full alert, borrowing our ARVs and booking the chopper for the rest of the day. They made arrangements to evacuate the station minutes before the London train arrived and dressed several officers in natty Railtrack uniforms. Marksmen were positioned around the adjacent platforms and steps taken to block-off all the exits and roads. ETA was 16:01, and Chilcott's feet wouldn't touch the ground.

At 15:06 the express stopped at Doncaster and Chilcott left it. The RCS detective got off, too, but had to hide behind a wall until Chilcott boarded the 15:40 to Manchester. That arrived at 17:00 hours and Chilcott and his faithful shadow then boarded the 17:12, Manchester Piccadilly to Newcastle.

'Could be Leeds, after all,' the super stated. He'd joined me in control when he realised that this one wasn't going away. Dave wandered in and I told him to collect as many bodies as he could, urgently.

'No, Boss,' I told Mr Wood. 'If there's one place he isn't going, it's Leeds. He could have stayed on the Kings Cross train if he was going to Leeds.'

The Met's RCS control room had managed to find someone in the railway business with the authority to spend some time talking to them, and were now being relayed times and destinations. 'That train stops at Heckley,' I told my contact. 'Where else does it stop?'

I wrote them down as he read them off. Oldfield, Huddersfield, then Heckley, Leeds, York and Newcastle.

'What time at Heckley?'

'17:54.'

'Six minutes to six. Struth, any chance of delaying it? I think he could be coming here and we're a bit depleted.'

They said they'd do what they could.

I sent someone to Heckley station to arrange things there. We needed parking spaces and easy access. Mr Wood rang the Assistant Chief Constable to organise the issuing of weapons. Our ARVs were in Leeds, so we improvised, borrowing two off-duty officers from the tactical firearms unit who'd missed the shout to dash to Leeds, in their own cars.

232

'Just the man,' I said when Jeff Caton wandered in. 'Did I see your crash helmet in the office, this morning?'

'I've come on the bike, if that's what you mean,' he replied.

'Good.' I turned to Mr Wood. 'Can we have a word, Boss?' I asked. He adopted his worried look and the three of us moved outside, into the corridor.

'So far,' I said, 'all we are concentrating on is lifting Chilcott. What I'd really like to know is: what is he doing over here? If he's up to something on my patch, I want to know what it is.'

'What are you suggesting, Charlie?' Mr Wood demanded wearily.

'Just that we don't arrest him straight away. I think we should follow him for a bit longer, find out who he's working for.'

'No,' Mr Wood stated. 'Definitely not.'

'He's been tailed for three hundred miles. Another twenty won't hurt.'

'I said no.'

I turned to DS Caton. 'What do you think, Jeff?'

He shrugged, embarrassed by the position I'd placed him in. 'Mr Wood's the boss,' he said.

'But could you do it, on the bike, working with someone in a car?'

'Yeah, no problem.'

'No, Charlie,' Mr Wood said. 'If he gets off at Heckley, you arrest him. And that's my last word.'

'It seems a shame, though, doesn't it?'

Gilbert heaved a sigh that would have blown a

small galleon off the rocks. 'Just ... just make it look good,' he said.

'Right,' I replied. 'Right.' I looked at my watch. It was 17:33. Twenty-one minutes to go.

We had a lightning rehearsal in the briefing room, with me drawing a plan of the station and slashing arrows across it. I designated who would ride with whom and appointed Annette as my driver.

'Code names?' someone asked.

'They're Batman and Robin,' I replied.

'Da-da da-da, da-da da-da,' they all chanted.

'Who's who?'

'Chilcott's Robin. Put my phone number in your memories, but we'll use the radio when the action starts, switched to talk-through but no chit-chat. OK?'

'OK,' they replied.

'And no heroics. He's dangerous, so don't forget it. There's enough widows in Heckley already.'

They strode out, talking too loudly and fooling around, but I hung back as Jeff zipped up his leather jacket and pulled his helmet on. Two others joined us and then Annette came over. 'What do you think, Jeff?' I asked.

'Always obey the last order, that's my motto,' he replied.

'And you two?'

'We're game,' one of them replied.

'OK,' I said. 'Nothing's decided, yet. We'll play it by ear if he gets off the train. Just listen for my instructions.'

'Of course,' one of them said, 'there's always the possibility that he has already jumped off, or he stays on it, isn't there.'

'He'll get off,' Jeff stated, his voice muffled by the gaudy helmet. 'I can feel it in my water.'

'What was all that about?' Annette asked as she jerked my car seat forward. The clock on the dashboard said 17:41.

I told her briefly what I had in mind. 'Does Mr Wood know?' she asked. 'Um, partly,'

'And he agrees?'

'Yes. Well, no, not really.'

'Oh, Charlie!'

I rang the RCS control on my mobile and gave them my number. Batman had commandeered a phone from a fellow passenger and was in regular communication with them. All along the line itchy-fingered policemen were assembling out-side the railway stations, wondering if the nation's most wanted criminal was going to grace their gunsights with his presence. The possible receptions varied. In some places he would be discreetly followed, in others shot on sight. We, I hoped, were doing it properly. As the train left each station Batman would pass a message back to the RCS and they would alert whoever was in charge at the next one down the line. At Heckley, that was me.

The train station is just down the road from the nick, so we made it with minutes to spare. A uniformed PC was at the coned-off entrance to the car-park, supervising a man in overalls who was working on the barrier. I thanked them both and told them to go for a cup of tea. We spread ourselves out, enjoying the luxury of all those parking places. Other cars, frustrated by having to drive round the block, started to fill the remainder.

'Presumably,' Annette said, 'if he is getting off here somebody will be meeting him. Taking a taxi would be risky.'

'Good point,' I agreed. We sat in silence for a few seconds, until I asked her if she was going away for the weekend. My mobile rang before she could reply, but her expression and the hesitation told me the answer. 'Heckley,' I said into the phone.

'Leaving Huddersfield,' the RCS controller told me. 'Still on-board.'

'Understood. Out.'

I turned to Annette. 'They've left Huddersfield. We're next.' I clicked the transmit button on the radio I was holding in the other hand and said a terse: 'Stand by, we're next,' into it. You can never be too sure who's listening to radio traffic.

'There's an interesting BMW just pulled in,' Annette told me.

'Where?'

'Behind us.'

I adjusted the wing mirror with the remote control, so I could see it without turning my head. It was R registered, silver, with four head-lights. 'Looks expensive,' I remarked as I made a note of the number.

'Series seven,' Annette stated. It sounded about right to me but cars aren't my strong point. She produced a tube of mints and offered me one. I shook my head. The clock changed from 17:50 to 17:51.

'Let's have some music,' she said, pushing the radio power button. A politician was sounding off about something or other. He used the expressions *spin doctor* and *mind set* in the same sentence, and would probably have slipped in a *sea change* had not Annette hit a station button. Two more tries and she was rewarded with Scott Walker's warm tones. 'That's better,' she said.

'We haven't been for a meal for a while,' I remarked.

'No,' she agreed.

'It's Thursday.'

'So it is.'

'If Chilcott's not on this train we could go for one.'

'A girl's got to eat,' she declared, throwing me a big grin.

I smiled at her and started to say: 'You should laugh more often. It suits you,' but the phone started warbling somewhere in the middle of it.

'Heckley,' I said.

'He's on his feet, heading for the door. Looks like this is it.'

'Understood. Out.'

I needed a pee. It's always the same: the least bit of excitement and I remember that I haven't been to the loo for four hours. 'This could be it,' I told her, and clicked the send button on the RT. 'Charlie to the Young Turks,' I said into it, 'it's looking good for us.' Three cars down in the facing row Dave raised a finger off the steering wheel in acknowledgement, and a face in a window to my left raised an eyebrow. I *wish* I could do that. Smoke puffed from the exhaust of

237

the car in front as he started the engine. I reached forward to kill Scott Walker and we both pulled our seatbelts on.

It all went off like a dream, exactly as planned, but you'd never have believed it. The Regional Crime Squad DCI was called Barry Moynihan, and he was one of the grumpiest little piggies I've ever come across. Now he was slumped in a chair in the corner of Mr Wood's office, elbows on his knees, face in his hands. He'd ranted and raved all the way to the station and plenty more when he was inside, but it's hard to take a bollocking from somebody wearing three-quarter length Burberry check shorts and a Desperate Dan T-shirt. Gilbert was lounging back in his executive chair, staring at the blank wall opposite. I was on a hard seat, left ankle on right knee, wondering if breaking the silence would be polite. I picked up my coffee cup and took a long loud slurp. Gilbert glared eloquently at me, but didn't attempt to put his feelings into words. I shrank into my jacket and placed my mug back on his desk as if it might explode.

Moynihan leapt to his feet and paced across the office. 'She might be in Le Havre now, for all I know,' he declared. He thrust his hands into the pockets of his shorts, then took them out again. 'God knows where she and the kids are.'

'Try ringing her again,' Gilbert suggested.

'How can I?' he snapped. 'How can I? The daft cow's got the friggin' mobile switched off.' He was back at his chair. He spun it round and crashed down on it, back to front, resting his chin

238

on his forearms. 'She's never driven the Frontera before,' he informed us.

'You should be able to join her tomorrow,' Gilbert ventured.

'Where?' he demanded. 'Portsmouth? France? I only popped across to arrivals to see if my parents were there.' He banged a palm against the side of his head, saying: 'And my friggin' passport's in the glove box.'

I had to admit it; he was in a predicament. No money, no credit cards, stranded in Yorkshire without a passport, in clothes like that. I must have smirked or sniggered, because suddenly he was on his feet again, pointing at me. 'You're history,' he snarled. 'You're fuckin' history.'

'That's enough,' Gilbert told him. 'I'll not have you talk to one of my senior officers like that.'

'He deliberately didn't arrest him,' Moynihan ranted. 'A target criminal, and he let him go.'

'He had his reasons,' Gilbert said.

'He deliberately disobeyed instructions.'

'Listen,' I said, looking at Moynihan. 'We had less than forty minutes notice that he was on a train that stopped at Heckley. Two minutes notice that he was getting off. RCS had taken all our firepower. We'd had no time to evacuate the station and I wasn't going to risk the lives of my officers and any civilians on your say-so. We contained the situation and have isolated the target. We have also identified his accomplices. I'd call that good work.'

'God!' Moynihan cursed, 'What a friggin' hole.'

There was a knock at the door and Mr Wood snapped: 'Come in!' so loudly my ankle slipped off my knee and my foot slammed down. The door opened and DS Jeff Caton emerged, leather jacket flapping, hair plastered down with sweat, grinning like a new dawn. He had a red line over his bloodshot eyes and down his cheeks, where the helmet had pressed.

'Good,' Mr Wood said. 'So what's the position, Jeff?'

'Pretty hunky-dory,' he replied, flexing the fingers of his right hand. 'We followed him over the tops and he turned off on to the old Oldfield Road, then down a narrow lane that goes right over towards Dolly Foss, past the dam. You know where I mean, Boss?' he asked, turning to me.

'I think so,' I replied.

'By the way, this is DCI Moynihan from the Met RCS,' Gilbert told Jeff.

'Pleased to meet you,' Jeff said, extending a hand. Moynihan ignored it and Jeff said: 'Suit yourself.'

Gilbert had acquired the appropriate OS map and we leaned over his desk as Jeff traced the route they'd taken. 'That's the house,' Jeff said, laying a finger on the map. 'It looks to have a name.'

'Ne'er Do Well Farm,' Gilbert read out, because the map was the right way up for him.

'Ne'er Do Well?'

'That's what it says.'

'Sounds appropriate.'

'What's the layout like,' Gilbert asked.

'Couldn't be better, I'd say,' he replied. 'It's an old farmhouse, with signs of some restoration work, so it's in reasonable condition. There's a

240

dry gill behind it and about five hundred yards away, on the other side of the gill, there's a rock outcrop, not far from a track. It's a perfect place for an OP.'

'We won't need an observation post,' Moynihan asserted. 'As soon as we've enough bodies we're lifting him. Where can I use a phone?'

He spent half an hour on the telephone in the secretary's office and Gilbert used the time to ring the Deputy Chief Constable. His advice was to let them get on with it. Give any assistance they might ask for, but otherwise leave it to them. Jeff told us about tailing Chilcott and I made some more coffee. He'd alternated with the Fiesta, hanging about a quarter of a mile behind, and was certain they hadn't been spotted.

'You did well,' I told him.

'*He* did bloody well,' Gilbert told us, nodding towards the adjoining office where Moynihan was brewing something. 'All that way, without being rumbled.'

'Dressed like that,' I added.

Moynihan came back in and we fell silent. 'Right,' he said. 'From now on it's an RCS shout. A team from the Met are coming up to lift him, probably on Saturday morning. In the meantime – tonight and tomorrow – number three district RCS will keep an eye on the farm. Thank you for your help, gentlemen, but we won't require any more assistance from you. If you don't like it, contact Chief Superintendent Matlock.'

With them it's personal. Chilcott was as good as a cop killer, one of their target criminals, and someone at the Met wanted the pleasure of feeling his collar. It would look bad if a bunch of hicks from Heckley did the job for them.

'Good,' Gilbert said. 'Good. That takes the pressure off us. All the same, we will keep a weather eye on things, if you don't mind. Just in case. We do like to know exactly what's going off in our little neck of the woods.'

Annette had vanished but didn't answer the phone when I rang her flat. I'd stayed behind to brief our local RCS boys, and it must have been after eight when I left the station. I drove straight to a pub up on the moors and had the landlady's steak and kidney pie. Friday morning I apologised to Annette and said I'd tried to ring her.

'I thought you'd be here until late,' she replied, 'so I went to the Curtain.'

'Aw, I am sorry. I wish I'd known. Did Mr Ho entertain you?'

'Yes. He was sweet. I said you might be along later, and when you didn't turn up he was all apologetic and filled with concern. He said you must have had a good reason for not being there.'

'Mmm, stupidity,' I replied.

I told her all about the RCS take-over and she said she'd enjoyed the shout. Her adrenaline was high and it had kept her awake all night.

'Maybe that was the monosodium glutamate,' I suggested. 'Yes, perhaps it was,' she agreed, but there was just a tinge of pink on her cheeks as she said it.

'This weekend...' I began. 'Are you going away?'

'Yes, unless...'

'Unless?'

242

'Unless you want me to work.'

'Er, no. No, I don't think that will be necessary.'

'Right. Thanks.'

I spent the rest of the morning on the word processor, typing a full account of the Heckley station caper in graphic detail. I even slipped in a few semi-colons, because I suspected it would be read in high places. I laid it on thick, saying that I thought it unsafe to approach Chilcott, a suspected killer, in a public place when we were ill-prepared. In fact, I made such a good job of it I decided that any other course of action would have been downright irresponsible. Ah, the power of the pen.

It gave me a headache. I found some aspirin in my drawers and washed a couple down with cold tea. I was rubbing my eyes with my forefingers when there was a knock at the door and it opened. I blinked and looked at my visitor. It was Nigel Newley, my one-time whizz-kid protégé.

'Hiya, Nigel,' I gushed. 'Sit down. Do you want a tea?'

'No thanks, Charlie. I was in the building, so I thought I'd call in.'

'You did right. So where's the famous moustache?'

'Ah.' He rubbed his top lip. 'You heard about that, did you? I decided it wasn't quite the part. Looked too frivolous.'

'For a detective on a murder case? Sounds a nasty job. How are you getting on with it?'

'Pretty good. We found semen samples on her, so we're going straight for mass testing, no messing about. That's why I'm here.'

'Nothing on the data base?'

'No, unfortunately. She was gorgeous, Charlie. Beautiful and intelligent. I wouldn't be surprised if somebody wasn't stalking her, but we haven't turned anything up yet.'

'Boyfriend? Ex-boyfriends?'

'Married last Easter to a childhood sweetheart who has a cast-iron alibi. He was building a bridge in Sunderland at the time. We haven't cleared him with the DNA yet, but we will.'

'And what does Les say about it all?' Les Isles was Nigel's new superintendent, and an old pal of mine.

'Oh, he's OK. A bit different from you, but he's OK. He wants to go ahead with the mass testing, soon as possible. Says there's no point in hanging about.'

'That sounds like Les.' I moved the computer mouse to cancel the screen saver, and clicked the save icon. I was playing for time, organising my thoughts. 'Tell me this,' I said. 'This girl...'

'Marie-Claire Hollingbrook.'

'...Marie-Claire. The reports say she was sexually assaulted. What exactly did that mean?'

'She was raped. Strangled and raped.'

'Post mortem?'

'Possibly.'

'Was she assaulted anally?'

'Why?'

'Because I want to know.'

'You want to know if there's any comparison with your case. Margaret Silkstone.'

'Yes.'

'I thought that was cleared up.'

'It is, but maybe this is a copycat.'

'Mr Isles has considered that. Yes, she was raped vaginally and anally, but I didn't tell you. We're not releasing that information.'

'We didn't release it for Mrs Silkstone, but the *UK News* got hold of it.'

'Maybe they were kite flying.'

'No, they knew about it. Someone spoke out of turn.'

'So,' he said, pointing to the little bottle on my desk and changing the subject. 'What's with the pills.'

I picked it up and placed it back in the drawer. 'It's nothing,' I said. 'I've just been staring at that thing for two hours. It's a bit bright for me. Do you know how to change it?'

'Just alter the contrast,' Nigel replied.

'How?'

'With the contrast control.'

I looked at the blank strip of plastic under the screen. 'There isn't a contrast control.'

'It's on the keyboard. You alter it on the keyboard.'

'There's nothing wrong with the contrast on the keyboard,' I argued. 'It's the display that's too bright. It's giving me spots before my eyes.'

'What sort of spots?'

'Just, little spots.'

'Do they go away when you stop looking at the monitor?'

'I don't know. I can't see them all the time.'

Nigel said: 'Turn towards the window and close your eyes.' I did as I was told. 'Can you see them now?' He asked.

'Yes.'

'Right. Cover one eye with your hand.' I did. 'Can you see them now?'

'I can just see two of the little buggers, close together near the middle.'

'Do they move when you look up?'

'Um, yes. Not straight away. They follow, quite slowly.'

'OK. Now the other eye.'

I swapped hands and the two spots vanished, but now I could see three others, spread about. 'I can see three now,' I told him.

'They're floaters,' Nigel informed me.

'Floaters? What are they?'

'Dead cells, floating about in the fluid of your eyeball.'

'Oh. What causes them?'

'Age. It's your age.'

'Well how come I have three in one eye and only two in the other? They're both the same age.'

'It's not that specific.'

The door burst open and Dave Sparkington was standing there. 'What do you want?' he demanded, looking at Nigel.

Nigel faced up to him, saying: 'I came to have a conversation with the *Big Issue* seller, not his mongrel.'

'We were talking about floaters,' I said to Dave.

'Floaters?' he queried.

'Yeah. Do you ever get them?

'Floaters?'

'Mmm.'

'Well, now and again. Especially if I've been

246

eating chicken chow mein.'

We agreed to meet on Wednesday evening and Nigel drifted off to organise a caravan in the market place where all the males of the town would have six hairs plucked from their heads, or would donate some other body sample, if they so preferred. It would be voluntary, but a close eye would be kept on those who didn't attend. Superintendent Isles would have prepared a list of the usual suspects, and they'd be encouraged along. I told Dave what Nigel was doing.

He said: 'Les Isles will have his balls for a paperweight if he finds out that Nigel's been talking to you about it.'

I said: 'There are certain similarities with our Mrs Silkstone job.'

'Copycat,' he replied. 'All the gory details were in the paper.'

'That's what I said.'

In the afternoon a superintendent from the Met RCS came in and introduced himself. He was obviously on a damage limitation exercise, shaking my hand, calling me Charlie, saying what a good job we'd done. I showed him Ne'er Do Well Farm on the map, then took him there, via the lane at the other side of the gill where the rock outcrop was.

Barry Moynihan was in charge, wearing a shell suit that somebody two sizes smaller had loaned him, with a decent growth of stubble on his face. Three others, from number three district, were also there; two of them permanently watching the farm. I had a look through their binoculars, but the place was as still and silent as a fog-bound airport.

Two more arrived, bringing flasks of soup, blankets and waterproofs. As they lifted them from their boot I glimpsed the dull metal of a Heckler and Koch rifle barrel. I had no doubt they had a whole armoury of weapons in their cars: H & K A2s for general purpose killing; Glock PT17s for close range killing; and perhaps a Heckler 93 sniper rifle, for long-range killing. I had an uneasy feeling that Kevin Chilcott would not be walking away from this one.

They were reluctant to discuss tactics in front of me and I began to feel like a rogue sausage roll at a bar mitzvah, so I glanced at my watch and said I'd better be off. It was just after half-past four when I left, and ten to five when I walked into the office, quietly whistling to myself: *The hills are alive, with the sound of gunfire*. At twenty-six minutes past five the phone rang. It was Superintendent Cox, the RCS super that I'd just taken up on to the moors.

'Did a motorcycle pass you, Charlie, on the way back to Heckley?' he asked.

'A motorbike? Not that I remember,' I replied.

'Shit! A bike left the house, about one minute after you. We clocked him heading that way, but lost him soon afterwards. He was probably in front of you.'

'You think it was Chilcott?'

'Yeah, didn't you know? A bike's his chosen mode of transport when he's on a job. He can handle one. Used to race at Brands Hatch in his younger days.'

'No, I didn't know that.'

'Christ, Charlie, I hope this is a dummy run and not the real thing. If it is the shit'll hit the fan.'

And I bet I knew who'd catch it all. 'Do you have a number for the bike?' I asked.

'No. Just those of ones stolen locally in the last couple of weeks.'

'You have done your homework. What make did he race?'

'What did he race? No idea, why?'

'Because bikers are often loyal to one make, that's why.'

'Christ, that's a thought, Charlie. That'd narrow it down. Well done.'

He was telling me that they'd asked traffic to look out for him when someone at that end attracted his attention. 'Wait a minute, Charlie,' he said. 'Wait a minute ... he's back. Thank fuck for that. We can see him, riding towards the house.'

I hung about for another hour, but no reports of gunshots or dead bodies came in, so it must have been a training spin. Cox didn't bother to ring me back so I went home via Sainsbury's and did a major shop. My favourite check-out girl wasn't on duty, which meant that the ciabatta bread and feta cheese were pointless purchases.

I had them for supper, toasted under the grill with lots of Branston pickle until they were bubbling. Welsh rarebit, Italian style, but it wasn't a good idea. I lay awake for most of the night, thinking about a man who was loose in society with the intention of killing someone. Thinking about Annette. Thinking about her friend.

What if ... what if ... what if Chilcott shot his target, who, by the type of coincidence that you only find in cheap fiction, just happened to be Annette's friend? Would I be pleased? Would she turn to me for consolation? Yeah, probably, I thought, to both of them. That's when I dropped off, just before the cold breath of a new day stirred the curtains and the bloke in the next street who owns half of the market and drives a diesel Transit set off for work.

Saturday is his busiest day, and I had a feeling that this one might be mine too. I had a shower and dressed in old Wranglers, cord shirt and leather jacket. I put my Blacks trainers on my feet, designed for glissading down scree slopes. You never know when you might need to.

According to the electoral role, the tenants of Ne'er Do Well Farm were Carl and Deborah Faulkner. According to the DVLA, the series seven BMW that picked Chilcott up at the station belonged to Carl Faulkner. According to our CRO, Carl Faulkner had a string of convictions long enough to knit a mailbag and Deborah had a few of her own. His were for stealing cars, bikes, household items and bundles of bank notes, plus GBH and extortion. Hers were for receiving, causing an affray, and a very early one for soliciting. The one thing that they certainly weren't was farmers.

'Nice couple, aren't they?' Dave said as I returned the printout to him. He sat in the spare chair and placed his coffee on my desk.

'He saved her from a life on the streets,' I

commented, sliding a beer mat towards him.

'Blimey, you're in a good mood,' he said.

'And why not? It's a new day, the weekend.'

'Chilcott might be the Met's,' he responded, 'but these two are ours.'

'They haven't done anything.'

'Well that'll make it harder, won't it,' he declared. He had a sip of coffee and continued: 'There's harbouring a fugitive, for a start. And conspiracy. And probably stealing a bike. And I bet they don't have a TV licence.'

'First time they poke their heads above a windowsill they'll probably have them blown off,' I said.

'Yeah, that's a strong possibility,' he agreed.

Word came through that strange policemen were congregating in our canteen and eating all the bacon sandwiches. They were the Met's Regional Crime Squad. At nine o'clock Mr Cox came in to my office on a courtesy call, to tell me that they were having a meeting in the conference room and they'd be very grateful if I could make myself available to answer any questions that might arise about local conditions, whatever they were. He looked as if he'd spent the night on a bare mountain, which he had. I said: 'No problem,' and followed him downstairs.

They were an ugly-looking bunch, chosen for their belligerence in a tight situation and not their party manners. Any of them could have moonlighted as a night-club bouncer or a cruiserweight. A couple wore suits and ties, some wore anoraks and jeans, others were in part police uniform, bulging with body armour. I gave

251

them a *good morning* when I was introduced and settled down to listen.

It was the usual stuff: isolate; control; maximum show of power, minimum violence. There was only one road going past the farm, with junctions about half a mile away to one side and two miles away at the other. A bridlepath crossed one of the roads. I told them that it was not negotiable by a car but a Land Rover or a trail bike might do it.

They would set up roadblocks on the lane, either side of the farm, and the local force would create an outer ring of roadblocks, just in case. This last comment raised a few sniggers, because they all knew it to be superfluous. Nobody would get past them. Mr Cox asked the various teams to acknowledge that they were clear about their duties and said: 'OK, gentlemen, let's bring him in.'

I was guest of honour, invited to ride with him. Our car-park was filled with their vehicles, haphazardly blocking the regulars in or out, and others were parked outside, straddling the yellow lines and pavement. We slowly disentangled ourselves and moved in a convoy out of town, towards the moors. I suspected that some of them had never seen a landscape devoid of houses, billboards and takeaways.

A steady drizzle was percolating through the atmosphere as we crossed the five hundred foot contour, blurring the colours slipping by our windows to a dirty khaki. Just how I like it. Superintendent Cox turned his collar up in an involuntary action and switched the windscreen wipers on.

'That's the lane to the other side of the farm,' I told him. He slowed and jabbed his arm several times through his open window. I swivelled round in my seat and counted five vehicles turn in that direction. Two miles further I said: 'And this is our lane to the farm.' He turned off the main road and set his trip odometer to zero.

'I reckon we make the block in about one point three miles,' he stated, slowing to a crawl. Three minutes later, with the farm still not in sight, he stopped and switched the engine off. 'This'll do,' he said.

Three vehicles from our side and two from the other were going to approach the farm and make the arrests. The others would act as roadblocks in case someone made a run for it. Our three moved ahead and parked in single file. Doors swung open and black looks were cast at the sky. Stooped figures opened boots, lifting out pieces of equipment: waterproofs; body armour; weapons. They donned hats and baseball caps, or pulled hoods over their heads. I stepped out and felt the cool rain on my face. Beautiful.

Cox was on the radio, calling up the observation post. I heard them report that the farm was as quiet as a grave. About half an hour earlier the curtains in an upstairs room had opened, and that was the only activity they'd seen. He made contact with the other section of our small army, code name T2, but they hadn't turned into the lane yet. The chopper was standing by, he informed us.

T1 was us, or more precisely the three cars that

253

would do the job. When the snatch teams were kitted up they squashed themselves into the cars and waited, steam and smoke rising from the open windows as they waited for the call. Every couple of minutes a cigarette end would come curling from one of the windows to *sizz* out in the wet grass. Our remaining three cars arranged themselves at angles across the narrow lane, completely blocking it.

'The trap is set,' Cox told me with a satisfied grin. He produced a half-empty hip flask of Famous Grouse from the depths of a pocket and took a long swig. I shook my head when he offered it to me, so he had mine, too.

He was on the radio again, chasing up T2 when there was a crackle of interference and a voice shouted: 'They're moving, they're moving!'

'Quiet please! Come in OP,' Cox said.

'Activity at the farm, Skipper,' came the reply. 'Three figures have dashed out of the house. In a hurry. I reckon they've rumbled us.'

'T2, acknowledge.'

'T2 receiving.'

'Are you at the lane end yet?'

'We're at a lane end, Skip, but it's only a dirt road.'

'That's the bridle path. The lane you want is about half a mile further on. For fuck's sake get there, now! OP, come in.'

'OP receiving.'

'What's happening?'

'They're in the garage, I think. Yes, the big door's opening and a motorbike's coming out.'

'My team, T1, did you hear that?'

'Yes, Skip.'

'He's making a run for it. Stand by.' Car doors opened and they tumbled out, brandishing their Heckler and Kochs.

'OP, OP, which way'd he go?'

'He's not reappeared yet from behind the house. A Land Rover and the BMW have also just come out of the garage and gone round the house. I can see the bike now. He's turned left, heading east.'

'That's towards us. Good.'

'And the other two are heading west.'

'Right. Did you clock that, T2?'

'Yes, Skip.'

'Are you at the lane end yet?'

'Not sure, Skip. There's a dam and a reservoir with a lane...'

'That's the wrong way!' I yelled at Cox. 'They've turned the wrong friggin' way!'

'You've turned the wrong way,' Cox told them, trying to read the map that was draped over his steering wheel. 'You need to be about three miles the other way, and get a move on.' He turned to me, saying: 'Fortunately Chilcott's coming towards us.' I rang Heckley control and told them to let our boys know that he'd made a run for it. It looked as if we might have to do the job for them after all.

The road ahead undulated like the spine of the Loch Ness monster and bent to the left. I climbed out of the car and peered at the furthest crest in the road. After a few seconds the bike appeared, rising into view then falling out of sight as it sank into a hollow. Then it appeared again, nearer and bigger, travelling quite cautiously, and dropped out of sight. In front of me the RCS crew spread out across the road and adopted kneeling positions, firearms at the ready. The bike rose into view again and fell away. One more brow left. We could hear it now. They pressed rifle butts against shoulders and peered down sights.

The rider's head appeared, then shoulders, windscreen, wheels: a splash of colour – red, white and fluorescent green – in the murky landscape.

'Here he comes,' a voice said at my elbow. It was Cox, his eyes bright with excitement. In the next few minutes he'd be reciting the caution to the most wanted man in Britain or zipping him into a body bag. Either would do. The bike stopped, a hundred and fifty yards down the road. I could sense the fingers tightening on triggers, and I desperately needed a pee.

'Easy boys, he's not going anywhere,' Cox shouted.

The biker tried to do a U-turn, but the road was too narrow. He paddled the bike backwards a few feet and completed the manoeuvre, driving off back towards the farm with a new urgency The engine note rose and fell as he went up through the gears, the bike and rider bright as a tropical fish as it crested the brows.

'T1 to T2,' Cox yelled into the radio. 'He's coming back your way Where are you?'

'T2 receiving, at the lane end,' I heard them confirm. 'Forming roadblock now.'

'Have you seen the other two vehicles?'

'Negative, Skip.'

'He'll be with you in about two minutes.'

The same thing happened at their end. The biker stopped, turned round, and headed back this way.

'OK, let's tighten the net,' Cox ordered. We climbed back into our seats and moved half a mile down the road, until the farm was clearly in view. We'd just reassembled into a roadblock when the biker came burbling round the corner, the rider sitting up, only one hand on the handlebars.

'He's a cool customer,' I said.

'Bravado,' Cox explained. 'He knows the show's over.'

The biker turned round, went back, saw the others blocking his flight and turned towards us yet again. He accelerated, front wheel lifting off the road, as if about to do an Evel Knievel over our heads, then slowed to a crawl. Cox was right: he could handle a bike. T2 moved forward, shrinking his playground.

There was a gate in the wall about a hundred yards in front of us, marking the beginning of the bridle path. The rider stopped, leaned the bike on its side stand and made a dash at the gate. Cars from both sides accelerated towards him, tyres spinning on the wet road. We held back, maintaining the roadblock. He pushed the gate open and leapt back onto the bike, gunning it towards the gap as the car from our side swerved to a standstill feet from him.

I'd started to say that he wouldn't get far on a bike like that when events made my words redundant. The motorcycle bucked, a leg tried to steady it but the bike spun sideways and shot from under its rider. Policemen were running towards him, guns pointing, shouting orders across each other.

The leather clad figure rolled over onto his back, one leg smeared with mud.

'Stay still!' Someone shouted.

He stayed still. In seconds he was surrounded by enough guns to blow a battleship out of the water, except we're taught that you can never have enough. And I'd proved it to be true, once, a long time ago.

'Don't move.' Hands reached down, pressed against him, passed over his limbs and torso, feeling for hard objects.

'Now, sit up, slowly.'

The figure sat up, very slowly.

'Now, very slowly, remove your helmet.'

A gloved hand moved deliberately towards the chinstrap and fumbled with the fastening. Then the other hand came up and started to ease the helmet over the rider's head, twisting it from side to side, forcing it upwards over flattened ears. A chin emerged, then a nose and eyes as it lifted clear. The rider's hair was still inside the helmet. When it was high enough the hair fell down, a cascade of shoulder-length peroxide-blonde locks that would have looked good on any Page Three girl. 'Was that slowly enough?' she asked with a smile.

'Oh fuck!' Cox exclaimed. I couldn't have put it any better myself.

I phoned the nick and told them what had happened. T2 stopped the BMW, driven by Carl Faulkner, which meant that Chilcott was in the Land Rover and had probably fled cross-country, bypassing our roadblocks. Deborah Faulkner, the motorcyclist, was handcuffed and taken to Leeds, her husband to a different nick in that city, but they both played dumb, refusing to answer questions. The helicopter came thumping over the hill, somewhere up in the clouds, and made a wide banking turn before heading back towards the valley and civilisation.

Cox liaised with our control, with number three district RCS and with the Met RCS before admitting: 'That's it. It's out of our hands, now.'

'I'm going to the house,' I said, walking in that direction. I'd almost reached it when the depleted convoy overtook me.

Barry Moynihan and the rest of the observation team had already arrived, walking across the moor from their overnight position. He'd borrowed a waterproof coat and leggings, but was still wearing the sandals with the rugged soles and more buckles and straps than an S & M salesman's sample case. His colleagues were brandishing guns as if they were no more lethal than walking sticks, and the whole scene could have been newsreel footage from the latest East European war zone.

'We've swept the house, Mr Cox,' a tall guy with a bristly moustache and a military bearing said as he came out of the front door, 'and it's clean.' He was carrying a Remington pump action shotgun, probably loaded with CS gas cartridges.

'Thanks, Bruce,' Cox replied. 'Let's see what we can find, then.'

'Gentlemen,' I called, raising my voice above the hubbub. They all turned to me. 'Can I remind you that this is a crime scene,' I continued, 'and ought to be inspected with that in mind, by the appropriate people.'

'Don't worry, Charlie,' Cox said. 'We'll be careful.' He wandered inside followed by his acolytes, and after a few gestures of helplessness I followed. They moved through the kitchen and into the living rooms. I headed for the fire burning in the iron range and stood with my back to it. They could trample on as much evidence as they wanted, but this was as far as I was going. The house had triple glazing, but any attempts at modernisation ended with that. The kitchen floor was stone-flagged, and ashes from the fire had spread away from the hearth, crunching under your feet as you moved around. All the furniture was bare wood, working class antique, and the sink was a deep stone set-pot.

Barry Moynihan came in and looked around. 'They're all through there,' I told him.

He joined me by the fire, saying: 'I'm perished,' as he balanced on one leg and tried to dry a soaking foot against the flames.

Suspended from the ceiling by a system of strings and pulleys was a rack filled with clean washing, hung up to dry. I pulled a wooden chair from beneath the table and stood on it. The washing was dry. I removed a threadbare towel and a pair of hiking socks from the rack and handed them to Moynihan. 'Put them on,' I told him, 'or you'll catch pneumonia.'

He took them from me and sat on another chair, drying his feet. When he'd finished he stood up, stomped around a few steps, then pronounced: 'That's better. Thanks.'

'We got off to a bad start,' I said.

'Yeah, well.'

'Have you contacted your wife?'

'Yeah. She went home. At first it sounded a daft thing to do, but I suppose it was for the best. I've spoken to her a couple of times and she's calmed down. Now I'm hoping the firm will recompense me.'

'They ought to,' I told him.

There was a shout from the next room that sounded like my name. We stood there waiting for it again, until Cox appeared in the doorway and said: 'We've identified Chilcott's target, Charlie. Come and look at this.'

We followed him through into what was the living room. It was gloomy, even with all the lights on, furnished with overstuffed easy chairs and flowery standard lamps. Centrepiece of the room was a highly polished table that was no-doubt worth a bob or two, and spread over it was a series of black and white photographs.

'We found them in this,' Cox said, showing me a cardboard folder. 'What do you think?'

The cops around the table parted to make room for me. There were six pictures, arranged in a big square. Top left was simply the frontage of a house, such as an estate agent might produce. Next one, a male figure was emerging from the door at the side of the house. After that it was his

261

car, focusing on the numberplate. Then the man himself, stooping to unlock the car, followed by two more of him behind the wheel.

I picked up the last print and held it towards the light. It was taken through the side window of the car, and the driver was completely unaware of it. Next time, it might be a gun, blowing his brains out. Somebody coughed.

'It's me,' I said, looking at Cox. He didn't reply. Everyone was silent, empty expressions on their faces. 'It's me,' I repeated. I placed the photo back on the table, carefully aligning it with its fellows. 'Why would anyone want to kill me?' I wondered out loud, and I swear they all shrank back a step.

Chapter 9

Four days is the magic figure. The chopper clocked the Land Rover entering the multi-storey car-park in Heckley and that was as much as they could do. It was later found neatly parked on the next-to-top floor, with the doors unlocked. It had, needless to say, been stolen two weeks earlier. From the car-park there are covered walkways leading to the shopping mall and the old town area, and other exits at street level. He could have taken any one of them. Within minutes the place was flooded with Heckley's finest, all twelve of them, but Mr Chilcott had vanished. We suspect he had a safe house somewhere, and was holed-up in that.

Back at the farm I'd requested assistance from Heckley nick, which didn't come because they were busy, and from the scenes of crime people, who never have anything better to do on a Saturday lunchtime. Having a *fatwa* on me earned a certain amount of respect from the RCS team, so when I ordered them all out of the farmhouse they did as they were told. They piled into their vehicles and hot-footed it to Heckley, desperate to salvage some credibility. I stayed behind and they kindly left a car and three men with me, just in case. We stoked the fire and made coffee.

Four days is the time a terrorist on the run is trained to stay concealed. The police employ psychologists who have worked out that a fugitive would stay underground for three days before making his bid for freedom. After that time, we assume we've lost him. So the terrorists enlist more expensive psychologists who tell them to hide for four days before legging it. Fortunately our anti-terrorist people have become wise to this, and they brought it to our attention. OK, Chilcott wasn't a terrorist, but they all download the same manuals.

Nigel extended his hands towards me so that I could extricate my new pint from between his fingertips. He placed another in front of Dave and an orange juice and soda on his own beer mat.

'Cheers,' we said.

'Cheers,' he replied, taking a sip. As Chilcott was still on the run and appeared to have a reasonable working knowledge of my movements, we had forsaken the Spinners and were having our Wednesday night meeting in the Bailiwick. 'So what time were you there until?' Nigel asked.

'Seven o'clock.' I said. 'We were stuck at Ne'er Do Well Farm until after seven. The SOCOs had left about four.'

'We were running about like blue-arsed flies,' Dave said.

'Flashing blue-arsed flies?' I suggested.

'And them.'

'Do you think he's still in Heckley?'

'God knows.'

'It's four days today. SB said he'd lie low for four days.'

'Don't remind us.'

I took a sip of beer and said: 'Well it proves one thing.'

'What's that?' they asked.

'That I'm not paranoid.'

'Just because someone *is* trying to kill you doesn't mean you're not paranoid,' Dave argued.

'Of course it does.'

'No it doesn't. He's only one man. It's not a conspiracy.'

'Of course it's a conspiracy.'

'No, it's not. He was doing it for money. It's not personal.'

'What difference does that make? The whole thing is one big conspiracy.'

'Against you? One big conspiracy against you?'

'Against everyone.'

'So someone's out to kill Nigel, too. And me. Is that what you're saying?'

'I might be.'

'You definitely are paranoid.'

'Is that what you think? Is that what you really think?'

'Yes.'

'Right,' I said. 'Right. Let me tell you something. You see this place?' I gestured towards the ceiling and they nodded. 'Good. And you see the names on all those labels behind the bar?' I read them off: 'Tetley's, Black Sheep, Bell's, Guinness, Foster's, and so on, and so on?'

'Ye-es,' they agreed.

'OK. Now let's look at what's outside. There's the Halifax opposite, and Barclays, and the Nat West. Further down there's Burger King and

Pizza Hut. There are jewellers, clothes shops galore, snack bars and ... oh, you name it and there's one out there.'

'So what's the point of all this?' Dave asked. Nigel grinned and took another sip of orange juice.

'The point is,' I told him, 'that it's all a big conspiracy. Why do all these companies exist? Go on, tell me that.'

'To do what they do,' he replied. 'To make beer or whatever, to provide a service, to employ people and to make a profit for their share-holders.'

'No they don't.'

'Well go on, then, clever clogs. You tell us why they exist.'

'They exist, every one of them, for one sole purpose.'

'Which is...?'

'Which is ... to convert my money into their money. That's what it's all about.'

'So that's why you're so reluctant to go to the bar,' Nigel commented.

'Cheeky sod!' I retorted.

'You are paranoid,' Dave concluded.

Shirley came to take us home and Dave bought her a tonic water. We were finishing our drinks when a familiar warbling tone came from somewhere on Nigel's person. 'Oooh, oooh,' we groaned, expressing our disapproval. Mobile phones are *verboten* on walks and in the pub. Nigel blushed and retrieved it from his pocket.

'Nigel Newley,' he said. I drained my glass and Dave did the same. 'Hello, Les.' Sounded like it was Les Isles, his boss. 'Hey! That's brilliant!' Good news. Lucky for some. 'Where does he live?' Sounded like Nigel had some work to do. 'Right. In the morning? Right. See you then. Thanks for ringing.' It would be an early alarm call for someone. He closed the phone and replaced it in his pocket, his face pink with enthusiasm.

'Guess what?' he said, 'We've had a match. One of the donated samples matches the DNA in the semen we found on Marie-Claire Hollingbrook. We're bringing him in first thing.'

'That was quick,' Dave said.

'It was, wasn't it.'

'So, er, where does he live?' I asked.

'Um, Heckley. He lives in Heckley.'

'Really? In that case he's one of ours, isn't he?'

'Oh no he isn't,' Nigel assured me. 'Oh no he isn't.'

I had a bodyguard, of course. It was all over the papers that we'd let Chilcott, Enemy Number One, slip through our fingers; if he still managed to complete his mission we'd really have egg on our faces. Well, they would; I'd have something else on mine. The two of them, Tweedle Dee and Tweedle Dum, sat patiently in the pub, backs to the wall, sipping soft drinks, while we tried to ignore them. I didn't like it, but knew better than to object. Shirley took me home first and they followed. I handed my keys over and one of them entered the house, casually, without making a drama out of it. 'You know where everything is,' I said when I was allowed in, waving towards the coffee ingredients, videos and sleeping bags that had accumulated in my front room. 'Make yourselves at home, gentlemen, I'm off to bed.'

'I've brought Terminator Two,' one of them told me as he filled the kettle.

'Seen it,' I lied. 'Early night for me. Keep it low.'

'Right. Tea?'

'Yes please. Will you bring it up?'

'No chance, you can wait.'

I felt like a guest in my own home. An unwelcome one at that. I took the mug of tea and trudged up the stairs to bed. Drinking doesn't suit me, and lately it had been creeping up a bit. I'd been thinking a lot, also, and the conclusions weren't good. I was at a funny age. From now on, it wasn't going to get much better. The good years, or what should have been the good years, were all in the past. Friday teatime Chilcott had gone on a dummy run, Superintendent Cox had said. I disagreed. I'd been up on the moors, watching the farm. Chilcott had come to Heckley looking for me, and he could have been out of the country again by the morning. Detectives are supposed to work regular hours, and on a Friday the whole world tries to get off home on time. It was his first opportunity to do the job, but my car hadn't been outside the nick, so he'd had to abort. A bullet through the brain, while I was sitting at the traffic lights; or here at home, sleeping, didn't sound too bad. I could live with that. It's all the alternatives that terrify me.

Annette took it badly. She'd sat there, white faced, when I'd announced that I was Chilcott's intended target. Afterwards she came into my office and asked what I was going to do. She thought I'd move away, stay in the country until things blew over, but I explained that it wasn't necessary. I had my minders, and Chilcott's number one priority, now, was making his escape. Even if he'd been paid in advance, nailing me would be off his agenda. I tried to sound as if I knew what I was talking about, as if the inner workings of an assassin's mind were my workaday fodder, but I don't think she believed me. I played safe and didn't suggest we go for a meal, that week.

Nigel and Les Isles arrested Jason Lee Gelder and charged him with the murder of Marie-Claire Hollingbrook. He'd walked into the caravan in Heckley market place, large as life, and donated six hairs and his name and address. Science did the rest. An arcane test, discovered by a professor at Leicester university as recently as 1984, reduced the DNA in Gelder's hair roots to a pattern of parallel lines on a piece of film that exactly matched the lines produced from the semen left on Marie-Claire's thighs. It was his, as sure as hedgehogs haven't grasped the Green Cross Code. It made the local news on Thursday evening and the nationals the next day. The people of the East Pennine division probably slept a little more contentedly in their beds, that weekend, knowing that a sex killer was safely behind bars.

'That was quick,' I said, when I spoke to Superintendent Isles on the telephone.

'I think he wanted catching,' he admitted. 'He

269

was hanging around as they set-up the caravan. He went for a burger then came back and made a donation. Wanted to know what it was all about. It was only about the fifteenth they'd taken at that point.'

Sometimes they do it to taunt the police, or to make the stakes higher. Ted Bundy killed more than thirty women across the USA. He moved to Florida because they had the death penalty. Trying to figure out why is like asking why a flock of birds turned left at that particular place in the sky and not right. Nobody knows. Maybe to-morrow they'll go straight ahead. We do tests to see if these people are sane: ask them questions; show them pictures; gauge their reactions. A man kills thirty women and they show him inkblots to decide if he's sane. Someone needs their head examining.

'So he's coughing, is he?' I asked.

'Oh no, he's not making it that easy for us,' Les replied. 'Say's he didn't do it; was nowhere near where she lived and has never been there.'

'Alibi?'

'Watching videos. He's classic material, Char-lie, believe me. We're waiting for the lab to do another test, the full DNA fingerprint job, but I haven't cancelled my holiday.'

'I'd like a word with him, Les,' I said.

'I thought you might. Why?'

'To see if there's anything to be learned about the way we handled the Margaret Silkstone case.'

'You mean, is this a copycat?'

'Something like that.'

'Has young Newley been talking to you? If he

has, I'll have his bollocks for a door knocker.'

'So when can I see him?' I asked. Not: 'Can I see him?' but: 'When can I see him?' It's what salesmen call closing. When I went to that sales conference I'd really listened.

'Give us two or three days for the reports,' Les said, 'then you can have a go at him.'

'Thanks. And he's called Gelder?'

'That's right. Jason Lee Gelder.'

'In olden times a gelder was a person who earned a living by cutting horse's testicles off,' I told him.

'Yeah, I know. It's a pity someone didn't cut his off.'

If you really want to ingratiate yourself with someone, you let them get the punch line in. I put the phone down and wondered what to have for tea.

The Regional Crime Squad paid renewed interest in the tapes Bentley prison had recorded of the conversations that led, we believed, to Chilcott being hired. Someone was willing to pay £50,000 to have me bumped off and they wanted to know who. We had the name of the people on both ends of the line, but it wasn't a big help. They were real nasties: professionals who'd tell you less than the Chancellor does on the eve of the budget. Except they'd do it belligerently, in language politicians only use when it slips out.

I had a passing interest myself in who was behind it all, so I made my own enquiries. I started by telephoning Gwen Rhodes, Governor of HMP Bentley. It took me all day to track her

271

down, but she was duly shocked when she learned what it was about, and gave me the freedom of her computer terminal, plus a crash course in using it.

On the morning I was there they turned the key on eight hundred and two inmates. That's screw-speak for the number of prisoners they had. In addition, a further one hundred and sixty-eight had passed through in the period I was interested in. Some had been released, some moved to less secure units, one or two possibly found not guilty. I printed out lists of their names and highlighted the ones that I thought I knew. One in particular leapt straight off the page at me.

'When you had Tony Silkstone,' I began, on one of the occasions when Gwen came back into the office, 'I don't suppose he could have had any contact with Paul Mann, could he?' It was Mann's phone calls that started the whole thing.

'Not at all,' Gwen assured me. 'Silkstone was on remand, Mann in A-wing, and never the twain shall meet. However,' she continued, 'you know how it is in places like this. Jungle drums, telepathy, call it what you will, but word gets around.'

'Who would Silkstone meet during association?'

'Fellow remandees. That's all.'

'What about the rehabilitation classes that Silkstone took? Who might he meet there?'

'Ah,' she sighed, and I swear she blushed slightly.

'Go on,' I said.

'Mainly cat C, with a few cat B. The ones making good progress, who we felt would benefit.'

'Is there always a warder present?'

'Yes. Always.'

'But he might have the opportunity to talk with them.'

'I doubt it, Charlie, but what might happen is this: he discusses his case with a fellow reman- dee, one who is about to go for trial and knows he'll be coming back. He leaves D-wing in the morning to go to court, but has a good idea that he'll be back in A- or B-wing by the evening. He could offer to have a word with someone he knows in there.'

I said: 'Not to put too fine a point on it, Gwen, the system's leaky.'

'Leaky!' she snorted. 'Of course it's leaky. We can't prevent them from talking amongst themselves. What sort of a place do you think this is?'

'It wasn't meant to be a criticism,' I replied.

I'd underlined four names, and we printed hard copies of their notes. Gwen showed me another file which showed who Silkstone had shared a cell with, and I printed their names and files, too.

Two of them were still there. Gwen used her authority and they both found they had a surprise visitor that afternoon. It cost me the price of four teas and four KitKats from the WVS stall to learn that Silkstone was a twat who never stopped complaining. He'd 'done over' a nonce, they said, and that made him all right, but half the time they hadn't known what he was talking about. He had big ideas and never stopped bragging about what he'd do when he was freed.

273

They were both looking at a long time inside, and soon tired of him. I thanked Gwen for her assistance and went home.

One of the other names was Vince Halliwell, who I'd put in the dock eight years ago. According to Gwen's computer he'd attended the same rehabilitation classes as Silkstone and had recently been transferred to Eboracum open prison, near York. He was nearing the end of his sentence, and considered a low risk, even though he was doing time for aggravated burglary. Halliwell was a hard case, but I remembered that there was something about him that I'd almost admired. He was tall, with wide bony shoulders and high cheeks, and blond hair swept back into a ponytail. I think it was the ponytail I envied. He had problems. All his life he'd lived in some sort of institution, and he had a record of binge drinking, paid for by thieving. The aggravated burglary – armed with a weapon – that we did him for was an escalation in his MO.

At first I hadn't considered talking to him, but that evening I started to change my mind. He'd refused to co-operate when he was arrested, but became garrulous when interviewed for psychiatric, social enquiry and pre-sentencing reports. They made sad reading, and he had a chip the size and shape of a policeman on his shoulder. It was hard to blame him. I rang Gwen at home and asked her to oil the wheels for me at HMP Eboracum. Next morning she rang me and said the Governor there was willing to play ball.

It was the probation officer I spoke to. She wasn't too keen on the idea, but the Governor was the boss... I assured her that Halliwell was a model prisoner, unlikely to blot his record at this late stage in his sentence, and I'd take responsibility if it all went pear-shaped. We settled for Friday morning.

When long-stay inmates are nearing the end of their sentences the prison authorities like to gradually re-introduce them to life on the outside; to give them a taste of freedom, in small doses. One way is by home visits, another is by what are called town visits. Vince Halliwell had no home to go to, so it would have to be a town visit. I knew he wouldn't talk to me in jail – somebody always knows it's a cop who's called to see you – but he might if I met him on neutral territory, away from screws and inmates and the gossip of a closed community.

The probation officer gave him strict instructions and a ten-pound note. It was a tough test. He had to catch the ten o'clock bus from the prison gates into York, walk to the Tesco supermarket, buy himself a pair of socks there, have a cup of coffee in the restaurant and catch the next bus back to the jail. He'd have to walk past all those pubs, all those shelves stocked with whisky and rum and beer from places he'd never heard of, with money jangling in his pockets. Anything less than superhuman effort and he'd be back at Bentley, category A again. At eight thirty, nice and early, I started the car engine and headed towards the Minster City.

I arrived with enough time to do my shopping, which was intentional, and to have a quick breakfast in the restaurant before he arrived, which was an afterthought. Their curries were a pound cheaper than Heckley Sainsbury's. At ten thirty I walked across the car-park towards the road he would come down.

It was a warm morning, with people strolling about in their shirt sleeves and summer dresses. Four-wheel drive vehicles with tyre treads like Centurion tanks slowly circulated, following sleek Toyota sports cars and chunky Saabs, all looking for a space near the entrance. In the afternoon they'd do the same outside the health club. The indicators flashed on a BMW like the one that met Chilcott at the station, and an elderly couple in front of me steered their trolley towards its boot. A few minutes later, out on the main road, they drove past me. The driver's window was down and I could hear the sound of Pavarotti coming from inside it. BMW spend countless millions of pounds and thousands of hours on wind tunnel tests. They install the finest music system money can buy with more speakers than an Academy Awards ceremony. They design a climate control – that's air conditioning to the rest of us – better than in the finest operating theatre in the world, and what happens? People drive around with the window down; that's what.

I hardly recognised him. Some thrive in prison, put weight on; others are consumed by it. Halliwell's time inside had reduced him to a shambling shell. Always a gaunt figure, he was now stooped and hollow and looked well into his fifties, although he was only about thirty-six. He crossed the road at the lights, waiting until they were red and then checking that the traffic had

276

stopped, glancing first this way, then the other, but still not moving until everybody else did. He was wearing grey trousers that had been machine-washed until they were shapeless, a blue regulation shirt that was almost fashionable, and cheap trainers. His jacket was gripped in one hand. I stood in the queue for the park-and-ride bus until he'd passed, then fell in behind him.

There were supermarkets before he went inside, but a man forgets, and the rest of us take progress, if that's what it is, for granted. He stopped to examine the rows of parked trolleys as if they were an outlandish life-form engaged in group sex, and stared at the big revolving doors as they gobbled up and regurgitated a steady stream of shoppers. Slowly, nervously, he made his way into the store.

The security cameras were probably focused on this suspicious, shabbily dressed character who wandered about aimlessly, occasionally changing direction for no reason at all, picking up packets and jars at random only to replace them after reading the labels, but nobody challenged me. How Barry Moynihan had followed Chilcott for eight or nine hours dressed like he was, without being spotted, I couldn't imagine. After a good look up and down the rows Halliwell selected a pair of socks and took them to the checkout. I replaced the jar of Chicken Tonight I was studying – 0.4g of protein, 7.7g of fat – and headed for the restaurant.

It was a serve-yourself coffee machine with scant instructions. Halliwell watched a couple of people use it before having a hesitant attempt himself. His first try dumped a shot of coffee essence and hot water through the grill, then a woman took over and showed him how to do it. He smiled and made an 'I'm only a useless man' gesture and allowed her to pass him in the queue at the till. For a few seconds I was afraid they would sit down together, but she had two cups on her tray and joined a waiting friend at one of the tables. Halliwell headed for an empty table in a corner. I collected a tea and joined him.

'It's Vince, isn't it?' I said, sitting down.

He looked at me, speechless, for a long time. His eyes were frosty blue, and the ponytail had given way to a regulation crop that still, annoyingly, looked good on him. He could have been a jazz musician on his way home from a gig, or a dissolute character actor researching a part. He had, I decided, that elusive quality known as sex appeal. His jacket was draped across his knees. He fumbled in the pockets until he found a tobacco pouch, and in a few seconds he was puffing on a roll-up.

'What you want?' he asked, eventually, as a cloud of smoke bridged the gap between us. A woman who was about to sit at the next table saw it and moved away.

'I was just passing,' I lied.

'Like 'ell you were. It's Priest, innit? Mr Priest?'

'Charlie when I'm off duty.'

'You still with the job, then?'

''Fraid so.'

'So this is all part of it, is it?'

'Part of what?'

'The test. This is all part of the test?'

278

'Oh yes,' I agreed. 'This is all part of it. All over York there are people from your past who are going to pop out in front of you, confront you with situations to see how you react. Then there are the markers. Women with clip boards and coloured pens, following you, giving you marks for style, difficulty and performance. So far you're doing well.'

He grinned, saying: 'They always said you were a bit of a card. Did you set all this up? If you did, you're wasting your time.'

He stood up to leave, but I said: 'Sit down, Vince, and hear what I have to say.' He sat down again. That's what eight years inside does to a man.

The roll-up was down to his fingertips. He nipped it and looked for an ashtray but there wasn't one, so he put the debris back in the pouch and made another.

'Could you eat a breakfast?' I asked.

'Not at your prices,' he replied.

'No charge. My treat.'

'No, thanks all the same.'

'It comes on a real plate, made of porcelain, with a knife that cuts.'

'I'll do without.'

I said: 'Listen, Vince. It's not going to be easy for you. You'll need all the help you can get, so if someone offers you a free breakfast, take it. That's my advice.'

'You weren't so generous with your 'elp and advice eight years ago,' he reminded me. 'You knew ... well, what's the point.' He left the statement hanging there, dangling like the rope from a swinging tree.

'I knew it wasn't your gun. Is that what you were going to say?'

'And the rest.' He twisted around in his chair until he was half-facing away from me.

'It wasn't my job to tell the court it wasn't your gun,' I said. 'It was your brief's. It was yours. You could have said whose it was.'

'And a fat lot of good it would 'ave done me.'

'It'd have got you five years instead of ten. Aggravated burglary's a serious offence.'

'You knew it wasn't mine. I've never carried a shooter, and you knew it.'

'There's always a first time, Vince. I wanted you to get fifteen years; keep you out of my hair for as long as possible. Now you're doing full term because you've refused to admit it was your gun. It's your choice all along, Vince. Take responsibility for your actions. Now, tell me this: How do you like your sausages?'

A youth in a white shirt was hovering near us. I looked up at him and he said: 'I'm sorry, Sir, but this is the no-smoking area.' Halliwell looked annoyed but nipped the tip of his cigarette.

I said to him: 'Go sit over there. I'll fetch you a breakfast,' and he carried his coffee to a table with an ashtray on it.

I kept a weather eye on him as I stood in the queue, but he sat patiently waiting, occasionally sipping the coffee, his glance following the succession of people who moved away from the pay point carrying trays and leading toddlers. I placed the plate of food in front of him and walked off towards the cigarette kiosk without waiting for a thank you. When I flipped the packet of Benson and Hedges on to the table, saying: 'If you must poison me, do it with something reasonable,' he grinned and said: 'Right. Cheers.'

I sipped the fresh tea I'd brought myself as he ate the first food he'd had in eight years that he could be sure nobody had dipped their dick in. When he'd half-cleared the plate he said:

'You not eating, then?'

'I had mine before you came,' I replied.

He manoeuvred a piece of egg white on to a corner of toast and bit it off. 'So this is all a fit-up, eh? You arranged the whole thing,' he mumbled.

'I thought you'd appreciate a day out,' I replied.

'You're wasting your time.'

I shrugged. 'It's a day out for me, too.'

'I'm sticking to my story.'

'That you didn't know the name of the bloke with you. You planned a burglary with him, did the job together, and never asked each other's names.'

He took a cigarette from the packet and lit it. 'Yeah, well,' he said, exhaling. 'That's how it was.'

'And you don't grass each other.'

'That's right.'

'He'd have grassed you. They always do.'

'Not always.'

'You were a fool, Vince. A twenty-four carat mug, believe me.'

'Yeah, well, I can sleep at nights.'

I changed the subject. 'How does Eboracum compare with Bentley?' I asked.

'It's OK,' he replied.

'Only OK? I'd have thought it would be a big improvement.'

'Oh, it is. It's just that, at Bentley, you knew where you stood, what the rules were, if you follow me. At this place, you're never sure. Some of the screws say one thing, then another will say summat different. 'Ere, what time is it? I'd better be getting back.'

'That's OK,' I told him. 'They know you're with me.'

'You sure?'

'I'm sure.' I decided to speed things up. 'Did you meet Tony Silkstone while you were in there?' I asked. 'He's one of mine, on remand.'

He grinned and said: 'Silko the Salesman? Yeah, I met him.'

'How come?' I asked. 'I thought you'd be on separate wings.'

'We were, but we had association. Well, not proper association, but we had these classes. Silko took one of them, sometimes, and we all joined. Well, it was an hour out of your room wasn't it? He couldn't 'alf talk, about, you know, motivation an' plannin' an' all that. We could all be millionaires, 'e told us, without breaking the law. Mind you, 'e did wink when 'e said that last bit.'

'That sounds like Tony,' I remarked.

'Yeah, well. He killed a nonce, didn't 'e? Good riddance, we all said. Come to think of it, we talked about you, once.'

'About me?'

'Yeah. We were in the classroom, me, 'im and

282

this screw, waiting for the others to arrive. I used to get the room ready, clean the blackboard an' tidy up. I'd just finished when they walked in. 'E was grumbling to the screw, saying that 'e'd be out, now, if it wasn't for this cop who was 'ounding 'im. This cop called Inspector Priest. I said that it was you that 'ad done me. That you'd ... well, you know.'

'That I'd fitted you up?'

'Yeah, well, summat like that.'

'So what did he say?'

'The screw laughed. He said that you'd just done someone you were chasing for twenty-odd years. It was in the papers, he said. Summat about a fire.'

'There was a fire in Leeds,' I explained. 'Back in 1975. Three women and five children were burnt to death. We just found out who started it.'

'Blimey,' he said, quietly. 'You got the bastards?'

'We got them. So what happened next?'

'Yeah, well, like I was saying. The screw thought it was a right giggle. 'E said that if 'e'd done summat wrong the last person 'e'd want on the case was you. 'E said that you never forgot, an' that 'e 'oped Silkstone was telling the truth, for 'is sake, 'cos 'e'd never be able to sleep at night if 'e wasn't.'

'Right,' I said. 'Right.' My tea was finished and Halliwell was chewing his last piece of toast. 'So did Silkstone have anything else to say?' I asked.

'No,' he replied. 'The others came in, then, an' we started. Come to think of it, though, he wasn't as chipper as 'e usually was, that lesson.'

283

I lifted my jacket off the back of the chair and poked an arm down a sleeve. 'Do you want a lift back?' I asked.

'No thanks, Mr Priest,' he replied. 'I 'ave to be careful what company I keep.'

'Scared of being seen associating with the enemy?'

'Summat like that.'

'I take it you are going back?'

'Dunno.' A little smile played around his mouth, the wrinkles joining up into laughter lines. 'Would it get you into trouble if I didn't?' he asked.

'No,' I lied. 'Nothing to do with me.'

'Then I might as well go back.' He stood up, uncurling from the chair and stretching to his full height with a display of effort. 'Thanks for the breakfast, an' the fags. Sorry you 'ad a wasted journey.'

'I'll give you a lift, if you want one.'

'No, Mr Priest,' he said. 'I want to walk down that road like all these other people. Past the shops, an' all. Enjoy my freedom while I can. It's been a long wait.'

'I hope it works out for you, Vince,' I told him. 'I really do.'

We walked across the car-park together. As we emerged on to the pavement I said: 'Vince.' He turned to face me, his face etched with worry, scared I was about to spring something on him. He'd already had enough excitement for this day.

'Tony Silkstone took out a contract on me,' I told him. 'He offered someone fifty thousand to kill me. Did you hear anything about it?'

'To ... to kill you?' he stuttered. 'Fifty thousand

to kill you?'

'That's right. Who did he talk to?' 'Dunno, Mr Priest. First I've 'eard of it.'

'He hired a man called Chilcott. You ever heard of him?'

'Chiller? Yeah, I 'eard of 'im, but 'e wasn't in Bentley.'

'I know. He was abroad. You didn't hear any talk?'

'No, Mr Priest, not a word. Honest.'

'If you remember anything, get in touch.'

'Yeah, right.'

'OK. Thanks anyway. Mind the road.'

I began to turn away but I heard him say: ''Ere, Mr Priest.'

'Mmm.'

'Is this what it was all about, an' not the other job?'

'That's right, Vince. The other job's history, as far as I'm concerned. We knew who was with you, just couldn't prove it.'

'So I told you what you wanted to know?'

'You gave me the reason that Silkstone had for wanting me dead. Yes.'

'You devious bastard.'

'I'm a cop,' I said, as if that was a full explanation.

'Fifty Gs, did you say?'

'That's right. Would you have taken the contract, if you'd known?'

'No,' he replied. 'Not my scene. But I'd 'ave chipped in.'

He had the grace to smile as he said it. I flapped a hand at him and we walked our separate ways.

Me back to the car and Heckley, him to his room in jail and the calendar on the wall that said that in two years he'd be let loose, with nobody to order him around, nobody to feed and clothe him.

The sun was in my eyes on the way back. I drove with the visor down, listening to a tape I'd compiled of Mark Knopfler and Pat Metheny. There'd been a shower and the roads were wet, so every lorry I passed turned the windscreen into a glaring mixture of splatters and streaks. I stayed in the slow and middle lanes, driving steadily, doing some thinking, my fingers on the wheel tapping in time with *Local Hero* and *The Truth Will Always Be*. These days, in this job, you rarely have time to think. Something happens and you react. Time to reflect on the best way to tackle the situation is a luxury.

Halliwell said he would have contributed towards the fifty thousand if he'd known about it. If he'd guessed the truth he'd have donated the full sum. We knew who his accomplice was because we'd arrested him the day before, and he'd turned informer, gushing like a Dales stream about the Big Job he was doing the following night. Halliwell was set up by the man he refused to grass on, and we were waiting for him. The gun was a bonus; we hadn't expected that. It was found afterwards, thrown behind a dustbin on the route Halliwell had taken as he tried to flee the scene. He denied it was his, and we admitted in court that we hadn't found his fingerprints on it. Because he wouldn't say who his accomplice was the judge credited him with the weapon and gave him ten years.

I'd give my right arm to be able to make music like that. Not to have to deal with all this shit. Nobody asked us about the bullets. The gun had been wiped clean but we found a fingerprint on one of the bullets. It belonged to the accomplice, who just happened to slip through our fingers. This was eight years ago, before the law changed, and like I said: nobody asked.

Gilbert had some good news for me. A British couple starting their annual holiday had been held up at gunpoint outside Calais and their car stolen. The hijacker answered Chilcott's description. As I had grumbled to him every day about my bodyguard Gilbert reluctantly agreed that Chilcott was probably making his way across France and Tweedle Dee and Tweedle Dum could safely return to their normal duties. I didn't point out that it would also help his staff deployment problems and overtime budget, but I did tell him about my confrontation with Vince Halliwell. Gilbert gave one of his sighs and peered at me over his half-moon spectacles. 'You're saying that Silkstone took the contract out on you because he wanted you off his case. You have a reputation for never forgetting, and he wanted to be able to sleep at nights. Is that it?'

'In a coconut shell,' I replied.

'Why?'

'Why what?'

'Why does he want you off the case? He's admitted killing Latham.'

'Because he's a worried man. He has something

287

to hide. Everybody else is saying: "Well done, Tony. You rid the world of a scumbag." I'm the only one saying: "Whoa up a minute! Maybe he was there with Latham when Margaret died".'

'You know what the papers are saying, don't you.'

'That he's a hero. Yes.'

'And that we're hounding him unnecessarily.'

'I haven't started hounding him yet.'

'You really think he was there, when she died?'

'Yes, Gilbert. I do.'

'OK, but play it carefully. Let Jeff take over the everyday stuff, and you spend what time you need on this. And for God's sake try to keep off the front page of the *UK News*.'

Gilbert's a toff. He listens to what I have to say and then lets me have my way. If I were too outlandish, way off the mark, he'd step in and keep me on track, but it doesn't happen very often. He protects me from interference by the brass hats at HQ; I protect him from criticism by giving him our best clear-up rate. If you want to commit a murder, don't do it in Heckley. Don't do it on my patch. I searched in my drawer for an old diary. I needed some information, the sort they don't print in text books, and I knew just the person to ask.

Peter Drago lives in Penrith now, but he was born in Halifax and was in the same intake as me. We attended training school together and got drunk a few times. He made sergeant when I did and inspector shortly after me, but he also made some enemies. With sexual predilections like his, that was a dangerous thing to do. He was even-

288

tually caught, *in flagrante*, by the husband of the bubbly WPC he was making love to in the back of her car, and they had a fist fight.

Next day Drago was busted back to PC and posted to Settle and the WPC told to report to Hooton Pagnell. That's how things worked in those days. Step out of line and you were immediately transferred to the furthermost corner of the region. It changed when the good citizens of these far-flung outposts discovered that the handsome and attractive police officers with the city accents that kept arriving on their doorsteps were all the adulterers and philanderers that the force had to offer. I found his home number and dialled it.

'Fancy doing Great Gable tomorrow?' I asked without ceremony, when he answered.

After a hesitation he said: 'That you, Charlie?' No insults, no sparkling repartee, just: 'That you, Charlie?'

'The one and only,' I replied. 'How are you?'

'Oh, not too bad, you know. And you?'

'The same. So how about it?'

'Great Gable? I'd love to, Charlie, but I'm afraid I won't be climbing the Gable again for a long time.'

'Why? What's happened?' This wasn't the Dragon of old, by a long way. His motto was: if it moved, shag it; if it didn't, climb it.

'I've just come out of hospital. Triple bypass, three weeks ago.'

'Oh, I am sorry, Pete. Which organ?'

'My heart, pillock,' he chuckled.

'What happened? Did you have an attack?'

'Yeah. Collapsed at work, woke up in the cardiac unit with all these masked figures bending over me. Thought I'd been abducted by aliens.'

'I am sorry,' I repeated. 'And was it a success? Are you feeling OK now?'

'I'm a bit sore, but otherwise I feel grand. *Right champion*, in fact.'

'OK,' I said. 'We'll take a rain check on the Gable, but only for six months. Next Easter we're going up there, you and me, so you'd better get some training in. Understood?'

After a silence he said: 'You know, Charlie, that's the best tonic I've had. Next Easter, and sod what the doctors say. It's a date.'

We chatted for a while, reminiscing about walks we'd done, scrapes we'd shared when we were PCs together. He asked about Dave and his family, and I told him that his daughter Sophie was about to start at Cambridge. Eventually he asked why I'd rung.

'Oh, it doesn't matter,' I replied. 'It was a bit personal, and I don't want to excite you.'

'Now you do have to tell me,' he insisted.

'Well,' I said, 'it really *is* a bit personal. Are you able to, you know, talk?'

'Yeah, she's gone for her hair doing. Tell me all about it.'

I didn't ask who *she* was; Pete's love life has more dead ends and branch lines than the London Underground. 'Well, it's like this,' I began. 'There's this bloke, and he's having an affair with a married woman.'

'He's shagging her?'

'Er, yes.'

'I just wanted to clarify the situation. Sorry, carry on.'

'That's all right. He sees her every Wednesday afternoon, at her house, while her husband is at work.'

'Presumably this is a purely hypothetical case,' Pete interjected.

'Oh, definitely. Definitely.'

'Right. Go on.'

'Thanks. Now, this woman is in her early forties, and she isn't on the Pill, so her lover has to take precautions.'

'As a matter of interest, is her lover married?'

'Er, no. As a matter of interest, he isn't.'

'Has he ever been?'

'Um, yes, as a matter of interest, he has.'

'I think I'm getting the picture. Carry on, please.'

I carried on, loosely describing what we'd found at Mrs Silkstone's house, speculating how things may have happened. I think – I hope – that he eventually realised that I wasn't one of the protagonists in the whole squalid episode. He gave me the benefit of his experience in these matters, and I was grateful.

It was a long phone call. As we went through the ritual of ending it he said: 'Did you ever hear what John Betjemen is supposed to have said on his death bed, Charlie?'

'Something about wishing he'd had more sex, wasn't it?'

'That's right, and I agree with him. Get it while you can, Charlie, you're a long time dead.'

I reminded him about Easter and put the

phone down, reflecting on the Pete Drago philosophy: get it while you can. He was a good bloke: intelligent, fair and generous; but something drove him, far harder than it drives most of us. And, God knows, that's hard enough. Bob Dylan included rakes in Chimes of Freedom, his personal version of the Beatitudes: *tolling for the rebel, tolling for the rake.* I'd never understood why, until now. Maybe he had it right.

We had a killing through the week. A youth was stabbed to death in the town centre, and my heart sank when I learned that he was from the Asian community I breathed again when it was revealed that his attacker was his brother-in-law, and it was all about family honour. I'm only interested in guilty or not guilty, and was relieved not to have a race war on my hands. Family feuds I can deal with. Saturday lunchtime I tidied my desk and fled, rejoicing at my new-found freedom, eager to be out in the fresh air. I drove to Burnsall, one of the most attractive Dales villages, and donned my boots. The route I took was loop-shaped, through Thorpe and Linton to Bow Bridge, then following the Wharfe back to the village. It's a beautiful river, sometimes rushing over boulders, sometimes carving deep languid pools and sandbanks. Dippers used to be commonplace, not very long ago, and I've seen the kingfisher there. The morning showers had passed over, and the afternoon sun made the meadows steam.

There were lots of people about. It's a popular place, and the last flush of summer always brings us out, determined to stock up on the beneficial rays before the dark nights close in. A group of people were vacating some rocks at the side of the water, packing their picnic remnants into Tupperware boxes and rucksacks. It was a good spot, in a patch of sunshine, with trees on the opposite side and the river gabbling noisily. Very therapeutic. I moved in after them, heading for a seat on a dry boulder, and as I sat down a dead twig, brittle as egg shells, snapped under my feet.

I'd called in Marks and Spencer's when I left the office, for a prawn sandwich and a packet of Eccles cakes. I wolfed them down with a can of flavoured mineral water, sitting there watching the stream go by. Swallows were skimming the surface, stocking up on flies before their long journey south, and a fish made ripples, out in the middle where it flowed more slowly.

There weren't many places that I would rather have been, but there's more to happiness than that. I wondered if Annette were doing something similar, picnicking with another man and his children as a different river slid past them. I leaned forward and picked up a piece of the branch I'd stepped on. It was about four inches long, dead as last week's scandal and encrusted with lichen. I tossed it, underhand, out into the stream.

It hardly made a splash and bobbed up and down, buoyant as a cork, until the current took hold and pushed it into the flow, heading towards a cleft between two rocks. I watched it accelerate towards them, turning as opposing forces caught and juggled with it. It entered the chute between the rocks, one end riding high, and plunged over the mini-waterfall.

The pressure held it down and the undertow pulled it back. There was a wrestling match between the flow of water and the buoyancy of the twig, but there could only be one result. After a few seconds it broke free of the water's grip and burst to the surface. I watched it rotate in the current like an ice skater taking a bow and nod away towards the North Sea, eighty miles down river.

I couldn't do it again. I broke another piece off the branch and threw it into the stream, but it was swept straight through the rocks and away. I tried bigger pieces and smaller ones, with variable quantities of lichen, but it didn't work. It was the balance that was important. Big twigs were more buoyant, but the water had more to press down on. On the other hand, the lichen provided drag, which should have helped the water. I tossed another piece into the stream and watched it slide away.

'My that looks good fun,' a voice said, behind me.

I turned, squinting into the sun, and saw an elderly couple standing there. They were wearing lime green and blue anoraks, and had two pale Labradors on extending leads, which they'd thoughtfully reeled in as they'd approached me.

'Hello,' I said. 'I didn't hear you. Isn't it a nice day.'

'Wonderful,' the man said. 'So what is it? Pooh sticks?'

'You need a bridge for that,' I told him. 'No, I

was just doing some experiments, studying elementary hydraulics.'

'Elementary hydraulics, eh. And I thought it was at least Life, Death and the Universe.'

'No, not quite. Are you going far?'

'Only to the footbridge and back. And you?'

'I walked up to Bow Bridge, and I'm heading back to Burnsall. Far enough for this afternoon.'

'Well enjoy your experiments,' he said. 'Hope we didn't disturb you.'

'Not at all. Enjoy your walk.' His wife gave me a special smile. She was attractive, had once been beautiful. Probably still was, when you knew her. I watched them stroll away, the dogs leaping about on long leads now, biting each other's necks. It was easy to forgive them their matching anoraks.

No, I thought, as I hooked my rucksack over my shoulder. Not Life, Death and the Universe. Just Life, Death and Elementary Hydraulics.

Chapter 10

Monday morning Superintendent Isles gave me permission to interview Jason Lee Gelder at HQ, where he was being held. I cleared my diary and reallocated a few tasks to accommodate him. Dave had driven to Cambridge over the week-end, to look at Sophie's room in the students' quarters. He was a lot happier now that he knew where she'd be staying, and told us all what a smashing place it was. Expecting displays of enthusiasm from him is normally like expecting impartial advice from your bank manager, but today he was full of it. I decided to attempt to harness the quality.

'And I've a special little job for you, Sunshine,' I told him.

'Like what?' he asked. From him, that's eager.

'One I wouldn't trust to anybody else.'

'I'll think about it.'

'Good. I want you to go to Boots and buy one hundred condoms.'

'A hundred condoms!'

'That's right. You can put them on your expenses.'

'You want me to buy a hundred French letters and put them on my expenses?'

'That's what I said.'

'You can cocoa!'

'I'm serious.'

'So am I! Go buy them yourself.'

I found a notebook with empty pages and put it in my pocket with a couple of fibre-tipped pens. 'You just can't get the staff,' I said standing up and sliding my chair under the desk.

Sparky had his cheeky grin on. 'So, er, things are looking up, are they?' he asked.

'No, they're not,' I snapped, adding: 'If you want a job doing properly do it yourself.'

'Why a hundred?' he asked. 'With your luck a packet of three would last you until the use-before date.'

'You can be very hurtful,' I told him, opening the door and switching the light off.

'Yeah, it was a bit. Sorry.'

'That's OK. How much are they, these days?'

'Johnnies? A pound for two from the machine in the Spinners' bog.'

'Is that plain or flavoured?'

'Plain. The flavoured are two quid for three.'

'You seem to know all about them.'

'I read the machine while I'm having a pee. What do you do?'

'Try to drown a fly. That'd be fifty quid, and I'd have to go to the bank for coins. And then the machine would run out and I'd have to ask the barman for my money back. It'll have to be a chemist's.'

'Are you serious?' he demanded.

'Never more. Want to change your mind?'

'No.'

'Fair enough, but I'll have to put it on your record. I'm off to HQ, to talk to young Mr Gelder. Try not to breach too many guidelines while I'm gone.'

I parked in town and went to Boots. The condoms were on the self-service shelves but there was a small queue at the pay counter, so I wandered around for a few minutes until it had gone. Fetherlites came in packs of a dozen, costing £8.85, so I'd have to buy ... I did the mental arithmetic ... six twelves are seventy-two, seven twelves are eighty-four, eight twelves are ninety-six ... nine, I'd have to buy nine packs, which would leave eight condoms over. Ah well, they might come in handy, some day.

The queue had gone so I gathered up a handful of packets. Dammit! There were only eight on display. Ninety-six. That meant I needed two packets of three to make up the shortfall. I added them to my collection and headed towards the counter.

A woman got there before me, but that was OK. I fell in behind her, my purchases clutched to my body, as she handed over a brown bottle of tablets and a ten pound note. The grey-haired assistant looked at the bottle and turned towards the glassed-off enclave where the pharmacist was busy counting pills.

'Paracetamol!' she shouted, and he raised his head and nodded his consent to the sale.

A wave of panic swept through me. Was she about to yell 'Condoms!' to all and sundry when she saw what I was buying? 'You know that they contain paracetamol, don't you?' she told the customer, who said that she did. Personally, I'd have thought that that was why she was buying them. And as it said *Paracetamol* in large letters across the label, it seemed not unreasonable to assume that she knew the chief ingredient.

'Can I, er, take those, please,' I mumbled, when it was my turn, half expecting her to warn me that I'd never make a baby if I wore one of these, on the off-chance that I was a lapsing Catholic. I passed the bundle two-handed across the glass-topped counter, followed by my credit card. She was counting them when the phone rang. 'Excuse me,' she said, placing my goods in a neat pile and turning to answer it. Unfortunately Durex packs are shiny and rounded, and don't stack up well. They slid over and spread-eagled themselves across the counter, fanning out like a hand of cards. I turned and smiled guiltily at the baby in the arms of the young girl who headed the queue that was forming behind me. The girl smiled back at me.

Seventy-six flippin' quid they cost. And thirty pence. I grabbed the bag that the assistant handed over and turned to flee, only glancing at the five women and two men in the queue behind me enough to notice that the last man looked suspiciously like my window cleaner. As I passed him he touched my sleeve. I turned to say hello, but he just said 'Receipt.'

'Pardon?'

'You forgot your receipt.'

'Oh, thanks.' I went back to the counter and the grey-haired assistant passed it to me. I felt as if I ought to make a witty remark, but she was already listening to her next customer.

Jason Lee Gelder wasn't what I'd expected. I try

299

not to be fooled by first impressions, but he took me for a ride. I shook hands with his brief, the duty solicitor, when he introduced himself, although we meet nearly as often as the swing doors down at the Job Centre, and sat down opposite them.

'Is it Jason or Lee?' I asked.

'Er, Jason,' he replied. He had the palest blue eyes I'd ever seen, short fair hair in a sensible style, a high forehead and a full mouth and jaw-line. When it came to looks, he was a heart-breaker, and I could imagine the girls falling for him like lemmings off a cliff. But nature gives with one hand and takes away with the other.

'Right, Jason,' I began. 'Are they looking after you well?'

'Er, yeah.'

'I see they've given you your own clothes back.'

'Er, yeah.'

'We were allowed to collect some from his home,' the solicitor explained, 'but most of his clothes are with your forensic people.'

'For tests,' I told Jason. 'We do tests on them.' Before either of them could speak again I said: 'This is an informal interview, to clear up a few things about this and another case. We are not recording or taking notes, but I have to tell you, Jason, that you are still under caution and anything you say may be taken down and used in evidence. Do you understand?'

'Yeah,' he said, which meant that he was probably the only one of us who did.

'Which newspapers do you read, Jason?' I asked.

He shuffled uncomfortably in his seat and stared down at somewhere near his navel.

'*The Sun?*' I suggested. 'Or the *Sunday Sport?*'

He shook his head and curled up even more.

'If I may,' the solicitor interrupted. 'Jason has reading difficulties. He doesn't buy a newspaper.'

'Oh, I'm sorry,' I said, taken aback for a moment. Then I remembered the magazines that were found in his room. 'You like pictures, though, don't you?' I asked. 'Which paper has the best girls in it? Tell me that, Jason.'

'Dunno,' he mumbled.

'But you look at them?'

'I suppose so.'

'Which ones?'

'Dunno.'

'Where do you see them?'

'All over.'

'Such as?'

'Anywhere.'

'Tell me, Jason. I'm trying to help you.'

He shrugged his shoulders and looked towards his brief for help. The solicitor waved a palm towards me in a gesture that said: 'For God's sake tell the man.'

'In the pub,' he replied.

'What?' I began. 'You mean, people leave them in the pub and you collect them?'

'I don't collect them. I just 'ave a look.'

'Where else?'

'Mates' 'ouses. All over.'

'Which papers do you like best?'

'I dunno. They're all the same.'

'*The Sport?*'

301

'Sometimes.'

'The *UK News?* Do you like the *UK News,* Jason?'

'Dunno if I do or not.'

'Where do you get your magazines from?'

'From mates.'

'Do you buy them?'

'No. We just swap them.'

It always looks good in the report of a trial: *Police found a number of pornographic magazines in the accused's house.* Of course we did, because they're all over the place. There isn't an establishment in the country that employs a majority of males where you couldn't find some sort of unofficial library of topshelf literature, and that includes most police stations. Jason would have been more interesting to the psychiatric profession if we *hadn't* found any sex books at his home.

'Tell me about your girlfriends,' I suggested.

''Aven't got one,' he replied.

'But you've had one, haven't you?'

'I suppose so.'

'Good looking lad like you,' I said. 'With a little car. Wouldn't have thought you'd have any problem pulling the birds. Am I right?'

'Sometimes.'

'Who was your last girlfriend?'

'Can't remember.'

'Can't or won't? How long since you last had a girl in the car, Jason?'

He thought about it, his brow a rubbing-board of furrows. ''Bout three weeks,' he eventually volunteered. 'Maybe a bit longer.'

'So that would be before Marie-Claire Holling-

302

brook was murdered,' I said.

'Yeah. 'Bout a week before.'

'How did you learn about her murder?'

'In the pub. They were talking about it in the pub.'

'Did you know her?'

'No.'

'Did you ever see her?'

'No.'

'So you didn't recognise her from her picture in the papers?'

'No.'

The solicitor leaned forward and said: 'Inspector, could you possibly explain where this line of enquiry is leading? My client has strenuously denied any knowledge of Miss Hollingbrook or any involvement in her death. There are several hours of taped interviews in which he answers all questions fully and satisfactorily.'

'There is some rather heavy evidence against your client,' I pointed out.

'Which is being contested,' he rejoined. 'There are precedents, Inspector, in which DNA evidence has been discredited. We are currently investigating the whole procedure for taking and examining samples from both the crime scene and witnesses.'

Here we go, I thought. O.J. Simpson all over again. O.J. bloody Simpson. It wasn't my job to give him lines of defence, so I just accepted what he said. I turned back to Jason and asked: 'What was this girl called that you last went out with?'

'Dunno,' he replied.

'You don't know? Didn't you ask?'

303

'Yeah, but I've forgotten.'

'Well try to remember. It could be important.'

'I've forgotten.'

'OK. Let's go through it. Where did you meet her?'

'At that club in Heckley with the daft name.'

'The Aspidistra Lounge.'

'Yeah, that's it.'

'Go there a lot, do you?'

'Yeah, I suppose so.'

'What nights?'

'Sometimes Thursdays, and most Fridays.'

'And what night did you meet this girl?'

'Not sure. Think it was Friday.'

'So what did you do?'

'What did we do?' he asked, looking even more bewildered.

'Did you dance?'

'Yeah, a bit.'

'Buy her a drink?'

'Yeah.'

'What did she drink?'

'Lager. And Blastaways.'

'Blastaways. Right.' I knew that was a sickly combination of cider and a ready-made cocktail called a Castaway. 'And did you ask her name?'

'I suppose so.'

'Which was?'

'Can't remember.'

It's at times like this that I wished I smoked. I could take out the packet of Sobranies, flick one between my lips, light it with my gold-plated Zippo and inhale a long satisfying lungful of nicotine-laden smoke. All I'd have to worry about was an early grave from cancer, not trying to keep an uncommunicative twerp like Jason from spending the rest of his natural being used as a trampoline in an open prison.

'Did you take her home?' I asked.

'Yeah.'

'Straight home?'

'Er, no.'

'Where did you go?'

'To the brickyard.'

Atkinson's brickyard was long gone, but the name lingered on. It was now a lawned-over picnic site, only the red shards poking through the grass indicating its industrial past. More people meet there after dark for sex than ever eat at the primitive tables during daylight hours.

'Did you have sex with her?'

'Yeah.'

'In the back seat?'

'No, in the front.'

'Really! Wouldn't you have found it more comfortable in the back?'

'Yeah, but...'

'But what?'

'We just started, you know, snogging, in the front, and that was it.'

'You were carried away.'

'Yeah. Well, she was. Dead eager for it, she was.'

'She took the initiative?'

'Yeah.'

I expected his brief to interrupt, but I think he was as fascinated as I was by the sexual mores of the young. I dragged the conversation back on course. 'Was she on the Pill?' I asked.

'No.'

'So what did you do? Risk it?'

'No.'

'You'd gone prepared.'

'Yeah.'

'Very commendable. So did you arrange to see her again?'

'Not really. I said I might see 'er in the ... the whatsit, the club.'

'You don't sound as if you were keen. Why not?'

'Because she was a slag, that's why.'

'But you must have asked her name.'

'Yeah, I suppose so.'

'Which was...?'

'Can't remember.'

I turned to the brief and told him that we were going to have a five-minute break. I said I was trying to help his client and the name of the girl might be of use in my line of enquiries. Jason was in hot water about as deep as it gets, and anything he told me could only help his case. I suggested they did some serious thinking.

Les Isles wasn't in his office, and Nigel was nowhere to be found, either. Two DCs were busy in the main office, working at computer keyboards that were in danger of being engulfed by the paperwork heaped around them. Who invented the expression *paperless office?* Woody Allen?

'Where's the boss?' I asked the nearest DC.

'Mr Isles?'

'Mmm.'

'Review meeting at Region. It's Mr Priest, isn't it?'

I didn't deny the fact and we shook hands. He'd attended one of my talks at the training college and said he enjoyed it. 'I'm interviewing Jason Gelder downstairs,' I told him, quickly adding: 'with Mr Isles' permission. Nobody told me he was ESN.'

'Who, Mr Isles?' he replied with a grin. 'That explains a lot.'

'I meant young Gelder.'

'Sorry about that. Strictly speaking, and according to the experts, he's not. Put in layman's language, he's thick, but he's not slow.'

'I see,' I said, 'or at least, I think I do. Where does he get his money from?'

'He works for a living, down at the abattoir. Spends his working day scraping flesh from animal skins. They pay him fairly well because nobody wants to do it, and he goes home stinking like an otter's arse.'

'Right. Thanks for your help. *Thick but not slow*, I'll have to ponder on that one.'

Down in the interview room Jason was slumped at the table and the brief was leaning on the wall, a polystyrene coffee cup in his hand. He shrugged his shoulders as I entered and resumed his seat.

'Where were we?' I asked, briskly, rubbing my hands together. 'Didn't you want a coffee, Jason?' and was rewarded with a shake of the head.

'So what was this girl called?' I demanded.

'I don't know,' he stated, staring straight at me. The brief must have given him a hard time because he looked as if he'd been crying.

'What did you talk about? If you did any

talking?' I asked.

'Not much,' he replied.

'How old was she? Did you ask her that?'

'No, I don't think I asked.'

I wasn't surprised. What was that other one from Pete Drago's list of sexual aphorisms: *If they're big enough, they're old enough.* 'How old did you think she was?'

'About eighteen. She was about eighteen.'

'So she wasn't under age.'

'No, definitely not. She'd left school.'

'Did she work or go to college?'

'I don't know.'

'So if she was over sixteen why won't you tell me her name.'

'Because you won't listen,' he sobbed. 'I keep telling you, I don't remember.'

'OK,' I said. 'Let's go through it again. You meet this girl at the Aspidistra Lounge, either on Thursday or Friday night...'

'Friday,' He interrupted. 'I think it was Friday.'

'But you're not sure?'

'No.'

'Right. You buy her a few drinks, have a dance and a smooch, and take her home. Did you stay right to the end?'

'No.'

'What time?'

'Dunno.'

'Before or after midnight?'

'About midnight.'

'Then you went to the brickyard, had sex with this young lady in the front seat because you were both too desperate to climb into the back, and that was that. You had ten minutes of passion but didn't bother seeing her again. Why not?'

'Because she was a slag. I've told you once,' he stated, almost shouting at me now. I decided to push him.

'A slag! Aren't all the girls you pick up slags?' I demanded.

'No. Not all of them.'

'But this one was?'

'Yeah.'

'Was Marie-Claire a slag, Jason. Was she another slag?'

'I don't know. I never met her.' Tears were running down his cheeks and he turned to the brief for help. 'Why won't they believe me?' he begged.

'Because you're not telling the truth, Jason.' I stated. 'This girl at the club; what was she called?'

'I don't know!'

'Why are you protecting her, if you think she was a slag?'

'Because you wouldn't believe me. You don't believe anything I say.'

He was cracking. I'd closed on him. 'What wouldn't I believe?' I asked.

'Anything.'

'Tell me what I wouldn't believe, Jason.'

'I can't.'

'Why? Why can't you tell me?'

'Because!'

'Because what?'

'Just because.'

He'd turned a ghostly white and was hyperventilating. The solicitor placed a hand on his arm, saying: 'Jason, if there's something you have to say, I think you should tell Mr Priest. It can't do you any harm.'

Jason stared at me, defiant, and I stared back at him. 'Go on, Jason,' I encouraged. 'Who was she?'

'I don't know her name.'

'You said we wouldn't believe you. What wouldn't we believe?'

'You'd 'old it against me. Gang up on me.'

'Why would we do that?'

'Because it's what you do.'

'Tell me what you know, Jason,' I asked.

'Tell Mr Priest,' the brief added.

Jason breathed deeply a few times, gathering his strength, then blurted the words out. ''Er dad's a copper,' he informed us.

'A copper?' I echoed. 'What sort of a copper?'

'A detective. He's a detective. At 'Eckley nick.'

It wasn't what I expected, or what I wanted to hear. Images of him having it away with his kid sister, or his probation officer, or some other unlikely person, were swirling around in my mind, but not this. 'Are you sure?' I asked, my voice a whisper.

'Yeah. She said 'er dad was a detective, in the CID at 'Eckley I didn't ask 'er, she just told me.'

'But ... you can't remember her name?'

'No.'

'Good,' I mumbled. 'Good. I think that will do for now.'

Chapter 11

I went into a sandwich shop, but when I saw them all lying there like shrink-wrapped museum exhibits waiting to be catalogued I decided I wasn't hungry. I bought a bottle of flavoured water, that's all, and sipped at it sitting on a bench in the town centre, because I couldn't think of anywhere else to go. It must have been a cold day because people were hurrying about with their collars upturned and I had the seats all to myself. I don't feel the cold.

O.J. Simpson was found not guilty of murder because his legal team declared that the DNA evidence was flawed. The jury accepted their claim because the police were a bunch of racists, and it was a glitch in the procedures for processing the DNA evidence that gave them the excuse to do so.

Blood samples from accused and victims were taken to the same laboratory, and O.J.'s thousand-dollars-an-hour attorney convinced the court that DNA could have floated about in the atmosphere and transferred itself from one sample dish to another. It's not as crazy as it seems. They'd used something called PCR, or polymerase chain reaction, to amplify a tiny stretch of DNA, too small to be useful, into a big sample. It's a procedure that a California scientist called Kary Mullis thought of while driving his car through the desert at night. It's a magical experience for anyone, but Mullis wove some real magic that night, enough to win himself a share in the Nobel prize.

He knew that if you took one single shred of a DNA molecule and gently heated it in a test tube, with an exotic brew of the right proteins and enzymes, the two strands would untwine, and as you cooled it down again each would create a copy of the partner it had just lost. In other words, you would now have two pieces of the DNA. How you knew that there was only one molecule in the tube to start with, and how you kept track of it, wasn't explained in the book I read. The heating and cooling process only took a few minutes, so do it again and you'd now have four pieces of DNA. It's a fiendishly complicated process – this was strictly the Ladybird version, intended for under-sevens and police officers.

Mullis stopped the car and did some sums. He calculated that in twenty heating and cooling cycles, which would only take until coffee break, you'd have over a million copies of your original sample. Still not enough to be visible on the head of a pin, but you were getting there. Keep going, and by the end of the week you'd be bringing in the enzymes by specially laid road and rail connections, and moving the DNA out by the barge-load. In a month you could fill the Grand Canyon and make a start on the Marianas Trench.

You don't need that much in a criminal case. O.J.'s lawyers said that with all the DNA being made, who could say that a spare flake hadn't floated into the wrong test tube or Petri dish or whatever they use, and nobody had enough clout to argue with a thousand-dollars-an-hour attorney. This DNA swirling about in the atmosphere could just as easily have belonged to Thomas Jefferson or Christopher Columbus, but nobody mentioned it. As the newspapers put it: *money talked, O.J. walked.*

Black spots were breaking out on the pavement in front of my feet, like some deadly infection, and a raindrop scored a direct hit on my neck. Jason Lee Gelder's solicitor was on the basic rate for the job, we had enough semen to do all the tests we needed and different samples are always processed in different labs. There was no comfort for him there. I took a sip of water and looked at the pigeons that had joined me, expecting to catch a few crumbs. They were all exactly alike, each a replicant of some distant ancestor, their lives pre-programmed in the genetic code. I wish I'd been a scientist. I screwed the top back on the bottle and went to find the car.

A solitary detective, David Rose, was at work in the office when I arrived back. He was in his shirtsleeves, surrounded by paperwork as he peered at the VDU screen on his desk, pencil behind his ear. He turned as I closed the door and said: 'Hi, Charlie.'

'No.' I replied.

'No what?'

'No, whatever it was.'

I went straight into my little office and gathered up all the papers put there to attract my atten-

313

tion. They could wait. I picked up the phone, dialled the HQ number and put the phone down again. Scenes of crime would have gone over Jason's car with the proverbial, in the faint hope of finding evidence that Marie-Claire had been in it and was therefore known to him. They'd failed, I knew that, but they must have found some evidence, like fingerprints, of other people who'd ridden with him. Like the girl he took to the brickyard. The detective's daughter.

I drummed my fingers on the phone, indecisive. I needed to know who he'd been with, not sure if I could face the truth. There are sixteen detectives at Heckley, and I knew all their families, had visited all their houses. I brought out a staff list and took the top off my pen, with the intention of writing their kids' names in the margin. The pen hovered next to the first name but I couldn't do it. I couldn't sully them by giving substance to Gelder's accusations. There was only one name that fitted, and I felt ashamed at even considering what was going through my mind. I tore the list into shreds and dropped them in the bin. But, I argued, someone was with him, somebody's daughter, and these were promiscuous times. Or at least, we were constantly being told they were. Myself, I wasn't too sure. Times had changed, of course they had, but people, including kids, made their own moralities and sometimes they were surprisingly high. I stood up and strode over to the window. It only took two.

I'd beaten the rain back, but it was catching up. Rooftops were glistening across the road, but this side was still clear. Even as that fact registered the first flurry dashed against the window and the street lights flickered on. We were in for a downpour. Black clouds were banked like pit heaps behind St Mary's Church, at the other side of town, blotting out the hills. A straggle of people was going in when I'd driven past, for afternoon mass or, perhaps, an organ recital. They'd get wet when they came out, but I don't suppose they'd mind. Not the faithful ones.

A report on the news had said that church attendance on Sundays was down by seven percent over the last ten years. A couple of spokesmen, Bishop Inevitable and Archbishop Complacent, said that it wasn't all bad news because attendance through the week was on the increase. I wasn't sure if going in to listen to a Bach fugue or buy mince pies from the WI stall counted, but it was good for the statistics and the offering.

Trouble is, nobody has any faith anymore. I'd never had any. Doubt, not blind belief in something I couldn't comprehend, was always my driving force. I wish it were otherwise, but it isn't. I returned to my desk and picked the top document off the pile I'd made. Would I like to contribute to Mr Pritchard's leaving present? I fished a ten-pound note from my wallet, placed it in an envelope with the letter and sealed it.

It wasn't true, I told myself. I did have faith. It might not be in a god, but it was there. I believed in the people around me, colleagues and friends, like I'd believed in my parents. Had faith in them. 'So prove it,' I told myself, picking up the telephone and dialling the custody sergeant at HQ. 'Sorry, Sophie,' I whispered as I waited for him to answer. 'Forgive me for doubting you.'

'This is DI Priest at Heckley,' I told him. 'I came in this morning and interviewed Jason Gelder, and I'd like to talk to him again, as soon as possible. Will it be alright if I come over?'

'You'll be lucky, Mr Priest,' he replied. 'We've just sent him to Bentley. You'll find him in the remand wing.'

'Damn,' I said. 'OK, thanks.' It would have to be tomorrow.

Gwen Rhodes wasn't there, so I had to use the proper channels, just like everybody else. The visits office said they couldn't possibly accommodate me on Tuesday, but after a pathetic display of subservience and respect for their difficulties they agreed to squeeze me in on Friday. They like us to know that they can't be pushed around. I said: 'Thank you, Friday will be fine.'

Tuesday, I went to court instead. After hanging about for two hours and another half-hour talking to a magistrate, I came away with a warrant to search Silkstone's house and a special circumstance attached to his bail conditions. He had to stay out of the way while we did so.

I rang him on his mobile and told him to bring his brief with him when he came to sign the book on Thursday. I wanted to do a substantive interview, to clarify his exact movements on the day his wife died. I didn't mention the search warrant.

'What if I refuse to stay?' he ventured.

'Then I'll arrest you,' I told him. The time had come to put pressure on Mr Silkstone. He'd had a long break, had probably grown complacent about his predicament. He was due for a wake-up call.

Wednesday I drove to the lab at Wetherton and had a long talk with one of the professors. He listened to what I had to say, sounded sceptical but agreed to loan me a scientist. At a price, of course. He followed me back to Heckley, where I held a briefing with Dave Sparkington, Jeff Caton and four members of the scenes of crime team. Compared to them, the professor had sounded jubilant and enthusiastic.

'So you were serious,' Sparky declared.

'I'm always serious, Dave,' I replied.

'What exactly are *we* looking for?' one of the SOCOs asked.

'You have the difficult bit,' I told him. 'Silkstone killed Peter John Latham with a kitchen knife, ostensibly belonging to Latham. It just happened to be available, on the worktop. If the murder was planned in advance Silkstone wouldn't have left anything to chance. What I want to know is whether Silkstone was aware that the block containing the knives would be there, or if he took it with him. Ideally, I'd like to link the knives with Silkstone. Had the block stood on his worktop before it went to Latham's house? We're talking micro-analysis stuff here; trace evidence. Look for marks, a faded patch on the tiles, an impression on the underside of the block, that sort of thing. Take some pictures in UV or

317

oblique light; you know more about it than me. My team will be looking for other possible links. Were the knives a present from the Silkstones, or were they bought specially for the job? Count the knives in both houses, does one of them have too many or too few? Look for a receipt, trace the supplier, who bought them?'

'Perhaps there are photographs taken in their kitchens that might show the knives,' the youngest of the SOCOs suggested. She was an Asian girl, with huge dark eyes. A SOCO's greatest asset is his or her eyes, and hers were belters.

'Good thinking,' I said. 'Find their photo albums. And while we're talking about photos, I'm going to ask Somerset to give the picture of Caroline Poole we found in Latham's bedroom a going over: does it carry any prints, inside or out, and what was used to trim it down to size? You know the score, so have a look at his scissors.'

'All this should have been done before,' Sparky declared.

'You're right, Dave,' I said, 'but Silkstone confessed to murder and we believed him. We believed what we saw and what he told us. Any tests we did were to confirm his story, because we had no reason to do otherwise. What we are saying now is that perhaps he was involved also with the death of his wife and the whole thing was premeditated. This is a murder enquiry, and not Confessions of a Salesman. Without witnesses the odds are stacked against us, but let's give it a try.'

They closed their notebooks and stood up, looking slightly more enthusiastic than before but not exactly overflowing with optimism. The young scientist from the lab hung back as they drifted away.

'So where are the, er, whatsits?' he asked.

'Here,' I said, passing him a manila envelope.

'There's a hundred in here?'

'A hundred and two.'

'Do you realise how long it will take?'

'It could be up to three hours,' I replied, 'but just do as many as you can. The more the merrier. What I mainly want from you is an unbiased report, nice and scientific, that nobody can argue with.'

He reached inside the envelope and extracted a dispenser of aloe vera liquid soap. 'And what's this for?' he asked.

'Um, use your imagination,' I replied.

'Present for you,' I said, opening the car boot.

'What is it?' Dave asked, coming over to me. It was seven thirty in the morning and a light drizzle was falling. We hadn't met for a pint the night before, so I'd spent the evening shopping and doing chores.

'My old microwave,' I told him. 'You can have it for Sophie, if you want. You said she needed one. The bulb's gone, but otherwise it's OK.'

He turned up his collar and looked at it for a few seconds before saying: 'And what about you? I thought you lived out of the microwave.'

'I bought a new one last night. A Mitsubishi. It does everything, including the washing up, so this is now going spare. Any good to you?'

'Charlie...' he began, 'I'd be annoyed if I

319

thought you'd gone out and bought one just so Sophie could have this.'

'I didn't,' I assured him. 'Sainsbury's have started doing these ready meals for the healthier appetite, like mine, and this isn't large enough for them. They get stuck corner-ways on when they rotate, so I bought a bigger one. Now I'm getting flippin' soaked, so do you want it or not.'

'Yeah,' he nodded. 'Thanks a lot. I believe you like I believe the Prime Minister, but thanks. It'll save me a bob or two.'

'And these are expensive times,' I said.

'You can say that again.'

I helped him carry it to his car and we walked into the nick, brushing the raindrops from our jackets. Dave is paid for the overtime he works, but it is strictly limited. I have to ration it out and try to be fair to everyone. The younger DCs have expenses, too: mortgages and young children if they're married; flash cars with big payments if they're single. 'What a miserable day,' I complained.

'Yeah,' he agreed with a grin. 'What we need is a nice juicy interview, to brighten it up.'

'I'll see what I can arrange, Mr Nasty,' I said.

'I'll wait for your call, Mr Nice,' he replied.

Jeff attended the briefing while I read the night reports. He was wearing blue trousers with a logo tab sewn to a pocket, a short sleeved white shirt and a green tie with multicoloured triangles in a random pattern. Annette waved a coffee mug at me across the office and I nodded a *Yes please* at her. She was wearing a lime green T-shirt that managed to look expensive, black trousers with a slight flair and chunky-heeled granny boots. She looked sensational and I let my eyes linger on her, catching the curve of her breasts as she reached to plug in the kettle. Jeff, in contrast, looked quite ordinary.

Just before ten, front desk rang to say that Mr Silkstone and Mr Prendergast had arrived and were now in interview room number one. We gave them five minutes to decide where they were sitting and went down to join them. Silkstone looked leaner than I remembered him, and had worked on his tan. He was wearing a stone-coloured lightweight suit that was inappropriate for the weather and made him look like Our Man in Havana. Prendergast was in solicitor blue, and two large umbrellas leaned in the corner, each standing in a small puddle. I wondered if they had licences for them.

'Nasty morning,' I said, brightly, as I sat opposite Silkstone. They both glanced at me without replying, Silkstone giving me the look he normally reserved for flat tyres and dodgy oysters. Dave placed two cassettes in the recorder and announced that we were off.

I thanked them for coming and did the introductions, adding that DS Sparkington would have to leave us in a few minutes to make a phone call. 'The principal reason we are here,' I continued, 'is to make what we call a definitive activity chart of Mr Silkstone's exact movements through the house on the day that Mr Latham died. It's not a new idea, but the prosecution service has started asking for it in all cases. Up to now we've only done one if we thought it relevant. I know you have told us most of it before, but I'd be very grateful if we could run through it again.' I extracted a plan of Latham's house at West Woods from the papers on the table in front of me, and slid it towards Dave. He squared it up and laid a pencil across it. 'So,' I went on, 'if you can describe your movements from when you parked on his drive to when the police arrived, DC Sparkington will mark them on the diagram.'

Prendergast looked as if I were trying to sell him a timeshare in Bosnia, which is about how I felt, but he stayed silent. Silkstone didn't know any better and leaned back in his chair, rehearsing his words as he drew on a cigarette. He had nothing to hide. He was the first person I'd met who could swagger sitting down.

'Er, Boss,' Dave said.

'Mmm?'

'Don't you think we ought to start before then?' he asked.

'Like when?'

'Well, when Mr Silkstone went home and found Latham with his wife.'

'You mean a week earlier, at Mountain Meadows?'

'That's right.'

'Why?'

'Because CPS will ask for it. It might not be relevant, but it's all part of the big picture. And then we want another one for a week later, when he found Mrs Silkstone's body. After that we can go to Latham's place.'

I clenched my fists and stared down at the desk,

breathing deeply. After a few moments I said: 'OK, OK, if you say so. Do we have drawings of Mr Silkstone's house.'

'It's The Garth,' Dave replied. 'There should be some in there.' I found one and pushed it towards him. 'Sorry about this,' I said to the other two, 'but my DC likes to do things by the book.'

Dave turned towards the tape recorder and said: 'I am now looking at a drawing of The Garth, Mountain Meadows.' He announced today's date and the date that Silkstone first went home early, writing them both on the diagram. 'Right,' he declared, looking expectantly at me and then at Silkstone. 'Let's go.'

'Where did you park the car?' I asked, and Silkstone leaned over the table and showed Dave exactly where he'd left his £40,000 Audi A8.

'And by which door did you enter the house?'

'The kitchen door.'

Dave traced a straggly line down the drive, around the corner to the side door.

'And then?'

'I walked through into the lounge,' Silkstone informed us, exhaling a cloud of smoke towards the ceiling, 'to where Margaret and Peter were sitting.'

'Which was where, exactly?' I asked.

'Margaret was on the settee and Peter in the easy chair nearest the fireplace.'

'And did you join them?'

'No. I was bursting to go to the toilet. That was mainly why I'd gone home. I put my briefcase down and went for a piss.'

'Which bathroom did you use?' Dave asked, his pencil hovering over the plan.

Prendergast yawned and twisted in his seat, trying to see out through the little window. Relax while you can, I thought. We'll brighten up your morning in a minute or two.

'Upstairs,' Silkstone replied. 'The family bathroom.'

'Why not the one downstairs,' I asked, 'if you were so desperate?'

'Never occurred to me,' he said. 'We only use that one when we entertain, and I don't suppose I was that desperate. Generally speaking, I use the family room all the time, and Margaret uses – used – the *en suite* one. I just went up there out of habit.'

'Inspector...' the lawyer began, his face twisted by a pain that expressed his disdain for what we were doing. 'Is this really necessary?'

I turned to Dave, saying: 'Isn't it about time you made that call, Sunshine?'

'Yeah,' he replied, pushing his chair back and standing up. ''Scuse me.'

'DC Sparkington leaves the room at ten thirteen,' I said, as if anyone cared, but it sounded professional. I reached for the incomplete diagram and turned to the brief. 'My DC is right,' I told him. 'It might all look unnecessary, but we have a list of forms to fill in and if any are missing the CPS start chasing us. It's nice if we can get it right first time: saves us having to bother you again. So, Mr Silkstone, you presumably came downstairs again and joined the others?'

I convinced them, I'm sure of it. We join the

324

police because we are honest, but it's a licence to lie through our teeth. You have to be careful, though. Evidence obtained by trickery is inadmissible, like almost anything else that works against the defendant. I don't care. Silkstone might get away with having been there when his wife died, and God-knows what else, but the newspapers would have a field day when they saw the pile of shit I'd bulldoze into court.

I galloped through the rest of his movements and was just at the point where he stabbed Latham when Dave returned. He handed me a manila envelope and I told the machine that he was back. When we'd finished we asked Silkstone to sign the diagrams and told him that he would be given photocopies, along with the tape.

'And finally,' I said, 'there's just a little matter of this.' I pulled the warrant from its envelope and slid it across the table.

'What is it?' Prendergast asked, as they both leaned forward.

'A warrant to search The Garth, Mountain Meadows, and make certain tests. A team of officers is there at this moment, waiting to start. You may go along to witness things, Mr Prendergast, but there is also a codicil to Mr Silkstone's bail conditions, saying that he must stay out of The Garth while these tests are being made. It expires at four p.m. today.'

Silkstone looked as if the MD had just had him in to say that from now on the company's cars would be Reliant Robins, and Prendergast did a passable impression of an oxygen-starved koi carp.

'This is preposterous!' the brief eventually opined.

'It's legal,' I stated, rising to my feet.

Dave said: 'I'll tell them to get on with it.'

'Yes, please,' I affirmed, and he left the room again.

'What you are doing, Inspector,' Prendergast spluttered, 'is ... is ... highly irregular and ... and ... of doubtful validity. First of all, there is the question of security.' He was getting himself back together. 'It is normal procedure for a responsible representative of the defendant be present when a search is made. My client may have large sums of money, or other valuables, in the house. And then there's the question of the admissibility of any so-called evidence your men may purport to have discovered. The situation is outlandish and should not have been sprung upon us in such a precipitate manner. I feel obliged to take this up with your superiors, and am considering a formal complaint. The whole thing is completely out of order.'

I turned to Silkstone. 'Are there any large sums of money in the house?' I asked, and he shook his head before Prendergast had time to advise him otherwise. 'My men, as you call them,' I continued, 'are accompanied by several civilian scenes of crime specialists and one of Her Majesty's scientists. I am confident that they will conduct themselves with their normal integrity and impartiality. As I have said before, their findings may corroborate your story and you will have full access to them. If you are concerned about your property you may go along and watch, but you will not be allowed in the house.'

'So what am I supposed to do?' Silkstone demanded. 'Stand in the garden in the rain?'

'I suggest you go about whatever you intended to do. Now, if you'll follow me to the front desk I'll sign a copy of the tape and photocopies of these diagrams over to you. Don't forget your umbrellas.'

Prendergast complained all the way there and was still berating the custody sergeant as I danced up the stairs, three at a time, towards my little kingdom and a well-earned pot of Earl Grey. All we needed now was some evidence.

Jason Lee Gelder said that the food at the remand centre was really good. It was next door to Bentley prison, catering expressly for under-twenty-ones, and still came under Gwen Rhodes' authority. They had sausages and beans for breakfast and something different every day for dinner. He shared a room with another youth and they got on well together. The duty solicitor joined us, complaining about his beaker of tea, and I said: 'Right, Jason. Let's talk about this girlfriend of yours. Have you remembered her name?'

'No,' he replied.

'Have you tried to?'

'A bit, but I can't.'

'I've checked the families of every police officer at Heckley,' I told him, 'and nobody has a daughter of that age who goes in the Aspidistra Lounge. Your girlfriend definitely wasn't a cop's daughter, so you have nothing to fear there. You are wrong about that, Jason, so who is she? Either you are lying to me or she was lying to you. Which is it?'

'Actually,' he could have said, 'it's you who are lying to me,' but he wasn't to know that. Instead he coloured up and shrank into himself, like a child scolded by a grown-up.

I eventually broke the silence by saying: 'Come on, Jason, start telling me about her. It can only help your case.'

'Tell the inspector what you know,' the solicitor urged.

'Let's start with a description,' I suggested, rising to my feet. 'How tall was she. You danced with her, so where did she come up to?' I took hold of his arm and helped him stand up. 'Up to here?' I said. 'Or here?'

''Bout 'ere,' he told me, holding his hand, palm down, level with his Adam's apple.

'About five feet four,' I said. 'Well done, that's a start. And what about her build? Was she slim, overweight, or in between?'

'She was a little bit fat.'

'Good. What colour was her hair?'

Simple questions that he could answer, that would have saved me a sleepless night if I'd asked them earlier. Sometimes even the toppest cops get the basics wrong. After they'd had sex he took her home, which was somewhere in the Sylvan Fields estate. Not right to the door, because she was afraid that her dad would see her coming home in a car and cause some grief. And he was glad to oblige because dad was a cop, wasn't he?

We went through the whole sordid scene, and

little flashes came back to him. She had a tattoo on her shoulder. He couldn't see it properly in the dark, but she said it was a spider. Her favourite group was Boyzone and her previous boyfriend drove a Mazda, but it was stolen and he lost it. She didn't go in pubs but went to the football, sometimes. Her mam and dad were always fighting and kept breaking up. She didn't think he'd stay much longer. They did it twice, and she helped him the second time. He only had one condom with him, but it was OK because she had one. Everything but a name. I could have asked him what I wanted to know, what I *really* wanted to know, but it would sound better coming from someone else.

'So you sat and talked for a few minutes before she got out?' I repeated for the third time.

'Yeah, a bit.'

'What about?'

'Dunno. This and that. What I just told you, I s'pose.'

'Did you arrange to meet again?'

'I told you, yeah.'

'Tell me again.'

'At the club, I think.'

'You just left it loose. You had brilliant sex with this girl and then you said: "OK, perhaps I'll see you again sometime." I don't believe you Jason. I don't believe that you are getting it so often that you can afford to be choosy. I think you desperately wanted to see her again, as soon as possible, and you arranged to do so. Maybe you promised to phone her. Was that it? Did she give you her phone number?'

Jason slowly straightened in the chair, his brow furrowed and his lips pursed. He had the looks of a film star, but he'd have needed a stuntman to do his dialogue. 'Yeah,' he said, the light of remembrance lighting his countenance with all the illumination of a male glow-worm. (It's the females that glow, wouldn't you just know it.) 'Yeah, that's what she did, she gave me her phone number.'

'Great,' I said. 'That's great.' Now all I had to do was prize it from him. Given the choice, I'd have preferred trying to take a banana from a rabid baboon. 'So did she write it down for you, or did you try to remember it?'

'We didn't 'ave a pen,' he told me.

'Well you wouldn't have, would you?' I replied with uncharacteristic understanding. With a combined IQ that was lower than the number of left legs at an amputees ball, it was unlikely that either of them would want to scribble down a sonnet, or even a haiku or two, after a moonlit shag in a Ford Fiesta. I waited for someone else to speak and wondered what to have for lunch.

'It wasn't then...' Jason began.

'Wasn't when?' I interrupted.

'Then. When I dropped her off. It was before that, at the brickyard, just after, you know...'

'Just after you'd had it?' My mind kept returning to the two of them bonking like a pair of ferrets in the front seat of his car. It was worrying.

'Yeah, then,' he confirmed. 'She told me 'er number and I asked 'er to write it down, on a parking ticket. Not a parking ticket, one from a

330

machine, you know.'

'A pay and display ticket,' I said.

'Yeah, that's right. Pay an' display. But she didn't 'ave a pen.'

'And you didn't, either.'

'No. So she wrote it on the win'screen, with 'er finger. Up at the top. It was steamed up, y'know. Then she pulled the sun flap down, "To protect it," she said. I'd forgotten all about it.'

'Alle-flippin'-luia,' I sighed, burying my head in my hands.

Chapter 12

Jason's car was still in our garage at Halifax, emblazoned with stickers saying that it was evidence and not to be touched. Fingerprints had found the last three digits of the number on the windscreen when they gave it a good going-over, hoping to find evidence that Marie-Claire had been in there. The numbers were meaningless, so no action was taken on them. 'It's a phone number for someone who lives in the Sylvan Fields,' I told Les Isles, over a coffee in his office.

'So it probably starts with eight-three, followed by an unknown number,' he stated.

'Which narrows it down to ten possibilities.'

An hour later BT had furnished me with five names and addresses, and after fifteen minutes with the electoral roll I found myself drawing a big circle around 53, Bunyan Avenue; home of Edward and Vera Jackson, and their daughter Dionne.

I rang the number, but it was engaged. Les had left me to have a meeting with somebody, so I wrote him a note and headed for the exit. They have a visitors' signing in and out book at HQ and a young man in a Gore-Tex waterproof was bent over it. He looked at his watch and entered his leaving time in the appropriate column.

'Could Mr Isles help you, Mr Hollingbrook?' the desk sergeant asked him.

332

'Not really,' he replied. 'He was very kind, as always, but said that all he could do was have a word with the coroner. He has to make the decision.'

He slid the book towards me and I put ditto marks under the time he'd written.

'I'm afraid that's always the case,' the desk sergeant stated. 'But the coroner's a reasonable man, and I'm sure he'll do what he can. I'd have liked to organise a lift back for you, but everybody's out at the moment.'

The visitor was Marie-Claire's husband, I gathered, come in to ask about the release of his young wife's body for burial. He only looked about twenty. I caught the sergeant's eye and said: 'I'll give Mr Hollingbrook a lift, Arthur. No problem.'

'There you are, then,' he said, and introduced me to the visitor. We shook hands without smiling and I opened the door for him.

His first name was Angus. He was twenty-four years old and a student of civil engineering at Huddersfield University, sponsored by one of the large groups that specialise in motorways and bridges. Marie-Claire had died on the Saturday or Sunday of the holiday weekend, while he was seconded to Sunderland to help in the replacement of an old stone bridge over a railway line by a modern pre-stressed concrete structure. He'd come home on Wednesday and found her body. I told him that I wasn't on the case, but I was interested because the assault was similar to the one on Margaret Silkstone at Heckley, back in June. I explained that we had somebody else for

333

that murder, but there was a possibility that Marie-Claire's was a copycat killing. That was the official line, so I stayed with it. No point in stirring up the gravel with my own private paddle just yet. There'd be plenty of time for that: there's no statute of limitations on murder.

'Lousy weather,' I said as the windscreen wipers slapped from side to side.

'Mmm,' he replied, not caring about it, his thoughts with the beautiful girl he'd loved, wondering if he'd ever forget her or find her like again.

'It's next left, please,' he said.

I slowed for the turn, then stopped to allow a bus out. It said *Heckley* on its destination board. The driver waved his thanks to me and when he was out of the way I turned into Angus's street.

'It's the last house on the left,' he told me.

They were Victorian monoliths in freshly sand-blasted Yorkshire stone, with bay windows and stained-glass doors, built for the middle-manage-ment of the day but now converted into flats or lived-in by extended families. The street was lined both sides with parked cars, because, like the pocket calculator, nobody predicted the advent of the automobile.

'This is rather grand,' I said, parking in the middle of the road.

'It is, isn't it. We just have the top floor. Marie loved it. Great big rooms and high ceilings. Lots of room for her hangings – she was in textile design – but a devil to heat. We...' He let it hang there, realising that there was no *we* anymore.

'Will you stay?' I asked.

He shook his head. 'No, no way. Our lease runs out at Christmas but I don't think I could stay that long. We'd wondered about buying it, but it didn't come off. Fortunately, now, I suppose.'

A car tried to turn into the street, but couldn't because I had it blocked. Angus opened the door and thanked me for the lift. 'No problem,' I replied, and drove round the corner, out of everybody's way.

John Bunyan would have loved the avenue they named after him on the Sylvan Fields estate, although the satellite dishes would have had him guessing. He'd have called it the Valley of Despondency, or some such, and had Giant Despair knocking seven bells out of Christian and Hope all along the length of it. I trickled along in second gear, weaving between the broken bricks, sleeping dogs and abandoned baby-buggies until I found number 53. At least the rain had stopped.

The front garden looked as if it had hosted a ploughing match lately, but the car that evidently parked there was not to be seen. I took the path to the side door and knocked. The woman who answered it almost instantly had an expectant look on her face and a Kookai carrier bag in her hand. She wore a tight leather jacket with leggings, and her halo of hair faded from platinum blonde through radioactive red to dishwater grey.

'Mrs Jackson?' I asked, holding my ID at arms length, more for the benefit of the neighbours and my reputation than the woman in front of me. I had a strong suspicion that male visitors

335

were quite common at this house.

'Er, yes,' she replied, adding, as she recovered from her initial disappointment: ''Ave you come about the fine?'

'No,' I replied, 'I haven't come about a fine. I believe you have a daughter called Dionne.'

'Yes,' she said. 'What's she done?'

'Nothing,' I told her, 'but we believe she may have recently witnessed something that will help us with certain enquiries. When will it be possible for me to speak to her?'

'You say she 'asn't done nowt? She's just a witness?'

'That's right. She may be able to clear something up for us. When will she be in?'

Mrs Jackson turned, shouting: 'Dionne! Somebody to see you,' into the gloom of the house, and stepped out on to the path. 'She'll be up in a minute,' she told me. 'I 'ave to go to work.'

'Well,' I began, 'I would like to talk to your daughter on her own, but because of her age she is entitled to have a parent with her.'

'But I don't 'ave to be, do I?'

'No, not really.'

'Right, I'll leave you to it, then. Bye.' She staggered off down the path, her litter-spike heels clicking and scraping on the concrete.

When daughter Dionne appeared she was wearing a tank top whose shoulder straps didn't quite line up with those of her bra and the ubiquitous black leggings. She was whey-faced, her hair hastily pulled together and held by a rubber band so it sprouted from the side of her head like a bunch of carrot tops. Hardly the sex bomb I'd expected. Her expression changed from expectancy to nervousness as I introduced myself.

'May I come in?' I asked, and she moved aside to let me through. I took a gulp of the chip-fat laden atmosphere and explained that she was entitled to have a parent present but as my questions were of a personal nature she might prefer to be alone. The carpet clung to my feet as I walked into the front room and looked for a safe place to sit. The gas fire was churning out more heat than an F14 Tomcat on afterburner and in the corner a grizzly bear was laying about a moose with a chainsaw, courtesy of the 24-hour cartoon channel. Dionne curled up on the settee as I gritted my teeth and settled for an easy chair. There was a plate on the table, with a kipper bone and skin laid across it.

'Kipper for breakfast,' I said, brightly. 'Smells good.'

'No,' she replied, her attention half on me, half on the moose who was now minus his antlers, 'that was me mam's tea, last night.'

I decided to axe the preliminaries. 'Right. Your mother said she was off to work. Where's that?' I asked.

'Friday she cleans for someone,' Dionne replied. The moose was fighting back, holding his severed antlers in his front feet.

'What else does she do?'

Dionne wrenched her attention from the screen and faced me. 'I don't know what they get up to, do I?' she protested.

'I meant on other days,' I explained. 'Does she

337

have a job for the rest of the week?'

'Yeah, 'course she 'as. She cleans for a few people. Well, that's what she calls it. Posh people. A doctor an' a s'licitor, an' some others.'

I looked around the room, taking in the beer rings on every horizontal surface and the window that barely transmitted light, and tried to recall the proverb about the cobbler's children being the worst-shod in the village. 'And what about your dad, Dionne?' I asked. 'Where's he?'

''E left us, 'bout two weeks ago.'

'Oh, I am sorry.'

'Don't be. 'E'll be back, soon as 'is new woman finds out what 'e's like.' The moose had gained the initiative and the bear was in full flight.

'Can we have the telly off, please,' I said, and she found the remote control somewhere in the sticky recesses of the settee and killed the picture.

'Thank you. Four weeks ago,' I said, 'on the Friday night of the holiday weekend, you were out with a boy He says you can give him an alibi for that night. Can you?'

'Dunno,' she replied. 'What was 'e called?'

'I was hoping you would tell me. You met him at the Aspidistra Lounge, and he brought you home.' She looked vacant, so I added: 'You called at the brickyard on the way,' not sure if that would narrow the field.

'Friday? Of the 'oliday weekend?'

'That's right.'

'Does 'e look a bit like Ronan in Boyzone?' she asked. 'Y'know, dead dishy?'

'He's a good looking lad,' I admitted.

'Yeah, I remember 'im. 'E's called Jason. I can

338

give 'im a nalibi for Friday night, if that's what you mean.'

'Good, thank you. Did you arrange to see him again?'

'Yeah, but 'e 'asn't rung me.'

'You gave him your phone number?'

'Yeah.'

'Did you write it down for him?'

'No, well, yeah. We didn't 'ave a pen, so I writ it on the front window of 'is car, in the steam. Mebbe it got rubbed off.'

'Perhaps it did. When you were talking to Jason did you mention your father at all?'

'No,' she replied. 'Why should I?'

'I thought you might have mentioned, for some reason, that your father was a policeman. Did you?'

Her podgy face turned the colour of my white socks after I washed them with my goalie sweater, and one hand went to her mouth to have its nails nibbled.

'It's not a crime, Dionne,' I assured her. 'You're not in trouble for it, but I'd like to know what you told him.'

''E's a bit dense, isn't 'e,' she stated.

'Jason? Yes,' I agreed, 'he does have a few problems in the brain department, like not being able to find one. Go on, please.'

'Well, it were like this. We were just passing 'Eckley nick – the cop station – an I said: 'Me dad's in there.' Someone, a cop, 'ad rung me mam, earlier that night to say that 'e'd been done again for drunk and disorderly an' they were keeping 'im in t'cells until 'e sobered up. 'E was

339

jumping up an' down in t'fountain, or summat, but I didn't tell 'im that.'

'And what did Jason have to say?'

''E got right excited, daft sod. "What, your dad's a cop?" 'e said. "Yeah," I told 'im. "'E's a detective." "Blimey!" 'e said. That's all. I think it ... you know.'

'Know what?'

'Nowt.'

She clammed up, and I knew she'd reached some indeterminate limit that I wouldn't push her past no matter how hard I tried. Everybody has one. I could only guess what she'd been about to say. That Jason became excited at the thought of shagging a detective's daughter? Probably.

'That's very useful, Dionne,' I told her. 'And then you went to the brickyard, I believe.'

'Yeah.'

'Right. Now this is where it gets a bit personal, I'm afraid. Not to put too fine a point on it, Dionne, and not wanting to pry into your private life, I have to ask you this: did the two of you make love that night, at the brickyard?'

'Yeah,' she replied, as readily as she might admit to sneaking an extra chocolate biscuit. 'We did it in the front of 'is car.'

'Right,' I said, nodding my approval at her answer, if not her morals. 'Good. And can I ask you if he wore a condom?'

'Yeah, I made sure of that.'

'Good. I don't suppose you remember if you did it more than once, do you?'

'Yeah, we did it twice. 'E was dead eager.' I

swear she blushed again at the memory, or maybe the gas fire was reaching her.

'And he had two condoms with him, had he?'

'No just one, but I 'ad one. We used mine the second time.'

'Very wise of you to carry one,' I told her. 'You can't be too careful, these days.'

'You're telling me,' she said, swinging her legs off the settee and facing me. 'You won't catch me risking it. Did you know,' she asked, 'that when you 'ave sex with someone it's like 'aving contact with everyone that they'd ever 'ad sex with? Miss Coward told us that in social health education. Put the wind up me, it did. So if you 'ave sex with, say, ten people, its like you've really 'ad it with a nundred.'

'Gosh!' I exclaimed.

'An worse than that, if you did it with twenty, that's like doing it with four 'undred. Four 'undred! In one go! Can you believe that?'

'No,' I admitted. 'It's frightening. But I'll say this, Dionne: you're good at maths.'

'Yeah, 's'my best subject. Nobody cheats me.'

'Good for you. So, when you'd finished, you know, doing it, what did Jason do with the condoms?'

'What did 'e do with them?'

'Mmm.'

'Well, what d'you think?'

'You tell me.'

''E just dropped 'em out of the window, that's all.'

And when you'd gone, I thought, somebody waiting in the shadows picked them off the dew-

341

laden grass, and the following day he smeared their contents on the rapidly cooling thighs of Marie-Claire Hollingbrook.

'Thanks, Dionne,' I said, rising to leave. 'You've been a big help.' I couldn't dislike her, or feel anything bad about her. Just sorrow for the world she'd grown up in. At the door I said: 'These condoms you carry. Are you embarrassed when you buy them, like I am?'

'No,' she replied. 'I pinch them out of me mam's 'andbag.' I smiled and flapped a wave at her, and walked back to the car, wondering how on earth I could have confused her with Sophie, my beloved Sophie. Cursing myself, hating myself, ashamed of myself. Les Isles wasn't surprised when I phoned him to say that he probably had the wrong man. He'd wondered about something like this, but Jason was still number one in the frame. 'Let's just say that our enquiries are continuing,' he admitted.

I could help you there, I thought, but I held my tongue. Instead, I drove all the way back to Halifax, to the street where Angus Hollingbrook expected to live happily-ever-after in a dream home, until his wife was murdered. He'd removed their name from the little space at the side of the bell, but there were only two of them and I assumed that the top one was for the upstairs flat. Sometimes you have to make these judgements.

I pressed the button several times, retreating to the gate after each burst and looking up at the windows. Eventually I saw a face and he gave me a wave of recognition. 'Sorry to trouble you,

342

Angus,' I told him when he opened the door, 'but a thought occurred to me. Can we have a word?' His eyes were rimmed with red and he was wearing a dressing gown over a T-shirt and jeans.

'I was having a snooze,' he said. 'Come in.' Halfway up the stairs he turned to say: 'It's a bit of a mess. They allowed me back in a week last Monday, but I haven't done anything. I'm still finding grey powder all over the place.'

He opened a door and we moved into a big white-walled room that could have been the annex to a gallery. Half of the wall opposite the window was covered with a hanging that had me spellbound. It was a kaleidoscope of textures in all the colours of the moors, changing and drifting as cloud shadows passed over the earth's surface and the wind stirred the heather. 'That's gorgeous,' I whispered as I stood before it, smelling the wet peat, hearing the call of a curlew.

'That's all I have of her now,' he said. 'That and some photographs.'

'Your wife was a very talented lady,' I told him, relieved that we'd brought her into the conversation but hating myself for it.

'Would you like a coffee, Inspector?' he asked.

'No thanks, Angus. I'll just ask you a couple of questions, then get out of your way.' He gestured for me to sit down and I sank into a chromium and leather chair that was surprisingly comfortable. How it would feel after an hour was another matter, because there was nowhere to hook your leg, loll your head or balance a glass. The room didn't have enough stuff in it to look untidy. Everything was clean-cut almost to the point of being clinical, but they'd started from scratch and stayed with a style. Only the wall hanging brought a touch of softness to the room, and I suspected the contrast was deliberate, to increase its impact.

'The grey stuff you keep finding is aluminium powder,' I explained, glad to be on familiar territory. 'The fingerprint people use it. The particles are flat, like tiny platelets, so they don't distort when it's lifted with sticky tape.'

'I thought it must be theirs,' he said, lowering himself onto a matching chair. 'So, er, what is it you wanted to ask me?'

'When we were sitting in the car,' I began, 'you said that you and Marie were considering buying this place. I'd like to know how far you went along that route.'

He looked puzzled, shrugged his shoulders, opened his mouth to speak and closed it again. He was upset because another cop was bandying his wife's name – his dead wife's name – as if he'd known her for years. I'm afraid there's no way around that one. 'It was Marie's idea,' he said. 'I wasn't keen because I'm not earning much, just expenses, and Marie's earnings were erratic, so we weren't a good risk for a mortgage.'

'So who did you approach?' I asked.

'Well, we, er, tried all the building societies,' he told me, 'but they didn't want to know.'

'Here in Halifax?' I asked. Home of the daddy of them all. Once they were a mutual society, existing for the benefit of members, whether they be investors or borrowers. Now they are part of the big conspiracy, doing it for shareholders and the Great God Profit.

'Yeah.' He gave a little smile at the memory. 'You know how it is,' he went on, 'these days they'll give you a loan to have the cat neutered, as long as they're sure they'll get their money back, or that you don't really need it. Everybody was very polite, but they were all sniggering behind their hands. We wanted a repayment mortgage, because of all the trouble we'd read about with endowment policies, but nobody would give us one. "Open an account and come back in two years" was the best offer we had.'

'So what did you do?'

'Nothing. Marie cut some adverts out of the papers and sent away for an application form, but when I explained to her that a secured loan meant that it was them that were secure, not us, she lost interest.'

'Who was that with?'

'No idea. Some company I'd never heard of.'

'Which papers do you take?'

'The *Telegraph*, usually, but I switch around a bit. Oh, and the *Gazette*.'

'The Halifax edition of the *Gazette*, I presume.'

'Yes, that's right.'

'No tabloids?' I asked.

'No, not usually.'

'And did she receive the application form?'

'Yes. I didn't want to send it back, but Marie said it couldn't hurt to find out what they offered.'

'And would they give you a mortgage?'

He shook his head. 'We didn't hear back from them, and then...'

And then all this happened. 'Do you still have any covering letter that came with the application form, or the advert from the paper?' I asked.

'I imagine so.'

'I'd be grateful if you could find them for me.'

'Why, Inspector? What's it all about. You've caught the ... the person who killed my wife, haven't you?'

'Yes,' I replied. 'A young man has been charged, as you know. Let's just say that I'm following a certain line of enquiry. These days it's not enough to prove who did the deed, we have to show that nobody else could have done it. We have to pre-empt any suggestions by the defence that another party, a mysterious unknown party, could be involved. You'd never believe the stories they'll concoct to sow a few seeds of doubt in the jurors' minds.' And I'm not bad at concocting a few of my own, I thought.

He believed me and went to find the documents. I wondered if there was a room next door where they kept everything: piled up to the picture rail with cardboard boxes, over-flowing bin liners and bulging suitcases, but he was back in thirty seconds, carrying a thin file. 'They should be in here,' he said, pulling a sheaf of papers from it.

They weren't. I recognised a couple of bank books, an insurance policy and what looked like their tenancy agreement, but there was nothing relating to a mortgage application. 'Sorry,' he said. 'Marie must have thrown it away. Like I said, I tried to discourage her.'

As I walked back to the car I saw another

346

Heckley bus leaving the kerbside, the front of it swinging out only inches from the car parked adjacent to the stop. I caught up with it on the climb out of town, and tucked in behind.

It did the grand tour, leaving the main road to call at every village, dropping off pensioners who'd strayed past the cheap fare deadline, picking up schoolchildren who had stayed behind and office workers carrying briefcases and shopping. When the bus stopped, I stopped. When it crawled up hills, I dropped into first gear and followed it. When it swooped down into the valley, swaying wildly and leaving a cloud of dust and gutter debris billowing in its wake, I hung back, waiting for the disaster that never came.

It took nearly an hour to reach the outskirts of Heckley, where I abandoned the chase, turning off the ring road near a fast bend where a tattered bunch of plastic flowers and a teddy bear marked the spot where young Jamie What's-his-name died, three months ago. Why would anyone want to commemorate such a place? It's one of those little mysteries that haunt my sleepless nights, like why do Volvo cars have their lights on during daylight hours, but Volvo lorries don't? I parked in a lay-by, near a fingerpost that said: *Footpath to Five Rise Locks*. It was twenty-five minutes past five, but good ol' Dave Sparkington was still at his desk when I rang him. A little bit of me was wishing that Annette would answer the phone, but it was Dave I needed right then.

'It's past your home time, Sunshine,' I said. 'What are you up to?'

'I'm doing police work. What are you up to is

more like it.'

'You'd never believe me. Listen, I'm at Five Rise Locks and could be in that pub called the Anglers in five minutes. It's two for the price of one before six. Did I hear you say that Shirley had gone to her mother's today?'

'I'll be about half an hour. See you there.'

Evidently she had. 'What about the kids?' I asked.

'Never mind them, I'm on my way.'

'OK, but don't be late, I'm famished.'

'I'm coming.'

I strode up the hill to the canal side, where five locks in rapid succession lift the waterway a hundred feet, and crossed over by the footbridge. A narrow-boat was waiting for a companion, before moving up to the next level and sending ten million gallons of water in the opposite direction. The people on the boat wished me a good afternoon and the smell of their cooking made me feel even hungrier. I hadn't eaten since breakfast. Turn left to the Anglers, a hundred yards away, right towards Mountain Meadows, home of Tony Silkstone, less than half a mile up the towpath. I looked at my watch and headed right.

There were two pot-bellied ponies in the paddock between his house and the canal, and one of his neighbours was using a strimmer or a chainsaw, or some other implement with an engine that made more noise than horsepower. Further along, four cormorants were perched in a dead tree, one of them spreading his wings to catch a brief burst of afternoon sun, the others hunched like judges. The fishermen are always writing to the *Gazette* to complain about the cormorants eating all the fish. The birds have been driven inland because there is nothing left for them in the coastal waters, their natural habitat, and the anglers are too dumb to realise that if there were no fish in the canal the cormorants would leave. The birds are just better at catching them than they are. I think they're cormorants, but they might be shags. I checked the time again and started back towards the pub. Halfway there I saw Silkstone's car coming up the lane at the other side of the field. Maybe he'd join us, I thought.

Dave pulled into the car-park at the same time as I arrived, and uncurled his bulky frame from the car. 'What's the difference between a cormorant and a shag?' I asked him as we walked in together.

'A cormorant and a shag?'

'Yep.'

'Um, is it that you don't feel like a cigarette after a cormorant?'

It was gloomy inside, but warm and friendly even though it was a large place, recently given a makeover, and we were the only customers. A young woman in uniform blouse and skirt greeted us as if we were an endangered species and asked what we'd like. *Here to serve you* said the badge on her blouse and a blackboard behind the bar told us that the guest beer was Sam Smith's.

'Pint of Sam's?' I suggested, and Dave nodded his agreement. 'Make that two, please,' I said, and she started pulling the pints, lifting them on to the bar after a few moments while the froth subsided.

'Will there be anything else, sir?' she asked.

I studied the chalked-up menu. 'Yes, please. We'd like to order some food. Is it still two for one?'

The young woman looked at the clock. 'Yes sir. Which table are you at?'

As we'd just walked in and were standing at the bar, I wasn't sure of the answer to that one. Dave came to the rescue. 'Over by the window,' he said, pointing, and the girl said it was table number twelve.

'Twelve,' I repeated. 'Remember that, Dave. Number twelve.'

'Twelve,' he said. 'Right. Twelve.'

'What would you like, Sir,' she asked, still smiling.

'Er, I think the gammon and pineapple,' I said, 'with a jacket potato, and, um, the half a chicken, again with a jacket potato.'

She tapped the order into the till. They don't have numbers on the keys, these days. Instead it says: *chicken and chips, egg and chips, ham and chips, ham eggs and chips,* and so on.

'Is that everything?' she asked, her finger poised over the *give them the bill* key.

'No,' Sparky interjected. 'I'd like some food, too. I'll have the steak and kidney pie and ... oh, half a chicken, both with chips.'

It's hungry work, being a cop, and we're growing lads.

Saturday morning we told Silkstone that we'd be interviewing him again on Monday, so come prepared. I had long conversations with Mr Wood and Les Isles and they both agreed with what I was doing. Les wanted to be present, but we haven't worked together since we were constables and I gave it the thumbs down. Besides, I wanted Dave with me. Dave and I go together like rhubarb crumble and custard, or mince pies and Wensleydale cheese. Mmm! There's none of this nice and nasty routine with us; we're both our normal, charming selves, most of the time. In the file I found an advert for Silkstone's company, Trans Global Finance, clipped from the *Gazette*. It said: *Can't get a mortgage? Low earnings? County court judgements? No problem! Secured loans available on all types of property. Send for an application form. Now!* More or less what I'd expected.

Sunday I went through it all, over and over again. Sometimes in my mind, sometimes scrawling on an A4 pad. I don't have hunches; I don't follow lines of enquiry. Not to start with. I gather information, everything I can, without judgement, as if I were picking up the shattered pieces of an ancient amphora, scattered on the floor of a tomb. Some bits might link together, others might be from a completely different puzzle. When I've gathered them all in I join up the obvious ones, like the rim and the handles, and then try to fill in the gaps until I have something that might hold water. Ideally, when I have a possible scenario in mind, it would be possible to put it to the test, devise an experi-

351

ment, like a scientist would. But liars and murderers are not as constant as the laws of physics, and it's not always possible. Instead, we turn up the heat and hope that something cracks.

'Did you know, Mr Silkstone,' I said as Dave and I breezed into interview room number one, ten o'clock Monday morning, 'that you have very good water pressure at Mountain Meadows?'

Prendergast looked up from the pad where he was adding to his already copious notes, shook his head and continued writing. Silkstone, sitting next to him, looked bewildered and reached for his cigarettes.

Dave removed the cellophane from two cassettes and placed them in the machine, watching them until the leader tape had passed through and nodding to me to say we were in business. I sat diagonally across from Silkstone and did the introductions, reminding him of his rights and informing him that he was still under caution. When prompted, Prendergast said that they understood.

'Let's talk about Margaret, your late wife,' I began. 'Word has it that you quarrelled a lot. Is that so?'

Silkstone drew on his cigarette and sent a cloud of smoke curling across the table. 'No,' he replied. 'We had an occasional argument – what married couple doesn't? – but that was all.'

'What, no vicious slanging matches? No slinging your clothes out of the bedroom window?'

'Inspector,' Prendergast interrupted. 'This

sounds like hearsay to me.'

'Of course it's hearsay,' I agreed. 'We talked to the neighbours: they heard it and they said it. It's a simple enough question, let Mr Silkstone answer.'

Silkstone sucked his cheeks in and licked his lips. 'That was nearly two years ago,' he replied. 'It only happened once, like that.'

'What was it about?'

'Money.'

'You were having problems?'

'No, not really. We just had to be a bit more careful than Margaret was used to.'

'But it's true to say that you stand to prosper by Margaret's death, is it not?'

Prendergast shook his head vigorously and banged his hands on the table. 'That's a preposterous thing to say, Inspector,' he exclaimed. 'My client did not profit in any way from his wife's untimely death.'

Addressing Silkstone, I said: 'But your mortgage will be paid off to the tune of a hundred and fifty thousand pounds, won't it?'

'Yes,' he hissed, 'but that's perfectly normal practice.'

'Indeed it is,' his solicitor affirmed. 'My own mortgage is covered by a joint life, first death policy as is anyone else's if they have any sense. You can't call that evidence.'

'No,' I agreed, 'but we can call it motive.'

'In that case, we all have motives to murder our spouses, and they us.' He sat back in triumph.

'Would you say, Mr Silkstone,' I asked, 'that you and Margaret had a normal sexual relationship?'

He looked straight at me, then said: 'I don't know, Inspector. How would you define a normal sexual relationship?'

'OK, let me put it another way. Were you and Peter Latham having joint sessions with your wife, three in a bed, that sort of stuff?'

'No.'

'You married sisters, didn't you? And you shared girlfriends, in the past. Latham had known your wife as long as you had. Was he the one who used to pull the birds, and you always ended up with the friend? Were you sharing her – Margaret – with him?'

'No,' he said, and crushed his cigarette stub into the ashtray.

Prendergast leaned forward, saying: 'This sounds like pure conjecture on your part, Inspector. Have you any evidence to corroborate these suggestions?'

'Evidence?' I replied, shaking my head. 'No. Not a shred.' I pulled the report that the lab scientist had done for me from its envelope, pretended to read the introduction, then pushed it back inside.

'No,' I repeated. 'We don't think you were having a three-in-a-bed sex romp that went wrong. It was a theory, but we have no evidence to support it.' I glanced sideways at the big NEAL recorder on the wall, seeing the tapes inside relentlessly revolving, making a copy of the words that passed between us. I'm a student of human behaviour, body language. When people lie they resort to using certain gestures: hands fidget and often cover the face; legs are restless;

brief expressions are quickly suppressed. But Silkstone was chain smoking, and that has a language all of its own, disguising his real expressions. I was relying on the tape to unmask him.

'We have another theory now,' I began. 'And this time we do have some evidence. This one says that Peter Latham wasn't present when Margaret died. He'd left, shortly before. This one says that you, Anthony Silkstone, killed her all by yourself.' They were both silent, stunned by the new accusation, wondering what the evidence could be. Sadly, it wasn't much. Prendergast shifted in his chair, about to come out with some double-speak, but I beat him to it. 'Let's go back a week,' I continued, 'To when you came home and found Latham and Margaret together. You are on record as saying that you went straight upstairs to the bathroom. Is that correct?'

'That's what I told you,' he replied.

'The family bathroom?'

'Yes.'

'And what did you do there?'

'I had a piss, washed my hands and went back downstairs.'

'Really? Are you sure you didn't see something floating in the water in the toilet, Mr Silkstone?'

He reached for his cigarettes and made a performance of lighting one. It wasn't a smooth performance, because the flame from his lighter was flickering about, magnifying the shaking of his hand. *My* hand would shake if I were being grilled for a murder. 'I don't know what you're talking about,' he replied.

'Are you sure you didn't see a used condom in there, Mr Silkstone? The one that Peter Latham had discarded and tried to flush away after having sex with your wife, earlier that afternoon?'

'Inspector,' his brief said, interrupting. 'You mentioned evidence. Will you be offering any, or is this another fanciful tale without any substance?'

I pulled the report from its envelope again. 'I talked to someone,' I said. 'A life-long philanderer, and he told me that when you deposit a French letter down the bog you have to be very careful to ensure that it goes right round the bend. He went into great detail on how to do it.' I smiled and said: 'We meet some terrible people in this job.' I didn't mention that I was talking about a fellow DI. 'So,' I continued, 'we did some tests. Last Thursday, while you were here, we dropped a condom down the toilet in your upstairs family bathroom and flushed it. Then we repeated the experiment a hundred times. To simulate used condoms we squirted a couple of shots of liquid soap into each one.' I slid the report across the desk. 'That's your copy. As you will see, it takes one minute and forty-three seconds for the cistern to fill again. That's very good. Each of the condoms went out of sight, round the bend, but then, lo and behold, a few seconds later thirteen of them popped back into view. Just like the one that Latham had used did.'

Prendergast looked across the table as if he'd just witnessed me kick an old lady. A very old lady. 'Is *this* what you call evidence?' he asked, waving the report. *'This!'*

'It'll do for the time being,' I replied.

'May we go now?' He rose to his feet. 'Or have you some other fairytale to amuse us with?'

Silkstone blew another cloud of smoke across the table. I held his gaze and refused to blink, although my eyes were watering. 'Sit down,' I said. 'I haven't finished.' Prendergast scraped his chair on the floor and sat down again.

'What did you do with it?' I asked Silkstone.

'Do ... with ... what ..., Inspector?' he asked, enunciating the words, chewing on them and enjoying the taste. He was growing cocky.

'The condom.'

'There was no condom.'

'I think you took it downstairs. After drying it off, of course. You wrapped it up in, say, cooking foil, and placed it in the fridge. At the back, behind the half-eaten jar of pesto and the black olives.' There was a flicker of recognition across his face as I recited the contents. I do my research. 'At that stage all it meant to you was proof of your wife's unfaithfulness. Maybe you were pleased to have the evidence or maybe you were devastated by it. Which was it? Pleased or devastated?'

'It didn't happen.'

'But as the days passed,' I continued, 'you thought of a better way to use it, didn't you? And a week later, after Latham had gone home, you murdered your wife, did things to her that she wouldn't let you do when she was alive – maybe you *couldn't* do them while she was alive – and then went round and stabbed Latham to death. After, of course, leaving the contents of the con-

357

dom on Margaret's body. That's what happened, isn't it?'

Now he looked nervous, scared, drawing on the cigarette before deciding it was too short and fumbling in the ashtray with it. Prendergast said: 'Your theories become more fanciful by the minute, Inspector. Now, if you have nothing to offer that bears the imprimatur of the truth, I suggest we bring this farce to an end.'

I gave Dave the slightest of nods and he leaned forward, elbows on the table, thrusting his face towards Silkstone. 'Tell us about Marie-Claire Hollingbrook,' he said.

'Never heard of her,' Silkstone replied, switching his attention to his new adversary.

'She was murdered in circumstances remarkably similar to Margaret's death. A month ago, on the Saturday before you did your sales conference.'

'I've read about it, that's all.'

'Bit of a coincidence, though, don't you think. Latham couldn't have done this one; he was dead.'

'Sergeant,' Prendergast interjected. 'The modus operandi of Mrs Latham's murderer was in all the newspapers. As you know, certain sick individuals often emulate murders they have read about.'

'It's constable,' Dave said.

'I'm sorry, Constable.'

'That's all right. And as you know, Mr Prendergast, sex offenders rarely stop after the first time. They get a taste for it, go on and on until they are caught.' He turned towards Silkstone. 'Is that

358

what you did? Get a taste for it? It was good was it, that way? You strangle them, I'm told, until they lose consciousness, then let them revive and do it all over again. And again and again. Is that what you did to Margaret, and then to Marie-Claire Hollingbrook?'

Silkstone looked at his brief, saying: 'Do we have to listen to this?'

Prendergast said: 'Let them get it off their chests. It's all they can look forward to.' He wanted to know how much, or little, we knew. And maybe, just maybe, he had a wife and daughters of his own, and was beginning to wonder a little about his client. Not that it would interfere with the way he handled the case. No chance.

'You'd done the perfect murder,' Dave told Silkstone. 'Got clean away with it. OK, you might have to do a year in the slammer for killing Latham, but the nation's sympathy was with you and it was a small price to pay for having all your problems solved.' He paused to let the situation gel in their minds, then continued: 'But the urge wouldn't go away, would, it? And when the application form from Marie-Claire plopped on your desk, it became too much to bear. What did it say? Name of applicant: Marie-Claire Hollingbrook. A lovely name, don't you think. Makes you wonder if she's as attractive as it sounds. Age: twenty-one; occupation: self-employed textile designer. Young and clever. It's more fun humiliating the clever ones, isn't it? Daytime telephone number and evening telephone number identical, so she must work from home. And then the same questions about her partner. Age: twenty-four; a student; and, would you believe it, not available during the day. You'd committed the perfect crime once, what was to stop you doing it again? Did you ring her at first, to see when her husband would be there? Or, hopefully, not there?'

'BT are checking all the phone calls,' I interjected.

'Or did you just visit her on spec? Which was it?'

'You're mad,' Silkstone replied.

'She invited you in and you asked to see the letter you'd sent her, and the advert from the *Gazette*. You carefully folded them, placed them in your pocket, and then the fun started. Except it wasn't much fun for that girl, because you were better at it by then, weren't you? And when you'd finished, you left your trademark: the semen you'd collected the night before, from the brick-yard.' Dave sat back and wiped his mouth with the back of his hand.

I said: 'On the day of the murder none of your neighbours saw you leave home in the car, but you were seen out walking. There's a bus route from the other side of the canal to near where Marie lived. We're tracing everybody who used the route that day. Also, we've appealed for anyone who was at the locks to come forward. Prints of your tyres have been taken and will be compared with those we found at the brickyard. If you've ever visited there you'd be wise to admit it, now.'

They sat there in silence, Silkstone with one

360

arm extended, his fingers on the table; Prendergast upright, hands in his lap, waiting. The smoke from his client's cigarettes was layering against the ceiling, drawn there by the feeble extractor fan, and shafts of light from the little armoured glass window shone through it like searchlight beams.

'Is there anything you wish to say?' I asked him.

'Yes, you're a fucking lunatic,' he snapped.

'Inspector,' Prendergast began, placing a hand on his client's arm to silence him. 'These are very serious allegations you are making. My client admitted killing Mr Latham, as we all know, but now he is being accused of these other crimes. First of all the death of his wife, the woman he loved, and now a completely unrelated murder. Either you must arrest my client and substantiate the charges against him, or we are leaving.'

'No,' I said wearily. 'We won't be arresting him.' I turned to the man in question. 'Do you remember Vince Halliwell?' I asked.

'Who?' he replied.

'Vince Halliwell. He was in Bentley Prison same time as you, doing ten years for armed robbery. Says you had a chat on a couple of occasions.'

'I never heard of him.'

'What about Paul Mann?'

'Never heard of him, either.'

'He's what we call a nutter. Poured paraffin over his girlfriend and hurled their baby out of a seventh storey window. Said it was an accident and is appealing against sentence. He got a double life, with twenty- and thirty-year tariffs.

Claims he dropped the baby, but unfortunately for him her body was found forty feet from the foot of the building. Kevin Chilcott, known as the Chiller, you ever hear of him?'

'No.'

'Never?'

'Never.'

'That's strange. Someone paid him fifty thousand pounds to kill me, and we thought it was you. Paul Mann arranged it, or is supposed to have done. Nasty people in prison. Wouldn't think twice about cheating a fellow inmate, especially one who thought he was a bit cleverer than them. Still, if it wasn't you there's nothing lost, is there? Fifty grand! Phew! I thought I was worth more than that.'

That's the bit we should have had on video. Silkstone's eyes narrowed and his face paled as all the blood drained from it. He crushed the empty cigarette packet in his hand and for a second I thought he was going to come over the table at me. Accuse him of rape, murder, buggery and he can handle it. Suggest that a bunch of no-hopers have cheated him out of his nest-egg and you really hit a nerve.

'Interview terminated at ... eleven-oh-two,' I said, and pushed my chair back.

Dave and I trudged up the stairs in silence. He went to fill the kettle and I sat at my desk. There was a note saying that the SOCOs had failed to find anything useful at either of the houses. I closed my eyes and leaned back, massaging my neck to ease the tension in it. The door opened and I thought it was Dave, but it was Annette's voice that said: 'Shall I do that for you?'

I grinned at her. 'I'd love you to, but it might look bad. People would get the wrong idea.'

'That's their problem.'

I shook my head. 'No, it's my problem. You leave this?'

'Yes. Came through ten minutes ago. Sorry.'

'Damn.'

'What did Silkstone have to say?'

'Nothing. We told him everything we knew, he told us nowt.'

'Everything?'

'Nearly everything. We didn't mention Caroline Poole.' I pointed at her note, saying: 'I was hoping this might give us some ammunition.'

Dave came in with two coffees and placed one in front of me. ''Spect you've been drinking all morning,' he told Annette, by way of apologising for not making her one.

'Most of it,' she agreed.

'So what do you think?' I asked him.

'About Silkstone?'

'No! About Annette drinking coffee all morning.'

He had a long sip, then said: 'He did it all, as sure as shit smells. There's no loose ends, no coincidences, no far-fetched theories. It all ties in, perfectly. You might not convince a jury, Chas, or even Annette and she hangs on your every word, but you've convinced me.'

Annette's cheeks turned the colour of a Montana sunset. I said: 'Well, that's a start. It gives us something to build on.' I felt like the Leader of the Opposition, after being wiped-out by a land-slide.

They fought back and they fought dirty. We had the tape transcribed and sent a copy to Super-intendent Isles. As I left the office that evening I was confronted on the steps by a reporter and a photographer. I referred them to our press office and fled. Tuesday, Dave and I had a meeting with Les Isles and Nigel at their place, and they made sympathetic noises but agreed that we weren't any further forward. Les's big problem was what to do with Jason Lee Gelder. He eventually decided to keep him inside for the time being, which I interpreted as a vote of no confidence. The HQ team was reconvened, however, and diverted to investigations that might place Silkstone near the lock or on a bus, that Saturday afternoon. As long as someone was in jail, the press would keep off our backs. That was the theory. As theories go it ranked alongside the one about the world being carried on the back of a giant tortoise.

Wednesday I decided to go in early and start the day with breakfast in the canteen. I wasn't sleeping well, too much on my mind, and it's a good atmosphere in there, early in the morning. The place is warm and steamy, loud with banter and fragrant with the smells of crispy bacon, sausages and toast. It's a good way of meeting the troops – the PCs who do all the real policing – and I always leave with high blood-sugar levels and a smile on my face, armed with a couple of new jokes to tell the boys. Except it didn't work out that way.

I was still at home, having a mug of tea and listening to Classic FM when the phone rang. It was Sparky. Sparky ringing me at six thirty means only one thing: he can't sleep, either. 'Tell me all about it,' I sighed.

'You seen TV AM this morning, Charlie?' he asked.

'No.' Sad though my life was, I still had a bit left before I was that low.

'Just before the news headlines they do a round-up of all the papers,' he explained. 'I usually watch it, just to catch up.'

'And...' I prompted.

'Well, this morning, you're all over the front page of the *UK News*.'

'Eh? Me? Why, what does it say?'

'I'll see you in the office, and bring one in with me.'

'I could collect one at...'

'No,' he interrupted. 'You'd better go straight in. Believe me, it's not nice.'

Chapter 13

There was a sprinkling of early birds in the office when I arrived. They raised their heads from their newspapers and followed me to my little enclave, where Dave was waiting. He closed the copy of *UK News* that he was perusing and spun it round for me to read.

One photograph took up most of the page. It was of Tony Silkstone, head bowed, tears glistening on his cheeks. But it was the caption that caught my attention. In the biggest typeface that the page could accommodate it said:

HOUNDED
BY KILLER COP

Inside was a photograph of me, taken when I left the office, Monday evening, with *World Exclusive* emblazoned across my forehead. A panel in large print informed the nation that I once shot dead an unarmed man, and now I was persecuting Tony Silkstone, the hero who did what the police had failed to do by ridding society of scumbag sex murderer Peter Latham, also pictured. On the next page but one, after a full-page special of a naked seventeen-year-old girl nibbling at a Cadbury's Flake, the editorial called me a renegade and a vigilante. *Is this the kind of police force we want?* it asked.

366

'The bastards,' I heard a voice behind me say.

'Yeah,' I agreed. 'The bastards.' I turned back to the photo of me and carefully folded the paper. 'Look,' I said, holding it towards the speaker. 'They didn't even get my best side.'

Willy O'Hagan was no-hoper mixed up in a drugs ring that we investigated. We raided a doss house one morning and he fired at me with a shotgun. Foolishly, I was alone at the time, and armed only with a little Walther two-two. There's a maxim among security forces that says minimum violence requires a maximum show of force. I got it wrong. I thought I knew best, but I got it wrong and I've reminded myself of that mistake almost every night since. O'Hagan swung his gun my way and blew a great chunk out of the chipboard wardrobe I was trying to hide behind, inches from my face. I loosed off three quick shots at him and he died a few minutes later. Then we noticed that his shotgun only had one barrel, and it wasn't a repeater. I'd killed an unarmed man.

The inquest was a whitewash, but I went along with it. He'd fired first, at an un-named police officer and that officer had returned fire. Lawful killing, justifiable homicide, call it what you will. I thought I'd heard the last of it, apart from the voices in the night, but Prendergast had done his homework. Like I said, they were fighting dirty.

Notoriety has its compensations. I laid low for the rest of the day, drinking coffee, catching up on paperwork and talking to our press office. They issued a statement, putting my case forward, and released a photograph that was used at the inquest, showing a uniformed PC standing where I'd been standing in O'Hagan's bedroom, with the corner blown off the cheap wardrobe. I blinked when I saw it, feeling the sting of debris hitting my face and eyes, seeing O'Hagan's form swimming before me, then falling to the floor.

I had a night in and watched the England game on TV, a couple of cans of Newcastle Brown at my elbow, like any good detective would do. The beer went down better than the football. With no goals scored and ten minutes to go our golden boy striker booted their dirty sweeper right in the penalty area and was sent off. One-nil to them, and that's how it ended. I bought a *UK News* on my way in next morning, but it was all football and ladies' chests; nothing at all about the Killer Cop. We were yesterday's news.

There was a big pink envelope on my desk, and the office was full. Was I missing something? I opened it and pulled out the card it held. It said: *Congratulations on your 100th birthday.* Inside, someone had written in a decent italic script: *To Charlie, just to let you know that we're all with you,* and everybody in the station had signed it. I walked out into the big office and flapped it at them. 'Thanks,' I said. 'I appreciate it.'

'Did you organise this?' I asked Annette, after the briefing and morning prayers, when she brought me a coffee. The big card was propped on my windowsill.

'Not guilty, Sir,' she replied.

'Well it was good of someone to go to the trouble. Tell whoever it was I said so, will you?'

'Will do.'

'Fetch your coffee and join me, please,' I said. 'I need some company.'

She came back and sat in my visitor's chair, crossing her legs at the ankle, like any well-brought-up girl should. She was wearing a pinstripe suit with a knee-length skirt and a white blouse but no jewellery. 'Don't suppose you watched the football last night?' I asked.

'No,' she laughed. 'Did you?'

'It was pathetic.' After an awkward silence I added: 'But at least it kept us out of the papers.'

'Charlie...' Annette began. I looked at her, inviting her to continue. 'Are you all right? We all know the truth about what happened, but it doesn't seem fair that ... you know, that only one side of it gets published.'

'Yeah,' I agreed. 'I half hoped that there'd be a more balanced report this morning, but I should have known better. Never trust the press, Annette. Never.'

'What you need,' she told me, 'is a really hot curry, with a few lagers to cool it down. It's Thursday – my treat, my car. OK?'

I shook my head. 'I'm sorry,' I replied, 'but I've something on tonight.'

'Oh,' she said. 'Well, never mind. Some other time, perhaps.'

'Yeah,' I said. 'Some other time.'

We finished our coffees and she picked up the mugs. As she left I said: 'The Deputy Chief Constable's coming to see me at eleven, so spread the word. Either be busy or be gone.'

I was waiting in Gilbert's office when the DCC arrived, a great bundle of newspapers under his arm. 'This is a pretty pass, Charlie,' he said, unrolling them on to Gilbert's desk. At least I was still Charlie.

'Anything in them?' Gilbert asked.

'Not a bloody sausage from our point of view. All flaming football in the tabloids and a couple of the broadsheets have picked up on the *UK News*'s original story. *The Mirror* and the *Sun* will pretend it never happened, because they didn't get there first, and the others might eventually print something if there isn't a more important scandal on offer, like a pregnant soap star.'

I grinned, saying: 'You have a highly jaundiced view of our free and fearless press, Mr Pritchard.'

'From years of experience dealing with 'em, Charlie. Now, what are we going to do?'

Don't you just love it when they ask you before telling you? He was retiring in a few weeks, so could afford to be generous and one of the boys. He'd come to the odd reunion or retirement party, but his authority would have gone and any influence he may have held would soon evaporate. What he'd like, all that he could hope for, was that people like me would talk about him with respect. 'He wasn't a bad old stick;' 'You always knew where you stood with him;' 'He was firm but fair;' or perhaps even: 'We could do with him back.'

He didn't take me off the case, he just destroyed the case. I'd done a good job, he said, had seen possibilities that were not immediately evident to other officers and pursued them with my usual diligence. The story, as I had related it, certainly had credibility. But the time had come to draw back, reconsider our position. Without forensics to link Silkstone with the death of his wife and Marie-Claire, we were leaving ourselves open to criticism. Silkstone had killed Latham, a known sex offender, and a vociferous amount of public opinion was behind him. We needed to channel that opinion so that it was with us, the police service, and not provoke it.

'We can only do our job with the consent of the people, Charlie,' he said. 'Never forget that.' I think he read it on a fortune cookie.

'So what do you want to do? Close the case?' I asked.

'*Close* is rather an extreme way of putting it,' he replied. 'Why not allow things to settle down somewhat and see what transpires, eh?'

'Put it on the back burner?' Gilbert suggested.

'Yes, put it on the back burner. And then, if anything else turns up, you can always re-open the investigation. But keep a low profile, the next time. I always find that the softly-softly approach has a lot going for it.'

'How long would you suggest before we looked at it again?' I asked.

'Oh, a couple of years?' he replied.

'And what about Jason Gelder?'

His smile turned sour for a moment, then returned in all its supercilious smarm. 'I think we should leave that for Mr Isles to sort out, don't you?'

I clumped down the stairs one at a time, dragging my hand on the polished banister, banging each foot on to the next step. I was hoping a friendly face would come the other way so I could shout at them, yelling: 'What's it got to do with you how I am?' but none came. I thrust my hands deep in my pockets and skulked back to the office.

Jeff Caton was the only person there, his head deep in that morning's *Gazette*. 'That all you've got to do?' I asked.

'Hi, Chas,' he said, looking up. 'Nothing in it, I'm afraid. Nothing about us, that is. The release will have gone out too late for this edition.'

'But?'

'But there's something in the free ads that might be worth looking at. Bloke selling a box of fifty King Edward cigars for fifty quid. Says they're an unwanted gift.'

'Maybe he's stopped smoking.'

'Maybe, but it's the seventh week the advert's been in.'

'Really? What are they worth?'

'About twice that.'

'I'm convinced. Let's go round in the morning and kick his door down. On second thoughts, let's go round now, just the two of us. I feel like some aggro.'

Jeff laughed. 'I'll call round later, posing as a buyer. What's brought this on?'

'Oh, Pritchard,' I told him. 'Wants me to drop chasing Silkstone. He hasn't taken me off the case, but I've to leave him alone. It's back to keeping the fair streets of Heckley safe enough for decent people to go about their business. Who cares if one of them just happens to be a psycho-path?'

'Maybe he's a fellow lodge member.'

'No, it's just bad public relations. I'm the ugly face of the police force.'

I went into my office and gathered up all the papers on my desk, piling them in the in-tray. I slumped in my chair and put my feet on the desk, pushing the chair back until the angle was just right. You can make yourself surprisingly com-fortable like that. I checked the position of the big hand on the clock and closed my eyes. With a bit of luck the phone wouldn't ring for ten or eleven minutes.

Three minutes, but it was Annette, so I didn't mind. 'Boss, I'm at the front desk,' she said, sounding breathless.

'Well, you see those stairs on your left? Go up the first flight and your...'

'I'm interviewing a girl in number two,' she interrupted. 'Says she was followed by a stalker. I think you should come down and hear what she says.'

'I'm a bit busy,' I lied. 'Can't you deal with it?'

'I can deal with it, no problem,' she replied, 'but I think you'd like to hear it for yourself. Believe me, Boss, you would.'

'OK, I'm on my way.' I swung my feet down on to the plain but functional carpet and reached for my jacket.

She was a big girl, with a bright, open face. Her hair was swept straight back into a ponytail and her complexion wasn't too good, but she had a nice smile and that makes up for a lot. Her school skirt was short, stretched tight around her crossed thighs, and she wore a blue V-necked pullover with a school badge on it. Apart from all that, she was sitting in my chair. I smiled at her and moved round the table to where the prisoner usually sits.

'This is Debbie Collins,' Annette said, 'and this is Inspector Priest. He's in charge of the case.'

'I know,' Debbie replied. 'I saw your picture in the paper.'

'That's me,' I told her. 'Now what can I do for you?'

Annette answered for her: 'I've recorded an interview with Debbie, but she said she doesn't mind going through it again.'

'OK. Let's hear it, then, Debbie, in your own words, at your own speed.'

She leaned forward, placing one hand on the table. 'It was one morning last June,' she began. 'I was going to school.'

'Which one?' I interjected.

'Heckley Sixth Form College. This man waved to me, from a car. I waved back, sort of instinctively, if you follow me. But when I thought about it I hadn't a clue who he was.'

'I know what you mean,' I said. 'Somebody waves and you wave back. It happens to all of us.'

'Yeah, well, a few mornings later I saw him again. I was waiting to cross the road and he drove by. This time he smiled and gave a little wave, like that.' She raised a hand, as if off a steering wheel. 'I didn't smile back, I don't think. Next time I saw him was in the afternoon, as I walked home, and he smiled again.'

'Did you take his number?' I asked.

'No, sorry. I didn't think too much about it. Then, a couple of weeks later, after we'd had our French exam, he stopped his car. I was smoking a cig. I don't normally, it's a stupid habit, but we were in the middle of exams and I was nervous. I took one of my dad's to school with me, to have afterwards, and I was smoking it on the way home and he asked me for a light.'

'He stopped the car and asked you for a light?'

'No, not quite. I saw him drive past and he pulled into the shopping precinct and dashed into the newsagents. He came out with a new packet of Benson and Hedges, and that's when he asked me. He sort of pretended he wasn't in a car and walked out on to the path, in front of me. Said he'd lost his matches and could he have a light.'

'Were you frightened?' I asked.

'No,' she replied. 'I was bigger than him. I'd've socked him if he'd tried anything.' Her face lit up in a smile, and she looked lovely.

'Did he say anything else?'

'Well, just something, you know, suggestive.'

'He propositioned you?'

'Not quite. He held the cigs out and said: "Can I give you one?" but it was obvious he didn't mean the fags.' She smiled again and this time Annette and I joined her. She'd done the right thing, coming to us, but fortunately her experience, if this was all there was, hadn't troubled her.

'And what happened next,' I asked.

'Nothing. I said no and he went off. After that

I started walking home with some other girls. I saw him once, the following week, but I ignored him.'

'Would you recognise him again?' From the corner of my eye I saw Annette smile.

'Oh, yeah,' Debbie replied, sitting up. 'I'd recognise him all right. It was him in the paper, with you, yesterday. Him who did that murder.'

'Oh,' I said, caught off guard. I hadn't expected this. I sat up straight and placed both hands on the table. It shows that I'm being honest and concerned. 'That must have been quite a shock for you.'

'It was.'

'Well, I'm pleased that your ordeal doesn't appear to have frightened you too much, Debbie, although it must have been pretty scary at the time. You handled the situation very well, but if it does start to bother you at all, have a word with us. Come and see Annette or myself, anytime. Meanwhile, as you know, he can't hurt you now, because ... well ... he's dead.'

Her eyes widened and I heard Annette clear her throat. 'No!' Debbie insisted. 'Not him! Not Peter Latham. It wasn't him who followed me, it was the other one: Tony Silkstone.'

I sat looking at her for an age, she returning my gaze from small blue eyes and her cheap scent spreading out across the rickety table. I glanced at Annette, whose grin looked as if it might bubble over into joyous laughter at any moment.

'When?' I managed, eventually. 'When did you see him the first time? You said it was June. June the what?'

Annette said: 'Debbie has checked when her French exam was, and believes it was on June the ninth.'

'One week before Margaret Silkstone died,' I stated.

'And probably the day Silkstone came home early and caught them together,' Annette added.

'Debbie,' I said, turning to her. 'What you have told us may be very important. Do your parents know you are here?'

'Yes. My mum told me to come. She wanted to come with me, but I said it was all right.'

'Good. I'm really pleased you did but I'd be grateful if you'd not discuss this with anyone else, OK?'

'Yeah, no problem.'

'Smashing. And meanwhile, DC Brown – Annette – will take you on a tour of the police station before driving you home. If you're hungry she might even call in McDonalds and treat you to a burger.'

'Great!' Debbie said, beaming one of her gorgeous smiles at me and uncurling those sapling legs.

I stopped at the front desk and dialled Mr Wood's number. 'It's Charlie,' I said when he answered. 'Is Mr Pritchard still with you?'

'No, he left about half an hour ago. Why?'

'There's been a development. Give him a ring, please, Gilbert. Tell him Charlie Palooka is back on the case.'

I rang my DI friend in Somerset and asked him to oil a few wheels for me. I wanted to see the file for the Caroline Poole murder, and then I wanted the files on all other associated cases. In a crime like that there are always similar offences which may or may not have been perpetrated by the same person. Caroline's death stood alone, shocking an otherwise safe community, but rapists and murderers go through a learning process, and usually have a few false starts before they hit the big time. I needed to know who might have had a lucky escape while the killer was developing his technique, and from them I needed a description.

Caroline's death pre-dated DNA fingerprinting by a couple of years, and there were no samples from her attacker that could be resurrected and tested, but the thought of sticking Silkstone in a line-up excited the Somerset DI. 'When were you thinking of coming down?' he asked.

'It will have to be Saturday,' I told him.

'Damn! I'm a bit tied up. I'll have to let you have Bob. You remember Bob?'

'I don't need any help,' I protested. 'Sit me in front of the files and I'll work my way through them.'

'No disrespect, Charlie,' he replied, 'but I'd like us to keep abreast of this one. We already have Caroline's file here in the office. I'll let Bob spend tomorrow on it and he'll identify the associated files and have them brought to Frome from HQ. He knows his way around them; with a bit of luck he'll have it done for you. What time will you be here?'

'Umm, ten o'clock,' I said, thinking that I'd work out the details later.

'Right. He'll be waiting for you.'

When I looked at the map I wished I'd said twelve noon. If I'd had the gift of second sight I'd have said: 'Make it Monday' but I don't, so I didn't.

It was microwave chicken casserole for tea, with pasta and green beans. After doing two-days worth of washing up I ran the car through the car wash and checked the tyre pressures and oil and water levels. My energy level was high, things were moving, looking good. I had a shower, put some decent clothes on and went out. It was nearly dark.

I drove to the brickyard, where the lovers meet. It was early for the normal trysts, but one car was parked up, windows grey with condensation. I drove to the opposite corner and parked so I could see it in my mirrors. It was a Vauxhall Vectra, brand new, with a mobile phone aerial on the back window. Later, after the pubs closed, the cars would be cheap Fords and Peugeots owned by the youth of Heckley who had no homes worthy of the name to go to, nobody to ask questions. Right now, it was the time for married men, having a drink with the boys or working late at the office.

I saw the interior light come on as a back door opened. A right-angle of white leg reached out, testing its strength before trusting it with the full weight of the attached body. Sex does that to your legs. A pale dress, flash of peroxide hair as she transferred to the front seat and made herself comfortable behind the steering wheel. Ah well, I'd got the details wrong. The man extricated himself from the back, glanced over towards me as he adjusted his clothing and took his place next to the woman.

They drove away back to their respective partners. 'Had a hard day, Darling?' 'Yes, you could say that.' Unless they were married to each other of course, and trying to recapture love's young dream. Whatever turns you on, I say. I didn't check to see if he'd dropped anything in the grass. I drove straight into town, not knowing why I'd been there, wondering if sometimes I take my job too seriously.

I couldn't park in my usual place because next week was Statis week. In mediaeval times it was the annual thanksgiving and excuse for a piss-up in celebration of another successful year's wool harvest. When nobody needed an excuse any more it fell out of favour for a while, but has recently been revived as part of the culture boom. The fair has been relegated to the park and the town square now hosts a series of open-air concerts, sometimes followed by a firework display across the canal. It brings money into the town and causes traffic havoc, but this is how they do things in Europe and our councillors like to show how cool and young-at-heart they are. Council workmen were busily erecting a stage and seating where I normally park, so I drove into the multi-storey. All leave would be stopped for the woodentops this weekend.

Buddy Holly was still on the door at the Aspidistra Lounge but his hair was growing again, and the ticket girl hadn't finished her gum. I paid my money, picked up my change and waited for him to open the door.

The steady boom-boom I'd heard outside threatened to do me brain damage now I was in. Blue whales in the South Atlantic probably had their flippers over their ears. The place was as empty as usual and Georgie was behind the bar, surveying his monarchy. In his position, I'd have considered abdication.

'My my, it's Mr Priest,' he said. 'Your usual, is it?' I nodded and he reached into the chiller cabinet for a Foster's Ice. He flipped the top off and slid the bottle towards me. 'This is getting to be a habit, Mr Priest,' he went on. 'Your little friends are in, not that they're little, of course. Young, perhaps, but not little. Like them young, do you, Mr Priest?'

'Glass,' I said, and he lifted one down from the rack above the bar. I carefully poured the over-priced, over-rated lager into it.

'Personally,' he said, 'I prefer them slightly older. More mature. But I can see what the attraction is. At their age they still have that innocence, don't you think? That openness, like a blank page that's waiting to be written on. I can understand how that might appeal to someone like yourself, Mr Priest.'

'George,' I began. 'I'd like you to know that you're talking family. If ever you or one of your goons as much as makes an approach to any of them, you'll be taking your sustenance through a tube for the next month.'

'Ooh, I love it when you talk tough,' he said.

I picked up my change and turned away. He called after me: 'You know what they say, Mr

381

Priest, *vice is nice, but...*' The rest of it was lost in the mindless drumbeat, but I knew what he meant: *Vice is nice, but incest is best.* It rhymes, which is the sole reason for its memorability.

There were only three of them. Shani saw me first and waved, causing Sophie to look up from her glass and give me a smile that did more for me than the lager ever could.

'Who's missing?' I asked, sitting down.

'Josie,' Sophie told me. 'She's doing a year in Italy before university.'

'And next week you'll all be gone, will you?'

'Week after is Freshers' week for me,' she explained. 'But this is our last night out.' Shani was going to London and the other girl, Frances, to Keele.

'Looks like I'll be here on my own, then,' I said, pulling a face.

'Aw!' they cried, in sympathy and Shani reached out and put her hand on mine. 'We'll make a special point of coming to see you during vacation,' she promised.

Sophie thanked me for the microwave and I mumbled something about having a new one. I offered to buy drinks but they said it was their turn and Frances went to fetch them. While she was gone Shani said: 'We're sorry about what it said in the papers, Charlie. They don't care what they print, as long as it sells.'

Sophie looked at me, blushing slightly. 'I told them what happened,' she began, 'when you and Dad ... you know.'

'That's all right, Sophie,' I told her. 'They have to print something.'

'But it doesn't seem fair,' Shani said.

'Fair!' I retorted with mock indignation. 'Fair! What's fair got to do with it? It isn't fair that you're all going to university while I have to stay here. It isn't fair that you have looks and brains, while I have to make do with just looks. And you're ten years younger than me. What's fair about that?'

We had a dance and another drink, staying longer than before because it was a special occasion. I politely asked if I was in the way, offering to leave them to it, but they glanced round at the local talent and begged me to stay, hanging on to my arms, making a production of it. We left when they started playing something called garage music, recorded in the panel beating shop by the sound of it.

It was the obligatory hot dogs at the stall outside, smothered in ketchup and mustard. I declined, sitting on the wall upwind of the smell until they'd finished. I watched them as they told stories about their teachers and boyfriends, and threw their heads back in girlish laughter.

We dropped Frances off first. She was a shy polite girl, and thanked me for the drink and the lift. I wished her well at Keele and told her that if she ever needed anyone sorting out she'd to let me know. She smiled and said she would.

Shani lived less than half a mile from Sophie. Outside her house she gave me a kiss on the cheek and said: 'I hope you catch 'em, Charlie, whoever they are.'

'Good luck, Shani,' I replied, 'and keep in touch.' I waited until she was safely inside before driving off.

We didn't speak for the last leg of the journey, both probably engrossed in our thoughts. At the top of Sophie's street I switched off the engine, doused the lights and coasted like a Stealth bomber towards her home, which was in darkness. I slowed on the brakes, very gently, and came to a silent stop outside her gate. I pulled the handbrake on and turned to face my passenger, my best friend's daughter, my goddaughter.

I could smell her perfume. It was Mitsouko by Guerlain, as used by Annabelle, my last love. Annabelle was accepted for Oxford when she was Sophie's age, but went to Africa instead and married a bishop. Sitting there, in the dark, it could have been Annabelle next to me.

'Sophie,' I began. She turned to face me, leaning her head on the back of her seat. I reached out and her hand found mine. I heard myself exhale a big breath, not knowing where to begin. 'Cambridge, next week,' I tried.

Sophie nodded. 'Mmm,' she mumbled.

'I just want to say that, you know, it's a whole new world for you. It is for anyone. If you have any you know, difficulties...'

'If I have any problems,' she interrupted, 'if anyone gives me any hassle, let you know and you'll come down and sort them out.'

'Well, that's part of it.'

'It's all right, Charles,' she continued. 'Nobody will give me any hassle, and Dad's said the same thing to me already.'

'It's not just that,' I told her. 'What I really meant was, well, money's bound to be tight. Impoverished students, and all that. Don't do without, Sophie. And don't keep running to your dad. I wanted to buy you something special, but I didn't know what. There'll be books you'll need, and other things. You're my family, too, you know, all I've got, so come to me first, eh?'

She bowed her head and put her other hand on mine. After a few moments she looked up and said: 'That's really lovely of you, Charles. Dad had told me that, too, but...'

'What?' I interjected. 'He told you to come to me if you were short of money? Wait 'till I see him...'

She squeezed my fingers, saying: 'No, silly, he told me to go to him first, not Mum.'

We sat smiling at each other in the dark, our fingers intertwined. After a while Sophie asked: 'Is it true you saved Dad's life?'

I shook my head. 'No.'

'He told Mum you did. She said he won't talk about it but that's why you are such good friends.'

'I hope we're good friends because we get on well together,' I replied. 'We've had a few adventures, like all policemen, that's all.'

'She said it was a long time ago, when you were both PCs.'

'Oh, I remember,' I declared. 'Yes, it was when we were both PCs. We were at Leeds Town Hall Magistrates' Court, and your dad had to go in the witness box to give evidence. Someone pinned a note on his back that said: *I am a plonker*. Everybody would have seen it when he went to the box, so I told him about it. He said:

"Thanks, Charlie, you saved my life." That must be what he means.'

Sophie squeezed my fingers. 'I don't believe you,' she giggled.

'Well it's true.'

'Charles...'

'Mmm?'

'I ... I love you.'

It was a tiny, hesitant voice, but the words were unmistakable, what we all long to hear: I love you. What do you say: 'Don't be silly' or 'You'll get over it'? I never subscribed to the views that babies don't feel pain, or that the emotions of the young are less valid than those of their parents. Love at eighteen is probably as glorious – or as agonising – as it gets.

'Yes, I know,' I replied, softly aware that I hadn't used the words myself for a long time, not sure how they would sound. 'And I love you.' There, it was easy once you took the plunge. The pressure of her fingers increased. 'I loved you when you were a baby,' I explained, but it was not what she wanted to hear and her grip loosened. 'And when you were a moody teenager.'

'I was never a moody teenager,' she protested.

'No, you weren't. You've never been anything less than delightful. And I love you now, as a beautiful young woman. Love changes, and it's a different sort of love.' She was squeezing my fingers again.

'But,' I went on, 'this is as far as it can go. You realise that, don't you?'

She looked at me and nodded. We held each other's gaze for a few moments until, as if by some secret signal, we both moved forward and our lips met.

We pressed them together, held them there, and then parted. I disengaged my fingers from hers and sat back. Her mouth had stayed closed, no tongue sliding out like a viper from under a stone to insinuate its way into my mouth and check out my fillings. She was still her daddy's little girl. 'That was nice,' I whispered.

'Mmm.' She agreed.

'Remember what I said.'

'Yes.' She reached for the door handle, then turned, saying: 'I think Annabelle is a fool.' From the pavement she added: 'And I hate her,' and reinforced her words by slamming the door so hard that the pressure wave popped both my ears. Why do women do that? I watched her into the house and drove home. I don't know why, but there was more joy in my heart than I'd felt in a long time.

Somerset Bob rang me Friday morning and I told him what I wanted. He was pleased and eager to be on the case and suggested I come down the A420, M4, and A350, but not the A361. I began to worry that we'd spend most of Saturday discussing the merits of the motorway versus those of A-roads, in which case I'd have to remind him of why I was there, but he was just being helpful and I needn't have worried. He invited me to stay the night with himself and his wife if we had a long day and I couldn't face the journey home, which was thoughtful of him.

I pulled everything that might be useful from

the Silkstone file and made copies for Somerset. I was extricating details of his early life in Heckley from the photocopier chute when Annette joined me, holding a letter she wanted duplicating.

'What's all that?' she asked.

'Stuff about Silkstone, for Somerset,' I replied. 'I'm going down there tomorrow to look at their files.'

'There looks to be a lot.'

'There is.'

'Why didn't you ask? I could have done it for you.'

'Because: a, you were busy; and b, you're a detective, not a clerical assistant.'

'Sorry,' she replied. 'Put it down to a hundred thousand years of conditioning.'

'Pull the other one,' I responded, lifting the original off the bed and gesturing for her to put her document on it.

'Thanks, I only want one copy.' I pressed the button for her. 'Are you driving down?' she asked.

''Fraid so. Early start, about six o'clock.'

'Do you want me to come with you?'

The light tube moved across and back again, and I lifted the lid. 'Why?' I asked. 'Aren't you going to York?'

'No. He's taking the girls to see their grandma. It's her birthday and I'm not invited.'

'Damn!' I cursed. 'I wish I'd known. I've arranged to stay the night at Bob – the DC's – house. It would have been a good day out, and you could have shared the driving.'

'Tell him there's been a change of plans.'

I thought about it. 'How were you going to spend the day?' I asked.

'Shopping in Leeds, and a hair-do,' she replied.

'Harvey Nick's? House of Fraser?' I suggested.

'That's right.'

'Treat yourself?'

'You bet!'

'Made an appointment for the hair-do?'

'Yes. What's all this leading to?'

'No,' I said. 'Thanks for the offer, Annette, but you have your day out in town. You've probably been looking forward to it, and you deserve it.'

'I don't mind cancelling,' she offered.

'No, but there is one thing.'

'What's that?'

'Don't let him cut too much off. I like it how it is.' She blushed, so I followed up with: 'And as it's an early start for me in the morning I won't feel like cooking tonight, so I might pop out for a meal somewhere. Some company would be nice.'

She tipped her head on one side and gave a little tight-lipped smile. 'Would I do, Mr Priest?' she asked.

'You'll do just fine, Miss Brown,' I replied.

I decided to splash out, demonstrate that I know how to treat a girl. Annette protested, said it was her turn, offered to at least split the bill, but I asked her to indulge me. I laid it on a bit thick, said I felt like a treat, something more special than our usual curry or Chinese. I drove us into Lancashire, to a place near Oldfield that Jeff Caton had discovered, run by a French-Persian couple and attracting rave reviews.

We started with kebabs and I followed them with lamb done in goat's milk and smothered in a spicy sauce. Annette had chicken in a fruity sauce with lots of chutneys, which I helped her with. We washed it down with a full-bodied Bordeaux. The proper stuff, all the way from France. The reviews, we agreed, were well deserved.

'Phew!' Annette exclaimed, dabbing her lips with her napkin. 'That was good.'

I finished my coffee. It came in tiny cups and was strong enough to drive a nuclear reactor. They didn't throw the grounds into the waste bin; they sent them to Sellafield for reprocessing. A waiter appeared with the coffee jug but I held my hand over the cup and shook my head. 'Any more of that and I'll be awake all night,' I said.

'And you've an early start in the morning,' Annette reminded me.

'Six o'clock,' I groaned. 'As much as I'd like to take you for a night on the town, it had better be some other time.' I paid the bill, which went a long way towards compensating the proprietor for the oil wells he lost when the Shah was deposed, and we left.

It was raining and dark, but I decided to take the scenic route back, over the tops rather than the motorway. I pushed the heater control over to maximum and pressed the Classic FM button on the radio. Rodrigues, excellent. I'd thought about pre-loading the cassette with a romantic tape, but it had felt corny, even for me. And what could be more romantic than Rodrigues? Annette wriggled in the passenger seat, making herself comfortable, and hummed along with Narciso Yepes.

A sudden flurry of sleet had me switching the wipers to maximum, but it only lasted a few seconds. 'Where does Grandma live?' I asked.

'Scarborough,' she replied.

'And does she know about you?'

'Yes. I think so.'

'So why aren't you going with them?'

'Because they're staying overnight, and there isn't room for me.'

'I see.'

More sleet splotched on to the windscreen, blobs of shadow that slithered upwards until the wipers swept them to the sides, where they clung to each other for security. 'Brrr!' Annette exclaimed. 'It looks a bit bleak out there.'

'Ah, but...' I argued, raising a finger to emphasise the point I was about to make, 'we're not out there.'

'Do you think...' she began, then stopped herself.

'Do I think what?'

'Do you think he is, out there?'

'Who?'

'Chilcott. Chiller.'

I hadn't forgotten him, just pretended to myself that he'd gone away. 'Somewhere, I suppose,' I replied. 'Probably where it's a little warmer than this, if he's any sense.'

'Have you heard anything about him, since he escaped?'

'No, not a word since the Calais sighting. When we interviewed Silkstone we made it clear that they'd conned him out of his money. That's probably what happened. Shooting me was never on the agenda.'

'I don't believe you,' she stated.

'Well I'll be off it now, that's for sure. All he'll want to do is survive. If the look on Silkstone's face was anything to go by he'd been paid in full, and there's no honour among thieves. None at all.' Apart from the odd fool like Vince Halliwell, I thought, doing ten years for someone whose name he 'couldn't remember.' Except that a hit man who ran off with the money without delivering the goods would very soon be an ex-hit man, but I kept that to myself.

I changed gear for the hairpin bend at the end of the reservoir and let the car drift over to the wrong side of the road. We were the only people up there, and it was easy to imagine, after just a few minutes, that we were completely alone in the world, snug in our private cocoon of warmth and music. Now it was Samuel Barber, Adagio for Strings. Someone was making it easy for me.

I slowed and turned off the road. A length of it, right on the top, has been straightened, but the old road is still there, used as a picnic place for day tippers from both counties, risking ambush by the old enemy.

'Don't panic,' I said as we came to a halt. 'I bring all my female friends here to admire the view.' Usually it's the sky ragingly beautiful as the sun sinks somewhere beyond the Irish Sea; or the lights of the conurbation, spread out below in a glowing blanket. Tonight it was a streak of paler sky marking the horizon, with indigo clouds bleeding down into it. Ah well, I thought, at least I got the music right. As I killed the lights I noticed the time. Twenty-two hours earlier I'd parked up with young Sophie sitting next to me. This was beginning to be a habit.

'I'm not panicking,' Annette said, turning towards me.

'I just thought we should talk more,' I began. 'It would have been really nice to have had you along, tomorrow.'

'We could have had a cream tea in the Cotswolds,' Annette suggested.

'Or Bath buns in Bath,' I added. The music paused, hanging there like an eagle over the edge of a precipice, held by the wind. It's moment, near the end of the adagio, when the silence grips you, forbidding even your breath to move. We sat quietly until the end of the piece, when I pressed the off button. Nothing could follow that.

'What will you do?' I asked, breaking the silence.

After a moment she said: 'He wants to marry me.'

The rain on the windows had completely obscured the view and a gust of wind rocked the car. Who'd believe we were just into October? 'Do you want to marry him?' I asked.

'Yes, I think so.'

'Will you leave the police?'

'Yes. If I go back to teaching we'd all have the same holidays. It would be an ideal situation.'

'You tried teaching, once.'

'I was twenty-two. I've learned a lot since then.'

'Like karate,' I said. 'How to disarm an attacker,

393

or use a firearm.'

She didn't reply. I said: 'I'm sorry, I shouldn't be trying to dissuade you.'

'What would you do, Charlie,' she asked, steering me away from the private stuff, 'if you weren't a policeman?'

'Same as you, I suppose,' I replied. 'I was heading for a career in teaching. Physical education and art. Non-academic, looked down upon by all the others in the staff room, with their degrees in geography and ... home economics. The police saved me from that.'

'What would you really like to do? If you could do anything in the world, what would it be?'

'Cor, I dunno,' I protested, my brain galloping through all the fantasies, searching for a respectable one.

'There must be something.'

'Yeah, I think there is.'

'What? Go on, tell me.'

'Swimming pool maintenance,' I announced.

'Swimming pool maintenance!' she laughed.

'That's right. In Hollywood. I'd have a van – a big macho pickup – with *Charlie's Pool Maintenance* painted on the side, and I'd fix all the stars' pools.' I liked the sound of this and decided to embroider it. 'When I'd finished checking the chlorine levels, cleaning the filters or whatever,' I continued, 'the lady of the house would come out with iced lemonades on a tray, and she'd say: "Have you fixed it, Charlie?" and I'd reply: "No problem, Ma'am." "What was the trouble?" she'd ask, and I'd say: "Oh, nothing much, only your HRT patch stuck in the filter again".'

Annette collapsed in a fit of giggling. When she'd nearly stopped she said: 'Oh, Charlie, I do...' Then she did stop.

'You do what?' I asked, but she shook her head. I reached out, putting my arm across her shoulders and pulling her towards me, meeting no resistance. I buried my face in her mass of hair, smelling it that close for the first time. 'You do what?' I insisted. 'Tell me.'

'I ... I ... I do enjoy being with you,' I heard her muffled voice say.

'That counts for a lot,' I told her, and felt her nod in agreement. I tilted her chin upwards and kissed the lips I'd longed to kiss for a long time. A grown-up kiss, tonight, with no holding back. She broke off before I wanted to.

As I held her I said: 'I've dreamed of that ever since I first saw you.'

She replied with a little 'Uh' sound.

'It's true. I'm not looking for a one-night stand, Annette, or a bit on the side. You know that, don't you?'

'Aren't you?' she replied.

'No. I want you to believe that.'

'Take me home, please.'

I started the engine and pulled my seatbelt back on. We drove most of the way to Heckley in silence. As we entered the town I said: 'If luck's on our side we'll find something tomorrow to link Silkstone with other attacks in Somerset.'

'Do you think you will?' Annette asked.

'Depends whether he did them,' I replied. 'And even then, it's a long shot.' As we turned into her street I said: 'I don't know what to think. About anything. Sometimes I wonder if it's worth bothering.' We came to a standstill outside the building which contains her flat. 'Here we are,' I said. 'Thank you for a pleasant evening, Annette. Sorry if I stepped out of line. It won't happen again.'

She shook her head, the light from the street lamps giving her a copper halo that swayed and shimmered like one of van Gogh's wind-blown cypress trees. 'You didn't step out of line, Charlie,' she told me.

'Honest?'

'Mmm. Honest.'

'Good. I'm glad about that.'

She reached for the door handle, like Sophie had done, then hesitated and turned to me in exactly the same way. 'What do you have against one-night stands and a bit on the side?' she asked.

'Nothing,' I replied. 'Nothing at all.'

I held her gaze until she said: 'Would you like to come in?'

'Yes,' I told her. 'I'd like that very much.'

Chapter 14

I blamed the traffic for being late. Bob asked if I'd come down the Fosse Way or Akeman Street, but I said: 'Oh, I don't know,' rather brusquely and asked him what he had for me. I realised later that it was an office joke, probably imitating one of the traffic officers who always swore that the *quickest* way from A to B was via Q, M and Z.

Plenty was the answer. I wanted to see the basic stuff first and then move on to the specific. I asked myself, as I looked at the ten-by-eights of poor Caroline's body if this was necessary. Couldn't I have gleaned the information I wanted from someone's report? No doubt, but this way was quicker. Caroline had been strangled and raped, from the front and not necessarily in that order. Also, the deed was done outdoors. Serial rapists develop a style, like any other craftsman. Some, who often have a record for burglary, prefer to work indoors. Others, quicker on their feet, strike in parks and lonely lanes. If Silkstone was our man he'd changed his style. Caroline's body was left in a shallow stream and not discovered for two days, hence the lack of forensic evidence.

Bob had extracted a list of statistics from the pile of information, to show how extensive the enquiry had been: fifteen thousand statements; twenty thousand tyre prints; eighteen thousand cars. He fetched me a sandwich and percolated some decent coffee while I read the statements made by the officers who had interviewed the Famous Four: Silkstone, Latham, Margaret, and Michelle Webster. What could they have said to differentiate themselves from all those thousands of others, short of: 'I did it, guv, it's a fair cop?'

But they didn't, and were lost in the pile of names just like others before them and a few since.

'Cor, that's good,' I said, taking a sip of the coffee. 'Just what I need.'

'Late night?' Bob asked.

'Yeah,' I replied.

'Working?'

'No, er, no, not really. It was, um, a promotion bash. Went on a bit late.' I liked that. A promotion bash. He was a detective, so he could probably tell that I was smiling, inside.

There were twenty-one reported attacks on women in the previous ten years that may have been linked to Caroline's death. Seventeen of them were unlikely, two looked highly suspicious. I started at the bottom of the pile, working towards the likeliest ones. Had I done it the other way round I might have become bogged down on numbers one and two. Some had descriptions, some didn't. He was tall, average height – this was most common – or short. Take your pick. He wore a balaclava, was clean shaven and had a beard. There were three of them, two of them, he was alone. He spoke with a local accent, a strange accent, never said a word. He had a knife, a gun, just used brute force. He was on foot, rode a bike, in a car.

Which would the good people of Frome prefer, I wondered? A serial rapist in their midst or twenty-one men who'd tried it once, for a bit of fun? Most of the attacks occurred on the way home from a night out, after both parties had imbibed too much alcohol. Some of the reports appeared frivolous, some hid tragedies behind the stilted phrases of the police officers. This was fifteen plus years ago, when the courts believed that a too-short skirt and eye contact across a crowded room meant: *take me, I'm begging for it.*

I'd placed the four favourites to one side. I untied the tape around the top one and started reading. She was a barmaid, walking home like she did every night. Someone struck her from behind, fracturing her skull, and dragged her into a field. She survived, after a December night in the open and three in intensive care, but never saw a thing of her attacker. One year, almost to the day, before Caroline.

Bob was busy at another desk. I raised an arm to attract his attention and he came over. 'He had full penetrative sex with this one,' I said. 'Do we know if she became pregnant?'

Bob lifted the cover of the file to look at the name. 'The barmaid,' he said. 'On the Bristol Road. She nearly died. Of these four she was the last and the only one where he managed it. We've thought of that so she can't have been.'

I didn't curse. I felt like it, but I didn't. It was good news for her. All the same, if he'd made her pregnant and she'd gone full term we could have done a DNA test, introduced someone to his or

399

her daddy perhaps.

The next one I looked at happened eighteen months earlier, in the summer of 1981, and he drove a Jaguar. 'Bob!' I shouted across the office.

'What is it?' he asked, coming over.

'This one,' I told him, closing the folder to show the name on the front. 'Eileen Kelly. In her statement she says that the car she accepted a lift in was a Jaguar. On the wall of Silkstone's bedroom is a photograph of him posing alongside a Mk II Jag. You can read the number and it's in the file somewhere.'

'I'll get on to the DVLC,' Bob said. 'When are we talking about?'

'She was attacked in August, '81.'

He went back to his telephone and I read the Eileen Kelly story. She was sixteen, and had just started work at the local egg-packing factory. At the end of her second week the other girls invited her out with them to a disco. They met in a pub and Eileen was disappointed to discover that they stayed there, drinking, until closing time. As soon as they entered the disco the other girls split up, each appearing to have a regular boyfriend, and Eileen was left on her own. The last bus had gone and she didn't have enough money for a taxi. The thought of rousing her parents from their bed to pay the fare didn't appeal to her.

An apparent knight in shining armour appeared on the scene and after a few dances offered her a lift home, which she gratefully accepted. Except he didn't take her home. He drove almost thirty miles to a deserted place called Black Heath, on Salisbury plain, and

400

dragged her from the car.

Eileen put up a fight and escaped. He chased her, but some headlights appeared and her attacker changed his mind and fled, leaving her to walk two miles down a dirt track in her stocking feet. She survived, and he graduated to the next level of his apprenticeship. He was on a learning curve.

The description she gave was fairly non-committal. Its broad terms certainly included Silkstone, who would have been twenty-five at the time, but it could equally have been anyone that you see at a football match or leaning on a bar. She was certain about the car, though: it was Jaguar.

'Bad news,' Bob said, placing a sheet of paper in front of me. 'Anthony Silkstone owned a Mk II Jag from September '76 to December '78, which is over two years too early for us.'

'Bugger!' I exclaimed.

'Steady,' Bob protested, 'I'm a Methodist.'

'Well sod and damn, too.'

'Maybe...' Bob began.

'Go on.'

'He'd be what, in his early twenties?'

'When Eileen was attacked? Twenty-five, maybe twenty-six.'

'But he'd only be ... what, twenty-one ... when he bought the Jag?'

'That's right.'

'A bit young, I'd say for a car like that, expensive to run. Maybe he couldn't afford it, and sold it to a friend, Latham perhaps, but still had access to it. And if you were up to mischief it

401

would make sense to use somebody else's car, wouldn't it?'

'I don't know,' I replied. 'I'm just a simple Yorkshire lad. Find out what happened to it, Bob, please. He may even have traded it in for another Jag. We need a rundown of every car he and Latham have owned, and a full history of the Jag after he sold it. Let's see if we can get some justice for Eileen, we owe her that much.'

I carried on with the file. Poor Eileen had been taken and seated in the passenger seat of every model that Jaguar, formerly Swallow Sidecars, had made. They changed their name at the outbreak of World War II, because SS, the abbreviated form, wasn't good PR in 1939. Eileen couldn't identify the actual model, but was adamant it was a Jag because it had the famous mascot on the bonnet and when she was little she'd seen a Walt Disney film about the animal.

I closed my eyes and leaned back in the chair. We were in the main CID office, but the place was deserted on a Saturday afternoon. I'd thanked Bob for his consideration but told him that I'd prefer to go home if we finished at a reasonable hour. Staying overnight would take another big chunk out of the weekend. Barber's Adagio is one of those tunes that I can hear in my head but can't reproduce with a whistle or hum. I imagined it now, with its long mournful descants and soaring chords. I saw a car, a Jag, revolving on a plinth. First it was sideways on, sleek and elegant; then it slowly turned to three-quarter view, radiating power and aggression with its rounded air intake and fat tyres; and then nose on, looking like it was coming at you from the barrel of a gun. People fall in love with their Jags, and I could understand why. Parting with it must have broken Silkstone's heart.

I collected Bob's mug and made us another coffee. He was talking on the phone and scribbling on a pad. I placed the replenished mug on his beer mat and tried to make sense of his notes.

'Thanks a lot,' he said. 'You've been a big help. I'll come back to you shortly.'

He pushed himself back and turned to me, throwing his pencil on the desk. 'According to Swansea the Jag was written off,' Bob told me. 'After that he owned an MGB, presumably bought with the proceeds, but three years later that was written off, too.'

'Writing off one sports car is unfortunate,' I said. 'Writing off two is downright careless. So he had an MGB at the time of the Eileen Kelly attack?'

'That's right.'

'According to the file she was shown and seated in every Jag produced, but couldn't recognise the precise model. I wonder if she was shown an MGB?'

'I don't know,' Bob replied, 'but we'll be on to it, first thing Monday.'

'Do you know where she is?'

'We'll find her.'

I pulled a chair closer to Bob's desk and took a sip of coffee. He shoved a sheet of paper towards me, to stand my mug on. 'I used to have a Jaguar,' I began. 'An E-type. My dad restored it

403

and it came to me when he died. It was a fabulous car, but wasted on me. I like one that starts first time, and that's about it. We used to go to rallies, and I was amazed at the attention and devotion that some owners lavished on their vehicles. Love isn't too strong a word.' I paused, remembering those good days, some of the best I'd ever had. 'Imagine, if you can,' I continued, 'that you are in your early twenties and you own your dream car. It's fast and desirable, it turns heads and it pulls birds. What more could a young lad want? Then, one day, you write it off. It's beyond repair, a heap of scrap. What would you do?'

'Look for another, I suppose,' Bob replied.

'There isn't another. They've stopped making them and those who own 'em aren't parting.'

'Look for something similar, then.'

'Yes, but what about the old car. How would you remember it?'

'Photographs?'

'Perhaps. What about something more substantial?'

'You mean, like a memento?'

'That's right.'

'The jaguar!' he exclaimed. 'The mascot off the bonnet. I'd save that.'

'Good idea,' I told him. 'And if you just happened to own an MGB? It's a very nice car, but not quite in the same class as the Jag you once had. Might you not be tempted to ... you know ... so you could relive your dreams...?'

'Put the mascot on the MG,' Bob suggested.

'Exactly. And Eileen Kelly said the car was a Jag

because of the mascot on the bonnet.'

'Fuckin' 'ell, Charlie,' he hissed. 'It's a bit far-fetched, don't you think?'

'I thought you were a Methodist,' I reminded him.

'Only in leap years.' We drank our coffee, reading the notes he'd made. 'A more likely explanation...' Bob began, '...is that it really was a Jaguar, driven by someone unknown to us.'

I nodded and placed my empty mug on his desk. 'I know, Bob,' I agreed. 'But humour me, please. We can either go back to the beginning and start all over again, which will take us nowhere all over again, or we can run it with Silkstone in the frame. So let's do it, eh?'

'That's fine by me, Chas.'

'Thanks. I'm going home.'

Sunday I stayed in bed until after ten, had a shower and went out for a full English breakfast. I brought a couple of heavies back in with me and spent the rest of the day catching up on the latest hot stories, a neverending supply of tea at my elbow. Heaven. Annette had said she might go to her mother's, in Hebden Bridge, and I'd said that I might stay overnight with Bob, so there was no answer when I tried her number. Another communication breakdown. The weather system had swung right round and the day was warm again, with just enough threat of rain to put me off doing some gardening. A quick run-around downstairs with the vacuum cleaner gave me sufficient Brownie points to justify an evening watching television and listening to music. I

405

brought the Chinese painting in from the garage and propped it in a corner, where it caught the light, so I could study it. You are supposed to leave oil paint for about a year to dry before varnishing it, but a month or two is usually enough. A few touches of black contour, I thought, on some of the images, and that would be that. I can't justify black contours, but they can transform a picture, and V. Gogh did it all the time so why shouldn't C. Priest? I was pleased with the painting and it was good fun having a whole day to myself. At nine o' clock I gave Annette's number another try, and this time she answered.

'You were lucky to catch me,' she said. 'I've only been in two minutes, and I've put my waterproof on to go straight out again.'

'Fate,' I told her. 'Fate, working in sympathy with our circadian rhythms as part of some great master plan to bring us together. On the other hand, I could have tried your number every minute for the last two days.'

'Oh, and which was it?'

'Fate, definitely fate. So where are you going, young lady, at such a late hour. Didn't you know that the streets are not safe in this town?'

'It's the start of Statis week,' she reminded me. 'There's a concert in the square, followed by fireworks. Why don't you come? I could see you there.'

'Who's playing?' I asked, as if it mattered.

'It's an Irish band, called Clochan. They're pretty good.'

'Right. Great. Where shall I meet you?' I like Irish bands, but I'd still have gone if it had been

406

Emma Royd and the Piledrivers.

Annette was standing at the edge of the audience, near the Sue Ryder shop as arranged, with the hood of her waterproof down even though it was raining. She looked pleased to see me, and I kissed her on the lips and put my arm around her.

'Good weekend?' I shouted into her ear, in competition with 'Whiskey in the Jar.'

'Mmm,' she mouthed in reply. 'And you?'

'So so. They are good, aren't they.' I sang along with them, to show how hip I'd once been: *As I was going over the Cork and Kerry mountains, I met Captain Farrel ... and I shot him with my pistol.*

We caught the last three songs, finishing with a *tour de force* rendition of 'Marie's Wedding' that slowly built-up and carried the audience along with it: first swaying to the tune; then clapping and foot-stamping; and eventually dancing wildly, arms and legs flailing. Annette and I looped arms and dozey-do'd, exchanging partners with the couple next to us, until the music stopped and we all ground to a breathless halt. I stood with my arms around her and the rain running down my face as she and the others applauded them from the stage. If the devil really does have all the best tunes he must be a Celt.

The bang startled me. I spun round, heart bouncing, but all I saw was a sea of upturned faces, washed in pink and then lilac as the firework filled the sky with spangles. Annette joined in the chorus of 'Ooh' and 'Aah' as chandeliers of fire blossomed above our heads, each burst of light a giant chrysanthemum, illuminating the smoke trails of its predecessor until it faded to make way for something even brighter. I looked around at the jostling crowd, their eyes shaded by hoods and hats, as explosions rippled and crackled through the sodden sky. The noise of a machine gun, never mind a .38, could easily have gone un-noticed amongst all that cacophony.

A single desultory bang signified the end, leaving us with fading images on our retinas and the smell of cordite in our nostrils. 'Thank you for the dance,' I said to the complete stranger that I'd been whirling around two minutes earlier.

'I'll save one for you next year,' she laughed, and her husband looked embarrassed, as if he couldn't believe it had all happened.

Annette and I picked our way through the crowd heading towards the car parks until I eased her into a side street and steered a course down towards the canal, where it was quieter. 'I'm in the multi-storey,' I explained. 'But let's take the romantic route.'

'I'd hardly call Heckley Navigation romantic,' she laughed.

'I know, but it's the best I can do. I think hot cocoa at your place is called for. How does that sound?'

'It sounds very inviting,' she agreed, squeezing my hand.

The alley down to the canal is the one where Lockwood and Stiles had come to grief, four months earlier. As we approached the end I sensed Annette looking around her, realising where we were.

'This is Dick Lane, isn't it?' she asked.

'Mmm' I replied.

'Where Martin Stiles got the panda stuck?'

'That's right.' Through the day it is blocked with delivery vehicles servicing the shops that back on to it, but at night only courting couples and glue sniffers use it, sheltering in the doorways and behind the dumpsters. Tonight the rain had kept them away, but it was still early. We'd reached the iron posts that prevent the egress of anything wider than a stolen Fiesta. 'And these,' I said, fondling one of the rounded tops, 'are the items in question.'

'Oh God!' Annette giggled, letting go of my hand.

'What?' I laughed.

'I just ... I just...'

'What?'

She shook her head and made gurgling noises.

I put my hand on her shoulder to steady her. 'You just what?'

'Nothing!'

I engulfed her in my arms and felt her body shaking as she tried to control her giggling. It was a pleasant experience. 'What?' I demanded, turning to shelter her from the rain.

'I just ... I just...'

Now I was giggling. 'You just what?'

'I just realised... I just realised why they call it... Why they call it...'

I completed the sentence for her. 'Why they call it Dick Lane? It was named after the Methodist minister who built this church.' I flapped a hand at the building to my left.

409

A respectable stream was running down the middle of the alley, and up at the top the cobbles shone yellow and orange with the lights from the square. Halfway along a movement caught my attention, so brief that I wondered if I'd imagined it. A figure stepped out of the shadows and stepped straight back into them.

'If you say so,' she replied, finding a tissue and blowing her nose. 'But I don't believe it.'

'I'm appalled,' I told her. 'I can't imagine what sort of people you mix with. C'mon, I'm soaked.' I grabbed her hand again and pulled her towards the towpath.

The canal was a black hole, devoid of movement or form apart from where an occasional rectangle of light fell on to it and the surface became a pattern of overlapping circles, piling on to each other as the rain increased in force. I stepped into a puddle and said: 'I think this was a mistake.'

Annette stopped, saying: 'That's where Darryl Buxton lived, isn't it?' She was looking at a mill across the canal, converted into executive flats. Buxton was a rapist that we jailed.

'That's right,' I agreed, looking behind us. I hadn't imagined it. A figure stepped cautiously out of the end of Dick Lane and merged into the shadows again. He was hugging the wall, gaining on us, and the next opening was nearly a hundred yards away. 'Do you have plenty of milk?' I asked, tugging at her arm.

'Milk?'

'Mmm. You know, comes from cows. I like my cocoa made with milk.'

'Oh, I think we'll be able to manage that. Except mine comes from Tesco.'

'That'll do. C'mon.'

'The canal looks spooky, doesn't it?'

'Yes. Not as romantic as I'd thought. Perhaps I was confusing it with Venice.'

'How deep is it?'

I looked back but couldn't be sure if he was there. 'I don't know.'

'Did you swim in it when you were a child?'

'No.'

'You didn't?'

'No. We went to the baths.' This time I saw him, and he was much closer, moving purposefully but still keeping to the shadows. I stopped to pick up a stone and tossed it towards the water. It splashed somewhere out in the blackness. When I looked, he'd stopped too.

We were nearly at the end of the next alleyway, similar to Dick Lane but without the dicks. It was another service road, cobbled and narrow, and not illuminated. I patted my pockets, feeling for my mobile phone, knowing I wouldn't find it. 'Do you have your phone with you?' I asked, but she didn't.

'Listen, Annette,' I said as we approached the end of the wall. 'When we reach this corner I want you to do exactly as I say.'

She sensed the urgency in my voice. 'What is it, Charlie?' she asked.

'Just do as I say. When we get round the corner I want you to run as fast as you can towards the town centre. There's a pub called the Talisman at the top of the street. Go in and go straight to the ladies'. Lock yourself in for five minutes. Then come out and order two drinks at the bar. I'll join you about then.'

'What are you talking about?' she demanded.

'Just do as I say.'

'Why? What is it?'

'We're being followed.' We reached the corner and turned it. Two big green dumpsters were standing there, just as I'd hoped. 'Now run!' I hissed, pushing her towards the lights.

'And what are you doing?' she asked.

'Just run!'

'I'm not running without you.'

I heard the *tch tch* of his trainers on the wet floor, fast at first, as if he were jogging, then slower, cautious, as he reached the corner. I grabbed Annette's arm and pushed her behind the dumpster, bundling her deep into the corner. A rat squealed a protest and scuttled away.

The footsteps paused as he surveyed the empty street, then started again, striding out. I heard his noise, sensed his shadow as I anticipated his position, predicting the exact moment he would emerge. As he passed the dumpster I took two rapid strides forward and hurled myself at him.

Priority was to stop him finding his gun. I threw my arms around him in a bear hug and knocked him to the ground. He kicked wildly and we rolled over, first me on top, then him, followed by me again. As he rolled over me I felt water running down my neck. He shouted something I didn't catch and Annette joined in, flailing at him with her fists, trying to hold his head. Next time he was on the bottom I risked

412

letting go with one hand for sufficient time to smash his face against the cobbles. He jerked and went limp.

Neither of us had handcuffs with us. I felt his clothing for a gun but he was unarmed. I rolled him over and moved to one side so my shadow wasn't on him. His lips were moving and a trickle of blood ran from his forehead until the rain diluted it to almost nothing.

'Oh shit!' I said.

'It's me,' he mumbled. 'It's me, Mr Priest.'

'Do you know him?' Annette asked.

'Yeah, I know him.' I grabbed his lapels and pulled him, still mumbling, into a seated position. 'I know him all right. I'd like you to meet Jason Lee Gelder: until recently chief suspect in the Marie-Claire Hollingbrook case.'

It was Les Isles' fault. We led Jason to where there was more light and cleaned him up. He was more apologetic than I was, and refused to be taken to Heckley General for a check-up. He wouldn't even let us give him a lift home. 'It's my fault, Mr Priest,' he kept insisting. 'I shouldn't have followed you like that.'

When they'd decided not to oppose bail, poor old Jason had interpreted this as implying that he was no longer in the frame for Marie-Claire's murder. He'd attempted to thank Les, who'd said: 'Don't thank me, thank Inspector Priest,' and told him that he owed me a pint. Jason took him literally. When he saw us at the fireworks he thought he would pay his debts, and followed us into Dick Lane. He said he was going to catch up

413

with us there, but when we stopped 'for a snog' he thought better of it and waited.

I believed him. Jason wasn't a crook, but he certainly qualified as a *client*, and some of them get funny ideas. They come into the station and see us in court, and start to see themselves as part of the organisation. We see them as the enemy, they regard themselves as our colleagues. I told Jason to call into the nick tomorrow and report the incident. He said it didn't matter, but I insisted. I'd do a full report, to keep myself and Annette in the clear. He was slow but well-meaning, and destined for a lifetime of holding the dirty end of whatever stick was offered him. I imagined him at the slaughterhouse, doing every obscene job that his sick workmates could find, and felt sorry for the Jasons of the world.

It was only a five-minute drive to Annette's, and we did it in silence. I doused the lights outside her flat and turned to face her. She stared straight ahead, unsmiling and pale in the harsh light. Under the street lamps the rain was falling like grain out of a silo.

'You're soaked,' I ventured, and she nodded in agreement. 'The, er, evening didn't quite turn out as I intended,' I said. 'No,' she replied.

'But the music was good. I enjoyed that.' Annette didn't respond, so I went on: 'We used to go to the Irish Club, years ago. Had some great nights there. It was the headaches next morning that put a stop to it.'

She turned to face me, and said: 'You thought it was him, didn't you?'

'Who?' I asked, all innocence.

'Him. Chilcott. The Chiller, whatever you call him. You thought it was the Chiller following us.'

'No I didn't.'

'I don't believe you.'

'I thought he was a mugger. He'd seen us and decided we'd be easy prey so he followed us. I thought we'd give him a surprise.'

'So I had to run as fast as I could to the pub and lock myself in the toilet? For a mugger? I don't believe you.'

'Yeah, well,' I mumbled.

'I saw the look on your face, Charlie,' she told me. 'When we were behind the bins. You were ... *eager*. You were enjoying yourself. You were about to tackle someone you thought had a gun, who wanted to kill you, and you were enjoying yourself.'

'I wasn't enjoying myself,' I protested. 'I was scared stiff and I was worried about you.'

'But you admit that you thought it was Chilcott?'

'It crossed my mind, Annette, in the heat of the moment. But now I see the idea as preposterous. He's a long way away and I'm just history to him, believe me.'

'I don't know what to believe.'

After a long silence I said: 'Shall we cancel the cocoa?'

'I think so,' she replied. 'If you don't mind.'

I shrugged my shoulders. I minded like hell. I minded like a giant asteroid was heading towards Heckley, and only a cup of cocoa in her flat, listening to George Michael CDs, would save the town. But who was I to make a decision like that?

As she opened the door I said: 'You're upset, Annette. It was a frightening experience. Go have a nice hot bath and stay in bed until lunchtime. I'll make it right. Have the whole day off, if you want.'

She looked at me and sighed. 'I think it's you who needs some time off, Charlie,' she said, opening the car door and swinging her legs onto the pavement. 'I'll be there,' she stated. 'Bright and early, as always.'

I braced myself for the inevitable door slam, but it didn't come. She held the handle firmly and pushed it shut, so it closed with a textbook *clunk*. She didn't slam it. I watched her sashay across the little residents' car-park and punch her code into the security lock. A light came on and she went inside. She didn't slam that door, either, but turned and held the latch. For a few seconds I could see her shape through the frosted glass and then she faded away as if she were sinking into a deep pool. She didn't slam the door, and that's the moment I fell in love with her.

On Tuesday afternoon, when Somerset Bob sat her in an MGB, Eileen Kelly went bananas. The poor woman had never really recovered from the attack and had drifted from one unhappy relationship to another. At the moment she was alone, living in rented accommodation and working in the kitchen of a department store in Bath. He said that she was pleased, at first, to have a change in her routine and go along with him to the house of a Bath traffic cop who had a much-cherished model of the car. On the way there she reiterated her story, glad that at last someone was listening, and no doubt encouraged by the change in attitude over the last eighteen years.

Her attacker's car had been parked at the roadside, and she hadn't realised which it was until he opened the door for her so she never really saw it from the outside. Bob said he opened the passenger door and beckoned her to get in. As soon as she dropped into the low seat she started shivering and shaking. He climbed in next to her and saw that she had turned white, her wide eyes taking in the instrument panel, glove box and everything else.

The traffic cop's wife made them tea and Eileen slowly regained her composure, sitting in their kitchen. 'I'm sorry,' she'd sobbed, blowing her nose.

'There's nothing to be sorry about,' Bob had assured her. 'What can you tell me about the car?'

'It was one of them,' she'd declared. 'Definitely, but it had a little animal on the front, like a Jaguar does.'

'Find it, Bob,' I ordered, when he finished his story.

'Might not be easy, it was written off.'

'Well find where the bits went. We need that car.' There was a note on my desk from the twilight detective, who just happened to be Rodger. Two of them alternate, afternoons and nights, because their wives work shifts at the General Hospital, and it suits them. I'd asked for a watch to be kept on Silkstone, when times were slack, and the note said that he'd fallen into the habit of strolling along to the Anglers for a meal, usually between six and seven. I grow restless when a case stagnates, like to jolly things along a little. It was time to go pro-active, I decided. We're big on pro-active policing at the moment. First thought was to take Annette with me, but I changed my mind. It would be better if I was alone, my word against his. Except I would have a witness. I rang our technical support people and asked to borrow a tape recorder.

Annette came into my office just before five, carrying a coffee. 'Hi, Annette,' I said, pointing to the spare chair. 'Sit down and talk to me.'

'Coffee?' she asked.

'No thanks.'

'You've been after me.'

'Yes,' I replied. 'I rang you because I'm going to accidentally-on-purpose bump into Silkstone, in that pub near his place, and I thought it might look more natural if you were with me.'

'No problem,' she replied. 'What time?'

'It's OK, there's been a change of plan. I've decided to be alone, in the hope that I can tempt him into the odd indiscretion.'

'But it won't be worth a toss,' she informed me.

'I know, but if it were he wouldn't say it, would he? We could have a drink after,' I suggested.

'Socially?'

'I suppose so. You've been avoiding me since ... since the weekend.'

'I don't think so, if you don't mind, Boss.'

'It's Boss again, is it?' I said.

'I'm sorry, Charlie,' she replied, shaking her

418

head. 'I don't know what to think.' She looked more unhappy than I've ever seen her.

'I cocked-up on Sunday,' I admitted. 'I know I did. Something just happened inside me. I was scared, but for you, not myself. I thought I'd got you into something. Maybe it was the music, or the words of the songs. I don't know. We need to talk, but this isn't the place. Let me come round to your place, later.'

'I don't know.' More head shaking, her hair covering first one half of her face, then the other, as it tried to keep up. I glanced out of the window across the big office. Nobody was watching us, trying to decipher the touching scene between the DI and the attractive DC.

'Friday night,' I began. 'I thought it was rather special. I thought that, you know, it said something about how we felt for each other.'

'So did I, but...'

'But what?'

She gave a violent shake of the head and started sobbing. I looked out and caught David Rose glance across. He quickly looked away. 'I'm sorry, Annette,' I said. 'Maybe I read too much into it. OK, it's back to strictly a working relationship, if that's how you'd prefer it. I don't want to lose you as an officer and I can switch it off, live a lie, if you can. Shall we just ... call the whole thing off?'

She sniffed and looked at me for the first time. 'Yes, I think we should,' she replied.

'Right.'

'I'm sorry, Charlie.'

'Me too, Annette. Me too.'

419

I did paperwork until just after six, then hared off to the Anglers. In the car park I tested the tape recorder, running the tape back to the beginning and pressing the play button.

Male voice: 'Hi, Annette. Sit down and talk to me.'
Female voice: 'Coffee?'
Male voice: 'No thanks.'
Female voice: 'You've been after me.'
Male voice: 'Yes, I rang you because...

I pressed the *stop* button and ejected the cassette. There was nothing there that I wanted to save for posterity; nothing I could play back to her later, and watch the colour rise in her cheeks until I reached out and cooled them with my fingertips. I hooked a thumbnail under the tape and pulled it from the spools, heaping it on the passenger seat until no more was left and ripping the ends free. I clicked the spare cassette into position and concealed the tape recorder in my inside pocket. The microphone was under my tie. It worked, and that was all that mattered. I locked the car and went into the pub.

I tried the steak and kidney pie but didn't enjoy it. I was stabbing a perfunctory chip with my fork – there's something oddly irresistible about a plate of cold chips – when a movement outside caught my eye. Another Ford Mondeo had joined mine in the car-park, and it was closely followed by a Peugeot. The place was getting busy. My phone rang and I grabbed it from my pocket. 'Charlie,' I whispered into it.

'He's with someone,' I was told, 'in a Ford like yours. I've done a vehicle check and it's owned by a Julian Maximillian Denver.'

'Cheers, I know him.' I looked up at the door as I slipped the phone back into my pocket and saw Silkstone, accompanied by Max Denver, ace reporter of the *UK News*, heading my way.

Denver, a grin on his face, was all for joining me, but Silkstone didn't want to. I'd never been formally introduced to Denver, but recognised him as the character who'd confronted me outside the station a week ago, and his name was plastered all over the articles. He was wearing a belted leather coat a size too big, faded jeans and a slimy smile on one of those faces that has *punch me* writ large across it. I scratched my armpit and switched the tape on. If Mohammed wouldn't come to the mountain...

They ordered drinks and food at the bar and took a table several places away from me. I waited until they were settled and wandered over, glass in hand.

'Well well,' I said, pulling a chair from an adjoining table and placing it at the end of theirs. 'I'd have thought this was a bit downmarket for a pair of hotshots like you two.'

'I was thinking the same myself,' Silkstone sneered.

'Sit down, why don't you,' Denver invited, somewhat superfluously as I already had done.

'Thanks. On the other hand, in your reduced circumstances, Silkstone, I'd have thought you'd have taken advantage of the two-for-one, before six o'clock.'

He turned to Denver, asking: 'Do we have to listen to this?' but Denver would listen to anyone, and the more aggro the better.

'Or is this little treat on your new-found friend's expense account?' I asked. 'Signed a contract with him, have you?'

Denver said: 'Killed any unarmed men today Priest?'

'No,' I replied, 'but there's time.' I turned back to Silkstone. 'How much is he paying you then? Enough to replace the fifty thousand you donated to the Kevin Chilcott holiday fund?' A red shadow spread from Silkstone's face, stopping as it reached his bald head, like the British Empire on an old map of Africa. Denver looked from me to Silkstone and back again, his brow beetled in mystification. 'What!' I exclaimed, 'hasn't he told you about the fifty thousand?'

'Because it's a pack of lies,' Silkstone hissed. 'Another of the stories you invented to blacken my name because ... because ... because you haven't got a leg to stand on and you know it. Why don't you leave me alone and ... and...'

'And go out and catch a murderer?' I suggested. I drained my glass and placed it on their table. Denver twisted in his seat and raised a hand to the girl behind the bar, but she turned away because they don't do waitress service.

'Ah, maybe you're right,' I conceded. 'It's this job.'

Denver got to his feet and shouted to the barmaid, asking if he could order some drinks, but she ignored him again. He wanted a drink in my hand, but he didn't want to leave my side, in case he missed something. 'Don't worry,' I told him, 'I'll get it.' I strolled to the bar and ordered myself another pint.

'You know,' I began, when I'd rejoined them, 'I took an instant dislike to you, Silkstone.' I looked at his companion and explained: 'You have to, when you're investigating a murder. But then, as I looked around your house, I decided that you had at least one redeeming feature.' I picked up my glass and drained nearly half of it, licking my lips and pretending it wasn't as unappetising as the cold urine it resembled.

'And what was that?' Denver prompted.

'He's a Jaguar man,' I replied. 'Had a 1964 Mark II. Great car, highly desirable.' I had another drink, before adding:

'Can't be much wrong with a man who owned a car like that, I said to myself.'

'It hasn't stopped you persecuting me,' Silkstone declared.

'Top brass,' I told him. 'You know how it is.' I finished my drink and Denver snatched up the glass almost before my fingers had left it.

'Another?' he asked.

'Why not?' I replied.

'Lager?'

'Please.'

'Which one?'

'Labatt's.'

He dashed off to the bar as I said to Silkstone: 'Once upon a time I had an E-type. A three-point-eight. Fabulous car. I loved it. Drove it to southern Spain, once. Boy did that machine turn heads. And pull birds. Felt like a bloody film star when I was in it.'

Denver placed the replenished glass in front of me and I thanked him. 'I was just telling Mr

Silkstone that I owned an E-type Jag, a long time ago. It nearly broke my heart when it was stolen. A scrote from Sylvan Fields took it and torched it. I'd have strangled the little bastard if I'd got my hands on him.' I took a sip of the Labatt's. It was a big improvement. I'd sold the car when prices were at their highest and made nearly ten grand profit, but they didn't need to know that. 'What happened to yours?' I asked.

'I crashed it,' Silkstone informed me.

'Crashed it? Were you hurt?' Some men are embarrassed if they have the misfortune to crash their car, see it as a mistake; others never accept the blame and enjoy relating all the gory details. I had little doubt which group our friend belonged in.

'No. I was lucky.'

'What happened?'

'Hit a patch of black ice on the A37. The gritters hadn't been out.'

'And it was written off?'

'Yeah. I rolled it over three times. Would have cost too much to repair, so it went for scrap.'

'And you walked away from it?'

'Without a scratch.'

'Blimey.' I had another drink.

'So what's the state of the investigation now?' Denver asked, trying to drag the conversation back to something he might be interested in.

'The file's with the CPS,' I told him. 'It's up to them.'

'But aren't you following any lines of enquiry?'

'No,' I lied. 'It's up to them, now,' and I gave a little belch, for emphasis.

'Why don't you charge Mr Silkstone?' Denver challenged me.

'What with?' I asked.

'You're the one making all the wild accusations. Saying he murdered his wife and that woman in Halifax.'

'Marie-Claire Hollingbrook.' I said. 'She has a name, Denver – God knows, you've typed it often enough.'

'So why don't you charge him?'

'I told you, it's the CPS's decision. Me, I'm just here for a quiet drink. Can I remind you that I was here first. But as we're all together I thought that talking about cars might be a pleasant diversion. I thought that was what people like us were supposed to do. You know, lads' talk. Did Silkstone ever tell you that he had an MGB after the Jaguar?' I turned to him saying: 'That's right, isn't it?'

'If you say so,' he replied.

'Not me, the DVLA,' I responded. 'I had to check your records. Was it any good?'

'The MG?'

'Mmm.'

'It was alright.'

'But not in the same league as the Jag?'

'No.'

I decided to backtrack, not pursue the MG. Maybe it was a mistake, bringing it into the conversation. I looked at my glass, studying the bubbles clinging to the sides, wondering whether they brought the lager all the way from Canada or just the name. Outside, a narrow boat glided by, heading for the open canal, fulfilling some-

425

one's long-held dream. I hoped it wasn't a disappointment. 'When my car was burnt out,' I began, 'I salvaged the little pouncing jaguar mascot from the bonnet. Actually, the garage where it went took it off and saved it for me, which was thoughtful of them, don't you think?' The expressions on their faces suggested they didn't, but I pressed on. 'I still have it. I mounted it on a piece of mahogany and had a little metal plate engraved for it. It stands on my mantelpiece, reminds me of the life I once led.' I smiled at the memory a little wistful smile, which was difficult because I'd just invented the whole story. 'What about you?' I asked, looking at Silkstone. 'Weren't you tempted to do something similar?'

'What's all this about?' he snapped. 'Why all this interest in my cars, all of a sudden?'

'It's just conversation,' I protested, turning to Denver as if appealing to him to intervene on the side of reason. 'I just wondered if he'd removed the mascot from his car, like I did.'

'Fuck off!' Silkstone growled.

'Nice friend you have,' I told Denver.

'He's right,' Denver said. 'Just what are you after, Priest?'

'He wants me to say something he can twist round, for his own purposes,' Silkstone declared. 'While my brief isn't here. Well, I'm not saying another word. Why don't you just piss off, Priest, and leave us alone. You're not welcome.'

I'd blown it, that was for sure. Ah well, I thought, if he wasn't going to say anything incriminating the least I could do was give him something to ruin his sleep, and maybe sow a few doubts in his new friend's mind. Perhaps I could provoke Denver into doing some investigating of his own. He had resources that I didn't possess, and could take liberties that would have me carpeted. With luck, he'd do my job for me. 'There was an attempted rape in Somerset,' I told Denver, 'two years before the girl called Caroline Poole was murdered; and another extremely serious assault just a year before. One of the victims has given evidence that suggests her attacker's car was an MGB.' I paused to let it sink in. So what? they were thinking. 'An MGB,' I added, 'that just *happened* to have a pouncing jaguar mascot screwed on the bonnet. Can't be many of those about, can there?' They didn't appear to have an opinion on that. Silkstone looked away and Denver was lost for words, so I pressed on. 'Silkstone and Latham gave each other alibis for Caroline's murder,' I said, addressing Denver. 'Margaret Silkstone and a woman called Michelle Webster verified their stories.' From the corner of my eye I saw Silkstone flinch at the mention of Michelle's name. 'She sends her regards,' I told him. 'She also says that she lied about the alibi. Her new story is that Margaret asked her to cover for you and Latham. I was being less than truthful a few seconds ago when I said that we weren't following any new lines of enquiry. We now think that you killed Caroline Poole, too, as well as Margaret and Marie-Claire.'

Denver shook his head and laughed. 'Kick a dog while it's down, eh, Priest?'

'He was besotted with Caroline,' I went on, 'after he saw a photograph of her in the local paper, as a twelve-year-old. He saved the photo, bought a glossy print from the paper and kept it as a souvenir, until he planted it in Latham's bedroom to throw suspicion on him.'

Denver said. 'Let's face it, Priest, you've got Tony for doing a scumbag like Latham and now you're trying to pin every unsolved crime on your books on him. Makes your figures look good but meanwhile the real killers go free. A confession for manslaughter isn't good enough for you, is it? No glory in that for Charlie Priest the Killer Cop, is there? You'll have to do better than that, Squire, you really will.'

'We'll see,' I replied, standing up to leave.

'You haven't finished your lager,' Denver said, eagerly gesturing for me to sit down again. He wanted more.

'I'd rather drink from the drip tray at the path lab, where I have to watch the results of his handiwork being dissected. You deserve each other.' I turned, then turned again. 'Think about this,' I said. 'Their marriage was on the rocks. Maybe he wanted to leave Margaret. Perhaps, just perhaps, she didn't want him to go. She suspected he'd done the Caroline job and was threatening to confess to lying about it if he did leave her. That makes another good reason for wanting her dead.' I found my car key in my pocket and pointed it at Denver. 'And just for the record,' I added before striding away from them, 'the first two pints were non-alcoholic, and they tasted like piss.'

428

On my way out I winked at the only other customer, sitting at a table near the door. Rodger, the shift 'tec, gazed implacably through me as he lifted a square of gammon towards his mouth. Outside, the rain had started again.

Chapter 15

Peddling drugs is a serious offence, as serious as it gets, and some people believe that tobacco is as pernicious as any. Jeff Caton posed as a buyer of King Edwards and brought their advertiser back in with him. We sat him in a cell for an hour and decided to let him off with a caution, this time. Selling tobacco isn't illegal but importing cigars, other than for your own consumption, is. He'd brought a thousand back from Spain and was a non-smoker.

I put on my jacket, straightened my tie, and went downstairs to give him his bollocking, arranging my expression to one of suitable solemnity. He stood to make about a tenner per box of fifty, which would give him a grand profit of two hundred pounds. Somehow, I just couldn't take it seriously. I told him that he was robbing the exchequer of their cut, reminded him that if he was prosecuted we could seize his assets, and suggested he didn't waste my time again.

'What about the rest of the cigars?' he asked. He was a real professional.

'How many do you have left?'

'Four boxes.'

'Well put them on the compost heap.'

Somerset Bob had left a message for me when I arrived back in the office. I tried his number but he'd gone out. 'After the Eileen Kelly attack,' I asked him, when we finally crossed wires on Wednesday afternoon 'was the information released that you were looking for a Jaguar?'

'Um, not sure,' he replied. 'I'll have to check the cuttings. Why do you need to know?'

I told him about my little talk with Silkstone. 'He clammed up as soon as I mentioned the mascot, as if he knew it had been a mistake. If he saved it, afterwards, we never found it when we searched his house.'

'I'll check. Want to know what I've dug up?'

'Yes please.'

'OK,' he began. 'I've checked his insurance records and discovered a bit about the accidents. It wasn't easy – they've had several take-overs since the time we're talking about. The Jag was written off and sent to the crusher. Apparently it was vandalised after the accident and set alight. The MGB went to somewhere called Smith Brothers Safe Storage, which is one of those places where insurance cases are stored until a settlement is made. They're at Newark. Silkstone's occupation is down as area manager with a company called Burdon Developments and he covered the Midlands, which is probably why he was over there.'

'Bet it wasn't his fault,' I said.

'No,' Bob agreed. 'He was dead unlucky. An old lady stepped off the pavement right in front of him and he skidded on loose gravel avoiding her. Lost control and side-swiped a telegraph pole.'

'Another write-off?' I asked.

'No, the electricity board straightened it up and

431

dabbed some creosote on and it was as good as new.'

'That's a relief. And what about the MG?'

'Oh, that was a write-off. Bent the chassis beyond repair.'

'It could happen to anyone. Have you taken it further?'

'Haven't managed to raise anyone at Smith Brothers, but I'll keep trying.'

'Do that, please, Bob,' I told him. 'Who knows, somebody may have bought the wreck and re-built it. We're getting warm, I can feel it.'

Nigel had a date with a sister from St James's, so he wasn't at the Spinners that evening. I assumed he meant the hospital, but with my luck she'd probably be from a convent of the same name. Dave brought Shirley to make up the number, and we sat looking miserable, hardly speaking. On the Saturday they were taking Sophie and her belongings to Cambridge in a hired Transit, hence their gloom. I had no excuse. I told them that Annette and I had decided not to have a future together, but didn't mention her other boyfriend; the one with the two daughters. I said that she wanted to stay with the CID and being linked romantically with the boss might not be a good career move. They made sympathetic sounds and Shirley said: 'Oh, Charlie, what are we going to do with you?'

I smiled, saying: 'Looks like I'll just have to wait for Sophie getting her degree,' and was rewarded with a growl from Dave as he picked up his glass. I'd touched his weak spot.

Bob rang me in the middle of Thursday morning, in a state of high excitement. 'The Smiths've still got records, Charlie,' he told me, 'after all these years. I talked to the son of the original proprietor. He found the file, eventually, and it said that the MGB was sold as scrap to someone called Granville Burgess-Jones, who owns a small motor museum just outside Newark. He's a regular with them, builds and restores vehicles. Sometimes they're not always roadworthy or might not have an engine in, but they look good. Most of them are just for show. We might be in with a chance, Charlie. You know what these collectors are like – never throw anything away. If the bonnet wasn't damaged,' he gushed, 'he might still have it.'

'That's fantastic,' I agreed. 'Any chance of you getting over there?'

'It's a bit awkward for me,' he began, 'and you're quite a lot nearer...'

'I understand, Bob,' I told him. 'Give me all the names and numbers and leave it with me.'

'There's a couple of other things.'

'Go on.'

'Well, after the Eileen Kelly assault we issued a statement saying that her attacker drove a dark sports car, possibly a Jaguar, so Silkstone would have known what we were looking for.'

'And destroyed the mascot.'

'Exactly.'

'Mmm. Did you say a couple of things?'

'Yeah. I've been thinking. Even if we find the actual bonnet, it won't have a serial number on it, or anything. The only link between it and

Silkstone is the paperwork. It's vital we maintain the integrity of that.'

'God, you're right,' I told him. 'Good thinking. OK, here's what we do. I'll set off for Newark in about, oh, an hour. Any chance of you ringing the local police and having someone meet me at the Smith Brothers' yard, just to witness things? It'll take me about two, two and a half hours to get there.'

'No problem. Good luck, and let me know what you find.'

'Thanks, Bob, you'll be the first to know. Meanwhile, I've another job for you. Put it all down in writing, particularly this conversation. Make it read as if we have a hypothesis, and all we have to do to prove it is examine the bonnet of that MG. That's what our entire case revolves around.'

Five minutes with the map can save you fifty on the road. I just made that up. It needs working on, but it's true. Head for the M1, A57 at J31 and then the A1 down into Newark. Smith Brothers were on a trading estate on the south side, as you left town, I was told. I memorised the route and set off.

I reached my destination half an hour earlier than expected thanks to clear roads and a reckless disregard of speed limits, but I was still overtaken by a procession of expensive cars on the motorway, heading for the next appointment. They can't all have believed that they'd be able to sweet-talk the traffic cops because they were on their way to nail a murderer, but they drove as if they did.

434

I lost the half-hour looking for the yard. It was well outside town, at an old World War II bomber station, and the business was based on the storage capacity of three huge hangars. There were wrecked cars everywhere: piled in heaps outside; stacked neatly on pallets inside. Multi-coloured conglomerates of twisted metal, chrome and glass; each one, I thought, bringing misery to someone. About ten people a day are killed on our roads, dotted about the country like a mild case of chicken pox, but this was where the evidence came together in one great sore. Some were hardly damaged, awaiting the assessor's go-ahead to repair; others – many of them – were unrecognisable, and you knew that people had died in there. Once these hangars had housed the bringers of carnage, now they housed the results. A corner was reserved for bent police cars, gaudy in their paintwork but strangely silent, like crippled clowns. Wandering down the first aisle, between the neatly shelved wrecks, I saw abstract images, paintings and photographs, everywhere I looked. I tore myself away and knocked at the office door.

A uniformed PC was inside, drinking tea with a man in a blue shirt and rainbow tie. A woman in a short skirt with a ladder in her tights, a small-town siren, was typing in the corner. 'DI Priest,' I announced to all present, 'Heckley CID. Hope I haven't kept you waiting.'

The PC stared at me, open mouthed, and the man in the shirt coughed into his hand. 'Lost your tongue?' I asked the PC.

'No, er, Sir,' he mumbled, reaching for his hat.

'Never mind that,' I said, turning to the other person and asking: 'Mr Smith, is it?'

'Um, yes,' he replied uncomfortably.

'Good. I understand you have some records for an MGB that was brought into here back in 1982.' I told them the registration number and continued: 'A colleague in Somerset has rung you, hasn't he?'

The PC unwound himself from the chair and stood up. He was only about twenty-two, but even taller than me. 'Could I, er, see your ID, Sir, if you don't mind, please?'

'Sure.' I already had it in my hand. He took it from me, studied it carefully, then said: 'Oh, heck.'

I pushed some papers to one side on a desk against the opposite wall and perched my backside on a corner of it, saying: 'I think you'd better tell me all about it.' I folded my arms in the pose of a patient listener and waited, except my patience was rapidly evaporating.

'I've just arrived, Sir,' the PC stated, and introduced himself. 'I came straight here when I received the message, but thought I must have missed you. Mr Smith had better explain.'

I turned to Mr Smith. When Bob had described him as the son of the proprietor I'd immediately formed an image of a young man barely out of college, but he was probably in his late forties. Another reminder of the passing years.

'Well,' he began. 'I, er, received this telephone call, yesterday, I believe it was, from the police about the MG. Nothing new in that, it's always happening, except usually it's about something that came in recently not twenty years ago. I said that we kept all the record cards and that we would probably have it somewhere if he gave me the dates.' He turned to the woman, who had stopped typing and was listening to our conversation. 'Glynis here found it, didn't you, duck?'

'Got black bright,' she complained. 'It's filthy in there, that far back.' She was wearing false eyelashes that a Buddhist monk could have raked the gravel with.

'And then what?' I asked.

'I was saving it,' Smith continued, 'here in my drawer. He rang me again this morning. Twice, in fact. First time I told him we'd found the card, second time he said that you,' – he showed me the pad he kept alongside his telephone, with my name written on it – 'would be calling to collect it. Then, about five minutes later, this man came in. Blimey, I thought, that was quick. Thought he'd said you'd be coming down from Yorkshire. This feller asked about the MG, gave me the number, and I said: 'Are you DI Priest?' and he said he was, so I gave him the card.'

'Can you describe him?' I asked.

'Well, he wasn't very tall. Didn't look like a cop, now you mention it. Dark hair, slim build, wore a leather raincoat.'

'I know him,' I said. 'He's a reporter.'

'A reporter!' Glynis exclaimed, clasping her hand to her mouth, as if I'd announced that the Son of Beelzebub had walked amongst them. I couldn't imagine what she might have told him.

'Did you ask for a receipt for the card?' I asked.

'No, I'm sorry,' he replied.

437

'Or make a photocopy?'

'No, sorry. After all these years…'

'Nothing for you to be sorry about, Mr Smith,' I interrupted. 'You were trying to be helpful and he took advantage. That's how he earns his living. He definitely said he was me, did he?'

'Yes. I said: "Are you DI Priest?" and he said: "Yes, that's right," just like I told you.'

'Can you remember what it said on the card?'

'No, not really, except that I remember telling the other policeman, the one who rang, that Mr Burgess-Jones had bought the MG from the insurance company. He's at Avecaster, on the Sleaford road, about fifteen minutes from here. Has a museum of vintage and classic cars. Used to buy a lot of stuff from us, but not so much these days.'

'OK,' I said, 'here's what I'd like you to do. Our young friend here,' – I gestured towards the PC – 'will take a statement from you, putting in writing exactly what you've just told me, and anything else you remember. I'll be grateful if you could do that for me.'

'Yes, glad to,' he agreed.

I stood up to leave. 'And Glynis can make a contribution, if she has anything to add. Towards Sleaford, did you say?'

'That's right.'

'It's just off the A17,' the PC explained.

'Then that's where I'm headed.'

It's a different landscape to the one I live in: kinder to its inhabitants but two-dimensional and undemanding. Neat and fertile fields stretch away into the distance, outlined by lush trees, and in every direction a church steeple punctures the sky. Underneath the signpost pointing to Avecaster was one for Cranwell, home of the famous RAF college. I'd considered going there, once upon a time. The thought of roaring up and down the countryside in the latest fighter plane, silk scarf blowing in the wind, had a great appeal to me, but they changed the uniform and I lost interest. Avecaster was a typical Lincolnshire village: yellow stone houses; ivy-clad walls and an understated air of prosperity. Close-cropped verges fronted walled gardens. In the main street the houses crowded the road but on the outskirts they stood back from it: some quite modest; others with stable blocks jutting out to balance the triple garage at the other side. Mr Granville Burgess-Jones and his museum were at Avecaster Manor, probably known locally as the Big House. The gates were open so I drove in.

It was a respectable driveway, curving and lined with ornamental chestnut trees to hide the house until the last dramatic moment. A sign pointed left to the museum and car-park, with the information that it was only open at weekends and bank holidays. I went straight on, through an archway in a high wall, to where I could see several parked vehicles.

Denver's car was parked at the end of the line and I turned towards the space alongside it, gravel crunching under the tyres, making the steering feel heavy and imprecise. Away to the right a group of people turned to see who the new arrival was.

I was in a courtyard, with the house facing me and outbuildings down the adjacent sides. The sun was out and I felt as if I'd wandered on to the set of *Brideshead Revisited*. Denver had reversed into his parking place, but I drove straight in, so my driver's door was next to his. Why people reverse into parking places mystifies me, unless it's so they can make a fast getaway. I climbed out and stretched upright. The little group of them – I counted six – were still looking towards me, over the roofs of the other cars in the line. Denver was there, and so was Prendergast, which was a surprise. I didn't know the others.

I glanced down into Denver's car and saw his mobile phone on the passenger seat, plugged into the cigar lighter to have its battery recharged. I also noticed that his keys were dangling from the ignition lock. It's a funny thing about Fords. Because of the activities of some of the younger members of our society, they, along with all the other manufacturers, have spent millions of pounds trying to protect our beloved vehicles against theft. War, they say brought about vast improvements in the field of aviation. Little scrotes like Jamie What's-his-name initiated the development of the car alarm and immobiliser, thus creating thousands of jobs in the security market. Thanks to him and his friends, the key I held in my right hand had a minute electronic chip built into it. It would only open a lock that had a certain combination of signals, and there were two hundred and fifty thousand possible combinations. My mind boggled at the thought of it. A thief had a 1-in-250,000 chance of his key starting my car, which made the odds against him guessing my pin number and emptying my bank account, at a mere 1-in-9,999, look a good bet.

What they don't tell you is that any Ford key will *lock* any Ford car. When it comes to locking the car, they're all the same. It was Sparky's sixteen-year-old son, Danny, that told me that. His dad had just bought an Escort, and Danny bet me a pound that his dad's key would lock my car. I lost the bet. That's what they teach them at school, these days.

The little group were still looking my way. Without taking my eyes off them I felt for the lock of Denver's car with the tip of the key for mine. Years of practise, opening the car day after day, give you an instinct for it. The key slipped home and I turned it away from the steering wheel. I heard the whirr of electric motors and the *chunk* of the bolts slamming across as a glow of satisfaction welled up inside me. Denver was locked out, and that was the best quid I'd ever lost.

Two of them were TV people. Freelancers, armed with cameras and sound equipment and presumably hired by Denver. The other two were wearing blue overalls with *Avecaster Motor Museum* embroidered on the breast pocket. The taller of them had a gaunt face and was puffing on a cigarette stub, the other had a handlebar moustache and the complexion of an outdoor man who enjoys a tipple. The type who never hunts south of the Thames nor services the wife in the morning in case something better presents

441

itself in the afternoon.

'Mr Burgess-Jones?' I asked.

'That's right,' he replied. 'I don't believe I've had the pleasure...'

'Detective Inspector Priest, of Heckley CID.' I looked beyond him. 'And that,' I added, 'is presumably the lady who brought us all here.'

It was the MG, standing there gleaming in the sun. Flame red, black and chrome, pampered and aloof, like a thoroughbred at Crufts or Ascot. She looked good.

'The police, did you say?' Burgess-Jones was asking.

'Yes Sir. I'm afraid you've been mixing with some bad company.' I turned to the others and pointed at Denver. 'This gentleman here is under arrest for impersonating a police officer and interfering with an investigation. He also impersonates a journalist, but that's not an offence. And this gentleman...' I looked at Prendergast, '...is a solicitor.'

Everybody spoke at once. Denver wanted to know why he was under arrest, Prendergast didn't know why he had been invited and Burgess-Jones was completely bewildered. I raised a hand to silence them. 'I don't know what you were planning to do,' I told them, 'but whatever it was, it's off. That car is evidence in a murder investigation and I am seizing it.'

'Hey man,' one of the TV people said. 'We still want paying, y'know.' He looked like one of the guitarists from Grateful Dead.

'The question is,' Denver stated, 'what will you do with the car?'

442

'We'll take it away and give it a thorough examination,' I replied.

'For holes in the bonnet,' he said, 'where you say Silkstone fitted the Jaguar mascot?'

'That's right.'

'In secret, and you'll fix it to suit your own ends.'

'That's not true. Everything will be done in the presence of independent witnesses.'

'Rubbish! You'll rig it.'

I ignored him and turned to Burgess-Jones. 'I'd be grateful, Sir,' I said, 'if you could move the car back into its garage until I can arrange for it to be either collected or examined here. You'll be fully compensated for any damage done to it.'

'Not my problem,' he replied. 'Just sold it to Mr Denver for a very good price. It's his, now.'

Denver smiled smugly. I resisted the urge to thump him and walked over to the MG. A Black and Decker angle grinder lay on the ground in front of it, ready to do business, with a bright orange cable snaking off into an outbuilding. I stooped to look inside the car and saw a thick photo album sitting on the passenger seat. 'Is that a record of the restoration?' I shouted to Burgess-Jones.

'That's right,' he replied, strolling towards me. 'We do a full photographic history of the entire process.'

'You built this car from two others, I believe.'

'Yes. This one had a damaged front end, so we grafted the front of the other on to it.'

'Is it roadworthy?'

'I think our work would be frowned upon now,

443

but at the time it was common practise. We've never tried to register it.'

'Do the pictures show the other car at all?'

'Oh yes. It's all there.'

'Was the bonnet from the other car? It's only the bonnet we're interested in.'

'It looks like it. It was a green one, so we must have resprayed it. I vaguely remember, but not the details.'

'Will there be any evidence of the original colour still there?' I asked.

'I would imagine so,' he replied. 'We'd fully strip all the top surfaces, but not underneath. The green paint should still be there, under the red, if it is the bonnet from the second car.' The paintwork was superb, glowing like rubies in the afternoon sun. He obviously employed a craftsman.

Denver had joined us. 'So let's do it,' he suggested.

Grateful Dead shouted: 'Look, you guys. We appreciate being here, an' all that, but we got places to go. Are we doing the fuckin' shoot, or what?'

'What's Prendergast doing here?' I asked Denver.

'I invited him.'

'Why?'

'Because I decided to. We're not a police state yet, you know.'

'You mean because you'd also invited Silkstone.'

'So what. He's a right to be here.'

'And it would have made a better story. State-

444

ments all round, from the injured party and his hot-shot lawyer. So where is he?'

'Don't know. Should have arrived an hour ago. We thought you were him.'

'I'll tell you where he is. Collecting whatever money you paid him and waiting for a ferry to warmer climes. The next time you see Silkstone he'll have a coat over his head.'

'So let's do it then, if you're so sure.'

'We're doing nothing. Go home. The show's over.' I shouted it, for the benefit of everyone: 'That's it folks. Go home, the show's over.'

'So what'll happen to the car?' Denver demanded.

'I've told you. We'll have it examined.'

'So why not do it now? You've got independent witnesses. There's Mr Burgess-Jones, and Mr Prendergast. What more could you want? And the crew can film the whole thing. What are you scared of, Priest? The truth? That you're hounding an innocent man? Or are you just scared that you won't be able to fix it, like you did when you shot someone?'

'It's the truth I'm after, Denver,' I told him. 'I'm not interested in a media circus and all this *the public's right to know* bullshit that you hide behind.'

'Then do it.'

'When we do it we'll do it properly, in the presence of a magistrate.'

Burgess-Jones coughed and took a step forward. 'Um, I'm a JP,' he announced. 'Been on the bench twenty-three years, if it's any help.'

The expression *painted himself into a corner*

445

flashed up in my mind. Strange thing was, Denver was right. This was the perfect opportunity to put the hypothesis to the test. The big problem was that if I was wrong, it was in public. I wouldn't have twisted the evidence in any way but I'd have sneaked off like a defeated stag and licked my wounds in private. What was my chief concern: the truth about Silkstone and the car, or my reputation? I remembered Sophie, and how I'd been scared to ask the right questions because I'd doubted her. Was I doubting myself, now? Everybody was looking at me.

'OK,' I said. 'We'll do it.'

Chapter 16

'Right!' Denver proclaimed triumphantly. 'Right! You lot ready?'

'We've been ready a fuckin' hour,' Grateful Dead told him.

'Not so fast,' I said. 'There's conditions.'

'Conditions?' Denver echoed.

'Jesus H fuckin' Christ!' Grateful Dead cursed, throwing his hands in the air.

'That's right. Conditions. First of all, it won't be a TV show, with you doing the narration. We do it from a forensic point of view, for use in court.'

'Well, fair enough,' Denver conceded.

'And secondly,' I added, 'you pay, so the tape is yours, but I'm impounding it until it can be copied. OK?'

'It's a deal,' he said. 'Let's get on with it.'

Prendergast, who hadn't spoken so far, decided to earn his fee. 'Gentlemen,' he said. 'I really do think this has gone far enough. As my client isn't here I have to say, on his behalf, that we do not accept the entire premise upon which this allegation is based. Whatever is found on the car, it can have little bearing on what happened twenty years ago. Who knows who has tampered with things since then.'

Burgess-Jones said: 'Nobody has tampered with things, as you put it, Sir. Everything is as it

447

was or as recorded in the photograph albums.'

'Good try, Prendergast,' I told him, 'but over-ruled. We'll tell Silkstone you did your best.' I turned to the film crew. 'Listen up,' I said, slipping my watch off my wrist. 'This is how I want it. Can you focus down on that?' I propped the watch behind one of the windscreen wipers and stood back.

'No problem,' Grateful Dead assured me.

'Good. I want to start and finish with a shot of the watch, close up. Then I want a wide angle, to include everybody present. After that you can zoom in and out as you like. The main thing is that I want the entire thing to be seamless, with one camera and no stops and no editing. Can you do that?'

'One take, beginning to end, starting and finishing with the time?'

'That's it.'

'You goddit, no problem.'

'Do we have sound recording?'

'Sure do.'

'Right. In that case, I'll do the talking. Let's go.'

I felt Burgess-Jones tug my sleeve and turned to him. 'Nobody goes anywhere without some protection for their eyes,' he said, placing a pair of safety spectacles in my hand. I put them on and the film crew found their Oakleys.

'OK, gentlemen,' Grateful Dead said, taking over the role of director because he realised that it was the only way to get things done, 'let's have you all together, at the side of the car. Take one, of one.'

Burgess-Jones picked up the angle grinder and

we stood there as the camera zoomed in at the watch and then encompassed us all in its impartial gaze. I introduced myself, feeling foolish, and invited the others to do so. Burgess-Jones's assistant was called Raymond, and he said he was chief mechanic and brother-in-law of the proprietor. He's married well, I thought.

'We will now lift the bonnet and attempt to establish its original colour, before any restoration work was done on it,' I said, and Raymond reached inside the car and released the catch.

We all stepped back to allow him to walk round to the front of the car. He poked his fingers inside the front grill for the lever and lifted the bonnet. I could see pipes and wires, a drive shaft and exhaust pipe, all pointing towards a big void where most cars have an engine.

'There's no fuckin' engine!' Denver gasped. He turned to Burgess-Jones. 'Hey! There's no fuckin' engine. You never said it didn't have an engine.'

'I told you it was a museum piece,' Burgess-Jones replied.

'Six fuckin' grand!' he ranted. 'I just gave six fuckin' grand for a car with no fuckin' engine.'

'Let's have a look at the underside of the bonnet,' I said, and Raymond held it upright so the camera could zoom in. Burgess-Jones pressed the trigger on the angle grinder and applied it to the paintwork.

He moved it gently back and forth and we watched as the scarlet paint shrivelled and flew off in a spray of debris and smoke. First a grey undercoat was revealed, then a dark colour and then more primer. He stood back and the machine in his hand whined to a standstill.

'That should do it,' he declared. 'BRG, I'd say. British racing green.'

Raymond stooped to look under the bonnet. 'Yep, BRG,' he confirmed.

Denver and I looked and agreed that the original colour was green. Prendergast declined.

'OK,' I said. 'Now lets have a look at the outside.' Raymond slammed the bonnet shut and Burgess-Jones stepped forward, brandishing the Black and Decker.

Denver restrained him with an extended arm and positioned himself in front of the MG, facing the camera. 'This,' he began, 'is a simple test upon which the life, the freedom, of a man depends.'

I was standing alongside Grateful Dead, who glanced sideways at me. Had I tried to stop Denver it would be captured on film, and he knew it. 'Keep filming,' I told him through gritted teeth.

'Tony Silkstone,' Denver continued, 'stands accused of a series of crimes – rape and murder – going back eighteen years. Some would say the police have been over-zealous in their pursuit of Silkstone, their enquiry based entirely on the suspicions of one officer. Whilst we wish our police to be diligent and thorough, there comes a point when these qualities become vindictive and mean spirited. Hounding the innocent should not be part of the police's role.'

I thought he'd finished, and took a step forward. Denver shot me a glance then looked back at the camera. 'The bonnet of this car might hold the clue to the killer who murdered and raped sixteen-year-old Caroline Poole back in 1983, and who had sexually assaulted young Eileen Kelly two years previously. Eileen says her attacker drove a Jaguar car. The police, or, more accurately, one police officer with a reputation for irresponsible action, say that the car was an MGB, similar to this one behind me...' he stepped to one side and gestured, '...that belonged to Tony Silkstone at the time in question. This officer says that Silkstone had fitted a Jaguar mascot to the bonnet of the car, thus causing Eileen to believe the car she was abducted in was of that make. Silkstone denies it. The proof, ladies and gentle-men, is awaiting discovery. If this car ever had the Jaguar mascot fitted, there will be evidence of two holes, somewhere about here.' He touched the appropriate place. 'Let's see, shall we?'

I thought about going out in a blaze of glory. They'd have put it down to post-traumatic stress, or something, and given me a full pension. And it would certainly have made good television, as I demonstrated how to reshape the front of an MG by battering it with a journalist's head. They might even have given me my own chat show. Instead, I just turned away and took a few deep breaths. I'm growing either old or soft, or both.

Burgess-Jones stepped forward again and the grinder in his hands leapt from zero to three thousand revs per minute with a yelp like a kicked dog. 'About there,' Denver instructed him, pointing to a spot just behind the MG badge. I walked forward to have a closer look.

He moved the spinning wheel across the pris-tine surface, barely skimming the top layer away.

We smelt burning paint and saw flakes of it melt and then fly off. He gradually enlarged the patch, revealing the grey undercoat and a darker primer edging the scar, like woodgrain, or an aerial view of a coastline.

Sparks flew when he touched metal. The patch of bare metal grew as he moved the wheel across it. Silver steel, that's all. 'Back a bit,' I shouted to Burgess-Jones above the whine of the grinder, and he expanded the area he was attacking. The patch grew longer, but it was blank and inviolate.

There was one aesthetically pleasing spot where you could fix the jaguar, and we'd covered that. Anywhere else and it would have looked wrong. Too far forward and the cat would have been leaping downhill, too far back and it would cease to be a bonnet mascot. But Silkstone knew nothing about aesthetics, and I clung to that fact.

'Keep going,' I said.

Denver gestured to Grateful Dead for him to move in with the camera and get a good close-up of the metal. Burgess-Jones was nearly halfway back to the windscreen when I saw him tense and stoop more closely over the car. 'There's something here!' he cried.

There it was. A dissimilar metal, to borrow a phrase from my schooldays, peering out from under the paint and growing by the second. First one brass-coloured disc was revealed, then another an inch behind it, like twin suns blazing in the silver sky of a distant planet. Burgess-Jones enlarged the sky, gave it a neat finish, then stepped proudly back.

'You did it,' I said to him. 'You did it. Thanks.

Thanks a lot.'

'My pleasure,' he replied, a big smile across his face.

Denver looked at where the holes had been, before some craftsman had filled them with braze and made the bonnet as good as new. 'Are they the right size?' he asked.

'Yes,' Burgess-Jones told him. 'About a quarter inch diameter at one inch centres. Exactly right, I'd say.'

'Wow!' Denver exclaimed, recovering his equilibrium and doing a U-turn that would have overturned a Ferrari but didn't make his conscience even wobble. 'Wow! Do I have a story! Do I have a fuckin' story!' He patted his pockets, feeling for his phone, then remembered it was in his car, being recharged.

Grateful Dead zoomed in at my watch and asked me if that would do. I nodded and he said: 'Cut!' and stopped the camera.

Denver was heading towards the cars, so I followed him. When I arrived he was emptying his pockets, piling coins and mints and tissues on the roof of his Ford. Everything but keys. I unlocked mine and reached into the glove box for my mobile phone. 'I've lost my keys,' Denver muttered. 'I've lost my keys.'

I tapped out the Heckley nick number and pointed inside his car, asking: 'Are they them?'

Denver stooped to look inside, pulling at the door handle. 'Aw fuck!' he cursed. 'I've locked them in. I've fuckin' locked them in. How'd I do that? I thought it was impossible. How'd I do that?'

453

'It's DI Priest,' I said into the phone. 'I want you to do two things for me. First of all I want an all ports warning issuing for the arrest of Tony Silkstone, and then I want to talk to the press department. I want a story circulating to Reuters and Associated Press, as soon as possible.'

Denver had decided to enlist help. 'Mr Burgess-Jones!' he called, turning and jogging back to the others. 'Mr Burgess-Jones, can you help me, please?'

A voice on the phone said: 'Heckley police station, how can I help you?'

'Hello George,' I replied. 'Where've you been? I've been talking to myself.'

'Feeding the cat, Charlie. Where are you? That's more to the point.'

'I'm down in Lincolnshire.'

'It's all right for some.'

'Work, George, work. Listen, there's two things. First of all I want an APW issuing for Tony Silkstone, and then I want to speak to the press officer.'

'Silkstone?' George replied. 'You got enough on him, have you?'

'Yes, George, I think we have. I really think we have.'

After that, I got mean. I made Denver sit in my car and when Prendergast started making objections I reminded him that he represented nobody there and threatened to chuck him in the duckpond, whereupon he made an excuse and left. Burgess-Jones thought it all a hoot. I rang the local CID and eventually handed everything

454

over to them, including Denver. The AA arrived with a set of Slim Jims, as used by the more professional car thieves, and opened Denver's car. Inside it we found the record card for Silkstone's MG, as made out by Smith Brothers and showing that it had been sold to Mr Burgess-Jones, so the chain was complete.

All the papers carried the story next day, but the *UK News* still claimed it as a world exclusive, even though we gave some of the best bits to the others. Lincolnshire police let Denver go, on their bail, and a week later he was given an official caution. No chance there of him claiming that we were heavy-handed with him.

Silkstone had made a run for it, as we thought. He panicked, and followed an elaborate plan to make it look as if he'd killed himself by driving the Audi over Bempton cliffs. Unfortunately several eye-witnesses and a few second's video footage revealed that he'd driven his late wife's Suzuki Vitara to York, travelled back to Heckley by train, taken the Audi to Bempton where he'd sent it over the edge, and then found his way back to York again and, he hoped, freedom. We picked him up two days later, lying low at a caravan site near Skegness. Dave and I went to fetch him – sometimes, I indulge myself.

Afterwards, in the in-between hours which are neither night nor day I thought that perhaps it might not stick. A clever brief might cast doubts on my methodology, declare some evidence inadmissible, get him off. It would all be down to the jury, but I didn't care. The first time DNA profiling was used in a murder case it indicated that the person under arrest was innocent, even though he had made a full confession. The local police were outraged and Alec Jeffreys, the scientist who developed the technique, must have been devastated. But he stuck to his guns, had faith in the system, and eventually the real murderer was caught.

Looking back on it, freeing that innocent man must give Sir Alec much more satisfaction than pointing the finger at a guilty one. About a fortnight after Silkstone was committed for trial I received a letter from Jean Hullah, matron of the Pentland Court Retirement Home. She said that Mrs Grace Latham, mother of Peter, had died, but she was aware that her son had been cleared of suspicion of murdering Mrs Silkstone and had wanted to write and thank me. And young Jason Lee Gelder was off the hook too. He was too dense to realise how close he'd been, but now he was free to earn his living skinning dead cows and spend his earnings on evenings of passion in the brickyard. Even if Silkstone walked, and I didn't think he would, it was still a result.

I was sitting at my desk, feet on it, reading a report from Germany about how changing the diet of the inmates of a children's home from cola drinks and fish fingers to organically grown sauerkraut transformed them all from rebellious louts into adorable little cherubs when there was a knock at the door and Annette came in. I let my chair flop onto all four feet and smiled at her.

'Oh, I thought you'd brought me a coffee,' I said, noticing that she was empty-handed and pushing the spare chair towards her.

'No,' she replied, without returning the smile. 'I brought you this. I thought you ought to be the first to know.' It was a long white envelope, addressed to me.

I took it from her and turned it in my fingers. 'Is it what I think it is?' I asked.

'Yes.'

'I hoped it wouldn't come to this,' I told her, and she shrugged her shoulders. I placed it on my desk, propped against a box of paperclips, and looked at it. 'You've some holiday to come,' I stated.

'Three weeks,' she confirmed.

'So you could be gone by the end of next week.'

'Yes.'

'You've accepted his proposal?'

'Yes.'

We only have to give a month's notice to resign. The last thing you want hanging round a police station is a demob-happy disgruntled officer spreading doubt and disillusion about the job. A week, though. We'd been jogging along quite nicely up to now. I'd behaved myself, Annette had done her job. We'd even had a drink together, after a particularly harrowing day and I'd enjoyed seeing her around, half hoping that her friendship with the teacher might grow cold. It obviously hadn't.

'There's an alternative,' I said.

She shook her head. 'No.'

'I could tear this up, drop it in the bin, and you could come to live with me.'

She hung her head, one hand on her brow. 'Don't, please, Charlie,' she mumbled. 'Don't make it more difficult than it is.'

I looked at her, seeing for the first time the worry lines in the corners of her eyes that hadn't been there before she started seeing me. Now somebody else would have to soothe them away. I opened my mouth to tell her that she was making a mistake, then changed my mind. I've been through all that, before. 'I'll miss you,' I said, 'and I hope it all works out for you.'

'I hope it all works out for you, too, Charlie,' she replied.

'Oh, it will,' I told her. 'It will. No doubt about that.'

So the following Friday we had a 'do' in the Bailiwick, with everybody there. Gilbert made a presentation and Annette said we were the best bunch of people she'd ever worked with. Embarrassing episodes in Annette's career were recalled and David Rose did his party trick, drinking a pint of beer while standing on his head. It's time to leave when David does his party trick.

I didn't have the opportunity to say a private goodbye to her, thinking that maybe I'd give her a phone call the next day but suspecting that I wouldn't. Dave Sparkington and I shared a taxi home and I asked him if they'd heard from Sophie this week.

'Yeah, she keeps in touch,' he told me.

'Is she enjoying her lectures?'

'She says she is. It's hard work, but she's coping.'

'And the flat's OK?'

'Hmm, bit of a problem, there. She says the

place stinks of garlic. The previous tenant must have eaten nothing else but.'

I remembered the microwave I'd given her, and the exploding chicken Kiev. 'Students,' I said, by way of explanation.

'Yeah, students.'

We rode the rest of the way in silence, apart from the hiss of the tyres on the wet road and the swish of the wipers. 'I reckon you missed your way there, Chas,' Dave said as we turned into his street.

'Where?'

'With Annette.'

'Oh. No, not my type.'

Rain, carried by a wind straight off the hills, was lashing at the windows as he slammed the car door and dashed for the shelter of his house. I gave the driver new directions and he took me home.

I over-tipped him and turned up my collar as he wished me goodnight. The postman had left the gate open and the bulb had failed again in the outside light. I'm sure they don't last as long now that we get our electricity from the gas people. I found the right key by the light of the street lamp then plunged into the shadow at the side of the house, shuddering with cold.

What was it to be, I wondered: a hot bath; some loud music; a couple of cans with my feet on the mantelpiece; or all three? Silkstone would probably be tucked up in bed in his nice centrally heated cell. Jason would be having it away with some totty he'd picked up at the Aspidistra Lounge. And what about Chilcott – the Chiller –

where would he be? In a bar in a warmer clime if his luck had held. Somewhere where you can live like a lord on ten grand a year. Cuba, or Mexico.

Unless, of course, he was still out there, wondering about fulfilling his last contract. I doubted it, but it gave life a certain piquancy knowing that somebody thought enough about you to pay money to have you killed. I was a cop, so I must be doing something right. The key found the keyhole third attempt and I turned it. I pushed the door open and reached inside for the light-switch. No doubt Mexico's fine, but there's no place like home.

The publishers hope that this book has given you enjoyable reading. Large Print Books are especially designed to be as easy to see and hold as possible. If you wish a complete list of our books please ask at your local library or write directly to:

Magna Large Print Books
Magna House, Long Preston,
Skipton, North Yorkshire.
BD23 4ND

This Large Print Book for the partially sighted, who cannot read normal print, is published under the auspices of

THE ULVERSCROFT FOUNDATION

THE ULVERSCROFT FOUNDATION

... we hope that you have enjoyed this Large Print Book. Please think for a moment about those people who have worse eyesight problems than you ... and are unable to even read or enjoy Large Print, without great difficulty.

You can help them by sending a donation, large or small to:

**The Ulverscroft Foundation,
1, The Green, Bradgate Road,
Anstey, Leicestershire, LE7 7FU,
England.**
or request a copy of our brochure for more details.

The Foundation will use all your help to assist those people who are handicapped by various sight problems and need special attention.

Thank you very much for your help.